Gun Digest

24th Edition 1970

Edited by

John T. Amber

ASSOCIATE EDITOR
Edw. Dams

ART EDITOR
H. Jasinski

TECHNICAL EDITORS
Bob Bell
John Lachuk
John Maynard
Ken Waters
A. M. Wynne, Jr.

EDITORIAL ASSISTANT
Lilo Orland

You'll find a great article by Pete Kuhlhoff in this 24th edition, a history of the Marlin Firearms Company and the scores of firearms designs produced by them in the past 100 years. Thoroughly covered also are the latest Marlins, their Presentation and Century Limited grades shown on our covers front and back.

The prize-winning, Townsend Whelen Award article in this issue is *Six Guns Since Sixteen Hundred* by Merrill Lindsay, with superb photographs by Bruce Pendleton. Yes, Virginia, there were revolvers before Sam'l Colt came along.

"Gun Proof in France," the third chapter in our continuing *History of Proof Marks,* will be found in this edition. Lee Kennett, the author, covers French proof and proof marks in a fully documented and detailed study.

OUR COVERS

Marlin Models 336 and 39 in Presentation Grade appear on our front cover, with a Century Limited Model 39 gracing the back cover.

MEMBER OF THE

Published by The Gun Digest Company

Chicago, Illinois

129L Printed in U.S.A.

SBN 695-80062-0 Library of Congress Catalog Card Number 44-32588

IN THE BLACK 

Free Ammunition!

Half a dozen bills have been introduced in Congress that would repeal the Gun Control Act of 1968. About the same number would impose Federal registration and licensing. Should the nation's organized sportsmen organize an all-out effort to pass a repeal measure? No, said Congressman Bob Sikes (Florida) at the recent N.R.A. meetings in Washington. He doesn't feel that repeal or registration has a Chinaman's chance in this Congress.

Sikes does recommend that sportsmen bend every effort to amend some of the most objectionable provisions of the Gun Control Act. The ammunition provisions would be a good place to start. Congressman Sikes is sponsor of a bill that would exempt rifle, shotgun and all 22 rimfire ammunition. It sounds like a great place to start, but let's ask Bob Sikes—and our own representatives—to enact repealers that will also remove all reloading components from GCA control.

Russians, Go Home!

In August of 1968 the Soviet Union and its vassalites—Poland, East Germany, Hungary, et al—invaded Czechoslovakia, murdering and pillaging, ending the Czech people's bid for new freedoms, for a lessening of governmental controls, for a free press. Now, nearly a year later, Russian subjugation of Czechoslovakia has increased, with perhaps worse to come.

There will be no Russian-made firearms shown in the 24th edition of the GUN DIGEST, nor in any subsequent issues if I have anything to say about it.

A small gesture, to be sure, but it does illustrate, at least, our condemnation of these vicious actions.

Townsend Whelen Award

Our annual $500 prize for the best contribution to firearms literature goes to Mr. Merrill Lindsay for his excellent "Six Shooters Since 1600," to be found in this 24th edition.

This is the fourth presentation of the Townsend Whelen Award, and we'd like to remind writers in this field that the award goes to that article published which meets the judges' criteria best — originality of material, clarity of presentation, readability and lasting value.

Our sincere congratulations to Mr. Lindsay and, if we may say so, the same to our valued readers.

Almost 15 Million Hunters

"Hunters and fishermen spent a record $168 million for licenses, tags, permits and stamps during the past fiscal year," the Bureau of Sport Fisheries and Wildlife announced in April, 1969, "an increase of almost $14 million over the previous high, in fiscal year 1967."

"Hunting license holders numbered 14,931,270, an increase of 245,538 from a year earlier. Fishing license holders increased 930,670 for a new high of 23,060,332."

License fees paid by sportsmen are a *major* source of funds for the States in carrying out their fish and game programs.

Such figures indicate that hunting and fishing has grown apace, but in view of the hardships imposed on hunters because of the passage of the 1968 Gun Control Act, will hunting continue to grow?

Shooting Preserves

A free copy of the *1969-70 National Shooting Preserve Directory* is available by writing: National Shooting Sports Foundation, 1075 Post Rd., Riverside, Conn. 06878.

The directory lists preserves which are open to the public, the address, telephone number and type of game stocked.

Weatherby Award 1968

Weir McDonald won the Weatherby Big Game Trophy for 1968, the 13th recipient of this famous award.

McDonald, a hunter and a great photographer, received the Weatherby award from Dr. Wernher von Braun, head of the space flight center at Huntsville, Ala.

Only 7 living Americans, McDonald among them, have taken Marco Polo sheep trophies. His, shot in 1967, is the largest taken in Afghanistan in modern times.

Townsend Whelen Trophy

Because of the loss of Camp Perry in 1968 as far as the full National Matches were concerned, the Townsend Whelen Trophy was not awarded. This memorial to the late Colonel Whelen is presented to the high ranking National Guardsman in the National Service Rifle Championships, an aggregate of seven matches. We hope the day will come when the National Matches are restored.

Questions and Answers

Far too many of the letters we receive ask about the addresses of the numerous individuals and firms mentioned—one place or another—in the GUN DIGEST. Often enough the information sought is in our Directory of the Arms Trade, when it concerns manufacturers and suppliers, or it is with the article or material itself. May we respectfully suggest that you check the DAT or the article *carefully* before writing—it may save time for both of us.

In general, however, we do our best to answer inquiries as to matters of information, but the demands on the editors' time are such that all letters cannot be answered, we regret to say, and replies to those selected may be delayed.

Please address all communications to The Editors, P. O. Box Zero (0), Chicago, Ill. 60690, and a stamped envelope must be included carrying the writer's return address.

Gun Digest Trophy

L. E. (Red) Cornelison of Seminole, Okla., won our annual award at Skiatook, Okla., in 1968—for the second time!

This trophy is given to the winner of the Heavy Varmint Rifle Matches, a part of the NBRSA Varmint and Sporter Rifle Championships.

Red's winning aggregate was .3903 M.O.A. (minute of angle), with .3008 at 100 yards and .4798 at 200. His rifle—stocked and gunsmithed by himself—was a Shilen-barreled Hart action, caliber 223-40, and he made his own bullets, too.

Our warmest congratulations to Red Cornelison for a great effort under trying range conditions.

Arms Library Notes

While we will be pleased to handle reader orders for our own titles—GUN DIGEST, HANDLOADER'S DIGEST, FISHERMEN'S DIGEST, GOLFER'S DIGEST, GUN DIGEST TREASURY, GUNS ILLUSTRATED, SINGLE SHOT RIFLES and CARTRIDGES OF THE WORLD—you will save time and energy if all orders for *other* books are sent to Ray Riling, 6844 Gorsten St., Philadelphia, Pa. 19119, or to N. Flayderman, Squash Hollow RFD 2, New Milford, Conn. 06776, or to Rutgers Gun Books, 127 Raritan Ave., Highland Park, N.J.

Winchester's latest bolt action rifle, the Model 770, made in standard and magnum calibers.

CONTENTS

FEATURES

DEPARTMENTS

SIX SINCE

by Merrill Lindsay

photos by Bruce Pendleton

There is no place in the world where the revolver is more appreciated, understood, or made better use of than in the United States. Nevertheless, when you ask the man in the street, or better yet, the man who owns one, "Who invented the revolver?," the answer nine out of ten times is "Colt." The tenth guy doesn't know. When you say that it wasn't, you get a "Would you believe" look and a tentative "Smith and Wesson?"

Of course it's true that Colt and Smith and Wesson mass produced more revolvers in the century after Colt built his first Paterson in 1836 than the entire world had made by hand before. Actually working specimens survive, however, which predate Colt by more than 200 years. I mean a revolver in the modern sense, a gun with a cylinder containing several charges which revolves behind a single barrel. An even earlier version of the "revolver," one in which three barrels "revolved," much like the Allen and Thurber pepperbox, was built for and possibly by the Holy Roman Emperor, Charles V, around 1530! Even before that, as far back as the 14th century, there were revolvers in the sense that three or four barrels were strapped together and fired separately. The whole gun was rotated, or revolved, for each shot.

There is a three-shot revolving matchlock pepperbox in the Palazzo Ducale Museum in Venice which was made around 1500. Nobody knows who made it, but it wasn't Sam Colt. In 1475, Roberto Valturio published an updated version of an old military text by Vegetius, who was living in 392 A.D. The updating included illustrations of the modern arsenal of weapons, including an 8-barrel revolving cannon, each barrel having what looks like about a one-foot bore, although this is hard to judge, as the scale is not exact.

The idea of having more than one shot for defense or hunting was a very early idea indeed. The need was great when one stops to think that a crossbowman could fire several deadly bolts

A revolving cannon (excellent idea when completely surrounded), from Vegetius, *De Re Militari*, p. 126, Paris, 1553.

SHOOTERS SIXTEEN HUNDRED

Sam Colt is usually credited with inventing the revolving-cylinder firearm, but in truth they are as old as guns themselves. Illustrated and described here are hand-cannon, matchlock, wheel-lock, flintlock and percussion—revolvers all.

while the primitive gunner was wrestling around trying to clean the bore and load a second shot in his hand-cannon. The hand-cannoneer was even at a greater disadvantage when trying to compete with an Englishman with a longbow. The longbowman could even outshot the crossbowman five to one, and he could put penetrating cloth-yard arrows into a target, such as the gunner, at distances that were as great as early guns could shoot. It is no wonder that the early guns were not very popular with the military. Nor is it a wonder that some quick moving gunner thought of putting a bunch of barrels together in order to give himself a chance to fight back as a flight of arrows showered down on his head.

The most primitive of the so-called revolvers was, then, a hand-cannon. This could be fired by turning the gun around with one hand while the other hand applied a burning match, a piece of smouldering bark, or a hot poker to the touch-hole of succeeding barrels. In order to do this without having the powder spill out of the priming pan, the pans had to have covers. There is an example of an all-iron three-barrel gun in Paris, at the Musee de l'Armee, made sometime before 1400 with three individual pan covers, these opened one at a time for the uppermost barrel. A German four-barreled hand cannon is reported by Dr. Leonid Tarassuk in the Hermitage Collection in Leningrad. He dates it only as "before 1500." There is also a four-barrel arm with a wooden handle like a piece of broomstick in the Winchester Gun Museum which dates from around the same period. All Tom Hall, the curator there, knows is that it came as a gift to the Museum from an old lady in West Virginia. It looks, and it may even be, older than the gun in Paris. It has no provision for keeping powder in the little dish-like depressions over each touch-hole, so the shooter not only had to rotate the gun, but he had to pour out a little powder into the exposed pan each time he wanted to shoot another of the four barrels. This particular gun may well be oriental, and it would certainly take all the skill of a Chinese acrobat to maintain any sort of rate of fire.

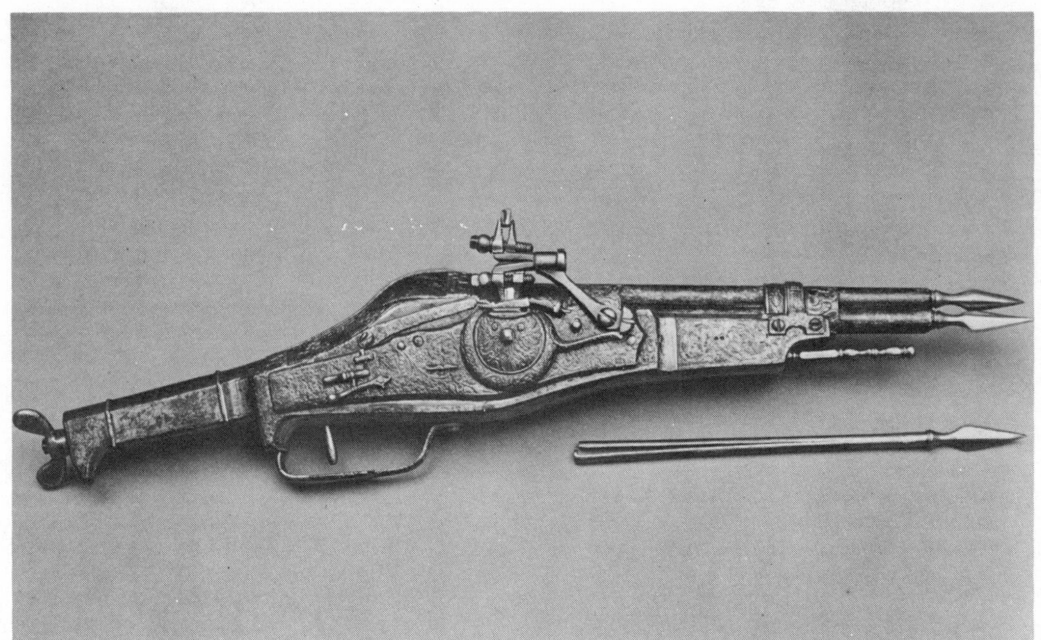

Three-barrel wheel-lock revolver with shoots darts, made in Nuremberg around 1530 for Charles V. The barrels are rotated by turning a wing nut on the butt. The breech of the barrel cluster carries the motto of Charles V, *PLVS VLTRA*, and his double eagles. 16¼" over-all, barrels 8", cal. 29. The arrows or darts are split and slightly sprung at the back to keep them from falling out of the barrel. No. N/49, Armeria Reale, Turin, Italy.

Under the circumstances, it's a wonder the infantryman of the Middle Ages didn't give up guns entirely, or carry with him a trunk full of single shots. Of course, this was done occasionally, especially in a fortified place, where a loaded rampart gun would be laid in each gun port or window and fired successivily by one man running around with a lighted torch. You have seen this effect in movies of the battle of the Alamo. Sometimes the U.S. cavalry did not arrive in time.

Inasmuch as a revolver was desperately needed, and Sam Colt hadn't been born yet, some early mechanical genius invented the muzzle-loading pepperpot. The idea had a lot of merit. The barrels revolved by hand, of course, on a spindle which was stuck into the stock of the gun. They were relatively simple to make as no precision fitting was required for the cylinder to fit tight against the barrel. About this time, between 1400 and 1450, another invention helped the revolver idea along. This was the matchlock mechanism. With a lit match attached to a serpentine trigger, successive barrels would be lighted from the same match in much quicker time. As this was a much better idea than going around borrowing matches all the time. the idea caught on, and matchlock revolvers were made in India and Europe as recently as the early 18th century. As well as the three-barrel matchlock in Venice, already mentioned, a matchlock revolving cannon, the Puckle gun, survives in the Tower of London, and an Indian matchlock can be seen in the Wadsworth Atheneum in Hartford, Conn. This last belonged to Col. Colt, and was left by his widow to form a collection in honor of her inventor-husband. Both of these matchlocks have separate cylinders. An earlier French matchlock musket with an eight-chambered revolving cylinder dating from the 1620s is in Leningrad. When the wheel-lock was invented around 1490-1500, the world finally had a gun which could be shot without carrying around a torch. Still the wheel-lock, at least the early ones, had to be primed with powder each time and wound up for the next shot. This was not a very promising mechanism to combine with the quick-firing possibilities of the revolver system. Just the same, a few revolvers were built on the pepper-box principle, and an outstanding example is in the Armeria Reale Museum in Turin, Italy. This is a most curious gun. In the first place, it shoots steel arrows instead of bullets. The arrows, each about seven inches long, are split half-way down the shaft and sprung a little bit. This provided enough pressure against the barrel to keep the arrows from sliding out when the muzzle was depressed or the pistol worn in the belt. The barrels, three of them, are held together by two sleeves, one at the breech, and one half-way down the barrels. The barrels are rotated into top firing position by a wing nut sticking out of the butt of the stock. This was a fine gun in its day, as can be seen not only by the ingenious revolving system but by the engraving, and a little bit of the gilt which still remains on the iron frame. The engraving not only helps date the gun, but tells who the owner was. There are Austrian Imperial eagles holding up the pillar of Hercules, which was Charles V's coat of arms, and on successive pillars which become visible as the barrels are rotated appear the words PLUS and ULTRA, Charles' motto. Now I am sure that some bright reader has figured out that with three barrels, there were probably three pillars. You're

14th century, 3-barrel hand-cannon with ramrod and sliding pan covers. 17" over-all, barrels 8⅜", cal. 40. No. 5917, Musée de l'Armée, Paris.

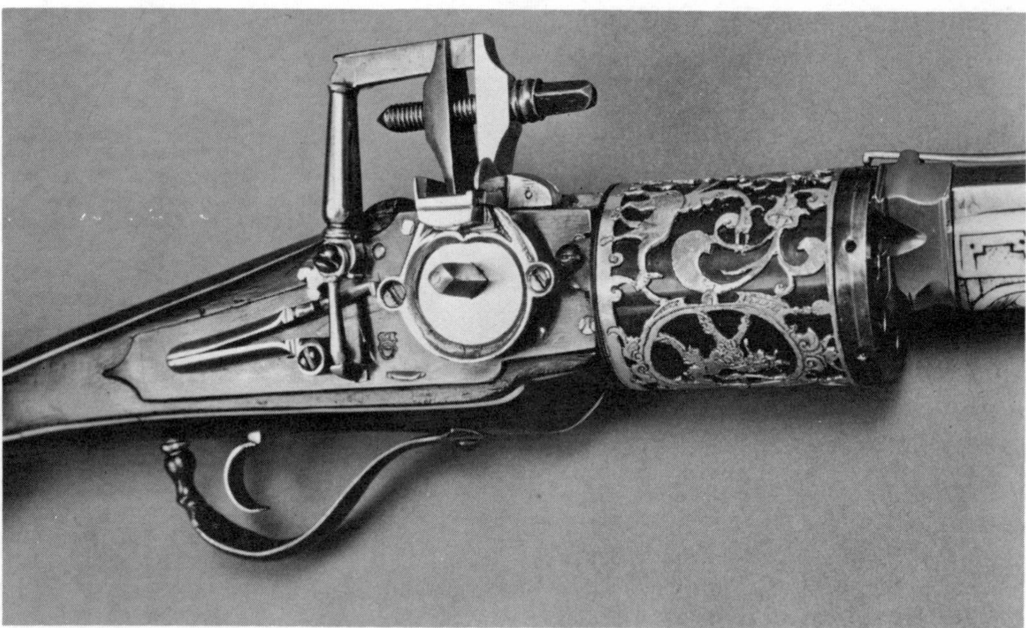

The oldest wheel-lock revolver. The two-tailed crowned lion in the gold lattice work on the cylinder is Bohemian. This 6-shot smoothbore revolver probably belonged to Matthias before 1606, when he became King of Hungary. Barrel has the mark of a kettle with a handle and the initials C-K. 29½" over-all, cal. 40. No. A-1145, Kunsthistorisches Museum, Vienna.

right. If you keep rotating the barrels, you read PLVS-VLTRA-PLVS, which was not Charles' motto, but what can you do with a three-barrel gun?

The wheel-lock was a pretty complicated invention with a lot more parts than most modern guns. While the parts were all cut and fitted and tempered by hand, they had to fit exactly for the gun to function correctly. For the next hundred years after the wheel-lock was invented, a craft developed of highly skilled mechanics in northern Italy, Austria, and southern Germany, who could do amazing things with steel, using only the most primitive hand tools. These are the mechanics who built the first tight fitting breechloaders. From being able to grind and polish two matching surfaces well enough to prevent the escape of violent gunpowder gases at the breech, it was an easy step to make revolver cylinders which rotated smoothly, and were in pretty tight contact with the breech of the barrel. The two earliest wheel-lock revolvers that I know about are in the Kunsthistorisches Museum in Vienna. They both belonged to the hunting cabinet of the royal family and have been in the same collection, now a museum, since they were made. There is little chance that they were faked or worked over. One is plain, but the fancier one, which is illustrated here, has a cut-out gold lattice decorative sleeve over the blued cylinder. The heraldic design, a two-tailed crowned lion, was the crest of the princes of Bohemia. The owner of the revolvers became King of Hungary in 1606 so that this insignia could not have been used after this, making the revolvers date somewhere *circa* 1600.

By 1600 there were other systems of firing guns. One of these, the snaphaunce, lent itself to a much more practical revolving firearm system. By using small sliding pan covers, which were automatically pulled forward out of the way as the cylinder was rotated, it was possible to fire the snaphaunce revolver with almost the speed of a modern cartridge gun. It wasn't perfect or fool-proof, and most of the surviving examples of this kind of mechanism have missing parts. Usually, what's missing is the delicate sliding arm which pushed the pans forward as the cylinder was rotated.

The snaphaunce, the earliest type of flintlock, has a steel (or frizzen) separate from the pan cover. In later models it also had an interior linkage which moved the pan cover forward when the hammer fell. This was the system which, borrowing somewhat from the wheel-lock, was first applied to single shot guns and pistols in about 1550. The first dated snaphaunce revolver is in the Tojhus Museum in Copenhagen. It was made in Nuremberg in 1597. It is rifled and has an eight chambered cylinder. Another revolving snaphaunce rifle, which John Hayward discovered, is in the Porte de Hal (Belgium) fortress, turned museum. It is a large bore five-shot piece dated 1634, and according to Hayward it may have been made by David Arnold in Liège. I am slightly dubious about this gun. I suspect that while parts of the gun are

Indian four-chambered matchlock revolver. Made in India in the 18th century. Wadsworth Atheneum, Hartford, Conn. No. 1905-1024.

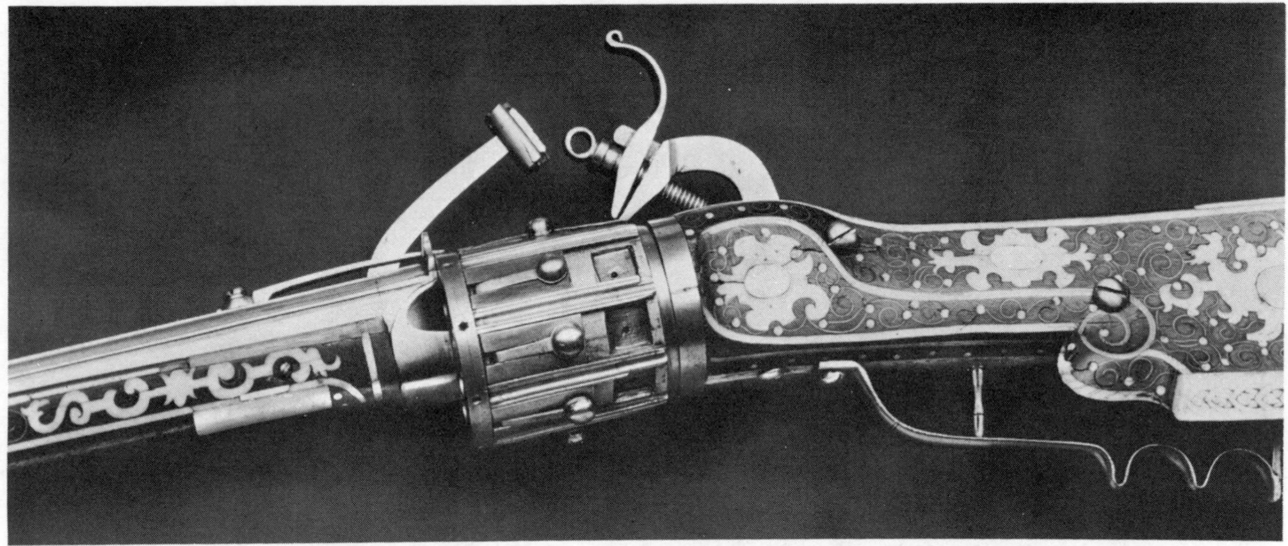

Oldest dated revolving firearm, this snaphaunce was made in Nuremberg in 1597. The barrel is rifled, and it has an 8-chambered cylinder. 41¼" over-all, barrel 27¾", cal. 42. One of a pair, No. 294-295, Tojhus Museet, Copenhagen.

old, the cylinder may have been lost and replaced at a later date in order to make a more complete exhibit. The bore of the rifle is 77 caliber while the five holes in the cylinder are only 62 caliber! Another six-shot snaphaunce revolver from the 1590s is reported by Tarassuk. A Russian four-barrel snaphaunce from the 1650s is reported in the English *Journal of the Arms and Armour Society* for March, 1959. The British built a small number of these snaphaunce revolvers, though at a later date than the ones on the Continent. I have seen two of these. One is in the Hartford Atheneum. As usual, the arm to open the pan covers is missing; the cylinder is brass and so are the sliding covers. It is signed: *John Dafte, Londini.* Dafte is listed as the Master of the Worshipful Company of Gunmakers, London, in 1694. His career as a gunmaker must have started a number of years before that in order for him to reach such an exalted position, so that it is possible to date the Hartford gun somewhere in the 1680s. The other snaphaunce revolver is in the Tower of London. As it is unsigned and undated it could either date from the same period as the Dafte pistol or it could have been made by a country gunmaker some years later. This is the theory of William Keith Neal, the outstanding English collector and Master of the Gunmaker's Company in 1953.

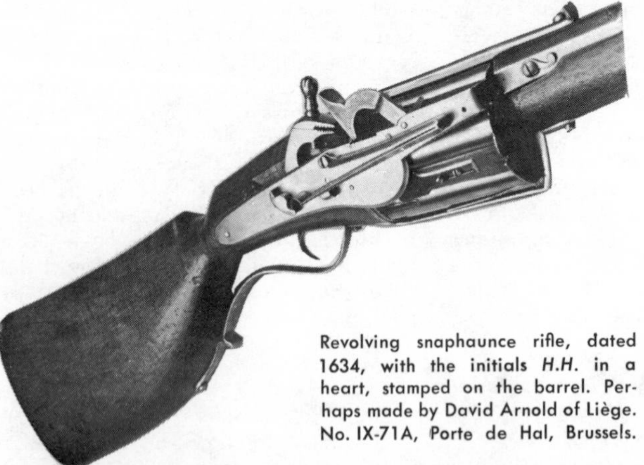

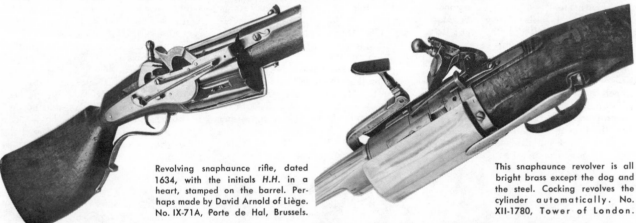

Revolving snaphaunce rifle, dated 1634, with the initials *H.H.* in a heart, stamped on the barrel. Perhaps made by David Arnold of Liège. No. IX-71A, Porte de Hal, Brussels.

This snaphaunce revolver is all bright brass except the dog and the steel. Cocking revolves the cylinder automatically. No. XII-1780, Tower of London.

During the first hundred years of revolver making most of the revolvers produced were hand-rotated. There was no mechanical device to rotate the cylinder automatically when the hammer was cocked. Instead, the cylinder was manually rotated to the next firing position after disengaging an indexing pin. These pins, with their spring usually on the top or bottom of the barrel, dropped into holes drilled into the edge of the cylinder to align each chamber. The pin, while in position, kept the cylinder from rotating out of alignment while the shot was being fired.

That is, all but the snaphaunce revolver, just mentioned, in the Tower of London. It has a cylinder which revolves automatically when the gun is cocked! This feature may make it later than the date first assigned to it. If it is contemporary with the signed Dafte pistol, it is perhaps the inventor's model of the first revolver having a cylinder rotated through the action of a pawl (or hand) attached to the foot of the cock. (As the cock was pulled back with the thumb, the foot of the cock below the axis moved upward, pushing the attached hand upward against a ratchet cut into the base of the cylinder, causing it to totate).

Here we come on a blank page in the evolution of the revolver. Fine hand-rotated revolvers were made in Spain in 1650. An example of a combination six-shot miquelet revolver and sword is in the Metropolitan Museum of Art in New York. A three-barrel French flintlock pepperbox, *circa* 1670, with sheet silver and wire inlays after the designer Berain, is in the Tower of London.

In the Victoria and Albert Museum in London there is another three-barrel pepperbox "revolver" which belonged to Cosimo di Medici. It was made in Florence, Italy, by Lorenzoni, who is credited with the invention of a repeating breech-loading system. This Italian revolver was made between 1695 and 1733. The Hermitage Museum has a hand-rotated cylinder revolver made in the Tula workshops

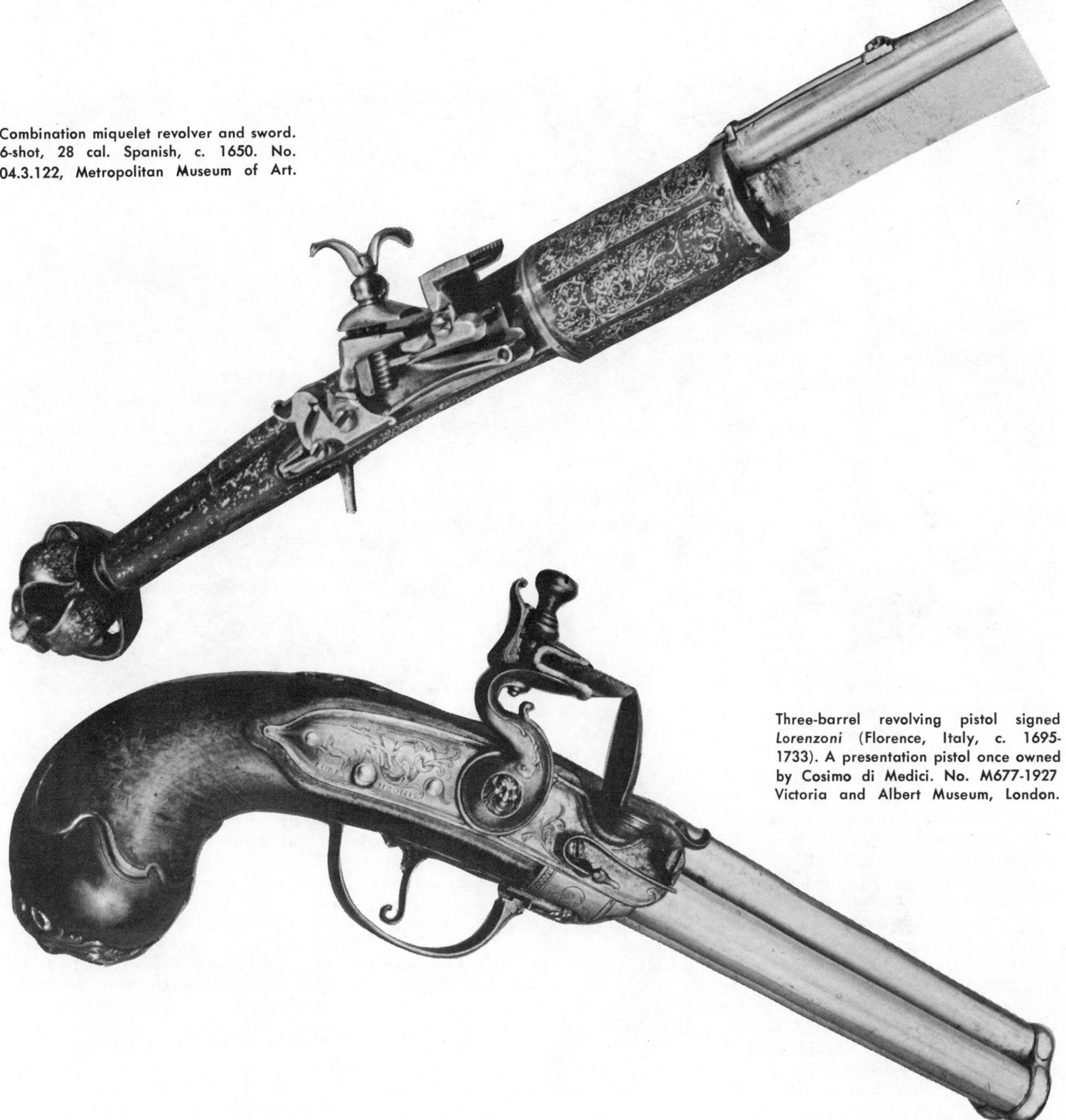

Combination miquelet revolver and sword. 6-shot, 28 cal. Spanish, c. 1650. No. 04.3.122, Metropolitan Museum of Art.

Three-barrel revolving pistol signed *Lorenzoni* (Florence, Italy, c. 1695-1733). A presentation pistol once owned by Cosimo di Medici. No. M677-1927 Victoria and Albert Museum, London.

by I. Polin in the late 18th century. Three Kalesnikov revolvers are in western collections; a carbine in Munich and a pair of gold mounted pistols are in Russ Aitken's collection in the U.S. These were made about 1770 to 1780 The fact that the Russians were well acquainted with revolvers is borne out by a set of four miniatures, the longest is about 22 inches over-all, and all six-shot revolvers. One is a long gun, one a carbine, the other two a pair of handguns. They were made in 1782 by a jeweller, gunsmith named Makarishchev for the fifth birthday of the Grand Duke Alexander.

As skilled gunsmiths in every European country were well acquainted with the principle of the revolver, there is no telling which one came up with the important invention of the mechanically rotated cylinder. If it wasn't Dafte, we will have to keep our eyes open for another 18th century revolver with a mechanical system for rotating the cylinder. I don't know of any, and am forced to jump a good hundred years 'till the beginning of the 19th century and the invention of the Collier flintlock revolver in 1820. The Collier revolver had a system for rotating the cylinder, but some surviving Colliers do not employ it. A further study of a number of Collier revolvers in Clay Bedford's collction on the West Coast should show whether the hand rotated models preceded the mechanically rotated ones or whether the mechanism was too complicated and was eliminated in later models. One of the features of the Colliers was a steel with a priming magazine built in behind the striking surface. This primed the single pan automatically each time the steel was dropped. The self-primer was not, however, a Collier invention. It first appeared on wheel-locks and the magazine repeaters of the Kalthoffs', and can be seen on the Kalesnikov revolving carbine made 40 years before Collier's patent was issued.

It is surprising to me that Henry Nock, who made flintlock pepperboxes in great profusion in London from 1750 on, did not concern himself with a mechanically rotated cylinder. However, the fact is that no such Nock revolvers exist. Perhaps one will turn up in a private collection. It might be

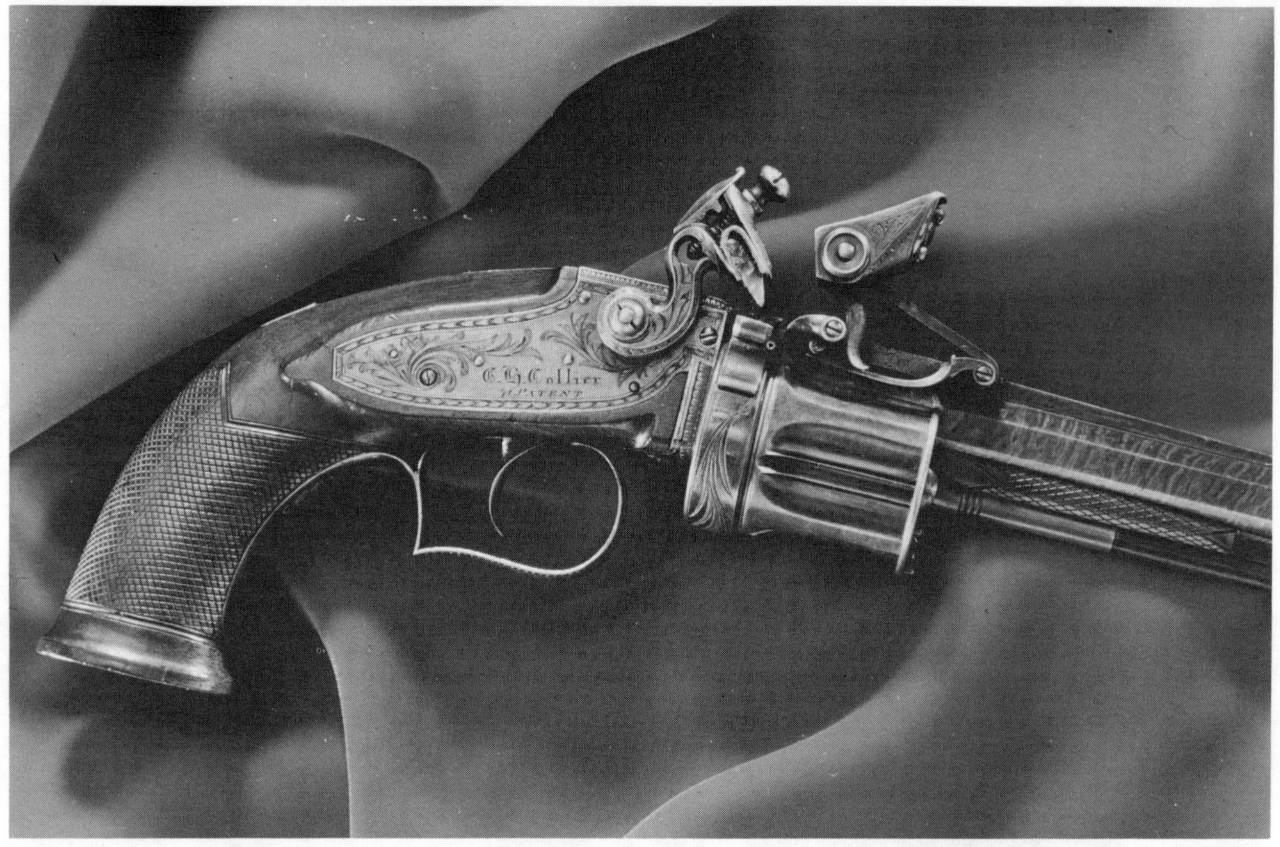

Elisha Collier's flintlock revolver, c. 1820. Made with primer magazine. Frizzen engraved *E. H. Collier/71 Patent.* 13⅞" over-all, barrel 6⁷⁄₁₆", 5 shots, cal. 46. Wadsworth Atheneum, Hartford, Connecticut.

signed by Twigg, Probin, Ketland or other English gunmakers of the period, as Nock seems to have made pepperboxes for the gun trade, and all do not carry his name.

John Nigel George in his book, *English Pistols and Revolvers,* says that it is a pity that the Collier invention came when it did. As a matter of fact, it was a fine revolver, but it was invented too late. Forsyth had already made all flintlocks obsolete 13 years before by his application of percussion powders to the firing of guns. A few years later, the Forsyth guns had magazine primers and a few years after that, in 1816, still before the invention of the Collier, the percussion cap had been invented by Joshua Shaw. The fate of the Collier flintlock revolvers was to be converted to percussion. Other Collier designed revolvers, made originally to use percussion caps, were made in France by Le Page.

Colt was not the only American to apply the new percussion caps to the revolver idea, but he was one of the first, and far and away the most successful. Billinghurst in Rochester (New York), Cochran from Enfield, New Hampshire and Porter in Memphis (Tenn.) built percussion revolvers before the 1850s were over. Eli Whitney and Remington began the manufacture of Beal's patent percussion revolvers in 1854 and 1856 respectively, and the Massachusetts Arms Co., commencing in 1849, manufactured revolvers until they were restrained by Colt for patent infringement just before Colt's patent expired.

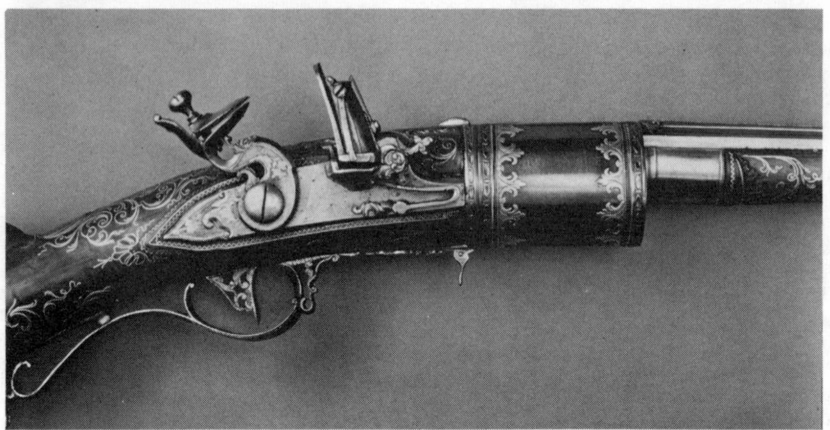

Russian revolving carbine. Made by B. Kalesnikov in Tula, before 1780, this well-made flintlock revolver has silver wire inlaid in the stock and gold and silver inlays in the blued cylinder and barrel. 6 shot, 44½" over-all, barrel 26", cal. 58 smoothbore. No. 2843, Bayerisches Nationalmuseum, Munich.

Both Colt and Cochran were born in the same year, 1814. In his recollections at the time of the Massachusetts Arms Co. trial, Colt tried to prove that he had invented the patentable feature in his revolver, the hand and the ratchet, when he was a teen-aged cabin boy in the 1820s. He introduced in court a wooden model which he said he had whittled at that time, as proof of the priority of his claim. Whether this model is as authentic as Colt claimed it was, it is a fact that Colt had a patent drawing of his revolver in 1835 and was busy making percussion revolvers in Paterson, New Jersey in 1836. Colt was then only 22.

The history of Sam'l Colt's ups and downs in well known. How he built the Walker pistol for use in the Mexican War is history. By the time his patents had expired, Colt had had more ups than downs. He was established with his own factory on Pearl Street in Hartford by 1847 and was producing military and civilian arms by the hundreds of thousands in the 1850s and 1860s. After the Paterson and the

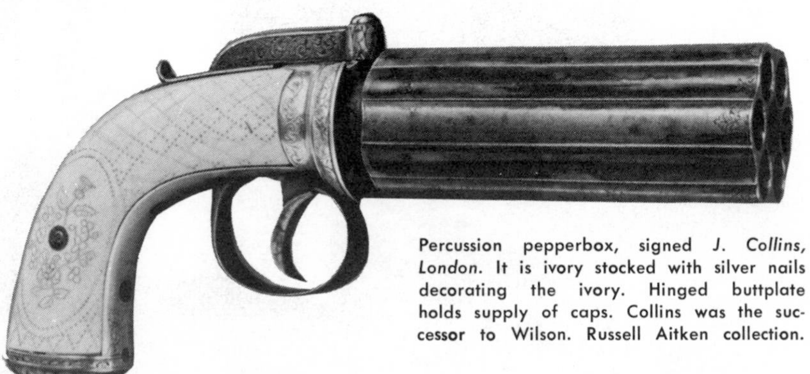

Percussion pepperbox, signed *J. Collins, London.* It is ivory stocked with silver nails decorating the ivory. Hinged buttplate holds supply of caps. Collins was the successor to Wilson. Russell Aitken collection.

Walker pistols, the Dragoons, the 1851 Navy, a variety of old and new model pocket pistols, and the 1861 Colt Army and Navy percussion pistols, in 44 and 36 caliber, poured out of Colt's factories in Hartford and London in such profusion that the name Colt became generic. It was applied to all revolvers, no matter who made them.

Colt was so busy and successful that he overlooked an important development that was taking place in his own factory in Hartford. One Rollin White, sensing or knowing the importance that fixed or metallic cartridge ammunition would have on the efficiency of revolvers, offered his design patent of a bored-through-cylinder to Colt officials. Not realizing that this was as much of a breakthrough as had been Colt's original application of the percussion cap to the revolver cylinder, they dismissed the idea. White then took his patent to Smith and Wesson, who had been experimenting with cartridges, and they snapped him up. They not only bought the rights to manufacture under the patent, they agreed in writing to defend the patent in court and pay all the expenses of defending it.

This is just what they had to do; fortunately for them the patent was upheld and Smith and Wesson were in the same favorable position that Colt had enjoyed 20 years before. While the life of the Smith and Wesson patents ran, they were able to keep competition pretty much at a standstill. There were, however, a number of ingenious attempts to get around the patent including Colt's own Thuer's patent cylinder. It had a cylinder with a removable rear end and, as such, was not bored all the way through! For a time the courts were full of patent infringement suits, but Smith and Wesson kept the lead that their foresightedness had given them. By the time their patents had expired, every pistol manufacturer worth his salt got into the cartridge revolver manufacturing business.

I have only touched lightly on the many ramifications of Colt and Smith and Wesson guns. For scholars and collectors of these valuable early weapons, the different models and the minor marking variations of a given model can be very important; in valuing a given gun, this knowledge can be worth thousands of dollars. The best books on Colt are Haven and Belden's *A History of the Colt Revolver;* John E. Parsons' *The Peacemaker and it Rivals;* James E. Serven's *Colt Firearms From 1836;* Larry Wilson's and John DuMont's *Samuel Colt Presents.*

There are two important books on Smith and Wesson. One is John Par-

Five-barrel volley gun. First model Forsyth detonator with "scent bottle" magazine, serial No. 3235. Probably made around 1820 though the Forsyth patent was issued in 1806. The primer flash discharged all barrels simultaneously when it entered the platinum-lined false breech. 41" over-all, barrel including false breech 24⅛", each barrel cal. 41. No. XII/1589, Tower of London.

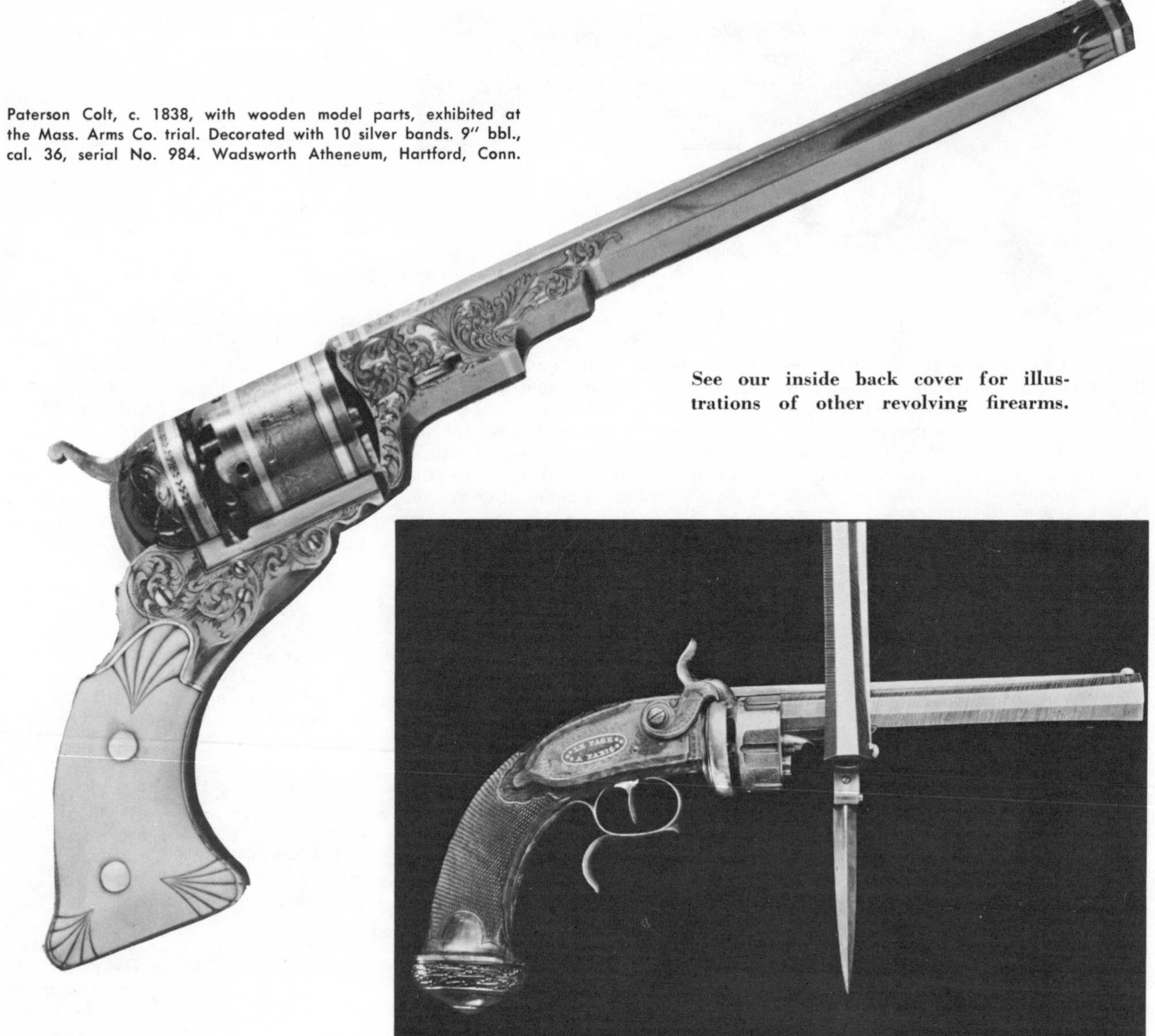

Paterson Colt, c. 1838, with wooden model parts, exhibited at the Mass. Arms Co. trial. Decorated with 10 silver bands. 9" bbl., cal. 36, serial No. 984. Wadsworth Atheneum, Hartford, Conn.

See our inside back cover for illustrations of other revolving firearms.

Pair of Collier type percussion revolvers with switch-blade bayonets, made by Le Page in Paris. Russell Aitken collection.

sons' *Smith and Wesson Revolvers.* The other is Robert Neal's and Roy Jinks' *Smith and Wesson—1857-1945* Charles and Carroll Karr wrote the classic *Remington Handguns,* reprinted many times, and lots of other books have been written on individual makers of the 19th century.* The British point of view is covered in a new book: A.S.F. Taylerson's *Revolving Arms.* Taylerson covers the 19th century, especially those English-made revolvers that were the direct result of Colt's attempt to win their market by building his London factory.

The British did make solid contributions to revolver design. While they had made a few percussion revolvers prior to Colt landing on their shore, the English shooting public had not taken particular notice of them. When the British gun industry was threatened by Colt who effectively exhibited his guns at the Great Exhibition, a trade fair which opened the Crystal Palace in London in 1851, their gunsmiths came up with a real contribution to revolver design. This was the first double-action revolver, built by the firm of Adams and Tranter, and it make its debut that same year, 1851. There were many famous names among English revolver manufacturers in the 19th century. Daw, Deane, Tranter and Webley being among the best known. Today only the Webley survives.

In France, far and away the best known of the revolver manufacturers was Lefaucheux. The Lefaucheux factory produced a large quantity of pinfire revolvers. Although the Frenchman Flobert was the inventor of the modern rimfire cartridge, it was the Americans, B. Tyler Henry at Winchester, and Smith and Wesson who improved the cartridge and exploited it.

Centerfire cartridges, as we know them today, were the inventions of Col. Edw. Boxer in England and Col. Hiram Berdan in the U.S., with bows, however, to Pauly (1812) and Houillier (1847 and 1850) of France. The adaptation from rim- to centerfire required modification of the location of the point of impact of the hammer, of

*See our Arms Library pages, elsewhere in this edition. for bibliographical data on these and many other titles.

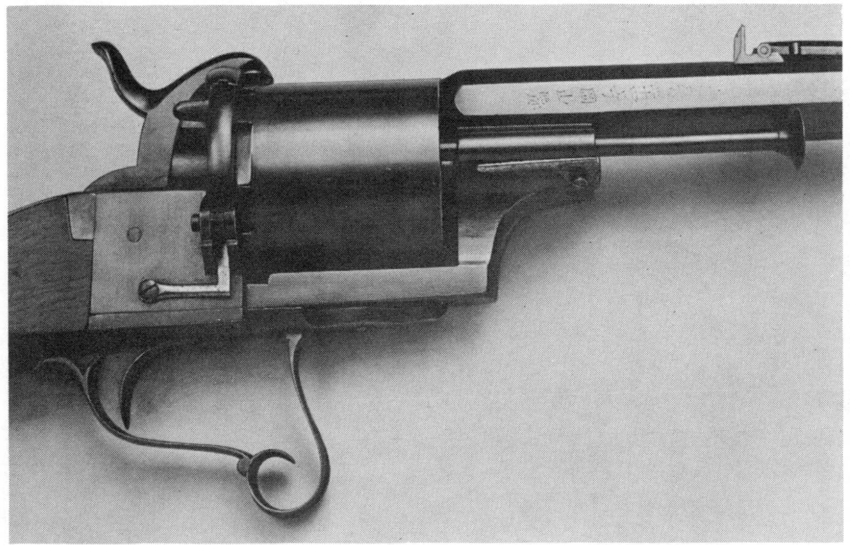

Lefaucheux pinfire revolving military rifle, made in France in the mid 19th century. Chinese markings on the flat of the 12mm octagonal barrel indicate that Lefaucheux had a contract to supply a Chinese warlord's private army. 44" over-all, bbl. 25¼". Bayonet fittings. Author's collection.

course. Rimless centerfire cartridges, which came later, presented extraction problems, but these were overcome.

The basic revolver has remained surprisingly unchanged from the late 19th century. It was a working, serviceable tool which took a lot of punishment and still functioned. It was not a subtle weapon and, because of its bulging cylinder, could not as easily be concealed as an automatic. It is still the safest of the hand weapons. With the hammer down a modern revolver is safe. With the hammer up, the gun is ready to shoot. There is no safety to worry about or concern for whether an unseen cartridge is in the chamber or jammed in the clip.

Anyway, the revolver is a most American weapon. In the early days of the percussion revolver, European shooters stuck to their boxed pairs of pistols. They just never did get the hang of a revolver in a holster or on the belt, and with good reason. The average European did not have to go around armed during peace time. Outside of the colonials, who learned to respect and use them, the average European had absolutely no need for a handgun.

Later on, when the 19th century and an era of frontier life was dying out, Paul Mauser, Georg Luger and John Browning each perfected his own breed of automatic. These guns were an instant success with the military, not only in Europe but all over the world, and our 45 Colt, invented by Browning, has been as American as apple pie since its introduction in 1911. Nevertheless, the revolver is a favorite side arm of hunters, many target shooters, the police and, in certain special uses, by the armed forces. The popularity of the revolver today can be judged by two facts. The single action Colt, considered so old fashioned by the Colt factory itself that they discontinued making it in the late 1930s, was revived by Sturm, Ruger and Co., with such success that Colt had to retool and start making them all over again. Both companies are still making single actions which a galloping horse couldn't tell from their granddaddy, the model of 1873—the original "New Army" or "Peacemaker." The other interesting phenomeon is the Hi-Standard Sentinel. When Harry Sefried designed this little potting gun, it was of interest because it utilized new methods of manufacture and new materials. No one, least of all Harry, dreamed that this gun would outsell all of the guns in total that old Col. Colt produced in his lifetime.

Cochran six-shot, 38 cal. turret revolver, c. 1837-8. Serial No. 62. Winchester Gun Museum, New Haven, Conn.

Probably the principle of the revolver will go on forever. Revolving cannon are being made today. The Vulcan and the Mini gun employ the multi-barrel revolver principle with such a cyclic rate that a single barrel machine gun barrel would burn up instantly. They are a valuable part of the armament of our current military aircraft. Not yet in production is Fred Steven's pepperbox, an underwater revolver made of stainless steel. This gun of the future shoots cartridges in the shape of darts. The unfired cartridges are about the same in appearance and in length as the projectile arrows which were used in the wheellock pistol of Charles V, made so many hundreds of years ago. •

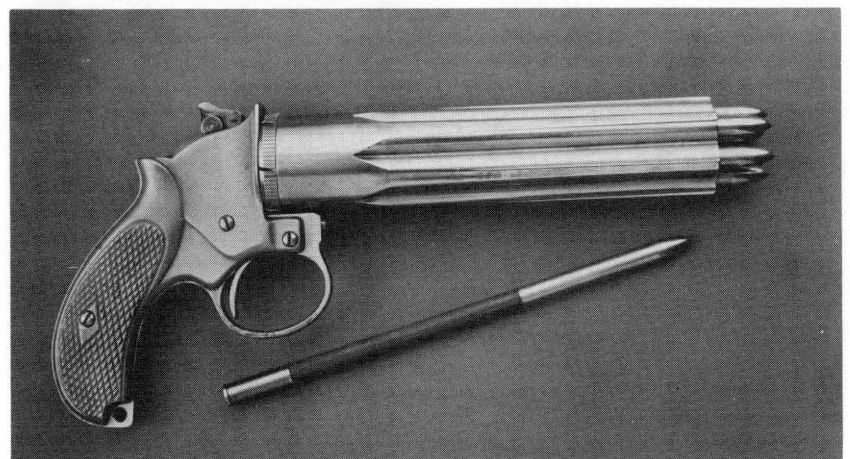

Fred Steven's stainless steel underwater 6-shot cal. 38 dart-shooting pepperpot.

Merrill Lindsay is the author of *100 Great Guns*, released in 1967, a valuable and colorful history of firearms as exemplified by his hundred-odd examples of the gunmaker's art.

Mrs. O'Connor, her gentleman shikari Prince Abdul Kyum, and a large tigress. Eleanor shot two tigers with a 30-06. In India those who have never used anything smaller say the 375 Magnum and the 450/400 should be used.

The Killing Power Controversy

by JACK O'CONNOR

Paper No. 1,319 in that old, old argument, with Jack insisting, rightly enough, that where you put it, not what you put in it, makes the big difference. True, yet it's better to be a bit over-gunned than not, right? Sure, but even the 22 Hornet has killed . . .

I HAVE BEEN following gun and shooting literature for many years and I have probably read many hundreds of articles on the subject of killing power. Some writers swear by lightning-fast bullets. Others whoop it up for large heavy missiles at moderate velocity.

There was a time when I read them all with starry-eyed innocence, but I must confess that in my declining years I find some of them difficult to follow.

One of the principal troubles with most of these articles is that they are based on testimonial evidence, and much testimonial evidence has a way of being pretty unreliable. When two amorous young men who have dated Susie Jones and who have spent many hours gazing rapturously into her luminous eyes cannot agree as to whether they are blue, green, gray, or hazel, what chance has the poor hunter to make a clear and objective report?

Not much! He is excited, untrained as an observer, prone to tall tales and alibis. Generally he is prejudiced. He is quick to jump at conclusions, and he almost never blames his own poor shooting instead of his rifle and his cartridge. Furthermore, even if a hunter with limited experience is a good observer, his conclusions aren't worth too much. Animals often react in different ways to the same placement of shots with the same bullets of the same caliber. Now and then animals are knocked flat with superficial wounds and occasionally they'll travel for considerable distance with hits that should have done them in.

As an example I once shot a very large buck mule deer squarely through the lungs with a 150-gr. 30-06 bullet. The buck ran around 300 yards and was still alive when I got to it. In this case the bullet had not opened up. If I had shot only one deer I might have thought the 30-06 a poor killer on mule deer. A few years later, with the same cartridge and exactly the same bullet, I shot another mule deer, running and perhaps 225-250 yards away. The buck went down so hard I expected to find it stone dead, but when I got up to him he got to his feet and started to wobble off. My shot had gone through one front knee. If that had been the only deer I had ever shot I might have thought it possible to hit a deer just about anywhere with a 30-06 bullet and knock it down. This last experience was genuinely cockeyed. My only explanation is that the buck may have had all of his weight on one leg. When the bullet hit it he may have fallen so hard he was stunned. Both of these are extreme cases but they happened!

In many years of hunting I have seen several hundreds of head of what passes for "big game" shot, and I have knocked off a bit myself. I have been in on the last moments of animals as small as the dik-dik, a tiny antelope about the size of large jackrabbits, and as large as elephants, which are the size of small houses. I am not quite as quick with my answer about killing power as I used to be.

Experience is a great teacher, and experience has often proved my notions wrong. Because of my poor shooting I once wounded a deer with a 30-30. The result was a long chase and for a time I looked down my nose at the 30-30. Then the occasion arose when I had to hunt with a 30WCF or not shoot. I killed three bucks with three shots and none of them went over 50 yards. Those three bucks don't make me an authority on the 30-30, but they did teach me that if a man owns a 30-30, knows its limitations, and can shoot it, he'll get himself plenty of venison; if it wounds only it is probably his fault and not that of the cartridge.

Ed Quinn, former Chrysler Corporation executive, killed this large East African leopard with one shot from a 7mm Remington Magnum. Kenya and Tanzania regulations say that for all dangerous game, including leopard, a 375 or larger should be used. The 7mm Magnum was more than plenty.

Magnum Malarkey

Much of the stuff written about suitable calibers for various big-game animals is, alas, malarkey of the purest ray serene. I sadly suspect that most of it is about as sound as the old notion that strong liquor made strong men. Some years ago a manufacturer was thinking seriously of bringing out a powerful 35 magnum cartridge for heavy American and foreign game. As an experiment some of the hired hands made a deal with a chap who owned a private buffalo herd to shoot 20 animals he was going to knock off anyway. They shot half of them with their powerhouse 35, half with a 7mm Magnum. They found one cartridge killed just as well as the other. They decided there was no crying need for the 35 and so shelved it. An American bison is heavier than the African Cape buffalo and almost as large as the Indian gaur. Would a 7mm Magnum kill these two just as neatly? Probably.

Not long ago I was talking to an old sourdough who for years shot moose, caribou, and sheep for the market in the free and easy days of the post-gold rush Alaska. He told me that articles listing proper calibers for this and that and giving figures of how many foot pounds of energy one needed to kill animals of various weights at various distances really threw him. He couldn't read one, he said, without becoming short of breath, breaking out in hives, and seeing spots before his eyes.

To save money this old boy used to cast lead bullets and load them to a velocity of about 1800 fps. He shot no end of caribou, moose, and sheep with these pip-squeak 30-30 loads, he said, and couldn't remember losing an animal he had hit well. He also told me of an Eskimo pal of his who used a 22 Hornet to feed a whole village with caribou and moose meat. This simple, untutored savage told this sourdough friend of mine that from the time he got a Model 54 Winchester in 22 Hornet until he had worn it out 20 years later, he had lost

416 Rigby rifle owned by Jack O'Connor. Metal work by Tom Burgess, Spokane, Wash., stock by Bob Johnson, also of Spokane. Brevex Magnum Mauser action, 24-inch barrel, ramp front sight, adjustable express rear. Weaver K2.5 scope on special Burgess bases with Redfield rings, Canjar trigger, special Burgess safety, front swivel base sweated to barrel. This 10½-lb. rifle is used with 416 cases made from 378 and 460 Weatherby cases with the belts turned off. Load is the 400-gr. Barnes bullet in front of 105 grains of 4831, velocity 2500 fps and energy is 5,652 ft. pounds.

exactly one animal hit with it—a grizzly.

I certainly wouldn't select a 22 Hornet for hunting deer, much less grizzly, but there is no doubt that a good shot with a 22 Hornet can keep himself in meat. Once in the course of a Mexican hunt, I left my 270 in camp and was out potting the big antelope jackrabbits with which the country abounded. I was armed with a single-shot rifle for the 2-R 22-3000 cartridge, a then popular wildcat with about the power of the 222. Suddenly I became aware that a very juicy buck mule deer had trotted out of an arroyo and was standing broadside about 200 yards away. The temptation was too much for me. I held the intersection of the crosswires for a high lung shot and squeezed off. The buck took one convulsive leap and piled up.

On an African trip a companion of mine brought along a rifle for the 222 Remington cartridge. We used it not only for varmints but likewise often for meat and bait animals like Grant's gazelle and topi (which are on the order of deer in size), and hartebeest, which are a bit larger, about the size of the smaller caribou. Mostly we used high lung shots. We never fired at an animal at over 200 yards and never pressed the trigger unless we knew where the bullet was going to strike. Almost every animal we shot at was dead within 10 ft.

Once when I was much younger and more sanguine I took a pop at a very large bull elk at a distance (measured not guessed) that left the 130-gr. 270 about as much remaining energy as a 25-35 bullet would have at 200 yards. The bullet went right through both lungs and I found it later under the hide on the far side. The bull wobbled around for 5 to 10 seconds on rubber legs and fell.

KPD Disputed

Actually I think differences in killing power between various comparable cartridges using bullets of similar construction lie largely in the imagination. I am often asked which is a better killer, a 270 or a 30-06, a 264 or a 7mm Magnum. The answer is that any of them is adequate with well-placed shots and inadequate with poorly-placed shots. In the spring of 1963 I saw a friend shoot a large Alaska brown bear with a 7mm Remington Magnum. The range was, as near as we could estimate, a bit short of 300 yards. A large Alaska brown bear weighs twice as much as a lion or a tiger and can be very dangerous when wounded. Generally the cartridge recommended for brownies is the 375 Magnum, and some have gone so far as to recommend elephant cartridges like the British 450/400 or the 458 Winchester. The 175-gr. bullet from the 7mm Magnum went through both of the bear's shoulders and was found under the hide on the far side. The bear didn't move out of his tracks. A 458 or even a 37mm anti-tank gun could not have done a better job.

My friend the bear slayer had previously been convinced that one needed at least a 375 for the big bruins. He had taken the 7mm along for black bears and seals and was in fact out after seals when we ran into the brownie.

The results radically re-oriented his thinking. Later he asked me just how far down the line could one go in the choice of brown bear cartridges.

I could only say that I'd be darned if I knew.

I suspect, though, that caliber, velocity, foot pounds of energy, and all the other hocus-pocus that we rifle nuts set so much store by is far less important than many of us think. Pioneer woodsmen and homesteaders killed off the deer, black bear, and elk east of the Mississippi with smallbore muzzle-loading rifles. Powder and lead were expensive so the boys were pretty sparing with it. As a consequence the rifles they used had about the power of the now just about obsolete 32-20 — and anyone tackling black bear or elk with a 32-20 today would by many be considered half-witted. I doubt seriously if these animals are any tougher today than they were 150-200 years ago. If Daniel Boone could knock off a big black bear or a whitetail buck with a Kentucky rifle firing a 78-gr. bullet at a velocity of 2000 fps and turning up 690 ft. pounds of energy at the muzzle, I see no reason why someone today couldn't do the same thing with the 80-gr. 32-20 bullet at 2100 with 780 ft. pounds. The pioneers didn't think they needed more power until they crossed the Mississippi and encountered the buffalo and the grizzly. Then they went to bigger calibers and heavier bullets.

A generation ago I sat in on a session of the Arizona game commission that set the minimum calibers for Arizona's big game. It was decided that the mildest caliber that would be allowed on deer was the old 25-35 with its 117-gr. bullet at 2300 with 1370 ft. pounds of energy and the lightest bullet legal on deer would be the 87-gr. bullet of the 250-3000 Savage. Elk, if I remember correctly, were to be taken with no bullet weighing less than 150 grains and with less than the power of the 30-40. The 30-30 at that time was outlawed on elk, as a great many elk had just been wounded by poor shooting with 30-30s during Arizona's first legal elk season.

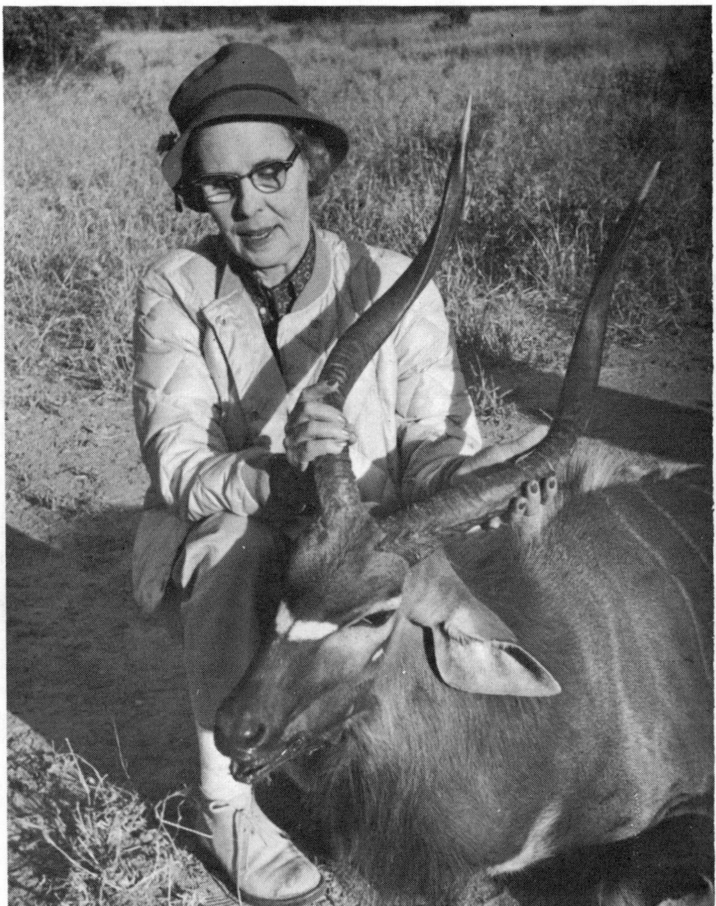

This rare and handsome Mozambique nyala was a one-shot kill with Eleanor's 7x57.

Minimum Calibers & Bullets

Probably this business of specifying minimum calibers is a good idea, as there is no doubt that a 30-06 (all things being equal) will make a more severe and extensive wound than a 30-30, and a 7mm Magnum will make a more severe wound, let us say, than a 243. I also believe that the setting of minimum bullet weights is a good idea, as, all things being equal, it is much less difficult to construct a reasonably heavy bullet that will get deep inside an animal than a lighter bullet.

A young engineer of my acquaintance is a long-gone gun nut but he is a naive type and has had scant hunting experience. Delving deep into the mysterious mumbo-jumbo of his trade, he has compiled an elaborate chart showing exactly at what range it is possible to kill certain game animals with various calibers. An elk is a dead duck, let us say, at a maximum range of 326 yards with the 130-gr. 270 bullet; at 411 yards with the 7mm Remington Magnum, and 506 yards with the 300 Weatherby Magnum.

If we follow this chap literally, the 270 would kill the elk at 326 yards but wound it with a hit in the same place at 327, while the 7mm Magnum would kill at 411 yards and wound a few yards farther — all with bullets of the same construction and the same placement.

Such stuff is, of course, the worst kind of nonsense. Animals are killed cleanly by putting properly-constructed bullets into vital areas and not by energy figures, fancy rifle stocks, gold plating on bullets, or anything else. If a bullet gets well inside an animal and ruptures both lungs the animal quickly dies. If the bullet goes through the heart, the animal quickly dies. If the brain is struck or the spine broken ahead of the shoulders the animal dies instantly. If the liver or kidneys are ruptured the animal seldom lives long.

But if an animal is shot in the guts, has a broken leg, a muscle wound anywhere, it doesn't make much difference what he is hit with. The result is a wounded animal.

Nor have I ever been able to convince myself that the size of the hole in the end of a rifle barrel had much to do with how well a weapon kills. I believe this notion that large calibers kill better than small is (like many other gun notions) a hold-over from the days of muzzle loaders shooting black powder and spherical lead bullets. In those days there wasn't too much difference in velocity

Eleanor O'Connor, famed lady hunter, knocked off this good Tanzania sable with a 7x57 Mauser.

with any of the muzzle loaders and since all bullets were round and made of soft lead, the only way it was possible to get more killing power was to increase the diameter and the weight of the bullet.

Today a bullet can be made to blow up quickly and violently, to expand to .35", .40", .45" or .50" and drive in deep. It can be made not to expand at all. Consequently I doubt if there is much magic in the initial caliber of the bullet.

Elk Hunting

I once read that a group of Idaho elk guides made the statement that when their hunters used rifles of 30 caliber or under they wounded on the average of three elk for every one they brought to bag. I have my doubts as to whether any large and representative group of Idaho elk guides ever made such a statement. The Idaho elk guides I know sing another tune. Most of them tell me that it doesn't make too much difference what their dudes shoot elk with just so they hit them right.

Many people have shot more elk than I have, but I have killed enough of the big deer so that I am not completely ignorant. If I can count right I have brought back 18 shot with the 270, mostly with the 130-gr. bullet. I have wounded one with the 270 — a gut shot. The bull lay down and I wouldn't have lost it except that my companion ran ahead of me, started smoking it up with a revolver, and got it traveling. Night came on and we had to give up the trail. Most of the elk I've shot haven't moved 25 yards after they were hit. One of the last elk I saw shot was killed with a 280 Remington and the 140-gr. bullet. Hit in the lungs, it collapsed at the shot, and rolled downhill. The last elk I killed was a big 7-pointer. Hit with the 150-gr. factory bullet of the 7mm Remington Magnum, he didn't move out of his tracks. Without exception the elk I have seen that went off wounded for any distance did so because they were hit in non-vital areas.

There are no pat answers to this business of making clean kills on big game, and it is of course better to be somewhat overgunned than undergunned. However, the two most important factors in getting quick and humane kills are the proper placement of the shot and the use of a bullet which is strongly enough constructed to get inside an animal, to break bones if necessary, and which will yet expand sufficiently to lacerate flesh and rupture blood vessels.

If a well-designed bullet is properly placed, it doesn't seem to make too much difference within limits what caliber is used. A well-placed 6mm bullet will do a much better job of bringing down a deer or an elk than a poorly placed 458 bullet. Likewise a well-placed 30-30 bullet of good construction is a better killer than a poorly placed bullet from a 300 Magnum.

Little Rifles

In 1962 my wife and I made safaris in Mozambique and in Angola. Between the two countries for trophies, bait, and meat we shot quite a bit of game. She used a little 7x57 Mauser for the most part and I the much more powerful 7mm Remington Magnum. The magnum shoots flatter, hits harder, develops much more energy. The shots were not difficult and almost all were well placed. The difference as far as results went didn't amount to much. The 7mm Magnum knocked some animals down in their tracks that might have gone 20 or 30 yards if hit with the 7x57. With the flat-shooting magnum and the fast-stepping 150-gr. bullets I felt justified in taking some shots at longer ranges than my wife did. I flattened a couple of bull kudu (antelope about as large as elk) with one shot each, but my wife with her less powerful rifle used two shots on one kudu and three on another. However, in either case the animal was vitally hit and probably would not have gone more than 100 yards after the first shot.

The most important factor in killing power then is a man behind the gun who can place his shot and the next most important factor is the use of a properly constructed bullet. If the hunter can shoot and if he uses a bullet which gets in deep enough and expands properly, he has no need of a cannon.

On a tiger hunt in India in the spring of 1965 my wife, who is allergic to recoil and not afraid to admit it, used a 30-06 with the 180-gr. bullet. Our professional hunter carried a double 450/400, which drives a 400-gr bullet at about 2150. He was badly shaken when he saw the small hole in the end of that 30-06 barrel. He had more respect for what he called the "little rifle" when she killed her first tiger so dead with her first shot that it didn't have time to growl.

W. D. M. "Karamojo" Bell shot well over 1000 elephants and no end of lions, leopards, buffalo, and antelope with the 7x57 Mauser, generally using the 175-gr. full metal-jacketed (solid) bullet. Charles Sheldon, the first man to collect all four varieties of North American wild sheep, not only shot dozens of rams and caribou but large moose, grizzlies, and Alaska brown bear with the 6.5 Mannlicher using a 160-gr. bullet at not much more velocity than that of a 30-30. He almost never used more than one shot on an animal, and if he had any close calls with brown bears or grizzlies he does not mention them in any of his books.

Animals may have got tougher than when Daniel Boone was knocking off black bears and whitetails with his Kentucky pea-shooters, and in the decades that have passed since Sheldon quit rolling over grizzlies and brownies with his 6.5. But I doubt it!

It has been my experience that if I hit an animal right with a good bullet from any reasonably adequate cartridge, he's almost always quickly in the bag. If I don't hit him right I am generally in trouble, no matter what I am using.

The longer I hunt and shoot the more I agree with the old Indian guide who said "Any gun good shootum good!" ●

Multum in Parvo—or the

HK 4 PISTOL

This small, light and compact autoloader offers four standard calibers — usable via one frame — and there's an optional 4mm insert-barrel unit for indoor shooting.

by LARRY S. STERETT

Production HK 4 Pistol

THE HK 4 Pistol System was first mentioned in the 1966/20th edition GUN DIGEST. However, it was not until late 1967 that production pistols were available for examination and testing.

The Model HK 4, of blow-back design, is aptly named. HK stands for the manufacturer—the German firm of Heckler & Koch GmbH—the "4" indicating the four calibers for which the pistol is chambered. With an auxiliary unit the HK 4 can actually fire cartridges of 5 different calibers, although the 5th cartridge must be loaded and extracted manually. That's not all—if "wildcats" are considered there are at least 5 others which will feed from the magazines to make a total of 10 cartridges for the HK 4—or was that HK 10?

Manufactured in Oberndorf am Neckar, W. Germany, the HK 4 is distributed in the U.S. by the Worcester, Mass., firm of Harrington & Richardson, Inc. As pocket automatics go the price sounds high, but when you consider what you receive for your $99.50 it is quite reasonable. Not only do you get a complete autoloading pistol, but 3 extra barrels and 4 extra magazines, all neatly packaged in dustproof plastic cases.

The HK 4 comes in one case, along with a combination cleaning rod and screwdriver, and in the other are the 25-, 32-, and 22 Long Rifle barrels and 4 magazines. A well-illustrated booklet of instructions is also included. The pistol is all set to go—except for loading—in 380 ACP caliber. Removing it from the case the left-side safety is placed in the "on" position by pushing the thumbpiece downward so that the white dot shows.

The magazine-release catch is on the bottom of the grip, behind the magazine. When the magazine is filled—the 380 holds 8 rounds—it is replaced in the pistol and pushed upward until the catch clicks, indicating it is locked in place.

The catch is an alloy casting and its arrangement shows thought. The coil hammer spring is also used to power the catch, thus reducing the number of parts compared to the push-button type ahead of the grip—as used on the M1911 Colt, Luger, etc. The push-button catch usually lets the magazine drop freely from the grip. However, the friction of the bottom catch on the HK 4 is such that the magazine must be pulled from the grip.

The HK 4 has a hold-open device which operates with or without the magazine in place, but there is no thumb-operated slide release. Instead, replacing the empty, or loaded, magazine will cause the slide to move forward. Or, if the magazine is removed, the slide may be caused to move forward by simply pulling on the trigger. The hammer will remain cocked, yet pulling the trigger, regardless of the safety position, will not unlock it. This is an additional safety feature, for the hammer cannot be lowered unless the magazine is securely locked in place—*almost* locked in place is not good enough.

If the slide is open, inserting the loaded magazine will release it, causing a cartridge to be chambered. The safety may then be released by pushing the thumbpiece upward, exposing the red dot, and the HK 4 is ready to fire. If the slide is closed when the magazine is inserted it is necessary to pull it back and release it. This will chamber a cartridge. The extractor, on the right side of the slide, at the rear of the ejection port, will protrude, indicating the presence of a cartridge in the chamber.

If the HK 4 is not to be fired im-

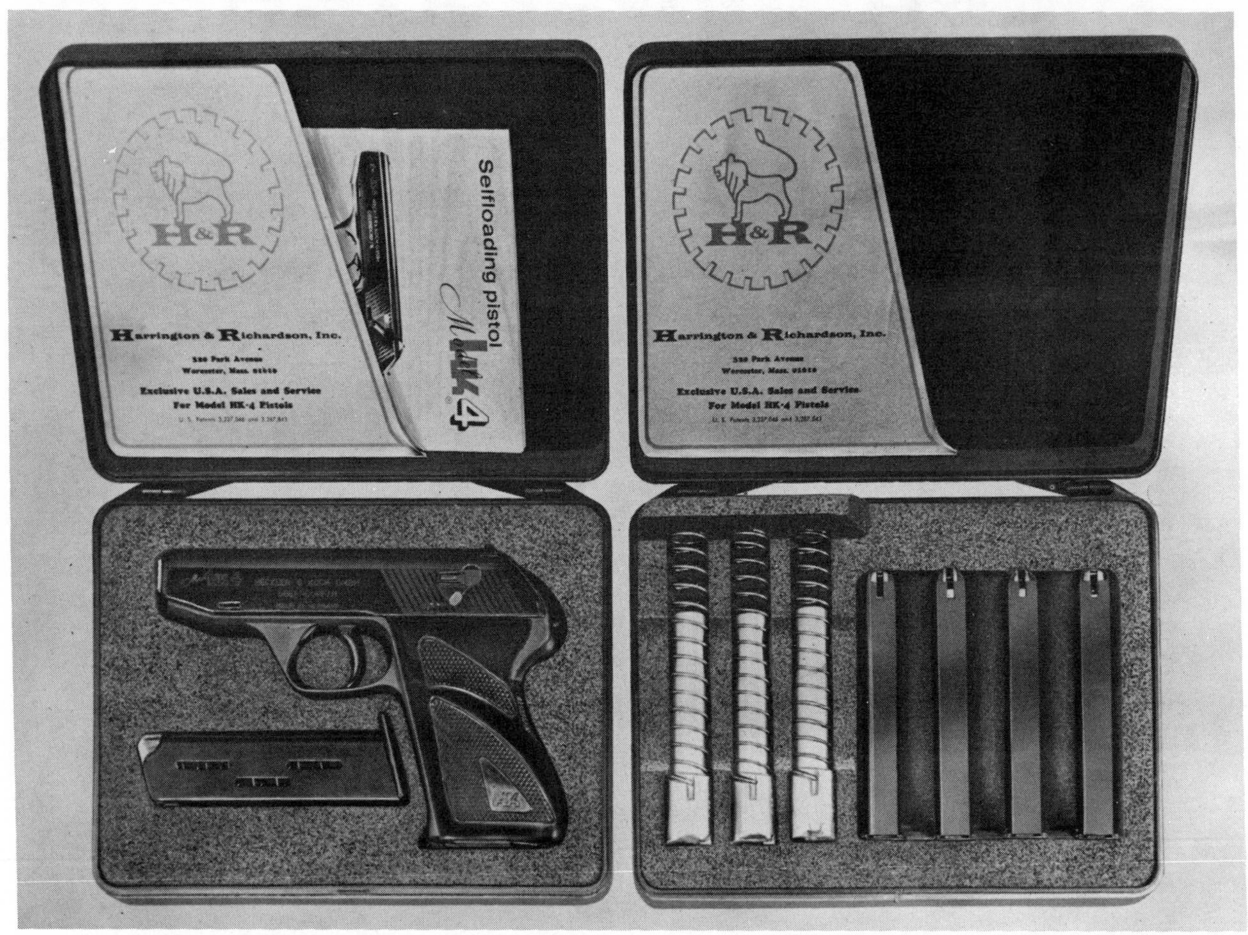

The HK 4 Pistol System comes in two sturdy, well-designed plastic cases.

mediately, the safety should be placed in the "on" position, and the hammer lowered gently with the thumb while pulling the trigger. (A not-to-be-recommended procedure consists of simply pulling the trigger.) The hammer may then be thumbed back approximately ⅛-inch to the safety-cock position.

The HK 4 may be fired single action or double action. With a cartridge in the chamber, the safety off, and the hammer thumbed back, pulling the trigger will fire the HK 4, and the cycle from this point is semi-automatic—ejecting the fired case and chambering a fresh round. On the model tested (No. 11055) the let-off was a creeping 4½ pounds. With the hammer down the HK 4 may be fired by simply pulling on the trigger—just like a double action revolver—after which the cycle will be semi-automatic. However, on the test gun the double action pull was over 15 pounds—the limit of the trigger scale—and it felt like twice this amount. In fact, if only the tip of the trigger finger is used it may require both hands; otherwise, by curling the trigger finger around the trigger the double action pull can be completed, but with the creation of another problem.

The shape of the trigger, and of the trigger guard, is not the same as on the prototype pistols, having been given a straighter shape with less curve. The relatively straight trigger causes the pad of the finger to bulge over the end of the trigger, pinching it against the flat portion of the guard. The inside curve of the guard has also been changed, leaving little room for even the slim ungloved finger of this writer; with gloves on it is worse. The double action pull definitely needs some improving, and so do the trigger and guard. Enlarging the trigger guard and curving it inside would help, but the trigger should also be given a greater bow or curve to the rear. In fact, duplicating the shape of the prototype pictured might be all that is needed.

Switching Barrels

The main theme of the HK 4 is interchangeability—being able to change from one caliber to another in seconds. To change to a different centerfire caliber first put the safety "on," remove the magazine, pull back the slide to eject the chambered round—if any—and close the slide by pulling the trigger. Now, grasp the slide in the right hand, push down on the barrel catch with the left thumb, move the slide forward ¼-inch and lift it off the receiver. Then hold the slide with the muzzle toward you, pull the barrel forward against the recoil spring until it clears the extractor, and lift it out of the slide.

Put on the other barrel by reversing the process, being sure the barrel breech is forward enough to clear the extractor before attempting to seat it. Place the slide on the receiver with the guide rails aligned with the receiver openings and pull it to the rear until it stops. (Note that the hammer must be cocked and the safety "on"). Inserting the loaded magazine closes the slide, chambers the cartridge.

Rimfire conversion is similar except for changing the firing pin position. With the centerfire barrel removed, remove the face plate screw—just above the holes for the firing pin—using the combination tool provided. Push the extractor outward until a "straight pin" can be inserted into the hole which appears. Now, remove the face plate and turn it so the side marked "R" is next to the barrel breech. Slip the face plate back into place and position the firing pin to go into the upper firing pin hole in the plate; this positioning is sometimes easier if the safety is put in the "fire" position. Replace the screw in the face plate and tighten. Remove the straight pin, allowing the extractor to return to the normal position and insert the rimfire barrel. The remainder

The HK 4 pistol in prototype form. The production gun has a smaller guard and a trigger with less curve.

of the re-assembly is the same as for the centerfire calibers.

A 4mm centerfire conversion unit can be obtained from the German firm of Waffen-Frankonia, Wuerzburg, W. Germany. Ours didn't arrive in time for the firing tests, but similar units have been used very successfully in other pistols. The 380 barrel is the best choice for the unit, but it may also be ordered to fit the 32-cal. barrel. The 4mm unit comes with insert chambers in the shape of the 380 cartridge, open at the rear to accept the special RWS 4mm bottleneck rimless centerfire cartridge known as the M 20 Marke U. The inserts, loaded into the magazine, are chambered and ejected like regular cartridges, except manually, since they do not have enough power to work the action. (The 4mm cartridges are available from Paul Jaeger, Inc., possibly others now.)

Recoil of the lightweight HK 4 slide is softened by a plastic buffer in the forward part of the receiver, ahead of the barrel catch.

For the rimfire 22 LR and the centerfire 25 ACP and 32 ACP cartridges the conventional blowback arrangement seems to be satisfactory, but the HK 4 designers took no chances with the more potent 380. Apparently they decided to further reduce recoil velocity of the slide by means other than the plastic buffer and a stiff recoil spring. HK also manufactures the 7.62mm G-3 rifles, which have a fluted chamber; this tends to slow down the opening of the breech. Three straight flutes or grooves are machined into the 380 chamber, 120° apart, each some .075-inch wide.

Fluted 308 Chamber

On firing the case wall expands into the grooves, slowing the case extraction rate, thus also the rearward movement of the slide. It does work, just as it does on the G-3 rifle. However, unlike the G-3, cases fired in the 380 chamber of the HK 4 are worthless for reloading. 380 case walls are thin, and their expansion into the grooves is just enough to cause cutting of the case; this cutting sometimes doesn't appear until the case is resized, at which time the edges start to overlap.

The HK 4, while designed for mass production, actually looks more expensively done. The receiver, an investment casting of lightweight alloy, is finished a dull charcoal-grey. Proofmarks appear on the left side of the trigger guard; the serial number on the bottom, ahead of the guard. Test gun surfaces were smooth with sharp edges—no burrs or uneven rounding—except for one irregular area on the tang. The mould markings are not visible until the one-piece wrap-around brown plastic grip is removed. The grip, well-checkered and with a slight thumb rest on the left, is attached with a single countersunk screw at the rear. The sides of the grip at the bottom are narrower than the top; a little more fullness would improve pointing qualities.

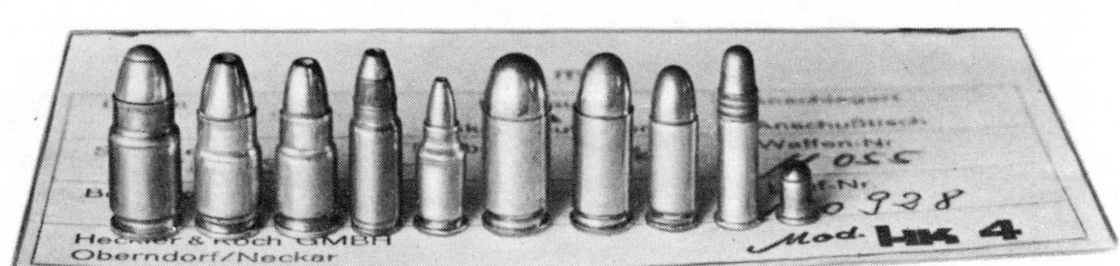

Cartridges for the HK 4, from left: A 30-cal. wildcat with 93-gr. soft point bullet. Another 30-cal. wildcat with 80-gr. HP bullet. 25-cal. wildcat with 60-gr. HP bullet; 22 JGR with 40-gr. HP bullet. 17-cal. wildcat with 18-gr. HP bullet. 380 ACP, 32 ACP, 25 ACP, 22 LR, and a 4mm. The 5 cartridges on the left could be fired in the HK 4 if chambered barrels were available, while the 5 loads on the right actually shoot in the present HK 4.

The stamped magazines, with removable floorplates, are well-finished. Caliber designations are stamped on the left side at the bottom. The only magazine improvement needed would be a finger-rest floorplate—a la Beretta—to provide some place to put the little finger; the grip is slightly short to accommodate all three fingers. This rest could be inexpensively done, and it would definitely be worth it.

The barrels, all alike externally, are chromium-finished. Their calibers are stamped on the right side, ahead of the extractor groove, along with a proofmark.

The internal mechanism of the HK 4 consists of coiled springs, pins and stampings of various shapes and sizes. When the P-38 was introduced 30 years ago it drew many comments regarding its alarm clock construction. It had nothing on the HK 4.

The slide is a heavy steel stamping —original thickness about 1/10-inch. Into this stamping are silver soldered the breech assembly (face plate, firing pin, safety, etc.), and a muzzle reinforcement. The fitting is excellent, and from the outside the slide appears to be machined from solid stock. The sides of the slide are mirror-finished a rich blue-black, while the rest of the slide has a matte finish with a slight sheen. The top of the slide is rounded with a shallow concave surface along the line of sight. The front sight is a low .075-inch blade; the rear of the slide is dovetailed to accept a rear sight having a square notch of approximately .075-inch.

Accuracy & Functioning

No matter how well a handgun may appear, it is the shooting and functioning qualities that count. The HK 4 was converted to fire the 22 LR cartridges first, and over a period of a few weeks several hundred rounds of assorted brands were put through it. Because the manual recommends the use of high speed 22s only, Western Super-X, Cascade Mini-Mag, J. C. Higgins Xtra-Range and Gevelot brands were used for the plinking-functioning sessions. To call the results disappointing is an understatement. Not only did the cartridges fail to feed and eject, but two brands—J. C. Higgins and Mini-Mag—did not even move the slide enough to cock the hammer. They had to be fed and ejected manually. The force required to retract the HK 4 slide was something over 15 pounds, while the effort on another autoloader designed for 22 LR high speed ammunition was only 12 pounds. Maybe German ammo has more zip than the U. S. brands, but it appears that the recoil spring is too stiff for our domestic rimfires. Super-X and Gevelot brands would feed and eject approximately 40% of the time, thus, for the most part, the HK 4 operated as a repeater—loading and extracting manually—rather than as an autoloader. A few old CCI Hy-Speed cartridges were available and these, tried out of curiosity, fed and ejected perfectly, 100% of the time.

A later session proved the HK 4 could compete with other pocket automatics for accuracy—nothing outstanding, but satisfactory. All firing—with rimfire and centerfire loads—was done from the bench, using sandbag wrist and forearm rests, at NRA slow-fire targets at 25 yards. Since the HK 4 is a pocket autoloader, 25 yards is about maximum for normal use, and generally it would be less. Three-shot factory test targets for each caliber, fired at 15 meters, accompanied each barrel, but it was decided that 5 shots at 25 yards would provide a truer picture of the potential of the pistol.

Eleven different rimfire cartridges were used, including those mentioned previously, plus CIL Pistol Match, Eley Tenex, F. I. Lapua, RWS and PIC Valor. The factory 22 LR test target had three shots in 31/32-inch, but the best 5-shot rimfire group at 25 yards measured 2¾ inches. This was using RWS Z-22 cartridges, having blunt-nose bullets. Intended for 50-foot indoor use, each round had to be loaded into the chamber manually since they contain almost no powder. They also shot some 6 inches high at this distance.

CIL Pistol Match loads shot closer to the point of aim than any of the other brands—½- to 1-inch above. Groups averaged just over 3 inches. This target load also partly-ejected fired cases—catching them between the barrel and ejector port. Some Valor cartridges — standard velocity loads imported by Precise Imports from Yugoslavia—ejected 40% of the time and cocked the hammer 40% of the time. These also shot close to the point of aim, but groups were over 5 inches.

The CCI Hy-Speed cartridges, which operated the mechanism perfectly, also produced groups that averaged an inch smaller than those the Mini-Mag produced, though the latter didn't even cock the hammer. Gevelot, CIL, Tenex and Lapua brands averaged groups over 3 inches, the others going over 4. Super-X and Mini-Mag loads averaged just over 5½ inches.

The HK 4 field-stripped.

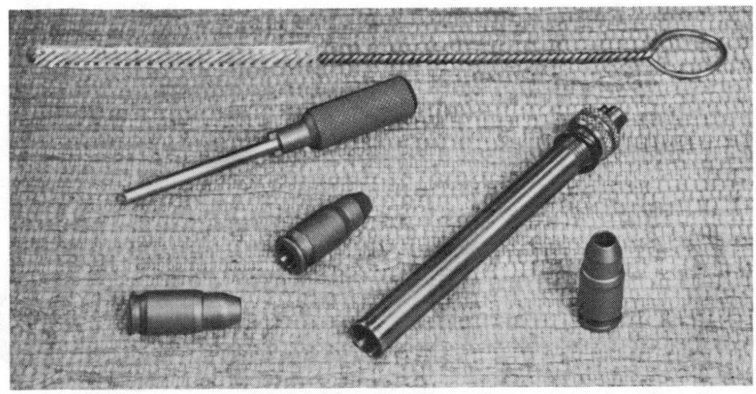

4mm conversion unit for the HK 4. Three of the auxiliary cartridges and the punch-out rod for removing the 4mm fired cases from them.

Unusual 4mm centerfire cartridges shown life-size with a couple of kitchen matches for scale. Used in the adaptor shown above left for practice, these M20 RWS cartridges should be available from Stoeger.

In order to compare the accuracy of the HK 4 with a conventional 22 LR autoloader, several brands were put through a Beretta Jaguar with a 6-inch barrel. The best group obtained measured 1 13/16 inches, using CIL Pistol Match ammunition. Western Super-X loads did almost as well, averaging just under 2 inches. The rest averaged around 4 inches, which indicates the HK 4, with its shorter barrel, is entirely satisfactory in the accuracy department when compared with ordinary plinking handguns.

The 25 ACP (6.35mm) barrel was next. Four imported ammos were used—Sako, Norma, Fiocchi and Hirtenberg. The last (made in Austria and imported by Mars Equipment), functioned perfectly—feeding and ejecting—100% of the time. Norma cartridges ejected about 80% of the time, but nose shape is important in these small calibers and this load would not feed into the chamber. Sako and Fiocchi brands ejected from 20% to 40% of the time. The Hirtenberg load was also the most accurate, averaging just under 4 inches, and these in the black. The other 6.35mm cartridges averaged just over 4 inches. No other 25 caliber autoloader was available at the time to check comparable accuracy, but the factory target measured only 9/16-inch for 3 shots at 15 meters.

The same four ammo brands were put through the HK 4 32 ACP barrel. Norma loads did best—4⅛ inches. The same brand produced the same size group in a Sauer & Sohn Model 38 being used for comparison. All four brands operated the mechanism of the Sauer perfectly, but Norma cartridges jammed about 40% of the time in the HK 4. Largest group fired with the 32 ACP HK 4 measured 8 13/16 inches, while the largest with the Sauer measured 7½ inches. Over-all there was no wide accuracy variation between the two ACP pistols, but the 5-shot groups were large compared to the 1¼-inch, 3-shot factory group at 15 meters.

Last to be checked was the 380 ACP, and only two brands of ammunition were available—Norma and Hirtenberg. No comparison pistol was available in the caliber, but the HK 4 groups averaged just over 6 inches, Hirtenberg ammo doing just slightly better than Norma. Both fed and ejected without malfunctioning. The 3-shot factory target measured 2⅛ inches at 15 meters.

The lightweight HK 4 (15 ounces in 22 caliber with an empty magazine) is a semi-automatic pistol, usually classified as a pocket automatic. Its basic design rates an A plus, the finish on the test gun is at least an A. For versatility it also rates an A, as it does for ease in changing barrels and field-stripping. However, it definitely flunked functioning. Accuracy, at least average, rates a C.

To be upgraded the HK 4 needs to have the strength of the recoil springs on the 22, 25 and 32 caliber barrels reduced, along with lightening the double-action trigger pull. The shape of the trigger and the trigger guard both need to be altered to provide more room for the trigger finger, particularly for the shooter with a chubby finger or for use with gloves.

Four other improvements would be worthwhile:

1. Widen the bottom of the grip slightly on the sides.
2. Put a finger rest on the magazine floorplate to provide room for the little finger.
3. Increase tang length—it is possible now to get the web between the thumb and trigger finger pinched by the hammer.
4. Change the safety to go "off" on the downward motion (as on the Sauer Model 38 H), instead of via the present upward motion. It is difficult—at least on the test gun—to push the small lever upward with the thumb, but not to push it downward.

The HK 4, a truly unique pistol system, would represent good value for the money if it functioned properly. ●

HK 4 Pistol Data

Calibers:	22 LR, 25 ACP, 32 ACP, 380 ACP
Height:	4.33″
Barrel length:	3.34″
Over-all:	6.18″
Weight:	15 ounces (22) with empty magazine
Magazine capacity:	10 rds. (22, 25); 9 rds. (32), 8 rds. (380)
Distributor:	Harrington & Richardson, Inc., 320 Park Ave., Worcester, Mass. 01610
Cost:	$99.50

Marlin A CENTURY OF

The Marlin Firearms Company, long considered one of this country's leading gunmakers, has a fascinating history. Though Colt and Winchester are usually associated with the winning of the West, Marlin supplied its full share of color to the American scene. Here are the facts and anecdotes of yesteryear, recalled to light and brought up to date . . .

JOHN MAHLON MARLIN, a journeyman tool and die maker, began making derringers and revolvers in New Haven, Connecticut, in 1863. He founded The Marlin Firearms Company in 1870 to begin a dynasty of gunmakers that has made the name synonymous with accuracy, dependability and fine workmanship.

There are "big doings" at The Marlin Firearms Company this year!

It was a century ago, in 1870, when John Mahlon Marlin founded the company — a company which, over the years, has made the name Marlin a symbol of accuracy, dependability and precision workmanship.

Marlin has gone all-out in production of lavish models to commemorate the first 100 years of Marlin firearms production—and every Marlin made during 1970 will be identified as a Centennial Model in one way or another. The piece de resistance of the series is the Presentation Matched Set. It consists of a special Model 39 in 22 Short, Long and Long Rifle, and a special Model 336 in 30-30 caliber (see photographs). The receivers of these straight grip, lever action rifles are beautifully embellished with fine engraving and have a centennial medallion inlet into the right-side surface of the receiver. The medallion (see photograph), made of cartridge case brass, has the familiar Marlin horse and rider in deep relief, with the word Marlin and the dates 1870 and 1970. Matching numbers are engraved on the upper tangs of each set. Stock and forearm are of selected American walnut, and the 20-inch octagon barrels are suitably engraved to identify these rifles as presentation pieces. Only 1,000 of the matched sets will be produced, these packaged in a special case.

Price of the matched set is $750.00, and I'm sure they will sell very quickly, especially to collectors.

Also, a special 100 year commemorative Model 39 (see photograph) is available. Engraved with "Century Ltd." on the 20-inch octagon barrel, it has the brass centennial medallion inlet into the receiver. It is similar to the Model 39 of the matched set, except it is not engraved. This special Model 39 sells for $150.

Marlin Beginnings

Although The Marlin Firearms Company is known throughout the world for its lever action rifles, the firm got its start producing small single shot pistols, followed by revolvers, and in 1875 by the famous Marlin Ballard single shot rifle. The first Marlin lever action repeating rifle was introduced in 1881.

John Mahlon Marlin was born in 1836 on a farm near East Granby, Connecticut. The Nutmeg State, then as it is today, was an important center of American gunmaking. As a young man, J. M. Marlin had learned the machinist trade the hard way, as an apprentice. In those days, when individual craftsmanship was a top requirement in practically all trades, the apprentice system was common throughout the world.

Young Marlin's working papers, covering the period of time until he was 21, were signed on November 14, 1853, by him, his father and Philos B. Tyler, superintendent of the American Machine Works. (Incidentally, this company, established by P. B. Tyler in 1843 at Springfield, Mass., made Smith carbines on a Civil War contract.)

By the terms of his contract, young Marlin agreed to work without pay during the first 6 months. He was to receive $1.50 a week during the second 6 months, $2.50 per week during the third 6 months, and a 50¢ a week raise every 6 months until his term of service expired at age 21. So, at the end of his service he evidently was receiving $4 a week. That wasn't

FAMOUS FIREARMS

by PETE KUHLHOFF—Gun Editor *Argosy Magazine*

really low pay at the time and, in effect, Marlin was being paid while learning his trade.

As the Civil War began John Marlin was working at the Hartford plant of Colt's Patent Fire Arms Company, where he remained until 1863. He then opened a firearms business in New Haven, his first shop on St. James street. Marlin moved around in New Haven quite a bit, having a shop on State street in 1864, then another on William street; 1865 saw him on Franklin street, then back to William street, and to Bradley street in 1866.

Very little is known about his gunmaking activities between 1863 and 1867. However, a 22 single shot pistol, a little over 4 inches long and marked "J. M. Marlin, New Haven, Ct." on top of the barrel, is believed to have been his first production arm. The better known OK model, similar but slightly larger, was 5 inches long, and made in 22 Short, 30 Short and 32 Short rimfire. The still larger 38 rimfire Victor model was quite similar to the OK model. These early Marlin pistols were without extractors.

Although most of Marlin's early efforts evidently involved pistol making, a Marlin patent dated February 7, 1865, describes an experimental autoloading 22 rimfire rifle.

In 1867 Marlin returned to Hartford, but details of his activities during the next 3 years are lost in the haze of time. However, on April 5, 1870, he was granted a patent covering an extractor, and he moved back to New Haven. In that same year he began production of the Never Miss pistols, making these in his State street shop until 1875. These pistols resembled the earlier OK models except that the barrel section over the frame is rounded instead of semi-octagonal, the frame is trimmed down with a strengthening ridge supporting the barrel; more important, they have Marlin's patented extractor. These pistols were also marked "J. M. Marlin, New Haven, Ct." but with the addition of "Pat April 5, 1870." Never Miss models are found in 22 Short, 32 Short and 41 rimfire.

Many companies started producing revolvers after the Rollin White patent on the bored-through cylinder expired on April 3, 1869. John Marlin, who was among these, made revolvers somewhat similar to the early Smith & Wessons.

The Marlin XXX Standard 1872 revolver, a 5-shot, tip-up type with 3⅛-inch barrel and non-fluted cylinder, was first made in 30 Short rimfire caliber. After July, 1873, the 30 Long rimfire was added along with several design alterations—a 5-flute cylinder and a 3-inch round barrel.

The Little Joker revolver, of 22 Short caliber, was introduced in 1873. It had a solid frame, non-fluted cylinder and octagonal barrel. The Little Joker, found in as many highly ornamented examples as in plain styles, was probably intended for the female market. Production lasted for only two years, maybe because the XX Standard 1873, in 22 Long rimfire, was the better gun.

As shown by variations in rifling design and introduction of new calibers, Marlin made continuous efforts to improve his products. The 32 Long rimfire XX Standard 1875 was offered in 1875, and 3 years later Marlin's first centerfire revolver, the XX Standard 1878, entered the picture. Chambered for the popular — and longer — 38 S&W cartridge, introduced in 1876, the gun was slightly larger than previous Standard models. This was the last version of the single-action Standard line, and all were discontinued in 1886.

The Marlin Model 1887, called simply "Double Action Revolver" in the old catalogs, is almost identical in appearance to the earliest Smith & Wes-

Only 1000 Marlin Presentation Matched Sets will be produced. An engraved Model 336 (left) in 30-30 and an engraved Model 39 in 22 rimfire, with matching numbers, are packed in a special case.

John Mahlon Marlin founded the Marlin Firearms Co. in 1870.

son double-action, top-break revolvers. A 5-shot handgun, it was made in 32 S&W and 38 S&W calibers, and it was produced from 1887 to 1899. This excellent revolver (see photograph) was the only double-action handgun manufactured by Marlin.

Marlin Ballards

As mentioned earlier, Marlin was interested in rifles before 1865, yet it was not until 1875 that he began making one—the famous single shot Ballard. Examples of this excellent rifle are still in use, mostly by target shooting single-shot buffs, but the great majority now are prized items in collectors' gun cabinets.

The basic Ballard patent was granted to C. H. Ballard on November 5, 1861. It was produced in many and varied forms for slightly over 30 years. The first type was a plain, simple, ruggedly constructed military carbine of 56 rimfire caliber, attributed to the Ballard Arms Co. of Worcester, Mass. This was followed by Ball & Williams Ballards, made in the same city; Ballards made by the Merrimack Arms & Mfg. Co., until 1869, and by the Brown Mfg. Co. (both of Newburyport, Mass.), until 1873. At that time Charles Daly, of Schoverling and Daly, a New York sporting goods firm, bought the rights to manufacture the Ballard. He approached J. M. Marlin with the idea of producing it.

(Daly evidently was to handle the business problems, with Marlin taking care of manufacturing. When the firm was incorporated in 1878, Daly became president. He sold his interest to Marlin in 1893 and, from then until 1915 the firm was owned entirely by the Marlin family.)

Marlin produced his first Ballard in 1875, the Hunter's model. This was followed over the years by a large number of versions including hunting, target and special Creedmoor types as well as light and heavy Schuetzen rifles. The Ballard was made in a large number of calibers from 22 rimfire to 45 centerfire, among them several special Ballard calibers. Also, Ballard actions were used by such famous barrelmakers as Harry M. Pope, Schoyen, Zischang and Petersen for building custom rifles. Many modern benchrest shooters are familiar with C. W. Rowland's 32-40 Ballard that made a 10-shot, 200-yard group measuring .725-inch—an amazing performance for its day, around the turn of the century.

Some 35 or more different Marlin Ballards were made, many of them handsomely engraved. Although the Ballard was discontinued about 1891-1892, Schuetzen and Creedmoor type single shot target rifles continued popular until well after 1900. With the coming of World War I, these special kinds of target shooting all but disappeared from the American scene. However, even today a fine Ballard rifle is seen now and then on the target range.

With the introduction of the Winchester 1866 lever action repeater—

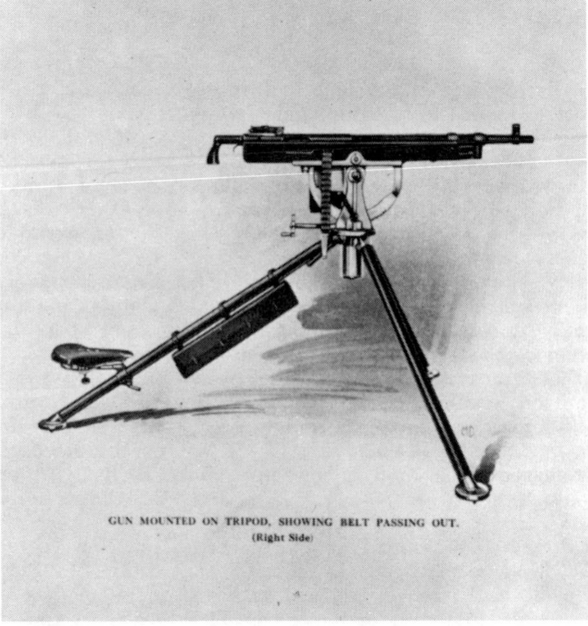

GUN MOUNTED ON TRIPOD, SHOWING BELT PASSING OUT.
(Right Side)

Colt Machine Gun, made by Marlin during World War I.

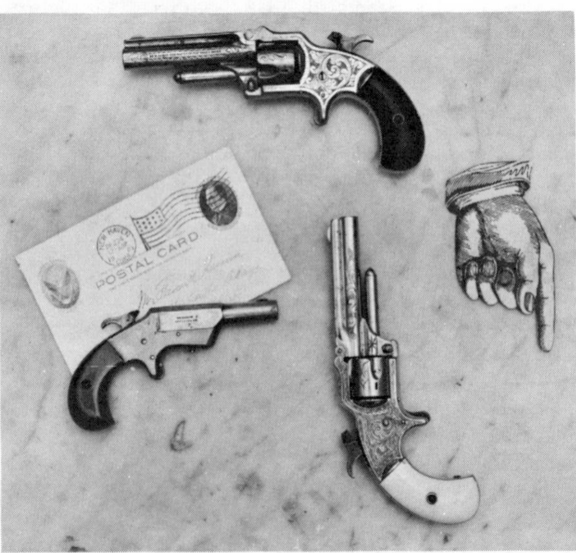

A Marlin OK derringer and two Model 1873 tip-up revolvers.

an improvement over its immediate predecessor, the Henry—the way was paved for the success of repeating rifles. The Winchester Model 1873, in turn, was a vast improvement over the '66. The chief problem was that cartridges for these early repeaters, principally the 44 rimfire and 44-40 WCF, were on the low-power side compared to the big 44 and 45 caliber cartridges developed for the single shots during the 1870s. The greater firepower of the repeaters was of tremendous importance to many shooters, and the heavy-caliber single shots went quickly into a decline. The introduction of the Winchester 1876 in 45-75 WCF caliber, with 350-gr. bullet at slightly under 1400 feet per second muzzle velocity and near 1500 foot pounds of energy, evidently inspired

Marlin to develop the Model 1881, his first lever action repeater. Its initial chambering was for the 45-70-405 U.S. Government cartridge. Eventually it was made in 45-85 Marlin, 40-60 Marlin, 38-55 Ballard and 32-40 Ballard calibers. The 45-85 Marlin case is virtually identical to the 45-70 case. Being loaded with 85 grains of black powder, instead of 70, and with a 285-gr. bullet instead of a 405-gr., the result was higher velocity. Marlin 45-70 and 45-85 rifles were marked "45 Government," as the cartridges were interchangeable.

The Marlin Model 1881 saw production for slightly over 10 years, with about 22,000 manufactured.

John Marlin developed into an astute businessman, with a keen perception in selecting key personnel. For instance, Andrew Burgess, holder of many patents involved with the Whitney-Burgess and Colt-Burgess lever action repeating rifles, worked with Marlin for a time; the Model 1881 incorporated Burgess patents, as well as those of Henry F. Wheeler. Then, in 1886, L. L. Hepburn joined the Marlin firm. Hepburn, a crack shot as well as talented inventor, had been foreman of Remington's mechanical department and a member of the comparatively inexperienced American rifle team that beat the veteran Irish team on Long Island in the famous Creedmoor match in September, 1874.

At the time Hepburn joined Marlin, Winchester had been enjoying excellent sales of repeating rifles chambered for the short-length 44-40, 38-40 and 32-20 WCF cartridges; these were doubly useful in that they were also revolver cartridges. Marlin wanted to tap this market. David Hall Rice invented a short-throw lever action in 1885 and assigned the patent to Marlin. Hepburn improved the action, covered by his patent of the following year. Marlin, in turn, improved the design, and a year later Hepburn put in the finishing touches and the rifle was introduced as the Model 1888. Weighing less than 7 pounds, the new rifle had an advantage over its competitors of 8 pounds and over.

Early awards won by Marlin. Left, 1892 Columbian Exposition; right, 1888 Centennial International Exhibition, Australia.

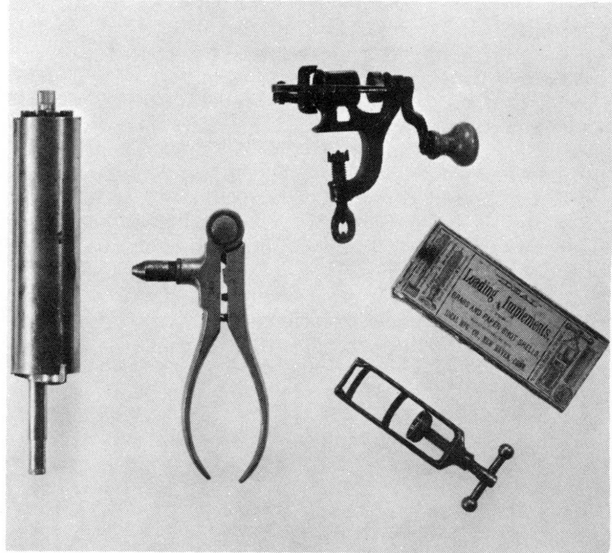

Early Ideal loading tools: From left, hand-held powder measure; Ideal No. 3 tong tool, shotshell roll crimper for bench mounting; hand crimper, with its box.

First Marlin Solid Top

Marlin lever action repeaters up to this point were of top-ejection type, but John Marlin was unhappy with them. The Model 1888, with less than 5,000 produced, was dropped in favor of a radically new type of lever action, the Model 1889. This rifle, with a solid-top receiver and side ejection, was called the "Marlin Safety." It would soon make Marlin world famous.

The Model 1889, advertised as "The strongest, easiest working, safest, simplest and most compact action yet devised," is attributed to the genius of L. L. Hepburn. It came out in September of 1889 and was produced in a variety of styles until May, 1895.

A special example of the 1889 was presented to Annie Oakley in 1890. Made with beautifully executed engraving, including her name, and with super-fancy walnut stock and forearm, Annie used it in her exhibition shooting.

Edward S. Farrow, in his book *American Small Arms**, had this to say about Marlin rifles:

"Marlin rifles have for years been celebrated for their strength, easy working and simplicity of action. The solid top receiver and superior mechanism insure absolute safety to the user. In all these arms, the top of the action, which is the portion coming between the cartridge and the shooter's head, is not cut in any way, but is left as a solid shield, making an accident to the shooter absolutely impossible. In using the old style system, opening on top, there is always

*New York, N.Y. 1904.

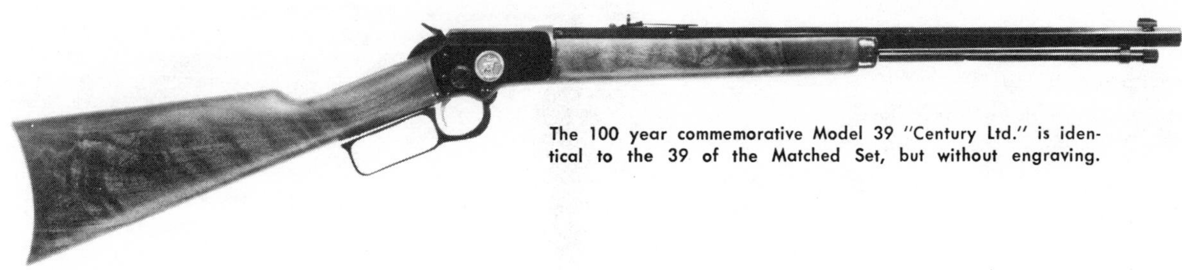

The 100 year commemorative Model 39 "Century Ltd." is identical to the 39 of the Matched Set, but without engraving.

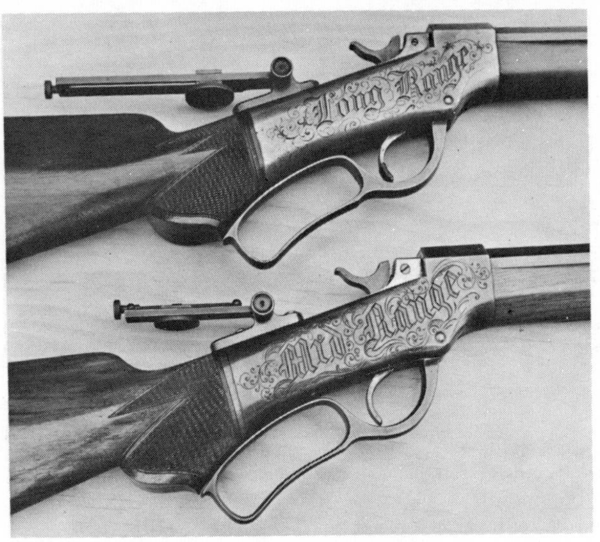

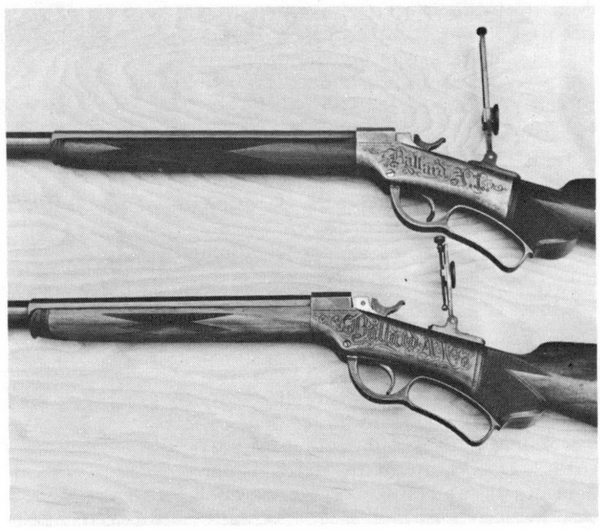

A pair of early, rare and now-expensive Ballard rifles. Above left, the A.1 Long Range, below the A.1 Mid Range, types used at Creedmoor Range on Long Island, N. Y. and elsewhere. Right, left-hand views of the same A-1 Ballard rifles.

a chance of accident and injury, either from defective cartridges giving out around the head, a "hang fire" (the cartridge not exploding immediately on the blow of the firing pin, but a fraction of time later, when perhaps the action is partly open), or some one of the many unaccountables for which guns and ammunition are proverbially famous.

"In this rifle there can be no accident from any of these causes. . . . The side-ejecting principal is a source of great comfort, as well as a matter of safety, for the empty shells never eject into the face; they never cross the line of sight; never interfere with the aim for the next shot; and the eyes and lungs are never filled with smoke and gases. The solid top makes it impossible for rain, snow, falling leaves and twigs, pine-needles, etc., to get into the action, as the top is always closed and consequently the action is protected; there are no crevices for rain, etc., to leak through, and there is no hollow to catch and hold rain."

The Marlin Model 1893 was introduced in 32-40 and 38-55 calibers, black powder cartridges introduced by Marlin in the early 1880s for the Ballard rifle. Winchester first loaded the 38-55 cartridge in 1884, the 32-40 in 1886, offering them in the Winchester Model 94 lever action rifle. The same Winchester was chambered for the smokeless powder 30-30 cartridge in August, 1895. This was a transition period, with smokeless powder loads starting to replace black powder cartridges.

Marlin quickly adapted the Model 1893 for the new 30-30 cartridge, with rifle production beginning in November, 1895. Also to be chambered for the 25-36 Marlin and the 32 Winchester Special cartridges, the '93 was made in a number of versions, including a musket with bayonet.

This famous rifle was revamped to become the Model 1936. The "19" was dropped in 1938, the new designation Model 36. The original square bolt was changed to a round one in 1948, at which time it became the Model 336. That rifle, of course, is still in production, going stronger than ever.

In the meantime, the first of the now-traditional Marlin solid top receiver rifles, the Model 1889, had been phased out in May, 1895. The Marlin 1894 was announced in July of 1894, made in 44-40, 38-40, 32-20 and 25-20. Made in several versions over the

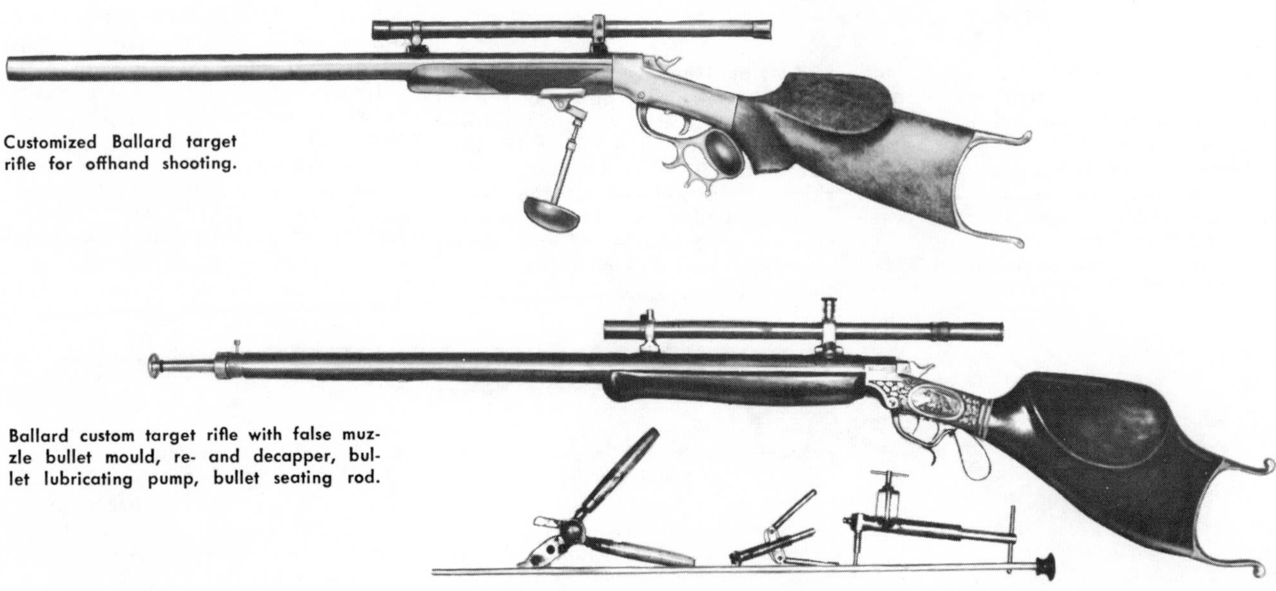

Customized Ballard target rifle for offhand shooting.

Ballard custom target rifle with false muzzle bullet mould, re- and decapper, bullet lubricating pump, bullet seating rod.

Early Marlin centerfire rifles. From the top, Model 1881 45-70, also made in several other heavy calibers. Model 1888, made in 44-40, 38-40 and 32-20 calibers. Model 1889, first Marlin with side ejection, solid top receiver. A fancy example of this model, presented to Annie Oakley, was used in her exhibition shooting. Model 1893, takedown version. The '93, in a number of forms, in calibers 45-70 to 25-36, was produced until the advent of the Model 1936. Model 1893 musket. Model 1894 half-magazine Baby Carbine, made in 44-40 and 38-40. Model 1895, larger-frame rifle or same system as Models 1893 and 1894, was made in early heavy calibers, with last production in 45-70 and 33 WCF in 1915.

years, the '94 was discontinued in 1917.

Revived Model 94

The Marlin Model 1895, made on the same system as the 1893 and 1894 models, had a larger and heavier receiver frame to accommodate a line of larger cartridges. During its 22-year span, until 1917, it was made in a number of calibers—45-90, 45-70, 40-82, 40-70, 40-62, 38-56 and 33 WCF.

In September, 1969, the Model 1894 became available again. This re-creation has the solid-top receiver, side ejection, hand-fitted action and stock of the old original. In fact, it has all of the quality features and traditional craftsmanship, even the square bolt, that made the original Marlin 1894 a favorite sporting arm. This new straight grip, 6-lb. Model 1894, complete with brass saddle ring, is chambered for the potent 44 Magnum cartridge, furnishing 10 fast brush-bucking shots for deer and black bear hunters.

Marlin's first 22 rimfire rifle, the Model 1891, was one of the most famous 22 repeaters ever made — the first to handle 22 Short, Long and Long Rifle cartridges interchangeably without adjustment to the rifle.

Early in 1892 the Model 1891 was also offered in 32 caliber. It was supplied with two firing pins, one for 32 rimfire cartridges, the other for centerfires.

The Model 1891 was discontinued in mid-1895, but Marlin had the Model 1892 ready for production at the same time. It was manufactured until 1916. Here is a quote from the 1915 Marlin catalog:

"The Model 1892 32 caliber Rifle is the only repeating rifle that uses the cheap but powerful and accurate 32 rimfire cartridges. It handles without changes in adjustment the 32 Short, 32 Long and 32 Long Rifle cartridge, and by substituting the extra firing pin (sent free with the rifle) it handles the 32 Short, Long and Long Rifle centerfire cartridges. It is especially recommended for rabbit, woodchucks, foxes and all small game up to 200 yards."

The Marlin Model 1897, similar to the 1892, had a take-down action and was made in 22 rimfire only, of course, taking Short, Long and Long Rifle cartridges interchangeably. The 1897 rifle was a bit expensive, for Marlin catalogs said: "It costs more to make and will cost you more than the other 22 rifles—but it's the best 22 caliber repeater in the world if you are willing to pay for it."

Model 39 Appears

After World War I the Model 1897 ceased to exist, but it was improved in 1922 to become the Model 39. Since then, the 39 has been manufactured in several versions, all retaining the time-proven drop-forged and machined receivers, and it still is in production. Besides the commemorative models, it is available in rifle form as the 39A, with pistol-grip stock and 24-inch barrel, and as the 39 Mountie, with straight grip and 20-inch barrel.

Over the years Marlin produced various other 22s—the pump action Model 18, called the Marlin Baby Repeater, had an exposed hammer and was made from 1906 until 1908. By changing carriers (two came with the rifle) it could handle 22 Short or Long Rifle cartridges. The Model 20, made from 1907 to 1922, looked like the 18 but was of take-down construction. The Model 27, 1910 to 1932, was an-

Early Marlin rifles. From the top—Model 1892 in 22 rimfire, a revamped 1891; Model 1891, 22 Short, Long and Long Rifle, also made in 32 Long rimfire and, with extra firing pin, for 32 Long centerfire; Model 1897, 22 rimfire, essentially the 1892, but a take-down. Replaced by the Model 39 rimfire 22 in 1922, next in its early take-down form; Model 20, a hammer-type pump action 22, Introduced 1907, discontinued 1921. Model 38, a hammerless pump action 22, introduced 1914, discontinued 1930.

other pump action made in two versions; one for the 25-20 or 32-20 centerfire cartridges, the other for the 25 Stevens rimfire.

Marlin's first hammerless pump action 22 was the Model 32, introduced in late 1914, followed after World War I by the hammerless Model 38.

The Model 25 was a single shot, bolt-action rifle, introduced in 1932. After that, a variety of bolt-actions, single shot and repeaters, as well as 22 autoloaders, were put on the market.

John M. Marlin entered the shotgun business with the Model 1898 (discontinued in 1905) a solid frame, hammer type, pump action of 12 gauge. The Model 16 (1904) was identical but in 16 gauge, while the Model 17 (1906) was a 12-gauge economy version. The Model 19 (1906) a 12 gauge take-down with pistol grip, lasted a year. Then came a number of models including the Model 21 Trap Gun.

The Marlin 1915 catalog lists hammerless pump-action Models 28 and 31 in 12, 16 and 20 gauge, and Models 24, 26 and 30 with exposed hammers. These shotguns were made in many versions, with numerous extras available.

When John Mahlon Marlin died in 1901, his two sons, Mahlon H. and J. Howard Marlin, took over the business as president and vice president respectively. During the period from 1901 until 1915, when they ran the company, a great many changes were made in the Marlin rifle and shotgun lines, and with some diversification. For instance, although evidence indicates that Marlin made bullet moulds as early as 1881, this end of the business was not vigorously promoted. The sons, desiring to expand this field, negotiated with John H. Barlow for the acquisition of the Ideal Manufacturing Co. Ideal, founded in 1884, made tools of all kinds for reloading ammunition.

As many shooters know, the name "Ideal" now belongs to the Lyman Gun Sight Corp., Middlefield, Conn. They acquired it from Marlin in 1925, and used it on their handbooks until the 41st edition appeared in 1957. Everyone who handloads ammunition knows the *Lyman Reloader's Handbook,* a direct descendant of the old Barlow and Marlin *Handbook of Useful Information for Shooters.*

With World War I in progress, 1915 proved to be a decisively important year for Marlin for it ended the family regime. A New York syndicate, headed by A. F. Rockwell, bought the company in December for approximately $1,500,000 and renamed it the Marlin Rockwell Corporation. The objective was to produce military arms, and during the war Marlin-Rockwell set records for machine-gun production for the United States, members of the Triple Entente and other Allies.

When the war was over and massive military production was at an end, Rockwell—with no interest in manufacturing sporting firearms — turned to fields that seemed more profitable. The gun operation slipped away by default.

In 1920, John Moran—former general manager of the Mayo Radiator Corp., also acquired by Marlin-Rockwell during the war—took over management of the old Marlin plant. His chief engineer and plant superintendent was A. W. "Gus" Swebilius, a brilliant engineer who later formed the High Standard Manufacturing

U-D (United Defense) 9mm submachinegun, first made by Marlin for the Dutch government early in World War II, later parachute-dropped to underground forces.

Co., maker of Hi-Standard guns.

It was a tough job converting back to peacetime production — but the Model 38 hammerless rimfire rifle, mentioned earlier, was developed. Soon, however, financing became a great problem, and the firm went on the auction block in 1924.

Kenna Regime

The story goes that on the day that the company was offered to the highest bidder, Frank Kenna was in the audience. Besides him, the group consisted of several curious children and a small dog. The New Haven County Sheriff is said to have asked, "Frank, why don't you bid this in?" Kenna replied, "I'll give $100" and a moment later the properties were his —complete with a $100,000 mortgage.

Frank Kenna, a leading New Haven lawyer and astute business executive with a long list of successful ventures behind him, entered the new field with his usual vigor. For an all-out effort to bring the company back to its former prominence in the production of sporting firearms, he eventually needed financing. He decided to offer stock to the public. Between 1926 and 1930 8% preferred stock at $25 par value was offered to investors with, as inducement, one share of common stock to be included with every four shares of preferred. Then, in 1931, when more financing was needed, the company offered 7% preferred stock, par value $25. This time the inducement was a Marlin rifle or shotgun free with a purchase of four or more shares of the preferred issue.

As a result of Frank Kenna's keen insight and great energy, Marlin made and sold more sporting rifles and shotguns during 1936 than at any other time in the company's history. In 1937 that outstanding record was exceeded!

With the sound idea that a manufacturer should have some degree of diversification, Kenna entered the safety razor blade field in 1936 with a production plant established in Newark, N. J. By 1947, one billion Marlin blades had been made.

Between the World Wars a great many new sporting firearms were designed, developed and produced at the Marlin plant. The Model 90, Marlin's only over-and-under shotgun, was introduced, with double triggers, in 1937. It was announced in single-trigger form just before World War II, but actual production was not achieved until 1954, at which time it was the only over-under shotgun made in America. In 1958 the single trigger gun sold for $139.95. In 1959 it was discontinued because of rising production costs and lack of interest among American shooters in double barrel shotguns. Today, those guns are known to bring premium prices.

With World War II on, civilian production of rifles and shotguns was halted. Marlin concentrated on production of aircraft fittings, M-1 rifle and carbine barrels, ammunition belts and a light 9mm sub-machine gun for the Netherlands Commission.

After the war Marlin, quickly retooled for sporting arms production, was one of the first American companies to convert from military to civilian production.

In late 1945 Marlin acquired the assets of the Hunter Arms Co. in Fulton, N. Y., and re-established the business as the L. C. Smith Gun Co. The new division produced some 56,000 L. C. Smith double-barrel shotguns before the gun was discontinued in 1950 because of the then-limited market.

The double gun has now regained some of its old popularity, and Marlin has re-introduced the famous side-

Early Marlin shotguns. From the top, Model 17 pump action shotgun, introduced 1906. This gun, as well as later Models 16, 19, 21 and 24, has the same general appearance of the original 1898 hammer gun. Take-down Model 30, in 16 and 20 gauges, was produced from 1911 to 1915. Model 44, a 20 gauge, is similar in appearance to the 43 (12 gauge), the 31 (16 and 20) and the Model 28, a 12 gauge, Marlin's first hammerless shotgun, introduced 1913. Model 60, a single shot; only 600 of these were assembled in 1923. Tom Mix's Marlin Model 90 over-and-under shotgun.

Frank Kenna, Sr., bought the assets and liabilities of the Marlin Co. for $100 at an auction sale in 1924.

Frank Kenna, Jr., President of the Marlin Firearms Co.

lock L. C. Smith shotgun in 12 gauge and sold with a written lifetime guarantee.*

Frank Kenna died in 1947 and was succeeded by his eldest son Roger. Following through with his father's policy—improving Marlin guns and vigorously developing new products to place the company in a strong competitive field — Roger's direction in sales and production programs led to more units being produced and sold than ever before.

Micro-Groove Rifling

In 1953 the company announced their new Micro-Groove rifling system, designed to spin the bullet effectively in flight for stabilization, but with less distortion during its passage through the barrel, resulting in increased accuracy. Instead of the usual 4 to 6 lands, a larger number of smaller lands of patented shape are used. Records of careful and extensive testing at the Marlin plant with 22 rimfire barrels show an average gain in accuracy performance of 20 to 25 per cent compared to results obtained with conventional-type barrels. Micro-Groove rifling was first made available in a Marlin semi-automatic 22 caliber rifle. Further extensive testing with the new rifling form in high velocity centerfire arms was concluded in 1956. Results were so highly successful that the company decided to make all Marlin barrels, centerfire and rimfire, with Micro-Groove rifling.

When Roger Kenna died in 1959, his brother Frank Kenna, Jr., took the guiding reins in hand. Now President of Marlin, Frank joined the organization in 1948, became a director in 1950, and was Plant Works Manager before assuming the Presidency.

Frank, an experienced shooter and hunter as well as a knowledgeable sporting firearms maker, knows both sides of the fence and has directed his efforts accordingly. He was responsible for the rebirth of the L. C. Smith shotgun, and new items for the shooter-sportsman are in constant development.

A major new project was the planning and building of a completely modern factory at 100 Kenna Drive in North Haven, Conn. The complex has some 250,000 square feet of working space, practically all of it on one level. Two indoor ranges, one of 100 yards, are used for checking function and accuracy of rifles.

An interesting feature of the new plant, from an efficiency standpoint, is the production procedure. Raw materials, entering the huge building at one end, are processed into finished shooter products by the time they reach the other end—all packaged and ready for shipment.

L. C. Smith double barrel shotgun, first made by Marlin in late 1945 or early 1946, shown with semi-beavertail fore-end, standard on Ideal and higher grades after July, 1949.

Back in 1958 Marlin introduced the Micro-Vue 4-power telescope sight for use on 22 rimfire rifles receiver-grooved for tip-off bases. The following year the company announced their Micro-Power scopes in 2½x and 4x for centerfire rifles. A plan was instituted that enabled the customer to save substantially with the purchase of certain rifle and scope combinations. The policy is still in effect with the new Marlin "Plus Power" line of scopes, affording a saving of from slightly under $5 to almost $13, depending on the rifle-scope combination.

Marlin currently lists nearly 30 models of rifles and shotguns, and for detail specifications of each see our U.S. Rifle and Shotgun Review pages as well as our Scope & Mount sections in this issue of Gun Digest. ●

*See Gerald R. Hunter's full-length article on the new L. C. Smith elsewhere in this 24th edition.

New Marlin complex, built on 23 acres in North Haven, Conn., has 250,000 square feet of working space.

SEATING DEPTH VS CHAMBER PRESSURE

Does deeper bullet seating—as we've long been told—result automatically in raised pressure? In all cartridges? We don't know all the answers yet, but here is a first step in controlled, laboratory determinations of pressure levels in relation to seating depth of bullets.

by GEORGE C. NONTE, JR.
and JOHN T. AMBER

I CAN'T remember when there hasn't been some sort of argument going on about the effect variations in bullet seating depth might have on chamber pressure. As old as this controversy is, one would think that some definitive testing would surely have been done at one time or another, and recorded for posterity.

A few months ago I was reminded of this lack of real data when John Amber told me of his long-time skepticism of the claim made by numerous writers in the past—that increased seating depth would automatically result in increased chamber pressure (hence increased velocity as well, one infers).

John said he believed that the *reverse* might well be the case, citing as one point of evidence that pundits on handloading generally warned against seating rifle bullets, at least, so far out that the ogive would be forced into the beginning of the rifling, thus *increasing* pressure.

John said he felt this situation made sense, in that the bullet in such case would require more force or pressure to get it moving than would be the case with the bullet some degree back from the rifling, when it could, in effect, get a running start. Ergo, if that *was* true, didn't it follow that a further increase in seating depth (the bullet farther into the case and farther removed from the rifling beginning) should result in lessened psi, not more?

At this point, it seemed like a good time to start digging into it. Surely someone somewhere had obtained a positive answer.

Not so. Poring through dozens of pamphlets and books, and hundreds of old shooting magazines produced not a single, *provable* statement on the subject. Quite a number of people had voiced their opinions, but there were no records of controlled tests conducted with proper equipment to find out whether they had the right idea.

Tests Started

John Amber and I decided to load up a batch of ammunition and run some pressure tests, using two quite different cartridges loaded with different powders and operating at considerably different pressure levels. The venerable 30-06 was chosen as representative of the modern, high-intensity, bottle-neck rifle type; the 357 Magnum as a relatively low-pressure number using a straight, cylindrical case. Differences in bullet type and configuration were also considered.

We publish this report, necessarily inconclusive at this time, with the hope that others will be induced to conduct similar tests. The Gun Digest will continue its own investigation.

Both were to be loaded to pressures and velocities closely approximating those of factory loadings. To this end, the 180-gr. 30-caliber (Hornady SP) bullet and 56 grains of 4350 powder was chosen for the '06. According to published data, this would give us about 2700 fps, approximating the standard factory load. Trouble was encountered immediately, in that this powder charge did not allow bullets to be seated deeply enough to conduct the tests we'd set up. A reduction to 54 grains solved the problem, allowing bullets to be seated as deeply as we wanted with only slight compression of the charge. With normal seating depth, this load produced just a wee bit under 2600 fps—high enough to make the tests valid. Dupont 4350 was chosen because of today's tendency toward using slow burning powder in charges that very nearly fill the case.

With this much settled, 10-round test lots were assembled in new Federal cases. Five lots were loaded, numbered 1 through 5. No. 3 was the "standard" load, with the bullet seated to the base of case neck. The two lots on either side of this had their seating depths varied by approximately .050", resulting in the following over-all cartridge lengths: Lot 1, 3.310"; Lot 2, 3.260"; Lot 3, 3.205", Lot 4, 3.160"; Lot 5, 3.110".

The shallowest seating depth (Lot 1) produced a loaded cartridge in which the bullet would just barely clear the throat of Bruce Hodgdon's Modern Bond Universal pressure barrel, while the deep-seated bullet (Lot 5) resulted in the case neck overhanging the bullet ogive. Certainly, this spread represents as much variation in seating depth as the average handloader is likely to produce, inadvertently or otherwise. The 0.200" total spread between seating depths may not seem like much on paper, but is difficult to exceed while still having a cartridge that will function in the average 30-06 rifle.

In the meantime arrangements had been made with Hodgdon for simultaneous recording of both velocity and pressure results with our test loads.

First Test Results

The test cartridges were shipped off to the Hodgdon lab, and, in due time, a complete velocity and pressure report was received. Hodgdon felt that the degree of shot-to-shot uniformity noted by them made it possible to settle for 5-shot tests, so he did not run the full 10 rounds of each lot. The results, extracted from the test report, will be found in Table 1.

The extreme pressure spread between individual rounds of the 5 lots was 3800 psi—from 40,800 (Lots 1, 3 & 4) to 44,600 (Lots 1, 2 & 4). Lots 1 and 4 contained both high and low pressures. The extreme spread between lot averages was only 800 psi—43,000 to 42,200. Now it has long been established that even finely accurate ammunition will often produce shot-to-shot variations greater than that.

These values showed far less pressure and velocity variation (average) than we expected. To determine if this test had produced fluke results, it seemed logical to go further. This time 20-round lots of each 30-06 load were made up (still from the same lots of components) and shipped off to the renowned H. P. White Laboratory, in Bel Air, Maryland. Instructions were to run simultaneous pressure and velocity tests of the full 20 rounds of each seating depth.

The test report received included both copper-crusher and Piezo-electric pressure values for each of the 100 test rounds. The complete report is too lengthy to reproduce here, but the averages and extreme spreads can be seen in Table 2.

Until receipt of this report we thought we had something going. The Hodgdon report, reading averages only, indicates that as seating depth increased, from the norm, so did pressure and velocity—and that decreased seating depth *also* produced increases in pressure and velocity.

Thus it will be seen that in this test, at least, no particular pattern emerged—as noted, MV and ME increased, if only slightly, with both increased and decreased seating depth.

The more extensive H. P. White test did not confirm this. Instead, except for Lot 5 producing a niggardly 1 fps more than Lot 4, velocity decreased as seating depth *increased,* and increased as seating depth decreased. With the exception of a similar reversal in the same lots, pressures reacted identically.

Since bullets could not be seated deeper with this charge, we couldn't extend the test. The fact that Lot 5 produced slightly greater pressure and velocity than Lot 4 indicates that, if extended to greater seating depth, the White tests would show the same pattern as the Hodgdon. This can be explained, perhaps, by some difference in throating and chambering between the two barrels. Where in the Hodgdon barrel lowest pressure and velocity were produced by Lot 3, Lot 4 did so in the White barrel.

Thus, when the curve of the White tests is projected, it assumes the same general shape as the Hodgdon curve shown on the accompanying graph. The quantitative difference in P and V values shown in the two graphs are due simply to the many minor differences between the two pressure barrels used. It is an established fact that no two barrels will produce identical results with the same load.

Having studied these tests and considered all other available information we have reached this conclusion: in a high-intensity bottle neck cartridge loaded to near-100% density with a slow-burning single base powder, a certain bullet-seating depth

TABLE 1—HODGDON TEST
CALIBER 30-06

Lot	Velocity, average	Velocity, ex. spread	Pressure, crusher	Pressure, ex. spread
1	2594 fps	61	42,400 psi	3,800
2	2590	30	42,800	3,200
3	2576	46	42,200	3,300
4	2587	28	43,000	3,800
5	2590	45	43,000	1,300

5 shots each lot.

180-gr. Hornady SP, Federal cases and primers (210). 54-grs. 4350 powder. Modern Bond 26" pressure barrel, .308" groove dia., 1-10" twist. 68° F. Pressures are copper-crusher values.

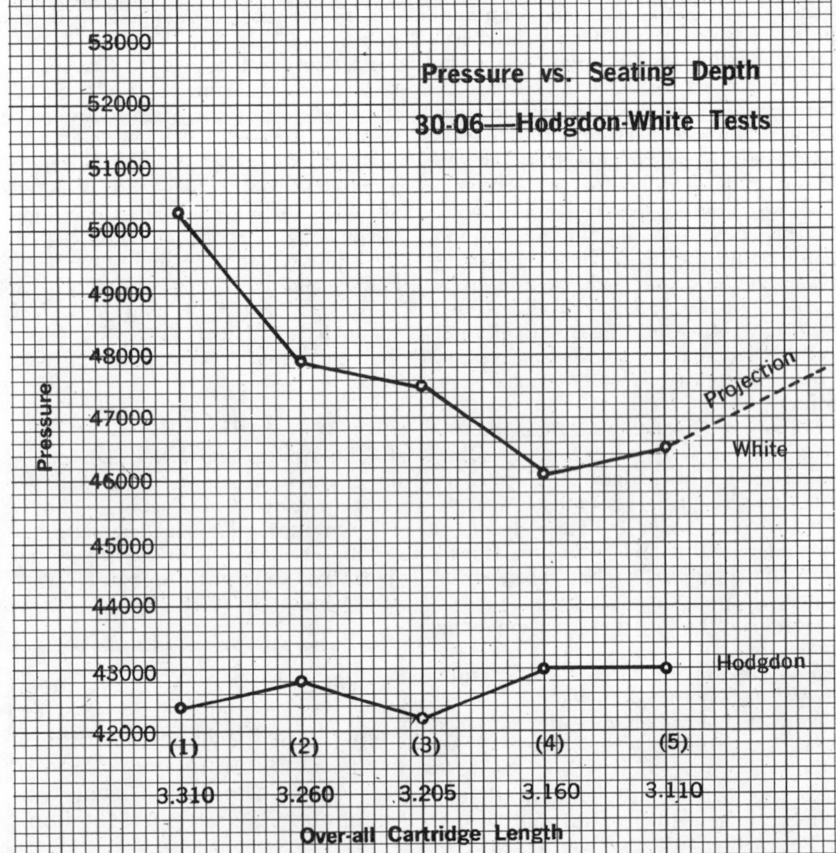

will produce minimum pressure and velocity in any given gun/load combination; that this seating depth will vary from gun to gun; that *either* increasing or decreasing seating from that particular seating depth will cause an *increase* in pressure and velocity.

Of course these conclusions apply only to cartridges of the 30-06 class and bullets and powders approximating those used. A 110-gr. bullet and a faster powder like 3031 might well behave in a different manner. A case with considerably different capacity/bore area relationship could probably be expected to behave somewhat differently. At this point we only *know* what this one load will do. Much more testing is required before any general statements can be made.

357 Magnum Tests

So much for the bottle-neck rifle numbers. Take a look at Table 3, which contains the results of similar tests of the 357 Magnum. The tests were conducted by Lee Jurras, of Super-Vel Cartridge Corp. Pressure/velocity was measured simultaneously in a 6″ one-piece (no barrel/cylinder gap) pressure barrel. Pressures were measured by a strain gauge setup, rather than the conventional copper crusher system. The strain gauge measures absolute pressure, while copper crusher measurement is based on long-ago arbitrary approximations. Consequently, copper crusher measurements, beyond a certain psi level, will indicate *less* pressure than a strain gauge. For our purposes here, this difference in values does not matter. We are interested far more in pressure/seating depth relationship than in actual pressures. The strain gauge system is more consistent and less dependent on the operator's technique for accuracy than is the crusher setup. Simply for comparison, Jurras ran concurrent tests on some factory 357 loads, the results showing his test setup to be working perfectly.

Five 10-round test lots were loaded in new Remington uncannelured 357 cases with SAC primers, 15 grains of Hercules 2400 powder and Speer 146-gr. jacketed hollow-point bullets. Cases were crimped moderately on the bullet. Seating depth was varied from the maximum cartridge length that can be accommodated by average 357 revolver cylinders (1.66″) to the maximum depth the bullet could be inserted and still be crimped in place (1.50″). This resulted in over-all lengths as follows: Lot 1, 1.66″; 2, 1.62″; 3, 1.58″; 4, 1.54″ and 5, 1.50″. Lot 3 at 1.58″ represents standard seating depth for this bullet. This load closely approximates factory-load velocity and is generally considered just a bit "warm," though the average pressure measured in these tests is below that of W-W and Norma factory loads.

Looking at the test results we see that the shallowest seating depth produced 1435 fps and 22,170 psi, the deepest, 1505 fps and 23,400 psi. However, the line graphs show that neither pressure nor velocity, followed a neat, simple pattern between the maximum and minimum seating depths. Pressure increased steadily as seating depth was increased through Lots 1, 2, and 3, then leveled off with Lot 4. Lot 5 showed a measurable drop in pressure, but of only 20 psi. That small a change (only 0.08%) can't be considered significant in only a 10-round test. A longer test, say at least 20 rounds (as in the White 30-06 test) would undoubtedly eliminate so minor an excursion from the established pattern. For all practical purposes, though, the tests indicate that increasing seating depth produces a corresponding increase in pressure.

Velocity follows essentially the same pattern except for Lot 2, which produced 10 fps less than Lot 1. Lot 2 produced the lowest velocity, but not the lowest pressure, as can be seen in the graphs. It seems strange that in producing 320 *more* psi than Lot 1, Lot 2 developed 10 fps *less*. In reality, though, these differences are very small percentage-wise (1.44% and 0.7,% respectively), and would probably be cancelled out in more extensive tests.

Subject to the same reservations made in the case of the 30-06, these limited tests lead us to conclude logically that in straight cylindrical cases used in revolvers, a decrease from the norm in seating depth, i.e., seating bullets farther out, will produce a corresponding decrease in both velocity and pressure. Increased seating depth produces an increase in both pressure and velocity.

We cannot, however, at this time, say whether this would hold true in the case of loads varying greatly in

TABLE 2—H. P. WHITE TEST

CALIBER 30-06

Lot	Velocity, average	Velocity ex. spread	Pressure, crusher	Pressure, ex. spread
1	2678 fps	93	50,280 psi	6,800
2	2647	94	47,975	7,100
3	2630	66	47,475	4,100
4	2602	65	46,150	4,500
5	2603	**109**	46,515	7,800

Same components as in Table 1.

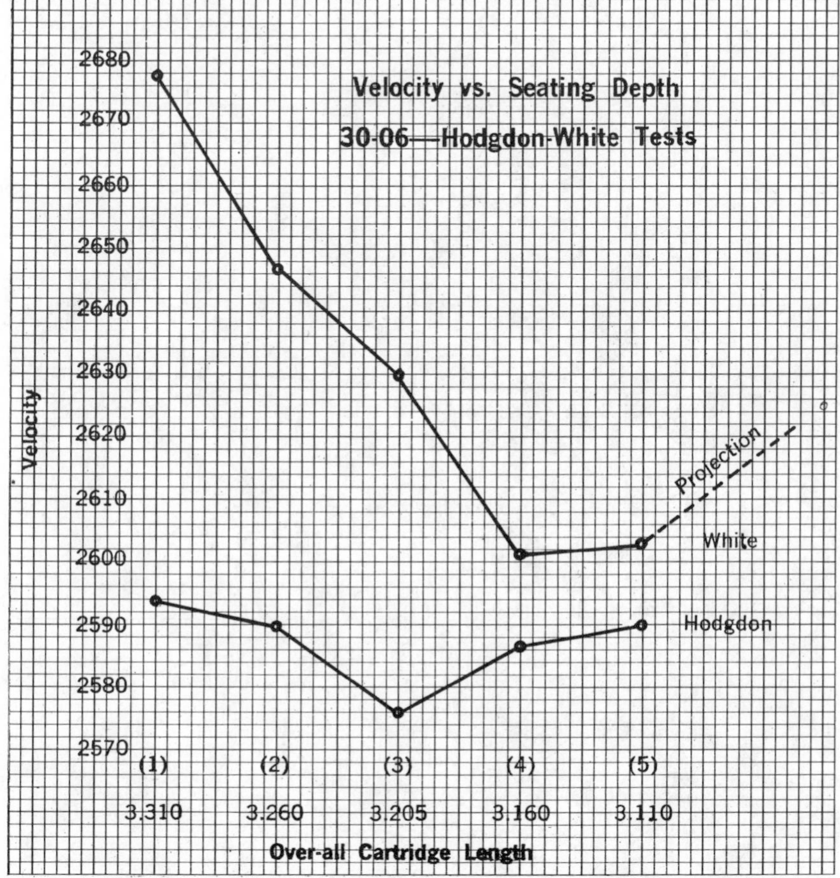

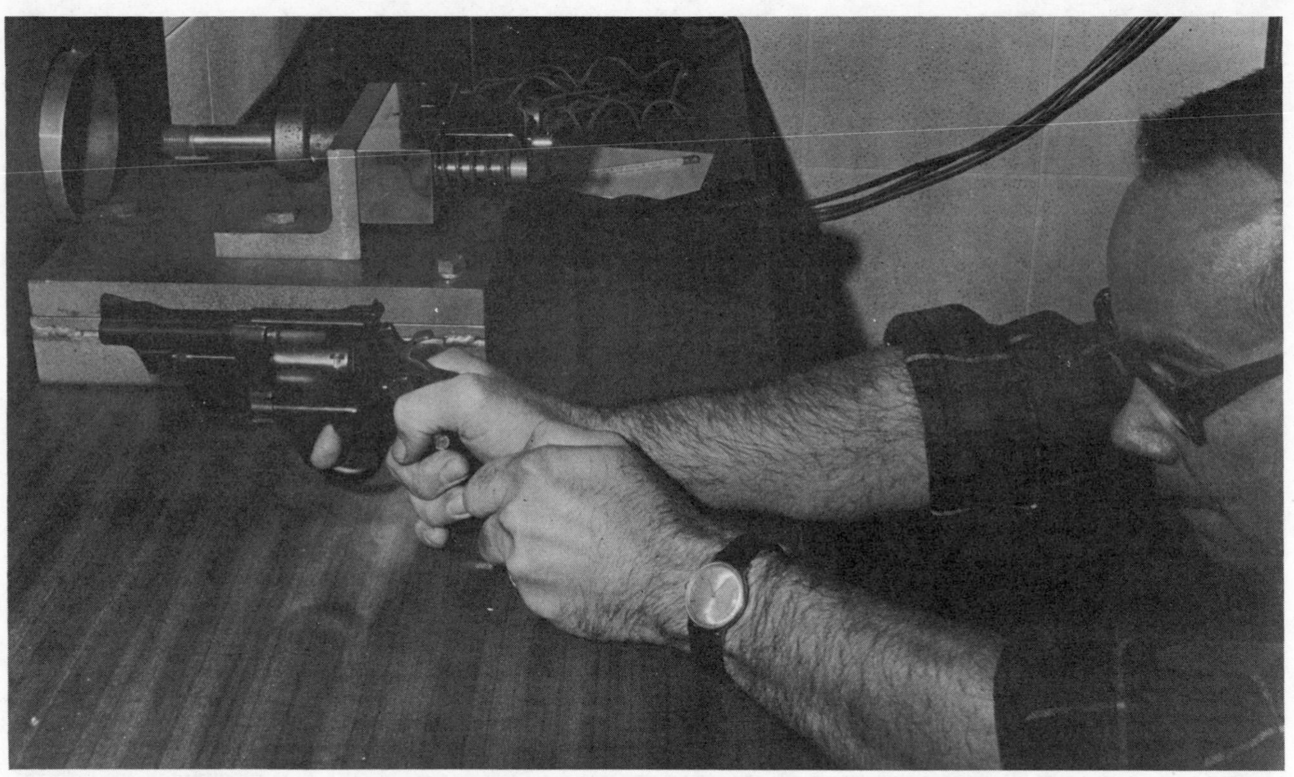

Above—Lee Jurras, President, Super Vel Cartridge Co., testfiring a S&W revolver in his lab at Shelbyville, Ind. Below—This view of the Super Vel lab shows the pressure barrel ready for testfiring.

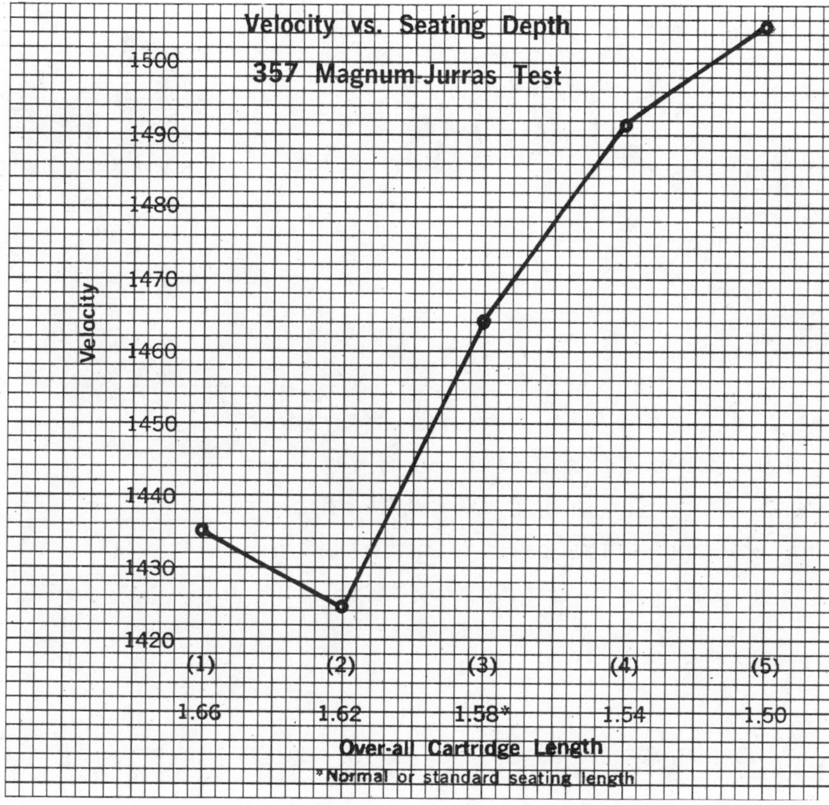

TABLE 3—JURRAS TEST 357 MAGNUM

Lot	Velocity, average	Velocity, ex. spread	Pressure, average	Pressure, ex. spread
1	1435 fps	66	22,170 psi	2,200
2	1425	65	22,590	2,300
3	1464	64	23,380	1,800
4	1491	64	23,420	1,200
5	1505	76	23,400	2,300

For over-all cartridge lengths, see graph.

146-gr. Speer JHP, Remington cases. 15-grs. 2400 powder, SacMag primers. 6" pressure barrel, .356 groove dia. 80° F. Strain-gauge pressure system.

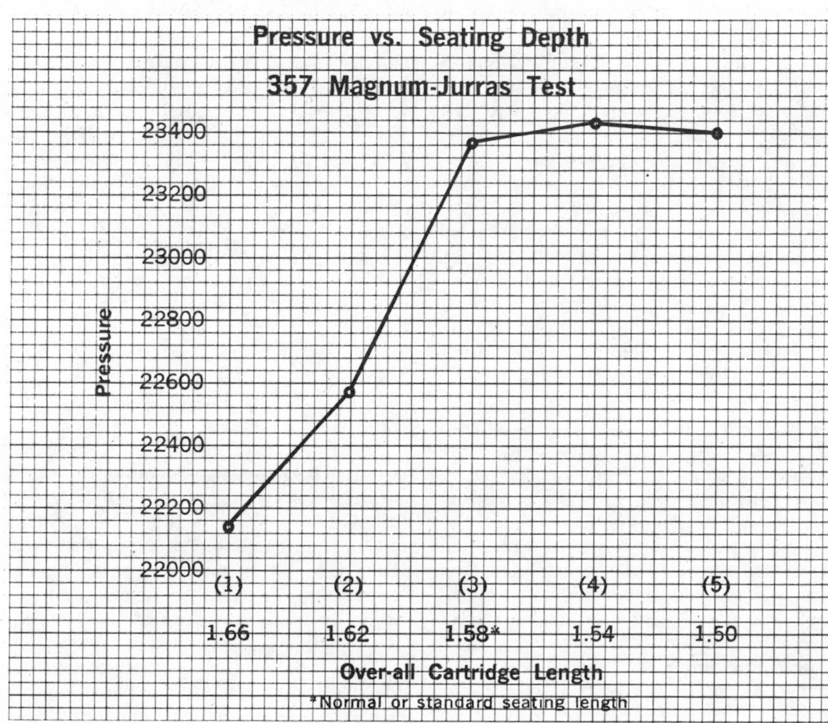

loading density, powder type, bullet type, etc., from the load tested. We do know now that it holds true for full-charge 357 Magnum loads with 2400 powder and jacketed bullets. We *may* safely expect it to hold true for similar loads in 38 Special, 41 Magnum and 44 Magnum, but that is as far as we'll stick our necks out.

While the results of these two series of tests did not prove to be as conclusive as we would like to present, two clearly defined, different patterns have emerged—one for the 30-06 class of cartridge; one for the magnum-type revolver cartridge, both loaded with relatively slow-burning powders.

Some Conclusions

By placing pressure and velocity curves for the two cartridges side by side and ignoring the minor excursions, two patterns are clearly evident. The '06 curve forms a wide "U," the low point representing the seating depth that produces lowest pressure and velocity and indicating that deviation *either way* from that point will produce increased pressure and velocity. On the other hand, the 357 curves show that pressure and velocity vary directly with seating depth.

While the effects of seating depth are certainly large enough to be seen clearly on paper, they are of considerably less magnitude than we had expected. For example, the spread between the five '06 lots is only 69 fps and 3800 psi in the Hodgdon tests, 76 fps and 4130 psi in the White tests. Greater variations than that are frequently encountered in single lots of the same load.

In a rifle cartridge of this class, the effects of such variations are not likely to show up at the target except from a finely-accurate bench rest rifle under good conditions. On game, I defy anyone to show me a visible difference in killing power produced by so small a velocity change. Even the maximum individual shot spread in the 100-round White tests was only 151 fps. Maximum individual pressure spread in the same tests was 11,600 psi, which seems rather high compared with the velocity spread. However, it is velocity, not pressure, that affects bullet performance.

Inasmuch as the 357 is a relatively short-range handgun proposition, the larger (percentage-wise) variations produced by seating depth changes are not likely to be noticeable on target. Nor are the pressure changes of sufficient magnitude to cause concern for the gun's safety.

In wrapping this up, we do want to express our appreciation to Bruce Hodgdon, Lee Jurras, and the H. P. White laboratories. Without their assistance and cooperation, we wouldn't have this data. ●

Sporting Arms of the

Today many of our old-line U.S. armsmakers obtain some of their models from abroad. The one-time clear distinction between those who made and sold firearms here and the gun importers has become nebulous and blurred. This year we mix 'em up, too!

by CHARLES ASKINS, BOB STEINDLER

Gun Controls

THE PASSAGE of the Gun Control Act of 1968 and the subsequent confusion engendered by the Alcohol, Tobacco and Firearms Division's efforts to interpret its provisions makes any discussion about imported firearms difficult.

Outlawed are all destructive devices, of course, and all military small arms, including rifles and pistols. While some importers of surplus arms still have a lot of interesting items to offer, once the warehouses have been emptied, there ain't going to be any more!

While the original draft of the import regulations drawn up by the ATFD appeared to restrict imports to those firearms for which no equivalents were made in the U.S., current rules (end of January, '69) seemingly permit importation of bolt action rifles, all types of sporting shotguns, even some handguns.

During the NSGA show in February, 1969, four top members of ATFD were present to discuss the legality of importing some handguns. At that moment, the rules were roughly this: no handgun with a barrel shorter than 4" would be permitted into the country. Barrel lengths would have to be 4 and 6 inches. One importer I talked with brings in handguns with barrels 4, 5, 6 and 7 inches long. Only the 4- and 6-inch guns were considered legal!

ATFD rules also rate imported handguns very much like a high school quiz, with points being given for each feature. One company has for years imported single action 22 RF revolvers. Since chamber pressure of such cartridges is not spectacular, there was nothing wrong with having some parts of the gun, such as the cylinder, machined from alloy castings instead of solid steel. First the ATFD accepted alloy castings, then reversed itself and outlawed the same features that had been accepted the day before.

Many importers have always dealt through the regular wholesaler-retailer outlets, but a number worked directly with the buying public. These importers no longer can sell to you, the consumer. Like all other gun companies, they must now go through a dealer, thus increasing the cost of the gun at your end. The consumer must now place his order with a local dealer, always provided the sale is legal in the state or other political division where the transaction takes place. The dealer must enter all guns received on his inventory sheet, by ATFD ruling, and then has to—after he sells the gun or guns to you—again enter all pertinent details of the transaction into his permanent firearms record book. In effect, any gun sold after 16 December '68 has been registered, and your name has been permanently recorded as the owner of that particular gun.

This record keeping of firearms sales has been in effect since the middle 1930s, of course, by federal law, so there's nothing really new about it except for the sharply increased number and type of questions the ultimate buyer is asked.

Whether the new law will be any more rigidly enforced than the old one remains to be seen. Did you know that the very *first* prosecution under the old—and quite stout—law took place only a year or so ago?

Imported ammunition, such as Eley's Tenex and Speer's line of DWM cartridges, may be more difficult to get. Ammo shipments can only be made from a licensed manufacturer or importer to a federally licensed dealer. Shipping small lots of ammo has always been expensive, and the service charge a dealer must tack onto the ammo price you want from an importer must be borne by you. Therefore, you should buy imported ammunition in larger lots—say 100 rounds of a metric cartridge rather than the 20 rounds you perhaps bought two or three times a year. Again, every ammo sale is recorded for posterity and the ATFD—and this is truly a *new* law. An amendment to the GCA '68 is now before Congress to remove or modify ammo restrictions, but what the fate of the amendment will be remains a question.

GCA '68 has had a profound effect on the firearms business, sharply curtailing many operations, shutting

World

▪ Browning ▪ Century ▪ Champlin ▪ Daly ▪ Fajen ▪ Galef ▪ Garcia/Beretta ▪ Ithaca ▪ Marlin ▪ Mossberg ▪ Navy Arms ▪ Remington ▪ Savage ▪ Sharps ▪ Smith & Wesson ▪ Weatherby ▪ Winchester plus—▪ Agawam ▪ American Import ▪ Apache ▪ ArmaLite ▪ Atlas ▪ Carter ▪ Centennial ▪ Davidson ▪ Europa ▪ Fessler ▪ F.I. ▪ Flaig ▪ Interarms ▪ J-K Imports ▪ Jana Int'l ▪ LAD ▪ McKeown ▪ Mowery ▪ Numrich ▪ Harry Owen ▪ Plainfield ▪ Ranger ▪ Replica ▪ Richland ▪ Tradewinds ▪ Universal ▪ Dan Wesson ▪ Rifle and Shotgun Gear

and the editors

down others completely. A few companies with larger dealer chains may have benefitted.

Imported sporting and target arms, rifled and smoothbore, will probably continue to be available.

Aside from barrel lengths and metallurgic requirements, handguns suitable only for competitive shooting or hunting are being let into the country, but defensive guns and plinkers are outlawed. Handgun plinking is the most popular way of burning up a couple of boxes of ammo, so if you still enjoy plinking and assaulting beer cans, you'll do it with domestic handguns.

Keep in mind that every ammo purchase is recorded for ATFD and that someday you may have to explain what you did with a box of 22s.

Another word of caution, Time was when an American abroad could buy a gun in a foreign country, and bring it back with him as personal property, providing he declared it and paid the necessary customs fee. If you now buy a foreign-made gun outside the U.S., you won't be able to bring it in unless you have a federal import license. Firearms import licenses are now procured through the ATFD, not the State Department, as formerly. Although import licenses are being granted, they are restricted to legitimate importers, though a dealer/jobber could obtain one under certain conditions. John Citizen may well find it impossible to get an import license.

In the past (before GCA '68) ATTU regional directors and, in some cases, even industrial agents, made and enforced decisions affecting the legal status of various guns *despite contrary* rulings or judicious decrees prevailing in other federal areas or in Washington.

This problem has been once again brought to the attention of ATFD top officials and, we understand, such regional aberrant decisions will no longer be permitted.

YOU SOMETIMES HEAR shooters voice the complaint that there are too many guns and too many calibers on the market these days. They contend the woods are now so full of models and cartridges that the average gunner can hardly keep up with all of them. There may be some truth to these bellyaches but I see little to complain about. It is a nice happy situation from the standpoint of the shooting man. I can well remember, before WWII, when you could hardly expect to see a new firearm more often than once in 5 years. Now there are a dozen brand new ones annually, and what a lot of fun that is!

The big arms companies keep whole bevys of gun designers at work year-long to whump up new models, each maker striving to outdo his competitors. This is tough on the manufacturer, and does not make the dealer very joyful, but it does resound to the benefit of the shooter. He is the recipient these days of the best shooting irons that our engineering brains can devise. The existing line is constantly under study today, and older models are retired in favor of improved types. Firearms technology has kept pace with our other engineering gains, and the 1970 model is, generally, an improved gun over its older brother. New manufacturing techniques, new materials, improved machines and a closer liaison between the designer and the man in the field have given us some of the best firearms the world has ever seen. (C.A.)

Complete gun specifications for most of the guns described in this article may be found in our catalog pages. The addresses of the companies mentioned are listed in the Directory of the Arms Trade. Generally, for those arms made abroad for U.S. firearms companies, such as the Italian-made Savage 440, refer to the company's complete listing under U.S. Rifles and Shotguns, Guns Foreign or in the catalog pages.

In the 23rd edition of the GUN DIGEST we went into considerable detail as far as individual guns were concerned, thus pre-empting a lot of space. This year we'll discuss primarily the new guns and model changes.

Beretta Quintet

Despite the cold winds and weather here in northwestern Illinois these past several months, my neighbor—Jerry Zwick—and I have been getting in a fair amount of shotgun shooting with a quintet of new Garcia-Beretta smoothbores. All are 12 gauge, all have ventilated ribs and 2¾ inch chambers, but there the similarity ends.

We decided to give the pump gun a trial first, the one designated the SL-2. The 26-inch barrel (actually 26⅜ inches) is Skeet bored and at our 40-yard pattern board it showed quite consistently uniform patterns with Remington 2¾-1⅛ 8s in the regular Power Piston loads—we hadn't yet received any of the new Remington "All-American" shells at that time.

With these loads 30-inch percentages ran about 63-64%, a result common enough these days with plastic cases and one-piece plastic wad columns.

Nevertheless, Jerry and I broke plenty of clays, both hand thrown and using a Trius machine.

I like the soft, matte receiver finish on this SL-2 slide action—which is the only one of the 5 Berettas that has it. The buttstock and fore-end show a nice figure, and the 12-line checkering is sharp and grabby—a good feature, and not always the case with fine-line checkering.

Stock dimensions run 14¼x1½x2¼ inches, about right for me at combnose and heel, but a bit short for my long arms. The extension-style fore-end (10½ inches long in the wood section) is a good handful, and there's a design feature very helpful on a pump gun—the front half of the fore-end tapers inward at the top, affording a good comfortable grip; just behind is a 2-inch section that is not tapered in, thus acting as a stop for the hand when the slide is pulled back, thus maintaining the same hold on the fore-end for each shot. Good thinking!

Some 200 rounds went through the SL-2 Beretta, and functioning of this 7¼-lb. gun was flawless—feeding, firing and ejection showed no problem. I'm not a pumpgun user ordinarily, and I did have a couple or so balks, but that was entirely my fault for failing to yank the slide back all the way.

In view of the hand-checkering on the semi-fancy stock and the vent rib, the SL-2 is highly competitive at its $185.00 price—and you're getting a truly quality shotgun.

The AL-2 Autoloader

Next Beretta tested was the AL-2, the gas-operated semi-auto shotgun that Garcia has now, for 1969, made available in 20 as well as 12. Also new will be a receiver with engraving, plus Skeet and trap models.

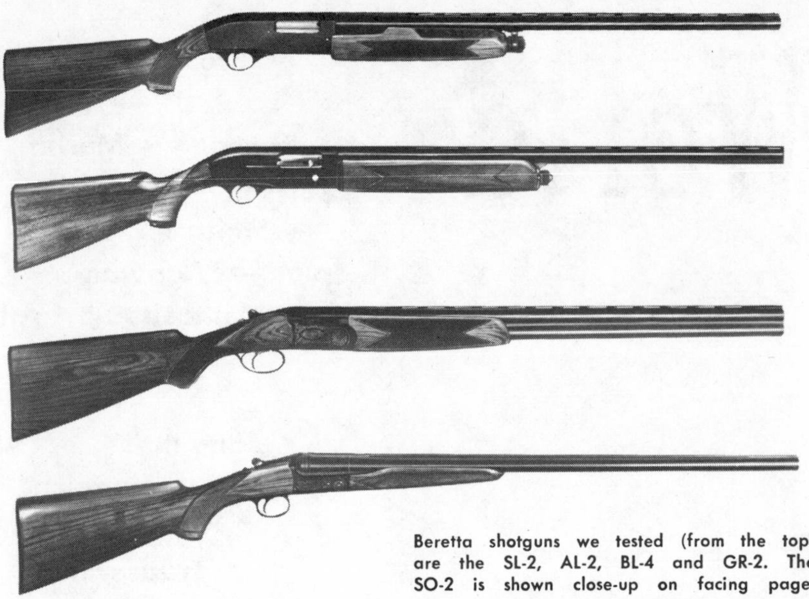

Beretta shotguns we tested (from the top) are the SL-2, AL-2, BL-4 and GR-2. The SO-2 is shown close-up on facing page.

Our sample 12-bore gun scaled a scant 7½ lbs., and its modified 28-inch barrel carries a low vent rib. Stock dimensions run 1⅜x2¼x14⅛ for this one; pistol grip and fore-end are hand-checkered, the fore-end showing a bit better workmanship in that the diamonds are larger, less square, than those on the grip. Lots of 'em too—the design runs almost the full length of the wood (12 inches long) and well up and under the pear-shaped handle. It feels good.

Receiver sides are semi-matte finished, as is the wood, while the top of the action is bright.

I did almost all of the test-firing of this AL-2 Beretta, Jerry being away. Using the same Remington P.P. loads I'd run through the SL-2 pump, it again came as no big surprise that the target 8s gave near-full choke patterns—a 5-shot average went 68%, with one shell showing 77%!

Functioning was 100% OK with the fresh Remington shells, but in shooting a handful of old paper case reloads I wanted to get rid of, I ran into extraction troubles, but that was all.

I didn't do as well on clays as I had with the Beretta pumpgun, but I was shooting alone—had to load the trap arm, cock it, yank the end cord and then fire. I'd give a couple of bucks for a trap that I could load with a dozen or so birds, hit a foot switch and shoot. Maybe even $5 if it had automatic angling!

The BL-4 Over/Under

The BL-4 is Beretta's next-to-the-top boxlock O-U—only the BL-5 is priced above it, and then the true sidelock O-Us start—in quality and cost.

The BL-4 carries a nice bit of hand engraving on receiver sides and bottom, with some on the barrel breeches and the guard. A selective single trigger, gold plated, is standard on this low-profile superposed, and the selected walnut pistol grip—a semi-p.g., really, with rounded-off bottom — and fore-end are well-checkered. The 9-inch fore-end has rather flat sides, with the bottom rounded, but it makes a good hand-filling grip, aided by the extensive checkering pattern—from within a quarter-inch of the top, across the bottom and up the other side. I like the roller-type fore-end release—it locks solidly too.

The comb nose is not fluted—as it is on the Beretta auto and pump—and I think I'd prefer the closer, capped pistol grip of those others as well.

Our specimen BL-4 is a 12, as were all the others, the weight going just under 7½ lbs. The 28-inch barrels carry a vent rib, and the boring is Modified and Full. Stock dimensions differed only a little on the BL-4, going 14⅛x1$\frac{5}{16}$x2½, but whatever the reason I wasn't able to bust the blue rocks too well with it.

This Ova-unda, as one British maker used to call his superposed guns, comes up nicely, however, with most of the weight lying between the hands.

The auto safety atop the upper tang also serves as the barrel selector —slide it to the left (on "safe" or off) and you'll fire the bottom barrel. A single sunken dot—bright—serves as an indicator. Moving the safety to the right reveals two dots, and the upper tube would go first.

All-in-all, a very nice job, the BL-4, and one that shot for us without a hitch or a bobble. The inertia-type single trigger gave no trouble at all but there's a fair amount of spring-loaded take-up before it lets go. The weight of pull is 4 lbs. for the bottom barrel, 6-plus for the top one, fired in that order, but 6 and 6½ when fired top barrel first. That's about right for normal sequence, but a bit heavy

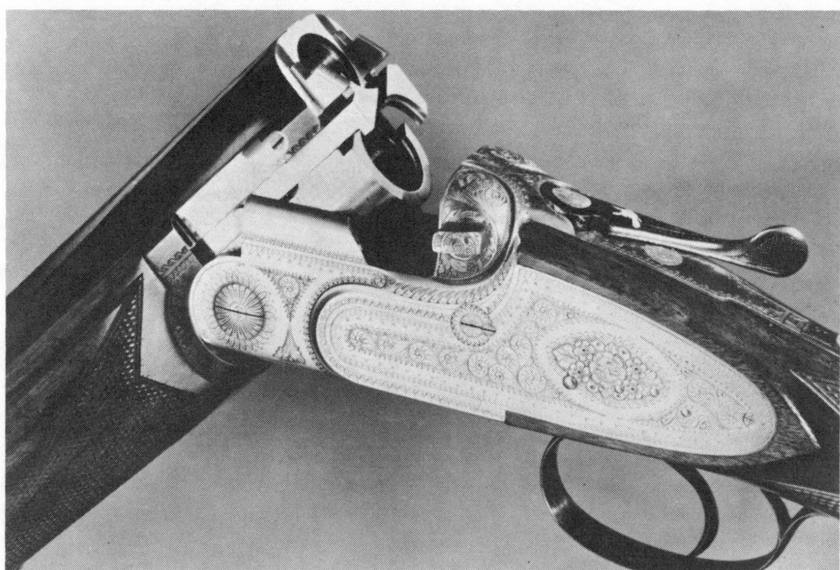

Close-up shows fine engraving on Beretta SO-2 action.

for the reverse order.

The BL-3, 4 and 5 shotguns will be available in 28 gauge this year, offered as Skeet-grades only so far. As with other Skeet guns in the BL series, the extra $12 buys a lot — Skeet-dimensioned stock, special sears, a manual safety and a middle bead sight, plus a bit more engraving than the regular grades have. Trap models, by the way, but in 12 gauge only, of course, carry these same extra features.

Beretta Sidelock

The other O-U of our 5 Berettas to be tested is their SO-2, a true sidelock smoothbore that is a handsome gun indeed. All receiver metal—tangs, top lever and guard as well—are covered with a combination of fine English scroll and rose engraving. A trifle stereotyped, perhaps, but well executed, and the silvery color of the receiver gives a bright contrast with the rich blue of the barrels. There's a silver pigeon inlaid into the top tang, a nice touch.

In addition to the chrome-plated bores, all internal mechanical parts are also chromed, and the barrels are made from famed Boehler rustproof steel. The trigger, safety and top lever are checkered.

Our sample SO-2 has an automatic non-selective single trigger and auto ejectors, but with this O-U the pull is very crisp — no play at all — and though the successive pulls weigh 5½ and 7½ lbs., neither seem quite that heavy.

The SO-2 is also a low-profile design, the pivot bearings being situated forward along the lower barrel sides. The locking up is on the double Kersten system, modified to a form of wedge-fast system, and top-lever actuated, of course. Both sides of the monobloc barrel breeches are finely engine turned.

These sidelock Berettas invariably carry well-selected walnut and our sample is no exception—it's a dense piece of striped French-style walnut, showing an attractive fiddle-back cross-grain also. The checkering on the moderately-close pistol grip is very sharply cut, aside from a few flat-top diamonds here and there. The semi-beavertail fore-end has an unusual checkering pattern—the fingertip area along the top of the wood is without diamonds, but the rest of each side and the bottom is fully covered. The pistol grip has a cap, apparently of some plastic in a fluted radial design, the color a deep red.

The Beretta SO-2 we've been shooting has 30-inch vent-rib barrels, choked modified and full, and the gun weighs 7 lbs., 5 ozs.

Stock dimensions are 14⅛x1½x2½ inches. That's a mite too much at the comb for me—though Jerry found it about right — and while we had no time to do any formal trapshooting, I'd have probably missed a number on the first go-round, at least. I judge that might have been the case because I did the same thing—missed 'em—when we used our Trius trap. I didn't seem to get enough elevation.

However, all of the SO series of Berettas can be stocked to order, with or without pistol grip, option of selective or non-selective single trigger, chokes to order, etc., and any of these at nominal extra cost.

At $875 the SO-2 is hardly inexpensive, but it is a sweet-handling, precision-made and fine shotgun of which anyone could be proud.

GR-2 Double Gun

In some ways this last Beretta I'm going to tell you about, the GR-2 side-by-side double 12 bore, appealed to me more than some of its higher-priced team-mates. It balances beautifully, for one thing, the muzzles of the 28-inch barrels neither too whippy or over-slow for me.

I also like the full beavertail fore-end, which looks and feels much like that on a Winchester 21 in Skeet grade. Nine inches long, it is profusely — and excellently — checkered, though I could wish that the stock finish hadn't filled up the cuts as much as it has. Checkering on the semi-pistol grip is almost as well-executed, but wood finish fills it up here, too.

The blued and lightly-engraved action is on the Greener crossbolt and underlug system, a well-tried design indeed — "tried" by just about all gunmakers at one time or another and still going strong!

The boxlock GR-2 has simple extractors and two triggers. The front trigger is hinged (pushes forward), a nice touch on a double in this moderate price bracket, and a worthwhile one for those whose trigger finger bumps the front trigger under recoil when the rear one is touched off.

Stock dimensions of our GR-2 are 14¼x1⅜x2⅜, length of pull to the front trigger. I ordinarily like a straighter stock at heel, and also one a little longer, but bundled up for cold-weather hunting—not clay busting—this Beretta fitted me quite well.

Fancy wood can hardly be expected in this price range ($260.00), but the genuine walnut is dense, tightly-grained, and has some contrast in the straight grain striping.

The 28-inch barrels are bored modified and full, and the gun weighs 6⅞ lbs. Both tubes proved on the too-tight side with the same Remington P.P. loads of 8s — 68% in the left, almost 79% in the right.

If they can deliver me one of these GR Berettas under 7 lbs., I think I'll buy one in the GR-4 grade. These have selective single trigger auto ejectors, a fully engraved receiver, full pistol-gripped stock, etc., and all of that for only $75 more! Sounds like a great buy, doesn't it?

GR-2 and 3 grades come in 20 gauge for 1969, same $260 price as the 12s. These 20s are also field guns, not offered in Skeet grade. None of the GR series are available in Skeet or trap configurations.

A brand new Beretta shotgun may be for sale by the end of 1969, but if not then it has been promised sure for 1970.

This will be a full de luxe side-by-side genuine sidelock, offered pretty much on a custom basis—any options or refinement the shooter wants can be had, including stock dimensions to his order, various single trigger setups, auto ejectors, of course, and so on.

It will be made in quick-detachable lockplate form, to retail at about $1500, and in standard sidelock style for some $1100.

For full details of the Berettas mentioned above, and for all of the other Berettas as well, see our catalog pages further on. (J.T.A.)

Remington

The most popular Skeet gun for some years has been the Remington 1100. It wins more of the big tournaments and is seen in greater numbers on the Skeet fields across the land than any other make or model. Still, Remington and the Skeet man had a problem. The 1100 was made only in 12 and 20, thus the Skeet shooter couldn't have a complete 4-gun battery. To shoot the 28 and 410 events he had to switch to some other make or model. Now that has all been changed.

There's a new 1100 in both 28 and 410, with the Skeet grade set up as matched pairs. As a matter of fact the Skeet gunner, at least for this year, *must* buy the matched pair. The Model 870 pump repeater is also now made in these light gauges. All of these 28/410 barrels run 25 inches, and the Skeet grade 410 is chambered for the 2½" shell. In the field grade guns (870 and 1100), the 410 chamber is 3 inches, and such barrels are interchangeable on the Skeet grades. There is also a "Match-Weight Skeet Cap," attachable to the fore-ends of both 1100 and 870 Skeet guns, which adds from 10½ to 12 ozs., giving these small bores the same feel and heft of the 12 gauge. The matched-pair Skeet guns carry that designation "Matched Pair" and "No. 1" and "No. 2," engraved on the receiver. Both carry Remington's attractive rolled engraving also, and all is gilded. Handsome looking pieces.

These 1100s and 870s have, until now, been offered only in 28-inch modified barrels. Trapshooters have been clamoring for a 30-inch barrel with a *modified* choke for two reasons —they wanted those other two inches of barrel length for better aiming, but they didn't want more than a modified choke, and here's why. Today's new shotshells, all packaged-up in a plastic container, shoot plenty close enough, too tight in many cases, especially in the traditional full choke barrels long-loved by trapshooters. Remington has now given 'em this boring and barrel length.

In 1966 Remington came along with a rifle called the Model 788, a marked departure from other rifles in the line. It has 9 locking lugs on the bolt—3 rows of 3—sort of like the Schultz & Larsen, the Danish rifle. The 788 has a very thick-walled receiver, the amount of metal over the locking lugs and in the receiver ring ample to hold any of our modern cartridges. It is chambered for 222, 22-250, 243, 30-30 and 44 Magnum cartridges.

This year the Model 788 has a left-hand bolt, a happy fact for the southpaw who always has trouble with the bolt action. Remington made a survey of the buying public and discovered that something like 12% of American gunners are port-siders. The new 788, chambered in 6mm Remington and 308, is the answer.

A companion piece to this centerfire highpower is the Model 581, a bolt action 22 repeater. Introduced at the same time as the 788, it has 6 locking lugs and other features of its big brother. Made with a 24-inch barrel, grooved for a tip-off scope mount, open iron sights and a weight of 5¼ pounds, the 581 may now be had with the bolt on the left side. Plainly finished—no checkering, no grip caps, no white line spacers—the 788 and 581 are intended to appeal to the budget-hampered buyer. The 788 sells for $94.95, the 581 for $49.95.

The 580 action has also been used for a new, moderately priced semi-heavy target rifle known as the Model 540X. It weighs 8 lbs. with a 26-inch semi-bullgun barrel. The 580/540 action has extremely fast lock time, and the new, fully adjustable trigger has a remarkably fine letoff—crisp, light and without after-fall vibration. The new target-type stock has a grooved thumb rest, and a 5-way adjustable buttplate. This can be moved to change the length of pull, shifted upward or downward or given a cant in any direction. There is a full length accessory rail that carries a front swivel-block and sling swivel. Those last two items, plus an oiled target sling strap, are optional at $6.95, installed, and iron sights (Redfield No. 75 micrometer rear, No. 63 globe front) are $20 extra. The receiver is grooved for tip-off scopes, and the barrel is tapped (7 inch separation) for target scope bases. Base price of the 540X is $89.95.

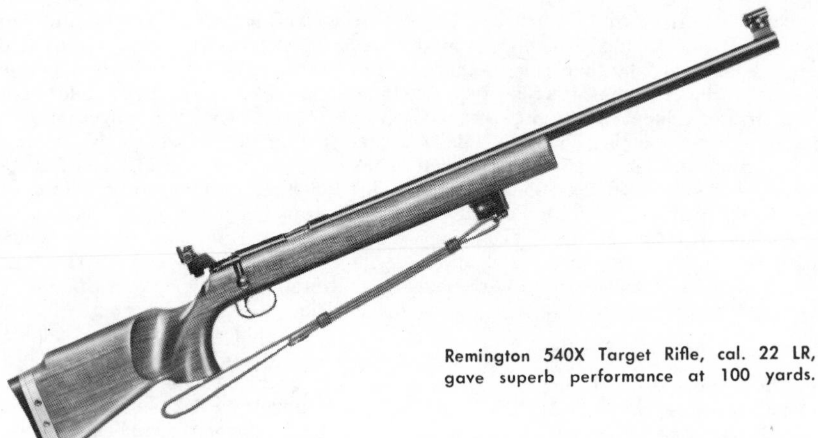
Remington 540X Target Rifle, cal. 22 LR, gave superb performance at 100 yards.

540X Bench Test

I bench tested our sample 540X with really surprising results. Shooting the Remington Rifle Match 22s that came with the rifle, lot no. KN40X3, I got a dozen or more 5-shot groups at 50 meters that went as small as ½-inch, and none larger than ⅞-inch. The weather was ideal, of course—no wind to speak of, and a high, bright overcast—and I was looking through an 8x Lyman scope, mounted on the receiver rails. My eyes are just too damned old for iron sights, to my vast regret.

We hear nowadays a lot of comments in the public prints—sporting and otherwise—about the decline in true craftsmanship, the disappearance of high quality, precision-made products. I've said as much myself, and it is indeed true that a great deal of the stuff we buy and contend with is shoddy and poorly made—junk, in a word.

Because this is the sad situation we often find ourselves in, I'm particularly pleased to be able to tell you how much I like the Remington 540X.

I'm not going to suggest that—at its popular price—it is the equal of, or even the near-equal, of such costly target rifles as the Savage-Anschutz, Remington's own 40-XB rimfire, et al. Nevertheless, I can't get over how very nicely done this 540X is—the buttstock is surprisingly well done, both in design for position shooting and in excellence of fit and assembly. The fully adjustable buttplate —which works perfectly—is hardly to be expected these days on a rimfire in this price range, anymore than is the full length under-rail.

The truly beautiful trigger pull I've already touched on, and I'll only add now that you must try it to believe it!

Which brings up a point—I hope that Remington will make a palm rest for this 540X, (necessary in the ISU offhand matches) and a pronged buttplate as well for the same type of competition.

Since then, and on a day equally good for shooting tight groups, I've had even more gratifying results with the Remington 540X.

I'd just finished firing a 308 match type rifle, using necessarily the micrometer peep rear and globe front sights that came on it—no scope could be fitted. Notwithstanding the iron sights, I'd done pretty well, so I thought I'd give the 540X a trial with its metallics as well.

To zero the newly-attached sights I grabbed a box of CCI 22 Mini-Mags —their high speed long rifles—and opened fire. The target frame was set up at 12½ yards—both to arrive at true zero and to make sure I was on—and the first 5 shots were in one small ragged hole. That looked promising, so after putting the point of impact where I wanted it, I swung over to the 100-yard targets.

The light was now darkish because of a low cloud cover, but still windless, and those Mini-Mag H.S. loads (Lot No. 765,001 A) gave me better groups than I've had from a 22 rifle in a long time, especially with having to use iron sights. I put three strings of 5 shots in ⅞", 15/16" and ¾" from the bench! I consider that a hell of a performance from an under $90 rifle, and you can believe that I was keyed up as I watched those groups forming.

I continued shooting, but the light was fast fading now, so I won't mention the names of the other two ammo brands tried. Unfair to them under the circumstances, but both were of match grade designation, and they didn't really do at all badly—one lot went into 1⅛", the other in 1¼".

(J.T.A.)

40XB-BR Bench Rest Rifle

The finest of all Remington target models, the 40-XB, has been revamped this season. This rifle, not only a target and benchrest piece but also a premier varmint rifle, now comes in 3 weights. The lighter (40XB-BR) version goes 9¼ pounds and, with the addition of the new BR scope, still comes within the benchrest rules for a 10½-lb. rifle. The other 40XB-BR weighs 13½ pounds with a 26-inch barrel, "legal" in the heavy varmint matches. With this year's changes the BR stock now has a pull length of only 12 inches. Benchrest shooters dictated this shortened stock, wanting to get their trigger finger in position without crowding the butt. Out in front the fore-end has been broadened and flattened, designed for the pedestal-type rest bench shooters use. The flat bottom eliminates canting. The regular 40-XB (9¾ and 11¼ lbs., sans sights) is offered in all the popular target and benchrest calibers.

There has been a demand for the highly popular M700 rifle to be chambered for the 6.5mm and 350 Magnum calibers, and that's now been done. There were calls also for the 760 pump to be chambered for the 6mm cartridge, and that's also now available.

Despite the wide acceptance and overwhelming popularity of the M700 rifle, Wayne Leek (chief firearms designer for Remington) has made some slight changes. The tail end of the bolt is now capped, the bolt body is engine-turned, and the stock has been slimmed down a fraction as has the cheekpiece. There is a white-line spacer at the buttplace and grip cap, and the now-serrated safety has been lowered slightly. There is a new skip-line checkering job at the pistol grip and on the forestock. The 700 comes in ADL, BDL and Varmint versions, and in 15 calibers. The 1969 M700 in BDL grade has been upgraded, too, and very nicely. A custom-styled scrolled checkering design is found on fore-end and pistol grip, even on the M700 Varmint Special.

New Remington Scope!

The most startling news from Remington this year is their entry into the scope sight business! Mike Walker, one of the design experts at Ilion, is also a ranking benchrest marksman. His influence is plain to be seen in the first of what we can only hope will be a series of telescopic sights.

The first model, to be known as the BR, is strictly for the benchrester. It comes in either 20x or 24x, with a length of 16¼", a weight with mount of about 20 oz., has ¼-minute micrometer adjustments in the external mount, a field of view of 7.5 feet at 100 yards in 20x, and 6.8 in 24x. In the benchrest game the rifle used in the Sporter and Light Varmint classes cannot weigh, with sights, more than 10½ pounds. The new Remington BR scope is the lightest of all the current crop of glasses. It was designed that way by benchrester Walker. It has also been engineered to position both mounts on the receiver of the rifle. The sharks have learned that it does some harm to accuracy to mount the optics on the barrel. The new Remington avoids this. The new glass is too powerful and the field too small for any kind of game shooting. It is to be expected that subsequent models will have less magnification, thus be suitable for varmint shooting and big game.

Remington Chain Saw

I've got a chain saw that has given me good service for nearly 10 years at Creedmoor Farm—excellent reliability, really, but less and less service as a matter of fact. Why? It's too damned heavy, and it seems to be getting heavier! That I'm getting older may have something to do with it, too.

We've got a lot of big trees at the Farm, oak mostly, and the fairly frequent tornadic winds we suffer from bring down wood in plenty. Nevertheless, despite two fireplaces to feed and the desire to keep the place looking halfway decent, our big 26 lb. chain saw hasn't been getting the exercise it should.

All is changed now, though. We've been giving a lengthy workout since last fall to a new—and lightweight, glory be—chain saw made by Remington Arms Co. (Power Tools Division, Park Forest, Ill. 60466).

This is their ultralight model, the SL-9, a mighty but little handful that goes less than 12 lbs., complete with the 15-inch roller-nose chain I selected. This little bomb is easier to get started, too, than my old saw—now retired—and I didn't have to make a single adjustment to get it rolling the first time out, either, aside from the usual tightening-up of the new chain tension as I broke it in.

The SL-9 handles very well, I found, and it's especially useful in reducing or trimming big limbs off their smaller branches. I found I can do this one-handed, leaving the left hand free to steady or support the main beams. With my old 2-hand saw that chore

Remington 40XB-BR rifle carries the new Remington 20x target scope.

could get tricky, particularly with a smallish limb down on the ground.

Nor was there any problems in cutting up main trunk sections—as big as 20-24 inches in diameter—which we use in lengths of 2-3 feet as part of our bullet backstop.

The SL-9 comes complete with an oiler for the roller nose and a takedown-adjusting tool, cost just under $170. It's a good product.

Other Remington chain saws range from the PL-4 at 12½ lbs. (engine weight) with guide bars up to 26 inches through the PL-5 and PL-6 (made also with automatic oilers) to their Super 754, a 19½ lbs. job that comes with a 31-inch guide bar if you want one that long, or with other lengths down to 13 inches.

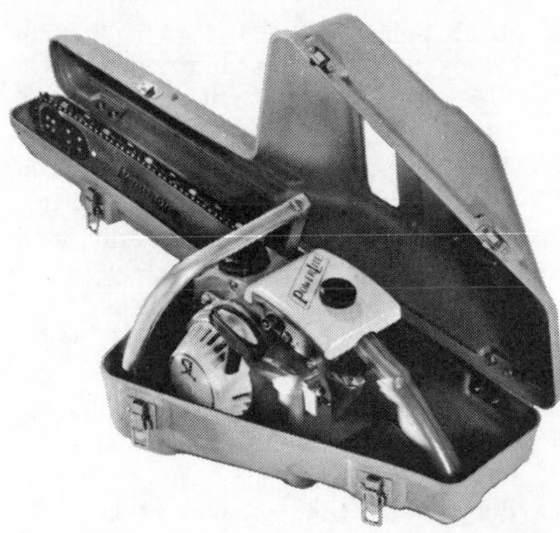

Our picture shows the SL-9 lightweight in a new storage-carrying case Remington calls the "Stash'n carry." Made of heavy-duty polyethylene, the hinges are riveted, there are positive luggage-type fasteners and there's a hole in the top that lets the saw's handle come through for carrying. Best of all, the new case is leakproof, so there's no chance of getting oil or gas onto anything else in your car or truck. New case is $19.95. (J.T.A.)

Sharps

GUN DIGEST announced the new Sharps rifle last year but production problems or something prevented the Sharps Arms Company from getting their kite off the ground. The new Sharps, to be designated the Model 78, is a thoroughly modernized version of the old original Sharps-Borchardt rifle. To be made entirely in this country there will be some 40 changes in the new action over the old original. Among the new features is a trigger mechanism which is part of the falling block mechanism. Single shot rifles generally have a length advantage of 5½ or 6 inches over the average bolt action rifle. In other words the Sharps M78 with a 30-inch barrel will have about the same overall length as a standard bolt action with 24-inch barrel. Obviously this could account for 200 or so extra foot seconds of velocity, and 36-inch barrels will be made!

The new rifle, when ready, will offer all the more popular calibers, from 17 to 50, including some revived old Sharps calibers, according to Art Swanson, company president.

A common fault with some older single shots was a tendency for the firing pin to hang up in the fired primer, a design fault usually because there was no camming-back of the firing pin before the block started to open. The M78 Sharps overcomes this completely, we're told.

Also unusual in any rifle is the incorporation in the M78 Sharps of Timken needle bearings, thus assuring extremely smooth operation of the finger level, great strength and high reliability.

The M78 Sharps safety offers the shooter his choice of automatic operation or manual—a quarter-turn of the adjustment screw effects the conversion.

The regular lever of the M78 will be the simple classic type pictured here, but full loop or English style lever will also be available. All will be spring-loaded, a desirable feature.

The trigger system of the M78 Sharps promises to be one of its most attractive features. These will be combination single stage and set triggers, made by the famed Canjar. Fully adjustable for weight of pull, sear engagement and travel, the new triggers may be used set or not at the shooter's immediate selection. The set trigger system may be adjusted to as low as ¼-ounce!

Two fore-end lengths and two styles will be offered, fancy American walnut being standard to match the buttstock. Two cheekpiece styles will be available in the latter, and any of these can be ordered with or without checkering. Solid rubber buttplates are standard, but other types are optional.

Last, but highly important, all M78 rifles carry a lifetime guarantee against defects in materials and workmanship.

The M78 will also be offered in a Golden Spike Centennial model, these in 3 grades at prices of $495 to $2500 for one rifle, with matched pairs up to $5,250, these with consecutive serial numbers in Grade VIII, the number sets within the 21 to 50 range.

All of these will be engraved and/or gold inlaid, stocks of fancy to fanciest woods, etc. I've got my numbers picked out but I don't know when I'm going to find the money!

Parker Ackley, the well-known barrel maker is one of the partners in the new Sharps organization, and undoubtedly barrels will be produced in his shop.

This is a commendable venture by the new Sharps Rifle Company—and a great gamble as well of time and money. We wish them every success.

Three versions of the new Sharps rifle. Note full loop lever of top gun, ball-end lever in center, and Winchester-type lever below. Receiver wall of center rifle is cut away to a greater degree than the other two, it will be seen.

Winchester

Winchester-Western has much to offer this year, with nothing probably more sensational than their entry into the air arm business. These 10 guns—8 shoulder arms plus 2 pistols—are not the BB kind. They're rifled, with good sights, and most of them with a man's heft. Calibers are 177 and 22. The precision air rifle game is catching on in this country, and the quick response on the part of Winchester indicates their faith in the game. More on the various models anon.

There is a new Model 70 rifle. Well, it's almost the 70 but the company calls it the Model 770. It is the standard rifle except not quite so finely finished. It stands midway between the 70 and the Model 670 announced last year. The 770 uses the regular action with all the strength, rigidity and dependability that you will find in the standard 70. The bolt isn't quite so slick and smooth, the finish on the receiver and barrel does not show quite the glossy finish, and the stock is a bit plainer selection of wood. Accuracy is just as good and dependability quite on a par with any Winchester made. The 770 is chambered for the 22-250, 222, 243, 270, 30-06 and 308, and there's a magnum variation offered in 264, 7mm Remington and 300 Winchester. Barrel length in the standard calibers is 22 inches ($139.95), while the magnums go 24. Magnum version sells for $154.95.

The Model 670, last year's offering, is an even slightly less costly firearm than the 770. It comes in rifle, carbine and magnum variations. The carbine lists at $114.95, in 243, 270 and 30-06 calibers. The rifle is chambered for calibers 225, 243, 270 and 30-06. These sell for $119.95, the magnums at $134.95.

There is a new and unusual Model 52 International rifle. It weighs 14 pounds and is intended for the free rifle game. It has a laminated thumbhole stock, an International buttplate movable for length of pull, drop and cant, and an International palm rest adjustable for height, reach and cant. The 28-inch barrel is precision rifled and lead-lapped. Steel scope blocks are attached. The fully adjustable trigger may be either the standard 52 type or the accessory Kenyon trigger. The latter runs the price up another $35. There is a full length, black anodized aluminum accessory track underneath, an aluminum fore-end stop assembly with felt base, a detachable swivel and clamping bar. The rifle is tapped fore and aft for iron sights. This 52, of course, has the Winchester speed action, a specially carburized receiver, bolt and firing pin. This is quite the finest Model 52 ever made, and with it Winchester intends to win in International competition. The company was stung during the '68 Olympiad because not only did our shooters shun the M52 but it was not used by any of the foreign competition either.

Winchester 1400 now with southpaw action.

Winchoke may be had on Winchester Models 1200 or 1400 shotguns.

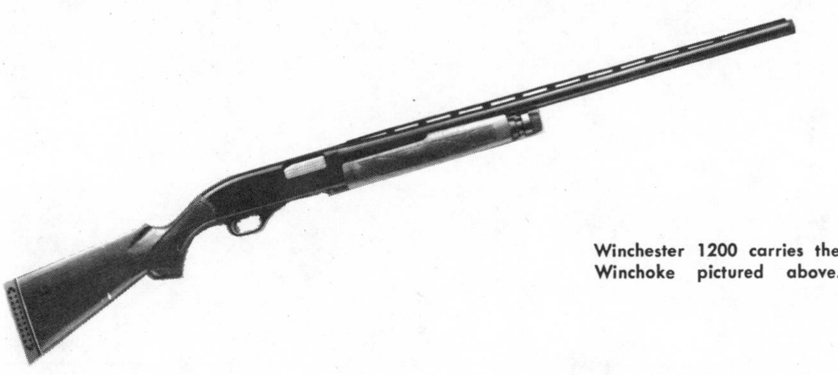

Winchester 1200 carries the Winchoke pictured above.

The Model 1400 Mark II left-hand autoloading 12 gauge is brand new. The ejection slot is on the port side, and the safety has been switched over to accommodate the southpaw. This is a considerable concession to the minority shooters, and marks the first time Winchester has taken note that there are any shotgunners except the right hander. Along with the left-hand M1400 is a new muzzle choke called the Winchoke, suitable for all M1400s and M1200s.

About 2½ inches long, the Winchoke screws down *inside* the gun muzzle. Made of lightweight alloy, the device can be had in any of the regular chokes, i.e., full, modified or improved cylinder, and in 12, 16 and 20 gauge. Certain Model 1400 and 1200 barrels are factory-adapted to receive it and it's only $4.95 per unit.

The beauty of the Winchoke is that it does not lengthen the gun muzzle. Also, being threaded into the barrel, it does not alter the muzzle profile. I tested the Winchoke on ringnecks, mallards and trapped live birds and found it works handsomely.

Each of the big arms companies must carry at least one low-priced single-barrel shotgun. This year Winchester offers the new Model 370, made in every gauge from 12 down to 410. Called the "Youth's Gun," it weighs some 6¼ pounds, depending on gauge. Barrels range from 26 to 36 inches, there is a top lever opener, auto ejector, exterior hammer and half-cock safety. The 12 carries a recoil pad, and all are a uniform $37.95.

In 1965, somewhat by accident, Winchester found out that commemorative guns are hot stuff. That year they made up a special Model 94 rifle to help the State of Wyoming celebrate its centennial. The gun sold well and Winchester has been at it ever since. This year there will be not one commemorative rifle but two —the Theodore Roosevelt and the Golden Spike.

The Roosevelt commemorative honors that great outdoorsman, statesman, naturalist and marksman. The beloved Teddy was our 26th President. There will be, actually, two guns to do the honors, a rifle and a carbine, both made up on the Model 94 action. Both have octagon barrels in 30-30 caliber only, and each has an American eagle engraved on the receiver, the words "26th President" and "1901-1909." Roosevelt's signature is reproduced on the upper tang. The receiv-

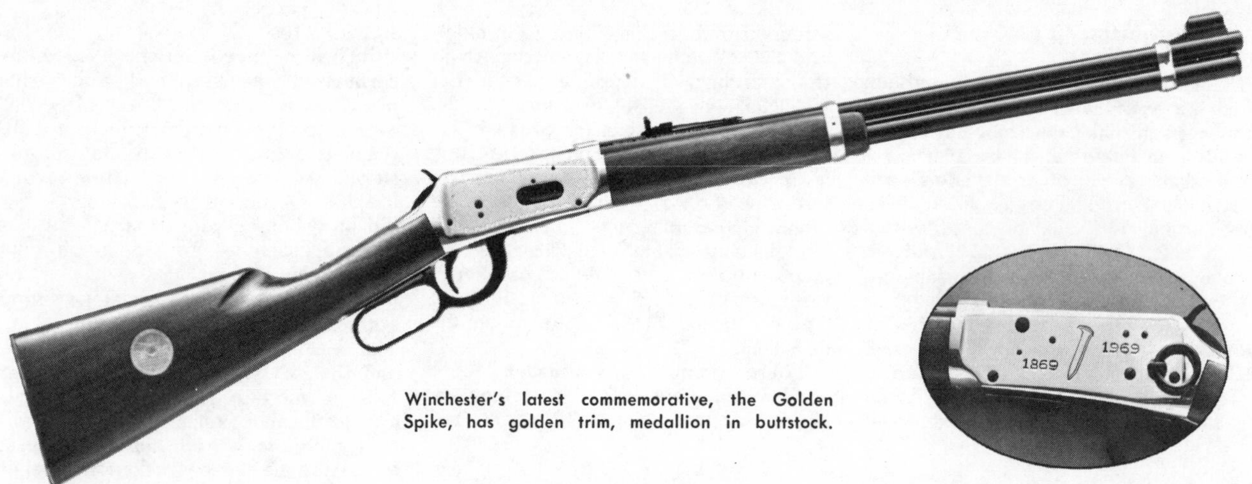

Winchester's latest commemorative, the Golden Spike, has golden trim, medallion in buttstock.

er, upper tang and fore-end cap are finished in white gold, and a commemorative medallion is imbedded in the selected walnut stock. The buttplate is the old-fashioned crescent type, there is a half-pistol grip and a matching loop lever. The rifle has a half-magazine, the carbine a full-length tube. Saddle or sling rings are on both.

The Golden Spike commemorative celebrates the 100th anniversary of the laying of the first transcontinental railroad. The Union Pacific and Southern Pacific railroads have joined Winchester in honoring the occasion. The Golden Spike rifle—really a carbine—contributes its share. This is another Model 94 with a golden receiver, tang and barrel bands. The U.S. Mint struck a special medallion to acknowledge the anniversary, and a replica of this medal is imbedded in the selected walnut stock. On the left side of the receiver are the dates 1869-1969 and an outline of the Golden Spike, the last driven to link up the two rail lines. On the tang is the wording, "Oceans United By Rail." The Golden Spikes will sell for $119.95.

As I've said, Winchester tried the commemorative thing first in 1965. It was an instant success. In 1966 the company celebrated its 100th birthday. It seemed only fitting and proper that a special gun be made up to mark the event. The new gun, the trusty old M94, was given the fancy-dan look and dubbed the Model 66. Made up first as a 40,000-unit lot, these were sold out in the first 30 days. Later 100,000 were produced and these also were gobbled up. The company planners kicked themselves that they had programmed for only this number. They could probably have sold a million!

During that same 1966, Alaska and Nebraska centennials were also staged and there were rifles to do both justice—1500 for the Alaska celebration, 2500 for Nebraska. Then Canada had a 100th anniversary and it required 90,000 Canadian centennial models for this one. About this time Illinois also turned the century mark and this necessitated 25,000 guns. During 1968, the rifle of the day was the Buffalo Bill commemorative. It sold to the tune of 100,000. In all probability the Roosevelt and Golden Spike models will do just as well.

New Air Arms

The new W-W air arms come from West Germany (Diana, at a guess), and here are the specs:

Winchester Air Arms

Rifles	Caliber	Barrel	Wgt./lbs.	Over-all	Price
333	177	Rifled	9½	43¼"	$169.95
450	177	"	7¾	44½"	84.95
435	177	"	6½	44"	54.95
427	22	"	6	42"	39.95
425	22	"	5	38"	32.95
423	177	"	4	36"	27.95
422	177	"	3¾	36"	22.95
416	177	Smooth	2¾	33"	15.95
Pistols					
363	177	Rifled	3	16"	49.95
353	177	"	2¾	16"	29.95

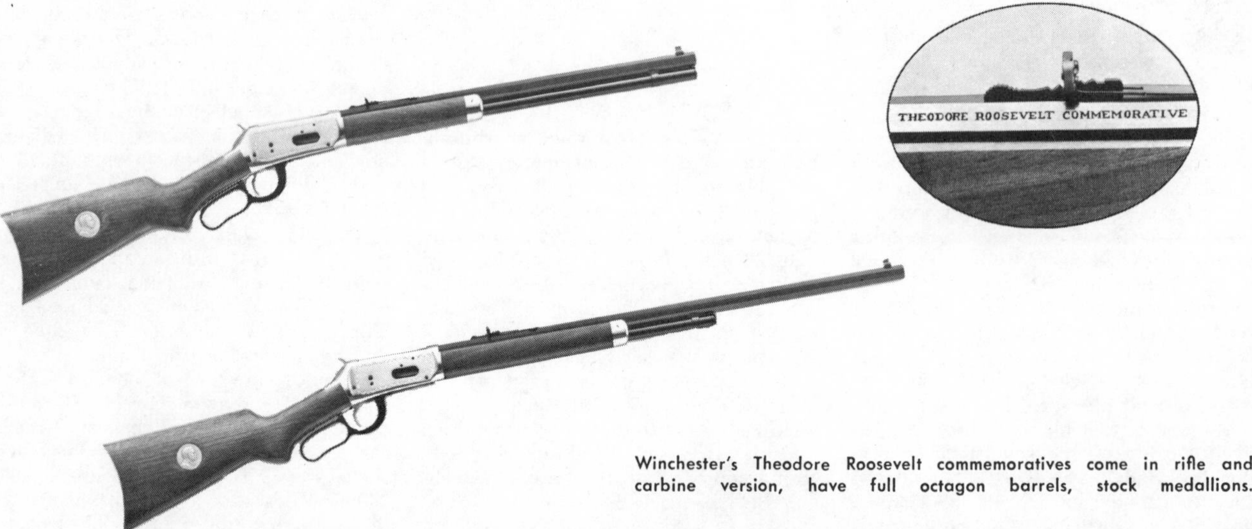

Winchester's Theodore Roosevelt commemoratives come in rifle and carbine version, have full octagon barrels, stock medallions.

Winchester 70 Mannlicher

My first shooting test of the new Model 70 Winchester in its Mannlicher- or full stock version was, I thought, a highly successful one. Mannlicher-stocked rifles have not been particularly noted for a high degree of accuracy, and I won't pretend that the new Model 70 that I've been recently shooting is anything like capable of one-hole groups or that sort of thing, but when I tell you that the first two groups—5 shots at 100 yards —from this brand-new rifle gave me 1" and 1⅝", both with Federal 130-gr. soft points, you see that it has about all the accuracy it needs as a hunting rifle.

I had mounted one of the new Redfield 3-9x variable scopes in a pair of the Bushnell 1-hole mounts, and commenced shooting by using up about 3 rounds to get just where I wanted to on the paper. I had used the Alley collimating device earlier, of course, to adjust the scope initially, and the first shot was well into the black, as it almost always is when an Alley collimator is employed. While there was no wind to speak of, it was a cold and heavily overcast day, and from the start I had some trouble with barrel mirage rising into the scope's field of view—not only with this Model 70 Mannlicher job, but with a couple of other rifles fired at the same session. I cured that problem, at least to some degree, by waiting about two or three minutes between shots.

By the time I was ready to shoot the last 10 rounds in the factory box, it was getting pretty dark, and whether that was the cause or not, the two last 5-shot groups opened up a bit, one going 1¾", the other just under that by a hair. Nevertheless, I certainly feel that such a performance for the first 20 rounds through a brand new rifle leaves nothing to be desired, conditions and components considered.

My next test, hopefully this weekend if the weather holds reasonably good for January, will be with some other factory loads and some handloads as well, if I can get them prepared in time. In the meantime, let's talk a little about the rifle itself, what it is and what it is not.

The new 19-inch barreled Model 70 Mannlicher is no exact match, certainly, for the well-beloved old Mannlicher-Schoenauer, in slimness and trimness, but from a practical, rugged-shooting standpoint it has some compensations. The buttstock carries the almost inevitable cheekpiece, in Monte Carlo style, of course, both of which seem to be at least in the manufacturer's eyes these days a stock adornment (?) that simply has to be put on any and all sporting rifles. In this case, as in the Monte Carlo cheekpieces of several other rifles as well, it is not as gracefully done as it might be, but offsetting that is its practicality for a scope-sighted rifle. Naturally, because of the height of the Monte Carlo comb, the optional iron sights (furnished by Winchester at no additional cost) are pretty high, and therefore don't add to the racy lines either.

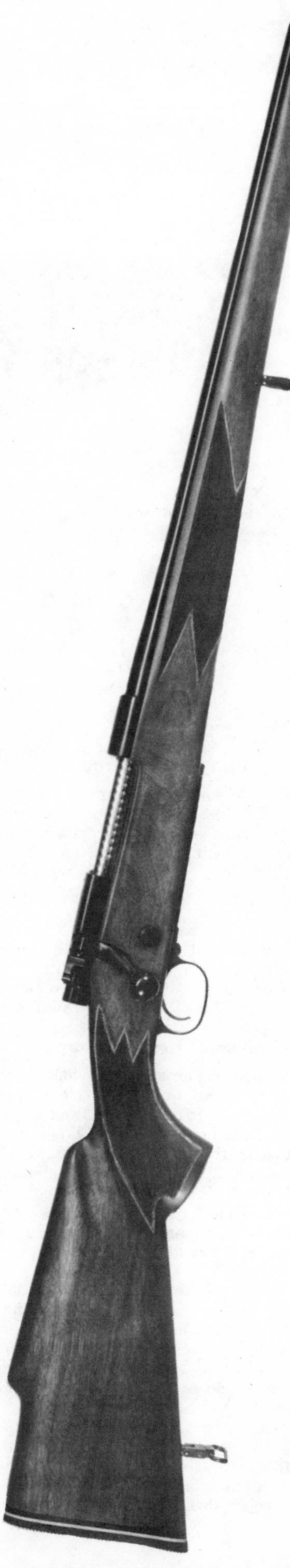

The forestock line, from the muzzle cap to the front of the trigger guard, is a quite flat one, and thus the Model 70 Mannlicher has a rather full fore-end if one compares it with the old upswept curve, in effect, of the early Mannlicher-Schoenauer. Nevertheless, I don't feel that this fullness detracts in any particular way from the grace or usefulness of the new Winchester — certainly it affords a good hand-filling hold for the shooter, particularly if he is hunting in rough country or in cold weather and is wearing gloves.

The complete rifle, with the Redfield scope and the Bushnell mounts on it as noted above, weighs just 9¼ lbs. The trigger pull is quite crisp and clean, but runs a little heavy for my taste, 5¼ lbs., which I'm going to lighten a bit if I can find the time before the next shooting session with it.

I like the 4-Plex reticle available from Redfield very much. The thin, intersecting crosshairs at the center permit a fine and accurate hold on the target, especially in a variable of 7 to 9 power, for long range shooting, whether it be for big game or varmints, while the thicker sections of the crosshairs are readily visible even in dull, dim light. While I've not had a chance to do any hunting under such conditions with this scope, I feel pretty sure that these could be made out on game under quite poor light conditions.

All of the full-stocked Model 70s carry a good job of hand checkering, by the way, and a rifle-type rubber recoil pad as well. Calibers available as of this writing are 243, 270, 308 Winchester and 30-06. It is not known at the moment whether others will be offered in the future or not. All of the comb noses on the 1969 Winchester Model 70s are fluted, and done in a very nice fashion. Much of the fluting seen nowadays on many sporting rifles appears to have been done with hardly anything more than a broad, round rasp, whereas the new Model 70 line shows that it has been handcut, I would guess, or at least hand-finished, and done with an increasing radius so that the bottom of the fluting flows handsomely into the buttstock. Quick detachable swivels are standard on the Model 70 Mannlicher also.

The iron sights I referred to above, an open barrel sight and a front bead mounted on the ramp, are furnished at the list price, but are not mounted on the rifle as received. They can, therefore, be used or not as the owner wishes. (J.T.A.)

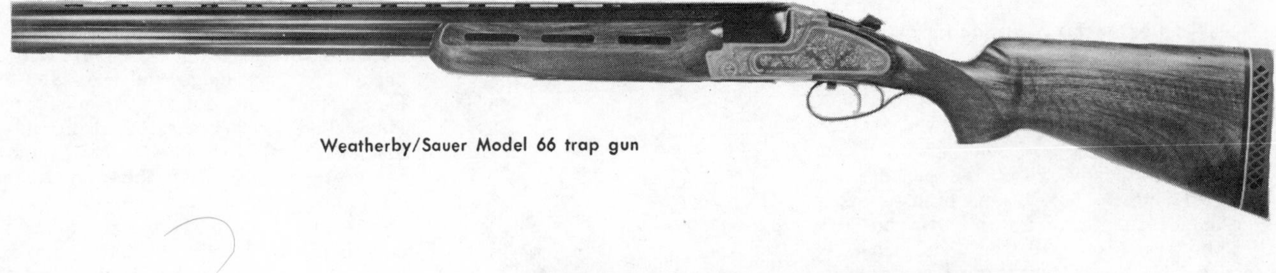

Weatherby/Sauer Model 66 trap gun

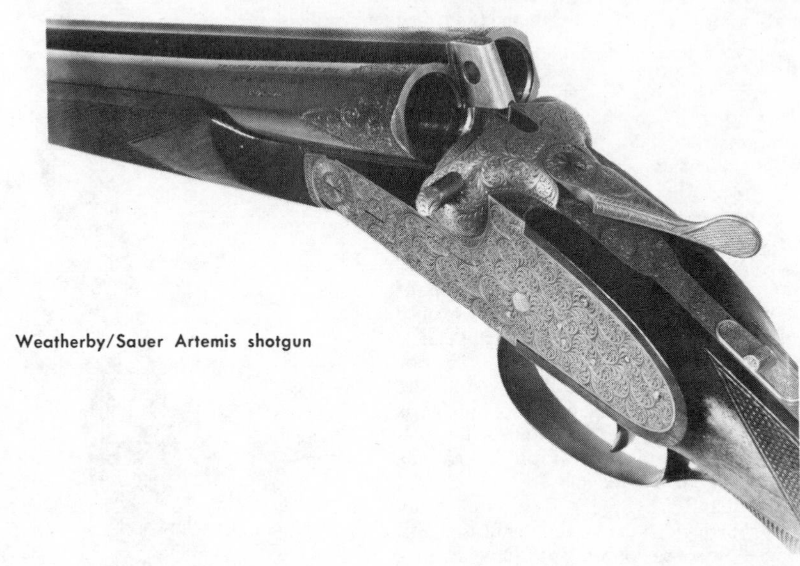

Weatherby/Sauer Artemis shotgun

Weatherby

J. P. Sauer shotguns will now be handled exclusively by Roy Weatherby. Let me say briefly that Sauer guns are of excellent quality, on a par with some British "Best" guns. The Model 66 sidelock trapgun (12 gauge only) I looked over is a beautifully made and a well-designed piece of clay busting ordnance. Detachable H&H-type sideplates and Greener crossbolting are standard. It costs $550 in Grade I; Grades II and III are $650 and $750, but available only on special order.

The "66" O-U field shotguns also come in three grades, $495 to $695. These guns feature nicely engraved metal and wood selected for good figure. Skip-line checkering on the pistol gripped stock is standard fore and aft and there's a recoil pad also. Barrels are of Krupp-Special steel, ventilated ribs standard on all grades.

The Royal Sauer, a scroll-engraved boxlock side-by-side double will be offered in 12 gauge for the 2¾" shell, in 20 for 3" loads. There is a single trigger, selective ejectors, a ventilated rib, and the price is $295.

Weatherby will also be marketing Sauer's rifle-shotgun combination guns and their drillings or 3-barrel guns. The former, called Model BBF, are O-U types, chambered for 7.65R or 30-06 and 16 gauge, the barrels 25 inches long. The action is the Blitz type, with double Kersten bolts, and the front (rifle) trigger may be "set." The pistol grip buttstock has an oval cheekpiece and that "hogback" comb line beloved of German shooters.

Two grades are offered; standard at $550, the De Luxe (with game-scene engraved action, skip-line checkering, etc.) at $645.

The Sauer 3000E Standard drilling has two 12 gauge bores on top, your choice of 222, 243, 30-06 or 7.65R in the lower barrel. The 3000E De Luxe comes in 30-06 or 7.65R only, the top tubes 12 bore as before. The price of the Standard is $625, the De Luxe $715. Both are engraved —scroll work on the regular grade, game scenes on the more expensive guns.

There has been no opportunity to shoot/evaluate any of these Sauer offerings, but Sauer quality may be taken for granted, I believe, and certainly Roy Weatherby has a high reputation to uphold. (S/A)

Dan Wesson Arms

Dan Wesson, with some 30 years of firearms design experience, imports two shotguns and two air rifles, and is now building a unique revolver. For the long arms, Dan went to Czechoslovakia for the justly-famed Brno products.

Because Mason Williams has a Testfire Report on all of these new Wesson guns in this 24th edition, I won't comment further on them here. (J.T.A.)

Universal Firearms Corp.

Universal's shotgun line has been expanded and improved. New this year is a group of autoloading shotguns called the Auto-Wing. The Model 2070 in this line is a 12-ga., 2¾" gun with a 26" vent rib barrel choked IC, M or F. Wood, finish, and checkering are good. The gun is also offered with 28" and 30" barrels, any of which interchange easily. All are $139.95.

The Duck-Wing, with 28" or 30" barrel, is just like the Auto-Wing, but all exposed metal parts have been factory coated with Du Pont's Teflon-S. This makes a lot of sense, since duck and goose hunting is rough on a shotgun; in tidal waters rusting is a considerable problem. Teflon-S prevents this sort of thing, and it also self-lubricates the gun parts. The Teflon-S coating is in camouflage olive-green color, thus disturbing reflections are eliminated, too. $164.95.

In the O-U, or Over-Wing line, 10 variations on a theme are imported. Offered in a wide variety of chokes and barrel lengths, these come in 12 and 20 ga., with single or double triggers, in plain or deluxe versions, all of them with vent ribs. Prices start at $199.95, deluxe guns sell for $249.95.

In the side-by-side or Double-Wing line-up, Universal offers 12 and 20 ga. guns, in several barrel lengths and chokes. Guns have rubber recoil pads, double triggers, and there's a special Magnum 10 goose gun with 3½" case 32" tubes. Those well-made doubles sell for $129.95, the goose blaster for an additional $20.

Three 12 ga. single barrel smoothbores, the Single Wing series, are offered. These are top break hammer guns with auto ejectors, 3" chambers, choked M or F, with 28" barrel. The checkered walnut stocks are hand rubbed. Price, $41.50.

Universal will also import the Mauser Model 66, a centerfire rifle with interchangeable barrels for 30-06, 270 or 243. Changing barrels can be done easily and quickly, and the rifles are tapped for scope mounting. The Mauser 66 starts at $269.95, a Presentation Set with three barrels, scope, bases and rings, all in a handsome trunk case, is $500.

Universal continues to bring in an extensive line of scopes—fixed- and variable powers, plus 22 rimfire types. (B.S.)

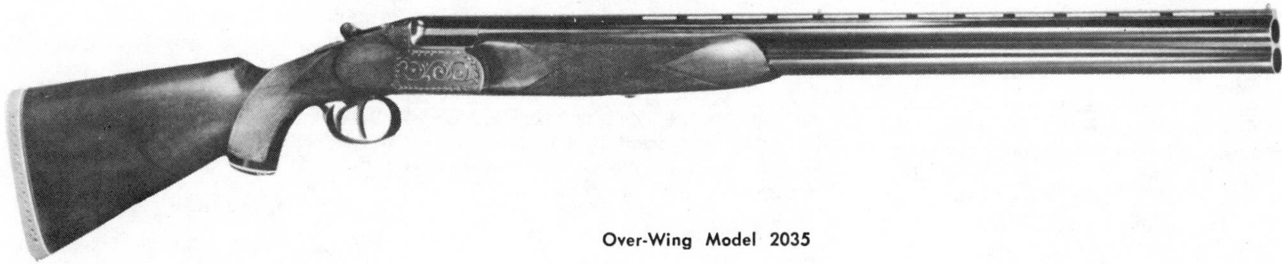

Over-Wing Model 2035

Universal Field Tests

We've recently been giving a couple of Universal's new shotguns an all-too-brief tryout. The winter has been a rough one, and now that the weather is easing up a bit we're too close to our deadlines.

Nevertheless, the Over-Wing 20 gauge we've been shooting — that's the Model 2055 — is an over-under that comes with single trigger but is without ejectors. A ventilated rib is standard on this model, the receiver is lightly engraved and the genuine walnut stock shows a nice bit of figure. We opted for the 26-inch barreled version, the choking improved cylinder and modified. Stock dimensions are about standard—14¼"x1½"x2½"—which means a mite too short to fit me just right, but the blue rocks have been busted with good regularity.

For this claybird shooting I didn't mind the lack of ejectors at all—in fact, being a shotshell handloader it was a convenience to be able to pluck the empties out and drop 'em into my pocket.

The editor tests a 20-ga. Over-Wing in some tall grass.

Tests at the pattern board were brief, too, but of several brands shot, Federal plastic-case 8s, their Monarch Target Loads gave me the most uniform pellet distribution, coupled with about 55% density, from the I. C. barrel. The same loads were almost as good in the modified tube, and the percentages averaged around 65%.

The inertia type single trigger of the Over-Wing balked only once in some 130 shots, and I think that was my own fault—I was swinging fast to my left, and I imagine the recoil-buildup was softened.

All in all, a good fast-handling, well-balanced over-under and one that I think will find good acceptance by a lot of shotgunners.

The other Universal shotgun received here is the striking new Teflon-coated autoloader, the one they call the Duck-Wing. I'd asked for—and got—this 12-bore autoloader in the Camouflage Olive Green coloration, and I'll have to say it takes a little getting used to. Yet I can easily see that this soft green finish is going to make a place for itself in the duck blind. Except for the small area of the bolt—which is bright metal—I can't see how this new camouflage finish is going to spook any wildfowl.

This new Duck-Wing is made only in 12 gauge, of course, with a choice of 28" or 30" barrel (with vent rib), both offered in full choke only. Ours came through with the shorter barrel, and because there weren't any legal waterfowl available, I tried the green gun at straight trap.

I'll have to admit that I didn't do as well as I'd hoped, and I think the standard stock dimensions of the Duck-Wing were getting me to shoot under the birds. As I've said, I take a long-pull stock—one needing a bit higher comb, too—and with the Duck-Wing gun I wasn't getting enough elevation usually.

A short session at the pattern board bore this out, too—my center of impact was several inches too far below the marker. Density and distribution were both excellent, however, and this time Winchester AA trap loads proved the best of the bunch, though by a scant margin over Brand X. Percentages ran high, the average for 5 shots going just under 79%. That fact may also help explain why I was missing more — I'm usually on the bird fairly quickly at the traps, so I was probably getting too tight a spread out there in addition to being a little low to start with.

Functioning was all I'd ask with all of the factory loads tried—four different brands, plus a couple of sizes within a given make—but I did have a couple of ejection failures with some odds and ends of handloads I put through the green gun. No fault of the gun, I know—just a result of my using a small number of loads that were, I'm sure, on the light side.

I like the pistol grip of this Duck-Wing—it's smoothly radiussed and snug—and the semi-beavertail fore-end makes for good control with the left hand. Handling and balance are quite good, though I find most autoloaders a bit muzzle light; the green gun is no exception, but I'd cure that with some fore-end weights if this new auto belonged to me. (J.T.A.)

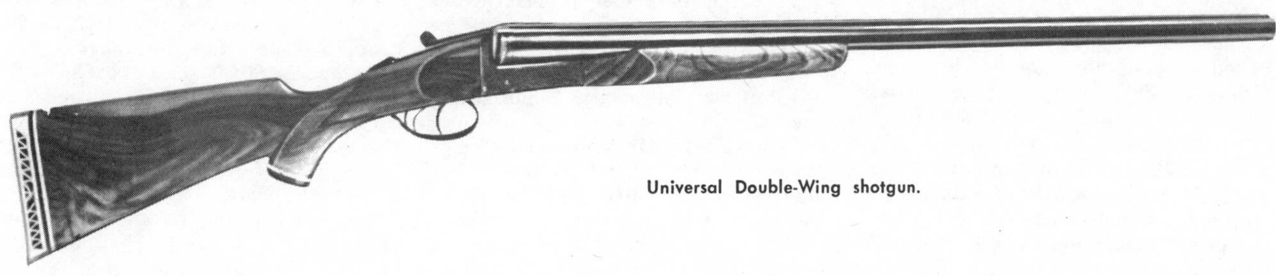

Universal Double-Wing shotgun.

Tradewinds

Long the prime importer of Husqvarna rifles, the company now offers two brand-new centerfire bolt action rifles, both bearing the Husqvarna name. The Series 9000 test gun mailed to me was stolen in transit, so I can't give you a first-hand report on its performance. It wasn't available for photography, either, but it is essentially a less expensive version of the Series 8000.

The S8000 features a completely new streamlined action and a redesigned stock. Skipline checkering and a semi-gloss finish is standard on both models. The lower priced 9000 ($172.50) features a good piece of European walnut, while the higher priced 8000 ($228.50) has a stock of selected wood. Both have a Monte Carlo stock with cheekpiece, a rosewood fore-end tip, and they're chambered for 270, '06, 7mm Rem. Mag., and 300 Win. Mag. The 8000 rifle has an engraved hinged floorplate, engine turned bolt, adjustable trigger, and carries no sights. The 9000 comes with an adjustable open rear sight and a hooded ramp front, but has a blind magazine and non-adjustable trigger. Both rifles are tapped for peep sights and scope mounts. Both have white spacers, 23¾" barrels, and weigh about 7¼" lbs.

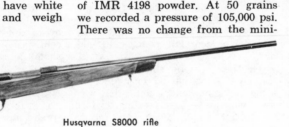

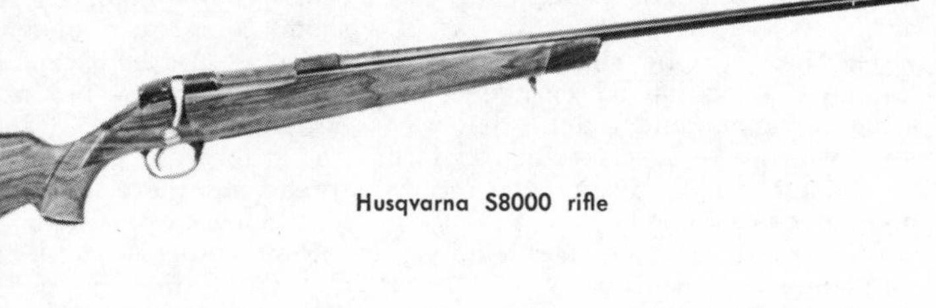
Husqvarna S8000 rifle

Here's a bit of good news! The three Mercury side-by-side guns and the single barrel smoothbore have new prices—lower ones! The 10-ga. side-by-side Magnum is now priced at $138.50 (was $159.95); the 12-ga. Magnum now goes for $108.50 (was $134.50); the 20-ga. Magnum now sells for $108.50 (was $134.50); the 10-ga. Magnum single barrel used to sell for $87.50, now costs $78.50. (B.S.)

Smith & Wesson

Smith & Wesson, who have not offered a rifle since 1890, now have an entire line. These are made-in-Sweden Husqvarna rifles, cataloged in 5 different variations. Two are offered with Mannlicher-type stocks. The Husqvarna action is essentially the Mauser 98, a good, sturdy, and time-tried turning bolt type. Calibers are 243, 270, 308 and 30-06. Weight varies from 6.6 to 7 lbs., depending on model and caliber. Barrels are 23¾" on the rifles, 20¾" on the Mannlicher-stocked carbines. All models are tapped for both receiver sights and scope mounts. Sling swivels are standard. An open rear sight and graceful ramp-type front bead are also found on all models. Now that Husqvarna has modernized the older 98 action it remains to be seen whether S&W will drop the current line in favor of the newer action. We'll watch to see how this one works out.

Schultz & Larsen Test

There's been a lot of conjecture about case stretch in bolt action rifles with rear locking lugs. Until recently, no one had done much to find out what happens when full loads are fired in one of these arms. The concensus has been that pressure exerted on the bolt face would cause compression of the bolt and slight stretch of the action, thereby producing a condition of excess headspace and case stretch.

A report made at H. P. White Laboratories for Fessler & Co. contains much relevant information and proves their Schultz and Larsen rifle action is a very strong one indeed. We quote, in part, the H. P. White findings using a Schultz and Larsen rifle, cal. 30-06:

"We began loading ammunition with 180-gr. Hornady Spire Point bullets with progressively higher loads of IMR 4198 powder. At 50 grains we recorded a pressure of 105,000 psi. There was no change from the minimum headspace existing when firing began. Having noted that the fastest burning IMR powder on the NRA loading chart for caliber 30-06 was 3031, we filled the case to the mouth with this powder (61 grains) and then compressed it with the bullet. The pressure was 120,000 psi. There was no change from minimum headspace.

"We continued the loads of 4198 powder until the case was full at 58 grains and the powder required compressing to make room for the bullet. The pressure was recorded at 129,000 psi. The bolt was so difficult to open that the handle was bent. There was no other damage and, again, the action maintained its minimum headspace.

". . .This phenomenal performance is due to the complete and precise support given the case by the bolt.

"At the high pressures of 100,000 and 129,000 psi in the Schultz and Larsen rifle, the case gave evidence of flowing into every crack provided. Since the case did not rupture, there could have been little momentary increase in headspace during any compression of the bolt. There was no permanent increase in headspace even after the highest pressure, 129,000 psi.

This is quite an outstanding performance by the Schultz and Larsen rifle, demonstrating the strength and quality of its action.

Savage

Two years ago Savage introduced a new 12 gauge over-under. It was a sturdy number and, along with its strength and plenty of good looks, it handled quite well. The price was also reasonable and the 440 instantly caught on. About the only complaint on it was the fact that it had no automatic ejectors, and was made only in 12 gauge. Savage this year offers the same gun with selective single trigger and auto ejectors, but still only in 12 bore.

This latest variation is known as the Model 444, and it comes with ventilated rib, chrome-lined barrels, stock and fore-end of selected European walnut, and in a variety of barrel lengths and chokes.

The original 440 is available now as a trap gun. It has a Monte Carlo comb, recoil pad, an extra wide trap-style ventilated rib, a semi-beavertail fore-end, 30-inch barrels bored full and modified or full and full, manual tang safety and, of course, the same simple extractors.

Savage has still another over-under this year, a comparatively inexpensive number as superposed guns go. It will sell for less than $200, and has a lockup similar to the fine old Model 32 Remington O/U. 12-gauge only, this new shotgun is equipped with a single selective trigger and plain extractors and is stocked in European walnut, checkered at pistol grip and forestock. A rugged field gun, in the best Savage tradition, it has been christened the Model 330.

Because of the fine acceptance of the Savage-Anschutz Model 54 sporter, a second rifle, somewhat less costly and not quite so lavishly turned out, has been announced this year. This is the Model 164, a custom grade sporter made in 22 caliber. It has the Anschutz Model 64 target rifle action, a man-size Monte Carlo stock of European walnut and is handsomely checkered. This 5-shot clip-loaded repeater has a glass-smooth bolt, an adjustable trigger pull, is tapped for a receiver sight and grooved for a tip-on mount. This latest Savage will sell for $87.50.

There are 3 other new 22 rifles from Savage, these autoloaders are the Models 60, 90 and the 88, which is a Savage-Stevens. The threesome all use the same blowback action, all are fed from a tubular magazine lying beneath the barrel. Best of the three is the M90 with Monte Carlo stock, a stock with a forward barrel band and sling swivels. It holds 10 Long Rifle cartridges, has a top tang safety and open sights. It is grooved for the installation of a Savage scope. Model 88 price is $47.50; M60 $59.50 and M90 $54.50.

Richland Arms

Tom Hoagland added one new shotgun to the Richland Arms lineup (covered in detail last year), and he also offers some special tools not available anywhere else. The new gun is the model 844, a 12-ga. O-U offered with 26, 28, and 30 inch tubes, a single non-selective trigger, ventilated rib, plain extractors and blued receiver. Furnished with a wide choice of chokes, the price will be about $190.

The new tools include a dial-indicator caliper, special pin vises, and a metric drift/punch set. Of special interest is their hacksaw and hacksaw frame for making European-type screw slots—and if you have ever tried your hand at that job, you'll know why I flipped over that new item.

Replica Arms

Black powder shooters can look forward to a very interesting time with the two new Replica Arms models. Ken Phelps now has a half-stock target rifle, caliber 38, that is a real beauty. Tagged at $360, I believe that this is the sort of gun a lot of fellows would find highly satisfactory, even if they are not super-distilled black powder buffs. The Berdan rifle in 44 caliber, with its double-set triggers and patchbox, is most attractive, but Ken anticipates a problem with his gun—more orders than guns available, hence it's going to be first come, first served. (B.S.)

Ranger Arms

First announced in these pages of our 22nd ed., Ranger Arms seems to be in full production on their Texas Magnum and Maverick rifles. The entire rifle is built in the U.S., including the actions. Model names have been changed—their best guns are called Governor's grade at $400, next down the line is the Senator's grade at $350, and last is the Statesman at $300. Magnum rifles are chambered for 270, 30-06, 7mm Rem. Mag., 300 Win. Mag. or 358 Norma Mag. Maverick's calibers are 22-250, 243 Win., 6mm Rem. or 308 Win. Prices and grades are the same for both rifles.

Magnum or Maverick barreled actions are $139.50; actions only at $97.50, delivered in the white. Left-hand actions may be had on all rifles, barreled actions or actions at the same price.

Ranger Arms' newest rifle is the Single-Shot Bench Rest/Verminter, made on their own side-port bolt action receiver. This one has a laminated walnut thumb-hole stock with a 13½" pull and a wide beavertail for end—all features appreciated when shooting from the bench. The action is fitted with a 24" match-grade stainless steel barrel chambered for 222 Rem. or 22-250. It's no lightweight, weighing 11¾ pounds, but it isn't too heavy for the purpose intended. Right- or left-hand models can be had at $450 in either chambering. Actions alone are $149.50, either standard (22-250) or "miniature" for the 222 Rem. Barreled SSBR actions bring $249.50, heavier barrels being available if desired.

Plainfield Machine Co.

The 30-caliber M-1 U.S. Carbine is one gun that refuses to die, even though the round it chambers has been condemned as worthless and ballistically unstable by many authorities. These arms were sold on the surplus market, but Plainfield saw fit to improve and manufacture their modified M-1 carbine some years ago in many forms. Newest of these is their presentation model, PPM 30, that has a hand-rubbed, oil-finished stock of American walnut with a Monte Carlo cheekpiece at $125. With the S&K mount and a 4x scope fitted, it becomes the model PPM 30T at $150.

If you like the M-1 carbine, but think it's just a plinker, here's the news you've been waiting for. Plainfield is now making these arms in 22 Long Rifle. The stock, receiver, barrel and price tag all look the same as the 30-caliber, only the bore size gives it away. We've been told that most models will be available, but check before you order.

Harry Owen

There has been an increased interest in barrel inserts, and you can look for some new ones from Harry Owen. Besides the original Lothar Walther 222/22 adaptor, made in Germany, there are now 22 rimfire adaptors for the 22-250, 220 Swift, and 22 Savage. A new adaptor to fire 30 U.S. Carbine rounds in 30-06 rifles is also coming, likewise for the 308 Win. and 30-30. These are $7.50 each.

Owen also imports adaptors handling the 4mm centerfire cartridge. A common cartridge in Europe, it's widely used there for indoor shooting. Noise level and velocity are on a par with those produced by pellet guns. Owen offers these adaptors for a number of pistols and revolvers. The 4mm ammo, obtainable from Liberty Arms, Box 309, Montrose, Cal. 91020, costs about the same as a box of BB caps. These pistol conversion units cost $24, and those I've worked with shoot very well.

Last year Owen introduced conversion units to fire standard 22s in 45 ACP and 9mm Parabellum pistols, and these are now to be had for the 22 WRM, the cost also $24.

Also available is an *Einsteckpatrone* (single shot case) for the M20 practice cartridge of 4mm caliber. As our photograph shows, these *rifled* steel cases simulate a given cartridge — 7x57mm, 30-06, et al—into which the little 4mm round is chambered. Accuracy is excellent at short range, say 10 meters, and there's virtually no noise; they're ideal for indoor shooting, to keep one's trigger finger tuned up.

There are two small drawbacks, maybe—the Einsteckpatrone is a bit slow to load and unload, though that could be cured by having 4 or 5 of them. Too, the 4mm cartridges won't be found everywhere.

All of these interesting and useful practice devices are made by Lothar Walther in West Germany. Construction is of top quality, too, the machining and rifling beautifully done.

Owen's engraved Krieghoff drillings have seen some changes, the 7mm Rem. Mag. caliber having been dropped. They're now offered for 243, and scope mounts for U.S. scopes can now be installed at the factory ($65 excluding the scope). (J. Neumyer)

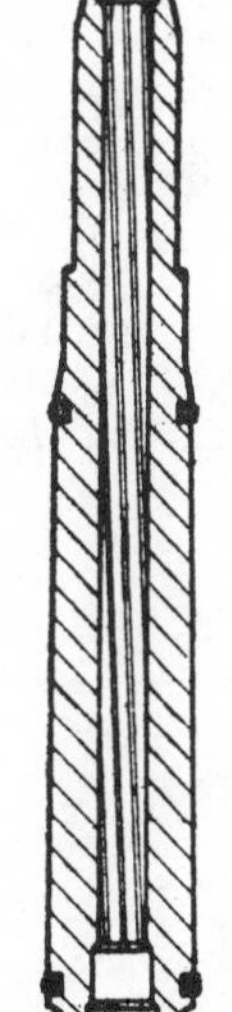

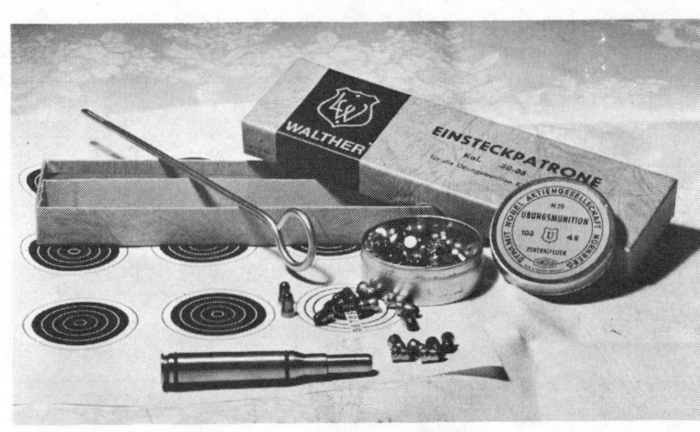

Left—Auxiliary cartridge for the 30-06 fires 4mm centerfire cartridges. Above—The *Einsteckpatrone* Kit is packaged with combination cleaning and expended-round ejector rod. 4mm ammo, not included with the kit, is shown for comparative scale.

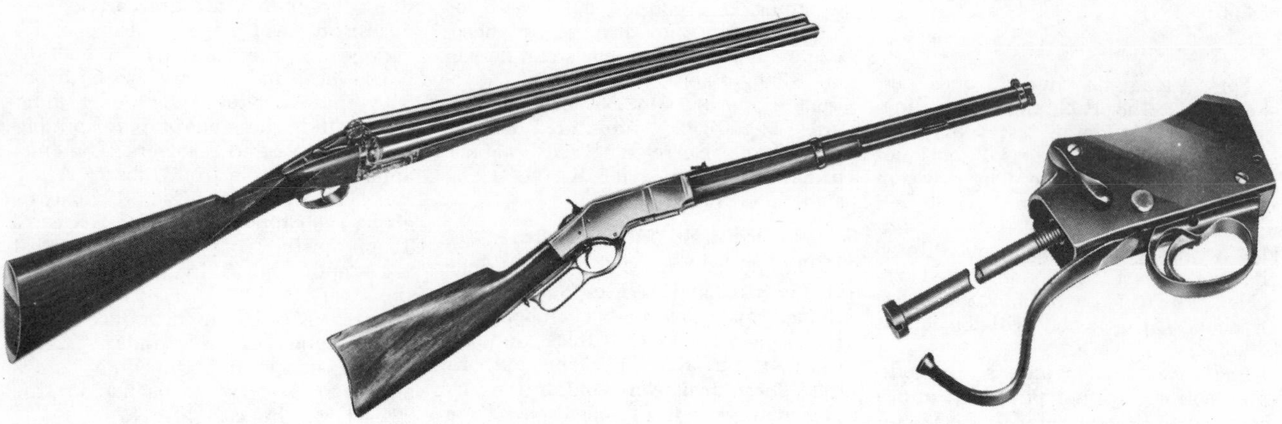

Webley & Scott Model 710 Yellow Boy 66 Carbine Greener GP Martini action

Navy Arms

The petite little beauty that stole the show at the British exhibit of the NSGA convention was the Webley & Scott Model 710 double barrel shotgun. Made in 28-ga. only, the 710 has a boxlock receiver covered with typical British scroll engraving. The straight-grip stock and semi-beavertail fore-end are of French walnut, hand-checkered and hand-rubbed oil finished. This lightweight shotgun (about 5½ lbs.) is fast pointing, should be easy to carry afield and will probably become the favorite of your wife or youngster if you let them practice with it—28-ga. shooting is virtually recoiless. Quality doesn't come cheap—the 710 costs $625.

W&S Models 700 and 701 are now made in 28-ga. also. These are not quite as small as the 710—the same receiver is used as on their 20-ga. 700 and 701 shotguns. Prices are $550 and $950 respectively.

Modern-made true sidelock shotguns are few and far between these days yet W&S introduced one this year, the Model 1100 Conquest. This bar-action double has intercepting safeties and is fully engraved in British style. Made in 12 gauge only, and with 2¾" chambers, 25", 26" and 28" barrels are offered, choked to your order. Auto-ejectors are standard. The straight-grip stock is of best quality French walnut, with "cast and bend to order." A beautiful shotgun, price $1750.

The Greener GP single barrel 12-ga. ejector shotgun, we feel, is really a bargain. The GP has an improved Martini action with automatic safety, and the take-down barrels, chambered for 2¾" shells, can be had in 26, 28, 30, 32 and 36 inch length. The straight-gripped stock and fore-end are of walnut-finished hardwood, hand checkered. A nice little single barrel trap gun for only $90. Actions only are available for building a varminter or a big game buster—it'll handle most cartridges from 22 Hornet to 45-70. This large Martini action is $49.50 blued; engraved and color case-hardened it's $59.50. We saw this action with a lever that was newly designed—recurved with a ball on the end for pistol grip stocks—but these may not yet be available.

Navy Arms will soon have a very fine replica of the Brown Bess flintlock musket, this to be the 2nd Pattern, the type that saw service in the Revolution. The full length stock of this famous 42" barreled shoulder arm will be of hard maple, while the "furniture" will be steel and brass to match the original in all respects.

Price of the musket is $225, and there's a Brown Bess carbine of the same period at the same cost. Bayonets, also exact replicas, will be $10 extra.

Knowing of editor Amber's interest in rifles with low or unusual serial numbers—he has a few numbered 00, 0, 1, 9 and so on—Val Frogett, president of Navy Arms, contributed one of his Yellow Boy 66s to this collection. This one is stocked in a good grade of walnut with nice metal finishing on both steel and brass. It has the crisp, light trigger pull of a target rifle and bears the serial number 00000. How's that for oneupmanship?

RWS is loading high velocity 38 Special cartridges for Val Forgett's 38 Carbine, said to offer 1635 foot seconds muzzle velocity from the 18-inch barrel. These loads, described as being made for hunting, show muzzle energy of some 930 foot pounds, about equal to the 30 M1 carbine round. (E.D.)

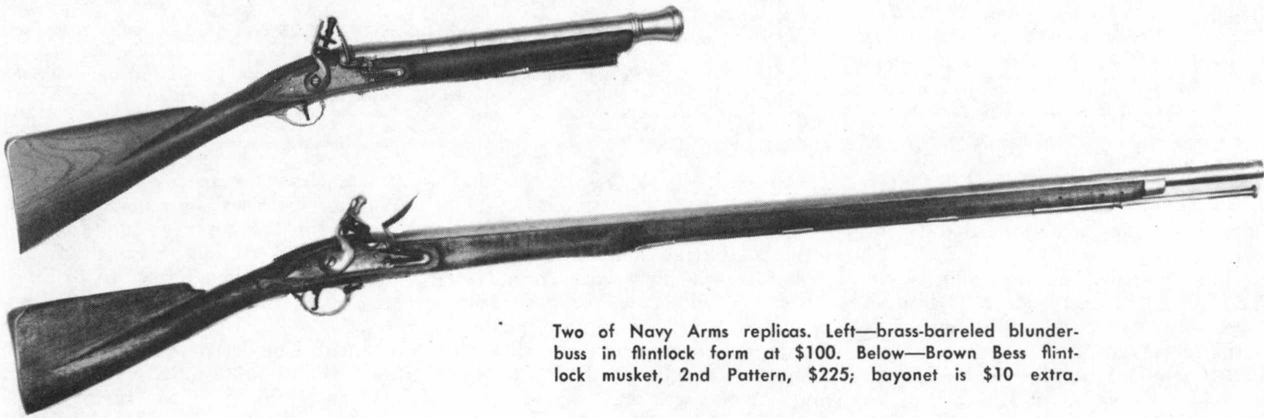

Two of Navy Arms replicas. Left—brass-barreled blunderbuss in flintlock form at $100. Below—Brown Bess flintlock musket, 2nd Pattern, $225; bayonet is $10 extra.

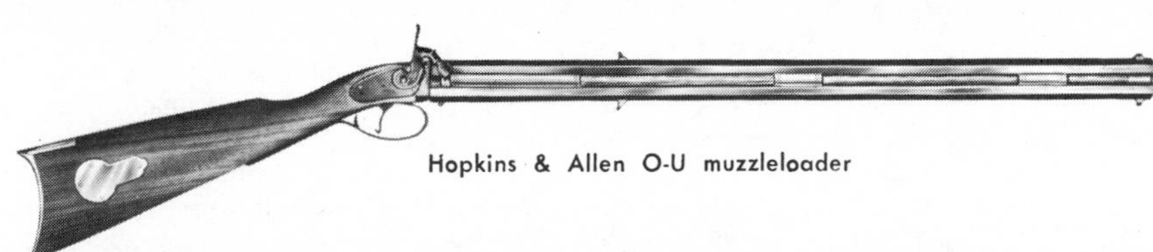
Hopkins & Allen O-U muzzleloader

Numrich Arms

The renewed interest in black powder shooting may not be entirely credited to Numrich Arms, but you can bet that a good part of the current trend is due to their stimulus. While continuing to produce the same line of good quality Hopkins and Allen guns, one new rifle has been added.

Unless you're a dyed-in-the-wool collector, you've probably never seen or heard of an over-under muzzleloader. They were made in both flint and percussion form, and now you can own one of the latter in replica for $125—it's the latest from H&A. The 28" barrels, 45-cal. and 11/16" across the flats, rotate on a pin fixed to the buttstock. Each barrel carries its own set of open sights, permitting the same point of impact to be hit with both shots. An American walnut buttstock, brass furniture and a brass-tipped hickory ramrod give attractive contrast to the blued steel barrels of this 8½-lb. front-feeder.

A new H&A 24-page catalog of muzzleloaders and accessories is available from Numrich for 25¢. It describes everything you need to get started in black powder shooting—everything but powder, balls and caps are available.

Allen & Thurber Replica

A replica of the Allen & Thurber percussion rifle is being made by W. L. Mowery Gun Works, P.O. Box 711, Olney, Texas 76374. The 32" barrel is 1" across the flats, of 50 caliber with a 1:60 twist. Buttplate, trigger guard, action and fore-end are all cast of high density brass. The buttstock is walnut and a striped hickory ramrod is brass tipped. Using a .498" ball and 100 grains of FFG black powder you have a nice plinker or target rifle—overlooking the open rear and blade front sights. Loading 125 grains of FFG, it can be used for hunting, as a velocity of 2300 fps is produced and a ME of 1985 foot pounds. This rifle (not a kit) sells for $149.50 complete—only powder, ball and caps are needed to feed this front-loader.

Mowery also has a Hawken Kit available—also with a 32" 50-cal. barrel. The fancy figured maple stock is machined outside to Hawken shape, a channel routed to fit the barrel and the ramrod hole drilled. All furniture is solid brass, as above, including the screws. Sights—iron front and adjustable rear—are specially made for the Hawken. Finishing materials are furnished, but lock and trigger must be acquired elsewhere—suppliers' names on request from Mowery. $125 FOB.

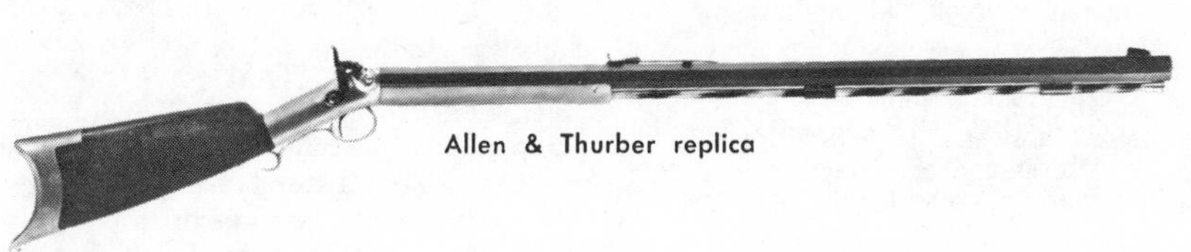
Allen & Thurber replica

Mossberg

Mossberg this year celebrates its 50th year as manufacturers of some of our sturdiest shooting irons. To do proper honors to its half-century of existence the company has offered a 50th Anniversary Pigeon grade Model 500 shotgun, a pump repeater. Made in 12 gauge only, this new shotgun will be offered in trap, Skeet and field styles. They'll carry specially selected walnut stocks with recoil pads, raised ventilated ribs, gold-inlaid receivers, with the "50th Anniversary" emblem in gold on the right side of the action. The pistol grip cap has another anniversary vignette in gold. There are two red bead sights on the vent rib and the buyer may have the C-Lect vari-choke if he likes. Price, $150.

Completely new this year at Mossberg is the Model 800 rifle in a Mannlicher-style stock. With a 20-inch barrel and a weight of only 6½ pounds, the latest Mossberg is a rakish and handsome addition. The bolt handle, styled to conform to the Mannlicher tradition, is not the old butter-knife styling, however; the new Mossberg has a semi-knob at its end to give the shooter a little more purchase. The stock, equipped with sling swivels, has hand checkering at pistol grip and forestock, and it's quite fetching. Calibers are 22-250, 243 and 308. Standard with open sights, the M800 Mannlicher is tapped for scope mounts, of course. Price, $135.

McKeown's Guns

Sold here under the name Allen, these Italian O-U smoothbores quite clearly show the influence of the American importer on the gunmaker. At present, 5 models are offered, with 3 or 4 more slated for later this year. The models available differ only in some minor features as well as wood selection and metal finish.

The MCK 68, the lowest-priced O-U in the Allen line, is offered in 12 ga. only, comes with vent rib, double triggers, case hardened finish, and chrome-lined barrels — price $198.95.

The S201 Allen American has double triggers, vent rib, extractors, chrome-lined barrels, comes in 12, 20, 28, and 410 and any choke combination desired. French walnut stocks with high gloss finish are standard on all Allen shotguns, as is good hand-checkering; with the exception of the M68, all carry some degree of engraving. The standard grade S201 retails for $249.95, while the S201 Deluxe costs 100 bucks more. Here you get a single, non-selective trigger, wide trap rib, ejectors, selected wood and more engraving.

The Mexico 68 model is a fancier version of the MCK gun, offered only in 12 ga., and sells for $385. The Olympic 68 model carries a vent rib, choice of extractors or ejectors, selective trigger, and the gun is offered with trap, Skeet or field chokes. $285. (B.S.)

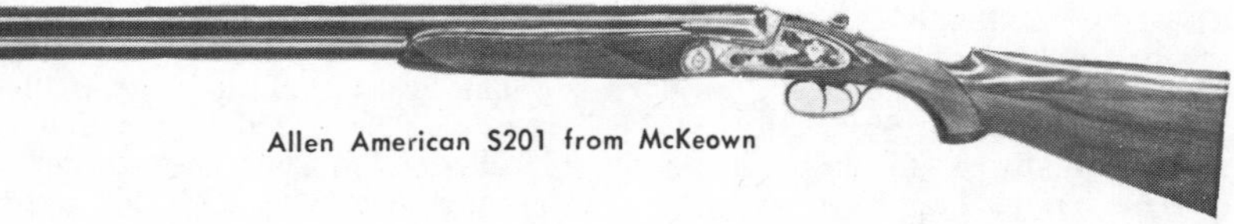
Allen American S201 from McKeown

Marlin

The two best known Marlin rifles are the Model 336, the centerfire high-power, and the Model 39, their 22 lever gun. Now there is a newcomer —if that's the right term! The Model 1894. Chambered for a 44 Magnum cartridge, the action is only about half the length of the 336, which happy fact adapts it most fittingly to the short 44 cartridge. The Model 1894 was first made by Marlin in that year, and production continued until 1917. The new rifle has a 20-inch micro-grooved barrel and the receiver has been tapped for both a receiver sight and scope sights. Like the other Marlins it has a solid top receiver, ejection to the side. It won't be available until after September, and the price will be about $99.95, perhaps.

You'll find a history of Marlin by Pete Kuhlhoff elsewhere in this issue. That story covers the new Century Limited models that Marlin will offer in 1969, these to carry commemorative medallions, and to be made in limited editions.

LA Distributors

In addition to last year's guns this importer will have a number of new firearms. When I looked them over the ATFD had just given the nod on importing some of them, but a few days later came word from ATFD that there was a question about some of their handguns. As of mid-March, 1969, I have not heard just what the ruling was. At any rate, here is the rundown planned by LA in the middle of February.

New to be offered by LA are: an O-U rifle in 22-250 with double triggers, extractors, top tang safety, the action to be tapped for scope mounting. The price will be about $300, very low for a rifle of this style. An O-U shotgun with two sets of barrels will be offered in three grades. The shooter who owns one of these will have his choice of using it as a 12-ga. gun on pheasants in the morning and as a 20-bore on grouse or woodcock after lunch. There's going to be a single selective trigger, selective ejection, top tang safety. The separated barrels will remind you of the old Marlin Model 90.

The Shikari bolt action centerfire rifle will be now offered chambered for the 300 Winchester and the 7mm Remington Magnums. Also in the hopper is a lever-action 22 RF tubular-fed magazine rifle. (B.S.)

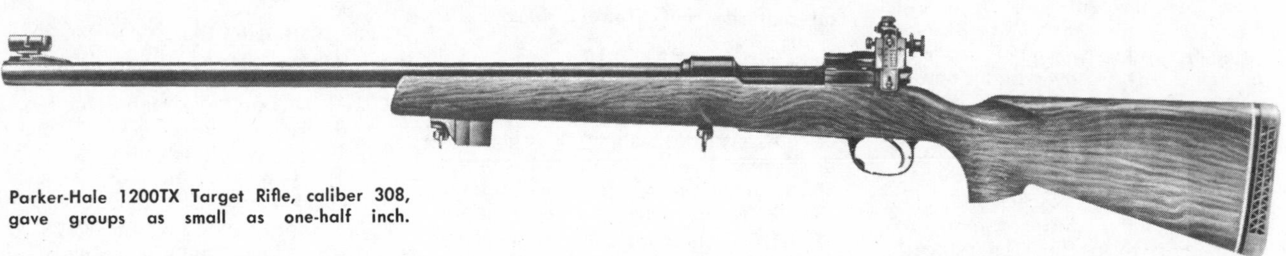

Parker-Hale 1200TX Target Rifle, caliber 308, gave groups as small as one-half inch.

Jana International

This importer handles the British Parker-Hale guns, but GCA '68 put a crimp into their line. P-H had been sporterizing the SMLE, calling it the P-H Custom No.1 303 Sporter. While the company was not able to revamp some of the more awkward features of the SMLE, they did a fine job on sporterizing the rifle. Although the 303 British cartridge has never become highly popular here, it's very big in Canada, naturally, where it is used for nearly all game the way the '06 is used here. Since the SMLE was originally a military arm, Jana can no longer import it.

The P-H Model 1200 Super Sporter is a well-made epoxy-bedded bolt action rifle on an FN-type Mauser action, tapped for U.S. scope mounts. The walnut stock carries skipline checkering and the pistol grip has a pronounced Wundhammer swell. The Super sells for $149.95 ($10 more for the magnums in all grades), and it's a hell of a good buy at that low price. Chambered for 243, 270, '06, 308 Win., 7mm Rem. Mag., 300 Win. Mag. and 308 Norma Mag., it will soon be ready in 22/250 and 6mm Remington.

The 1200V is a brand-new varmint edition of the above rifle. The 24″ 4 pound target grade barrel is free-floated, also glass-bedded and scope-mount tapped. In addition, you get target scope base blocks, but these are not fitted. There are no sights. Chambered for 22/250, 6mm Rem. and 243 Winchester, the M1200V is $169.95.

The M1200P is the P-H Presentation Grade 1200 rifle, and it's chambered for the same array of cartridges. Retailing for $199.95, the rifle comes with a select French walnut stock. The action, trigger guard and magazine floorplate are fully scroll engraved. Furnished without sights, the M1200P is an excellent example of British gunmaking skills.

All of these P-H rifles have adjustable triggers, sling swivels, and the floorplate release is in the trigger guard. Standard is a heavy rubber recoil pad, and the three-way silent safety locks trigger, sear and bolt. Bluing is top-notch, as is the stock finish, which appears to be some sort of epoxy. (B.S.)

The latest P-H rifle in the 1200 series is the 1200TX, caliber 7.62 NATO (308) only. A target style stock is used (13¼″x1¾″x2″ approx.), fitted with an adjustable hand stop below the beavertail fore-end forward, and a rotatable swivel/front guard screw at the rear for 1- or 2-point sling use.

The heavy 26″ barrel carries a globe front sight, and the famed P-H micrometer rear sight is attached at the receiver rear. Weight with sights is about 10½ lbs., and the price is $209.95.

The 1200TX has been signally honored! It's been selected as the rifle to be used exclusively in the Canadian Palma Trophy Matches in 1969.

Our sample 1200TX came along a bit late for a full-blown workout, but a fair amount of shooting was completed.

To give the rifle a fair chance—because I'm not that good anymore the iron sights—I screwed on target type scope bases to the rifle (the barrel and receiver ring are tapped for U.S. standard bases) and mounted my old but reliable 16x Fecker glass.

Forty rounds of factory ammo—20 each of an older lot of Sako cartridges were run through the barrel, 150- and 180-gr. soft point stuff. The results were not unexpected because these Sako loads had not in the past shown any spectacular accuracy. The 180-gr. rounds shot the best, a couple of 5-shot groups printing into 1½″-1¾″ spreads, but the average went close to 2″. The 150-gr. loads averaged 2¼″ plus, with only one string of 5 under 2″. This was at 100 yards, of course.

As with most brand-new barrels, I expect this Jana 1200TX will require some hundred shots or so to smooth it out and normalize it.

Nevertheless, when I put some target loads through it, the results were quite gratifying. Having still a fair quantity of HiVel 2 on hand, I loaded up 35 grains of that powder, Remington 9½ primers and the 180-gr. Sierra flat-base bullets. That gave me just over 2300 fps in another 308 not long ago, and it perhaps shows 2350 or so in the 26″ Parker-Hale barrel.

As I've said, they performed quite well—the first 3 groups of 5 went

Parker Hale 1200TX Specifications

Caliber: 7.62mm NATO
Barrel: 26″ free-floating
Over-all: 46¾″
Cartridge cap.: 5
Glass-bedded action.
Safety: Thumb slide locks trigger, bolt and sear.
Trigger: Single-stage, adj. for weight and backlash.
Stock: European walnut target stock with high comb, beavertail fore⅜end with adj. hand stop, full pistol grip, ventilated rubber recoil pad, oil finish.
Drop at comb: 1$\frac{11}{16}$.
Drop at heel: 1$\frac{5}{16}$.
Pull length: 13 $\frac{3}{16}$.
Weight (with sights): 10½ lbs. (approx.)
Sights: Mirometer-click/vernier rear; globe front with interchangeable posts/apertures.

Parker-Hale 1200TX being tested at Creedmoor Farm

7/8", 1 1/8" and 1" scant, but I goofed someway on the final 5, I think, opening the spread to 1 5/8".

There was just time, before final deadlines, to try a few more handloads in the 1200TX, but the wind and weather conditions weren't the best.

Nevertheless, in spite of a 12-15 mile west wind, I got some pretty good shooting from 39.5 grains of 4320 and the Sierra 165-gr. boat-tail H.P. bullet. Touched off with CCI regular primers, three 5-shot groups made 3/4", 13/16" and 1 1/8". That last one showed an even 1/2" for the first 4, but a strong gust of wind and/or my yanking put the last one out to the right.

Some older Speer 165-gr. and 150-gr. Centrix bullets—with the other components and the wind the same, gave me 5-shot strings running 1 1/2"-2". Obviously, this Parker-Hale rifle will shoot well, given the bullet it likes, and I'm looking forward to further trials with the Sierra 30-cal. match bullets and some other powder charges.

That was all I could get done at one shooting session, but it looks like this new match rifle is going to shoot fully satisfactorily. (J.T.A.)

Also new in the Jana line-up is an O/U shotgun called the Laurona. It has double triggers which, however, function like a single trigger. That is, *either* trigger will fire both barrels — alternately, of course — and some of you may be old enough to remember when the early Browning O-U guns offered the same system. Offered in 12-bore only, the gun will carry a vent rib, plain extractors, a checkered pistol grip stock and fore-end, plus recoil pad. Spanish-made, the Laurona will carry a price tag of $195. (B.S.)

Jana's Loyola side-by-side double, while not brand new with the importers, is a nice Spanish-made smoothbore in 12, 20 or 410 that sells for about $95. Checkering fore and aft is standard on the real walnut pistol grip stock, as is a rubber recoil pad. A vent rib version is also available at some $15 extra.

There's also a 10-ga. Magnum double in the Jana line, with 3 1/2" chambers in the 30" (M&F) or 32" F&F barrels. Price about $115 with matted rib, at $15 more for the vent rib model. (J.T.A.)

J-K Imports

J-K Imports (Box 403, Novato, Calif. 94947) is bringing over a new line of Italian-made over-under smoothbores that appear to be very well made and attractively styled. These are made by Mario Beschi.

The Condor, made in 12, 20, 20-3" and 28 gauge, has double side-lug lockup, Greener crossbolt, and chrome-lined bores. Two triggers and simple extractors are standard on this engraved boxlock (with dummy side-plate), while the stock is of choice Italian walnut, hand checkered. Straight grip or pistol, the Condor sells for $265.

The A.S.L. 206, quite similar to the Condor, has auto ejectors and unusual triggers; the front trigger acts as a single, firing both barrels in succession, while the rear trigger fires only the top barrel—a mite different in itself. Cost, $335.

The J-K Airone is identical but does not have false or dummy side-plates, and carries less elaborate engraving. Price, $224.95.

Mario Beschi side-by-side doubles are also imported. These run from a boxlock at $179.95 to a de luxe, fully engraved genuine sidelock at $365.

All of these imports have a frame size commensurate with the gauge, and most important, all of the J-K Imports shotguns described may be ordered on a full custom-fitted basis—stock dimensions, length of barrels, choice of chokes, type of fore-end and buttstock, etc., can be made to the customer's dimensions and taste at no added cost whatsoever. Write to the company for complete details, and ask also about their fine Spanish-leather gun case, etc.

J-K Imports' made-in-Italy Condor over-under can be custom ordered, without extra cost. See text for details.

Ithaca

Ithaca has a handsome new center-fire rifle. At first blush it appears to be a Sako, but it is made by Oy Tikkakoski of Finland. The short action is chambered for the shorter cartridges, the 22-250, 243, 6mm Remington and 308. Two styles are offered, standard and deluxe. The latter has a rollover comb, a rosewood fore-end tip and pistol grip cap, plus white line spacers. Barrels are 23 inches long, and the rifle weighs about 6 1/2 lbs. Furnished with open sights, the top of the receiver is milled to accept the scope without the usual screwed-on mounts, but so far no word on which mounts or rings these will be, nor when available. The single stage trigger is adjustable. Stock has the measurements and configuration that appeal to American gunners, This rifle looks like a real gem! All metal parts are forged from Bofors high-grade steel, including the barrels. The cartridge feed—from a detachable box magazine—is straight line, said to eliminate jams or malfunctions. We haven't seen one yet because delivery is scheduled for June, 1969.

Last year Ithaca commenced importation of the superb Perazzi (Italy) shotguns. These smoothbores, which hold many European trap and live-bird records, are about the best made anywhere. The 3 offered by Ithaca are all over-unders. The MX-8 Trap, the Competition I Trap and the Competition I Skeet, are all 12 gauge only. Barrels range from 26¾" for the Skeet gun to 32" for the trap models. Weight is in the 7¾-8 pound area. These Perazzis are custom built and can be had in any stock dimensions and any choke.

John Amber, squinting into the bright sun and wearing a pair of leather hunting breeches, holds the ZCZ Yugoslavian 30-06 rifle he used on his red deer hunting in Morovic Forest.

Interarms

Interarms has long been the prime importer of the fine Walther arms—pistols as well as their centerfire rifles and air guns. To that illustrious line of firearms has been added the name of Mauser.

In the centerfire, bolt action line, the Mauser Model 2000 is the latest Mauser design. Each action carries the Mauser "Banner" trademark, and precision machining is still the key word with Mauser. The new bolt has larger, re-inforced locking lugs and a recessed bolt face that wholly encloses the cartridge head for maximum support. Chambered (for the time being) only for the 30-06 cartridge, the magazine holds 5 rounds, and the magazine floorplate is hinged and embossed with a hunting scene. The Krupp steel barrel has a right-hand twist and 4-groove rifling, carries a gold bead ramp sight with removable hood and a folding U-notch rear sight adjustable for elevation. The receiver is tapped for most U.S. scope bases. The black walnut stock is hand checkered, has a Monte Carlo comb and cheekpiece and several eye-appealing frills. The gun comes with sling swivels, and the trigger is adjustable. Price of the M2000 Mauser is a low $139, and Interarms hopes to offer other chamberings in the fall of '69 or the following spring. (B.S.)

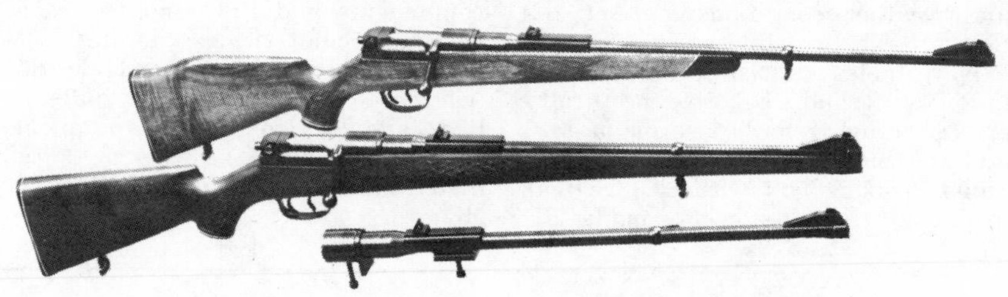

The new and improved Mauser 66 features quick barrel changing and a short-throw action.

The new Mauser 2000, a fine bolt rifle in 270, 308 and 30-06, selling for $139.

Zavodi Crvena Zastava of Yugoslavia, makers of excellent Mauser-actioned complete rifles, have entered into an agreement with Interarms (10 Prince St., Alexandria, Va. 22313), well-known importers of firearms.

Interarms will now distribute ZCZ rifles, actions and barreled actions on a world-wide basis. The new Mauser-type actions—improved over the regular 1898 form, Dick Winter of Interarms told me—should be available about the time you read this, and they'll sell for about $55.

At the moment (mid-May, 1969) prices for complete rifles have not been fully determined, but Winter says they'll be highly competitive; barreled actions will go for around $79.

Most modern U.S. calibers will be offered. Some of our readers will recall the article I wrote on my two hunting trips in Yugoslavia (Gun Digest 22), in which I used a ZCZ rifle in 30-06 to take a good stag in December of 1967.

I made other tests of the Zastava rifle after I returned home, and its performance at the target was quite satisfactory, as was functioning. My one criticism of the rifle was the factory installation of a semi-integral scope base, of special design, which necessitated the use of ZCZ-designed rings as well. The ZCZ receivers Interarms will bring over won't have these bases, I understand; instead they'll be tapped for the use of conventional mounts—Redfield, Weaver, Lyman, et al. (J.T.A.)

Galef and Son

As usual, this importer has a number of new guns for the American shooter. The old Monte Carlo stocked single barrel smoothbore now has a cousin—a trapgun. The easiest way to make a field gun into a trap or Skeet gun is to add a rib and straighten the stock to suit the particular requirements of the clay sport. Not so the Galef Monte Carlo—the gun has been revamped and redesigned from stem to stern and, for $149.95, you get a real, honest-to-gosh trapgun. Offered in 12-ga. only, the gun has an extractor, but the safety is still automatic—a feature some trapshooters could do without. Weight has been added, the new gun tipping the scale at 8¼ lbs., a comfortable handful for those long sessions at the traps.

Although it is not really new in the Galef line-up of imported guns, the Companion single barrel folding shotgun is now being made by a different Italian gunmaker. The handy little gun comes in all gauges, including 28, is offered with and without vent rib. Sans rib it's $49.95; with VR, $54.95.

A fine plinker, and equally at home on the casual target range, is the new

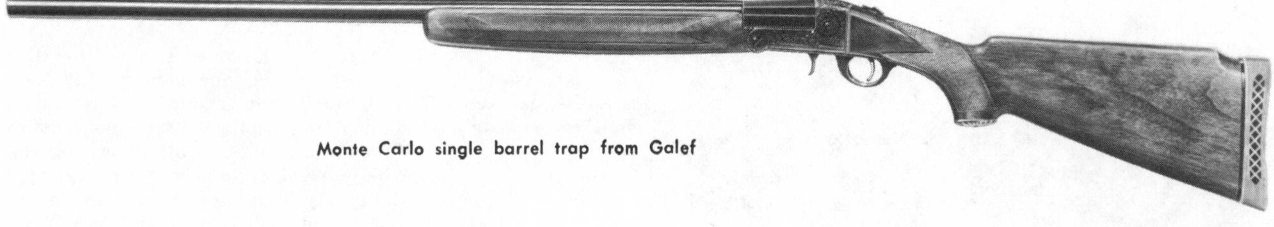
Monte Carlo single barrel trap from Galef

BSA Meteor Super air rifle in 177 or 22 caliber. This is a precision piece of machinery that did right well in my tests. The gun comes with a fully adjustable rear sight and the receiver is grooved for tip-off scope mounting. The trigger pull is excellent, and the performance as well as the feel of the gun is that of a sporting rifle rather than that of the usual air gun. Priced at $39.95, the gun reaches the consumer in a specially made box that even contains targets and a pellet trap.

The BSA Monarch deluxe hunting rifle is now tapped for standard U.S. scope bases. Offered in 222, 243, 270, 308 Win., 30-06, and 7mm Rem. Magnum in the hunting weight rifle (around 7 lbs.), the BSA is also made in a heavy-barrel version chambered for the 222 and the 243 (about 9½ lbs.). The walnut stocks are hand finished and moisture proofed. The safety, located to the right of the top tang, is really silent; the trigger is fully adjustable, and there's a hinged floorplate to make life easier. A handsome rifle that shoots very well, the hunting rifle will set you back $149.95, the varmint HB gun $20 more. (B.S.)

Flaig's Ace rifle, made in Ferlach, may be ordered in 25-06 caliber.

Flaig's

The Ace bolt action centerfire rifle is the latest addition to Flaig's line of fine imported sporting guns. The Ace, based on the Mauser 98 all-steel action, carries a 24" Boehler-steel, button-rifled tube with 6 grooves. The open rear sight is marked for 100 and 200 yards, and the hooded ramp front sight carries a gold bead. The bolt knob is knurled and the handle is forged low for scope mounting; the action is tapped for U.S. scope mounts. A side safety and Sako trigger are standard equipment.

The checkered pistol grip stock is of Circassian walnut, the grip cap and fore-end tip of rosewood. There is a good rubber recoil pad, and the gun comes with 1" swivels. Without scope the Ace goes 7½ lbs. This new offering is made in 243, 7x57, 270, 308, 30-06—and in 25-06! At long last, huh? In standard calibers, $135, in 25-06, including one fired case, $145. Made in Ferlach, the Ace carries Austrian proofmarks, of course. (B.S.)

Firearms International

This Washington, D.C., importer will be adding some fine arms to the line; after looking them over, I think you, too, will start figuring how you can float a second mortgage for some of these.

First of all, there is a Star copy of the S&W M39, the forged Duraluminum frame somewhat scaled down, and a fixed rear sight standard. Feel of the 9mm Parabellum pistol is excellent, and the price is a pleasant surprise—$89.95.

Remember the Winchester Model 62 of yesteryear? Well, you can have a copy of that fine "Gallery Model" from FI. Chambered for 22 S, L and LR, the gun feels and functions like the original—a nice item for $75.

Also new with F.I. is an O-U shotgun in 12 or 20, barrels 26", 28" or 30", all with ventilated ribs. The checkered stock has a pistol grip, and there's a handfilling fore-end. Two triggers and plain extractors are standard. Price, either gauge, $189.50.

Like the old hammer shotguns? Great, you can get three gauges—12, 20 and 410—in the new FI side-by-sides. Called the Overland, the guns carry beavertail fore-ends, double triggers, simple extractors and have 3-inch chambers. The 12s and 20s are also offered with 20½" tubes—real handy brush guns. $75 is the tab. (B.S.)

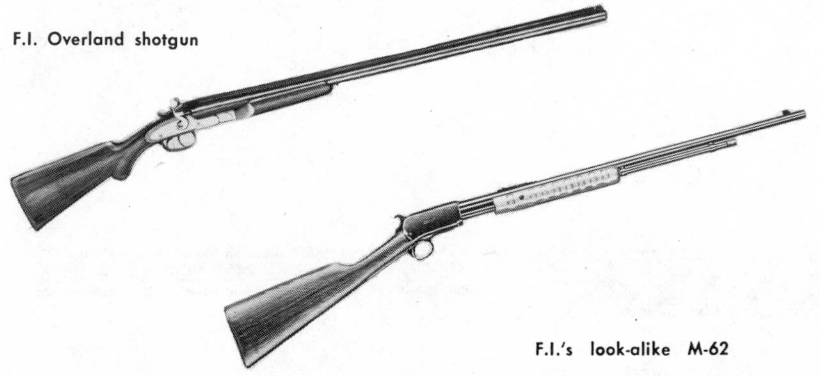
F.I. Overland shotgun

F.I.'s look-alike M-62

Fajen "Acra" Rifles

Just before we put this issue to bed I learned that Reinhart Fajen—manufacturer of the famous Fajen stocks—is now offering complete rifles in three styles. The "RA" model is his basic design at a low $119.95 for standard calibers (30-06, 270, 243 and 22-250) or at $129.95 for the two magnums, 7mm Remington and 300 Winchester. This is a hand-checkered, semi-classic styled half-stock sporter, using Santa Barbara of America Star-barreled actions.

(See my notes on S.B. of A. in this same section for details of their barrels and actions, which I won't duplicate here.)

Next up the Fajen scale is the Acra S24, made with better wood, rosewood fore-end tip and grip cap, rubber recoil pad and basket weave hand checkering. This one goes for $169.95, $10 more for the two magnum calibers.

Top of the "Acra" line is the M18, made with an 18" barrel and a full length Mannlicher-type stock, otherwise of the same fine quality as the S24, and selling for $189.95-$199.95.

No time or space for further dope—write to Fajen for more detailed information. (J.T.A.)

Krieghoff double in San Remo Grade carries nicely engraved action.

Europa

To say that some Krieghoff over-under shotguns are pretty fancy is an understatement. If the first look at the gun doesn't impress you, the price tag will—they're up 10% across the board from last year. The Standard grade now costs $595, San Remo $990, Monte Carlo $2450, Crown $2850 and the Super Crown is an even $3000.

Introduced at the NSGA show in Houston this year was the Krieghoff System, designed for clay-bird shooters. The "Systems" are cased sets for trap and Skeet using the same stock, fore-end, action and trigger while maintaining the same weight, weight, balance and swing—no matter which set of barrels are used. The Skeet set is delivered in a wood case, purple felt lined, the stock and fore-end strapped into its lid, the 4 barrels set in individual channels of the case proper. The Skeet System with 12, 20, 28 and 410 barrels is priced from $1750 for the Standard grade to $3500 for the Super Crown.

The Trap System has its 3 barrels fitted in the same 4-barrel case, but you can specify your preference on barrel length and choking for these. The Trap System begins at $1495 for the Standard grade and go up from there. (B.S.)

Davidson Firearms

This importer has added one new gun to the current list—the Model 69 SL. SL here means "sidelock," and I go along with Davidson's claim that this is the only sidelock within the reach of most shooters. Offered in 12 and 20, and chambered for the 2¾" shell, the gun carries a solid matted rib ⅜" wide at the breech and 7/32" wide at the muzzle. Two brass beads make up the sighting equipment. The sideplates are detachable, the firing pins are floating, and there are cocking indicators. The top tang safety is automatic. Extractors rather than ejectors are standard, and the two triggers are gold plated. The walnut stock is well finished, and the checkering is quite good. All Davidson guns are supplied with snap caps—a small but useful extra. O, yes, the price of the SL—a mere $129.50! (B.S.)

Charles Daly

This year Charles Daly offers five different O-Us, one side-by-side, and a single barrel trap gun. The latter, dubbed the Model 300, comes only in 12 ga., has a 32" full choke barrel. The gun is chambered for the 2¾" shell, has a manual safety and automatic ejector. The wide ventilated rib, specifically designed for the trapshooter, carries front and middle steel beads. Tipping the scales at 8 lb., it has a heavy duty recoil pad. A handsome gun with excellent balance, the Monte Carlo stock is designed to fit most shooters. The M300 retails for $329.

The Venture grade O-U was covered here last year, so we won't go into it now, except to note the new price—$249, up $13.

The Field grade, basically the Venture, has an automatic safety that is linked to the barrel selector and selective ejectors. On the Skeet gun the safety is manual. Like the Venture stock, the semi-pistol grip carries good hand checkering as does the hand-filling fore-end. Offered in all gauges except 16, the Field grade Daly is also available in 12-ga. Magnum with 30" tubes choked Full and Full. The 20 and 410s come with 3" chambers. This too is a lightweight gun, and the 12 Magnum comes with a heavy rubber recoil pad. This is a handsome gun, well finished, and certainly worth the $329-$349 asked.

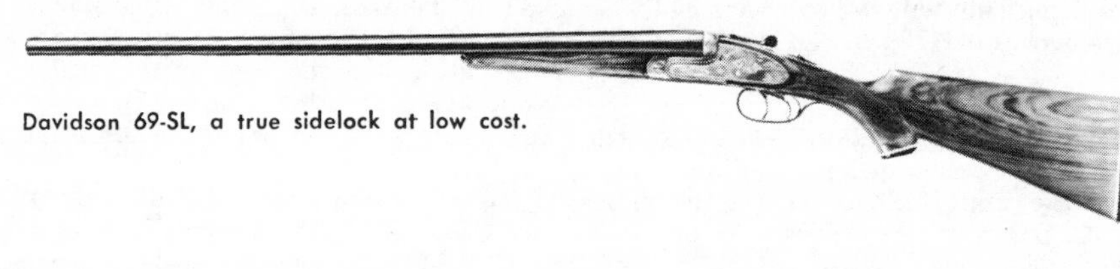

Davidson 69-SL, a true sidelock at low cost.

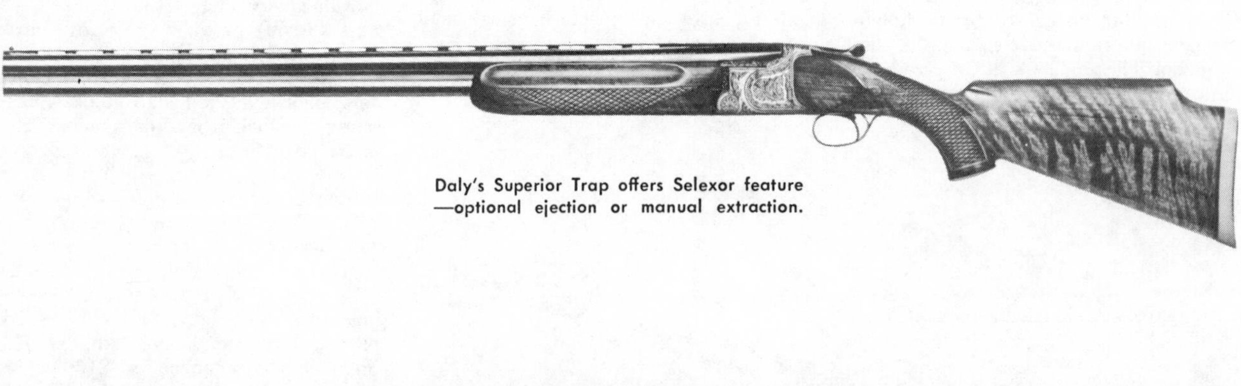

Daly's Superior Trap offers Selexor feature —optional ejection or manual extraction.

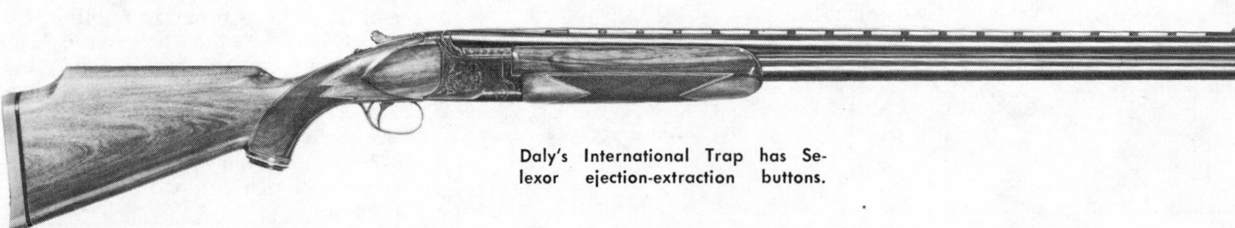

Daly's International Trap has Selexor ejection-extraction buttons.

Now, hold onto your hats—Daly has a new wrinkle which, though I haven't tried it, looks impressive! Offered only on the Superior and Diamond grade models in 12 bore, the *Selexor* permits the shooter to activate or deactivate the ejectors. With the ejectors working, you get selective ejection, with them shut out, you get manual extraction. A button on each side of the receiver provides the Selexor control—the right one takes care of the lower barrel, the left one handles the upper barrel.

The Superior grade field models are essentially identical to the previously mentioned Field grade, the only differences being in the wood figure, the amount of scroll engraving and in having full pistol grip stocks. The same barrel, gauge, and choke specs apply.

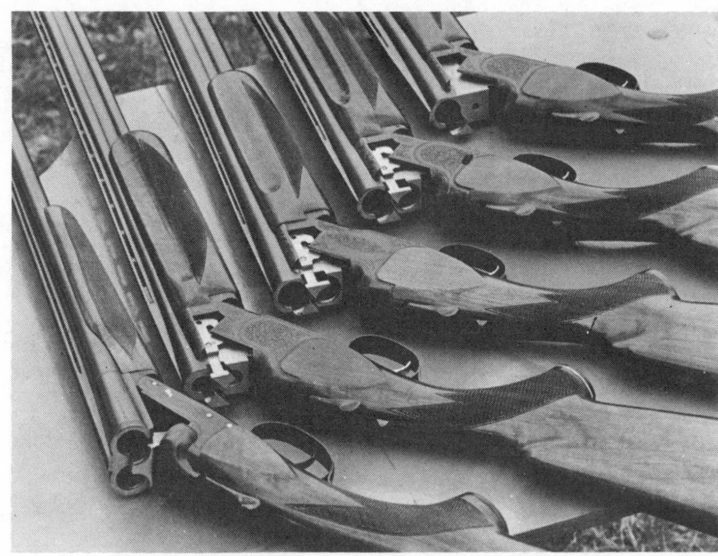

A battery of Daly doubles and the single barrel trap.

Close-up of the Selexor

The Superior trap model comes only in 12 ga. with 30- and 32-inch barrels, and all guns are chambered for the 2¾" shells. The new Flat Top O-U trap gun features not only the Selexor, but also a special ½-inch wide vent rib. The Flat Top O-U retails for $389, the Superior grade O-U for $349-$379, depending on regular or Monte Carlo stock, and whether or not the gun is equipped with the Selexor.

The Diamond Grade International Trap O-U is the top-of-the-line Daly with all the refinements a trapshooter could wish for, including a Selexor ejection. Price of that beauty is $575.

The new Daly side-by-side Empire carries a vent rib, auto safety and extractors. The single non-selective trigger is recoil activated, and the gun is offered in 12, 16 or 20 gauge with a wide choice of barrel lengths and chokes. All, except the 16, are chambered for the 3-inch shells; the price is $236. (B.S.)

Century Arms News

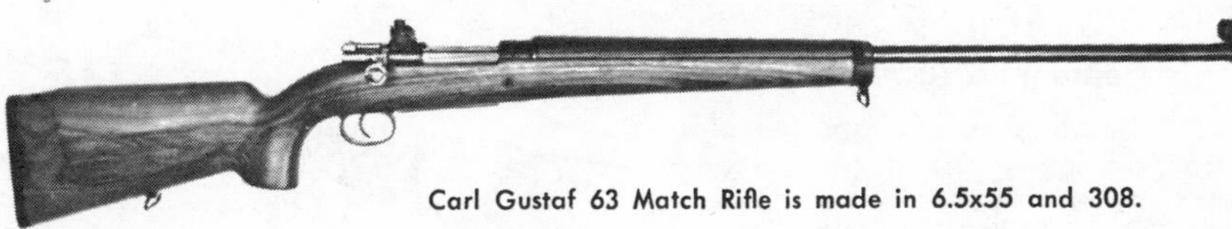

Carl Gustaf 63 Match Rifle is made in 6.5x55 and 308.

Century Arms of St. Albans, Vt., is importing the Carl Gustaf 63, a military-style competition rifle in 308 (NATO 7.62mm) caliber, and one of these was sent to us for trial recently. The rifle is also made in 6.5x55.

Our sample weighed just under 10 lbs., as specified, but the barrel was a trifle longer—29.25" versus 29.1" as listed. Over-all, the CG 63 is 49", the length of pull 13.5", and the weight of pull 4.5 lbs. There is the preliminary "military" take-up in the trigger, but the letoff itself is crisp, without creep.

The free-floating round barrel is 0.748" at the muzzle, and in 308 has a 12" twist. The front sight is a big globe type, with interchangeable inserts (1 post and 4 apertures), while the rear sight is fully adjustable for elevation and laterally. A scale on the "windage" knob is numbered 1 through 9, with click stops, and each division is equal to one centimeter at 100 meters, or about 0.4" per click. The elevation dial's scale is marked for 100 through 600 meters, with 25-meter divisions as well. Two interchangeable elevation rings are supplied—A for ammo giving 780 meter/seconds at the muzzle or 2560 fps, the other (B) for 800 m/s (2625 fps) ammo or higher MV. Four disks are furnished for the "GF-Diopter," from 1.5mm to 3.5mm, and there's a plastic hood that slips over the rear peep to shield the eye from stray light—it works well, too.

A small combination screwdriver-wrench is part of the kit—used for changing rings A and B, and for bringing the dials and windage marks to zero after that's been determined in shooting. A large plastic hood, covering the rear sight fully, protects against damage in transit or whatever.

As our picture shows, there's a handguard atop the barrel, and a pistol grip that is closely curled, quite deep, and a butt depth of 5.25". The comb is full, with a shallow cheek rest on both sides, but for me, at least, could be a fat ¼-inch higher. Rubber recoil pads are factory-offered to replace the shock-resistant plastic, or a vertically-adjustable buttplate may be had on special order.

A heavy-duty shooting sling is furnished with the CG 63. This has a good stay-put keeper for holding the loop snugly on the arm.

The CG 63 is made up on the Swedish Mauser action of 1896 vintage—a clip slot in the bridge and a thumb cut in the left sidewall are standard on this target rifle. Cocking is on closing, and a wing safety rides atop the rear of the bolt sleeve, which is open, not shrouded. The extractor is the long Mauser type, and the magazine holds 5 rounds. The steel follower is not angle-milled at the rear, thus locks the bolt open on the last shot.

Shooting the Carl Gustaf 63

A factory 5-shot target came with our sample rifle (presumably shot at 100 meters, though not so-marked) that was 1⅝" on centers. Most of our groups, with several brands and bullet weights of sporting ammo, ran a little larger than that on average, but 2½" from the bench was the biggest spread—and I'm not these days as good with peep sights as I am with a scope.

The best-grouping load was a mild one—41 grains of 3031 with 150-gr. Norma semi-boat-tail soft points. Several 5-shot strings went as small as 1¾", the largest of these loads just under 2¼".

For initial sighting-in for the handloads, some old components were used —7-year-old Herter 120 primers and 150-gr. Centrix SP bullets, using a start charge of 40.1 grains of 3031. These 5 (thrown-charged) went into 2⅞", conditions good, no wind, cloudy-bright.

Then, using the Norma bullets mentioned above, but all else the same, 5 went into 2½". Next the 3031 charge was set for 40.4 grains and, using the same Norma bullets but the powder weighed, I put 5 into 2⅛". The 41-gr. 3031 load, our best, was then shot.

A good, if not spectacular, performance for an iron-sighted rifle and me. I feel sure that our groups could have been 50% or more smaller had it been possible to use a scope.

Squibman 22 Autoloader

Squibman 22 Autoloader

Century Arms has another new import, a 22 rimfire semi-auto rifle that's made in the Philippine Islands. Why the name "Squibman?" I was curious, too, but when we unwrapped our sample the reason was clear—the Squires Bingham Company, located at Marikina, Rizal, in the P.I., are the manufacturers. I won't labor it!

Anyway, the S-22 is a neat little handful—19" barrel (21" including the muzzle brake), 40½ over-all yet with an adult-length pull of 14". The barrel carries conventional open sights—the rear a V-notch with 6-step elevator, the front a square blade that's less than 1/16" wide—it ought to be a bit fatter, and the rear notch would be improved by being square. It's called a Patridge, but it is not.

The steel magazine holds 15 rounds. There's a deflector device over the ejection port, and a safety lever is sited along the right rear of the receiver, where it's handy to the thumb of a right-handed shooter.

A protruding pin appears at the center rear of the receiver end cap when the rifle is cocked.

The pistol-grip, one-piece stock is nicely done — smooth finish on the Philippine mahogany, a shotgun style plastic buttplate in black, and the comb nose is fluted. Weight of the S-22 is 5¾ lbs., with the magazine attached but empty.

We had a spot of trouble with the first Squibman sample—it fired and ejected fully reliably, using a half-dozen brands of both high speed 22s and standard velocities — but every once in a while it failed to work the striker.

Accuracy, on the other hand, was quite good—at 25 yards, 5 shots went into ½-inch or so frequently. 50-yard groups were roughly an inch or so, but it was tough getting them because of the functioning hangups!

That sample was set aside and another one procured. The new one functioned perfectly with all HV brands—CCI, Western, Gevelot, Herter's, Remington and Hodgdon—and the accuracy was on the same order as before; half-inch groups or less at 25 yards were common, while 50-yard shooting gave me several of less than one inch.

That muzzle brake? I couldn't see where it had any effect, one way or the other. Certainly it might keep the muzzle down if this were a full auto rifle, but it isn't, of course. (J.T.A.)

As pointed out earlier, the day is not far off when you won't be able to buy a sportered military rifle. A Century Arms spokesman told me that, at best, there's about a year's supply of military rifles in the company's warehouse. So, if you want one, now is the time to order such a rifle through your local gunshop. Remember? You can no longer order by mail!

Centennial Arms Corp.

CAC is showing an imported blunderbuss replica. Have you, like so many other shooters, ever wondered how these old, bell-mouthed cannon really handled? I had for years, and some time back I took a whack at some tin cans with one. Man—that was a real handful of shooting iron. Going back into history, you might say that those hand cannons were the forerunner of our riot guns.

The replica I tried gave off a lot of satisfying noise and smoke, shredding tin cans with great regularity. Selling for $79.95, you have a handsome decorator as well as a shooter, and for another 25 bucks you can even have an engraved blunderbuss replica. (B.S.)

Champlin Firearms

Continuing to make the complete line of rifles announced here last year, Champlin Firearms has added some new arms. A left-hand model of the standard rifle is now available with prices beginning at $636.56.

Champlin is also importing a box-lock over-under shotgun in three grades. These will be made in Italy and stocked in the U.S. The standard grade will have a fully engraved receiver in either frosted or color case-hardened finish, with a straight (English-type) or pistol grip buttstock, and in a variety of barrel lengths and choke combinations. Available in standard grade, 12 gauge only, at $642.50, there's a deluxe grade also that comes with better engraving and wood at $847.50.

Custom grade shotguns, in 12 gauge only, will be just that. Custom stocks, barrel specifications and engraving by one of America's well-known engravers will be made to your order on a limited basis with prices beginning at $1100. (E.D.)

Carter's Gun Works

While not a gun importer *per se,* Carter has been able to supply many parts for French-made shotguns, including the Robust; numerous parts for that gun were completely unavailable for a while.

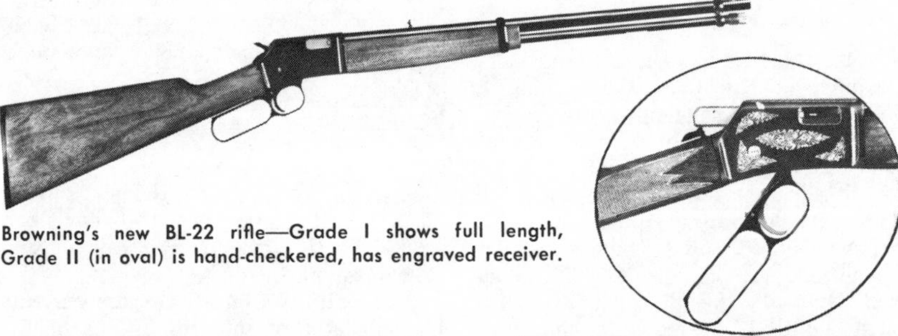
Browning's new BL-22 rifle—Grade I shows full length, Grade II (in oval) is hand-checkered, has engraved receiver.

New Browning Rimfire Rifle

Almost too late to get the mention into this 24th edition, we've just had a letter from Harmon G. Williams, vice-president of Browning Arms Company, announcing the BL-22, a lever-action short-barreled rifle or carbine in western styling. Made with the traditional straight-grip stock, and carrying a full-length tubular magazine under its 20-inch barrel, the new BL-22 looks like it might have been designed by the old master himself, John M. Browning.

The BL-22 weighs 5 pounds, is 36¾ inches over-all. The smooth-operating lever travels in a short arc, only 33°, thus the shooter can keep his grip on the stock while throwing the lever to full cock. The trigger is combined with the lever, travels with it, so there is no chance of a pinched finger. Trigger pull is quite crisp, I'm told, with no creep and has about a 5-lb. pull. A recessed muzzle prevents damage, so continued accuracy is assured. The rear sight is a fully adjustable folding leaf; the front is a raised bead.

The BL-22 handles 22 Short, Long or Long Rifle separately or in any mixed combination—15 LRs, 17 Ls, or 22 Shorts.

Safety was the watchword when the BL-22 was designed. The visible hammer has a half-cock position, and there is an inertia-type firing pin. In addition, a disconnect system prevents firing until the lever and breech are fully closed. Any pressure applied to the trigger while cocking must be released before the rifle is "off safe," thus accidental firing at the climax of cocking is prevented.

The BL-22 comes in two grades, both with selected walnut stocks and fore-ends. Grade II is hand-checkered fore and aft, the receiver and trigger guard hand-engraved.

Both receivers are of forged and milled steel, grooved to take most tip-off mounts or receiver sights.

Grade I will list at $67.50, Grade II at $84.50, and these BL-22s should be available by the time you read this. (J.T.A.)

The Super-Light Superposed shotgun was introduced a couple years ago for upland game hunters who wanted a light, straight-gripped field gun, but in 12 gauge only. Response to the Super-Light must have been good as Browning is now making it in 20 gauge also. Available at present in Grade 1 only, 12 or 20 gauge with the slender, solid rib is $465. (E.D.)

Blumenfeld

Some years ago, this company offered a most handy 20 gauge side-by-side, but something happened and only a handful of them ever got to the U.S. Now the gun is back with us, offered with 22- and 24-inch tubes in all choke combinations. There's a rubber recoil pad, double triggers, top-tang safety, and extractors rather than ejectors. Made in Spain by Arizaga, the gun carrries the straight stock of the British shotguns, and the case-hardened finish is pleasing. Price of this model is about $120.

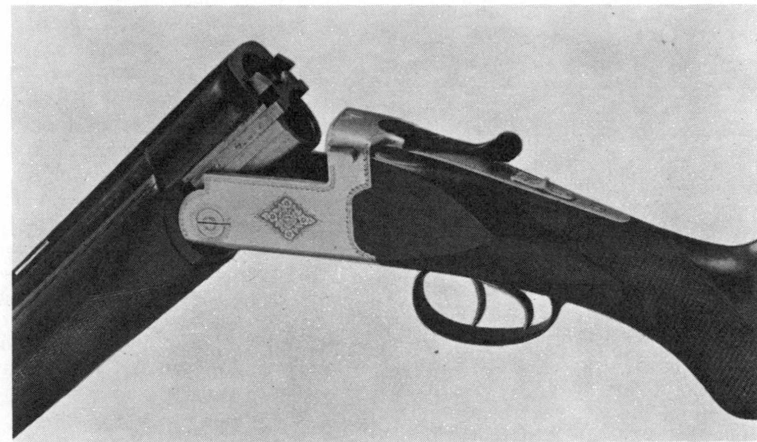

Atlas Arms Model 65 Over-Under

The Volunteer Pointer is the name given to the new 12-gauge semi-auto smoothbore. Based on the Browning design, the gun comes with 26, 28, or 30 inch barrel, in all chokes. This Japanese gun is destined to sell for about $150. The guns I examined were the first ones to come into the country. They appeared to be well made and well finished, but I didn't have the opportunity to shoot them. (B.S.)

Atlas Arms

This Chicago-based importer has dropped several guns from his well-established line—the De Luxe O-U Models 150, 160 and 170. Price increases were essential on the Model 87, now $235; the Model 95 is now $235; the Model 65 now sells for $195. The GCA '68 also lead to withdrawal of the Armi Galesi semi-auto pistols from the line. The Italian-made top quality Perazzi O-U doubles will continue, and Steve Polemus—boss at Atlas—says he will also bring over the superb sidelock Perazzi, these with beautifully engraved metal bringing about $1500. (B.S.)

ArmaLite

By now every firearms enthusiast is familiar with the M-16, 223 caliber, fully-automatic military rifle used in Viet Nam. A new development of this controversial arm, capable of firing 1200 rounds per minute, is now made by ArmaLite as the AR-18—available only to police and law enforcement personnel.

A similar model, the AR-180, is being made for the sportsman, but it has the automatic selector switch welded so it does not function, the auto sear deleted and some metal removed from the bolt carrier and hammer. Thus, it is virtually impossible for the basement gunsmith to easily convert the AR-180 to an AR-18.

Measuring only 29 inches with its fibreglass - impregnated stock folded, the AR-18 makes an easily stowable survival gun. With a sling, it can be comfortably slung over the shoulder and doesn't get in the way when on horseback. Weight empty is about 6½ pounds—a loaded 20-round magazine adds another 11 ounces. Magazines blocked to hold 5 rounds only will be supplied to the sportsman, but these can be converted where the law permits larger capacity.

As delivered at $237 both guns have front post sights adjustable for elevation and an aperture rear adjustable for windage. The receiver has an integral dovetail for a quick-detachable 3x scope, $68.75 extra. (E.D.)

Apache

Another new firearm that may be welcomed by fans of Elliot Ness and World War II arms collectors is the Apache. A near-replica of the Thomp-

Volunteer Pointer from Blumenfeld

Compact shotgun from American Import

son SMG, this is a semi-automatic weapon, and so-classified by the ATFD. While not truly a sporting arm, at least in our view, it may find a ready market with law officers and collectors.

The Apache fires the 45 ACP from a closed-bolt position, has an outside actuator at the left of the receiver for easier cocking, and a push-through thumb safety above and behind the trigger guard. Front sight is a fixed blade but the rear sight is adjustable for windage and elevation.

We looked one of these over—didn't get a chance to shoot it, though—and it appears to be well made where it counts most. The trigger pull was smooth and light. The bolt "clanked" like a Thompson and the over-all heft and swing seemed familiar. The Apache sells for $129.95 with one 30-round clip, extra magazines $10 each.

Note: This is not the Spitfire, which was made in Arizona. From what I've been told and seen, it doesn't look like *this* gun could be converted to full-auto—not that anyone is supposed to prove the point. (E.D.)

American Import Company

New on the company's list is a 12-ga. single trigger side-by-side known as the Dickson Compact; the 28" vent rib barrels are choked M/F or IC/M, are chambered for 3-inch shells, there is an automatic safety, and the single non-selective trigger works on the inertia system. The case-hardened Anson & Deeley action carries some light engraving in the Spanish manner. The walnut pistol grip stock is well-finished and hand-checkered, with the fore-end tailored to U.S. standards. In other words, here is an import that, for the reasonable price of $145, carries a beavertail fore-end rather than the splinter type traditional on the Continent. The gun weighs 6¾ lbs.

The Falcon side-by-side double trigger shotgun, a dependable stand-by with the company, is now made in 28 ga. and 410. The Falcons, despite selling for only $108.50, carry a 3-year guarantee!

A fine little knock-around gun is the 3-shot bolt action 410 with 25" full choke barrel. I have a spot where I can bang away at some quail, where a large gauge would be the thing to use except for the noise level. Next quail season I'm going to try one of these—should be a dandy, too, for pest birds and vermin. Only $32.50.

The $215 Gray Eagle O-U shotguns, made only in 12 and 20, now also carry a 3-year guarantee.

The Falcon Goose gun is a side-by-side Magnum 10, chambered for the 3½" shell, and this is a real handful of gun for $148.50. (B.S.)

Agawam Arms

Looking for a first gun for your off-spring, or for a pest plinker? Consider the M-68 from Agawam. This is so similar to the Ithaca 49 Saddle Gun it is hard to tell which is which— even the price tag reads $26.95.

Looking over the M-68 we find a cast alloy receiver, walnut finished stock, 18" barrel chambered for 22 Short, Long or Long Rifle and a blade front and open rear sights. A youth model with a shorter buttstock is the M-68Y with identical chambering and price tag. The M-68M, chambered for the 22 RF Magnum, is $32.95. (E.D.)

Rifle and Shotgun Gear

A&W Engineering

A new and interesting device called the Shotgun Diverter is being manufactured by A&W in Houston. Resembling a choke attachment—it does change the gun's pattern—this device is 2¾" long, 1⅛" in diameter and will add about 3¼ ounces to your shotgun's muzzle. That's not all it does! According to Mr. C. L. Ashbrook, president of A&W, "It changes the usual circular pattern to one that is *rectangular,* and of about 2 to 1 ratio.

We received a test barrel from A&W for a 12-gauge Remington M1100 and went to work on the pattern board. Test firing was done at 40 yards using 1⅛-oz. target loads of 8s. Patterns showed a horizontal rectangle of sorts about 30x60" at that range and by visual estimation about 80-85% of the shot. Dispersion within this area was smooth, showing few holes. A slight reduction of noise and recoil was also noted.

We canted the shotgun and caused canted patterns as a matter of interest. Time did not permit testing on clays or live game, but the Shotgun Diverter does offer some new experiences come fall—especially to those who are not the best of shots or don't get sufficient practice.

Two models of the Shotgun Diverter are available at $28.75—add $5.75 for factory installation. One is silver soldered onto the barrel, while the other must be threaded; both require that the barrel have a cylinder bore and that the existing choke be reamed out or cut off. We recommend factory installation, as our test barrel showed horizontal patterns when the shotgun was held in true vertical position. A military model giving a 4 to 1 ratio is also available for police use. (E.D.)

Amron—New Ammo Maker

Sometime early in 1970 you'll see a new brand name appearing on your dealer's cartridge shelves. This new ammunition will be completely American made by the Amron Corp. of Waukesha, Wis. The brand name hasn't been decided yet, but you can expect to see 30 U.S. Carbine, 7.62 NATO (308 Win.), 9mm Parabellum and 38 Special loadings first, with other popular calibers to follow as soon as production facilities permit.

Amron has been making 20mm and 40mm projectiles, cases and fuzes for the military for some years. They've built a well-respected name for themselves and their ammo quality in that area. Having been in business 42 years, they want to maintain that reputation as they expand into the centerfire sporting ammunition field.

Brass cases and projectiles are made by a new process right there at Waukesha. All machinery is brand new and 90% automated. Components may be offered handloaders later on. Powder and primers will be of U.S. manufacture other than Amron.

All ammo loading is being done at a new plant. "Quality control personnel will be in charge of all loading operations," says Dave Parsons, director of the QC department. It will be expensive to do it that way, but if it does make consistently better commercial ammo . . . who'll complain?

The ballistic test range is all new, too. Pressure guns fitted with crusher and transducer sensors, chronographing and accuracy testing facilities are housed in a sound proof, air-and humidity conditioned building. Four 100-meter bays are available for tests.

New packaging may include these ideas: Two sealed packets of 25 rounds each contained in the usual 50-round pistol-ammo box. 10-round "tobacco pouch" rifle ammo packaging. Unusual combinations of plastic and paper for easier ammo handling.

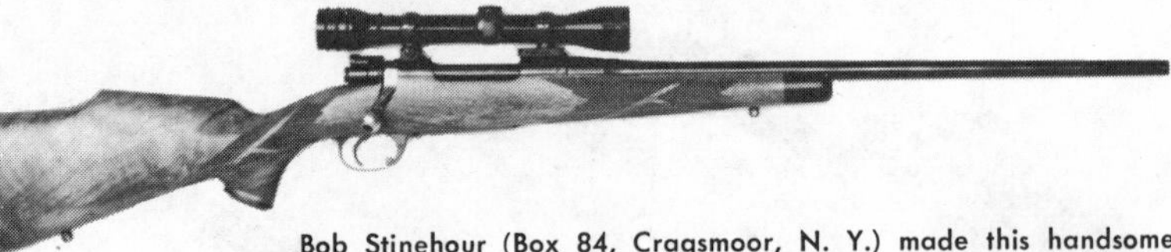

Bob Stinehour (Box 84, Cragsmoor, N. Y.) made this handsome stock, doing a superb job of checkering. A 270 on a Mauser action, with a barrel by Douglas, the metalsmithing is by John Van Patten of Milford, Penna.

Bob Brownell

Bob Brownell, compiler and distributor of that gunsmith's treasure trove, the big Brownell Catalog, has a new and highly useful small item.

The Brownell Dove-Tail Scope Base fits all *ungrooved* 22 rifles, thus allowing use of all standard tip-off rings. Two sizes are made—one of .840″ handles all small-ring 22s, with 1″ or less thickness, the other, 1″, fits 22s with receiver 1″ or wider.. Either one, $1.80, and well-worth it.

Clerke Technicorp

Bo Clerke, champion rifleman, is marketing a new receiver sight for match rifles. Called the Micro-Vernier, it is said to have zero backlash.

Windage and elevation adjustments are calibrated in ¼-minute clicks on the micro drum, the scales engraved for 3-minute divisions. Anti-backlash locks are provided for both w. and e. leadscrews, and there's an adjustable gib to remove any slacks that might develop in the elevation dovetails.

Factory literature directs the user to zero the rifle in (range not specified), then the "Vernier" elevation and windage scales can be set to that zero. Zero on the Clerke elevation scale is centered between 45 minutes up and down—if one zeroed in at 100 yards, of what use would be the 45 minutes below the zero point on the elevation scale?

Factory data refers to both w. and e. scales as being Vernier type, but if the Clerke sight corresponds in construction and engraving to the excellent illustration furnished, then there is no true V e r n i e r calibration on either. There are only, as noted, 3-minute graduations on the scales, with a single engraved line to indicate movement.

Usable on any receiver carrying target sight bases of standard form, the Clerke M-V sight sells for $59.95. The Merit eyepiece is suggested but not furnished.

Clerke's "Level" front sight is a globe type, furnished with 5 varying-diameter apertures (.070″, .085″, .095″, .100″ and .120″), and it contains a spirit level (visible while shooting) to reveal any canting—which can easily lead to target errors, especially at long range.

Cole's Recoil Suppressor Test Cradle

The "Level" sight mounts on standard dovetail blocks, sells for $19.95 alone or, with the Clerke M-V rear sight, at $75 for the two items. (J.T.A.)

Cole's Acku-Rite

Cole's Recoil Suppressor Test Cradle is designed to hold a rifle while it is being test fired, and to modify and absorb the recoil. It provides safety when testing max loads, as the rifle may be fired from a safe distance by a lanyard. This may well save your life or your face, and is the safest way to do your testing. The Cole Test Cradle is also of major help when loads are being chronographed, as it holds the rifle securely and, after firing, returns the rifle to battery, ready for the next shot.

Constructed of solid oak, it is 41″ long, 5¾″ wide by 10″ high at the barrel support. It weighs 13½ lbs. Built in two parts, there's a base section (on which the carriage glides) for fastening to the bench; the cradle or carriage holds the rifle and slides on aluminum rails. The recoil is absorbed by one, two or three compression springs as the need may be; these, recessed in the carriage, are readily removeable. An adjustable air check prevents the recoil springs from returning the carriage to battery too rapidly. The butt support and clamp are padded with soft leather, as is also the barrel clamp, to prevent any marring. The cradle carries Cole's own special finish, enhancing the rugged wood with a beautiful golden color. The complete Test Cradle costs $49.50, FOB Kennedy, N. Y., plus postage and insurance. The shipping weight is 19 lbs.

One of these Cole Test Cradles, furnished to the GUN DIGEST for trial, was installed on our heavy cement bench at Creedmoor Farm.

The first rifle tested in the Cradle was a Ruger M77 in 243, the load 38/3031/80-gr. Remington Power-Lokt bullets. To check the return-to-battery feature of the Cradle, the scope crosshairs were carefully centered on the bull, and the shooting began. Using only one of the three recoil springs furnished, it was observed that the rifle moved back smartly under recoil, then went forward again into position.

Looking through the scope—after each of 5 shots—showed the Cradle performing excellently. The crosshair intersection moved only a tiny bit from its original position on the target (about ¼-inch), and the 5-shot 100 yard group made 1.78″. Point of impact was higher than normal, as may be expected from the barrel itself being rested in the leather covered V-notch up front.

This was a fine performance, I feel, for a rest not designed for accuracy testing as such, and in view of the small movement of the rifle during the shooting. This 243 M77 will group, with good handloads, into 1¼″ on average for 5 shots, with some loads printing into ¾″-⅞″, so 1⅞″ from the Cole Cradle is highly acceptable, and proof of its good design and rigidity.

Our last test was with a 7mm Magnum, using Remington 175-gr. loads, and two of Cole's recoil springs. Recoil was easily absorbed, as before. The rifle returned to battery even better than had the Ruger M77, perhaps because the hold-down bolts were retightened between sessions. 5-shot strings ran 2.75″-3″, about par for that factory lot from the same rifle (Brand X) hand held.

The Cole Test Cradle will be an excellent tool for chronographing and load testing, obviously, especially when the heavier-recoiling calibers are being extensively fired. ●

Contra-Jet Muzzle Brake

Recoil—whether from rifle, shotgun or handgun—can be a problem for many shooters. It has been shown that felt recoil is highly subjective, for the same rifle and loads, let's say, that makes a big, strong guy cringe bothers his buddy—5½ feet and 130 pounds soaking wet—not at all. Really—I've seen just that many times, believe me.

Recently D. S. Tanabe (7920 49th Ave., Seattle, Wash. 98118) sent us a sample of his Contra-Jet Muzzle Brake, on which he holds U.S. Patent No. 3,187,633. This specimen was con-

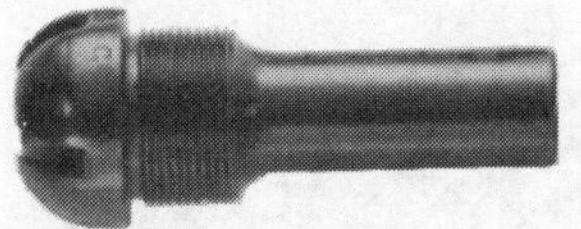

structed for 338- to 35-caliber barrels, and externally, at least, it resembles a couple of other such brakes on the market. Outside diameter is .825", length over-all just shades 3 inches, and the inside mikes .386".

It's the interior design that gained Tanabe his patent. The main sleeve attaches to the barrel by means of a 9/16"-28 V-60° thread, held in place by a hex lock-nut. The inner sleeve screws into the major sleeve, running back to within ¼-inch of the rifle muzzle.

The outer sleeve holds the secret of the Contra-Jet's effectiveness—8 series of gas deflection slots are cut into the sleeve, but each of these 3-part slots has a dividing wall in the middle. Thus there are 2 slots in one, and each of these openings (48 in all) deflects the powder gases sideways—not at the usual 90° to the bore axis. These emerging gases collide with each other, and the result is a distinct lessening of noise and blast for that reason.

Tests made by H. P. White Labs for Tanabe, using accurate recoil test equipment, revealed a reduction in free recoil of about 37% for a 308 rifle. That's an impressive loss, but in addition it was found that noise was little greater, if any, compared to unbraked muzzles—many muzzle brakes increase the noise level considerably —and that muzzle flash was also reduced noticeably.

Our 35-caliber Contra-Jet was installed on one of the new Remington Model 660 carbines, caliber 350 Magnum, but only after some delay. The M660 didn't reach us until a short time ago, and it then took our local gunsmith a couple of weeks to squeeze the job into his busy schedule.

For these reasons our test was not an extended one, but it certainly demonstrated the effectiveness and usefulness of the Contra-Jet. 20 rounds of Remington factory loads were put through the M660 without the brake, then 20 of the same lot with the Contra-Jet attached. These were the 250-gr. Pointed Core Lokt loads.

Breezy Wynne and I divided up this shooting, and while the reduced recoil was immediately noted by us both, Breezy experienced a greater reduction than I did. Perhaps this was so because I'm not sensitive to recoil generally, having learned long ago to swing with the recoil, to give a bit when it comes, and to shoot in a semi-relaxed manner. Breezy said he felt that recoil with the C.J. attached was about cut in half, but I can't go that far—I do know that it did make the 350 M660 more of a pleasure to shoot.

One surprising thing did appear. Both of us got rather better groups with the C.J. brake installed than without it, group averages dropping by some 25%. We're going to look into this further, but in the meantime I'm going to ask Tanabe to make his brake for the 458 Winchester. I'm going to be shooting one of those in Zambia next October, and the recoil of that one does make itself noticed!

The Contra-Jet we tested will work with the 340 Weatherby, 348 Winchester, 35 Remington and 358 Magnum, of course, in addition to the two calibers mentioned.

Tanabe makes two other sizes also —the Type 28 handles any caliber from 6.5mm to 7mm, the Type 30 any 30-caliber arms. In all installations the barrel OD must be within 0.5625" to 0.5560". All three sizes are priced the same, $24.95, installation not included.

Tanabe offers a fully-informative brochure on the Contra-Jet, and it's free. (J.T.A.)

Cureton Powder Horns

A short time ago, we inquired about Earl T. Cureton's powder horns, having seen an ad in another shooting publication. When they arrived, everyone at the office became so enthusiastic that two more sets were ordered immediately. We don't go that far overboard for many items received here, but this set is truly unusual.

The decorated (carved) set shown has genuine walnut fittings which are carefully turned, fitted and finished with a soft sheen. The horns themselves are of a mellow golden color and are nicely polished without being too glossy. The large horn is $15.50, the priming horn $7. Plain horns, which we've not seen, are $10 and $4 respectively. A small charger is also available for a dollar or two. If you're a muzzle-loading fan. these are for you—if not, they make a beautiful wall hanger for the den.

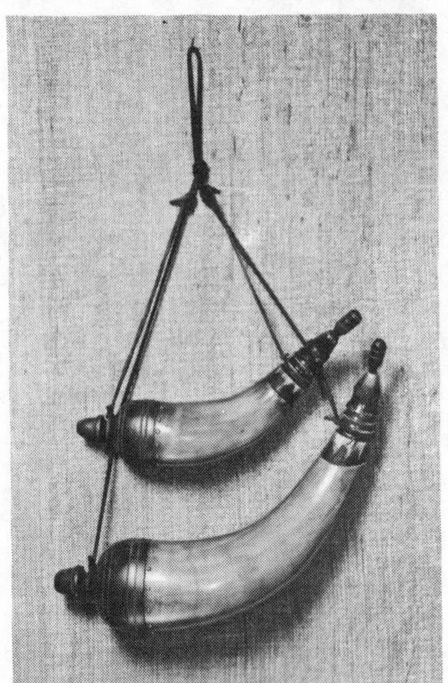

Edwards Recoil Reducer

Readers of our 22nd edition (pp. 74-75) will recall the comments made about this half-pound device that installs in the buttstock of a rifle or shotgun to reduce recoil. This same maker now tells us of another item—the shotgun counter balance.

Krieghoff or Winchester 101 shotguns can be changed from over-under to single barrel form, but obviously gun balance will change when this is done. Installing one of Edwards' units in the fore-end, which consist of 1- and 1½-oz. weights on a threaded shaft, permits the shooter to correct the problem by rotating a knurled knob until desired balance is restored.

A similar model, made for the Remington 870 and other pump guns, is installed in the magazine tube, adding a weight (adjustable) of 5 oz. Other models are available as well. For further information on these and other versions, plus prices, write Jesse Edwards, 269 Herbert St., Alton, Ill. 62002.

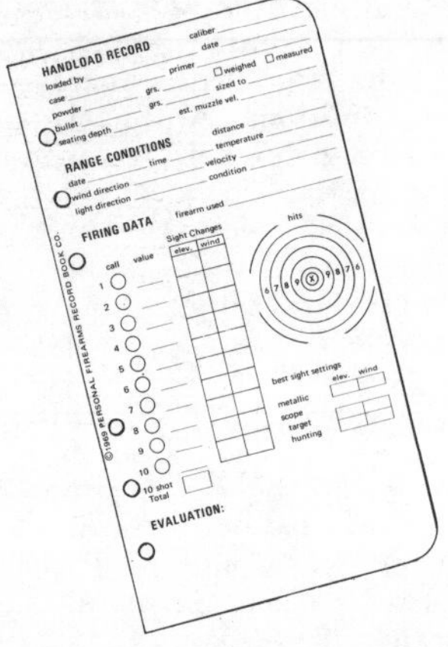

HANDLOAD RECORD
caliber
date
loaded by
primer
case
grs.
☐ weighed ☐ measured
powder
grs.
sized to
bullet
est. muzzle vel.
seating depth

RANGE CONDITIONS
date
time
distance
temperature
wind direction
velocity
light direction
condition

FIRING DATA
firearm used
call value
Sight Changes elev. wind
1 2 3 4 5 6 7 8 9 10
10 shot Total
hits
best sight settings elev. wind
metallic
scope
target
hunting

EVALUATION:

©1969 PERSONAL FIREARMS RECORD BOOK CO.

Firearms Record Books

The Gun Control Act of 1968 requires that records be kept of all gun and ammunition sales by dealers—it's a good idea for the individual gun owner as well. Personal Firearms Record Book Co. publishes two books to fill the requirements. The *Dealers' Firearms Record Book* has space for 500 gun transactions, showing both acquisition and disposition. The *Ammunition Disposition Book* has space for 850 entries. Size of both is 8½"x11" horizontal; plastic coated covers and pages of heavy, good-quality paper are spiral bound with wire so the book lies flat when open. $4.95 each, or both for $8.50 postpaid.

Handloader's Record Book is newest item, a small loose-leaf notebook (4½"x7") made of heavy red vinyl stamped in gold. It contains 35 special

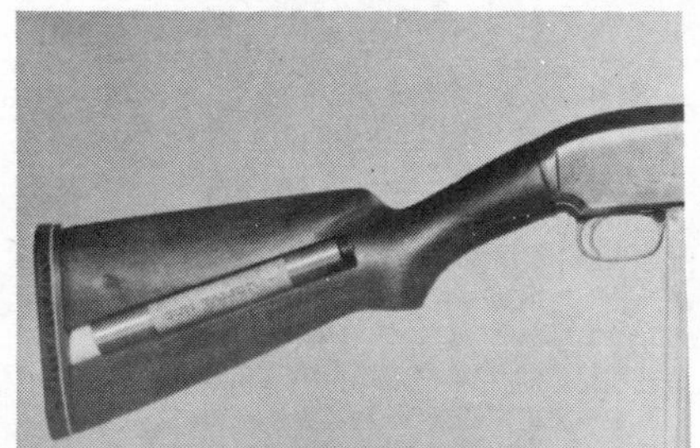

Gun Tamer device

forms on which to record load data, range conditions, performance at the range—a small target lets you record position and shape of group—and space for notes and evaluation. More notes can be made on the back of each page as they are printed on one side only. Five dividers serve to separate the forms by caliber or as you like. $3.95 postpaid from PFRB Co., Box 201, Park Ridge, Ill. 60068.

Gold Lode

Want to dress up that little bit of factory engraving and give your gun the look of a gold inlay job? Gold Lode (genuine 23-kt. gold) can do it with a bit of labor from you. Begin by cleaning the metal with their Agent No. 1, then brush Gold Lode into the engraved area. Clean the surface again with Agent No. 1 and polish with the felt block supplied, followed by a soft cloth—that's it, you're done! The kit, complete with all required materials, is $12.95, and this quantity will cover the most lavishly engraved gun. Available at your local dealer or from Gold Lode Inc., P. O. Box 31, Addison, Ill. 60101.

Gun Tamer

Muzzle whip, cheek slap and shoulder wallop are all reduced silently with the Gun Tamer made by St. Louis Precision Products, 902 Michigan Ave., St. Louis, Mich. 48880. A 6″x⅞″ sealed aluminum tube contains an air-vented lead cylinder with a spring at either end. This unit is installed in the through-bolt hole of the shotgun buttstock—a hole must be drilled at a 15° angle to the bore for best effect with rifles or shotguns having solid stocks. A special filler wad takes up the slack between Gun Tamer and buttplate. That's it—no adjustment is needed for gauge, caliber or load, all you do is shoot. Gun Tamer, priced at $18.50, is unconditionally guaranteed for life, unless you tamper with it.

Hunters' Hoist

After that long-stalked trophy is down, you've probably removed the rack and planned to cool the meat before quartering the critter. Needing two men and a boy, the project might end in the loss of good steaks if you can't find immediate help. The Hunters' Hoist—a small, pocketable, 12-oz. block-and-tackle that will lift 750 pounds—could save the day. The 5 to 1 mechanical advantage lets you lift any load with relative ease, but take along a couple of 2-foot lengths of wire or Nylon cord to attach the Hunters' Hoist to the beast and a tree.

The Flanders hoist has a lock—none of the others do—which permits the easy stopping at any point of the load being lifted. No need to frantically attempt to tie up the lifting cord.

Hunters' Hoist sells for $7.95.

Robert Hart & Son

In addition to the several styles of actions for which Bob Hart (401 Montgomery, Nescopeck, Pa. 18635) is deservedly famous—some 4 types, running from the No. 1 at $120 to the No. 4 for Unrestricted Classes at $160 —he also manufactures a sturdy and well-designed pedestal rest for bench shooters. Made of cast iron, the rest has dual vertical adjustments; a fast, sliding-rise and a threaded rise, both with individual T-handle locks. The rear leg holds yet another fine-threaded adjustment for height, while all legs have adjustable pins for leveling and enhanced stability. With the varmint-rifle bag (at right) the cost is $32; for the U.C. rest, left, add $2. Both will be sent for $36.

Herter's 22 Rimfires

Herter's new 22 Long Rifle ammo has demonstrated for us a fine level of accuracy in several rifles, the more noteworthy because of its relatively low cost.

In our Winchester 52 target rifle, with iron sights, 5-shot groups at 50 yards went into a 15/16" average, and that was beaten a little by our new Remington 540X rifle—an amazingly accurate rifle despite its moderate cost—groups ran ¾″ average for some 5 strings, also using iron sights. The wind was gusty, too—some 8-10 miles per hour—or I'm certain our groups would have been smaller.

Incidentally, Herter is setting up a Herter Dealership in every state to enable all non-licensed persons to obtain Herter guns, barreled actions, ammo of all types, etc., within their state borders. Write for the free Herter folder describing all this and many other aspects of the 1968 Gun Control Act.

Dean Lincoln

Custom Ammo & Gunsmithing, makers of custom metallic cartridges in over 50 calibers—rifle and handgun —cater to gun clubs and rifle ranges chiefly. Commercial canister powders are used exclusively (except for the target capacity cases), as are Hornady bullets unless directed otherwise.

They offer an attractive program for licensed clubs and dealers (write for their price list), with all 1000-lot orders shipped postpaid on an exchange basis for fired empties.

Bob Hart's pedestal rest

We've received 20-round samples of CA&G cartridges in several popular calibers, but there's been no opportunity to shoot these so far. They do look good—clean cases, uniform sizing and over-all length—and we'll try to insert a report on them before final deadlines.

I was able to testfire only the 243/100-gr. cartridges furnished, and the shooting had to be done on a chilly day, the wind out of the west at 12-15 mph, and gusty.

I got lucky for the first 5 at 100 yards—⅞″ using my Ruger Model 77, but apparently the wind caught me for the 2nd and 3d strings. 1⅜″ and 1⅝″, but not too bad for the conditions.

I then pulled bullets from 4 rounds to check powder charges and I was a little surprised—no variation at all for the first 3, all 42.2 of some large-grained propellant, with the fourth load 1/10th-gr. heavier. Excellent indeed, even for custom ammo.

Moderntools

Moderntools (K. A. Neise, Inc.) has several new tool designs of interest to the guncraftsman. One of these is their MT-19 Bevel Protractor of hardened stainless steel, offered in 6″, 8″, 12″ and 20″ lengths. These start at $27 in a wood case, and optional are a Base ($10.60), and a Square at $9.45, both stainless steel also. The extra we like very much is a Magnifier, its cost only $4.

Moderntools' MT-A Dial Indicators used with their MT-14A Magnetic Base are handy devices for the gunsmith or small machine shop user. The Moderntools MT-A style Dial Indicator has a 1¼″ dial size with graduations of .0005″ to a range of .030″. The MT-A costs $16 alone.

Moderntools MT-14A Magnetic Base, $15 alone in a wood case, has a 2¼″x1½″ base, and is 13″ high. Rod travel is 6″ with a 5/32″ scriber (furnished) opening.

We've commented in earlier issues on Moderntools full line of micrometers and dial indicators — well-designed and precision instruments all —so we won't cover them at this time. They're all described in Moderntools brochures, plus many other good items.

Ask Moderntools Corp., P. O. Box 407, Dept. GD, Woodside, N. Y. 11377 for their catalog.

Moran Knives

This Moran hunting knife — complete with heavy, top grain scabbard —has seen tough service on 5 hunting trips now, and it's still as new as the day it was made. I think it's just about indestructible.

See our Shooter's Showcase pages for more dope on Moran's other knives. (J.T.A.)

Olt Game Calls

P. S. Olt Co, of Pekin, Ill., makes an extensive line of mouth calls to tempt about anything you'd care to shoot. Just announced is the EL-45 Elk Call at $5.50. Made of red and black plastic to maintain tone and eliminate warping and splitting, the EL-45 is only 7⅜″ long and weighs just 2 ounces. There are no holes or sleeves to manipulate and is "easy to blow and master," says the catalog.

CP-21 is a close-range predator call meant to lure nearby fox and coyote even closer. It's 3½″ long and a raised rib lets you hold the call between your teeth harmonica fashion, while both hands are free to man the gun. A mylar reed, unaffected by moisture, is held in the plastic housing by non-corrosive rivets. Suggested for use with their T-20 or M33 long range calls, the CP-21 is only $2.50.

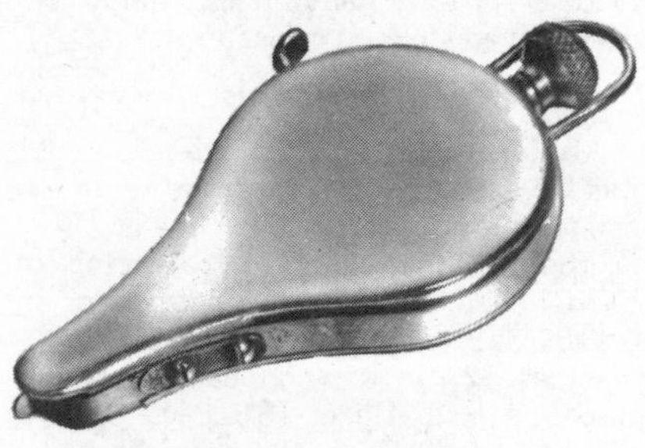

Mohawk Capper

Here's a practical and useful tool for the caplock muzzle-loader that holds 60 or more percussion caps, an ample supply for a day-long shooting session with the front feeders.

Made of sturdy brass throughout — except for minor elements — this capping device is less than 4 inches long by some 2 inches wide. The ring at its top is meant for a lanyard or thong, allowing the capper to be hung from the belt, alongside the powder horn or around the neck.

Pressing a side lever lets a cap drop into the top end, then releasing the lever locks the cap into position, all ready to be placed over the gun's nipple.

Designed for standard height caps, the Mohawk Capper sells for $8.50 postpaid, low for a virtually handmade product these days. Send your order to Pat Burke, 3339 Farnsworth Rd., Lapeer, Mich. 48466.

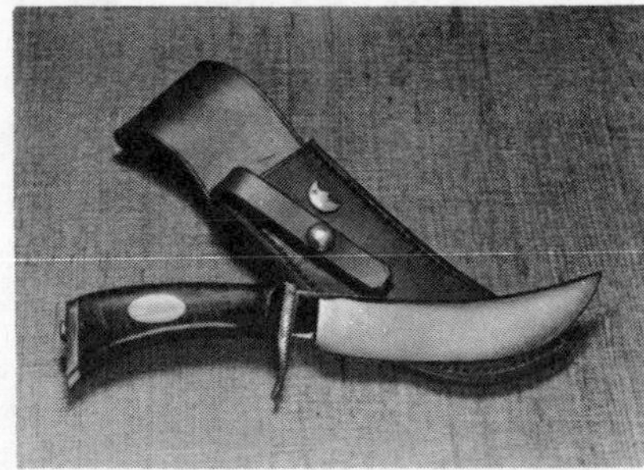

Our editor's Moran knife

Ormond Swing

Not a dance nor a radio announcer of the 40s, it looks more like a bandaged croquet hoop with a thyroid condition. Kidding aside, the Ormond Swing is a very useful gadget designed and patented by Clyde Ormond—the well-known outdoor writer—to fill his needs. He wanted a good, lightweight, portable vermint shooting rest for his rifle that was easily taken afield and relied on. He's solved the problem to our satisfaction, and at a price of only $1.50—we've spent more for gadgets that didn't work—this half-pound shooting rest is the least expensive of those commercially made.

Made and sold by Frontier Arms, Box 2593, 420 E. Riding Club Rd., Cheyenne, Wyo. 82001, it is a tempered 3/16″ steel rod formed into a "U," the top and sides wound with Nylon cord and tied between the legs. Push the legs of the Swing into the ground—or into two over-size 3/16″ holes drilled into the shooting bench —and lay the fore-end or barrel over the knot. The rifle will now swing back and forth, move side to side or—by retying the cord or changing hoop level in the ground—up and down. Shooting from the bench with a pistol it had the feel of a stretched-spring barrel rest. Tested with a rifle, no change of impact point was noticed —no tendency to shoot away from the rest.

Hunter's Hoist

PIC, importers of good spotting scope and other equipment for the hunter-shooter, now offer a heavy-duty Hunter's Hoist, this one the Model 2000. Rated at 1 ton for test purposes, the practical limit recommended is some 1400 lbs. Compact and powerful, the new HH features a 7x lift factor for easier weight lifting, Nylon line and pulleys, and two quick-release steel rings. Weighing only 1½ lbs., the HH does a first class job — we gave our sample a severe test recently. $7.95 is the price.

However, both PIC hoists lack a locking device, which would permit resting the load at any point, instead of scrambling to tie the Nylon cord!

The PIC Model 1000 is even smaller in size, will lift some 7-800 lbs., and costs $4.95.

One reminder, though—to use the M2000 HH you should have a couple of lengths of high test Nylon, steel wire, etc., along also—say 2- or 3-foot lengths. One is needed to attach the HH to a tree or whatever, the other to form a collar for your deer, bear or what have you.

Safe-T-Shell

Outwardly identical to a loaded 12-gauge shotshell, Safe-T-Shells are inserted into the chamber(s) of your shotgun to prevent accidents. Made of red, resilient plastic, just a peek at the chamber assures you that *only* the Safe-T-Shell is there, and that the gun is protected. Try to unload this device with the shotgun's extractor or ejector and the rear half only is removed—the front portion, with its post-formed center, remains in the chamber, preventing any standard length shotshell being inserted. Safe-T-Shell is easily removed by running a cleaning rod down the bore from the muzzle. While chambered, these gadgets can be used as snap-caps for dry firing. Available only from Safe-T-Shell Inc., 4361 Woodhall Rd., Columbus, Ohio 43221, or from Abercrombie & Fitch in 12-gauge only at $1 each.

Santa Barbara of America Ltd.

I looked over the barreled actions, actions only and the Claro walnut stock blanks on view at this firm's exhibit at Houston, and the picture was pleasing—so much so that a 458 rifle is being made up for my next African trip, using one of their actions, but more on that later.

The Mauser-type actions are entirely of steel, forged and/or machined as required, and very good looking indeed. Aside from such desirable changes as a streamlined bolt sleeve, a fully adjustable trigger and a side safety, these are still the same sturdy, rugged and classic Mausers of 1898—that's a hell of a long time for a rifle action to stay on top of the heap, isn't it? Or for anything else!

Traditionally—and with excellent reasons—the bolt is a one-piece forging, the extractor is the same, simple claw form as before, and ejection of fired cases is 100% dependable.

These well-made Mauser-style actions are priced at $59.95 for standard calibers, $10 more for magnums, and another $10 if you want a steel, hinged trigger guard—alloy guards are standard. Add another $20 if you want a barreled action.

The barrels—made by Federal Firearms Co., the well-known Star "diamond-lapped" tubes — are 24" long, and the calibers available are 22-250, 243, 270, 30-06, 7mm Remington Magnum and 300 Winchester Magnum. A fired test-case is furnished with each barreled action. Other calibers on special order.

Receivers are tapped for standard scope mounts, but no metallic sights are supplied.

The Santa Barbara stocks are 99% "pre-fit," and come with contrasting wood tip (angled form) and grip cap. Four grades are available, $29.95 to $59.95, and those I saw in Grades AA and AAA were handsome hunks of Claro.

The Santa Barbara-actioned rifle I mentioned earlier was made for me by Harold Waller (1288 Camillo Way, El Cajon, Calif. 92021) a fine custom gunsmith associated with S.B. of A. It's a handsome outfit, and the picture I'm showing doesn't do real justice to it. This 458 will go with me to Zambia next September, and I'll tell you about that hunt in our 25th edition, as well as the hunt to follow in India during November, 1969. (J.T.A.)

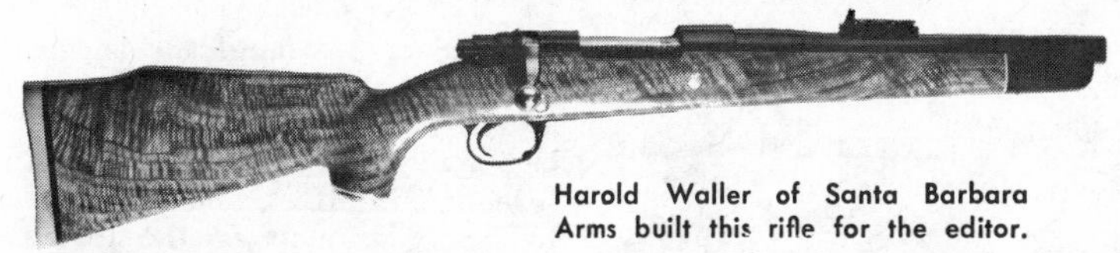
Harold Waller of Santa Barbara Arms built this rifle for the editor.

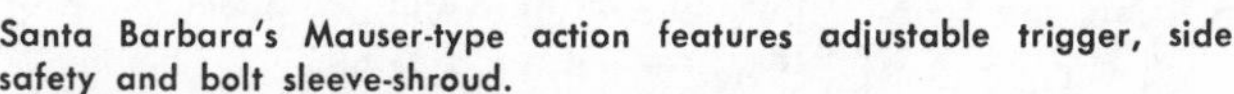
Santa Barbara's Mauser-type action features adjustable trigger, side safety and bolt sleeve-shroud.

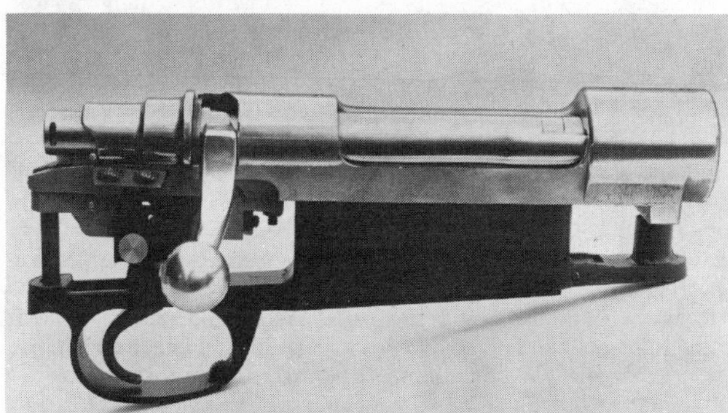

Sile Pre-Finished Stocks

Replacement stocks of European walnut, oil finished, checkered and with buttplate installed are to be had from Sile Distributors, 7 Center Market Pl., N.Y., N.Y. 10013. The stocks following are completely inletted and said instal as simply as the original. Available for Winchester 94 rifle; Model 97 or 12 shotgun (12, 16 and 20-ga.); Browning 5-shot auto (12 and 16-ga.) and the Remington Model 11 shotguns. Buttstock for any of the above is $19.95; fore-end is $14.95.

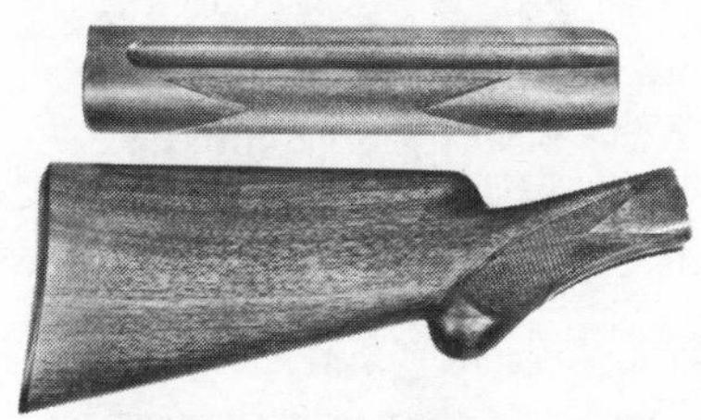

Skatchet

Skatchet is a patented tool that promises much—and delivers it, too! Made of well-tempered tool steel, the Skatchet is a truly unique product that combines a skinning knife and a hatchet in one compact forging. In addition, the hammer-head (a bonus) is threaded to accept any piece of wood (a branch, a sapling, etc.) of about one inch diameter as a handle. It's a few moments work to screw this into the Skatchet, and it's ready — and able — to chop through bone with ease.

Complete with a quality heavy leather sheath, the Skatchet is $9.95, and we recommend it.

Slug Site

Slug-Site—designed solely for shotgun and slug shooting—is an amazingly simple gadget that really works. A special adhesive attaches it to receiver (or barrel for the far-sighted), and it's easy to adjust for range. Easily removed, too, leaving the gun just as it was. $5.00 postpaid, satisfaction guaranteed or your money back.

Stock Lo-Kater

Earl Pellant offers an idea he's developed that should interest shotgunners generally, and certainly some rifle shooters.

Made from fine brushed leather, and usable by left- or right-handed shooters, this unusual item firmly locates the gunbutt, absorbs recoil to a degree, and lets the butt be brought to the shoulder without catching on the jacket or shirt folds. It's especially useful in warm weather, or any time you're in shirt sleeves.

Pellant's Stock Lo-Kater is $15, full instructions for fitting included. Write to Pellant, 1716 No. Serrano Ave., Hollywood, Calif. 90027.

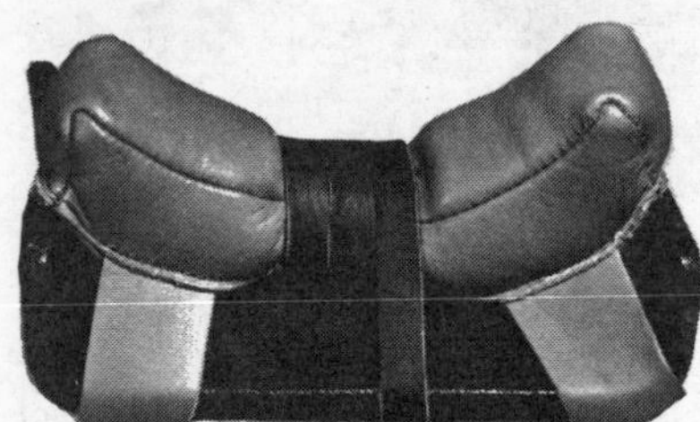

Tuller Half Moon sandbag

Tuller Protektor Products

I imagine that most of our readers are familiar with Basil Tuller's Protektor products—and to those who aren't, I suggest you write for his literature.

Tuller's most famous items are his Sand Bag Rifle Rests, used by bench shooters for many years, and seen everywhere, literally! His original No. 1 Buttstock Bag, first offered in 1953, is still in big demand, but Basil now has a variety of rifle rest bags—front and rear—that should satisfy any needs. They're too many to detail here, but his latest is the type pictured—the Half Moon—designed for the Beecher (or similar) fore-end rest, and wide enough at 6" to handle virtually any rifle.

The rawhide strapping shown is first soaked in water, then stretched out and tied around the curved-form bag, thus drawing it down tightly—as the rawhide dries. The result is a bag giving a 2-point contact with the fore-end, in effect, and to insure shot-to-shot alignment of the fore-end, a pair of leather straps can be buckled on either side of the rawhide.

Price of the Protektor No. 1 Bag with any Tuller front bag (including the new Half Moon) is $7.25 postpaid (no sand, though!). Write for Tuller's new folder—it describes and prices a new portable shooting bench, his line of rest bags—all of them top-grain cowhide and Nylon-thread sewn—and several other quality products for shooters.

Fred Wells

Fred F. Wells, 110 N. Summit, Prescott, Ariz. 86301, appears to be a competent and talented metalsmith. The picture shows a project he completed this last winter, starting with raw steel—it's a full left-hand version of the old double-square bridge/receiver Magnum Mauser, modified only by making the bolt handle in pre-war Winchester 70 style. Cost? We dunno, but probably not in the peanuts class!

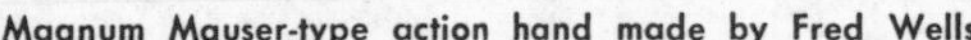

Magnum Mauser-type action hand made by Fred Wells

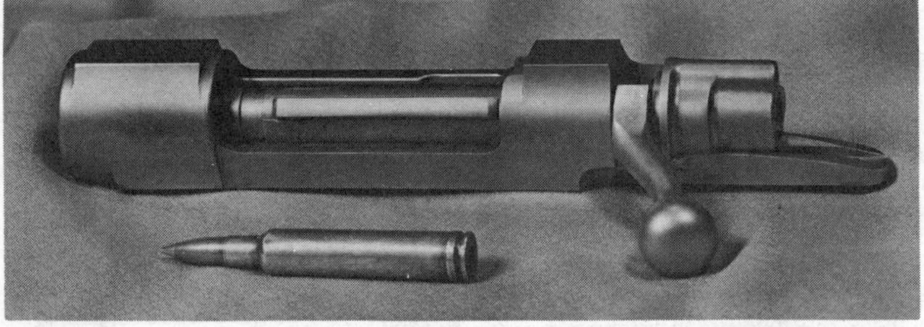

Williams Gun Sight Co.

Williams is now making special swivel adapters of rustproof alloy that clamp together about the barrel of rifles and shotguns. These lock securely with just one screw and a dovetail-mounted ball stud is provided to which standard or QD swivels can be attached. Five models fit most rifles and single barrel shotguns with a diameter between .700" and .825". For barrels from .405" to .700", the tubular magazine adapters are recommended. Write Williams for prices and further information.

Williams Swivel adapter

Y.O. Ranch

The Y.O. Ranch (Mountain Home, Texas) has a new brochure ready that fully describes the unusual and exciting hunting available there. The famed Y.O. Ranch "guarantees hunting every day of the year for animals from four continents," and that means Blackbuck, Sika, Fallow and American white-tail deer, as well as Aoudad and Corsican foreign sheep, wild turkeys, etc.

No special permit is needed to hunt on the Y.O. Ranch—just a Texas resident or non-resident license.

The Ranch is a little over 100 miles from San Antonio by car, and there's a 2200 foot air strip close to Ranch headquarters.

Write for the new folder, which includes a price schedule, or phone 512/654-2076 and ask for Bob Snow, Jr., the resident manager.

To Thwart a Thief

Gun thefts are on the rise. Many of the victims are gun dealers and collectors, but most are sportsmen. There's not much the honest, run-of-the-field hunter and shooter can do about it except insure, take certain precautions, and trust to luck.

Your guns may be fully covered in your home policy under "household contents"—but don't count on it. Check with your agent to be sure. You may even want to insure them under a special rider. In any case, be sure that an exact valuation is placed on each gun, by serial number, and that you have a full list of the serial numbers of your guns on file.

What can be done to keep guns from being stolen? Little enough—but these steps may help:

While on a hunting trip, even for the day, never leave guns or gun cases in a car where they can be seen. If you stay in a motel, always take your guns in with you at night. A thief can spot a hunter's car a mile away, and know it's a treasure trove of guns, cameras and binoculars. We know city shooters who won't even put sportsmen's club decals on their car windows.

If you have a gun cabinet at home, place it where it can't be seen from the outside. Better yet, keep your guns hidden. We know a hunter who keeps a full gun cabinet stocked with "loaner" guns as a decoy for burglars, and his good guns are stashed elsewhere. A farmer friend keeps only his work guns at home—a couple of 22s and an old shotgun. The rest of his muskets are kept hidden with a friend in town. One of our local trapshooters, who also lives on a farm, may take his best guns with him in the trunk of his car when he leaves home for the day.

Don't keep guns where they can be seen by casual visitors in your home, and never display them to strangers. It doesn't pay to advertise. In the past two years, three of our personal friends have had all their guns stolen from their homes. In each case, it was public or semi-public knowledge that they owned good guns.

1. A well-known outdoor writer and editor who works at home.
2. A hunter who displayed his guns on the walls of his family room.
3. A businessman who received publicity as a big-game hunter.

It doesn't pay to advertise. In fact, some of this increase in gun thefts may be a reflection of all the publicity that guns and gun ownership have gotten recently. And as restrictive gun laws increase and tighten, we can expect a corresponding increase in the underworld traffic of hot guns.

(John Madson, Winchester)

Hunting in Scotland

Stalking the wily stag over the rolling moors of Caithness County would be easy, I'd thought—I couldn't have been more wrong!

by JOHN T. AMBER

HUNTING in one of the Iron curtain countries is not an easy thing to arrange at any time, certainly not if the hunter wants to make the trip unencumbered by a gaggle of such attendants as tourist agents, petty government officials, et al.

I'd tried to set up a hunt in Russia several years ago, but after many months of correspondence and phone calls with the Russ tourist agency in New York, the Soviet Embassy in Washington and various parties in Moscow, I had to give it up—I was getting nowhere.

That wasn't quite the case with Czechoslovakia, though it wasn't accomplished rapidly, God knows. It took over 2 years to get everything ironed out. I wasted a lot of that time attempting to deal with Cedok, the Czech tourist agency (as one is ordinarily required to do), but I was told, quite firmly—not to say tersely and ungraciously—that I'd have to hunt their way, or else!

No going it alone, with only a guide and an interpreter, perhaps—I'd be told just where to go, for how long, and I'd be surrounded with the usual retinue.

Then, at a recent National Sporting Goods Association meeting, I met the BRNO arms people (see our 22nd GUN DIGEST for a report on the new BRNO ZKK series of sporting rifles) and after a few friendly talks with an Omnipol man I'd been in correspondence with, the hunt was set up. I would arrive in Prague about the end of August, spend a day or so there, then leave for the forests. (Omnipol is the Czech export organization.)

This would be an effort to shoot a really big European stag—or red deer—and I understood that I'd be able to hunt in high country, the famed Tatra mountains. Mountainous country stags in Czechoslovakia are famous throughout Europe for their massive, heavy-beamed antlers, and I'd be there for the whole rutting season! I'd taken a couple of stags in Yugoslavia in 1967 — which I wrote about in our 22nd edition — so I was looking forward with high hopes to stalking and taking a great stag in the Tatra—perhaps even a gold medal animal.

Then—as the whole world knows —the murderous Russians and their satellites invaded, pillaged and occupied Czechoslovakia in August of 1968. My visit to Bohemia was, of course, now out of the question, my plans for a memorable hunt destroyed, perhaps never to be resumed.

At this point I ran into Jim Rikhoff in New York—Jim is the Winchester-Western chief of public relations, an old and good friend, and we're fellow members of a very small, exclusive group, the 10-X Club!

Jim, hearing my tale of woe, had just the answer—how would I like to join him on a mixed-bag shoot in northern Scotland, where we'd be able to get in some good red grouse shooting, stalk the majestic monarchs of the lonely moors, maybe find time for the taking of a few salmon?

Under the sad circumstances, what could I say? I was about ready to leave for Europe anyway, and the three weeks or so that I'd scheduled for the Czech trip were now open and needing filling. I was going over to visit some gunshops and arms factories, later on in October going to Spain to hunt for the Spanish ibex—which is another story told elsewhere in this issue.

I told Rikhoff I'd meet him in London the last week in September, ready for the journey to Scotland, but what could he tell me now about the place we'd be staying, the game situation, and what the drill was?

W-W Adventures

Jim, as it happened, knew all about this particular Winchester World-Wide Adventure program in Scotland. He'd been there more than once —which I wondered about, for Jim had personally investigated many, if not most, of the other and numerous W-W Adventure's potential hunting/fishing operations, but one visit had usually been enough to satisfy him that the program offered, the facilities, etc., were first class—or that they were not.

Let me say here, parenthetically, that W-W Adventures has been at great pains to make sure that the trips they recommend and sponsor are everything they ought to be—that the accommodations are genuinely first class, that the sport offered will be what they promise; in short, that W-W clients will have really good sport, that they'll live well and enjoy themselves, to come back home satisfied in every important particular.

Sure, they've experienced a few hangups—or the guests have—but there are times when the weather and water won't cooperate, and it is a truism that "You should have been here last week!"

I can attest to the fine fashion in which Winchester-Western conducts some of these affairs—I was a member of the large writers/editors group that attended the W-W Seminar in Italy in 1967, where we all had absolutely unsurpassable sport — on grouse, pheasants and ducks—on the vast and ancient acres of the Marquis de Medici's game-rich estate. Following that, sub-groups of 4-5 fellows went on to Spain, Portugal, Morocco and elsewhere for further shooting. Some of this shooting, as later related, wasn't quite as good as we'd found in Italy, but what the hell could have been?

If these later hunts suffered at all it was only in comparison, and this was early-on in the W-W programming, when a few bugs could be expected.

Getting back to my talk with Rikhoff about the sport in Scotland, it was quickly apparent that he was wildly — repeat wildly — enthusiastic about the shooting to be had in Scotland, particularly over the stalking for stag. He'd done some of the finest hunting there that he'd ever done (Jim's been all over the world for game), he told me, and he was so very fond of it that he'd gone back several times.

He couldn't, he said, begin to tell me the way it really was—not that he didn't try! The people were warmly cordial, the food and drink were excellent, the ghillies were highly competent guides, skillful in locating and stalking stags on the great lonely moors—treeless for miles, though still called "deer forests," and with habitation scattered miles and miles apart.

I'd love it, Jim promised, and I'd also find stalking extremely hard work, tiring, and exhausting even, if the weather proved rough. Jim said he'd worked harder for a deer in Scotland than he'd thought possible, "that the hunting, mon, was rough, rugged." I secretly felt old Jim was putting me on a bit—you know how some guys like to impress you with how backbreaking their hunting is, thus letting you know just how *mucho hombre* they are—but little did I then know how damned difficult it actually would be. Rikhoff didn't tell it by half!

I noticed that Jim hadn't much to say about the grouse shooting or salmon killing, but I'd learn later that Rikhoff is a red deer man first, last and always—and I'd learn why.

Lochdhu house, far out on the Scottish moors, headquarters for shooting in Caithness County.

As arranged, the clan gathered in London on a bright Saturday in late September — Jack and Eleanor O'Connor, Jim and Jan Rikhoff, plus your reporter, on his own. We put in a hurried bit of shopping for a few last-minute possibles—Jack tried to find a knicker suit, *de regeur* for shooting in Scotland, bar the plaid—but they couldn't fit his long gangling frame. All of us spent an all-too-short couple of hours at the famed Holland & Holland shooting shool, near London, as guests of Holland's managing director, Malcolm Lyell — which is something else I've got to tell you about some day. For now, I can only say how truly accomplished their shooting instructors are—far more so than I'd believed—and that I wish I could get in a day's coaching there every week or so. They work wonders, I do assure you.

Our BEA plane set us down gently at Wick, a small city in the far north of Scotland—only John O'Groats is a little more north, and the North Sea is only a few miles away. Later in the week we'd be visiting Wick and Thurso for a look-around.

Loch Dhu

Robin Sinclair—Laird of Thurso, and owner of the far-flung moors we'd soon be shooting over—some 100,000 acres — and his wife, Margaret, whisked us away for the hour's run to the Loch Dhu Hotel—a Victorian-Gothic pile that'd be our home for the next week.

Already there and waiting for us were four men and their wives, all American and also guests of Winchester-Western Adventures. A brace of Englishmen were there, too, who had all but finished their shooting, and a charming girl as well, also a Britisher. In short order we were all on a first-name basis, tea was served and we were ready for some serious drinking, gun and shooting talk, plans for the morrow.

Actually, that was the only evening any of us did do any drinking to speak of, though the temptation was there in the form of a half-dozen brands of pure malt Scotches—heady, rich stuff. In the days to come we'd all be out on the moors, all day long (except me, worse luck), coming back to the Loch Dhu so beat that all we'd want would be a wash, a drink, some food and the hay—in that order. O, it wasn't all that rigorous really, at least not every day—the crowd usually got together in the saloon bar after dinner, changed into our finest, told a few lines and alibied our misses!

I'd caught a cold or a touch of the flu in Germany the week previous, and I felt so damned bad that I didn't get out on the moors except for two days of stalking, though Jack and I did manage to do some good grouse shooting for a few hours one afternoon, not far from the hotel.

Taking grouse in Caithness county—where there are only a few guns—is often done by "dogging." Setters, usually English or Gordons—are sent afield to locate the birds. Having done that, they'll set and wait for the guns to run over and get in position. Now the dog handler signals and the dogs flush the grouse. Sounds familiar, no? Well, this proved to be a bit different! These dogs range really far and wide, and it wasn't at all unusual for them

Jim Rikhoff has some Scotch in him—about two fingers, and very little water, please!

to make a set a couple of hundred yards away from the game.

That meant that Jack O'Connor and I would have to run—not walk—over to the dogs, otherwise the birds would be running away through the heather and the cottongrass, unseen and, of course, unshootable. That, in fact, was exactly what did happen many times—by the time we'd reach the dogs (neither Jack nor I are hundred-yard dash men any longer, if we ever were) the grouse had moved along, and rapidly. On our first few rises we'd taken a stand not far in front of the dogs, but we soon learned to run up well ahead of the setters, otherwise we'd have—and did have—birds getting up 40-50 yards away.

Nevertheless, it was a pleasant day of shooting—for me, who'd been holed up a couple of days, it was a joy—the smell of the heather and the peat, the soft wind bringing a touch of the sea across the moors, the stillness so profound when we'd be silent for a moment. It was amply rewarding, just to be outside.

Sick or not, I knew I wasn't going to leave Caithness county without doing some stalking for stag—not after having come several thousand miles to make my first attempt at Scotland's red deer.

Came the Rains

I told myself I'd go out next morning, even if I had to be hoisted to the flying bridge of one of their fat-bellied moor ponies. Having said that, I had yet another instance of what I've come to call Amber's Law—if there's going to be any rain, snow, sleet or hail, it'll happen on the days I plan to go abroad on the land. (Haven't you heard of the unprecedented 4-day rain that fell in Cabo San Lucas—at the extreme southern tip of Baja California—the year Winchester held their Seminar there? That lonely place hadn't had a quarter-inch of rain in the previous 7 years—or was it 11? Sure, I was blamed for that. We *fished* those several days; gun writers, mind you, instead of getting in the scads of white-wing dove shooting we'd been assured of!).

Monday had been clear and bright, and several stags had been shot by the other males of our small group. Tuesday—you guessed it—dawned dark, dreary and drizzling, nor was it to let up all day. It rained and it rained—not that something of that sort is unusual for Scotland.

My one piece of rain gear—a hip length rubber shirt — didn't help much. Within an hour we were all sodden, Jack O'Connor the least because he wore a short raincoat. The ghillies—youngsters both, and very nice boys—seemed to be in their element, so on we plodded, the moors we were heading for a long way off. As we slipped and stumbled over that knobby, hummocky ground, frequently going over our boot tops in the boggy stretches, I began to realize that Rikhoff hadn't been exaggerating about how wearying this stalking could be—and we hadn't even started "stalking" yet.

By this time we'd been tramping along for several hours, the few deer we'd seen being too far away, too small, too inaccessible—or all three. Jack and I had binoculars with us, of course, but in the mist and the dull, grey light we were unable to determine for ourselves what the stags seen offered in the way of racks. Our head ghillie carried one of those old and traditional draw-tube telescopes—with which he did as good a job as could be expected in the circumstances—but rain had soon got into the interior, fogging up the lenses, blurring his perception.

Across the rolling moors, here and there, small streams or "burns" make their tortuous way, winding slowly about in great looping curves and bends. Scotland had not had, in 1968, as much rain as usual, and these stream beds were often found nearly dry, the floor of the burn sometimes as much as a dozen feet below the level of the moorland banks.

Having located a shootable stag, perhaps two or three miles away—and that day we did finally spy a couple far off—the shooting party drops into one of the burns and begins to walk rapidly—or run—along the bottom in the direction the animal was last seen.

There are, obviously, several problems—first, while the stag now can't see you, you can't see him, either,

Jack O'Connor (left) and Jim Rikhoff look over Jim's new Winchester 70 Mannlicher-stocked 270 held by Robin Sinclair, our host on the hunt.

though a shift in the wind could waft your scent to him. For this reason the ghillie scrambles to the top of the stream bank at frequent intervals to make sure the stag hasn't winded the stalkers, that he has not disappeared, or to reassess his antlers—that early, long-range view might have been deceptive!

Three of my hunting partners in Scotland. From left—Scott Whitney, the writer, Jim Lacey and Ernest Moore. Only Jim Reinke is missing.

Remember I said that it was urgent to make time along the burn bed—the stag might well wander away, unseen, as I've noted. Yet, the party can't just tear like hell along the creek—the next bend might hold another stag or a bunch of them, heads worth shooting or not, so those blind curves must be approached cautiously, silently and prayerfully.

Sometimes it is necessary for the ghillie to climb the bank this side of a bend, get down on his belly and inch forward to peer over into the stream bed from above.

Rather late in that first wet afternoon we spotted a small band of deer, some 5 or 6, a long way off. Crouched over, half running, our ghillies led us to a burn a half-mile or so away, one that would let us approach the stags and hinds to within some reasonable distance, maybe within a couple of hundred yards—if we were lucky.

Then followed that succession of starts and bated-breath stops I've just related until we were—said the ghillie—about as close as we'd be able to manage. It wasn't 200 yards, either, but more like 350-400.

First Stalk

We left the burn, again bent 'way over, taking advantage of every rise we could, hurriedly trying to get within sure shooting distance. Jack, unfortunately, couldn't keep up the exhausting pace because of the painful hip joint resulting from an old auto injury. Now, having travelled for leagues, it seemed, on our hands and knees, we went down on our bellies, moving as rapidly as we dared through the wet, pungent heather, pushing and pulling our rifles along with us.

I was managing—though just barely—to keep up with our ghillie Robert, both of us some 50 yards ahead of Jack. At this tense moment, Robbie stopped—ahead of us the ground sloped away, making further progress impossible. Peering through the foot-high grass, my Winchester 70's scope trained on the deer some 150 yards off, we waited for Jack to come up and get a shot off—he couldn't have from where he lay. Jack had won the toss for the first shot as we started out. In that split-second the band took off, running rapidly, I fired, now that they were moving out, but I missed clear!

I felt badly about making that miss—and embarrassed as well—my only consoling thought the knowledge that the stags that had run off didn't have good heads. Tomorrow, too, was another day, and there'd be Thursday and Friday—what the hell!

That tomorrow dawned bright and clear, but I didn't. That soaking I'd got put me back in bed, feeling lousy. By dinner time I was a bit better, though, and I said to myself I'll make it on the moors next morning, come hell or high water!

The water part came true, of course. Thursday, a look out my window showed, was again going to be wet again—and wet, windy and chilly it was for the entire day.

The boys and I slogged over the moors, looking for a shootable stag, most of the long day. We did see, far off, a dozen or so beasts, but none worth taking off after. Then, in late afternoon, Robert saw three deer that he thought looked quite good and, equally important, might be got at if we'd hurry. They were several miles away, and the light would be getting no better fast.

The ghillies glass the far-flung moors, looking for a shootable stag. The telescope is the old-fashioned brass draw-tube type.

John Amber's stag, taken at the end of a long, wet day.

Into the Burn

We dropped into a burn bed, the rain still pelting down, and hurried along — our start-and-stop travel a repetition of the way we'd worked on the Tuesday. Robbie made the usual several clambers enroute to the top of the bank, returning each time to report that the stags were still where we'd first seen them, or thereabout.

Within some 30 minutes or so — though it seemed longer in my excitement—we cautiously left the stream bed, staying on our hands and knees as we topped to the bank—and there they were, some 300 yards away, golden coats gleaming despite the thin drizzle now gently falling.

My glasses showed one stag to be considerably better than his two companions—his rack was quite even, there were four points on either side and of about equal height; spread, too, was very good. At the moment we were lying atop a small rise, the deer a fair bit below us, but some 150 yards ahead of us was another low elevation, rising slightly toward the right.

Our job now was to make our way over the top of the small rounded hill before us without being seen—this would be the critical time. Happily, the light wind was almost directly in our faces, and—once we had gained the safety of the shallow depression ahead of us—we'd move a bit to our right, getting the wind dead ahead.

I was newly armed today—I'd lost a little faith in the 30-06 I'd missed with earlier, justly or not. I was now carrying Jim Rikhoff's rifle, one of the then just-announced Winchester 70s in the Mannlicher stocking, this one in 270 caliber. Jim had already accounted for two or three stags with it, he said, and it was printing right on the button at 200 yards using 130-gr. Silvertips. On top of it was a 4x Weaver scope, which I'd adjusted for my vision, but there'd been no chance to try a shot or two—I took Jim's word that it put them where it was looking.

Dropping to our bellies, we squirmed and crabbed our way over the first rise—getting thoroughly wet now—then ran in a crouch for the second knoll. Quickly, yet very carefully, we once more crawled up the slope and peered through the grass at the three stags, now some 150 yards away.

Bringing the rifle up into place I found I couldn't make the shot from the usual prone position. The grass, damn it, was too high. I'd have to raise myself and the rifle a little higher, it was obvious, and that might very well let the deer spot me.

The Stag at Bay

Hurriedly hoisting myself a few more inches—the steadiness of dug-in elbows no longer mine—I put the wavering crosshairs just behind the left foreleg and pulled the trigger.

The deer died where it stood—the 270 bullet, entering a trifle high, had pierced the heart and exited on the off side. The antlers measured 20 inches high, the spread some 25 inches, but not of heavy weight or beaminess. Certainly not a great head by any means, but I had my first Scottish stag and I was elated.

After the gralloching—dressing-out to you Yanks—the ghillies and I started the long haul back to Loch Dhu, the time now near 6:30 and the rain still with us.

We reached the hotel, wet and weary, almost too late for dinner. I had a couple of quick ones, then a bath and into dry clothes for the party being held that night—the top social event of the week, if not the season!

Robin Sinclair appeared in his dress plaid, his wife apparelled for a Scottish soiree — and very lovely — and they brought along a piper in full regimental regalia. Jim Rikhoff, who says he has Scots forebears (perhaps dating to Flodden Field), was in kilts as well.

That was a memorable evening—Margaret Sinclair led us all in dancing Scottish reels and hornpipes to the skirling of the piper. While I fancy myself as something of a dancer—they don't call me Twinkletoes for nothing—Robin and Jim put me in the shade. I consoled myself with the thought, "I'd been sick."

The next day was one of rest for just about all hands, though one of our men, Scott Whitney, went out and brought to bag another stag, the final one for the party. In all, we garnered an even dozen deer among us, a relatively small number really. Had the weather been better, and had Jack O'Connor and I been able to get out on all days, our take would undoubtedly have been a couple of dozen, easily. Caithness county has lots of deer, and I'm going back some day, preferably during the "roaring" time—a grand noise, ye ken? ●

Modern powders and bullets have given new life to old cartridges. Here is full detailed data for . . .

LOADING THE OLD ONES

TESTFIRE GD REPORT

...and some not so old

by KEN WATERS

READERS of the third edition of the HANDLOADER'S DIGEST may recall that this writer did a piece on reloading our more recently developed rifle cartridges, entitled "Loading the New Ones." Judging from letters received, this feature met with a favorable response, and one reader, S/Sgt. Donald R. Boyd of the United States Air Force, proposed that several of the more popular older cartridges be given a similar treatment.

Following that suggestion, the writer has selected four old and two not-so-old cartridges to discuss and talk about loading, in the hope that the information given will be interesting as well as helpful, especially to owners of rifles in these calibers.

Ours is a big country and the well-made rifles chambering these 6 cartridges are proving slow in wearing out. Countless thousands are still in use, many actively afield each year, continuing to bag game for their owners, and rifles are still being produced overseas for one of them. But whether the object of their shots be game, paper targets or just tin cans, they continue to deliver enjoyable outdoor recreation which, after all, is a primary function of sporting arms.

That enjoyment can be doubled and tripled, in both quantity and intensity, by reloading these cartridges. Thus, our objective is to show how this may be done, not only safely but with accuracy that equals or betters their original factory loadings. One of them is no longer commercially loaded, and two others can be handloaded to give considerably more power in certain rifles of adequate strength. For these cartridges especially, such a survey of reloading possibilities can have even greater significance.

The Not-So-Old

The first pair of cartridges to be scrutinized are not really old, yet they are obsolete. That is they simply failed to make the grade in the popularity department, so that although only 30 years old, no rifles in either caliber have been factory produced for some time now.

I'm talking about the 218 Bee and 219 Zipper—two dandy little varmint cartridges introduced by Winchester in 1938 and 1937 respectively, almost certainly as a result of the 22 centerfire craze spawned by the famous 22 Hornet, which had shown varmint shooters what could be done with light, fast-stepping and quick-opening jacketed bullets. The Bee and Zipper were both attempts to make the same sort of ballistics available to those preferring lever action rifles; oddly enough, both are better cartridges (in this writer's opinion) than the Hornet despite the way in which they have been allowed to languish into obscurity.

The reason usually advanced for this is that the light barreled Model 65 and 64 lever action rifles in which they were chambered lacked the fine accuracy required of a varmint rifle; to a certain extent this was probably true. However, having owned a Winchester 65 in 218 Bee and a Marlin 336 in 219 Zipper, it is my impression that the biggest share of the blame should have been placed on the absence of good telescope sights for top-ejecting Winchester lever actions. Varmint shooting, being a game involving small neutral-colored targets at medium-to-long ranges, demands more "seeability" and aiming precision than can be obtained with any kind of iron sights, so that no matter how inherently accurate a rifle may be, it is severely handicapped for this use unless fitted with a good scope sight.

Bad publicity, like a poor play review, is another thing that can damage a cartridge's chances for popular acceptance. I recall, for example, how two decades ago, some gun writers were saying that the Hornet was a more accurate round than the Bee, that being the era when all sorts of virtues, good and bad, were attributed to case shape. Doubting it even then, I purchased one of the inexpensive little Winchester 43 bolt actions in 218 Bee caliber and mounted a scope on it. Just as I had thought, accuracy proved fully as good as that delivered by 22 Hornet rifles of equal weight and barrel stiffness. For that matter, however, even my Model 65 lever action did as well, out to about 125 yards, as would most Hornets if iron sighted.

The Zipper, because it was expected to perform at still longer ranges and because it was factory loaded with a bullet of indifferent accuracy, suffered even more by comparison with scope sighted bolt action rifles. Substitute a known-accurate 50, 52, 53 or 55-gr. bullet of current manufacture for that old 56-gr. Winchester hollow-point, and your Zipper will shoot much tighter groups. Better still, fire them in a Marlin lever action or bolt gun with a scope sight, and you'll find it hard to believe you have the same cartridge.

Our approach to better accuracy in these two calibers can therefore be made along two or possibly three lines:

(1) Select the best suitable bullets available.

(2) Experiment with various powders and loads until the one best adapted to your individual rifle is found.

(3) If at all possible, mount a good scope sight.

Shooters lost no time in comparing it with the 22 Hornet, and they liked the almost 200 fs greater velocity which the Bee had at its muzzle, many failing to notice how this advantage dwindled to 100 fs superiority out at 200 yards. Nevertheless, there's no getting around the fact that the Bee delivers some 15% more bullet energy at that range than does the 22 Hornet and, but for the early (and mistaken) claims of better Hornet cartridge accuracy, the Bee might have won the popularity race. Both were rather prematurely killed off by the 222 Remington.

Once-fired 218 Bee cases of Winchester make have a capacity of 14.8 grains of water when filled to the base of case necks or, in other words, to the bases of seated bullets. By comparison, early thin-walled lots of Hornet brass averaged about 13 grains water capacity, while more recent and heavier Hornet cases hold only some 11.4 grains. This larger powder space is what accounts for the Bee's higher velocity, and it uses that limited capacity very well when it is noted that the 222, with room for 23.8 grains of water—or 60% more powder space—achieves only 12% higher velocity. Before leaving this subject of case capacity, however, it might be well to note that 218 Bee Remington brass—in some lots, at least — has an even greater capacity, which will have a direct bearing on developed pressures. Before making up any maximum loads, check the capacity of the cases to be used and adjust charges accordingly. At the very least, do not mix Winchester-Western brass with Remington-Peters.

As with practically all such small capacity cases, fast burning powders are indicated simply because they won't hold enough of the slower burning propellants to attain desired velocities. A corollary of this fact, of course, is that they are therefore quite sensitive to small increases of powder. Only ½-gr. more of 4227 or 2400, in some instances, will result in a gain of as much as 100 fs velocity. In the normal loading ranges, this may involve only a slight difference in pressure, but when working at or close to top psi levels, pressures may rise rather suddenly. Reasonable caution is therefore indicated.

218 Bee

Essentially a necked-down 25-20 with straighter body, longer 15-degree shoulder slope and shorter neck, the Bee is a small capacity, bottle-necked, rimmed cartridge intended for varmint shooting inside 200 yards. Because of its short case length of 1.345" and its rimmed form to control headspace, it is ideally suited for lever action rifles with short receivers, such as the Winchester Model 65 in which it was introduced, as well as rebarreled single shot rifles. In one of the latter, or in a suitable bolt action, it can be handloaded to give increased ballistic performance, but even its standard factory load of 46-gr. hollow-point bullet at 2860 fps MV the Bee offers a trajectory of 200 yards almost identical to that of the 300 Savage with the 180-gr. Silvertip factory load.

Factory loads in the 218 Bee develop about 44,000 psi, and I would advise that this level *not* be exceeded when loading for either the Model 65 lever action or the light Model 43 Winchester bolt action. Incidentally, these factory rounds chronograph at an actual 2760 fps in 24" barrels, or 2821 in a 26" length.

Du Pont 4227 and Hercules 2400 are the powders usually listed for reloading the 218 Bee, and they are probably the best for most purposes in this cartridge. However, there are at least two others which are useful under certain conditions. Hercules Unique has been found to give fine accuracy with cast bullets in light loads, and 4198 responds well in close to capacity loads with bullets of 50 grains or more weight, delivering good veloci-

LOADING THE OLD ONES

ties at lower pressures. I am of the opinion though, that factory load velocities cannot be exceeded, if indeed they can be equaled, with powders available to the handloader and still stay within our pressure limitation of 44,000 psi. To the best of my knowledge, none of the loads listed in our table exceed that figure, although I was unable to test them for pressure.

Any standard small rifle primer may be used with these loads, there being no need for a magnum primer with such fast burning powders in a small case like this. If pockets stretch so that primers fit loosely, color-code those cases and save them for very light loads only, or if too loose, discard them entirely—and reduce that load a little.

If your 218 Bee happens to be a bolt action or single shot, a really broad selection of bullets in all weights from 40 to 55 grains is available. Owners of lever action rifles with tubular magazines will have to be content with fairly blunt, round-nose bullets, either soft- or hollow-point, unless they are willing to use their rifle single-shot, loading cartridges with spitzer bullets directly into the chamber. Because of the jarring shock of recoil, rounds with sharp pointed bullets should never be placed in a tubular magazine where they bear against the primer of the round ahead of them.

One alternative would be to load a cartridge with a spitzer bullet into the chamber for the "shot that counts," then fill the magazine with blunt nose bullets. Before this is done, however, shooters should test both types on targets to ascertain whether the change in bullet shape will result in a different point of impact. If so, I would not consider this a good practice.

A better alternative would be to use a lever action as a two-shot rifle, loading one round only in the magazine, and the other directly into the chamber. In this way, both rounds could have spitzer bullets without danger, and the shooter would be assured of the same striking point for each.

The Sierra 40- and 45-gr. Hornet bullets expand well because of their thin jackets, and have sufficiently blunt soft points for use in the Model 65 lever action; also, I believe the 50-gr. Norma (No. 608) would be all right insofar as point shape is concerned. However, it should be borne in mind that unless case necks are tightly sized for a close friction grip on bullets, it will be necessary to select those having a cannelure for crimping. Also, the cannelure must not be positioned so as to cause too much of the bullet to project outside the case, making for too long an over-all cartridge length.

The Remington 46-gr. hollow-point is perhaps the best choice from this standpoint, although I personally prefer to use soft points and a heavy friction fit rather than crimping. Unfortunately, the lever action user doesn't have much to choose from in weights above 46 grains.

Standard specifications for the 218 Bee call for a barrel with .224″-.2245″ groove diameter, and a twist of 1-in-16″. Accordingly, jacketed bullets should be .224″, and cast bullets sized .225″. A good feature of the Bee was that barrels were not bored undersize as were many Hornets. I would not advise using bullets heavier than 53 grains though, partly because velocities will be lower, but mostly because the 1-in-16″ rifling twist then becomes marginal. If 55-gr. or heavier slugs are to be used, a steeper twist of 1-in-14″ would be preferable.

No particular trouble should be experienced in reloading the 218 Bee. Cases may stretch some if heavy loads are used or fired in a sloppy chamber and, when found to be in excess of the 1.345″ maximum length, they should be trimmed back to 1.335″ or thereabouts. Be uniform in this, especially if they are to be crimped, and again let me remind you to sort and segregate cases by make. Cases for the lever action may have to be full-length resized after every shot. My Model 65 was tolerant in this respect, neck-sizing being sufficient for about three loads.

Handled properly, there is absolutely no reason why a 218 Bee shouldn't be just as accurate and deadly as a 22 Hornet, given a barrel and bullets of equal accuracy and an equivalent sighting arrangement. This means that it will take all of the smaller varmints to about 200 yards, and the larger ones such as fox to around 150 or 160 yards. I once shot a very large hawk that was in the process of killing a chicken. The range was approximately 90 yards, and when the Bee cracked that hawk leaped about a dozen feet in the air and fell stone dead. Both wing butts had been shattered and a large exit hole caused instantaneous death. That was with the old 50-gr. Wotkyns-Morse bullet driven by 12 grains 4227, sighting with a Winchester No. 98 peep sight mounted on the rear of the Model 65's bolt. Best of all, the chicken survived!

I always had an affection for the 218 Bee, and wish I'd never been foolish enough to part with that fine little Model 65 rifle.

Here are some 218 Bee loads from my files:

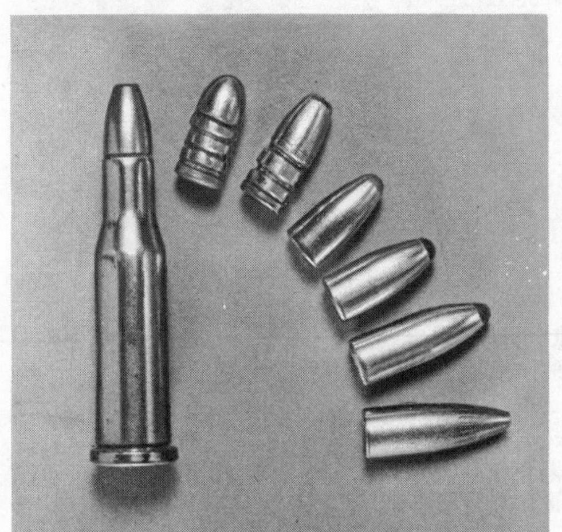

218 Bee Loads, Bullets and Factory Round

Bullet	Powder/grs.	MV	Remarks
43 Cast GC 225438	Unique/4.0	1750	Small game.
43 Cast GC 225438	2400/9.0	2192	
43 Cast GC 225438	4227/10.0	2227	Fast cast load.
48 Cast GC 225415	2400/8.5	2026	
48 Cast GC 225415	4227/9.5	2072	
40 Sierra Hornet	4227/13.4	2913	Accurate HS load.
40 Sierra Hornet	2400/12.0	2889	
45 Sierra Hornet	4227/12.0	2572	
45 Sierra Hornet	4227/12.7	2698	Accurate.
45 Sierra Hornet	2400/11.5	2673	
50 Speer SP	2400/11.0	2570	Good load.
50 Speer SP	4227/12.4	2653	Accurate
50 Speer SP	4198/14.5	2600	
52 Speer HP	2400/10.5	2490	
52 Speer HP	4227/11.7	2500	
52 Speer HP	4198/14.0	2516	Good load.

219 Zipper

Rimmed case—long sloping 12 degree shoulder—.224″ groove diameter—1-in-16″ rifling twist—and a reputation that belied its fine accuracy potential; all these things the 219 Zipper shares in some degree with the 218 Bee. But there are important differences too. Case capacity, averaging 33 grains (water) to base of neck, is more than twice that of the Bee, permitting the use of slower burning powders for higher velocities at reasonable pressures. Also, heavier bullets of greater sectional density suit this cartridge for work at longer range.

Most recent factory ballistics called for a 56-gr. hollow-point bullet with an MV of 3110 fps and ME of 1200 fp. Detractors will sneer that its 1550 fps remaining velocity at 300 yards is a full 200 fs less than that of a 50-grain soft point from the much smaller 222 Remington, but such derogatory comparisons ignore the true capabilities of the 219 Zipper cartridge when freed of its lever action restrictions. In a good bolt action or single-shot rifle, Hornady's 55-gr. spire-point bullet can be started out at 3400 fps and will still be traveling over 2000 fps out at 300 yards! This is not only better than anything the 222 can do—it is every bit as good as the 222 Magnum with its hottest handloads.

The Zipper must therefore be properly thought of, almost, as two separate cartridges—one with blunt nose bullets for use in lever action rifles at working pressures in the 40,000 psi class, and the other free to use ballistically superior pointed bullets at considerably higher pressures. It is only natural, therefore, that results should be drastically different. Not the least of possible improvements is a halving of deflection due to cross-winds. For these reasons, plus the fact that it is highly accurate in stiff barrels, tightly breeched and scope sighted, the 219 Zipper should not have been permitted to die a premature death.

The writer seldom presumes to take a great and respected manufacturer to task, but in this one instance I have always felt that Winchester displayed an unusual lack of consideration for shooters'—including recent customers'—interests when they abruptly discontinued production of this cartridge in 1962 without prior notice to allow stocking up (to my knowledge, anyway). Still worse, empty unprimed cases have not been made available either, despite the fact that Winchester rifles in 219 caliber were not dropped until after World War II, while Marlin chambered rifles for the Zipper up to 1961.

True, the 219 Zipper was based upon the old and still manufactured 25-35 case, necked down; and, with the proper dies, cases for the 219 can be formed from 25-35 brass. They can also, with a bit more effort, be formed from 30-30 and 32 Winchester Special brass, but non-reloaders and beginners are hardly up to this task, and I remain convinced that there is at least an implied obligation to produce ammunition and/or empty cases for a reasonable number of years after the last American-made rifle in a standard commercial caliber is discontinued.

Rim diameter and thickness are identical to those of the other cartridges named; case body varies by less than a thousandth at the base, body taper is very close, especially in the case of the 25-35, and the Zipper has the shortest case length, hence any of the others can be trimmed to 1.93″ following forming. Most reference sources specify 1.938″ as the case length of 219 Zippers, but the new Hornady Handbook gives 1.875″. I therefore measured new Winchester and Remington cases of late lots and found them to be 1.936″. Our trim-to-length of 1.930″ is thus correct.

Awhile back we mentioned the suitability of slower burning powders for this round. The writer has tried 3031, 4064, 4895, 4320, and all three powders of Hercules' Reloder series with bullets weighing from 45 to 63 grains in his 219 caliber Marlin Model 336. Excellent accuracy—less than minute-of-angle groups—was obtained with 4064, Reloder 11, 4895 and 3031 in the order listed. Actually any difference between these four has been minuscule and you wouldn't go wrong with any of them. (See the included table for our best loads to date, as well as a poor one for comparison). The Marlin 336 has an extremely stiff barrel, which may well account for much of its reliable accuracy performance. 4895 and 4320 produce about the best velocity/pressure ratios. At the same time, powders as fast burning as 4198 and Reloder 7 can be effectively used if desired, especially for lighter loads. The 219.Zipper is a flexible cartridge for reloading.

Primers indicated are the standard large rifle type, none of the above-listed powders requiring magnum priming. The bullet story, however, is an exact repeat of that told in connection with the 218 Bee. For lever actions with tubular magazines you'll need blunt nose projectiles — either soft- or hollow-points, unless they are to be single loaded or with not more than one in the magazine. Single-shot and bolt action rifles, however, free the handloader to use just about any .224″ diameter bullet.

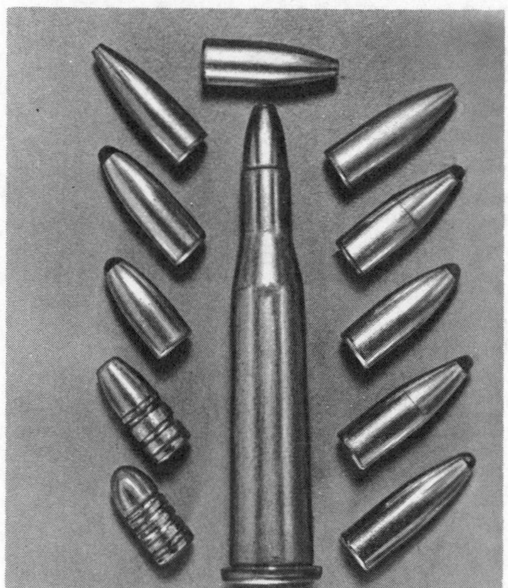

219 Zipper Loads, Bullets and Factory Round

Bullet	Powder/grs.	MV	Remarks
43 Cast GC 225438	2400/10.5	2010	
43 Cast GC 225438	4227/11.5	2022	
48 Cast GC 225415	2400/11.0	2070	
48 Cast GC 225415	4227/12.5	2150	
48 Cast GC 225415	4198/15.0	2200	
45 Sierra Hornet	Re #11/26.5	3570	Very accurate. Under MOA
45 Sierra Hornet	3031/27.5	3560	
50 Sierra SP	3031/25.5	3350	Accurate. Good load.
50 Sierra SP	Re #11/26.0	3444	
50 Sierra SP	Re #7/22.0	3300	
50 Sierra SP	4895/28.5	3428	
52 Speer HP	3031/25.0	3295	
52 Speer Silver Match	4064/28.0	3345	Most accurate load tested.
54 Gardiner HP	4895/25.5	3055	Accurate load.
55 Hornady SP	4895/25.0	3000	Average accuracy.
55 Norma SP	3031/25.0	3186	
60 Hornady SP	4895/24.5	2867	Good load in wind.
63 Sierra Semi-Ptd.	4064/26.0	3000	Poor load; see text.

My own experience with this cartridge verifies the findings of other experimenters in years past that the old 46- and 56-grain factory hollow-points are not too accurate, particularly the former. However, the 45-gr. Sierra Hornet round nose soft-point bullet gave us splendid accuracy when fired off by 26.5 grains of Reloder 11.

Speer's recently introduced 52-gr. Silver Match proved to be the most accurate of all bullets in my Marlin, and even the relatively heavy 60-gr. Hornady went into an inch for 5 shots. When the still heavier 63-gr. Sierra was tried, though, groups spread wide with evidence of bullet tipping on the targets. Evidently—and not surprisingly—this is just too much bullet for a 1-in-16″ twist, and if I were having a custom rifle made up in this caliber, intending to use 55-grain and heavier bullets, I'd specify a rifling twist of 1-in-14″.

Firing factory loads in the Marlin

LOADING THE OLD ONES

336 produced an initial base expansion of .0025", following which, successive reloads further increased case expansion by an additional .001"—.003". Ordinarily, I would consider any expansion of more than .0015" subsequent to the initial firing as excessive, and admittedly some of our loads do seem maximum in this rifle. But it should be remembered that we were working with a lever action rifle and only neck-sizing cases between firings. Cases did not suffer as a result, reentering the chamber readily. Thus, it would appear that, to a degree anyhow, the measured expansion was cumulative, occurring over a succession of shots. Accordingly, while I do not feel that any of our loads were excessive, I would consider the heaviest of them as being maximum in lever action rifles.

If there were such a thing as a varmint rifle match limited to lever action rifles, I'd use this Marlin 336 in 219 Zipper with handloads and a Weaver V-8 scope, and feel not in the least handicapped. The same goes for shooting live varmints of fox and coyote size in the field. It's a combination I trust and one that I wish was still available for today's varminters.

For our second pair of old cartridges, we turn back the calendar to 1892—the year both were introduced. They've been a fighting pair, literally, both starting life as military rounds and participating in more than one war, plus a rebellion and an insurrection or two. In the beginning they were even on opposite sides—that was the Spanish-American War of 1898—but that didn't take long to end, and about the same time sportsmen over a substantial portion of the globe became aware of their possibilities as big game hunting calibers.

Of course I'm referring to the 7x57-mm, often termed the "Spanish Mauser" in those early days, and the 30-40 Krag or 30 U.S. Army. Each is too well known to require our delving into their histories here, except to note that both were—and are—extremely well-balanced cartridges, and as such performed for their respective countries with an efficiency that might have been expected.

Two points in particular however, deserve noting. The Winchester High Wall single-shot rifle in 30-40 caliber was the first smokeless powder sporting combination produced in the U.S., dating from 1893 and thus preceding the 30-30 by a year or two. The 7mm Mauser is one of the oldest military and sporting calibers for which both rifles and ammunition are still being made (although only cartridges are made for it in this country). New rifles chambered for the 7x57 must be imported.

For all their 75 years of age, both the 30-40 and 7mm Mauser continue to serve shooters in America, especially those hunters who demand adequate killing power while shunning the newer magnums as excessively powerful. Present day ballistics of each are much improved over those of the 1900 era, modern powders making it possible to develop higher velocities without increasing pressures. Let's look at them individually.

The 30-40 Krag

Selected from over 50 different rifles extensively tested by a U.S. Army Ordnance Board, the Krag-Jorgensen was adopted as our new service rifle in 1892. With it came a new cartridge known as the "30 U.S. Army," and popularly referred since as the 30-40 Krag.

This was a drastic change for the military to make, previous service rifles having been of 45 caliber and larger, and reflected the changes brought about by the introduction of smokeless powder. Another "first" for the Krag was its use of metal jacketed bullets. That first 30-40 cartridge contained approximately 38 grains of an early issue smokeless, and a 220-gr. round nose bullet with cupro-nickel full metal jacket. Muzzle velocity ran from 1990 to 2005 fps, and effective range was considered to be about 600 yards.

Younger shooters may think it strange that this cartridge, specially designed for a bolt action military rifle, should have been given a rimmed case, but of course this was because the Krag did not employ a clip-type magazine. With a case length of 2.314", the 30-40 is both shorter and slightly smaller in diameter than a 30-06, resulting in an internal capacity (measured to base of case neck) averaging 22½% less. For today's denser smokeless powders, this is more of an asset than a detriment, and taken in conjunction with a case neck that is almost one-half inch long, it is practically ideal for reloading.

Over the intervening years, 30-40 loadings have undergone several changes of importance to today's owners. Adoption for sporting use brought soft nose bullets suitable for hunting big game, and along with the original 220-gr. weight, a sharp-pointed 180-gr. put in its appearance. Muzzle velocity for the Remington-UMC 180-gr. factory load in 1915 was given as 2320 fps. Still later, a 150-gr. loading with 2660 fps MV showed up. Peters offered a 225-gr. "Belted" for the biggest game, and there was even a special Short Range Winchester cartridge with 100-gr. bullet.

So much for background history.

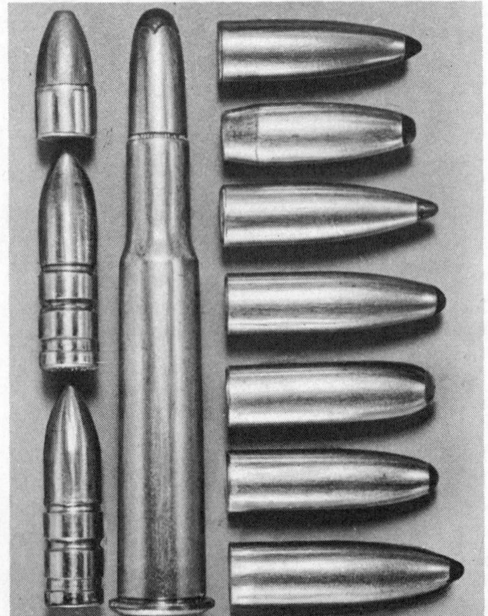

30-40 Krag Loads, Bullets and Factory Round

Bullet	Powder/grs.	MV (26" Bbl.)	Remarks
160 Cast GC 311375	4198/21.5	1790	Very accurate.
165 Cast GC 311413	4227/14.5	1374	Very accurate.
165 Cast GC 311413	4895/35.0	2108	Accurate.
100 Hornady S/J	3031/44.0	3000	Short range varmint.
150 Sierra Sptz.	HiVel #2/37.5	2543	
150 Sierra Sptz.	H-414/44.0	2455	
150 Sierra Sptz.	4895/44.0	2622	Vertical stringing.
150 Sierra Sptz.	4064/43.0	2588	Vertical stringing.
150 Sierra Sptz.	4350/49.0	2522	Vertical stringing.
150 Norma Match B.T.	4895/35.5	2269	Very accurate.
165 Speer sp.	4895/41.0	2433	
165 Speer sp.	4064/41.0	2472	Accurate.
165 Speer sp.	4350/47.0	2413	Best all-round load.
180 Sierra sp.	Re #11/36.0	2346	
180 Sierra sp.	4320/39.0	2243	Accurate.
180 Sierra sp.	Re #21/40.0	2177	
180 Sierra sp.	H 414/40.0	2240	
180 Sierra R.N.	HiVel #2/36.0	2363	Max. (42,000 psi).
180 Speer R.N.	4064/40.0	2359	Vertical stringing.
180 Speer R.N.	4350/45.0	2354	Most accurate load tested.
200 Speer sp.	4350/44.0	2230	Good load. (38,500 psi).

Today's 30-40 factory cartridges, while of decreased variety, offer increased performance. Winchester-Western lists their 220-gr. Silvertip at 2200 fps and a choice of either Silvertip or Power-Point in 180-gr. at 2470 fps Remington has only 180-gr. weights, but offers both a round nose and the pointed Core-Lokt traveling 2470 fps at muzzle. Canada's Dominion brand includes a single 180-gr. round nose number, likewise at 2470 fps. Unfortunately, there is no longer a factory 150-gr. loading. The 30-40 is thus a close competitor of the 303 British and 300 Savage, and not so far behind the 308 that any animal fairly hit would ever know the difference.

The most important point concerning the 30-40 Krag cartridge to be noted by handloaders is its pressure limitation, made necessary by many of the old rifles in which it was chambered. Loads in the 32,000 to 40,000 psi bracket are most common and to be preferred, but under no circumstances should they ever be allowed to exceed 44,000 pounds per square inch (psi). Consider 40,000 psi as normal max.

This is where that smaller case capacity averaging 47.5 grains (water) will be appreciated, it being possible to use charges that come close to filling the case without having so much that pressures climb above the established limits. The far more pleasant recoil of the 30-40 as compared to a 30-06 of equal weight, is also attributable to this lighter loading.

Optimum canister powders appear to be IMR 4064, and Hercules Reloder 11, which latter replaced the old and excellent HiVel 2. 4350 is likewise an excellent choice with 165-gr. and heavier bullets. With continued testing, it may develop that Reloder 21, Hodgdon's newest H-414 and Herter's No. 100 are also suited to use with heavy bullets. Vertical stringing of shots with 4895 would indicate a lack of uniformity in pressures, making it less desirable even though safe in recommended loads.

Considering both accuracy and power, 4350 has been outstanding in the writer's test rifles—an original military Krag with 30″ barrel, and a Model 1895 Winchester with slender 26″ barrel. Our two favorite loads to date have been: (1) The 180-gr. Speer RN with 45/4350, and (2) 165-gr. Speer spitzers and 47/4350. IMR 4198 is a good choice when cast bullets are to be used in moderate loads.

Being a true 30 caliber—that is, with bore and groove dimensions of .300″ and .308″ respectively — one would normally not anticipate any problem of bullets. However, there are a couple of things that should be pointed out in this connection, the first of which is that some of the early 30-40 caliber rifles—Krags especially—varied considerably in their groove diameters, running both under- and oversize (from .307″ to .313″). This could easily affect pressure development as well as accuracy, hence I suggest that handloaders slug and mike their barrels, thereafter selecting bullets which provide the best fit. Several bullets intended for 30-30s measure .307″ rather than .308″, and these would be practical for reloading a 30-40 with tighter-than-normal bore.

Secondly, it should be remembered that original 30-40 barrels were chambered with long throats to accommodate the old blunt-nose 220-gr. bullets. In such barrels, it is entirely possible that trouble may be experienced in getting lighter and shorter spitzer bullets to shoot accurately because they must jump across what is, in effect, a section of free-boring. It's common to blame the rifling twist for being too steep and over-stabilizing the bullet. Correct in theory, but seldom true in actuality!

The rifling twist of most 30-40 caliber rifles is 1-in-10″, as it must be to handle 220-gr. bullets, and by ample experience in a number of rifles, this is not at all too steep for even 150-gr. bullets. All that's necessary is to seat those lighter bullets as far out of the case as can be done and still permit them to function through the magazine and chamber properly. If you're content to single load, seat the bullet out to just miss the rifling.

It would be hard to find an easier cartridge to reload than the 30-40. That long neck helps in seating bullets correctly and holding them firmly without any need for crimping. Often cases can be reloaded time after time with only their necks being sized, and usually trimming won't need to be done too often. When it is, trim to 2.304″. Either standard or magnum large rifle primers may be used; personally, I seat magnums only when using 4350 powder.

Cast bullets perform especially well in most 30-40s, perhaps because of that generous throat which readily accepts the larger .311″ diameter often found, but partly also, I think, due to the long case neck that makes it unnecessary for bullet bases to project down into the powder space. If you have a Krag or other 30-40 rifle with a clean and not too worn barrel, cast bullets with gas check and long full-diameter bearing shank, such as Lyman's Loverin-designed 311466 and 311467, may well surprise you with their accuracy.

I'll not plug this oldie as "best" for any purpose, but I will say that an awful lot of fun can be had with it. Plenty accurate in a good barrel for big bore target shooting, it is also a game killing cartridge that was once hailed for its power, even on elk and moose. There's no reason it can't still deliver the goods as well or better than ever.

The 7mm Mauser

The Spanish-American War taught us the merits of the 7x57mm as a military cartridge, but the round was not a wartime surprise as has sometimes been intimated. Not only did we know of it beforehand, but it had actually been manufactured in this country from about 1896, or two years before the war.

Original specifications called for a round-nosed full-metal-jacketed bullet weighing 172.8 grains with a muzzle velocity (presumably taken in a 29″ barrel) of 2296 fps. Berdan primers and a charge of from 37 to 38 grains of a European smokeless powder created chamber pressures of just under 45,000 psi. Bore diameter was (and still is) .276″ with .284″ between opposing grooves. Four land rifling having a twist rate of 1-in-8.6″ were employed to stabilize this long bullet.

Several writers have referred to the 7mm Mauser as being much superior ballistically to the 30-40 Krag, but it is difficult to see this in their early loadings, especially when the Krag was used with 180-gr. Remington spitzer bullets. Comparable mid-range trajectory heights when shooting at 500 yards were:

30-40	220-grain	49.98″
30-40	180-grain	29.68″
7mm	175-grain	40.85″

They were, in fact, quite evenly matched, with most of the 7mms alleged superiority properly attributable to the Mauser's clip-loading feature, which enabled soldiers to reload faster.

Right now we're interested in the cartridge, however, and although the early sporting loads in the 7mm—which were virtually the military round with a blunt soft nose bullet replacing the FMJ—established an enviable record around the world for deep penetration, subsequent factory offerings were to make it a far more flexible hunting round.

Today, despite the unfortunate fact that Winchester and Remington only produce the 7mm Mauser in a single 175-gr. RNSP loading at 2490 fps, Federal has added a 139-gr. round whose MV is given as 2680 fps, Norma offers additionally a 150-gr. semi-pointed boat-tail at 2756 fps and a 110-gr. varmint load at a surprising 3067 fps, while Dominion lists both a 160-gr. at 2650 fps, and a 139-gr. at 2800.

Not having had an opportunity to try all of these factory loads, I can't help wondering whether they are actually capable of making those speeds in 22″ and 24″ sporting rifle barrels, but rather doubt it. Speer's laboratory tests in a 22″ tube revealed that while the Federal 139-gr. and Remington 175-gr. loads came very close to their claimed speeds, the Norma 150-gr. failed by almost 200 fs to make its published 2756 fps, and both Winchester and Federal 175-gr. loads were off by a substantial 110 to 235 fs. I

LOADING THE OLD ONES

can't seem to find any published ballistics for Sako's 155-gr. 7mm am*mo*, but in our 24" barrel Mauser it chronographed at an average 2456 fps.

Based upon these results, as well as our own tests and the reports of other reliable chronographings, it is the writer's feeling that reloaders shouldn't expect more than about 2770 fps with 139- or 140-gr. bullets, 2650 with 150-154 gr., 2600 with 160-gr., and 2420 fps with 175-gr. slugs. If these muzzle speeds are exceeded, pressures are almost certain to exceed the standard 45,000 psi.

The 7x57 Mauser has a conventional and quite modern appearing rimless case with very little more taper than a 270, and a shoulder slope that is some 3 degrees steeper. Best of all, from a handloader's standpoint, is its generously long neck—almost 3/8"—ideal for holding the long bullets of this caliber.

Case capacity averages about 53 grains (water), which is close to 7% more than most 308s, and 12% above most 30-40 cases. You're likely wondering then how come muzzle velocities aren't higher! Three reasons. Most important is that sectional densities of 7mm bullets are greater than those of 30-caliber bullets (under 180-gr.), while the area of a 7mm bullet's base upon which powder gases have to push, is smaller. A 154-gr. Hornady 7mm spire point, for example, has a sectional density of .273 compared to the .247 of a 165-gr. Hornady 30-caliber, and the 30-caliber bullet, like a larger piston, has approximately 17% larger base area.

Lastly, remember that 45,000 psi pressure limitation. With allowable pressures some 5000 psi higher in a 308, this is bound to have an effect on velocities. Reduce pressure in a 308 to 45,000 psi, and 180-gr. bullets will only be given some 2450-2475 fps—not too much more than the 2400 fps of a 175-gr. 7mm slug. Hence, these velocities are entirely reasonable. Then too, I fail to see any reason why loads up to 50,000 psi couldn't safely be used in a good commercial Mauser of recent vintage, or to Remington 30 and Winchester 70 rifles.

There's little doubt in my mind but that the medium-slow and slow burning powders are best in this case with bullets heavier than 150 or 154 grains. As will be seen from our table, Reloder 21, 4895, 4350 and even maximum loads of 4831 did very well, both as to accuracy and velocity. Somewhat contradictory to previously published reports, however, the same powders also performed excellently with bullets as light as 139 grains. Biggest surprise of all was our compressed load of 53/4831 behind 139-gr. Hornady bullets. While not as consistently accurate as 49 grains of 4350 or 42/4895, it did give slightly higher velocities, and grouping that couldn't be called poor.

If I were asked to name my favorite 7mm load, however, I'd have to say the 160-gr. spitzer with 52 grains of 4831. Averaging some 2700 fps with good bullet weight and superb accuracy, this seems an ideal combination of power and long range hitting ability. At reasonable ranges, there should be enough punch left in this load to down most species of game to be found in the original 48 states and Canada, assuming of course, that the shooter does his part.

Bullets and primers present no problem. Any .284" or .283" bullet can be used, and with a choice of weights from 110 to 175 grains, it's fairly obvious that the 7x57 is a versatile and highly useful cartridge. Standard large rifle primers will fire any of the powders named in this medium capacity case, but I prefer magnum caps when loading with 4350 or 4831.

I can't think of any particular problems connected with reloading the 7mm; it's almost a "natural" for this purpose. Barrel groove diameters will be found to vary some, especially in foreign made rifles, but in most instances this is readily taken care of by a judicious bullet selection from the size and weight variations offered. If a bore is extremely tight, it would be wise to reduce loads for that particular rifle, but this is a problem of individual rifles rather than criticism of the cartridge itself. In this connection, I would also warn that the heavier loads should *not* be used in the old Remington rolling-block single shot rifles. Loads shown are for bolt action rifles.

When case length goes beyond 2.235", trim to 2.225", and do not let over-all length of loaded cartridges exceed $3\frac{1}{16}$". Neck or partial resizing of cases should be sufficient, since these are mostly all bolt action rifles, unless cases from other 7mms are allowed to become mixed with yours. If that happens, it's best to play safe and full length size all empties.

As a final note, I suggest to those planning on using cast bullets, that they *not* choose any of the handsome spitzer shapes with long tapering noses and one or two grease grooves near the base. While pretty to look at, I've been disappointed in the way they shoot in this caliber. These long 7mms

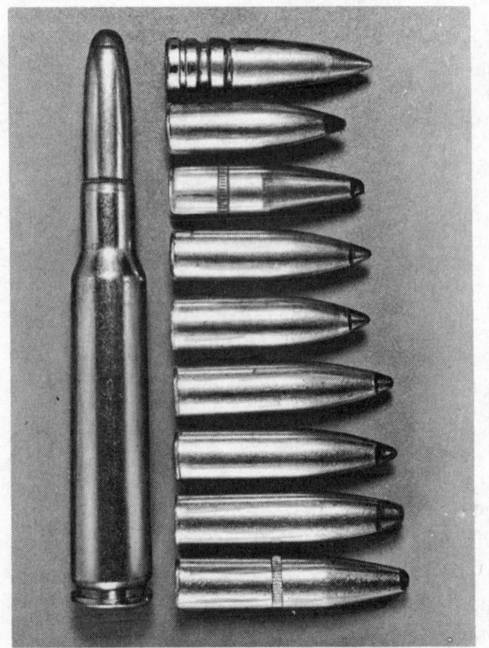

7mm Mauser Loads, Bullets and Factory Round

Bullet	Powder/grs.	MV	Remarks
150 Cast GC 287405	4227/19.0	1830	Accurate.
150 Cast GC 287405	4198/21.0	1722	Accurate.
120 Sierra spitzer	N-201/42.0	2814	Good load.
120 Sierra spitzer	4895/44.0	2921	Somewhat erratic.
139 Hornady	HP-101/42.5	2585	Accurate.
139 Hornady	Re #21/45.0	2694	Erratic.
139 Hornady	4831/53.0	2790	Compressed. (Max.).
140 Sierra spitzer	4350/49.0	2772	Excellent.
140 Sierra spitzer	4895/42.0	2687	Excellent.
145 Speer spitzer	4895/41.5	2602	Excellent.
145 Speer spitzer	4350/48.0	2708	Excellent.
150 Winchester P-P	Re #21/44.0	2570	Accurate.
160 Curry spitzer	Re #21/43.5	2480	
160 Curry spitzer	4895/41.0	2594	Some flyers (Max.).
160 Curry spitzer	4831/51.0	2646	
160 Curry spitzer	4831/52.0	2704	Most accurate. Compressed. (Max.).
160 Speer spitzer	4350/46.0	2569	Excellent.
175 Speer magnum	4895/40.0	2427	Excellent. Accurate (Max.).
175 Hornady	HP-101/41.0	2385	Very accurate.
175 Hornady	Re #21/42.0	2388	
175 Hornady	4350/44.0	2365	Excellent. Very accurate.
175 Hornady	4831/48.0	2460	

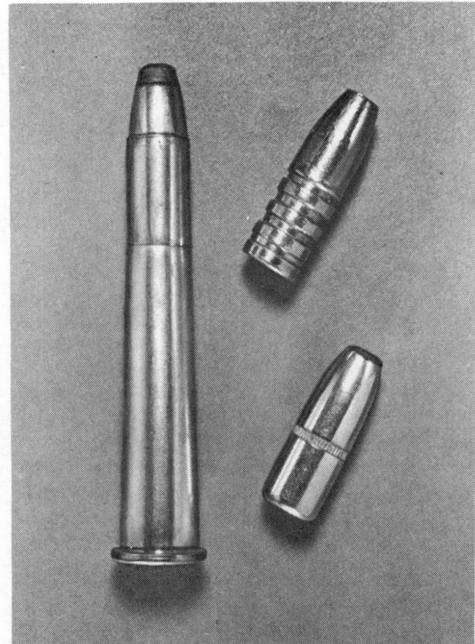

32-40 Loads, Bullets and Factory Round

Bullet	Powder/grs.	MV (26" Bbl.)	Remarks
(A) Target Loads (Low Pressure)			
181 Cast GC 321297	2400/13.0	1450	Very accurate.
181 Cast GC 321297	4227/14.0	1403	
181 Cast GC 321297	4198/17.0	1450	Good target load.
181 Cast GC 321297	HiVel 2/18.3	1295	Outstanding accuracy.
181 Cast GC 321297	HiVel 2/20.0	1430	
181 Cast GC 321297	Unique/7.7	1210	Short range target load.
170 Hornady .321" SP	Re 11/18.7	1334	Very accurate; low pressure.
(B) Medium Loads			
170 Hornady .321" SP	HiVel 2/22.0	1560	Approx. 20,000 psi.
170 Hornady .321" SP	Re 7/21.0	1583	
170 Hornady .321" SP	3031/23.0	1585	
(C) Heavier Loads for Strong Action Rifles Only			
170 Hornady .321" SP	3031/25.0	1721	
170 Hornady .321" SP	3031/28.0	1925	Max.—Best accuracy.
170 Hornady .321" SP	4895/29.0	1886	Good load.
170 Hornady .321" SP	Re 11/27.0	1923	
170 Hornady .321" SP	Re 7/25.0	1868	
170 Hornady .321" SP	4198/20.0	1718	

need to be stabilized, and a blunt nose gas check slug with full-diameter bearing section over most of its length, containing multiple grease grooves, such as Lyman's 287405 and 287448, designed by Guy Loverin, will generally be found to give far better accuracy. Our table gives a couple of starting points which, with a little luck, may result in a good practice and small-game load right off.

32-40 & 38-55

Our final pair of old cartridges go back still farther—to about 1884, in fact—yet many readers will be familiar with them even today since they are still with us, in certain makes at least.

Chances are, if you've ever fired a 32-40 or 38-55, it's been in a Winchester Model 1894, Marlin Model 1893 or Savage 99 lever action repeater. They're the rifles that seem to be around in the most numbers, but are in fact only a few of the many types and models that were produced in these calibers. Originally, both were Marlin-Ballard cartridges, introduced for their fine single shot match rifles, and were primarily intended for 200 and 220-yard off-hand target or Schuetzen shooting.

In this field they were eminently successful, both proving to be extremely accurate when properly loaded, while delivering mild recoil at the butt end. Understandably, it wasn't long before several folks got the idea that they should also make good deer hunting loads, and the late 1880s being the era when lever action repeaters were burgeoning, these two rounds found ready acceptance from a number of rifle manufacturers.

Some of these actions—particularly the early single shots and repeaters—were relatively weak, while others were quite strong. This is the reason background history can be important to reloaders. When we set out to refill 32-40 or 38-55 empties today, we must first know what rifles they are to be used in. Because the cartridge makers don't know which one that will be, this is precisely the reason once-available "high power" and "high velocity" smokeless loadings were dropped years ago, leaving only the mild-as-punch commercial offerings currently produced in this country.

So greatly different are the strengths of the various rifles available at one time or another in these calibers, that I decided the only safe approach to their reloading would be along the lines wisely adopted by Lyman for the 45-70 cartridge in the 42nd edition of their *Reloader's Handbook.* In that booklet, loads for the comparatively weak-action 1873 Springfield were kept separate from those for the strong Model 1886 Winchester. It made so much sense that I've done much the same thing here for the 32-40 and 38-55.

Naturally, any such listing as this is bound to be somewhat arbitrary, but dividing lines must be drawn somewhere so I've classified them as follows:

Strong Action

Winchester 1894 Lever Action
Marlin 1893 Lever Action
Savage Model 99 Lever Action
Remington-Lee Bolt Action
Remington-Hepburn S.S.
Stevens Model 44½ S.S.
Winchester High Wall S.S.

Medium Strong Action

Marlin 1881 Lever Action
Bullard Lever Action
Bullard Single Shots

Weak Action

Ballard Single Shots
Stevens 44 S.S.
Stevens Tip-Up S.S.
Maynard 1882 S.S.

Please note that we don't list every make and model ever chambered for the 32-40 or 38-55, but only those more likely to be encountered. Fortunately, those rated as having strong actions are the most commonly seen (with two exceptions) and, if in good sound condition with proper headspacing, are quite capable of handling pressures in the 35,000 psi bracket. Both cartridges use the same basic brass case as the 30-30 and 32 Winchester Special, so there is no reason why they shouldn't be able to. Indeed, with the 38-55 in particular, the greater expansion ratio provided by that large and generally long bore, causes pressures to drop rapidly once the bullet is in motion.

So that there is no chance of our being misunderstood, let me state unequivocally that if your 32-40 or 38-55 is *not* one of those rifles listed in our first column as having a strong action, you should stick with the light-to-medium loads listed in published tables, loads which do not exceed factory cartridge ballistics. If, on the other hand, you have a Winchester 1894, Marlin 1893, or one of the other strong ones, you can, by judicious handloading, turn that old rifle into a far surer killer of deer and black bear.

LOADING THE OLD ONES

TESTFIRE GD REPORT

The 32-40

First, a quick look at vital statistics. This is a rimmed case 2.130″ long, with .424″ and .506″ base and rim diameters, and straight-tapered sides to bottom of neck. Water capacity averages just under 34 grains to base of seated bullets, and standard U.S. factory ballistics call for a 165-gr. jacketed soft point bullet leaving the muzzle at 1440 fps. Canada's Dominion 32-40s are listed as giving a 170-gr. bullet some 1540 fps. Velocities for this caliber are commonly taken from 26″ barrels, and you'll probably be using this length or longer.

Winchester barrels in 32-40 have groove diameters from .320″ to .321″, while Marlins generally run .319″-.320″. Either will accept bullets from .319″ to .322″; in my tests I have used mostly .321″ jacketed and .3225″ cast gas check (G.C.) slugs. The standard rifling twist is 1-in-16″.

If a sufficiently hard alloy—say, 1-to-16 or harder—is used, plain cast bullets are entirely practicable at even the highest velocities reasonable in this cartridge. Above 1500 fps however, I have a distinct preference for those with gas checks to protect their bases and, despite the fact that cast bullet accuracy is excellent in 32-40s with clean, un-worn barrels, even at respectably high speeds, I always recommend the use of jacketed soft points for hunting reloads. This is because cast bullets alloyed hard enough to stand the higher velocities do not give as reliable expansion as soft points.

There will be many who disagree with me on this point, but after almost three decades of experimenting, I've come to prefer jacketed bullets when after big game, even including whitetail deer. This accounts for the lighter loads shown with cast bullets in our tables, but should *not* be taken to mean that cast slugs are less accurate. On the contrary, they make fine barrel-saving loads for target shooting in the 32-40s slow rifling twist, but may not open up on game unless bone is struck. Hollow-points help in this respect, but are by no means sure-fire when hard cast. 165- and 170-gr. flatnose soft points as produced by Winchester, Remington, Hornady and Speer in diameters of .320″ and .321″, are top choice when heading into hunting country. Don't worry about barrel life. You won't fire enough shots at game to wear out one of these barrels in a lifetime.

Back in 1914, Winchester listed a high velocity loading for the 32-40 with 165-gr. jacketed bullet at 1752 fps. By 1941, the speed of this load had been upped to 1950 fps. I wanted to see if I could duplicate those loads and yet, realizing they were much too potent for rifles with weaker actions, it was also desired to develop combinations which approximate present factory velocities while giving even finer accuracy.

In all, some nine different powders were tried, the fastest burning being Unique, and the slowest 4895. Charges were tailored to bullet type and acceptable pressure/velocity ratios, and experiments continued until the desired combinations of accuracy and bullet speed had been achieved.

For target loads with cast bullets in the 20,000 psi and under range, fast burning powders such as Unique, 2400, 4227 and 4198 appear to work well, and nothing slower burning than the old Hi-Vel 2 was used. Resulting velocities varied from 1200 to 1450 fps, and this first group proved to be OK, even in old Ballard and Stevens 44 rifles. Shooters wishing to accasionally use jacketed bullets in the older rifles —and they shouldn't be used as a steady diet—will find our load of 18.7 grains of Reloder 11 with Hornady 170-gr. flat-nose soft points, highly and consistently accurate with low pressures.

A second group, which might be referred to as "medium loads," were based upon these same 170-gr. .321″ Hornady bullets at moderate velocities of 1500-1600 fps. With these, I stepped down a notch in powder burning rates to 3031, also trying the recently developed Reloder Nos. 7 and 11. Actually, the loads in this bracket, as shown by our table, are very similar in performance to the Dominion factory rounds, and are good choices where something more powerful than U.S. factory loads is desired. They are *not* recommended for 32-40s with weak actions, however.

The third and final group stepped out at from 1700 to over 1900 fps, two of these loads coming close to duplicating the H.V. factory rounds of 30 years ago. Had we used 165-gr. rather than 170-gr. bullets, they should have been fully as fast. Although I do not have measured pressure figures on these heavier loads, they are conservatively estimated at not more than 35,000 psi. This is partially attested to by the fact that case expansion in the vital base area did not exceed .001″-.0015″ over miked diameters taken after initial firing of factory rounds in the same chamber. Case lengths remained exactly the same, a further good sign. Accuracy, while in most instances not quite as good as with the lighter target loads, was still of a high order once the load best suited to the individual rifle had been determined. 28 grains of 3031 with Remington 9½ primers and the 170-gr. Hornady bullets gave especially fine accuracy. I believe the average 32-40 rifle, if the bore is good, will be found to group better than most 30-30s.

Standard large rifle primers give entirely adequate ignition with any of the powders suited to the 32-40 and, as a matter of fact, for the lighter cast bullet and target loads I prefer those primers of a milder nature as giving still finer accuracy. For example, the writer has carefully saved his remaining supply of the discontinued Winchester 115 primers, which were less violent than the standard 120s and long known for their superior performance with light target loads. Today's Federal 210 and Remington 9½ primers have been proving good for such use.

Reloading the 32-40 is easy, but consists of two quite different procedures, depending upon the rifle being loaded for. In the case of lever action rifles, full-length resizing of cases is always called for to assure certain and uniform chambering, and to avoid unnecessary strain on the extractor. With a single-shot rifle, however, it is only necessary to neck-size cases, assuming no mix-up of cases from other rifles is allowed to happen. More than that, accuracy will be a bit better and cases last a little longer if only necks are sized.

For lever action rifles, bullets must be seated deep enough to keep overall cartridge length from exceeding the specified 2.50″, again to provide sure feeding and chambering. The seating die should be adjusted to turn a firm crimp of case mouth into the bullet's cannelure or crimping groove. In the single shots, I have obtained best accuracy by seating bullets out just short of touching the rifling lands, with nothing more than a uniform friction grip of case necks to hold bullets. Do *not* crimp when loading for single-shot rifles.

Finally, select only round or flatnose bullets, regardless of rifle type. Pointed bullets are dangerous in tubular-magazine lever action rifles (if placed in the magazine), and although quite safe in single shots, give greatly inferior accuracy due to their longer length in proportion to weight, making it more difficult to stabilize them with the slower twist rifling and at the lower velocities common to this caliber.

Recoil of the 32-40 is most pleasant, and barrel life will be long, especially if cast, lubricated bullets are used in the older single shots with their soft steel barrels. There's no reason why jacketed bullets shouldn't be loaded in the later repeating rifles. however.

If carefully loaded as explained, with due caution and attention to details, your 32-40 can be made to deliver either better accuracy or increased game killing power—possibly both—depending only upon rifle strength and condition.

Lyman's Ideal lubricant has always performed well for me at reasonable cast-bullet velocities, but more recently I have been trying the new Javelina

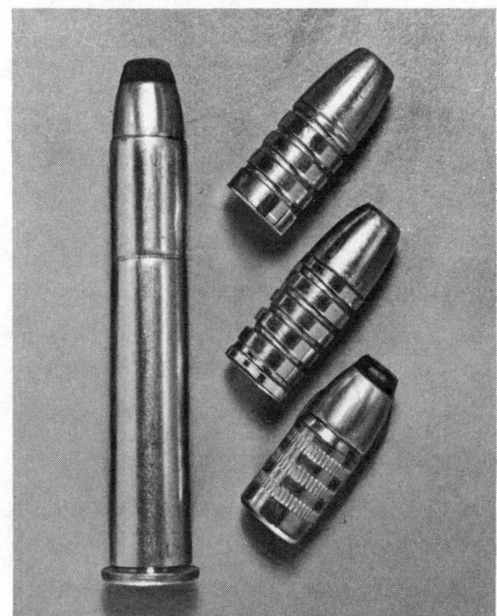

38-55 Loads, Bullets and Factory Round

Bullet	Powder/grs.	MV (26" Bbl.)	Remarks
(A) Target Loads (Low Pressure)			
250 Cast PB 375248	2400/15.0	1357	
250 Cast PB 375248	4227/17.0	1330	
265 Cast GC 375296	4198/20.0	1350	
265 Cast GC 375296	HiVel 2/23.0	1355	
(B) Medium Loads			
255 Winchester S.P.	HiVel 2/26.0	1455	
255 Winchester S.P.	4895/29.0	1415	Very accurate; mild pressure.
255 Winchester S.P.	4895/32.0	1560	Very accurate.
255 Winchester S.P.	3031/30.0	1601	
(C) Heavier Loads for Strong Action Rifles Only			
255 Winchester S.P.	3031/33.0	1760	
255 Winchester S.P.	3031/35.0	1866	Max.; powerful and accurate.
255 Winchester S.P.	Re 7/30.0	1684	
255 Winchester S.P.	Re 7/32.0	1796	Very accurate; best heavy load.
255 Winchester S.P.	Re 7/33.0	1852	Max.; powerful and accurate.

lubricant, a blend of 50% Alox 2138F and 50% pure yellow beeswax. This comes in brown colored "sticks" for use in lubricating pumps, but may be applied directly by hand, and is proving very effective in withstanding the higher temperatures of increased velocities.

The 38-55

Much that has just been said concerning the 32-40 applies equally to the 38-55, particularly our comments as to reloading procedures and techniques. This is because the 38-55 is not only the same type of rimmed, straight-walled case, but is even the same basic brass and has very nearly the same powder capacity. Too, both cartridges are used in precisely the same types and models of rifles. Fundamentally, only the caliber and bullet weights are different.

It should not be assumed from this, however, that there are no additional considerations. Merely increasing the bore diameter from 32 to 38 produces substantial changes in the expansion ratio and bullet-base area, thus inevitably affecting such things as powder burning characteristics, developed pressure, and the ratio of change-to-bullet weight. These factors influence both the choice of powder and charge weights and, in the 38-55 with its relatively high expansion ratio of 14 and low ratio of charge-to-bullet weight, medium and medium-fast burning powders in fairly small charges are indicated.

Thus, we find 3031, the old HiVel 2, and Hercules new Reloder 7 among the best propellants for full-power loads in this cartridge. Slower burning powders such as 4895 and Re 11 can be used, of course, but velocities will be lower in proportion to charge weight, and combustion will probably be incomplete. Going in the other direction, small amounts of fast burning powders, including 4198, 4227 and 2400 may be used with excellent accuracy in light target loads, but here it is imperative to guard against the possibility of getting in a double charge! If this happens with a powder such as 2400, the result will almost certainly be a blown-up rifle.

Note carefully the way in which the loads in our table have again been grouped in three different categories, and be guided accordingly. American factory loaded 38-55s develop only 1320 fps with 255-gr. jacketed soft point bullet, by way of comparison, while Dominion factory rounds are listed at 1600 fps, making these latter the most powerful commercially loaded 38-55s available. As will be seen, either of these are readily duplicated with handloads but again, as with the 32-40, the determining consideration must be the rifles strength and condition. If there is any doubt, play it safe, and *always* start below listed loads, working up gradually. Remember, the higher the velocity or the faster burning the powder is, the higher pressures will be.

Case capacity of the 38-55 averages about 37½ or 38 grains (water), and I consider 35 grains of 3031 or 33 Reloder 7 to be a maximum charge for *use in the best and strongest rifles only*. These loads are both powerful and accurate, driving the 255-gr. soft point bullet at better than 1850 fps for a muzzle energy of close to 2000 fp. Inside a hundred yards, the 38-55 with its heavier and larger diameter bullet is therefore a better game killing load than the 30-30 or 32 Special. Recoil, while heavier than that of a 32-40, is still quite mild—certainly not enough to induce flinching or other poor shooting habits.

The writer's favorite high power hunting load in a strong action 38-55 consists of 32 grains Reloder 7 with Remington 9½ primers and the Winchester 255-gr. soft point bullet. Accuracy with this load has been far better than with any other heavy combination; at almost 1800 fps we have an excellent woods hunting cartridge for deer and black bear. No hot loads with 4198 have been listed because pressures tend to mount rapidly and I found them inaccurate also.

Pertinent dimensions for the 38-55 cartridge consist of a case length of 2.128", which should be kept trimmed to a uniform measurement of about 2.118". Maximum over-all loaded cartridge length for repeating rifles is 2.44". Barrels in 38-55 caliber may vary, depending upon the maker, from .376" to .379" groove diameter, so it behooves reloaders to determine the actual diameter of ther rifle's bore before selecting a bullet.

Winchester factory soft points mike .376" and have given me splendid accuracy in several different 38-55s, but Lyman moulds can be obtained casting bullets of various dimensions from .377" to .382", so if your barrel has a groove diameter of more than .377", a better fit will be obtained with one of these. My own preference with cast bullets is for a .002" oversize slug that will positively fill out the rifling grooves and seal off the bore, preventing gas leakage past the bullet.

Cast bullet accuracy is especially good in this big bore with its slow 1-in-18" rifling twist, and I particularly recommend them for the fine old single-shot rifles whose soft steel barrels were never intended for jacketed bullets. With the right fit of bullet to bore, a good lubricant such as the new Alox-containing Javelina, and loads tailored to your individual rifle, I'm betting you'll be pleasantly surprised at the performance of a 38-55 or 32-40, either in the woods or on the range. •

TWO-FISTED HANDGUNNING

The pistol has always been a one-hand weapon — which doubtless explains why so few people can hit anything with one. Unless you're a top gunslinger, grab ahold with the other mitt, too, says Askins, and watch your scores zoom!

by Col. Charles Askins

THE COPS, who are pretty wise about such things, shoot their sixguns with two hands. Over at the University of Indiana, where the National Police Pistol Combat championships are banged out every year, the John Laws get a two-fisted grip on the 38 whenever the rules say they can. They shoot better that way.

Bill Jordan, whose book, *No Second Place Winner,* tells how to hit with the six-shooter when the chips are down, also advises the two-handed grip. Bill put in 30 years with the Texas Border Patrol, so you can be sure his advice about how to hit with the handgun is backed up by a plentitude of powder burning.

More lately, the Army has relented on a long-standing reg which insisted that all troopers when firing the high-bucking old 45 service gun had to use only one hand. Now our GI can double-grip it and to hell with stance. It may be the doughboys took a leaf from the Marines' book, for the USMC now shoots the big pistol two-handed. Their double-clutch is a recent change.

It stands to reason that the shooter—any shooter, whether the champ or the rawest dub—is going to shoot better, hit closer, score higher and step up his lethality with two hands. The pistol is a good deal like the rifle, and with the latter we shoot better because, among other things. it is held with both hands. It seems sort of stupid to me that someone hasn't pointed out long before this that all 10 fingers should be entwined around that sixgun stock.

Target match shooting, the kind the boys do in the competitive wars, is governed by an NRA rule which says the pistol has got to be supported by only the one hand. This rule is an archaic holdover from the days when the Code Duello was in flower. It specifically enjoined participants from gripping the pistol with both fists. The duellist took up the classic pose which saw his body edged to that of his adversary, thus presenting the smallest possible target. To have double-gripped the duelling weapon would have necessitated a full-face stance and given his opposition a lot more target to pink.

It might be well for the NRA fathers to give some thought to knocking this antiquated rule out of the book. It is apropos to point out that the National Rifle Association sanctions the National Police Matches, and here the gendarmes rap both fists around the stock in a number of the events.

Two-Handed Advantages

There are highly obvious advantages which accrue to the gunner who bangs 'em out two-handed. To begin with he faces his target squarely and brings the pistol onto the target directly before both eyes. If he is the kind of a shooter who aims with both eyes open he will like the two-fisted handgunning. It permits him to see gun and target just as freely and as easily with one eye as the other, and for this reason he is quicker and more sure of his aim.

A further advantage is that when the gun recoils it cannot buck so high. Since the up-flip is damped the marksman can get back on the mark faster for the follower shots. This can very well be a life-or-death matter with the law enforcement officer. With the casual shooter it is not nearly so critical, but he will instantly approve of a shooting style which allows him more time to aim and squeeze the trigger and which requires less time and effort to fight the recoiling handgun back down on the target again.

Apart from these major advantages there are some pretty obvious minor ones. Among these is the fact that the pistol can be held with a more steady aim in two hands than in one. Never is this more apparent than when shooting in the wind. Too, there is less fatigue in firing with two hands, and, as well, scores run higher and with less effort expended. Shoot all day, firing with one hand as we usually do, and you will wind up in the evening a very tired boy. Do the same stint two-handed and you will find your fatigue measurably less.

Sometimes I sit back and am a bit confounded that we did not swing over to two-fisted handgunning a long time ago. This reflection of mine will draw a lot of derisive snorts from the fraternity who hunt with the handgun. These gentry have always fired two-handed. An indication maybe that they are away ahead of the rest of us on the score of practicality.

I do not believe there is any argument but that we can all shoot better and hit closer with the handgun—any caliber, 22 to the magnums—using two hands rather than one. But just how much better?

Can the laddy-o who shoots an 8-inch group at 50 yards, one-handed, tighten that cluster to 4 inches if he double-fists the gun? Can the hotrock

Askins found he could get tight groups on the 7-yard silhouette target when firing with two hands, even though he banged out 6 shots in 3 to 4 seconds.

who knocks out a score of 95 out of 100 at rapid fire, sink 'em all and come up with a possible when he gets both hands on the gun butt? Can the police marksman who triggers off 6 rounds in 7 seconds at 7 yards on the Colt silhouette target—and puts 'em all in the "K" area—expect to two-fist the 357 and then put the group into the head portion of that target?

How Much Improvement?

If we grip the handgun with all 10 fingers, can we improve the group, or the score, or the hits by 50%? or 25%? Or is it only good for a 10% betterment? The fact is, no one seems to know just what the improvement may be. Everyone is in agreement that it is a surefire way to higher results, but no one seems to have pinned down just how much better. I determined in my own case to find out.

Each week for a lot of years I've shot the pistol two or three times. This has always been one-handed. Now when I swung around and squarely faced the mark, clamping my idle hand on the stock, I was thrilled at how steady the grip seemed. I have always been one of those gunners who pretty generously faced 'round toward the target, and to swing a little bit more was not difficult. The really satisfying part of the equation was the staunchness of the pose. I am a southpaw and so the left hand went first on the grip. I overlaid it with the right fist. The two together gave me a steadiness which I had never before attained, and I have been shooting with a monotonous regularity for the last 30 years.

I commenced to do a lot of dryfire practice, two-handed. I liked the experience right from the beginning. To shoot proficiently with the handgun it is essential that you not only stand almost perfectly still, but you must also be capable of holding the outstretched arm and hand practically motionless. Few people can do this, at least to the degree necessary to hit close, and do it round after round. Most handgunners shoot like the shotgun marksmen—they touch off the shot as the sights come winging by. The gun never really stops in the center of the mark long enough to achieve a decent trigger squeeze. The reason is, in great part, a continuous swaying movement in the body and a resulting lack of steadiness in the shooting arm and hand.

When dry firing with the two-fisted grip, I found that I was very much steadier. Not only did it seem to me that the gun rocked less but there also was a noticeable lack of body movement. It is the most natural thing in the world to squarely face whatever we are watching, with the feet widespread, and this was precisely the new stance with the pistol in both balled fists.

I could not do any rapid dry fire practice because I am a shooter of automatics, and when you get all 10 fingers wrapped around the stock there isn't any known method for yanking the hammer back in simulation of actual firing. Still, I was so elated with the feel of the gun, its steadiness and surety in the dry firing I'd done deliberately, I had no doubt the rapid fire would shape up all right. I was ready to move onto the range.

I proposed to fire 10 times over the Police Course, which is 10 shots at 25 yards slow fire, 10 shots timed fire and 10 shots rapid fire, on the Standard American target, first two-handed and then on the same day to go over the course with the one hand. I'd first shoot the 22, switch over to the 38 and wind up with the 45. This would amount to 900 shots with two hands and an equal number with one hand. It would cover our more common calibers and should tell me in exact percentages just how much better I could expect to be with the new two-fisted shooting.

After the strictly target shooting, I planned to do an extensive test on silhouette targets and here, too, I expected to spell out in percentages just how much advantage the one style had over the other.

Handguns Used

For this shooting I selected three good guns. The first was the High Standard Supermatic Trophy 22 with 7¼" barrel, 2¼-lb. trigger pull and standard factory stocks. For the stint with the medium bore I set aside S&W's 38 wadcutter automatic, the Model 52, with 3 lb. 2 oz. trigger and

In slow-fire, two-handed shooting, Askins found it easy to stay in the 10-ring of the 25-yard Standard American target with 45 ACP.

The double-grip helped hold the big 45 auto down during recoil, gave an average group of 5¼" for 6 shots at 7 yards, in only 3.8 seconds.

the as-issue stocks. The 45 was an Elliason-tuned job with Herrett's customized stocks. Federal cartridges were to be fired throughout.

The first 10 shots at 25 yards on the Standard American target, two-handed, resulted in a score of 100. It was easily done and I was elated of course but not at all surprised. If I'd shot any less score I'd have been disappointed—and surprised. The timed fire, 5 shots in 20 seconds in two strings, resulted in a score of 95. This was not so hot. The group had sunk into the 5 o'clock corner of the bullseye. I made a sight correction. It was a timely change for in the rapid fire, 5 shots in 10 seconds in two strings, I accounted for a very acceptable 99. The total score, 294. This is about all I can shoot and I was happy with the results. It looked to me like this two-fisted shooting really had something!

I immediately swung over and shot the course one-handed. The slow fire scored 97, the timed fire 96, and the rapid 97. Total, 290. Clearly the second hand on the stock was going to keep right on showing this difference. An improvement of 4 points may sound like very little, but when you intend to shoot over the Police Course 60 times, as I planned to do, a difference of 4 points each 30 shots would amount to a very considerable margin at the end of the stint.

Each day thereafter I fired once over the course using two hands and once over with the one hand. The totals totted up thusly:

	Slow	Timed	Rapid	Total
One Hand	97	96	97	290
Two Hands	100	95	99	294
One Hand	97	99	97	293
Two Hands	99	97	91	287
One Hand	94	98	98	290
Two Hands	98	100	100	298
One Hand	98	95	97	290
Two Hands	99	100	93	292
One Hand	98	97	96	291
Two Hands	97	98	98	293
One Hand	98	98	96	292
Two Hands	99	99	98	296
One Hand	99	97	97	293
Two Hands	98	100	97	295
One Hand	98	98	100	296
Two Hands	99	99	99	297
One Hand	99	96	100	295
Two Hands	98	96	100	294
One Hand	99	96	100	295
Two Hands	98	96	100	294
Ave. (one hand)	97.6	97.2	97.7	292.5
(two hands)	98.6	98.3	97.1	294.1

The difference here in favor of the two-handed hold was 1.6 points. This is only .5% and was a disappointment to me. I hadn't been so sanguine as to expect I was going to better my totals by anything like 10%, but I had, confidentially, thought I could prabably add not less than a 2% betterment. In my case this would have been considerable.

I immediately commenced with the S&W 38 wadcutter automatic and some finely selected Federal match. The routine was precisely the same as with the 22. I shot a slow fire string two-handed, and then the same string with one hand. This was repeated timed fire and then rapid. After 5 times over the course with each method, I stopped and took tally. I had an average of 291 with the one-hand and 291.2 with the two-fisted approach. I found I was shooting slightly better slow fire using both hands; the timed and rapid fire were running neck and neck. I had been quite certain in my estimate of the forthcoming shooting that as the recoil increased the two-handed clutch would show it was the better. However, in rapid fire with one hand I had an even 97 average; with two hands only 95.4.

I found, having by this time shot 450 carefully aimed shots with the two hands, that there were problems that did not show themselves in dry-fire practice. For instance, when you squarely face the mark and extend both hands before the body and those hands grasp a 40-oz. shooting iron, there is a tendency to tip over on your face. Or at least lean forward. This causes a swaying motion. In slow fire you can fight this but in rapid fire there isn't the time. Along with this back-and-forth sway there is a marked tendency of the knees to buckle ever so little in rapid fire. The gun kicks upward and the force has a more pronounced effect on the knees than on any other part of the body.

I learned, too, that it is just as easy to flinch with two hands as with one. Too, it seems that when you goose the trigger with both hands on the gun you can move it just a little bit farther out of the 10-ring!

I was disgusted with my firing of the 38. I'd had some theories about how it would perform and these had not proven out at all. I concluded that the 5 times over the course had given me usable averages both with the one hand and with the two, so I put the S&W aside and went to work with the 45. I shot it 10 times over the course with each grip. This was a full 600 shots and averages at the conclusion looked like this:

	Slow	Timed	Rapid	Total
One Hand	97.1	97.5	96.5	291.1
Two Hands	98.7	97.6	96	292.3

The only significant difference here was in the slow fire averages, where holding the pistol with both fists appeared to be a slight advantage. The timed fire and rapid fire showed no material differences. With the three guns the slow fire had usually been slightly ahead using both hands on the grip. At the same time the rapid fire was a mite the better with only one hand at the helm, a result which I had confidently expected would go quite the other way.

I now commenced to fire on the silhouette targets at 7 yards. In the police matches this is usually fired 6 rounds in 7 seconds. I shot considerably faster, using from 3 to 4 seconds for the string. I tried the 22 and then the 38 and finally finished with the 45. I shot the latter pistol 10 strings with the one-hand grip and 10 two-handed.

Here the advantages in favor of gripping the weapon with both paws became apparent. It was not evident in the 22 and barely perceptible with the 38, but with the 45 it was spelled out not only in a greater percentage of hits in the very center of the silhouette but also was fired in shorter time limits. Along with these obvious improvements were noticeably smaller shot groups. The sum total of the 120 45-cal. shots at 7 yards looked like this:

One Hand		Two Hands	
Time (Sec.)	Group (Ins.)	Time (Sec.)	Group (Ins.)
4.1	7.5	3.5	5.0
4.1	7.8	3.4	4.9
4.5	8.5	3.7	5.5
3.9	8.1	3.9	6.1
4.0	7.0	4.1	5.2
4.6	6.5	3.8	4.6
4.2	8.0	3.8	4.3
4.1	7.3	3.7	5.2
4.3	7.5	4.0	5.8
3.8	6.6	4.1	5.7
Ave. 4.16	7.48	Ave. 3.80	5.23

Here, then, I had, after a considerable amount of firing over an extended period, found what I was seeking. When the big-caliber pistol is fired really fast, as in defensive firing, it is a distinct advantage to double-grip it. Not only had it proven it was capable of tighter groups but the time limit was distinctly bettered.

It was obvious to me in an analysis of my shooting, however, that I was a poor guinea pig. Over the past 35 years or so I've probably shot away a million handgun cartridges—and almost all of them with the left hand. To have expected to noticeably improve my shooting by the double-fist grip was a bit too much. But what about some other handgunner? A fellow who was a good but not necessarily an expert marksman. How much would the two-handed approach help him?

I enlisted a couple of shooting cronies. M/Sgt. Ted Stafford, who made the landing with me in Africa in '42, one of the original 1st Rangers, a real hardcase character and a good pistol shot, was the first choice. With him he fetched along Bill Manual. Bill totes a sixgun all the time, using it on armadillos, jackrabbits and rattlesnakes. When I explained what I wanted, both of them snorted about holding a pistol in two hands.

"Sissy stuff," said Stafford, "but I'll do it just to humor you."

The Police Course was fired. Stafford went first and shot 231 with one hand. With two hands he got a 261. This really opened his eyes—and I was elated! "Maybe you've got something here," he grudgingly admitted.

Bill Manual then shot, getting 215 with one hand and 246 with two. The day following they again fired, Stafford turning in 227 with the one hand and 258 with the two-fisted grip. Manual came up to 237 with one hand and 259 with the two. The third and last day of the target work, Stafford had 240 and 268, Manual, 235 and 251, first with one hand and then with the two. Both were enthusiastic about the possibilities of the double grip by this time.

M/Sgt. Ted Stafford, one-time British Commando, upped his score from 231 to 261, using the two-handed grip for the Police Course.

Bill Manual, who likes to turn his handgun on jackrabbits, rattlesnakes and similar critters, cranked up his scoring by an average of 20 points when he fired two-fisted.

"I'm going to shoot a whitetail this fall with my 357 and this two-hand stuff," Manual enthused. "It ain't as good as a rifle, but it's sure a lot better than trying to make like Matt Dillon."

We then swung over to the Colt silhouette target and rapid fire. After 50 shots one-handed, Stafford had a group which showed 11 shots completely off the silhouette, 19 in the silhouette but outside the kill area. The remaining 20 were all K hits. Bill Manual had 24 K hits out of his 50 shots, one-handed.

Using two hands, Stafford, a short powerful man with strong hands and great muscular forearms, had all 50 hits in the K area. It was a spectacular show of good shooting. Time limits had run well under the 7 seconds prescribed for 6 shots. Bill Manual had 42 of his 50 shots in the K area and the remaining 8 had struck the silhouette but not within the vital zone. His, too, had been excellent shooting and indicated a marked improvement over his shooting with the one hand.

Here, then, was the place for the double grip. Though no great help to the hotshot, the average fair-to-good pistol marksman obviously can do markedly better if he will take a two-fisted grasp on the pistol or revolver. ●

IT'S NOT HOW LONG

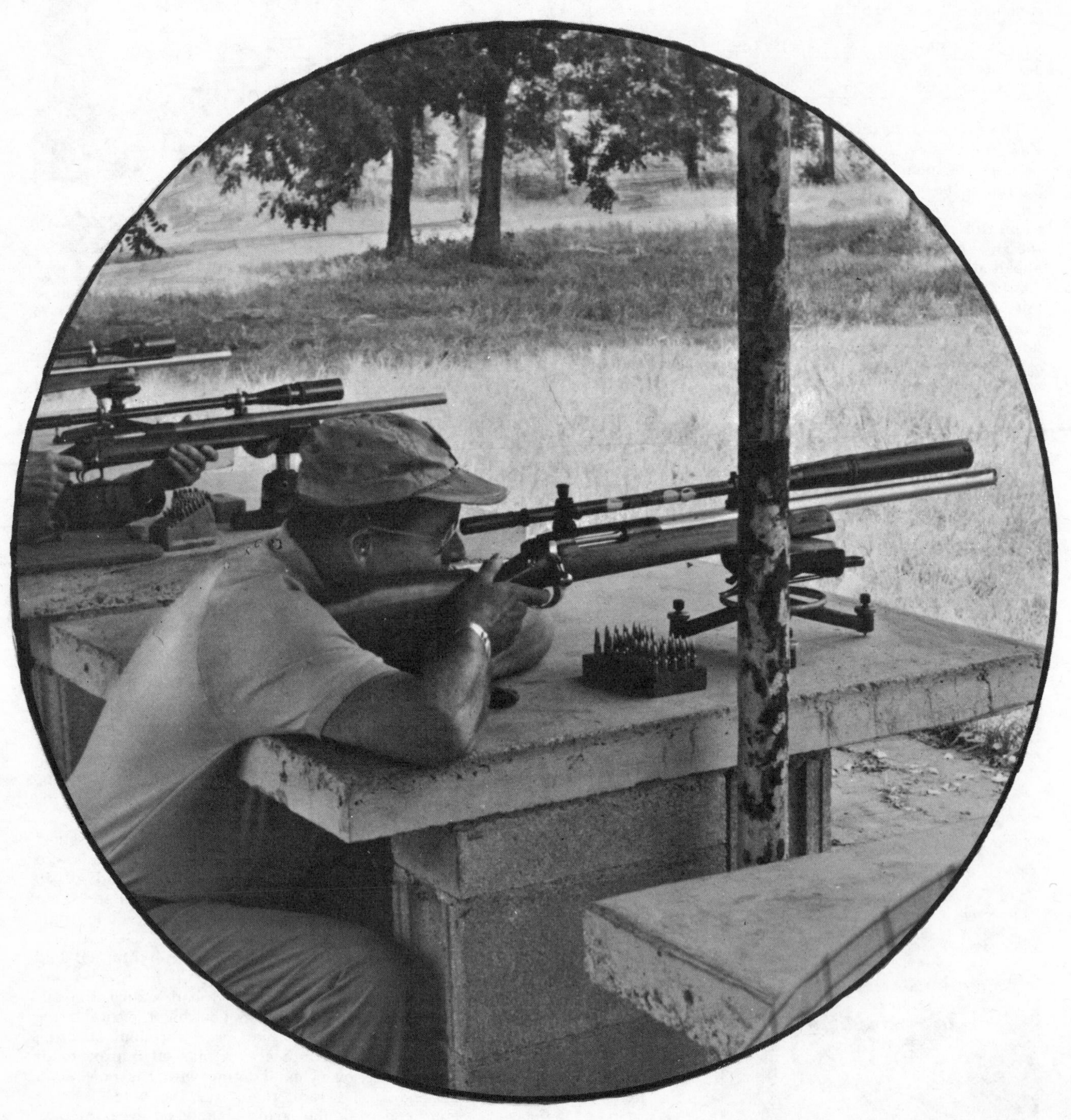

The author at the bench, his rifle one of the latest short-barrel types.

YOU MAKE IT

The current crop of bench rest rifle makers—and top shooters in that difficult game—want their barrels fatter and stiffer, and that means shorter if they're to meet NBRSA weight rules. Do they shoot? Here's Page.

by WARREN PAGE

THE FRONTIERSMAN'S long-tubed squirrel rifle swayed slowly, steadied, belched blue smoke and noise. Even the painted Wyandottes broke into a gobbling cheer at the result. Natty Bumppo's bullet had neatly split itself on the tomahawk blade. The long barrel had made a perfect shot.

Well, maybe a barrel half as long as a tall man was vital to accuracy, back in the days of Natty Bumppo and the scalping knife. But it certainly isn't today. In fact, on the evidence now at hand the most accurate rifle barrels are ultra-stiff and amazingly short. Length, within reasonable limits, has nothing to do with accuracy, however much it may enter into the velocity or energy equation.

This has to be so, since we have nowadays centerfire rifles achieving a level of accuracy only dreamed of two decades ago, and doing it with stubby tubes. At least that's the experience of NBRSA competitors, and there is today no development of rifle accuracy in which the National Bench Rest Shooter's Association is not directly concerned. Back around the time of the Sniper's Congress shoots in the Puget Sound area, and the first beginnings of the NBRSA by the varmint-accuracy bugs of Johnstown, New York, a bench shoot was held on the grounds of the Citizen's Rifle & Revolver Club of New Jersey. I recall that match. During it Bob Wallack, then a gunsmith and now a publicist, fired a phenomenal 5-shot group at 200 yards. It measured .714″ across. The millenium had arrived, thought some, and a great controversy arose as to whether or not this was indeed better than the legendary exploits of Rowland, famed experimenter of the black powder period.

Ridiculous. Today, a .714″ in any 200-yard match that isn't staged in a hurricane will, with 15¢, get you a cup of coffee. It takes much better than that to win. The all-gun record for 5 at 200 is .0630″—and that decimal point is in the right place. For a rifle dimensionally similar to the one Wallack used it's .1006″. That's like one-seventh the size of what they were excited about two decades ago. It's an only *slightly* lopsided hole!

The present levels of accuracy — and I'm talking about perfectly practical rifles, equipment you would not hesitate to take on a woodchucking expedition — are to the average deer hunter incredible. For example, at the National Varmint/Sporter Matches in Tulsa, Oklahoma, in 1968, on a range which admittedly baffles the best with its wind conditions, with the Heavy Varminter category of rifle (any centerfire weighing 13½ pounds or under with any scope power) to take an individual match required a group measuring about .174″. That's under 3/16ths of an inch, buddy. With the Light Varminter or Sporter classes (both of which heft 10½ or under including sight, the Light Varminter being any caliber, the Sporter 24-caliber or bigger) match-winning groups at 100 yards went anywhere between .169″ and .270″, averaging around .211-inch. Smaller than your pinky nail! Nor is this exceptional, limited only to the national matches. At almost any registered event, match winners in the Heavy Varmint category bulge single holes out of round by only about .20″, a fifth of an inch. It has to be seen to be believed.

Accuracy Today

Barrels, actions, bullets, and the ways of putting them all together, have improved so markedly that at this stage if a Heavy Varmint rifle won't, in still air, consistently average .25″, certainly no worse than .30″, you might just as well stay home with it—it can win only through sheer luck. If a Sporter or Light Varminter cannot, in your hands and under perfect conditions, average .30″ it is not likely to rate in the top guns. Not too long ago a half-minute Sporter wasn't too bad and one regularly good for .40″ to .45″ in dead air was a real dandy. I have one of those real dandies. It was for years good enough to keep me ticking as 3-rifle aggregate winner or runner-up, always in the race. It isn't good enough now, though it'll still average in the .40″ area somewhere. A replacement is being built, in accordance with the accuracy ideas we have developed during the lifetime of that "real dandy."

A handful of basic principles, elements common to all really and consistently accurate rifles, have become clear during the two decades since Wallack's group. First, the bullet must be perfect, absolutely even and dynamically balanced. Second, the bore must be a perfectly straight hole, smooth and dimensionally precise all the way. Third, the action, or whatever system is used to fasten the barreled action to the stock, must be stiff. There are a hundred other desirable points that have appeared, like fast lock time, stable stock bedding, powder charges right for the bullet and bore, matched and perfect cases, and so on, but most of these are details rather than principles and individual shooters have vastly different ideas about how to achieve them. You will note, however, that in the principles there is none that says the barrel must be long.

They were long at first. Heavy or unlimited class bench rest rifles used full length blanks — though nobody really knew why. Thus when the varmint and sporter categories came into competition they were also fitted with gracefully tapered tubes measuring about .75" at the 24"-26" muzzle for the 10½-pounders, and between .85" and .90" for the so-called Heavy Varminter. Barrels were often even 28 inches long.

New Stiff Barrels

Such equipment produced fine shooting. It was responsible for most of the crucial developments in what we today term an accuracy rifle, for savvy about case uniformity, bullet perfection, loading techniques, action stiffness, and so on. But these rifles had one great failing. They were goosy, inconsistent, prone to shooting hot one day and tomb-cold the next. Bedding shifts and sighting changes seemed to be root causes of the inconsistency. Hence came the *modern* accuracy rifle for the sporter and varminter categories.

Several custom action builders and action modifiers have sprung up in recent years — Hart, Gillman, Shilen, SS&D, actually moving into this limited field commercially — the idea always being to render an action ultra-stiff, its area of bedding into or onto the stock wood large and uncomplicated enough to make a close fit easy, its over-all length so increased as to permit mounting the optical sight, usually a target scope of Lyman, Unertl, or B&L branding, on the receiver alone. The first two reasons were logical extensions of the answers contrived for bedding problems by many gun builders. The third involved a new factor.

It has long been suspected, though it is extremely difficult to prove, that the target mount designs used today are not perfect. What had not apparently been realized for years is that when a very long telescope — the Lyman Supertargetspot is a full 24 inches, the bigger Unertls 2" longer— is mounted with one base on the receiver, the other out on the barrel, an act so simple as merely pulling the scope back into battery or firing position actually "loads" or puts slight strains into the barrel or into the scope tube. The end result is either an effect on optical alignment or a variation inserted into the patterns of barrel vibration as the bullet passes up the bore. Either or both will slightly alter the impact point of the bullet on the target.

When matches are won and lost in terms of a thousandth or two of an inch, even this theoretical factor is worth considering. As a matter of fact, this isn't so darned theoretical, as any half-baked mechanic with a dial micrometer and a scoped rifle can quickly discover. Tap a barrel even lightly and it may or may not vibrate back to its identical original position. Quite evidently, the longer and more willowy a barrel is, the greater its amplitude of vibration under firing stresses; the shorter and stiffer, the lesser the movement accorded the muzzle opening. Remember, the one basic secret of accuracy, with any form of rifle, is to get the bullet up the barrel and out the muzzle in the same period of time, so the muzzle is always in the same position at the instant of bullet exit. Evidently with the stiffened, and thus heavier actions, there was reason for a stiffened and so heavier barrel—and a better scope arrangement.

However, rifle weights under NBRSA rules are restricted — and there's no kidding about these rules, each rifle being weighed on a scale checked with NBRSA standard weights before each match series. Since the stock of a rifle can only be made about so light before it loses all stability, to accommodate weight increases in barrel and in action some heft had to be saved somewhere. To be stiffer, the barrel would also have to be shorter, and the optical sight would, if possible, have to be made lighter, preferably without sacrifice of optical quality.

New Design Stocks

Tom Gillman and Ed Shilen had been building short-coupled rifles for several years; other gunbuilders had been experimenting; no one experienced any accuracy problems with barrels that were much shorter than the old norms, some as short as 18 inches! At the 1968 Nationals the trend became evident. Of 63 Light Varminter competitors, 15 had barrels 23 inches or more long, but 18 used 21 inches or less. Similar percentages obtained in the other classes. Skirts had already gone up; now we had mini-barrels. Remington's gun designer, Mike Walker, unique among factory engineers (as I am among gun writers because we're both deeply involved in accuracy competitions), had long since started building rifles which, in the Light Varminter or Sporter types, featured a fore-end reshaped to be more angular and so steadier on sandbags; more important, on a barrel length of 20 inches or less, he achieved a muzzle diameter of .975", about all the fatness permitted under existing NBRSA rules. That's four inches less barrel than earlier 40XB rifles of this type had carried.

The Gillman and Shilen approach had also involved a very deep, chunky stock form, ugly but very functional for firing from rest, usually with a thumbhole shape. They, most particularly Shilen, put sleeves on actions of either the Remington 600 or 660 (even XP100 pistol) type, along with Remington's other M700 and M722 series. Shilen has three sleeve forms: one for Heavy Varminters which is a foot long and weighs 17 ounces; one of 13 ounces which employs a cantilever system for mounting the forward scope block up off the barrel; one of 11 ounces and a foot of length, which is square rather than round in cross section so that its bedding area is flat. All these are made of 2024 T3 aluminum, are epoxy-bonded onto the

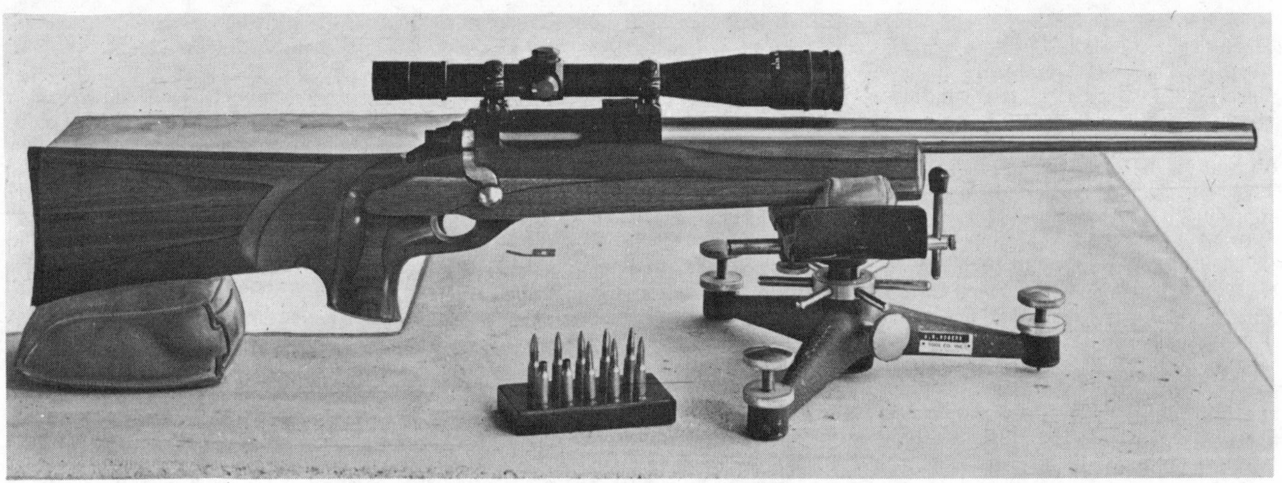
Here's one of the new short and stiff barreled bench rest rifles, mounted in a thumb-hole stock. Note action sleeve on this Ed Shilen rifle.

action after grinding to a glove fit. With the action thus beefed up and the stock actually on the stout side, the barrel has to be short! Now, with that shortness and consequent stiffness came accuracy improvement, as the competitive record of these two men and of others shooting their rifles quickly showed.

It must be admitted that Shilen had something more than the short-stiff concept going for him, since he has been turning out topnotch barrels from his shop at 4510 Harrington Road, Irving, Texas. Almost as many Shilens as Harts were on the line at the '68 Nationals.

Another Shilen rifle with short, stiff and heavy barrel, this on the Remington 600 action. The scope mounts on the receiver sleeve, not on the barrel.

If you'll go back a few paragraphs, you'll note that I made the point that A) with barrel weight kept up at maximum for stiffness; B) stock weight not to be sharply reduced and C) action — if not stable — then increased in weight by a sleeving technique, keeping the gross rifle weight down under NBRSA limits meant some tonnage had to be saved in the scope. The ideal weight of the sighting device — which all agree should be from 20X to 30X for this peculiar form of shooting — seemed to those of us engaged in these experiments to be around a pound, 16 ounces, *including* any mounts and bases. Now the Lyman glass weighs about 28 ounces, the Unertl a mite more, the new Redfield M3200 some 24 or 25 with bases, the Bausch & Lomb as much as 36. Cut one of these back to a pound? Even back to 20 ounces? Crazy, man.

Remington Target Scope

First attempts in this direction were with cobbled-up versions of existing hunting scopes. Walker hiked a Lyman 10X to about 16X by optical skulduggery; Shilen entered matches with a glass hotrodded to a full 20X but fuzzy as a San Francisco fog around the edges; I had Al Akin of the Bushnell establishment modify the objective of a 10X until it magnified 24 times, found it weighed as much as a target glass. There had to be some other than the hotrod approach.

By getting in some computer time and the advisory services of a skilled optical engineer, Walker worked up an answer, a scope just over 19 inches long, 19¾ ounces including Unertl-type mounts and bases, fully corrected at 20 or 24X to choice. To the surprise of many the Remington brass elected to put the design into production.

At expected mount spacing it will mount on a normal rifle receiver either with or without a sleeving extension and of course with no barrel contact. The overhang is short enough so that this rig will be amply rugged to work well on varmint rifles used in the field, the assembly being very evidently stouter than that of the usual run of target equipment. The glass must of course slide slightly forward on firing to protect your shooting eye, but any "loading" from its return to battery is on the receiver, with no effect, not on the barrel. Adjustments are clicked to the ¼-minute. The field of view is 6.8 feet for the 24X type, 7.5 feet at 100 yards for the 20X. The objective element focusses, of course, and the calibrations are correct, so that the glass will be in focus at the indicated yardage. This scope — and as this is typed only previews of prototypes, not actual usage for extended range periods, have been possible — bids fair to be the bench rest shooter's delight. It does, after all, give him about half a pound that he can put into barrel metal!

Remington's new 40X-BR rifle has short, stiff barrel, carries Remington's first target scope, also short for mounting on receiver alone.

One of the interesting sidelights of these barrel and sight trends is that while they produce a rifle that would render unhappy the classicist who dotes on Goens, burbles over Biesen, raves about Milliron, they still produce something that looks like a rifle. This is a tribute to the NBRSA rules, hammered out over years of competing with sea-lawyer types who fudged right to the limit of the law's letter, rules still not perfect but at least to some extent holding the line. Essentially they express the idea that an accuracy machine to be fired in Sporter or Varminter competition must have the general appearance of a rifle. The shorties may look a bit odd compared to a Griffin & Howe hunting rifle or even a Model 70 target job, but they are certainly recognizable as practical rifles and — more to the point — they shoot like crazy! ●

John Dickson (1794-1886), the founder of the company which bears his name.

A VISIT TO DICKSON'S

by Roger Barlow

You've never heard of this famed Edinburgh gunshop? You've never even heard of Edinburgh? Well, good old Charlie Gordon did — and here's your chance to come up to date on Scotland's greatest gunmakers

DON'T BE disconcerted that your reaction to the above title was, "Who or what in blazes is Dickson's?" You were not really expected to be familiar with the name. Had this piece been called a "Visit to Purdey's" or "Visit to Franchi" or "Visit to Sauer" you would have realized immediately that I had called upon one of the most famous gunmakers in England, Italy or Germany. Although mention of the name Dickson usually evokes but a blank look, when I *do* find someone familiar with it the response is generally overwhelming.

John Dickson & Son is the greatest name in Scotland's once-flourishing and famous gunmaking industry, and still considered one of the world's greatest gunmakers by those familiar with its products. Possibly the quickest and most convincing way to confirm the Dickson gun's high reputation is to point out that it is held in the highest regard by Holland & Holland, Westley Richards, Churchill, Purdey, et al. Many knowledgeable English shooters have, over the years, ordered guns from this Edinburgh maker, paying prices as high or higher than those of London's own famous "best" guns.

The Scottish firm of Dickson is not to be confused with that of Dixon, the English company specializing in various gun accessories.

My first encounter with a Dickson product took place in London only a year ago, when I was browsing through the secondhand weapons at Cogswell & Harrison. An old single shot 450 falling block rifle with a sidehammer took my fancy because of its unusually attractive lines and I bought it—for $27.50! Over the months, the more I handled this old rifle the more impressed I became with its excellent workmanship and remarkable balance and fit. Many large caliber rifles of the late 1800s were distinctly muzzle-heavy and generally clumsy. Continued acquaintance with this old Dickson rifle served to increase my respect for the makers and to whet my interest in learning more about them. I found out that the firm was still in business at 21 Frederick Street, Edinburgh, Scotland, and I had some correspondence with the managing director, Mr. A. Sinclair, who kindly delved into the firm's records to provide me with some of the history of my old 450 Dickson. "Your rifle," wrote Mr. Sinclair, "is described in our gun register as follows:

" '450 Single Express Breech-loading rifle, Henry's Patent.' Apart from stock measurements, weight, etc., the only other information given is that it was completed on August 16, 1873, to the order of Dr. P. A. Watson and intended for use with a powder load of 3½ drams of Curtiss and Harvey's #6 black powder."

Hmmm, a Dr. Watson . . . I wonder if a friend named Holmes ever used this rifle?

The Round Action

Some months later, in London again on my way back from St. Étienne, I went to Edinburgh to meet Mr. Sinclair, see the Dickson establishment and to examine at first hand some of the double barreled Dickson shotguns with the famous "round" action.

This unusual action is highly regarded by all connoisseurs of the break-action double. In *The Modern Shotgun,* Major Sir Gerald Burrard writes, "I have dealt with this Dickson action at considerable length because it is so unique and has such

John Dickson & Son, Edinburgh, Scotland

undoubted merits that I think it deserves description in detail. The workmanship is faultless . . . its great merit, however, lies in the strength of the bar; and on this account it is peculiarly well-adapted for the building of very light guns."

By which he meant a 12 gauge shooting the 2½" shell and weighing 6 lbs. (or even a couple of ounces less), fitted with automatic ejectors and carrying 28" barrels.

This is known as the round action because of a general absence of sharp corners or lines and because of the very clearly rounded shape of the under part of the bar of the action body. However, the real difference between this design and others is *internal* rather than external and therefore not readily understandable from a casual examination. In fact, without prior knowledge, even an experienced gun enthusiast might take this gun to have a conventional Anson & Deeley boxlock action, from a glance at its lines.

Far from it! Actually this Dickson is nearer to being a back action sidelock—except that the two locks are not fitted to the outside of the stock but rather in the *center,* directly above the trigger plate. In fact, each Dickson lock is built up on one side of a vertical plate integral with the trigger plate. Basically the Dickson locks are similar to normal sidelocks, but not identical. Ordinary bar action and back action sidelocks use V springs, while each Dickson lock uses what is, in effect, a single arm of a V spring, the base or foot of which is held in an anchorage on the rear of the trigger plate.

The forward end of this mainspring bears upon the tumbler (hammer) and provides the pressure for its blow upon the firing pin. Here is found another Dickson innovation—the forward end of each mainspring is fitted with a roller which itself fits into a

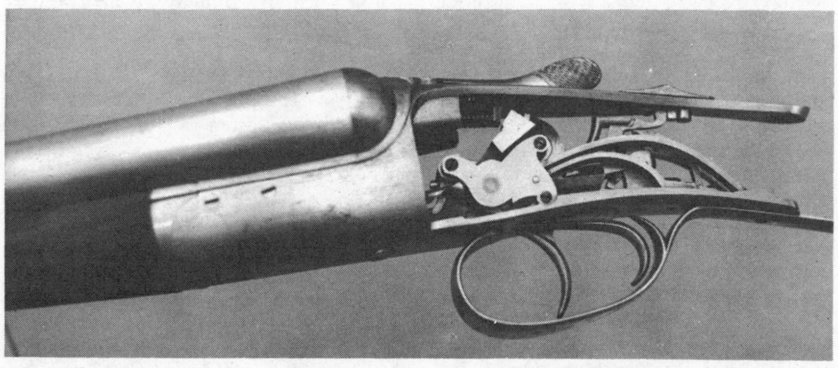

The Dickson round action—so-called because of the shape of the under part of the bar of the action—is a very strong one. Most internal parts are built up on the trigger plate, with locks gold-plated to prevent rusting. The large flat spring actuates the hammer, while the smaller one is the sear spring.

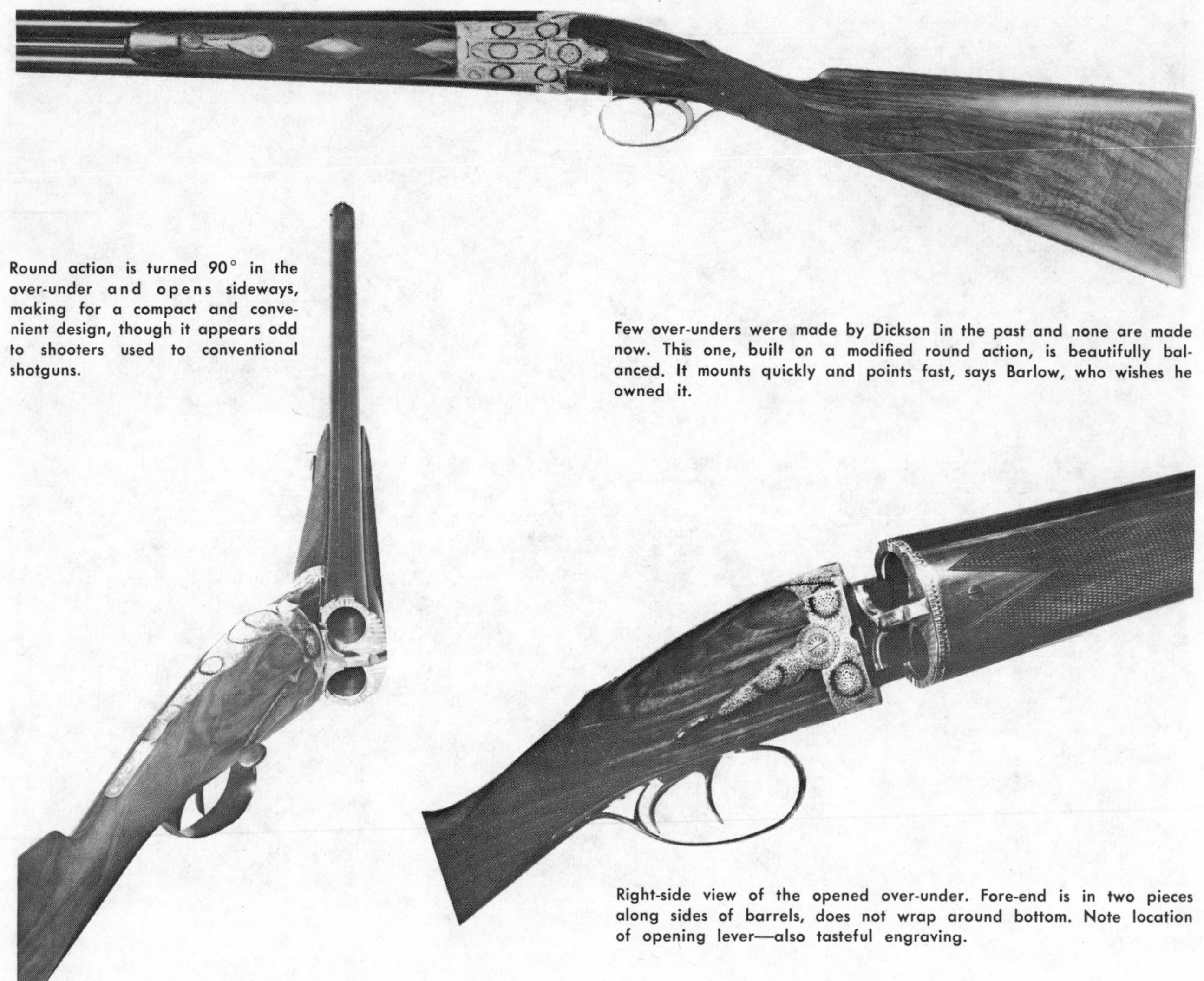

Round action is turned 90° in the over-under and opens sideways, making for a compact and convenient design, though it appears odd to shooters used to conventional shotguns.

Few over-unders were made by Dickson in the past and none are made now. This one, built on a modified round action, is beautifully balanced. It mounts quickly and points fast, says Barlow, who wishes he owned it.

Right-side view of the opened over-under. Fore-end is in two pieces along sides of barrels, does not wrap around bottom. Note location of opening lever—also tasteful engraving.

carefully engineered cam-like contour cut into the rear profile of the tumbler, in precise relationship to its pivot point. This enables the spring to exert the same amount of pressure at the *end* of the hammer's fall as at the beginning. (All pump and autoloading guns, as well as some present day doubles, utilize coil springs which, of course, exert maximum pressure at the start of the fall of the tumbler or hammer, and increasingly less power as they extend themselves. The older and seemingly more crude flat or V spring has—by many gunmakers—been mounted in relationship to the tumbler in such a manner as to maintain or even to increase its pressure as the hammer falls. The Dickson is merely one of the better and more efficient ways to achieve this highly desirable mechanical relationship.)

In the Dickson round action gun the mechanical efficiency is so high that the striker hits the primer with the required force while retaining the pleasing characteristic of an easy-opening and light-cocking gun.

Design Advantages

The action's unusual design also permits the trigger mechanism to be especially well situated in relation to the sear, thus achieving an exceptionally smooth and precisely regulated pull.

The complete lock mechanism is mounted *behind* the action body, which therefore has the minimum of cuts, slots and holes. As most of these which are necessary are circular, they have the least possible weakening effect. The round action thus combines high strength with light weight, something normally difficult to accomplish.

One other unusual feature of this Dickson is that the automatic ejector mechanism is contained in the action body rather than in the fore-end, thus improving balance by helping to concentrate even more of the weight between the shooter's hands.

This action was patented in 1880 and it is quite possible that no better or stronger action will ever be designed for the break-action double gun. Both Dickson's and the now defunct Edinburgh gunmakers, James MacNaughton & Sons, claimed to have developed this action. Some authorities credit MacNaughton but the courts found in favor of John Dickson. In truth this action quite probably came into being at both establishments, as there was a constant interchange between the two firms of workmen who most certainly carried ideas and techniques with them as they switched employers. In any case, this is now rather academic for the MacNaughton firm was ultimately absorbed by Dickson's.

The present day firm of John Dickson & Son no longer turns out the volume of guns it once did but I watched their few craftsmen carefully building up these fine actions just as they have been made for over three quarters of a century. Mr. Sinclair informed me that the present reduced output is not due to any lack of demand for these high quality guns but simply because as the old gunmakers have died off it has been impossible to replace them. Post-war apprentices learned enough in a couple of years to enable them to take less exacting jobs in the English automotive and aircraft industries at higher wages and with various fringe benefits. This problem has, of course, also affected the London and Birmingham gunmakers, and is a most serious matter for the entire trade. Dickson's are now selecting their new apprentices with great care—trying to avoid city types looking

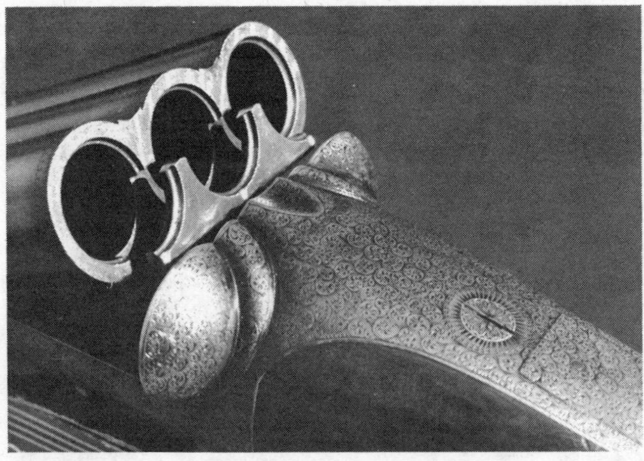

Side-by-side-by-side has conventional extractors and is built on the famed round action, with locks mounted on the trigger plate much the same as on normal Dickson double guns.

Front and middle triggers of a 3-barreled Dickson are hinged to give room even to gloved trigger finger. Opening side lever actually works from below the bar of the action. Note cocking indicators on tang.

Author shooting his 3-barreled Dickson, one of only 11 built. This gun was completed on June 9, 1882, the second of a pair for A. G. Murray, Esq. Weighing just under 7 lbs., it has excellent balance, is a delight to shoot.

for the most money for the least work and hoping to find country-bred boys with a deep-rooted and sincere love for guns. There is hope of again building up a labor force of sufficient size to substantially increase the production of new guns while still continuing the considerable amount of gun repair and rebuilding which is an important part of the firm's activity.

Five years is the official training period nowadays for a gunmaker, but it is only the exceptional young man who is regarded by Dickson's as being a real gunmaker at the end of that time. Mr. Sinclair states that only an extremely talented workman would, after five years' training, be good enough to work on the completion of new Dickson guns.

John Dickson established the firm bearing his name in 1820. It continued as a family business until 1925 when, upon the death of the third John Dickson, it became a corporation. Just before WWII the company amalgamated with Mortimer & Son, a famous old London gunmaking firm which had been founded circa 1735, receiving the Royal Warrant and being appointed Gunmakers to the King in 1822; later moving the business to Edinburgh. The history of Mortimer & Son informs us that it supplied a set of dueling pistols to the poet Byron and other weapons to Admiral Nelson.

The round action O-U shown in the accompanying photos is actually the first one of this type produced by Dickson's 60 to 70 years ago, and is not for sale. Only about 50 of these guns were made, and it is not contemplated that any more will be produced unless the work force of competent men can be increased.

Today Dickson's build only shotguns, whereas, at the turn of the century, they built pistols, rifles and smoothbores of all types and in large numbers. At that time they built a remarkably well-balanced 3-barreled side-by-side hammerless shotgun—this sounds better than an autoloader!

An Eccentric Collector

Mr. Sinclair told me of one of their

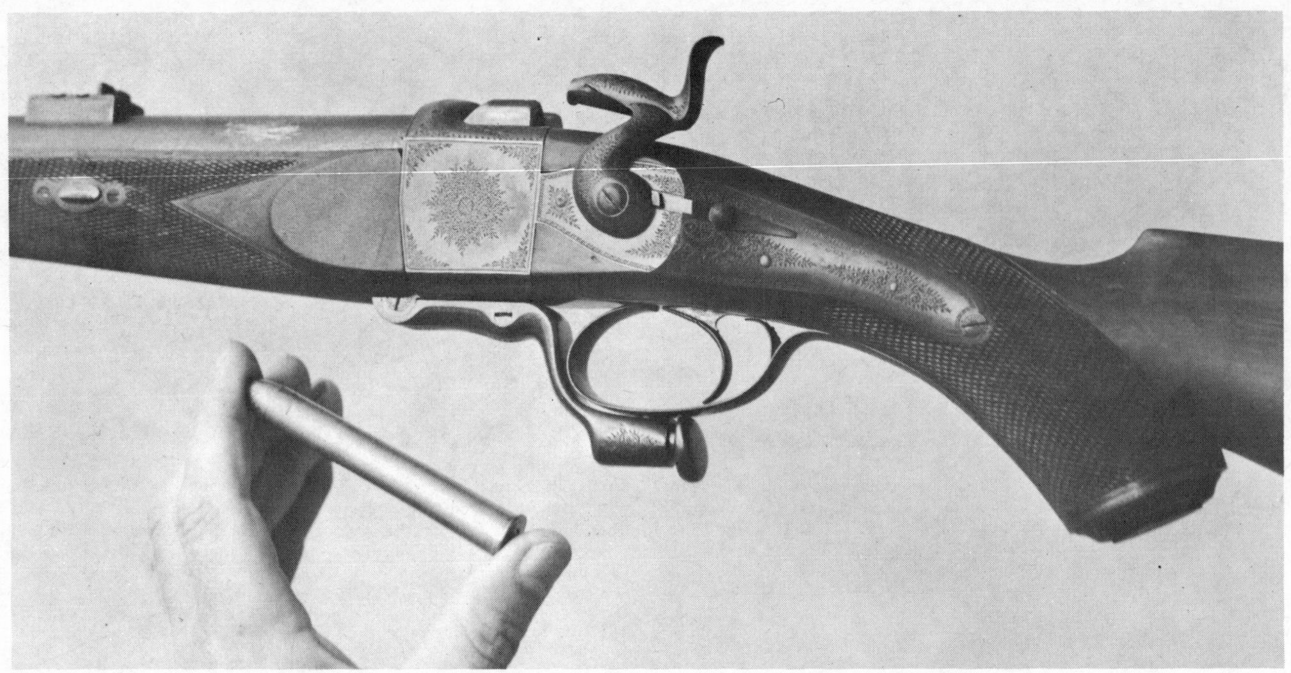

First Dickson encountered by author was this falling block 450-cal. black powder express, built in 1873 on Henry's patent action. Note that sidehammer, which can be locked at half-cock, is on left side. Most Henrys were made thus, though a few had hammers on the right side and a very few were hammerless.

customers of that period who had literally hundreds of weapons built specially to his order by Dickson's. This gentleman of means not only purchased *all* their standard models but would also order obsolete types to be made. Apparently he didn't like to collect old old guns but preferred to acquire *new* old guns! Dickson's made flintlock and percussion guns for Mr. Charles Gordon 25 years or more after cartridges were standardized. They made their last muzzle loader for him in 1903 and in 1904 completed a *pinfire* pistol for him.

Mr. Sinclair related that this Mr. Gordon was in the habit of paying unexpected visits to the workshops of John Dickson & Son and as soon as he arrived on the premises the word was quickly passed along from workman to workman, "Charlie Gordon's here," or "Pssst, Charlie Gordon," and they would put aside whatever they were working on at the moment, replacing it with something from under their work benches with a C.G. tag. As the genial old eccentric made his way slowly through the shop and peered over the shoulder of a stocker, commenting upon the grain of the walnut, the workman would reply, "One of yours, Mr. Gordon, finest piece of wood in Scotland," or an engraver working on a flintlock (the likes of which hadn't been made in Scotland for 50 years) would answer a query, "It's yours, Mr. Gordon, not many people appreciate fine guns like this anymore."

Two such Dicksons, one a muzzleloading single shot percussion rifle of 54 caliber, the other the same type but in 45 caliber and built more on the order of a light shotgun, are in the collection of the GUN DIGEST editor.

Mr. W. Keith Neal, English arms authority and writer, considers both of these caplock Dicksons to be among those ordered by Mr. Gordon.

Gordon died in 1904, undoubtedly convinced that he had personally kept the entire Guild of Scottish Gunmakers prosperous and happy—which, in truth, he pretty nearly had!

But Charlie Gordon's love for fine guns was to benefit gun fanciers all over the world for, upon his death, his family disposed of this vast collection (most of which had only been fired by the makers) piecemeal and Mr. Sinclair says that he can to this day tell that some of Charlie Gordon's guns have come into new hands when he receives a letter which starts out . . . "I have recently acquired a cased pair of Dickson guns in immaculate condition . . . ."

May God rest the bones of Charlie Gordon; there was a man after my own heart—but with money.

Few Over-Under Dicksons

After I had photographed a display model of the Dickson round action and visited the workshop, Mr. Sinclair showed me a number of fine Dickson guns. The round action most certainly does result in a beautifully balanced gun—fast mounting, quick pointing and with a "right" feel about it. Their grip is of the diamond-oval shape which is graceful to look at and firm to the hand. Lastly Mr. Sinclair brought out one of the very few Dickson over-under doubles ever built and no longer part of their program. This has a modified round action turned 90 degrees so the gun opens sideways, similar to the Belgian "Britt" action. This results in the most compact and convenient of all over-under designs. This Dickson O-U was almost like new but was being put through the shop prior to being offered for sale—and if the GUN DIGEST were to pay me £400 for this article the check would quickly be endorsed over to John Dickson & Son for this last of their O-U guns presently on the market! This happy situation being unlikely to come about, I pass this information on for the benefit of whoever can take advantage of it, for there is a gun worthy of joining any collection.

Should you want to order a new side-by-side Dickson round action 12, 16 or 20 bore the price is £800 ($2300) and time of delivery to 2 years—but if Charlie Gordon could wait so can you! Dickson's also make a "best" London-type sidelock gun for the same price and an excellent Anson & Deeley (boxlock) action gun for £200. They also make and sell fine fishing tackle plus carrying an extensive line of outdoor clothing and camping gear.

As Edinburgh is now more popular than ever with tourists, due in part to their annual Festival of the Arts, don't object if your wife suggests going there—you'll enjoy your visit to Scotland and in addition you can drop in at Dickson's, perhaps find an interesting gun you need or visit their extensive "shooting grounds," taking lessons in how to shoot grouse as the Scots do. ●

NEW HANDGUNS U.S. and FOREIGN 1969 — 1970

Earlier in the year we'd have guessed there'd be little handgun news for this edition, but then we got action—single and double! There's the new Colt Golden Spike and Mark III Trooper, the Beretta M-76, the Mauser Parabellum, the Dan Wesson 357 and the Sterling 22s — *plus the first Testfire Report on Ruger's new Double Action 357 Magnum.*

by Dean Grennell and the editors

LAST YEAR, in this same place, it was reported that earth-shaking developments in the handgun line a year ago were scarce and far apart. Much the same observation would be valid if made today.

A bit of reflection shows why this is not too surprising. The handgun field is ultra-conservative: an observation as obvious and indisputable as it is difficult to explain. Many, in fact most of the popular items in the lines of the major manufacturers have been made with no more than a few minor changes for half a century or longer. You could say that this is due to the high cost of tooling up for a radical departure in design but the comparable cost is much greater for certain other products, such as automobiles, where the situation is so fluid that some makers have trouble in waiting a year to bring out a dazzling new model.

As you page back through earlier issues of GUN DIGEST, it becomes apparent that radical departures rarely prosper in the handgun field. Guns such as the Dardick and the Gyro-Jet appeared upon the scene with much fanfare but quietly passed into oblivion within a year or two. It's obvious that sheer novelty is not the magic key. If you were asked to select the factors that get a new gun off the ground and selling well, a logical first choice would be buyer-appeal. A new gun, to excel its competition, can shoot harder, straighter, faster or oftener with a single loading. It can be cheaper, prettier or more versatile. It can offer superior reliability or durability. But if its prospective owners look it over and go on to buy something else, the new handgun is destined for the limbo that has swallowed countless entries of greater or lesser promise. If the handgun field is ultra-conservative, it is because most handgun buyers have that basic outlook and attitude.

All of which is by way of leading up to the observation that it may be several years yet before your friendly neighborhood gunshop offers any attractive bargains in good, second-hand laser pistols.

Other handgun *aficionados* in the audience will recall the peculiar situation of the single action revolver in the early 1950s. Colt had dropped this grizzled veteran from their line while reorganizing after WW II but, perhaps motivated by the burgeoning popularity of shoot-em-up westerns on TV, suddenly everyone seemed to want one of the old "hawg-laigs," and price was hardly any object. Battered relics of the previous century were changing hands for three-digit figures, with little regard to shooting condition. As usually happens, demand brought about supply. Bill Ruger built a thriving factory in Southport, Connecticut, on the appetite of the buying public for single action six-shooters and, perhaps a bit sheepishly, Colt restored the Frontier Model to the line, followed by their New Frontier.

For a report on the new Ruger double action revolver, see John Amber's article in this section.

A comparable set of conditions seems to have been building up with regard to the Pistole '08, or Parabellum, the brain-child of Georg Luger, Hugo Borchardt, et al. Perhaps spawned by the public's infatuation with spies and secret agents which boomed during the early 1960s, the slim-barreled Teutonic autoloaders have revelled in a bullish market. At the time of the single action craze, I recall buying an excellent DWM Luger with the 4-inch barrel for a fast 25 bucks—including a spare magazine and military holster. Its performance on targets was quite unimpressive in my hands so I cheerfully lined up a customer and felt gratified to unload it upon him for the full purchase price. Had I given it stable-space through the years, a modest amount of marketing effort might well return three to four times the original purchase price. But I didn't foresee the James Bond influence.

Browning

The Nomad and Challenger 22 caliber auto pistols have a new front sight. Blade shape is about the same, but it is now pinned to a nicely styled ramp which gives the pistol a streamlined appearance. Price is up $3 since last year, being $67.50 for the Nomad and $82.50 for the Challenger. This is not because of the new sight—all handguns are up in cost.

Conditions created by the new import laws have caused Browning to drop their 25 and 380 pistols, but the 9mm Parabellum and Medalist are still available. New prices on these are $108.50 and $134.50 respectively.

Having long since reconciled themselves to the re-adoption of their single-action, Colt has gone on to offer it in a profuse assortment of commemorative versions, absorbing the profits from such sales with a brave smile. The most recent of such souvenir editions is the "Golden Spike," a 6-inch barreled "Scout" model in caliber 22 Long Rifle to celebrate the centennial of the meeting of the Central Pacific and Union Pacific railroad lines at Promontory Point, Utah, on May 10, 1869. The metal of the Golden Spike is blued and gold-plated, with the walnut grips being sand-blasted to bring out the grain, producing an unusual weathered appearance. The presentation case, of simulated mahogany, is lined with plush green velvet. In the lid is a reproduction of an old tintype depicting the historic completion of the nation's first transcontinental railroad. Included in the case with the gold and blue gun is a gold-plated replica, full size, of the final spike which, like the right side of the gun's barrel, is inscribed with the legend, "1869 — Golden Spike — 1969."

As with all commemorative Colts, the Golden Spike has been issued in a limited edition and is available through registered Colt's dealers.

In a somewhat more modern vein, Colt announces the fourth and final edition of the 45 auto commemorating outstanding U.S. victories of the first World War. The first three were the Chateau-Thierry, Belleau Wood and the second Battle of the Marne. The last of the series observes the Meuse-Argonne offensive, which took place between September 26th and November 7th, 1918, effectively assuring victory for the Allied forces. The limited edition of the Meuse-Argonne Colt auto consists of 7,500 units, 25 custom-engraved at $1,000 a copy, 75 deluxe engraved at $500 and the remainder at $220, with standard engraving and the khaki-lined, glass-fronted display case.

Getting on down to the world at hand, it is reassuring to observe that the folks at Hartford are not neglecting the concept of handguns designed to be fired with live ammunition. Their newly announced "Trooper Mk III," caliber 357 magnum, appears to have been conceived by the realization that those people over in Massachusetts had been selling a lot of hardware to police departments without the benefit of hardly any gold plating. As with Colt's Python and Diamondback models, the ejector rod is protected by a solid metal shroud or housing, integral with the lower surface of the barrel. However, unlike the reptilian models, the Mk III's housing comes to a graceful end a short distance ahead of the rod rather than continuing to the end of the barrel. There are, somewhere, peace officers who still cover many miles

New Colts

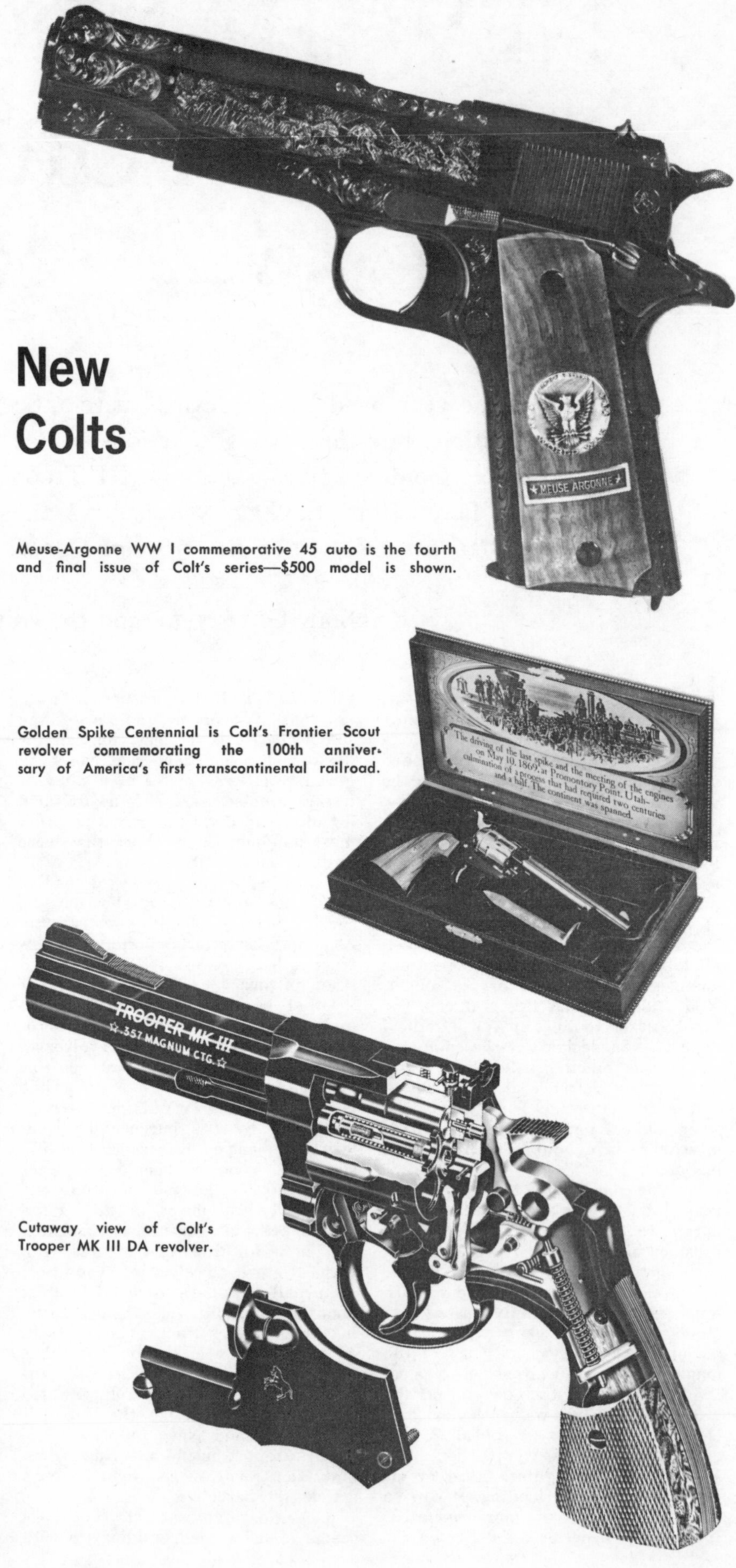

Meuse-Argonne WW I commemorative 45 auto is the fourth and final issue of Colt's series—$500 model is shown.

Golden Spike Centennial is Colt's Frontier Scout revolver commemorating the 100th anniversary of America's first transcontinental railroad.

Cutaway view of Colt's Trooper MK III DA revolver.

Colt's Diamondback revolvers in 22 caliber are now made with 2½- and 4-inch barrels and a choice of standard or target grips.

each day on foot, men who appreciate the weight saving of an ounce, or even a fraction thereof. Weight of the empty Mk III, with 4-inch barrel, is 40 ounces on the nose; an excellent compromise heft for the lusty 357 cartridge. The 6-inch version weighs in at two extra ounces.

Scanning the vital statistics for the Mk III (including such optional features as target hammers and stocks —improved, adjustable Accro rear sights are standard), the seasoned student of handgun lore encounters a really startling bit of data; the rifling pitch is one turn in 16 inches—quite normal for the caliber—but, *right hand twist?*

It's dim in the memory, but I think left-hand twist is said to have had something to do with the torque of bullets going up the barrel acting to tighten the threads rather than loosening them in the frame. At any rate, it's been traditional for Colt handguns to have left-hand rifling. As you view the fired bullet, with the nose away from you, the marks left by the lands start at the base and spiral to your left. Nearly all other handguns, and, for that matter, rifles, use right-hand rifling. Offhand, I don't know of anyone but Colt using left-hand rifling. I say "nearly" only as a hedge against the inevitable erudite reader poised to point out (crushingly) that they made three Rast-Gassers in 1911 with left-hand rifling when the polarity of the house current was reversed accidentally. For years, it has been a devastating ploy of the fairly well-versed ballistics expert to pick up a fired bullet and remark, "Hmm. Fired from a Colt." Or, "Obviously, not fired from a Colt," after a glance to see which way the rifling marks veered. But, alas, no more can this be pulled upon the open-mouthed layman. To me, this is the most startling piece of news in the world of handguns for this and several other years. Upon learning about it, I was surprised that the great metropolitan dailies didn't scarehead the news across their front pages in red ink: "COLT GOES NORTHPAW!" Ah well . . . .

In the meantime, levity aside, the Mk III looks like an excellent piece of ordnance when viewed from any angle. Its double-action trigger pull is a source of deep-dish delight and, with the growing realization that handguns that work for a living are apt to be fired that way in a clutch, that's worth a solid touchdown plus point-after in any evaluator's scorebook. Also to the good is the fact that Colt's hasn't been so carried away as to give up their clockwise cylinder rotation. What this means, in essence, is that the thing can be set up so that the notch that locks the cylinder can be offset slightly to bring it to one side of the thinnest spot in the chamber wall. Counter-clockwise cylinder rotation, for some odd reason, positions the little semi-circular notch right above the thin place, creating a weak spot. So long as the timing of hand and pawl is faultless, clockwise rotation is much to be preferred, though a small discrepancy can set off the primer with the chamber slightly out of alignment with the barrel; that state of affairs can knock out a hunk of cylinder wall. You pays your money and you takes your choice.

If the sample seen and handled is representative of production guns, the Mk III looks like a most promising entry in the sweepstakes for working handguns. It is an encouraging sign for those who believe that handguns are for shooting as much, if not more, than for admiring.

Architectural rendering of Colt's Rocky Hill plant.

The New Ruger Double Action Revolver—

A Rapid Fire Test Report

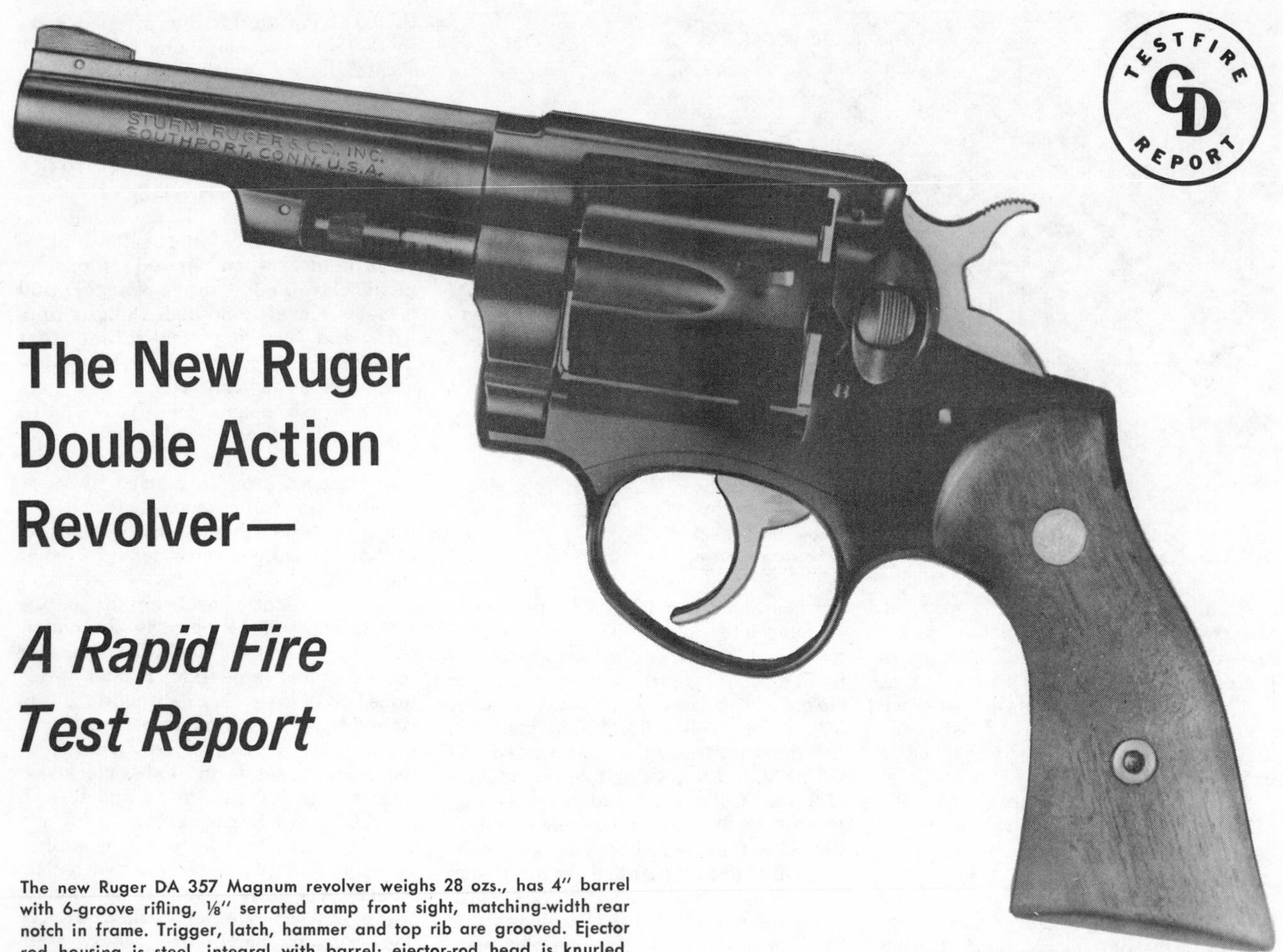

The new Ruger DA 357 Magnum revolver weighs 28 ozs., has 4" barrel with 6-groove rifling, 1/8" serrated ramp front sight, matching-width rear notch in frame. Trigger, latch, hammer and top rib are grooved. Ejector rod housing is steel, integral with barrel; ejector-rod head is knurled.

Bill Ruger introduced his long-rumored, much-anticipated double action revolver at the NRA meeting in Washington early in April of this year.

Made only in 357 Magnum so far—a caliber that could easily account for the great bulk of Ruger sales, even if he never offered it in any others—the new double action is a handsome gun indeed. Externally it doesn't depart materially from conventional styling—the cylinder holds 6 cartridges, swings out to the left, and the latch release button is just behind the recoil shield on the left side. This release, however, does not slide fore-and-aft, as has long been the custom, but is depressed at its rear edge by the thumb. It's a neat design, unobtrusive, and it won't dig into the thumb of the shooter who holds that member up alongside the receiver.

The inside of the new Ruger—the interior mechanism—is vastly different from any modern revolver. An examination of the frame design gives the first clue to an observant viewer that he's looking at a truly new handgun.

There is no sideplate! The frame shows a solid wall of metal on both sides, thus making the new Ruger an extremely rugged handgun. Without a sideplate there's no temptation here to lure the curious—and often inept and incautious user to explore the works; there are no sideplate screws either to shoot loose, to become lost.

All internal parts enter the Ruger receiver through the top of the bottom. Harry Sefried — a member of the design team responsible for this latest handgun from Southport — demonstrated at Washington the rapidity and ease with which the trigger unit the lockwork-guard assembly, etc., could be removed and replaced. Harry had *all* of the component parts spread across the table in about 30 seconds, including elements the ordinary owner would rarely—if ever—have to remove. Re-assembly, be it noted, was equally fast.

At no time did Sefried use a screwdriver, either! The checkered walnut grips may be removed with a coin, the one grip screw being so-designed. Once the grips are off the frame, the entire gun may be dismantled by the manipulation of a pin or two and the ready disjointing of various members.

The sample Ruger double action revolvers we handled were finished in a rich-looking blue; both had 4-inch barrels and, as noted, walnut grips nicely checkered.

The grip frame profile is the only area we'd criticize on the new Ruger, and that from a sales standpoint essentially. The backstrap flares out a bit rearward—where it meets the bottom flat of the grip frame—thus any grips fitted will carry this semi-single action style unavoidably. There are those potential buyers who will want, I'm sure, the more rounded grip form, the kind of handle that's more easily pocketable. This is particularly true of those people—law enforcement members generally—who want their revolvers to be as compact as possible. Perhaps Ruger will offer such a frame when the 2-inch barreled guns are made available.

So far we've not had a chance to assess and evaluate the new Ruger D.A., but if we can persuade Bill Ruger to send one here for a brief stay with us, we'll add a report below.

Our chance to look over the new Ruger 357 D.A. revolver came; Ed Nolan shipped No. X2, a toolroom prototype to us for a quick examination and trial—very quick, for we had the gun only 3 days.

Shooting was the first order of the day, done from rest and offhand, and both one- and two-handed. Some 200 rounds were put through our 4-inch barreled X2 with no malfunction of any kind.

Ed Dams and I set up a bench outdoors at the Farm, our target frame initially 20 yards away, then later at 50 yards.

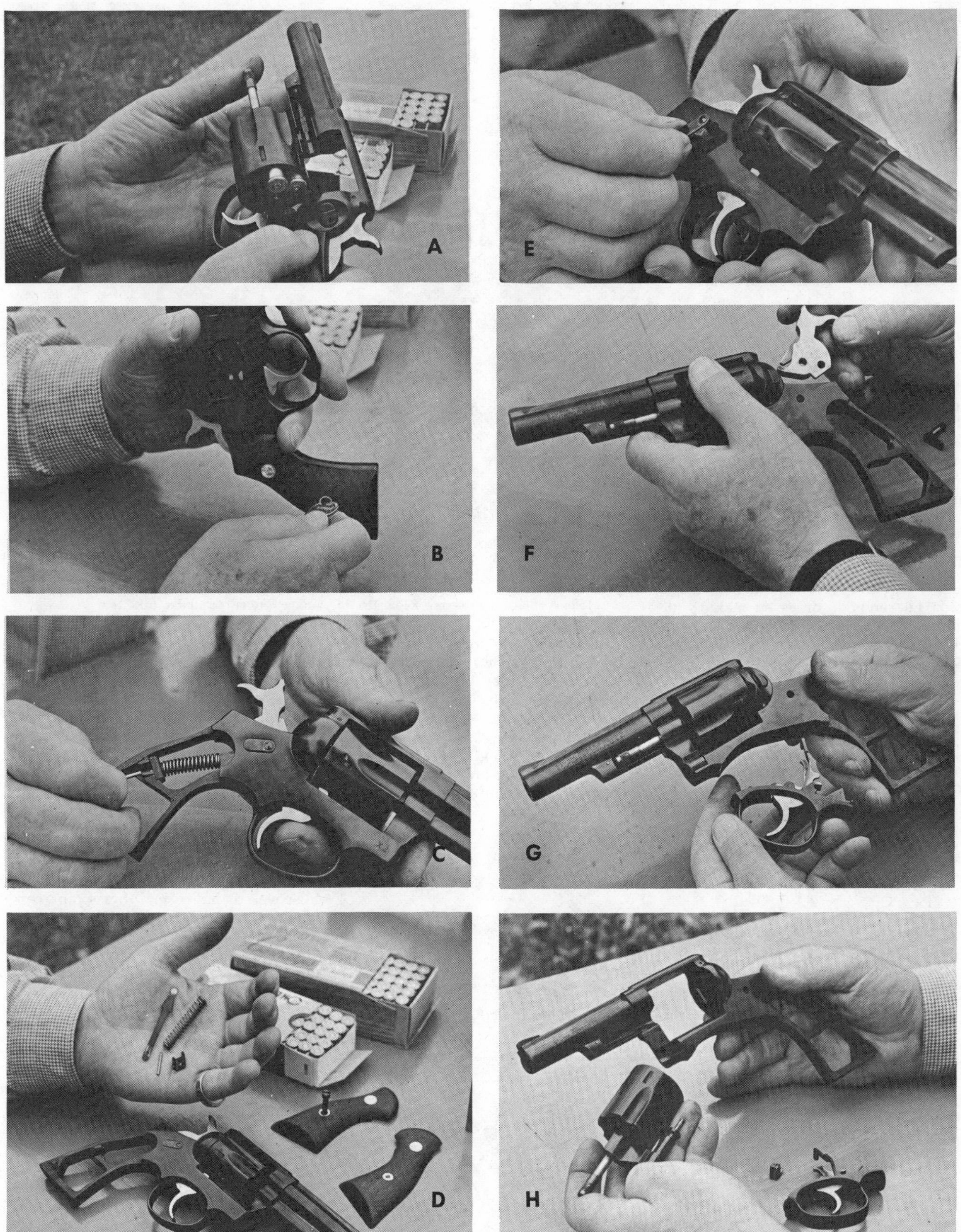

Ruger Double Action Takedown Data

A Before takedown the Ruger DA cylinder is emptied. Note latch position, which is pressed down, not slid, to release crane-cylinder.

B A small coin—a penny here—turns the grip screw out, allowing removal of the 2-piece handles.

C To remove hammer, cock it and insert small brass pin supplied into hole in bottom of thrust rod (inside mainspring). Now let hammer come forward and mainspring assembly may be lifted out.

D Mainspring, thrust rod, keeper comprise assembly; small brass pin aids takedown.

E Hammer pivot pin is L-shaped, removes by pushing from left side of frame, then lifting out.

F Trigger may now be lifted out of central slot in frame.

G Trigger-guard/hand assembly snaps out of frame bottom. Cylinder bolt, a separate unit, is removable.

H Crane-cylinder assembly pulls off forward. Cylinder bolt is pictured above guard.

First shooting was with 38 Special 148-gr. target wadcutters, including Federal, Remington and Sako brands. From rest at the shorter range all groups were one-ragged-hole types, though the Sako loads ran a bit bigger than the other two brands.

Both the Federal and Remington lots had given excellent accuracy previously in other target handguns, and these ten 5-shot groups with the Ruger D.A. were almost as good.

Next, to check point of impact, we fired Super Vel cartridges in 38 Special and 357 Magnum calibers at the 20-yard frame, again using the rest.

The Super Vel 110-gr. loads, in both 38 Special and 357 Magnum, were not especially punishing in this 28-oz. revolver, though there could be no doubt in the shooter's mind that he'd been firing a gun! Point of impact was a little bit lower with both Super Vel loads, and group size ran a mite bigger, too, at the 20-yard range, but all were well within the 10-ring area.

Velocity was not quite up to Super Vel figures—using the new Avtron photo-eye screens, and a 10-feet distance, from the muzzle, we got an average of 1304 for the 38 Special and 1601 for the 357 Magnum. These were only 5-round checks though—there was not enough time—so making allowances for the 4-inch barrel and the 10-feet range, we were probably getting 1350 and 1650 approximately at the muzzle.

Norma 357 loads in the new 158-gr. jacketed SPs, rated 1450 fps at the muzzle, did r'ar back a good bit in the Ruger D.A., understandably, and the gun tended to rotate in the hand under recoil. There was no chronographing done with the Norma loads at this time, but an earlier 10-round test with the Oehler Model 20 and his new photo-eye screens showed 1422 with a 10-foot instrumental distance.

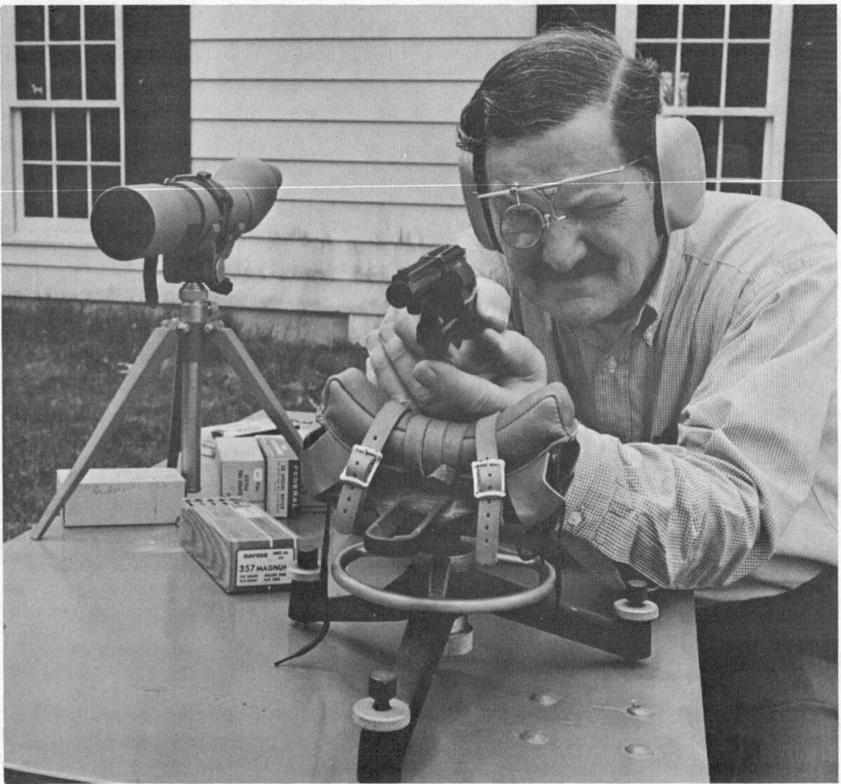
John Amber firing the new Ruger DA 357 Magnum from rest during brief test run.

Accuracy at 50 yards was still best with the Federal and Remington WCs, rest groups going about 3¼ inches average. Both Norma and Super Vel cartridges in 357 Magnum opened up to some 5-5½ inches, not at all bad, I think.

Trigger pull is crisp, weight of pull some 3¼ pounds, and the hammer fall is short and "dead," no vibration or jarring noted.

After we completed this shooting we disassembled the new Ruger—we didn't want to take it down before, not knowing whether we'd be able to get it back together properly or not!

In fact, stripping down and reassembly was easy and fast, once we'd discovered that a small brass pin (carried in the grip) was to be used in compressing the coil hammer spring.

I won't go into detail here on take-apart procedures—you'll find that information in our captions for the several illustrations. For now, I'll simply repeat that there's nothing tricky about it, and those who know me will agree that if I can take the Ruger down and put it back together then anybody can do it.

The lower rear profile of the grip frame, in our X2 sample, shows a change for the better, in my opinion. It differs from the examples seen at the NRA meeting in being somewhat more rounded, thus permitting a grip form more suited to a police revolver, especially by those peace officers wanting to use the Ruger D.A. as a hide-out arm.

In summary, a fine new addition to the handgun world, a gun that shows novel and enterprising design, a very high degree of ruggedness and reliability, first class performance and simplicity of disassembly. (J T.A.)

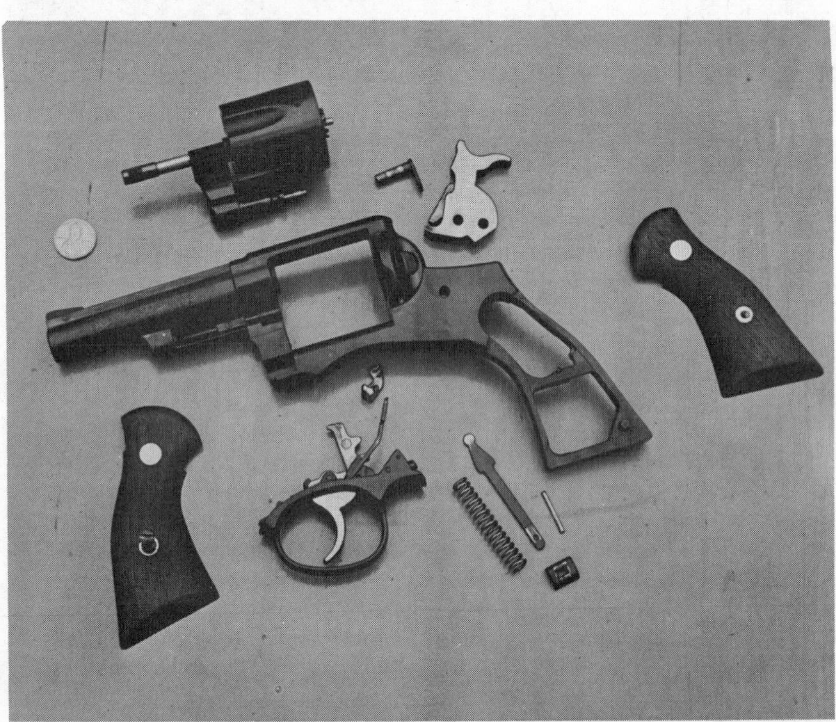
Ruger DA 357 Magnum revolver, fully disassembled except for separation of crane and cylinder.

Complete gun specifications for most of the guns described in this article may be found in our catalog pages. The addresses of the companies mentioned are listed in the Directory of the Arms Trade. Generally, for those arms made abroad for U.S. firearms companies, such as the Italian-made Savage 440, refer to the company's complete listing under U.S. Rifles and Shotguns, Guns Foreign or in the catalog pages.

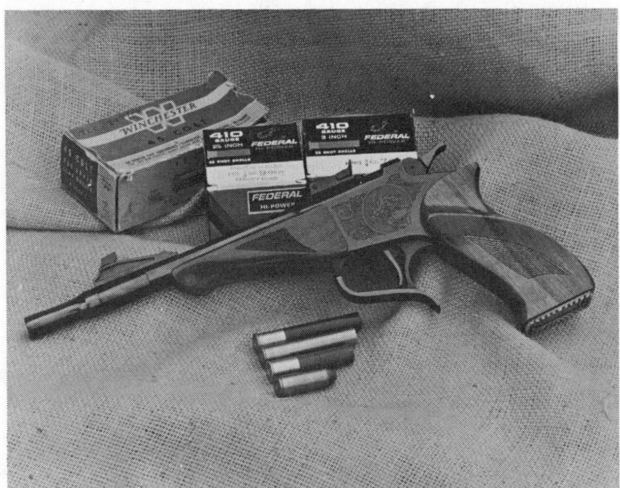

Thompson/Center Contender fitted with their 45/410 barrel having both muzzle brake and choke tube.

Thompson/Center

Up in Rochester, N.H., Thompson/Center continues to enjoy a cordial reception on the part of the fistgun public toward their super-versatile single shot Contender. Since last issue was locked up and sent to the printer, they have engineered a most remarkable coup in the handgun field: the production of a capable, legal, shot-pistol to handle the 410-bore shotshell. Once upon a time, it was a favored practice among assassins to chop down an old break-action single 12 to form a crude, rude, effective murder weapon. To proscribe the custom, legislation was enacted to make it illegal to make or possess a smoothbore firearm with a barrel shorter than 18 inches or with an over-all length of less than 26½ inches—thus tolling the death-knell for such useful and innocuous sporting arms as Marble's old "Game-Getter" over-under 22-410 with its folding skeleton stock. Rifled barrels gave any shot charge a swirling motion, creating a vortex effect which made shot load performance pathetically inadequate at anything beyond the shortest pointblank ranges. That is, it did until some inspired bright-eye at Thompson/Center conceived the idea of adding a perfectly legal choke device to the muzzle with straight, axial lands and grooves — fairly deep — to arrest the swirling motion of the shot charge, redirecting the pellets into straight forward motion. The resulting barrel is legal to the last letter of the law, since it's not a smoothbore. If you unscrew the choke device, you have a functional, highly accurate and efficient barrel to handle the 45 Long Colt cartridge, complete with an efficient muzzle brake to gentle down the bruising recoil of that monster round. In fact, it fires the 45 LC slug with incredible accuracy and notably less punishment than the shorter, plain barrel. Screw the choke tube into place and you can chamber and fire the 410 shotshell—standard or magnum length—with thoroughly respectable patterns out to a considerable distance. Again, the recoil is endurable but when the thing goes off you're aware of that fact with hardly any delay at all, especially with the 3-inch shotshells. Should you fire a 45 LC with the choke tube on, we're told by the Thompson/Center people that nothing comes unglued but the slug is considerably distorted and accuracy is nothing remarkable. Usually, switching from 45 LC to 410 requires rear sight adjustment to maintain zero.

The resulting handgun is remarkable, indeed. You haven't really lived until you have blown the hostility out of a coiled rattlesnake with a whiff of grape from the 410 configuration; it is a truly memorable experience. Especially for the snake. The bluff-bowed, 255-gr. slug from the factory load leaves the muzzle at a pace of right around 900 fps—slightly surpassing the optimistic factory specs for once—to offer quite respectable stopping potential in a single projectile, if required. All in all, its one of the most formidable combinations that anyone has dreamed up in a long, long while.

Apropos the preceding discussion of right- and left-hand rifling, the T/C 45 Long Colt barrel has a left-hand twist of one turn in 24 inches, a groove diameter of .453" and a bore diameter of .445". All other T/C calibers are rifled right-hand.

Specifications on barrel dimensions of other calibers previously listed as standard by Thompson/Center recently were released for publication in the monthly American Reloaders Association Bulletin, which listed them as follows:

Previously, all Contender calibers offered were in rimmed form, but T/C now has an extractor with a slight amount of spring which handles rimless cases with admirable ease. This innovation opens a broad new field so far as potential calibers are concerned. For spring 1969, optional calibers included the 22 K-Hornet, 222 Remington, 9mm Luger, 30 Carbine, 45 ACP and the 44/357 Bain & Davis; all are $45 each (barrels only), and are fully interchangeable with existing barrels and receivers. Research testing is under way toward the adoption of certain caliber 17 barrels into the line. An indication of the velocity potentially available is the fact that one experimental barrel, chambered for the 17 Bumblebee—a case based on the shortened 218 Ackley Bee — launched a 13.2-gr. .172" hollow point bullet made by Lee Baker at a velocity of 3546 fps for 367 foot pounds of energy with 8.3 grains of Hodgdon's H-110 propellant — respectable speed for a handgun in almost anyone's book!

In reviewing the accomplishments of this, one of the newest of the makers of handguns, there is a temptation to wonder what T/C can do for an encore. But past experience with this highly dynamic firm indicates that their entry in our 1971 edition will be something to watch for in anticipation. This is a group from which one comes to expect the unexpected.

Thompson/Center Barrel Data
(all dimensions in inches)

Caliber	Bore dia.	Groove dia.	Rifling	Twist
22 LR	.218-.219	.224	6 lands	1-14
22 WMR	.219-.220	.224	6 "	1-14
22 Jet	.219-.220	.224	6 "	1-14
22 Hornet	.219-.220	.224	6 "	1-14
256 Win.	.250-.251	.257	6 "	1-14
38 Spec.	.350 —	.357	6 "	1-18
357 Mag.	.350 —	.357	6 "	1-18
45 L. Colt	.445 —	.453	8 "	1-24

All twists are right-hand except the 45 Colt.

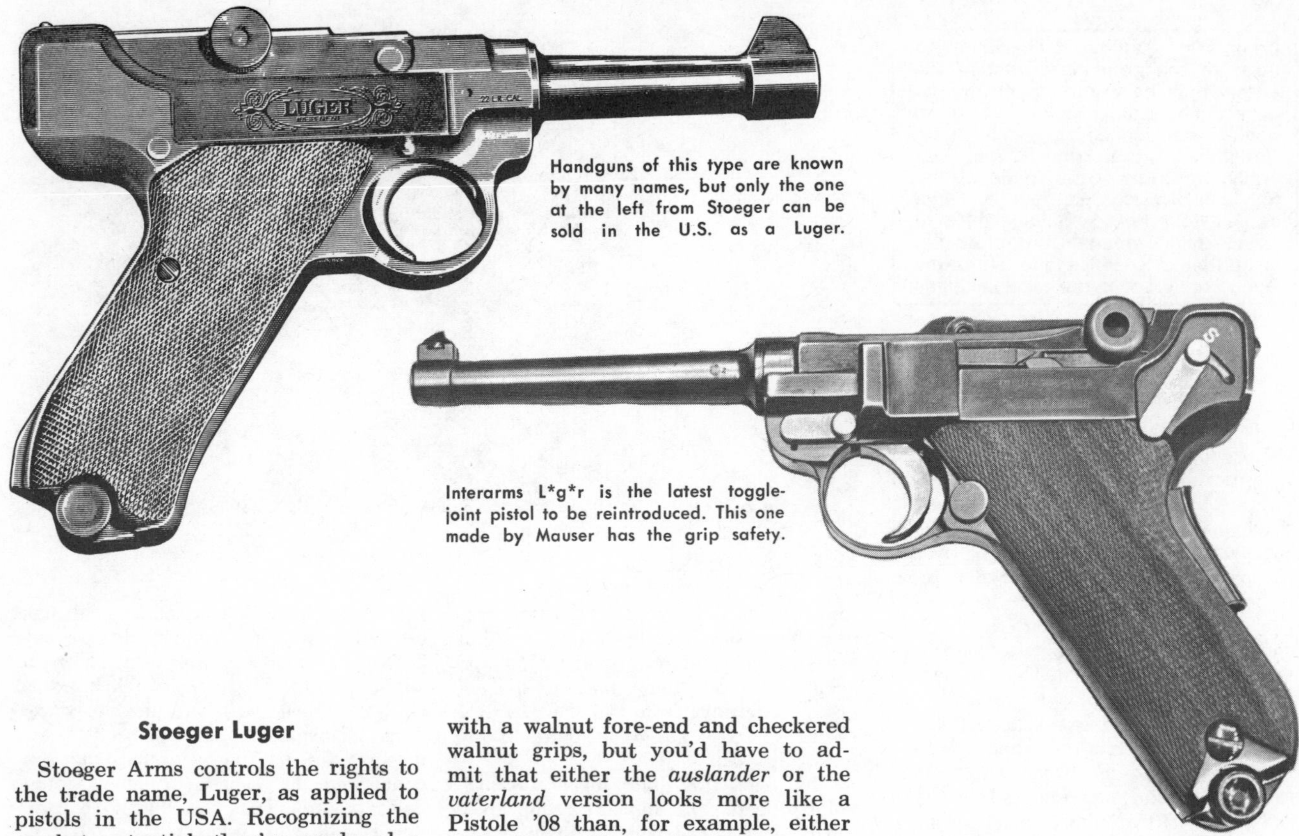

Handguns of this type are known by many names, but only the one at the left from Stoeger can be sold in the U.S. as a Luger.

Interarms L*g*r is the latest toggle-joint pistol to be reintroduced. This one made by Mauser has the grip safety.

Stoeger Luger

Stoeger Arms controls the rights to the trade name, Luger, as applied to pistols in the USA. Recognizing the market potential, they've produced a near-replica of the Pistole '08 in 22 Long Rifle. The name Luger is embossed on the right-hand side of the receiver, an embellishment the original Pistole '08 never offered. Examining the action, you might be tempted to coin a new term and call its design an "impeded blowback." On the original Pistole '08, the toggle knobs were kicked upward by an incline on the receiver after the barrel assembly had recoiled for a short distance, thus unlocking the action to complete the cycle of ejecting and reloading. The Stoeger Luger has the pivot point of its toggle assembly above the axis of the bore so that the puny push-back of the 22 round pushes against nothing more resistant than the inertia and mass of the sliding parts. Technically, it's a full-blowback design and, as such things go, by no means a bad one.

A moderate exposure to Stoeger Luger number 1099 indicates that it functions with notable reliability, using any of several typical brands of 22 Long Rifle high velocity ammunition. While it seems doubtful that it's apt to terrorize the competitors at Camp Perry or cop gold at the Olympics, the fixed sights of the test sample will put 10 holes in a cozy cluster, uncomfortably close to the point of aim, and it's hard to seriously fault a handgun that's capable of doing that. The Stoeger Luger looks at least much like a Pistole '08 as does its (forgive, please?) cousin-german from the old country. Yes, I know: the Erma Pistole is available in an assortment of versions such as the "Navy Model," with a walnut fore-end and checkered walnut grips, but you'd have to admit that either the *auslander* or the *vaterland* version looks more like a Pistole '08 than, for example, either looks like a Webley-Fosbery.

Interarms Parabellum

"Parabellum," in Latin, means "for war." Apparently no one has figured out how to corral the rights to this particular appellation because Interarms, Ltd., is importing the most convincing look-alike of all under the name of Mauser Parabellum. Harking back to the scarcer versions of the Pistole '08, the Mauser entry sports a functioning grip-safety, nicely milled parts and a genuine delayed blowback action commensurate with the lustier backlash of the cartridges for which it is designed. Initial production—hopefully available by the fall of 1969—will be in caliber 9mm Parabellum (or "L*g*r," as John Amber likes to call it), with barrel lengths of 4 and 5 inches. Later, the same barrel lengths will be offered chambered for the 30 Parabellum cartridge; the same round used in some of the Pistole '08 models.

With an eye to the Yankee market, the Mauser Parabellum has a safety lever on the left-hand side, with the upper or forward position marked by a white letter S. There's no more of the problem of trying to remember whether *gesichert* means "secured" or "watch it, bub!"

For obscure reasons which no one at Interarms could explain satisfactorily, the Mauser has followed most of the lines and contours of the Pistole '08 quite faithfully but they have planed away the sensuous little schnabel-like bulge at the lower front end of the grip, leaving the front surface a straight line from the bottom of the trigger guard to the butt. As a result, it looks and feels oddly not quite right—a bit like Raquel Welch with a luxuriant moustache. In the same vein, the prototype version that we examined had no checkering on areas where you expect it, such as the sides of the toggle knobs (where checkering fills a useful function), the magazine release button, the top of the safety lever and the little take-down lever ahead of the trigger on the left side. You can understand the elimination of features such as the tangs to accept a shoulder stock, but after going to a considerable amount of effort to create a detailed facsimile, it is puzzling that these points were changed.

Projected price-tag for the Mauser Parabellum is $160—which, as you might imagine, occasions a twinge on the part of a guy who once happily sold a similar gun for less than one-sixth that figure! However, at that price, you get freedom from such minor irritations as plastic and stamped sheet-metal parts: things which, while not detracting from the functional qualities of a handgun, must cause an ominous subterranean rumbling sound in the vicinity of Georg Luger's grave.

At this time (mid-May, 1969) we've just learned that the full-production Parabellum pistol will differ to a degree with the Interarms auto-loader described by Dean Grennell. J.T.A.

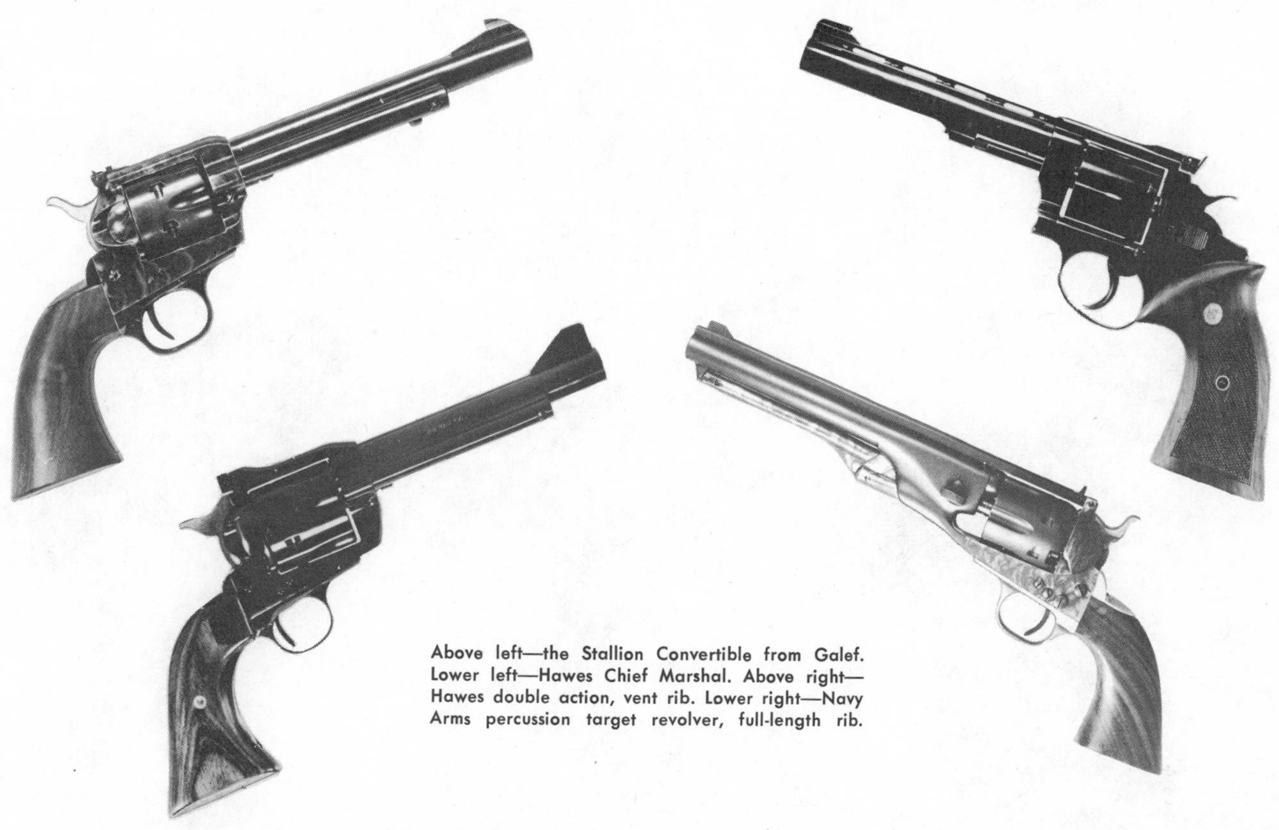

Above left—the Stallion Convertible from Galef. Lower left—Hawes Chief Marshal. Above right—Hawes double action, vent rib. Lower right—Navy Arms percussion target revolver, full-length rib.

Bob Steindler on some auslander

Galef and Son

The Beretta semi-auto pistols, long in the Galef line, have had a price increase, and a new gun has been added. Called the Cougar, the new pistol will be chambered for the 380 round, and is so new that we couldn't even get a picture. It is my understanding that the Cougar will have the identical features of the other Beretta pistols.

Brand-new is an Italian-made single action revolver called the **Stallion.** Convertible from 22 LR to 22 WRF, the gun features case-hardened receiver, fine bluing and a choice of barrel lengths—5½ and 6½ inches. The rear sight is fully adjustable for elevation and windage, the hammer has the conventional three notches. Including the second cylinder the gun retails for a very reasonable $87. I had a chance to give that gun a good handling, although I didn't fire it, and it is a solid piece of workmanship that should last a long time. (B.S.)

Gold Rush Gun Shop

This importer is now the sole U.S. agent for the guns produced by the *Schweizer Industrie Gesellschaft* — SIG for short. Of special interest to American shooters are the SIG semi-auto pistols. At present, only one model—the P210-6—is available, but two other models will follow shortly, may be available by the time you read this.

The P210-6 is the 4¾″ barrel version of the 6″ barreled P210-5, the well-known target pistol. Both guns have such target arm refinements as a trigger stop and fully adjustable rear sight, both are chambered for the 9mm or the 7.65 Parabellum cartridges. They are finely made and precision tuned guns, a joy to handle and shoot. The Model P210-1, utility edition of the P210-6, lacks the target refinements noted. P210-1 stocks are wood, and the gun is offered in the two Parabellum chamberings as well as in 22 LR.

Take-down of the gun is simple, functioning is perfect, and extra barrels to convert from one Parabellum caliber to the other will probably be offered, providing ATFD considers this a legal conversion. Also offered, for about $100, is a 22 LR conversion kit for the two match guns. In order to accomplish this conversion, the barrel, recoil spring, slide and magazine must be changed—yet a job that should take less than two minutes.

A vastly revamped SIG rifle, the AMT or American Military Target rifle is also being offered by this importer. This semi-auto rifle, based to a large extent on the SIG NATO rifle, and chambered for the 7.62 NATO (308) round, has an excellent accuracy potential. A bipod and/or scope will be offered with the gun (both optional) as well as a sling and one 5-shot magazine. The bipod and an extra magazine will bring the price of the SIG-AMT to $348—the gun with sling and 5-shot magazine is $299. The scope and scope mount, designed especially for this rifle, are top-quality products.

The Gold Rush Gun Shop also imports the French MAB pistols, and there is some talk that an MAB target model semi-auto pistol will be offered. This is the P-15 Competition grade, quite like the standard model except for having a ⅛″ Patridge front, a micrometer-click w. and e. rear sight and a smooth trigger pull. Somewhat oddly, perhaps, the 15-shot magazine is retained. (B.S.)

Hawes Firearms Co.

In last year's GUN DIGEST, Ken Waters reported in some detail on several of the Hawes SA revolvers. In the "Marshal" series of sixguns, the latest is a new super target model, the "Chief Marshal." To qualify for the target name, the new gun carries a ramp front sight and a rear sight fully adjustable for windage and elevation. To give greater comfort to the hand, the frame has been beefed up and the rosewood grips, on cursory examination, appear to be bigger and also better shaped than grips on the

Here's the new Walther PP auto pistol, available from Interarms in 32 and 380 auto calibers at $96.

Erma Pistole is now offered in an all-steel version. Insert above shows operation of toggle.

Interarms has revived the famed Mauser HSc auto pistol. Made in 32 and 380 auto calibers, cost is $96.

other guns in that series. The gun is chambered for 357 Mag., 44 Mag., 45 Long Colt, and 22 S, L and LR. The new model is $99.95. Like all the other Hawes handguns, excepting the well-made black powder numbers, the "Chief Marshall" is also made by J. P. Sauer in Germany.

New from front sight to backstrap is the J. P. Sauer-made double action revolver. The gun is chambered for only two cartridges—22 LR and 38 Spl., the latter with a ventilated rib on about a 6" barrel. The 22 LR version lacks the vent rib, and has a barrel of about 4 inches. The 22 DA is $104.95, the 38 Spl. an extra $15. Both guns carry fully adjustable rear sights, their heavy and well balanced frames reflecting the Sauer quality. The target hammer is amply knurled to prevent thumb slippage, and the wide and heavily-serrated trigger is of the target type. Stocks are walnut, offered with thumb rest or in regular style.

Here's another new item from Hawes—new, improved Red-Jet synthetic bullets, not to be confused with Red-Jets of yesteryear. These new Sampson Red-Jets won't melt or deform when fired at high velocity. When they strike a solid object, such as a pine board, they literally fall apart, thus no dangerous ricochets. Equally important, the new Red-Jets don't foul the barrel, and continued use of them, if the bore is cleaned after each 15-20 shots, will actually polish the bore. Offered in 30, 38, and 45 caliber, they are used with large magnum pistol primers. If more oomph is desired, they can be used with a propellant powder charge.

Also offered by Hawes are the Sampson aluminum 38 Spl. cases with slightly over-sized flash holes to give more certain firing of the Red-Jet. These cases can be used thousands of times according to Hawes, but it is emphasized that the cases *are not to be used with propellant powder charges* or with lead bullets. Also offered are special brass cases with enlarged flash holes, and primer pockets that accept large magnum pistol primers.

You can also use the Sampson Red-Jets in smoothbores (12, 16, 20) and a special shotgun adaptor and loading tool is offered for that use. (B.S.)

Interarms

The Mauser HSc of WW II fame, chambered for 32 ACP and 380, will be back with us shortly. The gun will retail for $92. And—hang on to your Stetsons—you'll be able to get a Mauser-made Pistole '08, commonly called the Luger in the U.S. The gun will be offered in 9mm Parabellum and 30 Luger, will sell for $160, and already Interarms has more orders for that pistol than they'll have guns for the first 6 months of production.

For those of you who have been hoping for the return of the Walther PP auot pistol—well, it's back again and Interarms has them. (B.S.)

LA Distributors

The Erma Pistole—the L-g-r look alike—will now be offered in an all-steel version, but still at $59.95. This 22 RF gun looks and feels quite like the original Pistole Parabellum; except for the markings on the gun, you have to look at the bore diameter before you can be certain as to what you hold in your hand. Also planned is a double action 9mm on the same principle, and a "Baby L-g-r" in 32 ACP and 380 Auto, price about $90.

Navy Arms

Brand new items Val Forgett lists are a handsome brass-barreled blunderbuss in flintlock form at $100, and a target model version of his popular 1861 Navy percussion revolver at $125. The important change is a full-length rib running back over the cylinder and locking into an extension of the recoil-frame. A rear sight is dovetailed into the rib. This "solid-frame" sixshooter cap gun should show improved accuracy.

Universal Firearms

Now in the mill is a 38 Special revolver, looking much like a well-known U.S. make. To be offered blued or nickel-plated (pending approval by the ATFD) there'll be several barrel lengths. Designed primarily for police use, these revolvers have fixed sights. The gun I examined was well made and seemingly worth the $65 asked.

Merrill Single-Shot

Newest entry in the single shot sweepstakes is the Merrill pistol, from The Merrill Co., Inc., Box 187, Rockwell City, Iowa 50579. Priced at $129.50 with one ribbed, 9-inch barrel, the Merrill is available in three rimfire calibers, 22 LR, 22 WRE and 22 WMR; also in 22 Hornet and "117 K. Hornet," probably a typographical error, for 17 K-Hornet. The 22 WRE is perhaps the all-but-obsolete 22 WRF cartridge. Spare barrels are offered at $25 each, interchangeable between the offered rimfire calibers and between the two centerfire sizes, though not switchable between rim and centerfire. A wrist brace is offered as an accessory item, price not given. Information given here is based upon the manufacturer's literature, only.

Smith & Wesson

In the 23rd edition of GUN DIGEST it was reported, complete with joyous calloos and callays, that Smith & Wesson soon would have a 22 LR pocket autoloader, about the size of a 25 auto and priced for less than $50. The report was a trifle premature. From the vantage point of an elapsed year, the promised pocket plinker has yet to be unveiled, although there is a grudging admission that such an item is in the works, toward an eventual parturition. Apart from that, all is quiet in Springfield as the shifts sprint to stay in sight of back orders.

Sterling Arms Ltd.

A new series of 22 rimfire autoloading pistols was announced early in 1969 by this new firm, full production being scheduled for June, 1969. If that proves the case, your dealer should have one or more of the four new designs on his shelves by the time you read this.

Still, in arms production as in so many other areas, there's many a slip —so don't bug your favorite gun dealer unduly if he shouldn't have the new Sterling "Cup" handguns on display all that soon.

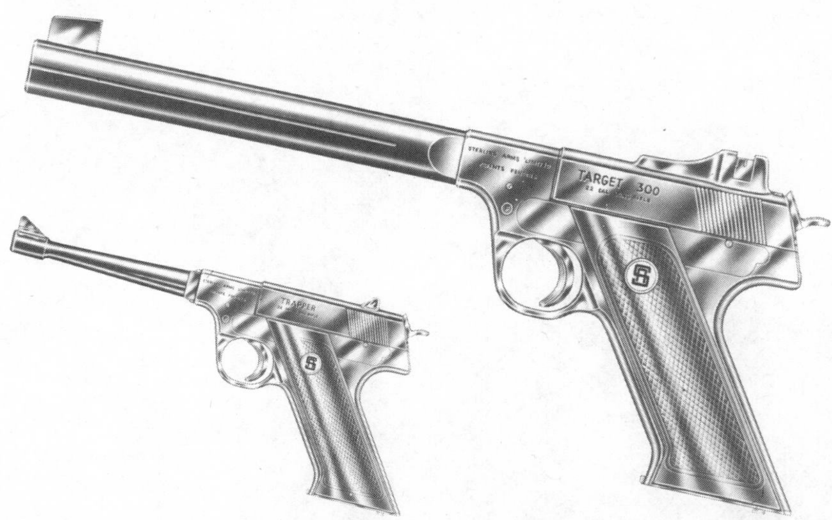

Sterling Arms Ltd. Trapper semi-auto pistol, cal. 22 Long Rifle, has fixed sights, sharply tapered barrel, external hammer.

Sterling Arms Ltd. Target 300 semi-auto pistol, cal. 22 Long Rifle, has heavy barrel, adjustable rear sight, external hammer.

What are these new auto pistols like? Well, judging from the well-prepared brochure furnished (we have not seen any sample gun so far), the general outline appears very much like the Hamden, Conn. gun used to look. The Sterling autos all have external hammers, though, and barrels are fixed, not quickly removable, and the adjustable rear sights on two Sterling models are carried in a heavy housing.

The Target 300, made with 4½", 6" or 8" heavy barrels and "microtype" rear sight, is the top of the Sterling "Cup" line, selling for $105.

The Target 300L, offered only with a 6" Luger-looking barrel, but quite like the gun just described, is $89.

The Sterling Husky has a 4½" heavy barrel, fixed sights only (cost $49.95), while the Trapper model carries the Luger-like barrel of the Target 300L, but with fixed sights only, and sells for $69.

All of these Sterling pistols are of all-steel construction, have a safety of push-through type that may be reversed for left-handed shooters, and 10-shot magazines.

Eight other models are said to be available—or should be soon—but no information on these has been offered to us. (J.T.A.)

Dan Wesson Arms

Dan Wesson Arms, of Monson, Massachusetts, offers a new revolver with several novel features, the most remarkable of which is a system of quickly interchangeable barrels. Offered only in 357 Magnum, barrels to be offered are 2½", 4", 5" and 6", each being secured by a barrel nut at the muzzle, and each requiring its own shroud. The ramp-type, front and rear sights are adjustable, and the latch for the swing-out cylinder is located *ahead* of the cylinder for positive lockup. The trigger is adjustable for weight of pull and travel, while the broad-spur, target hammer has an unusually short throw in both single or double action. For a full-length article on the new Dan Wesson firearms, including his air guns and shotguns, see Mason Williams' article elsewhere in this issue.

The Merrill Sportsman single-shot pistol fitted with a Bushnell 1.3x Phantom scope and folding wrist support. Cartridges (from left) are 17/222 and 17 K-Hornet, are Merrill's own chambering; 17 Ackley Bee and 17 Bumble Bee are suitable but not factory produced.

Dan Wesson's Model 12 DA revolver and some of the 38 Special and 357 Magnum cartridges it can digest.

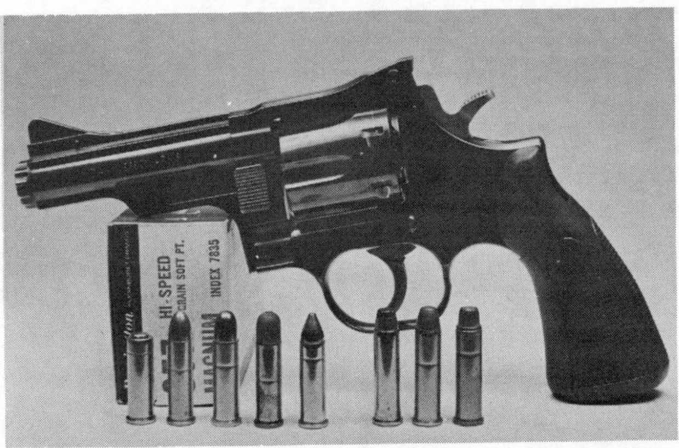

Two models of Bushnell Phantom scope mounts—one for revolvers with adjustable sights, the other for fixed sights.

Handgun Accessories

Among handgun accessories there are a few noteworthy items—Bushnell has a new series of scope mounts to adapt their Phantom optical sight to the more popular designs. After several attempts to come up with a mount that requires no modification in the existing gun, they have bowed to the inevitable and introduced a mount that requires tapping of a single hole in the top strap of revolvers equipped with an adjustable rear sight. The resulting mount, at last, offers the necessary rigidity to cope with the recoil of all the hairy handgun chamberings up to and including the 44 Magnum without the undesirable shifting of the scope in the mount. At the same time, unlike earlier efforts, there is no interference with cylinder rotation. Should you desire to return to iron sights the extra hole remains but is not a serious detraction to the appearance of the gun. An all-purpose dual mount is offered for those handguns without adjustable rear sights, requiring the tapping of two holes in the top strap. List price for either is $5. The upgrading of performance made possible by putting a scope on a handgun previously equipped with fixed iron sights can be most impressive. Many an owner has discovered, to his delight, that a so-so shooter is capable of excellent groups, once fitted with sights that take a close look at the point where the bullet is due to land.

As further assistance toward the handgunner's eternal dream of enhanced accuracy, there is a new device to correct a basic design flaw in the anatomy of the human animal. The original blueprint for *homo sapiens* incorporated a fully articulated wrist joint; which is handy for many purposes but somewhat of a handicap when it comes to the accurate firing of handguns. To improve the situation, a device called a "Wrist-Loc" can be attached to the gun to weld gun, hand and forearm into one solid unit. While this does nothing for the wobbles that stem from elbow, shoulder and the oscillation of two-legged creatures, it does effect an amazing improvement in the steadiness of the sight picture. Attachment is by means of one aluminum plate beneath each grip, with an aluminum wire loop extending to the rear and over the forearm, with a neoprene sponge pad to cushion recoil shock. Besides enhancing accuracy, either offhand or from rest, the performance on rapid fire is much improved. Two versions are offered: one that attaches by screws at $9.95, and a spring-clip type at $11.95. Further information from Mr. Roger A. Smith, 19320 Heber St., Glendora, Calif. 91740.

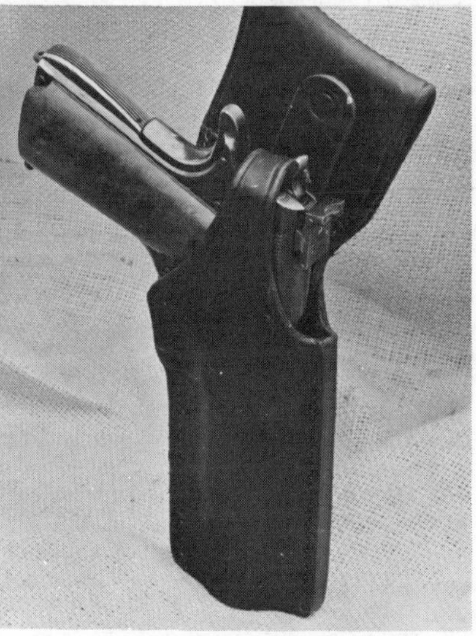

Safariland M-55 holster for Colt 45 Auto or Commander, S&W M-39 and M-35 Browning Hi-Power.

New holster items include a remarkable unit for autoholders from Safariland, Inc., called the Model 55. Primarily intended for police use, it positions the muzzle forward for convenience in automobiles and, just incidentally, offers extreme speed and reliability on the draw—leading to a wide acceptance by the competitive combat shooting enthusiasts. A thumb snap at the top secures the pistol in the holster, either cocked-and-locked or with hammer down. In drawing the weapon, the natural gesture of the thumb toward the safety lever releases the securing strap in the same motion. Incorporating Safariland's "Sight Track" feature, the holster can be used with pistols that carry the higher, target type sights. As a side benefit, the design makes it quite difficult, if not impossible, for another person to snatch the pistol from the holster from the front or side of the person wearing it. Price is $16.95 for the plain version in black leather. At the same figure, Safariland's Model 19 now is available for 4-inch barrel revolvers up to the S&W Highway Patrolman or Colt's Python. The Model 19, made also for 2-inchers, carries the revolver inverted under the arm. The longer version offers the plain clothes officer the advantage of the longer barrels without loss of concealability.

Also new within the past year from Safariland is a system of no-buckle leather goods for police and other

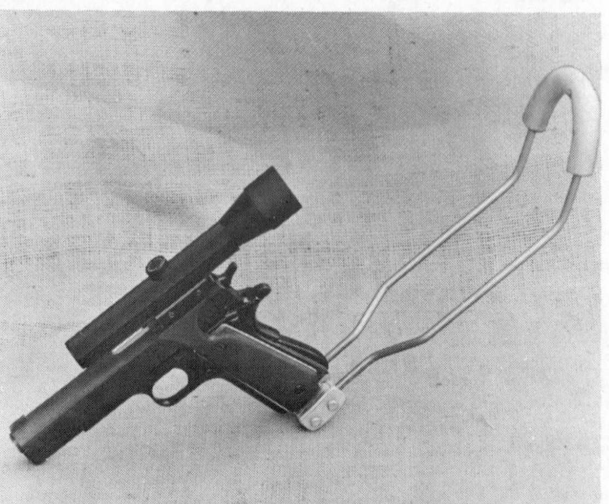

Smith Wrist-Loc device installed on Colt 45 auto fitted with Bushnell Phantom scope using the old discontinued mount.

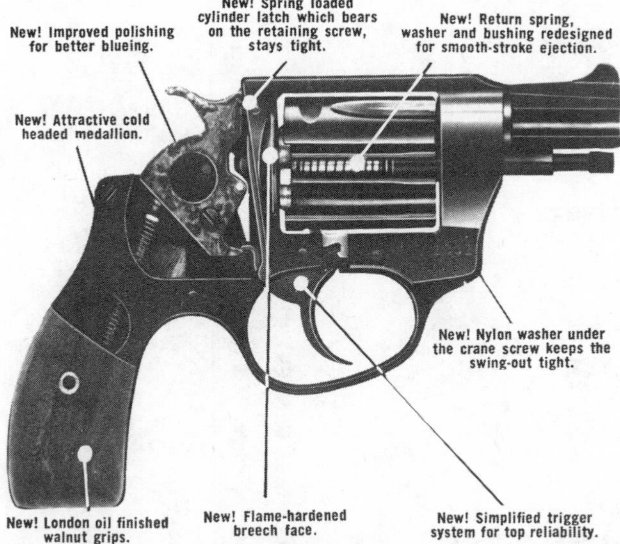
New! Improved polishing for better blueing.
New! Spring loaded cylinder latch which bears on the retaining screw, stays tight.
New! Return spring, washer and bushing redesigned for smooth-stroke ejection.
New! Attractive cold headed medallion.
New! Nylon washer under the crane screw keeps the swing-out tight.
New! London oil finished walnut grips.
New! Flame-hardened breech face.
New! Simplified trigger system for top reliability.

Improvements recently made in Charter Arms Undercover revolver. Not shown is the new 8-groove rifling with 1:17" twist.

purposes. The obvious advantage is the elimination of those reflecting surfaces that offer natural aiming points in dim light, plus a considerable reduction in weight and bulk. The secret lies in a material called "Velcro," which provides two adhering surfaces of great strength and durability.

Which seems to represent the gleanings as to what's new in handguns. A canvass of the other manufacturers at recent shows elicits the response that, "We don't have anything new but all of the old stuff is as good as ever."

Bianchi Holsters will—by the time you read this—have a new catalog available, price $1, which will carry something new — a 100-point questionnaire or evaluation chart that will let you determine the relative quality and usefulness of virtually any holster made—theirs as well.

The catalog will also, of course, carry full information on the excellent Bianchi holsters, belts, carbine stocks, etc.

Wasson Tip-Up Apertures

For years I used a piece of black plastic with a tiny hole I'd punched in it to sharpen up handgun sights and the target. I bent the edge over so it would hang on my shooting glasses. It worked well, but it was far from convenient—it was not easy to position the one hole properly, and I'd have the same problem every time I used it.

Now there's an adjustable optical attachment available that is easy to use and it's far more efficient than my old home-made gadget. The Wasson device clips on the shooter's glasses, offers a choice of 6 different-sized apertures in combination with the 2 master holes in the non-rotating element, and the whole thing can be quickly lifted up, out of the way, when desired.

The rotating front piece of plastic is quite thin, thus the holes—all hand reamed—take a sharp edge that's non-reflecting, while the back of the device is matte-finished for the same reason. The attaching hinge is well-padded and attaches the aperture firmly to the eyeglasses, but without any danger of scratching or damage.

The adjustable clip-on aperture is $3.50. A blank clip-on, especially useful to those who close one eye in shooting, is $2.00. Both may be had for $5 a set. Order from H. P. Wasson, Box 181, Netcong, N. J. 07857.

X-Ring

X-Ring Centrifugal Bullet Traps are so well known that a detailed description of them and their high degree of usefulness might seem superfluous, but they're now 3 times stronger than they were before!

Having an outdoor range at Creedmoor Farm, I'd never felt the need for a bullet trap until the new barn went up late last year. I intended to set up an indoor range inside it, mostly for handgun use, so the 18-inch Pedestal Model of the X-Ring line was ordered, complete with a pair of lamp holders.

The funnel of the trap is made from ¼-inch boiler plate, 100% electric welded to the heart of the trap—the centrifugal section—using special high-tensile welding rod. This rugged and sturdy setup makes any X-Ring trap virtually indestructible if it's used as it should be.

Bullets impinge against the trap funnel at a shallow angle—18 degrees—and are then guided into the rotary-path trap casting. As the illustration shows, the bullet follows a circular course, its energy absorbed by the high friction the centrifugal forces develop. This energy absorption is so great that the bullet's velocity, as it drops into the removable receptacle, won't break a piece of paper!

Unlike many backstop arrangements, the X-Ring design for low-angle impact tends to keep the striking bullet whole until it reaches the trap proper. There's no fragmentation on impact, hence there is no danger of bullet pieces flying back to endanger the shooter.

A big advantage of the new construction lies in the dust-free, clean condition of the lead fragments collected in the trap. Bullets can be cast from this supply without any further attention.

We've been using the new 18-inch X-Ring for a couple of months now, and into it—at ranges varying from 10 feet to 10 yards—have gone handgun bullets up to 45 ACP caliber and even some light rifle stuff as a sort of proof test. No damage, no problem, but the X-Ring traps, please note, are designed to safely absorb only handgun bullets or such other bullets as develop no more than 600 foot pounds of muzzle energy.

X-Ring trap prices start at $24 for their 12-inch table model, and on through intermediate sizes to a $48 cost for the 18-inch pedestal type we've been using. Lamp holders are $6 each. X-Ring Centrifugal Bullet Traps are supplied now by Outers Laboratories, Inc., Onalaska, Wis. 54650. They'll send a free brochure giving full details. (J.T.A.)

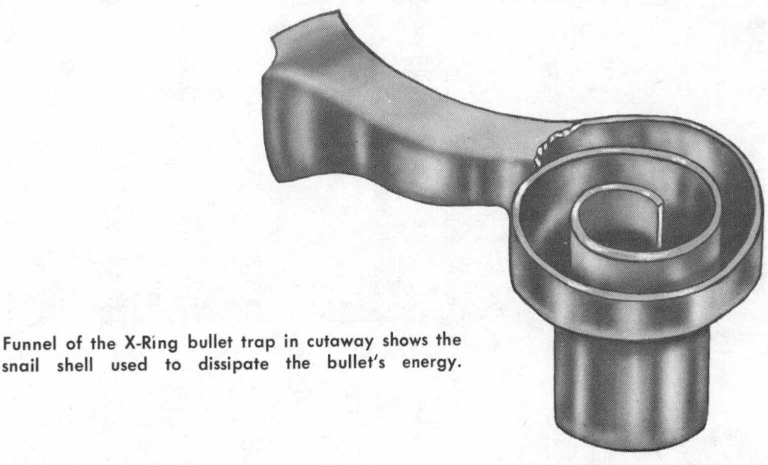

Funnel of the X-Ring bullet trap in cutaway shows the snail shell used to dissipate the bullet's energy.

CHECK CHART OF U.S. RIMFIRE HANDGUNS

Make	Model	Sights	Price	Barrel	Notes
AUTOLOADERS					
Browning	Nomad	adj.	67.50	4½-6¾	22 LR, also 2 target models
Browning	Challenger	adj.	82.50 up	4½-6¾	ext. trigger adj. screw
Browning	Medalist	adj.	134.50 up	6¾	target; dry-fire device
Colt	Huntsman	fix.	71.50	4½-6	10-shot
Colt	Targetsman	adj.	82.50	6	10-shot
Colt	W'man Sport	adj.	100.00	4½-6	10-shot
Colt	MT Woodsman	adj.	115.50	4½-6	10-shot
H. S.	Duramatic	fix.	64.50	4½-6½	quick takedown
H. S.	Sport-King	fix.	72.50	4½-6¾	22 LR or 22 S (Flite King)
H. S.	Sup. Tour.	adj.	90.00	5½, 6¾	also with bull barrel
H. S.	Sup. Citation	adj.	110.00	5½-6¾-7¼	Cit. Military, $110.00
H. S.	Olympic (ISU)	adj.	130.00	5½, 6¾	22 S only (Oly. Mil. 22 LR)
H. S.	Sup. Trophy	adj.	125.00	5½-7¼	Trophy Mil. $125.00
Ruger	Standard	fix.	47.50	4⅝-6½	first Ruger model
Ruger	Mark I Target	adj.	67.50 up	6⅞	9-shot, comp. extra
S & W	46 Target	adj.	102.50	5, 7	22 LR. Heavy bbl. $108.00
S & W	41 Match	adj.	120.00	5, 7⅜	22 LR or 22 S (5½ HB)
Sterling	Target 300	adj.	105.00	4½-6-8	22 LR
Sterling	Target 300L	fix.	89.00	6	Luger type bbl.
Sterling	Husky	fix.	49.95	4½	10-shot
Sterling	Trapper	fix.	69.00	6	interchangeable safety
REVOLVERS					
Colt	Frontier Scout	fix.	65.00 up	4¾	22 RF, also 22 RFM
Colt	Buntline Scout	fix.	75.00 up	9½	22 RF, also 22 RFM
Colt	Official Police	fix.	110.00	4-6-5	also in 38 Spl.
Colt	OM Match	adj.	143.00	6	also in 22 RFM
Colt	Cobra	fix.	98.00	3	38 Spl. also
Colt	Diamondback	adj.	125.00	2½-4	also in 38 Spl.
F. I.	Regent	fix.	34.95	3-4-6	8-shot-Swingout cyl.
H & R	622	fix.	36.50	2½-4-6	solid frame
H & R	900	fix.	41.50	2½-4-6	snap-out cyl.
H & R	949	adj.	47.50	5½	9-shot
H & R	929 Side Kick	semi	47.50	2½-4-6	swingout cyl.
H & R	925 Defender	semi	62.50	2½-4	top break, 38 S&W also
H & R	Ultra S'Kick	adj.	62.50	6	vent. rib bbl., safety lock
H & R	999 S'man	adj.	67.50	6	9-shot, top-break
H. S.	Sentinel	fix.	63.00	2⅜, 4, 6	nickel, $70.00
H. S.	Double-9	semi	70.00	5½-9½	frontier style
I. J.	55A, Cadet	fix.	42.50 up	2½-4½-6	solid frame, both models
I. J.	57A	adj.	42.50 up	4½-6	now with loading gates
I. J.	Sidewinder	fix.	44.25 up	6	frontier style
I. J.	Trailsman 66	adj.	49.95 up	6	rebounding hammer
I. J.	Viking 67	adj.	53.25 up	2¾-4½-6	snub model—67S
Ruger	Bearcat	fix.	44.00	4	engr. cyl. walnut-grips
Ruger	Single Six	fix.	64.25	5½	22 RF, 22 RFM, walnut grips
Ruger	S.S. Conv.	fix.	69.50	5½-6½-9½	2 cyls. (9½" bbl. $78.00)
Ruger	S.S.S. Conv.	semi	78.00	5½-6½	2 cyls. New frame profile
S & W	Combat M'piece	adj.	89.00	4	also in 38 Spl.
S & W	22/32 Kit	adj.	90.00 up	2-4	also 3½" Airw'ght & 22 RFM.
S & W	22/32 Target	adj.	97.00	6	small frame
S & W	K22 Magnum	adj.	98.00	4, 6, 8⅜	22 RF Magnum
S & W	K22	adj.	98.00	6, 8⅜	also in 32 and 38
MISCELLANEOUS					
Chgo. Derr.	Derr.	fix.	34.95	2⅝	22 LR, 4-shot (Sharps)
H. S.	Derringer	fix.	45.00	3½	O-U, 22 LR or 22 RFM
Savage	101	semi	21.95	5½	single shot
T. C. Contender	Single Shot	adj.	135.00	10"-8¾"	extra barrels ($36 ea.) convert to 22 WMR, 22 Rem. Jet, 22 Hornet 22 K-Hornet. 256 Win., 357 Mag., 38 Spl., 45 Colt & 45-410 ($144), 9mm Luger, 30 Carb., 222 Rem.

CHECK CHART OF U.S. CENTERFIRE REVOLVERS

Make	Type	Model	Calibers	Sights	Barrel	Price	Notes
REVOLVERS							
Char. Arms	Belly	U'cover	38 Spl.	fix.	2-3	75.23	round or square butt.
Colt	Belly	Det. Spl.	38 Spl., 32 NP	fix.	2-3	93.50 up	nickel, $114.25
Colt	Belly	Cobra	38 Spl., 32 NP	fix.	2-3-4	98.00	nickel, $112.70
Colt	Belly	Agent	38 Spl.	fix.	2	98.00	with hammer shroud $104.00
Colt	Med.	Diamondback	38 Spl.	adj.	2½-4	125.00	also in 22 LR
Colt	Med.	Pol. Pos. Spl.	38 Spl., 32 NP	fix.	4-5	93.50	nickel, $107.50
Colt	Med.	Off. Pol.	38 Spl.	fix.	4-5-6	110.00	nickel, $126.50
Colt	Med.	Trooper MKIII	38 Spl., 357 M	adj.	4-6	135.50 up	target, $142.00
Colt	Tar.	O.M. Match	38 Spl.	adj.	6	143.00	
Colt	Lge.	Python	357 Magnum	adj.	2½-4-6	175.00	nickel, $200.00
Colt	Lge.	S.A. Army	357, 45C	fix.	4¾-5½-7½	175.00	also 44 Spl.
Colt	Lge.	Buntline	45 Colt	fix.	12	200.00	
Colt	Lge.	New F'tier	357, 44 Spl., 45C	adj.	5½-7½	210.00	flat-top, Royal Blue
H&R	Small	G'man 732	32 S&W Long	fix.	2½-4	52.50	new "Safety Lock"
H&R	Belly	925	38 S&W	Semi	2½, 4	62.50	
I.J.	Belly	55S-A	32 & 38 S&W	fix.	2½	39.50	
I.J.	Belly	67S Snub	32 & 38 S&W	adj.	2¾	53.75	
Ruger	Lge.	Blackhawk	357, 41 Mag., 30 US	adj.	4⅝-6½	98.50	41 cal. new
Ruger	Lge.	Blackhawk	357/9mm Convert.	adj.	4⅝-6½	100.00	2 cyls.
Ruger	Lge.	Super B'hawk	44 Magnum	adj.	7½	125.00	brass guard
S&W	Belly	Terrier	38 S&W	fix.	2	76.50 up	
S&W	Belly	Chiefs Spl.	38 Spl.	fix.	2-3	76.50 up	airweight, $79.00 up
S&W	Belly	M60 Chiefs Spl.	38 Spl.	fix.	2	100.00	stainless steel
S&W	Belly	B'guard	38 Spl.	fix.	2	78.50 up	airweight, $79.00 up
S&W	Belly	C'tennial	38 Spl.	fix.	2	82.50 up	airweight, $88.00 up
S&W	Small	Reg. Police	32 & 38 S&W	fix.	2-3-4	76.50 up	
S&W	Small	Hand Ejec.	32 Long	fix.	2-3-4	76.50 up	
S&W	Med.	Mil. & Pol.	38 Spl.	fix.	2-4-5-6	76.50 up	2",4"airweight,$79.00 up
S&W	Med.	H. B. M&P	38 Spl.	fix.	4	76.50	heavy barrel
S&W	Med.	Mil. & Pol.	41 Magnum	fix.	4	96.00 up	
S&W	Med.	Combat Mas.	38 Spl.	adj.	2, 4	89.00	
S&W	Med.	Combat Mag.	357 Magnum	adj.	4, 6	132.00	target stocks
S&W	Med.	CF Magnum	22 Magnum	adj.	4, 6, 8⅜	132.00	inserts for 22RF
S&W	Tar.	K-32	32 S&W Long	adj.	6	98.00	
S&W	Tar.	K-38	38 Spl.	adj.	6-8⅜	98.00	S.A. type, $109.00
S&W	Lge.	H'way Patrol	357 Magnum	adj.	4-6	98.00	
S&W	Lge.	357 Magnum	357 Magnum	adj.	3½, 5, 6, 8⅜	143.00	
S&W	Lge.	41, 44 Mag.	41, 44 Mag.	adj.	4-6-8⅜	165.00	target grade
S&W	Lge.	1955 Target	45 Auto	adj.	6½	126.50	

CHECK CHART OF U.S. CENTERFIRE AUTOLOADERS

Make	Type	Calibers	Sights	Barrel	Price	Notes
AUTOLOADERS						
Browning	Mil.	9mm	fix.	4⅝	104.50 up	13-shot clip
S&W	Mil.	9mm	adj.	4	100.00 up	double action
S&W	Tar. 52-1	38 Spl. WC	adj.	5	180.00	new trigger, sear, etc.
Colt	Mil.	45, 38, 9mm	fix.	4¼	115.50	Commander
Colt	Mil.	45, 38	fix.	5	115.50	
Colt N.M.	Tar.	45, 38 Spl.	adj.	5	175.00	Gold Cup 45, 38

New Beretta Pistol

Beretta's latest target pistol is the moderately-priced Model 76, a new handgun that functions and performs well.

by RAYMOND CARANTA

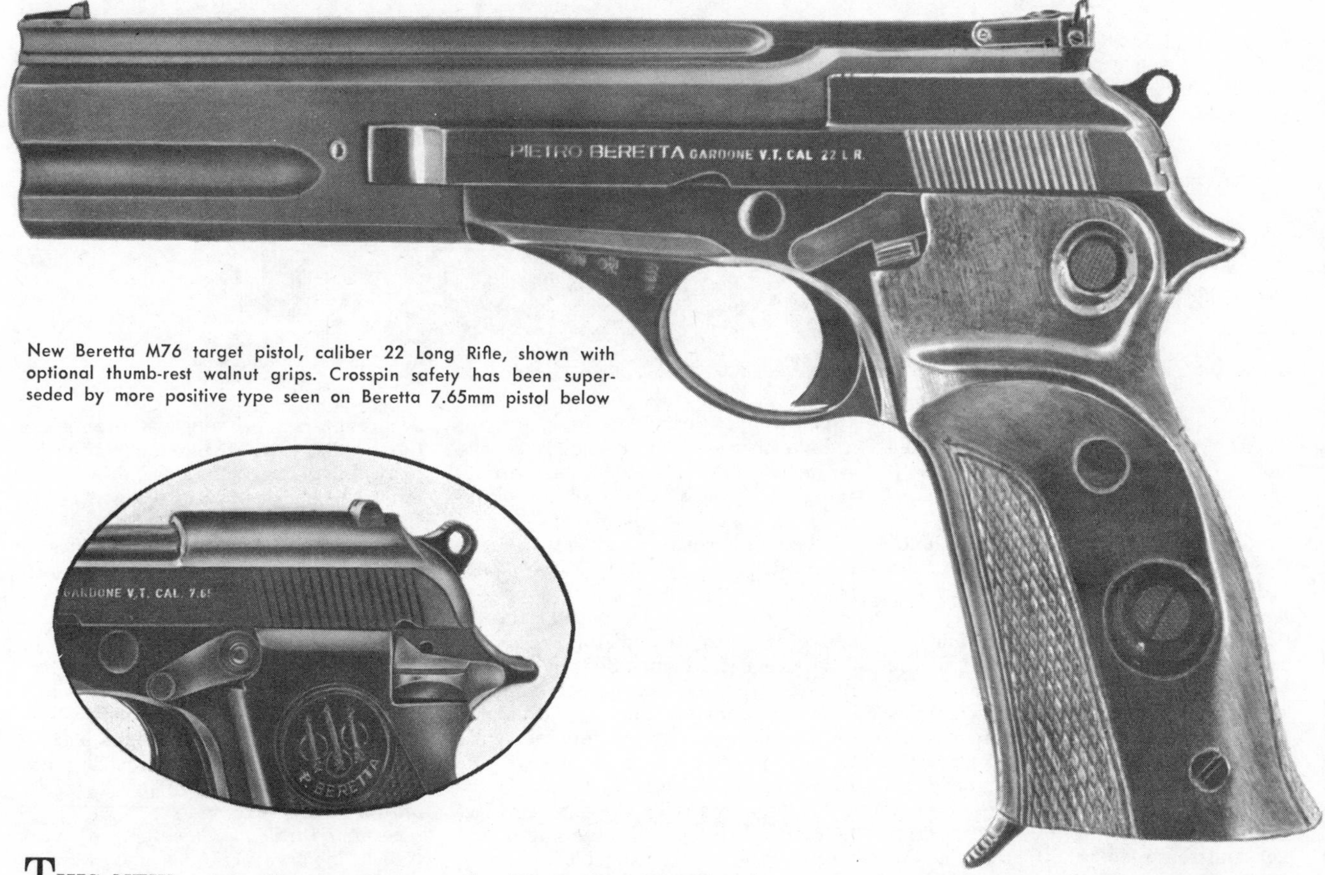

New Beretta M76 target pistol, caliber 22 Long Rifle, shown with optional thumb-rest walnut grips. Crosspin safety has been superseded by more positive type seen on Beretta 7.65mm pistol below

THIS NEW autoloading target pistol was introduced in October, 1968 (Galef & Son, importers for the U.S.) for general target use and, principally, for the "Standard Pistol" class of shooting as set up by the International Shooting Union during their meeting of September 21, 1967, at Bologna (Italy).

According to these new regulations of the ISU, to which the NRA is affiliated, this competition is very similar to the U.S. small-bore pistol program. It consists of firing (at 25 meters or 82 feet) four 5-shot strings in 2½ minutes, four 5-shot strings in 20 seconds, then four 5-shot strings in 10 seconds at the international free pistol target, which has a 50mm (1.97″) 10-ring. This match will be mandatory for the world championships.

The guns used shall conform to the "Centerfire Pistol" rules except for caliber, which will be 22 Long Rifle only.

ISU Requirements

Caliber	22 LR
Barrel length, max. (chamber included)	150 mm (5.9″)
Sight radius, max.	220 mm (8.66″)
Grip thickness, max.	50 mm (1.97″)
Trigger pull, min.	1 kg (35.27 oz)

M76 Specifications

Caliber	22 LR
Barrel length	5.9″
Sighting radius	6.8″
Grip thickness:	
wood stocks	1.57″
plastic stocks	1.18″
Trigger pull	38-48 oz
Weight, empty	33 oz
Length over-all	9.2″
Height	5.6″
Mag. capacity	10

The Beretta M76 is not intended to compete with the best pistols of that category, such as the High-Standard Trophy and Citation, the Smith & Wesson M41, the Hammerli M208 or the Browning Medalist. It is, rather, a medium-priced handgun specifically designed for beginners and for those who cannot afford the more expensive models.

This external-hammer Beretta is based on the conventional blow-back action of the time-proven Model 71, known in the U.S. as the "Jaguar." It is provided with a barrel sleeve, an all-steel receiver, interchangeable front sights and a rib-mounted adjustable rear sight.

The standard plastic stock version is quite handsome in its all-blue appearance, and the general barrel outline is not unlike that of the Colt Woodsman Match target. However, for serious target work, the optional thumb-rest stock, made of checkered French walnut, should be selected. Beside helping the shooter to master the gun, which is decidedly muzzle-heavy, the wood stock improves the looks. The M76 is too slab-sided in the standard configuration.

The Beretta M76 consists of four main components:

The *receiver* with two-piece wrap-around stocks, the *magazine*, the *slide* with its recoil spring and recoil-spring guide, and the *barrel-sleeve* assembly.

Field stripping is performed thus:

Remove the magazine by pressing the magazine catch in the left-hand stock. Clear the chamber if required.

Draw the slide to the rear until the notch on the right side lines up with the top of the latch marked *Smontaggio* on the receiver.

Rock the latch forward while holding the slide.

Draw the slide-barrel assembly forward, off the receiver.

Remove the recoil spring and its guide. Separate the slide from the barrel.

Receiver The steel receiver carries a conventional single action lock, originally fitted with a small set-screw for trigger pull adjustment, down to about 45 oz. Now, because of very close manufacturing tolerances, trigger pull is factory adjusted in the 38-48 oz. range for use with standard velocity ammunition.

The hammer safety notch has been omitted so as to improve the letoff and to avoid possible interference. On the sample pictured with this article (delivered at the end of 1968 in Italy) the cross-bolt safety was de-activated. A positive Colt-Browning swinging safety lever will be substituted for it on the export models to be delivered in 1969. (The 32 ACP Beretta pistol pictured is fitted with such a safety.)

Anyway, this problem is purely academic for a target arm provided with a slide stop and an external hammer.

Magazine The single row 10-shot magazine features a plastic follower with a stud acting as an aid for loading and a light alloy extension bottom plate, typical of the Beretta line of handguns. Proper alignment of the cartridge rims is easily checked through the slots of the spot-welded magazine rear wall.

Slide The steel slide is fitted with a floating firing pin and a rocking extractor located at the rear. The bolt recess is protected by a step projecting around the breech so as to blow powder particles forward at the instant of firing.

Barrel The 5.9″ carbon steel barrel has 6 grooves with a 13.78″ right-hand pitch. It is fastened to the receiver for one inch and is firmly locked in place by the knurled dismounting latch marked *Smontaggio* (disassembly). The barrel is housed in a Zamak (light alloy) fluted sleeve, acting as a balance weight for the 10-second stage; two flats are machined on both sides, and there's an integral glare-proof rib carrying the sights.

The gun has a removable 1/8″ square front sight as standard. Two spare front sights, 1/10″ and 5/64″ wide, and a multi-purpose tool are part of the kit delivered with the pistol.

The rear sight, installed on the barrel sleeve extension, has micrometer elevation control, and is adjustable for windage by alternately screwing two side screws in and out, in the Browning Challenger fashion.

Two specimens of the first production run of this pistol, plus one of the second type (with fixed trigger pull), were tested at our shooting range.

Reliability was perfect with all handguns in the firing of 1000 rounds each of standard velocity RWS and Winchester Leader cartridges. With low velocity ammunition, such as the Fiocchi (Italian) CarBeretta, the power available to operate the slide is only marginal, and the gun is apt to jam when dirty. No testing was carried out with ultra-high velocity cartridges since this pistol is intended only for target practice. However, the fixed-trigger-pull sample performed well with the Fiocchi "Ultrasonic" ammo.

Using standard velocity ammunition, the Beretta M76 groups easily in the 10-ring (1.97″) at 82 feet from a bench rest. According to the Beretta engineering department, all guns are test fired for .55″-.74″ groups at that range.

The removable barrel assembly should not become loose during normal operation since, in addition to its conventional breech attachment, the lower section of the sleeve bears against the receiver's front surface.

When tested under actual match conditions, all of the three Beretta samples had trigger pulls cleaner than that of most Browning Medalist pistols, but not as crisp as that of a good High Standard or of a typical Smith & Wesson M41.

Shooting this gun with both styles of stocks led to the following conclusions:

The plastic stocks are too flat for a target arm, bringing on premature fatigue because of the gun's muzzle-heavy aspects. Moreover, they are much too arched and (contrary to Browning's grips, which suffer from the reverse defect), they produce a finger position suitable only for such short-handed people as youngsters or women.

The wood stocks correct most of these faults by being fatter, and are a must for shooters wanting to take full advantage of this pistol. The thumb-rest position is perhaps a little low, at least for my hand. A palm shelf, a la the Margolin pistol, would improve the grip.

Summed-up, it may be said that this M76 Beretta is a very accurate and dependable automatic pistol, capable of taking a good bite of the popular target pistol market—if the prices are kept reasonable! ●

Galef has the M76 available—or at least catalogued—the GCA '68 permitting! Galef calls the M76 the "New Sable," and the retail price is $87.

Galef also lists for 1969 three other new pistols, or at least new treatment of previous models. One is the "New Jaguar," in 22 LR (on which the M76 is based) while the others are the "New Puma" and "New Cougar," in 32- and 380 Auto caliber respectively.

All show the streamlined trigger-guard treatment seen on the M76 pictured here, and all four in Galef's line have 2-piece wrap-around and checkered plastic grips.

Prices run from $69.95 to $87 for the centerfire Berettas. (J.T.A.)

M76 rear sight windage screw has Nylon insert to prevent loosening. Small screw is micrometer elevation control.

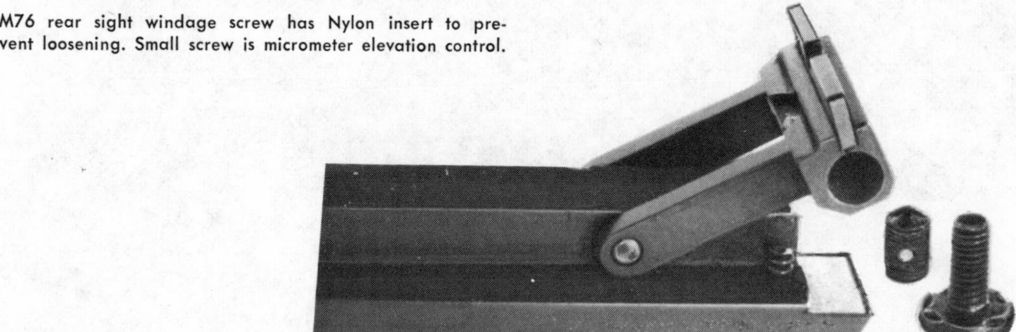

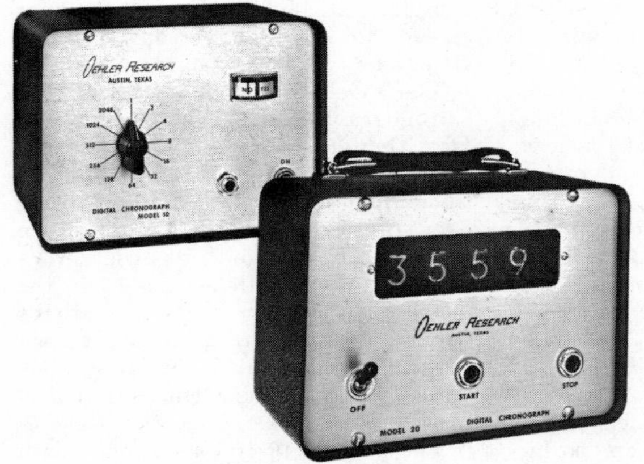

Oehler Model 10 (left) and new Model 20

NEW CHRONOGRAPHS NEW PHOTO-EYE BULLET SCREENS

by JOHN T. AMBER

Tired of jumping up to change your chronograph screens? Want to shoot faster, speed things up? The tools are here—at a price!

New Oehler Chronographs and Photoelectric Screens

The ballistic chronograph offered to the amateur has come a long way since our first article on them appeared in the Gun Digest (14th ed., by Edward M. Yard). Complete reliability was hardly a strong point with the earliest chronographs, and a further trouble often met was faulty or erratic readings. Those early decade counter tools were usually constructed with vacuum tubes in their make-up, so they were subject to "microphonics;" muzzle blast, high noise levels and other jarrings brought about aberrant and unreliable readings.

Progress was made, of course, and the serious firearms researcher has been able to buy chronographs in recent years that offer excellent reliability, portability and long life within a wide price range. Some dozen machines can be had today, from a low of about $60 to well over $500.

Until quite recently all of these chronographs used break-type screens—wire, foil tape, printed-path paper or plastic. These work perfectly satisfactorily of course—rarely is a dud screen found nowadays. There's no denying, however, that it is something of a chore using such means of recording a shot, especially if a lot of chronographing is to be done—place the pair of screens in their holders, go back to the bench, sit down and shoot, then get up and remove the shot-up screens and start all over again!

Now, however, there's an easier way—far easier—at least for those who can afford the new photoelectric-eye systems recently announced.

Late in 1968 Dr. Kenneth L. Oehler made available his latest development, the Model 50 Photoelectric Screens. These professional quality screens are intended for use with the Oehler new Model 20 chronograph.

Dr. Oehler offers these new photo-eye screens in two forms: the ready-to-go units are made of reinforced plywood, black vinyl covered, exterior dimensions 19"x19"x6" deep. Lumiline lamps are housed at the top, inside, of course, while the electronics are at the interior bottom. The shooting opening is 12"x12". Setting up takes only a few moments—insert the separate 120-volt AC 3-wire plug into a mating receptacle, connect the Model 20 chronograph to the screens, then throw the switches to On.

No adjustments of any kind are needed, and the screens are usable under any light conditions from bright sunlight to darkness. Fluctuations in the prevailing light will not accidentally trigger the screens, either, which is a big and important advance over earlier types. The Potter professional screens were subject to this.

The Model 50 units can be had in kit form at $219, complete except for the plywood housings, while the fully assembled Model 50 screens sell for $299 FOB Austin, Texas.

The new Oehler chronograph, his Model 20, is a true digital, crystal-controlled unit giving a direct reading in miscroseconds, to four places. Two forms of the Model 20 instrument are available; one with a 400,000 cycle oscillator, the other with 1,000,000 cycles per second.

As our illustration shows, the Model 20 chronograph presents a compact, highly portable machine, gratifyingly simple in appearance—and equally simple to use. (If the Model 20 is used with paper screens, velocity checking can be done anywhere, inasmuch as its power source, a 12-volt lantern battery, attaches directly to the back of the instrument.) One moves the one toggle switch—there's no other control of any kind—from Off to On, and the Model 20 is ready to go to work. Such convenience and ease of operation demands a toll, understandably—the Model 20 is about 4 times the cost of Dr. Oehler's earlier chronograph, the Model 10, about which more later.

The Model 20 uses solid state (silicon/integrated) circuits for trouble-free operation, and a voltage regulator is employed to insure that uniform voltage is supplied to the critical timing-counting system despite battery weakening. Some 400 shots can be fired before the battery fails if the operative switch is turned off between shots.

I asked Dr. Oehler to send us a trial Model 20 with the 1,000,000 cycle crystal rather than the 40,000 cycle unit because I wanted to experiment with an ultra-short screen separation. We've got a new barn here at Creedmoor Farm, erected mainly to do test shooting indoors in bad weather and I wanted to place a chronographing layout in as short a length over-all as could be managed. Many other chronographs have 100,000 cycle oscillators, their makers suggesting a 10-foot screen separation. With the 1,000,000 cycle Oehler, I figured, I should be able to get equivalent accuracy with one foot between screens.

Dr. Oehler disagreed, pointing out that there were other factors present that could—and would—prevent attaining high accuracy if I used the short screen distance mentioned. First, there'd be the difficulty in maintaining an exact one foot interval between screens, for a 1/16-inch error at one foot is more serious than a half-inch discrepancy at 10 feet. Second, the Lumiline tubes used in the Oehler Model 50 photoelectric screens (and used in others) do not have filaments (single wire) tautly stretched in a straight line. They describe, rather, a wavy or curved path, thus unless each shot through the screens is made at exactly the same place, some error will occur. Last, if the first screen were placed rather close to the muzzle (as would be the case in our barn), muzzle blast and/or bullet shock-wave could contribute to erroneous readings.

All quite true, of course, but generally not insurmountable, and I wasn't, in any case, all that interested—or convinced—that *absolute* accuracy is needed. I think that most of us are concerned with *comparative* accuracy. We can't possibly hope to observe on our chronograph the same muzzle velocity figures printed in factory tables—we're not using the same barrels or necessarily the same ammo used by the factory. Checking factory cartridges is a small part of chronographing anyway; handloads are our chief interest, and the main interest of this chronographer, at least, is to put together loads as uniform as possible, thus potentially, at least, accurate loads. This is where the chronograph offers help, clear evidence of good workmanship. In other words, I'm not usually concerned with velocity *per se,* nor ordinarily with maximum speeds. I don't care if my chronograph figures show 2950, for example, or 3025, but rather that each shot sent down range has the same velocity as those before it and after—the ultimate goal—or as nearly so as I can achieve.

Getting back to valid arguments offered by Dr. Oehler, I think I can say that I licked 'em! I made a pine box, very carefully dimensioned, that holds the Oehler M50 photoelectric screens exactly one foot apart — or my fine steel tape lies — using wedge blocks to tension them in that position. Then, to obviate point 2 above (the Lumiline tube problem) I arranged bench, cradled sand bags, screens and a target to insure I'd be shooting through the screens at exactly the same location with every shot.

Because 22 Long Rifle ammo is made to give long-standard velocities, several brands were tried in our all-too-brief tests. Fresh Super-X HS loads were shot first. Low reading was 1208 fps at the 5-feet-from-muzzle distance, high was 1250, average 1232. This is well below advertised MV for the load (1365), but our shooting was with a Winchester M-141 bolt action, its barrel 20¾ inches long. I think these figures speak for themselves, for I've never got much better uniformity with any high speed 22s. Next, 10 rounds of Herter's 22 LR HS were used in the same rifle for an 1158 average, setup exactly as before. Then, moving the screens farther away to avoid blast (first screen at 7½ feet), 10 rounds of 100-gr. 6mm loads were sent over the electric sensors. Except for one shot, results were again respectably uniform—9 averaged 2765, the one shot showing 2840. These were shot in a M600 Remington, its barrel of 18-plus inches being 8 inches or so shorter than factory test barrels often are. Finally, Jerry Zwick put six of his last 264 Magnum loads through the screens—53.5 of Du Pont 4320/120-gr. Speer bullets—using my Winchester 264 with 20-inch featherweight barrel. These 6 shots gave excellent uniformity, with the fastest shot reading 3076, the slowest 3058; average 3067. Again low for the load, and Jerry said he used to get about 3200 in his 24-inch barreled Browning 264, now with a 270 barrel.

That ended the session with the new Oehler equipment, and I'll only add that I can't fault it in any way. Its simplicity and rapidity of operating is a real pleasure, and the only trouble I had (which the Oehler manual warns about) was caused by my not inserting the first screen jack firmly. The signal for this is a jumble of digits when the switch is moved to On instead of the row of 4 big bright zeros normally seen.

Price of the Oehler M20 is $375 complete, including all cables, paper screen holders, 100 screens, full instructions, velocity tables, etc.

The Oehler Model 10 Digital Chronograph, mentioned earlier, was Dr. Oehler's first offering in this field, and it's an excellent value at the $91.95 price. Its maximum error—guaranteed—with a 5-foot screen spacing ranges from 2 fps at low MVs to a maximum of less than 15 in the 4,000 foot second area—and that's with a ⅛-inch error in the screen separation. The same low-error guarantee holds for the Oehler Model 20 instrument also.

The Model 10 is usable only with printed screens unless ordered with a pair of the new Oehler M50 screens (or, a Model 10 can be returned to the factory for such modification when the photo-eye screens are bought).

The Model 10 is a compact unit, only 8"x5"x4", and the power source is 3 D-size batteries. With its 400,000 cycle crystal, it handles MVs from 500 to 5,000 fps when a 5-foot screen spacing is used. Solid state components are used throughout.

Operation of the Model 10 differs from the Model 20 Oehler chronograph, the former using a switching system coupled with a "Yes-No" indicator. The switch is rotated after the shot through 12 positions—1, 2, 4, 8, 16 and so on to 2048—and the "Yes" figures are put down in succession and added up to arrive at the microsecond readout. Reference then to the Model 10 manual reveals the velocity in foot seconds of the shot just made.

A little time-consuming, certainly, compared to reading off microseconds directly, as with the Oehler Model 20 and others, but it is a reliable system, and the price is right!

To speed things up a bit, and to avoid having to write down the "Yes" figures on each shot, I set up the 12 figure sets in a column, then check them off as indicated—it works well.

New Avtron Products

T973 Chronograph

Dwain Fritz produced the first commercial digital chronograph of popular price some 10 years ago—and his Avtron instruments have been at the top of the heap ever since. True, they've been getting some real competition in recent years, but Avtron chronographs are still the standard of comparison throughout the country.

Now, for the man who wants a reliable, well-built chronograph at a price well under the $350-$520 range of the Avtron Models T333A and T333C, Fritz has available a brand new machine, the Model T973.

The T973 is a true digital-counter instrument, featuring a 100,000 cycle

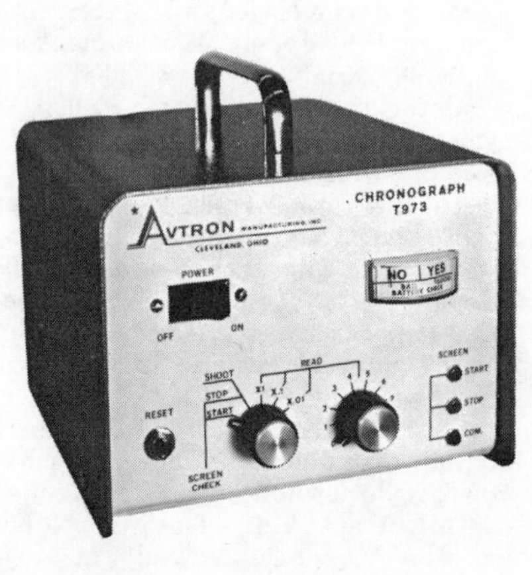

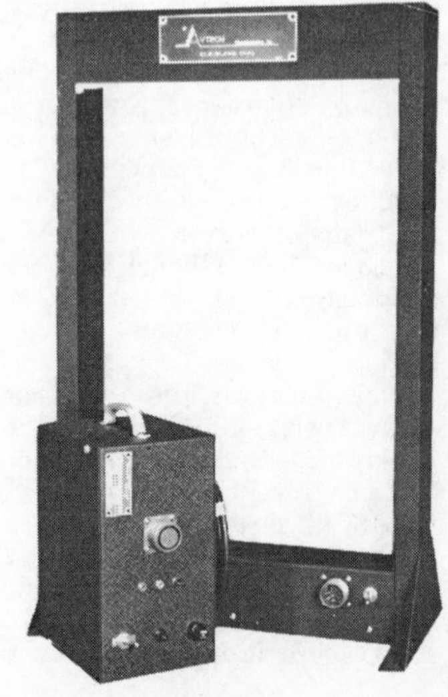

crystal-controlled oscillator, with accuracy guaranteed to 0.00001-second plus or minus. All circuits are solid-state components.

The new T973 differs from the other—and more costly Avtrons—in not having a direct readout in microseconds. Instead that left hand knob you see pictured is turned to X for the first decimal place, and with it in that position, the right-hand knob is rotated from 0 to 9. At some one figure—and only one—a single numeral will get the "Yes" or "No" signal from the dial at top right. These steps are then repeated through knob positions X^1 and X^2, rotating the right-side knob at each stage. This done, you now have a set of three figures, these in microseconds, standing for the time it took your bullet to pass through the screens. The Owner's Manual contains a conversion table, and it's a moment's work to read off the answer in foot seconds of velocity.

Actually, this knob twisting is faster than it sounds, as we found out in operating the test T973 Dwain Fritz sent to us. There's no requirement to set down a group of figures, to be added up for the elapsed time, as there is with some other chronographs.

Power for the T973 is a 6-volt lantern battery, contained within the chronograph housing, so the new unit is completely portable. There is no provision for 110-volt AC operation.

Printed screens are used, these the same aluminum-on-clear plastic supplied with the other Avtron units. Battery drain is very low, and the instrument is compensated to eliminate errors that might otherwise occur with temperature fluctuations.

It took only a few minutes to set up the T973, our screen-holders being permanently mounted, and there wasn't the slightest bit of trouble, even when the rifle's muzzle was fairly close to the chronograph. Such freedom from dud readings didn't use to be the case, by the way. In the days when tubes were used, microphonics was a not-infrequent problem, and 100% reliability was seldom attained.

The T973 is furnished with battery, 100 screens, two screen holders (improved type) and cables for $159. While it isn't as fast-operating as the more expensive Avtron, it's fully as accurate and just as reliable as the other two.

Photo Eye Screens

At about the same time as the T973 chronograph was announced, Dwain Fritz told us during a phone talk that he had a set of new photo-eye screens ready, these for use with his Avtron T333A and T333C instruments.

This was big news for me because Dwain and I had discussed just such an offering by his company many times. I had pointed out a marked disadvantage in the design of the old Potter professional-use screens, suggesting that Fritz ought to eliminate this hazard if he ever decided to produce photo-eye chronograph screens.

Sitting atop the Avtron T333A chronograph (on bench at left) is the sturdy metal housing that contains the major electronic circuitry for the new photo-eye screens (left background) now offered by Avtron in two sizes. Hookup is simple, fast. At right is the new Avtron digital chronograph, Model T973, offering highest accuracy at the comparatively low price of $159. The K101 Electronic Screen system sells for $400 complete, the great convenience and saving in time and energy justifying the extra cost for many users.

The undesirable aspect of the Potter screen—and perhaps of others as well—had to do with the proximity of the electronic components to the line of fire. In the Potter screen a metal box is located immediately below the apex of the inverted V that forms the Potter configuration. This box (on both screens, of course) contains the vital components of the system—and it's an easy trick to get a shot right through one or both boxes! Exactly that has happened, too, including one such accident in a large bullet plant on the first day they'd installed the Potters.

The new K100 and K101 electronic screens by Avtron completely eliminate that problem. There's a sturdy metal box, all right, but in this system it's tethered to a long cable that permits siting the box well away from the screens themselves. There is only one box, too, and it's connected to the screen by a twin-lead cable through Amphenol pin-jacks (look at the photograph of the Avtron units set up on my outdoor bench for a clearer idea of how they're interconnected).

The new Avtron electric screens must have an AC power source for their operation because 110-volt Lumiline tubes are used for exciters, but they can be used with the Avtron T333A or T333C chronographs whether these are battery or AC operated.

The new K-series electronic screens are completely solid-state constructed, with special circuits and optical filters installed to prevent accidental triggering by muzzle blast and flash—a well-recognized bugaboo with several other systems. Fritz tells me that they have tested, during the extensive development period, extremely small calibers and big ones as large as 40mm, and that "Even the muzzle flash from a 25mm cannon in a dark room will not cause false triggering." Well, I'm not about to touch off any ordnance that big, but that's a pretty impressive statement!

The K101 screen set has a sensitive area of 170 square inches, which should be ample for the amateur ballistician, while the K100—intended for professional use—offers 213 square inches. In both the sensitive area is in the form of a keystone; in our sample K101 the useful screen dimension at the bottom is some 4-5 inches wide, and about 15 inches across at the top.

This quite big area was, of course, easy to use, with little or no danger of shooting too close to the photo-eye tubes. In the photograph you'll see that the K101 screens are positioned on top of our 20-foot chronograph framework, but that was a temporary setup.

When permanently fixed in place, by means of the extension plates at each side, the top of the lower cross-member will lie below the level of the 2 by 6 planks, thus affording full protection for the photo-eyes.

Shooting tests with the K101 screens went very smoothly—no miscues at all. To test their ability to withstand muzzle blast and flash, I shot my 22-inch barreled 264 with the muzzle only one foot from the first screen. I got perfectly normal readings on the 10 trials I made.

Good, solid quality, these Avtron screens, and I think this demonstrated insensitivity to muzzle disturbance is an important step forward. For those who can afford the $400 price tag, they're a great convenience, a great time saver—and they work.

A History of

This is the third installment of the new and fully up-to-date series "History of Proof Marks" initiated in our 22nd edition. The author, Mr. Lee Kennett, is highly qualified to have undertaken the definitive research required, and we feel certain his comprehensive and detailed work will prove reliable, interesting, instructive and valuable.

While Mr. Kennett used the framework of the late Baron Engelhardt's "The Story of European Proof Marks" as a structural guide, he personally visited and talked with Proof House officials in many countries in his research. He will continue to do so until all nations in the survey have been covered. When that time arrives, we will publish the complete book.

With this issue we present "Proof Marks in France." The completed and published book will carry a full account of the origins and historical back ground of proof marks.

FRANCE
Origins to 1810

THE CITY OF SAINT-ETIENNE was both one of the earliest and one of the most important arms centers in France; it remains today as the chief seat of arms production. A long tradition credits King Francis I (1515-1547) with starting the serious manufacture of firearms there in 1535. If a similar legend is to be believed, the water at Saint-Etienne possessed mysterious qualities which helped to temper the iron. Unfortunately, records for the 16th century are rare, and it is not until the following century that Saint-Etienne's arms production can be documented. The town's artisans did a particularly lively business supplying the armies of Louis XIV at the end of the 17th century. By 1665 the King had named a royal official to accept delivery and to verify the quality of the arms.

The origins of proof in Saint-Etienne are equally sketchy. According to Gras, gunmakers for the civilian market did their own proving, or delegated one of their number to do it. The proof charge was usually triple the normal one.[1] The practice was well established by 1700. In that year an important change occurred. The Count of Verdun, acting for the royal government, insisted that all civilian barrels be submitted to proof by royal controllers who proved military arms. Moreover the heavier military proof was administered, requiring a powder charge equal in weight to the ball. Although no law expressly required this, the Count brought pressure to bear on local gunmakers through his power to grant or refuse licenses required to export arms from the town. The gunmakers gave in, but not without strong objections. They argued with some justice that military proof was too strong for the lighter civilian barrels; moreover they argued that the government proof mark was not respected or even known: "No one has confidence in the Saint-Etienne proof mark," said one of their petitions.[2] In truth, the governmental proof marks changed frequently, probably being designed to suit the fancy of each successive government controller. The marks which date from this period are many; they usually contain the controller's initials, in conjunction with a fleur-de-lis, a crown, or crossed palms, part of the Saint-Etienne coat of arms.[3]

From 1700 to 1782 the gunmakers waged a seesaw battle with the crown over rules of proof. In 1726 compulsory government proof for sporting arms was abolished, only to be restored in 1741. Violations were undoubtedly frequent, for gunmakers were reminded of the regulations in 1746 and 1751. A more stringent reminder appeared in

Proof Marks

Gun Proof in France

by Lee Kennett

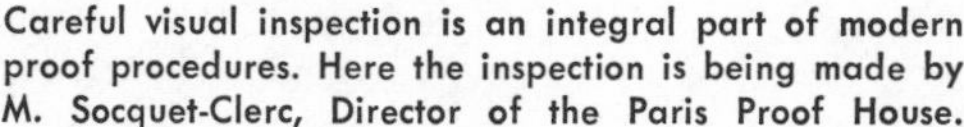

Careful visual inspection is an integral part of modern proof procedures. Here the inspection is being made by M. Socquet-Clerc, Director of the Paris Proof House.

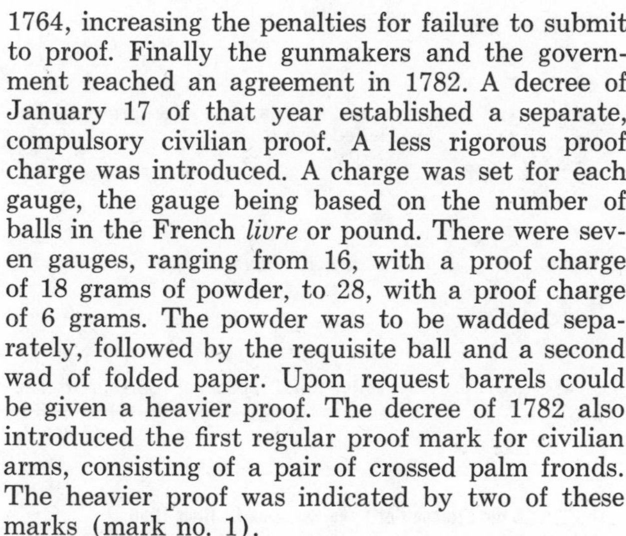

1764, increasing the penalties for failure to submit to proof. Finally the gunmakers and the government reached an agreement in 1782. A decree of January 17 of that year established a separate, compulsory civilian proof. A less rigorous proof charge was introduced. A charge was set for each gauge, the gauge being based on the number of balls in the French *livre* or pound. There were seven gauges, ranging from 16, with a proof charge of 18 grams of powder, to 28, with a proof charge of 6 grams. The powder was to be wadded separately, followed by the requisite ball and a second wad of folded paper. Upon request barrels could be given a heavier proof. The decree of 1782 also introduced the first regular proof mark for civilian arms, consisting of a pair of crossed palm fronds. The heavier proof was indicated by two of these marks (mark no. 1).

Saint-Etienne had been using its new proof system for only seven years when the French Revolution broke out. The strife and confusion which followed ruined for a time the sporting gun trade. Indeed, the Revolutionary government, at war with most of Europe, banned production of civilian arms in 1792 and turned Saint-Etienne into a vast arsenal.[4] The law of 1782 had become a dead letter. When civilian production began again in the mid 1790s, the gunmakers did their own proving, firing their guns in alleys or even out of open windows; the town fathers replied to this dangerous practice by banning the discharge of any firearm in the city. A solution was reached in 1797, when proof was reestablished under the 1782 rules.

1810-1868

Napoleon brought order to the proof system, as he did to almost every other aspect of French life. His decree of 14 December, 1810, followed the 1782 rules in several matters, but the Napoleonic decree was much more detailed. It even specified the diameter of the proofmaster's ramrod, and the exact size of the wads — a paper 8cm square for the larger calibers and 5cm square for smaller ones. Rationally, proof was according to a scale of calibers or gauges. But the new gauges were unusual in that they were based on the number of balls per kilogram. Thus 32 gauge in this system approximated our 12 gauge. The scale was as follows:

Kilogram gauge	Normal gauge	Powder (grams)
32	12	20
36	14	18
40	16	17
44	18	16
48	20	15
52	22	14
56	24	13

Larger pistols were proved by the pair, with the

A shotgun mounted in the firing cradle ready for definitive proof. The gun is fired from an adjacent room by means of the long cord attached to the trigger. The cradle is lined with foam rubber to prevent damage to the gun's finish.

French Proof Marks 1782-1969

In this table the mark numbers at left are those assigned by the author, and keyed by him to the text for reference. The 2nd column shows the true form of the proof mark and gives the period of its use. The last column tells of the marks' significance.

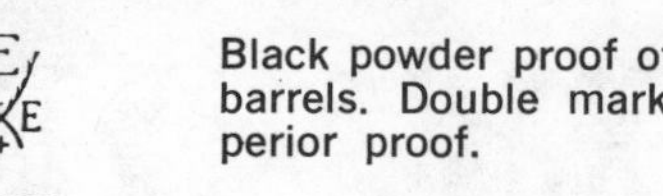

1	1782-1811	Proof of barrels at St.-Etienne (double marks for superior proof).
2	S E 1811-1824	Same as above.
3	1811-?	Same as above, at Charleville.
4	1811-?	Same as above, at Souilhac.
5	1824-1856	Replaced mark no. 2.
6	1856-1869	Replaced mark no. 5.
7	1862-1885	Commercial reproof of reworked surplus military arms.
8	E S E 1869-1879	Black powder proof of semi-finished barrels. Double marks indicate superior proof.
9	ST ETIENNE 1879-	Same as above, Since 1924 proof pressure at 14,200 psi.
10	ST ETIENNE 1879-	Superior black powder proof of semi-finished barrels. Since 1924 at 16,500 psi and called double proof.
11	A F 1879-1897	Same as no. 9, but for arms made elsewhere in France than at St.-Etienne.
12	A E 1879-1924?	Same as no. 9, but for foreign-made arms. (Goddard shows a variant without the oval).
13	E F 1886-1893	Black powder proof of finished arms.
14	E.F 1893-1897	Same as above.
15	Es F circa 1893	Superior black powder proof of finished arms.
16	S E.F 1894-1897	Same as above.
17	1892-1962	Provisional proof of barrels in the rough, at 16,500 psi. after 1924.

Saint-Etienne (left) and Paris marks from 1896

18	1897-1962	Provisional proof of barrels in the rough at Paris, at 16,500 psi. after 1924. St.-Etienne equivalent is mark no. 17.
19	EP 1897-	Black powder proof of semi-finished barrels at Paris, at 14,200 psi. since 1924. St.-Etienne equivalent is mark no. 9.

20 — 1897-

Superior black powder proof of semi-finished barrels at Paris, at 16,500 psi. after 1924 and known as double proof. St.-Etienne equivalent is no. 10.

21 — F — 1897-

Black powder proof of finished arms. See text for pressures.

22 — S — 1897-1962

Superior black powder proof of finished arms (smoothbores) at 11,400 psi. after 1924.

23 — ST ETIENNE — 1897-

Proof in finished state of pistols, revolvers, and sub-caliber long arms. See text for details.

24 — NA — 1901-

Supplementary mark for unjoined barrels. Used with marks 9, 10, 19, 20, 25 and 26.

25 — 1901-

Double proof (black powder) of semi-finished barrels at 20,500 psi. until 1924. Presently called triple proof at 18,000 psi.

26 — 1901-1924

Triple black powder proof of semi-finished barrels at 27,000 psi.

27 — PJ PJ — 1896-1914

Definitive proof with smokeless powder "J."

28 — PS PS — 1896-1914

Definitive proof with smokeless powder "S."

29 — PM PM — 1898-1914

Definitive proof with smokeless powder "M."

30 — PR PR — 1898-1914

Definitive proof with smokeless powder "R."

31 — PT PT — 1900-

Definitive proof with smokeless powder "T."

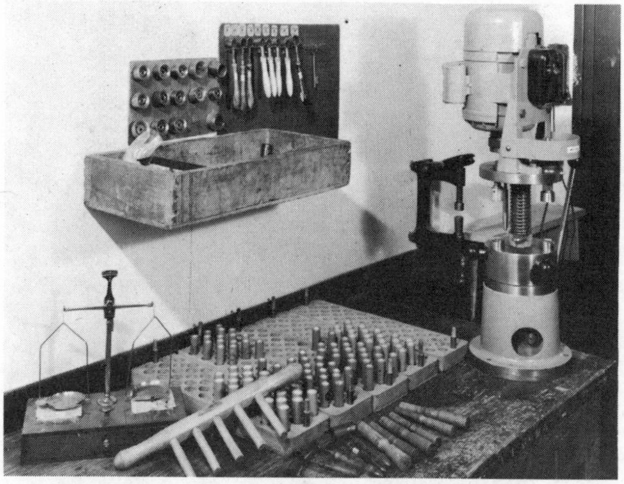

A proof house loading room. Proof cartridges prepared here are frequently checked for pressure by means of the pressure gun.

32 — PT PT — 1924-

Superior definitive proof with powder "T." See text for pressures.

33 — AR ST ETIENNE — AR — 1924-

Definitive proof of rifled shoulder arms at 30% excess pressure.

34 — NORMAL — 1924-1962

Supplementary mark to designate a shotgun with 65mm chamber length.

35 — 1924-

Supplementary mark for definitive proof in completely finished state.

36 — ARME ETRANGERE — AR.ETR — 1924-

Supplementary mark for foreign arms submitted to proof. Not used at St.-Etienne since 1962.

37 — R R — 1960-

Black powder reproof.

38 — R — P.T. R — 1960-

Smokeless powder reproof.

39 — P. T. R — 1960-

Superior smokeless powder reproof at Paris.

NOTE: Those periods not showing a closing year indicate continuing use of the mark indicated, up to the time of publication of this book.

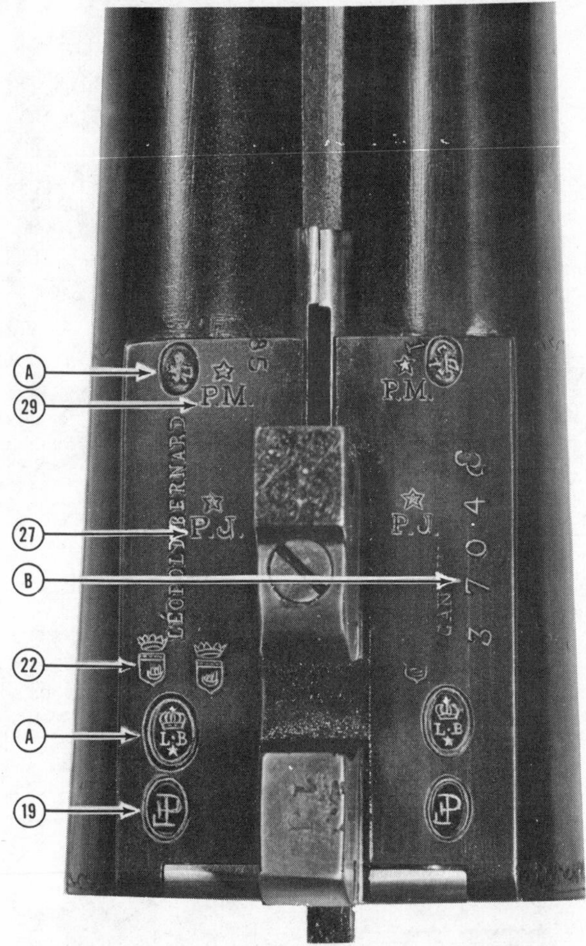

French shotgun proved at Paris in the period 1897-1914. The marks tell an interesting story. Made c. 1880 by Leopold Bernard of Paris and proved by him, using private proof marks (A). Its owner must have been a stickler for safety, as he sent it to the Paris proof house for four separate proofs. (B) Indicates gun's serial number. Refer to text for explanation of numbers shown.

proof charge divided between them. Thus a pair of 44-ga. pistols were proved with 8 grams of powder each. Pocket pistols were proved with 4 grams. All proofs were to be made with wadding over the powder, followed by a lead ball of requisite size and a second wad. Incidentally, the decree reinforced a law of 1799 banning civilian guns of service caliber, then 17.7mm, or within two millimeters of that caliber. This provision, a curious example of restrictive firearms legislation, is still retained in France today.

The decree followed its predecessor in providing for an optional superior proof designated by double proof marks. Superior proof for a 32-ga. barrel was the ordinary proof charge for 44 gauge, superior proof in 36 gauge consisted of the ordinary proof for 48 gauge, etc., these added to the standard proof charge for the gauge. Any barrel failing proof was returned to its maker, who could rework it and submit it again. If it failed a second time, the proofmaster was to break it before returning it.

In the matter of proof marks, Napoleon's law authorized a proof house with distinctive marks in each arms center, and permitted the use of the town's coat of arms for this purpose, though it appears that only Saint-Etienne, Charleville and Souillac devised such marks (nos. 2, 3, and 4). Marks were to be placed at the breech so as to be clearly visible. Barrels were also to be stamped with their caliber at the time of proof, and it was illegal to enlarge the caliber subsequently. This measure was designed to end a practice, common in the 18th century, of submitting barrels to the heavy military proof and then reaming them out afterwards, lightening the gun but reducing the safety margin.

Napoleon's decree remained in force long after his downfall; indeed, it survived, with some modification, until 1868. The proof mark underwent several minor changes. In 1824 a crown was added, probably symbolic of the restoration of the monarchy in 1814 (fig. no. 5). In 1856 the proof house passed under the control of the Saint-Etienne Chamber of Commerce, and the proof mark was enclosed in an oval (fig. no. 6). In 1862 a proof mark was introduced for the proof of reworked military surplus arms (fig. no. 7). By the mid-19th century gunmakers desired more profound changes in the old law. According to Ronchard-Siauve, writing in 1864, the proof charges were excessive. The proof table did not cover many gauges subsequently introduced, so that the proofmasters were obliged to make these up. Finally, the kilogram gauge system had never caught on outside of France. Foreign purchasers were confused by the gauge designations, to the detriment of the French gun trade.[5]

On June 19, 1865, new proof regulations were issued, but instead of being an improvement, they were even worse from the gunmaker's point of view. The proof charges were heavier than before; so high, in fact, that 85 per cent of the barrels submitted failed to pass. The only valuable feature of the new legislation seems to have been a provision granting free entry to foreign arms bearing official proof marks. In any event, the gunmaking trade petitioned, apparently with success, to have the 1865 regulations set aside and to continue under the 1810 system until another law could be drafted. The new law appeared in 1868.

1868-1897

The decree of 22 April, 1868, retained obligatory proof, but overhauled completely the proof charges and bore designations. The Saint-Etienne arms industry had requested a separate proof of finished arms, or definitive proof, but the new regulations only introduced a double proof system for rifled barrels, to be tested before and after rifling. Smoothbores were still submitted to a single proof, administered to the barrel in a rather advanced state of manufacture — completed except for breeching, polishing, and bluing. The proof tables were among the most elaborate ever devised. No longer would the proofmaster be obliged to invent charges for odd calibers. Both smoothbore and rifle tables are given for bore diameters graduated in 2/10mm steps. Table B, for rifled arms, provided 140 separate sets of proof charges, for arms ranging in bore diameter from 9mm to 37mm. Table C, for smoothbores, provided 215 charges for bore diameters from 10.6mm to 53.6mm. This latter diameter — something over two inches — was proved with a half-pound of black powder and five pounds of shot!

The tables, which are far too long to be reproduced here in their entirety, may be found in Polain's *Recherches historiques*, (1891 ed.), pp. 351-358. See Tables B and C for illustrative selections.

Table B — Proof Loads for Rifled Barrels

Caliber in mm	Proof Charge — Grams 1st proof	2nd proof	Diam./Wgt. of Lead Ball mm	grams
9	7.0	4.5	8.5	27.5
10	8.5	6.0	9.5	36.0
11	10.0	6.5	10.5	44.0
12	10.5	7.0	11.5	46.0
13	10.5	7.0	12.5	46.0
14	10.5	7.0	13.5	46.0
15	11.0	7.0	14.5	47.5
20	17.5	12.0	19.5	98.5
25	35.5	23.5	24.5	196.0
30	61.5	41.0	29.5	344.5
35	100.0	66.5	34.5	550.0
37	118.0	78.5	36.5	660.0

Table C — Proof Loads for Shot Barrels

Gauge Nominal	mm	Proof Charges — Grams Powder	Soft #8 Shot
410	10.6	6.0	20.0
32	12.8	7.0	30.0
28	14.0	7.5	35.0
24	14.8	8.0	40.0
20	15.6	8.5	45.0
16	16.8	9.0	50.0
14	17.6	10.0	60.0
12	18.6	11.0	70.0
10	19.6	12.5	85.0
8	21.2	14.0	100.0
4	23.8	20.5	165.0
1 in.	25.4	23.0	190.0
2 in.	50.8	174.0	1700.0
2.2 in.	55.4	218.0	2140.0

Some other features of proof according to the 1868 rules are as follows: Smoothbores of bore diameter of less than 10.6mm were all proved with 3 grams of powder and 20.8 grams of shot. Smoothbore pistols of 10.6mm and less underwent this same proof. In the event that their barrels were too short to contain the charge, they were filled to half their length with powder and the remainder with shot, a wad being placed just inside the muzzle. Pistols with bores of from 10.6mm to 11.4mm, and with barrels under 15cm in length, took a proof charge equal to half of that in Table C. Pistols with a bore diameter of over 11.4mm and/or a barrel length of over 15cm underwent proof as prescribed in Table C. Revolvers were proved once in each chamber, but only with the service load, which seems a curious weakness in an otherwise stringent law. Another feature of the 1868 rules was the inclusion of a table of charges for military muskets, whose manufacture by private enterprise had been permitted in 1860. Finally, the law retained an optional superior proof of smoothbore barrels. The

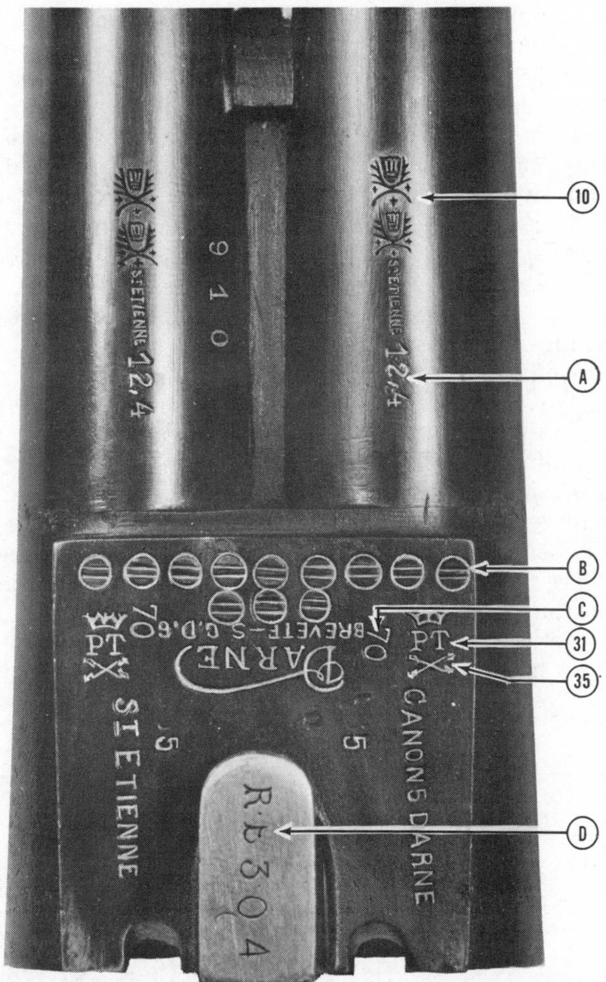

Darne shotgun of recent manufacture, proved at Saint Etienne. (A) Shows 12.4mm bore diameter. (B) Darne quality stamps; twelve stamps indicate highest quality made except for special order. (C) Chamber length — 70mm. (D) May be gun's serial number. Refer to text for explanation of numbers shown.

superior proof charge contained 50% more powder than that in Table C. As before, this proof was indicated by double proof marks.

It was thought advisable to introduce a new proof mark to reflect the new changes in proof. This was introduced sometime in 1869 (fig. no. 8). In 1879 this mark was abolished, to be replaced by three new ones. One mark contained the palms of Saint-Etienne, a mural crown and the words "St.-Etienne" (fig. nos. 9 and 10), and was reserved for the products made in that locality. The letters A. F., signifying *arme française*, placed in an oval with palms, formed a new mark for arms of other cities in France proved at Saint-Etienne (fig. no. 11). A third mark, composed of palms and the letters "A. E." (*arme étrangère*) in an oval was used for foreign guns (fig. no. 12). Any of these marks stamped twice signified superior proof.

On August 5, 1885, the French parliament passed a law designed to give the arms industry greater freedom to manufacture military arms. The law was badly worded, and a subsequent ruling in 1889 held that the law had abolished compulsory proof of civilian firearms entirely. Although there were many protests, particularly from gunmakers, the government decided in 1895 that proof was official but *voluntary*, a situation that continued for the next 65 years. The results of this accidental end of obligatory proof were actually not very serious, as arms manufacturers generally continued to submit guns to proof. Small caliber rifles, very small bore shotguns, Flobert-type arms and small caliber pistols sometimes were not submitted, and so may not bear proof marks. Finally, one ambitious producer of arms ran his own proof house for a few years. As a general rule, however, any gun generating relatively high pressures was officially proved.

The 1868 law had required only proof of barrels of shotguns and rifles, though in advanced state of manufacture. To supplement this proof — obviously inadequate with breechloaders — a true definitive proof was introduced by a decree of 2 December 1885, put into effect early in 1886. The charges were among the first to be set with the aid of the pressure gun, and were supposed to yield something in the neighborhood of 14,000 psi. The new proof was for shotguns only; some of the charges were as follows:

Gauge	Chamber Length (mm)	Powder (grams) Strong Black #2	Shot (grams) No. 8
20	65	4.50	30
16	65	5.75	31
16	75	5.50	50
12	65	6.75	42
12	70	6.50	55

The proof mark for this proof was the letters "EF" (fig. no. 13). In 1893 the mark was changed slightly (fig. no. 14). The two letters represent the words *épreuve* (proof) and *fini* (finished).

A superior definitive proof followed in 1893, probably to meet the higher pressures of early smokeless powder shotshells then coming into use. This proof was supposed to generate pressures of about 16,000 psi, though the figure is open to doubt, given the problems of accurate pressure readings on the early pressure guns. This pressure was thought to be about 40 per cent in excess of normal operating pressures. Some representative charges are as follows:

Gauge	Chamber Length (mm)	Powder (grams) extra fine black	Shot (grams) No. 8
20	65	6.50	29
16	65	6.50	30
16	75	7.50	40
12	65	7.00	39
12	70	8.75	36

The proof mark was composed of the letters "EF," to which was added an "S" to designate superior proof. There are two variants, of which the first (fig. no. 15) was probably a makeshift used in 1893. By 1894, the second (fig. no. 16) became standard.

In 1892 still another proof was devised to meet the demands of gunmakers for a preliminary proof of barrels *en jambes*, or in the rough, hitherto lacking in the French system. Representative loads for this proof were as follows:

Gauge	Powder (grams) Strong black #2	Shot (grams) No. 8
20	9	50
16	10	60
12	11	70

The proof mark assigned for this proof was a mural crown (fig. no. 17).

So far, we have mentioned proof only at Saint-Etienne. There were of course other arms centers, notably Paris. Did they have proof houses? The answer seems to be that they did not. Most 19th century writers on the subject say quite explicitly that Saint-Etienne had the only proof house. Mangeot, writing in 1856, says that barrels were being

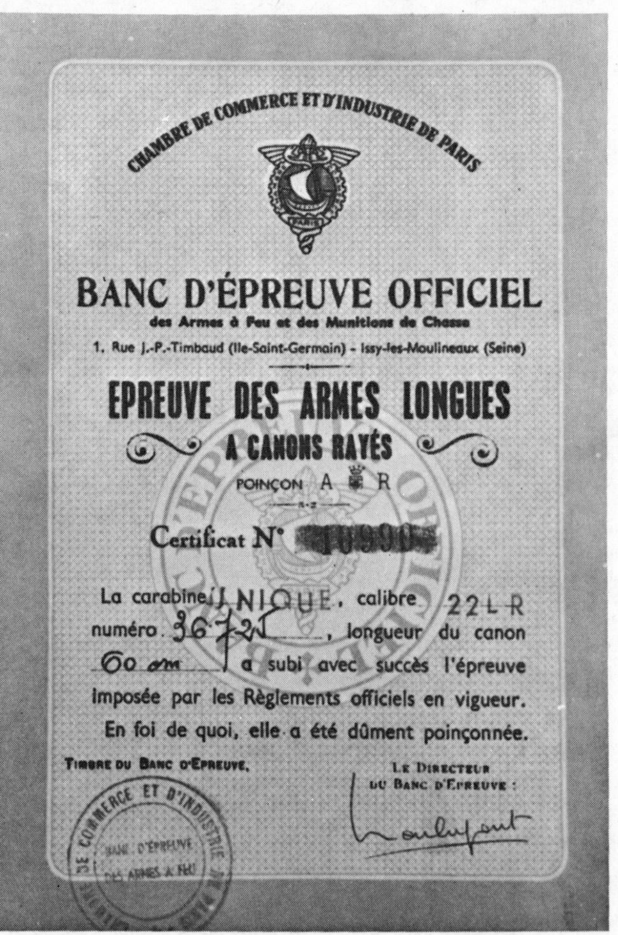
CHAMBRE DE COMMERCE ET D'INDUSTRIE DE PARIS

BANC D'ÉPREUVE OFFICIEL

des Armes à Feu et des Munitions de Chasse

1, Rue J.-P.-Timbaud (Ile-Saint-Germain) - Issy-les-Moulineaux (Seine)

EPREUVE DES ARMES LONGUES

A CANONS RAYÉS

POINÇON A R

Certificat N° [illegible]

La carabine UNIQUE, calibre 22 L R numéro [illegible], longueur du canon 60 cm a subi avec succès l'épreuve imposée par les Règlements officiels en vigueur.

En foi de quoi, elle a été dûment poinçonnée.

TIMBRE DU BANC D'EPREUVE.

LE DIRECTEUR DU BANC D'EPREUVE :

Proof certificate indicating proof at Paris of a 22-cal. rifle.

made in Tulle, Paris, and Chatellerault, but adds: "Only Saint-Etienne possesses a mark of guarantee for its sporting barrels; the barrelmakers of other localities simply put on their barrels a private mark, reserved for their own use." He goes on to say that Paris gunmakers proved on the purchaser's request, their marks being their own initials, in most cases within an oval and accompanied by a crown or a pair of palms.[6] From all of this the logical conclusion is that whatever the law said, proof was compulsory only at Saint-Etienne. That the government was aware of this situation is clear. A directive of 11 August, 1865, ordered arms manufacturers and dealers to take their unproved arms to the local bureau of weights and measures, where they would simply be stamped with the letter "M," in lieu of proof.[7] It was not until 1895 that Paris gunmakers set to work to establish a proof house there, which opened in 1897.

The law of 7 November, 1895, which authorized the establishment of a proof house in Paris, also afforded an opportunity to overhaul once more the much amended rules of 1868. As early as 1892 the Saint-Etienne Chamber of Commerce had created a commission to examine the question. Its report, completed in 1894, was adopted in the new series of rules issued by the Paris and Saint-Etienne houses on 30 July, 1897. The 1868 proof tables for smoothbore barrels were revised in order to lessen charges for bores of 16.6mm and under, judged to be excessive. Thus the proof load in 28 gauge dropped from 7.5 grams of strong black powder #2 and 35 grams of shot to 5 grams and 32 grams respectively. All arms of "small dimensions" were now to be proved in finished state. Pistols of below 11.4mm bore diameter were proved with 2 grams of black powder and 10 of lead; those of larger bore with 3 grams and 20 grams respectively. Revolvers were tested with the service ball loaded in front of sufficient black powder to extend cartridge length to that of the cylinder. The most important changes, however, were in the proof marks. Paris devised a set for its new proof house, while several of the Saint-Etienne marks were changed. Paris adopted a pair of script "Ps" to signify proof of rough barrels (fig. no. 18), an "EP" monogram within an oval (fig. no. 19) for proof of nearly finished barrels, and the same mark twice for superior proof of this type (fig. no. 20). The Saint-Etienne marks for these proofs were unchanged (fig. nos. 9, 10 and 17). Both houses devised new marks for ordinary and superior proof of finished arms. Saint-Etienne used an "F" surmounted by a crown for ordinary proof and Paris used the city coat of arms (fig. no. 21). For superior proof Saint-Etienne introduced a crowned "S" and Paris applied the coat of arms twice (fig. no. 22).

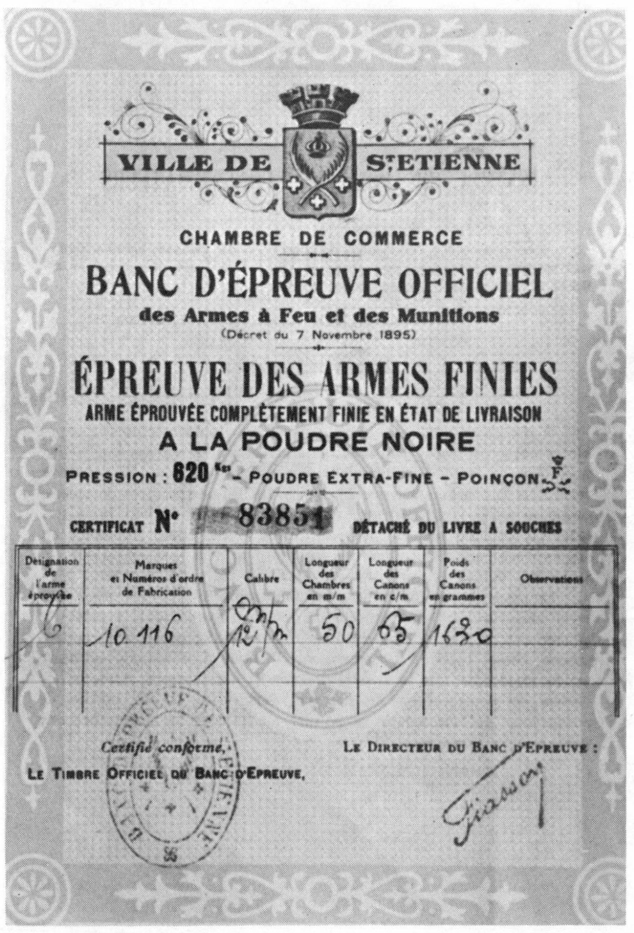

VILLE DE ST ETIENNE

CHAMBRE DE COMMERCE

BANC D'ÉPREUVE OFFICIEL

des Armes à Feu et des Munitions

(Décret du 7 Novembre 1895)

ÉPREUVE DES ARMES FINIES

ARME ÉPROUVÉE COMPLÈTEMENT FINIE EN ÉTAT DE LIVRAISON

A LA POUDRE NOIRE

PRESSION : 620 kgs – POUDRE EXTRA-FINE – POINÇON

CERTIFICAT N° 83851 DÉTACHÉ DU LIVRE A SOUCHES

Désignation de l'arme éprouvée	Marques et Numéros d'ordre de Fabrication	Calibre	Longueur des Chambres en m/m	Longueur des Canons en c/m	Poids des Canons en grammes	Observations
6	10 116	9m/m	50	65	1620	

Certifié conforme,
LE TIMBRE OFFICIEL DU BANC D'EPREUVE,

LE DIRECTEUR DU BANC D'EPREUVE :

Saint Etienne proof certificate for a black powder proved 9mm shotgun.

For proof of small bore arms, pistols and revolvers, Paris employed its coat of arms depicting proof of finished arms, while Saint-Etienne used the mural crown followed by the words "St.-Etienne." Both of these were in reduced format (fig. no. 23).

In 1901 three more marks were introduced. The first of these consisted of the letters "N.A.," signifying *non assemblé* or not assembled, to be added to the customary proof mark for finished barrels when these had not yet been joined. A second innovation, and a very confusing one, was the introduction of a "double" and a "triple" proof for finished barrels, to supplement the ordinary and superior proofs already in existence. The ordinary proof was rated in 1900 at 14,200 psi, and the superior at 16,500 psi. The new proofs were much higher. Double proof, indicated by triple marks (fig. no. 25), attained 20,500 psi. Triple proof, which was designated by four marks (fig. no. 26), was rated at 27,000 psi.

So far, all proof charges we have mentioned are with black powder; indeed, the superior proof of finished arms, designed to meet the increased pressures of early smokeless loads, was done with black powder. Since powder production in this country was, and still is, a monopoly of the French government, and the varieties developed were few, the proof houses developed a smokeless proof load for each powder as it was introduced. These were Powder J (and its derivatives, J^1 and J^2) and Powder S in 1896, Powders M, R, and S^2 in 1898, and Powder T in 1900 (fig. nos. 27-31). These represent proofs administered to the finished gun, and they varied considerably in their pressures. Very often the proof charge was stamped on the gun in addition to the proof mark; the practice was more common in Saint-Etienne than in Paris. The basic problem with most of the powders was that pressures were insufficient to meet the 12,000 psi minimum set by the Brussels Convention. As a result, all but Powder T were dropped as proof powders in 1914, though several continued to be available commercially.[8] Powder T is the only one of these early smokeless propellants still being manufactured, and is still by far the most widely used in France today.

Rules of 1928

France was obliged to change her proof system in order to conform to the Brussels Convention; the new rules, known often as the rules of 1928, were initiated by decrees of 18 December, 1923 and 4 June, 1926. Most of the new rules were actually being applied in both proof houses by 1924. The most notable change occurred in provisional proof of finished barrels. Triple proof was abolished; double proof was revised. Neither of these, with their extremely high pressures, had served a very useful purpose. Of the thousands of barrels proved at Saint-Etienne in 1923, only 54 had been given double proof and only 24 triple proof.[9] Considerable confusion arises from the fact that in 1924 the old superior proof (fig. nos. 10 and 20) became double proof, keeping the same marks and pressures. The previous double proof (fig. no. 25) now became triple proof, but with pressures dropped from 20,500 psi to 18,000 psi. About the only clear conclusion that can be drawn from this is that a gun bearing the four marks of triple proof was proved between 1901 and 1924, and is made of a very rare piece of steel indeed.

The 1924 rules retained the proof and marks for barrels in the rough, rated at 16,500 psi. Standard black powder proof of finished shotguns was set at 8,800 psi, and superior black powder proof at 11,400 psi. Marks were not changed. In addition to smokeless proof with Powder T (12,000 psi) a superior proof was offered (fig. no. 32) at 15,600 psi. Rifles and handguns were proved with 30 per cent excess pressure loads, and new marks were introduced for rifles, containing the letters "A.R.," for *arme rayée* or rifled arm (fig. no. 33).

Shotguns were stamped with chamber size and length in millimeters, or with the enclosed word "NORMAL," which signified a shotgun with chambers 65mm long (fig. no. 34). Finally, two sets of supplementary marks were introduced: one designated arms submitted to definitive proof in completely finished state and ready for delivery (fig. no. 35); the other set was used to designate *arme étrangère*, or foreign guns (fig. no. 36).

Present Proof Regulations

Proof in France is today governed by the decree of 12 January, 1960, and by the internal regulations of each proof house drawn up in conformity with it. The most recent Saint-Etienne rules are those dated June, 1962; current Paris rules, virtually identical in wording, were drawn up in June, 1964. The most striking change in the 1962 law is the reestablishment of compulsory proof for all civilian firearms. While there are still only two proof houses, they both operate branches in various arms centers, though the proof practices and marks are identical with those of the parent installations. A synopsis of the present regulations is as follows:

Category I: Long or Short Barreled Smoothbores. These must have one of three proofs: black powder proof, ordinary smokeless proof or superior smokeless proof (note that smokeless proof is not obligatory). Two proof cartridges are fired in each barrel; in case of superior smokeless proof, the first cartridge is that for ordinary smokeless proof. Pressure requirements, which are more elaborate than previously, are as follows:

	Chamber length (mm)	Pressure (psi)
Black powder proof	65	8,800
	70	9,200
	75	9,600
Ordinary smokeless proof	65	12,000
	70	12,800
	75	13,500
Superior smokeless proof	65	15,500
	70	17,000
	75	17,000

All arms must be finished, but may be "in the white." Arms completely finished receive the supplementary mark indicating this (fig. no. 35).

All arms are carefully inspected upon reception, and may be refused proof if found defective. If the barrel already bears the mark for optional provisional proof of finished barrels, its caliber must be at least equal to that marked on the barrel at time of provisional proof. Chamber length and chamber and bore diameters must fall within the limits established by the Permanent International Commission on Firearms. After these verifications, each barrel is stamped with chamber length in millimeters, and bore diameter in millimeters and tenths of millimeters. Arms are inspected again after proof. Those judged to have passed are stamped with the requisite mark (fig. nos. 21, 31 or 32) on barrels and breech. A certificate of proof is delivered with each gun, identifying it by factory number and indicating proof type and pressure.

Category II: Long or Short Barreled Rifled Arms. These are proved with two ball cartridges in each barrel, or in the case of revolvers, in each chamber. Proof pressures must be at least 15 per cent in excess of those of maximum commercial loads. For salon type, small caliber arms, the proof cartridge is to be loaded with enough extra fine black powder to obtain the requisite 15 per cent excess pressure when loaded behind the service ball. As with smoothbores, inspection precedes and follows proof. Arms are stamped with marks 23 or 33. Caliber is stamped if it does not already appear.

Category III: Optional Provisional Proof of Barrels. These must bear the mark of the maker, and be in a sufficiently finished state that "their completion after proof will not compromise their solidity, not chambered but with barrel walls polished and dry." After preliminary inspection, bores are calibrated at a point from 15 to 50 centimeters from the breech. Diameter is stamped on the barrel in millimeters and tenths of millimeters. In their subsequent finishing operations, gunmakers may not enlarge the bore diameter by more than 0.2mm. In consequence, on instructions from the maker, barrels may be stamped 0.1mm or 0.2mm larger than they measure, to account for this subsequent enlargement. Barrels may be submitted to one or more of three separate proofs, all of which are made with fine black powder, No. 8 shot and linen paper wads.

Ordinary proof is at 14,200 psi, double proof at 16,500 psi, and triple proof at 18,000 psi. They are then stamped with marks 9, 10, 19, 20 or 25, and with mark 24 if unassembled. Gunmakers may also request higher proofs. In this case the proof charge is indicated on a certificate of proof, but no special mark is used.

Category IV: Reproof of Arms. All imported arms fall into this category, save those from signatory nations of the Brussels Convention and Great Britain. For arms of unusual caliber, proof charges are left to the discretion of the proof master. Guns which have undergone alteration sufficient to compromise their safety must be reproved. Any shotgun whose bore diameter is enlarged by 0.2mm or whose chamber is lengthened by 5mm or more, or whose barrel has been lightened by 6 per cent of its weight must be reproved.

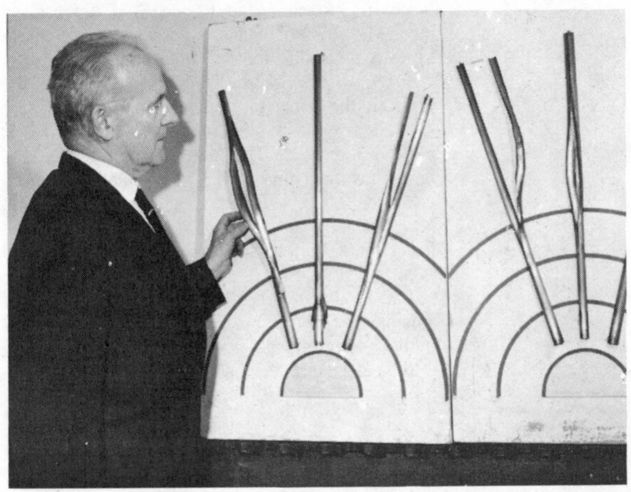

Though such split barrels as these are now less common in European proof houses, they are eloquent testimony of the value of proof.

To indicate reproof five new marks have been devised, all incorporating the letter "R," signifying *rééprouvée* or reproved. Both houses offer a black powder reproof (fig. no. 37) and a smokeless reproof (fig. no. 38). In addition, Paris offers a superior smokeless reproof (fig. no. 39).

The 1960 legislation created no other proof marks. On the other hand, it has dropped certain marks and proofs. Most notable of these was the proof for barrels in the rough. In actual fact, Paris has not proved any of these in a good many years, the barrel making trade having disappeared there. The superior black powder proof of finished shotguns has been dropped, along with its marks. Saint-Etienne no longer applies a special mark to designate foreign guns, though Paris has retained it. One final note on present proof is the substitution of "bars" for kilograms per square centimeter, in expressing pressure. Thus the certificate of proof for a shotgun with 70mm chambers will show proof pressure of ordinary smokeless proof as 900 bars, rather than 900 kg/cm^2. The result is, of course, a slight increase in proof pressure, the bar being equal to 1.02 kg/cm^2. This change was made in 1965.

References

1. J.-L. Gras, *Historique de l'armurerie stéphanoise* (history of the arms trade in Saint-Etienne), St.-Etienne, France, 1905, p. 52.
2. *Ibid.*, p. 34.
3. For these early marks see Stockel, *Haandskydevaabens Bedommelse,* I, 192-193; II, 427-437. For the names of gunprovers before 1782, see Gras, *Historique,* p. 175, who reproduces two lists which are not in complete agreement.
4. Yearly production of military muskets varied from 10,000 to 26,000 before the Revolution. By 1805 production was 45,000 and by 1810 it reached 97,000. These figures make it clear that by Napoleon's time Saint-Etienne had become the unquestioned leader in arms production. Marcel Arbogast, *L'Industrie des armes à Saint-Etienne* (The arms industry in Saint-Etienne), St.-Etienne, 1937, pp. 56-58.
5. According to the same author, the proof charge in 32 gauge (our 12 gauge) was *seven* times the normal hunting charge. M. Ronchard-Siauve, *Traité des canons de fusils* (Treatise on gun barrels), St.-Etienne, 1864, pp. 66ff.
6. H. Mangeot, *Traité du fusil de chasse et des armes de précision* (Treatise on the shotgun and precision arms), 6th ed., Brussels, 1856, p. 198.
7. Gras, *Historique,* p. 163.
8. Information supplied by M. Fiasson, present Director of the Saint-Etienne Proof House.
9. All of the triple proofs and 94 per cent of the double proofs were administered that year for the famous Darne Company, a fact which the company still cites in its catalog of double barreled guns.

Bibliography

R. Dubessy, *Historique de la manufacture d'armes de guerre de Saint-Etienne* (History of the military arms factory of Saint-Etienne), St.-Etienne, 1900.

J.-L. Gras, *Historique de l'armurerie stéphanoise* (History of the arms trade in Saint-Etienne), St.-Etienne, 1905.

Marcel Arbogast, *L'Industrie des Armes à Saint-Etienne* (The arms industry in St.-Etienne), Saint-Etienne, 1937.

Henri Manceau, *La manufacture d'armes de Charleville* (The Charleville arms factory), Charleville, 1962.

Alphonse Polain, *Recherche Historique sur l'eprouve des armes a feu au pays de Liége* (Historical research on the proof of firearms in Liége), Liége, 1891.

Capitaine Languepin, *Histoire de la manufacture d'armes de Tulle* (History of the Tulle arms factory), Tulle, n.d.

M. Ronchard-Siauve, *Traité des canons de fusil* (Treatise on gun barrels), St.-Etienne, 1864.

Report of the proof commission of the Saint-Etienne chamber of commerce, *Etudes sur la differentes poudres employées, sur la résistance des métaux, et sur les charges à adopter pour les épreuves des armes non reglementaires* (Studies of different powders used, of the resistance of metals, and the charges to employ for the proof of non-military arms), St.-Etienne, 1894.

———, "French Nitro Proofs" in *Arms and Explosives,* London, March, 1894, p. 102.

———, "Gun Proving in France" in *Arms and Explosives,* London, September, 1894, pp. 210-212.

Lee Kennett, "Gun Proving in France" in the *American Rifleman,* Washington, D.C., August, 1965, pp. 24-25.

* * *

The author is indebted to M. Socquet-Clerc, Director of the Paris Proof House, and to M. Fiasson, his counterpart in Saint-Etienne, both of whom were extremely helpful, and to Mr. Sealtiel, Proof Master of the London Proof House, who very kindly put his register of foreign proof marks at the author's disposal.

Gras Model 1874 Rifle

Historical Notes

Artillery captain (later brigadier general), Basile Gras originally designed this rifle as a conversion for that grand-daddy of French militaries, the 1866 Chassepot needle gun, from needle fire to metallic cartridge. His conversion, popularly called "fusil (rifle) Gras" was later adopted as the "Fusil Model 1874." It was also adopted by Greece in 1878.

Although the Gras was not used in a European war, it was the backbone of early French colonial expansion—North Africa and Morocco, the first Dahomey and Madagascar wars, Indo China, and many smaller actions, where it was used by such legendary troops as the Zouaves (pictured), the Foreign Legion, Turcos, etc.

Many of the 1874s were slightly modified in 1880 and will be marked "M 80" on the left side of the receiver. Like the earlier Chassepot, and all French bolt-action militaries since, it does not provide a safety device. The barrel, receiver, bands and band springs were blued; all other parts were left bright. Also issued as a carbine (musketoon), which has a flat, turned-down bolt handle and brass mountings.

An excellent gun in its day, it was faster to operate and more dependable than most of the falling and rotating-block rifles used by most other armies. It fires the 11mm Gras cartridge, which is comparable to our 45-70. However, the cartridges are far more scarce than is the rifle.

Disassembly

Caution! Be sure the rifle is not loaded, then remove the bolt. This may be done by raising bolt handle into its vertical position, then removing bolt stop screw (5). Next squeeze the trigger (6). This compresses the sear and allows the entire bolt to be withdrawn to the rear.

The rest of the rifle is easy to disassemble. Unscrew cleaning rod (29). Unscrew tang screw (18), remove barrel bands (25 and 27), and lift barrel from the stock. The ejector screw (4) may be unscrewed from the receiver floor. Unscrew set-screw (10) from the sear (8), then the sear screw. (Note: some of these old rifles may have the sear screw "frozen" in place. If this is so, it is best to leave it as forcing the screw may break it, and the trigger mechanism is so simple as to be easily cleaned.) Remove trigger guard (20).

To disassemble the bolt, push the bolt head (16) ¼-turn counterclockwise until slot on the firing pin nut (15) aligns with slot on the cocking piece (12). Remove bolt head (16). Twist cocking piece (12) ¼-turn counterclockwise. It will move forward, removing tension from firing pin spring, and rest flush against the bolt. Make sure the slots on the firing pin nut and cocking piece are still aligned. On a block of wood, push bolt (11) and cocking piece (12) down on firing pin (13), until the firing pin nut (15) is completely exposed and can be removed from the firing pin (13). Remove cocking piece (12) to the rear, then the firing pin (13) and firing pin spring (14) forward from the bolt.

The extractor (17) may be removed from the bolt head (16) by pushing up and to the rear until it is unseated. Then it may be pushed forward and out of the bolt head.

Gras Model 1874 Rifle

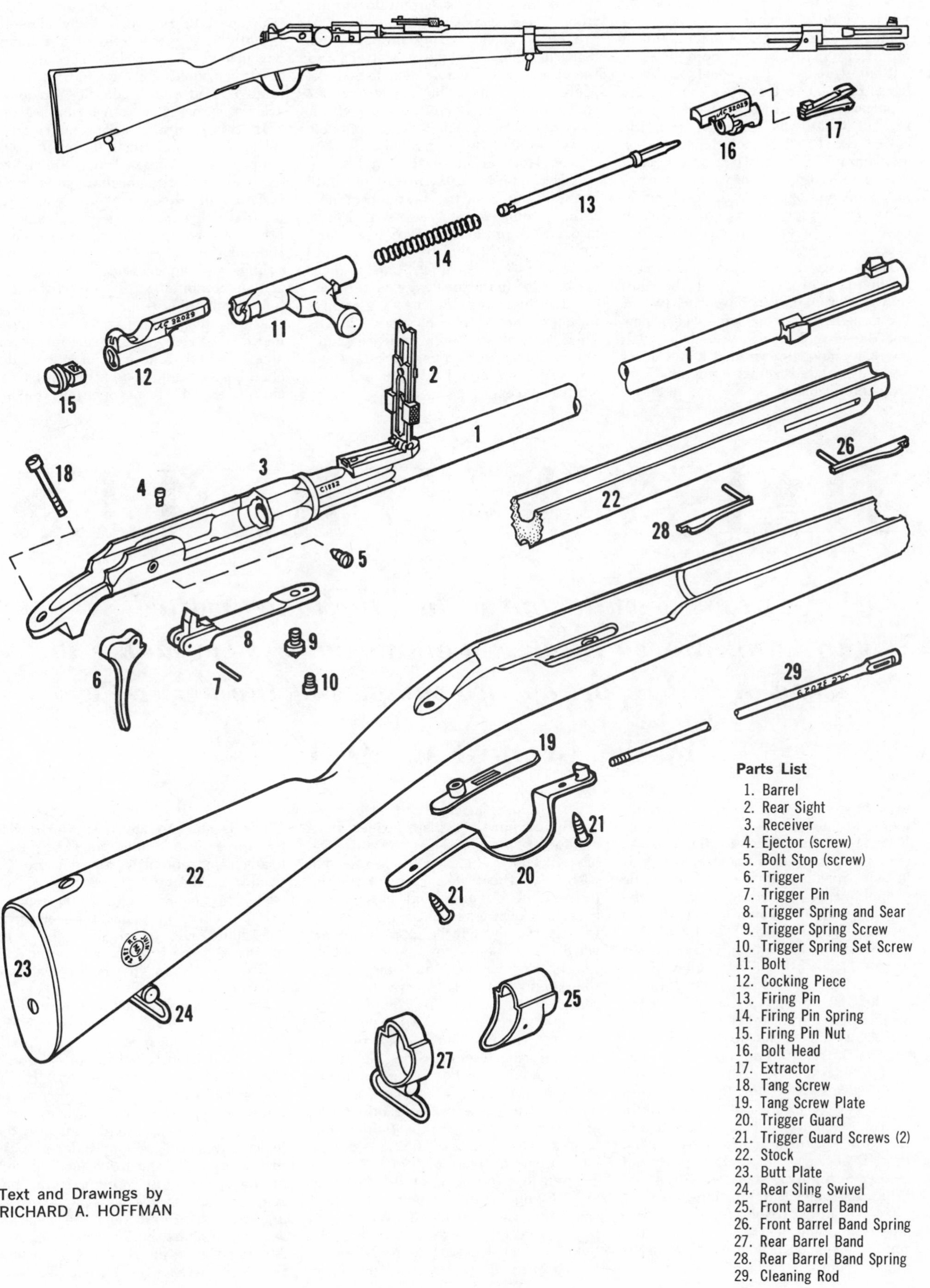

Parts List

1. Barrel
2. Rear Sight
3. Receiver
4. Ejector (screw)
5. Bolt Stop (screw)
6. Trigger
7. Trigger Pin
8. Trigger Spring and Sear
9. Trigger Spring Screw
10. Trigger Spring Set Screw
11. Bolt
12. Cocking Piece
13. Firing Pin
14. Firing Pin Spring
15. Firing Pin Nut
16. Bolt Head
17. Extractor
18. Tang Screw
19. Tang Screw Plate
20. Trigger Guard
21. Trigger Guard Screws (2)
22. Stock
23. Butt Plate
24. Rear Sling Swivel
25. Front Barrel Band
26. Front Barrel Band Spring
27. Rear Barrel Band
28. Rear Barrel Band Spring
29. Cleaning Rod

Text and Drawings by
RICHARD A. HOFFMAN

DAISY V/L RIFLES

It took a while, but at last the long-awaited Van Langerhoven caseless ammunition-system makes the scene. A full report on two samples of the new rifle.

by Maj. GEORGE C. NONTE, JR.

NEARLY FIVE YEARS ago, we received our first information on a new caseless, primerless gun/cartridge shooting system being developed by Daisy/Heddon (now a division of Victor Comptometer Corp.). Initial reports by many writers were glowing, but all were based on brief exposure to a few laboratory test guns, test reports, and various artists' renderings of what was to come from the basic idea. Practical, marketable guns and ammunition that could be bought across the counter were long in coming, long enough after the early publicity that many people had doubts they would ever be generally available.

Both guns and ammunition are now in volume production and distribution is national. We have had two of the guns in hand for some weeks now and have put them through enough paces to have determined a few facts and formulated some opinions.

Ammunition is as shown, a 29-gr. lead bullet (dry-lubricated) virtually identical in form to the common 22 Rimfire Short bullet, to the base of which is attached a short rod of yellowish-white solid propellant. The propellant is formed in place on the bullet, extruded around a teat formed on the bullet base. Weight of the complete round is 30.3 grains (average of 5); length 0.535″; bullet diameter 0.224″; propellant 0.200″ diameter at its rear. Performance is listed as 1150 fps muzzle velocity—in the same range as the high-velocity 22 Short. Daisy prefers not to call the complete round a cartridge, though there seems to be no other term adequately descriptive. It does contain all the elements that must be fed into the gun in order to fire a shot, even though it lacks both the case and primer normally associated with a metallic cartridge. Ammunition boxes are labeled simply "caseless ammunition." The slim, flat carton contains 100 rounds, packed 10 each in translucent plastic tubes.

The rifle, the Model 002, is mechanically identical to conventional lever-actuated spring-air guns. Externally, it resembles a sleek semi-auto rimfire rifle. Lines of both stock and metal are quite good (in my opinion, this being a highly subjective matter) and the rifle weighs a hair over 5 pounds. Metal finish is a blue-gray lacquer that clings well. It *can* be scraped off, but normal abrasion and impacts don't seem to do it much harm. The plastic stock is more than a bit unusual; plastic is pretty much "old hat" by now, but it is the best job of imitating wood we've yet seen. Pores, grain, and random surface irregularities are faithfully reproduced, and even the feel is much like that of wood. The main giveaway is the lack of variations in color that are always found in wood. The moulded shell is filled with plastic foam to give rigidity and weight and carries black fore-end tip, grip cap and buttplate, all with white spacers.

Functioning is just like that of most spring-air guns. A piston rides in a cylinder behind and in line with the barrel. The cylinder itself is movable within the sheet steel receiver for the purpose of opening and closing the breech. Cocking is accomplished by forcing the cylinder and piston rearward together—the latter being caught by the sear and the former then being returned forward after a round is placed in the chamber.

Pressing the trigger disengages the sear and the piston is driven forward by its spring, compressing the air in the cylinder. At the instant of maximum compression, a special ball-type check valve in the cylinder face opens and the compressed air (which has heated to as high as 2000°F.) is directed against the base of the propellant.

The propellant is ignited by the hot air jet and begins to burn like most smokeless type powders, producing a large quantity of gas which pushes the bullet down the barrel. As pressure begins to build up, action of the check valve is reversed by that pressure, sealing the chamber off from the interior of the cylinder. At the same time, the cup-shaped seal forming the front part of the valve body expands radially sealing the rear of the chamber just as the cartridge case does in a conventional gun. From this point onward, internal ballistic functions are the same as in conventional arms.

In this manner, the Daisy/Heddon "V-L System," named after its Belgian inventor, Jules Van Langenhoven, combines the mechanical characteristics of the spring-air gun with the ballistic characteristics of smokeless powder ammunition. At the same time, it eliminates the costly case and primer of the metallic cartridge.

The combination is not without a few disadvantages all its own. First is the fact that at this state of development, only single-shot arms are available. Second, ammunition once fully chambered cannot be extracted by the simple expedient of opening the action as with a metallic cartridge. There is no case rim or similar device by which the round may be withdrawn. Consequently, there is no extractor in the gun. If, perchance, you wish to unload, it can be accomplished only by firing the round in the chamber, or by pushing it out by means of a rod inserted at the muzzle. Neither is always the most convenient thing to do.

Operation of the 002 is quite simple. The cocking lever is housed in the underside of the fore-end when in the stowed position. Hook a finger under the end of the lever and pull it out and rearward until the sear can be felt to engage the piston head and the lever will remain rearward. As the lever moves back, the cylinder is withdrawn, opening the large loading port at the upper right receiver front. The rear of the chamber is clearly visible and a V-L round may be inserted with the fingers, bullet first, of course. Moving the lever back to the stowed position carries the cylinder forward and the seal in its face surrounds the propellant portion of the round and seats it solidly in the chamber. The automatic safety moves to "safe" during cocking and must be shoved forward to disengage before firing. It's very simple and nearly as fast as loading most cartridge single shots.

Report is light; smoke and recoil non-existent for all practical purposes. Accuracy thus far has been on a par with the average rimfire plinking rifle shooting high-velocity 22 Shorts. In firing several hundred rounds we've not yet had a malfunction of any sort. It has become apparent, though, that people who have forgotten how to clean guns will have to learn all over with V-L. Since chamber walls are not protected by a cartridge case, they are exposed directly to the hottest portion of the propellant gases. Consequently, they are scoured totally dry by firing. Subsequent exposure to atmospheric humidity causes fine rust to form fairly rapidly unless the chamber and valve face are wiped with

The author loads the V/L rifle, leaning over to let the underlever clear the ground.

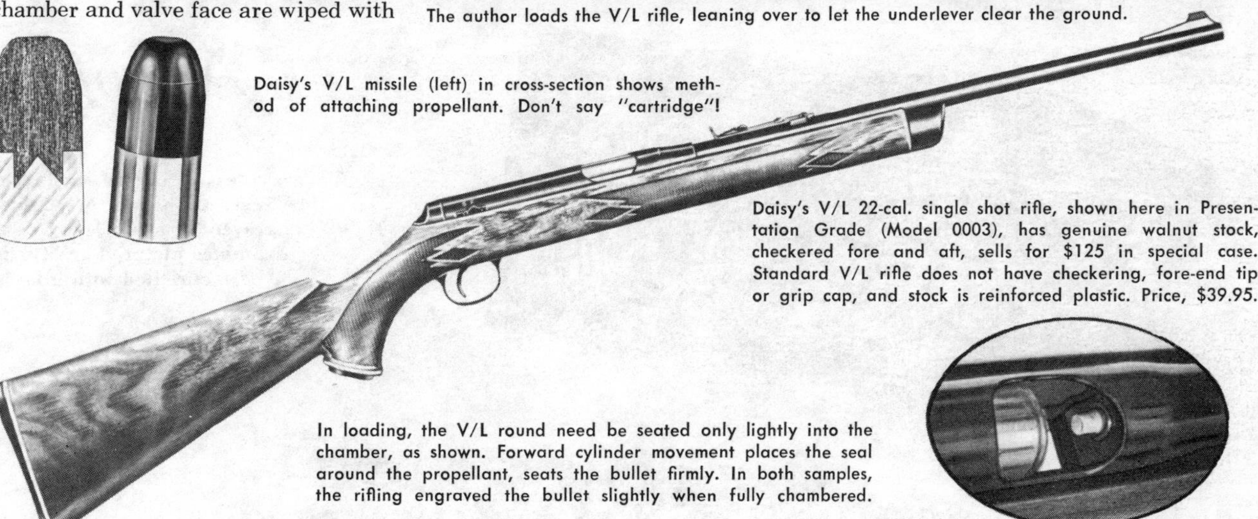

Daisy's V/L missile (left) in cross-section shows method of attaching propellant. Don't say "cartridge"!

Daisy's V/L 22-cal. single shot rifle, shown here in Presentation Grade (Model 0003), has genuine walnut stock, checkered fore and aft, sells for $125 in special case. Standard V/L rifle does not have checkering, fore-end tip or grip cap, and stock is reinforced plastic. Price, $39.95.

In loading, the V/L round need be seated only lightly into the chamber, as shown. Forward cylinder movement places the seal around the propellant, seats the bullet firmly. In both samples, the rifling engraved the bullet slightly when fully chambered.

Working the V/L cocking lever forces a cylinder and piston to the rear, compressing a heavy-duty spring. The breech, now open, accepts a V/L round. Closing the cocking lever brings the cylinder forward, closes the breech, the piston held in cocked position by a sear. Pulling the trigger releases the sear, the spring driving the piston forward. Air in the cylinder is rapidly compressed, forced through a small hole and around a ball check-valve. This compression causes an extreme rise in temperature, the heated air jet igniting the bullet's attached propellant. The ball check-valve instantly closes, the burning propellant forces the bullet down the barrel, the 29-gr. bullet reaching 1150 fs muzzle velocity.

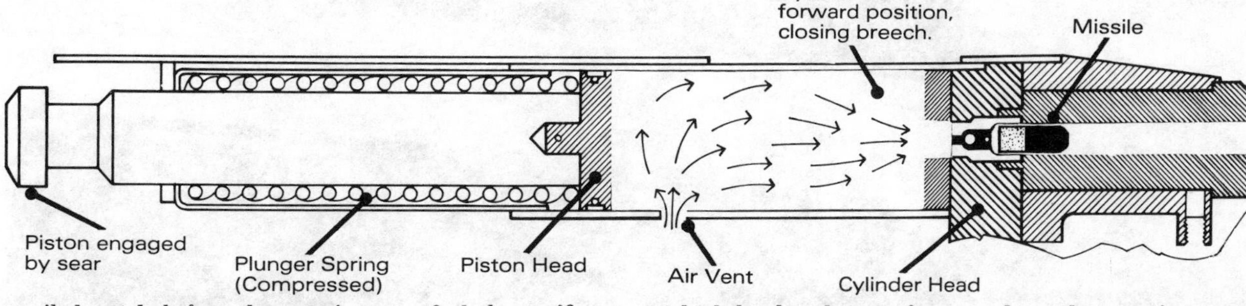

an oiled patch before the gun is put away. Here, in average midwestern winter climate, we found that very light rust would form overnight, becoming quite evident after three days. None formed in the barrels of our sample guns, probably because a light film of bullet lubricant remained there. Even after 6 days exposure without cleaning or oiling, we did not find that sufficent rust had developed to interfere with normal correct functioning. The first new round left the surface clean and bright again. Some lazy people might consider this a major deficiency, but we didn't. After all, every gun *should* be cleaned after use, especially in the chamber area.

The standard Model 002 sells for $39.95. Should you feel inclined to get fancy and go the prestige route, you may opt for the "Presentation" model. It is essentially the same gun, dressed up with a nicely finished walnut stock with engraved brass plate, a rigid plastic foam-filled carrying case, a pair of brass wall hangers and a certificate of ownership bearing the gun's serial number. This handsome package is sold for $125. •

A. A. White

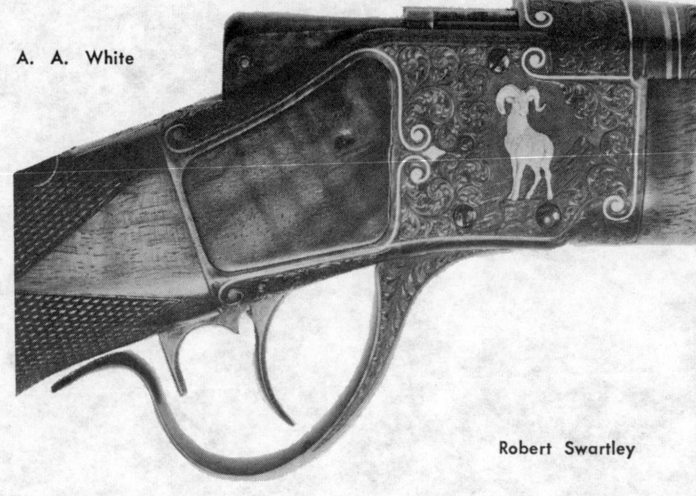

Robert Swartley

Pachmayr Gun Works

Art of the

We are pleased indeed to present, this year, the work of eighteen engravers in steel. Many of the examples pictured are further enriched with inlays of

Pachmayr Gun Works

Paul Jaeger

A. A. White

Arnold Griebel

Engraver

gold and silver, some in relief, some not.

The addresses of the artists displayed here will be found in our Directory of the Arms Trade.

Pachmayr Gun Works

Pachmayr Gun Works

Paul Jaeger

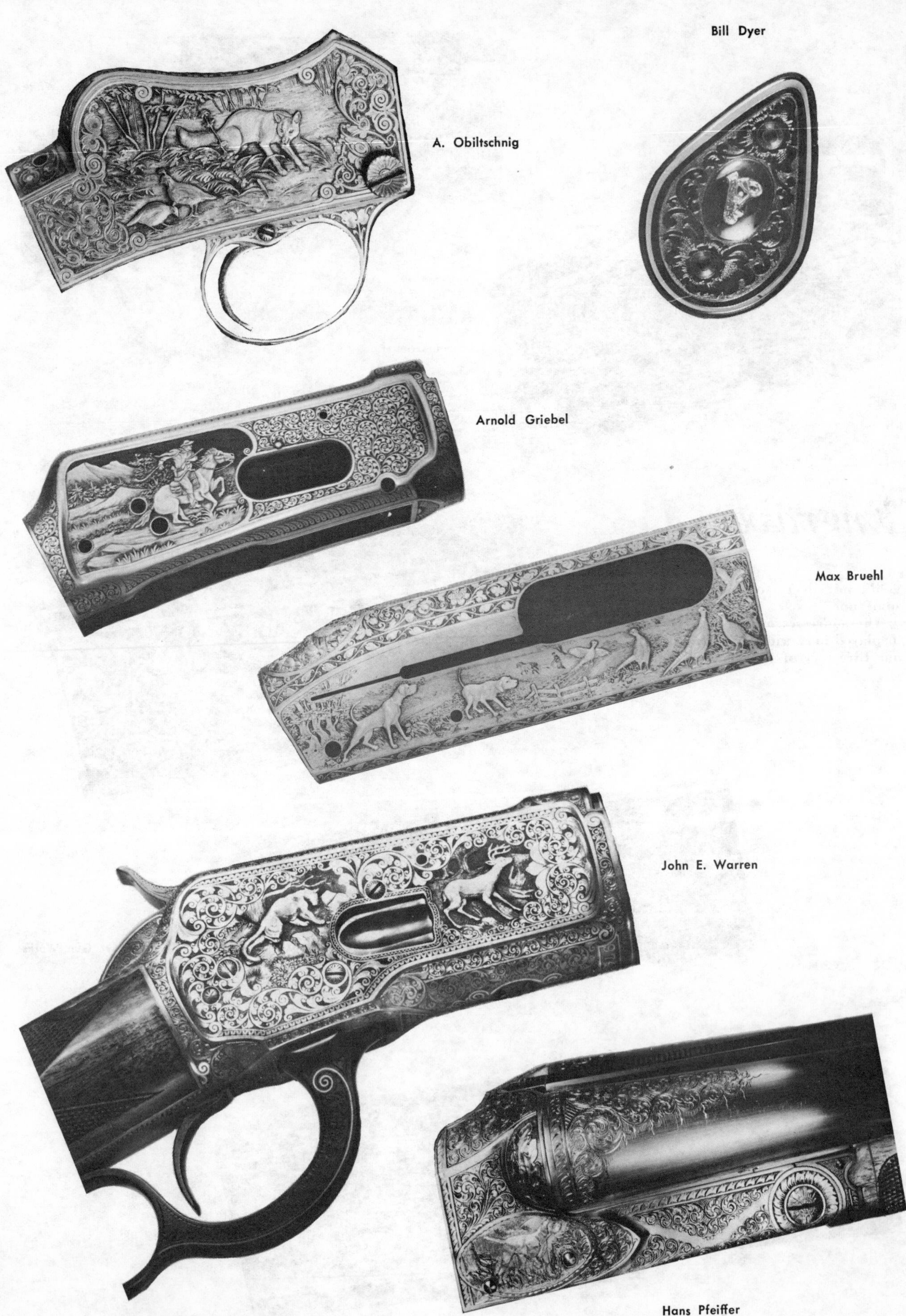
Bill Dyer

A. Obiltschnig

Arnold Griebel

Max Bruehl

John E. Warren

Hans Pfeiffer

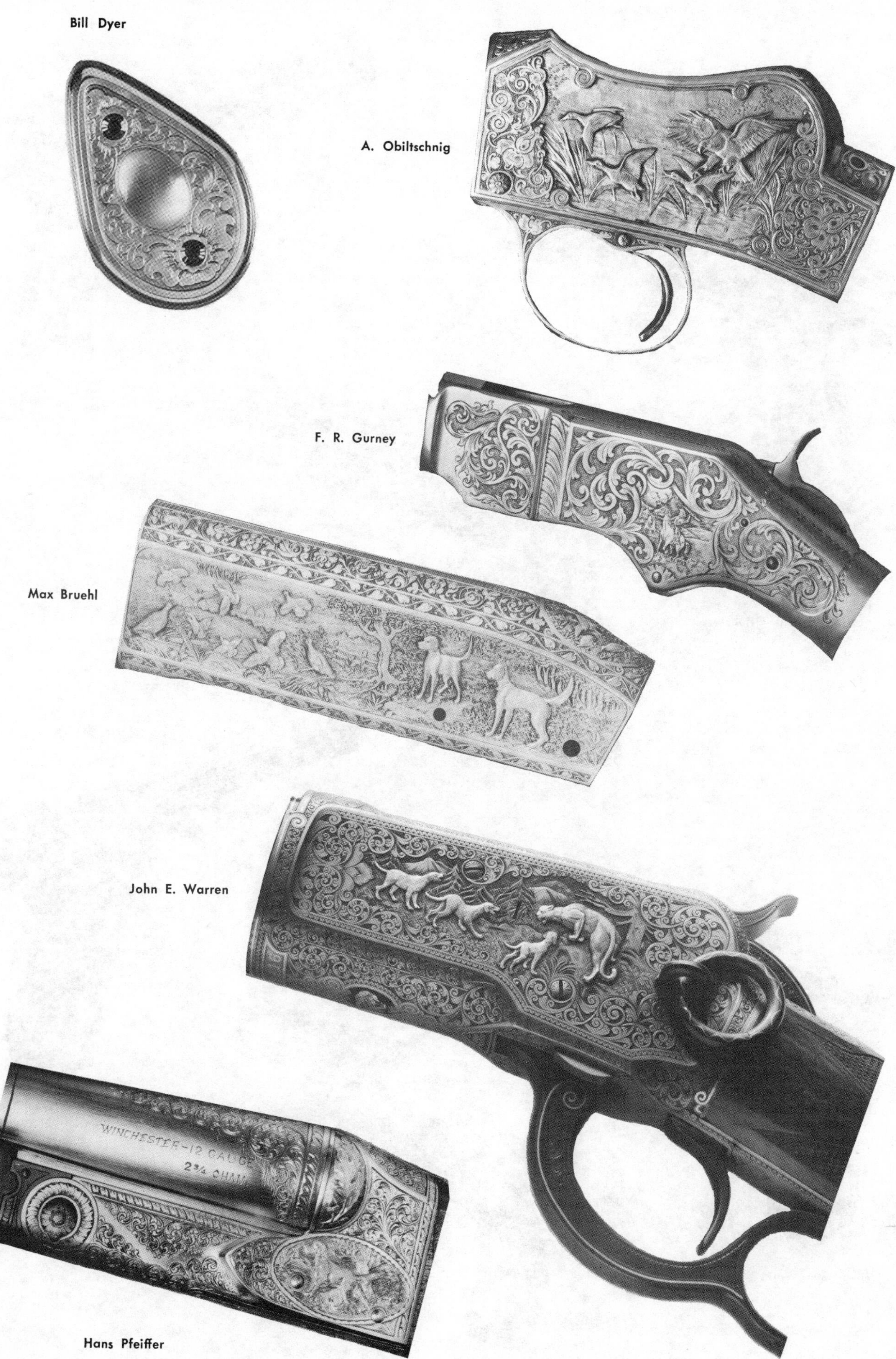

Bill Dyer

A. Obiltschnig

F. R. Gurney

Max Bruehl

John E. Warren

Hans Pfeiffer

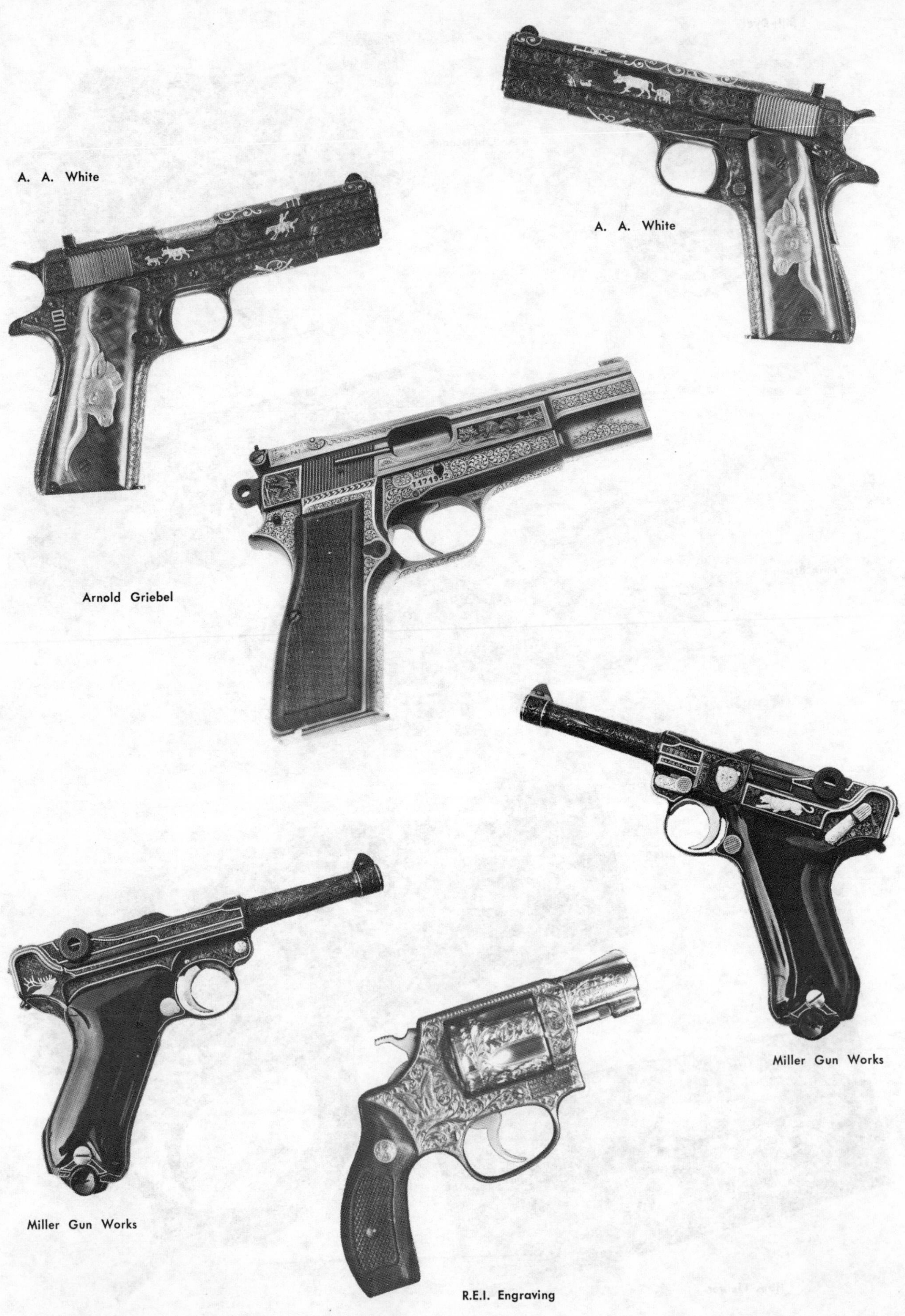
A. A. White

A. A. White

Arnold Griebel

Miller Gun Works

Miller Gun Works

R.E.I. Engraving

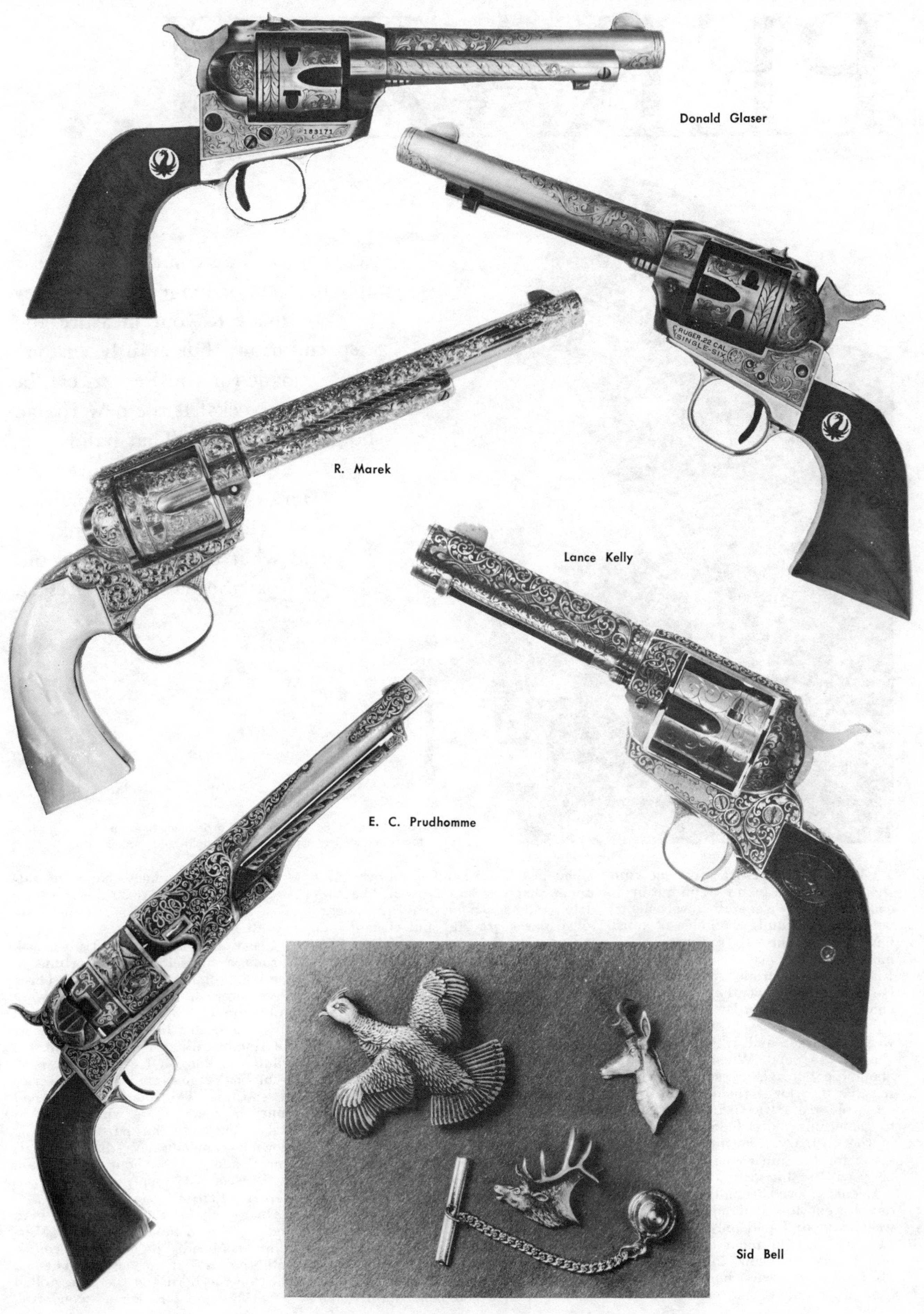

Donald Glaser

R. Marek

Lance Kelly

E. C. Prudhomme

Sid Bell

PERAZZI...

You could wait up to a couple of years or longer for a Purdey made to your measure and specifications, but a fully custom-made-for-you Perazzi can be had in a few weeks! Is the new Italian shotgun that good? That handsome, functional, trouble-free? Here's what a top competition claybird buster thinks — and what the editor found out at the factory in Brescia.

Hand engraving of Perazzi guns is carried out in a special top-floor atelier under full daylight illumination.

AFTER 20 YEARS of shotgun shooting, amateur gunsmithing, coaching and general involvement with firearms, quite a number of guns have passed through my hands. As most of those years were spent in England and Europe, many of them bore the names of the elite of the shotgun world: Purdey, Boss, Franchi, Beretta, Merkel and Sodia, as well as Parker and Ithaca from this side of the pond. When I first read about the Perazzi, my senses, including that monitor of them all, the sixth one, told me I was being introduced to something more than a little out of the ordinary. The author's enthusiasm for the gun shone through and between the lines.

Events moved rapidly. The next day I went to see if all the rhetoric was justified. I had only to take the Perazzi over-and-under trap model in my hands to know instantly that, after those 20 years, here was a gun that truly rated the term different. I had just never handled an over-and-under that was so .... well, "handle-able" and "self-pointable!" In appearance it was graceful and elegant, yet very practical in the simplicity of its design and craftsmanship. Was it possible that I had stumbled across my dream gun? A gun that might, perhaps, shoot as well as it looked, and satisfy the fussy, perfectionist nature of an International Trap clay buster? When you have to deal with 100 mph targets hurtling out in any of 15 unpredictable angles and heights, I feel justified in being a fussy perfectionist!

The man who helped design the gun Perazzi constructed was Ennio Mattarelli. He held the unequalled record of winning the Italian, European, World and Olympic Games International Trap Championships. Even to a skeptic like me, there seemed a fair chance the man knew what he was doing! "Think I'll try one," I told myself nonchalantly, but I had about as much chance of getting one of these $1,000 masterpieces as a snowball had of surviving in — we all know where.

Every now and then, Lady Luck throws a morsel of good fortune to the traditionally starving actor. Three days later my Perazzi-dreams were interrupted at 3:30 A.M. and I found myself dazedly listening to a cheerful Italian calling me from Milan. He wanted to know if I would come back from Los Angeles and repeat a series of sporting TV commercials I had done the year before when living in Italy. Through the haze came the glowing remembrance that Perazzis were made just one hour from Milan, at Brescia. My reply was swift — Perazzi, here I come.

One week later I closed my eyes and prayed. Daniele Perazzi's Mercedes was headed on a collision course with the steel factory gates. Then, a blast on the horn and the gates rolled smoothly back. I remember wondering

Ferrari of Shotguns

by DEREK PARTRIDGE

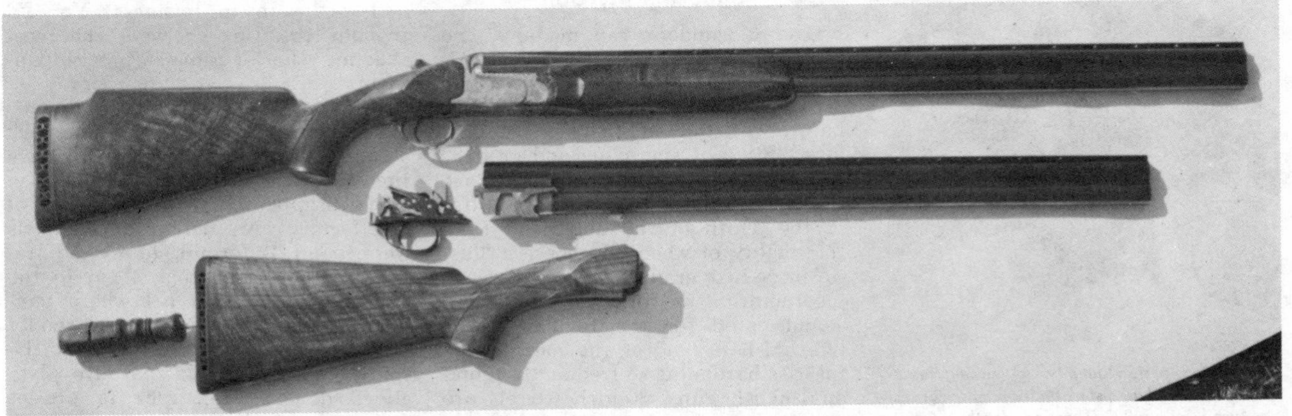

Partridge's all purpose, de luxe Perazzi Trap Model with extra trigger assembly, Skeet barrels and stock, all fitting the same action. Stocks are changed with tool projecting from recoil pad. Slots in end of Skeet barrels reduce recoil.

if he made guns with the same flourish and precision—and then I remembered he did—which was why I was here. Grinning broadly at my reaction like a mischievous schoolboy, Perazzi ushered me past the attractive receptionist and on to further pulchritudinous delights.

At The Factory

The showroom housed a breathtaking collection of over-and-unders; singles; combination interchangeable over-and-unders with singles for the American Trap market and lateral doubles; all in different models for International Trap and Skeet, regular trap and Skeet, live pigeon, game and wildfowl hunting. Beautifully engraved game scenes, English scroll work and finely figured walnut root stocks dazzled my eyes, reminding me of Bob Petersen's and Frank Pachmayr's collections. There were such refinements as a combination over-and-under Skeet/Field model for the rough shooter who likes the occasional round of Skeet. The Skeet barrels are unusual in having built-in muzzle brakes which, along with the special chokes, help give wider patterns and stretch the shotstring. There was even a prototype of a single trap gun with a standby hammer and firing pin built into the action!

Mattarelli was showing the MX8 (for Mexico 1968) to a group of Italian International Team members. I didn't like the look of the high, stepped, elevated rib, but it was designed to overcome the increased heat-dissipation problems encountered in Mexico City's high altitude. This was his personal gun for the Olympics and an interesting feature was an experimental, interchangeable screw-in choke for the lower barrel. I had read that nearly all Perazzi stocks and their unique detachable trigger assemblies were also interchangeable with any of their guns. A mass-produced gun like Browning didn't have interchangeable stocks, so I found it hard to believe that this purely custom-built thoroughbred could achieve it.

Mattarelli's demonstration took care of that. He also pointed out that there were single and double trigger assemblies, set to fire lower or upper barrel first and with release/release or release/pull. There was certainly no lack of customized versatility.

We turned to the job of producing my gun and although I thought I had been very thorough in my specifications, as we went along, I was made further aware of the wide choice available in the Perazzi line. To pick the stock blank, they were kind enough (or unwise!) to allow me my choice from their entire collection. The result does not have to be described—the pictures bear eloquent testimony to the superb piece of Yugoslavian walnut. Franco, the chief stocker, started the task of shaping it entirely by hand—normally, they are

Fine hand-polished finish of interior of action face is clearly shown here.

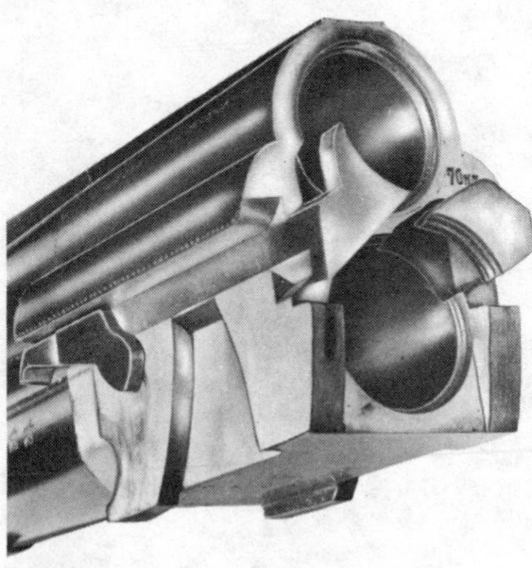

By having a side-lump barrel locking mechanism, instead of usual under-lumps, Perazzi reduced over-all O-U action depth to minimum, resulting in gun's slim, graceful lines.

part machined into rough shape and then hand finished. Apart from obvious choices like having a Monte Carlo comb and a pistol grip; setting the length of the pull to the heel, center and toe of the butt; drop at comb and heel; cast at comb, heel and toe and down pitch, there were also width of the stock at the cheeking point and at the butt; depth of the butt, thickness of the recoil pad; distance from the face of the action to the comb; distance from the trigger to the front of the pistol grip and the width and thickness of that grip. Having weathered all that, I thought I could just have an ordinary beavertail fore-end (as opposed to a standard field one), but no—"What length please?" I settled for the standard 9¾-inch unit. Their beavertail has unusual sloping finger grooves—as against the normal parallel indentations. It is both comfortable, an aid to good pointing and very attractive.

Choosing My Gun

Over-and-under, trap model — no problem. "Sidelock or boxlock?" Although many prefer the slightly more ornate and luxurious sidelock, I was happy with the simplicity of the boxlock. "Style of engraving and grade?" Apparently several of the grades have the same engraved scenes, but differ in the depth of the engraving (and the quality of wood). I choose a "lusso" or de luxe grade with a game scene incorporating partridges — naturally, —and opted for the regular silver-like finish instead of the more colorful case-hardening so frequently found on English guns. 30-inch barrels are my favorite for International Trap, not too short to flip, not too long to be difficult to maneuver accurately at speed. A concave, parallel ventilated rib — it could have been flat and/or tapered — is deeply file-cut to practically eliminate reflection problems. They recommended a fluorescent post front sight. In time I found myself so mesmerized by this huge glowing creature, that I reverted to a standard gold bead—and started looking at my targets again! You can also have silver, white or red for front sight or middle bead.

Although momentarily attracted by the internally goldplated trigger mechanism, I settled for two standard, non-selective, lower-barrel-first sets and then customized them by having my initials engraved in gold. I advise anyone getting a Perazzi to have a spare trigger assembly. This is not because they are likely to cause any trouble (my gun had remained malfunction-free after firing some 7,000 trap loads), but simply because this is the weak area in any gun. To have the security of knowing you can be back in a competition within seconds, should anything go wrong, is well worth the extra $75. Finally, I confirmed the over-all weight of 8 lbs. and we were in business. Yet I'd thought the English were the most exacting when it came to precise gunfitting.

Franco was rasping away with visible effort at the tough walnut stock and it was obvious he wouldn't have time to do the fore-end, so the chosen piece disappeared to another part of the factory. An action and barrels were found conforming to my requirements, and Bruno took them to the underground test tunnel where temperature and humidity are rigidly controlled. He pressed a button on the control panel and a pattern plate glided down a rail-track to pre-set distances, which may range from 17 to 50 yards. Once there, it stops and a spotlight hits a red disc which glows luminously in the center. He fired from behind the protective screen and on impact, the plate automatically reversed itself. After the second shot,

Quick-detachable Perazzi trigger assembly. This entire unit is removed by simply pressing safety fully forward and pulling down on rear of guard.

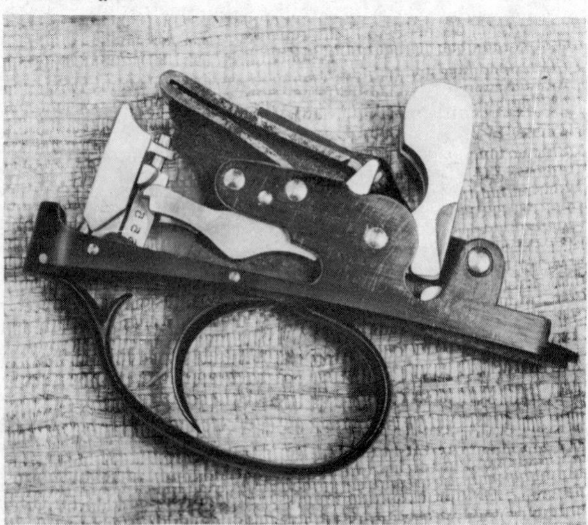

The Leonard Mews 5/16" clear epoxy comb was created to avoid covering the beautiful grain of author's stock.

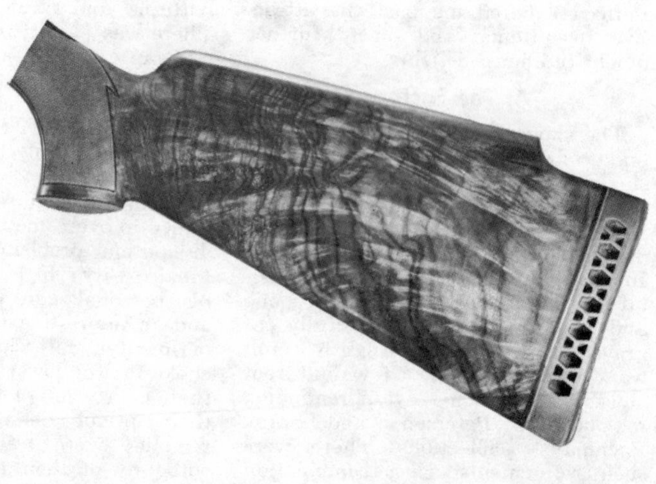

Fine engraving is a feature of de luxe grade Perazzi shotguns.

Partridge happily holds his completed dream gun, created by the combined talents of Daniele Perazzi (center) and Ennio Mattarelli (right). Behind is Mattarelli's 1964 Olympic Victory, on which the firm was founded.

the plate returned to us for pellet counting and percentage calculation. The patterns were a bit on the tight side, so up they went to Lucio who has the delicate and highly skilled job of removing just the correct amount of metal from the right place in order to give the desired percentage and retain the all-important even distribution of the pellets in the 30-inch circle.

Testing and Patterning

Normally each barrel is tested with the exact load and make of shell specified by the customer. I don't like to be so fussy, because in International shooting, you often find yourself in another country without your favorite shell and so your confidence may suffer. Consequently, we tried eight different International loads from five countries and when the patterns were consistently showing around 70% first barrel and 80% second with all the shells, I was satisfied. I would have been happy with 65/75 or even 60/70 as I shoot extremely fast. However, the pellet distribution was so excellently uniform in spread, that I decided not to risk spoiling a good thing. The wisdom of this decision was proved later. The tight choking has never seemed to be a handicap and the satisfaction of completely pulverizing second barrel shots at International targets around 45 yards is both rewarding and psychologically reassuring.

While in the tunnel, Ennio Mattarelli drew my attention to one of his pet "toys." He and Perazzi have rigged up a trap synchronized to a firing stand for the gun and set to throw a clay towards the pattern plate at 35 yards. This is about the distance most shooters fire first at an angle target from the International Trench — 40 yards and over being the approximate distance for second shots. Shotstring has a span of roughly 8-12 feet from leading to trailing pellets. By setting microsecond delays in the firing of the gun, they can break the target with any part of the shotstring. It just goes to prove that you can "miss" a clay a long way in front and still break it, but just one inch behind — forget it! On the way up, Perazzi mentioned that after the Italian proof authorities have subjected barrels to a double charge proofing test, he then makes them undergo a triple charge—just for our safety.

The interchangeable trigger assem-

Chief members of the team that built the author's Perazzi: from left — Franco, Bruno, Pietro, Lucio and Aldo.

Perazzi stock blanks are rough-turned on this machine. The metal master stock is at top.

Action cuts are made with this high speed router, but ample wood is left for hand fitting.

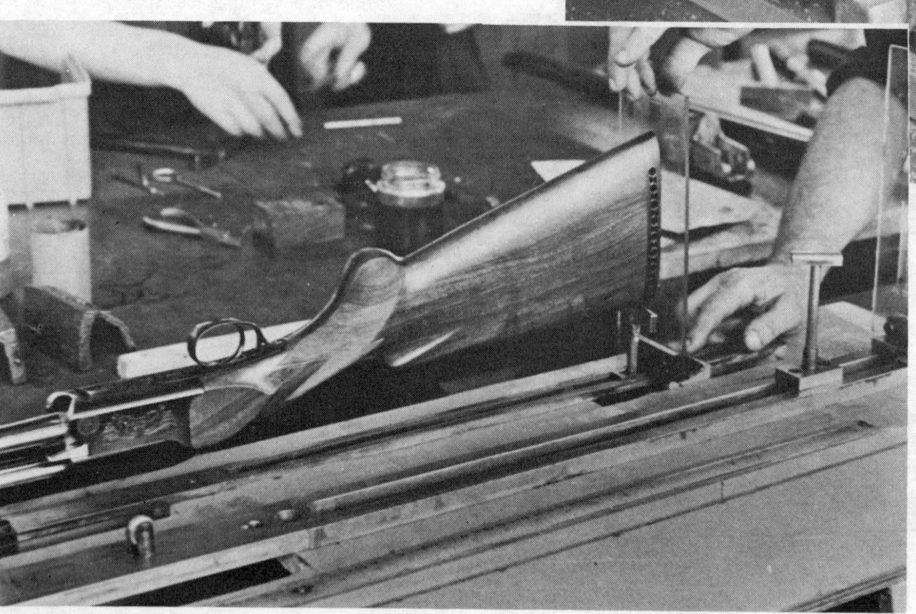

The completed stock is being checked to make certain it conforms in dimensions to the customer's specifications.

blies are of the inertia type, requiring recoil to set the second pull. They are removed simply by pushing the safety fully forward. Triggers are Daniele Perazzi's specialty, as he started making them as a boy. These have an extremely fast lock time and can be safely set to very light, crisp pulls, which do not vary once set. Pietro, the works foreman, set mine to about 2½ lbs. and 3½ lbs. second—and they really were crisp and sweet. From there to Aldo, who let in the gold initials while I watched his companion, the only other engraver, working on a delicate Renaissance scroll pattern. Their engraving is of a very high standard, comparable to the best English and German work. All too often other engraving looks like something I might have scribbled in 5th grade. On the next bench, the sole checkerer and polisher was cutting the fine 24-line to-the-inch diamond-shaped islands.

The completed gun weighed exactly the 8 lbs. asked for, but to me and almost every other shooter who has handled it, the weight seems a whole pound less, so perfect is the balance. This is one of the secrets of the phenomenal success of this gun; the weight is so well-distributed between the hands that one has this impression of effortless, therefore easy, pointing.

The slim, graceful lines of the gun are due in part to the basic simplicity of its over-all design and in particular to reducing the frame depth to a minimum by doing away with under-locking lugs. Instead, they are set in the sides of the lower mono-bloc barrel. The mono-bloc construction means that the barrels are brazed into the chamber end, which is a solid forging.

Perazzis Virtually Handmade

Their present output is around 100 guns a month and it requires the same number of workers to produce them. Although much previously time-consuming handwork has been taken over by ultramodern machinery they designed, all parts are still hand-finished. After compressed-air cleaning, parts are submitted to inspection by ultraviolet light which shows up any internal defects and also surface dirt that could not otherwise be detected even under high-power magnification. Perazzi, through his happy, informal but highly efficient personality has succeeded in imbuing his workers with a tremendous sense of pride in their work and an air of cheerful dedication pervades the place. Having a master craftsman and an Olympic Champion for bosses obviously means a great deal.

In the design room the two architects amazed me when they told me that any new model involves around 500 drawings for the 112 parts and that's in addition to hundreds of sketches illustrating the machining processes of each part. I was then not so surprised to learn that the creative cycle is a good 2½ years. They use an optical comparator to verify the accuracy of each new part—the magnified outline of the part is projected onto a glass screen and compared with the original drawing.

During the next few days, I studied these two remarkable men and in the evenings, I learned about their backgrounds and how their company, the *Manifattura Armi Perazzi* came into being. Perazzi is only 35, but looks so much younger that clients frequently ask for his father, unwilling to believe that he could be the famous Perazzi. Laughingly, he asks if they want their shoes repaired—his father was a cobbler! Although of so-called humble origin, Daniele is a true gentleman with a warm, open, honest manner, and one who applies the same cheerful dedication to living and to his work.

Early Training

When only 14, he started working for a gunmaker, doing unpaid menial tasks, but profiting from the experience by study and observation. The first results were single-trigger mechanisms he created and produced while working after hours. These mechanisms, which he sold to the world-renowned artisan gunmakers of Brescia, turn up from time to time in guns which have gone throughout the world. A spell with the Franchi firm convinced him that mass-produced guns were not his line. Working on his own, he completely made his first shotgun. Traveling the country, he eventually sold it. That enabled him to make two guns, which were again sold by the same method. The pattern was repeated until he was able to take on a few workers, train them and form a small company. Not being in a position to pay good wages, he frequently found himself the recipient of a back-handed compliment when well-established firms took his workers from him. Never discouraged, he managed to recruit new ones as fast as he lost the others. Today, the situation is reversed. Those same employers

About a quarter of the Perazzi shop is shown here. The man in the foreground works on buttstocks and fore-ends.

now come asking to study his methods. He doesn't hesitate, but is happy to show them around. I hope his generosity is not taken advantage of again.

Ennio Mattarelli shares Perazzi's humble beginnings and like him, had to start work at 14, becoming an electrician. Showing outstanding skill at hunting, he was persuaded to try competitive clay busting where his successes drew the attention of Bashchieri & Pellagri, famous ammunition manufacturers. They took him on as a salesman and developed his shooting abilities. The two met in '63 when Perazzi came to learn more about shells with a view to improving the choking and pattern regulation of his guns. Mattarelli, having a very practical knowledge of exactly what he felt he needed in a gun, had asked several gunmakers to produce what he wanted. None had succeeded.

Perazzi did. With the gun he built, Mattarelli won the Italian and European titles, the Moscow Tournament and the highest honor any individual can win — an Olympic Gold Medal. This victory clinched it. Between them, they could start the world's first company dedicated exclusively to the making of custom-built, top-qualtiy competition shotguns. Backing was provided by Doctor Pasquale, a keen shooter and important industrialist, who had already shown interest in their efforts. The *Manifattura Armi Perazzi* became a reality.

In common with many other shooters whose performances have improved from using Perazzis, my scores almost immediately started exceeding those I had put up six years ago when I last did any serious International Shooting. I made one change in my style and cheeked the gun much more firmly than before. This was to try to eliminate the shooter's worst enemy and cause of most lost targets — the fatal desire to lift your head and look at the clay. It meant raising the comb. I couldn't bear the thought of covering any part of the beautiful wood and delayed the necessary work for some time — to the detriment of my shooting!

Then I was fortunate enough to meet that master stockmaker, checkerer and all-round gun genius, Leonard Mews, who was working at the Hollywood Gun Shop. I put my problem to him. Over the next few weeks he worked under the constant pressure of my taking the gun back at weekends to use it. But after much painstaking experimentation, he was able to find a particular epoxy which would bond to the wood, keep its shape and most important of all, be so transparent that it was impossible to tell that a whole 5/16" had been added to the comb. Even people who know of its existence are often hard put to believe it has been done—un-

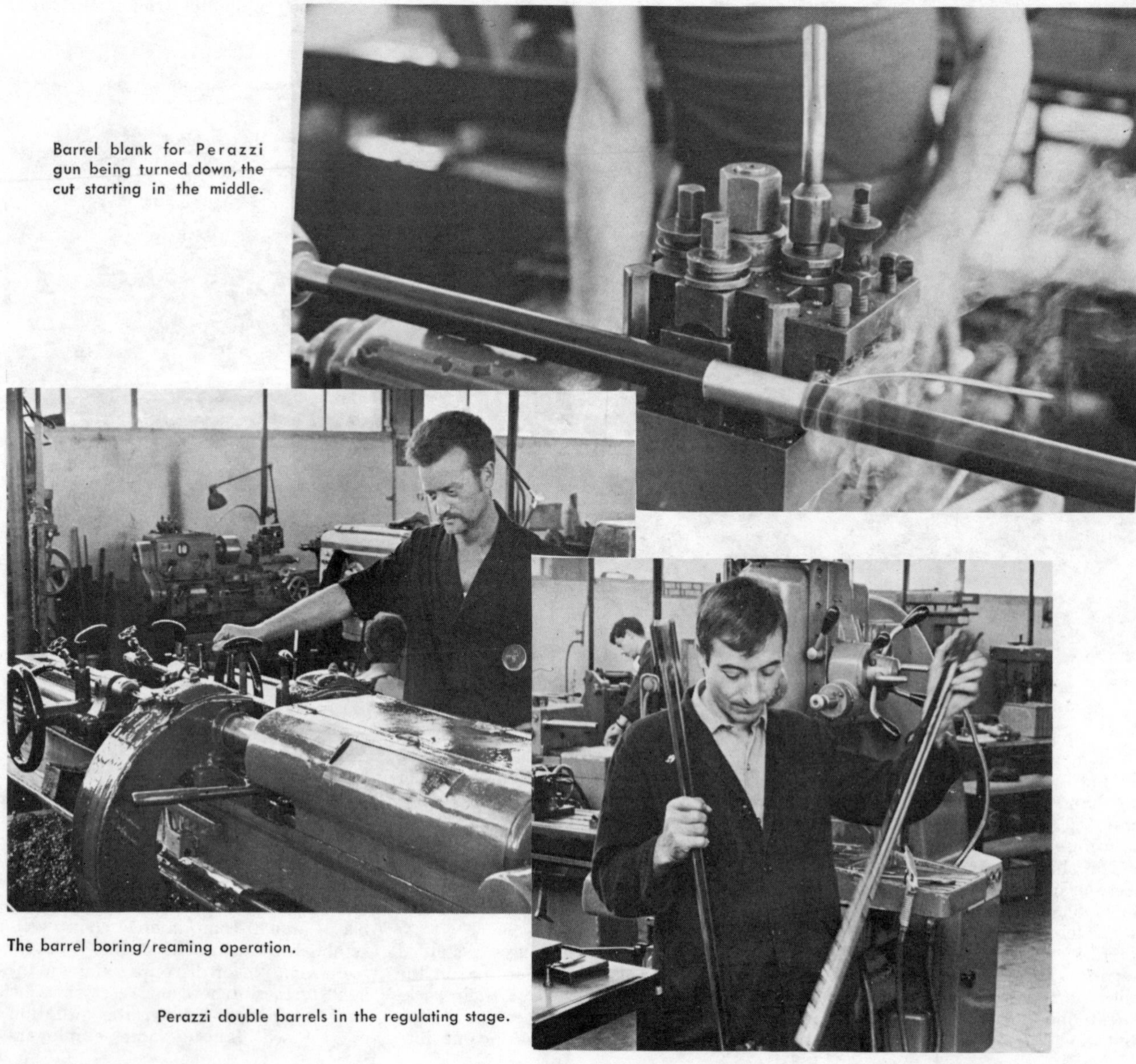

Barrel blank for Perazzi gun being turned down, the cut starting in the middle.

The barrel boring/reaming operation.

Perazzi double barrels in the regulating stage.

Barrel straightening takes a trained, long-experienced eye.

The master action-filer at Perazzi's is one of their oldest workmen.

Making the final and critical action fitting is this man's job.

til it is held against the light as in the picture here.

Watching and listening to Leonard Mews over those weeks, I gained more knowledge about guns and shooting than I thought existed — and I had devoted much of my life to studying the subjects! He is a mine of information on all aspects of shooting and gunsmithing and their practical interapplication. It is not widely known that at one time he was also one of the nation's leading Schuetzen-style rifle shooters. After 40 years of working on most of the world's top-quality guns, Leonard can only think of one gun which he considers comparable in quality to the workmanship of the Perazzi — the renowned English Boss. High praise from a man who knows what he's talking about.

Thanks to the Mews comb and the Perazzi, my International scores are now averaging consistently in the low to mid-90s. Previously I used to shoot the occasional score in the 90s, but averaged in the mid 80s. For those of you more familiar with the 99-plus averages common in the upper echelons of American Trap, it would put International/American Trap averages in proportion to mention that England's Bob Braithwaite, who won the Gold in Mexico with 198/200, runs an annual average in the 92-93 area.

Recently, thanks to the Ithaca Gun Company who import Perazzis into the States, I was able to try out the Skeet model and found (not really to my surprise) that it too was a very sweet-shooting, good-handling gun designed specifically to meet the demands of Skeet. In fact, as I finish this, I am looking forward to leaving for Italy in a couple of days, where I will renew my friendships with all at the *Manifattura Armi Perazzi*—and get myself a Skeet model! For those of you who can get over there, I recommend the trip, as a visit to the factory is very worthwhile. For those of you unable to at this time, you can get your Perazzi from Ithaca. The trap models start at $825, Skeet at $900 and the MX8 at $1500.

(If I can help anyone interested further in a Perazzi, I'll be delighted to do so. Write to me care of the GUN DIGEST editorial office, P. O. Box Zero, Chicago, Ill. 60690.)

My dream gun was no let-down in reality and every time I use it, Perazzi takes me a little nearer to realizing my highest shooting ambitions. From my own experience and that of other delighted Perazzi owners, I feel confident it can do the same for you. If the number of shooters who come up to talk to me about Perazzi is any guide, it seems that many of them are already thinking this way. Perazzi advertises that his guns are as personal as your finger print — he means just that! ●

BROUHAHA IN BRESCIA

Your editor finally got his beautiful Perazzi, but not without some delay and disappointment along the way.

by JOHN T. AMBER

I FIRST MET Derek Partridge on a trip to California a year or so ago. At that time the Perazzi guns were even less well known than they are today, but Derek was so enthused about them that I asked him to do the story he's written in the preceding pages. In addition, a good deal of his admiration and high regard for these new Italian shotguns was transferred to me—perhaps through that sort of osmosis that occurs between those of us who have a feeling for superb craftsmanship, for the grace and flowing lines that distinguish the best firearms from the mediocre, the less-well-done.

Because I was going to Europe for some factory visits and some hunting —which I've told about elsewhere in this issue—I made it a point to go to Brescia, the city where Perazzis are made. Brescia, lying in the hills of northern Italy, has been a gunmaking center for centuries. There are scores of arms factories in and around that old city today—some large, others very small.

My TWA plane touched down at Milan's Malpensa airport one morning early in September, the beginning of a train of serio-comic events that didn't end until months later!

I had only a couple of days to spare for the visit to the Perazzi factory—where I meant to see how the guns were made and, most interesting of all, order a Perazzi over-under trap gun to my specifications and dimensions. Signore Daniele Perazzi had told me by letter that he'd have me picked-up by car at the Milan airport, sending one of his drivers and Miss Maria Teresa—his secretary and the only person in the company who spoke English. I waited at the airport for over an hour, then called the factory to find out what had happened. No one, I seemed to gather, knew where the car was, but it had gone to the Alitalia office in Milan to pick me up —not to the airport. Learning that, I grabbed a taxi and sped into Milan and the Alitalia office. "Yes," said a young man who could speak English, "the Perazzi people were here, but they've just left for Malpensa airport, expecting to find you there." That was great, but I stayed put, Maria Teresa phoned from the airport in a half-hour or so, and in another 30 minutes we got together. It took another hour or so to reach Brescia, where we didn't arrive until almost 1:00 p.m. By the time I'd registered at my hotel, had a bit of lunch, and got out to the factory it was well into the afternoon.

That day was virtually lost—about all I got done was to meet the volatile, dynamic bundle of nerves called Daniele Perazzi, a surprisingly young man of only 34. I did manage a hurried trip through the spacious, one-story factory, prowled through Perazzi's showroom briefly—marveling at the rows of finished shotguns softly gleaming in the racks—but the pictures I wanted to get of the many and varied gunmaking operations would have to wait for the following day. So would my getting fitted for the gun I was going to order.

I spent the next day looking over the many steps it takes to make the Perazzis. The start is actually made with a billet of square steel, some 3 by 4 inches in section. This is fed to a power hacksaw, and the resulting blocks are rough-machined to general form. From then on there's a very great amount of hand-filing and stoning before the action is ready for engraving and coloring. The customer may have, by the way, his choice of blued finish, case-coloring or a silver-grey appearance, plus a wide choice indeed of engraving. The 100-odd workers in the metal shop—men all —range in age from the apprentice youngster to those of 50 and 60 years, and everyone is under the watchful eye of the maestro himself—Perazzi is constantly running up and down stairs, from his office into the shop, seeing to this and that.

The woodshop is in a separate place, the rough blanks piled high. There's a copying lathe for rough-turning the blanks, and there are many ingenious jigs and fixtures for roughing out the inletting cuts in the various models —over-unders, side-by-sides, different gauges, and so on.

I would say that at least 75%-80% of all Perazzis are handmade, and certainly all critical work, on wood and metal, is done by hand. It was a pleasure to watch the older workmen, the master craftsmen, filing away with delicacy and precision at the various bits and pieces of the actions, on the actions themselves, the quick-detachable trigger assemblies, etc.

These readily removable triggers work beautifully, be it noted, and each assembly receives the most meticulous and critical scrutiny before being approved. The design, as has been noted, is Daniele Perazzi's own, but if you'd like to see who first came along with a center-mounted trigger-lockwork arrangement—also ready detachable—read *The Modern Shotgun**, pp. 146 *et seq* of Vol. 1 for the author's detailed comment on the John Dickson "round actions."

The woodshop was the source, as it happened, of another contretemp! As you might imagine, I made it a point to look for as nice a piece of wood as I could find for my Perazzi—and I found it. It was a beautiful piece of walnut, in the Circassian type, the contrast between light and dark areas very high. Take a look at the photograph of it—that'll tell you more than I can here.

By now, having completed my inspection of the plant and made the pictures I wanted, I took my fancy buttstock and matching fore-end blanks to Perazzi, and the dimensions of the stock I'd be getting were made and recorded. These figures are carefully noted on the work card that accompanies each gun on its trip through the work, and it remains on the finished gun when the customer receives it. No slipups, huh?

That evening, bidding Daniele and Maria T. goodbye, I left Brescia for Germany, telling Perazzi I'd be returning in about four weeks to pick up my completed gun.

My hunting in Scotland and Spain ended, I went back to the Perazzi shop early in October, a day or two ahead of schedule.

Not only was the gun not quite ready—Daniele remarked on my being a bit early—but my beautiful hunk of magnificent walnut had not been made up. Instead—and it *was* ready—the stock I was expected to take showed as much figure as a piece

* By G. Burrard, 3 vol. ed., London, 1951, revised.

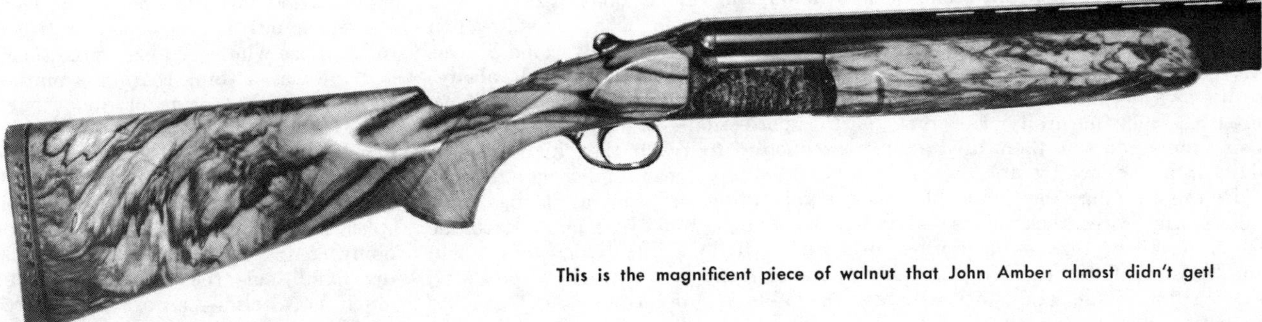

This is the magnificent piece of walnut that John Amber almost didn't get!

of white pine, and from three feet away it looked like a solid mass of brown stain.

I'll pass lightly over the ensuing three-way jabbering that took place between D.P., Maria T. and me, but I eventually learned that my special wood had been rejected because it wouldn't—in its rough state—meet the dimensional standards required!

I'm afraid I got a bit adamant at that point! I'd just seen that the calipers indicated that the buttstock blank *was* within limits, even if on the scant side, so I insisted I'd have that original handsome wood or else!

Perazzi said he'd do his best—though no promises—but I couldn't wait the several days or more that making another stock would take. That inability to take the gun with me was a big disappointment for more reasons than one—at that time it was legal to bring back into the U.S. up to three guns, no import license needed as long as the gun or guns were carried through customs by the traveler. Now I'd have to get a permit, the gun would have to be shipped via Italian and U.S. customs brokers both, and I'd be worried as to what might happen to the gun en route—it could be damaged or even stolen. Anyway, I left clear shipping instructions and departed for home.

A couple of months went by, and I began wondering what had happened—I'd called various airline freight offices, but could learn nothing. Then, because Derek Partridge was going to Italy again, I asked him to see what the trouble was. Amazingly, he learned that the gun had been shipped all right, by air, but with only an address—my name had been left off the labels!

Several more phone calls finally located the gun, lying in a customs warehouse—it had been there for some 40 days—and my bill for air freight, broker's fees, storage charges and duty came to about $90.

All—at long last—was well, however, for my extra-fancy wood had been found suitable, oddly enough, and I've now got one of the world's great shotguns.

Its performance on clays has been superb—I've been shooting way over my head—and the pattern board shows a remarkably uniform density, especially with Winchester trap loads. The pull length is a trifle too long, but that's entirely my fault—I asked for it. The single trigger sets — I bought two — have operated without a single bobble.

Maybe those various hangups have endeared it to me all the more—the goal achieved after adversity and all that?

There will be other Perazzi's ready in 1969-70, I was told—and I saw one of the prototypes.

This was a beautiful 20 gauge over-under, made up in Perazzi's best quality. The buttstock was straight-gripped, the fore-end a relatively slender field type, and a handsome hunk of walnut was used for both. There was no buttplate as such—instead the back surface was fully checkered. Weights will be around 5½-5¾ pounds.

These new over-under 20s will be identical mechanically to the Perazzi 12 bores — quick detachable trigger assemblies, interchangeable buttstocks, and so on. They'll be made only in three fancy grades, however, and the price, even in Italy, won't be cheap!

The De Luxe will bring about $700, the Super De Luxe just under $1,000, while the Extra De Luxe will fetch some $1300. The one I looked over had been made up for S. Mattarelli, and it was worth all of $1300—magnificent!

Another new 20 will be a side-by-side double, same high grades and prices as above. This will also be a field gun, the fore-end a semi-beavertail type a la 21 Winchester.

A single barrel 12-gauge trap gun should also be available in 1969, and Perazzi is also working on O-U and side-by-side double rifles, no less. I saw several in-the-rough examples of these, but I think they're a couple of years away, worse luck. ●

Styles and Fashions

If what I've written here carries a touch of arrogant belief in my own taste, I can only add that it derives from some 40 years of exposure to firearms of all kinds. Over that long span I've learned that the simpler elements of good line, deftly-handled proportions, economy and tautness of line and curve, blended together form a functional whole, make for a shotgun—or rifle—that epitomizes the ultimate in handling, shooting and visually attractive qualities.

These truly handsome examples of the gunmakers' art—the best gunmakers, to be sure—elegant in their rich simplicity, their restrained and subdued finishes—are not, as you might suppose, at all new. Far from it. Flintlock-ignition shotguns—the fowling pieces of the late 18th century—show a grace of form and style, a degree of functionality the equal of today's very best guns. The stock dimensions of early Mantons, for example, differ in no important degree from the standards found acceptable and useful today. True, the drop at heel is often rather more than American shooters find correct, but that's because of a stance and shooting style situation prevalent here in recent years. British and continental shotgunners shoot with the head held higher—more erect—than is our practice, and more drop at heel is required by them.

I realize—all too well—that the U.S. is full of garish and gaudy guns, more particularly rifles—guns bejeweled and bedizened, guns showing carving and/or checkering, often intermingled in ill-designed, even more ill-executed patterns, replete with exaggerated combs and roll-over cheekpieces, flared pistol grips, oddly-slanted fore-end tips, blinding piano finishes and other alluring aspects.

Alluring they must be to many. Thousands upon thousands are sold, almost all of them paying homage to Roy Weatherby in their adoption of style points he pioneered years ago. Some of them, indeed, are far more ostentatiously styled than Weatherby ever intended.

These things, too, will pass away—or so I keep telling myself! Styles and fashions change, though it may take years, but I'm confident that these glittering, glaring guns will eventually disappear—at least in good part—leaving the classic, traditional style once again pre-eminent in the field.

DALE GOENS
Stockmaker Supreme

This great artist in wood shows a magnificent command of line, proportion and classic form. Here is what he has to say about his work.

DALE GOENS comes from a long line of German-Dutch ancestors. Just about all of his immediate forbears had a great interest in guns and hunting—shotguns, rifles and handguns—so his own life-long attachment to fine firearms came naturally. He grew up using guns and saw them used almost daily in his boyhood years.

Before joining the rank of top-notch, first rate stockmakers — and Goens is all of that — he worked in the musical field, repairing and restoring fine violins and other stringed instruments.

His first work on guns was in 1949, and he's been completely involved in that field ever since.

His work is so well-liked and sought after these days that a wait of many months for one of his superb stocks is not uncommon. That's true, of course, of fine craftsmen in any field—there's no rushing the artist.

Here is what Goens himself has to say about his work, gunstocking in general and the rewards of his chosen field:

"My first serious work on gunstocks was in checkering and such other ornamentation as inlays and carving. I soon found that I preferred the pure classic form of gunstocks over any other, and I soon found myself making the complete stock, as well as doing checkering. Although some of my very first stocking efforts were on semi-inletted blanks, I quickly learned that full satisfaction came to me only if I did my work from the raw blank, starting from scratch.

"Producing a fully hand-made gunstock must be, in good part, a labor of love—few, if any, workers will find this the most lucrative way to make a living! On the other hand, the work has its compensations, for it is a real and deep pleasure to make something that brings so much pleasure to others, to know that one's efforts are admired and cherished.

"To the young man wanting to become a gunsmith or stockmaker, I would say this:

"With all the technological advancements being made today, a really good education should be a "must." When a person becomes truly good in his chosen field his services will always be in demand, so my advice is to strive for perfection—and he will need good schooling to reach that high goal. A really good gunsmith has got to be a combination of several things, but above all he must be a good mechanic with artistic ability. A custom stockmaker must have a world of patience, be able to determine and execute proper proportion as well as the line of beauty, and yet the finished stock must be fundamentally a sound, strong and practical tool.

"I can assure the aspiring stockmaker that, even if he possesses all the attributes I've described, success does not come quickly. It takes time to become a good craftsman, and it takes time for his work to grow in demand.

"I would encourage young men with a feeling for metal work to take up that specialty, and to become truly skilled and adept at first class metalsmithing on custom guns. This field is wide open, with a strong demand, and the man who can do it will get more work than he can handle."

When asked about some of the problems facing the custom stockmaker, Goens said this:

"A reliable source of fine gun stock blanks is and has been a big problem. The customer almost always wants a fancy blank—with which I heartily agree—for when 70 to 80 hours are spent making a stock the very best wood to be had is my chief desire, too. It costs no more to make a stock from a highly figured blank than it does to construct a plain one. In fact, the plain walnut blank, usually of less quality, is often harder to work with.

"Most of the problems with checkering tools have been solved since the introduction of good tools by such men as Bill Brownell and Dembart. Both are to be highly commended on their outstanding job of making *excellent, reliable* tools. I'll confess that I once tried to design better checkering tools, but I'm now well satisfied to let those who specialize make them.

"However, I think there is a market for a good checkering cradle, though designing a really good one has its problems. Checkering is usually done with hand tools or an electric tool. (I still use the hand tools; Brownell spacers and Dembart V tools for pointing up the diamonds.) When using hand tools the cradle has to be much more solid—because of the force required to do line spacing and final pointing—than is needed when using the electric tool. Not nearly as much pressure is required with the latter. Alvin Linden once said that the base of an anti-aircraft cannon would be about right for a checkering cradle!

"Finishing causes more problems than any other one thing that I can think of. Whenever stockmakers get together, almost always the first question asked is, "What are you using for stock finish now?" I've had the pleasure of visiting the shops of some of the finest stockmakers in our fair land, and if the first item of conversation isn't on stock finishes at those bull sessions, the second certainly is. Several years ago, when I was fighting the finish problem, I wrote to the dean of custom stockmakers, Tom Shelhamer, and asked his advice. That fine gentleman wrote me a three-page typewritten letter on the *Whys and Wherefores of Stock Finishing,* going into great detail to explain the fine oil finish he is famous for. Needless to say I've taken his advice to heart, and I use it. One thing he said, which really stuck, is that what works for one man does not always produce identical results for the other. Each one has to do his "own thing," to borrow a present-day expression.

"A minor problem in stock finishing is whether the finish is to be in the wood or on it, then to choose from the many types of finish available. In my work, I use the Flecto Varothane plastic oil sealer and Lin-Speed oil for final finish." ●

At top—This Mauser-actioned sporter caliber 243 Winchester (shown in left and right side views), was made by Goens for Sol Levine of Columbus, Nebraska. The engraving of the floorplate, guard and grip cap is by Albin Obiltschnig of Ferlach, Austria.

Center—Goens made this handsome rifle for Fred Quintana of Albuquerque, N.M. It is a 270, the action a pre-1964 Model 70 Winchester. The full fancy Claro walnut carries 24-line checkering in a ribboned fleur-de-lis pattern.

Below—Right and left sides of a pre-WW II Model 70 Winchester, caliber 270, made by Goens for James Reeves of Woodland Hills, Calif. The superb stock wood is top quality French walnut, the fleur-de-lis checkering 24 lines per inch.

AIR ARMS I.Q.

Interest in air arms continues to expand at a sharply increased rate. Here is much-needed information on types, terminology, the use and care of air guns—plus their strange historical background.

by LADD FANTA

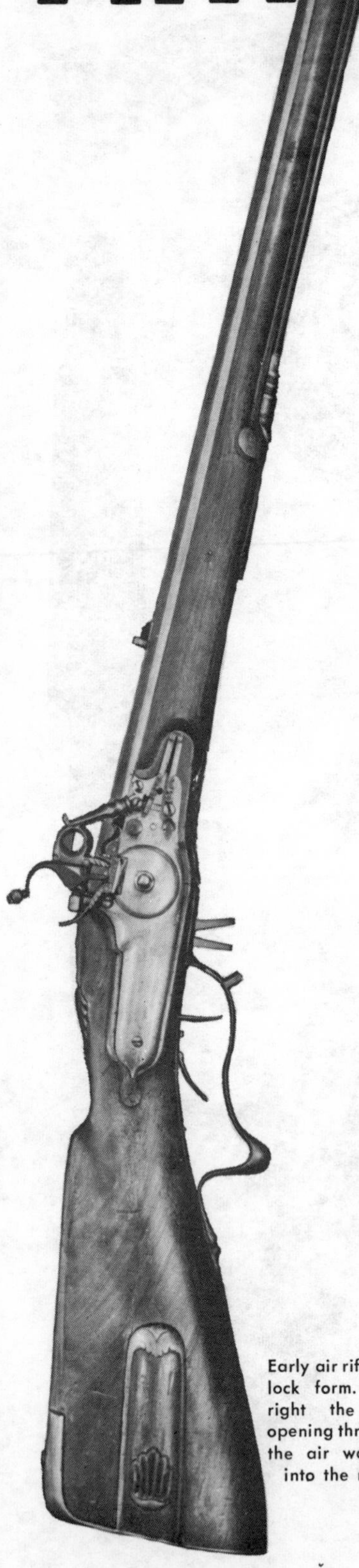

Early air rifle in wheel-lock form. At upper right the buttplate opening through which the air was pumped into the reservoir.

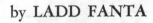

THE SPIRALING number and variety of new air-arms on the market indicates increasing interest, ownership and discovery that the air guns of today are "something else" than the familiar BB gun of yesteryear. Indeed, the degree of present-day air-arm sophistication often shows the culmination of brilliant gunmakers' knowledge and advanced engineering with newest materials.

An undeniable fact is that whether he is young or old, shooting BBs or the ISU Match Course, air-arms have a degree of fascination for nearly everyone. The world of air-arms has its own nomenclature and idiom; history, gun types, calibers and rewards all its own. This can include: unbelievably accurate target shooting; up to rabbit size hunting and pest shooting; endless variety in guns, ammo and scaled-down ballistics experimentation; last but not least, whole new vistas for plinking fun. For pistol buffs, there are almost as many pistol counterparts as there are different air rifles.

Because of the many prevalent half-truths and misconceptions concerning air guns, it is no small wonder that many otherwise knowledgeable firearms-oriented shooters turning pneumo-bug get somewhat confused. For example, a timely shooting magazine editor writing about a line of spring-air rifles calls them "single *pump* guns . . . closing the gun forces the air into a *tightly sealed* chamber." Only pneumatic air guns are "pumped" and have a sealed air chamber or reservoir. Further on he wrote: "Pull the trigger and the air is suddenly released through a needle valve." CO_2 and pneumatic air guns employ valves, but there are none whatever in any standard spring-air arms. Another popular gun magazine says that 177 pellets "weigh 3.2 grains." Average weight of typical Diabolo 177 pellets is 8.0 grains. Such errors are all too frequent, and much air-arm terminology is incorrectly applied. As with word usage for firearms, some erroneous references are made so consistently that they become a part of the accepted way. For example, there's the wrong but common practice of simply calling all autoloading, full-automatic or semi-auto arms "automatic." With "air guns" certain terms are also apropos. Here are a few common definitions:

An *air gun,* specifically, is an arm (or toy) with smoothbored barrel, discharged from the shoulder normally, and in which the expanding force of compressed air or gas propels the projectile. In a general way, "air gun" is often used as an all-inclusive term.

An *air rifle* is as above except that it must have a rifled barrel. This term is subject to its share of confusion since, as a toy, it is smoothbored, as in *BB air rifle*.

An *air pistol* is an arm (or toy)

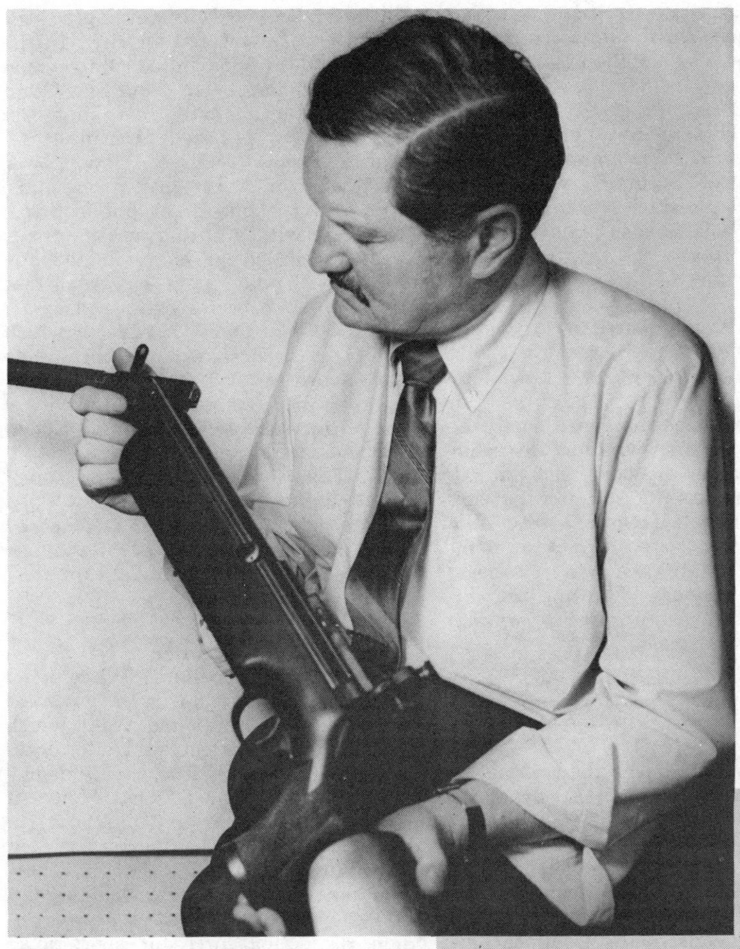

This is the Winchester Model 363 air pistol the editor is holding, designed for competition shooting and made in 177 only. Fully adjustable sights are standard, as is the adjustable trigger system. About $50.

Winchester's new line of air arms offers something for every purse, from the Model 416 smoothbore 177 at $16 to the 9½-lb. ultra-accurate Model 333 at $170, complete with fully adjustable peep sight. In between are 6 other air rifles from about $23 to $85 for their Model 450. This last is the only solid-barrel type in the group, operating by an under-lever. Two air pistols are also available.

Editor Amber here looks over the Model 333 Winchester — note small lever, at his right thumb, which locks the barrel and receiver rigidly together in the ready-to-fire position.

normally discharged with one hand. The adult or advanced air pistol may have a smoothbored or rifled barrel. The toy variety is not rifled.

An *air shotgun* is a smoothbored shoulder arm using compressed air or CO_2 gas to propel a small quantity of round shot in the manner of the common shotgun.

Air-arm is the preferred term for serious-use adult-size air guns, whether CO_2, pneumatic or spring, rifled or not, hand held or shoulder mounted.

A *pneumatic* is the compressed air type of air-arm requiring successive pump strokes to build up the desired shooting force. Also, less frequently, called *pump gun, pump action* and *pump up*.

A *gas gun* uses a CO_2 liquid-vapor power supply as the propellant, in disposable or refillable cylinders. Also called *carbon dioxide arms, CO_2 guns,* etc. (Note: not to be confused with the German "Barakuda," a spring-air rifle using an *ether gas* booster attachment, giving an explosive force for added power).

A *spring-air* arm is one in which the released power of a heavy, compressed spring is used to drive a piston

AIR ARMS I.Q.

in a tube, compressing and propelling the air in its path through a small vent to drive the pellet down the barrel. Also called *spring piston* or *spring gun*. The basic forms are the *barrel-cocking* or *barrel break-down* type. Improved forms are the *underlever* and *sidelever* types. The latest technological refinement is the *recoilless* kind, which uses opposing spring-piston assemblies or other means to eliminate the slight, so-called "recoil" (spring piston surge at moment of firing) common to other spring-air arms.

Dieseling is an inevitable though undesirable occasional occurrence (usually after oiling) in nearly all spring-air arms. It happens when the compressive action produces (sometimes) a temperature high enough to ignite some of the oil vapor, resulting in added velocity, louder noise and a flyer for that shot.

Air lock is a condition which can occur in those pneumatic air arms, using an impact hammer, which are over-pumped, and the hammer-fall upon the outlet valve is insufficient to overcome the great internal pressure and thus let the compressed air be released. (One hears of stories, which will never die, such as: "A trusty old pump-up I used to have could be pumped up 30, 40, even 60 times! Shot through 2 or 3 two-by-fours! Like a 22 Long Rifle yet!" Dear reader, tales like these are all in the realm of popular myth and fallacy.)

Air Arms Classified

The imported match target air rifles, mostly specialized spring types, are designed to let target shooters punch impossible looking one-ragged-hole groups at the ISU 10-meter range. Usually furnished (or optional) with the finest accouterments, their chief characteristics are: heavy weight, 177 caliber, triggers finely adjustable in several ways, curved buttplates; Swiss, Bavarian or Tyrolean cheekpieces with massive, well-checkered stocks; micrometer peep sights and low power for minimum firing disturbance. The best of these are of the newer recoilless types.

Sporting air rifles are usually of lighter weight (than Match models), of any caliber or propulsion system, and of higher power. In 177 caliber this invariably means 660 feet per second muzzle velocity (fps MV) and up compared to the usual 550 to 610 of the match-target varieties.

Diabolo pellets are the familiar indented-waist air-arm ammunition. The name originated in Europe from resemblance to the juggling or throwing spool used in the ancient game of Diabolo. Also called *hour glass, wheat stack, spool shaped, skirted* or *waisted* because of their general outline.

Q. What special appeal do air-arms have to shooters in general?

A. Much of their appeal lies in the challenge for accuracy with limited power and the single shot. Just as big bore enthusiasts also enjoy 22 rimfires, shooting with air-arms is also a pleasurable and rewarding logical step.

Q. What other attributes does the air-arm have?

A. There are many. Low noise. Greater relaxation. Landowner permission for shooting more easily obtained. Shooting without disturbing nearby game or domestic animals. Easily carried, almost unlimited supply of ammo. Greater safety. Low shooting cost. Safer storage at home. Easy ownership (nearly everywhere). Shooting indoors. Hunting or just plinking in areas unsafe or impracticable for firearms.

16th Century Air Guns

Q. How far back in history do air-arms go?

A. Air-arms have their basis in primitive blow guns. Air-arms appeared as early as 1530*, and quite early types with as many as 6 and 7 barrels were not uncommon. Repeating air-arms were also invented in the early 1600s. Many of the early air-arms were constructed to appear just like wheel-locks and flintlocks. The means of storing the air varied greatly —hollow spheres attached underneath the gun or above; reservoirs in the buttstock or around the barrel, and so on. More recent use was with pneumatic air rifles, between the Austrian forces and Napoleon's armies around the end of the 18th century. The Austrian army used a secretly developed 44-caliber multi-groove repeating air rifle capable of shooting 150 paces, these being assigned to certain selected marksmen. (Collectors' specimens show good effectiveness at 100 yards. poor accuracy at 200 yards.) This was a secret weapon of the first order, setting fear in the hearts of lonely sentries and other soldiers. Some say that so great was the effect that Napoleon ordered immediate execution of enemy soldiers caught with one of the new "noiseless" guns. Compressed air for these air rifles was stored in the detachable shoulder-stocks, refilled at horse-drawn base stations using large two-man pumps. Extra portable reservoirs were also used. About 2000 pump strokes were required for full capacity charge.

Q. What about the beginning of the CO_2 and spring-air rifles?

A. In 1889 a Frenchman named Giffard succeeded in developing the first CO_2 gas-powered air rifle. In the same era, in the United States men like Quakenbush, Haviland and Gunn were experimentally working on spring-piston powered air rifles. Because of the relatively low power available from these early spring guns, they did not find great public favor; anything with a spring was automatically regarded as being in the toy category. Today, it is no great feat for the high power sporting spring-air rifles to lob Diabolo pellets, which are basically designed for short range use, in excess of 100 yards.

Q. So how come Europe produces the spring jobs and the United States the pneumatic and CO_2 guns?

A. That is paradoxical, and somewhat similar to the English-developed Boxer primer and the U.S. invented Berdan primer popularity exchange between the U.S. and Europe.

CO_2 Air Arms

Q. Is carbon dioxide (CO_2) gas an ideal air-gun propellant? What is it?

A. Carbon dioxide is a chemical anhydride—a compound from which water has been extracted. Under cryogenic conditions it is easily liquefied, requiring less than 500 psi. Hence it is cheap to produce and purchase (in the U.S.). At room temperature, it maintains a confined reservoir or accumulator gas pressure over the liquid CO_2 of 1080 psi. CO_2 is an excellent projecting force for short-range pellet guns since it is colorless, non-toxic, odorless and won't burn—but it has some drawbacks too.

Q. If I buy a CO_2 type air rifle, what are its advantages and disadvantages?

A. Some advantages are: Conventional appearance, the compact power source allowing manufacture with closer resemblance to typical firearms. Easy operation and fast rate of fire, valuable for group participation, and training in particular. Fairly uniform velocity; until pressure begins to drop off, CO_2 arms give reasonably consistent velocity without any direct attention on the shooter's part. Good accuracy by the average shooter without physical effort. In contrast, the pneumatic requires pumping and the spring-arm a fairly stiff cocking stroke.

Some disadvantages are: Increased shooting cost. With any CO_2 arm, you not only have ammunition to consider but continual replenishment of CO_2 gas. Also, delicate valves and seals will require some attention. Lower penetration. The multi-stroked pneumatic and the high power spring-air rifle can both produce higher velocity. Temperature changes, both external and within the arm, considerably affect CO_2 operating efficiency. In hot weather or warm climates, velocity will be higher than normal. During cold weather use outdoors, the velocity can drop disappointingly. Depen-

---

**Air Guns and Air Pistols*, by L. Wesley (London and New York, 1955). A good small volume, well-illustrated, and the first devoted exclusively to air-arms.

dency on separate power supply. Sooner or later, very likely at a most inopportune time, the CO_2 supply has a disconcerting way of running out; and with no CO_2, there's no shooting.

Q. Do CO_2 rifles using the dual CO_2 cartridge system produce double velocity?

A. No. They produce only about 10% greater efficiency.

Pneumatic Types

Q. What are some of the pros and cons with the pneumatic air rifles?

A. The pneumatic has one important and outstanding feature: versatility. With power flexibility, it can cover the widest range of possible uses. Indoor, outdoor; small game and pest; plinking; penetration and power comparisons with other types of air arms and, with rear peep sight added, for accurate target shooting. In short, it can perform all of the *general* requirements of the CO_2 and spring-air rifle. The pneumatic design presents a light and very compact self-contained power package, the short overall length made possible by its unique configuration. With air chamber and pump below, the barrel attached on top has an added stiffness, which gives it good accuracy stability without weight. The lack of disturbing jump produces better shooting by beginners, the occasional or average shooter. For some, the mere thought of highest power capability (even if by considerable exertion) holds a definite rapture. In actual practice, however, this high power shooting is seldom used because putting 8 to 10 pumps into a good pneumatic rifle produces an accelerated heart-beat.

Experience generally teaches the proficient pneumatic rifle shooter to stay within the 4- and 5-pump velocity level. Rifling-twist rates of the pneumatic are such as to produce optimum accuracy in that region. As a sage old shooter once observed: "It's shore better to *hit* with less power than to miss with a lot of that there magnum power."

Q. There are several makes of pneumatic air rifles available. Would you comment on each? Can they be scope mounted? Can they be accurized?

A. One at a time, please! The Crosman Series 140 air rifles feature self-cocking and air-lock prevention. However, the "blow-off" system used for compressed air release involves varying pressures on the sear block. With this design, trigger pull becomes harder with each successive compression stroke, intolerable for accurate shooting. This aspect disqualifies these models as a possible top choice.

Sheridan air rifles use the time proven "impact-hammer" system for compressed air release. With this design, trigger pull remains constant regardless of compressed air charge. Sheridan 20-cal. pellets are a good compromise between 177 accuracy and 22 power. The limitation to only one brand of pellets may, to the uninitiated, appear as a drawback because they cost more than regular grades of Diabolo pellets, and no optional style (until recently) was available. Realized or not, this is of direct benefit to the shooter since Sheridan pellets are of match quality and comparably priced. To use one excellent pellet for all forms of shooting has distinct advantages:

No alteration in group point of impact through changing pellet style and weight.

Consistently shooting the same pellet will let the shooter obtain performance knowledge difficult otherwise, thereby allowing him to obtain the best capability from his air-arm.

I cannot recommend scope mounting on any pneumatic air rifle, but the Williams 5D-SH rear peep sight made for the Sheridan is very worthwhile.

Putting a scope on the Sheridan interferes with efficient bolt-handle operation, for one thing, and the mounting itself is rather precarious.

The Benjamin Series 300 air rifles are also of impact-hammer design. Salient features are light weight, power capability and dimunitive size in the hands of an adult. Despite the small stock which can easily be lengthened with wood or rubber spacer, they have a strong appeal to many adult shooters.

The following modifications are simple and, if all are done, will give better handling, accuracy and enjoyable use of the Benjamin 312, 310, 317 and, in part, to other makes and models.

1. Pump handle. Build up to comfortably massive size to serve as a beavertail fore-end, ease pumping effort and prevent pinching fingers.

2. Bumper. Add small patch of rub-

Right—Weihrauch Model 55T spring-air rifle, made in 177 caliber only, for precision match shooting, has fully adjustable click rear sight and trigger, globe front with 4 inserts, genuine walnut stock, hand-checkered fore and aft, with high Tyrolean cheekpiece. About $110.

Left—The BSF Model S60N air rifle shown here is offered in 177 and 22 calibers, the former with extra high muzzle velocity, some 728 foot seconds. The S60N has adjustable sights and trigger and genuine hand-checkered walnut stock. About $57.

Center—The BSF B55 (similar to the S60N) also features high velocity, light weight, and shortened barrel. MV is 700 fps and more with a single cocking stroke, whereas the average pneumatic air rifle requires 7 to 9 pumps to produce the same speed.

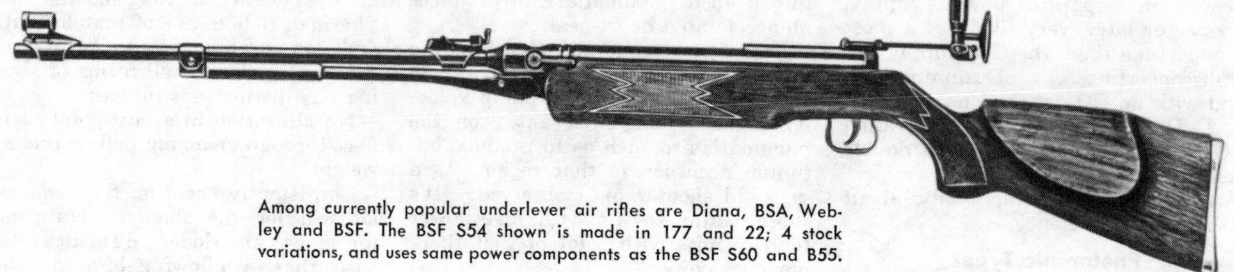

Among currently popular underlever air rifles are Diana, BSA, Webley and BSF. The BSF S54 shown is made in 177 and 22; 4 stock variations, and uses same power components as the BSF S60 and B55.

ber or felt to underside area where pump handle touches pump tube in closed position.

3. Upper grip. Press a 3¼" long piece of slit ¼" (inside diameter) thick-walled rubber hose over barrel section between receiver and rear sight mount boss.

4. Trigger guard. Inlet into stock or remove and deburr, feathering out edges for comfort of middle finger during firing position.

5. Sight, front. Bevel a 45° flat on upper rear corner of existing bronze blade front sight. This simulates the Redfield Sourdough.

Sight, rear. Remove original open rear and install the Benjamin No. 273 rear peep into receiver slot provided. No tapping required.

6. Trigger. Make adjustable by soft-soldering a 2-56 nut on edge to either side of the one-piece trigger-sear. Install 2-56 screw to contact pump tube body, allowing fine adjustment of sear engagement.

7. Lubrication. Thoroughly lubricate area of hammer travel, hammer and hammer spring with mixture of Lubriplate and MoS_2 powder (Molykote) or Molykote G paste.

8. Power. Stretch or replace hammer spring to provide strong enough hammer fall to exhaust 8- or 9-pump compression charge with one hammer blow.

(Fanta Air Rifles, the firm headed by Ladd Fanta, is no longer able to do custom work or modification of Benjamin air guns, but he offers for $1.00 a 4-page pamphlet fully describing and illustrating the alteration described in his article.)

Q. Why are some pneumatic rifles equipped with bronze barrels instead of steel?

A. Pneumatic arms operate on the principle of *decompression*. The act of air release is a cooling one and can produce moisture in the barrel, producing rusting in steel barrels. On the other hand, spring-arms operate on the principle of *compression*, generating heat.

Q. Sometimes I pump my pneumatic more times than usual and get less power. How come?

A. A pneumatic arm which is overpumped will, if it functions, have lower, not higher, power, because the chamber air pressure will be too great; thus the hammer blow, which opens the outlet valve, will not be heavy enough to fully overcome the extra pressure. This prevents release of the entire air charge, which in turn means less power and unused air remaining in the chamber.

Air Arm Tips

Q. How beneficial is the loading technique of pushing a pellet into the rifling (beyond the breech) to overcome friction?

A. Tests show that in some instances velocities can be increased as much as 27% and group size *decreased* 30%!

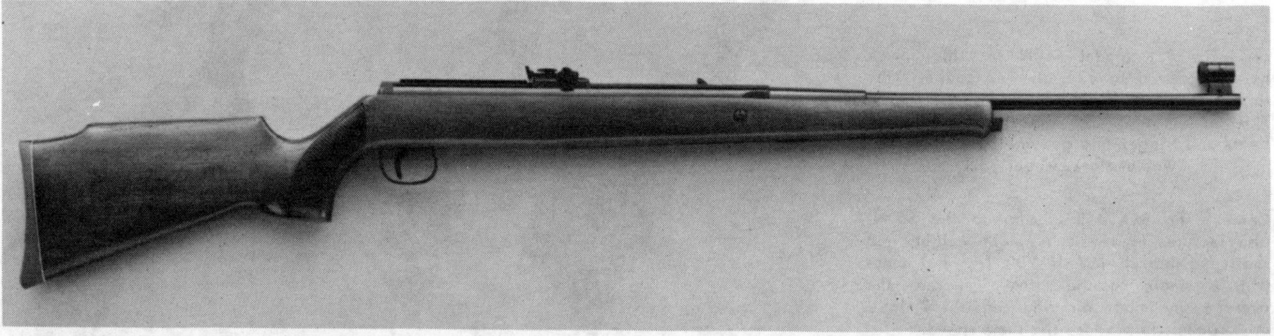

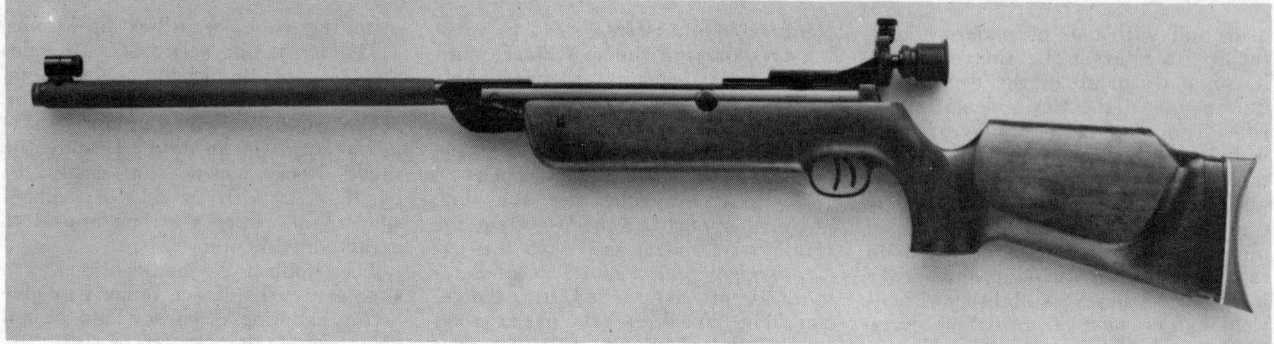

For serious competition, the new line of Winchester Precision Air Rifles includes these two top performers. The Model 450 (top) has a precision-rifled fixed barrel, underlever cocking, adjustable trigger, interchangeable-post/apertures front sight and fully adjustable rear sight. The Model 333 (bottom), top-of-the-line match rifle, has a double-piston action that eliminates all trace of "recoil." A 2-stage trigger, adjustable for weight, pretravel and let-off, has a safety that automatically locks the trigger when the barrel is open. The M333 features a micrometer peep rear sight, interchangeable front sight assembly and hand-checkered walnut cheekpiece stock.

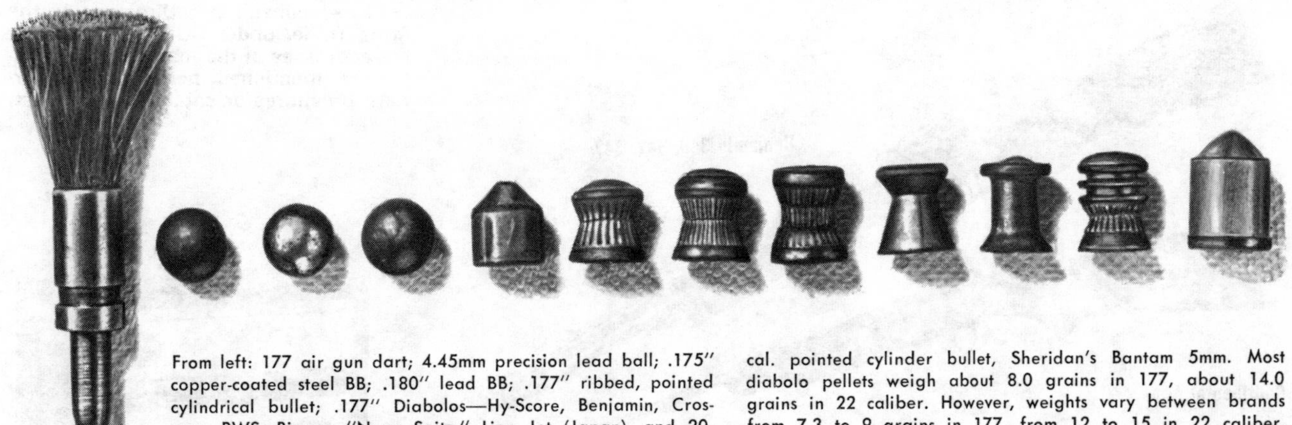

From left: 177 air gun dart; 4.45mm precision lead ball; .175" copper-coated steel BB; .180" lead BB; .177" ribbed, pointed cylindrical bullet; .177" Diabolos—Hy-Score, Benjamin, Crosman, RWS, Bimoco "Neue Spitz," Lion Jet (Japan), and 20-cal. pointed cylinder bullet, Sheridan's Bantam 5mm. Most diabolo pellets weigh about 8.0 grains in 177, about 14.0 grains in 22 caliber. However, weights vary between brands from 7.3 to 9 grains in 177, from 12 to 15 in 22 caliber.

Q. Are bedding and stock-screw tightness critical on a spring-air rifle?

A. Yes, very. The spring-air rifle *must* have all stock screws firmly locked in place. A quarter-turn loosening of a major (fore-end) screw will cause a definite change in zero. New gun screws should always get careful Loc-Tite treatment. For troublesome areas, to ensure proper Loc-Tite hardening and adhesion, first apply Locquic Primer. In some cases toothed lock washers can be effectively used. The more high powered the spring-piston assembly is, the more closely the bedding hold-down screws (and sights) have to be watched.

Q. Should my new spring rifle have an adjustable trigger? How can I make my old air-arm trigger work smoother?

A. The trigger section on the spring-air rifle must do a tremendous job to effect a reasonably easy let-off and still keep the powerful mainspring in check. Cheap guns with no trigger adjustment should be avoided. They will have an oversimplified hard trigger pull, precluding any accurate shooting. There are also some with a next-to-useless form of adjustment which only varies trigger spring tension; not the sear engagement.

Some remarkable results can be easily achieved with most trigger mechanisms by judicious application of MOS_2 powder to already present lubricant or use a 60% MOS_2 paste called Molykote G.

Air Arm Noise

Q. Is there any difference in firing noise between the 3 different air gun propulsion systems?

A. Yes. In a CO_2 or pneumatic air gun, firing produces sudden depressurization, accompanied by a distinct "pop." In a spring-arm, the opposite occurs. The powerful spring-piston produces instantaneous high compression, generating hundreds of pounds pressure. For equal power involved, the spring-air rifle has a noise level several times less than a comparable CO_2 or pneumatic. This can be a very useful advantage where a minimum report is desired.

The noise level even with the highest powered spring-air rifle is so low that one can sometimes get several shots off at pests before the quarry is alerted.

For indoor or backyard shooting (where allowable) this low noise level can also make the difference between shooting acceptance or not by family or neighbors.

Q. What are some of the spring-arm sight problems?

A. Medium and better grade spring-air rifles have satisfactory open sights. Those who have difficulty seeing an open rear sight clearly may find they can get a fairly clear sight picture with the spring-air rifle factory rear sight, some 4" to 8" farther from the eye than those customarily found on a firearm.

Until recently, many spring rifles have had no provision for scope mounting. When one can be mounted, successful use requires: A) A good quality scope whose lenses won't shake loose. B) Very competent installation so that scope and mount will remain in place. C) In the barrel-cocking types, selection of the individual rifle for barrel and receiver axial straightness. You can check this by holding the rifle at arms length, on its side, and sighting of an angle from the receiver to barrel tip. If the usual slight down-tilt is considerable, forget the scope. Lateral alignment can also be amiss.

Peep sights are a better choice and just as accurate for normal air-arm ranges. But some of the same problems applicable to scope mounting exist. The sidelever and underlever type air rifles with their fixed barrel-receiver relationship offer better conditions for peep and scope use, along with freedom from zero changes in sight settings.

Q. Authoritive sources have diametrically opposed views on holding the spring rifle to the shoulder. One says tight, the other loose. Which is better?

A. Whether held tight or loose, *consistency* of developed shooting form is the most important factor.

Shooting the standard spring-air rifle with its small recoil-like effect requires a more careful hold than when shooting a conventional 22 firearm, since any alteration of hold or even shooting position can vary the pellet point of impact. This ability is easily acquired with practice and will pay off with better scores when shooting regular firearms.

Q. Which is the more accurate, the barrel-cocking or the side-lever under/lever type?

A. The fact that all top makers offer under- or sidelever models, with fixed-barrel/receiver relationship, should answer the question. While some hinged-barrel models may equal fixed-barrel models in accuracy *during individual tests*, the fact remains that the fixed-barrel design will maintain a stable peep or scope sight setting, while the barrel-breakdown type invariably has small but continual zero changes.

Pellet Choice

Q. There are many different makes of air-arm pellets on the market. Which are best?

A. Changing brands and styles of pellets promiscuously can cause endless confusion. In some air rifles, various brands of pellets may group as much as 1¼" from each other at 20 feet. Repeater models always require sole use of manufacturer's recommended pellets; to do otherwise causes jams. The inherent accuracy of the flat-headed match pellets makes them just as valuable for the casual plinker and pest shooter. The expert air-arm target shooter pays strict attention to his pellets. By careful experimentation, he has found the brand which performs best in his particular gun. He handles and loads his match pellets with fastidious care. He knows that no air rifle can be any better than the ammunition used in it. Regardless of caliber, exclusive use of one thoroughly tested brand and style

Please consult our Directory of the Arms Trade, under GUNS, PELLET, for the addresses of the manufacturers/importers mentioned here. All will forward brochures or catalogs on request.

Benjamin 340, 342, 347

Continental Arms

Crosman Pumpmaster

Precise Imports air rifle

Marksman MFT target

Pneu Pellet Arms

Benjamin

New air guns for 1969: the No. 340, a BB smoothbore; the No. 342, a rifled 22, and the No. 347, a 17-cal. rifle. All are lever-pumping arms, looking quite like the older Nos. 310, 312 and 317 models, but with such new features as a thumb safety, handy to either hand; new and improved sights, plus grooved receiver for scope mounting. All are single shot, all are $34.95 each, and scope bases cost $7.50 a pair.

Continental Arms Corp.

Czech made, this 17-cal. spring-air rifle has a 10-groove steel barrel and a muzzle velocity of 500 fps. Metallic sights are standard. Price, $32.00.

Crosman Pumpmaster 1400

Crosman's first lever-action 22-cal. pellet rifle features a full size stock, variable power (depending on number of strokes), automatic cocking, adjustable trigger, a right- or left-hand safety, etc., and weighs a full 6 lbs.

Crosman 451 Auto Pistol

Designed to simulate the G.I. 45 pistol, the new 22-cal. 451 holds 6 pellets, uses CO_2 power, weighs a whopping 45 ozs., and has a 4¾", button-rifled barrel. The slide functions realistically on every shot, automatically recocking the gun—and it feels very much like the 45 Colt auto. The rear sight is adjustable, the front is an undercut blade.

Galef-BSA Meteor

We've enjoyed shooting the new 22-cal. air rifle—it handles well, it shows very good velocity (500 fps), and accuracy has been entirely satisfactory. That doesn't mean that I've made any one-hole groups at the prescribed 10 meters, but I put a Weaver 4x scope on the Meteor's grooved receiver and had no trouble making hits on plinking targets at 25-30 yards.

The stock is well-proportioned—though a mite higher comb would be helpful, especially with a scope—and the adjustable trigger pull is excellent. The letoff is crisp and **right now** —no initial take-up as with some other air arms. Our sample has a 3-lb. pull, and I'll leave it there.

17-cal. Meteors are also available, identical with the 22s, and both come with nice rubber recoil pads—I don't know why!

Furnished with a box of pellets, targets and target holder, plus lubricant—and all in a permanent case — the Meteors are a good value at $39.95.

Marksman Products

The Model MPR, a 20-shot BB repeater that also handles 17-cal. pellets, has about the same feel and appearance of the Colt 45 auto pistol. No CO_2 cartridge needed; power is built in. Price, $9.95.

Marksman's new Model MFT Flashing Target, 6-volt battery operated, signals instantly whenever a hit is made in the green, amber or red area of the target; a light of the same color flashes on to show the ring value. Usable with any kind of air pellet, the MFT costs $19.95, complete with instructions, a liberal number of paper targets and a parts list.

We like the MFT target—it worked well.

Precise Imports Air Arms

PIC has a new bolt action 22-cal. pellet rifle ready, one that uses two CO_2 cartridges —not just one—for extra velocity and longer time between changes. Open sights are standard, cost $24.50.

The other PIC air gun is the Roger BB pistol, an autoloader that "will fire 100 shots as fast as you can pull the trigger," if that's your bag. Small or large CO_2 cartridge can be used, a good point, and the Roger looks like an attractive, hand-filling pistol, should make a good training arm. $19.95, including 100 BBs and a CO_2 cartridge.

Service Armament Co.

This new 17-cal. single shot air pistol, used by West Germany as a police training arm, has the feel, weight and handling qualities of a Mauser cartridge pistol. The slide of the LP-210 lifts up for cocking. Price, $20.00.

Stuart Industries

Brand new among U.S.-offered air arms are the Champions, made for 17-cal. and 22-cal. pellets, and looking rather like machine rifles. The break-open-cocking barrel is 12-groove rifled, tested at the factory for accuracy. Rear sight is fully adjustable, the front is a hooded bead.

Loading can be done from the shooting position, and the special trigger design prevents firing while loading. Price, $29.95.

Stuart's Sharpshooter air gun, caliber 17 and 22, while lacking some of the Champion's refinements, is a fully rifled pellet gun at a low cost—$19.95.

Galef-BSA Meteor

Crosman 451 pistol

Stuart Sharpshooter

Stuart Champion

Marksman MPR pistol

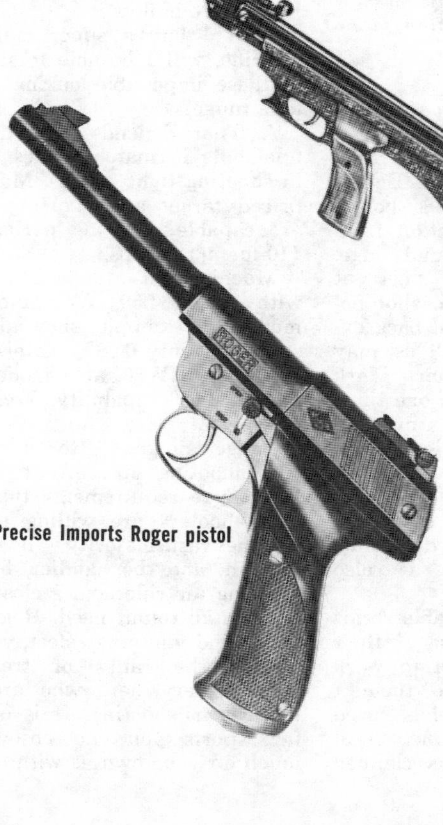

Precise Imports Roger pistol

Service Armament LP-210 pistol

of pellet in your air rifle will result in reliable accuracy for target, plinking and hunting.

Q. Just how strong are the mainsprings in the spring-air rifles? Are they easy to replace? Subject to frequent breakage?

A. Although stressed to the limit, if made of music wire the mainspring is very long-lived. The regular carbon steel springs normally give very good service if common sense precautions are observed: 1. When cocking, stop when a click is heard. Strong-arm banging to the limit is also harmful to leverage mechanism. 2. *Never* "dry fire" a spring-air arm without a pellet in the chamber. 3. Do not store the gun away in cocked position for protracted periods of time; like overnight.

Ease of mainspring replacement varies with design from fairly easy to quite difficult. Some of the high powered models require 150 lbs. *initial* compression pressure merely to install in un-cocked position. Well-engineered leverage allows cocking this brute force with a nominal 25 to 30 pounds.

Q. Is it good to oil a spring-air arm cylinder frequently? How much and how often?

A. Recommended frequency varies with different manufacturers, who after all should know what's best for their product. About 2 or 3 drops every 1000 rounds is a good average. Silicone oil is excellent since it is unsurpassed for leather treatment, which is what the majority of spring-arms use for a piston seal or washer. In contrast, the highly publicized Feinwerkbau air-arms use an all-metal ring and piston construction with factory installed Molykote (MOS_2) lifetime lubrication. Since no oiling is needed, no dieseling ever occurs to plague the shooter. Introduction of MOS_2 powder/compounds into cylinder and mainspring area of conventional spring-air arms can likewise produce very significant cocking ease, velocity increase, wear-free longevity and more freedom from conventional lubrication. Some manufacturers advise plentiful oiling to give a "diesel effect." This not only *increases* velocity but hampers *uniformity* of velocity, which can adversely affect accuracy.

Air Arm Testing

Q. Is there some simple way for accurate air-gun power testing?

A. Penetration testing with air guns has a fascination that few shooters can resist. Very often these impromptu shooting sessions become the basis for future exaggerated stories.

Actually, there are not many sound methods by which the average air-arm enthusiast can make easy but meaningful comparison tests at home. Shooting into or through tin cans, wood and books is fun, but a long way from obtaining repeatable and valid penetration tests. There are many pitfalls in empirical do-it-yourself penetration testing, and I would like to describe at least one method based on some semblance of quasi-scientific common ground.

If you have a good pneumatic air rifle of recent vintage, this can be used as a standard since published velocities with known pellet size and pump strokes are available. Naturally the pumping must always be done in a positive manner from fully open to fully closed.

It is most important to have a material of uniform, non-changing consistency to shoot into for accurate results. The variety of materials chosen is endless, but wood is perhpas the most popular. Wood is also the reason for most conjecture over penetration results. At best, tests against wood are far from conclusive because of its moisture content, grain structure, density, etc.

17-caliber pellets fired into Ballistic Putty at 10 and 5 feet show these results: top, RWS match grade, below Crosman. Note that flat-head RWS pellets become rounded while round-heads flatten out.

Old phone directories or catalogs should have the unbound edge taped or held flat so that the same resistance is offered to each shot. Equal-powered shots fired near the bound edge will differ in penetration from those fired near an unbound edge. Resist the temptation to peek at penetrated pages after each shot because the pages will not fall back exactly in the same place. This may affect next-shot penetration. Mark entry holes and check all at one time.

Metal is also poor for air-arm penetration tests. With incomplete penetration, trying to "read" the dents is misleading, and rebounding projectiles are hazardous. Use of a solid steel splash plate to determine amount of fragmentation is also guesswork and dangerous.

Bars of soap and re-meltable resins are not very useful because of their size, cost and messy clean-up work needed after shooting into them.

For years, Benjamin has used "penetration of (so many inches) of soft pine" for their various claimed power qualifications. Crosman would merely say "maximum carrying range of (so many) yards."

Webley and Scott list ratings by firing through 3⁄64″ strawboards (cardboard) placed ½″ apart.

BSA rates their air-arms by firing into .006″ aluminum sheets of controlled hardness placed ½″ apart.

Regardless of material used, many other things such as shape; weight and design of the pellet; lubrication; power consistency; rifling, etc., can affect penetration.

Some years ago, I discovered an excellent penetration-test material called "dum-dum." It is an asbestos-base plastic sealing compound. Brought to the attention of Air Rifle Hdqtrs., they now use this material for all of their air-arm power testing, and call it "Ballistic Putty."

Like a heavy putty, dum-dum is reusable for penetration tests; is non-toxic and non-shattering; can be formed and reformed to any size; lasts indefinitely and has a homogeneous texture throughout. It is easy to recover pellets from dum-dum to study deformation and rifling engraving. The one I use is called "Duxseal," which belongs to a whole family of similar products made by the Johns-Manville Co.

The material is generally supplied in "pugs" weighing 1 or 5 lbs. A 1½- to 2-lb. piece can be repeatedly formed in minutes between 2 boards to a 2″x2″x10″ bar or other suitable size. Air-arm penetration will seldom exceed 1″ and hits can be spaced closely together without affecting results. A 3″ thickness (backed up) of this dum-dum is also sufficient for any 22 Long Rifle bullets.

Q. If I buy a super match grade air rifle, will I be able to shoot some of those impossible-looking groups at long range?

A. That depends. The deluxe refinements in match grades only *help* in shooting tight groups. Many lower-priced target and sporting air arms are capable of firing perfect 33-foot (10-meter) groups.

Machine-rest groups at 10 meters with the $64.50 Weihrauch HW55 model, for example, show an extreme spread of only 0.08″, center-to-center. The little HW30, at a modest $36.50, has an 0.18″ capability. *You* may not do so well!

Long range (40 to 50 yds.) air rifle shooting of really tight groups has severe requirements that few casual shooters are willing to pursue. To the vast majority, an air-arm is for fun; and the handier, high grade sporting air rifle comes closest to filling the all-round need. Regardless of what kind you may select, you will be joining the ranks of trend-setting people everywhere who are turning to air-arm shooting. It is one of the few sports you can enjoy just as much on your own as with others. ●

Ibex in Iberia

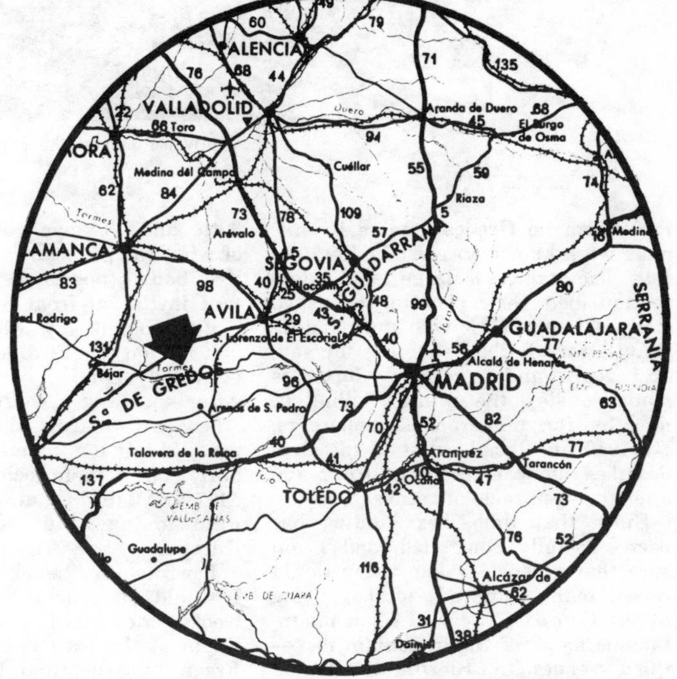

Cabra Montes—the long-horned goat that is unique to Spain—travels the wind-swept ridges of the high and rocky Sierra de Gredos. Finding a big one in three days was the challenge.

by JOHN T. AMBER

THE NINTH WINCHESTER Seminar for writers and editors was held in Europe in December of 1967 (see GUN DIGEST, 23rd ed., p. 30), and during our week's stay in Spain for red-legged partridge shooting there were a few evening entertainments—despite the fact that we never got back to Madrid from the shooting area near Toledo until 9 or 10 o'clock. From then to midnight is the fashionable time for dinner in Spain, however, so we didn't really miss much—after shedding our hunting clothes, followed by a quick bath and an equally quick drink or two, we'd be ready for whatever the agenda offered.

One of these affairs was a cocktail party given by Herb Jerosch—then manager of the Castellana Hilton in Madrid — followed by a great dinner in the grand manner in that famous hotel. The cocktail party was well attended—in addition to our small group of Jack O'Connor, Pete Barrett, Bill Talley, Bob Petersen, et al, there were many figures from the world of sport and Spanish government present, among them his excellency Don Manuel Fraga Iribarne, the Minister for Touring and Sport.

Senor Iribarne is a great enthusiast for sports in general, and for hunting in particular, we soon learned after being introduced to him. With the welcome help of Senor Max Borrell—who speaks English fluently—acting as an interpreter, we were deep in gun and shooting talk with Don Manuel. The upshot was that Jack O'Connor and I were invited to visit Spain in the fall of 1968 to hunt the famed Spanish ibex — *Capra hispanica* — in the Cote de Gredos some hundred miles west of Madrid. Sometime before the hunting season opened in September we'd receive the formal invitation, we were told, a choice of dates in September and October would be offered and, having selected a suitable time, we'd receive by mail the hunting license itself.

The Spanish ibex (locally, Cabra Montes) has been held by Abel Chapman* to be an animal found only on the Iberian peninsula, and nowhere else. He wrote "To this splendid game-animal, the Spanish ibex, we allot place of honour in our list [of game available in Spain] not only because he represents the supreme prize in Spain to the cragsman-hunter, but also by virtue of the species being peculiar to the Peninsula. . . . The ibex of Spain stands out clean cut and distinct from all of his congeners (family) the world over, as a lion differs from a leopard, or a grouse from a blackcock."

**The Gun at Home and Abroad,* Vol. III (London, 1914).

Cabra Montes

The Spanish ibex is a small animal, about 30-34 inches at the shoulders, average weight some 70-80 pounds. In summer the back shows brownish-grey, shading off down the flanks and legs into tannish-white. There is the usual beard, typical of the goat family, long and thin in an old ibex.

The horns are quite different from other ibex; the triangular-section horns start upward and outward from the head, then go backward and, at the tips, inward, thus performing a half-spiral. The front surface of the horns is divided into ridges, but nothing like the prominent knobiness of other ibex.

At the turn of the century the Spanish ibex was almost extinct. In

Early morning at the Parador de Gredos.

the Sierra de Gredos a mere 15 animals were known to exist in 1905. At that dire stage, the large landholders relinquished their shooting rights to King Alfonso XIII, who immediately shut down all ibex shooting for several years, and a serious effort was made to stop the wanton killing of ibex by the numerous sheepherders. By 1910 an official count of the Gredos ibex alone showed well over 400 animals—a miracle of recovery.

Since that time ibex hunting has been carefully controlled, and I am sure that a census taken today would reveal many hundreds of ibex living in the Gredos. Several other mountainous areas of Spain contain ibex—the Pyrenees, the Sierras de Cazonia y Segura and de la Serrania de Ronda, et al.

For the reader who might like to do some hunting in Spain, let me point out that the invitational procedure I've touched on earlier is the preferred way of going about it. True, organized partridge shooting—which can be arranged through Winchester's World Wide Adventures—and other hunting can be arranged after one's landing in Spain, but to bring a gun in without having an invitation means visiting a Spanish consulate or embassy here, describing the gun in detail, getting a special firearms entry permit, and the applicant must show his State hunting license as well.

Spain, like most European countries, keeps firearms under strict control, which perhaps explains why those entering Spain carrying firearms should have an invitation to show the police and customs agents on arrival.

In due course I received my invitation and list of dates to choose from, so I selected October 3d to 5th. Jack O'Connor received his invitation also, and we were planning on hunting the Gredos together. Unfortunately, Jack had to forego the ibex hunt, but I left London for Madrid on September 30th, and I'll give you an idea now of what the problems would have been if I hadn't possessed that all-important invitation from Sr. Iribarne.

I'd brought my Model 77 Ruger bolt action to Europe, which 308 I eventually carried on the ibex hunt. After spending a short time in Italy, I flew to Frankfurt, the rifle still with me (I'd left it in bond at Milan's airport), but I then decided to send the M77 to Madrid by air freight. I didn't want to lug it all over the rest of Europe.

I wrote on the shipping tag that I would be reaching Madrid a few weeks later, that I was coming to Spain at the express invitation of Sr. Fraga Iribarne, and that I'd collect the gun on my arrival.

Trouble at the Pass

Despite these precautions, it took me almost 2 hours to obtain the rifle, and I was aided by the secretary of a Madrid friend, a girl fluent in English and Spanish. We had to talk to the police and customs men—pay a few small fees—before I got that rifle. It would have gone faster, I learned, had I carried the rifle with me.

I'm not complaining, I'm just telling it like it was—when in Rome and so on, of course, and U.S. frontier agents can put just as many obstacles in the way of the foreigner entering this country, to mention not the troubles a returning citizen sometimes has.

So—with my Ruger rifle and my cartridges at last in my hands — I set off for Madrid. I planned to spend a couple of days there, get settled in at the hotel, shop for a couple of last-minute things I wanted for the hunt, then make the drive to the Gredos mountains.

I'd been warned that the Gredos were rough and rocky in the extreme —no cover of any kind, the scattered vegetation thin and low—so I wanted to get a pair of moderately heavy work gloves, preferably of leather, and perhaps a pair of lightweight leather chaps. There'd be a lot of scrambling up and down the boulder-strewn slopes, and plenty of crawling about on my hands and knees, I'd heard.

Maybe I went to the wrong stores, but I could not find one glove shop that had the kind I wanted! Never heard of 'em, I was told, so maybe the Spanish laborer does his stuff barehanded. In any case, I bought a pair of pigskin dress gloves—for which I was thankful later—but passed up the only *chaparejos* I saw; thin, too-dressy types and all quite short. I could have brought the right kind of gloves with me, of course, but I'd thought Spain—famous for leather goods, and justly so — would have work gloves!

On October 2nd I rented one of the little 850 Fiats—a 2-door coupe with a rear engine, 4 on the floor and no guts. Matter of fact, it was fun to drive, though the gearbox was in constant use—it handled well, no power steering needed, and on the last 50 miles or so of winding, twisting gravel roads that led upward toward the Gredos, I found it cornered nicely, too. The heavy rear end was a little twitchy on the loose-gravel bends once in a while, but there wasn't enough power in hand to break it loose—and lose it.

Parador de Gredos

I reached the Parador de Gredos late in the evening. Spain's secondary or country roads aren't any better marked then some of ours, and I made a miscue a couple of times. These paradors—or tourist hotels—are scattered over much of Spain now, invariably at or close to some national park or other attraction for the visitor. The parador at Gredos is a long structure of weathered grey stone, two stories high, with a long and inviting verandah open to the sun. From this southern exposure the valley drops away, then gradually rises, first gently, then steeply into the immensity of rocks and boulders great and small that make up the Cote de Gredos. It's a grand view at any hour. For those who appreciate a quiet, restful holiday, basking in the sun or walking through the countryside, the Parador de Gredos offers a charming and soothing environment. There is, thankfully, no radio or television in the rooms—nor in the library or lounges—no entertainment of any kind. The service is excellent, though, the food and wines very good indeed. The rooms are ample and delightful, the furnishings simple but adequate, with much handsome wood panelling.

I was to enjoy my too-brief stay here, but now to bed for I'd be getting up at about 6 in the morning. I had been expected, of course, so even though I got there too late for the regular dinner period, some food was made available through the gracious help of a waitress and the cook.

The next morning, under a brilliant blue sky, I drove about 10 miles to my meeting place with the *guardas* who were going to find me an ibex. My lunch and theirs, stowed in huge saddlebags, had been handed to me at the parador, and included was a full liter of local red wine—*tinto*—for each of us.

Two of these deeply-tanned, weather-beaten men were to be my guides, the third one acting as horse wrangler. Our mounts were already saddled, and in a moment we'd left this end-of-the-road rendezvous—already well up into the foothills of the mountains—and were on our way. It was a beautiful day, my new companions were friendly and jovial fellows, and I was looking forward, keyed up and excited, to my first glimpse of Cabra Montes — I felt great.

I'd been briefed in Madrid by a man who'd been hunting in the Gredos recently, so I already knew what the general strategy would be. In good weather we'd climb the horses a few thousand feet, then dismount and make our way to the top of the ridges. There we would be in a position to glass the rocky slopes below, to clamber down on foot if ibex were spotted far below or descend also to see if any bucks were lying up underneath the overhanging cliffs.

By 8 o'clock we had reached the first mountain top, eroded away to a fairly broad, roughly rounded area, broken here and there as we moved forward by great, jagged masses of solid rock jutting up into the sky. These formed good vantage points for scanning the country below, but were usually impossible to get around without our scrambling several hundred feet down to easier, shale-covered slopes. Here we could skirt the base of the great rocks, then climb back up again to the tops.

Sierra de Gredos

The Gredos peaks there are not extremely high, some 7000-8000 feet or so, but I suppose we must have climbed up and down their steep and boulder-strewn slopes a score or more times during that day's hunt. Getting down was much harder work usually, leaps having to be made of 5 or 6 feet onto the next big rock below, but the climb back up was almost as bad. I was soon puffing and blowing, but I'd at last make the ridge again. I was to lose 12 pounds in that short time, and I became so dehydrated that I drank water endlessly at the end of the day—or so it seemed.

About 10 o'clock that first morning, after we'd gone down the rock

The guardas of the Sierra de Gredos are rugged, hard working men, good at their job and fond of it.

face for the 5th or 6th time, my two guides had moved in behind a huge boulder to glass the area underneath it and to see the section to the left as well—ibex could be concealed here, asleep or lying up, which we couldn't have located from the top.

Suddenly they began whispering excitedly, and I knew they'd found ibex. Both men were stretched up on tiptoe, peering over the rounded mass of rocks at a steep angle, for the ibex were lying asleep on a ledge almost vertically below them. All this I sensed instantly, of course, but I'd learned long ago that in European hunting you generally wait for a signal from the guide before moving up for the shot. I stood there, wondering what was going on for what seemed like several minutes but was doubtless much less, when Paco motioned me forward, indicating by gestures that I was to shoot.

I squeezed in between them, my glasses ready to locate the ibex below me, but I'll be damned if I could find them. Frantically I swung the binoculars, trying to see almost straight down and everywhere else, but not until they moved did I see that there were three ibex, running at top speed out of there. My rifle was propped up against the rocks! In another movement, some hundred yards away, a band of 16 or 17 ibex jumped up and ran. The first 3 had been lying some 200 yards from us.

This larger bunch the guides had not mentioned, indicating to me by their raised hands only the 3 first seen, but there was the usual frustrating language problem. I've got only a smattering of Spanish, so perhaps they had seen the others and said so, but that wasn't what bugged me then and during the next couple of ibex sightings.

Sleeping Ibex

I had never seen an ibex before, of course, and I had no real idea of what they would look like. Not until I saw the 3 running did I realize how beautifully their brown-tan-white coloration blended in with the rocks and brown soil we were on. Those 3, too, had been lying asleep, Paco told me finally, but I hadn't known that earlier.

I now tried to explain that because I was unfamiliar with the game, that because I'd have trouble again, no doubt, in spotting any ibex located, that I wanted to get my glasses working as soon as their's were onto an animal.

I didn't get the message over, I could see that, for on the next couple of times that ibex were located, the same damned thing happened—I'd be called into position at the last moment, just before the ibex moved out, it seemed, for my own locating of them. True, I was finding them now a lot more rapidly, but I still wasn't all set to shoot. Fortunately, on these first several small bands, I saw nothing worth shooting, and the guides agreed.

Still, I was getting in some good practice at identifying ibex—which was to prove invaluable later—and I was now shoving my way up to the lookout point just as soon as I could see that ibex had been located. If a good head did show, I was going to be a lot better prepared than I had been.

The day wore on, sunny but nicely cool, and about 2 o'clock the guides, the wrangler and I sat down to eat, a cold, clear spring close by. I was, of course, kicking myself a bit for not having got a shot at the first trio—two of them had good horns, I'd thought, and Paco agreed—but the hunt wasn't over yet. The meal break was welcome, and I had my fill of water, wine and thick cheese sandwiches. It was good to be up in the mountains again.

Evening came, and while we saw several bands of ibex through the rest of the afternoon, none had horns I was going to settle for this early in the game. I was hopeful of taking a gold medal goat, a record-book ibex—which my ticket permitted—though I might change my mind about that on the third and last day if I'd been unsuccessful.

The horses were tired at the end of our first long day, and so was I.

It was a long haul back to the meeting place, much of the ride in darkness. I was bone-weary, again extremely thirsty, and glad that my poor old horse knew the way home without strong guidance from me.

I reached the parador about 8 o'clock, changed and showered, then sat down in the pleasant dining room to a good dinner—over which I almost fell asleep.

Hundreds of Ibex

I got to the guide's corral next morning, not quite as full of energy as I had been the day before. I had got a good night's sleep, but yesterday had been tough—too tough maybe—but I was still keyed up about finding a really big ibex, and the whole day stretched before me.

That entire day was pretty much the same as the day just passed—we climbed up and down interminably, we got back on the horses now and then to move to another range, and we saw, I suppose, at least a hundred ibex—mostly females and youngsters, with none of the bucks presenting a first class rack. In the two days we must have looked over some 200 ibex, I think.

At about 5:30 or so we were toiling back up to where the horses stood. The three of us had dropped down into a steep-sided narrow canyon, one that stretched downward and away at about 90 degrees to our main ridge. The western edge of this canyon rose high and sharp-edged, its other side sloping away to a broad valley far below. We had been unable to see anything of that offside slope, so we'd descended into the canyon floor, then scaled the wall to peer through the vertical cracks and openings in it hoping to find game somewhere on the other side. Nothing—we three looked through our glasses slowly and carefully, handicapped at this hour by the sinking sun at our backs. The broken, jagged rocks below our eyes were filling with shadow, growing more inpenetrable by the moment. Nothing moved.

Ernesto and I scrambled down to the canyon's floor, then started climbing back up among the stones, headed for our main ridge and the horses. The hunt was over for the day. Paco, however, had not descended to the bottom of the canyon; instead, still searching for an ibex, he'd continued to move along the steep canyon wall, stopping to use his glasses as he went. Then, as Ernesto and I were well up the mountain—and well away from Paco at an angle—he whistled softly. I didn't hear him, but Ernesto did, and because he was in front of me I could see him motioning to me to turn around. Paco was beckoning to me urgently. Quartering my way to him as fast as I could over the tangle of rocks, my rifle loaded and safe, he pointed steeply down as I reached his side. Far below, just inside the shadow line stood a big ibex in a narrow cleft in the rocks. Only his back and fore-quarters were visible, his magnificent horns looming over his withers as he fed, head down.

Muerte!

Leaning way out from the opening in the rock, I raised the rifle and fired, remembering as I did to hold low on the animal's shoulder. At the report Paco shouted *"Muerte, muerte,"* clapping me on the back and pumping my hand in congratulation. By this time Ernesto had reached us, and we began a 3-man celebration. The ibex was indeed dead — Paco said he'd never moved after the shot — but now came the job of getting to him. I'd made the shot at about 200 yards, but the open valley floor was far below that, the course up to the dead ibex filled with great rocks—and steep. Night, too, would be on us in a half-hour or so.

By this time our wrangler had started toward us, leading one horse for me, but the guides waved him off, shouting that he was to bring the horses down the other side of the ridge and around to the valley floor below our ibex.

I'm willing to confess that I sat and rested where I was. I wasn't about to scramble down to that ibex —he wouldn't go away—then have to climb back up again, perhaps. I'd had just about all of that I could handle in two days, and the successful *cazadore* has some privileges, no?

The men soon reached the ibex, dressed him out and tied him behind a saddle as I watched. I'd changed my mind, of course, and after resting a few minutes I'd also made my way down to the ibex. His horns measured just 77 centimeters each (30.3 inches), neither one damaged or broomed, and I was pretty damned well pleased with myself and my very good ibex. No, not a gold medal trophy, but at the time I made the shot I'd have settled for an ibex showing a lot less horn! I'd about had it.

We had hunted a range this day much farther off than before, and the ride back took nearly four hours. Happy hours, though, riding under a brilliant moon, singing and laughing—I was sorry to have it come to an end as we reached my little car.

The horns of this Capra hispanica measured 77 centimeters, well above average.

I drove back the next morning to collect my horns and make a few pictures—it had been too dark at the time I'd shot—and said goodbye to my guides. Hard-working, game-wise, competent and friendly *companeros,* and if it had not been for those last-moment efforts of Paco's I might well have left for Madrid empty-handed. ●

SCOPES & MOUNTS 1969-1970

A mount 'em and shoot 'em evaluation of the year's scopes and mounts crop—we're getting good glasses today, mostly, says the author.

by BOB BELL, Editor of Pennsylvania Game News

● **Bausch & Lomb.** No additions have been made to the popular B&L line of scopes this year—understandable after last year's announcement of the full line of Trophy scopes and mounts. One deletion has been the Balvar 24, the large 6-24x variable power target scope. It's our understanding that this big scope, a favorite with a number of benchrest riflemen who liked the way its variable magnification let them adapt to different mirage problems, was so expensive to make that its price couldn't be maintained. Since it was already by far the most expensive scope in America, apparently it was felt that an increase was not in order and it was discontinued. This is not to say that it, or a revised version, could not appear in the future—and somehow this wouldn't surprise me.

Howard Palmer, B&L's product administrator, tells me they have some new items under study, but nothing will be announced in the near future.

During the past year we have had the opportunity to do rather extensive shooting with the two Trophy scopes mentioned here in GD-23, the 2½-8xBalvar B and the 4x Balfor B. The most obvious difference between these and the Custom line are their internal adjustments. These have ½ MOA value and are accurate. We tested for this by mounting the scopes on an accurate 222 heavy barrel rifle and shooting. Such results could be determined by mounting the scope solidly, cranking adjustments and watching reticle movement against a target of known dimensions, of course, but we've always found it more interesting to actually shoot and watch how points of impact responded to reticle adjustments. Point of impact does not change when power is changed—highly important in any variable design scope.

The Balvar B is currently on a 7mm Magnum, where it seems right at home, and the Balfor is awaiting the completion of a lightweight 7mm/308 rifle, which should make a fine deer outfit with this gin-clear glass aboard.

All B&L scopes have external finishes of aluminum oxide, a very tough material. I don't know how much usage it takes to get them to show wear, but this pair is still gleamingly unmarked. (I think it would be an interesting experiment to offer dull-finished scopes for hunters such as myself who are always expecting highly polished surfaces to spook game; but maybe I'm the only one who worries about this.)

These scopes are bedded in the bridge-type Trophy mounts described last year. Their outstanding feature is the Allen screws used to secure the ring halves and to fasten the rings to the bases. All of us seem to eventually mar screw heads with conventional screwdrivers; Allen wrenches eliminate this problem. We wish the same type of screw would be used to fasten the base to the receiver. In the four samples we have, slotted screws are used.

We've used this mount with perfect success on the M70, M700 long and short, and the Sako action which has integral male dovetail blocks. A friend had some trouble with the Trophy base on the Remington M760, apparently through an imperfect fit on that curved action; this gave an out-of-flat top surface when the base was snugged down, reportedly enough to spring the scope tube slightly. It's the only adverse comment I've heard on the Trophy mount.

A useful accessory from B&L is the Quiet-Ear hearing guard—an earmuff type sound deadener, made in top- and back-band models. I prefer the latter, as it permits wearing a hat at the same time. The Quiet-Ear has a lining of polyurethane and seals tightly around the ears. It's comfortable to wear for reasonably long periods of time, and it really takes the *crack* out of shooting. If I'd had one of these 25 or 30 years ago my hearing doubtless would be a lot better now than it is. Price, $7.95.

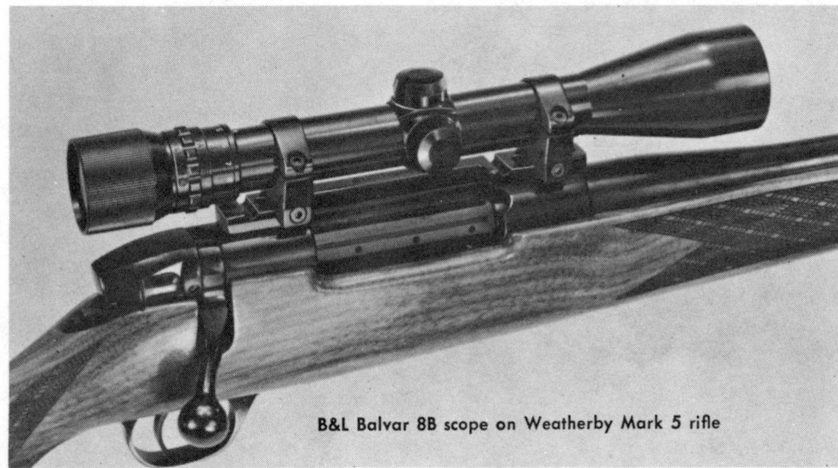
B&L Balvar 8B scope on Weatherby Mark 5 rifle

● **Browning Arms Co.** continues to market three scopes, all of high grade. For their high power rifles they list a 2-7x variable and a 4x, with a small-diameter 4x for their 22 rifles. The latter has crosswire reticle only; while the others may be had with crosswire, flat-top post or dot. Their bridge-type mount has split rings in three heights: .142", .272" or .402". A special barrel mount base is made for the Browning 22 auto rifle, and split-ring mounts that fit the grooved receiver of the T-Bolt 22.

● **Buehler, Inc.** has for many years offered strong, extremely well made bridge-type mounts. Several designs —one-piece bases in two lengths, two-piece bases, and the Micro Dial with integral ¼-minute windage and elevation adjustments—permit any kind of shooter, stock-crawler or turtlenecker, to install whatever suits him best. The Forward Mount for Remington's 600 and 660 hooks over the top of this carbine's recoil lug to help prevent scope movement, though this has never been a problem with any Buehler mount.

General manager Bob Ray tells me they've been getting quite a few requests for mounts to fit Herter's U9 round receiver rifle, so two-piece bases are now offered. Also, since some lucky riflemen have somewhere found a few Brevex Magnum actions, a limited supply of two-piece bases have been turned out for this outfit, at a slight price increase. If demand warrants, it will be added to regular inventory. Buehler mounts are also available for the new Smith & Wesson and Series 1200 Parker-Hale rifles.

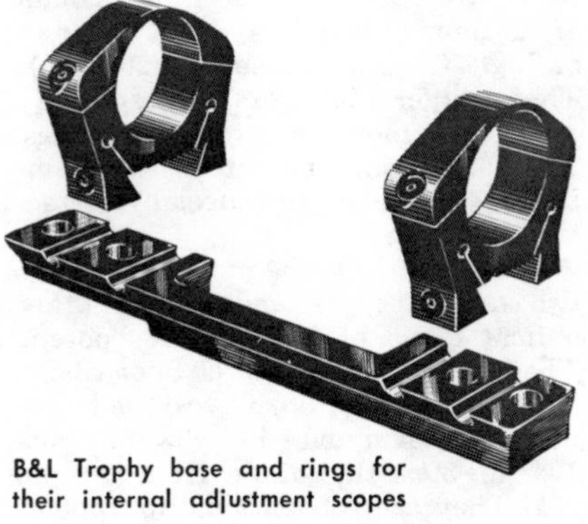
B&L Trophy base and rings for their internal adjustment scopes

● **D.P. Bushnell & Co.** also has taken a breather, after introducing a boatload of new items last year. This is understandable—in fact, seems a wise thing to do. We've never felt a scope company had to bring out a lot of new stuff every year. It's a better procedure to improve what's gone before, if necessary or possible at a given price.

Bushnell's Scopechief IV series has a 20-year warranty, against 10 for the Custom line and 5 for the Banners. The two higher-priced lines are still made with built-in blocks that fit the Universal mount studs, now available to fit the 8-40 threading of the Remington 788, Marlin 44 and new Marlin 336, as well as the more common 6-48 holes.

A new economy version of this mount sells for $9.95, against $12.95 for the basic model and $14.95 for a streamlined unit. This mount consists of a set of 1" rings and the necessary studs. A high 6-48 stud is made for the rear position on the Savage 99, and this mount would seem to be a good choice for this rifle—much more easily installed than a mount requiring holes in the side of the action. A tiny error there leads to all sorts of elevation problems.

Because the mount blocks are movable along the scope tube, either on the built-in or separate designs, they easily adapt to different action lengths. This is more important than it used to be, with so many manufacturers now making rifles of different lengths, and some, such as Remington, making several sizes. Studs of three heights permit basic adjustment for elevation, and an oversize base hole for one stud has opposing locking screws which give preliminary windage adjustment.

For awhile I was a bit leery of this mount, I must say. Those two dinky little screws just didn't look strong enough to hold glass and rifle together when the going got tough. But I've had one on a hard-kicking outfit for a long time now, and it works. Thus this somewhat late comment on the Universal mount.

There isn't a lot new to say about Bushnell's Scopechief scopes. They've often been reported on here through the years. Now in their fourth generation, they were darn good to begin with and they've been improved regularly. No hunter is likely to find fault here.

Those who enjoy hunting or plinking with 22 rifles should consider the Scopechief 22 in 3-8x ($19.95) or 4x

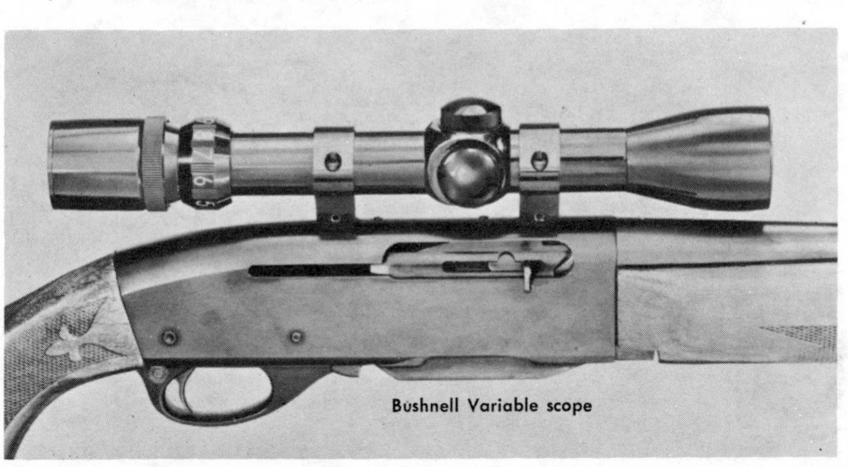
Bushnell Variable scope

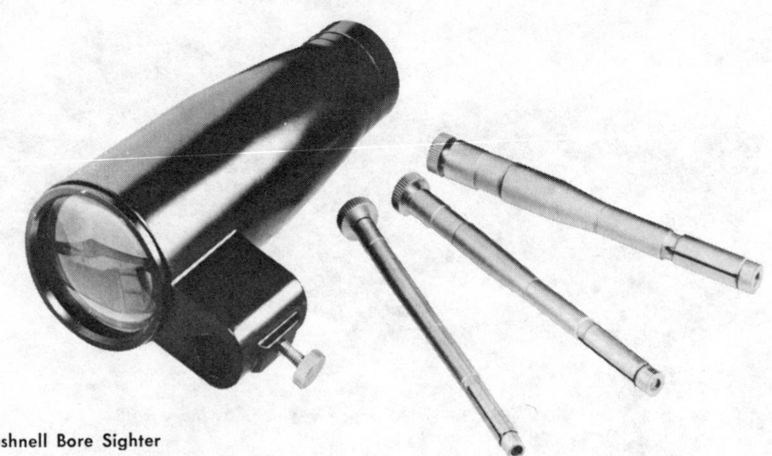

Bushnell Bore Sighter

($14.95), or the Custom 22 in 3-7x ($15.95) or 4x ($10.95). Both are built on 7/8" tubes with integral mounting rails, internal adjustments and eye relief long enough for the rimfires or Hornet-Bee class.

Bushnell is now offering a Bore Sighter—a collimator for aligning the optical axis of a scope with the rifle bore. A number of these are now on the market. This one is different in that two types of arbors are made—single calibers in 9 sizes (22 to 375) at $2.25 each, or expandables at $3.95. There are 3 sizes of these, one for bores of 22 to 7mm, the second 7mm to 35, and the third 35 to 45 caliber. I prefer the single caliber style. Bore Sighter price, $24.95.

● **Collins Co.'s** Bulittco scopes are unchanged from last year. Since then we've had a lot more time to use them and can report very good results with the 6x on a lightweight 6mm. This makes a good combination for the times when you are tramping the back meadows rather than cruising back roads. The 6x is not too much power for offhand shooting, but high enough for average work on chucks.

Collins now offers an unusual mount for 22 rifles with grooved receivers. It is adjustable for height, permitting use of iron sights by aiming beneath the scope. Appearance seems odd to one used to low-mounted scopes, but doubtless this will appeal to some. It's made for 1", 7/8" and 3/4" tubes. $4.98.

Also distributed by Collins is the West German-made Steiner Model BS-30 E binocular. An 8x30 glass, it is contoured to fit the hands, has a Fiberglas case and individual focusing. Less than 4" tall and 7" wide, it is the sort of binocular a hunter would be inclined to carry, rather than leave in camp. Price, $44.95.

● **Compass Instrument & Optical Co.** markets a line of aluminum tube scopes for high power rifles—2½x, 4x, 6x 12x, 3-9x and 2½-10x—as well as a 4x and 3-7x for 22s. The big scopes are on 1" tubes, the small models on 3/4". Choice of crosswire, post or dot in most.

● **Conetrol's** super-streamlined mounts continue to build a following among hunters who want a strong outfit with no projections whatsoever. They are made for all rifles which will accept a conventional screw-attached top mount low over the receiver. The two lines, Custum and Huntur, each come with bridge or two-piece bases. Rings are solid or split, in 1", 26mm or 26.5mm diameters, low, medium or high (no low version in 26.5mm). These larger diameters are especially useful in mounting foreign scopes. The short bridge mount for the Remington 660 makes an especially attractive outfit, we feel.

● **Davis Optical Co.** manufactures two target scopes and several other optical items of interest to shooters. The target models, called Spot Shots, have 1½" or 1¼" objectives, the larger diameter available in powers from 10x to 30x, the other from 10x to 20x. They are conventional in appearance.

Davis also makes long eye relief eyepieces which can be installed on most American scopes. These cut magnification approximately in half and greatly lengthen eye relief, thus permitting use of the scope on a handgun. $15.

At the other end of the glass, Davis also makes Targeteer attachments in 1½" and 1¼" objective diameters. Installed on low power hunting scopes, these increase magnification to 6x or 8x, thus converting a big game hunting scope to one suitable for general varmint shooting. The owner can install these units, which employ the threads already in the scope tube for attachment. Field of view is reduced when power is increased, of course. Prices run from $18 to $29.50.

We've never used a Davis attachment, but in years past did considerable shooting with Litschert modifications of apparently similar design, and found them well worth their cost.

● **Firearms International Corp.** can supply excellent ring mounts for the Sako rifles which have integral dovetail blocks. Split rings are made for 1" and 26mm tubes, in three heights for the smaller diameter. An extension ring is available if additional eye relief is wanted. Knurled rings tighten these mounts onto the tapered dovetail blocks, making a design which recoil only tightens. They're beautifully finished. We've used them and like them.

● **J. B. Holden Co.,** Box H-1495, Plymouth, Mich. 48170, recently came into the scope mount market with a design called the Ironsighter. The design makes possible the instant choice between scope and iron sights, as it raises the glass sight some 3/8" and provides "look-through" ovals in the bottom of each mount ring. The Ironsighter mount is made for many popular high power rifles, as well as some rimfires and shotguns.

How much demand there is for such a rig we cannot guess. Shooters who grew up using iron sights often don't completely trust scopes until they've used them several seasons. These people frequently try to use both sight types at once—and not infrequently end up using neither, as they frantically switch from one to another, trying to make up their minds. The vast majority of scope users want nothing to do with iron sights. Nevertheless, there can well be occasions when a drenching rain or an accident puts a scope out of action, and at times like this, the Ironsighter mount could save the day.

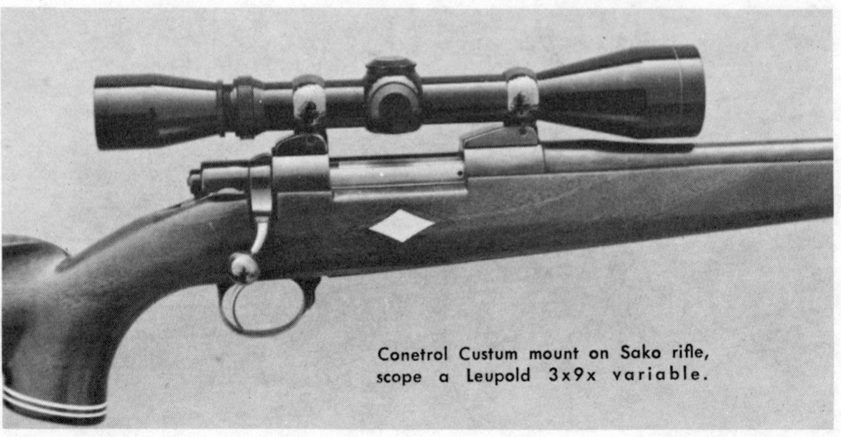

Conetrol Custum mount on Sako rifle, scope a Leupold 3x9x variable.

● **Jason Empire** has added a pair of competitively priced scopes for 22s to its line, a 4x at $7.95 and a 3-7x at $14.95. Their 4x, 6x and 3-9x for high powers are now said to be waterproof (samples not in yet, so no direct report can be made), and a high luster finish replaces the brushed satin of last year.

● **Kuharsky Bros.** A note from Tom Kuharsky says everything they make in this line now has the Bausch & Lomb name on it. Pretty good name, huh?

● **Kwik-Site** (27367 Michigan Ave., Inkster, Mich. 48141) is the name of a new mount ring style designed, if we interpret the photos correctly—and that's all we've seen so far—to fit Weaver style bases. The unusual aspect of these is their stilt-like appearance. They position the scope an inch or so higher than normal, thus allow instant use of iron sights. $11.95.

● **T.K. Lee Co.** has been installing Tackhole Dot reticles in scopes since the early 1930s, and reportedly has over a half-million such aiming points in the field at present. A *very minute* percentage of these are mine! Others belong to top shooters like benchrester Red Cornelison, who has turned in some record groups using his, and numerous members of the Army's Marksmanship Training Unit. I was interested to see that for hunting Lee advises rather large dots (9″ - 3″ in the 1½-4x variables, for instance), and this agrees perfectly with my comparatively limited experience. Bench shooters can get Lee Dots as small as 1/32″, if desired, but most prefer ⅛″ to ¼″, even in a 30x scope.

● **Leupold & Stevens,** perhaps because of their Portland, Oregon, location, where it's been known to rain on occasion, have for years turned out a line of scopes as weatherproof as any we've seen—and more so than many. But this is only one of their qualities. Their Golden Ring glasses are tophole all the way, with brilliant lenses that give excellent definition and accurate adjustments, as proved by tests over a period of years. Jack Slack tells us that the 10x and 12x varmint models announced a year or so ago have been in short supply, but are expected to catch up. Two models, the 7½x and 2x, have been boosted $5 in price, to $74.50 and $46.50.

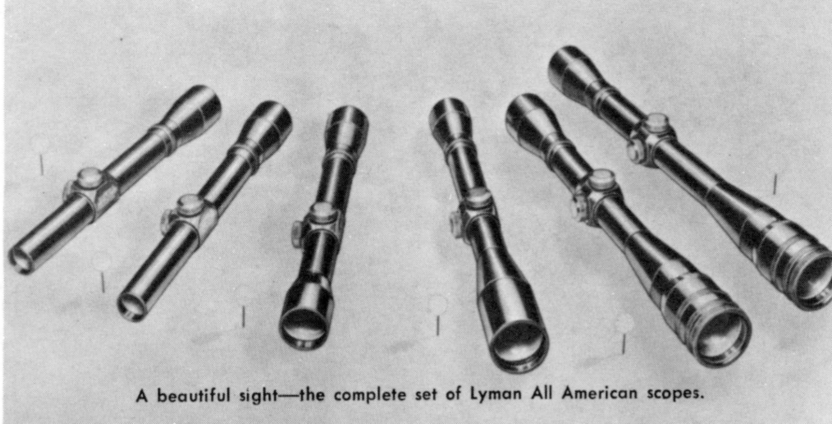
A beautiful sight—the complete set of Lyman All American scopes.

L&S continues to test their scopes on a machine that duplicates the recoil effect of a 375 H&H, as well as submitting every scope to a water test at 120 degrees F. and a vacuum of minus 10″ of mercury—a procedure that reveals the smallest leak. That explains why a leaking Leupold is hard to find!

Leupold-Stevens Detacho mount

● **Lyman Gun Sight Corp.** Some months back, J. A. Widner arranged to have a complete set of Lyman's All-American hunting scopes sent along for full testing for this Scope Review. Usually we get only samples of new items each year. However, this seemed an interesting project and we were glad to give it a whirl. The line includes 2½, 3, 4, 6, 8 and 10 powers, the latter two having movable objective lens units for range focusing, which of course eliminates parallax as well as giving the best optical qualities possible with a given scope.

To begin with, we tested each scope for leakage in the normal manner—submerging it in a pan of fairly hot water. This heats the air inside the scope, causing it to expand; bubbles escape at any unsealed point. No bubbles appeared in the low power models. In the 8x, a very few escaped from a point beneath the rear of the movable objective lens housing. This was not a steady stream of bubbles as sometimes is seen, but only 3 or 4 slowly emerging singles. Whether this would be important to a shooter depends mostly on his mental attitude. In a practical sense, it's of no consequence.

Shooting on several rifles — a 222 and a 6mm—indicated that w. and e. adjustments were as advertised. These, incidentally, are different in each power and different than most other scopes; i.e., 2½x, 1″; 3x, ⅞″; 4x, ¾″; 6x, ½″; 8x, ⅓″ and 10x, 3/10″. A shooter used to making corrections in ¼ or ½ minutes can get mxied up here if not careful.

These All-Americans have unusually long eye relief—at least 4″ in all powers—making them ideal for heavy-recoiling rifles.

We've used a 10x for years on a favorite 6mm varmint rifle with never a complaint. Some benchrest shooters also have chosen this model in matches where weight is important, and this indicates a quality not achieved by many hunting style scopes.

Metal finish is a solid looking black, not the super-glossy shine so typical of many makes — which I'm always expecting to spook game long before I get into range, if a vagrant sunbeam hits it.

All in all, these All-Americans are fine scopes, suitable for any rifle.

The Lyman Tru-Lock mount is made to fit 1″, 26mm, ⅞″ or ¾″ tubes. One- or two-piece bases are available for over 40 popular rifles. Notches in the bases prevent slippage due to recoil.

● **Noble Mfg. Co.** has discontinued its scope line.

● **Numrich Arms** has redesigned their mount to fit original GI 30-cal. carbines as well as commercially manufactured ones. This mount, which fits 1″ tubes, is positioned centrally over the bore, has a deflector for the empties being squirted out. $6.95.

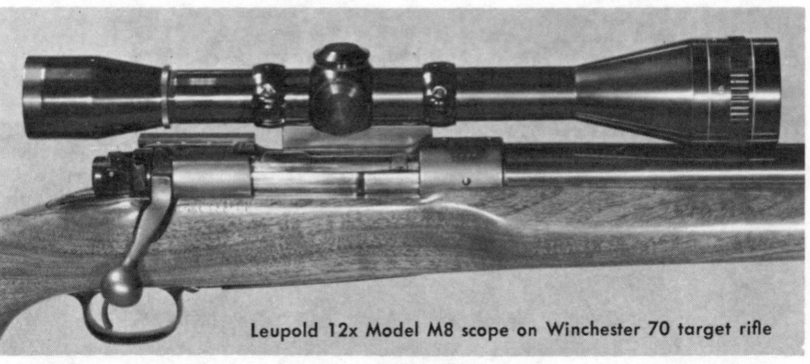
Leupold 12x Model M8 scope on Winchester 70 target rifle

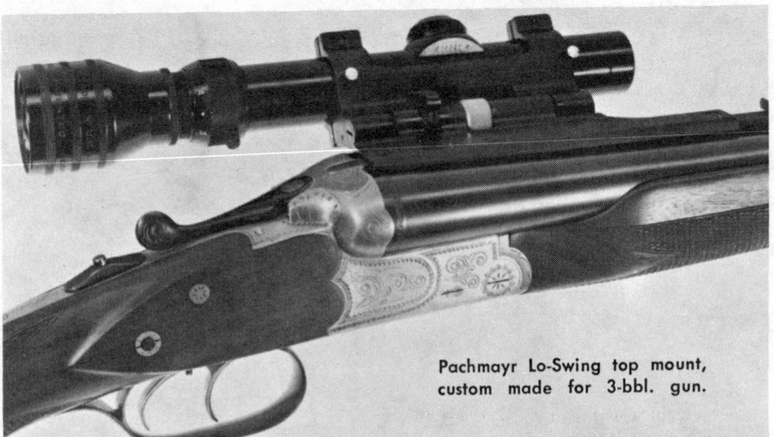

Pachmayr Lo-Swing top mount, custom made for 3-bbl. gun.

● **Pachmayr, Inc.,** has redesigned all their Lo-Swing top mounts to allow more latitude for eye relief. This was accomplished by moving the hinge point farther forward on the base. Probably everyone knows by now that this Pachmayr mount permits swinging the scope aside to use iron sights, whenever such might be felt necessary, then returning it without loss of zero. It should be mentioned that the top mount version fits factory holes, while the side mounts require tapping.

Windage and elevation adjustments normally permit close correction in the mount, leaving only final zeroing for the scope's adjustments. This is important with the older scopes having non-centered reticles, and is a good idea even with the new ones, as you're then using the best-corrected portion of the lenses for aiming.

In recent years, Pachmayr has been making quite a few custom mounts for double rifles, and for some double shotguns used primarily with slugs. This design has a tapered, spring-loaded release pin to prevent backlash on these monsters. It reportedly performs very well, which indicates this Lo-Swing mount will work on anything . . . which we never really doubted. It's a good rig.

● **Pacific Gunsight Co.** Four big game models are currently offered by Pacific, a 2½x32, 4x40, 6x40 and 3-9 variable. Called the Supreme line, all are on standard 1" tubes and have ¼-minute clicks. The large objective lenses in relation to power in the straight-mag models give large exit pupils, which make fast aim easy, and good light transmission. Two lower priced 4x scopes, the Standard and Deluxe, have been discontinued.

● **Realist, Inc.,** has added two new Camputer scopes, both variables, to their selection of Auto/Range models. Last year's GD described the method by which this line of Realists works; that is, the method by which a pair of movable stadia wires in the reticle is adjusted to bracket the 18" vital area of a deer or antelope, at the same time raising or lowering the scope by means of a precisely machined cam to bring the aiming crosswire to dead-on zero. A different cam is necessary for each load, of course, because of variations in trajectory.

The first scope offered was a 6x, and later a 4x. Now a 3-9x and 1½-4½x are available. In these, the computing/camming/compensating is accomplished by rotating the power change ring. In these variables, because of changes in field of view when power is switched, the stadia wires will bracket an 18" target at approximately 150 yards when set at 3x. At 9x they bracket 18" at 450 yards. Thus the power generally suited to the range is the one you automatically get. The maximum range to which this unit will work in the variables is 450 yards—and that's far enough for any reasonable hunter to try shots, in my opinion.

The Realist mounting system has been strengthened this year with a steel mounting rail for the A/R models, and scopes have been beefed up internally for continued use on magnum rifles.

Test shooting on an accurate target weight 30-06 indicates this Realist Auto/Range system works; however, under field conditions, it's not a simple chore to hold these stadia wires on a live critter off in the distance and at the same time try to twist the cam to make the unit just bracket said animal.

The 3-9x model is slated to appear with 9" stadia wire separation for varmint shooters.

● **Redfield Gun Sight Co.** is another organization that constantly updates and improves its scopes without changing model numbers, designations or whatever. Through the years, we learned firsthand that the popular variables were redesigned to incorporate improvements. During the past year, the low power models were altered to even stronger one-piece tubes and bells, with a general beefing up inside.

We've been using one of the latest 4xs for some months now, and it's a great scope. (I know some friends are gonna be shocked that I even comment on a straight power job; I've plugged the switch-powers so long that several even call me "Variable." But truth is, if I had to use a good 4x for all of my big game shooting, I wouldn't feel at all handicapped.)

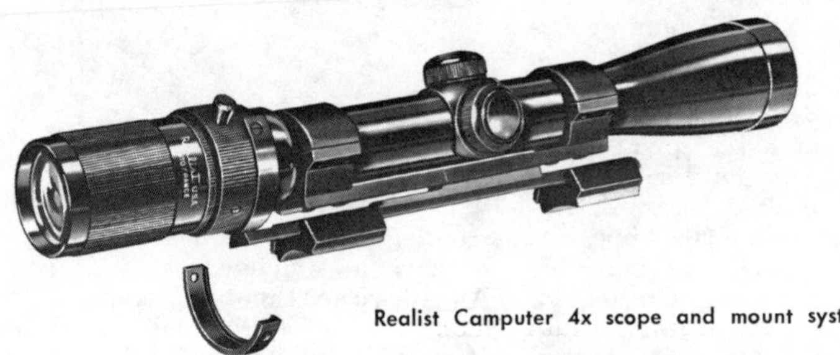

Realist Camputer 4x scope and mount system

The Redfields with 1" tubes are now called "Magnum" scopes. Most come with a choice of half a dozen reticles. This 4x has a 4P CCH, meaning 4 posts with center crosshair. Actually, it's a 3-diameter reticle, the outer ends subtending 3.2 MOA, the intermediate portion 2.1 and the center, .8. (This is different in each power of scope.) This reticle would seem a complicated gizmo to manufacture, but it's very fast in use, and doesn't disappear in bad light as some stan-

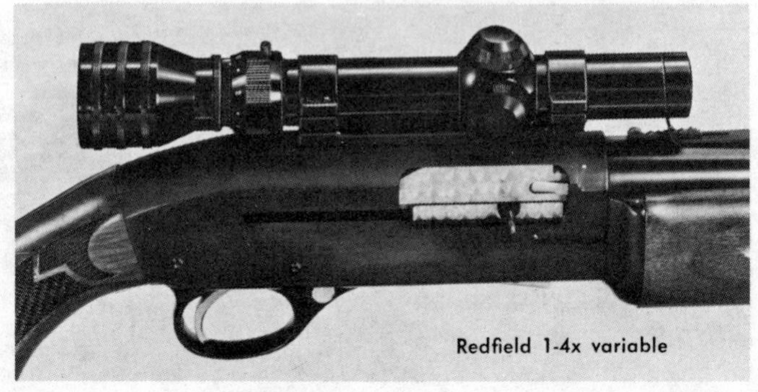

Redfield 1-4x variable

dard crosswires do.

As normal with Redfields, the adjustments are accurate and dunking in warm water reveals no leaks.

The 1-4x variable, brand new as we went to press last year, has received a good workout since. It seemed an ideal choice for the 338 Magnum, and that's where it's been riding this past twelve-month. I long ago settled on one load in this lengthened-mag gun—the 275-gr. Speer ahead of 77/4831. This disassembles even larger elk neatly, wraps them up and delivers everything to the freezer, with energy left over. It also shakes glassware up a bit, since the whole caboodle weighs maybe 8½ lbs. So far, the little Redfield variable has come up smiling, which is more than I can say after a long morning at the bench. Here is a scope that belongs. Only questionable aspect is that the w. and e. adjustment marks are awfully close together, which makes zeroing in a bit more time consuming than it might be. But this is checked only a few times a year, so it's no great sweat. With the same reticle as the 4x, this is a fine scope.

At the other end of Redfield's size range is their 3200 Target Scope. It was described at length in this review last year, but deserves further comment. We had a 20x then—serial number 11, as I recall—and it was returned after a couple of months for other writers to play with. Some time later a second one arrived for more extensive shooting. This one is a 24x.

Redfield's VARD, an optical 1½ power rear sight attachment, focusable by the shooter.

For new readers, it should be mentioned that the most unusual design features of the 3200 are its internal adjustments and its solid mounting. No other genuine target scope has these. It takes a helluva lot of self-confidence to believe you can manufacture inside-working w. and e. movements accurate to a quarter-minute, but someone out Colorado way obviously has that confidence—and ability—for these work. Tell you how I know. I retired an old 6mm Cobra barrel from a pre-WW II M70 action and had Al Wardrop fit and chamber one of Clyde Hart's fine stainless bull barrels in 308 caliber. Then I shot it, with this 3200 aboard. The thing about an outfit like this is, it makes you wish you could shoot well enough to do it justice. Suffice it to say, the scope works. If you're interested, so does this Hart barrel and those 168-gr. Sierra International projectiles.

This 3200 has excellent resolving power, its field is flat to the edges, with no color distortion, and the target image is clear and sharp. Eye relief is long enough so that there's no problem with recoil, and the exit pupil is large enough—about 1.7mm—that the scope has good light transmitting characteristics. Our sample has a fine crosswire reticle which subtends .125 MOA and makes it simple to aim at a smallbore bullet hole at 100 yds. if desired. The medium crosswire covers .187″ and a ¼″ dot is available. All in all, this is quite a scope.

Among other interesting reticles at Redfield (and the aiming device in a scope is awfully important, as you'll soon realize if you try to use a rifle scope without one!) are the 4-Plex, which is essentially a less-complicated version of the 4P CCH, as it has only two diameters in the reticle, and the CH Peep, which is a tapered crosswire having a hollow dot or circle at the intersection. This has most of the virtues of the well-known center dot, but never conceals your exact aiming point. I haven't used one long enough to make a choice between it and the dot. Regardless, it gives riflemen another choice. No extra charge for the 4P CCH, 4-Plex or CH Peep.

● **Remington Arms.** Biggest scope news of the year comes from a company not at all known for telescopes—but certainly one of the world's great gun manufacturers. We're speaking, of course, of Remington Arms Co.

For quite some time now, doubtless due in part to the influence of Mike Walker and other top riflemen and designers at Bridgeport, Remington has been turning out extremely accurate bolt action rifles in various categories—hunting, varmint and bench. It seems likely that the M700 in one weight or another is as accurate as most "custom" jobs that anyone is likely to meet, whether in big game bush or varmint meadows. The M40-XB turns in one-holers so often that it qualifies as a benchrester.

With all this going for them, it apparently was only a matter of time until they decided to take a look at the glassware that goes on top of these shooting machines. Since total rifle/sight weight is important in bench shooting, it's obvious that the lighter the glass is, if there's no sacrifice in optics, the better, for this allows additional barrel weight while staying within weight limits. Also, to eliminate any effect on grouping ability due to part of the scope's weight being applied to the barrel via the front block, it's advantageous to mount the scope elsewhere. This is difficult to do, resulting in extended action-sleeves—an expensive proposition.

Remington's 40XB-BR and 20x Scope, both brand new.

Considering all desirable aspects, the Remington people decided to build a scope that would embody as many as possible. This, they've done. At this writing, a few have been produced and they should be available everywhere soon. The scope is a 20x, weighing just 19⅜ oz. and measuring 16¼″ long. Objective lens diameter is 36mm, eye relief 2¼″, and field of view 7½ feet at 100 yards. Optics are top grade. The scope's short length permits mounting on the action of the 40-XB. At present, Unertl micrometer-adjustable external mounts are used. These are longtime favorites of most bench shooters; still, I wouldn't be surprised if Remington came out with their own mounts shortly. This would give them a complete bench-grade outfit—rifle, scope and mount. As far as that goes, I wouldn't be surprised if they offered the scope in 12x or 14x for varmint shooters too, though this might not take place immediately.

The 40-XB has been redesigned in some aspects for bench shooting, but I'm certain that will be covered elsewhere in this edition, so I won't go into that here. I do feel Remington has come up with a winner in this scope.

● **S & K Mfg. Co.** has added Insta-mounts for the FN 1949 Auto rifle and the AR-15, Sid Haight tells me, making a baker's dozen of military rifles which these popular mounts are adapted for, including various SMLEs, Springfields, Mausers, etc. These mounts certainly have been a boon to the hunter using a surplus rifle. The more conventional steel ring mount announced in last year's GD is being continued, and by the time this sees print a new alloy ring of the same design should be available. Projected price, $7 per pair.

● **Sanders Custom Gun Service** carries a full line of Japanese-made scopes called the Bisley Deluxe. They cover the power field from 2½x to 10x, including three variables, one being an unusual 5-13x with 40mm objective. Tubes are aluminum alloy.

● **Savage Arms** has come out with a bunch of new guns this year, but no new scopes. We've had one of their 3-8x variables for a couple of years now, and it still is performing flawlessly.

● **Scope Instruments** has boosted what was an extensive line of hunting scopes—19 Target Master models last year—by the addition of 3 Target Master Ultra scopes. The 2½x and 4x models have 32mm objective lenses, which give good light transmission, while the 6x has a 40mm objective. Tubes are one-piece aluminum, reticles Perma-locked, optics "amber" coated. Crosswire or post reticle.

● **Southern Precision Instruments** has added a 1½-5x and 2-7x variables to a selection of hunting scopes which also includes all regular powers from 2½x to 10x. All these are on standard 1″ tubes, with CH, post or tapered crosswire reticle. For rimfire rifles they have a 3-7x and a 4x on ⅞″ tubes.

● **Stoeger** currently is offering three fixed power hunting scopes, 4x, 6x and 8x, and a 3-9x variable, the last being the highest priced at $46.95. All are on 1″ tubes. Specs are similar to other scopes of this power. For use on heavy recoiling rifles, eye relief is a minimum of 3″. Clicks are ½ MOA.

● **Swift Instruments'** 2½-8x Zoomsight continues to lead this company's sales, followed closely by their 4x Gamescope, which would seem to bear out our contention that these powers are about what most hunters want. The Zoom model has a 40mm objective, which gives more than enough light even at top magnification, while the 4x uses a 32mm lens. Exit pupil here is 8mm—more than the human eye can take advantage of. The Swift line is rounded out with the variable Yukon 2½-8x and straight power Grizzly, Stag and Bighorn glasses, in 2½x, 4x and 6x.

● **Tasco** lists 23 scope models, far too many to cover here in any kind of detail. A half-dozen of these are for 22 rifles (all have tip-off mounts), the remainder being low- to medium-priced hunting models. The Target Marksman 4-12x, at $49.95 with Opti-centered crosswire, post or dot, is the top of the line. This is a big scope with a 40mm objective and a 10-lens optical system. Most models come with haze-filter caps.

Author Bob Bell examines Al Wardrop's bench outfit that carries a 2″ Unertl 24x scope.

● **Tops.** This lineup of scopes is unchanged from last year—five models in the standard powers from 2½x to 10x. New this year from Ed Paul is the Parallel Scope Corrector, a collimator for making the basic adjustments for zeroing a scope. Similar to several others on the market, it sells for $32.50 with two bore plugs; extra plugs, $3.

● **Unertl Optical Co.** At $192, the Unertl Programmer-200 seems to be the most expensive scope in America. At 45 oz. it's certainly one of the heaviest. And no matter how you look at it—or through it—it's one of the best. For new shooters we'll say that this is an extremely high grade target scope having a 2″ objective lens, 1″ tube, and external mounts featuring ¼ MOA adjustments. It's made in most even powers from 8x to 36x, this unusually high magnification being useful only to a few bench-rest shooters. 18x to 24x is probably the most common power bracket.

Two design features are of interest. First, a linearly spaced cam which has dwell positions at all the common target ranges, plus a secondary graduated ring for final precise focusing. This eliminates the tedious focusing via fine-pitch threads common to most target scopes. Second, the Posa-Mount system. This uses split frame mounts with a binder screw in each that engages a notch in the mounting block to form a recoil lug. Combined with the full-surface contact made possible by the split frame, this system is far superior to the older cup-shaped screw engagement.

This scope is a favorite of shooters who don't have to be concerned about weight and who want a sighting instrument second to none.

All Unertl scopes are noted for their ruggedness (seamless steel tubing makes up the main units) and optical efficiency. They're made in all common powers for big game or varmints, as well as for all kinds of target shooting. About the only style not available is the variable power . . . and somehow it seems hard to imagine one of these coming from Unertl.

Unertl also makes several fine spotting scopes, the most interesting, perhaps, being the 100mm Team Spotter. It's intended for team coaching primarily, but I've always been fascinated by the idea of using one of these tripod-mounted glasses—preferably in 32x—on the range. But somehow I always seem to be a few bucks shy of the $450 price tag. Oh, well. . . .

● **Universal Firearms Corp.,** probably best known for its 30-cal. carbines, is now offering a full line of hunting scopes under its own name. They come in all straight magnifications from 2½x to 10x, 3 different variables and 4 models for rimfires (these have tipoff mounts). The UI-40, a 10x with 40mm objective, is their most expensive straight power at $34.95. In variables, a 3-9x and 1½-5x retail for $42.95 each. Both have 40mm objectives, which seems a bit unusual in the lower power, but the large exit pupil should make it fast to use. Another 3-9x and a 2½-8x are offered with 32mm objective.

● **Weatherby, Inc.** As announced here last year, Weatherby now has two complete lines of scopes, the well-known Imperials which have internal adjustments, and the newer Olympians, which are near duplicates optically but which have no adjustments. Each line comes in 2¾x, 4x, 6x, 2-7x and 2¾-10x. The Olympians have crosswire reticle only, while the Imperials may also be had with Lee Dot or Open Dot ($12.50 extra for either), as well as the post or CH design.

Since the Open Dot is the newest, we obtained a 4x81 Imperial with this reticle for testing. This style actually is two concentric circles, the inner one very small for precise aim at tiny targets in good light, the outer one large and heavy enough to be immediately seen under any conditions that could be called normal for hunting. A thin vertical line runs from the bottom of the scope's field almost to the outer circle. In use, I found this line a bit distracting, but it is apparently necessary to insure that the scope is mounted plumb (which in turn is necessary if windage adjustments are not to affect verticals, and

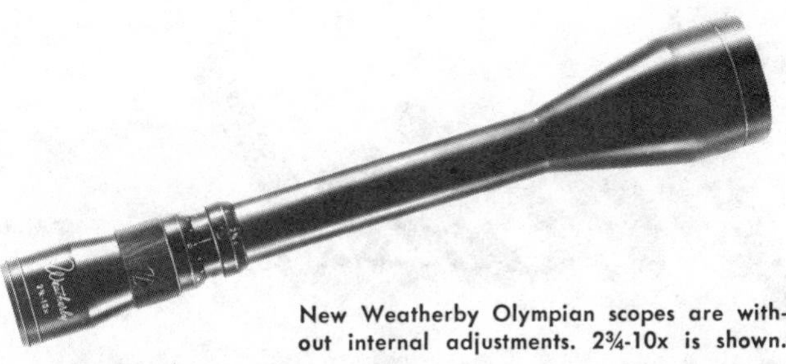

New Weatherby Olympian scopes are without internal adjustments. 2¾-10x is shown.

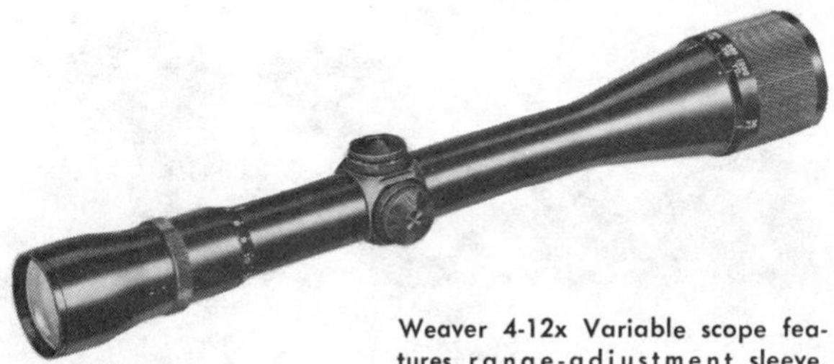

Weaver 4-12x Variable scope features range-adjustment sleeve.

vice-versa). Nevertheless, I'd personally prefer to have no vertical line here. This Weatherby Open Dot does not hide the target at all, is beautifully simple in appearance, and extremely fast to use—quite a change from some manufacturers who seem to believe that the more complicated a reticle is, the better.

As with the other Imperials, the 4x81's w. and e. adjustments are protected under one weatherproof cap, with focusing arrangement under another. Elevations are via ¼-minute clicks, while windage corrections are made by a coin-movable friction ring. These German-made Weatherby scopes are clear and sharp in use, as well as attractive in appearance. We like them, and particularly this Open Dot reticle.

New from Weatherby is a 20-45x zoom spotting scope having a 60mm objective lens. Complete with case and tripod, price is $114.50; scope alone, $99.50, or with fixed-power eyepiece, $85. At this writing, we have not had a chance to use this spotter, so cannot comment directly. Knowing that Roy Weatherby has an intense interest in maintaining high quality in anything that carries his name, we expect it to perform very well.

● **W. R. Weaver Co.,** the outfit that really started the swing to scopes in this country, has added one new glass to their line this year—the V12. Actually, there just isn't room for many additions, as the K series currently extends from 1½x to 12x and the Vs from the small 1½-4½x up through the 2-7x, 3-9x and now 4-12x, not to mention the rimfire models, V22, C4 and C6. About the only type missing in the Weavers is a true target scope . . . and who knows—maybe one of those is on the drawing board now. The ¾″-tube A2.8 and A4 are not listed in the latest Weaver catalog.

Getting back to the new V12, this is the same size and weight (13″ long, 13 oz., 1″ tube with a front end diameter of 1.86″ and eyepiece diameter of 1.48″) as the earlier V9. Adjustments are ¼-minute clicks, focusing is via a fast-moving objective housing, and power switch is accomplished by turning the complete eyepiece. Eye relief on our sample measures 4″, which is more than adequate even on a heavy recoiling rifle. Field is 24-9 feet, per specs and tests both. This is less than a straight 4x would give, by about 13%, but that's part of the price you pay for the variable's other conveniences. Properly mounted on a well-stocked rifle, this is enough for woods use, more than enough for open country.

Weaver Dual-X reticle, an excellent hunting type.

One of my most accurate rifles is a M700 Remington Varmint 22-250. With the 55-gr. Power-Lokt bullet and 36/4895, ½″ groups are common. I mounted the V12 on it to test the adjustments and its use for general varmint shooting. The testing indicated each click was worth a scant ¼ minute. Even when moving only one or two clicks, as during final zeroing of a load for field use, the reticle responded precisely, indicating no lost motion in the machinery. This is important, as it can be hellishly frustrating to sit at a bench and shoot and shoot and shoot, trying to get a group centered exactly where desired, and have it ping-pong across that point but never settle there. The V12 didn't do this for us.

Don't know how rugged this scope is, for to tell the truth it takes quite a bit of shooting even on a hard-kicking gun to shake a good scope apart. We haven't had time to go that far with this one, and don't expect to. If there's one thing we've noted about Weavers through the years, it's that they ain't delicate!

The V12 is available with CH, Dual X, P-CH, Range-Finder and, at extra cost, Center Dot. These reticles are offered in most K and V models. The Dual X, which has fine crosswires at the aiming point coming out of 4 posts, is now made in the V22 scope for rimfire rifles. This is a very useful reticle, one I'm coming to prefer to conventional crosswires, as it's more usable in dark woods, gloomy weather, etc.

Strictly for big game shooting, the little V4.5 is still one of my favorites. This past hunting season I switched mine to my wife's lightweight 257 M722, which has been cut to a 20″ barrel and restocked, and used it for deer. It again proved ideal on Pennsylvania's hardwood ridges, the big dot proving fast and accurate on a short range brush shot. The load, incidentally, was Hornady's 100-gr. bullet ahead of 41/Reloder 21, for some 2850 fs. It went in the top of the shoulders and exploded in the lungs for an *instant* kill, no fragment of bullet exiting or even marking the opposite side of the rib cage.

Weaver 4-12x variable

the 38 Special - -

new life or last gasp for police use?

A pipsqueak load, says the author, with—at one and the same time—too much penetration and too little shocking, stopping power. There'll be those who don't agree, but . . .

by JAN A. STEVENSON

The 38 revolver, rejected by the Army in 1904 as too ineffective for combat use, is to be found today on the hip of practically every cop in the country. Police experience over the past 50 years proves the Army was right. 38 Colt Official Police (bottom) compared to the gun it replaced, the 45 Colt New Service. The New Service was the standby of such hell raisers as the Border Patrol. The Canadian Mounties stuck with it for 13 years after it went out of manufacture. Note difference in size of the 38 and 45 cartridges.

THE 38 SPECIAL is America's favorite centerfire handgun cartridge by such a large margin that comparisons become ludicrous. As a police service round, the 38 is the standard and standby of practically every North American police agency,* most of whom require it to the exclusion of all others.

Additionally, it is the nearly unanimous choice of private police and security agencies, guards, couriers, armored transportation agencies, many branches of the military, householders, storekeepers, and practically everyone else who carries a handgun for defensive purposes.

*True, a small handful of departments use the 9mm M39 S&W, the M1911 45 ACP, the 41 and 44 Magnum, but these few hardly make a dent in the 40,000-odd police organizations estimated operating in the U.S.

All Specials—Far left, the standard 158-gr. round-nose service loading—a notorious pipsqueak. Next, the 200-gr. blunt-nosed "Super Police," an over-rated round. Last three cartridges are attempts to get the 38 on its hind legs. Square-shouldered bullet (center) gives good shocking power, penetration for car bodies. Cup-point bullet expands immediately, minimal penetration. Best for urban use, but generally taboo for publicity reasons. Square-shoulder hollow point (right) is excellent compromise.

Thousands of target panners will use nothing but the gilt-edged accurate 38 for centerfire competition. And finally, far more 38 Specials are reloaded annually than all the other pistol and rifle cartridges combined.

With such an enthusiastic following, and such long established acceptance, it would seem that the eternal popularity of the round would be as universally recognized and unchallenged as the 10 Commandments. So it often seems.

Admittedly, the 38 has a lot going for it. If you are shopping for a gun, the weapon you want is chambered for the 38 Special, whether it be a flyweight, snub-nosed belly gun small enough to be concealed in the palm of your hand, or a 3-lb., foot-and-a-half long, scope mounted hunting pistol, or a super-accurate target automatic.

If you buy your ammo over the counter, with no other caliber do you have as wide a choice of loads as with the long-time favorite 38 Special. Approximately 15 different factory loads are available, ranging from blank cartridges to wadcutters, with just enough power to drill a clean hole in a paper target, to high velocity armor-piercing rounds.

If you reload, no other cartridge offers so many convenient possibilities. Brass is always plentiful. The cartridge is a wonderfully flexible one with which to work. It contentedly gobbles up every powder in the book from ultrafast burning Bullseye to slow simmering 2400 rifle powder. Swaged bullets, ready-cast bullets, and dies or molds for making your own are available in endless profusion. The round can be loaded down to be less objectionable than a 22, or upward to equal 357 factory ballistics. Plastic or wax bullet loads are readily gotten.

Police instructors love the 38, because it is superbly accurate, and its mild recoil makes it easy to train recruits with. It has been hailed as "the perfect pistol cartridge." Indeed, the 38 Special is more popular than the Beatles.

With a set of qualifications like this, badmouthing the 38 Special sounds about as level-headed a thing to do as objecting to the institution of motherhood. Yet a lot of level-headed people are doing it these days — the former, not the latter.

Forty yars ago, Elmer Keith was almost alone in proclaiming what knowledgeable police firearms men are now coming to recognize—that as a police cartridge, the 38 Special stinks. Back about the turn of the century, A. C. Gould, writing under the pen name, "Ralph Greenwood," was a voice in the wilderness editorializing against the pipsqueak round. He was in good company with such combat seasoned officers as U.S. Cavalry Lt. Eben Swift, and the British empire-taming army officers, Maj. Gen. H. E. C. Kitchener and Lt. Col. G. W. Fosbery, V.C., of the Bengal Staff Corps. But no one was listening; least of all America's police, who were busy climbing on the 38 Spl. bandwagon.

In a few instances, the adoption of the 38 was a step in the right direction. New York City, for instance, known as one of the world's finest departments, used the 32 before they got in step with the times.

For most agencies, though, the switch to the 38 was a great leap backwards, to borrow a phrase from pseudo-political scientists. The U.S. Border Patrol, as gun savvy an outfit as ever enforced the law, used M1917 45 revolvers until, sometime in the 1930s, they decided to swing with the times. The New York State Police, in the late 40s, abandoned the magnificent New Service 45 Long Colt when they made the changeover.

The last outfit to toe the mark was the renowned Royal Canadian Mounted Police, who reluctantly turned in their old glory-encrusted 455 New Service in 1954—thirteen years after the weapon went out of manufacture. It was a sad day for the student of police ordnance when the Mounties buckled on the insignificant looking 38s. Compared to the hoary old New Service, the shiny new M&P seemed a slender reed with which to *Maintien le Droit*.

How did we get stuck with the abomination in the first place? In retrospect, it seems like a prime case of group feeble-mindedness—a cruel melange of follow the leader and blindman's bluff, the results of which unnecessary game has been the death of many a fine officer in the line of duty.

The Army, spurred on by Cavalry Col. Elmer Otis, started the trend to the small bore handgun in April, 1892, when they adopted the 38 Long Colt.

However, the forthcoming Philippine Campaign of 1899-1901 proved in gory and incontrovertible fashion that, as a manstopper, the 38 was a fraction better than hopeless. Posthaste, the Army ungreased a quantity of old single action 45s sitting in stateside storage, and shipped them out to the Philippine field units. After their arrival, there was a marked reduction in the number of headless officers to be crated up after each engagement.

As far as the Army was concerned, that did it. The famed Thompson-LaGarde Committee was convened to analyze the elements of stopping power in handgun cartridges, and their report, submitted in March of 1904, recommended that no pistol round of less than 45 caliber be considered. The conclusion was a sound one, and the

the 38 Special--

Army has yet to budge from it. The current service automatic, Model of 1911A1, was adopted shortly thereafter in 45 caliber as a result of the Thompson-LaGarde Report.

That the U.S. Air Force issues 38 Specials in some numbers doesn't alter the basic facts. The U.S.A.F. has for long been concerned with ultra lightweight arms—unduly of lives, as witness the debacle with their aluminum-cylinder, small-frame revolver.

Meanwhile, back in the States, Smith & Wesson began diddling around with the discredited 38 Long Colt cartridge. The bullet weight was increased from 148 to 158 grains; the powder charge was upped from 18 to 21 grains of smokeless powder. This raised velocity from 785 feet per second to 870 fps, and muzzle energy from 205 to 266 foot pounds. The result was christened the "38 S&W Special."

By any logical evaluation, the improvement in performance was negligible, but for some incomprehensible reason, the nation's police decided that the new round was the total answer, and the rush was on.

The current 38 Special load with 158-gr. round nose lead bullet is even less potent, while the 1090 foot second load—using the same weight bullet—is not, I believe, in general police use. In any case, this faster load would produce gross over-penetration, an aspect already in bad odor.

The lessons of the Philippine campaign were forgotten, if they were ever considered, and the findings of the Thompson-LaGarde Committee went unheeded. Most surprising of all, no collection and statistical analysis of evolving data on cartridge performance was undertaken for the next 60 years.

Even the FBI, a sage outfit which commands the respect—or perhaps awe of even its most vehement and intractable critics, the organization which has been responsible for the steady upgrading of police training in this country, and who were first to institute training of officers under combat conditions, a crew always in the lead in availing themselves of the means of physical science in police work, never bothered to organize or study the available data on the combat performance of handgun cartridges.* Nor did the FBI, so far as I can learn, make a formal study of the conditions prevailing in armed encounters between officers and felons. If they did, I couldn't run it down, and I dug extensively.

Because of this strange disinclination to consider or believe the results of the military's experience or tests, because of this disinterest in studying the problem from the viewpoint of statistical analysis, because police combat is a fragmented and widespread affair, and it has taken half a century for the cumulative weight of individual tragedies to force themselves into the general consciousness, the love affair with the 38 Special continued unabated until it was the standard of nearly every department in the country.

Only the unheeded John the Baptists mentioned earlier, together with a few knowledgeable and experienced officers, continue to rock the yacht. In 1959, however, Professor Allen P. Bristow, a former Los Angeles County Sheriff's Deputy, and later of the Department of Police Science at Los Angeles State College, undertook an organized study of cases in which an officer was shot in the line of duty. His report was released in 1961, and appeared in the highly respected *Journal of Criminal Law, Criminology, and Police Science*. It created an immediate ruckus.

Actually, Bristow hadn't intended to consider cartridge effectiveness at all. He was interested primarily in tactical studies, but the data he assembled forced him to conclude that the police use of the 38 Special cartridge was a primary causative factor in officer fatalities.

Typical of the cases Bristow discovered is the following:

At 1:25 AM, an officer forced the suspect, who was driving a stolen car, to the curb; in the following hoopla, the suspect was shot 4 times with the officer's 38 Special, before escaping down an alley on foot, having wounded the officer in the meantime. The suspect was shot through each arm, solidly through the right side, and sustained a flesh wound at the base of the rib cage.

At 2:10 AM, the same suspect robbed a motorist whom he had just forced from his vehicle, but had to flee from the scene on foot before he could make off with the automobile. He was spotted 20 minutes later in a field two miles from the scene of the original shooting, and was again chased by officers on foot, but eluded them.

At 3:00 AM, the same suspect stole a car and was busily engaged in covering ground when he was spotted an hour later by a state patrolman. There followed a 30-minute high-speed chase which ended when the suspect wrecked the car. The suspect crawled out of the wreckage, and high-tailed it for the woods with the trooper hot behind him. When the suspect whirled to fire on the trooper, he was felled by a single 357 Magnum through the head from the state patrolman's service weapon.

In another case, a suspect who had just killed an officer was shot 5 times in the center of the chest at off-the-muzzle range by a second cop's 38. The suspect fell to the ground, as was seemly and proper under the circumstances, but when the officer turned his back to minister to his partner, the suspect stood back up and started shooting again. Five 38s in the chest killed him eventually, but they didn't stop him when he should have been stopped. And that is the purpose of a police sidearm—stopping a sequence of actions immediately.

Killing is not the job of the police, it is a function of the courts. That police bullets kill is simply a regrettable side effect. Their purpose is to stop whatever action forced the officer to shoot in the first place. If the suspect does not stop what he is doing when shot, the police cartridge has failed its duty, and if that failure costs the life of an innocent person, or of the officer himself, then that failure is doubly a tragedy.

This is the kick with the 38 Special. It's a great cartridge, but depending on it to stop a determined man is rather like trying to turn back a gale wind with a windowfan. You will notice that most of the advantages we listed for the round at the beginning of this article are purely matters of convenience stemming from the 38's widespread and unwarranted popularity. A lot of people buy 38s. Hence there is a wide range of weapons available from which to choose. The same reason holds true for the choice and availability of many types of loads and components.

We've said other good things about the 38 Special, but we can't say it's a manstopper, at least not the way the factory loads it; and if it's not a manstopper, it is logically not what the police need.

This then is the problem facing every thinking police firearms specialist in America today. Should the department face up to the facts, scrap the 38, and shoulder the burdens involved in adopting a round with more slap-'em-down spunk?

The problems this courageous course of action would entail (not considering that all important one of finances) present themselves in plentitude. Training officers to handle heavier guns is a problem: it's no use adopting a round if it results in a serious decline in practical accuracy. Usually the recruit is expected to reach minimum proficiency with a big bore on the same amount of training expended on the 38. Thus both training and ballistics are involved. Let's look at the 41 S&W. The low speed 41 load's recoil is only a bit less than the 357 gives, both fired in equal-weight guns.

*The FBI issues the Colt OP, 4" barrel in 38 Special, perhaps the 38 M&P as well. Their regulations permit the 357 Magnum, and back in the 30s they were a popular arm with the FBI.

The two up-and-coming rivals to the 38 as a police service arm are S&W's new 41 (top) and Colt's old Government Model 45 automatic (bottom). Colt's 38 Official Police shown center for comparison.

Handloading is the answer, and no department can provide adequate training in any caliber with factory ammunition.

True, the officer should be able to handle full-charge factory service ammo. Our best departments give 50 hours of intensive firearms instruction, and require every officer to fire at least 500 rounds a year to qualify. Some departments train even more extensively. Professionals like these will turn in a creditable performance with any service sidearm, and need only a cartridge that does its share of the job.

However, many departments train rarely, if at all. A 20-man force was recently found with 4 guns that would not fire, one frozen shut by rust! Such departments, invariably armed with 38s, are a hazard to all. Happily, their number diminishes each year.

Educating officers to lug more iron is a problem that inevitably follows the adoption of a heavier sidearm.

It is a serious step for the department to undertake, this ditching of the inefficient old slingshot. More and more police agencies, though, are taking the plunge. On the west coast, a number of departments have gone so far as to abandon not only the unreliable 38, but the revolver itself, and have adopted that old tried and proven battle-ax of many wars, the 45 Automatic.

This shows a refreshing appreciation of the lessons of long combat experience, and was brought about by the very enlightening reports of a vociferous little group known as the Southwest Combat Pistol League, a coterie of combat-competition hobbyists who number among their members many Golden State lawmen.

League competition over the past decade has proven beyond much doubt that in the hands of a *highly trained man,* the 45 Auto is without peer as a combat handgun. Whether it is the answer to the needs of the police is still a moot question, and the rest of the profession will be observing with interest the practical experiences of those pioneering departments that have adopted the old warhorse.

Amarillo, Texas, was the first of a number of departments to adopt the new 41, which Smith & Wesson brought out in 1964 in answer to the requirements of the police for a man-stopping cartridge tailored specifically for them. However, Smith's was a somewhat timid venture, and the offering to date is hardly versatile enough to proclaim itself as the final answer. For instance, the lightest weapon Smith offers weighs in at a rather portly 41 ounces, when compared to the 35-oz. displacement of the average service 38. It's bulky too, being built only on Smith & Wesson's big N-frame.

That "mere" 6-ounce difference doesn't sound like much, but it is noticeable hanging on the belt, loaded as the latter is with department gadgetry.

There is another objection too, as regards the two cartridges offered for this revolver. The Magnum loading is a real rip-roarer—a hot, highly accurate round, and excellent for its purpose. The milder "city" load is also excellent, though a bad bore leader if enough rounds are fired without cleaning.

The hitch is that even the lighter of the loads recoils too much for training purposes, or for general use in an as yet unobtainable lighter weapon, though mass reloading equipment is available for this round. However, if it is brought out on Smith's lighter K-frame in a 5-shot version, and a third and less emphatic cartridge is offered, it will be the hands-down obvious answer to police needs that it was intended to be.

For such a weapon I would favor a 200-gr. or lighter *semi-wadcutter* bullet as slow as 700 fps even—anything that was comfortable to fire. Such a weapon would be comparable to the 38 only in ease of portability. It wouldn't be much on penetration, but stopping power should be excellent. You'd have, in addition to a heavy bullet of proper nose configuration, all that additional cross-sectional area working for you, transmitting maximum impact energy to the target.

Smith & Wesson offered, until recently, a number of other man-stopping sidearms which, although on the big frame, are light enough not to be objectionable on the hip. These are the 44 Special, and the 45 Auto rim. The fine old 45 Colt is no longer available in a practical double-action weapon, either.

Many departments recognize the deficiency of the 38, but are unwilling to junk the old pipsqueak for one reason or another. Sometimes their reluctance stems from a fear of innovation, an unwillingness to grapple with the problems a change of calibers would entail, or a sheer ignorance of the ballistic behavior of large bore handguns and bullets, and a groundless apprehension of them.

Often the reasons for retaining the 38 are more laudable than these, such as an awareness of the financial, training, and logistical problems involved, and a belief that the 38, in the long run, is still the best gun for the cop.

These departments concede that the 38 Special in its standard service loading, is a farce as a manstopper, ricochets badly, and overpenetrates, with the danger that an innocent person on the other side of the target will be hit. On the other hand, they contend that with proper loads, these faults can be cured, resulting in a weapon-load combination far better suited to police duty than any bigbore.

Some advocate that the 38 be replaced by the 357 Magnum, which offers the advantage of firing 38 ammunition for practice, as well as heaving some excellent armor-piercing projectiles for roadblock or barricade tactics.

The standard 357 Magnum load is a pretty good manstopper. On the other hand, it's a real hollering horror on penetration, which is a disadvantage, and it recoils as fiercely if not more so than a big-bore, so the training problem is no more easily resolved (save by the availability of 38 ammo) than with the large caliber weapons. To top it off the 357 can be a really intolerable bore leader.

Having ruled out the 200-gr. round nose 38 load, and the 357 Magnum option, what then can be done with the 38 Special to make it an adequate round for police use?

Obviously, we have to achieve maximum stopping power with minimum penetration and recoil, and the way to do it is to up the velocity and use light, pure lead, semi-jacketed bullets with wide cavity hollow points, cup points, or hydraulic expansion mechanisms built in, or else depend on extremely high velocity to expand a solid slug without assist from an expansion-inducing nose configuration.

Yet here we tread on tender toes. Super-expanding bullets for police—dum-dums if you will! There is no reason, legal, moral, or tactical not to use them; their employment will save the lives of officers and innocents who might otherwise perish—sacrificed on the cruel altar of bureaucratic timidity. But it cannot be gainsaid that super-expanding bullets are potential dynamite for anti-police propagandists.

Nevertheless, the department which opts to retain the 38 has little choice, if it recognizes its moral obligation to its officers and the public, but to continue the already substantial amount of experimentation with expanding 38s that has been carried out by private parties, and to eventually consider adopting them.

Probably the most impressive formal research into the use of expanding bullets undertaken to date by an enforcement agency is that of the Phoenix, Ariz., Police Department.

Contrary to the norm, the Phoenix program was brought about not by their dissatisfaction with the 38s' stopping power, but because of its excessive penetration. An officer was forced to fire on a felon, and did a good job of it, keeping all his shots squarely on target. However, the 38s zipped right through, felling a window-shopper on the next block.

This caused some consternation down at headquarters, and the Phoenix brass-hats determined to load them up a 38 that would stay in the target. This either means dropping velocity still further, making the 38 scarcely more emphatic than a threat, or else, as Phoenix chose to do, upping the velocity to near sonic speed to ensure expansion of soft lead, and adopting a bullet designed to expand in the target, with its concommitant risk of ill publicity.

The chief down there is a cautious man, and in order to build an irrefutable case for the department's new cartridge being the last word in the

38 Special (center) with contending 41 rounds at left, 45 autos right. 41s and 45s give good knock-down punch without necessitating use of hollow points—also give healthy recoil. 41 Magnum (far left) is a rip roarer (210-gr. bullet at 1400 feet per second—almost twice the 38's velocity. Standard 41 is more sedate. 45 comes in hard ball (4th) and expanding (5th).

public's best interest, an impartial, blue-ribbon panel was chosen to conduct the tests. Members were Capt. Gordon Selby of the Phoenix Police, one of America's top combat shooters; a lieutenant, a sergeant, and two crime lab technicians from the Phoenix Police; Ben Avery, outdoor editor of the *Arizona Republic,* and Pete Brown, arms editor of *Sports Afield* magazine.

This illustrious panel of experts, following the extensive tests, suggested that the Phoenix police "adopt a high-velocity cartridge with a bullet designed to mushroom on impact." The department did just that, turning to the Super-Vel Cartridge Corp. (Shelbyville, Ind.), as have 300 other police units.

Super-Vel produces ammunition in four calibers (9mm to 44 Magnum), but most popular are their improved 38 Special loads. The Super-Vel 158-gr. semi-wadcutter is a tremendous improvement over old-school loads, but the one that really breaks with tradition is the 110-gr. ¾-jacketed bullet (solid or HP) at 1370 fps. These disrupt violently when they hit, field and test reports confirming their ample stopping power. These put the final cure on the over-penetration problem.

This then is the painstaking course which must be followed if the department insists on making the 38 perform as it must, and would still protect itself from the specter of unjustified public condemnation.

As an indication that something along these lines must be done if the 38 Special is ultimately to survive as a police cartridge, experimentation similar to the Phoenix program is being carried out all over the country, either formally by department arms units, or informally by individual officers and private experimenters.

An increased knowledge of terminal ballistics, or the action of the bullet within the target, is the result, and this can only be to the good. However the danger is (and it's a very real danger) that through poorly conducted, inapplicable experimentation, a body of misconceptions will be established resulting in the adoption of a cartridge that will not behave in combat as expected.

Usually, the result will be overpenetration, a la 357 Magnum, and the reason is that the medium chosen for terminal ballistics studies does not duplicate human flesh.

Let's face it—cops are human, and in none of them does the scientific zeal for accurate data overcome a very strong, normal, natural, warm, and emphatic human squeamishness. No police unit in the country has the desire to do things as thoroughly and impassionately as the Thompson-LaGarde Committee, and conduct firing tests on live steers in slaughter houses, and on suspended human cadavers. Yet, there is no way to pass the buck and get the Army to test the loads in battle zones, because expanding bullets are militarily taboo since the Hague Accords.

The old 45 auto is getting a lot of attention from police these days. Plenty of firepower and a slap-em-down cartridge—two virtues the 38 Special lacks.

So we're back to the firing range, and the results are ludicrous. One experimenter tests his bullets in "dry, clean playground sand." Another uses moist sand. Why? No one knows. It's meaningless. Other popular mediums for test firing are moist clay, modeling clay, and "wetpack"—compressed, waterlogged phone books and newspaper. Criminals are made of none of these. Nor do criminals resemble steel drums filled with water and tightly capped.

Firing into substances such as these is an interesting game, and good for comparing the conduct of one bullet with another. But to say that the results will predict the action of a bullet in flesh is a farcically naive approach.

The only way to compile predictive terminal ballistic data, other than the long term project of studying the results of ensuing individual police combat affrays over a period of decades, or by hunting light game with test bullets and performing field autopsies after it is felled, is to conduct range tests with a target medium more closely resembling flesh than those above.

Commercial arms plants usually conduct their bullet expansion tests on blocks of gelatin compound, and if the police intend to precede the adoption of expanding bullets by a body of scientific data that will withstand criticism, it's time they got serious and did likewise.

The next few years will bear watching. That the 38 Special is virtually ineffective and was a bad bill of goods from the start has been well-proven and is no longer a matter for serious discussion among knowledgeable police firearms specialists. What to do about it is.

Foreign ammunition makers such as the Swedish Norma Projektilfabrik and the Canadian CIL are already marketing or are considering introducing high velocity 38s with improved bullet designs, and there is some experimental stirring about in the large American plants. Custom ammo loaders, and new commercial operations such as the Super-Vel Company, are doing a booming business in expanding bullet, hot-loaded 38s. Cautious but intense experimentation by police agencies across the country is becoming more and more the thing.

The result of all this will and must be that either the 38 Special, that notorious old pipsqueak, now in its second half-century of service, and until now all but unchallenged, will come up with the goods and gain a new lease on life, or else it's breathing its last, unlamented senile gasps, and will soon be buried alongside the image of the Keystone Cop. May they both rest. •

WHEN GD EDITOR Amber asked me to take on the "Testfire" project this year, I began to lay in the supply of guns selected plus sample scopes and ammo, the latter from Remington, Federal and Winchester. Two guns are among the missing and can't be reported on thanks to the new Gun Control Act which says I can't be shipped a gun—or ammo.

One of these is a Browning auto rifle in 338 caliber, sure to be the hottest hunting rifle in years. I was really looking forward to trying this one out; the 338 is one of the finest long range cartridges—with bigger smash than Weatherby's 300 and with nearly equal ballistics.

At the outset I think it might be wise to spend a few moments telling you how and why these guns are evaluated as they are. For a 12-year period I was a custom gunmaker; since then I've been in the advertising agency business. I've also been contributing books and articles to the gun press for about 20 years, thus my background is a combination of technical, practical, sales, marketing and advertising.

Many things in the evaluation of a firearm are purely personal opinion and many others are plain fact. For example, if a trigger pull weighs over 4 pounds and is creepy as an old rusty farm gate, it's too poor to be considered right. This is fact, plain and simple. If the lines of a stock don't please the reviewer that's personal opinion. Similarly, an experienced shooter and tinkerer can often make a rifle shoot well by fiddling with it—even though it doesn't shoot at all well as received. The procedure I've followed is to first test the gun as it comes out of the box. Just wipe the bore clean, mount the scope and bang away at the range just like the ordinary purchaser would. Then, if necessary, I've tinkered and tuned to get it perking better. By the same token, the average hunter shoots factory ammo; there's not much point in writing a glowing report about how a rifle can be tuned to win a bench rest match with carefully assembled handloads since the average guy won't ever use his rifle that way.

Another interesting fact often not disclosed is the way most rifles will shoot better with one brand of factory ammo over another. A year ago, when Jack Smart and I sighted our hunting rifles in at his club in Winthrop, Maine, his remodeled Springfield 30-06 wouldn't shoot for sour apples with Remington ammo. I was just about to suggest that he take an extra rifle of mine and leave his pet back home when I discovered two boxes of Federal 150-gr. factory loads in my car. When we tried these in Jack's rifle they closed his groups from 3 inches to one! That's some difference but it's no freak; the reader is advised to try another brand before he gives up in disgust—or writes a nasty letter.

Testfire Report

A field-test evaluation of several rifles and shotguns, covering their handling, shootability, quality factors and styling. A critical report . . .

- Beretta BL-4 Over-Under
- Charles Daly Venture Over-Under
- Galef Golden Snipe Over-Under
- Harrington & Richardson Auto Rifle
- Ithaca 500 SKB Over-Under
- Mossberg 500 Pump Gun
- Ruger 77 Bolt Rifle
- Smith & Wesson Bolt Rifles

by BOB WALLACK

Smith & Wesson Rifles

Some said S&W ought to have produced its own action when they decided to market a bolt action sporter. Instead, the company took a route followed by others in the past. They imported the S&W rifle from Husqvarna in Sweden. The HVA action is an altered Mauser, very lightweight, mine going 6⅞ pounds with a Leupold 2-7X scope installed in Leupold mounts. Whether Smith & Wesson should have produced their own bolt action or taken the course they did is not for me to say. It's none of my business. I'm going to talk about the S&W rifle that's here.

The HVA action has been around this country for some 15 years and has proved itself pretty well. It has a better shaped bolt handle and smaller receiver ring than the FN. The trigger is basically a single stage military one with a surprisingly good pull — averages 3¾ lbs. It has some noticeable creep, however, and something I've never found in an S&W handgun. I think the sliding HVA safety leaves something to be desired. It locks trigger and bolt, does not lock the cocking piece (though the latter can't be released when on safe). This doesn't imply there's anything wrong with the safety, I prefer the handy simplicity of the old Enfield type as used on the Remington 700.

I'd like to meet the Swede who wound up the guard screws on this rifle! I had to use a wrench on the screwdriver to remove them and dismount the stock.

This rifle employs a light-metal cast guard, with a hinged floorplate. The lines of this guard are bulky and cumbersome to my mind and eye.

The stock is made from a fairly good piece of European walnut, checkering is of the old cut style though a bit coarse, and the diamonds are not brought to a point. S&W's Model C is as close to classic stock design as any of the S&W models, but I think it lacks the pure elegance of what I call "classic." I suspect that's the European influence because virtually no European gunmakers, save the English, seem to know (or are willing to make) a classic stock shape. In any event, the S&W has a schnabel fore-end tip, somewhat popular in America during the 1930s until gunwriters of that day criticized them so merrily and constantly that they finally disappeared. S&W and Husqvarna may feel the time is right for another go at the schnabel, and surely it will appeal to some (Mr. R-g-r uses it, too!)

The entire butt section of this stock is too low, starting from the comb and running back to the heel. The comb nose is about 5/16ths below the cocking piece, and it should be 1/4-inch higher, which would correct the whole shape. If the whole stock could just be raised this quarter-inch, and the awkward-appearing grip improved, it would be much better. I'd also prefer to see the comb considerably wider; it has the usual European knife edge.

S&W has used a fairly nice piece of European walnut (to the uninitiated, European walnut is far superior to American, being harder, denser and much more handsome) and its finish is of the luster type and very good.

The proof of any gun is in the shooting and the little S&W 270 performed extremely well. All shooting was done at 100 yards at the Angle Tree Stone Club in Attleboro, Mass., from bench rest; only 3-shot groups were fired, OK for any light hunting rifle. They quickly prove a rifle's inaccuracy since no number of additional shots can better a lousy 3-shot group, and a tight 3-shotter is enough shooting to prove a good hunting rifle.

Starting with 130-gr. ammo, this light rifle shot groups averaging 3 3/16" with Winchester, 3" with Remington and 1 1/8" with Federal. (Federal ammo was far and away the best in this rifle, the largest group being 1 7/16" and the smallest a tight 5/16" group! I wouldn't say that one tiny group was representative of the gun's potential by any means, but it does indicate excellent shooting when the rifle is given the ammo it likes).

Using 150-gr. loads it didn't do quite as well, but the accuracy was quite acceptable for hunting. Averages were: Winchester, 3 7/8", Remington, 3 1/2" and Federal, 2 1/4". All shooting was done with a Leupold 2-7X variable set at 7X, and mounted in a Leupold two-piece mount.

Summing up, this new S&W 270 Model C bolt action rifle shoots like blazes when given the proper ammo, and it'll make a fine sporting rifle for any game suitable for the caliber selected. Most of the criticism I have is directed toward the stock, which I believe could be vastly improved.

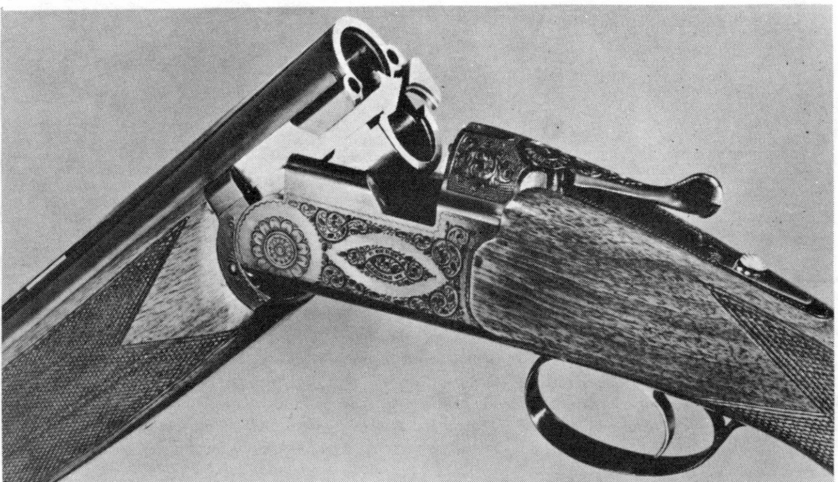

Garcia's Beretta BL-4 over-under shotgun, a trim and handsome boxlock-actioned design, is light, low-profiled and nicely engraved. Single selective trigger and auto ejectors are standard on the BL-4, made in field, Skeet and trap versions.

The H&R Auto Rifle

I doubt whether the general shooting public has much awareness of H&R's vast capabilities in automatic weapon design and manufacture. It dates 'way back. H&R developed and manufactured the Reising submachine gun during World War II. Since that war, the company has a fine track record with the M-14 rifle, which it helped design and produce, and its plants are now producing M-16 rifles, the first of which was recently delivered ahead of schedule. H&R president, C. Edward "Ted" Rowe, Jr., spends much of his time in his Worcester and Gardiner, Mass., plants, as well as Washington and abroad.

H&R's semi-auto sporting rifle was a long time coming. Prototype models existed a couple years before production numbers finally started coming off the line. Ted Rowe bagged a Boone & Crockett caribou with one of these early prototypes in 243 caliber in 1965—he bagged an even bigger one in Quebec's Ungava district the following year when I accompanied him. The rifle was pretty well tried out in these early stages.

The H&R autoloader is a gas-operated system which locks as the bolt's rear end moves up into a recess in the receiver top. Essential parts are forged. The gas piston moves rearward about 1/2-inch before unlocking begins; locking is positive and foolproof. The removable box magazine holds 5 cartridges, and extends 1/2-inch out of the bottom of the rifle, right at the balance point; this makes carrying the rifle in one hand a little bit awkward. This is a penalty in using a removable box, however, since the shooter must be able to grab it for

Garcia's top-of-the-line Beretta is the superb Model SO-5, a true sidelock over-under that is virtually 100% custom made. This beautiful shotgun can be ordered with single or double triggers, selective ejectors or not, with full pistol-grip stock or not. The Crown Grade engraving complements the fancy walnut in the stock and fore-end.

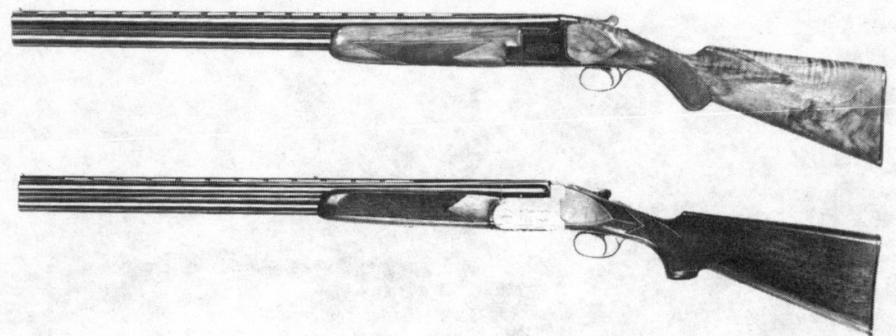

Charles Daly's Venture Grade 20-gauge over-under (top) is made in Japan by Miroku. Offered with single trigger and plain extractors, the new Venture is a well-turned out double that handles and points well. The buttstock and fore-end show a warm, reddish-toned finish; the receiver is lightly engraved. ● Galef's line of shotguns are made by Antonio Zoli in Italy. The Silver Snipe model pictured features a streamlined, low-profile frame by virtue of its side-hinging. Made in 12 and 20 gauges, standard are 3" chambers, single trigger and simple extractors. The Golden Snipe tested by Wallack differs only in having auto ejectors.

removal. The magazine catch is located directly behind the magazine. Behind this catch is an action-bar catch which can be used to hold the bolt back for cleaning, inspection and the like. The new H&R's safety is a front-back, push-pull affair located in front of the trigger guard. It's pushed forward to fire the rifle by the trigger finger from inside the guard.

I have three criticisms of my 308 sample rifle's action; first, when you pick the rifle up and shake it, you hear an odd rattle. This may or may not disturb you. It does disturb me. The blame lies with the gas piston, which moves around in its housing. I don't imagine this is very serious, but if I'm buying a gun I don't want it to rattle like a gourd filled with dry beans. Second is the trigger pull, which weighs more than 9 pounds (which is as heavy as I could measure), and third is the necessity (?) of a 5½-inch long by ⅛-inch wide gap in the right hand side of the stock to allow the operating rod to fly back and forth. This gap is ideally sited to collect rain, snow, leaves, twigs, pine needles, dirt and all manner of trivia.

Aside from these comments (the trigger pull being the most serious) the action is sound, excellent and dependable. It should be noted in passing that its design requires an action one-inch longer than a standard Mauser bolt action. Which, translated into gun-handling terms, means you'll sacrifice an inch of barrel length for a gun of the same over-all length as a standard bolt gun.

I don't know what beginner designed this stock. It appears to be a marriage of what's necessary to hold the action and some attempt to follow designs pioneered by Weatherby. The result isn't a total success. A flared pistol grip is capped with a flared grip cap of chocolate-brown wood, with a white spacer between. The comb nose is almost non-existent and a cheekpiece lays over the comb like a wet pancake; the underside of the cheekpiece on the left hand side of the stock is cut in a straight line extending nearly to the toe of the butt. I suspect this is an attempt to be different. It is different — but I don't think it is pretty.

I also believe the comb ought to be higher. My rifle has a Bushnell 3-9x variable in the new Bushnell mounts; it's mounted about as low as any scope. My face tends to err on the pudgy side rather than the slim, and the comb is far too low for me. Moreover, a straighter stock (that is, one with much less drop so the center of the butt is closer to a line drawn from the center of the bore) would reduce jump in recoil.

H&R manufactures its sporting rifles in a new, modern plant in Gardiner, Mass., center of some of the nation's furniture industry. As a result, there are many skilled woodworkers in the area. The H&R standard of workmanship is very high; it's the design I'm quibbling about. Otherwise, the stock is executed well, the checkering is ample and nicely cut (not impressed). The American walnut is nicely finished. I have to rate the gun a little heavy; my sample goes 8 lbs. 10 oz. with scope and mount.

The H&R will deliver acceptable hunting accuracy, no more than that. Using all tree brands of ammo, as before, best groups went roughly into an average between 2 and 3 inches. That's no great shakes, but certainly is adequate for the ordinary hunting rifle where shots won't be much over 100 yards at the outside.

It is my own opinion that this basic rifle might well be redesigned for a 2-piece stock. Like the Model 100 Winchester auto, it is tricky to get the metal into and out of the stock and, more important, the inletting requires removal of all the wood save two side panels. Some shooters believe a one-piece stock has some magical qualities of accuracy, but this is false. A case in point is Remington's line of high-power auto rifles, which deliver excellent accuracy. Another is the Model 336 Marlin lever gun, which shoots even better. I think employment of a 2-piece stock would help this H&R significantly.

The Ruger Model 77 Rifle

We had hoped to report on this rifle in either 6.5 or 350 Remington Magnum but Ruger could not supply either caliber in time. It may seem redundant to report on another Model 77; the rifle has been well-covered by this time, but I have some things to say that haven't been said.

Let's first stipulate that Bill Ruger has designed a fine rifle, that he has the courage to introduce a classic style stock — something that's been ignored too long. As great a rifle as this is, I believe there are some shortcomings. For example, I wish Ruger had made this with a long action. No matter how highly touted, the 308 is no 30-06 nor 300 Winchester Magnum, and the 350 Remington is no 338 Magnum. The adoption of a short action rules out many finer cartridges. Ruger may make a standard action later, I do not know.

The rifle has a few points I can't get enthused over; one is a piece of bent wire about $\frac{1}{16}$th-inch diameter, and some 2 inches long, that's hooked to the safety on one end and into a little locking device on the front end. This serves to communicate the safety motion from the sliding tang thumb piece to the trigger mechanism. While I'm sure it's reliable it has the looks of a jury rig; furthermore, it tends

Harrington & Richardson's gas-operated autoloading rifle (top) has detachable box magazine, roll-over cheekpiece, white spacers at buttplate and grip cap. ● Sturm, Ruger & Co.'s Model 77 bolt action sporter displays graceful classic stock form, well-executed checkering. Bolt design is new, built to withstand great pressures.

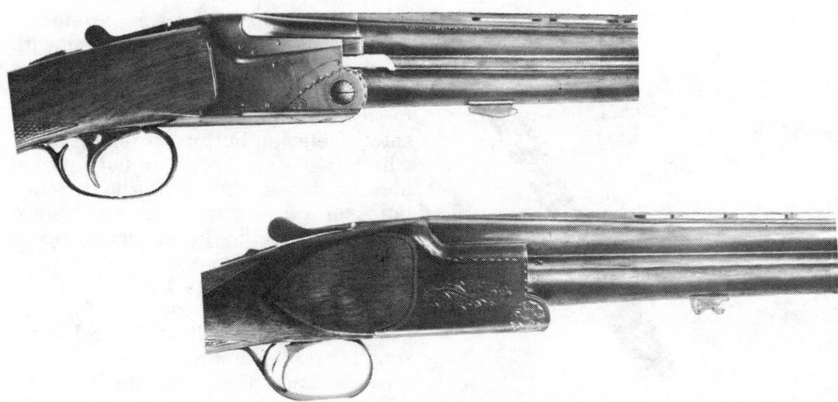

Over-under frame depth of SKB Ithaca (top) compared with conventionally-hinged Charles Daly Venture grade below. The side-hinged Ithaca permits a shallower action, more of an advantage in 12 gauge than 20.

to fall out of place when the rifle is disassembled. The inletting is good, but certainly not what I'd been led to expect; there is a good, wide flat under the receiver ring, but it doesn't bear fully in the wood and, in spite of that highly-touted slanted guard screw, the recoil lug doesn't bear fully on the sample I have. Incidentally, the slanted-screw principle has received lots of publicity but I don't believe it makes any contribution—assuming a properly bedded receiver in the first place. The sample rifle also had a heavy trigger pull of 7 pounds, plus some creep.

The very first thing my eye caught on the Ruger 77 was the bolt handle. It may appeal to Bill Ruger, but it doesn't appeal to me. My idea of the handsomest bolt handle ever made was the original pre-WW II Model 70 Winchester, and the Ruger 77 would be a better looking rifle if this handle had been copied.

So much for personal and subjective (remember?) nit-picking. This is still a handsome rifle, one of the best to arrive. The stock design merits considerable praise, chiefly because its maker had the courage to produce a classic stock—not only that, but one without a cheekpiece! Any experienced stockmaker knows a cheekpiece is strictly non-functional—you control the shooter's eye elevation by the width of the comb.* Even though the Ruger 77 comb is a bit low (about 1/8-inch below the cocking piece) the eye is still in line because the comb is wide and full.

Total absence of a Monte Carlo comb also brings tears of joy to any lover of the classic stock. For too many years another school of gunmakers has wooed the public with silly falsehoods about combs sloping away from the cheek, Monte Carlos that reduced the feel of recoil and other such racket that a whole generation has grown up thinking it's so. Now along comes the new Ruger with no Monte Carlo and no cheekpiece—and you're going to learn that these things aren't necessary! And if you have any eye for stock design, you'll learn that the absence of a Monte Carlo, 1) makes a better-looking stock, 2) a better-shooting stock and 3) a stock with straighter lines, thus a rifle that doesn't jump as badly.

*Your editor doesn't agree with Wallack on this point, our view being that comb height is the more important factor, but this shows the leeway we give our writers!

Note the absence of cheekpiece (and Monte Carlo) on the Ruger 77. When you cheek this gun at your local store note that you need neither cheekpiece or MC! A cheekpiece does dress up a stock, if that's what you want, but the Monte Carlo has no useful function, should never have been introduced on a rifle. In the writer's opinion, this Ruger stock would look a little better with slightly higher comb, but its generous width is what really counts.

Stock wood is a nice piece of quarter-sawed American walnut with a finish that I assume is oil; it is nicely filled and finished. The return to an oiled finish is also nice to look at rather than the bright, shiny finishes so common today.

This stock is also nicely checkered, the old-fashioned kind of cut checkering, done without borders to cover up runovers of the tools. It's a nice job, neatly done.

I wish Ruger would offer optional lower scope mount rings. I've mounted one of the new Bausch & Lomb variable sights with internal adjustment on this rifle and it could be 1/8-inch lower. Complete with scope, the sample rifle weighs 7¾ lbs.—nice and light.

Only Remington offers 6mm ammo so all shooting was done with this brand. Model 77 accuracy has been reported often enough already; suffice it to say, accuracy was excellent, with my groups running around one inch. Handloads didn't show enough improvement to be startling. Summing up the 77 Ruger, I'd say it's a very welcome addition to the bolt action field and I'm especially impressed with the classic style. This is a well-engineered, well-executed rifle.

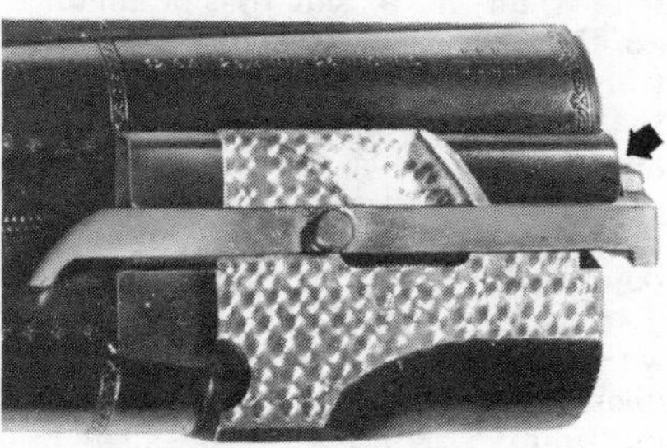

Italian Beretta from Garcia shows very good workmanship. Solid lug at rear of top barrel (arrow), just over ejector bar, acts as a "dolls head," helps lock gun at moment of firing. Drooping projection at front of ejector bar is caught by a sear inside fore-end when barrel is fired. Ejector is then held back until gun is opened and, just as bottom barrel clears the frame, ejector is allowed to snap fired shell out of the gun.

The Beretta BL-4 Over-Under

Here's one very elegant O-U, with single trigger and ejectors, that scales an even 7 pounds, balances right, handles fast, points and shoots true. Not much more to ask for!

Beretta guns are imported from Italy by the Garcia Corp., the same people who have been such big operators in the fishing tackle business. Available in several grades in both sidy-by-side and over-under styles, and in pump guns and autos, they would seem to cover the shotgun market like a blanket—if I may coin a phrase.

When over-under guns were much younger (and an almost exclusive province of the fine London makers) two guns existed that had a very low silhouette. These were the Boss and Woodward brands. Boss guns are still made; Woodward was bombed out of business in the last war and its over-under business was bought by James Purdey, and they're also made today.

Boss and Woodward guns reduced the depth through the action by installing the locks and hinge at either side of the barrels rather than underneath, as is common in side-by-side doubles. If they were to use bottom locks on their over-unders, the depth through the action would have to be deep enough to accommodate two 12-bore barrels plus the locks. In such case, they realized, the bottom locks would be located a long way below the top barrel, much farther from the bore than in a side-by-side double. So they positioned their locks about two-thirds of the way up the sides of the lower barrel. In double gun language, the locking recesses are known as "lumps," and in English gun lingo the separated lumps on these O-U doubles are called "bifurcated lumps." The net result of the Boss and Woodward systems is to move the locks up about an inch closer to the top of the gun and to reduce the over-all depth through the action by about ½-inch.

In a 12-gauge gun, this reduction of action depth is very noticeable, and it adds a great deal to the appearance of the gun. Seen next to each other, the gun with bifurcated lumps is much trimmer and more graceful than a bottom-locking gun. Many over-under Continental gunmakers, including Beretta, have adopted similar systems.

Beretta has placed his locks about ⅓ the distance up the top barrel, and the recesses in the breech face consist of two round, tapered holes. The locking bolts are also tapered, and are moved in and out of the standing breech by the top lever. The system is excellent and the tapered surfaces should, as they are designed to, accommodate wear, thus not shoot loose.

The deep U of the bar in an over-under gun has great strength in itself. Its disadvantages are that it is more expensive to make, it is heavier and, if bottom locked, there is more strain on the action when the top barrel is fired. Reducing the action depth reduces all these disadvantages except the first. There being less strain on the action when firing the lower barrel, over-under guns should always fire this barrel first. It's also true that the lower barrel produces straighter recoil, being located nearer the centerline through the butt—thus the gun jumps less and when the lower barrel is fired first, it is easier to stay on target than the other way around.

Ithaca's Model 500 SKB (shown at top) a box-lock over-under made in Japan, has selective single trigger, auto ejectors, and is another O-U with a low-profile frame. The 20-gauge model tested by Wallack performed and handled well, showed good workmanship and an attractive appearance. The Beretta Models BL-4 (center) and SO-5 are described elsewhere.

Beretta's gun comes equipped with a selective single trigger which means you can choose which barrel you wish to fire by moving the combination safety/selector button to left or right whether it's on "safe" or not, a good idea. I think this is without much point on a field gun, where you almost always want the lower, more open-bored barrel first.

A word should be said about the packaging used by Beretta for this gun. It's a standard cardboard shipping container and a good one. To impart elegance, the boxmaker has coated the inside of the box with green "flocking," a wood fiber product that can be had in any color and is blown onto a glued surface. It looks like felt when done right. Unfortunately, the flock job in the box I got didn't stick and the whole gun was covered with green dust. Lacking an air hose, which would have been ideal, I spent more than an hour with pipe cleaners and an old toothbrush getting this stuff off of and out of the gun.

It's doubtful that added strength is needed for lockup in this gun, but Beretta adds two lugs on either side of the barrels that drop into notches in the U-frame These offer additional support to the strain of firing by the same method that a "doll's head" top extension adds strength to a side-by-side action. These additions do not *appear* to have any function since they move in and out freely as the gun is swung open On firing, though, the recoil tends to make the barrels pivot at the bottom of the U below the face, not at the hinge pin. Just as the doll's head works so do the extra side lugs on this BL-4 make a strong lock-up even tighter

The engineering on this gun is extremely good; its selective single trigger appears trouble-free, and an inertia block is used to prevent doubling. (Any single trigger requires either a block or some sort of "extra" pull because you always pull a trigger *twice*. The second pull, known as the "involuntary" pull, occurs during recoil. If a second pull is not provided as a "waste" or extra pull, the gun will double, or fire both barrels. Use of an inertia block prevents the second pull by swinging into the path of the trigger during recoil. It also activates the selector to fire the second barrel You can detect an inertia block single trigger by dry-firing! Pull the trigger once, snapping one barrel; you can't fire the second barrel until you rap the butt sharply with the heel of your hand toward the muzzle. This moves the block and activates the mechanism.)

Like most of today's gunmakers, Beretta has avoided the English ejector systems of Southgate or Anson and Deeley, which use separate locks very similar to firing mechanisms, in the fore-end. Instead, Beretta uses coil-spring ejectors fitted to the barrels; ejector sears are located in the fore-end. It must be said that this system performs as well as a Southgate ejector for all practical purposes, even though it lacks the niceties and refinements of the latter.

Over-under guns using bifurcated lumps also require a different hinge arrangement since, if the object is to make the action shallower by removal of the lumps, it makes no sense to deepen it to put a hinge there. Beretta's hinges are two short stubs set into the front of the U-frame where ordinarily a single hinge pin would extend clear through the frame.

The BL-4 (at $325) is nicely engraved on the receiver and guard. This is tastefully done except that I think it unnecessary for the maker's name to appear three times on the receiver! Since the name also appears on the barrel, there isn't much doubt as to who made the gun. I consider the metal parts of this gun extremely good.

I wish I could say as much for the wood. The gun comes up nicely and points smartly, but it still could do that and look better. First, the piece of wood on my sample is ordinary, not good enough for a gun of this grade. Its inletting is very good, but the outside shaping doesn't bring the wood down to the metal surface — where the buttstock joins the receiver, the wood sticks out noticeably on the sides and even more so at the bottom. The gun's appearance would be helped considerably had the wood been taken down to the same plane as the metal.

I'm a firm believer in a straight-grip stock for double guns, either side-by-side, over-under, one trigger or two. Yet I'm aware that many prefer a pistol grip, and it is to this market the Beretta is obviously addressed. Even so, this isn't a full pistol grip but a modified type called a "half" grip. (The BL-5, top boxlock Beretta, and $100 more, has a full pistol grip.) The comb is too knife-edged, and a very ordinary hard rubber buttplate is fastened on with Phillips-head screws. The fore-end is a better piece of wood, but it's also away from the metal and has a perch-belly sag that could be improved by being straight. In fact, if straight, it would help the over-all lines of this gun significantly. The line from toe to grip would look better if straightened, too.

The checkering could be better. The diamonds are flat in some areas, pointed in others, and so much finish has been added that the whole checkered area is clogged with it.

Using Federal, Remington and Winchester ammo, I shot a few rounds of Skeet and a few birds in Maine with the Beretta. It's a lot of gun indeed and one that can be highly recommended. I like it but it can be improved with better stock work.

The Mossberg Model 500 Pumpgun

I read someplace that the shooting world really shouldn't mourn the loss of Winchester's Model 12 because we now have the Mossberg 500. There is a lot of truth in that, and it is just as valid to say the new 410-bore 500 Mossberg replaces the Winchester 42 pump action 410.

Neither gun is an equal replacement since the 12 and 42 were pretty superb models. But the new Mossbergs probably come closer to filling that gap than anything else. I've got a 42 Skeet model, which could make me more critical of the 500 than I ought to be. Since you can't buy a 42 today, there isn't much point in making any more comparisons.

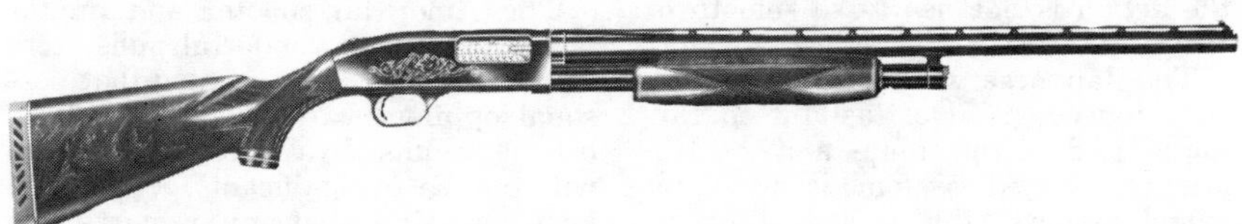

Mossberg's new 50th Anniversary Pigeon Grade Model 500AA slide-action shotgun is made in 12 gauge only, but trap, Skeet and field grades are offered in limited numbers. Buttstock and fore-end are of selected genuine walnut, hand checkered, and the receiver carries gold-lined rolled engraving. Ventilated rib is standard. Mossberg's 500EKR 410-gauge model is similar but is without engraving and fancy wood.

Mossberg has done a fine job on this new 410 Skeet 500. It has a 26-inch vent rib barrel, walnut stock with impressed checkering. The pistol grip is very full and comfortable. I think a slimmer, trimmer trigger guard and trigger would improve the looks but that's no serious criticism. Safety is on top of the receiver, operates fore and aft like a double gun. Some internal parts are stamped which seems a fact of life today. Weight is an even 6 pounds, just right for clay-bird shooting, and that's all any 410 is made for.

A Look at Three Twenties

Twenty-bore shotguns are getting more and more popular, as well they should, because they toss enough shot today to make anybody happy—and do as much good as a 12 for nearly any purpose. The over-under double is also rapidly becoming more popular here, too, so we decided to explore three of the better imports to see what makes them tick.

Those chosen were (listed according to price) Zoli's Golden Snipe from Italy at $274.95, Ithaca's SKB Model 500 from Japan at $239.95 and Daly's new Venture grade by Miroku of Japan at $236.00. I've had a lot of good shooting from all three, mostly on the clay target range, but with a great day of preserve shooting using the Golden Snipe, a wonderful old pointer named Duke, three good companions and the excellent cover provided by Henry Bernard near Colchester, Conn.

I used the Galef Golden Snipe only because it arrived ahead of the other guns; once I got the hang of the gun I never missed a shot—including two "shots to remember."

Both the Snipe and Ithaca guns employ the bifurcated lumps I described earlier in the Beretta discussion. However, the resultant shallower frame depth isn't nearly so important in a 20 as it is in a 12-bore gun. Both of these guns have automatic ejectors while Daly's Venture does not. Reloaders are said to prefer the non-ejector gun but, although I'm a reloader, too, I believe a good field gun ought to have ejectors.

There's a great deal of similarity between the Golden Snipe and the Beretta we've already discussed, which indicates that Antonio and Pietro obviously speak to each other. Zoli uses a crossbolt lock; two lugs located on the barrels drop into frame recesses and are locked down in place by the crossbolt. The Zoli lacks the additional dolls-head-type bolting, but that shouldn't be necessary in a 20-bore. Zoli also uses his cocking bars to operate the ejectors in a slightly different manner—equally effectively and possibly more compactly, but it is hard to fault either system. Zoli finishes his frame for this model in a silvered finish (apparently an acid etch), which provides an interesting contrast to the other blued parts. Some very tasteful engraving is used and, although minimal, it is pretty. His name, however, is stamped on both sides; it would improve the gun's looks if he engraved the name (or at least used a script roll stamp) just once on the bottom!

Woodwork on this gun is below par for a gun of such grade. The wood itself looks more like pine than walnut, the buttstock is grey in color while the fore-end is non-matching and walnut colored. Checkering is cut, but poorly done, with run overs along the border. Diamonds are not cut to the same depth consistently, and many are not brought up to points. The general shape of the stock is reasonably good to my eyes, and it feels good when shooting the gun. Zoli's buttstock is bored out drastically to reduce weight. In my opinion it has been cut out too much, comes perilously close to the edge in one place. The stock *feels* hollow and it shouldn't.

This Golden Snipe is a good gun,

The Smith & Wesson rifles, made by Husqvarna: Top, the standard-stocked sporter (tested by the author) with schnabel fore-end tip. Center, the Mannlicher-styled rifle in straight-comb form. Below, the de luxe grade S&W sporter with Monte Carlo comb, contrasting-wood fore-end tip. The two rifles above it may also be had with MC combs.

but better stock work would effect a vast improvement.

Ithaca Model 500

A product of SKB in Japan, this gun represents Ithaca's offering to the American market for its modern line of double guns (side-by-side doubles are also offered).

Like the Zoli, this gun uses a cross bolt lockup but with slightly different configuration. SKB also employs what appear to be "dolls-head" extension lugs alongside each upper barrel, but these are at such angles that they cannot assist in locking. It must be assumed that these extensions serve to obtain barrel/frame alignment. Like Beretta, SKB's ejector sears are contained in the forearm.

I've never seen a gun open so easily as this one, that is, when the gun is cocked! Push over the top lever and the barrels snap down as though propelled. This seems to be a combination of very smooth movement and an actual propelling action by the ejector springs. After the SKB's locks have been snapped, however, opening the gun is far and away another story. It now has to cock the hammers and the action is not nearly so smooth or easy.

The Japanese workmanship is very good indeed, a bit of tasteful engraving is used on the frame, and the Ithaca roto-forged system is used for barrel making (this is a cold-forging operation; Ithaca has had large and long experience in making excellent shotgun barrels).

Though a very plain piece of walnut is used, the stock has quite good lines—the best of the three in this department. Checkering is coarser than it should be and there are imperfections in the depth and diamonds.

Ithaca's SKB 500 is a good gun. I'd rate the Golden Snipe a bit ahead of it, but this is natural since the latter also costs more. The SKB has a selective single trigger.

Daly Venture

This 20-bore O-U is a new addition to the fine line of Daly doubles imported from Japan and made by Miroku. It's a bottom-hinging, bottom-locking gun that outwardly much resembles the Browning. That's probably not an accident. Over the years Charles Daly guns have made a very good name for themselves both at Skeet and trap and in the field. Their new Venture 20 ought to add to that fame. This is a good gun, simple in design and well-executed.

Miroku uses a reddish-colored grade of wood that offers warmth and is quite attractive. Like the Browning, stock dimensions are bulky; I think these could be improved by slimming, yet still giving enough to offer a good hold.

Here's another case where the checkering could be much improved; many of the diamonds are not brought up to points, and there are numerous runovers. These criticisms of such things as checkering don't diminish the shooting or handling qualities of any gun, but I consider them very important. I prefer a gun with no checkering to one with poor checkering. Daly's checkering patterns are excellent, and provide generous grip, but their execution leaves something to be desired.

Inside workmanship on this gun is very good — and you can tell that readily since the gun cocks with ease. Examination of the parts shows quality of both design and execution.

The Daly Venture is a very solid gun. I'd prefer to see it with ejectors but others will like it as is. If this were a 12-bore gun I would have to rate it below the others because of its bottom lockup and deeper frame, but this isn't important in a 20 simply because the bores are smaller.

Make no mistake here, all three of these 20s are fine guns. I think they could all be better as I've noted, but when you compare features, workmanship and prices, they represent fair and honest value.

The American shooter and hunter has a wealth of wonderful guns from which to select. Bear in mind that personal opinions vary widely and some of the points I've objected to here will not be a significant factor. Also keep in mind that my remarks are based on one sample of each gun and that others will vary somewhat. But I sure wish Tony Zoli had found a better source for walnut than he did!

Literature

A word is in order about the literature accompanying some of these imported shotguns. Many come with a formidable document in some foreign language, impressive looking. But you can't read 'em! The Italians, for example, use a system of crosses to designate choke where a single cross indicates full choke, two mean improved modified, three modified and four are used to indicate improved cylinder. Beretta encloses an English language guarantee and, on the one that came with my over-under, it says the *right* barrel is four-cross and the *left* three. They might have lessened the confusion by printing another sheet for their O-U models, and they could have lessened it further by saying what the crosses meant! The Beretta crosses appear prominently on the top barrel, except that you still have to know what they signify. Zoli puts the crosses on the barrels and under the fore-end, no problem. His literature also tells you what they stand for.

These fancy guarantees are nice and it's good to have them, but it also seems to me the importer ought to supply more detailed information in English for the American market. ●

DAN WESSON ARMS

by MASON WILLIAMS

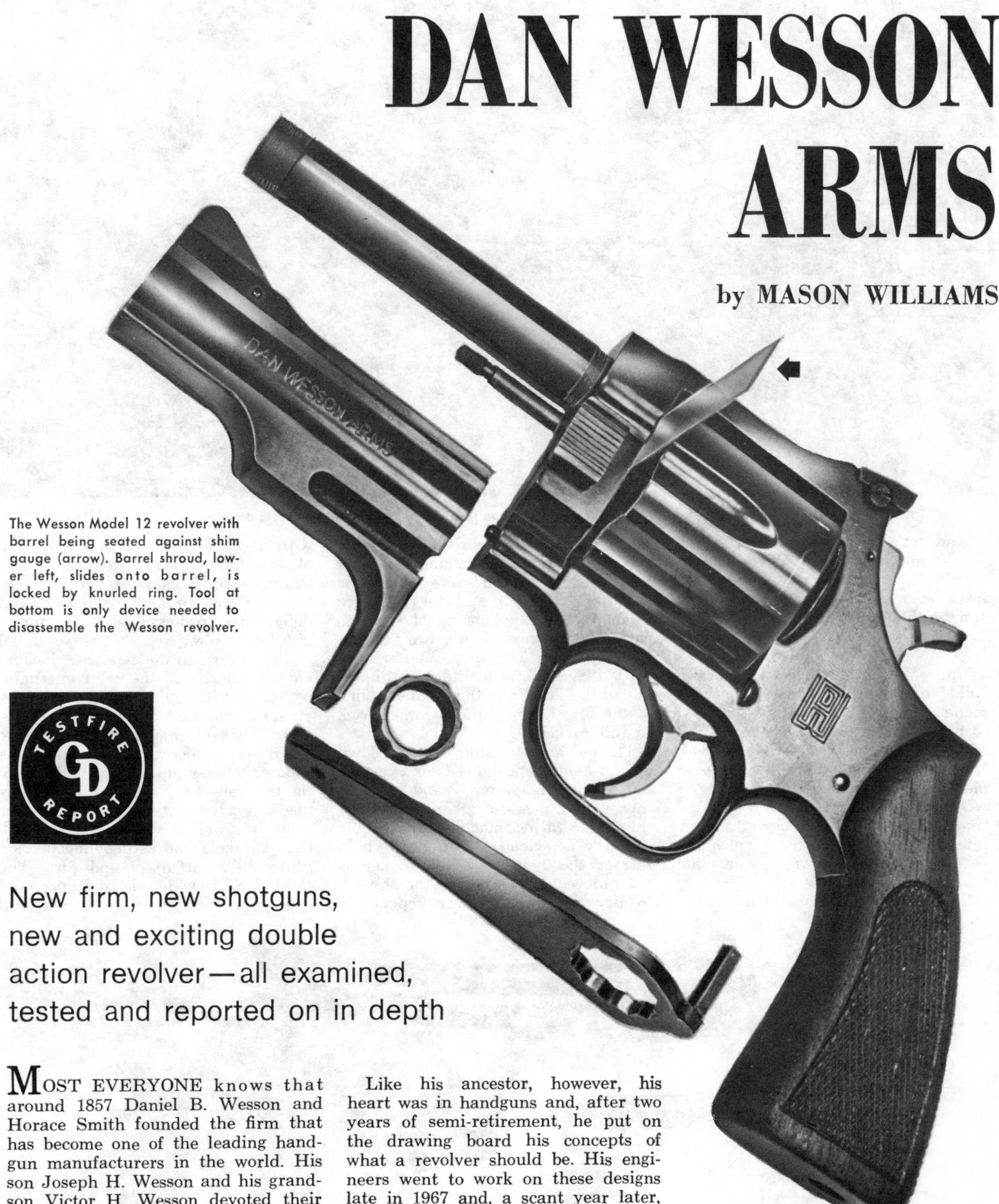

The Wesson Model 12 revolver with barrel being seated against shim gauge (arrow). Barrel shroud, lower left, slides onto barrel, is locked by knurled ring. Tool at bottom is only device needed to disassemble the Wesson revolver.

New firm, new shotguns, new and exciting double action revolver—all examined, tested and reported on in depth

MOST EVERYONE knows that around 1857 Daniel B. Wesson and Horace Smith founded the firm that has become one of the leading handgun manufacturers in the world. His son Joseph H. Wesson and his grandson Victor H. Wesson devoted their lives to the company.

About two years ago, the great grandson of Daniel B. Wesson left Smith and Wesson shortly after its takeover by the Bangor Punta Corporation. This 4th generation Wesson, the second member of the family to bear this famous name, is a man who could, once again, perhaps, execute a great forward step in the firearms industry. For some years Dan's firm, Daniel B. Wesson Company, Inc., manufactured screw machines.

Like his ancestor, however, his heart was in handguns and, after two years of semi-retirement, he put on the drawing board his concepts of what a revolver should be. His engineers went to work on these designs late in 1967 and, a scant year later, in August of 1968, these new handgun ideas were being converted from drawings into steel, and from steel into finely finished prototype firearms.

As soon as he knew that the manufacture of his handguns would be feasible, Wesson leased an old public school building in Monson, Mass. At this time the building is being ripped to pieces to create a modern production plant for the new Dan Wesson Arms Co., a subsidiary of Daniel B. Wesson Co., Inc. Because Wesson's long-range plans called for a complete line of firearms—rifles and shotguns as well—he set aside two huge warehouse rooms to store a complete line of imported long arms. Early in 1968, Dan spent several weeks in Europe visiting various arms factories, finally selecting the huge arms works in Brno, Czechoslovakia, as his source of air rifles, shotguns and sporting rifles. We'll describe these later.

Fred Haines (left) shoots the new Wesson revolver while Dan Wesson looks on.

Now let's take a close look at the new — and startling — Wesson handgun. It has some truly unique features, even if it isn't the handsomest gun in the world.

The New Dan Wesson Revolver

Dan Wesson's interesting brainchild, a remarkable revolver that's made only in 357 Magnum — at least so far — has features that could well make it the most versatile revolver, with the widest potential use, ever placed on the American market.

This handgun must be evaluated commencing with the receiver and its integral parts; the base on which the shooter creates his own, his personal handgun.

This unit contains one of the shortest — if not the shortest — double action revolver mechanisms I've ever handled, yet at the same time it is without the tension and the resistance so many short actions must have to correctly and consistently fire the cartridge primer. The single action is so short that I found it difficult to operate until I realized that a mere flick of the finger brings the hammer back to full cock.

The low hammer spur lies well down on the hammer, coming back over the top rear of the frame to aid in cocking when necessary. In place of thumb-lacerating machine checkering it has wide, clean serrations to help retract the hammer. The trigger is not grooved. This enables the shooter to dry fire the revolver repeatedly without rubbing the skin off the tip of the trigger finger during double action work. This plain trigger, plus the silky smooth double action, should delight the professional handgunner.

Allen screws replace conventional slotted screws in the sideplate, located on the left side of the receiver, thereby eliminating 90% of the screwdriver scratches that ultimately mar so many revolver sideplates. I like these Allen screws because they allow the shooter to draw up the sideplate more tightly, thus keeping them tight during a long firing session. The rear sight lies well down in its cut with the windage adjusting mechanism protected from abuse and dirt. The sight itself is wide, big and open and comes in two types — target and

Above—Dan Wesson's new Model 12 double action revolver, caliber 357 Magnum.

Left — Interior of Model 12 Wesson shows marked departure from conventional designs.

combat.

The hammer rests against the solid steel of the frame so that it cannot fire or even reach the firing pin — housed within the frame — unless the trigger is pulled back raising a bar into position between the hammer and the firing pin. The receiver does not have the conventional recoil plate surrounding the firing pin; rather there is only a firing pin hole through which the firing pin protrudes when struck by the hammer block. There is nothing fitted, driven or pinned into or around the firing pin that can loosen or come out.

A spring-loaded ball bearing, inserted into the receiver below the firing pin hole, snaps into and locks the recessed rear of the ejector rod. This eliminates the complicated and sometimes delicate ejector rod assembly that normally slides a rod back into the frame.

All springs, of stainless steel coil type, reduce the chances of breakage or rusting; no flat springs are used. One spring handles the hammer, another takes care of the hand that revolves the cylinder, and a third keeps pressure against the cylinder lock bolt. With this type of design, each part has the correct spring tension it requires to work correctly.

The rear of the receiver ends in a square, hollow lug that contains the hammer spring. In addition, this lug acts as an anchor for the one-piece grips, which slide onto and over the lug. A heavy Allen screw runs through the center of the grip, screwing into the base of this lug to hold them on. Because of this design, there's plenty of wood around the lug, thus the shooter can file and alter the grip shape to suit his particular hand, even altering the angle of the grips if he likes. However, Wesson furnishes three different types and styles of grips, checkered or smooth, for those who don't feel like cobbling their own.

Because the cylinder latch lies *forward* of the cylinder, both sides of the receiver are clean, which means that grips may be shaped to fit the shooter's hand or to meet his special requirements. The ability to literally fit any style or type of grip to this handgun gives it a versatility seldom found in the firearms business.

The new-design cylinder latch is an integral part of the crane; under spring pressure it snaps its locking stud up and into a matching cut in the receiver, directly below the barrel throat. Therefore a slight but definite downward motion of the left thumb will release the cylinder, and I found that a coordinated push with the finger tips of the left hand against the right side of the cylinder will snap it open and, in the same motion, the thumb will easily move to the end of the ejector rod to dump the fired cases. Either hand may do this alone. This is important for both combat and law enforcement work.

The bottom part of the crane that fits into the front of the receiver beneath the cylinder carries the cylinder lock spring and plunger which spring, as I mentioned above, is a stainless steel coil spring. The ejection rod assembly consists of the ejection rod extension that lies within the barrel shroud and which screws onto the actual ejector rod and head. This head has a lug that fits into a recess in the cylinder and is held by spring pressure. As I mentioned before, the rear end of the ejector rod head has an indent to receive the ball bearing that lies in the recoil face of the receiver to securely lock the rear of the cylinder into place. This design locks the cylinder front and rear.

The crane, with its accompanying cylinder, is locked into place by a steel or aluminum barrel shroud. The buyer can opt for either. Barrels will be made first 2″ and 4″ long, later on in 5″ and 6″ length. Each barrel will require a shroud mated to that particular barrel length. These barrels are quickly exchanged in the following manner, using the barrel-nut wrench and Allen screwdriver furnished with each Wesson revolver. First make certain the gun is unloaded; then—using the wrench—unscrew the barrel nut at the muzzle, pull off the barrel shroud and unscrew the barrel. The replacement barrel is then screwed partially into the front of the receiver, but it must have correct clearance in relation to the front of the cylinder. This is regulated by means of a gauge furnished with the revolver. Slip this gauge in flat against the front of the cylinder and turn the barrel up finger tight against the gauge. Now slide the mating shroud on over the barrel and fasten it tightly into place with the barrel nut. Remove the gauge and the revolver is ready to fire. This entire procedure takes less than a minute—once you have done it a couple of times. This versatility makes this Dan Wesson handgun an extremely desirable revolver for all classes of handgun users from match target shooters to trappers, hunters and law enforcement personnel.

The shroud itself carries the front sight, located deep in a front sight base that is integral with a rib that runs full length of the shroud. The front sight, protected against abuse and dirt, is adjustable for elevation only. While I haven't dropped the revolver on the sights or hit them, they appear to be ruggedly constructed, able to withstand constant, daily use.

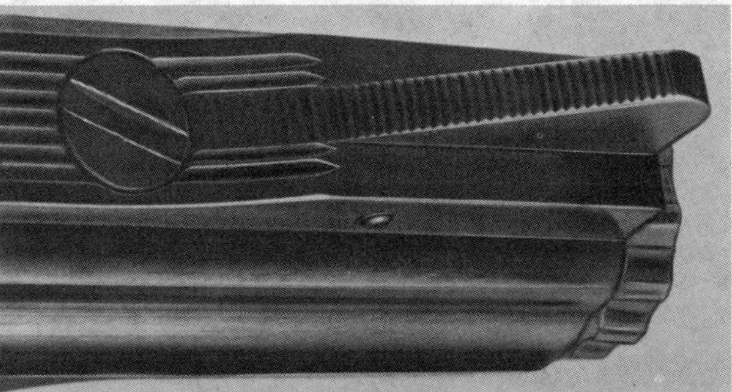

Rugged rear sight of Model 12 (left) Wesson revolver is windage-adjustable. Serrated ramp front is adjustable for elevation.

Why 357 Magnum only? Well, with that chambering, the owner can cover the field—from low velocity 38 Special match wadcutter ammo through the high velocity heavy-bullet Magnum handload—all in one handgun and at a price that's only a few dollars more than a top quality 38 Special.

The wide hammer and wide trigger are standard—no extras. All Model 12s will carry one of the two sight patterns—combat or target. Both will be adjustable for windage and elevation, but there is talk that another model will carry fixed sights designed specifically for law enforcement work. The construction of the ejector rod head and its specially designed relationship to the individual chambers just about eliminate any binding or jamming of fired cartridges during extraction—providing, of course, that excessive charges have not been used.

Dan Wesson tells me that the price will run between $100 and $125 and that his revolvers should be on your dealer's shelves by the time you read this.

DAN WESSON ARMS

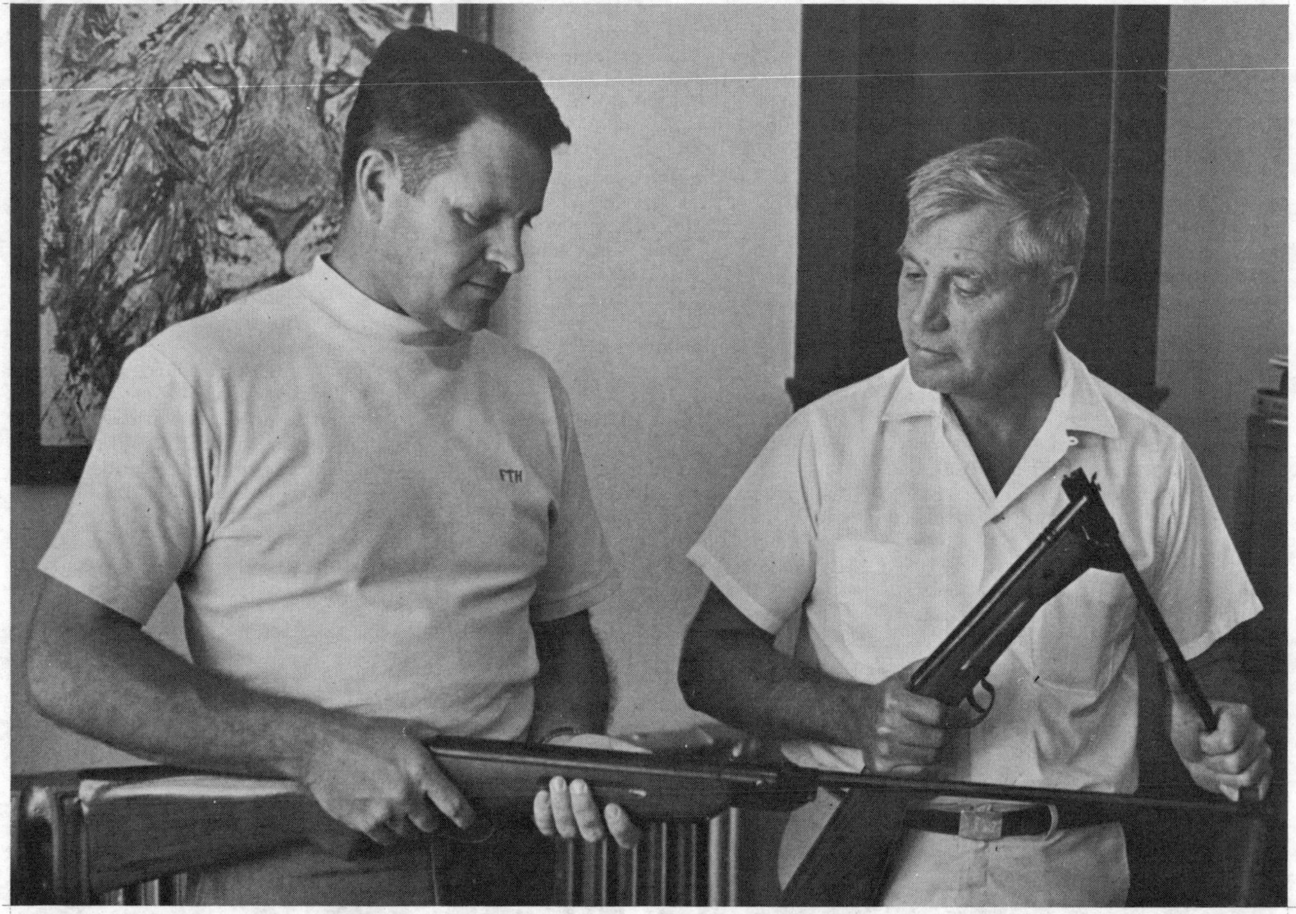

Fred Haines, sales manager for Wesson Arms (left) and Dan Wesson looking over the two Wesson air guns.

Wesson-Brno Arms

One of the great firearms manufacturers of the world, Brno has earned the admiration and respect of shooters and hunters everywhere regardless of nationality. Brno, once well known in the U.S. for its high quality firearms, will be a new name to many of our sportsmen. Only a trickle of Brno arms came into this country after 1939, and printed information on them was negligible.* Brno is something like General Motors, manufacturing many precision products for industry and civilian use.

Brno agreed to produce arms subject to Dan Wesson's approval, these aimed specifically at the American market so that our sportsmen would have an American-type firearm, but one crafted by old-world artisans. By the time you read this, all of Dan Wesson's imports will carry the stamp: CUSTOM BUILT FOR DAN WESSON ARMS—the buyer's guarantee of quality and value. The first few long arms shipped to dealers, however, do not carry this stamp! Wesson won't permit the stamp on any firearms that do not meet his specifications. The first shipments had minor European details that he wouldn't accept as standard—sling swivels and cheekpieces on the double shotguns, and trigger assemblies not quite good enough on the big air rifles. In addition, as soon as an inspection room is set up, Dan Wesson Arms inspectors will open cartons and check each firearm, repack it, enclose American instruction sheets and literature and only then OK shipment to dealers.

The first arms to arrive from Brno were 17-cal. air rifles. Spring operated, these are cocked by a single down stroke of the barrel that, at the same time, exposes the breech for reloading. The front sight is a fixed blade sight; the rear sight has a conventional notch that may be filed, enlarged or altered to suit the shooter's wishes; it permits of ample elevation adjustment, allowing the rifle to be fired at greater ranges than the regulation 30-foot distance.

Two air rifle models are imported: the 620 is an adult-size arm giving the shooter the feel and heft of a full scale rifle for accurate shooting. The barrel is 19½" long, over-all length 43½". Not a toy at all, this is a well-built, accurate air rifle that retails for a mere $19.95. Included in this price is a target, stamped with the rifle's serial number, showing a 5-shot test group and the inspector's name. My sample rifle, not specially picked out for me, has a trigger pull that is clean, sharp and light. As a matter of fact, I selected it myself from many hundreds that had arrived while I was in the warehouse; one of the packages had been partially broken open, and I got my 620 air rifle from this bundle.

The Model 624, a Junior version of the 620, is 38½" over-all and has a 16" barrel. This little air rifle should prove ideal for teaching youngsters the fundamentals of safe rifle shooting—its light weight and easy cocking are perfect for this work. This 624 Junior also comes with a 5-shot target and has a serial number. Its trigger pull is long and creepy, but at a retail $14.95 I consider it a darn good buy.

All rifles have individual characteristics that can often mislead the novice into believing his particular rifle —or air rifle—is not accurate. Few people appreciate the importance of using pellets that are best suited to their particular air rifle. As an example, neither of my two Wesson air rifles would shoot well with Crosman pellets, yet when Hy-Score pellets were used both gave excellent accuracy. Anyone buying an air rifle should try out all of the various types

---

* See the GUN DIGEST, 22nd ed.

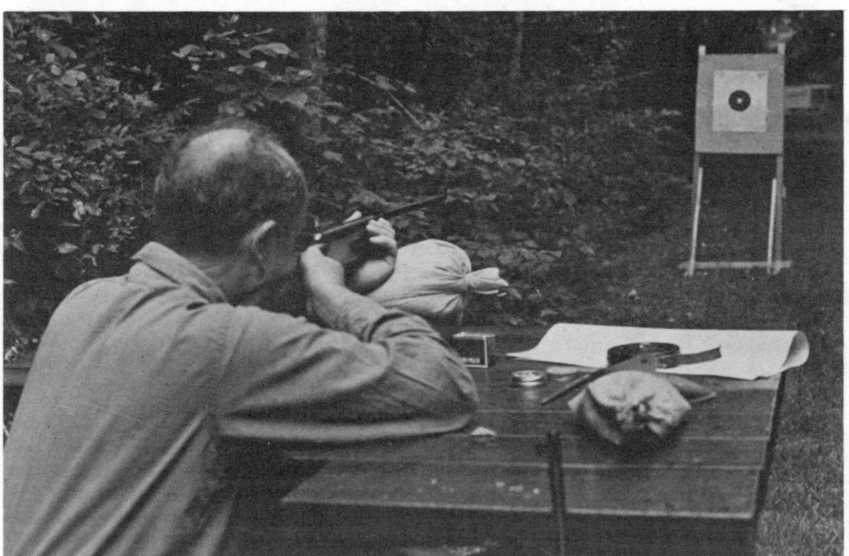

The author firing a Dan Wesson air rifle in an accuracy test at 10-meter range.

and makes of pellets available to him, then settle on the one brand or type that gives the best accuracy in that rifle.

The 620 air rifle has a factory-specified velocity of 540 fps. As far as I have been able to determine, using my Avtron chronograph, velocities show good uniformity. Here are the figures for 10 shots from the M620 rifle, using Hy-Score pellets:

650	661	632	623	620
635	622	622	615	628

Note that maximum variation amounts to only 46 fps, and that average velocity runs some 90 fps higher than the published factory velocities. I am inclined to believe that velocities will probably even off at around 590 fps once the air rifle has been well-broken in. This is surprisingly good and consistent velocity for an under $20 air rifle.

I then checked out both rifles for accuracy, using Crosman and Hy-Score pellets. I used a benchrest and sandbags, resting the air rifles on my hand and my hand on the sandbags. The range was an exact 30 feet. The 620 rifle turned in 5-shot groups that ran ¾″ to ⅝″ with the Hy-Score pellets. Crosman pellets opened up the groups to around ⅞″ to 1½″ indicating that this brand is not suited to my particular rifle.

The 624 Junior rifle averaged 5-shot groups of 1½″ to 1⅛″ with Hy-Score pellets and, surprisingly enough, 1½″ to 1¾″ with Crosman pellets; perhaps the Crosman pellets are more suited to lower velocities or will give more consistent accuracy with this particular air rifle.

In any event, it would appear that both of these air rifles are highly accurate for the price and—in my opinion—the 620 is a lot of fine machinery for $19.95. I've had no problems with either air rifle.

Dan Wesson hopes to develop a better trigger mechanism for the 620 in order to obtain more of the potential accuracy built into the rifle, and I would not be surprised to see the open rear sights modified before long.

Wesson-Brno Shotguns

Dan Wesson Arms is bringing in two models of shotguns from the Brno factory to help fill the demand from American hunters and claybird shooters for well-designed, soundly built and honestly assembled shotguns at a price that the average American shooter can afford to pay. I believe he has succeeded. Let's start with the double.

The ZP49 12 gauge, a sidelock double, reminds me of the famed Parkers. The balance is about the same, and the gun comes up with a clean single motion that gives the shooter the correct sight picture for shots on rising birds. The locks are patterned after the Purdey system, the firing pins are spring loaded, there are two triggers and an automatic tang safety. The pistol grip stock is walnut, nicely hand checkered, and the wood has a soft oil finish I like. It has European sling swivels, plus a cheekpiece, but Dan Wesson is dropping both of these details in favor of an American style stock. At present the ZP49 comes through with 2¾″ chambers, a correct length for this lovely little double; the gun is too light—6½ lbs.—to handle 3″ Magnums comfortably!

This fast-handling gun has 28½″ barrels, with over-all length 44½″. From the moment I got my hands on this ZP49 I fell in love with it, but I also wanted to find out if its beauty was skin deep or if it was a truly rugged, lifetime investment. A phone call to an avid hunter in Montreal who owns just about every type of rifle and shotgun made, dug out the information that Brno makes firearms the way they should be built and that their repair and maintenance is almost non-existent. They just go on, year after year. Brno firearms, my friend revealed, have been sold in Canada for over 20 years.

When I visited Dan Wesson Arms, the warehouse was filled with hundreds of shotguns. Fred Haines, Dan's Sales Manager, asked what choke I'd prefer, pointing out that each shotgun is individually factory checked out and shot for pattern, the results in percentages then stamped on each shipping carton. I said I'd like to browse around, and that I'd choose my own double. I went down row af-

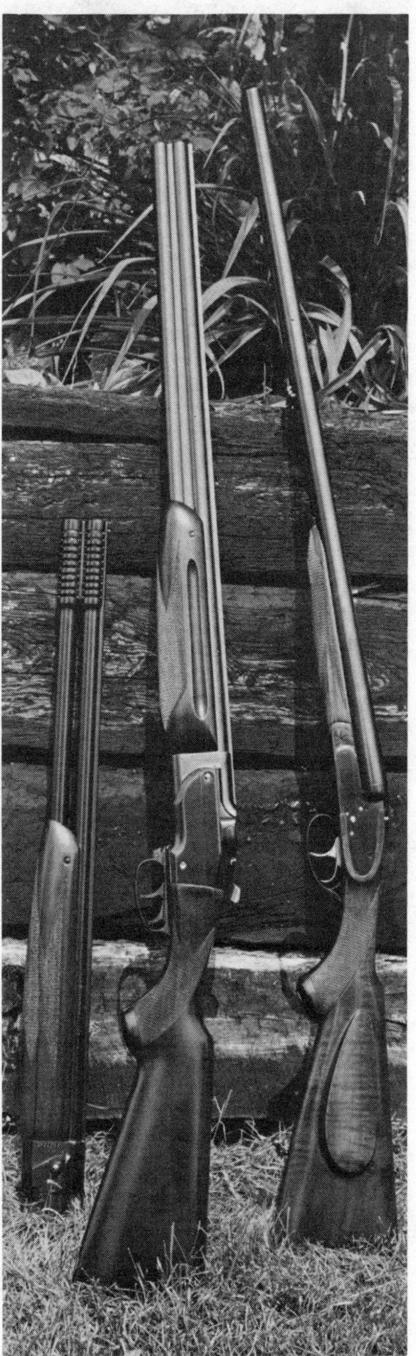

The new Dan Wesson shotguns. Left, spare Skeet barrels for the over-under in the middle; right, the side-by-side double.

ter row of ZP49s in their sealed cases and, sure enough, it appears possible to practically name the combination you want and get it. These stamped choke figures, of course, represent patterns shot at the factory with the particular loads in use on that day, and should be considered as a guide only. As all experienced shotgunners know, different sizes of shot, different loads, different shells and different makes of shells, all contribute to changes in shot patterns, but the ZP49 carton figures will give the purchaser a pretty good idea of the barrel potential. I picked out a right barrel with 69% and a left barrel with 75% figures, both percentages for the standard 30" circle at 40 yards.

My ZP49 has automatic ejectors, ideal for a field shotgun, and allowing the hunter to reload quickly. (The ZP47, at $169.95, has extractors.) The ZP49 sells for $199.95 and, when you consider the workmanship and quality lavished on them, their design and balance, I believe you will agree with me that they're a real bargain.

Roger Leroux and Les Morrow checking patterns, using a 30" hoop for convenience.

Wesson's Over-Unders

The Wesson over-under shotgun is known as the Model ZH201 and, since the last war, has earned a world wide reputation for sheer ruggedness and reliability both in the hunting fields and as a trap and Skeet gun.

One Canadian Trap and Skeet Club has around 30 active members, and eight 201s are generally on the line each week.

For my test shotgun I choose a ZH201 with a 76% top barrel, the bottom 73%. With its 27½" barrels the gun stands just under 45" over-all. Blueing on all metal is excellent. The pistol grip buttstock and fore-end are hand-checkered. Like the double, this shotgun goes together with a tight smoothness that is a joy to work with. The receiver and breechblock design breaks up the smooth continuity of the flowing lines of this shotgun so that the average American may, at first glance, wonder why Brno did not stick with the conventional lines of the ordinary over-under. Brno could not do this and still give the buyer the benefit of their unusual breeching up. This Brno design fits the breechblock assembly directly to the rear of the barrels in such a manner that—if desired—the barrels and breechblock may be removed from the receiver and actually fired by striking the rear of the firing pins with a hammer. This means that when these two assemblies are together nothing can affect their fit or tightness — a breech lock-up that should never shoot loose. The breechblock assembly moves back about ¾-inch within the receiver itself to permit the barrels to swing open and cock the hammers — all in the same movement. The barrels pivot on two solid side lugs that fit into the top front section of the receiver, bringing both chambers into full view for easy and sure loading. Two heavy lugs below the bottom barrel cam back the spring-loaded breech assembly, which travels on machined guide rails. As the action is closed two springs force the breech assembly forward and, as the opening lever snaps shut, the breech assembly locks onto the rear of the barrels to provide a completely sealed—ready to fire—unit within the receiver.

When this shotgun is new, I suggest you open the action only with the safety in the *on* position. Otherwise excessive stress is placed on the unlocking lever and its associated parts. My 201 has now eased up so that the safety snaps back automatically into the on position without strain, but it has taken quite a bit of firing to achieve this. This is the only detail I can fault in the entire shotgun. The safety, located in the front of the trigger guard, may be pushed off with the trigger finger. Wesson will furnish the ZH201 with a disconnected safety for use in trapshooting.

The extractors move the fired shells back about half an inch to allow the shooter to pluck them out, ideal for reloaders and trapshooters. The stock design, ideal for upland bird hunting, handles recoil so well that I've fired this shotgun day after day without any discomfort.

You can buy the ZH201 as a field shotgun only at $199.95 or, as I did, you can choose one with an extra set of 26" Skeet barrels with built-in compensators. The barrels, designated ZH202, cost an extra $60. My top Skeet barrel throws 68% into a 30" circle at 22 yards, the bottom barrel 72%.

The ZH201 also takes a wide selection of other barrel combinations, but the one I'm anxiously waiting for is the rifle/shotgun set, which pair explains the chief reasoning behind the unusual double/single triggers of the ZH201. When firing the ZH201 as a shotgun, the rear trigger fires both barrels in the conventional manner, or the shooter may fire the top barrel with the front trigger and the bottom barrel with the rear trigger. This lets the shooter selectively fire the 7x57 rifle- or the shotgun barrel at will.

When assembling the ZH201 receiver and barrels it is *first* necessary to press back the breechblock in order to cock the hammers. This is done quite simply by pushing the face of the breechblock against a flat surface (preferably not metal), moving it back about ¾-inch. At the same time push the opening lever over to the right.

Shooting the Wesson Shotguns

Regardless of how well shotguns are built and designed, and in spite of all of the praise heaped upon these Brno shotguns, I still wanted to put them through a lot of shooting in the hands of many shooters. I also wanted to verify the choke patterns assigned to the guns.

The Mawcook Shooting Club, Inc., about 30 miles from Montreal, is the only place I know where benchrest, rifle, shotgun and handgun shooting can go on at the same time, while families picnic and relax nearby. Roger Leroux, Club President and an old friend, told me to come on up. We spent all of Saturday and Sunday firing the two Dan Wesson Arms shotguns.

The Mawcook patterning board is a 4x4 foot quarter-inch steel plate mounted on a steel frame, all welded into a single unit. A heavy, pointed steel screw in the center of the plate takes a black cardboard 6-inch disc as an aiming point. After each shot, the surface of the plate is painted over with a non-drying solution of white lead and oil, readying it for the next shot. This is an ideal arrangement, far superior to large sheets of paper.

During our two full days of firing over 18 experienced Canadian shooters saw, handled and fired these two shotguns, and all commented favorably on their quality and workmanship. Winchester, CIL and imported Czech-made Sellier & Bellot shells, the latter widely used in the Montreal area, were shot in these tests.

The Wesson-Brno over-under disassembled. Safety is in front of guard. Rear trigger acts as single trigger. Guard bow could be a little roomier.

We started with the side-by-side double, the barrels stamped 75% and 69%. Using a 30″ hoop to rapidly work out the number of shot *outside* the 30″ circle, we not only exceeded the factory percentage figures but shot some amazingly uniform and consistent patterns with the Winchester shells. Throughout the tests the Winchester loads were remarkably uniform, far more so than CIL or Sellier & Bellot shells.

The Wesson-Brno over-under shotgun. Note double extension lugs, locking crossbolt and rearward movement of breech on opening.

CIL shells averaged out at just about the factory figures. The Sellier & Bellot loads were erratic, but these were an extremely low-priced type, probably not up to standard S&B quality. They also gave off a great deal of smoke.

The ZH201 over-under with the field barrels, choke figures of 76% and 73%, was an eye opener. Winchester shells gave patterns so tight that we had to move back to 50 yards to shoot the factory figures with #6 shot. The ZH202 Skeet barrels proved deadly with #8 shot, giving such wide, full pattern at 22 yards that it was almost impossible to miss a bird — but I did — with the Winchester shells unless the targets get out to 40 and 50 yards. The CIL and S&B shells gave their usual performances.

As a result of this firing I've concluded that, based on a price-to-quality relationship, Brno shotguns compare favorably with shotguns that sell for a lot more money.

On my return from the Mawcook Shooting Club I called my old friend Johnny Spucches, who runs the Ring-Neck Lodge Game Preserve in Amenia, N.Y. John has all types of birds plus somewhere around 30-odd highly trained dogs, so that it would be a relatively simple matter to test fire these Brno shotguns on actual upland game. I took my young son Jeff with me and the two of us spent an enjoyable day working with John's great dogs on pheasant, partridge, chukars and quail. Once again, the Wesson shotguns gave good and consistent performance with the Winchester shells. As far as I am concerned Dan Wesson can stamp his name on either of these shotguns with pride and confidence. ●

RELOADING FOR

An extensive and fully detailed treatise on this specialized phase of cartridge making.

Left—Author recently picked off this coyote with 240 Weatherby Magnum, shown here. The new 6mm round is an instant killer, offering the largest case capacity and velocity practical with the 6mm bore size. Better sectional density and high coefficient of form help buck the wind better. Right—Laramie gunsmith,

RELOADING FOR varmint hunting differs from run-of-the-mill home ammo assembly, mainly in the extra care required to squeeze that cone of fire down as close to one bullet diameter as possible, plus the proper choice of cartridges and bullets.

Varmint rifles are generally small bore from 17- to 25- caliber, launching comparatively lightweight bullets at high velocity. The object is to kill harmful or nuisance vermin humanely. Since no effort is made to save meat, as with deer or other game animals, varmint shooters seek the most explosive effect possible — to achieve instant kills.

Certainly it's possible to kill varmints with deer-class rifles, but calibers above 25 cause quakelike concussions that sorely tax the good hospitality of farmers or ranchers in the area. Also, big bores don't often exhibit that sub-minute-of-angle accuracy so earnestly sought by varminters. Even if inherently super accurate, where is the man who can hold a belching cannon with the precise nicety required to hit a coke bottle-sized ground squirrel at 300 yards or so, for 100 or more rounds? By the time he'd triggered off a day's prairie dog hunting with say a 7mm Remington, the average nimrod would be punchy.

Wildcat 17 calibers go "spat" instead of "boom," spitting 20- to 25-grain pellets, that have a bomb-like effect all out of proportion to their diminutive size. The demand for this mini-caliber appears to be growing at a great rate. Joyce Hornady made up a biggish batch of 25-gr. 17-cal. bullets and they were sold out overnight! He's now busy making a lot more.

Centerfire 22s are legion, but currently most popular are the 224 Weatherby, 225 Winchester and 22-250 Remington. All share similar velocity figures, and any one is a good choice for every phase of varminting, from squirrels to coyotes and bobcats. Still tops in velocity, killing power and *barrel erosion,* is the 220 Swift, with many advocates in the field, but few in print.

Way out West, where we got a name for wind, and it isn't always "Maria," 22 rifles sometimes adopt two trajectories, one down, the other sideways. That's when the 6mm and 25s take over. The most popular wildcat among predator hunters out here is the formidable 25-06, an '06 case necked down to 25-caliber. Some writers decry it as "overbore capacity," but it puts down critters out as far as you can see them, with all of the conviction of Thor's thunderbolts storming down from Mount Olympus. My 257 Weatherby has more of the same "wrath of the Gods" effect. However, most hunters would as soon pass up the boisterous bang and vigorous push on the shoulder.

Surveys show the 243 Winchester topping popularity polls among California varmint hunters, and the 6mm Remington has a substantial fan club, but I expect the new, super-potent 240 Weatherby to make inroads on both. A couple of wildcat 6mm cartridges, popular nationwide, are the 240 Page Super Pooper, a 28°-shouldered, blown out version of the 244 Remington, sired by gun writer Warren Page, and the 243 Super Rockchucker, developed by Fred Huntington, manufacturer of "Precisioneered" RCBS reloading tools, years before the 243 Winchester and 244 Remington fostered popular interest in the 6mm. The 243 SRC is a 30-06 case, necked down to 6mm, with the shoulder pushed back to 28°, leaving a slightly longer neck. No fireforming is required. (RCBS, Oroville, California, chambers barrels for both of these cartridges).

The key to varmint loading, regardless of caliber, is proper bullet selection. Squirrel-chuck hunters and predator hunters both want light, fragile bullets, but the latter must avoid those that are too light. One day I watched a friend, shooting 60-grain bullets in a 243 Winchester, lose three coyotes and a bobcat. All went down, apparently with well placed hits, but got up and left the country. We trailed one coyote for over an hour, before it disappeared into thin air. Using 75-grain or heavier 6mm bullets, I have never lost a coyote that was well hit. Recently, I caught a desert wolf through the flanks, as it crossed in front of me, full bore. I watched in wonder as it barreled on, hardly faltering, but recovered in time to correct my lead and drill the fleeing animal through the shoulders

VARMINT HUNTING

by JOHN LACHUK

Anderson, and author look over some chubby Rockchucks shot by the latter during Wyoming trip. Author discovered that his 240 PSP far outranged high velocity 22 centerfire, and held up much better in gale-like winds. He recommends use of heavier bullets for long range shooting with 6mm or 25 caliber.

with a 75-grain Sierra HP from my 240 Page Super Pooper. Traveling at 3400 fps, ahead of 41 grains of 4895, this bullet left a 3-inch exit. It's a tribute to the coyote's stamina that it continued to run with such a wound.

Another coyote, standing head-on, was hit in the chest with my 243 Winchester, pushing an 80-grain Speer spitzer at 3350 fps with 40.3 grains 4895. The animal dropped like a stone. There was no exit wound, but the coyote gurgled like a half-empty fifth of whisky when I picked it up, indicating extensive internal damage.

Sierra's 6mm "Total Destruction" 85-grain boat-tail, with its tendeı .018" jacket, tapering to .009" at the hollow point, makes an excellent long-range chuck or squirrel bullet because it bucks wind and retains velocity better than a flat-based bullet. On a recent rockchuck hunt in Wyoming with Fred Huntington and *Shooting Times* editor, Robert Steindler, I used this bullet in my 240 PSP while Bob used a high velocity 22 bore with 55-grain slugs. An excellent marksman, Bob got more than his share of fat, far-ranging chucks—until the wind started to blow. Then he found himself handicapped by the 22's proclivity to follow the beckoning call of the whistling siren.

Adding five grains to the popular 55-grain weight improves both the 22's long range ballistics and its wind bucking ability. The largely overlooked 60-grain Hornady spire point zips out of a 22-250 at a respectable 3500 fps ahead of 33.7 grains of 4320. The 55-grain spire point, with 34.9 grains of the same powder, takes off 100 fps faster. However, when they both reach 100 yards the 60-grain bullet's 2740 fps almost equals the 55-grain's 2760 fps. At 300 yards, the 60-grain leapfrogs its lighter competition, with 2410 fps against 2390 fps for the 55-grain. The 55-grain has a ballistic coefficient of only .246, while the 60-grain boasts .269, better than a 70-grain Hornady 6mm at .260.

Ballistic coefficient (BC) measures a bullet's wind bucking and velocity retention capabilities. The oft-quoted sectional density (SD) is a fair barometer of bullet performance but it fails to take into account the nose shape of the projectile. To illustrate, compare Speer's 6mm 90-grain spitzer, sectional density of .217, with their 105-grain round nose, SD .254. Looks like the heavy bullet easily bests the light one, but wait! The 90-grain has a ballistic coefficient of .323, the 105-grain's BC is .256. Why? Because the blunt bullet has far greater air resistance.

For the 257 Weatherby and the 25-06, I prefer the heavier bullets, with high ballistic coefficients. They offer super wind bucking plus high velocity retention at long ranges, and that's really what you're buying with a quarter-bore. The 6mm kills varmints as dead as they can get, so you don't need greater killing power. What the 25 has to offer is exemplified in the 100-grain Hornady spire point, with an impressive BC of .357. Launched at 3500 fps from a 257 Weatherby, it retains 62% of its original velocity at 500 yards. Contrast this with 57% for the 87-grain Hornady 6mm, starting at 3300 fps from a 6mm Remington, and 52% for the 60-grain Hornady 22 with a muzzle velocity of 3500 fps from a 22-250.

I've never experienced ricochets using heavy 25 caliber bullets, and they are grossly destructive. I once loaded my 257 Weatherby down to about 3100 fps, using 117-grain Sierra spitzers, hoping to shoot bobcats without too much pelt damage. I caught one cat full in the chest, and the bullet left a saucer-sized exit, luckily far enough back to allow a fine shoulder mount.

Bores larger than 25 require light weight bullets to avoid ricochets near inhabited areas, and to offer explosive effect on small animals. Sierra's 90-grain hollow point is good in the 270. For the 308 or 30-06, use the 130-grain Speer hollow point or the Sierra 110-grain HP.

Despite the extensive lineup of current factory cartridges, some wildcats have assets worth considering. The 25-06 uses cheap, plentiful brass, requires no fire forming, merely a quick trip through a 270 sizing die and a 25-06 sizer, thence to the powder measure. With today's slow burning powders, it's a more efficient round than when it was created by A. O. Niedner, after World War I.

Not all wildcats have it so easy.

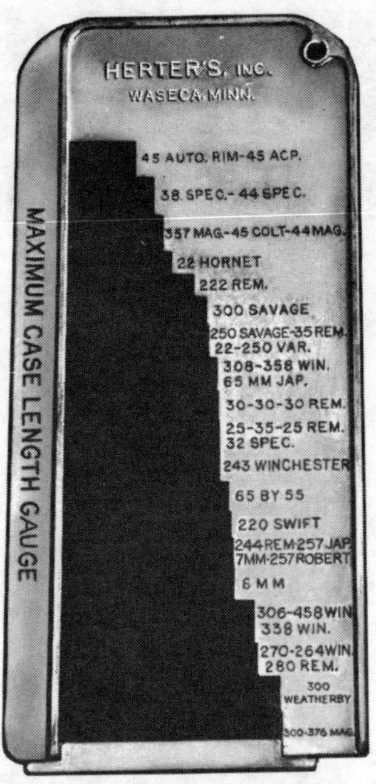

A case-length gauge is an important asset to reloaders. Most varmint cartridges are high intensity rounds that tend to lengthen in firing, especially such as the 243 Winchester, 220 Swift, etc. Frequent trimming is essential to accuracy and safety. Long case-necks may squeeze into the throat, run up high pressures.

Some go through several reductions in length and/or diameter. It's important that case forming dies support case walls, as they exist, while sizing down the case neck. If die walls are a larger diameter than the case, case walls will buckle before neck sizing occurs. That's why file trim dies can seldom double as forming dies. When die-forming wildcat brass, adjust your final sizing die so cases offer a crush fit in your rifle, to prevent headspace problems. If cases start out too short for your chamber, seat bullets well out, to hold case heads back against the bolt when firing. Another method is to run a slightly oversized expander plug through the case neck and size it back just enough to chamber.

Use near-full loads, never sub-loads to fire-form rimless cases. With light loads, an apparent "bouncing" phenomenon can occur, yielding perfect-appearing cases, that none-the-less possess excessive headspace, often as much as .040" to .050". Reloading and firing such cases is dangerous in the extreme!

Never die-form or resize cases without lubricating with commercial lube supplied by various die makers, or use machinist's soluble oil. Apply just enough lube to give an oily feel to cases. An excess around the shoulder area will result in oil dents.

Reloaders still wage a bitter debate over the relative merits of full-length resizing versus neck-sizing. Being more hunter than target shooter, I usually full-length size, for easy chambering in the field, where a stuck case has more than once cost me a fine trophy. However, when I got my test copy of the new 240 Weatherby Magnum, the cartridge was so new that reloading dies weren't yet available. I sent fired cases to Fred Huntington, and in due course had a full set of RCBS dies, but meanwhile, I had to neck-size using my 240 PSP die. Groups resulting from that exigency were no worse but certainly no better than those fired later after full-length resizing with the proper dies, tending to discount claims that neck-sizing improves accuracy.

Another pro neck-sizing argument states that brass becomes more brittle as it is repeatedly expanded by firing and then resized. Full-length sizing works the body of the case more than neck-sizing, thus logically should shorten case life. However, few failures occur in the body of the case. Normal fatality results from lengthwise cracks in the neck that most often occur during firing. The greatest enemy of long case life is not the sizing die, but high pressure, usually resulting from too much powder. Cartridge cases, like people, die young when they become gluttons.

The sensitive Lachmiller priming tool helped the author in getting primers seated perfectly square with the case head, and neatly to the cup bottom. Proper primer seating is important to accuracy.

To demonstrate how tenacious cases really are, Fred Huntington held a shooting/reloading marathon with four random selected cases, two Remington and two Winchester. They were full-length resized for each loading, in a standard RCBS 30-06 die: Cases were lubed outside only. Leaving the necks dry on the inside, deliberately subjecting them to added strain. Loads were standard velocity and pressure, and the Model 70 Winchester had a normal chamber. Results: One Remington case split at the neck on the 36th firing, the other ditto on the 52nd. The Winchester cases failed in like manner at the 50th and 55th firings. Inasmuch as all failures occurred in the case necks I fail to see how neck-sizing only could have made the cases last longer.

There is at least one disadvantage to neck-sizing. Wall thickness around the circumference of individual case necks can vary .003" to .004". Neck-sizing dies, which can't support the case body adequately, tend to offset the necks toward the stronger side. The bullet, held cockeyed to begin with, gets off to a bad start in the rifling and accuracy suffers.

If you don't care to stick with your brass through thick and thin, try inside neck reaming with a line-ream die offered by RCBS, that guides the reamer concentrically, helping to even out wall thickness. Or use the Forster Outside Neck Turner, that trues-up case neck O.D. over a mandrel for about the same effect. Both tools reduce variations between cases for a more consistent bullet pull, further improving accuracy. Full-length

Armory C-H case trimmer is easy to use and fast, keeps cases trimmed, after using case gauge or caliper to set proper length. The chamfering tool (right) is used to remove burrs left inside and outside of the case mouths after trimming.

RCBS case-forming dies provide cases for many wildcat and standard calibers, using cheap, plentiful GI or commercial 30-06 brass. Dies shown form 22-250 brass. Be careful in final sizing of any formed case to make it a crush fit in your rifle, to avoid headspace problems. Use normal, not reduced loads, for fire-forming rimless cases.

This RCBS line-reaming die helps make case necks of uniform wall thickness after they have thickened from brass flowing forward during firing. Be sure to size cases full length, and pull the case necks back over the expander button before reaming.

resize and expand necks before trimming and reaming.

Check case length periodically with a vernier caliper, Pacific's "Big Mike," or a case length gauge from Herter's, McKillen & Heyer, Wilson, etc. Some cases such as the 220 Swift and 243 Winchester, grow .003" to .006" each firing with high intensity loads, simultaneously thickening at the neck and require frequent trimming and reaming.

When case necks start splitting, it can be like a plague descended upon your brass. I've lost as many as 8 cases out of 20. To save the rest of the lot of 100, I pulled the bullets and powder, ejected the primers, and annealed the case necks. I'm still using those cases ten reloads later. If you keep track of the number of times your cases are reloaded you can learn to anticipate split necks, and anneal before attrition sets in.

It pays to practice neck annealing with reject brass the first time. I use a common method, as follow: I stand six or eight cases in a ten-inch cake tin, in water within a ¼-inch of their shoulders and play the flame of a Bernz-O-Matic torch inside of each case mouth in turn. When the neck turns red, I tip the case over. The water prevents heat from drawing the hardness of the body and head, where strength is essential to safety. It takes only ten to fifteen seconds per case. Time yourself, so the annealing will be even on all of the cases.

For tapered cases such as the 22-250, "partial sizing" offers most of the advantages of both full-length and neck sizing. Instead of adjusting your full-length sizing die to a firm contact with the shell holder, stop about ⅛-inch short. The diameter of case walls will be reduced but slightly. The neck will be fully sized and held concentric with the body. The shoulder area, controlling headspace on rimless cases, will be untouched. Partial sizing reduces cold working of the case body but cases chamber without hesitation and bullets start concentric with the bore. Cases with only a slight taper, such as the 243, won't accept partial sizing because case walls are almost completely sized, squeezing in the shoulder and buckling it outward, in effect lengthening headspace, so the bolt can't close.

All reloaders desire accuracy, but to varmint hunters, it's more than a tender sentiment, it's an absolute necessity! Any load that groups much over an inch at 100 yards makes poor varmint ammo. Frank Snow, president of Sierra Bullets, Inc., and Ferris Pindle, Sierra research engineer, have made some interesting discoveries anent reloading accuracy. They spot check every lot of bullets coming off the line by actually loading and firing them in a heavy bench rifle, mounting a 2-inch, 30x Unertl scope. Shooting is done in Sierra's own 200-yard, underground tunnel. A $3000 counter chronograph automatically reads off instrumental velocities at ten feet and 200 yards simultaneously. Groups average around .200", for five shots at 100 yards. "If they run over a quarter-inch," says Pindle, "we start to worry!"

Powder charges are metered directly into the cases from a Lyman powder measure, and not weighed, but velocities and pressures are in the low to medium range, where a slight variation in powder weight has less effect. Snow and Pindle use Wilson and RCBS neck-size-only dies most of the time, with a periodic run through an RCBS full-length die. Bullets are seated in a Wilson straight-line die, and concentricity, which they consider very important is checked on a Wilson cartridge spinner.

Bullets are seated .010" into the lands, a practice that I don't recommend to varmint hunters loading at or near maximum because it runs up pressures erratically at high pressure levels. Accuracy does improve if bullets are not obliged to leap a wide gap from case to rifling, but the bullet ogive should not actually touch the lands. Your rifle magazine likely limits overall length anyway, so the discussion is largely academic, unless you want to single-load—OK for chucks and squirrels, too slow for a coyote darting through distant prickly pear and sage. Seat short bullets at least one caliber deep, to prevent their working loose in the field.

Accuracy depends to a surprising degree upon good primer action. Superior automobile performance requires a hot spark. The same is true of rifle cartridges. Magnum primers, from CCI, Federal and Remington, assure proper ignition of heavily deterent-coated powders such as 4350, 4831 and the Hodgdon ball powders, even in large capacity cases. Intensely cold weather makes powder harder to bring up to kindling temperature. Magnum primers overcome this reluctance to ignite plus helping to keep velocities more uniform and nearer normal in spite of the cold.

Magnum primers also improve accuracy by making up for deficiencies in the rifle's firing mechanism. Frank Snow discovered that short-action bolt rifles shot better when heavy firing pin springs were installed. Coincidentally, ballistician Edward M. Yard found that a heavy blow of the firing pin causes increased flash energy from a primer. Says Mr. Yard, "The difference between a normal and a light blow can be enough to drop a magnum primer to the level of a standard one."

Seat primers uniformly to the bot-

224 Weatherby Magnum has about same ballistics as 225 and 22-250, the latter also offered in Weatherby Varmintmaster rifle, on scaled down Mark V action. Use of 60-gr. bullets in any of these three 22s will make them stand up better in the wind. Ease of deflection by wind is the major failing of 22 caliber varmint rifles.

tom of the primer pockets, both for firm support of the anvils and to prevent a cushioning effect upon the firing pin, making it seat the primer cup fully before it can crush and ignite the primer pellets. No harm will come to primers from seating them well below the case heads. In fact, sensitivity is improved by placing primer pellets under "dry compression."

In the interests of accuracy, I clean primer pockets every fifth or sixth loading, using a Herter's brass bristle brush in a drill press. I also check primer flash holes with a Herter's flash-hole gauge, discarding atypical cases. All of my cases are segregated by make and lot.

A bullet is inherently accurate when its center of gravity coincides with its center of form. In the bore, a bullet is forced to rotate around its center of mass, but once free of confinement, it can wobble at will around a misplaced center of gravity, and miss the place that you want it to go. Bullets of modern manufacture are, almost without exception, uniform and well balanced, but individual rifles often evidence a strong preference for a particular brand or bullet weight. You must discover the optimum bullet/powder combination for your rifle.

The trick in working up loads for any varmint rifle is to get the job done without wearing out the barrel before you get to take it hunting. Eliminate as many alternatives as possible with theory, before testing. You may have to consider three or four powders, and perhaps a dozen bullets. Astute study of various reloading tables will reveal which powder offers the best velocity/pressure ratio. Bear in mind that ball powders, BL-C2, H375, H450, the new W-W powders, etc., cause less bore erosion and also cooperate wondrously well with almost any powder measure. For data see *Hodgdon's Manual* 20. For long barrel life, load under maximum. You won't miss 100 fps or so in the field. Narrow down the bullet list by considering the game you'll hunt. For varmints, you need lighter weight, explosive bullets.

Eliminate unnecessary variables. For instance, I always use CCI 250 Magnum primers—one variable removed. Change only one component at a time, so you know what to blame or credit for a change in performance. Don't mix powder lots or bullets. Stock up on lot numbers that perform well.

Load initial tests of only three rounds each. This is enough to show which loads are grossly inaccurate or show pressure signs. These you abandon without wasting more time and material. Promising combinations are loaded again, in ten-round groups for more decisive testing.

If comparisons are to be valid, accuracy must be tested from a solid benchrest, over a 100-yard range, with no wind. Sandbags fore and aft eliminate muscle tremors. Fire 5-shot groups, allowing 30 seconds cooling between rounds, with the bolt open. Cooling improves accuracy and reduces bore erosion. To assure fair comparisons of various components, scrub the bore with solvent and wipe dry, between strings.

Metal and powder fouling both seriously affect accuracy. Once I took my 300 Weatherby to the range, preparatory to an Idaho elk hunt. Sighting groups at 100 yards printed 3"-4" patterns. The gun had shot much better the year before but, I reasoned, the stock fore-end might have warped slightly during storage. Then, remembering what a cursory cleaning I had performed after the last hunt, I dipped a brass brush in Hoppes, thoroughly scrubbed out the bore, and dried with a patch. The next three shots went into one hole, 12 o'clock-high, right where I zeroed it the year before!

When accuracy testing, take a notebook to the range and record group size and position for each load. If you get a real flyer, and your hold was good, mark the case head with nail polish. If that case delivers a flyer the next time it's loaded, retire it to a second-string batch, reserved for barrel warmups and plinking. Benchrest shooters use this system to weed out bad brass, often winding up with only

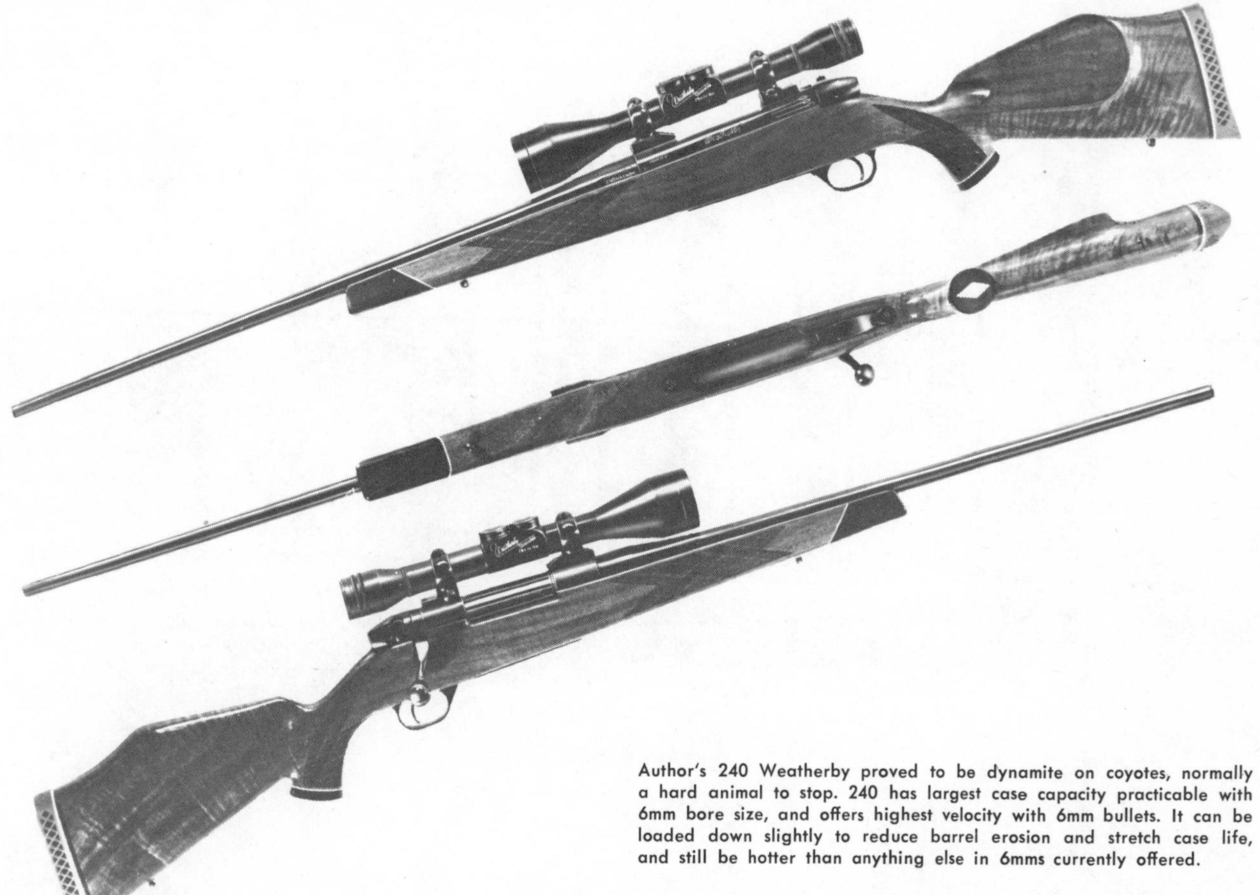

Author's 240 Weatherby proved to be dynamite on coyotes, normally a hard animal to stop. 240 has largest case capacity practicable with 6mm bore size, and offers highest velocity with 6mm bullets. It can be loaded down slightly to reduce barrel erosion and stretch case life, and still be hotter than anything else in 6mms currently offered.

about ⅓rd of their cases eligible for match competition.

Many home experimenters have acquired one of the remarkably accurate, and reasonably priced, Avtron, Herter's B-Square, Oehler, etc., chronographs now available and are blowing primers, separating case heads, and otherwise scaring themselves half to death, vainly trying to match published factory velocity figures. Chances are those numbers were never read off a chronograph! They were interpolated by adding a few fps to convert actual chronograph velocities to "muzzle velocities," plus a little more to equate the elevation to sea level, and an adjustment for temperature, etc. Then, for good measure, the technician subtracts his wife's age and adds his mother-in-law's. Well, it isn't really all that bad, but let's face it, pressure barrels are often 28 to 30 inches long, and usually of tighter bore than production barrels. How can you hope to emulate factory velocities with your super-lightweight 20-incher? (Also remember that two rifles leaving the assembly line the same day, may record velocities as much as 50 fps apart, with the same ammo.) For a candid view of factory velocities, see page 80 of *Speer's Manual For Reloading Ammunition 7*.

Chronograph owners should also buy Homer Powley's P-Max pressure gauge ($49.95), to keep track of pressure as well as velocity in a scientific manner. The 1968 22nd ed. of the GUN DIGEST carried news of a new, easy-to-use pressure measuring system developed by Michael W. York and Don Cantrell. This valuable instrument, which measures absolute pressure—not crusher gauge psi—will be available by the time you read this at less than $300.

A practical way to detect excess pressure is to "mike" the case head just in front of the extractor groove, or on the belt, before and after firing your reloads, to see if expansion has occurred. Some head expansion *may* have taken place on the initial firing, assuming you're getting your brass via factory cartridges. As little as .0005" expansion indicates that your load has exceeded the elastic limits of the brass. This calls for a 5% or more drop in the powder charge. Don't measure the case in front of the solid head portion. Expansion from that point forward is quite normal, even with mild loads. Another excess pressure indicator is expanded primer pockets. Acc-U-Ream provides a set of Go-NoGo gauges for easy detection.

While you can't read primers like tea leaves, they are weather vanes of safety. In his book, *Rifles and Shotguns*, Jack O'Connor offers these guidelines: A primer leak, evidenced as a black smoke ring around the primer, often indicates pressure of some 70,000 psi. Blown primers, that is, primers that *fall out* of the expanded primer pockets when the bolt is opened, warn of about 80,000 psi!

I once had a 243, Savage 110 that handled 41 grains of 4895, behind a 75-gr. Speer bullet, without a whimper. Later, I got a 243 Winchester Model 100, semi-automatic rifle. The identical load displayed severely flattened and cratered primers, most times a red alert for pressure. Examination through a jeweler's loupe disclosed that the case head had pushed back into the hole in the bolt face holding the spring-loaded plunger-type ejector, leaving a round raised spot on the base head. Obviously pressure was far too high. It's not uncommon for one rifle to regurgitate loads that another digests with relish, but I wanted to know why, so I continued firing. On the 6th round, the bolt failed to close fully. With considerable difficulty, I pulled the cartridge, and on the bullet ogive, I saw deep engraving from the rifling lands. Seating the bullets deeper stopped all indications of pressure. However, to be on the safe side, I dropped the charge by one grain, to compensate for the reduced case capacity occasioned by seating the bullets deeper.

Caution and patience should be the handmaidens of handloaders, the patience to start below and work up to maximum loads, and the caution to

High-power 22 centerfire calibers were lacking after WW II. The 220 Swift fell into disfavor, leaving a vacuum that went unfilled for years, until the 224 Weatherby, 225 Winchester and 22-250 Remington appeared. Their only disadvantage is wind-sensitivity that can be improved by using 60-gr. bullets. From left: 222 Rem., 222 Rem. Magnum, 223, 219 Zipper, 22-250, 224 Weatherby, 225 Win., and 220 Swift.

Left—25 caliber is the largest practicable bore size for varmint hunters. Larger bores are troublesome in terms of recoil, noise and possible ricochets. Potent 25s are best with 87/100-gr. bullets. From left: 250-3000 Savage, 257 Roberts, Wildcat 25-06, and 257 Weatherby Magnum. Right—The author considers the 6mm bore size the all-round best compromise for varmint hunting. It combines the low recoil and low noise level of 22 centerfires with potent killing power and boardinghouse reach of quarter-bores. From left: 240 Page Super Pooper, 243 Super Rockchucker, 243 Win., 6mm Rem. and 240 Weatherby Magnum.

drop back again every time a new component is introduced into the formula. Tests by Remington demonstrated that changing the primer mixture alone could vary pressure readings as much as 21,000 psi. How many home loaders reduce charges when they try a new primer?

Reloading errors have a way of compounding themselves. Combine a new, hotter primer with a thick or overlong case neck, plus a bullet seated into the lands, and pressure starts upward. Temperature escalates, causing the powder to burn faster than normal, and pressure leaps, in a vicious cycle that builds on itself, perhaps with disastrous results.

Even simple reloading goofs sometimes have dire consequences. On the range one day, I met a fellow whose face resembled a well-peppered egg, with two white ovals around his eyes. "I was shootin' my '06 Enfield," he said, "when all hell broke loose! If it weren't for my Ray Bans, I'd be in the market for some pencils and a tin cup." (Moral 1: Always wear shooting glasses when testing loads.) His load of 55 grains of 4350 teamed with a 180-gr. bullet, sounded mild enough, but a subsequent lab test revealed, in addition to 4350, generous doses of faster-burning 3031 and 4064. (Moral 2: Dump the powder from your measure back into the correct, *clearly labeled* can as soon as you've finished loading!)

Excess pressure isn't the only rifle wrecker. Normal operating pressures of 50 to 55,000 psi (crusher gauge) can splinter a rifle, if turned loose by a head separation, resulting from excess headspace. If a rimless cartridge is too short for its chamber by as little as .020, the firing pin will drive it forward to solid shoulder contact, then set off the primer. Pressure pushes case walls aganist the chamber where they cling. The case head retreats to the bolt face as pressure mounts, pulling free from the body of the case. 50,000-plus psi will wrench and tear at steel and wood, never intended to withstand such an onslaught.

The author's reloading bench. Convenient layout offers speed and minimum of confusion. Tools, left to right rear: Akro-Mills steel cabinet for holding dies; Fitz cartridge boxes; Lyman Spar-T turret tool; Lyman-Ohaus D-5 scale, with RCBS Powder Dripper. In front, C-H Armory case trimmer; Wilson case gauge; vernier caliper for checking case length; C-H chamfering tool; plastic loading block; RCBS lube and lube pad; Fitz Flipper with primers; Lyman 55 powder measure.

Excess headspace can result from a sizing die screwed down until it sets the case shoulder back too far. Well made dies, mated with same-make shell holders, should not allow this to happen, but some dies are too short for some rifle chambers. Forcing a Mauser-style extractor over a case rim instead of feeding ammo from the magazine can push a cartridge forward hard enough to shorten it and cause headspace. Some bolt actions, especially old military rifles, have considerable end play. Hurriedly slamming a round into the chamber can actually "resize" it, to the extent that the bolt can move forward before encountering the barrel, again setting up dangerous headspace.

The most methodical experimentation is for naught if the data are not dutifully recorded. Even a superior memory is a poor reference for technical detail. In the long run, record keeping saves many hours of aggravation. My own method is a simple card file, broken down by calibers and bullet weight. Each 5"x7" *caliber* card lists case length, maximum cartridge length, and shell holder numbers for my various tools. Following *load* cards, subdivided according to bullet weight, list caliber, case brand, bullet weight, brand, style and lot. Below is listed chronographed velocity, date taken, temperature, benchrest accuracy, rifle used and wind conditions. I label all boxes with the labels included in bullet packages, or the excellent and detailed gummed labels available.

For final advice: Gather a library of reloading manuals. Besides the Speer and Hodgdon books, Lyman, Norma and Pacific all publish clear, informative manuals. The new *Hornady Handbook of Cartridge Reloading* boasts a section, devoted to ballistics tables, that is alone worth the $3.50 price of admission! These comprehensive tables enable direct comparisons of velocity, energy, drop and trajectory for all calibers and bullet weights made by Hornady. Tables for over 7,600 loads are among the most complete and easy to follow that I have seen. •

VARMINT LOAD CHART

Powder/grs.	Bullet/grs.	MV/fps
Caliber 222 Remington		
25/BL-C(2)	50/Speer SP	3309
24/BL-C(2)	55/Speer SP	3187
Caliber 222 Remington Magnum		
26.4/4064	50/Horn. Sp.P.	3400
26.2/4064	55/Horn. Sp.P.	3300
25.5/3031	55/Sierra SP	3350
Caliber 223 Armalite (5.56mm)		
29/H380	50/Speer SP	3113
28/H335	50/Speer SP	3353
27/H335	55/Speer SP	3238
Caliber 225 Winchester		
34/N203	50/Norma SP	3685
33/N203	55/Norma SP	3500
33.5/4895	52/Speer HP	3776
33/4895	60/Horn. Sp.P.	3500
Caliber 22-250 Remington		
35.5/4895	50/Horn. Sp.P.	3800
34.4/4895	55/Horn. Sp.P.	3600
34/4895	60/Horn. Sp.P.	3500
33/3031	63/Sierra	3500
Caliber 224 Weatherby Magnum		
31.5/3031	50/Speer SP	3827
31/3031	52/Speer HP	3679
30.5/3031	55/Speer SP	3650
31.3/4895	60/Horn. Sp. P.	3400
Caliber 220 Swift		
43.5/H380	50/Speer SP	3947
42.5/H380	55/Speer SP	3839
41/H380	63/Sierra SP	3580
Caliber 243 Winchester		
48/4831	80/W-W Power Pt.	3288
45/4831	100/W-W Power Pt.	3104
40.8/4064	75/Horn. HP	3400
36.2/4064	87/Horn. Sp.P.	3100
Caliber 6mm Remington		
49/4831	85/Sierra HPBT	3318
46/4831	100/Sierra SP	3050
44.2/4320	75/Horn. HP	3500
43.7/4320	87/Horn. Sp.P.	3300
50.6/N204	75/Norma HP	3650
47.7/N204	90/Norma SP	3300
41/4895	75/Speer HP	3400
41/4895	80/Speer SP	3368
39/4895	90/Speer SP	3234
Caliber 240 Page Super Pooper		
48/4350	85/Sierra HPBT	3446
45/4350	100/Sierra SP	3191
Caliber 243 Super Rockchucker		
58/4831	85/Sierra SP	3708
55/4831	100/Sierra SP	3353
Caliber 240 Weatherby Magnum		
58.4/N205	70/Horn. Sp.P.	3850
55.2/N205	90/Norma SP	3500
54.2/N205	100/Norma SP	3395
Caliber 250 Savage		
33.7/3031	75/Horn. HP	3200
38/4064	87/Speer SP	3210
Caliber 257 Roberts		
48/H380	75/Sierra HP	3563
47/H380	87/Speer SP	3364
Caliber 25-06		
61/4831	75/Sierra HP	3618
60/4831	87/Speer SP	3576
55.7/4831	100/Horn. Sp.P.	3300
52.4/4831	117/Horn. RN	3000
Caliber 257 Weatherby		
73/N205	87/Sierra SP	3750
71/N205	100/Horn. Sp.P.	3530
69/N205	117/Sierra SP	3350
67/4831	120/Speer SP	3344
Caliber 270 Winchester		
54/4895	90/Sierra HP	3600
Cailber 308 Winchester		
62/4831	100/Speer HP	3370
43/4198	110/Sierra HP	3200
Caliber 30-06		
53/4320	130/Speer HP	3162
57/4064	110/Sierra HP	3400
54/4895	130/Horn. Sp.P.	3200

Custom Guns

Walter Abe
Lightweight (6-6½ lbs.) Mauser, cal. 243, in the classic style, has ebony fore-end tip and grip cap, Dayton-Traister trigger, 23" Apex barrel, fine English walnut stock, Pachmayr de luxe pad with edges rounded.

R. E. Anderson
22-250 on Brno commercial action. Douglas barrel machined to ½-octagon form, top file-cut at 75 l.p.i. Exhibition grade Claro walnut has horn buttplate and grip cap, 22 l.p.i. checkering, classic oil finish. Metal parts matte-satin finished.

Gus Butterowe
25-284 on Sako action, Apex barrel, stock has high rollover cheekpiece, 2-line white spacers, recoil pad. Leupold 3-9x scope in Conetrol Custum 2-piece mounts.

Aaron T. Gates
A 375 H&H, the barrel by Titus on an F.N. Mauser action. All metal work by Tom Burgess. The Claro walnut stock is oil finished, the 3-panel checkering 24 lines per inch. Built for Dr. J. A. Johnson of High Point, N. C.

Russell R. Zeeryp
7x57 on G33-40 Mauser, metal work by A. R. Pryor of B'ham, Ala. Plasti-Kote finished French walnut stock, Redfield 4x scope in Weaver mount.

Jerry A. Fisher
224 Weatherby Magnum rifle, restocked in handsome French walnut, the borderless fleur-de-lis checkering 24 lines per inch. Fisher made new steel guard and floorplate.

Walter Abe

300 Super Apex magnum, made by Gilbert Van Horn for Abe on M1917 Springfield action using Bastogne fiddleback walnut. Hand polished, rust blued, barrel has 3-leaf English express sight, straightened bolt handle.

R. E. Anderson

257 Roberts has ½-octagon, one-third ribbed barrel on Mauser action altered to left-hand. Safety, bolt stop, floorplate release and rib hand checkered, 50 lines per inch. Exhibition grade walnut is fully checkered in multi-point 24-line pattern, has oil finish.

Mike Conner

270 Winchester on Mauser G33-40 action. The classic fancy grade French walnut stock carries extensive multi-point checkering, recoil pad. Scope is a Leupold variable in Redfield mount.

Aaron T. Gates

Left side view of 375 H&H rifle shown opposite. Note forward point of cheekpiece terminating in checkering area and treatment of wood around bolt-release lever. Scope is a Redfield 2¾x in Redfield mounts.

Russell R. Zeeryp

30-06 on an F.N. Mauser, 18¼" light barrel. Stock is curly maple, fancy checkered at grip and fore-end. Rifle with K2.5 Weaver and Weaver mount weighs 7½ lbs.

Jerry A. Fisher

Left side view of the restocked and altered 224 Weatherby Magnum pictured across the way. Note graceful schnabel treatment of fore-end. Scope is a Redfield variable in 2-piece Buehler mount.

Roberts Wood Products
Weatherby Mark V action, supreme grade myrtle stock with ebony fore-end and grip cap, rosewood and ebony inlays.

Clayton N. Nelson
7mm Remington Magnum, made on the new Champlin action for Warren Page. 22" barrel is octagon, French walnut stock carries 24-line hand checkering.

Jon R. Sundra
BSA-actioned sporter using a Douglas barrel, the stock a Fajen Regent grade of fancy American walnut.

Smitty's Gun Shop
277 Smith Magnum, F.N. action, Canjar trigger. Walnut laminated stock and stainless barrel for use in arctic conditions.

Paul Jaeger
270 Winchester on F.N. Mauser; receiver, grip cap, guard, scope rings, etc., engraved and gold inlaid, with Bighorn sheep in raised gold on floorplate. Bolt knob is fully checkered.

Wells Sport Shop
Unusual vent rib barrel, cal. 460/510, milled from the solid blank on a magnum Mauser action. Checkering combined with excellent carving at grip and fore-end.

Hal Hartley
30-06 Springfield on a Winchester Model 70, stocked in hard curly maple, the checkering at the fore-end running full around the bottom. (Vertical rifle above)

Paul Jaeger

7mm Remington Magnum on F.N. Mauser action, the metal of receiver, guard, floorplate, grip cap and buttplate engraved and gold inlaid. Leupold scope is held in Jaeger quick detachable side mount.

Clayton N. Nelson

Left-side view of Nelson-made Warren Page rifle seen across the page shows graceful cheekpiece. With 4x Leupold scope in Redfield mount, weight is just over 7¾ lbs.

Frontier Gun Shop

7x57mm on a Mauser action by Duane Wiebe, the stock of fancy Claro walnut. A lever-released floorplate and engraving were done by Wiebe also.

Talmage Enterprises

A Texas Magnum action with Douglas barrel, the all handmade stock carrying a high roll-over cheekpiece. Redfield scope in Buehler mount.

Edw. O. Hefti

358 Norma Magnum on a Texas Ranger action and barrel has French or skip-line checkering, angled fore-end tip, with white spacers at tip, grip cap and buttplate.

Keith Stegall

6mm Remington on a Peruvian Mauser, Shilen stainless steel match barrel. Finest French walnut stock, Biesen steel buttplate, engraved grip cap. Leupold scope in Redfield mounts.

Hal Hartley

Left-side view of the Model 70 in 30-06 caliber pictured across the page. Cheekpiece flows into pistol grip nicely, and no Monte Carlo comb is needed on this high-heel design. (Vertical rifle above)

Hal Hartley

Full stock 40-cal. percussion Kentucky-Pennsylvania rifle, stocked in fiddleback maple, the barrel a 1-inch Douglas. Hartley, who also made the locks and triggers, will furnish such rifles in flintlock and Hawken plains type.

Pachmayr Gun Works

Model 70 Winchester, pre-1964 type, stocked in superb Circassian walnut in the classic fashion. All metal parts, including barrel, are fully engraved and gold inlaid in relief.

Carl E. Swanson

Sako L61 actioned sporter, Douglas Premium barrel. Presentation quality Claro walnut, skipline checkered. Redfield 3-9x in Redfield mounts.

R. J. Maberry

270 Winchester on an F.N. Mauser, the barrel by Douglas, the stock with skipline checkering. Receiver, floorplate, bolt and rear of barrel engraved and gold inlaid. Leupold scope in Leupold mounts.

Wilson "Bill" Crook, Jr. of Dallas, Texas, used a 300 Winchester magnum to take a bull which scored 114 Boone and Crockett points.

BUFFALO HUNTING TODAY

The long-ago mainstay of the plains Indian's economy, these great shaggy beasts still offer a degree of sport for the astute—and affluent—hunter.

by BERT POPOWSKI

Time was when a huge hunk of the United States and Canada wore a living buffalo robe. The great shaggy beasts ranged from the Appalachians to beyond the Rockies, and from Texas up to Canada's huge granite shield exposed by the retreat of the last Ice Age.

When white settlers started stalking the retreating frontier they first encountered the woods bison, remnants of which are still living in the world's largest herd on a preserve straddling the Alberta-Northwest Territories boundary. This largest branch of our North American wild cattle always liked forests adjacent to grazing meadows which furnished shelter, food and water. The smaller plains bison were most numerous on the enormous grass seas of the Great Plains to the west of the Mississippi river. But, whether woods or plains bison, these huge bovines were the mainstay of many Indian tribes before the first firearms reached North America.

White men got along pretty well with their round-ball muskets and Pennsylvania-made Kentucky rifles for squirrels, turkeys and deer. But when they broke out into the spacious prairies they needed rifles of longer range, shooting cylindrical bullets enormously greater in weight and killing power. Muzzle loading was fine for harmless Eastern game, but a man often didn't have time to load, prime and cap his rifle for a second shot when he was dealing with a ton of bison, or the far more fearsome plains grizzly bears. Also, on the Great Plains, there were far too few trees to climb in such a tight.

Thus were born the Spencers, the Henrys, the Remingtons and the Winchesters, all breechloaders with their own partisans. Bill Cody, who shot enough buffalo to qualify as an expert in rifle choice, preferred the 50-caliber, single-shot Springfield, the one he called Lucretia Borgia. Then, when buffalo hunting reached the hide- and meat-hunting era the preferred rifles were the Sharps big 40s, 45s and 50s, the Remington rolling blocks and others. Their long range accuracy made them especially effective for killing buffalo from stands and their strong actions allowed them to be loaded with from 120 grains and more of black powder, in cases originally intended for 90-grain loads. Bullets, paper patched, ranged from 370 to 550 grains, generally of pure lead so they would upset to fill the rifling and mushroom rapidly to produce quick kills. Sharps of from 14 to 18 pounds in weight also helped to damp the recoil of such massive loads.

Most of the meat and hide hunters shot from stands, ranging from 100 to 200 yards from the herds. If they got too close the buffalo might be stampeded by gunfire and hugely increase the butchering and skinning chores. When the herd leaders were downed the others, often smelling the blood welling from lungs and nostrils, would paw, circle and bellow to drown out the sound of subsequent shooting.

Historic Hunters

The daily kills often depended chiefly on how many animals the skinners and butchers could process, or how much meat and how many hides the wagons could haul. Kirk Jordan, with three 4-horse teams and 20 men in his outfit, shot 100 buffalo at his best stand along the Santa Fe railroad. Even this figure was occasionally bested by such killers as Frank Collinson, who downed 121 with a Sharps .45 weighing 15 pounds; and Tom Nixon, who dropped 204 head with a single stand.

Nixon once used two rifles in killing 120 head in 40 minutes. When one got too hot to handle he'd open the breech, run a wet cloth through it and let it cool while he used his other Sharps. During one 45-day stretch of shooting strictly for hides he totaled 2,173 buffalo. Orlando "Brick" Bond killed 200 in a single day and 5,855 from mid-October to mid-December of 1876. Wright Mooar estimated he shot 20,500 during his nine years of hunting. Bill F. "Doc" Carver once claimed he dropped 10 buffalo from horseback one winter day in Nebraska in 1875. He estimated he shot at least 30,000 during his hunting career before turning to Wild West show business.

Wright Mooar probably left more written records of his buffalo hunting than any other man. He never used a shooting stick on which to rest his rifles. He would tie his horse out of sight and crawl up on a herd, wearing pads and gloves to protect his knees and hands from cactus. Once in good range he'd pick the herd leader and shoot it through the lungs, his favorite shot. It would back up a few steps, fall over and die. A heart-shot buffalo would often run 300 to 400 yards, taking the herd with him, and require a second approach.

All meat- and hide-hunters were careful to avoid startling the animals. Mooar wore a hat as near the color of grass as he could find and other clothing to match. Whenever possible he used rocks or sagebrush to help in concealment. He generally shot off his knee but occasionally sat and rested both elbows on his knees. Where cover was light on a ridge overlooking a herd he would flatten out on his stomach and shoot from the prone. The only thing buffalo would see were occasional puffs of gun smoke, the only sound the heavy boom of the Sharps.

There were two Mooar brothers: J. Wright, the experienced rifleman, hide-and-meat salesman and, much later, recording historian; and John Wesley, who commenced his career as a camp tender at $50 per month. But it must be noted that camp tending — cooking, reloading, staking out hides and defending the premises against marauders, with hunters and skinners many miles away — was a very responsible job. The Mooar camps, like many others, frequently had thousands of dollars worth of gear, curing meat and drying hides on hand between selling trips. Indians, furious at the whites' wasteful butchery of their wild cattle, were a recurring and deadly hazard. Camp tending wasn't Sunday school.

Once the great herds reached a certain point of decline their populations dwindled rapidly. Railroads poked their way into areas previously difficult of access and furnished rapid means of replenishing supplies and funneling meat and hides to hungry Eastern markets. There were still lots of buffalo at the mid-1870s. But a decade later, when the National Museum at Washington wanted a typical habitat group for mounting, it had difficulty in acquiring satisfactory specimens. Fewer than 1,000 head of buffalo were believed left surviving by 1886.

From this fragmentary stock, now fiercely protected by conservationists in both the United States and Canada, the species recovered to safe numbers. By 1926 there were 4,376 buffalo in the United States and 11,957 in Canada, all of them on protected preserves. By the early 1960s they had increased so satisfactorily that surplus animals were being annually harvested to save the ranges on which they were confined. When taken on national lands the meat was usually distributed to reservation Indians for their traditional ceremonies. But when on state lands or in private herds they were available for hunting. Buffalo are now found in some 15 states, from Alaska to Texas, and about 300 head are annually taken by sporting hunting.

Buffalo Hunting Today

During 1968 South Dakota offered $500 permits for taking ten mature surplus bulls from its Custer State Park herd of 1,500 head. These were promptly snapped up by hunters from Texas, Ohio, South Dakota and Nebraska. All participating hunters were so pleased with the hunt that it's possible, even probable, that the hunt will become an annual affair for the harvesting of surplus mature bulls of trophy potential. It was especially gratifying to this writer, who had pressed for sporting elk hunting in this Park nearly 20 years ago. In reporting on the first elk hunt within Custer State Park, held in 1926, I hinted that a few buffalo offered to sportsmen wouldn't be amiss. Now that a pilot hunt has been held I hope it will become an annual affair.

If the South Dakota Game Commission authorizes another such hunt the permit applicants should wire, phone (605-255-4515) or write to Custer State Park Superintendent Virgil Johnson, Hermosa, South Dakota 57744. During the past season the permits were offered on a first-come first-served basis. But, in future years, if there are more applicants than available permits, a drawing will have to be held to determine the winners. Pre-payments for permits should be made by bank draft, money order or cashier's check. The fee is refundable if the applicant's name isn't drawn.

Custer State Park also offers 192 $100 licenses for elk (residents only), and 120 $20 antelope licenses to both

Tourists in South Dakota's Custer State Park often see herds of American bison.

residents and visitors. Additional charges are $5 daily for four-wheel transportation by guide-drivers and cooling the meat carcasses at the Park cooling locker plant.

The $500 permit fee is actually quite reasonable since the hunters get the whole animal, gutted in the field and skinned, quartered and cooled out in the Park locker plant. The price was set on the basis of how much live animals had brought at previous auctions to buyers who were starting their own private herds. Another consideration was the income derived from buffalo which are butchered and sold as meat carcasses, usually in quarters or multiples thereof.

Park personnel provides guiding, transportation in four-wheel-drive vehicles and all of the work involved in retrieving kills. Hunters thus have a chance to choose from among several trophy bulls. All ten participating hunters professed themselves well satisfied with the handling of all hunt details and the subsequent condition of their kills. Those who do not want all the meat may either sell it or contribute it to friends or charity. Since South Dakota's Legislatures have never declared buffalo a game species the sale of such meat, if taken under permit, is both ethical and legal. But its disposal is entirely up to participating hunters. The Park will not act as middleman after its locker plant has skinned, quartered and cooled the carcasses.

Sending experienced guides with the hunters was simple insurance against mishap to either hunters or game. Between them these guides — Wes Broer, Fred Mathews, Harry De Vries and Harvey Lancaster — have shot thousands of buffalo over many years of annual herd reduction. They can provide expert advice on where bulls should be hit for quick kills. Their favorite meat-saving kills are two: at the butt of the ear, where the skull joins the neck vertebrae; and at the center of the forehead, where diagonal lines from eyes to the horns on the opposite sides intersect. For the latter shot there's a whorl of hair, somewhat smaller than a baseball, which must be hit for an instant kill. Oldtime meat- and hide-hunters didn't like this shot. Their soft lead bullets often flattened out on mud imbedded in the forehead hair and failed to penetrate the two skull plates which protect the brain. But modern soft-point jacketed ammunition drills right on through even on tough bulls.

Buffalo bulls are notoriously short-tempered. If carelessly shot they may blame nearby herd members for their sudden pain and gore them in retaliation. Only when a bull is off by himself is a hunter privileged to shoot his game wherever he wishes. But foot-stalking to extremely close range is discouraged since a lone bull, whether shot or not, may be aggravated to the point where he may choose the hunter. The more elderly and solitary the bull the more crochety he may be. That's why all guides carried back-up 30-06 rifles, loaded with 150-grain Silvertip ammunition, the same combination they use in their herd-reducing chores, to deal with any unforeseen emergencies.

Guide Wes Broer, who is in charge of the buffalo herd and doubles as assistant superintendent of Custer State Park, and Louis Meyer, who has processed thousands of carcasses through the locker plant, told me that buffalo lose about 55 per cent of their live weight in being reduced to meat carcasses. Thus a 1600-pound bull produces a meat carcass of about 725 pounds. All bulls taken during the hunt were in the seven-to-nine-year or older class, probably averaging out around 1700 pounds. Bulls mature at five and do grow bigger with age. But, even if pen fed, the occasionally advertised weight of 3000 pounds in live weight is a bit doubtful. The largest bull ever handled in Custer State Park went just a bit over 2100 pounds, which is very close to maximum for strictly grass-fed animals.

Buffalo taken strictly for meat are generally younger and thus lighter than those cited above. These animals reduce down to hind quarters averaging at 100 pounds apiece and front quarters of 150 each. When these quarters are sold, at 70 cents per pound for hinds and 60 cents for fronts, they bring somewhat under $300 per animal. Green hides, suitable for tanning for rugs are also occasionally available at $10 each; if skinned to include the cape for full-body rugs they cost $35. Naked weathered skulls, sometimes used for display purposes, sell for $12.50 but if they still wear the horn shells they come to $16.50. Buyers of all such items must also pay for transportation.

One of the 1968 hunters belatedly wished he'd had his bull skinned out by splitting the hide along the back. He intended to turn his trophy into a full-body mount and such skinning would have helped hide the taxidermy seams. Oddly enough, when Indians and whites were hunting strictly for meat during primitive and pioneer times, that's the way they exposed the choice cuts of hump, tenderloin

Such signs do not always keep visitors from approaching short-tempered bison for picture purposes. The breeding and calving seasons are especially dangerous.

and hams. When these slabs of solid meat were cut out, without the need of gutting the animals, the rest of the carcasses were abandoned to the wolves. Of course, when hides were to be salvaged the skinning procedure was to cut along the belly as is done nowadays, but without gutting the animals in the process. This made for easier, neater and much faster handling.

Buffalo Cuisine

Buffalo meat is superb table fare; darker and coarser than grass-fed domestic beef but owning a flavor all its own. The elderly bulls taken by hunting were undoubtedly tougher than the meat of animals in the two-to-five-year-old class taken strictly for eating meat. But their game flavor—as is the case with all males of big game species — is more robust than that of young stuff of either sex or of mature females. And when ground up into buffaloburger it produces some very flavorful food, identifiable at a bite from common hamburger.

Indians and pioneer whites esteemed it so highly that, even when other game was available, they preferred buffalo. Of course during those days a lot of western big game was handled quite wastefully. Due to unwieldy size buffalo were often stripped only of the choice tenderloin and hump. This produced about 60 to 80 pounds of superb meat. If weight, space and storage presented problems this was cut into slender strips and hung on trees, bushes, ropes and crude drying racks exposed to the hot sun and wind. After a day of such dehydration each strip was covered with a natural glue-like glaze, both insect and dust proof.

This was the famous cured jerky. It could be safely transported and stored for use some months later. During cloudy or damp weather such meat was sheltered under buffalo hides or canvas and smoked over green-wood fires. If wood wasn't readily available buffalo chips would do nicely for drying the meat. They do not smoke and produce very little flame. They burn with an ember-like quality that is ideal for small compact cooking or heating fires in sheltered camps. Indians didn't go for the huge roaring camp fires which white camps favored and often used buffalo chips in their tepees for both cooking and comfort.

For immediate eating fat ribs were broken or chopped out in sections and broiled over campfires. Slabs of juicy hump were similarly cooked. Tongues were a delicacy but took more cooking time. They were usually parboiled, then peeled, sliced and fried in "buffalo butter" — the marrow pushed, cleaning-rod fashion, out of the large leg bones. The whole tongues were also dried for later use. During the hide-hunting era hundreds of thousands of buffalo were completely wasted except for their pelts and tongues. When there was later need for meat in considerable quantities, especially in Indian camps, the muscular hams and shoulders, so prized by today's steak eaters, were cut across the grain into long ribbons and dried into jerky. Some Indian women were so skilled with their knives they could turn a ham into one continuous red ribbon of meat. When dry, this was wrapped into roughly spherical balls and lashed so for convenience in handling.

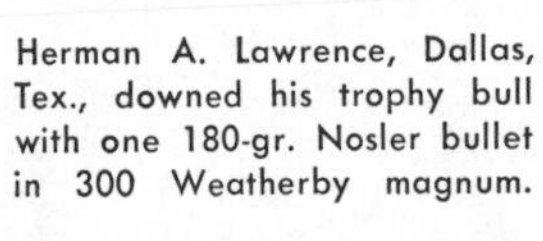
Herman A. Lawrence, Dallas, Tex., downed his trophy bull with one 180-gr. Nosler bullet in 300 Weatherby magnum.

Space forbids further exploration of how completely Indians utilized whole buffalo carcasses for food, robes, hides for cordage, ropes, tepees and luggage bags, paunches for kettles, intestines for pemmican sacks, bones for marrow and tools, hoofs for glue and scrapers, even the gall and bile for condiments.

The buffalo was the complete Indian commissary, from birth to the robes in which they were wrapped at death. They lived on other game during the easy months of the year. But when buffalo grew fat during the late summer and early autumn months whole tribes went out to "make meat" on which to subsist during the rough half of the year. It was a time of feasting and dancing combined with stern and often dangerous harvesting of the literal wherewithal of existence. It's no wonder that when the buffalo were gone many Indian tribes felt as if life itself had been torn from them.

270 Rifles Minimum

In combination the first ten licensed South Dakota buffalo hunters in the state's history had quite a composite story to tell. All of them had plenty of rifle for the job. In fact they had been advised that nothing lighter than the 270 would be permitted. They were also told that Custer State Park butchers usually shot buffalo behind the ear or directly into the brain. Exactly half of them put down their bulls with single shots; the rest needed from three to seven shots to collect their game. Since this was the first buffalo hunt for all of them that's about par for such tough and burly game. Hunters' ages ranged from 15 to 58 and their previous big game experience from deer and antelope up to a score of North American big game species, from Alaska to Mexico.

Rifle calibers ranged from single copies of the Winchester 7-mm magnum, custom 308 Norma and Winchester 375 H&H; two 300 Winchester magnums, though one was a Remington-made rifle; two 30-06s — a Remington pump and a Savage bolt lefty; and three Weatherby 300 magnums. Only two hunters used handloads: 63 grains of 4350 behind 150-grain Hornady bullets in the 7-mm, and 80 grains of 205 pushing 180-grain Hornady bullets in one Weatherby 300 magnum.

Weaver scopes led all other brand names, three of them in four-power and one of 2¾-power magnification. There were also three Redfields in use, one each in 4x, 2-7x and 3-9x. Weatherby 3-10x, Bausch & Lomb 2½-8x and Leupold 2-7x were represented by one each.

Most of the bulls were killed at from 35 to 85 yards, only three being taken at ranges from 125 to 175 yards. Those hunters who used multiple shots on their game were simply in too much of a hurry to precisely place their first shots, or expected to see their bulls fall instantly upon being hit. When they didn't they just kept right on shooting, whether the chosen bulls were standing or moving off. Four of the five one-shot kills were spotted at the butt of the ear on in the brain. The lone exception was a severed spine in the hump area at a shooting range of 150 yards with the 308 Norma using 220-grain Norma bullets. That was a tricky shot since the backbone is located well below the top of the hump and must be hit precisely to avoid crippling.

The best time of year to take bulls with prime pelts for mounting the heads and tanning the hides for hair-on rugs is in December and January. The winter coat of hair is luxuriant and fully grown then and firmly seated in the hide. Buffalo, both bulls and cows, then also wear a much heavier mantle of heavier hair over the front halves of their bodies and are much more impressive in appearance. The hair starts to slip in April and, during the next few months, sheds off in big ragged patches into the short summer coat. During this procedure the animals acquire a moth-eaten appearance. If rugs or mounts are made then all such loosened hair must be combed out during taxidermy.

300 Head Annually

In addition to South Dakota's Custer State Park, buffalo may be hunted from many other state herds, in state and national parks and from private herds requiring annual reduction. About 300 head are annually taken by sporting hunting and a good many more for meat use. Many of those taken from private herds are primarily taken for meat on a continuing cycle much like raising domestic beef. However, such meat is chiefly sold through specialty shops at substantially higher prices than those charged for comparable beef cuts. This merely reflects the more costly operation of fencing in and raising wild game than it does to produce domestic cattle. They are both susceptible to the same bovine diseases and the inoculation and vaccination problems and costs are substantially higher on nimble wild buffalo.

Where buffalo meat is offered for home consumption it usually runs from 40 to 50 per cent over comparable cuts of domestic beef. One Denver market offers T-bones at $1.98 per pound, rib steaks at $1.59, round steaks at $1.48 and ground buffaloburger at 79 cents. Since the meat is usually bought in carcass quantities and then processed into serving portions, this higher price reflects the considerable waste of the large and heavy buffalo bones.

Restaurants which offer meals of buffalo often vary considerably in their prices. Some of them use it for its novelty value, just so their customers can say they've eaten buffalo. The T-bones run from 10-ounce to half-pound portions and are served at from $3.95 to $4.50, as compared to $3.50 for beef T-bones. Buffaloburgers are dressed up with olives, pickles and potato chips to sell for 75 cents while plain beef hamburgers go for 45 cents. Of course these prices vary, mostly up, depending on the class of clientele served and their distance from areas where eating buffalo meat is no special novelty.

The South Dakota Custer State Park office is served by phone and postal facilities via Hermosa, S. D.

Special Gear Needed

The sheer size of buffalo requires special gear for handling the massive carcasses. Animals taken strictly for meat are drained of gallons of blood by severing the main veins and arteries of the neck. Custer State Park has a homemade winch to gradually lift each animal by the hocks for ease in gutting. The field-dressed carcass is then lowered onto a truck bed and hauled to the locker plant. There it is hung on an overhead trolley so it can be hosed out with cold water and all free blood washed off meat and hide. It is then skinned, quartered and hung in a cooling room to rid it of all animal heat as rapidly as possible. However this must be done gradually, at a temperature of slightly above freezing, which requires about 24 hours.

Hunting buffalo by the most sporting means available can't be classed as a thrill-packed sport. Although the animals are on large and spacious range they are not free to stampede off to dim horizons. They're also comparatively stolid critters, only faintly secretive by nature and are readily located for observation, examination and harvesting. Abundant pasturage has made it needless for them to migrate from grazed-out areas as sheer numbers forced them to do in the past.

Some of today's buffalo hunters add a novel and nostalgic touch to the sport by using the historic rifles which felled so many buffs during the hide-hunting era. Bob Benton, a collector of Sharps rifles of historic significance in and around the Black Hills area of South Dakota, used one of the Big 50s, shooting 550-grain lead round-nosed bullets. Shot behind the ear the bull dropped in its tracks on a 50-yard standing shot in Custer State Park.

Editor Bob Elman of *Guns and Hunting* magazine borrowed a Winchester 45-90 falling-block wearing a 30-inch octagonal barrel. Handloads of 405-grain lead bullets ahead of 48 grains of RelodeR 7 produced a velocity of 1850 fps. Bob shot off a forked shooting stick at around 80 yards for a clean behind-the-ear one-shot kill. He was hunting on the Marquiss Little Buffalo ranch southwest of Gillette, Wyoming. Starting with only one bull and two heifer calves, two generations of the family have been raising buffalo there since the 1920s. Not far away is the Durham Meat Company spread which also annually harvests the animals to supply restaurants and West Coast novelty meat outlets.

Today's hunters who want to add bison heads to their trophy rooms can do so at nearly two-score locations along the western length of the United States. Since the harvestible trophy surplus varies from year to year it's wise to nail down preliminary arrangements well in advance of any prospective hunts. But anyone who has the equivalent of a 270 or 30-06 —or access to an oldtime buffalo rifle, a steady hand and a spare $500 can bag the makings of a historic trophy species.

Thereafter he will have to ante up another $150 to $250, or more, depending on how extensive a mount he wants from his taxidermist. Even a mount that takes in only the head and the pendulous dewlap takes up considerable space, both in width and projection into the trophy room. The mounted head off a 1500-pound buffalo bull is sure to crowd things in the average city apartment. But it will furnish a novel conversation piece of a long-gone time when some 75,000,000 of these great shaggy bovines roamed our western plains. ●

SHOOTING A BUFFALO

They're big and heavy, but killing one is an easy matter with the right shot—it can't really be called hunting.

by JOHN T. AMBER

I've moved to about 125 yards (lower left), from the small herd—something I probably couldn't have done in the 1870s with really wild buffalo. Now (center), using a set of modern cross-sticks, I'm about to shoot—and miss! The great shaggy animal (top) went down to the second shot, sans cross-sticks, from my old Winchester 70 in 30-06 caliber.

George Nonte and I went deer hunting in South Dakota in the fall of 1968 (which is another story) and because we were going to hunt on one of the largest cattle and buffalo ranches in the state—if not in the U.S.—I asked Keith Wilcox to see if he could arrange for me to shoot a buffalo while we'd be there.

Keith Wilcox—who is executive director of the Great Lakes of South Dakota Association—wrote back that he'd fixed it, and that I'd be able to shoot a buffalo before the deer hunting began.

George and I reached Pierre, S.D., on a clear and brilliant day, parked the Chevy 4-wheel-drive Carryall and our Franklin Trailer, and drove out to the Triple U Ranch with Keith Wilcox.

Some 40 miles from Pierre, the Triple U spread stretches as far as the eye can see over those rolling prairies. Roy Houck, the genial and dry-humored man who operates the big sprawling place was waiting for us and ready to go buffalo "hunting."

With about 1500 buffalo on his acres, and scores of them visible soon after we'd left the ranch building, taking one of these mighty animals can hardly be called hunting!

I'd thought—or at least hoped—that some real hunting and stalking might be possible, but Roy explained that it just wasn't practicable. In the first place, there was virtually no cover, and because Roy wanted only certain "meat" animals shot, he'd have to point one out. That meant getting pretty close, say a maximum of 150-

200 yards, and preferably less. Roy also said that the shot could be made only when the selected bull was far enough away from the herd to insure a well-placed shot, one that would put the buffalo down now! If merely wounded, a troublesome melee could well develop, the bulls fighting and injuring themselves, With a bull in the herd worth $400-500, that's a no-no!

In a short time we came up on a small herd, some 25 animals, and Roy indicated 3 or 4 bulls that could be shot.

I jumped out, carrying my old Winchester 70, a 30-06 plain-grade sporter I'd bought in 1937, but now fitted with a truly handsome stock of fiddle-back maple that Hal Hartley had whittled out. Attached to the barrel was a modern version of the old buff runner's crossed sticks — a spring-loaded bipod that was almost my undoing.

Moving away from the small cluster of men and pickups, I got into a prone position at about 125 yards, the wooden legs of my bipod supporting the rifle barrel.

Waiting for what seemed like 15 minutes—but which was probably not over 5—until one of the bulls had moved a few feet from the herd, I fired at the butt of the ear. I saw a little dust fly, but that was all—the bull I'd shot at stood there, staring in my direction. I suddenly realized that I'd forgotten entirely about the raised point of impact the bipod—attached to the barrel—would cause. Roy Houck, though, concerned that maybe I had hit the buffalo, slowly circled the herd, looking for signs of blood. There were none, however, and I again steadied down in the grass, having yanked the bipod off. At this shot the bull collapsed, dead instantly or in seconds from the impact of the 165-gr. Speer bullet through his ear. 47.1 grains of 4064 did the work.

In a few minutes a heavy farm tractor, fitted with a special welded box-frame, rolled out to hoist the heavy bull—some 1500 pounds—into the pickup, and it was all over.

Roy Houck had permitted a few hunters on his place in the past, his charge for shooting a buffalo $300. However, as of this year, Roy has set up a membership plan for hunting, fishing, camping and recreation in general. Charter members will pay a $500 fee that includes their families and guests, good for ten years and virtually unlimited use of the vast Triple U Ranch and its planned facilities. There's to be a 100-room motor lodge, an 18-hole golf course, a great swimming pool, and other aspects too numerous to recite here. Roy Houck will gladly send you a fully descriptive folder on this attractive operation—write to L. R. Houck, P.O. Box 1076, Pierre, S.D. 57501. ●

That's about 1500 pounds of buffalo being hoisted into Roy Houcks' pickup.

The latest Chevy carryall wagon, a sturdy 4-wheel drive job, carried Nonte and I out to South Dakota and back without a speck of trouble. We slept and ate in the Franklin trailer we toted behind.

Time out for a smoke and a look around on the rolling grasslands of north-central South Dakota.

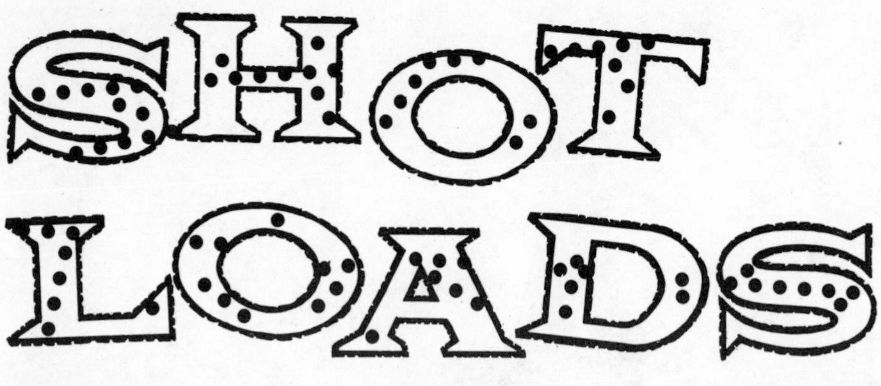

SHOT LOADS For Revolvers

Handloaded shotshells are easier to prepare than many suppose—here's how to make 'em for 45 Colt, 44 and 357 Magnum, 38 Special.

by EDWARD DAMS

IN A PINCH, a shotshell cartridge in your revolver is a very handy item to have. Hearing the rattle of a snake, if your side arm is loaded with shotshells, you can feel confident of knocking it off with the utmost dispatch. Because of its wide and successful use against snakes, the handgun shotshell cartridge is usually called a "snake load."

There are other useful applications, however. They may be used for shooting pests or very small birds and game for the pot. In aerial target practice, where a bullet's range might be dangerous, shot loads may be used to build the shooter's skill and confidence.

The idea is not new. Flintlock pistols are said to have been loaded with shot, scrap metal, small gravel or rock salt. At one time Peters Cartridge Co. manufactured 45 ACP shot cartridges for use in the Thompson submachine gun. Such cartridges were to be fired over the heads of rioters or a mob—the noise and small shot falling would encourage the crowd to disperse in haste. These rounds could be used in the 1917 Colt or S&W Army revolvers if half-moon clips were provided. They could also be fired from the 1911 Colt automatic, but had to be singly loaded as their over-all length was too great to permit their use in the magazine.

Until some years ago, too, shot loads were factory made in 44-40, 44 Russian, 45 Colt and other calibers. The 44 Marble Game-Getter shot load, made for Marble's over-under pistol-carbine, was a highly popular shell for years.

Before they became unlawful, smoothbore revolvers were made by a few gunsmiths. Some of the barrels had chokes machined into them and good patterns—a 20″ circle at 20 yards—were not unusual. These smoothbore revolvers could, of course, also fire bulleted rounds safely and fairly accurately, but beyond 40 yards or so the bullets would keyhole.

Today, according to law, we must have a rifled barrel on the revolver. This complicates the efficient loading of shotshells, but we can produce acceptable loads which will more than discourage a snake at reasonably short range.

Let us consider what we have to work with—shot, powder and wads. Powder and lead don't pose any problem, but those wads take up a lot of space. Then, too, the lead being loose shot, the charge will have to be contained within the cartridge. Solid bullets will often project 50% or more from the case mouth.

The problem is logically resolved if we use the longer cartridge cases. 45 Long Colt, 44 and 357 Magnum cases were chosen for this reason. We'll also cover the popular 38 Special in connection with a new device that makes it as efficient for our purpose as the 357 Magnum.

Wad Specifications

A good wad must possess a number of desirable qualities. Most importantly, it must form a good gas seal between powder and shot, not only while it is in the case, but as it pushes the shot out the cylinder and down the bore. The wad should be able to hold the powder under pressure so that good and consistent ignition results. At the same time, it should lubricate the bore to reduce the possibility of leading—a big job for a thin wad less than one-half inch in diameter.

Most of these problems have been solved by shotgunners, and we'd be foolish if we didn't avail ourselves of what they have learned. The best thing, then, is to use the same wads.

The Alcan Co., probably the best-known manufacturer of conventional wads, graciously contributed a quantity of wads in their "Special Sizes" (see catalog section) for use in our tests. Before the advent of these products it was necessary to use a Lyman Kake Kutter of appropriate caliber, using it to punch wads from old felt hats and chip board. The special Alcan wads are a great convenience and time saver.

Anyone who has ever loaded a shotshell knows the procedure: powder, nitro card, felt wad, shot and over/shot card. That's exactly how I began, using 357 Magnum brass. First, I made up a dummy round with one .070″ nitro card, ¼″ felt wad and shot, but less primer and powder. There was room for only 71 grains of shot, so that idea was scrapped. My next move was to try the same thing using a .135″ nitro card only—ah, much better—now the case held 123 grains of shot with room for an over/shot card.

Shotshells generally produce less pressure than a bulleted round, so since 3 grains of Bullseye is a suggested starting load for the 357 Magnum with lead bullets, that charge was assumed safe with less weight in front of it. Six cases were sized, primed and their mouths belled, just as you would prepare any handgun cases, using the usual metallic cartridge dies. The cases were charged with powder, the .135″ nitro card seated with a new pencil and 123 grains of shot poured in, then topped off by an over/shot card. All went wonderfully well.

Retracting the seating stem from

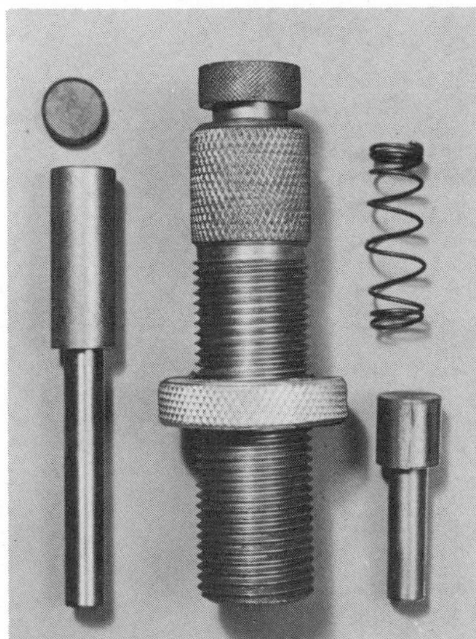

Component parts of the SAS die. At left are the parts needed to seat wads; right, those used to hold wad and shot in place while cartridge is being crimped; both sets fit die body in the center.

the crimp die, I attempted to crimp the newly-made shot cartridge. What a mess! The crimp could not be made heavy enough to hold the card without multiple manipulations of die and press handle—even then it wasn't really strong enough to hold the shot against the heavy recoil of a magnum bulleted load fired from the same cylinder. This problem was easily solved by using water glass (sodium silicate, obtainable from your drug store). The top wad was "glued" in place with this stuff, and allowed to dry overnight.

Firing these first loads was a disappointment. The water glass wasn't hard enough and, even though the crimp held on a few cartridges, the 30″ wide roll of wrapping paper used as a target showed the pattern to be inconsistent. Back to the drawing board!

Two dozen rounds were made and allowed to dry thoroughly. Meanwhile, I wrote to Ted Smith of SAS for one of his shotshell pistol dies I'd seen advertised. The die arrived just about the time that an opportunity arose to do some shooting. In haste, two dozen more rounds were assembled using Ted's die and what a charmed day that was. Components just about flew together.

Some people have a knack for solving others' problems, and Ted Smith is one of those people. The die he sent convinced me that I'd want others in 44 Magnum and 45 Long Colt for the work that lay ahead. Ted's die comprises one die body, two punches, a spring, a rubber pad and a screw top for each caliber. The long punch is used to seat the wads with the rubber pad between it and the screw cap. When wads have all been seated firmly upon the powder the long punch and pad are exchanged for the short punch and spring. The die is turned down until it touches the case, then given an extra ¾-turn to form a crimp that rivals the factory product, while the short punch and spring hold the wad and shot in place. Fast and simple, if only the cartridges work—they looked highly professional.

357 Magnum Loads

Back at the range, I was surprised to find that both groups of cartridges performed about the same. The ones made with the SAS die were just a bit more consistent, if a bit spread out. At 20 feet, the shot charge covered the 30″ paper. The question now was how to tighten up the pattern and close up the holes. There were 5 or 6 places where a snake could slip by unscathed.

Since patterns were just about the same, and the SAS die made loading so easy, I took the path of least resistance and made up a couple dozen more rounds. These were in groups of 6 with the powder charge changed by increments of 2/10-gr. each. When these were fired the result was unusual. The best load in the 6″ barreled Python test gun was 3.4 grains of Bullseye. The load either side of it (3.2 and 3.6 grains) spread wider. A few more rounds were loaded at 3.3, 3.4 and 3.5 grains. The 3.5 grain load proved best, showing no holes that a snake's head could slip through!

Demonstrating the nice 20″ pattern at 20 feet to a friend one day made everything look wrong again. That 20″ circle spread out over the 30″ paper like fly-specs. I couldn't believe it, not until it was realized that it wasn't the Python being fired, but a 357 S&W Combat Magnum with a 4″ barrel. This is not to imply that the Colt is better; it's just different. Working up a load for the Smith, I got the best patterns with 3.2 grains of Bullseye, about the same spread and density as before. Number 9 chilled shot was used in all tests.

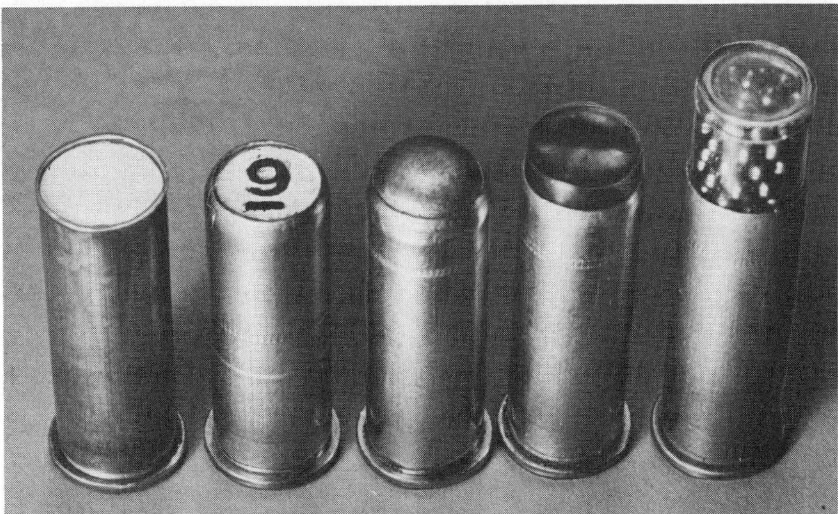

Five ways to finish shot cartridges. From left: top wad held in place with water-glass; top wad crimped in place; gas check for top wad; Hodgdon plastic half-jacket allows more shot; Shot Cap carries the largest shot weight of these shown.

44 Magnum-45 Colt Loads

Having achieved success with the 357 Magnum, the same procedure was followed in working up loads for the big 44 and the 45 Colt. Progress was swift, success almost instantaneous. The best load, using a 7½″ barrel Super Dakota single action 44 Magnum for a test gun, worked out at 5 grains of Bullseye, .135″ nitro card and 165 grains of shot. For the 45 Long Colt, with a Colt S.A. with 5½″ barrel, the best load was 4.5 grains Bullseye, .135″ nitro card and 172 grains of shot produced very tight, evenly spaced patterns at 20 feet, usually less than the 20″ circle drawn.

This story could end right here, but being a dyed-in-the-wool handloader, I hated to see those nice new felt wads sitting on the shelf. Both the 44 Magnum and 45 Long Colt

Three sizes of Shot Caps now available; 44 Mag., 38 Spec.-357 Mag. and 45 Long Colt. Note small cup in the base, which should be in contact with the powder for best results.

were throwing quite a charge of shot, so even if some pellets were sacrificed in favor of a felt wad, I reasoned there would still be enough left to do in a snake. Then, too I had a can of Hodgdon's new Grey B powder that hadn't been opened—no loading dope was available for anything that I shoot often. Teaming up these components did effect the desired result, and a few surprises, too.

Starting with the 44 Super Dakota, a load of 5.8 grains of Grey B, .70" nitro card, and a 1/4" felt wad still left room for 144 grains of shot and an over/shot card. The surprise was that the group tightened up even more—showing about a 16" circle—and the pellets were more evenly spaced. Muzzle blast sounded more like a shotgun and less like a pistol, making this load easier on the ears.

The 45 Long Colt gave best results with only 5.3 grains of Grey B, using the same combination of wads, and the average load held 147 grains of shot. For some reason the barrel of this old timer (it has a three digit serial number on the frame) showed traces of lead in the bore but a Speer half-jacket reduced this problem to some extent. It is common knowledge among shotshell pistol cartridge loaders that a gas-check or a half-jacket works well as a shot cup, but I didn't find that out until after I began to brag a bit.

Here is another way to cut down on the lead which gets scraped off the shot by the rifling: Before placing the over/shot card, spray the shot in the cartridge with Dry Gun Lube, a product of Nutec Inc., P.O. Box 1187, Wilmington, Del. 19899. This lube has fine particles of Teflon suspended in a vehicle and is dispensed from a spray can making it convenient to use for coating the loaded shot. Just a quick spray cut the leading to darn near nothing. In retracing my steps with the other loads, the same result was always shown.

These two guns, a S&W Combat Magnum and Colt Python, used in developing 357 Magnum loads gave different patterns; probably because of differences in bore, cylinder gap and barrel length.

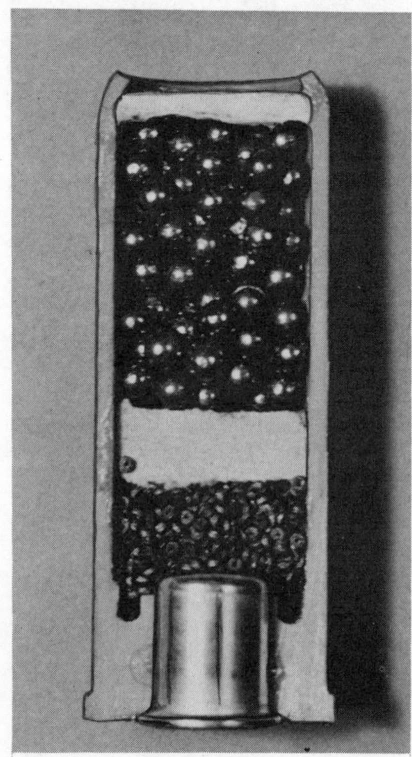

Alcan's 45 Long Colt shot cartridge in cutaway view. Shot shell primer is used to ignite the 3.5-gr. charge of a special single-base powder. The .135" O/P wad and 142½-gr. charge of No. 9 shot is similar to the load we worked out.

Shot Caps

A new approach to the shotshell revolver cartridge problem of poor patterns and not enough shot is the Remco Shot Cap. These are caliber size plastic tubes, sealed at both ends, and containing a pre-measured quantity of #9 shot. This makes the loading of shot cartridges easy—you prepare the cases as usual using the loading data supplied. The shot doesn't touch the bore and you gain about 30% in shot-charge weight. Shot Caps are packed 50 to a box, are available for 38 Special and 357 Magnum at present, and sell for $4.95 per box postpaid from Remco, 1404 Whitesboro St., Utica, N.Y. 13502. Other sizes to come are 44 Magnum, 45 Colt and 45 ACP at $5.95 a box.

The Shot Caps are very easy to assemble and less critical of the powder charge used. Patterns were as good or better than any that I was able to build from loose components and, in the 38 Special, more shot is thrown than is possible out of the 357 case when loaded with loose shot. The Remco shot cap contains 145 grains of #9 shot—the best I could cram into the 357 case was 129 grains, using two of Hodgdon's plastic half-jackets, one over the powder and the other over the shot. If you only intend to shoot shot cartridges occasionally or would rather not bother to work up a load for aerial practice, the Shot Caps may be for you. However, if any amount of shooting is anticipated 10¢ a round may be considered a bit expensive.

These plastic tubes of shot are loaded just as you would load a bullet. No wads are necessary and the shot projectile is seated easily with the thumb. The cartridge is inserted in the seating die of the press, and the bullet seating die adjusted to seat the shot capsule to slightly less than the cylinder length of your gun while giving the case mouth a slight crimp at the same time. Don't use the SAS die for crimping as it will crush the capsule.

Rocking Chair Reloading

For those who want only a few 45 LC shotshell cartridges for a hunting trip, there's another alternative. Alcan makes 45 Long Colt plastic cartridges, for one time use only; they carry a shotgun type primer have a fast-burning single base powder which I can't recognize, and carry a healthy charge of #9 shot. They're packed 50 to the box and sell for $5.15. They can also be used in your shotgun with a brass adapter available from Alcan for a dollar (specify gauge).

A number of custom reloaders make up shot cartridges, and perhaps one near you might be willing to make them for your revolver. Their names and addresses will be found in the Directory section of this book, or write to Howie's Shooters' Supplies, Pine Plains N.Y. 12567 or Montana Custom Handload, 408 S. Bozeman Ave., Bozeman, Mont. 59715. •

IT'S HIGH TIME, I feel, to burst the illusory bubble that has so long engulfed the rifled slug-shotgun combination for deer-sized animals. For too many years now, too many people including a few gun writers, have given the erroneous impression that this bulky little missile is the best invention since four corners were chiseled off the square wheel. In fact, the shotgun-slug duo, when employed in the fashion of the average deer hunter, leaves a great deal to be desired as an efficient deer slayer.

Right off the bat, I want to make it emphatically clear that I harbor no personal resentment or ill will for the rifled slug. Perhaps because I have never asked this deer load to exceed its capabilities, it has always performed admirably for me. But I certainly do take exception to the often stated claim that rifled slugs and shotguns are a magic potion, a cure-all combination that will deliver the death blow with the slightest touch. This simply isn't true. To the contrary, its use requires greater skill, better marksmanship and a more thorough knowledge of shotgun and slug performance than that needed by the average deer caliber rifle hunter.

RIFLED SLUGS --HOW GOOD ARE THEY?

Do they have that fabled knock-down power, will they anchor a deer right now? Here are the facts, derived from a detailed questioning of 150 Illinois whitetail hunters—successful ones!

by ART REID

Those of you who at the moment are recalling a number of one-shot kills on whitetails are no doubt already taking exception to these words. If so, you are counted herein among an elite group, an overwhelming minority of thousands of hunters in the many states requiring slug-loaded shotguns for deer. More about you folks later.

Consider the information I recently read concerning advice a writer offered Missouri deer hunters. The article was comprehensive because Missouri residents are permitted to hunt deer with rifles as well as shotguns and slugs.

The opening statement about slugs was highly complimentary because they had "terrific knockdown power." However, in a later paragraph the author said that a rifle caliber such as the 30-30 was a poor choice for whitetails. This caliber, he said, does not have the power to put a deer down to stay unless hit in just the right spot. He explained further that even though a deer were hit in the lungs or heart with the 30-30 bullet, it might run for a quarter-mile before dropping. It is significant to remember that nothing more was said of rifled slugs, as to gauge, etc., except that they possessed terrific knockdown power.

Rifled Slug vs. the 30-30

To the novice and many average hunters who may be a bit fuzzy on ballistics, this information clearly implies that rifled slugs of any gauge are the berries as a venison procurer and the venerable old thutty-thutty rates the thumbs-down gesture; a caliber so nasty no one should touch it.

There's no question but what the various 30-30 loads do leave a great deal to be desired in the velocity-energy department in comparison with the 270, 30-06, 308, etc., but for just plain knock-'em-down-for-keeps power what qualifications do rifled slugs offer? How do they stack up against the mediocre 30-30, using standard ammo tables for our comparsion?

The conglomeration of tiny ballistic figures tells us that the 150-gr. Winchester 30-30 bullet leaves the muzzle at 2410 feet per second (fps). One of the best rifled slug loads available (the imported Brennekes) gives a muzzle velocity of 1593 fps for the 12 gauge, 817 fps slower than the 30-30 bullet mentioned.

At 100 yards this 30-30 bullet is still humping along at 2020 fps while the 12-ga. slug is lumbering along at a mere 977 fps. In muzzle velocity the 12-ga. slug is not in the same league with the 30-30. Relative effects, of course, are argumentative, because of the difference in weight of these respective loads; the 12-ga. slug weighs approximately 341 grains more than the 30-30 bullet. Thus we are projected into the energy department, the whomping power.

Muzzle energy of the 30-30/150 is listed as 1930 foot pounds (fp), and is still delivering 1360 fp at the 100-yard marker. The slug surpasses the smaller projectile at the muzzle, with just over 2700 fp, but I have yet to hear of a documented case where a deer was killed at the muzzle of any firearm. The distance many deer are hit tells a more accurate story. At 50 yards the slug has shed energy to 1606 fp and at 100 yards it plunges to 1049.

Continuing this ballistic binge, let's not forget the 20- and 16-ga. rifled slugs, because a slew of them are used on deer each fall. I've never used any size but the 20 gauge on whitetails. Velocity and energy of this little stinger almost reach the "plumb ridiculous" stage when compared with the 30-30.

The 20-ga. slug leaves the muzzle around 1530 fps. Its making only 890 at 100 yards. Energy at the muzzle is 1852 fp. At the century stripe it struggles for 637.

The crux of this whole ballistic trade

is that more than a few authorities, including the Sporting Arms and Ammunition Manufacturers' Institute, do not recommend a load that develops less than 975 fp of energy at 100 yards for deer, etc. The meager effort of the 20 gauge doesn't approach that energy, and the 12 gauge is just over the hump.

Forgetting all about figures, since I doubt if anyone has ever beat a bounding deer to death with a ballistics loaded piece of paper, we'll get to the practical application of rifled slugs on deer.

Knockdown Nothing

In January, 1966, a friend of mine shot a young doe in the left shoulder with a ⅞-oz. 16-ga. rifled slug. The deer was about 15 yards from the muzzle. Although a fifty-cent piece would fall through the entry hole made by the slug, the lead remained inside after penetrating the lung area. Before dropping, the doe ran 84 long-legged paces. I stepped it off. The deer field-dressed at 75 pounds. This—at 15 yards—was knockdown power? Hardly.

After taking 5 rifled slugs in the boiler room this whitetail ran over 50 yards.

My friend was but one of more than 150 successful deer hunters I had the unusual opportunity to work with and interview over a 10-day period during a special deer hunt. The hunt took place on a 16,000-acre section of the Crab Orchard National Wildlife Refuge in southern Illinois. During that time I also talked with dozens of other deer hunters who shared in the bag of 1109 whitetails taken with shotguns and rifled slugs during the hunt. As well, I had personally killed four deer with this combination prior to the time Crab Orchard officials permitted Illinois hunters to thin this overpopulated area.

Dave Wolfe, editor and publisher of *The HANDLOADER*, spent three days with me in the field during this special deer harvest. We had both drawn permits to take deer, either sex.

Dave carried a Hi-Standard pump action 12-ga. slug gun with adjustable sights. I was packing my Browning 20-ga. autoloader with a slug barrel.

With Dave Rose, assistant manager of the Crab Orchard Refuge, we spent the first day interviewing hunters in Rose's jurisdiction and supervision. Many questions were asked of these men: amount of deer hunting experience; number of deer killed with shotgun and slugs; type of shotgun with or without special slug shooting barrels with rifle type sights; brand of ammunition used; number of deer seen and shot at; number of shots required to fell deer; area of body where deer was hit and approximate distance deer ran after being hit with slug, etc.

In many cases the answers were startling. Of 150 specific cases I recorded, only eight hunters had a gun equipped with adjustable sights. The majority of these men, obviously laboring under the delusion that to point at a deer was to hit it, had never test-fired the ammunition they expected to take vension with. It was evident they merely assumed their slugs would hit the point of aim.

Also shockingly apparent was the misconception of the rifled slug's effective range. Some expressed the opinion that they could easily hit and kill at 100 yards or more—with the conventional shotgun barrel and no sighting device.

The bulk of these interviews can be summed up in one man's terse statemnt: "What makes the difference anyway? You hit 'em with one of these bowling balls and they've gotta go down."

A 12-gauge slug hit this buck high in the lungs, a certain death blow, but deer still ran over 100 yards.

This, to be sure, was an extreme attitude and would be quickly repudiated by the experienced deer hunter, but to emphasize how radical such thinking really is about the potency of rifled slugs, let's check further into the so-called "bowling ball knockdown power."

5 Hits and 50 Yards

The day my license was filled, a large 8-point buck unexpectedly broke from the timber as Dave Wolfe and I were crossing an open pasture. As ridiculous as it may sound, the whitetail's attention was diverted from us, standing there in the open, by the hunter

A doe with neck band ran off to die after being hip shot with rifled slug that gave no visible clue of connecting.

who had spooked him from hiding. He trotted right toward us.

About 50 yards away the buck started to change course. Swinging right on his brisket, I fired the first shot and the ⅝-oz. 20-ga. belted him. The buck reacted as if being attacked by a swarm of hornets; he virtually catapulted into flight going full out.

Dave let off a shot with his pump action 12 gauge and I hurried my second shot. Dave fired again but there wasn't the slightest indication that any of these slugs were connecting as the buck scorched real estate. I fired my third and last shot as Dave emptied his shotgun. Our target was still running without any slack in stride.

Incredibly lousy shooting? Yes, that did enter our minds for a second—until the 8-pointer skidded on his nose 52 yards farther on. He was dead when we reached him, *with five hits that ruined his heart, lungs and liver.* One 20-ga. hole was just behind the rib cage. Knockdown power indeed! The buck weighed in at 180 pounds.

In another case, a permit holder hit a spike-horn three times in the boiler room with 16-ga. slugs. The buck didn't give up the ghost for 70 yards.

582 deer were taken with slugs during the first three days of the special ten-day period. Most of these were hit at least twice, one slug generally in a vital area. Many of these successful hunters admitted to me the deer gave no immediate indication of being hit. Almost to an animal it was necessary to blood trail them, often as far as 100 yards, to where they lay dead. The only exceptions were when the deer were hit in the spine or the neck. Most of these dropped on the spot, figuratively speaking.

Besides our experience with the big buck, the most vivid indication of the rifled slug's lack of knockdown power occurred when Dave Wolfe shot a mature doe on the third day.

As the deer approached Dave's position in the timber, he fired from about 40 yards. The slug entered at the point where the neck meets the brisket. It traveled straight in through the lungs, passing through the chest and into the stomach cavity.

Dave told me the deer gave no indication of a hit, but quickly disappeared in the dense thickets. There was only a single telling sign, one the less experienced deer hunter might not know of or think about at the critical moment—Dave was positive she had not flared her white tail-flag skyward. As well, he knew his shotgun and loads and had confidence in his ability to use them. He followed the deer's path.

To me, a few hundred yards away, one shot from his area meant that Dave had a deer down and could use help in getting it out. I slowly worked my way in that direction.

I found Dave bending over the fat doe, but instead of the successful deer hunter's usual expression of delight; Dave seemed troubled. His explanation also disturbed me, and added weight to my growing conviction that the efficiency of rifled slugs on dee should be re-evaluated.

No Blood Trail

Dave explained that the doe ran more than 100 yards from point of impact. This wasn't so bad, he pointed out, but the fact that he couldn't find the smallest drop of blood had almost convinced him he'd missed cleanly.

When we inspected the 12-ga. slug wound in the doe's chest there wasn't a speck of blood to be found on hide or hair. Shock power from this massive hunk of lead? It didn't even slow her down until she bled to death internally.

Knowing of my interest in all details of slug performance, Dave Rose looked me up after getting a report on a dead 8-point buck. When we found it, we saw its only apparent wound was in the left rear hip. Rose and I loaded the buck into his pickup truck and took it to Don Autry, a biologist of the Cooperative Wildlife Laboratory of Southern Illinois University. Autry was running one of the two check stations on the refuge where all deer are recordd.

Autry meticulously inspected the dead deer; there were no other wounds. Then he dissected the one damaged hip area, carefully following the course of the slug that had entered directly from the rear. A deformed 12-ga. slug (determined by weight) was located only ten inches from point of entry. The hipbone was broken, but with only ten inches of penetration the slug was a long way from vital internal organs. Not a very impressive performance.

In the days that followed we investigated a number of similar cases in which slugs were fired at deer running directly away. In each case penetration was always slight, even though a long shot in this heavily forested area would be 50 yards.

However, on the credit side of the rifled slug ledger, it should be noted that one-shot kills were made, many of them in fact. I personally guided hunters to whitetails that were dropped in their tracks with all three gauges of rifled slugs. During the 1965 deer season in southern Illinois, Barney Delmore popped a 125-lb. forkhorn twice in the neck with 12-ga. slugs. The deer made a single jump. That same season a friend from Springfield, Ill., dropped a doe with a 12-ga. slug that shattered the spine.

During the 1966 Illinois season, Wayne Long and Cleo Bunting both took nice whitetail bucks with neck shots requiring but a single slug each. The consistent one-shot kills, though, where deer drop on the spot or nearly so when hit with rifled slugs, are usually executed by above-average hunters who know where, when and how to point their shotguns. These people have no preconceived notions about near-miracle performances from this load. Further, I've seen too many deer shot by too many hunters to be convinced that any hit other than in the spine, neck or head will drop them on the spot.

Contrary to what you may have been led to believe, few deer will actually show the hunter an unmistakable sign of being hit with a rifled slug, even one in the boiler room, so be prepared to follow up after you squeeze your shotgun trigger. •

An 11-point whitetail, shot with a 12-gauge slug in the lungs by Lee W. Rose (left), ran 125 yards before falling.

The L.C. Smith Resurrected!

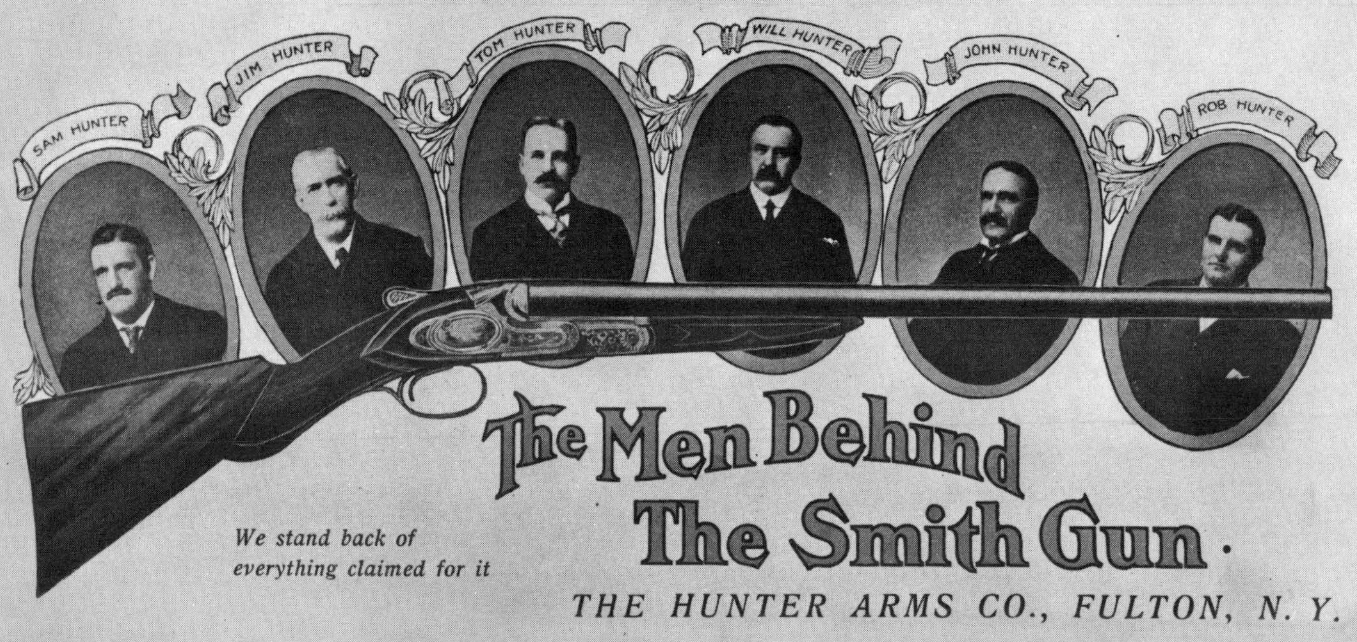

Long dead these many years, the L.C. Smith is born again. Like the Phoenix, this attractive birdgun is again available to please the eyes and gladden the hearts of those who appreciate fine shotguns.

by GERALD R. HUNTER

A CLASSIC AMERICAN shotgun has been reborn—and if I reported simply, "The new L. C. Smith is just like the old one," I'd be substantially correct, for the original jigs and specifications are employed.

But there are differences—and some surprises—worth attention. It may hurt my family vanity to admit that the modernized Marlin-made replica is better than the original built by the Hunters, but it's true. Still, I'm going to pick the new gun apart, but first, a very brief background for those young shooters who've come along since a fine double was the "in" gun.

For more than half a century the L. C. Smith was built by Hunter Arms Co. at Fulton, N. Y., during which time we also produced the less expensive boxlock *Hunter Special* and *Fulton* shotguns. As early as 1935, L. C. Smiths had won a majority of the competitive world championships. The old company made some half-million of these "guns that never shoot loose," and most, we believe, are still shooting. (So are a lot of Ithaca and Fox guns which copied its lockup system). Due to imprudent speculation in unrelated fields, the L. C. Smith enterprise went into receivership and was bought by Marlin Firearms Co. at the end of World War II. During this period, increasing production costs killed off virtually every fine American-made double shotgun, but Marlin, by assembling another 60,000 Smiths from Hunter-made parts, managed to hang on until 1951.

Today, the only Hunter remnants interested in the Smith have no financial connection with its production; these are Verna Hunter Wadsworth and Clair Wadsworth, of Fulton, and the writer. Clair, who designed the famous Smith single-barrel trap gun, among his other patents, was production manager of the old plant. Hunter Arms Co. survives as a small diversified firearms facility but no longer builds guns nor solicits business. Anyone interested in a detailed history may inquire of E. F. Buehlman (389 Flynn Creek Dr., Barrington, Ill.) who, since a tornado blew away our family records, is the best living authority on the Hunter/Smith saga. He is planning a book on the subject.

For nearly two following decades no traditional sidelock double guns were produced here. In fact, the only American-made double to span the breech was the boxlock Winchester Model 21—which jumped its standard grade from around $400 to $1500, so middle class young America forgot the honest joys of a good double gun.

Then along about here—I'd done some gun designing for Marlin as long ago as 1943—a funny thing happened: I approached Marlin (on behalf of the Hunter family) and offered to buy back the L. C. Smith and put it into production. Marlin said they'd ponder my offer. Instead of furnishing me the requested inventory and making me a price, president Frank Kenna, Jr., countered by announcing that Marlin would reintroduce the gun! Just how significant the effect of my offer was we'll never know, but I suspect it was the deciding catalyst that precipitated the new L. C. Smith. I wished them well, was invited up to New Haven in a consultant category, and expect to continue offering my services in the new project on a purely personal, avocational basis.

The new Smith was announced for very limited public offering as of June, 1968, at a list price of $225. It is the only hand-fitted American double ever to rise from the economic grave, and it sells for about 1/7 the cost of the vanity-priced Winchester 21. The initial model is a field grade 12 gauge with double triggers, plain extractors and 28-inch barrels bored modified and full. 44½ inches long, it weighs about 6⅝ths pounds. Emile W. Clede of Marlin sent me the first of these new guns, and here's what I found.

Barrel Assembly

The modern steel barrels, bored as specified, are properly Englished-in for convergence of patterns at 40 yards. Finish and bluing, as on all metal parts, is superb. The bores, nicely polished, show no tool marks.

The lower rib is conventional, but topside is an innovation: a Poly Choke-made, wide, scalloped, aluminum alloy ventilated rib, cemented above a rudimentary steel jointer. The rib adds only 2 ounces of weight. There's a large front bead and a small middle bead, both ivory and highly visible. The scalloping kills glare even when aiming close to the sun. I recall that Tom Wotherspoon of Poly Choke discussed this rib cementing problem with me when I was on a visit to the Poly plant 10 years ago. The gun I tested has now been fired thousands of times, and Tom is a very dependable fellow, so presumably the cemented rib will stay put. Spacing of the integral studs on this rib is closer than any I've seen, 1.234″ between centers, so accidental denting of the bridges will be minimized. The alloy rib is wedge-anchored under a short steel terminal at the rear which extends to become the dolls-head, the latter slotted for the familiar rotary crossbolt.

How's this for a shocker: The muzzles are *flared.* That's right—maximum choke comes ½″ *behind* the muzzles.

Using upland loads, the chokes perform as expected. Then comes a real jolt: With wildfowl and turkey fodder (heavy loads in shot sizes 6 to 2) they do a compound *reversal.* The modified (right) barrel consistently tosses tighter patterns than does the full choke. *Both* throw groupings that considerably skin the standard 70% full-choke criterion, the right barrel averaging 82% and the left 76%! Though ballistically inconsistent, this switching phenomenon with large *versus* small shot is a unique premium, since in each case the gun, almost as if with a mind of its own, adapts for the game at hand.

Between the forcing cones and the chokes are bores precisely .7310″ in diameter—.002″ larger than the traditional .729″ standard, and .001″ above even the modern .730″. The full choke tube tapers to .6924″, the modified to .7083″. There's no mandatory size for a 12 gauge bore, however, and the diameter means little except as it relates to choke constriction.

A notable point to ponder is that the left forcing cone is 1⅛″ long, while the right cone is only ⅞″. Teaser: Can this considerable variation be responsible for the astonishingly tight groupings of large shot

Verna Hunter Wadsworth, Clair Wadsworth (center) holding the only 28-gauge L. C. Smith ever made, and the author.

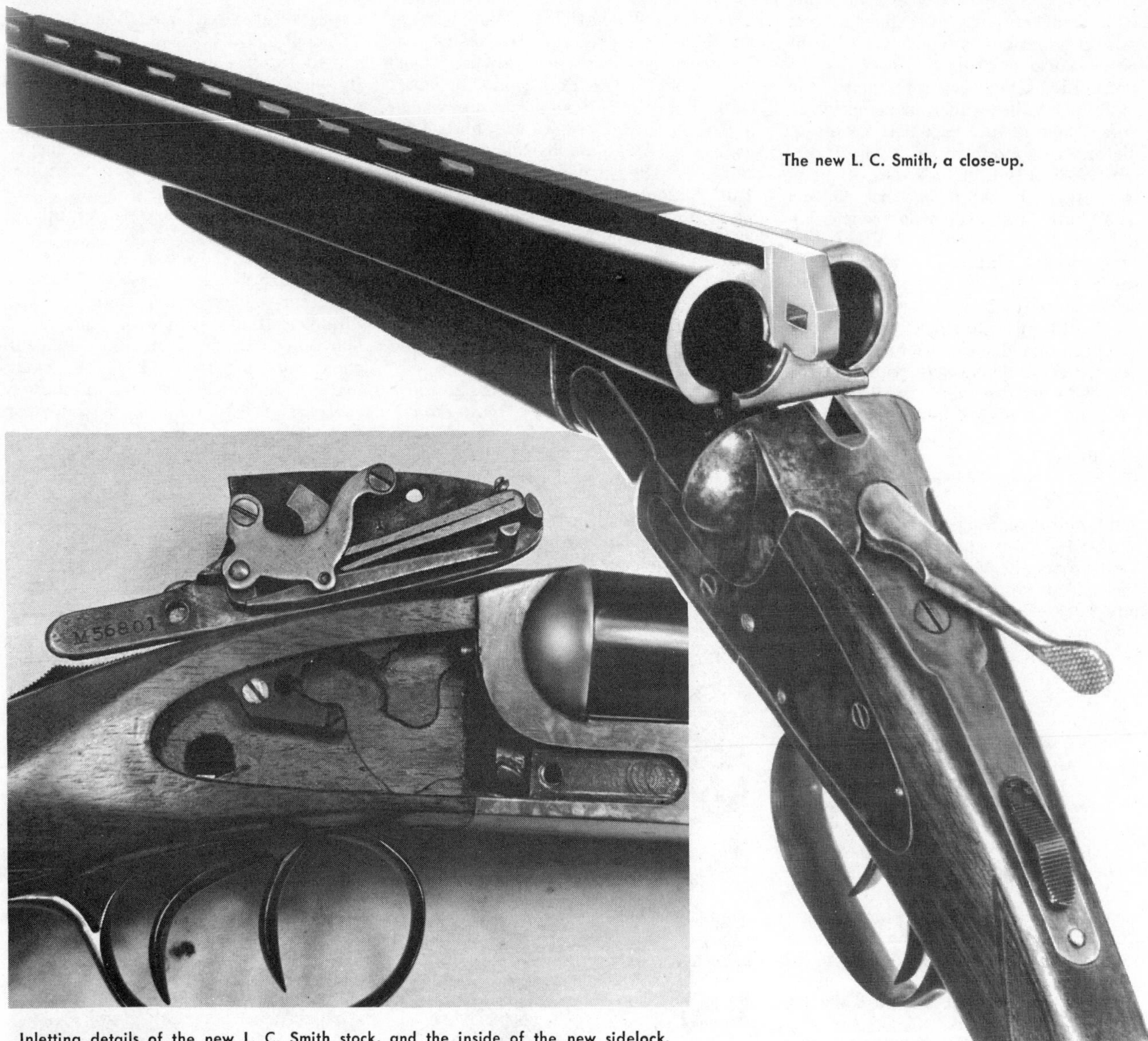

The new L. C. Smith, a close-up.

Inletting details of the new L. C. Smith stock, and the inside of the new sidelock.

from the starboard barrel?

Chambers are exactly .8118″ diameter for the initial 2½″ of their length. Then they taper slightly for another ½″, to a degree that just allows standard 2¾″ hulls to unfold properly upon firing. No measurable pressure is required to insert 3″ shells into these chambers, though there's a definite, if slight, resistance for the final 3/16″ of their travel to warn the shooter that he's got some overly hot fodder in hand.

Barrel walls are noticeably thicker than those of earlier models, so weight control obviously is achieved elsewhere in the arm. In fact, the muzzle walls are so thick (.055″ and .057″ respectively) they remind me of a top grade European shotgun—an astute defense against the careless new-generation shooter used to the virtual indestructibility of the bellowing autoloader. Chamber wall thickness is .175″ (exception: the outboard right chamber wall is .190″). Average chamber wall 3″ ahead of the breech is still .151″ which, especially with the new steel, is ample to allow rechambering for 3″ shells. A caution on that later. The barrels are 1.235″ outside diameter at the breech.

Marlin has retained the traditional double-cam dolls-head, thus has the strongest lockup in current production. Heart of this strength is the crossbolt which hooks through and across the dolls-head. Granted, several current doubles have crossbolts or longbolts, but none except the Smith have an ascending-taper bolt that not only locks, but also wedges the lock ever tighter with wear. A rimcracked shell, particularly an old handload, will peel the rib from most guns—or worse—but never on a Smith.

The fore-end latch lug retains the concave centering depression designed by Clair Wadsworth, to positively center the fore-end and add stoutness to the snap. Instead of the former airbleed holes in the lower rib, a tiny gap is provided next to the fore-end lock. Fitting of the extractor is precise, as are the firing pin cam slots.

Frame Design

A necessary shortcut in the new manufacture is investment casting of the main frame. An investment casting is one made under pressure in an incredibly expensive super-precision die, so accurate as to require no shaping cuts and usually no milling, as compared with conventional molds which merely roughout a product to shape and size. Consequently, the new frames, even in this "field" grade, show tool marks in only two internal areas. Except for the dolls-head seat, the new frame (it's 7⅜″ long compared with the prewar 8″) is identical to the old, to accommodate prototype working parts. Lockplates are of the later austere contour (compared with the flowing lines of earlier models) and the forward anchor screws go straight in instead of at the former oblique angle. Frame and lockplates are shallowly case hardened in the oldtime colors.

The right sear falls at 6 pounds and the left at 7. But these trigger pulls are comfortable due to stiff sear-springs and very hard, smooth sear points that use a full 7/32" width of bearing surface—and they're *safe*.

Any gun can "double" because of bad sears. Doubling in the new Smith is virtually impossible, for these carefully mated hard sears aren't likely to wear appreciably. The other cause of doubling—unwanted friction of one sear extension (the arm activated by the trigger) against the other due to sinking-in of the lockplates—has been positively eliminated by two precautions. Crux of this is a flatheaded jackscrew sunk into the stockwood under each sideplate, and adjusted so the sears cannot touch. The other safeguard is glass bedding of the entire perimeter of the lockplates, plus glassing of every point at which the plates and frame touch the stock. When you install one of these new sidelocks and begin tightening the throughbolt, there's no doubt about when to stop: the bolt (a machine screw) practically bumps to a sudden stop as it finds "home." All screws go "home" with their slots neatly fore-and-aft in the oldtime tradition of craftsmen.

Glassing technique used in the revived Smith gives me a meditative pause. The well-read shooter knows that a glass thickness of at least 1/16" between wood and metal is recommended by all makers of bedding compound. In the Smith, all stock-to-metal contacts are so-bedded (except for the triggerplate), but this glassing is almost microscopic in places, and never thicker than 3/64". Will this skinny smear of glass crack out with use and time? Frankly, I don't know. I do know that L. C. Smith No. FWM 56801 has been fired a lot of times with no failure of the glass and no cracking of the wood.

Safety

The Smith safety is still just a trigger block (as is the case with virtually all guns other than bolt actions) but it's well-fitted and positive. Gone is the sometimes dangerous (for neophytes) non-automatic rear position. The safety slide exhibits a conventional, positive, automatic, two-position, foolproof choice.

Another eyebrow lifter is the trigger guard. Remember how the Smith often either skinned your finger, nearly broke your second finger, or both, from recoil? Well, you've a pleasant surprise in store. The new version doesn't hurt, even with magnum loads. Although there's no obvious change in the guard, a thorough inspection reveals that its inside clearance has been lengthened to 2 13/32", deepened to 1⅜", and its tang reshaped for a much more gradual rear angle. The triggers have been respaced to exactly 1" apart, for a length of pull of 14" front and 13" rear. The new liberal dimensions will especially delight cold weather hunters who must wear gloves.

Tumbler pivots extend out through the lockplates and are brightly polished. They're not indexed, but it wouldn't be much of a chore for an owner to slot these as both visible and sensory cocking indicators. Firing pins are polished, with perfect hemispherical ends. They strike the primers soundly and dead center, just as the hammers center the firing pin bases.

If there's any fault in the frame-to-barrel fit, it's a microscopic gap between chamber face and standing breech. This gap is inconsistent but runs around .003". While such a "chasm" might horrify bookworms who've been brainwashed on guns that "wont close on a cigarette paper," the separation isn't visible unless viewed crossway to a light. I'd like to toss in, from experience, the observation that such a peripheral vent would prevent a lot of damage from an overloaded shellburst, not to mention its needed allowance for expansion when the tubes heat up from repetitive shooting.

Stock and Fore-end

Fore-end wood is standard size, checkered to match the stock. The latch is a simple compression, modified leaf spring. Both extractor cam spring and latch spring are of helical design, assuring long life. The Wadsworth latch point is well hardened and

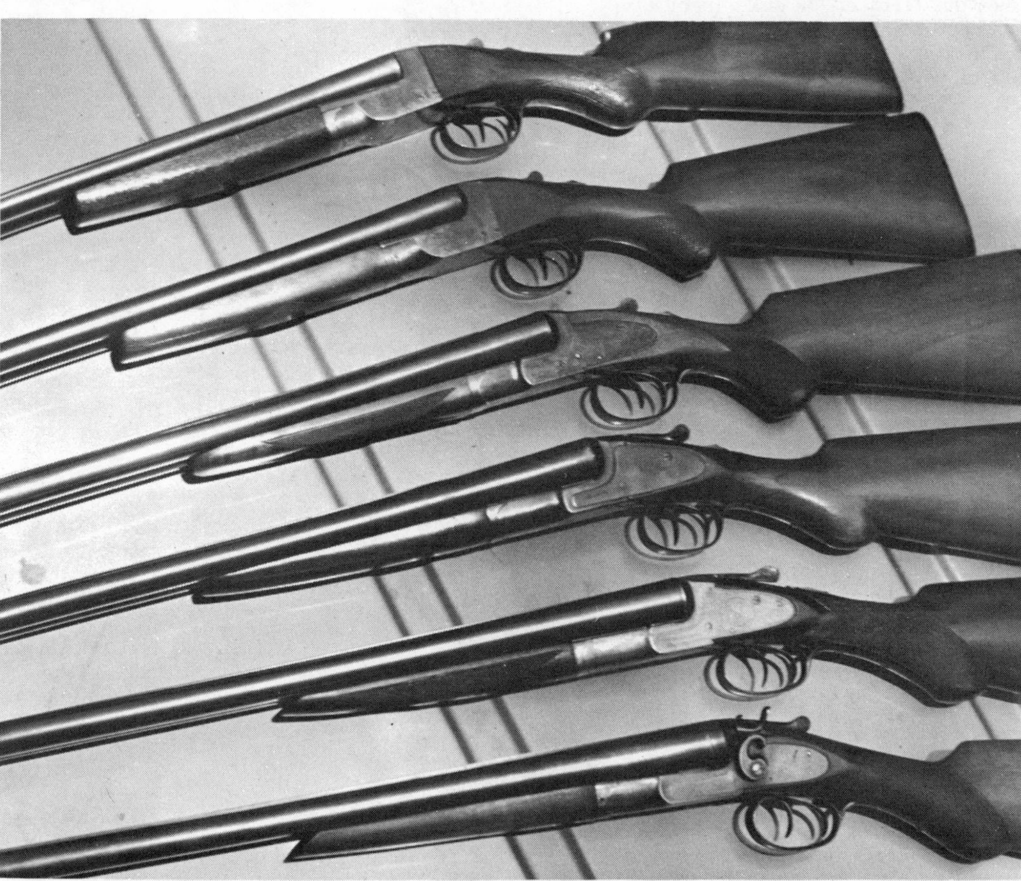

Some shotguns in the Hunter family. From the top: Fulton; Hunter Special; new Marlin-made L. C. Smith; old Crown Grade L.C.S.; old Field Grade L.C.S.; hammer model.

doesn't flop around in its slot. Metalwork is traditional L. C. Smith, but inletting of wood for the barrel channels is substandard.

The first thing I noticed about the new stock floored me! It has approximately 1/4" of *cast-on*—a remarkable variation for a standard arm, and even more so for an American-made one. Nearly all production shotguns have straight stocks. A few continental ones have cast-off. But, cast-*on*? This means that if you hold the gun out before you in sighting attitude, the stock seems to bend to your left. The new Smith, for the stock-crawler with an average face (like mine) puts the sighting eye nicely dead-in-line with the two sights. But the southpaw is going to find he "overshoots" the stock, and natural snapshooters—who usually aren't aware of the sights anyhow—may have a bit of feathering at first.

Five other innovations appear.

The stock is inherently stronger. At the wrist, the part gripped by the shooting hand, thickness has been increased to a full 1 1/4". Former Smith stocks usually ran about 1" here, and an old Crown grade of mine is only 7/8". There's more wood around the sideplates. Both additions are achieved without visible bulk. The illusion of slenderness is augmented by reducing the butt too radically: New butt dimensions are only 4 13/16" by 1 1/2", and this skinny area of shoulder contact becomes painfully noticeable when shooting high velocity or magnum loads. The stock is considerably "straighter," which should reduce apparent recoil; precisely 1 1/2" drop at comb and 2 1/2" at heel. Any armchair engineer will perceive, however, and any shooter will learn empirically, that these dimensions (plotted against line of sight and direction of recoil) let this comb kick back *into* one's cheek at about an 8° blow, instead of comfortably along it or away from it. Anything less straight could kill you! Ordinary slug loads will make you cry. Unfortunately, inherited aesthetics seem to demand this engineering mayhem. It would be simple enough to offer a parallel comb, a la Monte Carlo, or even a rudimentary cheekpiece that wouldn't make one's jaws ache and his ears throb.

Parenthetically, this is why I couldn't recommend rechambering this gun, as offered, for 3" waterfowl shells. The sustained punishment would be prohibitive. A hot 3" shell inadvertently fired in this light, unaltered gun, by adding the extra pressure of a severely constricted shotshell fold, would just about knock the unseasoned shooter into the Happy Hunting Ground.

The expectedly rather plain walnut of this field grade gun is attractive and shows care in placing the run of the grain properly through the wrist. Hand-cut checkering of 16 lines per inch provides substantially better gripping surface than the more ornamental 18 to 22 lines demanded by the showcase trade. It's first-class checkering—better than that in the posh Winchester 21, for instance—and requires a really pessimistic inspection to locate runovers. Buttplate and grip cap are of a plain black material. Enough lip of wood is allowed behind the floating firing pins to prevent the nuisance of having a pin drop out, unnoticed, during reassembly.

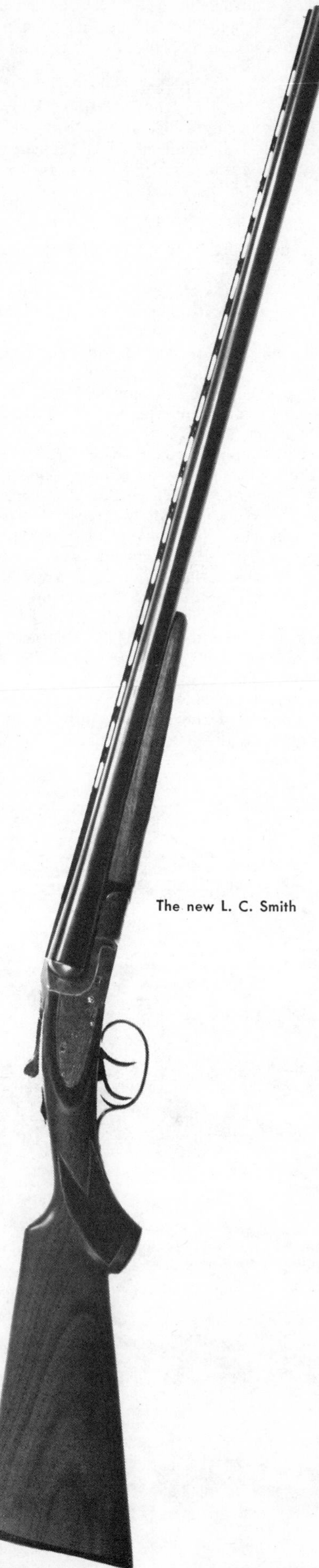
The new L. C. Smith

Fitting of wood to metal, and metal to metal, is tops.

Summary

A unique resurrection has made available, at popular prices, a genuine American-built sidelock double gun. Like everything this side of heaven, the new L. C. Smith has its undesirable features, but these few shortcomings are heavily outweighed by its plus qualities.

This first-offering model makes a fine upland gun that does what it's supposed to do. At the expense of heavier recoil, it's a better than excellent waterfowl, turkey and deer gun, phenomenally changing its performance characteristics to conform with the load used. 26" barrels, bored improved cylinder and modified, are planned as optional or extra or an even better bird gun. Yet even in present length, the center of balance, falling precisely at rear of the fore-end wood, provides an arm so *apparently* light and pointable that even small women and boys can handle it with ease. "Handle," yes, but they'll need a good recoil pad or considerable experience with stiff recoil.

I'd guess this present model will find hurried acceptance in my adopted South, for several reasons.

The old L. C. Smith always has been a highly favored deer gun but, like most guns, usually patterns only a single size of buckshot well. The new Smith is the only gun I ever saw, double or single tube, that will put the *whole load* of any size of buckshot in precisely the desired place.

Its instant choice of triggers means that the southern hunter, often a "swamp rambler," can call for buckshot from one barrel or a turkey load from the other.

Dependability is high on the rambler's list, and the Smith's completely independent firing systems insure integrity. In such a sidelock gun, the odds of having a mishap to one side preventing proper functioning of the other, are nil. In fact, you can take one entire firing mechanism off and throw it away without any effect on the other.

One particular niche has been crying for such a gun: The tent camp hunter who goes off for several days after a variety of game. If he takes more than one gun, those he isn't using must remain in the unprotected camp at the mercy of thieves. Range tests of these astonishing new tubes tell him that all he has to do to "change guns" is to switch shells.

In a different direction, the new production offers a valuable bonus. I've never seen a properly lubricated L. C. Smith worn out from use, but many have become inoperative from abuse. Since new parts, including barrels, are being made on the original Hunter jigs and to original specifications, they'll be available to repair or rebuild older L. C. Smiths. Parts will still require hand fitting, of course.

Changes I'd like to endorse would include a comb that doesn't abuse the shooter, a merciful buttplate of greater contact area, offerings of a 20-bore single trigger ejector model, and a heavier 3″ wildfowl buster. As a gunsmith, I'd like to see the toplever post pivoted on the frame (like the old Fox) instead of on the triggerplate, and a hinge joint takeup screw (like the old Lefever). No one could improve on the warranty: every new L. C. Smith comes with a written lifetime guarantee.

Ultimately, by what criterion does an owner judge his personal firearm?

In the vast silences that overtake the lone hunter as he pauses and waits for game or sits back against a tree at the twilight rendezvous, he scans the sky for coming weather. He sniffs nostalgic woodland odors. He remembers other pleasant days afield —and he looks down at his gun with an unusually critical eye. These are the moments when he wonders whether or not his gun is what it ought to be. If it happens to be a modern L. C. Smith, how is he going to feel about it?

I think his reaction could be summed up in the comments of Clair Wadsworth, from his wealth of experience and observation:

"I'm really delighted to see this gun," Waddy told me. "You know, the ancestral Hunter motto is 'The Eagle Does Not Catch Flies.' I'm glad Marlin held to this integrity. I don't mean to criticize Savage for sneaking the Fox label onto its Stevens, or Winchester for overbraining its Miroku, or Ithaca for lending its name to the SKB. But somewhere down in the heart of every American shooter survives a personal pride in our national heritage, one that clearly tells him he'd *rather* have a traditional gun made in this country. I'll sleep better, knowing he can again have one at a reasonable price."

I couldn't express it better. •

PELLETS & PATTERNS—BUCKSHOT & SLUGS

Test results with a new model L. C. Smith*

Load	Pellet size	Barrel	Pellet Hits in Quadrants NE	SE	SW	NW	Pellets/load	Pellets/circle	Pattern %	E.H.S.[1]	E.V.S.[2]	P.I.[3]
Western Super-X Mark 5 Mag	1B	R	1	9	4	4	20	18	90	19½″	16″	1″ @ 6:00 o'cl.
Western Super-X Mark 5	1B	L	2	2	7	4	16	15	94	15½	13½	2¾″ @ 9:30
Western Super-X Mark 5	0B	R	1	6	1	3	12	11	92	9½	15	1″ @ 5:00
Western Super-X Mark 5	0B	L	1	6	5	0	12	12	100	18	10	3½″ @ 5:00
Western Super-X Mark 5	00B	R	1	3	4	1	9	9	100	14	18½	2½″ @ 6:00
Western Super-X Mark 5	00B	L	0	6	1	2	9	8	88	16	13	3″ @ 5:30
Western Super-X Slug	Slug	R			1		1	1	100			5″ @ 7:30
Western Super-X Slug	Slug	L		1			1	1	100			7½″ @ 5:00

All shooting was done at 40 yards, using the standard 30-inch circle. No ammunition was selected or bought especially for these tests. All were loads picked up at random in the shop.

*Made by Marlin Firearms, serial No. FWM 56801.

[1]E.H.S.—Extreme horizontal spread

[2]E.V.S.—Extreme vertical spread.

[3]P.I.—Center of pattern relative to target center.

PELLETS & PATTERNS—WILDFOWL LOADS

Test results with a new model L. C. Smith*

Load	Pellet Size	Barrel	Pellet Hits in Quadrants NE	SE	SW	NW	Pellet/load	Pellets/circle	Pattern %
Western Super-X Mark 5	6	R	32	64	83	62	281	241	86
	6	L	29	70	92	36	281	227	81
Western Super-X Magnum	4	R	17	42	66	32	202	157	78
	4	L	28	37	51	23	202	139	69
Peters High Velocity	2	R	14	27	24	26	112	91	81
	2	L	6	21	39	20	112	86	77

All shooting was done at 40 yards, using the standard 30-inch circle. No ammunition was selected or bought especially for these tests. All were loads picked up at random in the shop.

*Made by Marlin Firearms, serial No. FWM 56801.

Handloading—1969-70

A full and comprehensive review of all the new and useful tools and reloading helps—with complete coverage of the latest in components.

**by Maj. Geo. C. Nonte, Jr.
and the Technical Editors**

Part 1—Equipment

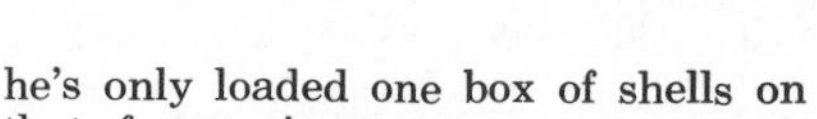

AT THE RISK of being repetitious, I have to begin this dissertation by saying that handloading continues to grow steadily. Since this time last year we've seen an ever-increasing interest in the subject, just as in many years gone by. Probably the best index of interest—and of money being spent — is the continually-increasing number of products that are being placed on the market. No business firm offers new items except in anticipation of a tidy profit. Further evidence is clear in the "back-order" status of many component producers. I can't recall a single time during the past year that the major makers were able to ship immediately dealer requirements of more than half to three-quarters of their lines. The boys in the field, their C-presses busy, have simply been buying more than the factories could produce.

Even new items are snapped up immediately. One bullet maker found his first full production run of a new bullet sold out by the time it was completed—all without a single piece of advertising or publicity. At least two other bullet firms and one primer maker have been struggling for nearly two years just to catch up on deliveries of new items introduced that long ago. This, even with continued expansion of production capabilities.

A few years back many of us felt that the handloading boom would last only a few years, then level off. But the leveling-off point hasn't yet been reached, and we wonder now if it ever will be. We've come to the conclusion that the average handloader doesn't load primarily for economy, though many of them begin for that reason. After a bit of exposure, loading becomes more an end unto itself than simply a way of saving a few bucks. In some instances, it has even become a sort of status symbol. The professional man who can show cocktail guests a shiny, four- or five-hundred dollar shotshell loading tool and say casually, "sure, I load my own, like it better than factory stuff," accounts for some slice of the action—even if he's only loaded one box of shells on that fancy rig.

In any event, handloading and the business of supplying the wherewithal for it continues to grow. As a result, lots of new goodies have been introduced during the past year, and we present them here for your enlightenment.

Armory C-H as such is out of business. Owners of their tools who require parts or reloaders who choose to buy tools of that manufacture can obtain them from C-H Tool & Die Corp., Box L, Owen, Wisconsin 54460. Write them for your needs—perhaps a new catalog will be available as you read this.

Acme The extensive Acme shotshell loading tool line continues in production and popularity. With increased interest in economy and in loading Canadian cases, Acme has introduced a Cap Conversion Tool modification on each of its standard models. These tools incorporate a simple mechanism which can be switched to either cap or battery cup priming. Changeover requires only moments. Individual tool prices vary only slightly above those of the standard models and run from the $25 range to nearly $90.

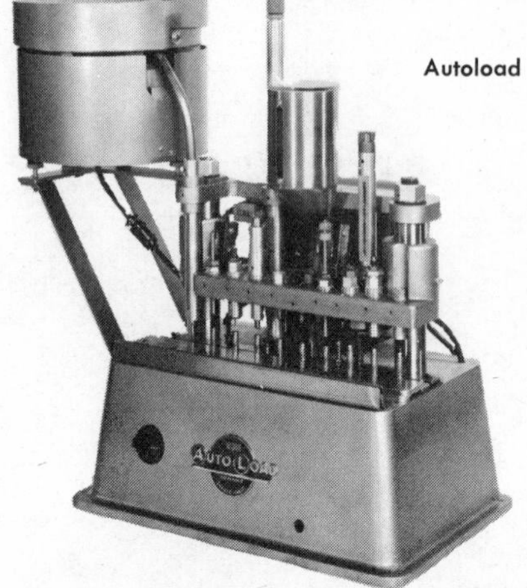

Autoload

Automatic Reloading Equipment Inc. produces only high-speed production-type equipment suitable for the commercial reloader or police departments. The original Autoload machine has been available for a number of years and has progressed through numerous improvements. In its latest form it appears to be highly reliable.

Essentially it is an electrically driven, 10-stage, straightline, progressive loader with automatic feeding of all components. Cases are fed from a vibrating, orienting hopper; bullets and primers from pre-loaded magazine tubes; powder from an automatic disc-type volumetric measure. The Autoload shows good workmanship and can be had in most pistol and some small rifle (such as 30 U.S. Carbine) calibers. Most units are built to order and prices vary widely according to the customer's requirements. Price can run as high as $5,000, but for a production rate of 5,000 rounds per hour, that isn't really too bad. An accessory, their Automatic Primer Tube Filler, helps to maintain the high production rate. Cost—a mere $450.

Autoload also offers a large-capacity case cleaning barrel tumbler which may be used to prepare cases for loading, as well as to clean and polish loaded ammunition. This is priced at $435 and can be delivered within 30 days as can the other tools above.

Bahler Die Shop is now offering 17-caliber bullets in 20-, 22-, 25- and 30-gr. weights at $4 per hundred, $30 per M. Jackets in the same caliber are $12.50 per M.

New and simpler bullet-making dies in handgun calibers (so far no rifle sets) are available for the RCBS Rockchucker press only. They function with half- or ¾-jackets and are priced at $60 for solid point, $65, hollow point.

Bair Machine Co, mentioned for the first time in these pages last year, now offers a very extensive line of handloading equipment of all sorts—virtually everything except bullet-making items. The line consists of 5 metallic-cartridge presses ranging from $27.50 to $74.50, and three shotshell tools at $59.50 to $149.50.

New in the metallic line is the Brown Bair series H-type presses. BB #I is a single-station press with a cast riser bar sliding vertically on two ground steel posts, carrying a standard detachable shell holder head. Dies are carried in a cast top bar threaded ⅞x14, and all are tied together by a massive cast base. An unusual fully automatic primer feed is mounted behind the riser on the base. A vertical primer arm passes through the riser to seat the primer to a positive stop. The arm is cammed rearward as the tool handle is fully depressed. This serves to keep ejected, fired primers and their debris from falling into the seating bushing—which is a common source of annoyance in most other H-type presses. This simple solution works beautifully and seems foolproof.

BB #III is essentially the same press with riser and top bar reshaped to hold three dies and shell holders, permitting a complete die set to be installed simultaneously. This allows cases to be processed through all loading operations without die changing. You can even process three cases at once, moving each one step to the right, producing a loaded round with every stroke of the handle. Both Brown Bair presses are capable of performing all reloading work including full-length sizing and case forming.

Brown Bair #1 costs $44.50 with primer punch only; $54.50 with auto-primer feed and two primer tubes added; $64.50 complete with dies and shell holder for one caliber. BB #III prices are $54.50, $64.50, and $79.50 as above. Since Bair dies are $13.50 per set and shell holders 2.50, the package prices represent a substantial saving over the piece-by-piece price.

Bair continues to offer primer trays, bullet pullers, powder dribblers, reamers, trimmers, funnels, scales, measure, primer feeders and other accessories.

Newest Bair shotshell loader is the Honey, reported capable of 225 rounds per hour by an experienced operator. This $74.50 tool is an up-graded, more compact version of last year's Panda and uses the same dies. It has a vertical sliding die head riding on a square steel column attached to a heavy round base. It features positive rod ejection of cases from the resizing die; a drawer in the base to catch fired primers; and a nylon bushing in the sizing die. This bushing greatly reduces friction and sizing effort, and also removes one more area susceptible to rust. Powder and shot flow may be cut off by rotating the transparent hoppers. In addition, the hoppers are slightly tapered, permitting stacking to increase capacity. Gauge conversion kit costs $26.50, but does not include powder and shot bushings.

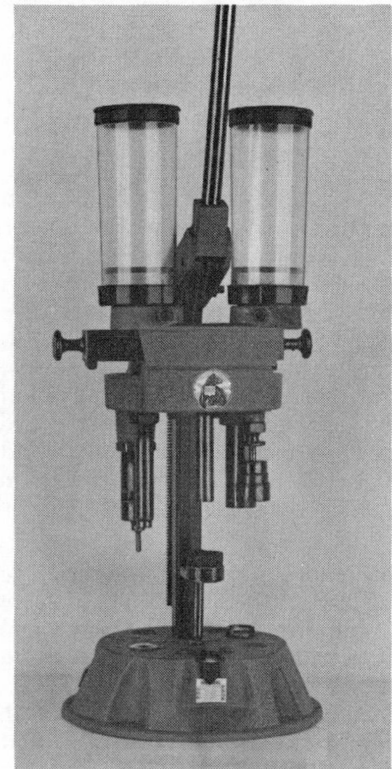

Honey Bair

Bair has also added a cam-actuated wad guide to its big Polar shotshell tool. The guide swings over the case only when required. The $7.50 primer tube filler is now included in the Polar's $149.50 price.

New Bair accessories include a powder dribbler at $2.85; replacement nylon spring fingers to fit most shotshell tools at $1.00; and popular-gauge shotgun snap caps at $2.00 per pair.

The Magna Damp powder scale at $18.50 has been introduced, apparently replacing the Auto Damp of last year. Aside from a base of somewhat unusual profile, this is essentially a conventional beam balance with magnetic damping.

Brown Bair #1

B-Square has just announced a hand-cranked lathe that uses standard hand-held chamfering and deburring tools. This tool speeds up production, ends the roughness produced by usual stop-start motions. The lathe is $4.95 (plus 25¢ shipping); a chamfer/deburr cutter if you need one is $3 postpaid. An accessory primer pocket reamer is also $3 postpaid. It can be used in the lathe or hand held.

Brown Precision Co. has a case spinner with some unusual features called the Little Wiggler. Complete with a 1″ dial indicator, the Wiggler will measure case neck thickness and variations or bullet tilt of completed rounds. The case or cartridge is inserted between two precision-machined mandrels. The small mandrel fits all pointed bullets—round nose bullets require a special mandrel. The dial indicator, with .001″ divisions, is set to zero over the small mandrel, the case is inserted and the large coned mandrel positions the case head. By rotating the case wall thickness can be measured at any point on the neck.

When measuring bullet tilt, the round is inserted first and then the dial is zeroed. If bullet run-out is detected, a small screw jack is raised from the cast base to better align the bullet. Straightening ammo in this way will make it straighter shooting, but you can use the Little Wiggler to detect out-of-round or egg-shaped chambers and seating/sizing dies. Available only by mail, the Little Wiggler costs $34.75, including dial indicator.

Barotta Sports Ltd., a Canadian firm, now handles a complete line of American reloading tools and components. Firearms, ammunition and a large assortment of sporting and camping goods are also stocked. This bit of information is included especially for use by our good neighbors to the north, but when U.S. hunters travel that area they might want to stop in at 605 - 7th St. S.W., Calgary, Alta., and see what domestic (Canadian) products are available other than CIL.

Blackhawk Small Arms Ammunition offers a die exchange service. Used dies are purchased, inspected, cleaned, repaired, packaged and labeled. They are then offered for sale or exchange. Customers may ship a serviceable die set, paying an exchange fee which varies from $2.00 upward according to type and caliber, and receive a refurbished set. The same dies may also be purchased outright. A minimum stock of 2000 die sets is maintained at all times, often making it possible for Blackhawk to deliver faster than regular distribu-

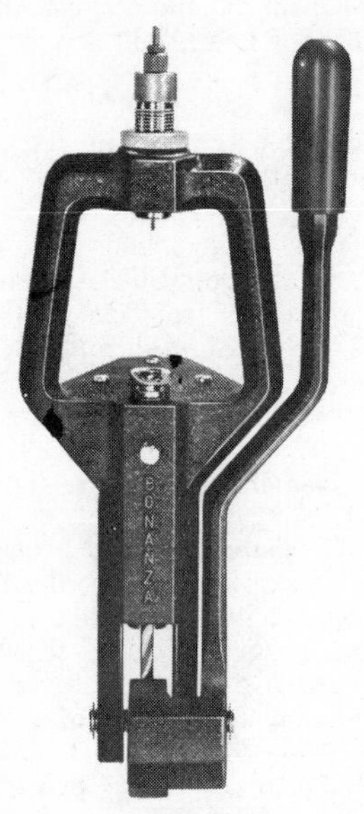

Bonanza 68

tors. This is particularly true of dies in calibers that would normally have to be special-ordered from the factory. That takes months, while Blackhawk may have the desired caliber in stock.

The *Blackhawk Bugle* is a periodical listing of dies available, along with other useful information. A subscription costs $2.75, and it'll be useful to any handloader.

Bonanza Sports Co. got off to a good start in handloading two years ago. Nearly all of the initial line was covered in GD-23, but new developments have taken place.

Bonanza 68 is the name of their new, medium-price loading press. It is a heavy casting of what is sometimes called "machine iron"—because of its use in massive machine-tool bases. Of O-type design, it sits vertically on the bench, which we prefer to rearward cant so common among earlier tools. The work opening narrows toward the top, formed by two heavy, hexagonal uprights. Opening is 3¾″ wide, 4″ high and 3″ wide at top, providing plenty of hand room. The vertical ram accepts standard detachable shellholder heads. Heads supplied with the tool have a beveled front edge to ease insertion of cases.

The priming system of this tool is similar in principle to that of the Co-Ax, but different mechanically. A hardened pin is inserted into the frame and passes through an elongated hole in the ram, permitting about ½″ vertical ram travel. A separate loose priming punch unit is then dropped into the central hole in the ram and the ram raised to the limit of its short stroke. A primer is placed in the guide sleeve of the punch; a case slipped into the shell holder. Lowering the ram now presses the case over the primer, because the punch unit is resting solidly on the pin first mentioned. Both pin and priming punch must be removed for resizing and bullet seating. Priming punches are easily changed without tools.

The handle is cast integrally with the link and is offset to the right, fitted with a large, smooth plastic grip. It is balanced so as to remain at rest in either up or down position —no more skinned knees. The price seems good at $31.55 with shell holder and universal type priming device.

A new cartridge case preparation kit includes Bonanza's Cricket, Case Graphiter, Case Lubricating Pad with a bottle of Case Sizing Lube conveniently packaged for $6.95.

Eagle Reloading Products makes the Cobra press, now at $39.90. A new turret type press is in the works to be released later this year, but we've not yet seen a sample. Eagle's One-Stroke bullet puller, priced at $9.00, continues to be the most convenient on the market.

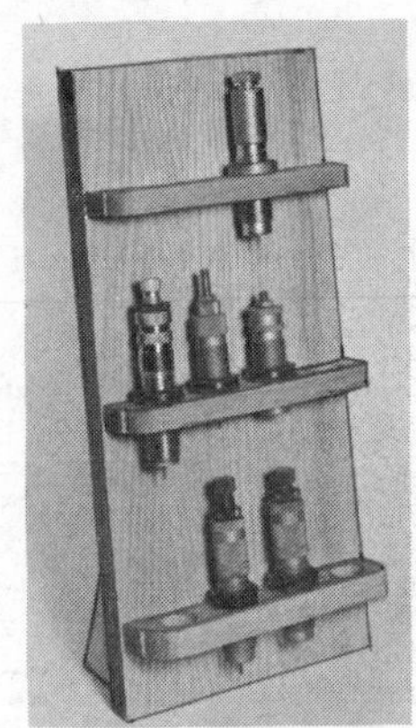

Cole's Acku-Rite Products offers a handsome rack to hold 12 dies. Made of ¾″ solid oak throughout, the dies fit into three tiers of four each. Oak is heavy wood, the weight stabilizes this upright rack with or without dies. The finish is beautiful and natural. Bill Cole tells us that no stain or filler is used to produce the satin-smooth sealed surface. Here is an attractive, serviceable piece of furniture for the reloading bench at $3.95 plus postage.

Forster-Appelt, makers of an extensive line of precision products for the handloader, the shooter in general and the gunsmith, have just announced a line of headspace gauges for *rimmed* cartridges, each with a pilot for easy use. Attractively priced at $4.50 each, these will certainly fill a long-felt want—as far as I know, such gauges have not been generally available previously. Write for the F-A catalog—it's free.

Fall Sales Co. is a new organization in the handloading game, though its products aren't entirely new. Fall has taken over the existing small line formerly sold as "Precision" and has plans for considerable expansion.

Fall Sales PR-7

At present a single press, the PR-7, is offered at $24.95. It is of general C-type configuration with an integrally-cast reinforcing bar closing the "C." This makes it, in effect, an O-type. The entire press is vertical when mounted, eliminating case lean, and the ram accepts standard detachable shell holder heads. A universal-type primer arm is standard; die hole is ⅞x14; power is applied on the downstroke and linkage is conventional. Provision is made for installation of standard auto-priming devices.

Fall Precision Reloader dies and shell holder heads are also offered in about 70 popular calibers. Dies are conventional in design; 3-unit sets for straight cases; 2-unit for bottle necks. Finish is good inside and out; external finish is dull grey from heat-treat, not blued or plated; single, knurled, setscrew-equipped lock rings are used. Price is $10.50 per set, shell holder $2.

Both press and dies performed well for us in 357 Magnum caliber and represent good, sound—though not unusual—equipment well worth the price.

Two additional items now in development stages are a primer remanufacturing kit and a swaging tool that will stamp and form bullet jackets. It will be interesting to see what these tools look like. Those processes have always been considered beyond home-shop capabilities.

Frank A. Hemsted "Hemp," as he prefers to be called, has been making his excellent bullet-swaging dies for a good many years in a wide variety of calibers, as mentioned last year in these pages. With 17-caliber popularity increasing, he tells us he will now

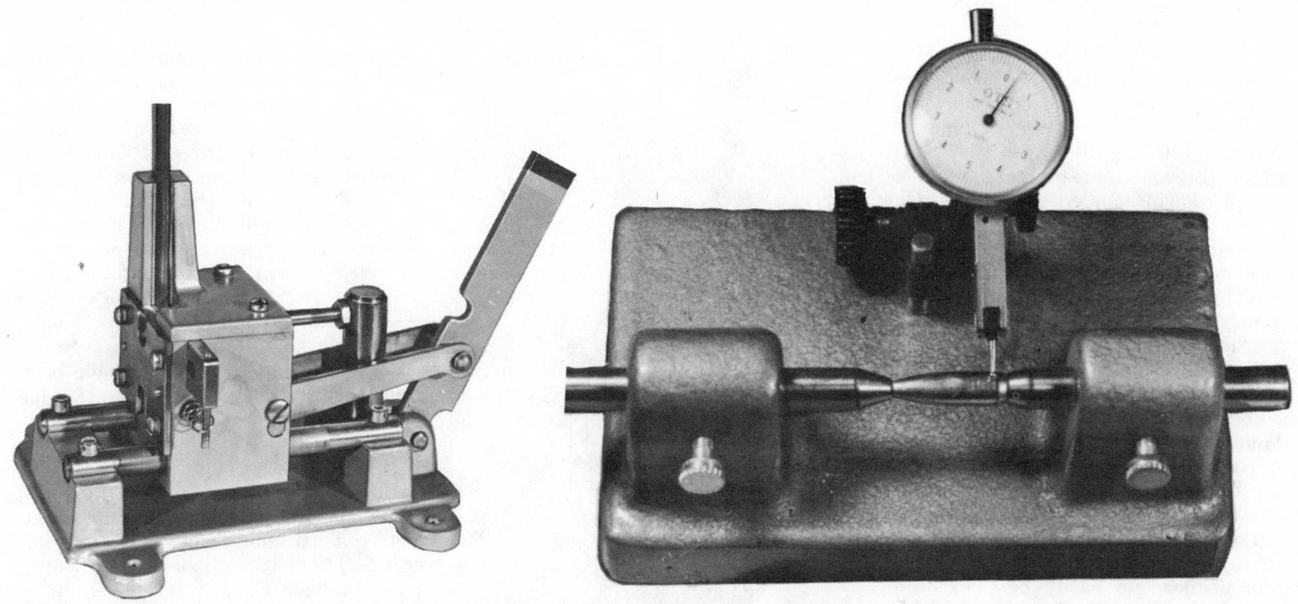

Gun Clinic priming tool

Hart Bullet Spinner

supply complete die sets in that caliber. I've also heard that he's made a set or two in 14- and 20-caliber on special order. Frankly, Hemp is a good man to go to for special bullets. He can—and will, time permitting—make dies to turn out about any bullet you need. Workmanship is excellent, but don't expect overnight service on off-beat jobs. They take time.

Bob Hart, best known for his top accuracy achievements at the bench—and for his sleeved action—now offers a bullet spinner that will reveal bullet runout—flat base or boat-tail—of as little at .0001". Covering calibers from 22 to 30, this new tool has a heavy base of fine-grained cast iron, and is delivered complete with a precision-quality dial indicator for $52.95. A sturdy walnut box, to transport and protect the instrument, is available at $7 extra.

Hart also supplies cleaning rod guides—for most bolt action centerfire rifles and calibers — that effectively protects the rifle's bore and throat from damage. Cost, $5.25, and a must item if you want to preserve your rifle's top condition.

Herter's Inc. For many years handloaders have been accustomed to ordering components and tools from Herter's by mail. Since federal law now makes that impossible, Herter's is now setting up a nationwide dealer organization. At least one dealer will be appointed in each state. That dealer, then, will be able to supply the Herter line by mail within that state, as well as through regular across-the-counter sales. This applies, incidentally, to all the other Herter lines—guns, shooting accessories, etc.

The Gun Clinic The Model 46 Precision Priming Tool is not new, but is efficient and unusual in its construction. A sliding block contains all moving parts, the vertical primer magazine, and the plate-type shell holder. This block is moved fore and aft on two guide rods by a vertical handle. A post, mounted on the base, carries the primer seating punch which passes through the sliding block. The tool is sturdily built and may be operated very rapidly. It features a double shell holder—a square place notched on opposite sides to fit different calibers. The M46 must be screwed or clamped to your bench for proper operation. We've used this tool for years and find it quite good. Primers are easily "felt" into pockets, and seating depth and pressure can be easily controlled by punch adjustment. Price is $28.50.

Hollywood Gun Shop A new top plate now available for Hollywood turret presses. It carries three ⅞x14 and five 1½" die holes—the latter for special dies like the shotshell re-forming die to size plastic cases inside and out to original specs at $37.50. The new plate will fit most older Hollywood turret presses and is a desirable replacement because it provides more positive indexing and alignment.

The big Hollywood 12-hole turret press, made with an alloy frame, was phased out some years ago. Now, I've learned, an all-steel model of this massive and excellent tool may be made available; price unknown at this time, but probably around $225 stripped. Weight will be 100 lbs.!

I was fortunate enough to get one of the older 12-hole tools some 10-12 years ago, and I use it constantly. It is mounted so I can work with it standing up.

The Hollywood "Automatic" tool—shotshell or metallic—and able to produce 1800 shells an hour, now does everything by automation — primer, powder, cases and shot or bullets are fed to the turret automatically. $995 is the price complete, and older "Automatics" may be updated by buying one or more of the new accessories. Write for their latest folder and price list. (J.T.A.)

The Hutton Rifle Ranch has two load tables for the asking. One shows 50,000 psi loads for a variety of wildcats based on the 284 case, the other a like listing for 348 wildcats. All loads were worked up using the Powley Computer and PSI Calculator, were then tested via chronograph and pressure gauges for verification. I find the 6mm/284 and 25/284 data especially interesting.

Kenru Reloading Service, long known among bench rest shooters for top quality bullets and jackets, is succumbing to the effects of the G.C.A. of 1968. H.K. Hayward, operator of Kenru, states that the new restrictions make it impossible for him to continue the business primarily conducted by mail with individuals all over the country. That's impossible under the new law.

Lachmiller Engineering Co., like many other loading tool firms, has been forced to raise its prices, though the line remains the same. Representative new prices are $13.50 now for die sets and $38.25 for the 707 Olympian press and die set kit. Production has been increased at Lachmiller to provide faster delivery.

Jim Bell, bossman at LEC, has just told us that he has a couple of new items—one is a cast iron lead pot, capacity 10 lbs.; with both a lip and an "ear" opposite to facilitate pouring the melt into ingot moulds. $2.50 only.

The other tool is a Primer Pocket Swage set, this one for such small-primer cases as the 30 Ml Carbine, 223 and 9mm Luger. Usable in any standard press with ⅞"-14 threading and 13-16" ram, the cost is $6.95.

Write for the new 1969 LEC catalog—it's free.

Lee Engineering manages to introduce a new, useful, low cost item about every year. For '69, it's their Priming Tool; no fancy name. A simple, palm-size tool, into the top of which screws a detachable shell holder. A spring-loaded punch passes through the holder to seat the primer. A thumb lever is pivoted to the other end, and moves the punch through a cast link. The spring retracts the punch and holds the lever in its open position.

In use, drop a primer (anvil up) in the hole in the shell holder, insert a decapped case, then press the lever. That seats the primer. Seating depth and/or pressure can be varied by the depth to which the shell holder is screwed into the tool body. This all works nicely and doesn't require any great amount of pressure on the lever. The primer can easily be "felt" into its seat. Price is $2.45, including .175" and .210" primer punches, plus $1.50 for your preferred caliber shell holder.

Biggest new Lee item is the Target Model version of the well-known Lee Loader. While of the same general type and operation as the latter, it contains the unusual Lee chamfering tool; primer pocket cleaner; case trimmer; neck reamer; a micrometer-adjustable bullet seater, plus the priming tool already mentioned. The various components of the set are available separately and may, to varying degrees, be used with existing loaders. Of particular interest is the simple chamfering-deburring tool which consists of a slotted steel cone, squashed slightly oval so the slot forms cutting edges. The case trimmer is equally simple, but is made in two parts; the cutter proper fits on the decapping stem and automatically reduces the case to its proper length.

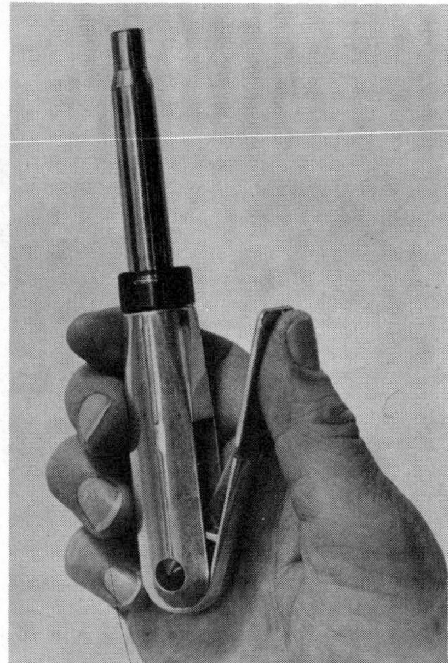

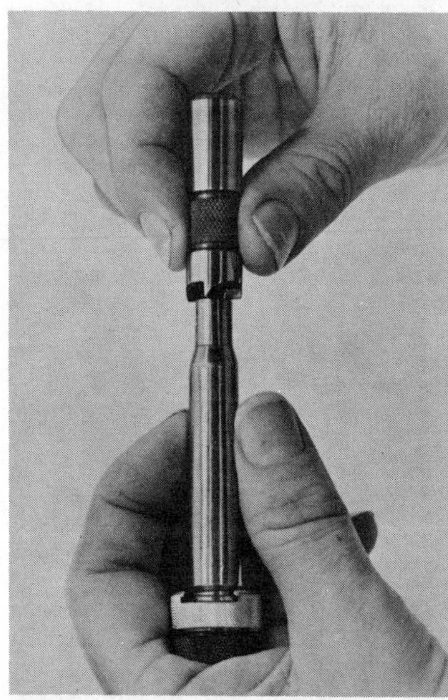

Normington & Co. makes Jim's Powder Baffles which fit into most powder or shot measures. Another form (with a threaded plastic sleeve) fits between the poly-bottle hopper and shotshell press. These are nicely made of aluminum and are said to maintain a constant height powder column (about 1") on the measuring chamber. In most powder measures accuracy of 1/5-gr. can be expected no matter how full the hopper is. Mention the measure you have and for $1.50 you'll get an appropriate baffle in a blister pack, with instructions.

Jim Normington told us of an experiment some readers may like to try. An opened 25-lb. bag of shot was set into the shot tube of a Texan II. Because of the excess weight, the spring-loaded bushing plate would not return to battery. After a baffle was installed, the same bag of shot was again put into the hopper and the press functioned perfectly. The baffles might not help with large-sized shot (bridging) but with small shot and powder your measure operates like it was just greased.

Pacific Gun Sight Company's all-new and very extensive line was covered in detail in these pages in GD-23 last year. Unfortunately, production didn't get under way as quickly as planned. It has been only in the past few months that the complete line has become available in quantity and without delay. A complete new plant is now in operation, turning out thousands of Pacific items. If you've been waiting for something from Pacific, that wait should be over.

Even so, some new items have been added, others improved, and some prices changed. Verelite wads have dropped in price to $10.50 per M. "Durachrome" dies in rifle and pistol calibers are plated externally with hard chrome, and file-type case forming and trimming dies are now offered. The carbide-insert type 3-unit pistol caliber die set has gone up to $28.50, the carbide resizing die to $19.50. Die sets are packed in a convenient plastic, compartmented storage box.

The Deluxe powder measure is now supplied with a ⅞x14 threaded body which screws into a loading press, or into a bench bracket. A stand is supplied with the measure and must be bolted or clamped to the bench in order to function.

Of particular interest to shooters using the older Canadian 12-gauge cases is a cap conversion kit for the DL-155 loader, priced at $4.95. It allows punching out the fired cap without disturbing the battery cup in the case. A new cap is then seated, thus priming the case. Those cases whose primers are, in effect, crimped in place cannot be conveniently primed any other way. Standard cases may also be processed with this kit, for a substantial saving, caps being considerably less costly than complete battery cup primers.

Pacific's new *Rifle & Pistol Cartridge Handloading Manual* made it off the press at the end of '68. This long-awaited volume is quite extensive in its coverage of the subject. It may not contain as much loading data as some other books, but it has more than enough for all popular wildcat and standard cartridges to suit a reasonable person. The data is clearly presented and, generally speaking, contains a moderate and max load for each *suitable* bullet/powder combination in each caliber. I'll wager that there is no reasonable requirement that can't be met by this data.

Of special interest is the detailed, well-illustrated coverage given of the metallic cartridge as a whole, and of each of its components. This is one manual that contains a great deal of "why," as well as "how" information. Load development is set forth clearly, as are all reloading operations.

Naturally this $3.50 book promotes Pacific products, but we consider that a virtue, rather than a fault.

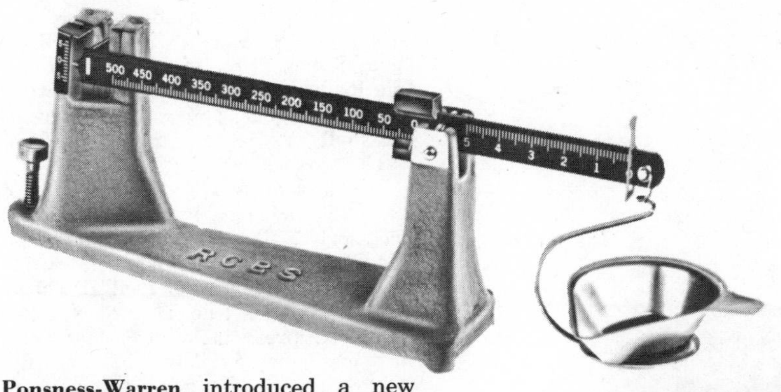

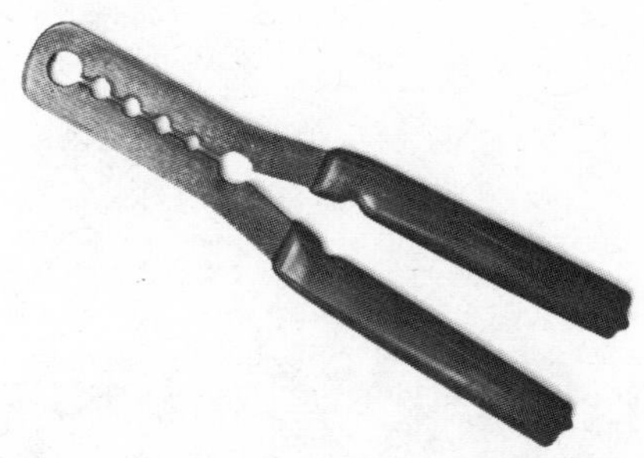

Ponsness-Warren introduced a new sizing chamber for use on their Duo-Matic press only. This die re-forms the Wanda all plastic shotshells to original dimensions making insertion of wads as easy as when cases were new. Price $6.

RCBS: Apparently business at RCBS has been so good there wasn't enough time to develop and introduce any excitingly new products. One recent release is a $19.95 powder and bullet scale. For several years RCBS has attempted to develop an advanced form of scale especially adapted to the handloaders' needs. We've seen several prototypes, even commented on them here, but none made the grade with Fred Huntington. The new 505-grain capacity scale is of fairly conventional beam balance design, has heavy magnetic damping and is typical of RCBS quality. It rounds out the RCBS line.

Also new is an RCBS-green molded-plastic 3-compartment die storage box. There are similar die boxes on the market but they don't fit all makes of dies, nor will they accept dies with lock rings at extremes of adjustment. The RCBS box will, and that makes it mighty handy. Available at $1.00 each, or get one free when you buy a set of RCBS dies.

The well known A-2 loading press has been improved and the new model is the A-3. It uses the basic frame and linkage design of the A-2. The die hole is now fitted with a 1½″ bushing threaded ⅞x14 for standard dies. It may be removed to allow use of large diameter dies or special tools. The ram accepts standard shell holder heads, but is stepped and beveled directly below the holder for more convenient insertion and removal of cases. A more substantial mounting bracket is supplied and the press may be bolted to it either canted or vertically. This appears to be a most worthy successor to the A-2. Price is $73.50, complete with one shell holder head and universal primer arm.

Redding-Hunter has no new items to offer, however, the Model No. 16 shotshell loader is now available in 28 and 410 gauge at $62—as opposed to $58 in the other gauges. Small gauge conversion kits are $22, and a new self-indexing crimp die is $4.50. Other R-H item prices have increased slightly from last year.

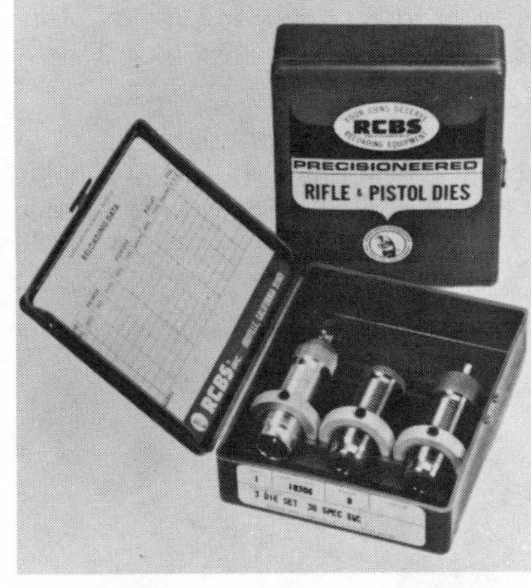

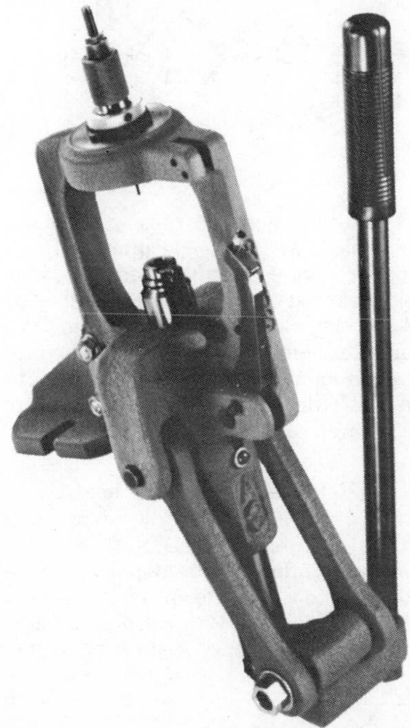

SAECO We ran into Bob Modisette, Jr., owner of SAECO, at the NRA meeting in Washington. Bob has big new plans for SAECO, a firm that hasn't been very active in recent years. Bob explained that he'd been tied up in aircraft products, and that he'd soft-pedalled his reloading tools because of his NRA work.

Now SAECO—famous for top quality in their loading tools, bullet moulds, electric lead pots and a superb bullet lubricator—will enter the field again in a big way.

He'll have a new plant at Carpinteria, California (P.O. Box 778) and the firm will be called SAECO Reloading Inc. In addition to his older products, Bob said several new items are in the mill, one being a truly straight-line seating die for handgun bullets, one that won't permit canting or lead-shaving. A long-needed product.

SAS Ted Smith now offers a new bullet puller, a simple spring-steel block with holes for 6.5, 7 and 8mm, plus 30 caliber. Run a loaded round up through your press die hole; drop correct hole over the bullet; squeeze tool handles; reverse press handle movement pulls the case off the bullet. $5.95, other sizes to order.

Ted's Mity-Mite bullet swaging press is now $225! I don't think Ted really wants to sell 'em.

Schulz & Korfmann The Alzey reloading tool is unusual in that it is of current German manufacture and is among the very few such items produced in Europe. It is a simple arbor press type design, reminiscent of some U.S. designs of the 1920s and 30s. It performs the basic functions of reloading in such calibers as 9mm Parabellum and 38 Special. Also supplied is a one-piece mold for casting cores. Their hollow-base half-jackets and the cast cores are then swaged to final form in a very basic punch and die set.

It doesn't seem likely this tool will be made available here, the price in Germany of nearly $50 being far above that of comparable domestic items.

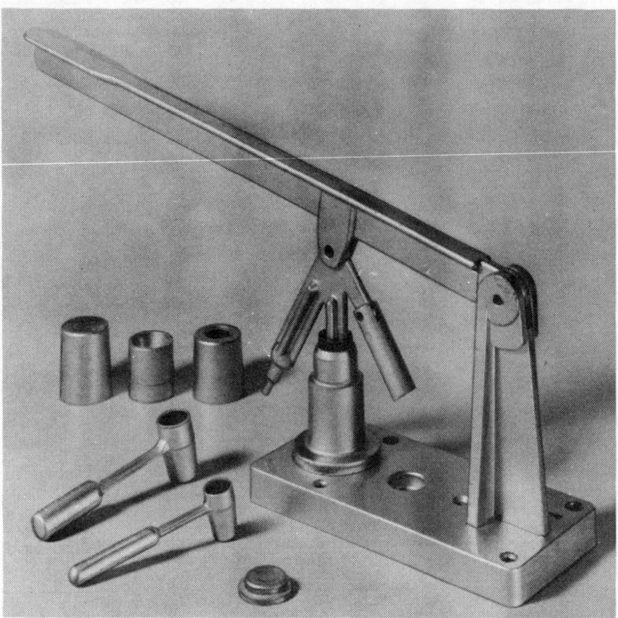

Safari Shotshell loader

Swanson Co., Inc. The Safari 12-gauge shotshell loader is an unusual simple tool that produces entirely satisfactory results with both paper and plastic cases. It is complete with all dies and powder-shot dippers at $19.95.

A long handle is pivoted to an upright on the flat base. Attached to the handle is a multiple punch with separate legs for decapping, repriming, and crimping. After de- and repriming, a sizing die is forced over the case by the handle; powder, wads and shot are inserted by hand; then a crimping head is placed over the die and the crimp is formed by means of the handle and appropriate punch. The die is then lifted and rotated slightly to stand on 3 pegs, and the loaded shell is ejected by the crimping punch. Operation is simple and easy, and not as slow as it sounds.

Sport Ammo Corp. Everything these days must be mini to be good, and for the shotgunner Mini-Skeet (or trap if you prefer) may be the answer to low-cost practice or training. Fired from your shotgun and producing virtually no recoil and a low noise level, Mini-Shells of cast metal alloy are reloadable indefinitely at about 1½¢ per shot. Available in 12, 16 or 20 gauge, all have an inside diameter of .410"—you use 410 shotshell wads. A box of 10 are $3.95.

Mini-Kit is a complete reloading set-up for these shells and includes a small arbor press, powder/shot dipper, wad cutter and 5 Mini-Shells. Only No. 209 primers are needed to break Mini-Birds with the 50-gr. shot charge, however loading dope with powder is supplied for moderate loads useful for shooting pests or frogs. Mini-Kit sells for $14.95 and only a set of correct size Mini-Shells are necessary to change gauge.

Mini-Trap is a target launcher that handles Crosman-type plastic or Moskeet (clay) birds. $29.95 delivers one, ready to throw Mini-birds that are said to simulate the regulation size clays in appearance and flight. Mini-Birds are packed 25 per box at $3.95 and are reusable.

All these goodies are put into one package—the Mini-Target System at $49.95 — containing the Mini-Kit, 10 extra Mini-Shells, 25 Mini-Birds and the Mini-Trap, a saving of some $4.

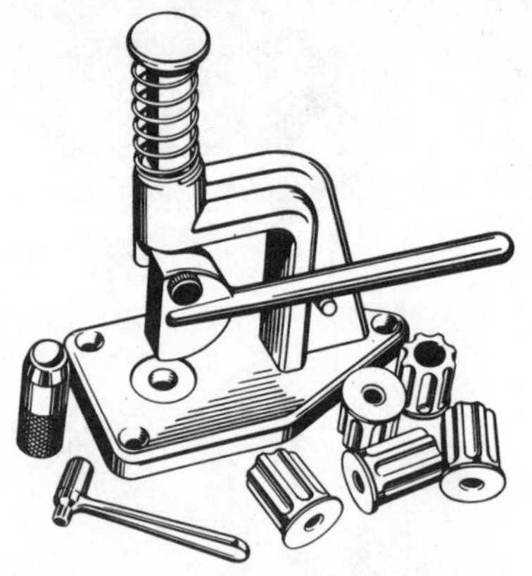

Sport Ammo Mini-Kit

TNT bullet swaging dies are made and sold by the designer, Reed Thacker. They are intended for making jacketed bullets and sell for $67.50. Thacker operates under the name Independent Gun & Machine Shop, and also handles a complete line of rifle bullet jackets, calibers 22 through 308.

Texan Reloaders Inc. has been with us for quite a number of years now, and its progressive MII virtually became a standard large-capacity loader. That tool has been continuously improved and today represents an unusually fine balance of quality, durability, capacity, convenience, as the MIIA at $249.50. Many a Skeet shooter has three or four of these fine loaders, each permanently set up for a different gauge. Three other shotshell tools are available from $48.50 to $89.50.

Texan also produces a variety of metallic cartridge loading tools and accessories. Top of the line is the Model 101-T-II, a 7-station turret press with auto primer feed at $99.50. Newest in the line is the No. 256 Double-C press introduced last year, but just now available in quantity. At first glance it appears to be a conventional C-press, but a close look discloses *two* thick, vertical reinforcing ribs running up the back of the "C," making for a very rigid channel section. Theoretically it is the stiffest, most rigid, C-press available. According to the designers, it possesses as much rigidity and freedom from load-induced distortion as the average O-type. without the inconvenience inherent in that design. The handle and link are cast in one piece, bent to the right for convenience. Price is $29.50 with ram and universal primer arm. Shell holder head is $2.50.

Texan has finally begun using its unusual new die production method. Rough-drilled blanks are *bored* to precise cavity shape and dimensions. In this process a boring tool is controlled by cams and programming to cut the die cavity to shape and size, eliminating the use of shaped reamers. In theory, at least, this allows greater die-to-die uniformity than is possible with reamers. The reamer must cut each cavity ever so slightly smaller than the last, until, finally it will no longer produce a hole large enough. In addition, boring is reported to permit easier control of surface finish quality in the cavity. These new Micro-Bore dies look very good and are priced at $13.50 with double, hexagonal lock nuts.

Texan also offers a new plastic powder funnel in two sizes at 75¢, and a new and improved funnel holder which may be screwed to Texan and several other powder scales at $1.25.

Texan shotshell tools now use a single, standard wad guide for all gauges. An interchangeable plastic spring-finger bushing is placed in the guide for each different gauge. The basic unit price is $3.50, additional bushings $1.00 each. Model of press must be specified when ordering, as three units are available to modify older presses.

Texan wad guide

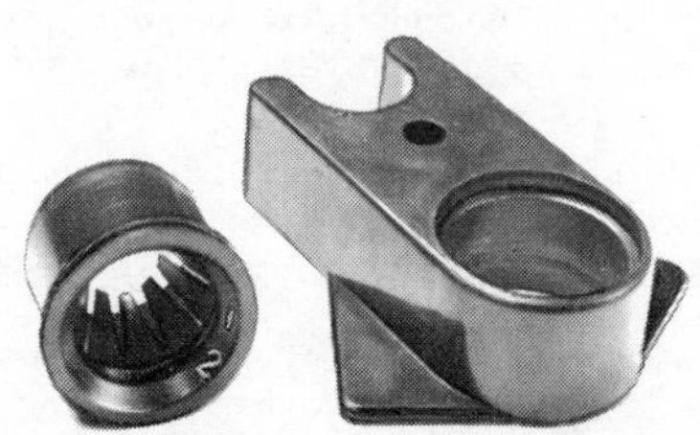

Part 2—Components

Bullets, Cases, Powders, Primers, Shot, Wads, etc.

HANDLOADERS ARE generally careful people. However, after reading *Properties and Storage of Smokeless Powders,* a SAAMI brochure, my opinion has changed a bit. It is doubtful that we are all as safety-minded as we think!

Do you know that the powder storage cabinet should be of insulated material with *weak,* that's right weak walls, seams and joints, and not be closely confined? That's what SAAMI says, and after some thought you'll understand the logic. Also, it is not safe to store powder in the same cabinet with solvents, flammable gases or other highly combustible material—like primers, perhaps?

Write SAAMI at 420 Lexington Ave., New York, N.Y. 10017, for the brochure. After reading it through, you'll have to agree that their recommendations are sound.

Alcan has lots of new items coming up, though some can't be revealed at this time. We do know, though, that lots of expansion and behind-the-doors work has been going on at the plant.

The new Unisleeve plastic one-piece wad column is now available in A height for R-P plastic shells, in B height for AA, Alcan, and Federal cases. Price is $12.30 per 1000. Of special interest in this area is the new Alcan process for lubricating plastic wads, giving smoother passage through the bore. Later this year all Alcan wads will be so-treated, a process that produces a smoky grey color, rather than the usual white.

Alcan plastic empty shotshells are now available in both low- and high-brass styles. Twelve-gauge is $5.67 and $7.41; 16-gauge $4.67 and $7.17; 20-gauge $4.59 and $7.08 per hundred respectively.

The 45 Colt blank, of brass-colored plastic, is now loaded in black and smokeless powder versions, both with a compressed granulated cork closing wad which disintegrates on firing.

Of big interest to some handloaders are the non-corrosive European Berdan primers regularly supplied by Alcan. Sizes normally available are: 217B (6.5mm, 7mm, 8mm Mauser, etc.); 250B (303 British); ERB (the long German combination gun cartridges such as the 9.3x72R); and 645B (for Fiocchi brass shotshell cases. Loading with Berdan primers isn't all that difficult—get one of the Lachmiller Berdan decappers; fresh primers can be seated with an ordinary tool.

Due later this year is a low-priced, 200 page reloading manual, and a magnum-type large rifle primer for handloaders.

DuPont's current issue of their *Handloader's Guide to Powders for 1968-69* is very much worth having. Up to 24 pages, 10 more than the previous issue, there's a tremendous amount of valuable data in the new booklet, especially for shotshell stuffers — for whom some 14 pages are devoted. 4 pages cover centerfire metallics, but all popular calibers are shown, and one page gives handgun loads. Write for your copy.

Federal Cartridge Corp. has introduced an important new item for the hitherto-ignored 410 shotshell reloader. Until now, the 410 lover was forced to use old-style wad columns and to do without shot protection, unless he wanted to cut his own wrappers.

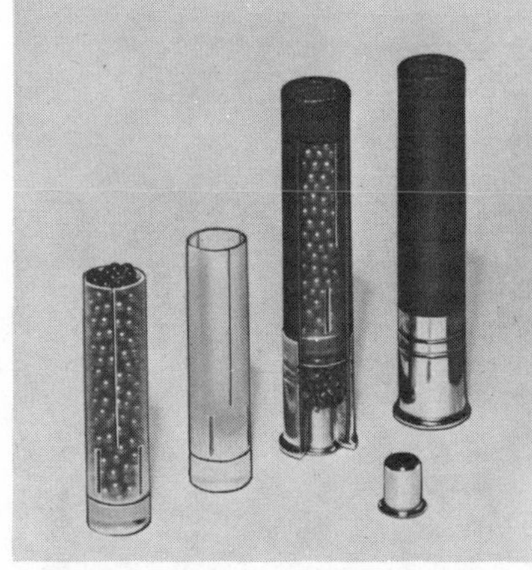

Federal 410 components and shell

Federal has eliminated this with a polyethelene, single-unit wad column/shot cup unit. White in color, this wad is of conventional split-cup design, and made for use in 2½-inch shells with the standard 2½-dram, ½-ounce Skeet load. A most welcome addition to our shotshell components at $11.80 per 1000.

This new wad cannot be seated properly with many existing 410 loading tools, but most tool makers are now making replacement seating punches to handle it. They should be available by the time you read this.

Companion to this wad is a plastic 2½-inch 410 shell, available empty or loaded. It replaces the paper 410 Skeet load in the Federal line, other 410s continuing in paper cases. This case requires a special Federal 410 primer, these at $14.95 per 1000.

A new Triple-Plus plastic wad column is being used in Federal 12-, 16-, and 20-gauge game loads for '69. It consists of a deep cup-type over-powder wad from which a mushroom-shaped compression post protrudes. The plastic shot cup seats on this post—upon firing the post collapses, reducing the acceleration load on the shot charge. Later, this wad column will be supplied in magnum loads.

The shot cup used in the Triple-Plus column will be offered to handloaders this year. Three 12-gauge sizes will hold 1 oz., 1¼ oz., and 1½ oz. of shot. Single 16- and 20-gauge sizes hold 1 oz. and ⅞ oz. respectively. Cups are color-coded for easy identification.

G.J. Godwin supplies a wide variety of cast lead bullets, lubricated and sized, ready to load. Most popular diameters and weights are available at prices ranging from $1.85 to $2.55 per hundred. All are made from a relatively hard lead/tin/antimony alloy. A softer alloy may be specified on orders of 500 or more. Godwin will tool up for any Lyman bullet if you buy 2000 or more. These bullets look good, are cleanly cast and sized, and grooves are well filled with an Alox-type lubricant.

Green Bay Bullets, well-known suppliers of an excellent line of cast, lubed and sized bullets—rifle and handgun —now offer a size-die and bullet swage lube that makes these chores easier and smoother. Eze-Size is only 60¢ a bottle, and it does work well.

B.E. Hodgdon, Inc. now has an Alox Bullet Lube, the same mixture of beeswax and Alox 2138F that the *American Rifleman* recommended so highly. It's 75¢ per hollow stick.

Hodgdon Case Cleaner is a mild acidic solution that you dilute with water for soaking or tumbling dirty cases. Said to clean cases bright and shiny, without etching them, a 4-oz. poly bottle costs $1.50.

Another item we've received here for testing is Tect-Her, a protective device designed for women. The purse-sized flip-top poly bottle contains 1¼ oz. of non-lethal chemicals —supposedly sufficient to discourage "attackers, molesters, muggers and purse snatchers." Price, $3.95.

Data Book #21 will be published this fall. According to Bob Hodgdon, a lot more loading dope, including the Weatherby calibers, will be covered in a book about the same size and price as No. 20—a real buy these days at $1.50.

Hornady Mfg. Co. Joyce Hornady doesn't introduce a new product as often as some people. When he does, it has normally been tested and researched to an unusual degree. Consequently, the two new bullets announced during the last twelve months are expected to perform very well, indeed.

First came the 25-gr. 17-cal. hollow-point. In the hands of various shooters, this scribe included, this bullet has produced excellent varmint accuracy at velocities as high as 4200 fps. At those velocities it performs well in clean, smooth barrels but, according to Hornady, may blow up or become erratic in tubes not so smooth or, perhaps somewhat fouled. These ultra-small calibers are highly susceptible to fouling. In any event, these were the first *production* 17-cal. bullets available—and they perform very well. As this is written, a second production lot, these with a bit heavier jackets, is underway — the first having sold out immediately — so you'll be able to get what you want at $4.20 per hundred.

Introduced at the NSGA show was a new 158-gr. .357" diameter cannelured, jacketed soft-point bullet for use in 38 Special and 357 Magnum calibers. The same bullet is also offered containing a cavity in the exposed lead soft point. This bullet, in both forms, is designed to produce good expansion at reasonable handgun velocities. The hollow-point will, of course, expand to the greatest degree, all other factors being equal. Shape is conventional round-nose, with jacket coming forward well into the ogive. They're $4 a hundred in either form.

Of special interest to those who'd like to know just how sharp (or dull) their handloading knowledge might be, is the Hornady Reloading/Shooting Test. It consists of 43 questions requiring 55 answers, for a total possible score of 110 points. A score of 62-70 is considered fair, 52 minimum passing. A passing score qualifies you for a Hornady brassard when the completed test is mailed in. Many handloaders could benefit from taking this test.

Hornady's new bullet board, containing one of each bullet in the line, makes an excellent den or shop wall display. Frame in weathered wood, the background is reproduced with an early United States map. Price is $11.50.

Price on all bullets (except 30-cal. 110-gr. RN) is up about 5% as of March 1st. Crimp-on gas checks have gone up about 30%.

KTW bullets are a newly-developed item intended purely for police use. They are a unique combination of gilding metal jacket, Kennertium (tungsten alloy, 50% denser than lead) core, and Teflon. The very hard core is coated with Teflon to improve penetration, the entire unit is then encased in a conventional short jacket. Since the hard core cannot upset or be engraved by the rifling, the soft gilding metal jacket serves to seal the bore and impart spin to the bullet. Various people who have tested them report metal penetration with the 200-grain KTW 38 Special bullet far in excess of that produced by commerical armor piercing loads. This performance is attained at 700 fps and 14,000 psi chamber pressure.

At present, loaded ammo is available in 38 Special, 357 Mag., 9mm Parabellum and 350 Rem. Mag. The price is high—$4.00 per box of six rounds in 38 Special. Cartridge collectors may obtain inert rounds at $1.00 each from the manufacturer, Dr. P.J. Kopsch, 710 Foster Park Rd., Lorain, Ohio 44053.

Leon's Reloading Service now offers Speedy Bullets, a new line of lighter weight ¾ (or is it ⅞ths?) jackets that show impressive velocity figures—and expansion to match. Leon (and Jim Horton, demon pistolero) recommend these Speedy Bullets be loaded by the advanced handloader only, for max velocity is required to get max shooting power.

These Speedys—made in 9mm/110-gr., 357-38/112-, 120-, 130-gr. and 44/210-, 240-gr.—will positively not lead the barrel, and the cores are guaranteed 100% pure soft lead for best expansion.

These precision-made bullets are at their best with such loads as 10.5 Unique/110-gr. Speedy JHP for 1830 fps in the 357 Magnum, or 7.5 Unique/120-gr. Speedy JHP in the 38 Spl. case for 1375 fps or so. These are recent Hercules-listed loads, and pretty impressive, yes?

In our own tests with the Speedy 120-gr. 38 Spl., shot in a Colt OMT, I couldn't get beyond 7.1 grains, but the barrel on that Colt is on the tight side.

Two-hand rest groups ran pretty good, I thought—at least for me—2¼"-3" at 25 yards. Expansion in soft black dirt was excellent, recovered slugs going almost the size of 2-bit pieces. These Speedys perform.

9mm, 38 Special and 357 KTW

112 gr. J. H. P.	120 gr. J. H. P.	120 gr. J. S. P.
$4.60	$4.60	$4.40

Some 38-357 Speedy bullets

Lyman Gun Sight Co. has not introduced any new tools, however, a .445" Minie bullet mould is now available for use in the Hopkins & Allen muzzle-loading rifles. Of typical Minie, hollow-base form, this bullet weighs 249 grains and should be much superior to round balls for hunting. Blocks only cost $7.50, handles $3.50 extra. This mould will also be available from Numrich Arms.

John S. Miller, operating SWM Bullets, offers a line of 17-cal. bullets in 22- to 26-gr. weights, these in hollow-point form—and seemingly very well made. Regrettably, the samples were received in January, and there's been no chance to try them out, the weather being what it is. SWM 17s are $5 per hundred, and we'll report on their performance later.

Miller Trading Co. offers numerous cast bullets for rifles and handguns, sized and lubed, or not, as you like. All bullets are shipped in wood boxes, and they're all sent out prepaid and insured too. Their list is yours for a post card.

Norma-Precision continues to make inroads into the market with new handloading products. Since the last GD, three new double-base propellant powders have been announced and are now available.

N2010 is a shotshell powder designed for light and standard 12-bore loads, and is apparently aimed at Skeet and trap shooters. Reputed to produce lower flame temperatures than competitive domestic powders, its disc-type granules flow freely through volumetric measures. We can vouch for the latter and for its general good performance in standard Skeet loads. Offered in both 8-oz. cans and 8-lb. kegs.

N2020 is generally similar to N-2010 but slower burning and, therefore, intended for magnum-type and heavy hunting loads with relatively large shot charges. This one is offered in 10-oz. cans and 8-lb. kegs.

N1010 is a pistol powder of the same basic general characteristics as above. It is intended for light-to-medium loads, being particularly suitable to 38 Special target loads, and hence it's considered fast-burning. Packaged in 9-oz. cans and 8-lb. drums.

Another new Norma powder, N1020, intended for high-velocity, magnum-type pistol and revolver loads may be available as you read this, but we have no samples yet.

Norma Boxer primers (many people use the term, anvil-type today) are currently in good supply in all standard U.S. sizes. They carry the Superflash label and are packed in the usual 100-piece trayed boxes. Prices are competitive.

We've used Superflash primers for some months now in both rifle and pistol loading. No misfires or other ignition difficulties have been encountered and accuracy has been excellent. Loads ranged from light 38 wadcutters through hot 357 Magnum and 222 Remington and 264 Magnum. Ignition was fine with the slowest powders in the latter caliber. Dimensional control seems excellent and all primers seated smoothly with the proper amount of pressure in standard commercial cases.

Some handloaders have the idea that these primers are of the magnum type. This isn't so. According to Evan Sheldon of Norma-Precision, Superflash primers have "a little more zip than standard, but are definitely not in the magnum class."

Omark-CCI There isn't much new one can come up with in primers, aside from internal product improvement. However, CCI primers do *look* new—they are now in colorful packages designed to help avoid confusion. In all sizes, green boxes contain standard primers, red boxes contain the magnum type.

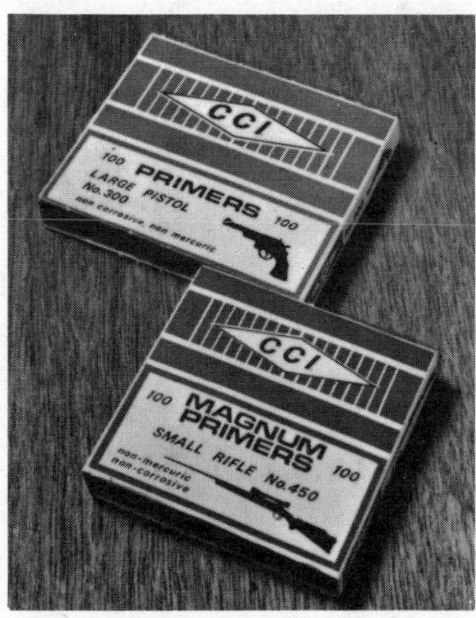

During the past year Omark-CCI introduced a new 22 caliber CB cap as an extension of its rimfire line. Selling for 77¢ per box of 50, they use an unplated lead 22 Short bullet and —contrary to old CB practice—contain a reduced charge of powder which produces a uniform 650 fps. This load gives better accuracy than early CBs and is unusually quiet in rifle-length barrels. They're ideal for informal indoor shooting.

Nosler Bullet Company John Nosler has sold his bullet-making operation to an equally high quality house —Leupold & Stevens, makers of as fine a line of scope sights as the world produces, and better by far than many others.

John Nosler will still direct and manage the bullet-making division, I was glad to learn. Now, with new L&S capital available, we can expect to see the Nosler line expanded, I feel sure. John will continue to see that Nosler Partition Bullets maintain their famous game-taking quality, I know, and that has always been at the very top.

Peterson's Labels makes very nice pressure sensitive fluorescent-red aiming bulls called Targ-Dots. They are available in 1", 1½", 2", and 3" diameter and can be stuck on any reasonably smooth surface to form an excellent aiming point. Depending on size, they are available in rolls of 40 to 300, price ranging from $1 to $4 per roll. Peterson also offers nicely printed pressure sensitive labels for pistol and rifle cartridge boxes. Two sizes are made, both in rolls of 250 to 1000, which may be fed through your typewriter, too. $2 to $6 per roll.

Remco Shotshell loads are popular for revolvers carried afield, especially for potting small camp game and to eliminate pesky varmints and an occasional rattler. Most standard cases are, however, restricted in the amount of shot they can contain. Remco offers a neat solution to this in a plastic shot capsule which extends beyond the case mouth. Called Shot Caps, they are quite easy to load and make it possible to get over ½-ounce of shot in the 45 Colt. Shot Caps are supplied sealed and pre-filled with No. 9 shot. Other shot sizes available on request. Standard reloading procedures apply. Prices are $4.95 for 357 Mag. and 38 Special and $5.95 for 44 Mag., 45 ACP and 45 Colt per box of 50.

Sharps Arms Co. is a new firm formed primarily to produce and sell a modernized version of the revered Sharps-Borchardt rifle of the 1880s. This development is covered elsewhere in this volume. However, this firm has also entered the bullet business. Its announced intention is to produce several sizes, from 17- to 50-caliber, all in jacketed form.

First is a hollow-point boat-tail 25-gr. 17 (.172″) caliber game bullet. It is designed to provide controlled expansion at velocities up to 4500 fps. Second is a flat-base, 17-caliber 22-gr. target bullet, also hollow-point. Samples show excellent workmanship and a good point shape. We haven't tried either yet, but preliminary reports indicate good performance. Prices are $4.50 and $4.25 per hundred, respectively. A welcome addition, making *two* factory-produced 17s available.

Speer Inc. Three new handgun bullets have been introduced by Speer. Dave Andrews, ballistician there, shook his head sadly and told us they simply couldn't introduce any more items until production caught up with demand for their existing line.

In 9mm (.355″) caliber, last year's 125-grain jacketed soft-point bullet has been revised, adding a knurled cannelure. This provides the correct cartridge length when the 9mm Parabellum case mouth is crimped into it. The same basic bullet is made in .357″ (38-caliber) diameter, the cannelure positioned farther forward for correct over-all cartridge length when the 357 Magnum case is crimped at the cannelure. In 38 Special, 15.0 grains of Hercules 2400 powder drives this 125-gr. bullet at 1212 fps from a 6″ revolver barrel. Extensive 38 Special and 357 Magnum loading data will soon be available.

The third bullet is of conventional lubricated, swaged lead construction in .358″ diameter. It weighs 158 grains and is of semi-wadcutter form, with two lubricating and one crimping groove. A good general-purpose bullet, far superior to round-nose types for hunting, defense or target use. It can easily be safely driven at velocities up to 950-1000 fps.

Speer-DWM ammunition and components are still in short supply. Unprimed cases in 38 Special and 357 Magnum are to be available in March; 7mm and 8mm Mauser cases in mid-'69. Currently available are 222, 270, 30-30, and 30-06 unprimed brass.

Of special interest to handloaders is the fact that new ammunition will be packaged in yellow plastic, divider-type boxes of the same style many of us buy separately. No more ragged, falling-apart cardboard boxes. This "Hunter's Ammo Pack" will also be sold separately (empty) for use with any caliber, 22-250 through 8x57mm. It assembles 4 ways to hold most cartridges snugly, minimizing rattle.

Incidentally, customers buying Speer-DWM ammo in the old paper boxes may ask the dealer for (and receive) the new pack to replace those old-style containers on a one-for-one basis. But, only to the extent of purchases made *now*—no back-dating, Charlie!

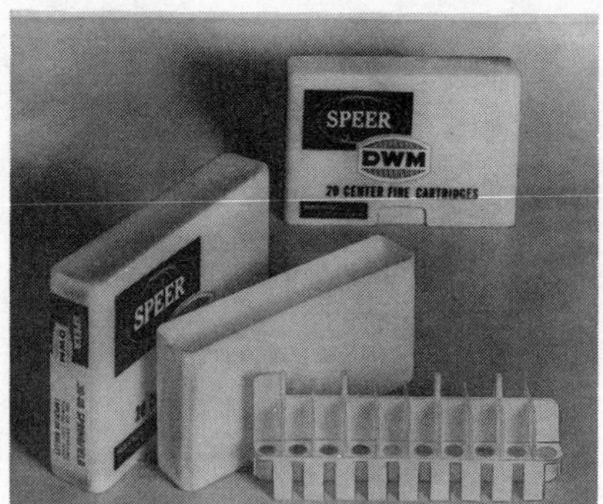

Speer 4-way cartridge box

Those who use and rely on the *Speer Reloading Manual* will be happy to know that Dave Andrews and his crew are hard at work on issue No. 8, available this fall.

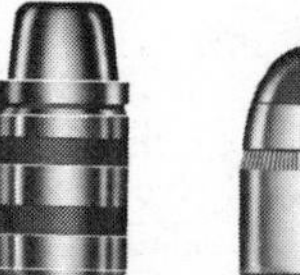
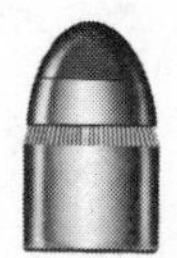

Speer 38 SWC, RNSP and 9mm RNSP

Stoeger Arms Co. now imports the very good RWS primers. From the catalog we've seen, a series of 21 primers is used to cover the needs of pistol, rifle, shotshell and percussion arm shooters. These are available in Berdan, Boxer and battery cup form and as winged musket caps.

Using the "ring-anvil" construction, these primers are said to offer sure firing, shortest bore time, high sensitivity and uniformity. They are, of course, non-mercuric and non-corrosive—the Sinoxid priming compound being used. Primers we've inspected have shown good quality control in maintaining outside dimensions.

Sullivan Arms now offers a 20-gauge plastic Sacwad in three heights, for all standard shells and loads. Of one-piece construction, at first glance it resembles the 2-piece Variwad. Base and shot cup are connected by 3 posts which collapse on firing, thus reducing inertia load on the shot charge.

SAC shotshell primers are again available in quantity, as are the several other shotshell items upon which the company was built.

Sullivan Arms 20-ga. Sacwad

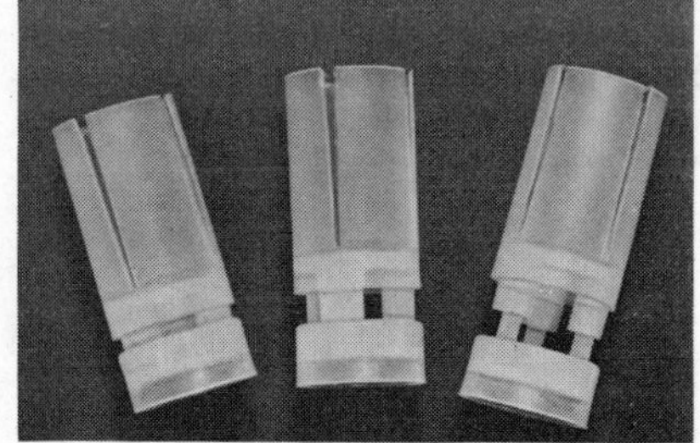

Super Vel Cartridge Corp. has now achieved sufficient production volume in their commercial ammo operation to spare bullets for the handloader. While some conventional bullets are offered, the specialty is a lightweight, thin-jacketed type, hollow- and soft-point, in 9mm, 38 and 44-caliber. More are in the making, including one for the 45 ACP. Here are a few on their list.

80-gr. .355″ JHP (.380)	$2.55
90-gr. .355″ JHP (9mm)	2.55
110-gr. .3565″ JSP (.38, .357)	2.45
125-gr. .3565″ JHP (.38, .357)	2.55
180-gr. .429″ JHP (.44)	3.10
180-gr. .429″ JSP (.44)	3.10

Lee Jurras, of Super Vel, tells us he has compiled a mass of loading data using these bullets, including pressure values. He expects to be able to make it available as a manual some time this year.

Popularity of Super Vel loaded ammunition in 38 Special, 357 Magnum and 9mm calibers has grown tremendously, especially among law officers. I just interviewed one officer fresh out of a gun fight in which he'd used full-jacketed 9mm Parabellum (Luger) ammunition—"Never again will I carry anything but high-velocity hollow-points. That guy didn't even know he'd been shot until the cuffs were on him," were his closing words.

Super Vel intends to offer unprimed cartridge cases to handloaders as soon as production is great enough. Small pistol primers are already available at $8.00 per M.

Xelex, Ltd. We thought Canadian shooters would like to know a distributor determined to give reloading a shot in the arm up there. Drop a line to them in Hawkesbury, Ontario, and they'll send a comprehensive list of tools and components.

At present Canadian reloading is only 1% that of the U.S. according to Thomas Higginson of Xelex. No wonder—IMR powder is $4.25 per can. But this company is promotion minded. Buy a keg of CR17 powder at 90¢ a pound and load 1000s of 303 MK VII cartridges so popular there. They give 2 lbs. of CR17 with each C-press, die set, scale, etc. A beginning reloader could keep himself in free powder for some time acquiring his tools this way. An unheard of practice in the States, huh?

The manufacturers listed below have not reported anything new for 1970, at least not to us. However, any of them will send catalogs and/or brochures on request. Complete addresses will be found in our Directory of the Arms Trade, located at the back of this book.

Belding & Mull, Milton Brynin, Flambeau, Hercules, Hulme, LLF Die Shop, McKillen & Heyer, Paul McLean, Mayville Eng., N.E. House, Southern Lead Co., Potter Eng., Roman Products, Vickerman, Webster, Wilson, Zenith, Zimmerman.

Parker Safety Hammerless with tang safety at top of backstrap. In forward position, the trigger was locked; moving it to the rear prepared gun for firing.

AMERICAN REVOLVER SAFETIES

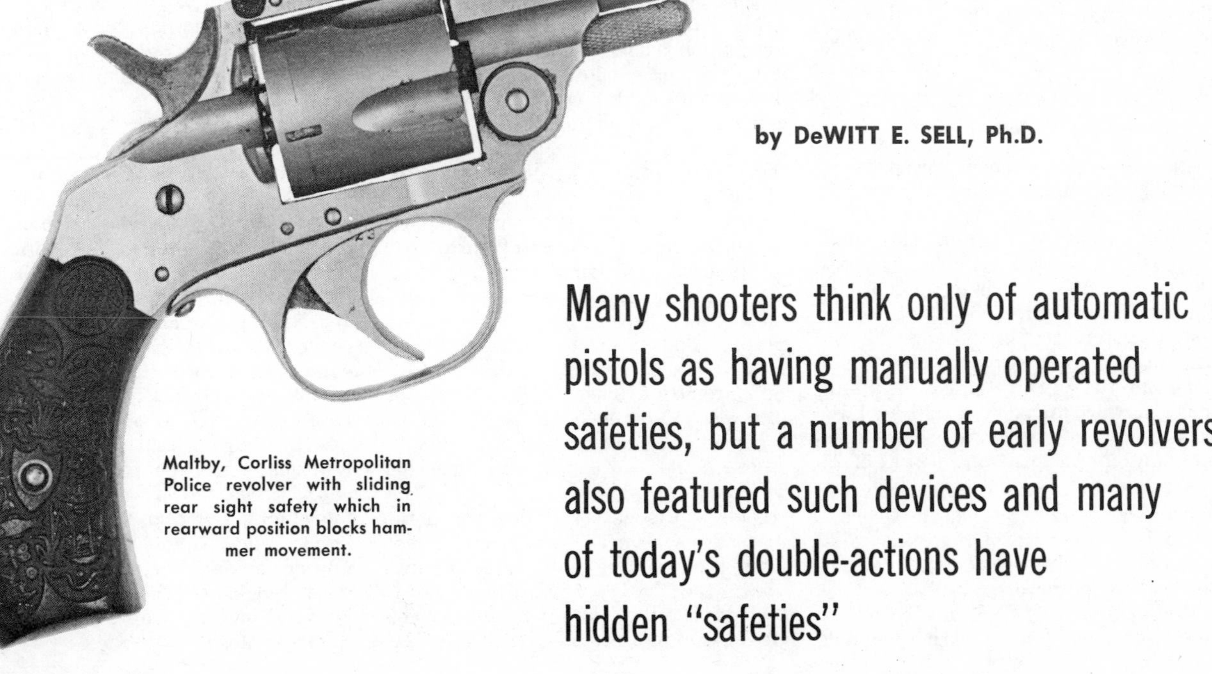

Maltby, Corliss Metropolitan Police revolver with sliding rear sight safety which in rearward position blocks hammer movement.

by DeWITT E. SELL, Ph.D.

Many shooters think only of automatic pistols as having manually operated safeties, but a number of early revolvers also featured such devices and many of today's double-actions have hidden "safeties"

IN ALL LIKELIHOOD, the term "safety" in reference to handguns is exclusively associated with semi-automatic pistols by the majority of firearms publications readers. Safeties have been a standard feature on virtually all autoloading handguns (there are a few exceptions) from the inception of their history. This has not been nearly so true in the case of revolvers, yet a number of safety devices have been produced for them. They were intended not only to render their operation safer for the owner-shooter but also to prevent their being accidentally discharged.

This article will review a variety of safeties that have been incorporated on American cartridge revolvers since 1858 — the year following Smith & Wesson's introduction of their Model No. 1, or Seven Shooter, revolver chambered for their 22-cal. rimfire short, which launched the cartridge era in American handgun history. As its name suggested, the cylinder of this revolver contained seven chambers.

The Smith & Wesson No. 1 had no safety feature whatever. The only certain manner in which it could be carried safely was with the hammer nose at rest opposite an empty chamber. This, in effect, reduced its firepower potential to six shots. Although "fathers" of the American cartridge handgun industry, Smith & Wesson failed to provide a safety-notch on their first three commercially produced rimfire revolvers—their No. 1 (3 issues), No. 2, and No. 1½ (2 issues). They rationalized this omission by the following statement in their loading directions: "A half-bent is entirely dispensed with, as it is found to be much more convenient and safe to carry the hammer resting between two cartridges; when so placed it is impossible to be accidentally discharged." Smith & Wesson did not alter their stand in this respect until 1870, when they provided a safety notch on their No. 3 American model.

Allen & Wheelock

In 1858, Allen & Wheelock marketed cartridge revolvers in calibers 22 RF (rimfire) and 32 RF based on Ethan Allen's patents of September 7 and November 9 of that year. These side-hammer models—infringements of the Rollin White patent — featured a safety notch for the hammer. By drawing the hammer back slightly, a notch in the sear retained the hammer's forward movement and kept its nose clear of any cartridge head which might be lined up in front of it.

This safety notch is sometimes erroneously referred to as a "half-cock," although seldom located at the midpoint of the hammer's arc. Some later revolvers incorporated both a safety notch and a half-cock notch, as in Colt's Single Action Army model. Finger pressure on the trigger will not release the hammer from the safety notch, thus affording a significant measure of safety from unintentional discharge even when all cylinder chambers are loaded. This safety notch remains effective throughout the remaining distance of the hammer's arc until it reaches the position of full cock. Should the thumb slip off the hammer while drawing it back to full cock, the hammer's forward fall will be arrested by the safety notch.

While this safety notch apparently was not a patented feature, it seems unequivocal that the Allen & Wheelock side-hammer models of 1858 were the first American cartridge revolvers to employ this safety principle.

Hopkins & Allen

A "safety cylinder" patented by Henry H. Hopkins on April 27, 1875 (Patent No. 162,475) was incorporated in a number of the Hopkins & Allen models and fully exploited via advertising. This safety cylinder featured raised sections on the periphery of the cylinder's base between each chamber; these were milled through in the center to provide a secure resting place for the hammer nose. The thickness of these sections approximated that of the cartridge rims and they were virtually flush with the recoil shield, thus providing the secondary gain of increased stability during the cylinder's revolution. Despite the fact that Hopkins & Allen described this cylinder as foolproof against accidental discharge, they nevertheless provided a safety notch on the sear. The engraved Hopkins & Allen XL 3 model illustrated has both the patented safety cylinder and a safety notch.

Hopkins & Allen made their most noteworthy contribution to revolver safety in the perfecting of their Triple Action Safety Police revolver. Patented August 21, 1906, this revolver marked the acme of this firm's handgun development and was, if the company's subsequent catalogs are to be given credence, phenomenally successful. As Hopkins & Allen contended, their triple action revolver was not, like other "safety" revolvers, an ordinary double action with safety appliances. It embodied its safety principle in its basic construction and action. The piece is cocked, as in other double action revolvers, by thumb or pulling the trigger (first action); upon release of sear by trigger, the hammer falls directly against the floating firing pin (second action). Here the similarity to other double action revolvers, whose action stops with the drive of the hammer, ends. Upon releasing the trigger of the Safety Police, the hammer rises via an eccentric cam to rest flush against the solid steel frame above the firing pin (third action). Neither blows against the hammer nor the snapping of the hammer, accidental or otherwise, can affect the firing pin or discharge a cartridge.

Smith & Wesson

Daniel B. Wesson's and James H. Bullard's patent No. 198,228 of December 18, 1877, covered specifications for a "rebounding hammer." The first revolver to utilize this feature was Smith & Wesson's New Model 32 (also known as No. 1½, New Model) which was introduced during March,

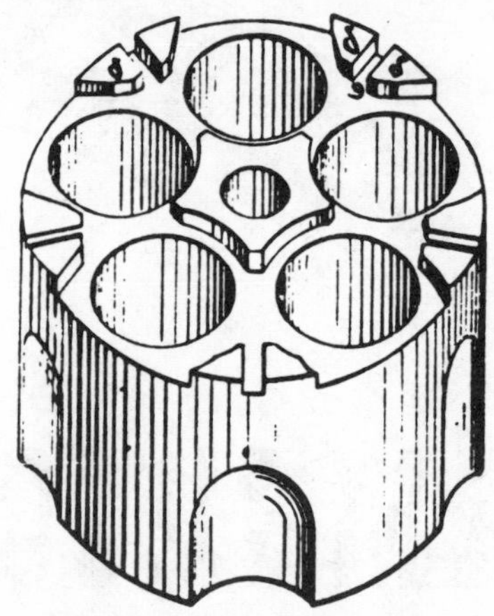

Hopkins safety cylinder. The raised sections between chambers were milled out in the middle to provide a secure resting place for hammer.

1878. This was the firm's sole single action model chambered for their 32 S&W centerfire cartridge. An advertisement of the New Model 32 appearing in July, 1878, described the rebounding hammer feature as follows: "These arms are provided with simple automatic rebounding locks, so arranged as to prevent the point of the hammer coming in contact with the cartridge at any time except at the instant of intentional discharge. By this means, accidents arising from a chance blow upon the hammer are absolutely prevented. The value of this improvement will be readily recognized."

The first 500 of the New Model 32s produced also had a safety notch, but this feature was thereafter eliminated as superfluous and confusing in conjunction with the rebounding hammer. The rebounding lock cannot be released by the trigger before the hammer is drawn back to full cock. Rebounding hammer locks were incorporated in all Smith & Wesson revolvers developed after the New Model 32. It is impossible to discharge modern Smith & Wesson revolvers unless the trigger pull is completed intentionally, as the hammer is otherwise prevented from full forward movement by two safeties—the rebound slide upon which the lower end of the hammer rests and the solid steel block which lies between the hammer and the frame just below the hammer nose.

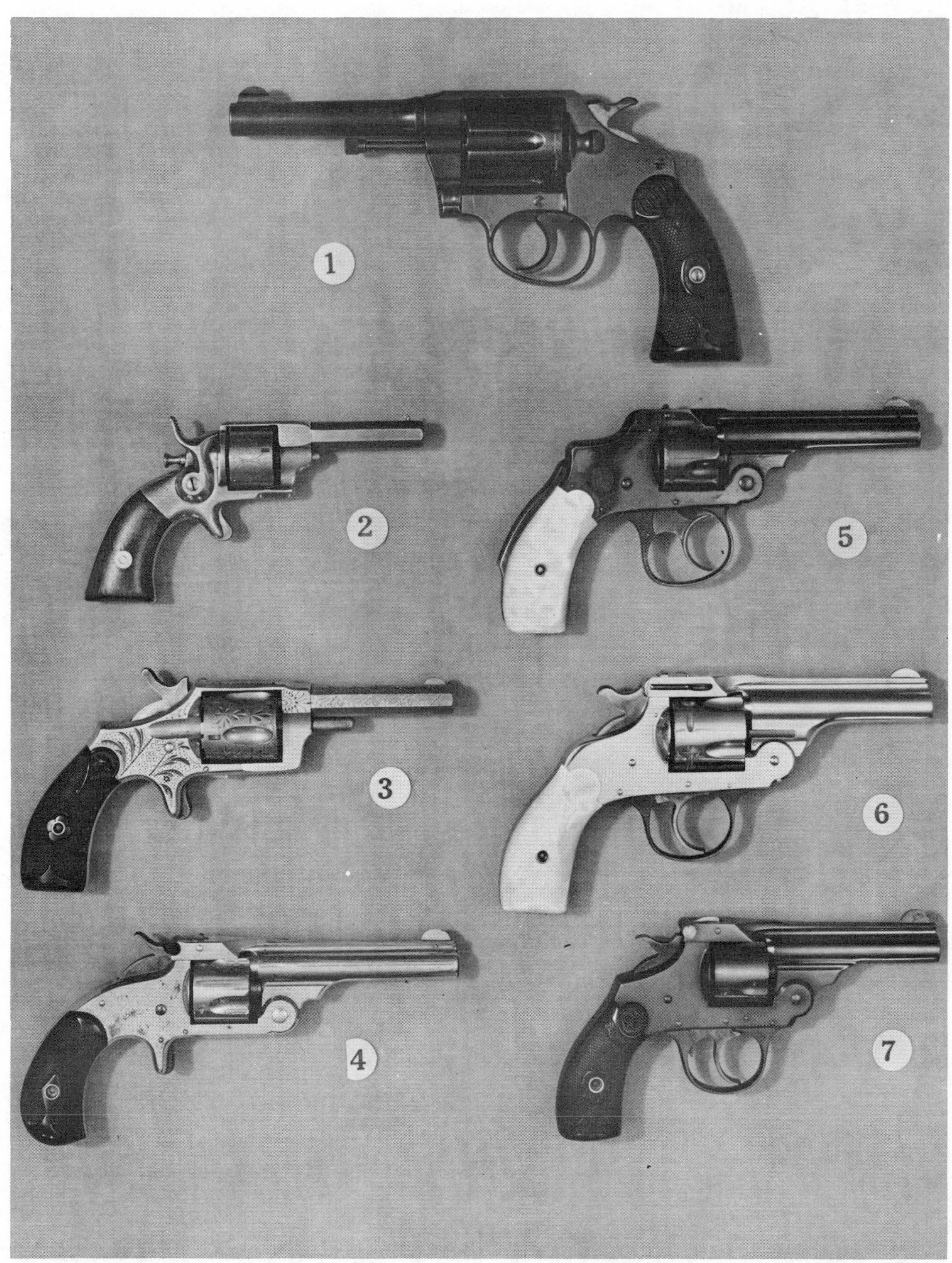

1—Colt Police Positive Special, cal. 32-20; 2—Allen & Wheelock sidehammer M1858, 22 rimfire; 3—Hopkins & Allen engraved XL-3, with safety cylinder, 32 rimfire; 4—Smith & Wesson New Model 32 (No. 1½, New Model), cal. 32 S&W; 5—Smith & Wesson Model 32 Safety Hammerless, 2nd issue, 32 S&W; 6—Hopkins & Allen Triple Action Safety Police Model, 32 S&W; 7—Iver Johnson Safety Automatic Hammer Model, 32 S&W. Each of these revolvers has an interesting and unusual safety; all are discussed in detail in the text.

AMERICAN REVOLVER SAFETIES

In 1887, Smith & Wesson brought out their initial Safety Hammerless cartridge revolver—also known as the New Departure and unofficially, to collectors, as the Lemon Squeezer. The Safety Hammerless is actually a double action revolver whose internal hammer is prevented from being cocked by the trigger unless the lever projecting from the backstrap is squeezed in when gripping the arm. This safety lever was another ingenious invention of Daniel B. Wesson and was patented in his name. The safety lever locks the hammer in its rebound position until grasped firmly and held flush with the backstrap. No blow nor fall can occasion discharge. The action has a somewhat long and heavy trigger pull but is unique in that, while double action, a distinct pause occurs just prior to let-off of the hammer in full cock position. This action allows the accuracy and deliberate let-off characteristic of the single action and again is contributory to safety. Smith & Wesson stated in their 85th Anniversary catalog in reference to the Safety Hammerless that, "Another most valuable feature obtained by the long and firm trigger pull required—combined with the grip—is that a child cannot discharge the arm, the distance to the trigger is too great and the strength required too much for its hand."

While the Smith & Wesson Safety Hammerless revolvers were discontinued about the time the United States entered World War II, postwar demand for a grip safety hammerles revolver induced Smith & Wesson to revive this feature in their Centennial model, introduced in 1952. The Safety Hammerless was of topbreak construction—the last S&W of that design to remain in production—while the Centennial is of solid frame construction with swing-out cylinder.

Iver Johnson

One can state categorically that no firearms manufacturer has given more prominence to the concept of revolver safety than has Iver Johnson's Arms & Cycle Works. For more than half a century (1892-1950) this firm plugged its "Hammer the Hammer" safety feature until it became virtually a household slogan.

Iver Johnson introduced his Safety Automatic revolvers in calibers 32 S&W and 38 S&W in 1892, adding 22 RF in 1895. This was the first model to employ the Hammer the Hammer safety. Its principle involved incorporation of a "safety lever" between the hammer and the spring-actuated firing pin located in the frame. The safety lever and pawl are hinged together at their bases, fitted within the frame just to the rear of the trigger, and they rise together as the trigger is pulled. The hammer nose is cut away so that when at rest it lies flush against the frame above the firing pin—hence it can literally be hammered upon without fear of detonating a cartridge. However, when the trigger is fully pulled, it holds the safety lever up so that it is interpreted between the hammer and the firing pin and transmits the falling hammer's force to effect ignition. With the release of the trigger, the safety lever again drops below the firing pin with the hammer nose at rest against solid steel above the firing pin. In 1908, the Safety Automatic revolvers underwent major modification. Flat springs were dispensed with and the coil mainspring was fitted with an adjustable mainspring tension bar; also, ball and socket mainspring plunger and hammer contact with the safety lever were fashioned of vanadium steel.

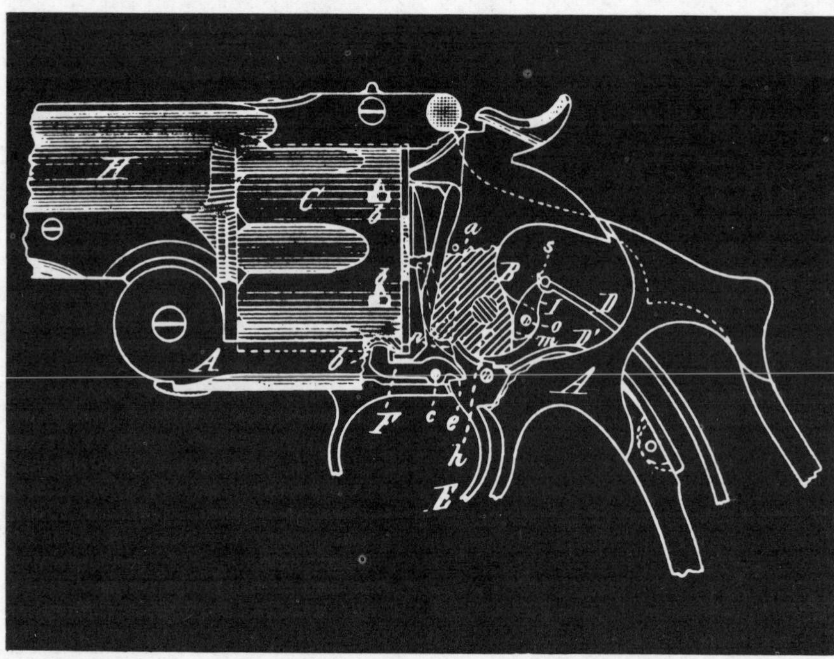

Patent drawing of S&W's rebounding hammer feature, which prevented the hammer from contacting the cartridge except at the moment of discharge.

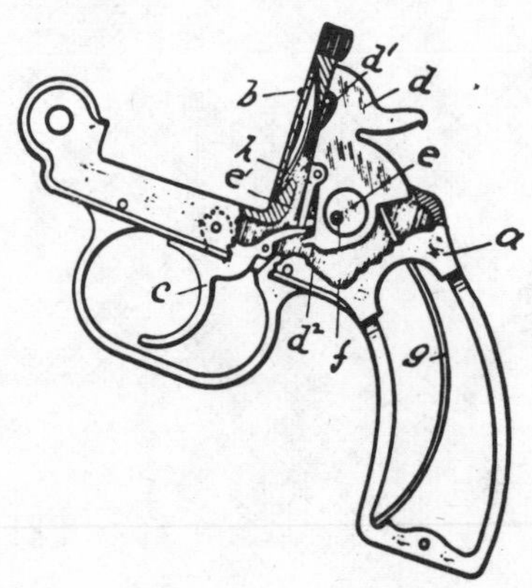

Hopkins & Allen Triple Action safety. In this design the hammer rested against the steel frame rather than on the firing pin. Letters are patent references.

A "safety trigger" is also found on some early Safety Automatic models. It consists of a hinged projection extending approximately half way down the front of the trigger proper. It must be drawn back flush with the trigger's surface in order to free the trigger for retraction. How this superfluous gadget provided an additional safety factor is an enigma to this writer, and apparently the manufacturer soon became disenchanted with this innovation as it was of short duration. Although the Safety Automatic revolvers were discontinued in 1950, Iver Johnson's retained the Hammer the Hammer safety feature on their Supershot Model 844 of the mid-50s and it was again revived on their current double action hammer revolver, the Model 67, Viking.

"Flash Control" Cylinder

The venerable firm of Iver Johnson's was to make yet another contribution to revolver safety.Their patented "Flash Control" cylinder, introduced in 1954, is recessed at the front to provide a flange at the circumference for deflecting gases and possible lead shavings away from the shooter or any persons who may be standing in close proximity to the shooter's side or rear.

Colt

From 1905 on, several of Colt's model designations included the word "Positive;" e.g., Police Positive. This was a result of the Colt firm patenting in that year their "Positive Safety Lock," which they incorporated in most of their revolvers and highligted in their advertising from then on. They described this feature in the following words: "The expression 'You can't forget to make a Colt safe' has often been heard, due to the fact that all Colt double action revolvers are equipped with the Colt Positive Safety Lock—which makes accidental discharge absolutely impossible." (Author's note: The above statement became true after 1910, when the original Colt Double Action Model of 1877, with bird's-head grips, was discontinued). The Colt Positive Safety Lock consists of a solid bar of steel, 1/10″ thick, which automatically places itself between the hammer and the cartridge head, remaining in this position at all times except when the trigger is intentionally pulled to the extent that the hammer reaches, and is released from, full cock.

Harrington & Richardson

Harrington & Richardson, who have been manufacturing handguns as well as shoulder arms since 1871, patented a unique (if a dubious merit) revolver safety which consisted of a casehardened cross-bar of oblong shape incorporated in the frame just above the trigger guard. When this cross-bar is pushed flush with the left side of the frame, the trigger cannot be pulled. Conversely, when the cross-bar is flush with the right side of the frame, the safety is nonfunctional. The patent date, May 22, 1917, is stamped on the left side of this cross-bar, which has been noted on both hammer (the Automatic Ejecting) and hammerless models. Inasmuch as models featuring this safety are seldom encountered, it is assumed that its employment was of short duration.

As late as 1959, Harrington & Richardson introduced yet another safety —their exclusive "Safety Lock," with key. Appearing initially on the Ultra Side-Kick model, it was also available optionally on the Guardsman model. This Safety Lock is incorporated in the bottom of the grip frame, a turn of the separate key rendering the action inoperable.

Miscellaneous Safeties

Several other types of revolver safeties developed by minor manufacturers are worth noting. Maltby, Henley & Co., who apparently were distributors rather than manufacturers, marketed a hammerless revolver under their name which incorporated a tang safety at the top of the backstrap. This safety functioned in a manner analogous to the typical tang safety found on many shotguns—the trigger was locked when the knurled safety was moved forward; moving it rearward freed the trigger.

The Columbian New Safety Hammerless and the Parker Safety Hammerless revolvers also feature a tang safety identical to the one found on the Maltby, Henley referred to above. It can be assumed they were produced by the same manufacturer, inasmuch as both bear the date, (January 24, 1888), of a patent issued to John T. Smith of Rockfall, Connecticut, and both have black rubber grips embossed at their apex with three interlocking circles of floral design, which identifies them as handguns distributed by Maltby, Henley of New York, N.Y.

Corliss replaced Henley as a partner of Maltby during the '80s, the Metropolitan Police double action hammer revolver, which featured an odd type of safety, being marketed under the name of Maltby, Corliss & Co. An independent rear sight which slides back and forth on the flat topstrap serves a dual function as a safety. With the rear sight in its rearmost position, the hammer is blocked from retracting, rendering the action inert. When the rear sight is slid forward, the hammer is free to be cocked by thumb or finger pressure on the trigger.

The pertinence of either of these above described safeties—tang or siding rear sight—is obscure if their purpose was to prevent accidental discharge by a child or other unauthorized person, since their method of operation is readily disclosed via trial manipulation. Nevertheless, it appears that many manufacturers of revolvers during the closing decade of the last century and the opening decade of the present one were under competitive pressure to develop some gadget he could label a "safety" and publicly acclaim as such.

The Cody Thunderbird, a double action hammer revolver introduced in 1957, featured a thumb-safety located on the left side of its frame. This safety operated in a vertical plane, blocking trigger movement when in its "up" position and ineffectual when "down." The Cody was unique inasmuch as the original issues of this revolver were all aluminum with the exception of a rifled steel barrel liner and internal parts. Later issues were furnished with steel cylinders prior to their discontinuance in 1959. The Thunderbird was of top-break construction with cylinder counterbored and chambered for six 22 long rifle cartridges.

Around 1930, most manufacturers producing revolvers in 22 RF caliber began utilizing "safety cylinders" whose chambers were countersunk to permit seating the cartridge rims within a wall of steel, the cylinder's base being virtually flush with the recoil shield. This safety measure was necessitated by the introduction of high velocity 22 RF ammunition which posed the potential danger of blown rims if used in earlier type cylinders designed for standard velocity ammunition.

The acquisition of revolvers featuring the wide variety of safeties delineated in this article can constitute a fascinating sub-specialty in gun collecting. The author believes it worthy of pursuit. ●

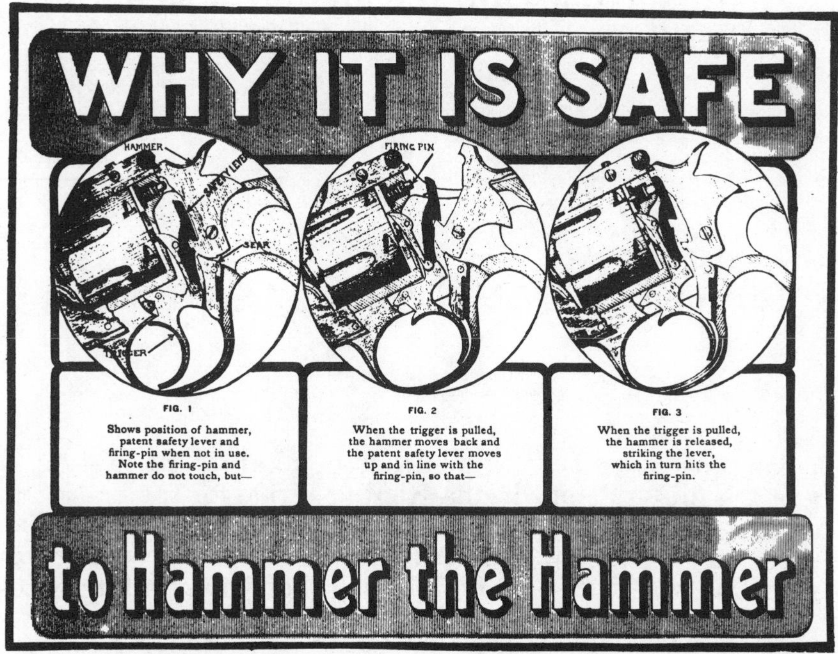

WHY IT IS SAFE
HAMMER
SAFETY LEVER
SEAR
TRIGGER
FIRING PIN
FIG. 1
Shows position of hammer, patent safety lever and firing-pin when not in use. Note the firing-pin and hammer do not touch, but—
FIG. 2
When the trigger is pulled, the hammer moves back and the patent safety lever moves up and in line with the firing-pin, so that—
FIG. 3
When the trigger is pulled, the hammer is released, striking the lever, which in turn hits the firing-pin.
to Hammer the Hammer

PENNSYLVANIA LONG RIFLES

An explanation into the mystery, the enigma, of their inlaid and engraved decorations.

Text and art by Major R. O. ACKERMAN

A long and graceful flintlock rifle hangs over a mantel. In the flickering light from the fireplace, the soft patina of its worn surface glows. The light also picks up high points of an engraved patchbox, curiously-shaped metal inlays and perhaps some raised or incised carving of the beautifully-grained curly maple stock.

To the uninitiated, examining a typical Pennsylvania-Kentucky rifle for the first time, the primary questions would probably be, "How was it fired?" and "How accurate was it?" Closely following these standard inquiries would come another, "What do those odd decorations mean?"

Any reasonably well-informed gun enthusiast can answer the first question. With the growing popularity of muzzle loader shooting, we are better qualified to answer the second one than were the preceding couple of generations.

The third question is a different matter.

Did you know that virtually no information will be found anywhere on the origin or significance of these bizarre designs? That standard reference books will tell which area favored certain motifs, but never mention their source? That only two serious attempts have been made to write a detailed article on the subject—both many years ago, so that even Xerox copies could not be obtained from the publisher, museums or central exchange libraries?

During two years of research upon this symbolism, these are just a few of the things this writer found out. I also learned that many of the nation's collector-specialists had just two answers to my questions: (A) They did not know, and (B) They would like to.

Why an 8-pointed star, instead of the more conventional 5-pointed one? Why is the point of a heart twisted sideways? Why is a fish inlayed in a rifle more often than appropriate game? Why does the date of a rifle seem to govern whether a serpent is more likely to be a plain snake or a rattlesnake?

The primitive flavor of so many of these designs, plus the mystery surrounding them, made an intriguing challenge which could not be ignored.

Today, after exploring every avenue and following every lead which presented itself, the writer can say one thing with certainty—this is the dadblamedest, most controversial subject I have ever attempted to research! Invited to at least voice their personal opinions, many correspondents proved to have very definite ones! It was interesting to note the widely conflicting theories, and the reasons behind them.

Among the leading recognized authorities on the muzzle-loading long rifle, there is the widest possible difference of opinion. Several have an honest conviction that the familiar designs had no significance, but were mere decoration reflecting the whim of the rifle maker or his customer. Others believe just as strongly that early Christian symbolism influenced many of the motifs. Additional theories are also supported, but not by these particular sources.

Divergent Theories

As objectively as possible, let us examine each major theory which has presented itself.

1. Total absence of significance sounds logical until one looks carefully at the opposing arguments. We must discard this theory as leaving far too many unexplainable coincidences.

2. Study of every available reference upon early Christian history and symbolism disclosed many startling parallels. It must be remembered that the originators of this rifle were deeply religious people—a fact which would naturally be reflected in every facet of their everyday life, and more particularly in their decoration of familiar objects.

3. By the same token, these people were also supersititious by nature. The "Pennsylvania Dutch" had immigrated from the Palatinate, the upper Rhine, Swabia and Switzerland. With them they had brought certain art motifs, which to this day have changed but little from generation to generation, and which still show the European influence. Some of their stylized designs were known as *hexafoos* (witch's foot), designed to ward off the devil and bring good luck. This superstitious connotation has been denied by some and exploited by others. Some ally it with witchcraft, others more with religious faith. There can be little doubt that original meanings have largely been lost in time, and that the "hex signs" on Pennsylvania barns today are, as they claim, "just for fancy." However, 200 years ago these folk art motifs were not far removed from their European origins, and there is much basis for belief that they influenced the decoration of the Pennsylvania-Kentucky rifle. Again, detailed study of Pennsylvania Dutch folk art revealed many startling similarities, as will be seen. These similarities were noted more often in the embellishment of their furniture, china, birth certificates, etc., than in the barn motifs, which were more universally geometric in design than the ones we are discussing.

4. Twice the theory was raised that all of the rifle decorations were symbols of Freemasonry. An entire history of the order, replete with symbols, failed to indicate any evidence of this. Of course, Freemasonry symbols are seen, but not that often.

5. The belief was advanced that these are basic symbols which have been used from the time of Neolithic Man, and have outlived such civilizations as the Mycenaean, Egyptian, Minoan, Hittite and the later Etruscan, Mayan, Aztec, etc. They are part of a common heritage and do not consciously represent nature. This ties in with the strong mythological flavor that some of these designs possess.

What conclusions may be drawn from all this? Probably none that will change any minds or lessen the controversy. However, isn't it possible that no one theory is entirely right or wrong, but that the motifs upon our American rifle came from many sources? This is definitely the writer's feeling, after long immersion in a whirlpool of conflicting theories, theologies, cultures and mythologies.

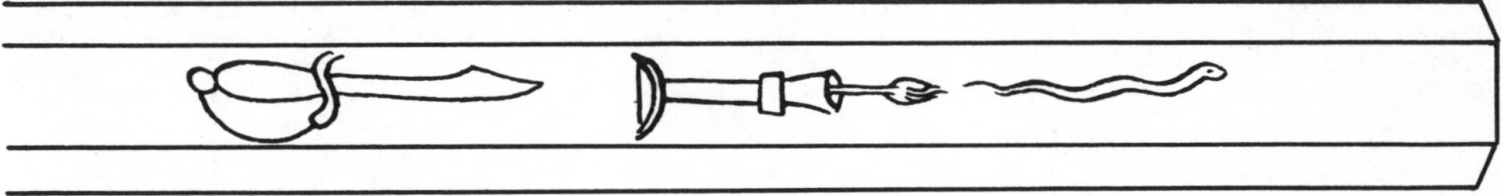

Quite frankly, more support was found for theories number two and three than for any other. It is a significant fact that some symbols are disguised (like a tiny serpent as the center line of a flower petal), while others are completely hidden from view. Examples of the latter are seen on rifles made by J. P. Beck and Nicholas Beyer, both of whom often engraved "INRI" on the under side of the barrel where it was covered by the stock. Another rifle has J. Deo Beck on the under side—the "Deo" probably signifying "With the help of God." Some rifles are reported to have an "X" on the bottom flat, right underneath the sight, to guard that member from any evil spell.

Albert Sullivan, president of the Kentucky Rifle Association, sent me a picture of three engraved symbols from the underside of the barrel of a George Schreyer rifle he owns. This piece was made in Hanover, Pa., about 1765. The symbols (see drawing) are of a sword, a candlestick and a serpent. They are believed to be of a religious nature. Mr. Sullivan is anxious to get the opinions of others on the exact meaning of this combination, so I will gladly forward to him any letters which may be received on the subject.

One might ask, why sneak these symbols onto a rifle so surreptitiously if they held no special significance for the owner?

Following is a listing of various motifs which have been used in the decoration of the Pennsylvania-Kentucky rifle. Each one has been noted on one or more examples—many of them quite a number of times. There were undoubtedly many others which the author's research failed to disclose.

This list of symbols is from many sources, from the ancient Druids to the Pennsylvania Dutch, from early Christian signs to heraldic emblems. These possible origins are spiced with some of our own frontiersmen's quaint "lucky omens" and beliefs, such as their admonition to always fire the first shot from a new rifle at the moon. This relaxes the barrel and allows the rifleman to shoot straighter and farther from then on!

Eight-Pointed Star This was, almost without question, the earliest design used on these American rifles, and certainly one of the most popular. Stars are noted in various forms, as inlays or even patch box finials, but the 8-pointed version far outnumbers all others. They're seen most often on the cheekpiece, sometimes as barrel-pin escutcheons, more occasionally as an independent inlay and, rarely, in the engraved design of the patch box. Some call it the Hunter's Star, but with strong opposition from other schools of thought.

The 8-pointed star is a popular motif in Pennsylvania Dutch folk art, in which it signifies "abundance and goodwill." From this source, it quite possibly derived from the "Rosenkreuz" or Rose and Cross, which was a 15th century German symbol of religious freedom and private land ownership. The latter is also the emblem of the philosophic order of Rosicrucians.

Dillin* insisted this star was born with the American rifle, ignoring the fact that it occurs on central European rifles and even crossbows which pre-date our American firearms.

Archeologists attribute the star to an ancient sun cult, to whom it meant fertility.

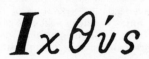

Religion and science (often at odds) combine forces to suggest the most interesting origin of our 8-pointed star. Legend says it is the Star of Bethlehem, and thus was used as a talisman to guide the rifleman along the proper path—through life, as through the wilderness. Astronomers say that a remarkable conjunction of Mars and Saturn in Pisces occurs once every 794 years, and that this may have a direct relationship to the star of the wise men. That "star" was abnormally bright, and could have been the two planets shining side by side. This could also account for the usual elongation of the rifle star, although this most likely was just to conform with the shape of the cheekpiece or forestock.

*J. G. W. Dillin, *The Kentucky Rifle*.

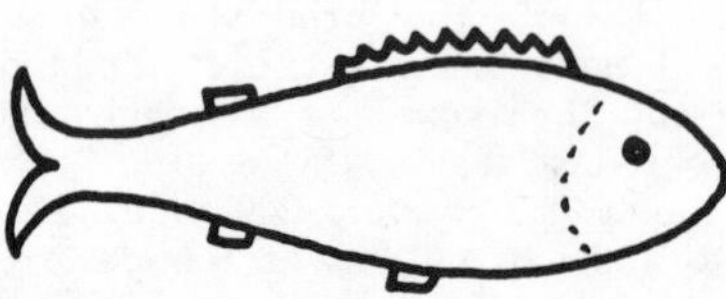

Ιχθύς

Crescent or Quarter Moon This was almost as popular a motif as the star, but probably not quite as early in its appearance on our rifles. Many of the first rifles were devoid of decoration, but the earliest inlays were most likely to have been either the star or the crescent.

A widely accepted theory about the crescent is that it is our talismanic hope for a bountiful life. It is symbolic of the harvest moon, a bumper crop and fertility. An interesting aspect of the fertility theme is that crescents on rifles are sometimes distinctively male and female. One particular pair of long rifles is known which clearly illustrates this point. This is a rare feature.

The crescent, with or without face, was often used as a cheekpiece inlay on rifles from south-central Pennsylvania. It was the early Christian symbol for the Virgin Mary and for God's creation. The American pioneer said that the rifle crescent should be mounted with the points down, and signified a wet moon. This meant dampness of ground and of fallen leaves, so that he could stalk game quietly. Four crescents represented the four seasons.

Naturally, the changing phases of the moon intrigued and mystified ancient man, so it is natural that we should find it as a talisman for .any different early cultures.

Distlefink The good luck bird of the Pennsylvania Dutch settlers was the thistlefinch, or "distlefink." This was the goldfinch, which gained its other name by eating thistle seed and using thistle down for its nest. The goldfinch was also the Christian sign for the Passion of Christ, due to its fondness for thistles which related to Christ's crown of thorns.

Distlefinks are seen on rifles of the later and more highly decorated types. A number of birds are observed on these Pennsylvania-Kentucky rifles, many of them too stylized for identification. We know that Pennsylvania folk art also popularized the dove, parrot and peacock.

Fish The fish is not seen on very early rifles; it is usually found on those made after 1800, and from central

Pennsylvania.

It was an insignia of the early Christians, who used it when they met secretly in the catacombs. The Greek word for fish (ichthus) is spelled with the initial letters of the phrase, *Iesus Christos Theou uios, sotor* (Jesus Christ, Son of God Saviours). There was closer agreement upon this origin for the fish inlay than I found for any other design, among serious students of the rifle. One fish refers to Christ and three fish to the Holy Trinity.

The fish was also an ancient Oriental symbol, although that is not considered relevant to our subject. The backplate of the axe holder on Conestoga wagons was often shaped as a fish. Those covered wagons, from Lancaster County's Conestoga Valley, were part of the same culture which produced the long rifle.

Frontier folklore had it that a fish inlay made the rifle shoot straight.

Another superstition was that if the rifle was not hitting, the barrel must be removed, unbreeched, and placed in a stream with the muzzle upstream. The running water would wash out evil spirits, poor shots, etc. As a fish usually faces the current, the fish inlay should point toward the muzzle.

Eagle There is an interesting theory concerning the eagle on long rifles. When the bird appears as a patriotic American emblem, possibly signifying ownership of the rifle by a military man, the arm probably is a late one. The eagle on our Great Seal was not adopted until the early 1790's. A few earlier rifles with eagles indicate a mark of respect to the makers' of former country—Germany. Even the double-headed eagle of Imperial Prussia is occasionally seen. This was the *doppel adler* of the Pennsylvania Dutch. Before Germany adopted this royal bird, it was the symbol of the Holy Roman Empire.

After the American eagle was adopted, it became quite popular on Pennsylvania-Kentucky rifles. Bedford County gunmakers still used the decoration into the third quarter of the 19th century, being the last of their breed.

Ancient beliefs attributed unusual powers to the eagle, such as periodically renewing its plumage by flying near the sun and then plunging into water. It thus signified renewal or rebirth to the Pennsylvania Dutch, and this also could have influenced its appearance upon their rifles.

Heart The heart was not generally used as a decoration until just after the turn of the 19th century. It was probably first placed upon long rifles made in Maryland—then later it became popular in lower-central and lower-western Pennsylvania.

There is real disagreement upon its original meaning. It is preferable to believe it signified love of God and of

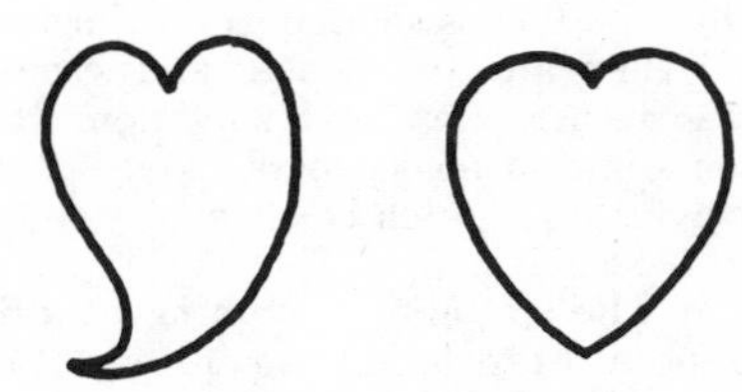

one's fellow man. However, another school of thought calls it a protective talisman against evil forces which would lure the soul away from the body. When the point of the heart is twisted to one side, it is termed the Bleeding Heart. This design traditionally represents the Fifth Wound of Christ.

Our pioneer forefathers wanted this crooked heart inlaid upon the wrist of the rifle. There the shooter's hand would cover it, symbolic of protection of loved ones—or the rifle and the man, between family and danger.

Acorn This one really goes back in time! The ancient Celtic cult of Druids worshiped the oak. It was later absorbed into Christian symbolism and became emblematic of Christ or the Virgin Mary. It denotes strength in body, mind and character.

Alternately several have mentioned that it stands for the lumber to erect a cabin. It is seen as an inlay, engraving or finial.

Flower In the decoration of the long rifles, flowers were much used. These are highly stylized rather than naturalistic, and like the birds, are seldom recognizable. They have acquired various names from collectors, though it is doubtful what flowers the maker actually had in mind. It is felt that by the 19th century, a number of the designs had no significance other than as ornamentation. However, certain flowers were among the earlier motifs and will be included here.

Tulip The tulip, sometimes called the German lily, had a special meaning to the Pennsylvania pioneers. It was the emblem of their exodus to escape the tyranny and persecution of the Old World. It still is to them what the shamrock is to the Irish, and it is a favorite art motif. They say the tulip stands for faith in yourself, what you do and your fellow men. Oddly, this has not been seen as an inlay, but as piercings or in the engraving of patch boxes.

Diamond The diamond is probably just a geometric shape. It is seen frequently on long rifles from North Carolina and Virginia.

Scroll This implies a letter or a message. One correspondent remarked that a bullet often delivers a message.

Squirrel, Deer, etc. With certain exceptions, such animals simply represent the game normally hunted.

Teardrop This could also be a raindrop—a Chinese Yang motif for fertility of the soil—but was probably used merely because it was a geometric shape and easy to draw.

Serpent A Christian symbol of the

devil, or a warning against temptation. It could also represent the brass serpent of Moses for healing the people.

Entirely different is the meaning of a rattlesnake, the Revolutionary War period symbol of American independence. As it occurs on rifles made 50 years after that war, its presence does not guarantee that an arm is of Revolutionary vintage.

Anchor A Christian sign of hope and steadfastness. It could also be on a rifle at the request of an ex-seafaring man.

Dolphin This is seen more in Christian art than any other fish, and symbolizes resurrection and salvation. It is sometimes seen as highly stylized engraving on a patch box.

Fox The epitome of cunning or guile. General Francis Marion of Revolutionary War fame was nicknamed the "Swamp Fox," and such inlays could conceivably be a tribute to this popular patriot.

Shell The shell, notably the cockleshell or scallop, refers to a pilgrimage or travel. Sometimes seen as a finial.

Fleur-de-Lis Emblem of the kings of France, first chosen by King Clovis. Also the emblem of the city of Florence. Used as a finial.

Daisy The most-used flower among those identified by name, the daisy is sometimes seen as an engraving. More often it is a patch box finial, particularly popular with Lancaster County makers. Tradition calls it a daisy, but it bears closer resemblance to a wild rose. It is the symbol of innocence.

Thistle The thistle stands for earthly sorrow and sin, with an added religious connotation because of its thorns. It is the heraldic and national emblem of Scotland. Seen chiefly as a finial.

Skull Signifies the transitory nature of life on earth, or it could have had a more macabre meaning for a rifle's owner. Seldom noted, and only as an inlay.

Bell Sometimes serves as a warning to demons, from St. Anthony Abbot having carried one attached to his crutch.

Bow Strangely, a bow stands for war and worldly power, while an arrow is considered a spiritual weapon. Both are seen occasionally on the rifles, with the arrow occurring more often of the two.

Scales Equality and justice are the obvious meaning of the scales. This inlay was reported on just one rifle, possibly made for a frontier magistrate.

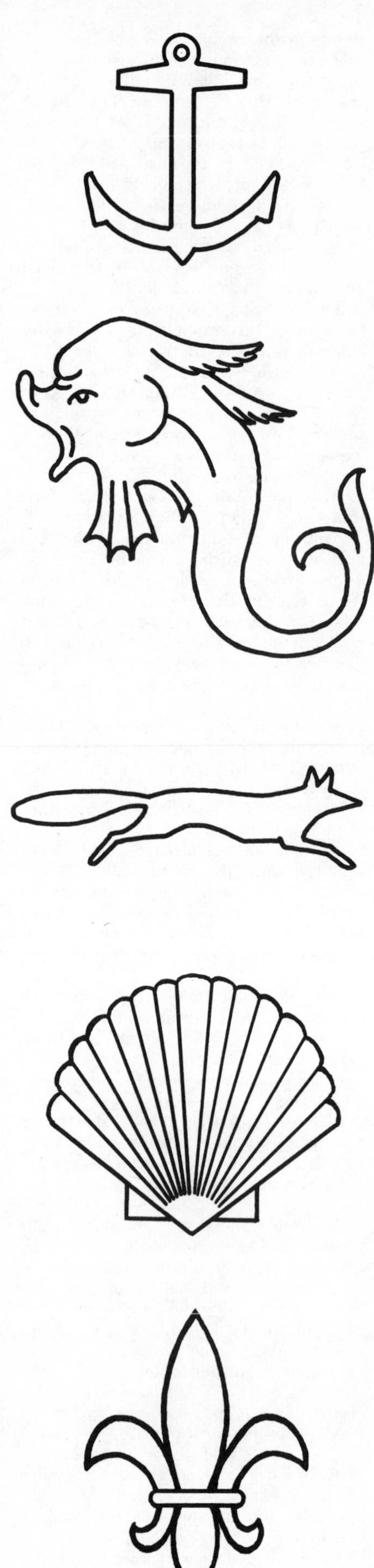

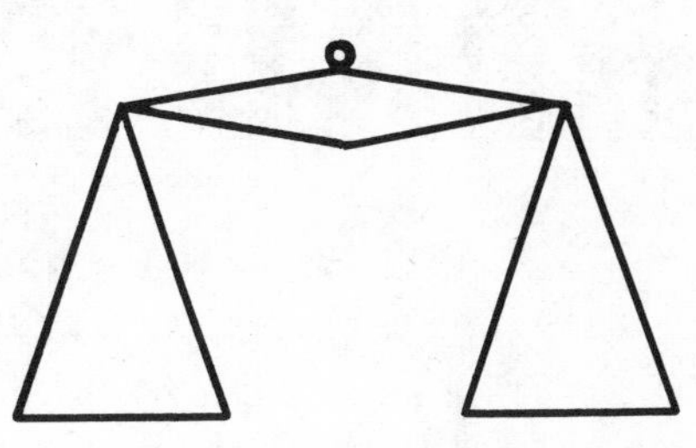

Sword A sword or knife signifies martyrdom in the early Christian code. It also might only indicate a military owner.

Torch This was one of the emblems of the Betrayal of Christ. On a rifle it was more likely to indicate the bringing of light to the wilderness.

Wheel This is a symbol of divine power, especially if it has flames all around its circumference. Otherwise, it indicates a traveler.

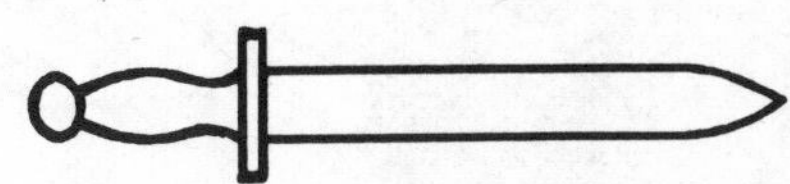

Pineapple This occurs almost exclusively on firearms made in Philadelphia. That city's gunmakers had to compete with those of England, therefore adopting the pineapple motif quite popular on English guns. In the writer's collection are a British percussion rifle and a Philadelphia Deringer, both bearing the pineapple design on their trigger guard finials. Thus, even arms of the following era support this observation from an authority on the American flintlock rifle.

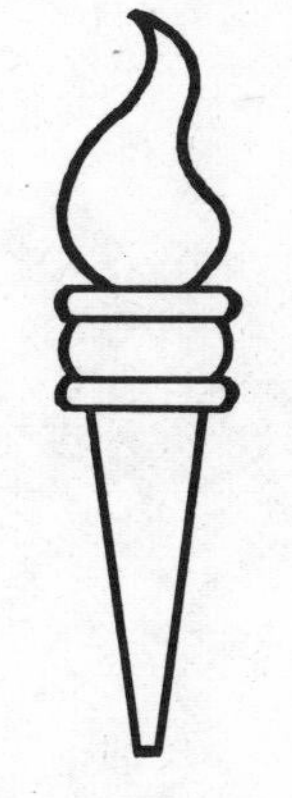

There are a number of others, not shown here because of the rarity of their occurrence. These would include the unicorn, all-seeing eye (Masonic), strawberry, harp, crown, horse, lion, centaur, etc.

In spite of the research represented by this list, plus the carefully considered opinions of leading authorities, the writer realizes it will not prove anything or convince anyone against his will. However, if it only stimulates interest in a sadly neglected facet of our American heritage, it might encourage further research by others who come after. •

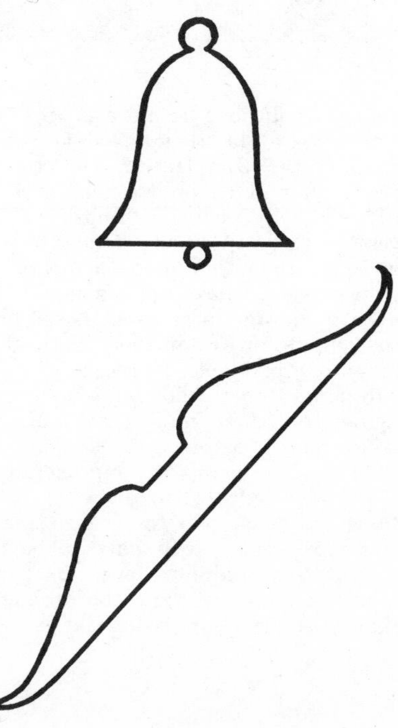

Gratefully acknowledged are the contributions to this research by the following persons and organizations. Their differences of opinion are respected, and each one has been reflected here:

Albert M. Sullivan, President, Kentucky Rifle Association.
Wes Kindig, Log Cabin Sport Shop, Lodi, Ohio
George Shumway, York, Pa.
Dr. J. T. Herron, Canonsburg, Pa.,
Jacob Zook, Paradise, Pa.
Henry J. Kauffman, Lancaster, Pa.
Joe Kindig, Jr., York, Pa.
Stephen V. Grancsay, Metropolitan Museum of Art, New York, N.Y.
Herschel C. Logan, Tustin, Calif.
M. L. Peterson, Smithsonian Institution, Washington, D. C.
Dr. John J. Stoudt, Kutztown, Pa.
Dr. Thomas T. Hoopes, St. Louis, Mo.
Richard Yarman, Mt. Vernon, Ohio
William Hout
The Historical Societies of Lancaster, York and Berks Counties, Pa.
William Penn Memorial Museum, Harrisburg, Pa.
Eagle Americana Gun Museum, Strasburg, Pa.
The Pennsylvania German Society, Allentown, Pa.

and others too numerous to mention.

HEAD HUNTING in B.C.

This vast Canadian province, half again as big as Texas, offers a great variety of big game—and plenty of it. Record heads—moose, caribou, grizzlies and blacks, elk and mountain goats—are still to be had in the Northwest. Go get 'em!

by Bradford Angier

THE HEAD HUNTERS in British Columbia are taking more big game trophies than ever. One of the reasons? In this 366,000-square-mile slab of western wilderness, an area more than 39 times larger than New Hampshire, only some 150,000 resident and 6,500 non-resident hunting licenses are sold annually even during these record years. In other words, there's plenty of room.

This is all the truer because most residents are more interested in top sirloins than in rocking-chair racks. Add to this the facts pointed out to me by game director, Dr. James Hatter, that 85 per cent of these residents are located on the lower mainland, that more than 90 per cent of them hunt within a 300-mile radius of their homes, while more than 60 per cent stay within a 100-mile radius, and that few pursue the mountain species. Thus you can better appreciate why so many of the really big trophies await the non-resident sportsman who is laying it on the line for something to go in the den rather than on the dining room table.

There's considerable difference, too, in the behavior of that top-heavy sheep or caribou when you're maybe the first human he's ever seen or scented. As I can personally testify after being exposed to a quarter-century of such action, a lot of other top game regions lose much of their glamor once you've hunted in British Columbia mountains where, as the saying goes, the hand of man has seldom set foot.

"We are making better use of our game populations as more people become aware of their existence and availability," Jim Hatter, Director of the Fish and Game Branch, said in his offices in Victoria. "Improved access in the way of new roads, use of aircraft, and other modern means of transportation have opened up to the average hunter large areas heretofore too remote for exploitation. Naturally, many non-residents, by reason of their willingness to spend large sums of money on their hunts, are able to reach more pristine game areas.

"The time is rapidly approaching," Hatter leveled, "when pioneer conditions will fade from the scene. Intensive management will have to be resorted to to maintain large and productive game herds, and the problems that arise from under-utilization will

A strange, but not unusual sight, is this hunter and his triple trophy—caribou, moose and mountain goat.

be replaced by those of control of use to a level compatible with the productive capacity of game herds."

In the meantime, though, what Jim Hatter calls "the most liberal wildlife harvest regulations to be found anywhere on this continent" still prevail. To state it another way, don't keep putting off that dream trip too long.

What reasonable man could? After all, who wouldn't like to hunt in a vast big-game reservoir, nearly half again as big as Texas, where there is one moose for every two deer. As for deer, there are so many on the sprawling Queen Charlotte Islands, just south of Alaska, that there is no closed season and no limit. In much of the remainder of British Columbia two deer may be collected, while in a large part of the Province the limit is three.

Moose

A couple of hundred million or so North Americans think that the only good moose hunting was back in pioneer days. They have the idea that the moose have been just about shot off. That's not true by a long way. Settlement and development have resulted in moose becoming scarce in many regions, especially near and below the U.S.-Canadian border. But farther north settlement has actually aided these all-time giants of the deer family.

British Columbia is an outstanding example. Moose were unknown in the central interior of this province until about half a century ago. Moose then started their southward march, advancing about 15 miles a year. Why? Logging, burning, and otherwise clearing the dense forests created ideal range for the huge mammals which can eat 40 to 50 pounds of browse in a day. Moose were first sighted south of Prince George in 1905. Now they've moved down to the International Boundary. The densest British Columbia moose populations are in this newly invaded area.

The sportsman has a chance at three different species including the largest of them all, the Alaska Moose, which ranges north from Telegraph Creek through the Yukon drainage basin including Atlin and Teslin Lakes. The British Columbia Moose roams throughout most of the remainder of the Province's largely un-

Not only blacks, but grizzly bear too, are common in the B.C. hunting grounds. About 300 are bagged annually.

settled wilderness except for the Pacific slope and some areas in the south. In the extreme southeast tip there is the smaller Yellowstone Moose.

Hunters will find more moose than ever, at least 250,000 of them. With seasons opened on all sexes and ages, there isn't the drain, either, there would otherwise be on trophy animals. The majority of the natives, as might be expected, prefer the tenderer cows and calves. Besides providing more moose for more people, the antlerless law is also paying off by cutting down feeding pressures.

"As every rancher knows," explains the Game Department, "it is good animal husbandry and range economy to sell his animals before he has fed and maintained them for too many years. If he markets two-year-old steers, he can produce twice as many in the same time it would take him to grow four-year-olds; and, certainly, the two-year-old is almost as valuable as the four-year-old. The more times the moose population is turned over, the more times the surplus is realized."

If, like a few million other sportsmen, you get a thrill out of the ultimate moment when you knock over a deer, then you haven't really lived until you look down the sights at a half-ton or more of moose. With seasons opening as early as late August, if you want to enjoy some unforgettable backsteaks before lugging home that spread, the secret is to hunt early, before the bulls start rutting at about the time of the full moon in September. That way they'll still be fat enough to make even the most skeptical realize why such trophies remain far and away the heftiest game animals in the New World that are widely hunted for their meat.

Grizzly and polar bear grow bigger, it's true. But neither is famous for its steaks. Moose meat is something else again. To put it briefly, it has been my main sustenance for better than a double handful of winters in northern British Columbia, and by choice.

Bears

Speaking of bear, the blackies in their various color phases are so numerous that you are allowed two of them. They run big and long-furred, too, and in a trail stove cook up into sizzling roasts so succulent that you have to eat them to believe them. With the cook trimming off most of the fat, the mulligans are something to write about in your diary, too.

As for their big cousins, about one-fourth of the 1,300-odd grizzly still bagged in North American annually fall to hunters in British Columbia. No reliable estimate of the number of grizzly bear in the Province has ever been made because of their peculiarly sensitive range requirements, but they number in the thousands.

"Grizzly are about as plentiful as ever in most British Columbia areas," the Department of Recreation & Conservation advised me recently.

This is plenty good. Outside of Alaska, British Columbia has long afforded the sportsman the best grizzly hunting in the world. Grizzly are found throughout most of the mountainous areas of the province and down as far as tidewater, although they are strangely absent from Vancouver Island and the Queen Charlottes. The head of nearly every inlet along the thick and wet Pacific coast mainland, a magnificent continuation of southeastern Alaska's, supports appreciable grizzly populations. Productive, too, are the thousands of square miles of open alpine country still seldom touched by human boot. British Columbia's most pro ductive grizzly areas today? According to the official surveys and statistics, they include the Bella Coola region, Knight Inlet, Owikeno Lake, and the Rockies.

Old Ephraim is no pushover. You're going up against an adversary who has been sharpening his survival skills since the day of the saber-toothed tiger. Some scientists figure that grizzlies were doing all right for themselves on this continent a million years before the first human being started making footprints here. It wasn't until the appearance of the white man himself that the self-reliant giant met any serious challenge.

The major threat confronting the grizzly today, say the experts, is the rapid change of the environment in which the big bear lives. Wilderness-type range represents the most important requirement of present-day grizzly habitat. The rapid shrinking of this type of country throughout much of the West has brought about the most serious condition the grizzly has yet encountered in its struggle for survival.

That's where British Columbia's largely unoccupied vastness pays off again. Although you have to ride four or five days straight into the wilderness with a pack train to begin really to appreciate the country's tremendous emptiness, you can get some comprehension of its bigness by realizing there's room in B.C. for all California, Oregon, and Washington, plus most of Idaho. The British Co-

Although not trophy size yet, these yearling elk are a promise of good hunting in the years to come.

lumbia season, depending on the area, is from August 13 to December 31.

Caribou

Some of British Columbia's best caribou hunting, for my money, is when you take after them during late summer and early autumn in tall country. This time of the year they're still up among the grizzly and sheep and goat above timber line. Climb a peak where you can glass the mountain slopes and high plateaus where they're ranging during the hot months, and within an hour you can often see a dozen-odd single and small bunches.

Caribou feed desultorily on such tidbits as willow and ground birch throughout such days. It is at dusk and dawn that they really begin moving around. I've lounged in the shadow of my horse in caribou country west of the Alaska Highway during August and September afternoons. Nothing much would be stirring except maybe some whistlers, a few ptarmigan, perhaps some ewes and lambs grazing beside a glacial lake, and maybe in the metallic ribbon of a stream half a mile below the darkness of a partially submerged moose. Then a ridge lifts in front of the sun, and a breeze starts trumpeting a cool blue note. All of a sudden, caribou who've also been escaping the heat appear in every direction.

British Columbia's Mountain and Osborn Caribou, two subspecies of the true mountain caribou, come down into the timber during the winter months. They do not bunch together on any very large-scale migrations, however. The Osborn, the taller-antlered and larger of the two, inhabit the high country of the Finlay, Liard, and Stikine River drainages in northern B. C. and range up into the Yukon Territory. The so-called Mountain Caribou are scattered to the south.

Like that of the mountain goat, the distribution of caribou in British Columbia is discontinuous, its areas of mountain habitat being separated by hundreds of miles of unsuitable plateaus and valleys. But where they abound, a sportsman with the time and persistence can be almost certain of a trophy. Either the Fish and Game Branch in Victoria, B.C., or the outfitters can give you the best steer.

As far as potential success is concerned, the best time in British Columbia to hunt this Stone Age animal —whose general appearance, judging from the carvings of cave men, hasn't changed for hundreds of years—is early in the season. The sportsman able and willing to pack well back above timber line early in September, with caribou hunting a major objective, is just about sure to collect after picking what he wants.

One reason? This most ruggedly beautiful of all North American game animals, with the most spectacular rack of any game on this continent, is on the increase in British Columbia, although its numbers are decreasing elsewhere in northern Canada. An estimated 20,000 caribou are now thriving in the remote regions of B. C. The fact that any size or sex is legal means a saving for the non-residents of those with real trophies—bulls with the magnificent spreads, frequently longer than the animal is tall, often fantastic in size, shape, and number of points.

Elk

There are approximately 2,000 elk on Vancouver Island, several hundred on the Queen Charlotte Islands, and at least 15,000 in that part of the Rocky Mountain Trench commonly called the East Kootenay area. Scattered bands of this largest and grandest of North America's round-antlered deer, once the most widely distributed in the New World when only Indians hunted here, also enliven the Peace River country. With only between 2,500 and 3,000 being harvested each year in B.C., most of the herds are maintaining their numbers, with increases noted in some districts of the East Kootenays.

Ever hear the bull elk's sweet, reedy *a-a-ae-e-eeeee-eaugh-ee-waugh eee-waugh?* The high, organlike notes still lift from many of British Columbia's bush peaks and forested draws, especially at dawn, and again at sunset, although they sound more desultorily throughout many days. The nearer you are to the bull, the more you can appreciate the resonance that deepens at the culmination in a series of mooselike grunts. However, elk, like people, have different voices. It's the old-timers that hit the depths. Youngsters among these smartest of all deer tend toward squeakiness, another tip-off on what you're stalking.

Although two or three thousand elk are harvested each year, their population is increasing in some areas.

"The most productive elk hunts in British Columbia come in the early part of the season, during the rut, and during the extreme end of the season when wapiti are moving onto winter ranges," points out Director James Hatter, who was taken on his first elk hunt by my old friend, Frank Butler, now resigned veteran game director whom Jim has succeeded. "If a hunter really wants to bag an elk, any elk, the best time for him to hunt is toward the latter part of the any-elk season. If what the sportsman wants is the best chance at a real trophy, the likeliest time to hunt is during the middle two weeks of September, when the rut is in progress."

Mountain Goats

Although mountain goat have disappeared from much of their former range in the southern Rockies, and in the United States, except for Alaska, are found only in Montana and Idaho in any numbers today, they are plentiful in British Columbia and abound throughout most of the mountain ranges. Numbering at least 25,000 and very possibly 50,000 here, they thrive in country so magnificently primitive and remote that they are comparatively unaffected by hunting.

In fact, man has had no apparent effect upon the British Columbia environment of this relative of the Swiss chamois, found in B. C. (except on the coast islands) wherever there are mountains of sufficient height and ruggedness for its preferred habitat. Since most of this habitat is situated above timber line, even the effect of fire has not been important. One of the breath-quickening spectacles on any pack trip in the Province is when a white dot first catches your eye up among the isolated vegetated patches and bare rocky faces and, all tiredness suddenly disappearing as you reach into a saddlebag, you finally get the glasses on the spot. All of a sudden, you pick out perhaps a half dozen dazzling white goat high among the clouds.

"Yep," the guide nods, "that old fellow with the long beard ought to look good on your wall. That's where we'll be tomorrow morning. There's good graze for a camp around the next bend."

Wild Sheep

British Columbia is also one of the world's sheep-hunting paradises, a fact that brings in a considerable proportion of non-resident trophy seekers. Stone sheep, usually so dark that it's often difficult to pick them out among the cliffs unless you catch them against the skyline, inhabit the Omineca and Cassiar portions of northern British Columbia, ranging down to the Peace River. The first two I ever shot, as a matter of fact, were within walking distance of my log cabin on the river.

The Stones mingle with Dall sheep near the Yukon border, producing the dramatic varied-colored Fannin sheep common to the Atlin Lake area. Isolated bands of pure Dall sheep occur near the Alaska Panhandle in the Saint Elias Range west of Atlin Lake, giving the Province three district varieties of thinhorn sheep in all.

As if that didn't furnish enough action for one $25 non-resident hunting license, Rocky Mountain bighorns occur on their native ranges in the Rocky Mountains from approximately the 55th parallel, below the Peace River, south to the U.S. border. This subspecies was also introduced into three areas in south-central B. C. in the 1920's.

British Columbia, too, has the last sizable herds of California bighorns in the world. Recent transplantings in Washington, Oregon, North Dakota, and most recently, Idaho came from here.

In other words, you can take your pick. This is the excuse that not a few of the head hunters grab onto to bring them back to British Columbia during succeeding sheep seasons which, varying with districts, run from August 13 to November 13. Another reason? Sheep roasts and chops are far and away the finest eating you'll ever come across in this hemisphere's game meat realm.

One of the best things about all hunting in British Columbia, in fact, is the large number of different trophies that are available, the Province having long been famed for the diversity as well as the abundance of its big game.

"The reason for this," as Jim Hatter says, "is that British Columbia itself is a Province of great physical and climatic diversity. With the Rockies on the east, sagebrush desert to the south, and rain forest on the coast, you can imagine some of the variations. But this is not all. Narrow fingers of grassland penetrate heavy forests in the central interior. This gives way in the north to typical Canadian spruce forest and muskeg. To add even greater variety, the topography is complicated by numerous river valleys and high mountain ranges. For example, at one point a traveler may be surrounded by dry sagebrush, while in another half hour he will be on top of a mountain beside a dark spruce forest. In most provinces one travels north to observe arctic and sub-arctic vegetation, but in British Columbia, you have only to climb a mountain.

"This variability of environment explains the great variety of game animals native to British Columbia. Every species of animal has its particular habitat requirements. With such a diversity of conditions, the Province is able to meet the requirements of life for most of the big game animals native to our continent."

What Does It Cost?

All this is yours for a $25 non-resident hunting license. This now even includes pheasants. With non-resident fishing licenses going for $7, you'll generally be well advised to pick up one of these, as casting a fly over virtually virgin waters is a fine way to fill in a lazy afternoon when you make camp early.

The non-resident *trophy* fee, which formerly varied depending on whether you were hunting north or south of the 56th parallel, has now been standardized throughout the Province. Rates for moose, elk caribou, and grizzly are $60 each. Mountain sheep run $75 each and goat $40 apiece. Any deer costs $25; each and every black bear is $5. This is only for trophies actually killed.

You can take home one of these sheep trophies on that $25 B.C. big game license, too. There are a great many to choose from—may as well get a good specimen like this.

With one registered guide being required for every two non-resident sportsmen, the hunt of a lifetime, therefore, can cost as little as three or four hundred dollars if you're willing to settle this time for maybe a moose, deer, and a couple of black bear obtained near the home ranch. This can be easily expanded up to several thousand dollars for an extended trek back of beyond, where the recordbook busters live, with you perhaps meeting the pack train at a mountain lake by plane.

A couple of final tips? If you're going big game hunting in British Columbia, get in shape first. This is particularly important if you are heading in by horse. But no matter how you travel, take a little more time at this stage if possible, and really get back into wild country. There, if you want a trophy badly enough to work for it, the odds are that you'll connect and collect big. ●

The Shooter's Showcase

● *There have been* several rifle rests offered in recent years — we've commented in past issues on most of these — but the latest to arrive is, we feel, one of the best. Perhaps we should say "two" because the Harris bipod comes in a couple of styles, though they're essentially similar.

All-metal made, the Harris rest carries two spring-loaded legs that fold back along the fore-end for easy transportation or may be instantly snapped into position for supporting the rifle. Attachment to the rifle is via a double-pin system that enters each side of the front sling-swivel base; tighten a slotted screw underneath and the Harris bipod is firmly fixed.

Model 1A has legs that may be extended from 7″ to 12″ plus, and in between as well; Model B, suitable for sitting or kneeling, has longer legs, these extending from a 12″ minimum to about 24″, and also lockable in between.

These Harris bipods, very sturdy and solid, attach to the fore-end, *not the barrel.* Normal point of impact is almost always raised when a barrel rest is used, but no change should occur with the Harris bipods.

The short version is $14.50, the Model B $16.50. A well-thought-out idea, and a highly practical one.

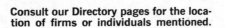

● *Another award* for "The Farm." Introduced early in 1968, Remington's 16mm sound-and-color motion picture, "The Farm," has garnered an impressive list of awards. Produced by Larry Madison, its latest honor was a "Teddy" as the best "How-To-Do-It" film at the National Outdoor-Travel Film Festival of the Michigan OWA, named after Theodore Roosevelt, the nation's first great conservationist president.

Other honors include a "Golden Eagle" presented by the Council on International Nontheatrical Events (CINE); a 3-star award in the annual conservation film contest of the Outdoor Writers Association of America, and the highest award in the educational division at the Columbus (Ohio) Film Festival. The CINE award qualified the film for entry in foreign festivals where it is expected to earn further acclaim.

"The Farm" tells the story of Remington Farms, the company's wildlife management demonstration area located near Chestertown, Maryland, on the Eastern Shore of the Chesapeake Bay. By tracing activities on the farm for the four seasons of the year, this 28-minute film shows how professional agriculturalists and game biologists are working together on research projects designed to demonstrate that good wildlife management and sound farming are compatible activities.

28 minutes long, prints for use by TV stations or for live audiences may be obtained free of charge from Modern Talking Picture Service, 1212 Avenue of the Americas, New York, N.Y. 10036.

Consult our Directory pages for the location of firms or individuals mentioned.

● *Rampak No. 334* is a new pack frame we've enjoyed using on a couple of hunting trips. Made by Himalayan Industries and sold by Bear Archery Co., this lightweight tubular aluminum frame holds their Hunter's Duffle No. 23 and is comfortable to wear. The design raises the load above the waistline and the padded harness clings to the shoulders. Side zippers make it convenient to get to articles in the main pack, and there's also a readily-accessible small zippered bag to hold ammo, etc. Leave the duffle at camp, fold Rampak's platform upward for woods mobility, and you're ready to pack out your trophy head comfortably. $28.90 buys Rampak and Duffle.

● *Tote-Seat,* a desirable combination of a back-pack, portable seat and shooting platform, is made of 3/8″ steel rod and 1/2″ plywood. The canvas knapsack provided measures 4″x10″x14″, large enough for your lunch, extra ammo and survival gear. Having located a spot you'd like to hunt, the Tote-Seat is positioned quickly by lashing the chains, used as a harness when backpacking, around a tree. The platform will support 300 lbs. $19.95 postpaid from Sportsgear, 4909 Fremont Ave. S., Minneapolis, Minn. 55409.

• *Waffen Frankonia,* the greatest distributor of firearms, ammunition and related items in West Germany, has just released the latest edition of their world famous and highly popular catalog, *Der Ratgeber für den Jäger* (The Hunter's Counsellor). This big (8¼"x11½") 290-page book is overflowing with attractively displayed wares for the sportsmen. Arms of every kind are listed, scopes, mounts, ammo, clothing, leather goods, you name it, it's there in profusion and frequently in 4-color presentation. We have just received a limited number of these German-language catalogs, complete with prices in Deutsche marks, which we can send anywhere in the U.S.A. for $2.50 postpaid. Write to P. O. Box Zero, Chicago, Ill. 60690. No CODs, please.

• *Cartridge collectors* must have a tough time adding new pieces by mail. While revising the 2nd edition of *Cartridges of the World* we needed some ammo for picture purposes—finding the correct rounds was difficult due to poor documentation. However, we ran across one catalog by Peter Bigler, 291 Crestwood Dr., Milltown, N.J. 08850, that's worth the $1 he asks. Mr. Bigler says he is a 30-06 military specialist, but he does deal in other areas—metric, British, shotshell and handgun. His listing makes selection precise and easy with a break-down on headstamp, primer material, sealer color and bullet identification. There's a lot of information in this book.

• *Dr. Edward L. Kozicky,* Director of Conservation for Winchester-Western, has been elected president of The Wildlife Society.

The Wildlife Society is an international professional organization comprised of some 4,000 game managers, research biologists, conservation educators and administrators, and other specialists in the wildlife field. The Society's objectives are to establish the highest possible professional standards; to develop all phases of wildlife management along sound biological lines; and to issue publications and other information. The Society publishes the *Journal of Wildlife Management* and *Wildlife Monographs.*

Dr. Kozicky, a native of Elberon, N.J., has written over 100 publications on game birds, and is the coauthor of the book *Shooting Preserve Management—The Nilo System.*

Consult our Directory pages for the location of firms or individuals mentioned.

• *Coleman* stoves and lanterns are as familiar and reliable as the Winchester 94. Coleman's latest catalog shows they've extended their line of outdoor recreational equipment to include sleeping bags, tents, catalytic heaters, insulated jugs and camp coolers.

Coleman's Model 5257 Convertible Cooler has been used by the staff and can be recommended as one of the best. On a hunt in Texas, where it gets hot, 25-lbs. of ice took almost three days to melt. For ultimate economy, there's a tap inside, below the ice compartment, that dispenses (you guessed it) ice cold water. The Convertible Cooler was so named because it can stand on either end, for left- or right-hand door opening, or as a chest by lying on its back. No matter how you pack the camper, car, truck or boat you can always make the contents of the Convertible Cooler accessible.

Since last year we've had time (and need) to use Coleman's catalytic Dial-Temp heater. Model 515 has a maximum output of 8000 BTUs and a minimum of 5000, dial any comfort level in between, yet it's only a foot in diameter and weighs 11 lbs.

A catalytic heater produces no smoke or carbon monoxide, but one word of caution, a bit of ventilation is always needed with or without a heater. Warming cold air causes moisture to condense and it's best to have warm, dry, fresh air rather than wet, stale air whatever shelter you use. Initial burn-in (carbonizing the heater's element) and lighting the heater should be done outdoors. The raw fuel poured over the element is not so completely consumed and does produce some smoke.

• *Repairing* broken or splintered gunstocks may be more reliable and predictable using Centerline Adhesive. Packaged in two graduated plastic units resembling large hypodermic syringes, this pure epoxy compound can be measured out precisely as needed and can be reclosed preserving it for later use.

There are literally thousands of epoxies, but this one should prove "just right" for general use around the shop. It provides high tensile, impact and peel strength, a high wetting action and has an unusual insensitivity to oil soaked wood. Stocks that were formerly considered beyond salvage can now be put back together if you still have the pieces. The kit is $1.95 postpaid from Centerline Products, P.O. Box 14074, Denver, Colo. 80214.

• *Bernz-O-Matic,* well-known propane-stoked lantern and campstove maker, has a new product that, ironically, makes other combustible materials (like wood) easier to set afire. "Fire Starters" are small, solid-fuel pellets about an inch square that light easily with a match but burn slowly without flaring up. Each Fire Starter burns for about 10 minutes, giving sufficient time to ignite most materials. Not as romantic as birch bark, perhaps, but they're handy out in the field. At home they can start the Bar-B-Q grill or the trash burner. Inexpensive, too, a package of 24 is 98¢.

• *Foredom Electric Co.,* Bethel, Conn. 06801, makes a variety of miniature power tools than can do many small jobs very efficiently. These electrically powered, variable speed, flexible-shaft tools sell for $39 up. Add collets, abrasive points, burrs, brushes, sanding drums, buffs, carving bits, saws, drills, mandrels, arbors and chucks best suited to your needs. A variety (14) of handpieces is available—all run quiet, virtually vibrationless and do not heat up in operation.

Those owning a good motor may equip it with the "Flexade"—a flexible shaft best operated between 1500 and 14,000 RPM. Flexades, less expensive, start at $14.25, and will accept the same range of accessories as the basic flex-shaft tools.

Foredom's miniature bench grinder is only 1/15 HP but has a completely variable speed range from 0 to 14,000 RPM. Selecting proper peripheral speed is usually overlooked when grinding, polishing or buffing but should be considered for best results. The grinder is $30 and a Flexade may be attached for greater utility. Write for their catalog describing these tools and a wide range of accessories in greater detail.

• *Guns Illustrated 1970.* This big 224-page volume, the 2nd edition, is a complete guide to current firearms of all types, foreign and domestic; to loading tools, ammo components, scopes, sights, etc. A valuable reference, the cost is $2.95, and it's available at your gunshop, sports store or bookseller.

• *Cartridges of the World.* 2nd edition, has been enjoying a very good sale indeed. Brought fully up to date, this new and revised issue has 32 extra pages more than the first edition, these containing all new material on the several cartridges announced since 1964, and the few minor errors of omission and commission found in the original book have been cleared up. Prepaid, $7.95 or at your favorite gun- or bookshop.

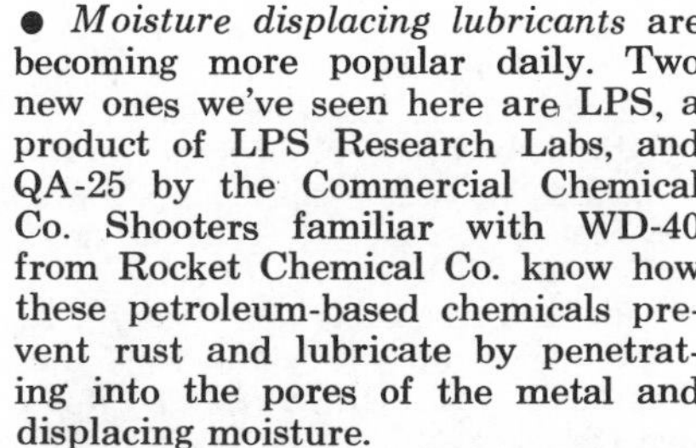

• *Moisture displacing lubricants* are becoming more popular daily. Two new ones we've seen here are LPS, a product of LPS Research Labs, and QA-25 by the Commercial Chemical Co. Shooters familiar with WD-40 from Rocket Chemical Co. know how these petroleum-based chemicals prevent rust and lubricate by penetrating into the pores of the metal and displacing moisture.

LPS is made in three grades—#1 and #2 are similar in forming a .0001″ transparent oily film, but #2 has greater viscosity, stays on better. #3 (much like RV-2 by Silicote Corp.) forms a .0002″ transparent, soft, waxy film said to protect metal *outdoors* for two years or more against salt, acid or chemical fumes, and moisture as well.

WD-40 is now packed in a 2¾ oz. "take me along" can—handy in the field. QA-25 oil; Anti-Rust (Riel & Fuller) and 7-11 (Silicote Corp.) are similar products, and there are undoubtedly others available.

• *A simple-to-install,* inexpensive and useful item is the Paulin conversion unit. Attachable in seconds, literally, to Coleman and other gasoline-burning 2- or 3-burner stoves, the Paulin fitting allows use of clean propane gas — or a quick return to gasoline at any time.

Propane gives off a clear, hot flame instantly, of course, and because white gasoline is getting harder to find all the time, the Paulin can come in very handy indeed — propane cylinders are available everywhere.

The standard Paulin converter is $7.95; a 6-ft. hose and fittings for a large propane tank is $9.60 extra.

Among numerous other Paulin products of interest to campers is their *refillable* propane cylinder ($3.50) and the refill adaptor for it at $3.00. With disposable cylinders selling for $1 or more usually, this pair of units soon pays for itself.

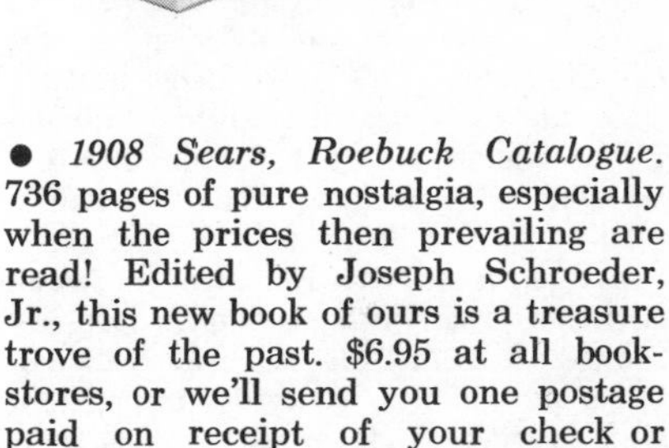

• *1908 Sears, Roebuck Catalogue.* 736 pages of pure nostalgia, especially when the prices then prevailing are read! Edited by Joseph Schroeder, Jr., this new book of ours is a treasure trove of the past. $6.95 at all bookstores, or we'll send you one postage paid on receipt of your check or money order.

• *Single Shot Rifles and Actions,* by Frank de Haas, covers 55 different actions in great detail. Photographs, line and sectional drawings to scale, history and development, suitability or not for modern ammunition, etc. A truly great work of 288 pages, 8½″ x 11″, postpaid anywhere in the U.S. for $7.95.

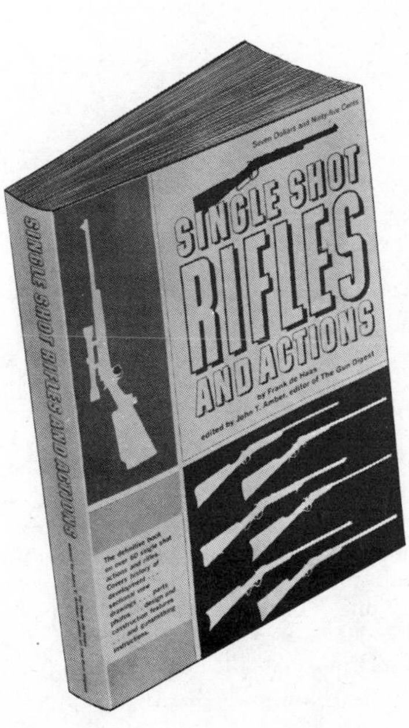

• *Armite Laboratories,* makers of Rust Buster and 12/34 (another moisture displacing lube) have a new product of interest: Led-Plate No. 250 is an anti-seize compound of 70% pure lead powder and 30% non-volatile vehicle. The anti-seize feature prevents a corrosive weld between metal surfaces—the lug bolts holding the wheels to your car are an example—eliminates galling and freezing, and provides a lubricating film between surfaces. Led-Plate is unaffected by temperature and pressure as well. On telescope sights, where adjustment caps seem to lock or an eyepiece is a bit rough to turn, No. 250 may solve the problem—it did for us in a couple of instances. Their No. 250-F is a filler for every high-pressure application.

• *Tex Wirtz,* 1925 W. Hubbard St., Chicago, Ill. 60622 makes realistic decoys of tough, moulded plastic. Ducks and geese decoys are oversize, expertly done, show good color and plenty of feather detail. Write for a brochure—not only can you use these as decoys, they would make pleasant lawn decorations also.

• *Tent pegs* have been the curse of campers for years. I can recall *trying* to drive GI types into the concrete West Texans call sand. Reliance Products, Ltd., 1830 Dublin Ave., Winnipeg 21, Canada, has a solution. Their Power Peg is made of strong, yellow impact plastic.

On first inspection, they looked nice but I doubted their usefulness. No sharp edges, not even the point, but tests proved their strength and utility. We've used these as tent pegs, of course, but guyed lines and wedged wood blocks with them; beat them with an entrenching tool and sledgehammers, but we've yet to break one. Three to a card the 9" Power Pegs are $1; three 12" for $1.15. One day I'll return to West Texas for the acid test.

• *Genuine Arkansas Stones* are available from Russell's, P.O. Box 474, Fayetteville, Ark. 72701. Technically, Novaculite is a rare mineral found in the Ouachita mountains of central Arkansas. Slabs are cut with diamond saws and hand-polished to size using a revolving cast iron table and emery grit. Most of the work is done by hand, thus labor makes them rather expensive.

However, don't compare Russell's stones with emery — Arkansas stones don't wear down as rapidly, they'll slick an edge quicker and with reasonable care (don't drop one, they shatter) one will last a lifetime. If you haven't used one, you don't know what you've been missing.

Having sold you one, let me try for two. One Russell stone is hard, extremely hard, and should be used only for razor-sharp edges—surgeons please note! The other, not as hard, is still highly durable, being more useful to the hunter for skinning knives, etc.

I'm enthusiastic about Russell's Arkansas stones because, having lost one handed down to me, they're almost impossible to find elsewhere, and nothing commonly available produces a finer edge. They're cut in a variety of sizes and shapes, but WCP-0515, a 3¾"x1⅜"x⅜" pocket-sized stone in a soft plastic sheath at $2.40, is our choice.

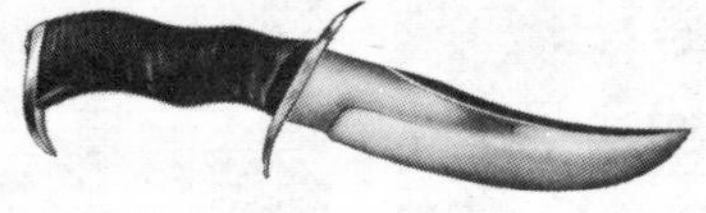

• *W. F. Moran, Jr.,* the custom knife maker, has designed a new combat knife—the M23. Meant especially for the serviceman in Viet Nam, Moran says it incorporates the best features he's forged into his knives over the years. The hand-filling, comfortably shaped handle has a hooked pommel to pull the knife out should it become stuck — for this is a combat knife. However, it has proved itself in the field as a survival and utility knife as well. Blade is 7" long and 1¾" wide. Price $95.

All of Moran's 22 other models—everyone individually hand forged, shaped and stocked—are still available, priced from $20 to $450! The blade finish is superb, resembling first class chrome-plating, but it's not, there's only the handsome steel. A life-time investment, all Moran knives are made to order, either in stock patterns or to your own design. Delivery time at present is 18 months.

• *Shooting glasses* are a necessary expense for safety's sake. Many shooters may have put off buying a pair because the $15 or so could buy a new set of scope rings or a few boxes of ammo. You can't evade the issue that way any longer—now you can easily afford to protect your eyes and see the target better too!

Davis Aircraft Products makes smartly styled glasses that are shatterproof, glareproof and distortion free. A special ridge spanning the top lets them fit over regular eye glasses, too. Side shields cut out cross-light and reduce reflections. Four colors, yellow, green, grey and a special hunter's amber are available. The amber hue filters out all colors except red, brown and green for better vision and additional safety in the woods. Buy some eye safety for $2.98 per pair.

• *Yield House* publishes a 64-page catalog of furniture and decorative accessories to help turn that spare room into a first class sportsman's den. Cabinets for 6 to 16 guns are made as finished units or in kit form for you to assemble and finish. Wall and floor racks are also available. Too many "goodies" to describe here, so write Yield House, Dept. 228, North Conway, N.H. 03860.

• *Keep It Clean* A Winchester-Western rep was recently threatened with mayhem after a game manager field-tested the new HD Magnum shotshell.

This revolutionary new shell features a shot charge packed in powdered polyethylene. The cushion of white plastic "sawdust" prevents deforming of shot pellets and gives amazingly uniform patterns.

Some HD Magnum loads were shipped to state game departments for field testing, and one game manager wrote back: "I cut open one of the shells and it appears to be packed with laundry detergent. What's the deal?"

The unofficial reply from W-W was: "Well, you want clean kills, don't you?"

● *Proper footwear* is extremely important to the hunter. If your feet hurt or your boots slip and leak water, the hunt you've looked forward to may not be much fun. Wisconsin Shoe Co., 1039 S. 2nd St., Milwaukee, Wis. 53204, makes the "Game Warden" boot (style 8406), an excellent choice for most purposes short of mountain climbing. Made of tan glove leather, this 8″ boot is fully leather lined, including its cushioned insole. A bellows tongue, storm welt and one-piece crepe sole and heel should keep your feet dry and comfortable. They're $24.95, sizes 7 to 12 and 13 and in D, E or EE widths. Mine have given me full satisfaction, and several other styles are available.

● *W. Kneubuhler* makes fine, hand-crafted knives of historic American patterns. The eleven knives bearing the "WK" trademark are fully guaranteed against any defects in materials or workmanship. Designed as replicas of famed frontier knives, they're good, sturdy, serviceable tools — they'll last a lifetime with reasonable care.

We've had the Popo Agie (standard and little models) knives here for inspection and trial. They are well-executed, handsomely fitted and polished, and are beautifully sharp. Big Popo is heavy, having a 5½″ blade 1¼″ wide and ¼″ thick — just what is needed to cut through the joints when quartering a big critter. Little Popo has 4¾″ blade 1¼″ wide and ½″ thick, which makes this smaller version a good skinner and suitable for most general chores afield. Both have stag handles. Prices are quite reasonable, considering that each WK knife is hand-made; $30 for Little Popo Agie, $32.50 for the big one. Prices include a sole leather sheath, hand-stitched and snug fitting.

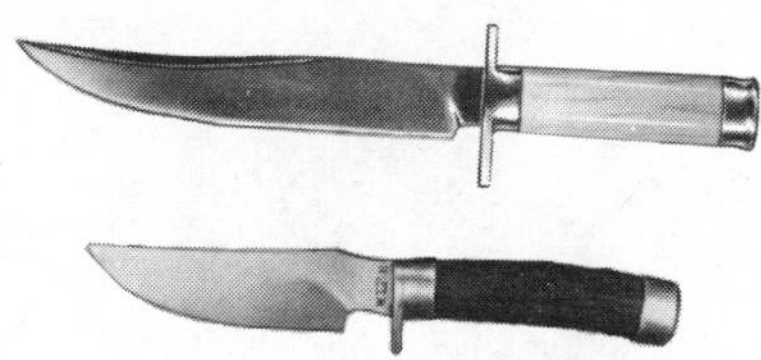

W.K. patch knives, hunting bags, hatchets and other authentic muzzle-loading accessories — as well as his hunting knives — are described in the W.K. catalog, cost 25¢. There's a bit of history on the men who originally styled these knives and information on how they're reproduced today.

● *Firearms enthusiasts unite!* When the government saw fit to close the Springfield Armory in 1964, the citizens of Springfield, Mass., united to preserve this historic landmark and superb 10,000-piece collection intact. There was a proviso, however; the government agreed to donate the collection—the Main Arsenal and the Commandant's house, to form a museum complex on the 5 acres these buildings occupy—if sufficient funds could be raised to maintain the collection and museum.

The Springfield Armory Museum, Inc., is a non-profit organization created to operate these facilities. The officers and board of directors are a group of historically oriented citizens interested in preserving this historic landmark. They donate their time and effort without pay.

At present the two buildings do not conform to city and state regulations for public use. Extensive alteration and restoration is necessary. New stairwells and a heating system need to be installed. Elevators need renovating, parking facilities and grounds work will be needed. This work will require about $650,000 minimum.

Donations are being sought, but this is more than a gift, it's an investment. Your donation can be a single payment or pledge to be paid over a 3-year period. The amount you send is deductible, so be as generous as possible to help preserve our heritage for the generations that follow. Send check, money order or pledge to Springfield Armory Museum, c/o Safe Deposit Bank and Trust Co., P.O. Box 38, Springfield, Mass. 01101. Acknowledgment, membership card and insignia lapel pin will be forwarded by return mail.

Members and their families are entitled to free admission to the museum, the museum bulletin and may avail themselves of the research and information center. A good investment even if you don't need the extras.

● *John M. Olin,* honorary chairman of the board of Olin Mathieson Chemical Corporation, was named recipient of the First Annual Award of the North American Game Breeders and Shooting Preserve Association at the association's recent convention at Callaway Gardens, Pine Mountain, Ga.

Presented by Gov. Lester Maddox of Georgia, the inaugural award cited Mr. Olin for his contributions to the game breeding and shooting preserve industries. A pioneer of the modern shooting preserve concept of quality shooting in natural surroundings, Mr. Olin was responsible for the development of Nilo Farms, the first demonstration and experimental shooting preserve.

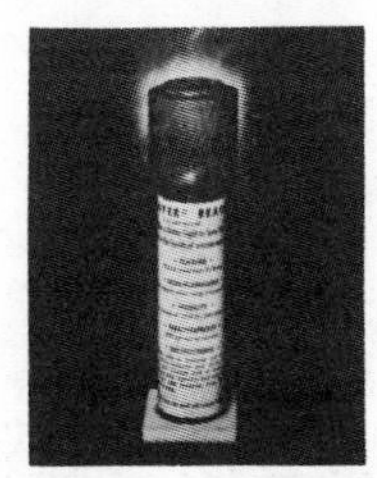

● *Lifesaver Beacon* is a red, battery-powered emergency flasher to be used on the highway to prevent accidents. The flashing light can be seen 1000 yards or more at night and is an approved highway safety device. Made of plastic and weighing 8 oz., it is weatherproof and should last for years. The two batteries included will power the Lifesaver Beacon for 30 hours of continuous service. Lifesaver Beacons are available for $1.98 at auto suppliers, service stations, drugstores and supermarkets.

● *Gun cases* of moulded plastic, urethane-foam lined, are now made by many firms. However, Challanger Mfg. may have a really big winner, their No. 4100 Carbine Case. Designed to fit *any* popular carbine made in the U.S. today with or without scope, it measures 41″x9″x3¾″ and is compact and handy like the carbine it protects. A full-length piano hinge and three draw-bolt locks make it rugged. The metal bead with walnut grained trim compliments the brush brown or Moroccan green exterior. The Challanger Carbine Case is $36.95 and unconditionally guaranteed. If No. 4100 is anything like their earlier models we've tested, both consumer and manufacturer should be satisfied.

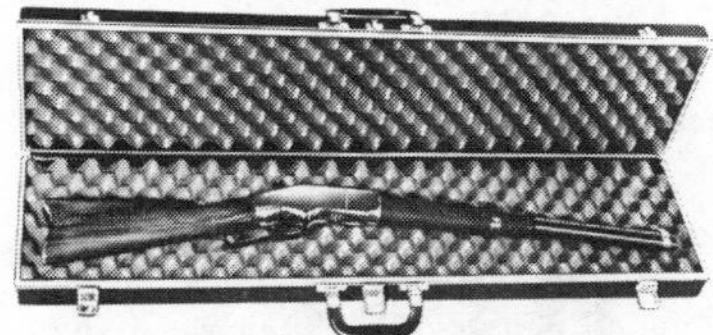

Here's a switch—Challanger built their reputation by making sturdy, durable, hard-surfaced gun cases. Their newest case, of genuine leather (green rough-out), is made to carry shooting accessories and associated gear. Resembling a photographers gadget bag, the Sportsman Field Case (TGL-29) is well made with a full zipper around three sides of the main bag's top. A large outside pocket, expandable to hold smaller items, is secured by two straps.

The Sportsman Field case proved its worth on a number of hunts—being handy for ammo and cleaning gear, camera and film, etc. Of airlines carry-on size, the TPL-29 will look at home in the field or aboard a trans-oceanic jet. $39.95. (E.D.)

● *Walle-Hawk* "is a metal survival tool better than knife or compass, because it's both," (and a couple dozen other things too) says Jessie Morrison, its inventor. Among the uses suggested are: cutting, wire forming, signaling, lighting matches, stripping wire, and as a can or bottle opener, a screw and nut driver, leather punch or as a fishing lure. That's a lot of utility from a tool small enough to fit in your wallet—about the same size as a credit card. The one that's been floating around the office since the last edition has been used by everyone. For opening packages and pulling those treacherous, heavy staples from cartons it can't be beat by any two larger tools. Send $5.95 to Walle-Hawk, P.O. Box 1024, Burlington, Vt. 05401.

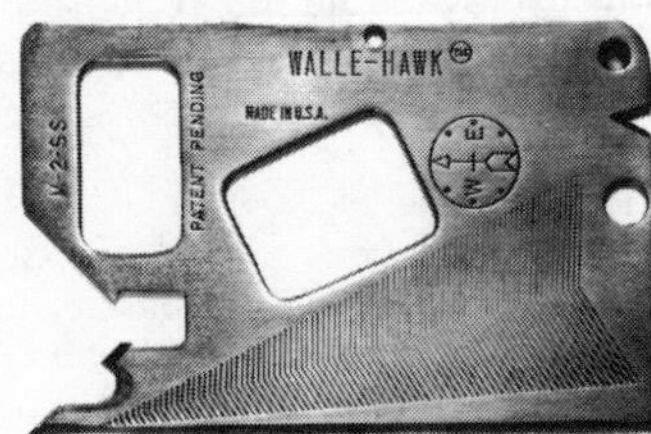

● *Field Guide for Trophy Hunters* is a pocket-size book available from Denver Jonas Bros., 1037 Broadway, Denver, Colo. 80203 for 50¢. These 24 pages are crammed full of dope explaining exactly what to do after the game is downed. Animals, birds and fish are covered and directions for shipping your trophy to the taxidermist are explicit—even from overseas. A good booklet for every trophy hunter to carry on the hunt.

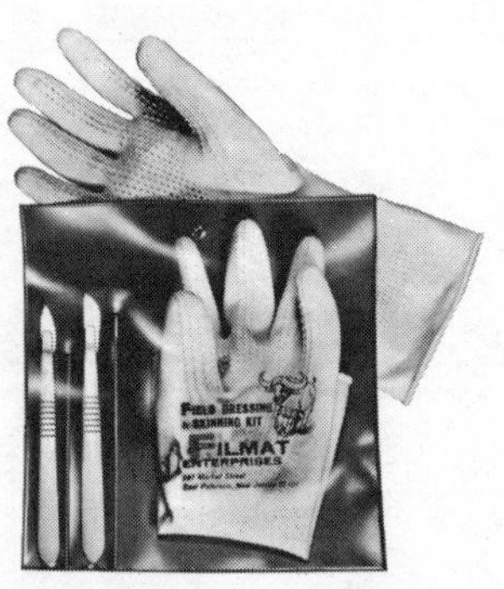

● *Carbon monoxide,* suffocation, asphyxiation — it usually happens in that order — will become prevalent terms again this fall as sportsmen take to the field with their portable heaters. When these are used in trailers, campers, fishing shacks, converted buses or cabins and tents, there is always a chance of doing yourself in unless you provide some ventilation. Even with the new catalytic heaters, tightly enclosed areas should be provided with fresh air ventilation—the human body burns oxygen too! Heed this advice and we'll see you again next year.

● *Teflon*—now a household word—has finally found its way into the gunshop. Nutec, Inc., developed Dry Gun Lube as a dry, stainless lubricant with all the slippery properties of Teflon. Dry Gun Lube can be sprayed from its aerosol can and will stick tenaciously to most surfaces, but is easily removed, if desired, by cleaning fluid or gasoline.

We've used this product for about a year and can recommend it for lubricating surfaces where oil is especially unsuitable. Used between the slide and frame of a Browning Medalist and a 1911 Colt made them feel like they've been accurized.

Dry Gun Lube stays put—one application is generally sufficient—and it has many applications at the reloading bench, too, from the press ram to a sticky cabinet drawer. A 4-oz. can at $1.98 will go a long way —only a light film is necessary.

● *17-caliber* enthusiasts needed rifle cleaning gear desperately last year. Here's good news from Outers Laboratories: just released is a 3-piece *steel* rod (still packed in a steel box) with tips, brushes, solvent, patches and oil. The kit price is about $4.25, while the 17-cal. rod alone will be $2. 17-cal. brushes of brass, bronze, Nylon and bristle are also available.

Outers Electric Smoker is a compact (11½" x 12" x 24½") portable smokehouse. It loads from the front, is made of aluminum, and weighs 16 lbs. A flavor pan (for the hickory sawdust supplied) is inserted above the electric heating element—the sawdust or chips just smolder. Urban hunters and gourmets can now do-it-themselves, be it in the backyard, patio or on the balcony of a high-rise.

● *Checkering* a gunstock yourself may provide personal satisfaction and save money, but arriving at a good design can be a rough nut to crack. Stan de Treville, P.O. Box 2446, San Diego, Calif. 92112, makes decal checkering patterns varying from simple diamond form to quite intricate designs with carved borders—pick one best suited to your gun and skill. If you appreciate the work of Leonard Mews or Monty Kennedy, you'll find their designs represented, too. At $1.50 to $1.75 each, these checkering patterns take much of the sweat out of stock checkering.

● *Cleaning* lead and plastic from the shotgun's bore isn't a quick or pleasant job. Schmid & Ladd, P.O. Box 4066, Clearwater, Fla. 33518, will help speed this task if you buy their new chamber cleaning brush. A sturdy, oversized (1"x4"") bronze wire brush is mounted on a 10" rod of ⅜" aluminum with a T-handle (Model 10-H), without the handle (10-NH) for use with a ¼" drill or with a 32" (32-NH) rod to run completely through the bore from the breech end. Any one of the three is $4.95 postpaid.

● *Storing guns* safely, while keeping them out of the hands of kids and unauthorized persons, has been a problem difficult to solve at low-cost. Lundy's Gun-Locking Chain offers a simple solution that's as good as any, aside from a walk-in vault. It is very strong, made of two lengths of steel, forged-link chain, enclosed in a flexible plastic sleeve to prevent marring your guns. Easily installed by epoxying the attached wood blocks (available in decor-matching finishes) to the wall — screws/bolts and wood plugs included for permanent, more secure attachment — the chains run through the trigger guards and are locked with the padlock supplied. Lundy's chain may also be used inside gun cabinets or racks. Complete package is $20.95.

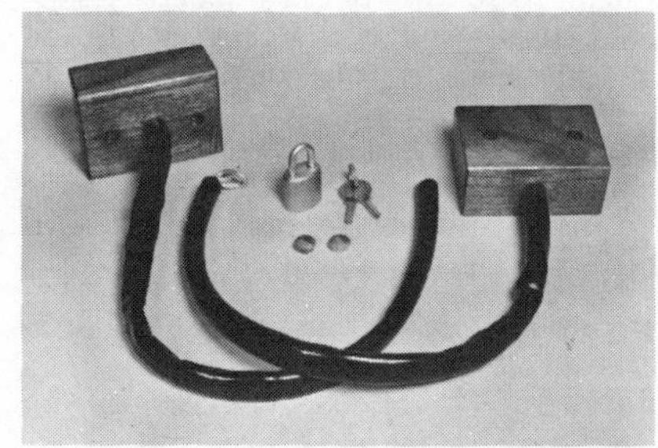

● *Field dressing* and skinning kits, available from Filmat Enterprises, 287 Market St., East Paterson, N.J. 07407, eliminate much of the dressing-out mess, and are designed especially for the job. The compact plastic case holds two scalpels with stainless steel blades and a pair of sure-grip skinning gloves. It's easy to pack the kit along, and after use it can be replaced in the pouch to be washed later. Get yours for $4.95.

● *East Tenn Mills,* makers of athletic garments, enters the gun world with their Gun Sock. Looking like something that went wrong at the plant, the Gun Sock is the longest (3 ft.), one-size-fits-all piece of hosiery we've ever seen. Knitted of 100% Nylon and silicone treated, it stretches long enough for most shotguns or rifles — some with scopes mounted too. Gun Socks may be had in solids, stripes or checks at $2 each. When was the last time you bought one sock?

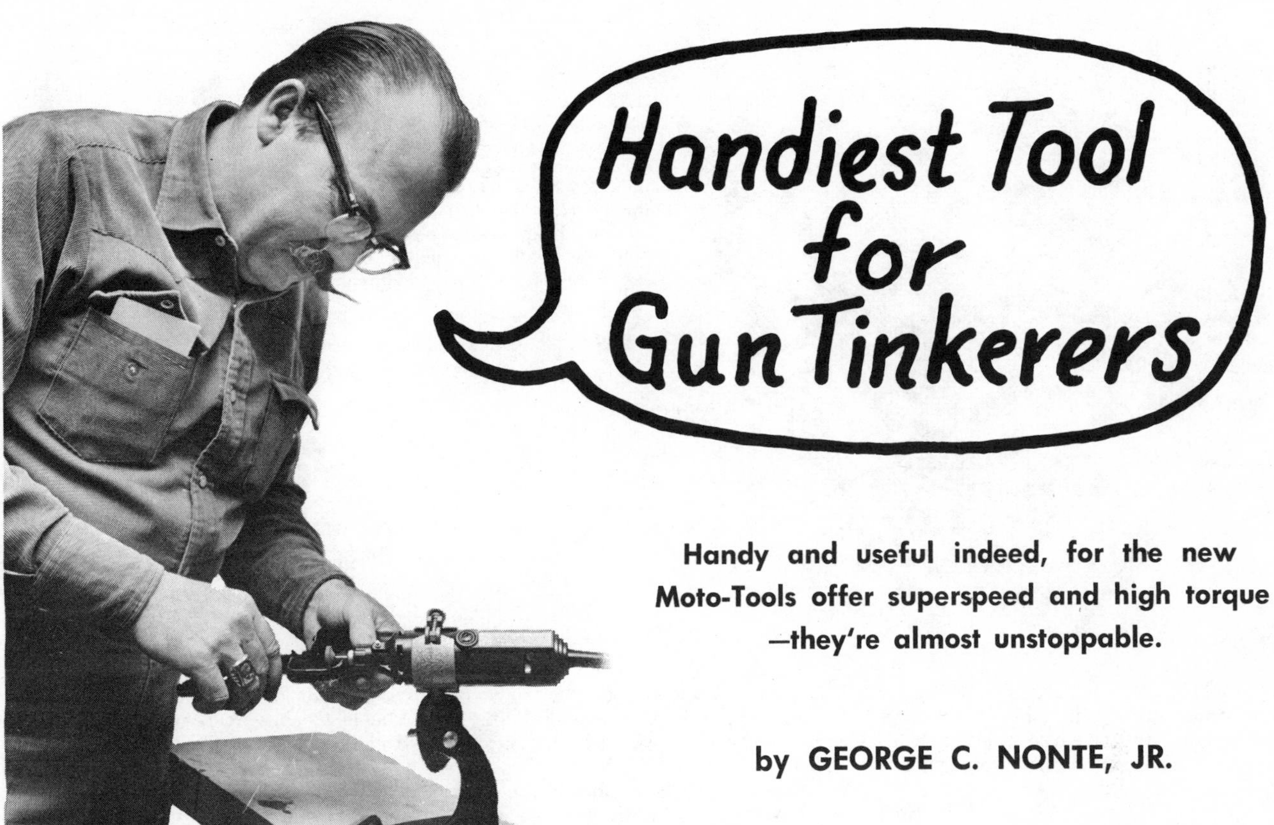

Handiest Tool for Gun Tinkerers

Handy and useful indeed, for the new Moto-Tools offer superspeed and high torque —they're almost unstoppable.

by GEORGE C. NONTE, JR.

DURING the score of years that I bounced around the world as a member of our military establishment, I learned to pare the weight and bulk of my outfit to the bare minimum. Yet, like many other gun buffs, I always had to keep enough tools handy to repair, refurbish and, sometimes, completely rebuild whatever interesting, worthwhile guns could be acquired along the way. It didn't take long to find out that hauling heavy equipment around in a footlocker or bedroll is entirely out of the question. But, I did discover a power tool that could be carried in a coat pocket, if necessary. It would drill, grind, shape, and polish to the extent usually necessary in barracks gunsmithing. Slower and less efficient for some jobs than bench-mounted tools, I must admit, yet its low cost, portability, and versatility far offset those minor shortcomings. Also, it could do a lot of jobs that big tools couldn't handle at all.

That item was the Dremel Moto-Tool Electric Hand Grinder; I've been using various models of it now for over 25 years. I'd sure hate to have to get along without it, especially in the little shop off my office. While the older No. 1, 2, and 3 models gave (and still do) fine service, the new No. 270 and 280 models are by far the best yet.

Basically, the Moto-Tool is a hand-held grinder measuring 1½" in diameter, 6" long, weight 11 ozs. The durable Lexan plastic housing is shaped for easy control and handling and contains a direct-drive motor that spins the ⅛" collet chuck at 30,000 rpm. Now, that's fast! In the process it develops, at stall speed, 16 inch-ounces of torque, 5 times that of some other popular grinders. To produce this performance, the new tool uses a direct-current, permanent-magnet motor running off rectified household AC, and draws just under one ampere. A heavy-duty shaft-mounted fan cools the tiny motor so it doesn't heat up during sustained use. The No. 280, incidentally, differs from the Dremel 270 in that it is fitted with ball bearings, insuring longest possible life under heavy use. Frankly, I've never had one of the sleeve-bearing models give any trouble in this respect.

An almost endless variety of accessories adaptable to gun work is available with the Moto-Tool — shaped grinding and polishing wheels, buffers, wire brushes, slitting and cutoff saws, rotary files, and routing (wood) bits. Other accessories most useful in gun work include a drill press stand, a bench stand, variable speed control, and a routing attachment. Shank sizes of all the mounted accessories run up to ⅛", which is maximum capacity of the largest chuck furnished for the Moto-Tool. Over 20 different grinding wheel shapes are available, each in several sizes; a dozen shapes in rotary files; and a lesser number in sanding drums, felt polishing wheels, engraving cutters, saws (both wood and metal), cutoff discs, mandrels, etc.

Here the Moto-Tool is clamped in a bench stand for better control while narrowing a trigger guard. Incidentally, safety glasses are a must for *any* grinding or cutting operation with *any* power tool.

This wide variety of tools and accessories makes it possible to do virtually any gun job requiring removing, reshaping, or smoothing wood or metal. There are many jobs which cannot, in fact, be done properly or efficiently with any other type tool. Moto-Tool's small size gets it into places that can't be reached by bigger outfits.

One of the first jobs my Moto-Tool did (many years ago) was fitting a Smith & Wesson target sight to a battered but good 1917 revolver. All the slots and cuts in the top strap and frame were roughed out with shaped grinding wheels, and then trued up with files. The blind slot for the elevation screw head was made with a small-diameter cutoff wheel. Had a milling machine been available, the job could have been done quicker, but slow is a lot better than not at all. That is one feature of having a tool like this—you'll find yourself accomplishing repair and alteration jobs that would not otherwise get done.

Gunsmithing Jobs

It's hard to say just which jobs are most likely to be handled with a

Left — The new Dremel Moto-Tools also come in kit form with 34 accessories, all housed in a moulded polyethelene storage case. Prices run from $32.95 to $49.95. Right — The Dremel No. 229 Router Attachment sells for $9.95, uses any of the current Moto-Tools for power. High speed router bits cost $3.00 each.

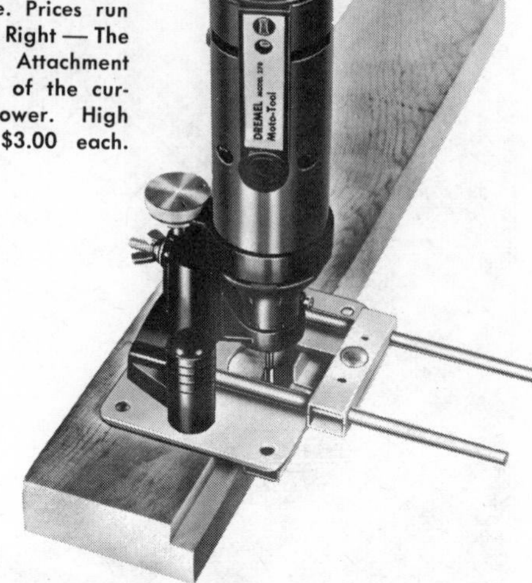

Moto-Tool. If you are a working or part-time gunsmith, doing odd jobs for friends and the like, the list is almost endless and will certainly include the following:

Spotting holes: Fitting scope mounts or receiver sights on military surplus rifles requires accurate drilling and tapping of several holes, often through hard surface skins. It is difficult to centerpunch or start drills accurately until the skin is ground away. A ⅛"x½" silicon wheel or, better yet, a silicon small-ball "point" in the Moto-Tool makes very short work of grinding a starting spot. This will prevent drill "walk."

Altering extractors: In converting so-called standard-caliber bolts to one of the belted magnums, the extractor claw must be cut back and carefully reshaped — a job that takes endless hours if done with files and stones. The Dremel tool and a couple of mounted wheels can do the job in a few minutes. Special care is required to insure that enough extractor tension is retained to hold a loaded round against the bolt face, while at the same time providing sufficient clearance for the cartridge to feed smoothly into the bolt face from the magazine. Particular care must be taken to shape the claw to match the groove in the case; a sharp edge on the extractor is bad. Then, with the Moto-Tool used as a tool post grinder you can open up the bolt face for the larger case head.

Reshaping feed rails: When rifles are rebarreled to new calibers, the magazine often fails to feed the new cartridge correctly. This is particularly true of the belted magnum cases. I know of no practicable way to reshape the inside of the rails other than with a hand grinder. The ⅜"x½" mounted emery wheel works well for this, and the job should always be finished by polishing the rails with a felt or hard rubber wheel. Feeding in almost any gun will usually be improved by such polishing. This is a cut-and-try job and should be done in slow stages, checking to see where cartridges bind and/or are misdirected.

Bolt alterations: When forging or welding a bolt handle to scope height, a lot of hand filing and polishing can be avoided by using the Moto-Tool with wheels and sanding drums. For this purpose, it is even better than a bench grinder because of its smaller size and ease of control. Fitting a scope safety often involves removal of small amounts of metal from the bolt sleeve or cocking piece, and these parts are usually too hard to cut with a file. The Dremel Moto-Tool does the job in seconds. Cocking effort can often be reduced considerably by carefully polishing the cocking cams and, sometimes, the extractor cam which may also bear during bolt lift. Lapping of these surfaces in traditional fashion takes hours, but very nearly the same result can be obtained by careful application of rubber polishing wheels in the Moto-Tool. It takes only a few minutes.

Receiver alterations: Grinding a slight downward taper on 98 Mauser receiver tangs makes them easier to inlet smoothly. A groove must be cut in the right side of most receivers when reinstalling a bolt whose handle has been altered. This can be done with round files and patience, but is a quick, simple job with a ⅜"x½" wheel in the Moto-Tool. Likewise, the corresponding stock groove can be formed much quicker with a rotary file than by chisel and gouge. Many times a 1903A3 Springfield rifle's looks can be greatly improved by streamlining that gross cutoff housing extending from the left side of the receiver. It doesn't take long with an assortment of grinding and polishing wheels to convert that eyesore into a slim torpedo-shape that flows smoothly into the rest of the gun's lines. Tang reshaping is simple with a hand grinder and certainly improves appearance. Rough bolt ways can be polished with rubber wheels, greatly smoothing bolt operation.

Trigger work: I've known shooters to spend literally days carefully cut-and-try stoning and polishing various surfaces to improve a trigger's pull. The metal is usually quite hard, and it takes hours with a slipstone to remove tool marks and roughness. A couple passes with the Moto-Tool will accomplish the same thing, provided you use some form of holding fixture or clamp so that critical sear-engagement angles aren't changed.

When installing commercial triggers on military rifles, it is often necessary to remove metal from the receiver, enlarge the sear recess, or open up pin holes. Here again, Dremel does in seconds what would require much hand filing. Maybe you've somehow acquired a rifle with a guard screw broken off in the receiver and don't have a set of screw extractors handy. Simply cut a driver slot across the broken end with a small-diameter cutoff wheel, and then turn the screw out. The same procedure may often be applied to sheared sight screws, though their smaller size makes it a ticklish job. There are numerous areas on most guns which can be slightly reshaped to customize or personalize them — tangs, bolt sleeves, receiver edges, trigger guard bow, sight bases, etc. The Moto-Tool and assorted wheels make this sort of work quick and easy, just as long as you've a steady hand and use a bit of taste in deciding what cuts to make. Another interesting job on smooth military triggers is a series of parallel grooves

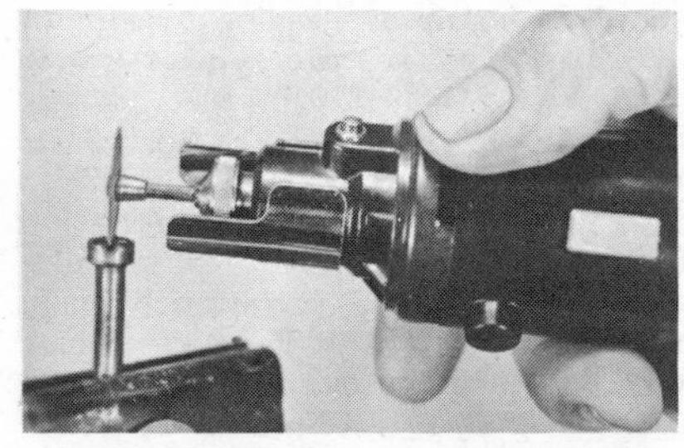

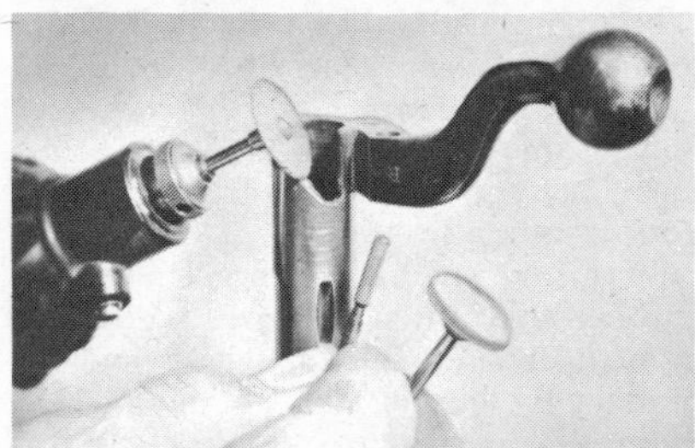

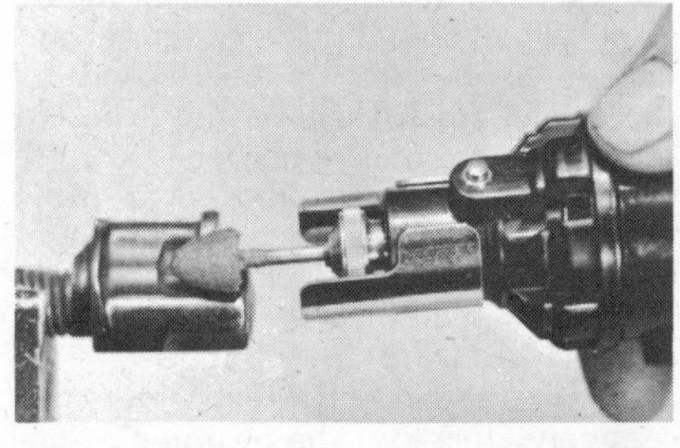

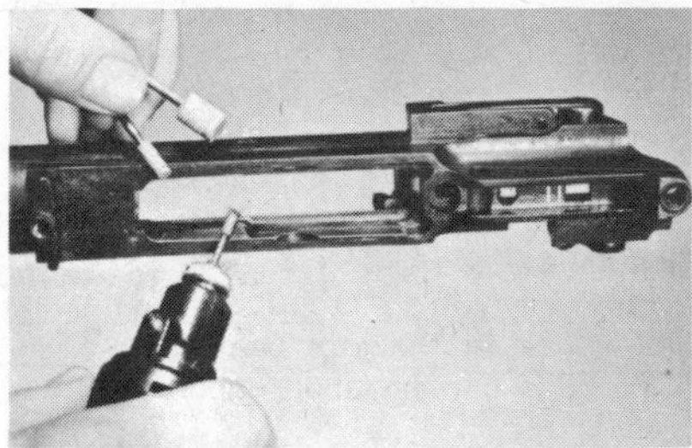

These pictures show only a few of the many gunshop jobs easily handled by the new Dremel Moto-Tools.

to improve control. Just use the edge of a cutoff wheel to make them. Clamping the trigger down and using a strip of wood as a guide makes for a neater job. In fact, almost anything short of a barrel amputation or complete repolishing job can be accomplished with the Dremel Moto-Tool.

Woodworking Tips

The Tool's woodworking capabilities are also useful. I've just inletted a caplock pistol stock from scratch. The octagonal barrel channel was cut to within a few thousandths of an inch of final dimensions with router bits in the Moto-Tool. A guide was clamped to the stock blank and the Dremel router base was moved along it to make a straight cut. Subsequent passes after repositioning the guide and varying depth of cut completed the job. The entire lock was inletted by guiding the router base freehand inside the traced lockplate outline. After that the router base was removed and the rest of the wood cut away freehand with rotary files to clear internal lock parts. The latter process was also used to inlet the trigger plate, trigger, and **side** plate.

The only hand work required was minor chiseling to clean up some edges in the freehand areas, and that was more the fault of the operator than the tool. Those who have reservations about the smoothness of cut haven't reckoned with cutters moving at 30,000 rpm. Any cut made at that rate is *smooth.* At no time did we encounter any motor stalling, even in that hard maple blank.

Using the Dremel Moto-Tool does take a little learning. The motor must be allowed to reach full speed before the cutter is touched to the work. This only takes a fraction of a second, in reality, but during that time, there is considerable torque reaction, which causes the tool to rotate slightly in the hand. If the cutter is touching the work, this can cause it to jump and hit the wrong place. Once it is up to speed, the tool is quite stable and easy to control so long as you don't try to force the cutter or wheel hard against the work. A light touch actually cuts faster and smoother. Some form of guide or rest is often desirable, if not necessary. Clamping the work to the bench, and then resting the wrist on a bag of shot will keep those morning-after tremors from fouling up the job. In some instances, it's better to mount the tool in the accessory bench stand and move the work piece over the cutter. When a long, straight cut is required, use the stand, then clamp the work to a block of wood and slide it slowly under the cutter. This resembles a surface grinder in miniature. The drill press and the router base with a separate fence may also be used in this fashion with either metal or wood-cutting tools.

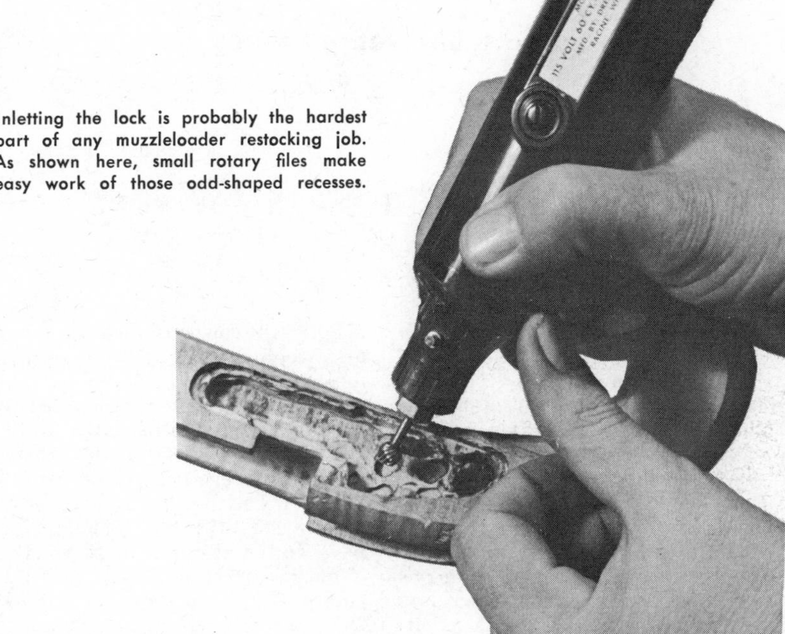

Inletting the lock is probably the hardest part of any muzzleloader restocking job. As shown here, small rotary files make easy work of those odd-shaped recesses.

While we must admit that the Moto-Tool can't take on the heavy jobs such as drilling sight mounting holes, it is still by far the single, most useful hand or power tool the average gun tinkerer can own. That may sound rather biased, but after using one in its several forms for nearly a quarter-century, I feel qualified to make it.

As a matter of interest, Dremel produces other useful items for the gun buff — a power jig saw and a vibrator-type engraving tool, the latter very useful for marking or decorating.

Lock, Stock and Barrel—
and profit too!

Stock as in stock market, that is, with particular application to the arms manufacturers and their issues. You could make some money.

by GERALD R. HUNTER

HOW WOULD YOU like to acquire the Remington, Winchester and Savage Arms companies? Or maybe you'd prefer Colt and Smith & Wesson?

Now, hold on — I'm not fooling. While it isn't likely that any individual shooter will ever entirely own one of these big gunmaking firms, it's entirely practical for *the average shooter* to own, and profitably, a substantial part of most of this country's major firearm and ammunition factories. You can get started for as little as ten dollars — and perhaps revolutionize the relationship between the American gun owner and the industry which supplies his shooting irons.

You do this by buying common or preferred stock in these companies. While word of this opportunity may be no startling revelation (I myself own at least a little stock in the major producers) my recent survey shows a startling unawareness, among the vast majority of sportsmen, as to what goes on here.

In the first place, did you realize that more than 22½ million Americans own common stock in industry? That more than half of these stockholders have annual household incomes of less than $10,000?

As to where the gun industry fits in, consider these figures.

The year 1966 saw the over-all stock market fall some 20%, one of the worst bear markets in years. Of the 50 most popular stocks, 21 increased in value nevertheless, but 29 actually lost money for their owners. Yet the people who owned stock in the firearm companies generally came out nicely ahead despite the break.

Typical examples of these are Winchester (Olin Mathieson), Colt and Daisy, representing, for instance, widely different types of guns.

If you had bought a share of Winchester stock at the 1966 low, you'd have gotten it for $46. If you'd sold it at the 1966 high point you'd have gotten $64.25, a profit of $18.25, or 29% interest on your investment. Had you held it until March 10, 1967 it would have brought $66.75; and by March 30 it had climbed on to $68.00 — and is still going up at this writing.

You could have bought Colt at $13.63 and sold it at the high point of 1966 for $29.50, a profit of $15.87, or more than 100%. By March 20, 1967 Colt had risen to $36.50 and by March 30 to $37.75. Of course, had you chosen to sell your share of Colt on December 31, 1966, which happened to be a very bearish day, you'd have gotten only $18.87 for it, or a profit of only $5.24 — but still way ahead of what finance companies are allowed to charge their worst suckers. The point of this last illustration is this; when and if you plan to sell your stock, you have to watch the market more closely than you would if you planned to hold the stock for a long term investment.

Daisy was a bit more erratic — and no one can ever be sure of exactly why a stock fluctuates as it does. You might guess, in this case, that varying publicity on Daisy's combustible cartridge development validly influenced the attractiveness of investment in Daisy. This veteran plinker-maker went from $15 to $26 in 1966, closing the year at $18.50 bid. In 1963-64 it ran the gamut of price from $7.50 to $26. Stocks with such wide variation fall more nearly into the "speculative" rather than investment class. But remember, in 1966, while Daisy was wandering around on the price scale, it paid a per-share dividend (or *extra* bonus on your investment) of 3.2%. And Daisy has paid its owners a dividend every year since 1893.

In making yourself a part owner of one or more firearms making firms, most of you will properly consider your buying-in to be a long-term growth investment. Neither I nor anyone can guarantee that you will make money, or even that you will not lose money, by buying the common stock of some sound gun company. We can only go on history, and, historically, these firms have been in business a long, long time. Over the years they've made their owners a tidy profit out of both sporting and military guns. Most of them are even further diversified. I expect this profit-making to continue. Fully as important, ownership of common stock means your dollar doesn't lose its purchasing power due to inflation — as savings do, for instance — but keeps pace with inflation as industry and the economy grow. This last, but very important factor, is one usually overlooked by those who stash their cash in the old sock only to find some years hence that the cash, whose value never grows or changes, won't buy very much of anything at the new inflated prices.

A hard example: A 22 rifle today costs twice what it did a few years ago, twice as many *dollars;* while your common stock in the company that made the rifle, which cost you X-bucks long ago, is now worth in dollars more than the rifle now sells at, even at the new and higher price. Whether you're losing or gaining depends on whether you're buying stock or goods.

How do you go about buying common stock in the gun companies?

Well, it can be about a one-minute transaction. I'd suggest you approach one of the major stockbroking firms, such as Merrill Lynch, Pierce, Fenner & Smith (home office 70 Pine St., New York, N.Y. 10005, and branches all over), or some other reliable firm, or even many local banks. An account executive will be interested in even your smallest investment, for that's how he makes his living, and will explain anything about it you want to know.

One of the best starts you can make is to buy (some brokerage houses give them away free) the Bantam-published paperback book *How to Buy Common Stocks* by Louis Engel. You'll find it a complete beginner's guide, as well as fascinating reading.

You also need to mull through one of the full summaries, published by a number of investment firms on an annual basis, such as Standard & Poor's *Stock Guide—1966 Year-End Prices* (345 Hudson St., New York, N. Y. 10014) at a dollar or two. These summaries discuss every actively-traded stock — thousands of them, together with a complete working history of each firm over the past several years. It tells you how solvent a firm is, ranges of its stock values, amount of dividends paid and for how far back, and a wealth of solid facts upon which to base your decisions.

For the average investor, the stock market isn't the frenzied, complicated Wall Street he has been led to picture. Sure, there are million dollar fliers taken every day; ancient firms fool the experts; public reaction to publicity releases shake up prices by the hour. There is still a lot of selling short and buying on margin, putting and calling. But this need not concern you, for these manipulations almost exclusively concern traders in "round lot" volumes—lots of 100 or more shares at the time.

Although 500,190,600 shares of the most popular 50 stocks were traded in 1966, there were also 83,982,178 shares traded in "odd lots" (from 1 to 99 shares), and this is where you fit in. Not only fit in, but are very welcome, perhaps necessary.

There are two ways in which you can begin buying stocks in a gun company, or in more than one company, if you like. You can buy any number of shares you want, from 1 share on up, outright, just as you'd buy apples or gasoline. For this, you pay the quoted price of the stock, plus a small brokerage fee.

Or you can buy on one of the monthly or quarterly plans, in which you invest (usually) multiples of $40 either each quarter or each month. There's no front-end "loading charge."

In either case, your contact at the investment firm will give you full details. Whether you buy stocks listed on the New York Stock Exchange, the "big board," or the American Stock Exchange ("curb market") or "over-the-counter," you may win or — let's face it—you may lose; but you'll get a fair shake for your money, for they are all regulated by the Securities Exchange Commission, under which a bust like the 1929 crash is virtually impossible. Unless, that is, the entire U. S. economy breaks down—in that case, what good would even cash be?

I wouldn't put more money into stocks, not even into a reliable old firearms company, than I could afford to lose, for stock buying is a risk, calculated if you like, not a guarantee. I can't think of anything that offers a potential profit that doesn't also imply a risk. Those are the facts of life.

With this in mind, you can pick a stock that appreciates very slowly, and also very safely. Or you can choose a middle ground type. Or you can latch onto a wild one that may depreciate rapidly, may stabilize, or may make you a thousand per cent profit.

Nobody can tell you for sure which one will do *best.* If they could, everyone would own the same stock. That's where your own foresight and intuition come into play. That's what makes it fun.

One thing seems certain. As more shooters come into ownership of the companies which make the guns they're using, a sounder future will be built for the shooting sports in this age when pressures to suppress the entire gun business grow ever louder. ●

Summary of Common Stock Replies From 36 Major U.S. Manufacturers

Manufacturer	Exchange	Firm Owned by**	Price	Date	Spread - 1966		Spread - 1967		Performance Samples Price	Performance Samples Date	Performance Samples Change‡
ArmaLite	CH	Same	NA		NA		NA			NA	
Browning Arms	OTC	Same	9⅜	3-9-67	7⅝	13⅛	7½	17½	25¾	9-10-68	275%
Buddie Arms	CH	C.D. Hibbs	NA		NA		NA			NA	
Charter Arms	CH	Same	2½	3-1-67	No Change		NA			NA	
Colt Ind.	NYSE*	Same	37¾	3-30-67	13⅝	29½	19	65¾	66	9-20-68	74%
Daisy	OTC	Daisy/Heddon, 53%	18½ bid	1-1-67	15	26	NA			NA	
Charles Daly	CH	Family	NA		NA		NA			NA	
Harrington & Richardson	OTC	NA	9½	5-12-66	4	11	4	18	14½	12-31-67	53%
Healthways	OS	Same	NA		NA		NA			NA	
Ithaca	CH	Family	NA		NA		NA			NA	
Marlin	CH	NA	NA		NA		NA			NA	
O.F. Mossberg	CH	Family	NA		NA		NA			NA	
Navy Arms	CH	Same	NA		NA		NA			NA	
Noble Mfg.	OS	NA	NA		NA		NA			NA	
Nu-Line Guns	CH	J. Stevens	NA		NA		NA			NA	
Winchester	NYSE	Olin Mathieson	66¾	3-10-67	46	64¼	56⅞	81¾	35†	9-20-68	NC
Remington	ASE	E.I. DuPont, 60%+	16	3-6-67	13⅛	17¼	13⅞	24½	19¼	9-20-68	8.3%
Savage-Anschutz	NYSE	Emhart Corp.	28⅝	3-3-67	23¾	39⅜	24	40⅜	46½	9-20-68	61.55%
Sheridan Products	CH	Same	NA		NA		NA			NA	
Smith & Wesson	NYSE*	Bangor Punta	27½	3-31-67	18⅝	36¼	23⅞	55	44¼	9-20-68	61%
Stoeger	CH	Family	NA		NA		NA			NA	
Thompson/Center	CH	K.W. Thompson Tool	NA		NA		NA			NA	
Tingle Mfg. Co.	CH	Same	NA		NA		NA			NA	
Weatherby's	CH	Same	NA		NA		NA			NA	

NYSE—New York Stock Exchange ASE—American Stock Exchange OTC—Over-The-Counter
OS—Other Sources CH—Closely Held NA—Information Not Available NC—Not Computed

*Preferred stock also available.

†Instead of a split, Olin distributed .6695 shares of Squibb Beechnut on 1-12-68 for each share of Olin, similar to a stock going ex-dividend.

**All stock 100% owned except as shown.

‡Average price increase (profit) of 6 reported stocks between March, 1967 and September, 1968 was 88.8%.

All firms listed offered comment except Colt, H&R, Marlin, Buddie, Navy Arms, Noble and Stoeger.

No data is available on the 12 firms which did not reply. Only Daisy and Winchester actively urged that shooters buy their stock.

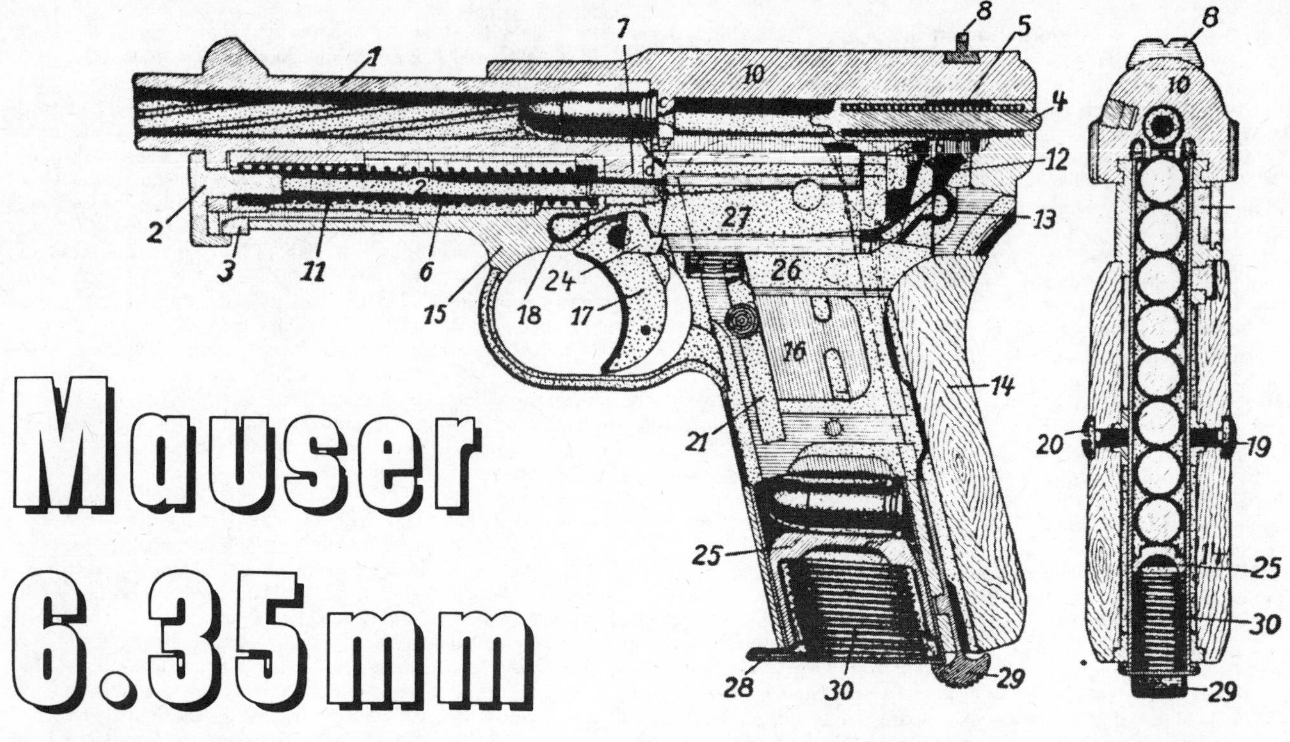

Mauser 6.35mm Pistols

A thoroughly detailed and highly informative study of the Mauser 25 caliber pistols. Periods of manufactures and serial number ranges are included.

by JAMES B. STEWART

AMONG 25-caliber semi-automatic pistols perhaps none are more sought after than the pre-World War II products of the Mauser Werke at Oberndorf in south-western Germany. Despite the great popularity and worldwide sales of the Mauser 25s, how many know that this was the *first* widely marketed German 25 auto, or that Mauser vestpocket pistols were made by the French? Surprisingly little factual information is available concerning their history or the variations in which they occur.

Although Paul Mauser had been one of the pioneers in the automatic pistol field, the factories at Oberndorf were, prior to the First World War, almost exclusively engaged in the production of their world-famous military bolt action rifles for many of the world's armies. Comparatively small quantities of the M1896 pistol were also made for commercial and limited military contract sales. The considerable commercial success of this M1896 Military Pistol, known to many as the "Mauser Broomhandle," had not been the result of conscious effort to capture civilian markets. The pistol had been designed, as its name implies, as a potential military pistol-carbine. Although no major power had officially adopted the design, the publicity it received from various military tests, and during the Boer War, coupled with its obvious sound design, reliable functioning and excellent cartridge, combined to assure, for the times, a brisk commercial sale. Still desirous of capturing the large military sales that had so far eluded the M1896, Mauser continued to experiment. With the advent of the 9mm Parabellum cartridge for the Luger in 1902, and its subsequent adoption by the German Navy in 1904, Mauser turned his efforts to a pistol to use this round. The first effort, the so-called 1906/08 pistol, never progressed beyond the pre-production stage. This locked-breech design was followed in 1909 by a massive, blow-back pistol called the M1909. This pistol, patented on Christmas Eve, 1908, is known only from factory records and photographs. It is here, with the advent of this unsuccessful military blow-back pistol that the story of Mauser's 25s really begins.

The manufacturing facilities of Waffenfabrik Mauser, on the banks of the Neckar river in the beautiful Black Forest region of Baden-Württemberg, had been engaged in the manufacture of fine military arms for 35 years by 1905. In that year the Fabrique Nationale d'Armes de Guerre of Herstal, Belgium, introduced John Browning's new concept in personal protection, the vestpocket automatic pistol. Browning's system consisted of a miniaturized, much simplified version of his successful M1903 "F.N. Grande Modele" military pistol, resized to use a scaled-down rework of his 1900 7.65mm cartridge. This new round became known first as the 6.35mm Browning and, later, as the 25 ACP.

Paul Mauser was not especially interested in the commercial market, so that three years elapsed before any work was undertaken concerning the new 6.35mm round. Finally, no doubt due to the fantastic success that F.N. and its imitators, both licensed and not, were having with the vestpocket pistol, the conservative Mauser organization began work on a 25-caliber pistol. The direction taken was the scaling down of the unsuccessful blowback M1909 military pistol to accept the new cartridge. This process, while producing an arm more aptly described as pocket, rather than vestpocket, worked out very well indeed.

In construction the pistol is of simple striker-fired design (Fig. 1). The 9-

Fig. 1 (above) Section of early Mauser Model 1914, cal. 7.65mm. Model 1910 and Model 1914, cal. 6.35mm, are similar in construction.

shot magazine fits in a conventional well in the grip frame. The removable barrel is secured to the frame, at muzzle and chamber, by the recoil-spring guide pin. The slide, which is cut away over the barrel from muzzle to chamber, compresses the recoil spring by means of a front cross piece located below the barrel and behind the front barrel-securing point. The lockwork consists of a trigger/interrupter assembly, a disconnector, a long trigger bar and sear combined, and a pivoted ejec-

Fig. 2—First type Model 1910 Mauser, cal. 6.35mm.

Fig. 3 — Early Model 1914 Mauser, cal. 6.35mm.

Fig. 4—Model 1914/34 Mauser, cal. 6.35mm.

tor, all located under an access plate on the left side of the frame. An unusual two-piece safety-lever arrangement blocks motion of the trigger bar/sear and locks the slide closed.

The safety lever protrudes from under the front edge of the left grip and operates in the normal manner to engage. To release, one must push the spring catch button located immediately below the lever. This somewhat cumbersome system is of doubtful value, but it was on the ill-fated M1909, so it was incorporated! Like its predecessor, the M1896, the new design minimizes the use of pins or screws, being assembled as a Chinese puzzle of interlocking parts.

The only pin is used to hold the interrupter into the hollow back of the trigger. Two screws hold the grip on. The grip is unusual in that it is of one-piece wrap-around design, slipped on from the rear of the frame. This construction allows a very skeletonized grip frame, making for an arm quite light for its size.

The True Model 1910

The pistol reached its final form early in 1910, and by late 1910 was in production (Fig. 2). This original 6.35mm pistol is the only true Model 1910, and differs considerably from later models. The head of the recoil-spring guide pin recesses into a notch on the underside of the barrel. It is removed by pushing the head in to disengage it from the notch and rotating it 90 degrees. The pin can then be pulled out, freeing the barrel. The lock-work cover plate on the 1910 is dovetailed into the frame with parallel dovetails and locked by a special take-down lever/trigger pin combination. This system is another legacy from the M1909 design. In this early model the cocking indicator is a separate, spring-loaded pin in the rear of the slide. When the arm is not cocked the pin is flush. When the striker is cocked the rear of the firing pin forces the indicator pin to protrude from the rear, where it may be seen and felt. The magazine of the M1910, unlike later models, is of conventional design having a stamped sheet-metal follower and a pinned-in floorplate. The floorplate recesses up into the bottom of the frame. Most magazines are nickel plated. The magazine catch is quite small and is of solid machined construction.

Serial numbers for the first type M1910 apparently start at 100 and run to about 15,000. The full serial number on all the Mauser pocket models is carried on the left front of the slide. The last four digits are usually also carried on the rear of the frame. The last two digits are stamped on most parts. As with all Mauser pistols, the M1910 carries the "double crown U" proofmark of the Oberndorf proofhouse. The first type M1910, in fact all pocket models, have the Mauser "football" trademark rolled into the lockwork cover plate. The left side of the slide has the legend WAFFENFABRIK MAUSER A.-G. OBERNDORF A.N. MAUSERS'S PATENT, in block, serif style capitals, with oversized initial letters, rolled into it. No markings other than proof occur on the right side. The second variation begins at about serial number 15,000 and runs to about 60,-

000. There is some intermixing of the two types in the 14,500 to 15,500 range. This variation has the typeface on the slide legend changed to a block, sans-serif style with all characters the same height except for the "A" in "A.N.," which is smaller. This run brought production up to early 1914, and an end of the Model 1910.

The Model 1914/34

Early in 1913 Mauser personnel decided to improve some of the shortcomings that had become evident in the M1910, and to offer the design in 7.65mm Browning as well as in 6.35mm. The M1910 had sold well and, with the loosening of Paul Mauser's conservative grip on marketing policy, the company began to look seriously at the large domestic and export markets for sporting and protection arms. The improved version of the M1910, christened the Model 1914, emerged early in 1914, with promises, soon fulfilled, of "a new pocket pistol 7.65mm Browning incorporating all of the advanced features of the latest 6.35mm model, to soon be available."

Several mechanical improvements and production economies were made in the new model. The recoil-spring guide pin is provided with a separate catch in place of the under barrel notch. This catch, located on the underside of the frame front, must be pushed up before the pin can be rotated prior to removal. On the M1914 the lockwork cover plate is held in place by means of asymmetrical dovetails rather than the takedown lever/trigger pin of the M1910. The M1914 trigger pin is staked into the lockwork well in the frame. In place of the separate cocking-indicator pin of the M1910, the M1914 simply has an extension on the rear of the striker (Fig. 1-4). In the cocked condition this protrudes to the rear as does the separate pin of the M1910. When the striker is released it travels far enough that the extension goes completely into the slide, leaving an open hole. Another minor change is the wider spacing of the finger grooves on the slide (Fig. 3).

The big changes from the M1910 occur in the magazine and its relation to the lockwork. In place of the standard type magazine the M1914 has a magazine with a large, rugged follower machined from solid stock, and an oversize, removable floorplate. The latter does not recess into the frame and grip but protrudes below. The magazine catch, except in very early production, is no longer a machined piece, but is a return bend in the bottom of the stamped mainspring. The heavy follower is part of a slide hold-open system. The pivoted ejector is redesigned to accomplish hold-open and magazine-safety functions. The ejector is strongly springloaded to tip forward. When the magazine is inserted, the right lip tips the ejector backward so that its rear is flush with the frame and the front is up to eject spent shells. When the last round is ejected the heavy follower rises into the path of the breech face, blocking the slide back. As the magazine is removed, the ejector-spring portion of the mainspring re-asserts itself, tipping the ejector forward and raising its rear end into a cutout in the underside of the slide. The slide moves forward slightly during this process before relocking on the ejector tail. When the magazine, either empty or loaded, is re-inserted the follower no longer can block the slide. The lip lifts the front of the ejector, freeing the slide and allowing it to run forward. When the ejector is tipped forward, that is, when the magazine is removed, a projection on the bottom of the ejector blocks motion of the sear creating an effective magazine safety. M1914 slide markings differ by the omission of MAUSER'S PATENT and the changing of the typeface to uniform-height italic capitals. Numbering picks up where M1910 serials ended.

After commercial introduction of the 7.65mm M1914 both calibers were produced in the same serial numbering series. To avoid confusion, from about serial number 265,000 on, the right side of the slide of 6.35mm arms bears the legend, in large italic typeface, *Mauser 6.35*. Because of WWI almost all of the pistols in the range from 65,000 to over 200,000 are in 7.65mm caliber. Many of these saw service as substitute standard side-arms with the German Army.

In 1922, because of changes brought about by the Versailles Treaty, the firm changed its name to Mauser-Werke. Although the company name was officially changed, the pistols continued to carry the old name until late 1929. This occurs at about serial number 360,000, from which point on the left-side slide legend reads MAUSER-WERKE A.G. OBERNDORF A.N. in sans-serif italics. Production of the M1914 continued after introduction of the true vestpocket models, and to help distinguish it, was referred to in factory literature as the "Neun Lader" or nine-loader.

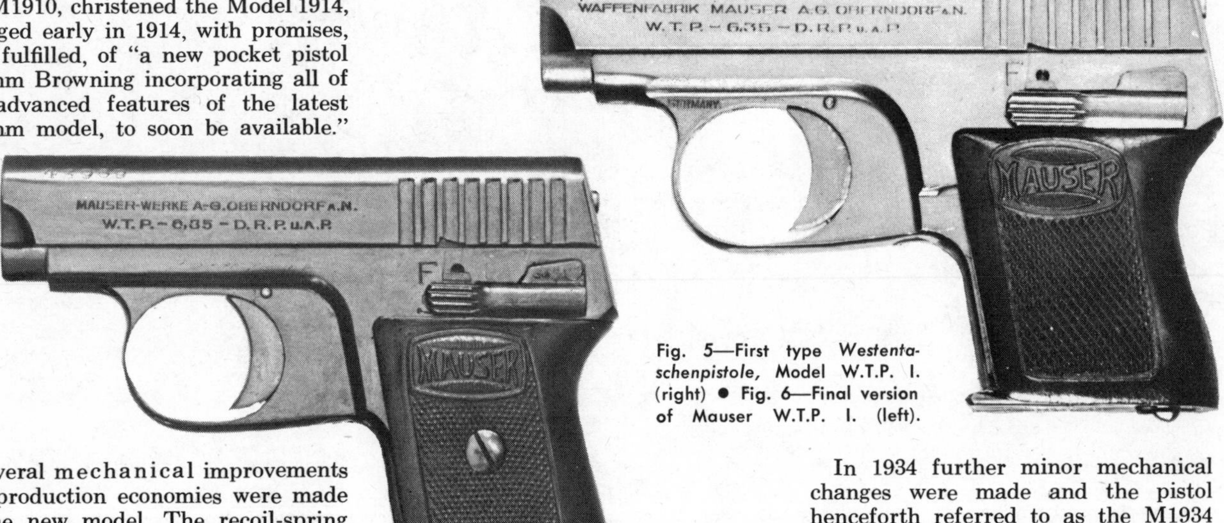

Fig. 5—First type *Westentaschenpistole*, Model W.T.P. I. (right) • **Fig. 6**—Final version of Mauser W.T.P. I. (left).

In 1934 further minor mechanical changes were made and the pistol henceforth referred to as the M1934 or Neues Modell." The magazine-bottom design is simplified and the magazine catch reformed. The most noticeable change is in the grip shape (Fig. 4). A considerable swell is added at the rear to improve fit and pointing characteristics. The right-side slide inscription is changed back to block letters, reading: Cal. 6,35-D.R.P.u.A.P. The initials stand for the German equivalent of "patented in Germany and foreign countries." Previous models are low-luster rust blued with brilliant heat-blued triggers, extractors, and recoil-guide pins. The M1934 pistols, not as nicely machined, are highly polished and chemically dark blued all over. When the M1934 pistols were discontinued is not known, but probably not until 1939 or 1940. The M1934 6.35mm is uncommon, and serial numbers seem to range mostly between 420,000 and 430,000.

M1910 and M1914/34 pistols were usually provided with a walnut, machine-checkered grip. They could also be had with a checkered, monogram, hard rubber grip. The 1910 and 1914 rubber grip has a shield with an intertwined script WM for Waffenfabrik Mauser as the monogram. The

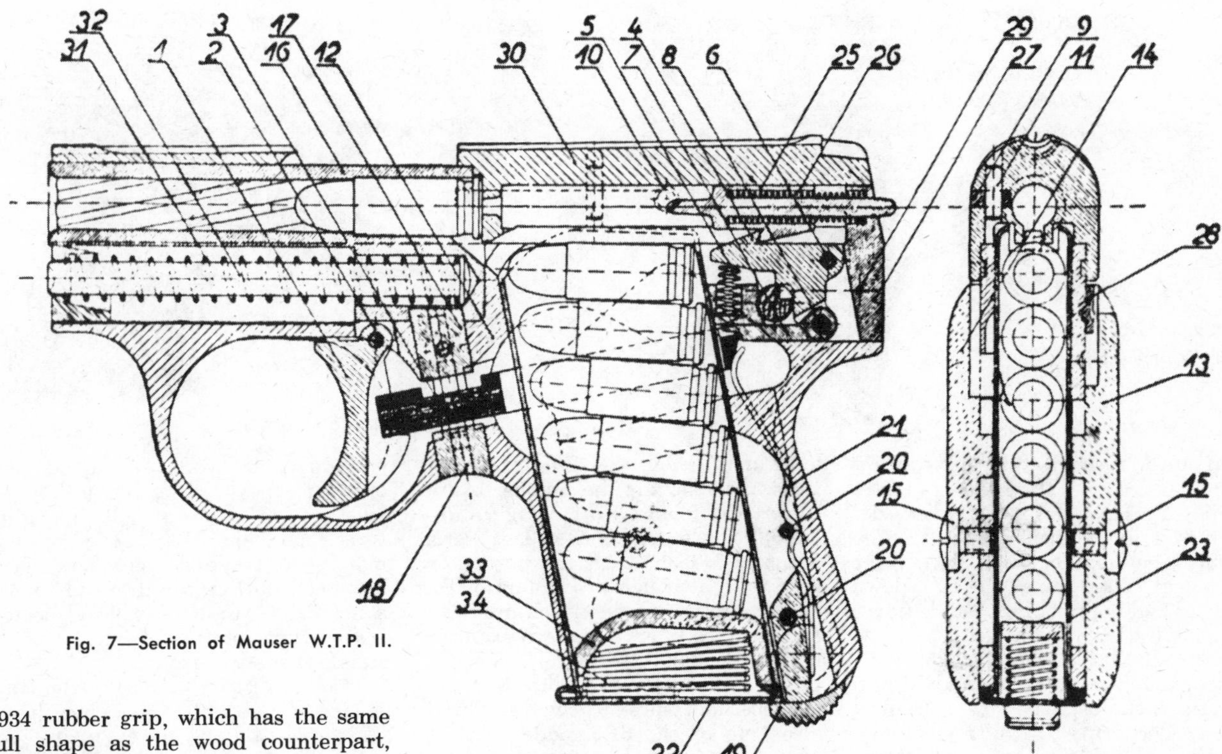

Fig. 7—Section of Mauser W.T.P. II.

1934 rubber grip, which has the same full shape as the wood counterpart, has the Mauser "football" in place of the monogram.

The Westentaschenpistole

By 1918 F.N. had sold more than a half-million of their vestpocket model. In order to compete more favorably with F.N., and the rising flood of models in competition to them, Mauser began work in early 1919, on patents granted in 1918, to produce a true vestpocket pistol. The new pistol was introduced in late 1919 or early 1920 as the "W.T.P.," or *Westentaschenpistole,* German for vestpocket pistol. Aside from the familiar wraparound Mauser grip, it bears little resemblance to the previous pocket models (Fig. 5).

Like the earlier pistol, the W.T.P. is striker fired. Being smaller, its magazine capacity is only 6 rounds. The general appearance of the weapon is similar to the standard Browning pattern, but the lockwork is typically Mauser and the takedown system is unique. The barrel is held in place, in a channel in the frame, by a plunger that passes up through the frame, between the grip and trigger, and engages a hole in the underside of the barrel-mounting lug. The plunger has a spring catch on its right side. When this catch is pressed in it can be used to pull the plunger down, releasing the barrel and blocking trigger movement to prevent accidents. With the plunger down, the barrel and slide can be slid off the front of the frame. The lockwork is similar in operation to the M1914, except there is no hold-open action. The lockwork parts are cleverly shaped steel stampings, a very modern concept for the time. The long thumb safety blocks the sear and locks the slide. The typical, oversized floorplate Mauser magazine is used. Also, in accordance with previous practice, the bent end of the mainspring serves as the magazine catch. Because of the bulk of the grip and contour of the catch, which is not grooved, it is very difficult to release the magazine. This fault was not corrected during the life of the model. The button which protrudes from the rear of the slide serves as a non-visual cocking indicator. When the striker is cocked, it abuts the inside of the button, making it impossible to push in. When the gun is uncocked, the button floats against the striker spring and is easily pushed in. The sights are recessed into a groove in the top of the slide. The vertical slide grooves are very wide, shallow, and of rectangular cross section.

The grip is of moulded hard rubber, shaped to fit the hand. It slides into a wide, machined dovetail on the frame sides, and is secured by a single screw in the rear. The grip carries a large Mauser "football" trademark at the top of the checkering. The left side of the slide is marked in block (Roman) sans-serif extended-style letters WAFFENFABRIK MAUSER A.-G. OBERNDORF A.N. over: T. 6,35. Only the first few hundred production pistols are marked in this manner. Subsequently the second line is changed to read: W.T.P.—6.35—D.R.P.U.A.P.

The serial is carried on the left top of the slide, near the muzzle. Most parts carry the last two digits. Serials start at some low number, presumably one, and pertain only to the vestpocket model.

When the change in company name markings on pistols was made in late 1929, the W.T.P. left side marking was changed so that the first line read: MAUSER-WERKE A.-G. OBERNDORF A.N. This change occurred somewhere below serial 35,500. At the same time the grip was changed from hard rubber to plastic and made thinner to reduce the over-all thickness of the pistol. Sometime later, but prior to serial number 44,000, the grip was again changed. The dovetail grooves were removed from the frame and the grip redesigned to be attached by two side screws in the normal manner (Fig. 6). How many of the first model W.T.P. were made is not known, but serials extend to at least 46,000.

This model W.T.P. is of uniformly excellent finish. Most parts are nicely rust blued. The grip screws, extractor, cocking indicator bushing, takedown plunger and, on some late examples the trigger, are brilliantly heat blued. The barrel, recoil-spring guide rod, and cocking indicator are polished.

The Second Model W.T.P.

In 1936 a new, improved version of the W.T.P. was announced, but apparently didn't actually reach the market until sometime early in 1937. Although strikingly different in external appearance from the old W.T.P., the new pistol is internally very similar (Fig. 7). The lockwork, takedown and safety systems are identical. The cocking indicator is simplified to the same system used on the 1914/34 pocket models. Complaints of the difficulty of using the magazine release on the old model resulted in its change to a conventional, separate catch in the second W.T.P. The slide grooves are

Fig. 8—Mauser W.T.P. II, initial type.

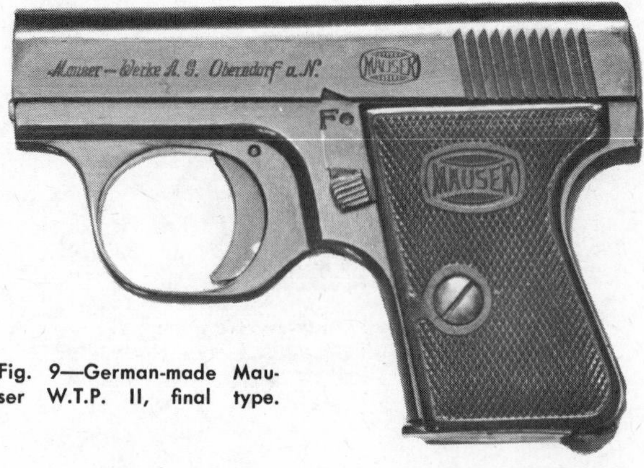

Fig. 9—German-made Mauser W.T.P. II, final type.

most un-Mauser-like, being conventional narrow "v" grooves, slightly angled. Perhaps the most radical departure is in the grip and frame. The frame is cut out between the trigger and grip, shortening the takedown plunger and providing more finger room on the grip. In the grip itself, the traditional Mauser wrap-around style is abandoned in favor of standard grip plates, each held on by a central screw. The grips are fully checkered plastic, and bear a large Mauser trademark near the top. Unlike the early model, the grips extend all the way up to the slide, covering all except the tip of the safety lever. The barrel is shortened over the older model, resulting in a very compact arm, smaller in most dimensions than its predecessor (Table 1). It is probable that the introduction of the ultra-compact Walther Model 9 in 1922 and the equally small F.N. Browning Baby in 1935 forced Mauser to redesign its old W.T.P. to maintain some semblance of competition.

The first W.T.P. II pistols are marked, in block sans-serif style lettering, on the left side of the slide: MAUSER-WERKE A.-G. OBERNDORF A.N." followed by a smallish Mauser "football" (Fig 8). The right side of the slide is marked, in the same style characters: W.T.P. — 6,35 — D.R.P. The serial numbers are carried at the same location as on the early model. Both are apparently numbered in the same series. Whether the numbering is consecutive with the early model, or whether a block of numbers was skipped, is unknown, but no serials have been observed below 57,000 for the W.T.P. II. At about 58,000 the typeface used in marking both sides of the slide is changed to a flamboyant script, in upper and lower case, in place of the all captial block lettering used in the first few hundred pieces (Fig 9). The size of the Mauser trademark is also increased.

Shortly before serial number 62,000 the numbers move to the right side of the slide, between the slide grooves and lettering. The bulk of production is of this style. At about serial number 73,000 a final change appears in the form of widening the slide grip serrations and reducing the number of finger grooves from 17 to 11 (Fig. 9). Production continued up to at least serial number 74,000. It is interesting to note that, although production of this model surely proceeded well into 1939, and perhaps later, no known examples carry the 1939, Nazi era, "eagle N" proofs. All retain the "double crown U" Oberndorf pre-1939 mark. This is also true of the 6.35 model 1914/34. Mauser 7.65mm HSc pistols produced after the new law went into effect do carry the new proofing, as do some very late 7.65mm 1914/34 pistols. The significance of this is yet to be explained.

A final, and most unexpected, chapter in the story of the W.T.P. II was written in 1945. At the end of the war France occupied Oberndorf, and the Mauser works. Like the Walther factory, in the usual post-hostilities fervor, the plant was wrecked. It is not known whether the French worked the plant before destroying it, or whether they moved materials elsewhere. They must have done one or the other, because they assembled from un-serialed parts, or made from scratch, at least 750 W.T.P. II pistols! These pieces are fully as well made and finished as prewar German manufacture, but are easily recognized by two differences. First, they carry no proofmarking of any kind. Second, the serial numbers are stamped into the rear of the frame, below the end of the slide. These pieces are especially good items for the collector to be on the lookout for. Not only are they scarce, but in 1964 at least 50 of these pistols, including serial numbers one through 8, and many in two-digit numbers, were brought into this country and sold at a meeting of the Ohio Gun Collectors Association, intermixed in a lot of the standard pre-war model.

Mauser pistols, especially the early models, could be had in luxury finish. This consists of full engraving and relief carving in scroll and oak leaf patterns. Some minor gold and silver wire inlay is also included. The grip is usually of ebony inlaid with silver wire and mother of pearl chips. Both M1910 and W.T.P. I pistols have turned up finished in this manner.

This then is the guided tour of Mauser's 25's. Although at the present moment Mauser is again planning production of automatic pistols, there is no intention to produce any in 25 ACP. Mauser never was really competitive in this caliber. The M1910 and M1914/34 were too large and heavy for the mass personal protection market. The vest pockets were, because of their rather complex design and quality manufacture, more expensive than most of the competition. In a market where many purchasers were looking for either the least expensive or smallest weapon the Mausers, unfortunately, were neither. In the final analysis, the Mauser 25s sold in quantity only because of their excellent materials and fine workmanship; in short, because they were *Mausers!* •

TABLE I
Dimensions of Mauser 25-cal. Pistols

	M1910	M1934	W.T.P. I*	W.T.P. I†	W.T.P. II
Over-all	137	144	115	115	102
	5.5	5.67	4.53	4.53	4.02
Height	100	105	78	76	71
	3.94	4.13	3.07	2.99	2.80
Thickness	22	24	22	20	20
	0.87	0.94	0.87	0.80	0.80
Sight radius	115	117	100	97	90
	4.53	4.60	3.94	3.82	3.54
Barrel length	78	76	61	61	52
	3.07	2.99	2.40	2.40	2.05
Weight, empty	445	448	320	318	290
	15.6	15.7	11.2	11.0	10.1

Dimensions: millimeters, grams; inches, ounces
* Early versions
† Late versions

AMERICAN BULLETED CARTRIDGES

A new check list of modern U. S. ammunition, plus a guide to cartridge performance and usefulness.

by KENNETH L. WATERS
and the Technical Staff

LATEST DEVELOPMENTS IN METALLIC CARTRIDGES

Use of and interest in firearms manufactured in Europe and chambered for metric cartridges has never been more widespread in this country than it is today. That this is understandable, considering the influx of both foreign military surplus and commercial sporting arms during the years following World War II, goes without saying. The point is that sale of these guns created a parallel market for ammunition to shoot in them. For many years this demand was at least partially satisfied by the huge stocks of surplus military cartridges, likewise imported, plus the fact that a few of the more popular calibers, such as the 7x57mm, 8x57mm and 303 British are produced commercially in the U.S.

Certain foreign ammunition makers have also sought to serve this enormous potential clientele, including Norma of Sweden, Sako of Finland and CIL Dominion (Canada). In past issues of the GUN DIGEST *we have reviewed their respective lines. These products have been a very real benefit to American shooters of foreign arms. They are, in fact, a far better answer to our metric ammunition needs than are surplus military cartridges for a number of reasons, despite the lower cost of the latter.*

First, they come loaded with the proper soft point bullets suitable for hunting purposes. Secondly, they are primed with American-type Boxer primers, making them easily reloadable. Third, they are constructed of fresh brass, whereas many of the military rounds are now as much as 20 or 25 years old.

Inevitably, too, stocks of military ammo are sure to be used up one of these days and when that happens, demand for the commercial products is certain to increase.

SPEER-DWM

With commendable foresight, a new combine has been formed under the name of Speer-DWM, linking together two famous names in the ammunition and cartridge component fields. Purpose of this report is to show what is being offered in this new line, and what our tests revealed concerning its performance.

While not privy to Speer-DWM's policy decisions, it would appear that this operation consists basically of two parts. The first, and most actively pursued, involves the offering of both loaded cartridges and empty cases for handloaders in such popular calibers as: 222, 243, 270, 7x57, 7mm Remington Magnum, 300 Savage, 308 Winchester, 30-30, 32 Special, 30-06, 300 Winchester Magnum and 8x57, plus the 38 Special and 357 Magnum revolver cartridges. This, the "bread-and-butter" line, is expected to involve the bulk of sales, being loaded with American-made primers and Speer "Hot Core" bullets.

The second part is their European metric line—a gratifyingly comprehensive listing ranging from the little 5.6x35R Vierling to the big 10.75x73, and including not only such well-known numbers as the 6.5 Manlicher-Schoenauer, 7x57 and 8x57, but also less frequently used ones: 5.6x61 vom Hofe, 6.5x57, 6.5x57R, 7x57R, 8x56 MS, 8x57J and 8x57JR (.318"), 8x57JRS (.322"), 8x60, 9.3x64, 9.3x72R and 10.75x68mm. Amongst them too are several outstandingly effective cartridges, noted for their excellence in the world's game fields. I refer to the 7x64, 7x65R, 7mm vom Hofe Super Express, 8x64S, 8x65RS, 9.3x62, 9 3x64 and 9.3x74R.

As we go to press, word has just reached us from Speer, Inc., that many changes are being made in the Speer-DWM line. Some cartridges are being abandoned, others are being reduced in the range of loadings offered. See our Ballistic Tables for the current Speer-DWM offerings or write to Speer for the latest information. (J.T.A.)

Speer seems to look upon this second part of their DWM operation as primarily a service to American shooters owning rifles in these calibers — for which a good many of us can be grateful. However, I have a strong hunch that they may be in for a big surprise when the word gets around. Something tells me this metric part of their cartridge line will prove far more popular than anticipated, partly for reasons already outlined, but possibly because American shooters may well become sufficiently interested in some of these European calibers to order rifles specifically for them.

As one example, take the shooter who wishes to have a rifle taking a modern, high performance *rimmed* case of medium caliber. In the standard U.S. domestic cartridge line-up there are none, unless you are willing to settle for the 30-40 Krag or 303 British. From the Speer-DWM group though, he could select the 7x65R with 139-gr. bullet at 3000 fps MV, the 7x75R vom Hofe Super Express with 169-gr. Torpedo Stopring bullet at 3070 fps, or the heavier 8x65RS Brenneke with 198-gr. at 2830 fps.

It's like adding a couple of dozen new cartridges to our present factory listings, and not having to wildcat this or that to do it! It's bound to have an impact, and I'm betting it will be a sizable one.

Several additional factors are expected to contribute to the popularity of this ammunition. Most important is the fact that many of the Speer-DWM metric cartridges are already coming through primed with American-type (Boxer) primers rather than the European (Berdan) caps so troublesome to reloaders in decapping. Also, Speer has announced that DWM intends to change *all* cases to Boxer-priming in the near future. This is a tremendous advantage that shouldn't be minimized.

Discontinuance of certain calibers from the Norma line of imports, including the 9.3x62, 9.3x72R and 9.3x74R, should also affect the demand for these same Speer-DWM items, especially since the last two named cannot be readily formed from American brass. The writer has a 9.3x62 Husqvarna Mauser, and while I could form cases for it from 30-06 empties, I prefer to use those with the proper headstamp.

Speaking of cases with reloading in mind, Speer claims their DWM cases are made so durable they'll last up to twice as long. Frankly, I can't say whether this will prove out or not, but I've yet to discard a single one of these cases for any reason. To date there have been no splits, no cracks, no excessive stretching, nor even any overly-expanded primer pockets, despite continued reloading. Speer explains this by saying modern extrusion techniques are used in drawing the virgin brass, after which cases are induction annealed.

Trials have been conducted for accuracy with Speer-DWM cartridges in direct comparison with other brands, both domestic and imported, in calibers 222, 243, 30-30, 308, 30-06; 8x57JRS and 9.3x62mm, with the following results:

(1) The Speer-DWM 222—from our lot at least—has proven to be the most accurate factory ammunition of that caliber the writer has tested. Only the Remington Power-Lokt has come close to it among factory loads. Grouping from a Model 788 Remington with Unertl 10x target scope has varied between 7/16″ and 13/16″ for 5 shots at 100 yards. It is so good, in fact, that only the very best handloads will equal it. Of course this may not be typical of all lots.

(2) Tests of the 30-30 Speer-DWM were run twice, using two different rifles—a Winchester '66 Centennial with 26″ octagon barrel, and a Savage Model 340-C carbine. The Winchester lever action didn't like this ammo as well as either Winchester-Western or Remington-Peters, averaging 3″ groups. In the Savage bolt action with 3x scope though, it went into 1⅛″ to 1⅜″, establishing it as fully up to par for 30-30 fodder.

(3) A Winchester 70 standard scoped sporter in 243 held groups of five 100-gr. Taperlok bullets to about MOA, equaled by 100-gr. Winchester soft points, but beaten only by Sako's 90-gr. factory loads.

(4) In 308 Winchester caliber, an extremely light-barreled Browning sporter placed series of five 165-gr. Speer PSP bullets into 1½″, and a particularly accurate Winchester 70 HB target rifle repeatedly made groups of five shots in ⅞″, with four only 11/16″ apart. This is only slightly inferior to what the same rifle will do with LC National Match ammo.

(5) Another Model 70 target rifle, this a 30-06, duplicated the performance of the 308, though not as uniformly so. That is to say, there was a greater variation between 30-06 groups than there had been with the 308. A best group measured only 7/16″. These DWM cases were also loaded with 165-gr. Speer PSP bullets.

(6) A new double rifle by Josef Just in 8x57JRS caliber has turned in some fine targets with 196-gr. DWM rounds, firing

right and left barrels alternately, but we didn't have enough of this ammunition to make really conclusive tests.

(7) Our 9.3x62 Husqvarna with 293-gr. Torpedo Universal soft points in Boxer-primed cases has produced smaller groups than any of the handloads I've made up so far! 1⅛″ for 5 shots is good shooting for a sporter firing such heavy bullets at 2515 fps.

I've concluded, therefore, that Speer-DWM ammo is indeed a quality product. It should be especially welcome to owners of metric-caliber rifles and handloaders generally, for whom Speer is also offering empty, un-primed cases in a number of American and European calibers. However, their offerings in our own standard calibers are equally good; so much so, that they should be given a trial by all serious riflemen seeking to find the loads which perform best in their individual rifles.

I guess I should have referred to this combined operation as that of a triumvirate: Speer of Lewiston, Idaho; DWM of Karlsruhe, West Germany, and NWM of Holland. Those cartridges produced in Germany are loaded with the famous DWM bullets, and those from Holland with their "Taperlok" design.

For 1969, Speer added an attractive and useful plastic cartridge box that should stand much use, with reversible interior divisions to enable them to hold cases of different lengths and shapes.

The only suggestions this reviewer can offer are that they expedite the complete changeover from Berdan to Boxer primers in the metric line, and gradually add other much needed calibers difficult to duplicate here, such as the 280 Ross, 333 Jeffery and 8x68S.

Part I. RIFLE CARTRIDGES

The Centerfires

22 HORNET One of the most useful smallbore cartridges, and the first standard 22 specifically for varmint hunting. Since its appearance in 1930 it has earned a reputation for fine accuracy, flat trajectory, and quick bullet expansion. Effective to 175 yards on foxes, woodchucks, and jack rabbits, excellent for wild turkeys, it should definitely not be used on deer.

218 BEE Introduced in 1938 for the lever action Model 65 Winchester, its use was extended to bolt actions where its greater powder capacity, higher velocity and flatter trajectory from a stronger case made it a better choice than the Hornet. Effective on the same game species as the Hornet. Not available in any rifle today.

219 ZIPPER Introduced by Winchester in 1937, this rimmed cartridge acquired a poor reputation for accuracy in the Model 64 lever action, but in custom bolt action and single shot rifles, it groups excellently. Bullets are same diameter as Hornets and Bees regardless of name. Powerful enough for coyotes but still not adequate for deer. Discontinued 1964.

22 REMINGTON JET See Part II — Handgun Cartridges.

220 SWIFT Highest velocity standard rifle cartridge ever commercially produced in the U.S., its 48-grain bullet leaving the muzzle at 4110 fps is virtually a bomb, unfit for use on big game animals. As a long range varmint cartridge it is one of the finest, needing only a longer, heavier bullet less sensitive to wind. With full power loads cases stretch and bore wear is accelerated — which would occur with any cartridge of similar intensity. Popularity of the Swift has accordingly declined to the point where Winchester has discontinued chambering rifles for it, although factory cartridges are still produced.

222 REMINGTON One of our newer and most accurate cartridges, the 222 has climbed rapidly to fame as a bench-rest target and varmint load. Its bullets are better shaped than its predecessors, extending the range to about 225 yards, and it is chambered only in strong bolt action rifles. Production of this cartridge has resulted in decreased sales of Hornet, Bee, and Zipper ammo.

222 REMINGTON MAGNUM Big Brother to the standard 222 Rem., this newer and slightly longer cartridge has nicely combined power and wind-bucking ability with the fine accuracy of its forerunner to give varmint hunters one of the best balanced, most practical 'chuck cartridges ever developed. 55-gr. bullets of factory loads have a resistance to wind deflection superior to the 50-gr. standard 222 bullet, and handloaded 60-gr. bullets are still better in this respect. Also these heavier Magnum bullets arrive at a 200-yard target with some 25% more energy than the 50-gr. standard 222's.

222 SUPER RIMMED Developed in Australia, this rimmed version of our 222 Remington emigrated first to Canada and thence to the U.S. An ideal choice for chambering in single shot rifles, case dimensions (except for the rim), ballistics and loading data all duplicate those of the standard 222. Velocities may be somewhat higher however, in the longer barrels common to single shot rifles.

223 REMINGTON Adopted by the U.S. military forces as the 5.56mm with full metal jacketed 55-gr. bullets, its civilian name is 223 Remington, under which headstamp a soft point bullet is loaded. Identical ballistically to the 222 Magnum, the 223's case dimensions differ enough so that they should never be fired in a 222 Magnum chamber; they'll go in, but hazardous excess headspace will be present with a probability of case separations. Rifles for the 223 have a twist rate of 1-in-12" rather than the 1-in-14" of most 22 centerfires, this to insure bullet stability all the way out to 600-yards. Case capacity is about a grain less than the 222 Magnum and its neck is about 1/16" shorter, making the 222 Magnum a better choice for handloaders. Future government surplus ammunition will probably be available for the 223, however.

225 WINCHESTER Intended as a successor to the 220 Swift (in Winchester rifles), this new high performance cartridge has done more than that; it has also superseded the discontinued 219 Zipper in its role as the most powerful rimmed 22 centerfire. Although officially classified as "semi-rimless," the 225 does have a rim, easily sufficient to permit its use in single shot rifles while still fitting the bolt heads and extractors (of 270, 30-06 dimensions) of modern standard rimless cartridge repeaters. Closely similar in design to the 219 Improved Zipper (but differing in certain vital dimensions), the 225 Winchester is loaded to higher pressures than the old standard 219 Zipper, developing 540 fps greater muzzle velocity for a trajectory that is almost twice as flat. Factory cartridges in this new caliber are loaded with outstanding uniformity and provide excellent accuracy.

22/250 REMINGTON A long time favorite wildcat with both varminters and benchrest shooters, the 22/250 was standardized by Remington in 1965 and shows signs of rapidly growing popularity. Generally considered to be better designed than the Swift, it will give nearly as high velocities with bullets of the same weight. Because it is slower, case and barrel life are longer. Case capacity to bore ratio in the 22/250 is most favorable, and its short over-all loaded cartridge length of 2.35" makes it readily adaptable to short-action box magazine repeaters. Either new 22/250 Remington or Norma cases, or reformed 250 Savage brass may be used for reloading.

243 WINCHESTER One of the new 6mm or 24 caliber compromises between 22 and 25 calibers, having in large measure the best features of both. A 100-gr. bullet with high sectional density at 3,070 fs for deer and antelope, and an 80-gr. at 3,500 for long range varmints, provide accuracy equal to the Swift and far better wind-bucking and killing power. Excellent for the one-gun hunter of game not larger than deer.

244 REMINGTON Another new 6mm, but because of Remington's 1-in-12-inch rifling twist, bullet weights are restricted to 75 and 90 grains. Thus the 244 is not considered quite the equal of the 243 on big deer, despite the greater powder capacity of the 244. On targets or varmints however, it is doubtful if the shooter — or the chuck — would notice any difference, assuming rifles of equal accuracy. In custom barreled rifles with 10" twist, 100- or 105-gr. bullets can be handloaded to give 243 power.

6mm REMINGTON Identical in case dimensions to the older 244 Remington, this newer cartridge is loaded with the 100-gr. bullet demanded by deer hunters. Remington lists MV as 3190 fps, and barrels have a rifling twist of 1-in-9" to stabilize the longer bullet. Despite the fact that 75- and 90-gr. 244 cartridges can also be used in 6mm rifles, shooters wanted a varmint round bearing the 6mm headstamp. Hence, in 1965 Remington announced an additional load using their new 80-gr. Power-Lokt bullet, which has proven exceptionally accurate and flat shooting. The 6mm is therefore an even better dual purpose cartridge than the 243.

25-20 WCF Prior to the coming of the Hornet and Bee, this was the top combination small game and varmint cartridge, dating back to 1893. Today, a choice of 3 loads is available, (requiring different sight settings), including the older 86-gr. lead or soft point bullets at 1,460 fs, and a later 60-gr. H.P. at 2,250 fs. The slower, heavier bullets are good for game from squirrels to turkey, while the 60-gr. is strictly a varmint cartridge. Neither should ever be used on deer.

25-35 WINCHESTER Another cartridge from the 1890's, this one **can** be used for deer. Currently obtainable only as a 117-gr. soft point at 2,300 fs, the 25-35's chief claim to fame lies in its reputation as one of the most accurate cartridges ever developed for lever action rifles, and one of the lightest recoiling.

250 SAVAGE Popularly known as the "250-3000" because of its velocity with an 87-gr. bullet, this fine cartridge appeared in 1915 as one of our earliest really high speed loads. 100-gr. bullets are loaded to 2,820 fs. Quick killing power, flat trajectory, and light recoil have kept this cartridge popular for over 40 years. Use 100-gr. bullets for deer and 87's for varmints. In wind-swept areas, the 100 grain is preferred, even for varmints.

256 WINCHESTER MAGNUM See Part II—Handgun Cartridges.

257 ROBERTS Named for its famed originator, Ned Roberts, this was to be an extra-long-range varmint cartridge, but with its adoption by Remington for factory production, loaded with both 100- and 117-gr. bullets, it was recognized as an excellent medium game cartridge as well. The 87-gr. at 3,200 fs is for varmints. It is thus a speeded-up 250 for bolt actions, with greater powder capacity and a 10-inch twist, permitting the heavier 117-gr. factory and 125-gr. custom bullets which make this the finest all-around cartridge where game no larger than deer will be hunted. Biggest fault of the 257 is its deep-seated bullets, loaded thus for short actions. Seated out for custom long-throated chambers, accuracy improves noticeably.

6.5 REMINGTON MAGNUM Second of the short-case belted magnums. This cartridge is available only with the 120-gr. Pointed Soft Point Core-Lokt bullet so far. MV lists as 3030 foot seconds for the 20" barreled Remington 660 carbine. With a powder capacity very close to that of the 270, ballistics are also similar in barrels of the same length. In game killing power, it stands midway between the 6mm Remington and the larger 7mm Remington Magnum.

264 WINCHESTER MAGNUM This is the third in a series of short belted cartridges designed to deliver magnum velocities and power from standard length bolt actions. The 264 Magnum is a cartridge with a specific purpose—the delivery of a controlled-expanding bullet with flat trajectory and high residual energy at ultra long ranges. This it does exceptionally well. At 500 yards the 140-gr. bullet has 1370 fp of energy, 37% more than the 270 WCF 130-gr. and 23% more than a 30-06 180-gr. Velocity at that far-out point is still 2100 fps—close to 30-30 muzzle speed, and bullet drop is about 6" less than the 270. The 100-gr. 264 varmint load is even flatter-shooting, dropping some 9" less than the 140-gr. The 140-gr. loading should be adequate for medium soft-skinned game up to and including elk and moose.

270 WINCHESTER Superior to the 257 and 6mms for western use and for game larger than deer, the 270 has earned a good reputation among open country hunters. Its flat trajectory and high velocity with 130-gr. bullet at 3140 fps makes hitting easier over long, difficult-to-estimate ranges. Thus, as a mule deer, sheep and goat cartridge it is all anyone could ask for. For larger and heavier game of the caribou, elk and moose species, Winchester loads a 150-gr. Power-Point bullet to an increased muzzle velocity of 2900 fps, while Remington offers a 150-gr. round nose Core-Lokt at 2800 for woods hunting. The 100-gr. load is excellent for varmints, and is a good choice on antelope, too.

7mm REMINGTON MAGNUM Rifle cartridge of 1962, this short-case belted magnum mates the striking power of a 180-gr. 30-06 with the velocity and flat trajectory of a 130-gr. 270. The 175-gr. load has 21½% greater muzzle energy than the 180-gr. 30-06, and the 150-gr. is traveling 12% faster than the 130-gr. 270 bullet out at 300 yards. Various "wildcat" 7mm Magnum cartridges have evidenced their game killing ability in all corners of the globe, and now we have a factory standard cartridge capable of doing the same.

In 1965, Remington added a 175-gr. factory loading having a pointed Core-Lokt bullet designed to retain high velocity over longer ranges. Starting out at the muzzle with the same 3070 fps as the round-nose bullet, remaining velocity of the new spitzer slug is 340 fs higher at 300 yards and 460 fs faster at 500 yards, even equaling the 150-gr bullet by the time 300 yards is reached.

In 1967, Remington added still another loading, this time a 125-gr. PSP at 3430 MV, thus making available a lightweight, high speed bullet with correspondingly flat trajectory for use on the smaller species of big game under long range conditions. This load should **not** be used in taking really large game, especially at short to medium ranges where velocity is still high.

280 REMINGTON Competitor of the 270 Winchester for open country hunting, and challenger of the 30-06 for "all-around cartridge" title in U.S. hunting fields, the 280 combines the best features of the 270 and the 7mm Mauser, providing slightly better ballistics **with factory loads** than either of those two. Four bullets—100-, 125-, 150- and 165-gr.—make the 280 "right" for a large variety of game; it combines flat shooting, a choice of either quick expansion or deep penetration, and easy recoil. This is one cartridge that is suited for practically any kind of hunting country or terrain, open or wooded, long or short range. For larger game such as moose, its 165-gr. bullet makes it preferable to the 270 unless the latter cartridge is hand-loaded to equal bullet weight. This is a "true" 7mm, bullets measuring .2835", and any 7mm bullet with a diameter of .283" to .284" may be used.

284 WINCHESTER Unusual for American cartridges, this short-cased round has a body diameter larger than its rim, giving it a powder capacity only about 1 grain less than the 280 Remington, even though ½-inch shorter, while retaining a "standard" size rim (common to such calibers as the 270, 280, 308 and 30-06), in order to permit use of the 284 cartridge with existing bolt face dimensions. Designed to give short action rifles (specifically the Winchester M88 lever action and M100 autoloader) ballistics equaling the longer 270 Winchester and 280 Remington cartridges, there is no reason why bolt action rifles shouldn't be chambered for it.

7mm MAUSER Originating as the Spanish military cartridge of 1893, the 7x57mm became popular the world over and today's factory loadings are better than ever. It will handle any game that the 270 will, but if used for antelope or other plains game at long range, either Federal's or Dominion's 139-gr. at 2900 fps, or Norma's 150-gr. load at 2756 fps should be specified. For varmints, Norma offers a 110-gr. bullet loading at 3068 fps MV. These modern high velocity versions have given the 7x57 new appeal However, the standard U.S. cartridge with 175-gr. round-nose bullet of high sectional density is still the best choice for big game, especially when hunting in brush or woods.

30 CARBINE Commercial jacketed SP cartridges are loaded by both W-W and R-P for the 30 M-1 carbine. Remington's 110-gr. is a round nose SP whereas Winchester's is a hollow point SP. MV is 1980 fps, for only 955 fp energy. At 100 yards only 575 fp energy remains, so this cartridge should not be used on deer or any other big game species. As a small game load it is of course adequate, but may ricochet badly if fired at varmints in open fields.

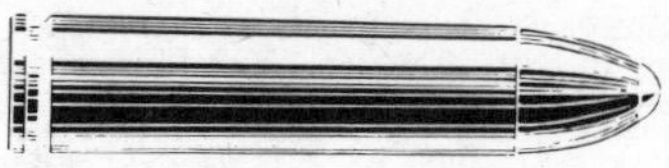

30-30 WCF & 32 WINCHESTER SPECIAL Old favorites of the deer hunter and rancher, these cartridges continue to be popular more because of the light, handy carbines which use them than because of any attribute of the cartridges themselves. For the indifferent marksman they are wonders, having neither great bullet weight nor high velocity. These are deer cartridges and should not be "stretched." They're neither flat shooting nor accurate enough for varmints, nor do they have the power to be good moose killers.

30 & 32 REMINGTON Rimless versions of the 30-30 and 32 Special for the Remington line of autoloaders and slide action rifles (Models 8, 81, 14 and 141), bullet weights and velocities are the same (except no 150-gr. bullets), and there is no difference in killing power. Depends solely on which rifle action the shooter chooses as to which cartridge he uses.

300 SAVAGE Developed by Savage to approximate early 30-06 ballistics in their Model 99 lever action, this cartridge had a phenomenal acceptance for a time. It has an extremely short case neck, making it difficult to reload, but with 150- and 180-gr. factory loads it is a quick killer on deer. The lighter bullet should be chosen where flat trajectory and rapid expansion counts, but for wooded country, or for bear, moose and caribou, use the 180-gr. bullet.

30-40 KRAG Generally called the "Krag", this old military cartridge looks good in "civies." Rifles are no longer made for it, but the Krag bolt actions and Winchester Model 95 lever actions just don't seem to wear out. 180- and 220-gr. bullet loadings are available, with the former as best choice for deer, or mountain hunting requiring the flattest possible trajectory, while the latter is a long brush-cutter slow to open up and offering deeper penetration on heavy game than the faster 30-06, assuming like bullets.

308 WINCHESTER Commercial version of the 7.62mm NATO cartridge, the 308 is a big stick in a small bundle. A stubby cartridge, resembling the 300 Savage with a longer neck but still half-an-inch shorter than the 30-06, this hot little number comes within 100 fs of equaling 30-06 velocities. When first brought out, only 150- and 180-gr. bullets were available in factory loads, but now there is a 110-gr. varmint load and a dandy 200-gr. for the heavier stuff. As the new service cartridge, it will prove increasingly popular for target work as well as hunting.

30-06 SPRINGFIELD American military cartridge since 1906, this has been the standard by which all other big game cartridges were compared. Many have called it our most versatile all-round cartridge, for there are many bullets available, from the 110-gr. for varmints, through the flat-shooting 150-gr. to the 180-gr. "all-purpose," and finally up to a 220-gr. for big game and timber hunting. Except for Alaskan brown bear, buffalo, and rear-angling shots on elk, it is probably adequate for any North American game.

300 H&H MAGNUM Introduced in 1925 as the "Super-Thirty," this was the first factory cartridge giving a velocity in excess of 3000 fps with a 150-gr. bullet. Re-named "300 H&H Magnum" by Americans, it soon demonstrated its superiority as a big game cartridge and, starting in 1935, as a long range target load in the Wimbledon Cup Match at Camp Perry. By virtue of its larger belted case and heavier powder charge, the 300 H&H moves 180-gr. bullets 220 fps faster than the 30-06 with an additional quarter-ton of energy. This gives the shooter who is able to handle the increased recoil flatter trajectory with less wind deflection and more remaining knock-down power. Match Target loads are also offered.

300 WINCHESTER MAGNUM Recognizing the average American hunter's prediliction for 30-cal. rifles as the favorite all-round bore size, Winchester in 1963 introduced this modern 300 Magnum, thereby spelling the doom of the fine old 300 H&H after 38 years. MV of the new round runs 150 to 200 fps higher than the 300 H&H with equal bullet weights, delivering almost 24% greater remaining energy at 400 yards (180-gr. bullet), and 13% flatter trajectory at the same range. Ballistics also exceed by a considerable margin those of smaller bore magnums. The 300 Winchester Magnum with proper bullet weights is adequate for all our big game from deer and antelope to elk, caribou, moose and even the great bears, plus African game of similar weight.

303 BRITISH British service cartridge for over half a century, the 303 has long been popular in Canada, and now with thousands of surplus military rifles in the hands of U.S. shooters its use on this side of the border has increased enormously. Consequently, a wide variety of factory loads have been made available including the old standard 215-gr. round-nose from Remington, Norma and Dominion at 2180-2200 fps; a 180-gr. from Remington, Winchester, Federal, Dominion and Norma averaging 2540 fps (Dominion, 2610); 150-gr. Dominion and Norma at 2720 fps. and even a 130-gr. Norma load traveling 2790 fps. The 303 has thus become a quite effective multi-purpose cartridge for North American game.

303 SAVAGE Another light deer cartridge of the 30-30 class, but in this one some velocity was traded for more bullet weight, 180- and 190-gr. bullets being given 100 to 200 fs less speed. 30-30 killing power, with penetration slightly increased at the expense of a more arched trajectory.

32-20 WCF An almost obsolete little shell which simply refuses to die, it should have been named the 30-20, for it uses a 30-cal. bullet. Too light and under-powered for deer. OK on turkeys, and up to 100 yards it will do a good job on 'chucks. Use the 80-gr. high-speed H.P. for varmints and the 100-gr. "standard" for edible game.

32-40 WINCHESTER Another old timer for which rifles are no longer made, this one began life as a single shot target cartridge, but was soon adapted to repeating hunting rifles. Its 165-gr. bullet lacks the velocity and punch of a 30-30, especially since the high velocity loading was discontinued, but it is still sometimes seen in the deer woods.

8mm MAUSER Underloaded by American ammunition makers because of the wide variations in quality and bore diameter of foreign rifles chambering it, this cartridge has ballistics about like the 30-40 Krag and is a good deer slayer. As loaded by Norma and imported into this country it is quite different, acquiring 30-06 powers. Caution here is to make sure of your rifle. Strength and accuracy vary widely with the individual rifle. Given a good one, this can be a fine big game cartridge using the stepped-up loadings. Do NOT mix with 30-06 rounds!

8mm LEBEL French Army cartridge for many years and until now loaded (only) by Remington, the Lebel has surprisingly good ballistics but is only used in sporterized military rifles or carbines and hence has never found wide favor in this country. Its fat rimmed case is not well adapted to modern bolt actions, but it is a powerful deer load. Discontinued 1964.

338 WINCHESTER MAGNUM Long awaited by many big game hunters, the 338 has shown itself to be a leading contender for the all-round rifle crown, killing large game such as brown bear and bison with the aplomb of a 375 H&H, or whitetail deer with less meat destruction than a quick-expanding 270 bullet. This is a modern, high-efficiency cartridge with flat trajectory slightly bettering the 30-06-180 gr. and 270-150 gr. loads, while delivering about 25% more striking energy at 200 and 300 yards than the 30-06. The great sectional density of the heavier bullets insures penetration and resistance to deflection by wind or brush, especially when the 275-grain Speer bullets are handloaded. Recoil is greater than with lesser cartridges, but not excessive for the shooter used to firing heavy 30-06 loads in light sporting rifles. The 338 will become increasingly popular with hunters who mix elk and moose with their regular deer menu.

348 WINCHESTER Lever action cartridge for really big game as well as deer, this is one of our most powerful rimmed cases. It appeared in 1936 for the Winchester Model 71 and was chambered in that one rifle only. Some versatility is provided by a triple range of bullet weights—150, 200, and 250 grains—but the heavier pair are best bets and all that are really needed. While more powerful than necessary for deer, it will do a sure job without wasting any more meat than an explosive 270 or 30. The 250-gr. bullet has ample stopping power for our largest American game. With its flat-nose bullets it is a deadly cartridge whose principal limitations are a rather heavy recoil and medium range.

35 REMINGTON With 200-gr. bullet, the 35 has been found to have considerably more anchoring power than the smaller 30's and 32's. Then too, it's good for getting through brush without deflection, and leaves a better blood trail. To 200 yards there's little difference in trajectory from the 30-30 and it has the advantage of being effective on larger game such as moose at moderate ranges, without excessive recoil. Highly recommended for Eastern deer and black bear, this praise does **not** include the pointed 150-gr. load. Stick to the 200-gr. for best results.

351 WINCHESTER SELF-LOADER Chambered only in the now-obsolete Winchester '07 autoloading rifle, the 351 hangs on because of its widespread use by police departments. For close wood ranges it can be used for deer and will kill with a proper hit.

358 WINCHESTER New and rimless brother of the 348, this one develops almost the same ballistics at the muzzle but its more pointed bullets retain that punch further out. The 358 is simply the 308 Winchester, neck-expanded to take 35-cal. bullets. The 358 is a splendid cartridge for moose and elk, and even the large bears can be tackled with it using the 250-gr. Trajectory is the same as that of the 30-40 Krag with 220-gr. bullet.

350 REMINGTON MAGNUM First commercial cartridge to deserve the term Short Magnum, and one of the most practical big game rounds to appear in recent years, the 350 Magnum is especially notable for the restraint built into its design. Either standard length or short actions will accommodate its squat hull and deep-seated bullets, and its power is an almost perfect compromise, for American big game, between too much and not enough. This stems directly from its powder capacity, about 7% more than that of a 30-06 when both cases are filled to the base of their necks. 200-gr. bullets have a MV of 2710 fps, while 250-grainers reach 2410 fps, both from only a 20" carbine barrel. The old 35 Remington is thus hopelessly outclassed and the 35 Whelen challenged by a cartridge that is still within the recoil limitations of once-a-year hunters. Deer hunters and those who are recoil-shy should use the 200-gr. load, which delivers noticeably less kick.

375 H&H MAGNUM World-wide big game cartridge and champion of the "mediums," the 375 H&H dates back to 1912 but can still boast no peer as an all-round load for big and dangerous game. It will dispatch the largest American game as well as most African species. If necessary, it will kill an elephant, and yet its big 270-gr. slug will travel over long ranges as flat as a 180-gr. 30-06 to kill mountain game without excessive meat destruction. There is also a 300-gr. bullet turning up over 2 tons of muzzle energy. Cartridges may be purchased in almost all of the big game regions of the world. Its one disadvantage is its quite heavy recoil.

38-40 WINCHESTER This "38" actually measures 40 caliber and should have been named "40-40." Many deer are still killed yearly by its 180-gr. bullet, loafing along at 1,330 fs, mostly because it punches a big enough hole to let out a lot of blood. It's obsolete and there are a lot of better cartridges, but for short ranges (under 100 yards), it will still do the trick.

38-55 WINCHESTER Like the 32-40, this cartridge started out as a target load for single shot rifles, in which it quickly established a reputation for fine accuracy. Its use spread to repeating hunting rifles where the 255-gr. bullet proved to be a more sure stopper than the 30-30. It tends to ignore brush, but its low velocity means a rainbow-trajectory and so it lost the popularity race. No rifles are made for it.

44-40 WINCHESTER Big brother of the 38-40, this is the same type of short, low-velocity cartridge, varying only by being slightly larger in bullet diameter and weight (200 grains). Under 100 yards it will kill as well as a 30-30.

44 REMINGTON MAGNUM See Part II—Handgun Cartridges.

444 MARLIN In essence a "super" 44 Magnum since it uses the same 240-gr. .429" jacketed SP bullet but in a long, straight 2.22" case, the 444 Marlin provides 30% higher MV with 88% greater ME! At the muzzle its energy is greater even than that of the 30-06, at least on paper, but the blunt, relatively short bullet sheds velocity so fast that at only 100 yards it is down to the power level of the 7mm Mauser and 300 Savage. However, the 444 will be hitting as hard at 200 yards as the 35 Remington at 150, making it a fine deer and black bear cartridge to this range, while at 100 yards or less it is capable of handling just about any North American big game. Its biggest need is for a heavier constructed bullet that will not break up on the tough muscles and bone structure of such game or any intervening brush. Such bullets are already available to handloaders.

45-70 Stil potent after 85 years, some of which was on the battlefield, but even more in the hunting fields, this old timer asks only to be used within ranges where its trajectory isn't too steep. Other than that, its user can count on a kill (if he does his part) whether the game be a small deer or a big moose. Excessive drop makes hitting tough beyond 150 yards, despite its ability to kill well-beyond that distance.

458 WINCHESTER Most powerful commercial American cartridge, the 458 has already won its spurs in Africa; the special Model 70 rifle chambered for it is known as the "African" Model. It is well named, for the massive 500-gr. full-steel-jacketed and 510-gr. softpoints are an "over-dose" for practically all other game with the exceptions of Indian tiger, Asian gaur, and Alaskan brown bear. Heavy bullet weight and high speed for its caliber combine to make this more than just a good killing cartridge—it is a "stopping load," designed to break down the most ponderous and dangerous beasts, and this it will do. For an American going to Africa for elephant, buffalo and rhino it is top choice. The soft point should be used on even the largest soft-skinned game, for the solid bullet is a specialized number for elephants. Has greatest recoil of all American cartridges.

THE WEATHERBY CARTRIDGES

Weatherby Magnum cartridges have been factory produced for many years now, and are sold at sporting goods stores all over America and in many foreign countries. The brass cases are produced in Sweden, but all other components are American-made and assembled. They therefore qualify as American ammunition and merit inclusion in this analysis of cartridges on the U.S. market.

224 WEATHERBY VARMINTMASTER Smallest of the Weatherby's, the 224 also has the smallest capacity of any belted case. Despite its modest size, however, velocities over 3700 fps with 50-gr. bullets and 3600 fps with 55-gr. have been chronographed, making it a close competitor of the 22-250. It is thus an efficient case which, in combination with the added safety features of good base thickness and positive headspacing provided by the belt, rates as an impressive performer. For those varminters who feel a need for more velocity than the 222 or 222 Magnum, but are willing to settle for less than the 220 Swift, the 224 Weatherby is an outstanding choice.

240 WEATHERBY MAGNUM Highest velocity of all factory-loaded 24 calibers, with the single exception of Holland & Holland's 244 Magnum, this medium capacity Weatherby features an entirely new belted case of reduced dimensions, capable of driving 70-gr. 6mm bullets to 3850 fps, 90-gr. to 3500, and 100-gr. to 3395 fps. It is thus some 200-300 fs faster than the 6mm Remington, and 300-400 fs ahead of the 243 Winchester. With loads giving sufficiently fine accuracy, this should prove to be an outstanding cartridge for open country deer and antelope shooting in combination with summer use as a long range varmint round.

257 WEATHERBY MAGNUM For varmint shooting at extremely long range or for the lighter species of big game in open country, where a premium is placed on flat trajectory and rapid bullet expansion, this cartridge is outstanding. Offering the flattest trajectory of any known 25-caliber cartridge, it utilizes the maximum loads of present-day powders that can be efficiently burned in this caliber to provide the highest striking energy for its bore size. In these combined respects, it is exceeded only by the 264 Winchester Magnum in cartridges under 270 caliber, and even there the difference is negligible.

270 WEATHERBY MAGNUM Next step up in the Weatherby line, the 270 WM is also a better choice for those who place more emphasis on big game hunting, but would still like to use the same rifle for off-season varminting. Bullets of 100, 130 and 150 grains are available with energies and trajectories close to Winchester's 264 Magnum with, however, a somewhat better bullet selection for greater flexibility. While 270 WM muzzle velocities are around 300 fps faster than the standard 270, at 300 yards the speed differential is little more than 100 fs with he lighter bullets but some 270 fs ahead in 150-gr. loadings.

7mm WEATHERBY MAGNUM This cartridge so closely parallels the 270 WM in almost all respects that little more need be said about it, except to note that there's a .007" bigger bullet and heavier bullet selection (to 175 grains) in the 7mm. In any event, there is little to choose between the 7mm WM and the newer 7mm Remington Magnum.

300 WEATHERBY MAGNUM Weatherby says this is his most popular and versatile caliber, and it's not hard to see why. With equal bullet weights, the 300 Weatherby develops from 285 to 355 fps more muzzle velocity than the 300 H&H Magnum for a noticeable increase in power. This cartridge is also liked for the nice balance it strikes between the large and small bores. For example, the 180-gr. 300 WM load offers some 500 fs velocity advantage over the 270-gr. 375 H&H Magnum with a consequent flattening of trajectory by 27%, and yet when loaded with a 150-gr. spitzer bullet it is both faster and flatter shooting than either the 270 or 7mm Weatherby Magnums. Despite some rather extreme claims for it the 300 Weatherby Magnum is doubtless one of the finest all-round big game cartridges.

340 WEATHERBY MAGNUM This is Weatherby's newest big game cartridge, produced to satisfy those hunters who want still more bullet weight than the 300's 220 grains, but at the same time wish to retain the 300's velocity and trajectory characteristics. This it does, giving a 250-gr. bullet only 55 fs less muzzle velocity than the 220-gr. 300 WM. Recoil is up, however, and the man who selects the 340 in preference to a 300 should be reasonably sure he needs its extra punch. For the great Alaskan bear it would appear to be a better choice, but for an all-round rifle involving mostly smaller game, the 300 would get the nod. The 340 WM uses the same bullets as the 338 Winchester Magnum, but boosts bullet speeds by 150 to 210 fps. An excellent moose, elk and bear cartridge.

378 WEATHERBY MAGNUM With this truly "magnum-size" cartridge we enter the field of specialized big game calibers. The latest Weatherby catalog states that it was "designed for the purpose of killing thick-skinned animals where extremely deep penetration is needed." With bullet weights of 270- and 300-gr. at velocities of 2900 to 3180 fps, it should be obvious that while striking power is unquestionably great, so is its recoil; entirely too much, in fact, for the average hunter not used to handling such heavy comeback. Experienced African and Arctic hunters, however, accustomed to the slam of the 375 H&H and larger rifles, report the 378 WM to be a most effective cartridge for the big stuff. With the adoption of the 378, Weatherby has discontinued production of the 375 WM, although ammunition for the older caliber is still being made. Despite its designation, the 378 uses the same bullets as the 375 Weatherby and the 375 H&H Magnum.

460 WEATHERBY MAGNUM Comments made on the 378 WM apply with even greater force to this largest and most powerful of all American cartridges. Using the same oversize belted case as the 378 Weatherby, its energy of 8000 fp with 500-gr. bullet is so great that it would normally be selected for only the very largest and dangerous game including elephant, rhino and buffalo. Some authorities feel that the 378 Weatherby would be adequate for such animals were it not for African game laws requiring rifles of 40 caliber or over for those species. Here again the name may be misleading, since the 460 WM uses the same size bullets as the 458 Winchester, only at a phenomenal increase of 570 fps muzzle velocity and nearly 3000 foot pounds of ME.

AMERICANIZED IMPORTED CARTRIDGES

We include here summaries on some of the popular and significant cartridges produced in Europe for the U.S. market. Some were actually designed in this country, others of overseas origin were specifically intended for export to the States; since most of them are encountered with increasing frequency, it is reasonable to think of them as "American" by use if not by manufacture. Only those loaded with American-type "Boxer" primers are included.

6.5x54 MS An old but still liked cartridge for the Mannlicher-Schoenauer carbines, Norma offers five different versions with bullet weights of 77, 139 and 156 grains at muzzle speeds of 3117, 2580 and 2461 fps. A modest capacity round, the 6.5 MS built its reputation as a game cartridge **not** on velocity, but rather on the deep penetration of its long pencil-like round nose bullets. In its heaviest bullet weight, it has been well-liked in Maine as an effective black bear load.

6.5x55 SWEDISH Long the military cartridge of Sweden and Norway, the 6.5x55 has become quite common in the U.S., partly because of thousands of imported surplus military rifles and the fine Schultz & Larsen target rifles. With its light recoil, resistance to wind deflection and excellent accuracy, it has justified its Scandinavian reputation and is seen increasingly on our target ranges. Norma offers 6 different loadings with bullet weights of 77, 93, 139 and 156 grains at velocities somewhat above those of the smaller Mannlicher cartridge. The 139-gr. load is probably the most popular here.

7x61 S&H A modern high velocity big game round with Norma short belted case, the brain-child of Americans Phil Sharpe and Dick Hart, this shell is only 4mm longer than the old 7x57 Mauser case but velocity with 160-gr. boat-tails is 3100 fps at muzzle of a 26" barrel, according to the Norma table.

In 1968, Norma improved the 7x61 case by changing its interior dimensions to provide thinner but stronger case walls. Known as the Super 7x61, exterior dimensions remain exactly the same as formerly, hence the new version will fit all rifles chambered for the older 7x61 S&H, but due to a slightly increased powder capacity, velocity is rated 50 fs higher; (3150 with 160-gr. bullet from 26" barrels).

30 U.S. CARBINE To satisfy the demand for 30 Carbine ammo, Norma produces one with full metal jacket, the other in soft point, both 110 grain. This last, the one hunter-owners most sought, is at best little more than a small game cartridge, since velocity and energy are down to 1595 fs and 622 fp respectively at only 100 yards. Fast repeat shots should not be counted on to make up for inadequate power; this cartridge should not be selected for deer or other big game hunting.

308 NORMA MAGNUM A short magnum tailored to American big game fields. Its 180-gr. bullet steps out at a velocity 400 fs faster than the 180-gr. 30-06, is 180 fs ahead of the great 300 H&H, equals the new 300 Winchester Magnum and even approaches the much larger 300 Weatherby. Advantage of the Norma cartridge (true also of the 300 Win. Mag.) is that it has the same over-all length as a 30-06, hence will fit in '06 magazines and only requires re-chambering the barrel and opening up the bolt face, plus an extractor alteration, to convert an '06 to 308 Magnum. Pressures run pretty high in this case, so only rifles with strong actions should be converted to the new cartridge. Only factory load is with 180-gr. "Dual-Core" bullets, but the cases may be reloaded with American primers and any 30-cal. bullets from 110- to 220-gr. weight. It is thus a versatile as well as powerful high performance cartridge.

NORMA 7.62mm RUSSIAN Imported by Norma-Precision for American owners of Winchester Model 1895 and surplus military rifles in this caliber, the 7.62mm is furnished with the Tri-Clad soft point 180-gr. bullet developing 2625 fps muzzle velocity and more than 2750 fp energy. This is a rimmed bottle-necked case, ballistically almost identical to our 308, thus only slightly inferior to the 30-06. Formerly loaded in this country with either 145-gr. or 150-gr. bullets at 2820 fps, those ballistics may be reproduced in these new cases by handloaders desiring a lighter, faster bullet loading.

303 BRITISH HV Another modernized old cartridge is Norma's high velocity loadings of the 303 British. As loaded by Remington with a 215-gr. bullet and by Winchester with a 180-gr., pressure limitations of the Lee-Enfield action have held velocities to a sedate 2180-2540 fps, and owners of surplus 303's have wondered how they could obtain higher speeds. The safest way is to decrease bullet weight, and this is just what Norma has done. Two Norma factory loads include a 150-gr. bullet at 2720 fps and a 130-gr. at 2789, either of which will shoot flatter and open quicker on impact than the heavier bullets. If you use a 303 for open country hunting of deer or antelope, give these new loads a try.

7.65 ARGENTINE Originally known as the 7.65mm Belgian Mauser, this cartridge was once loaded in the U.S. and chambered in such popular rifles as the Remington 30-S and Winchester 54 and 70, but was discontinued about the time of WW 2 for lack of demand. Importation of surplus Argentine military Mausers has reversed the picture and there is once again a need for this surprisingly efficient round. Norma offers a single 150-gr. soft point with 2920 fs muzzle velocity and 2105 fs at **300** yards for a midrange trajectory height of only 5.8". Regardless of the fact that this cartridge was designed over 70 years ago, in its modern version it is still an excellent deer cartridge. Bullet (not cartridge) size is the same as a 303 British—.311"-.312".

8x57-JR and 8x57-JRS Rimmed versions of the famous 8x57 Mauser cartridge, the 8x57-JR is loaded by Norma with a 196-gr. .318" bullet, while the 8x57-JRS has the same weight but in .323" diameter. Post-war rifles generally have the larger bore size, while pre-war rifles usually (but not necessarily) have the .318" bore. In any event, the proof markings on the barrel should be carefully examined and only those cartridges with the proper size bullets used. Both of the 8x57 rimmed rounds are good deer and black bear cartridges.

358 NORMA MAGNUM First of the new line of Norma Magnums, this 35-caliber number was offered to the market in 1959 and since then has steadily gained favor among big game hunters here and abroad. In the Scandinavian countries, the 358 Norma has become a favorite of moose hunters, a use for which it is well-fitted almost anywhere. A 250-gr. bullet at 2790 fps from a 23" barrel gives 4322 fp energy—some 1500 more than a 220-gr. 30-06—and energy close to the 4500 fp of a 375 Magnum. With a 200-gr. bullet, 3100 fps can be reached with permissible pressures, so that the 358 Norma may be thought of as a direct competitor of the 338 Winchester, both ballistically and as concerns adaptability to game species. It should fill the bill as a powerful "medium" bore for African hunting, and of course is a natural for Canadian and Alaskan large game.

RIMFIRE CARTRIDGES

5mm REMINGTON RIMFIRE MAGNUM Although announced in the fall of 1967, this 20-cal. bottle-necked rimfire cartridge had still not been offered for sale by spring of 1969. Various troubles are said to have been experienced with early production runs. If eventually able to meet predicted ballistics, calling for a 38-gr. jacketed soft point at 2100 fps MV, performance at 50 yards will about equal that of the 22 WMR at its muzzle, and still deliver as much punch at 150 yards as does the 22 Long Rifle High Speed at the muzzle. Object of this round is to provide lower cost small-game stopping effectiveness with fine accuracy to 150 yards from light, relatively inexpensive rifles.

22 SHORT The economical shooting gallery cartridge. Accurate to 50 yards, this old load is still a popular number. Three loadings—Standard, High Speed and Gallery—give it a usefulness second only to the indispensable 22 Long Rifle. It is **not** a game cartridge, however, and its use on live targets should be restricted to rats, snakes, starlings and the like, since even in the high speed load its light bullet gives but half the energy of the Long Rifle.

22 LONG Only the High Speed loading of this little "betwixt and between" cartridge survives. Having neither the accuracy of the Short nor the power of the Long Rifle it is not recommended except for those few old repeating rifles chambered especially for it.

22 LONG RIFLE Finest and most versatile rimfire cartridge ever developed, it is today better than ever. Four loadings fit it for just about everything except big game hunting. This is everybody's cartridge, with the gilt-edged accuracy of the special Match loads for serious competition, the Standard rounds for economical practice, the High Speeds for small game hunting (with hollow-point bullets), and the Shot cartridges for pest destruction. The High Speed with plain bullet is not recommended for **any** of these uses. For hunting, better use the hollow-point for humane kills, and even try for a head shot. Pass up shots beyond 75 yards and be content with squirrels, rabbits and birds.

22 WINCHESTER AUTOMATIC Useful only to owners of the old Winchester Model 1903 autoloader, it is less powerful than the Long Rifle.

22 WRF (or REMINGTON SPECIAL) More powerful than any Long Rifle load and a far better hunting cartridge, it deserves to be more popular. Its flat-nose bullet, of slightly greater diameter and 5 grains more weight than a Long Rifle, is faster, and turns up a third more energy. For squirrel hunters it is hard to beat, and rifles for it should again be made.

22 WINCHESTER MAGNUM RIMFIRE This newest and most potent rimfire cartridge offers the highest velocity, flattest trajectory and greatest striking power of any rimfire cartridge currently available. Its ballistics in a 6½" barrel exceed even those of any other rimfire when used in a rifle. This new cartridge is a top-flight choice for the 100-125 yard varmint shooter who doesn't handload; similarly, for the farmer's gun kept against raiding hawks, foxes, etc., **and** for the handgunner who prefers to use his "short gun" for hunting.

Part II. HANDGUN CARTRIDGES (Rimfire & Centerfire)

22 SHORT RF This little cartridge is currently experiencing a revival of popularity because of its adaptability to rapid-fire International-type shooting in the autoloading pistols made especially for it.

22 LONG RF See Rifle Cartridge Section.

22 LONG RIFLE RF Just as with rifles, this cartridge has done more than any other to popularize shooting and training with the handgun. In either revolver or "automatic" it is highly accurate and makes a fine companion for hunter and trapper. Ammo is easily carried, yet will kill small game better than some larger centerfires. Use high speeds for hunting and standards for target work.

22 REMINGTON JET First of the CF handgun cartridges to appear, this little bottleneck was introduced in March of 1961 when Smith & Wesson announced their Magnum M53 revolver. Besides the 22 Jet this gun handles (via cylinder inserts) 22 Shorts, Longs and Long Rifles. The factory-announced muzzle velocity of 2460 fps (obtained in closed-breech test barrels) has not been achieved in revolvers with their open gap between cylinder and barrel. However, the 1870 fps reached with 6" barrels (2100 with 8⅜") makes this a respectable handgun varmint cartridge in any man's language.

221 REMINGTON FIREBALL The second 22-cal. CF cartridge to be introduced by Remington, it established a precedent in 1963 by being chambered in the first American commercial bolt action pistol. 2650 fps has been reached with a 50-gr. bullet from its 10½" barrel, equal to a factory 22 Hornet with 45-gr. bullet fired in a full-length rifle barrel.

256 WINCHESTER MAGNUM Winchester's entry in the high speed, flat trajectory handgun cartridge field had trouble getting off the ground after it was announced in April, 1961, but it has finally developed as **both** a handgun and rifle cartridge. Early published factory velocities were **lower** than those actually attained, first tables saying 2000 fps for the 60-gr. SP bullet, whereas independent chronographs registered 2350 fps from the 8½" barrel of a Ruger Hawkeye.

25 AUTO Smallest of production centerfires, this is strictly for use in defensive weapons—tiny automatics lacking both power and accuracy, firing 50-gr. metal case bullets with less energy than even the standard velocity 22 LR.

30 CARBINE In producing his Blackhawk revolver chambered for the 30 Carbine cartridge, Bill Ruger has made this round properly classifiable as a handgun load. For the considerable number of today's pistol shooters seeking a high speed, flat-shooting revolver cartridge without the heavy recoil of a 44 or 41 Magnum, but with more bullet weight and diameter than a 22 caliber, the 30 Carbine may provide the answer. Factory and GI loads produce velocities varying from 1400 to 1530 fps from our 7½" barrel test revolver, giving them some 40% more muzzle energy than the 22 Jet. As a revolver load it will be liked particularly by owners of carbines in the same caliber as a companion piece.

30 LUGER A bottle-necked cartridge for automatic pistols firing a 93-gr. metal case bullet at 1,220 fs. Flat shooting with high paper energy, expansion is lacking due to bullet construction, severely limiting its game-killing or man-stopping capabilities. However, it far out-classes the 32 ACP.

30 MAUSER Early high velocity champion, this is still one of the world's hottest cartridges, boasting 1,410 fs with 85-gr. metal case bullet. Like the 30 Luger, it makes long range hitting easier but the bullet falls short of adequate killing power, and it must be used in the awkward Mauser pistol.

32 AUTO Next step up in the caliber scale for automatics, this is a very popular cartridge here and abroad for pocket pistols. Many are used by foreign police where it is known as the 7.65mm, but again a small (71-gr.) round nose metal case bullet gives energy only in the high speed 22 Long Rifle class and no bullet expansion. Not recommended for hunting or defense use.

32 S&W & 32 S&W LONG These are the most popular of the 32's for revolvers, the shorter load used in innumerable old "bureau-drawer specials," the accurate Long in target and light police revolvers. The Long should always be chosen if the gun will handle it. A good small game cartridge but lacks power for police work.

32 COLT SHORT & LONG A pair of "obsolete" cartridges used in old-model Colt pocket revolvers, they are less accurate and less powerful than the 32 S&W Long, and will not chamber in modern 32-caliber revolvers.

32-20 WINCHESTER Best of all the 32's for revolvers, using 100-gr. bullets in both lead and soft point types with flat nose, this is the smallest caliber practical for serious police and defensive use. Trajectory is also flatter due to higher velocity, making this a good hunting cartridge for varmints and small game. Do NOT use the "High Velocity" rifle loads in revolvers.

38 AUTO and 38 SUPER AUTOMATIC The 38 Automatic cartridge is intended to be used in the original Colt 38 Automatic pistols, Models of 1900 and 1902. When the Colt Super 38 appeared about 1925, a new, more powerful loading was offered under the name of Super 38 for this stronger pistol. These Super 38 Automatic cartridges should not be fired in the early model Colt pistols in view of their system of slide attachment and the higher pressures of the Super cartridge. Even the regular 38 Automatic is closely comparable to the 9mm Luger in power, and the 38 Super will give the 357 Magnum a run for its money in barrels of equal length. If loaded with soft point bullets, both of these 38 Auto cartridges would make good game killing loads. Either cartridge will function properly in the Super automatic pistol.

380 AUTO Designed to give more power in a straight blow-back automatic pistol than is provided by the 32 ACP cartridge, and yet keep down chamber pressure and recoil to stay within the limitations of small pocket pistols, it is the smallest auto pistol cartridge which can be recommended for defense.

9MM LUGER This is a more practical load for automatic pistols, using a heavier (124-gr.) bullet at good velocity (1,120 fs), and with considerable accuracy. It is the closest thing to a world or international military pistol cartridge and its popularity here is on the increase with the new S&W automatic and the Colt Commander chambered for it.

38 S&W A favorite cartridge for pocket revolvers, with 146-gr. bullet, and adopted by the British military during World War II, when it was known as the 38-200 (as it was loaded with a 200-gr. bullet). Nothing smaller is recommended for defensive use.

38 COLT SHORT & LONG The 38 Short was used in early Colt house defense guns and the Long was the cartridge which failed to stop fanatical Moros during the Philippine Insurrection. Either may be used in a 38 Special revolver, but both are out-classed by that cartridge for any purpose, hence seldom used.

38 SPECIAL Known as the "S&W" when loaded with round nose bullets, and as the "Colt Special" with flat-points, this is undoubtedly the most popular revolver cartridge in existence. Highly accurate for match shooting, adequately powerful for police and defensive work, yet light enough in recoil to permit its use in small, featherweight belly guns.

357 MAGNUM A high velocity revolver cartridge ideally suited to the needs of police officers and field shooters, its 158-gr. bullet travels at a far higher velocity and delivers an even greater increase in striking energy than the same weight bullet from a 38 Special of equal barrel length. With metal piercing bullet it will penetrate an automobile body, and with the flat-point lead bullet it will kill game of considerable size. An even better choice of bullet for field use is the soft point Remington or Norma half-jacket which will not lead up barrels as do the ordinary lead bullets at high velocity. One of our three best long range revolver cartridges, a gun in this caliber has the added advantage of chambering all 38 Special cartridges for target work.

38-40 WINCHESTER See Part I—CF Rifle Cartridges.

41 LONG COLT Chambered only in old model Colt revolvers, this slow moving, heavy bullet (195 grains) load is suited only for short range shooting where the blunt shape of its lead bullet makes it a good stopper.

41 MAGNUM Produced by Remington for Smith & Wesson revolvers in response to demands for a more potent police cartridge, this new 41 Magnum fills the gap between the 357 and 44 Magnums. Two loads are offered, one a 210-gr. SP at 1500 fps, the other a 210-gr. lead bullet at 1050 fps, both MV figures from 8¾" bbls. In the more common 6" bbl., velocities run 1342 and 986. A potent and accurate cartridge in SP version, trajectory is practically as flat as the 44 Magnum is; it penetrates even deeper, though bullet energy is less. Recoil, only 75% of a 44 Magnum's, makes it a much more pleasant load to shoot. It may well find more use in the game fields than on the policeman's beat. Recoil and gun weight are both heavy for police use, and so far the lead bullet loads have shown only mediocre accuracy. Bullet diameter is .410" and will not interchange with the old 41 Long Colt.

44-40 WINCHESTER See Part I—CF Rifle Cartridges.

44 S&W SPECIAL Developed as a target cartridge from the earlier 44 S&W Russian, the 44 Special has never been loaded by the factories to its velocity potential. The 246-gr. lead bullets travel slowly (755 fs), which is of no matter on target ranges where their high accuracy is paramount. Only when properly handloaded is its true power capacity realized.

44 REMINGTON MAGNUM 44 Special and 44 Russian cartridges may be used in 44 Magnum revolvers when light loads are desired, but for a serious mission afield or on the highway, the new Magnum load is in a class by itself. A flat point, copper-base bullet of 240 grains at 1,570 fs gives the unprecedented muzzle energy of 1,310 fp or nearly **twice** that of the 357 Magnum. Power, recoil and cost are all high, making this a cartridge for specialized use by veteran handgunners. A 44 Magnum is now available specifically designed for use in rifles and carbines. Remington uses a jacketed soft point bullet with a muzzle velocity of 1750 fps claimed; Winchester's ammo has a hollow, soft point that leaves the muzzle at 1750 fps.

45 COLT Most famous of all American revolver cartridges and still one of the best, whether the target be criminal or beast. For close range work we would prefer its big 250-gr. bullet to the 357 Magnum. Now that new guns are again being made for the old 45, its historical background as well as its effective power should ensure a continued popularity and long life.

45 AUTO (or ACP) Official U.S. Army sidearm cartridge for over a half-century and spanning three wars, this largest American cartridge for automatic pistols has thoroughly proven itself both in combat and on the target range. Difficult load to control, but inherently accurate, it has now been given assists in the form of a new light wadcutter target loading, and in late 1957 a new target model pistol of the Colt Model of 1911. There is even a metal-penetrating load for highway patrolmen. This is a good choice for the bigbore shooter, but needs a soft point bullet for field work on game.

45 AUTO RIM Companion of the 45 ACP, this thick-rimmed cartridge was developed for use without half-moon clips in revolvers chambered for the automatic cartridge. For either game shooting or police work it is a better choice than the ACP because of its 230-gr. lead bullet.

CENTERFIRE RIFLE CARTRIDGES — BALLISTICS AND PRICES

Winchester-Western, Remington-Peters, Federal and Speer-DWM

Most of these centerfire loads are available from Winchester-Western and Remington-Peters. Loads available from only one source are marked by a letter, thus: Winchester (a); Western (b); Remington (c); Peters (d); Speer-DWM (f). Those fewer cartridges also available from Federal are marked (e). Contrary to previous practice, W-W and R-P prices are not necessarily uniform, hence prices are approximate. Federal prices are generally slightly lower.

Cartridge	Bullet Wt. Grs.	Bullet Type	Velocity (fps) Muzzle	Velocity (fps) 100 yds.	Velocity (fps) 200 yds.	Velocity (fps) 300 yds.	Energy (ft. lbs.) Muzzle	Energy (ft. lbs.) 100 yds.	Energy (ft. lbs.) 200 yds.	Energy (ft. lbs.) 300 yds.	Mid-Range Trajectory 100 yds.	Mid-Range Trajectory 200 yds.	Mid-Range Trajectory 300 yds.	Price for 20*
218 Bee*	46	HP	2860	2160	1610	1200	835	475	265	145	0.7	3.8	11.5	$7.75
22 Hornet*	45	SP	2690	2030	1510	1150	720	410	230	130	0.8	4.3	13.0	7.45
22 Hornet* (c, d)	45	HP	2690	2030	1510	1150	720	410	230	130	0.8	4.3	13.0	7.45
22 Hornet*	46	HP	2690	2030	1510	1150	740	420	235	135	0.8	4.3	13.0	7.45
220 Swift	48	PSP	4110	3490	2930	2440	1800	1300	915	635	0.3	1.4	3.8	4.25
222 Remington (e)	50	PSP, MC, PL†	3200	2660	2170	1750	1140	785	520	340	0.5	2.5	7.0	3.50
222 Remington Magnum (c, d)	55	SP, PL†	3300	2800	2340	1930	1330	955	670	455	0.5	2.3	6.1	3.80
223 Remington (c, d, e)	55	SP, PL†	3300	2800	2340	1930	1330	955	670	455	0.5	2.1	5.4	3.80
22-250 Remington (a, c, d)	55	PSP, PL†	3760	3230	2745	2305	1730	1275	920	650	0.4	1.7	4.5	3.80
225 Winchester (a, b)	55	PSP	3650	3140	2680	2270	1630	1200	875	630	0.4	1.8	4.8	3.80
243 Winchester (e)	80	PSP, PL†	3500	3080	2720	2410	2180	1690	1320	1030	0.4	1.8	4.7	4.80
243 Winchester (e)	100	PP, CL, PSP	3070	2790	2540	2320	2090	1730	1430	1190	0.5	2.2	5.5	4.80
6mm Remington (c, d)	80	PSP, HP, PL†	3450	3130	2750	2400	2220	1740	1340	1018	0.4	1.8	4.7	4.80
6mm Remington (c, d)	100	PCL	3190	2920	2660	2420	2260	1890	1570	1300	0.5	2.1	5.1	4.80
244 Remington (c, d)	90	PSP	3200	2850	2530	2230	2050	1630	1280	995	0.5	2.1	5.5	4.80
25-20 Winchester HV*	60	OPE, HP	2250	1660	1240	1030	675	365	205	140	1.2	6.3	21.0	6.60
25-20 Winchester*	86	L, Lu	1460	1180	1030	940	405	265	200	170	2.6	12.5	32.0	5.90
25-20 Winchester*	86	SP	1460	1180	1030	940	405	265	200	170	2.6	12.5	32.0	6.60
25-35 Winchester	117	SP, CL	2300	1910	1600	1340	1370	945	665	465	1.0	4.6	12.5	4.10
250 Savage	87	PSP, SP	3030	2660	2330	2060	1770	1370	1050	820	0.6	2.5	6.4	4.50
250 Savage	100	ST, CL, PSP	2820	2460	2140	1870	1760	1340	1020	775	0.6	2.9	7.4	4.50
256 Winchester Magnum* (b)	60	OPE	2800	2070	1570	1220	1040	570	330	200	0.8	4.0	12.0	7.05
257 Roberts (a, b)	87	PSP	3200	2840	2500	2190	1980	1560	1210	925	0.5	2.2	5.7	4.95
257 Roberts	100	ST, CL	2900	2540	2210	1920	1870	1430	1080	820	0.6	2.7	7.0	4.95
257 Roberts	117	PP, CL	2650	2280	1950	1690	1820	1350	985	740	0.7	3.4	8.8	4.95
6.5mm Remington Magnum (c)	120	PSPCL	3030	2750	2480	2230	2450	2010	1640	1330	0.5	2.3	5.7	6.55
264 Winchester Magnum	100	PSP, CL	3700	3260	2880	2550	3040	2360	1840	1440	0.4	1.6	4.2	6.55
264 Winchester Magnum	140	PP, CL	3200	2940	2700	2480	3180	2690	2270	1910	0.5	2.0	4.9	6.55
270 Winchester	100	PSP	3480	3070	2690	2340	2690	2090	1600	1215	0.4	1.8	4.8	5.30
270 Winchester (e)	130	PP, PSP	3140	2880	2630	2400	2850	2390	2000	1660	0.5	2.1	5.3	5.30
270 Winchester	130	ST, CL, BP, PP	3140	2850	2580	2320	2840	2340	1920	1550	0.5	2.1	5.3	5.30
270 Winchester (c, d)	150	CL	2800	2440	2140	1870	2610	1980	1520	1160	0.6	2.9	7.6	5.30
270 Winchester (a, b, e)	150	PP	2900	2620	2380	2160	2800	2290	1890	1550	0.6	2.5	6.3	5.30
280 Remington (c, d)	125	PCL	3190	2880	2590	2320	2820	2300	1860	1490	0.5	2.1	5.3	5.30
280 Remington (c, d)	150	PCL	2900	2670	2450	2220	2800	2370	2000	1640	0.6	2.5	6.1	5.30
280 Remington (c, d)	165	CL	2820	2510	2220	1970	2910	2310	1810	1420	0.6	2.8	7.2	5.30
284 Winchester (a, b)	125	PP	3200	2880	2590	2310	2840	2300	1860	1480	0.5	2.1	5.3	5.30
284 Winchester (a, b)	150	PP	2900	2630	2380	2160	2800	2300	1890	1550	0.6	2.5	6.3	5.30
7mm Mauser (e)	175	SP	2490	2170	1900	1680	2410	1830	1400	1100	0.8	3.7	9.5	5.30
7mm Remington Magnum	125	CL	3430	3080	2750	2450	3260	2630	2100	1660	0.6	1.8	4.7	6.55
7mm Remington Magnum (e)	150	PP, CL	3260	2970	2700	2450	3540	2940	2430	1990	0.4	2.0	4.9	6.55
7mm Remington Magnum (e)	175	PP	3070	2720	2400	2120	3660	2870	2240	1750	0.5	2.4	6.1	6.55
7mm Remington Magnum (c, d)	175	PCL	3070	2860	2660	2460	3660	3170	2740	2350	0.5	2.1	5.2	6.55
30 Carbine*	110	HSP, SP	1980	1540	1230	1040	950	575	370	260	1.4	7.5	21.7	8.40
30-30 Winchester (c, d)	150	CL	2410	1960	1620	1360	1930	1280	875	616	0.9	4.5	12.5	4.15
30-30 Winchester (e)	150	HP	2410	2020	1700	1430	1930	1360	960	680	0.9	4.2	11.0	4.15
30-30 Winchester (a, b)	150	PP, ST, OPE	2410	2020	1700	1430	1930	1360	960	680	0.9	4.2	11.0	4.15
30-30 Winchester (e)	170	PP, HP, CL, ST, MC	2220	1890	1630	1410	1860	1350	1000	750	1.2	4.6	12.5	4.15
30 Remington	170	ST, CL	2120	1820	1560	1350	1700	1250	920	690	1.1	5.3	14.0	4.85
30-06 Springfield	110	PSP	3370	2830	2350	1920	2770	1960	1350	900	0.5	2.2	6.0	5.30
30-06 Springfield	125	PSP	3200	2810	2480	2200	2840	2190	1710	1340	0.5	2.2	5.6	5.30
30-06 Springfield (c, d)	150	BP	2970	2710	2470	2240	2930	2440	2030	1670	0.5	2.4	6.0	5.30
30-06 Springfield (e)	150	PP	2970	2620	2300	2010	2930	2280	1760	1340	0.6	2.5	6.5	5.30
30-06 Springfield	150	ST, PCL, PSP	2970	2670	2400	2130	2930	2370	1920	1510	0.6	2.4	6.1	5.30
30-06 Springfield	180	PP, CL, PSP	2700	2330	2010	1740	2910	2170	1610	1210	0.7	3.1	8.3	5.30
30-06 Springfield (e)	180	ST, BP, PCL	2700	2470	2250	2040	2910	2440	2020	1660	0.7	2.9	7.0	5.30
30-06 Springfield	180	MCBT, MAT	2700	2520	2350	2190	2910	2540	2200	1900	0.6	2.8	6.7	7.25
30-06 Springfield	220	PP, CL	2410	2120	1870	1670	2830	2190	1710	1360	0.8	3.9	9.8	5.30
30-06 Springfield (a, b)	220	ST	2410	2180	1980	1790	2830	2320	1910	1560	0.8	3.7	9.2	5.30
30-40 Krag	180	PP, CL	2470	2120	1830	1590	2440	1790	1340	1010	0.8	3.8	9.9	5.30
30-40 Krag	180	ST, PCL	2470	2250	2040	1850	2440	2020	1660	1370	0.8	3.5	8.5	5.30
30-40 Krag	220	ST	2200	1990	1800	1630	2360	1930	1580	1300	1.0	4.4	11.0	5.30
300 Winchester Magnum	150	PP, PCL	3400	3050	2730	2430	3850	3100	2480	1970	0.4	1.9	4.8	6.70
300 Winchester Magnum	180	PP, PCL	3070	2850	2640	2440	3770	3250	2790	2380	0.5	2.1	5.3	6.70
300 Winchester Mag (a, b)	220	ST	2720	2490	2270	2060	3620	3030	2520	2070	0.6	2.9	6.9	6.70
300 H&H Magnum (a, b)	150	ST	3190	2870	2580	2300	3390	2740	2220	1760	0.5	2.1	5.2	6.70
300 H&H Magnum	180	ST, PCL	2920	2670	2440	2220	3400	2850	2380	1970	0.6	2.4	5.8	6.70
300 H&H Magnum	220	ST, CL	2620	2370	2150	1940	3350	2740	2260	1840	0.7	3.1	7.7	6.70
300 Savage (e)	150	PP	2670	2350	2060	1800	2370	1840	1410	1080	0.7	3.2	8.0	5.15
300 Savage	150	ST, PCL	2670	2390	2130	1890	2370	1900	1510	1190	0.7	3.0	7.6	5.15
300 Savage (c, d)	150	CL	2670	2270	1930	1660	2370	1710	1240	916	0.7	3.3	9.3	5.15
300 Savage (e)	180	PP, CL	2370	2040	1760	1520	2240	1660	1240	920	0.9	4.1	10.5	5.15
300 Savage	180	ST, PCL	2370	2160	1960	1770	2240	1860	1530	1250	0.9	3.7	9.2	5.15
303 Savage (c, d)	180	CL	2140	1810	1550	1340	1830	1310	960	715	1.1	5.4	14.0	5.30
303 Savage (a, b)	190	ST	1980	1680	1440	1250	1650	1190	875	660	1.3	6.2	15.5	5.30
303 British (e)	180	PP, CL	2540	2300	2090	1900	2580	2120	1750	1440	0.7	3.3	8.2	5.30
303 British (c, d)	215	SP	2180	1900	1660	1460	2270	1720	1310	1020	1.1	4.9	12.5	5.30
308 Winchester	110	PSP	3340	2810	2340	1920	2730	1930	1340	900	0.5	2.2	6.0	5.30
308 Winchester (a, b)	125	PSP	3100	2740	2430	2160	2670	2080	1640	1300	0.5	2.3	5.9	5.30
308 Winchester (e)	150	PP	2860	2520	2210	1930	2730	2120	1630	1240	0.6	2.7	7.0	5.30
308 Winchester	150	ST, PCL	2860	2570	2300	2050	2730	2200	1760	1400	0.6	2.6	6.5	5.30
308 Winchester (e)	180	PP, CL	2610	2250	1940	1680	2720	2020	1500	1130	0.7	3.4	8.9	5.30
308 Winchester	180	ST, PCL	2610	2390	2170	1970	2720	2280	1870	1540	0.8	3.1	7.4	5.30
308 Winchester (a, b)	200	ST	2450	2210	1980	1770	2670	2170	1750	1400	0.8	3.6	9.0	5.30
32 Winchester Special (c, d, e)	170	HP, CL	2280	1920	1630	1410	1960	1390	1000	750	1.0	4.8	12.5	4.25
32 Winchester Special (a, b)	170	PP, ST	2280	1870	1560	1330	1960	1320	920	665	1.0	4.8	13.0	4.25
32 Remington (c, d)	170	CL	2120	1800	1540	1340	1700	1220	895	680	1.0	4.9	13.0	5.00
32 Remington (a, b)	170	ST	2120	1760	1460	1220	1700	1170	805	560	1.1	5.3	14.5	5.00
32-20 Winchester HV* (1)	80	OPE, HP	2100	1430	1090	950	780	365	210	160	1.5	8.5	24.5	7.35
32-20 Winchester*	100	SP, L, Lu	1290	1060	940	840	370	250	195	155	3.3	15.5	38.0	5.90
32-40 Winchester	165	SP	1440	1250	1100	1010	760	570	445	375	2.4	11.0	28.0	4.65
8mm Mauser (e)	170	PP, CL	2570	2140	1790	1520	2490	1730	1210	870	0 8	3.9	10.5	5.30
338 Winchester Magnum (a, b)	200	PP	3000	2690	2410	2170	4000	3210	2580	2090	0.5	2.4	6.0	6.80
338 Winchester Magnum (a, b)	250	ST	2700	2430	2180	1940	4050	3280	2640	2090	0.7	3.0	7.4	6.80
338 Winchester Magnum (a, b)	300	PP	2450	2160	1910	1690	4000	3110	2430	1900	0.8	3.7	9.5	6.80

CENTERFIRE RIFLE CARTRIDGES—BALLISTICS AND PRICES (continued)

Cartridge	Bullet Wt. Grs.	Bullet Type	Velocity (fps) Muzzle	100 yds.	200 yds.	300 yds.	Energy (ft. lbs.) Muzzle	100 yds.	200 yds.	300 yds.	Mid-Range Trajectory 100 yds.	200 yds.	300 yds.	Price for 20*
348 Winchester (a)	200	ST	2530	2220	1940	1680	2840	2190	765	509	0.4	1.7	4.7	$7.15
348 Winchester (c, d)	200	CL	2530	2140	1820	1570	2840	2030	1470	1090	0.8	3.8	10.0	7.35
35 Remington (c, d)	150	CL	2400	1960	1580	1280	1920	1280	835	545	0.9	4.6	13.0	4.80
35 Remington (e)	200	PP, ST, CL	2100	1710	1390	1160	1950	1300	860	605	1.2	6.0	16.5	4.80
350 Remington Magnum (c, d)	200	PCL	2710	2410	2130	1870	3260	2570	2000	1550	Not Available			6.55
350 Remington Magnum (c, d)	250	PCL	2410	2190	1980	1790	3220	2660	2180	1780	Not Available			6.55
351 Winchester Self-Loading*	180	SP, MC	1850	1560	1310	1140	1370	975	685	520	1.5	7.8	21.5	10.45
358 Winchester (a, b)	200	ST	2530	2210	1910	1640	2840	2160	1610	1190	0.8	3.6	9.4	6.20
358 Winchester (a, b)	250	ST	2250	2010	1780	1570	2810	2230	1760	1370	1.0	4.4	11.0	6.20
375 H&H Magnum	270	PP, SP	2740	2460	2210	1990	4500	3620	2920	2370	0.7	2.9	7.1	8.40
375 H&H Magnum	300	ST	2550	2280	2040	1830	4330	3460	2770	2230	0.7	3.3	8.3	8.40
375 H&H Magnum	300	MC	2550	2180	1860	1590	4330	3160	2300	1680	0.7	3.6	9.3	8.40
38-40 Winchester*	180	SP	1330	1070	960	850	705	455	370	290	3.2	15.0	36.5	8.75
44 Magnum* (c, d)	240	SP	1750	1360	1110	980	1630	985	655	510	1.6	8.4	—	9.25
44 Magnum (b)	240	HSP	1750	1350	1090	950	1630	970	635	480	1.8	9.4	26.0	3.70
444 Marlin (c)	240	SP	2400	1845	1410	1125	3070	1815	1060	675	Not Available			5.15
44-40 Winchester*	200	SP	1310	1050	940	830	760	490	390	305	3.3	15.0	36.5	10.60
45-70 Government	405	SP	1320	1160	1050	990	1570	1210	990	880	2.9	13.0	32.5	6.50
458 Winchester Magnum	500	MC	2130	1910	1700	1520	5040	4050	3210	2570	1.1	4.8	12.0	15.65
458 Winchester Magnum	510	SP	2130	1840	1600	1400	5140	3830	2900	2220	1.1	5.1	13.5	10.30

* Price for 50 HP—Hollow Point SP—Soft Point PSP—Pointed Soft Point PP—Power Point L—Lead Lu—Lubaloy ST—Silvertip HSP—Hollow Soft Point MC—Metal Case BT—Boat Tail MAT—Match BP—Bronze Point CL—Core Lokt PCL—Pointed Core Lokt OPE—Open Point Expanding †PL—Power-Lokt (slightly higher price) (1) Not safe in handguns or Win. M73.

WEATHERBY MAGNUM CARTRIDGES—BALLISTICS AND PRICES

Cartridge	Bullet Wt. Grs.	Bullet Type	Velocity (fps) Muzzle	100 yds.	200 yds.	300 yds.	Energy (ft. lbs.) Muzzle	100 yds.	200 yds.	300 yds.	Mid-Range Trajectory 100 yds.	200 yds.	300 yds.	Price for 20
224 Weatherby Varmintmaster	50	PE	3750	3160	2625	2140	1562	1109	1670	1250	0.7	3.6	9.0	$4.95
224 Weatherby Varmintmaster	55	PE	3650	3150	2685	2270	1627	1212	881	629	0.4	1.7	4.5	4.95
240 Weatherby	70	PE	3850	3395	2975	2585	2304	1788	1376	1038	0.3	1.5	3.9	6.60
240 Weatherby	90	PE	3500	3135	2795	2475	2444	1960	1559	1222	0.4	1.8	4.5	6.60
240 Weatherby	100	PE	3395	3115	2850	2595	2554	2150	1804	1495	0.4	1.8	4.4	6.60
257 Weatherby	87	PE	3825	3290	2835	2450	2828	2087	1553	1160	0.3	1.6	4.4	6.60
257 Weatherby	100	PE	3555	3150	2815	2500	2802	2199	1760	1338	0.4	1.7	4.4	6.60
257 Weatherby	117	SPE	3300	2900	2550	2250	2824	2184	1689	1315	0.4	2.4	6.8	6.60
270 Weatherby	100	PE	3760	3625	2825	2435	3140	2363	1773	1317	0.4	1.6	4.3	6.60
270 Weatherby	130	PE	3375	3050	2750	2480	3283	2685	2183	1776	0.4	1.8	4.5	6.60
270 Weatherby	150	PE	3245	2955	2675	2430	3501	2909	2385	1967	0.5	2.0	5.0	6.60
7mm Weatherby	139	PE	3300	2995	2715	2465	3355	2770	2275	1877	0.4	1.9	4.9	6.60
7mm Weatherby	154	PE	3160	2885	2640	2415	3406	2874	2384	1994	0.5	2.0	5.0	6.60
300 Weatherby	150	PE	3545	3195	2890	2615	4179	3393	2783	2279	0.4	1.5	3.9	7.70
300 Weatherby	180	PE	3245	2960	2705	2475	4201	3501	2925	2448	0.4	1.9	5.2	7.70
300 Weatherby	220	SPE	2905	2610	2385	2150	4123	3329	2757	2257	0.6	2.5	6.7	7.70
340 Weatherby	200	PE	3210	2905	2615	2345	4566	3748	3038	2442	0.5	2.1	5.3	7.70
340 Weatherby	210	Nosler	3165	2910	2665	2435	4660	3948	3312	2766	0.5	2.1	5.0	9.70
340 Weatherby	250	SPE	2850	2580	2325	2090	4510	3695	3000	2425	0.6	2.7	6.7	7.70
378 Weatherby	270	SPE	3180	2850	2600	2315	6051	4871	4053	3210	0.5	2.0	5.2	15.00
378 Weatherby	300	SPE	2925	2610	2380	2125	5700	4539	3774	3009	0.6	2.5	6.2	15.00
460 Weatherby	500	RN	2700	2330	2005	1730	8095	6025	4465	3320	0.7	3.3	10.0	17.50

Trajectory is given from scope height. Velocities chronographed using 26" bbls. Available with Nosler bullets; add $2.00 per box. SPE—Semi-Pointed Expanding RN—Round Nose PE—Pointed Expanding

RIMFIRE CARTRIDGES—BALLISTICS AND PRICES

Remington-Peters, Winchester-Western, Federal & Cascade Cartridge, Inc.

All loads available from all manufacturers except as indicated: R-P (a); W-W (b); Fed. (c); CCI (d). All prices are approximate.

CARTRIDGE	BULLET WT. GRS.	BULLET TYPE	VELOCITY FT. PER SEC. MUZZLE	100 YDS.	ENERGY FT. LBS. MUZZLE	100 YDS.	MID-RANGE TRAJECTORY 100 YDS.	HANDGUN BARREL LENGTH	BALLISTICS M.V. F.P.S.	M.E. F.P.	PRICE FOR 50
22 Short (a, b, c)	29	C, L*	1045	810	70	42	5.6	6"	865	48	$ .77
22 Short Hi-Vel.	29	C, L	1125	920	81	54	4.3	6"	1035	69	.77
22 Short HP Hi-Vel. (a, b, c)	27	C, L	1155	920	80	51	4.2	—	—	—	.88
22 Short (a, b)	29	D	1045	—	70	—	—	—	—	(per 500)	6.85
22 Short (a, b)	15	D	1710	—	97	—	—	—	—	(per 500)	6.85
22 Long Hi-Vel.	29	C, L	1240	965	99	60	3.8	6"	1095	77	.82
22 Long Rifle (a, b, c)†-1	40	L*	1145	975	116	84	4.0	6"	950	80	1.39
22 Long Rifle (b)†-2	40	L*	1120	950	111	80	4.2	—	—	—	1.39
22 Long Rifle (b)†-3	40	L*	—	—	—	—	—	6¾"	1060	100	1.39
22 Long Rifle (d)†-4	40	C	1165	980	121	84	4.0	—	—	—	.88
22 Long Rifle Hi-Vel.	40	C, L	1335	1045	158	97	3.3	6"	1125	112	.93
22 Long Rifle HP (Hi-Vel. (b, d)	37	C, L	1365	1040	149	86	3.4	—	—	—	1.03
22 Long Rifle HP Hi-Vel. (a, c)	36	C	1365	1040	149	86	3.4	—	—	—	1.03
22 Long Rifle (b, c)	No.	12 Shot	—	—	—	—	—	—	—	—	1.70
22 WRF [Rem. Spl.] (a, b)	45	C, L	1450	1110	210	123	2.7	—	—	—	2.21
22 WRF Mag. (b)	40	JHP	2000	1390	355	170	1.6	6½"	1550	213	2.95
22 WRF Mag. (b)	40	MC	2000	1390	355	170	1.6	6½"	1550	213	2.95
22 Win. Auto Inside lub. (a, b)	45	C, L	1055	930	111	86	4.6	—	—	—	2.21

†—Target loads of these ballistics available in: (1) Rem. Match; (2) W-W LV EZXS, Super Match Mark III; (3) Super Match Mark IV and EZXS Pistol Match; (4) CCI Mini-Group. C—Copper plated L—Lead (Wax Coated) L*—Lead, lubricated D—Disintegrating MC—Metal Case HP—Hollow Point JHP—Jacketed Hollow Point

NORMA C.F. RIFLE CARTRIDGES—BALLISTICS AND PRICES

Norma ammunition loaded to standard velocity and pressure is now available with Nosler bullets in the following loads: 270 Win., 130-, 150-gr.; Super 7x61 (S&H), 160-gr.; 308 Win., 180-gr.; 30-06, 150-, 180-gr.; 375 H&H, 300-gr., all at slightly higher prices. All ballistic figures are computed from a line of sight one inch above center of bore at muzzle.

Cartridge	Bullet Wt. Grs.	Type	Velocity, feet per sec. V Muzzle	V 100 yds.	V 200 yds.	V 300 yds.	Energy, foot pounds E Muzzle	E 100 yds.	E 200 yds.	E 300 yds.	Max. height of trajectory, inches Tr. 100 yds.	Tr. 200 yds.	Tr. 300 yds.	Price for 20
22 Hornet*	45	SPS	2690	2030	1510	1150	720	410	230	130	Not Available			$7.25
220 Swift	50	PSP	4111	3611	3133	2681	1877	1448	1090	799	.2	.9	3.0	4.20
222 Remington	50	PSP	3200	2660	2170	1750	1137	786	523	340	.0	2.0	6.2	3.40
223	55	SPP	3300	2900	2520	2160	1330	1027	776	570	0.4	2.4	6.8	3.70
22-250	50	SPS	3800	3300	2810	2350	1600	1209	885	613	Not Available			3.70
	55	SPS	3650	3200	2780	2400	1637	1251	944	704	Not Available			3.70
243 Winchester	75	HP	3500	3070	2660	2290	2041	1570	1179	873	.0	1.4	4.1	4.65
	100	PSP	3070	2790	2540	2320	2093	1729	1433	1195	.1	1.8	5.0	4.65
6mm Remington	100	SPS	3190	2920	2660	2420	2260	1890	1570	1300	0.4	2.1	5.3	4.65
250 Savage	87	PSP	3032	2685	2357	2054	1776	1393	1074	815	.0	1.9	5.8	4.35
	100	PSP	2822	2514	2223	1956	1769	1404	1098	850	.1	2.2	6.6	4.35
257 Roberts	100	PSP	2900	2588	2291	2020	1868	1488	1166	906	.1	2.1	6.2	4.80
	120	PSP	2645	2405	2177	1964	1865	1542	1263	1028	.2	2.5	7.0	4.80
6.5 Carcano	156	SPRN	2000	1810	1640	1485	1386	1135	932	764	Not Available			5.65
6.5 Japanese	139	PSPBT	2428	2280	2130	1990	1820	1605	1401	1223	.3	2.8	7.7	5.65
	156	SPRN	2067	1871	1692	1529	1481	1213	992	810	.6	4.4	11.9	5.65
6.5 x 54 MS	139	PSPBT	2580	2420	2270	2120	2056	1808	1591	1388	.2	2.4	6.5	5.65
	156	SPRN	2461	2240	2033	1840	2098	1738	1432	1173	.3	3.0	8.2	5.65
6.5 x 55	139	PSPBT	2789	2630	2470	2320	2402	2136	1883	1662	.1	2.0	5.6	5.65
	156	SPRN	2493	2271	2062	1867	2153	1787	1473	1208	.3	2.9	7.9	5.65
270 Winchester	110	PSP	3248	2966	2694	2435	2578	2150	1773	1448	.1	1.4	4.3	5.15
	130	PSPBT	3140	2884	2639	2404	2847	2401	2011	1669	.0	1.6	4.7	5.15
	150	PSPBT	2802	2616	2436	2262	2616	2280	1977	1705	.1	2.0	5.7	5.15
w/Nosler	130	SPN	3140	2884	2639	2404	2847	2401	2011	1669	Not Available			6.20
	150	SPN	2800	2616	2436	2262	2616	2280	1977	1705	Not Available			6.20
7 x 57	110	PSP	3068	2792	2528	2277	2300	1904	1561	1267	.0	1.6	5.0	5.15
	150	PSPBT	2756	2539	2331	2133	2530	2148	1810	1516	.1	2.2	6.2	5.15
	175	SPRN	2490	2170	1900	1680	2410	1830	1403	1097	.4	3.3	9.0	5.15
7mm Remington Magnum	150	SPSBT	3260	2970	2700	2450	3540	2945	2435	1990	0.4	2.0	4.9	6.35
	175	SPRN	3070	2720	2400	2120	3660	2870	2240	1590	0.5	2.4	6.1	6.35
7 x 61 S & H (26 in.)	160	PSPBT	3100	2927	2757	2595	3415	3045	2701	2393	.0	1.5	4.3	6.65
w/Nosler	160	SPN	3150	2927	2757	2595	3415	3045	2701	2393	Not Available			7.65
30 U.S. Carbine	110	SPRN	1970	1595	1300	1090	948	622	413	290	.8	6.4	19.0	3.25
30-30 Winchester	150	SPFP	2410	2075	1790	1550	1934	1433	1066	799	0.9	4.2	11	4.05
	170	SPFP	2220	1890	1630	1410	1861	1349	1003	750	.7	4.1	11.9	4.05
308 Winchester	130	PSPBT	2900	2590	2300	2030	2428	1937	1527	1190	.1	2.1	6.2	5.15
	150	PSPBT	2860	2570	2300	2050	2725	2200	1762	1400	.1	2.0	5.9	5.15
	180	PSPBT	2610	2400	2210	2020	2725	2303	1952	1631	.2	2.5	6.6	5.15
	180	SPDC	2610	2400	2210	2020	2725	2303	1952	1631	0.7	3.4	8.9	5.65
w/Nosler	180	SPN	2610	2400	2210	2020	2725	2303	1952	1631	Not Available			6.20
7.62 Russian	180	PSPBT	2624	2415	2222	2030	2749	2326	1970	1644	.2	2.5	6.6	5.65
308 Norma Magnum	180	DC	3100	2881	2668	2464	3842	3318	2846	2427	.0	1.6	4.6	7.25
30-06	130	PSPBT	3281	2951	2636	2338	3108	2514	2006	1578	.1	1.5	4.6	5.15
	150	PS	2972	2680	2402	2141	2943	2393	1922	1527	.0	1.9	5.7	5.15
	180	PSPBT, SPDC	2700	2494	2296	2109	2914	2487	2107	1778	.1	2.3	6.4	5.15
	220	SPRN,	2411	2197	1996	1809	2840	2358	1947	1599	.3	3.1	8.5	5.15
300 H & H	180	PSPBT	2920	2706	2500	2297	3409	2927	2499	2109	.0	1.9	5.3	6.50
	220	SPRN	2625	2400	2170	1986	3367	2814	2301	1927	.2	2.5	7.0	6.50
7.65 Argentine	150	PSP	2920	2630	2355	2105	2841	2304	1848	1476	.1	2.0	5.8	5.65
303 British	130	PSP	2789	2483	2195	1929	2246	1780	1391	1075	.1	2.3	6.7	5.15
	150	PSP	2720	2440	2170	1930	2465	1983	1569	1241	.1	2.2	6.5	5.15
	180	PSPBT	2540	2340	2147	1965	2579	2189	1843	1544	.2	2.7	7.3	5.15
7.7 Japanese	130	PSP	2950	2635	2340	2065	2513	2004	1581	1231	.1	2.0	5.9	5.65
	180	PSPBT	2493	2292	2101	1922	2484	2100	1765	1477	.3	2.8	7.7	5.65
8 x 57 JR	196	SPRN	2362	2045	1761	1513	2428	1820	1530	996	.4	3.7	10.6	5.65
8 x 57 JS	123	PSP	2887	2515	2170	1857	2277	1728	1286	942	.1	2.3	6.8	5.15
	159	SPRN	2723	2362	2030	1734	2618	1970	1455	1062	.2	2.6	7.9	5.15
	196	SPRN	2526	2195	1894	1627	2778	2097	1562	1152	.3	3.1	9.1	5.15
358 Winchester	200	SPS	2530	2210	1910	1640	2843	2170	1621	1195	.4	3.1	8.8	6.20
	250	SPS	2250	2010	1780	1570	2811	2243	1759	1369	.6	3.9	10.4	6.20
358 Norma Magnum	250	SPS	2790	2493	2231	2001	4322	3451	2764	2223	.2	2.4	6.6	7.10
375 H & H Magnum	300	SPS	2550	2280	2040	1830	4333	3464	2773	2231	.3	2.8	7.6	8.15
44 Magnum	240	SPFP	1750				1640				Not Available			3.65

P—Pointed SP—Soft Point HP—Hollow Point FP—Flat Point RN—Round Nose BT—Boat Tail MC—Metal Case
DC—Dual Core SPS—Soft Point Semi-Pointed NA—Not announced *Price for 50

CENTERFIRE HANDGUN CARTRIDGES—BALLISTICS AND PRICES

Winchester-Western, Remington-Peters, Norma and Federal

Most loads are available from W-W and R-P. All available Norma loads are listed. Federal manufactures only four — two each in 38 Special and 45 ACP — marked with an asterisk. Other loads supplied by only one source are indicated by a letter, thus: Norma (a); R-P (b); W-W (c). Prices are approximate.

Cartridge	Bullet Grs.	Bullet Style	Muzzle Velocity	Muzzle Energy	Barrel Inches	Price Per 50
22 Jet (b)	40	SP	2100	390	8⅜	$7.25
221 Fireball (b)	50	SP	2650	780	10½	3.35
25 (6.35mm) Auto	50	MC	810	73	2	4.70
256 Winchester Magnum (c)	60	HP	2350	735	8½	7.05
30 (7.65mm) Luger Auto	93	MC	1220	307	4½	7.50
30 (7.63mm) Mauser Auto	85	MC	1410	375	5½	7.50
32 S&W Blank (c)	No bullet		—	—	—	3.60
32 S&W Blank, BP (c)	No bullet		—	—	—	3.60
32 Short Colt	80	Lead	745	100	4	4.05
32 Long Colt, IL (c)	82	Lub.	755	104	4	4.25
32 Colt New Police	100	Lead	680	100	4	5.00
32 (7.65mm) Auto	71	MC	960	145	4	5.35
32 (7.65mm) Auto Pistol (a)	77	MC	900	162	4	5.20
32 S&W	88	Lead	680	90	3	4.05
32 S&W Long	98	Lead	705	115	4	4.25
7.5 Nagant (a)	104	Lead	722	120	4½	7.25
32-20 Winchester	100	Lead	1030	271	6	5.90
32-20 Winchester	100	SP	1030	271	6	7.35
357 Magnum (b)	158	SP	1550	845	8⅜	7.15
357 Magnum	158	MP	1410	695	8⅜	6.90
357 Magnum	158	Lead	1410	696	8⅜	6.05
357 Magnum (a)	158	JSP	1450	735	8⅜	6.95
9mm Luger (a)	116	MC	1165	349	4	6.50
9mm Luger (c)	115	JHP	1140	330	4	
9mm Luger Auto	124	MC	1120	345	4	6.70
38 S&W Blank (c)	No bullet		—	—	—	3.70
38 Smith & Wesson	146	Lead	685	150	4	5.05
38 S&W (a)	146	Lead	730	172	4	4.90
38 MK II (a)	180	MC	620	153	5	
38 Special Blank (c)	No bullet		—	—	—	5.85
38 Special, IL (c)	150	Lub.	1060	375	6	5.30
38 Special, IL (c)	150	MC	1060	375	6	6.25
38 Special	158	Lead	855	256	6	5.15
38 Special	200	Lead	730	236	6	5.35
38 Special	158	MP	855	256	6	6.40
38 Special WC (b)	148	Lead	770	195	6	5.35
38 Special Match, IL (c)*	148	Lead	770	195	6	5.35
38 Special Match, IL (b, c)*	158	Lead	855	256	6	5.25
38 Special Hi-Speed	158	Lead	1090	425	6	5.00
38 Special (a)	158	RN	900	320	6	5.00
38 Colt New Police	150	Lead	680	154	4	4.90
38 Short Colt	125	Lead	730	150	6	4.55
38 Short Colt, Greased (c)	130	Lub.	730	155	6	4.55
38 Long Colt	150	Lead	730	175	6	5.05
38 Super Auto (b)	130	MC	1280	475	5	5.65
38 Auto, for Colt 38 Super (c)	130	MC	1280	475	5	5.65
38 Auto	130	MC	1040	312	4½	5.65
380 Auto	95	MC	955	192	3¾	5.45
38-40 Winchester	180	SP	975	380	5	8.75
41 Long Colt, IL (c)	200	Lub.	730	230	6	5.65
41 Remington Magnum (b)	210	Lead	1050	515	8¾	7.80
41 Remington Magnum (b)	210	SP	1500	1050	8¾	8.90
44 S&W Special	246	Lead	755	311	6½	6.85
44 Remington Magnum	240	SP	1470	1150	6½	9.25
44 Remington Magnum	240	Lead	1470	1150	6½	9.05
44-40 Winchester	200	SP	975	420	7½	10.60
45 Colt	250	Lead	860	410	5½	6.85
45 Colt, IL (c)	255	Lub., L	860	410	5½	6.85
45 Auto*	230	MC	850	369	5	7.30
45 ACP (a)	230	JHP	850	370	5	7.75
45 Auto WC*	185	MC	775	245	5	7.60
45 Auto MC (a, b)	230	MC	850	369	5	7.65
45 Auto Match (c)	185	MC	775	247	5	7.40
45 Auto Match, IL (c)	210	Lead	710	235	5	7.40
45 Auto Rim (b)	230	Lead	810	335	5½	7.30

IL—Inside Lub. JSP—Jacketed Soft Point WC—Wad Cutter
RN—Round Nose HP—Hollow Point Lub—Lubricated
MC—Metal Case SP—Soft Point MP—Metal Point
LGC—Lead, Gas Check JHP—Jacketed Hollow Point

SUPER VEL HANDGUN CARTRIDGES—BALLISTICS AND PRICES

The cartridges listed below are perhaps the most powerful and destructive of these calibers commercially manufactured. Bullets listed can be had as components — other weights (not loaded by Super Vel) are also available.

Cartridge	Bullet Gr.	Bullet Style	Muzzle Velocity	Muzzle Energy	Barrel Inches	Price Per 50
380 ACP	80	JHP	1026	188	5	$6.45
9mm Luger	90	JHP	1422	402	5	7.45
38 Special	110	JHP/SP	1282	399	6	6.45
38 Special*	147	HBWC				5.35
38 Special Int.	158	Lead	1090	414	6	5.85
357 Magnum	110	JHP/SP	1690	697	6	7.45
44 Magnum	180	JHP/SP	2005	1607	6	†4.10
45 Auto*	170	JHP				8.45

*Ballistic data not available †Price per 20
JHP—Jacketed Hollow Point SP—Jacketed Soft Point
HBWC—Hollow Base Wad Cutter

SHOTSHELL LOADS AND PRICES

Winchester-Western, Remington-Peters, Federal & Eley

In certain loadings one manufacturer may offer fewer or more shot sizes than another, but in general all makers offer equivalent loadings. Sources are indicated by letters, thus: W-W (a); R-P (b); Fed. (c); Eley (d). Prices are approximate.

GAUGE	Length Shell Ins.	Powder Equiv. Drams	Shot Ozs.	Shot Size	PRICE FOR 25
MAGNUM LOADS					
10 (a[1], b)	3½	5	2	2, 4	$8.10
12 (a, b, c)	3	4½	1⅞	BB, 2, 4	5.30
12 (a[1], b)	3	4¼	1⅝	2, 4, 6	4.90
12 (a[1], b, c, d)	2¾	4	1½	2, 4, 5, 6	4.50
16 (a, b, c, d)	2¾	3½	1¼	2, 4, 6	3.90
20 (a, b, c)	3	3¼	1¼	2. 4, 6, 7½	4.00
20 (a[1])	3	Max	1 3/16	4	3.65
20 (a[1], b, c, d)	2¾	3	1⅛	2, 4, 6, 7½	3.55
28 (a, c)	2¾	Max	1	6, 7½, 8, 9	3.55
LONG RANGE LOADS					
10 (a, b)	2⅞	4¾	1⅝	4	4.75
12 (a[1], b, c, d)	2¾	3¾	1¼	BB, 2, 4, 5, 6, 7½, 9	3.90
16 (a, b, c, d)	2¾	3¼	1⅛	4, 5, 6, 7½	3.60
16 (a[1], b, c)	2¾	3	1⅛	4, 5, 6, 7½, 9	3.55
20 (a[1], b, c, d)	2¾	2¾	1	4, 5, 6, 7½, 9	3.40
28 (a, b, c)	2¾	2¼	¾	4, 6, 7½, 9	3.50
FIELD LOADS					
12 (a, b, c)	2¾	3¼	1¼	7½, 8, 9	3.45
12 (a, b, c, d)	2¾	3¼	1⅛	4, 5, 6, 7½, 8, 9	3.30
12 (a, b, c, d)	2¾	3	1⅛	4, 5, 6, 8, 9	3.25
12 (a, b, c, d)	2¾	3	1	4, 5, 6, 8	3.10
16 (a, b, c, d)	2¾	2¾	1⅛	4, 5, 6, 7½, 8, 9	3.10
16 (a, b, c)	2¾	2½	1	4, 5, 6, 8, 9	2.95
20 (a, b, c, d)	2¾	2½	1	4, 5, 6, 7½, 8, 9	3.00
20 (a, b, c)	2¾	2¼	⅞	4, 5, 6, 8, 9	2.75
SCATTER LOADS					
12 (a, b, c)	2¾	3	1⅛	8	3.40
16 (a, b, c)	2¾	2½	1	8	3.10
20 (a, b, c)	2¾	2¼	⅞	8	2.95
TARGET LOADS					
12 (a, b, c)	2¾	3	1⅛	7½, 8, 9	3.25
12 (a, b, c)	2¾	2¾	1⅛	7½, 8, 9	3.25
16 (a, b, c)	2¾	2½	1	8, 9	2.95
20 (a, b, c)	2¾	2¼	⅞	8, 9	2.75
28 (a, c)	2¾	2¼	¾	9	3.50
410 (a, b, c, d)	3	Max	¾	4, 5, 6, 7½, 9	3.10
410 (a, b, c, d)	2½	Max	½	4, 5, 6, 7½, 9	2.60
SKEET & TRAP					
12 (a, b, c, d)	2¾	3	1⅛	7½, 8, 9	3.25
12 (a, b, c, d)	2¾	2¾	1⅛	7½, 8, 9	3.25
16 (a, b, c, d)	2¾	2½	1	8, 9	2.95
20 (a, b, c)	2¾	2¼	⅞	8, 9	2.75
BUCKSHOT					
12 (a, b, c)	3 Mag.	4½	—	00 Buck—15 pellets	6.10
12 (a, b, c)	3 Mag.	4½	—	4 Buck—41 pellets	6.10
12 (a, b, c)	2¾ Mag.	4	—	00 Buck—12 pellets	5.30
12 (a, b, c)	2¾	3¾	—	00 Buck— 9 pellets	4.70
12 (a, b, c)	2¾	3¾	—	0 Buck—12 pellets	4.70
12 (a, b, c)	2¾	3¾	—	1 Buck—16 pellets	4.70
12 (a, b, c)	2¾	3¾	—	4 Buck—27 pellets	4.70
16 (a, b, c)	2¾	3	—	1 Buck—12 pellets	4.70
20 (a, b, c)	2¾	2¾	—	3 Buck—20 pellets	4.70
RIFLED SLUGS					
12 (a, b, c, d)	2¾	3¾	1	Slug	5.85
16 (a, b, c)	2¾	3	⅞	Slug	5.55
20 (a, b, c)	2¾	2¾	⅝	Slug	5.35
410 (a, b, c)	2½	Max	1/5	Slug	5.05

W-W 410, 28- and 10-ga. Magnum shells available in paper cases only, as are their scatter and target loads; their skeet and trap loads come in both plastic and paper.

R-P 410 and 28-ga. shells are available in paper only: their 12-ga. trap and skeet loads have Power Piston wads (in both plastic and paper cases); their 12-, 16-, and 20-ga. target loads have H wads.

Federal magnum, long range and field loads are available in both plastic and paper in 12 gauge; other gauges and all target and scatter loads are paper; 12-ga. buckshot and slug loads are plastic only.

Eley shotshells are of plastic-coated paper.

1—These loads available from W-W with Lubaloy shot at higher price.

CIL Ballistics

BALLISTICS

KKSP—'Kling-Kor' Soft Point
PSP—Pointed Soft Point
SP—Soft Point
CPE—Copper Point Expanding
MC—Metal Cased (Hard Point)
PNEU—Pneumatic
HP—Hollow Point
ST—'Sabretip'

DESCRIPTION	Bullet		Velocity in Feet per Second						Energy in Foot Pounds					
	Wt. Grains	Type	Muzzle	100 Yds.	200 Yds.	300 Yds.	400 Yds.	500 Yds.	Muzzle	100 Yds.	200 Yds.	300 Yds.	400 Yds.	500 Yds.
22 HORNET	45	PSP	2690	2030	1510	1150	—	—	720	410	230	130	—	—
22 SAVAGE	70	PSP	2800	2440	2110	1840	—	—	1220	925	690	525	—	—
222 REMINGTON	50	PSP	3200	2600	2170	1750	—	—	1140	785	520	340	—	—
243 WINCHESTER	75	PSP	3500	3070	2660	2290	1960	1670	2040	1570	1180	875	640	465
243 WINCHESTER	100	PSP	3070	2790	2540	2320	2120	1940	2090	1730	1430	1190	995	835
244 REMINGTON	75	PSP	3500	3070	2660	2290	1960	1670	2040	1570	1180	875	640	465
6.5 x 53 MM MAN.-SCH.	160	SP	2160	1950	1750	1570	—	—	1660	1350	1090	875	—	—
6.5 x 55 MM	160	SP	2420	2190	1960	1760	1580	1420	2080	1700	1360	1110	885	715
25-20 WINCHESTER	86	SP	1460	1180	1030	940	—	—	405	265	200	170	—	—
25-35 WINCHESTER	117	SP	2300	1910	1600	1340	—	—	1370	945	665	465	—	—
250 SAVAGE	100	PSP	2820	2460	2140	1870	—	—	1760	1340	1020	775	—	—
257 ROBERTS	117	PSP	2650	2280	1950	1690	—	—	1820	1350	985	740	—	—
270 WINCHESTER	100	PSP	3480	3070	2690	2340	2010	1700	2690	2090	1600	1215	890	640
270 WINCHESTER	130	PSP	3140	2850	2580	2320	2090	1860	2840	2340	1920	1550	1260	1000
270 WINCHESTER	160	KKSP	2800	2530	2280	2050	1840	—	2790	2270	1850	1490	1200	—
7 x 57 MM MAUSER	139	PSP	2800	2500	2240	1990	1770	1580	2420	1930	1550	1220	965	770
7 x 57 MM MAUSER	160	KKSP	2650	2330	2040	1780	1550	1350	2500	1930	1480	1130	855	645
7 MM REMINGTON MAGNUM	175	SP	3070	2720	2400	2120	1870	1640	3660	2870	2240	1750	1360	1040
30-30 WINCHESTER	150	PNEU	2410	2020	1700	1430	—	—	1930	1360	960	680	—	—
30-30 WINCHESTER	170	KKSP	2220	1890	1630	1410	—	—	1860	1350	1000	750	—	—
30-30 WINCHESTER	170	ST	2220	1890	1630	1410	—	—	1860	1350	1000	750	—	—
30-30 WINCHESTER	170	MC	2220	1890	1630	1410	—	—	1860	1350	1000	750	—	—
30-30 WINCHESTER	150	ST	2410	2020	1700	1430	—	—	1930	1360	960	680	—	—
30 REMINGTON	170	KKSP	2120	1820	1560	1350	—	—	1700	1250	920	690	—	—
30-40 KRAG	180	KKSP	2470	2120	1830	1590	1400	—	2440	1790	1340	1010	785	—
30-06 SPRINGFIELD	130	HP	3150	2730	2470	2170	1920	1690	2870	2160	1770	1360	1060	820
30-06 SPRINGFIELD	150	PSP	2970	2670	2400	2130	1890	1670	2930	2370	1920	1510	1190	930
30-06 SPRINGFIELD	150	ST	2970	2670	2400	2130	1890	1670	2930	2370	1920	1510	1190	930
30-06 SPRINGFIELD	180	KKSP	2700	2330	2010	1740	1520	—	2910	2170	1610	1210	920	—
30-06 SPRINGFIELD	180	CPE	2700	2480	2280	2080	1900	1730	2910	2460	2080	1730	1440	1190
30-06 SPRINGFIELD	180	ST	2700	2470	2250	2040	1850	1670	2910	2440	2020	1660	1370	1110
30-06 SPRINGFIELD	220	KKSP	2410	2120	1870	1670	1480	—	2830	2190	1710	1360	1070	—
300 WINCHESTER-MAGNUM	180	ST	3070	2850	2640	2440	2250	2060	3770	3250	2790	2380	2020	1700
300 HOLLAND & HOLLAND MAGNUM	180	PSP	2920	2670	2440	2220	2020	1830	3400	2850	2380	1970	1630	1340
300 SAVAGE	150	PSP	2670	2390	2130	1890	1660	—	2370	1900	1510	1190	915	—
3C0 SAVAGE	150	ST	2670	2390	2130	1890	1660	—	2370	1900	1510	1190	915	—
300 SAVAGE	180	KKSP	2370	2040	1760	1520	1340	—	2240	1660	1240	920	715	—
300 SAVAGE	180	ST	2370	2160	1960	1770	1600	—	2240	1860	1530	1250	1020	—
303 SAVAGE	190	KKSP	1980	1680	1440	1250	—	—	1650	1190	875	660	—	—
303 BRITISH	150	PSP	2720	2420	2150	1900	1670	1470	2460	1950	1540	1200	930	720
303 BRITISH	150	ST	2720	2420	2150	1900	1670	1470	2460	1950	1540	1200	930	720
303 BRITISH	180	KKSP	2540	2180	1860	1590	1360	—	2580	1900	1380	1010	740	—
303 BRITISH	180	CPE	2540	2330	2130	1940	1760	1600	2580	2170	1810	1500	1240	1020
303 BRITISH	180	ST	2540	2300	2090	1900	1730	1580	2580	2120	1750	1440	1200	1000
303 BRITISH	215	KKSP	2180	1900	1660	1460	1250	—	2270	1720	1310	1020	750	—
308 WINCHESTER	130	HP	2930	2590	2290	2010	1770	1560	2480	1940	1520	1170	905	700
308 WINCHESTER	150	PSP	2860	2570	2300	2050	1810	1590	2730	2200	1760	1400	1090	840
308 WINCHESTER	150	ST	2860	2570	2300	2050	1810	1590	2730	2200	1760	1400	1090	840
308 WINCHESTER	180	KKSP	2610	2240	1920	1640	1400	—	2720	2010	1470	1070	785	—
308 WINCHESTER	180	ST	2610	2390	2170	1970	1780	1600	2720	2280	1870	1540	1260	1010
308 WINCHESTER	200	KKSP	2450	2210	1980	1770	1580	1410	2670	2170	1750	1400	1110	875
8 MM MAUSER	170	PSP	2570	2300	2040	1810	1600	—	2490	2000	1570	1240	965	—
32-20 WINCHESTER	115	SP	1480	1220	1050	940	—	—	560	380	280	225	—	—
32 WINCHESTER SPECIAL	170	KKSP	2280	1920	1630	1410	—	—	1960	1390	1000	750	—	—
32 WINCHESTER SPECIAL	170	ST	2280	1920	1630	1410	—	—	1960	1390	1000	750	—	—
32 REMINGTON	170	KKSP	2120	1800	1540	1340	—	—	1700	1220	895	680	—	—
32-40 WINCHESTER	170	KKSP	1540	1340	1170	1050	—	—	895	680	515	415	—	—
35 REMINGTON	200	SP	2100	1710	1390	1160	—	—	1950	1300	865	605	—	—
351 WINCHESTER SELF-LOADING	180	SP	1850	1560	1310	1140	—	—	1370	975	685	520	—	—
358 (8.8 MM) WINCHESTER	200	KKSP	2530	2210	1910	1640	1400	—	2840	2160	1610	1190	870	—
38-40 WINCHESTER	180	SP	1330	1070	960	850	—	—	705	455	370	290	—	—
38-55 WINCHESTER	255	SP	1600	1410	1240	1110	—	—	1450	1130	880	700	—	—
43 (11 MM) MAUSER	385	LEAD	1360	1150	1030	940	—	—	1580	1130	910	750	—	—
44-40 WINCHESTER	200	SP	1310	1050	940	830	—	—	760	490	390	305	—	—
44 REMINGTON MAGNUM	240	SP	1850	1450	1150	980	—	—	1820	1120	710	510	—	—

Short Range Sighting-in—It is preferable to sight-in a rifle at the "recommended sighting" range. However, it is sometimes necessary to sight-in a rifle at a distance shorter than the "recommended sighting" range because you don't have the necessary yardage available. To do this, find from the range table at what distance the bullet will first cross the line of sight. Put up a target at this distance and from a firm rest fire

and Range Table

RANGE TABLE—Values shown in this table are based on a sight height 1½" above line of bore. RECOMMENDED SIGHTING: ⊕ Indicates the most favourable sighting range in order to minimize the sighting problem at shorter and longer ranges. + Indicates inches high; − Indicates inches low.

RANGE

First Crosses Line of Sight App. Yds.	50 Yds.	75 Yds.	100 Yds.	125 Yds.	150 Yds.	200 Yds.	250 Yds.	300 Yds.	400 Yds.	500 Yds.	Bullet Wt. Grains	Bullet Type	DESCRIPTION
29.0	—	+1.5	—	—	⊕	−4.0	—	—	—	—	45	PSP	22 HORNET
25.0	—	—	+2.0	—	—	⊕	−4.5	—	—	—	70	PSP	22 SAVAGE
30.0	—	—	+2.0	—	—	⊕	−3.5	—	—	—	50	PSP	222 REMINGTON
30.0	—	—	—	+2.5	—	—	⊕	−3.0	−15.5	−36.5	75	PSP	243 WINCHESTER
27.5	—	—	—	+3.0	—	—	⊕	−3.5	−16.5	−35.5	100	PSP	243 WINCHESTER
30.0	—	—	—	+2.5	—	—	⊕	−3.0	−15.5	−36.5	75	PSP	244 REMINGTON
25.5	—	+1.5	—	—	⊕	−4.0	—	—	—	—	160	SP	6.5 x 53 MM MAN.-SCH.
21.0	—	—	+3.5	—	—	⊕	−5.0	−13.0	−39.0	—	160	SP	6.5 x 55 MM
16.0	+2.0	—	⊕	−4.0	—	—	—	—	—	—	86	SP	25-20 WINCHESTER
23.0	—	+1.5	—	—	⊕	−4.5	—	—	—	—	117	SP	25-35 WINCHESTER
27.5	—	—	+2.0	—	—	⊕	−3.5	—	—	—	100	PSP	250 SAVAGE
24.0	—	—	+2.5	—	—	⊕	−4.5	—	—	—	117	PSP	257 ROBERTS
31.5	—	—	—	+2.5	—	—	⊕	−3.5	−14.5	−33.5	100	PSP	270 WINCHESTER
27.5	—	—	—	+3.0	—	—	⊕	−4.0	−16.0	−35.5	130	PSP	270 WINCHESTER
28.5	—	—	+2.0	—	—	⊕	−4.0	—	−25.0	—	160	KKSP	270 WINCHESTER
27.0	—	—	—	+4.0	—	—	⊕	−4.5	−18.5	−41.0	139	PSP	7 x 57 MM MAUSER
29.0	—	—	+2.5	—	—	⊕	−4.0	—	−28.5	—	160	KKSP	7 x 57 MM MAUSER
25.0	—	—	—	+3.5	—	—	⊕	−4.0	−18.0	−43.0	175	SP	7 MM REMINGTON MAGNUM
27.0	—	+1.5	—	—	⊕	−4.0	—	—	—	—	150	PNEU	30-30 WINCHESTER
23.0	—	+1.5	—	—	⊕	−4.5	—	—	—	—	170	KKSP	30-30 WINCHESTER
23.0	—	+1.5	—	—	⊕	−4.5	—	—	—	—	170	ST	30-30 WINCHESTER
23.0	—	+1.5	—	—	⊕	−4.5	—	—	—	—	170	MC	30-30 WINCHESTER
27.0	—	+1.5	—	—	⊕	−4.0	—	—	—	—	150	ST	30-30 WINCHESTER
20.0	—	+2.0	—	—	⊕	−5.0	—	—	—	—	170	KKSP	30 REMINGTON
21.0	—	—	+3.0	—	—	⊕	−5.5	—	−41.0	—	180	KKSP	30-30 KRAG
27.0	—	—	—	+3.0	—	—	⊕	−4.0	−19.5	−47.0	130	HP	30-06 SPRINGFIELD
25.0	—	—	—	+3.5	—	—	⊕	−4.0	−17.5	−41.0	150	PSP	30-06 SPRINGFIELD
25.0	—	—	—	+3.5	—	—	⊕	−4.0	−17.5	−41.0	150	ST	30-06 SPRINGFIELD
24.0	—	—	+2.5	—	—	⊕	−4.0	—	−32.5	—	180	KKSP	30-06 SPRINGFIELD
21.0	—	—	—	+4.0	—	—	⊕	−4.5	−20.5	−46.0	180	CPE	30-06 SPRINGFIELD
20.0	—	—	—	+4.0	—	—	⊕	−4.5	−21.0	−48.5	180	ST	30-06 SPRINGFIELD
21.0	—	—	+3.0	—	—	⊕	−5.5	—	−41.0	—	220	KKSP	30-06 SPRINGFIELD
27.5	—	—	—	+3.0	—	—	⊕	−3.5	−14.5	−32.5	180	ST	300 WINCHESTER-MAGNUM
25.0	—	—	—	+3.5	—	—	⊕	−4.0	−17.5	−39.0	180	PSP	300 HOLLAND & HOLLAND MAGNUM
26.0	—	—	+2.5	—	—	⊕	−3.5	—	−29.0	—	150	PSP	300 SAVAGE
26.0	—	—	+2.5	—	—	⊕	−3.5	—	−29.0	—	150	ST	300 SAVAGE
20.0	—	—	+3.5	—	—	⊕	−5.5	—	−43.0	—	180	KKSP	300 SAVAGE
21.5	—	—	+3.0	—	—	⊕	−5.5	—	−35.0	—	180	ST	300 SAVAGE
17.5	—	—	+3.0	—	—	⊕	−5.5	—	—	—	190	KKSP	303 SAVAGE
22.0	—	—	—	+4.5	—	—	⊕	−5.0	−23.0	−53.5	150	PSP	303 BRITISH
22.0	—	—	—	+4.5	—	—	⊕	−5.0	−23.0	−53.5	150	ST	303 BRITISH
23.0	—	—	+3.0	—	—	⊕	−5.0	—	−41.0	—	180	KKSP	303 BRITISH
19.0	—	—	—	+4.5	—	—	⊕	−5.0	−23.0	−52.5	180	CPE	303 BRITISH
17.5	—	—	—	+5.0	—	—	⊕	−5.5	−26.5	−71.0	180	ST	303 BRITISH
16.0	—	—	+4.5	—	—	⊕	−7.0	—	−54.0	—	215	KKSP	303 BRITISH
23.5	—	—	—	+3.5	—	—	⊕	−4.5	−23.5	−59.0	130	HP	308 WINCHESTER
25.0	—	—	—	+3.5	—	—	⊕	−4.5	−20.0	−47.5	150	PSP	308 WINCHESTER
25.0	—	—	—	+3.5	—	—	⊕	−4.5	−20.0	−47.5	150	ST	308 WINCHESTER
23.0	—	—	+3.0	—	—	⊕	−5.5	—	−38.0	—	180	KKSP	308 WINCHESTER
22.0	—	—	—	+4.5	—	—	⊕	−5.0	−21.5	−51.5	180	ST	308 WINCHESTER
22.0	—	—	+3.0	—	—	⊕	−5.0	−12.0	−35.0	−48.5	200	KKSP	308 WINCHESTER
22.5	—	—	+3.5	—	—	⊕	−5.5	—	−33.5	—	170	PSP	8 MM MAUSER
16.5	+2.0	—	⊕	−3.5	—	—	—	—	—	—	115	SP	32-20 WINCHESTER
23.0	—	+2.0	—	—	⊕	−4.5	—	—	—	—	170	KKSP	32 WINCHESTER SPECIAL
23.0	—	+2.0	—	—	⊕	−4.5	—	—	—	—	170	ST	32 WINCHESTER SPECIAL
20.0	—	+2.0	—	—	⊕	−5.0	—	—	—	—	170	KKSP	32 REMINGTON
21.0	+1.0	—	⊕	−2.5	—	—	—	—	—	—	170	KKSP	32-40 WINCHESTER
19.5	—	+2.5	—	—	⊕	−6.0	—	—	—	—	200	SP	35 REMINGTON
16.0	—	+3.0	—	—	⊕	−7.5	—	—	—	—	180	SP	351 WINCHESTER SELF-LOADING
20.5	—	—	+3.0	—	—	⊕	−5.0	—	−38.5	—	200	KKSP	358 (8.8 MM) WINCHESTER
14.5	+2.5	—	⊕	−4.0	—	—	—	—	—	—	180	SP	38-40 WINCHESTER
13.5	—	+4.0	—	—	⊕	−8.5	—	—	—	—	255	SP	38-55 WINCHESTER
16.0	+2.0	—	⊕	−3.5	—	—	—	—	—	—	385	LEAD	43 (11 MM) MAUSER
12.5	+3.0	—	⊕	−4.5	—	—	—	—	—	—	200	SP	44-40 WINCHESTER
13.0	—	+4.5	—	—	⊕	−8.0	—	—	—	—	240	SP	44 REMINGTON MAGNUM

a three-shot group. The centre point of the group is the "centre of impact"—the average spot where the bullets strike. Adjust sights to bring the centre of impact to the centre of the target then fire another group. If the centre of impact is on target the rifle will be sighted in at the range recommended in the range table. It is, however, desirable to fire a target at that range as soon as possible as a double check.

SPEER-DWM C.F. RIFLE CARTRIDGES—BALLISTICS AND PRICES

These DWM metric calibers are imported by Speer, Inc. The Starkmantel (strong-jacket, soft-point) bullets have apparently been discontinued. Metric cases and bullets for calibers listed may be special-ordered from Speer. U.S. calibers offered by Speer-DWM will be found elsewhere In this section.

	Bullet		Velocity				Energy				Mid-Range Trajectory			Price
Caliber	Wt. Grs.	Type	Muzzle	100 yds.	200 yds.	300 yds.	Muzzle	100 yds.	200 yds.	300 yds.	100 yds.	200 yds.	300 yds.	for 10
5.6 x 35R Vierling*	46	SP	2030	1500	1140		418	224	130		1.2	7.5		$5.80
5.6 x 50R (Rimmed) Mag.*	50	PSP					Not Available							
5.6 x 52R (Savage H.P.)	71	PSP	2850	2460	2320	2200	1280	947	846	766	.3	2.3	6.5	4.10
5.6 x 61 SE	77	PSP	3700	3360	3060	2790	2350	1920	1605	1345	.1	1.1	3.4	10.30
5.6 x 61R	77	PSP	3480	3140	2840	2560	2070	1690	1370	1120	.1	1.3	4.0	10.30
6.5 x 54 MS	159	SP	2170	1925	1705	1485	1660	1300	1025	810	.5	4.1	11.5	3.50
6.5 x 57 Mauser	93	PSP	3350	2930	2570	2260	2300	1760	1350	1040	.1	1.7	4.8	3.80
6.5 x 57 R	93	PSP	3350	2930	2570	2260	2300	1760	1350	1040	.1	1.7	4.8	4.10
7 x 57 Mauser	103	PSP	3330	2865	2450	2060	2550	1890	1380	977	.1	1.7	5.2	3.50
	162	TIG	2785	2480	2250	2060	2780	2200	1820	1520	.3	2.4	6.7	4.10
7 x 57 R	103	PSP	3260	2810	2390	2000	2430	1820	1320	920	.1	1.8	5.3	3.70
	139	SP	2550	2240	1960	1720	2000	1540	1190	910	.3	2.9	8.6	3.70
	162	TIG	2710	2420	2210	2020	2640	2120	1750	1460	.3	2.4	6.9	4.55
7 x 64	103	PSP	3572	3110	2685	2283	2930	2230	1670	1190	.1	1.4	4.4	3.80
	139	SP	3000	2570	2260	1980	2780	2040	1570	1200	.2	2.2	6.4	3.80
	162	TIG	2960	2603	2375	2200	3150	2440	2030	1740	.2	2.0	6.0	5.30
	177	TIG	2880	2665	2490	2325	3270	2820	2440	2130	.2	2.0	5.6	5.90
7 x 65 R	103	PSP	3480	3010	2590	2200	2770	2100	1540	1120	.1	1.5	4.7	4.25†
	139	SP	3000	2570	2260	1980	2780	2040	1570	1200	.2	2.2	6.4	4.25†
	162	TIG	2887	2540	2320	2140	3000	2320	1930	1650	.2	2.2	6.3	6.05†
	177	TIG	2820	2600	2420	2255	3120	2660	2300	2000	.2	2.1	5.9	6.60†
7mm SE	169	ToSto	3300	3045	2825	2620	4090	3480	3010	2600	.1	1.4	3.9	10.30
7 x 75 R SE	169	ToSto	3070	2840	2630	2430	3550	3050	2620	2240	.1	1.6	4.5	10.30
30-06	180	TUG	2854	2562	2306	2077	3261	2632	2133	1726	.2	2.2	6.3	4.50†
8 x 57 JS	123	SP	2968	2339	1805	1318	2415	1497	897	477	.2	2.7	8.8	3.35
	198	TIG	2732	2415	2181	1985	3276	2560	2083	1736	.3	2.5	7.1	3.95
8 x 57 JR	196	SP	2391	1991	1742	1565	2488	1736	1316	1056	.5	3.9	11.2	3.20
8 x 57 JRS	123	SP	2970	2340	1805	1318	2415	1497	897	477	.2	2.7	8.8	3.50
	196	SP	2480	2140	1870	1640	2680	2000	1510	1165	.4	3.3	9.4	3.50
	198	TIG	2600	2320	2105	1930	2970	2350	1950	1620	.3	2.7	7.6	4.25
8 x 60 S	196	SP	2585	2162	1890	1690	2905	2030	1560	1245	.4	3.2	9.2	3.95
	198	TIG	2780	2450	2205	2010	3390	2625	2130	1770	.3	2.4	6.9	5.00
9.3 x 62	293	TUG	2515	2310	2150	2020	4110	3480	3010	2634	.3	2.8	7.5	5.15†
9.3 x 64	293	TUG	2640	2450	2290	2145	4550	3900	3410	3000	.3	2.4	6.6	7.60†
9.3 x 72 R	193	FP	1925	1600	1400	1245	1590	1090	835	666	.5	5.7	16.6	5.25†
9.3 x 74 R	293	TUG	2360	2160	1998	1870	3580	3000	2560	2250	.3	3.1	8.7	6.95

*Price for 20 †Boxer Primed FP—Flat Point SP—Soft Point PSP—Pointed Soft Point TIG—Brenneke Torpedo Ideal TUG—Brenneke Torpedo Universal ToSto—vom Hofe Torpedo Stopring

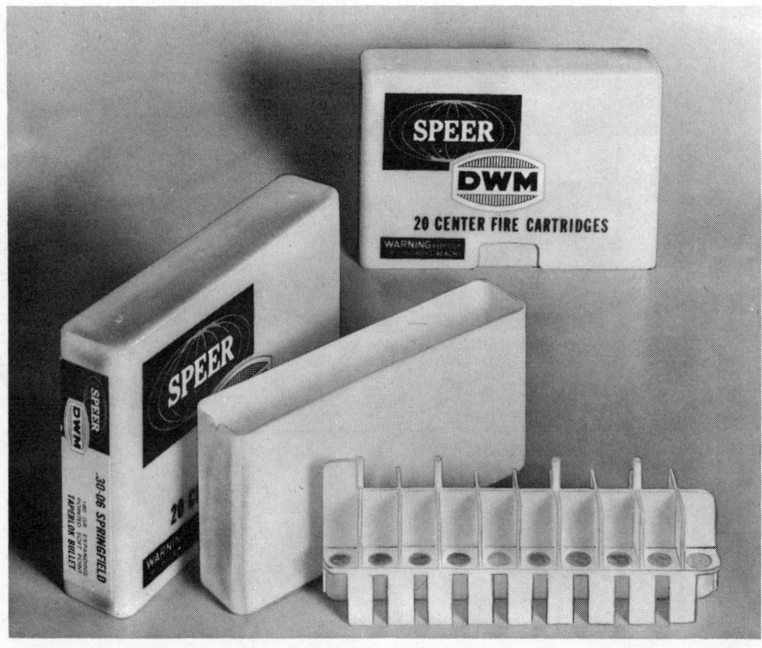

The new reusable 4-way cartridge box in which all Speer-DWM ammo will be packed.

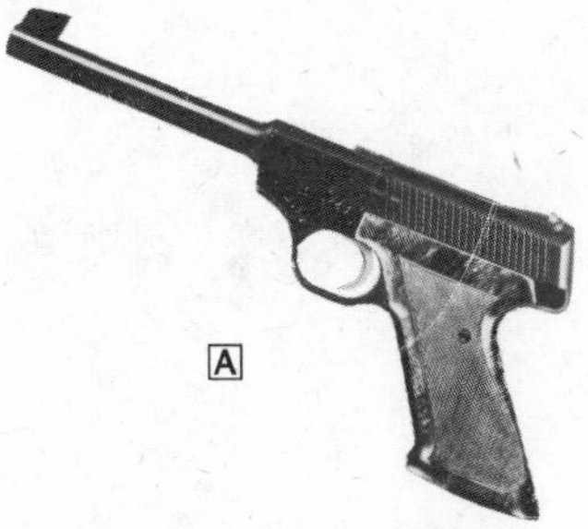

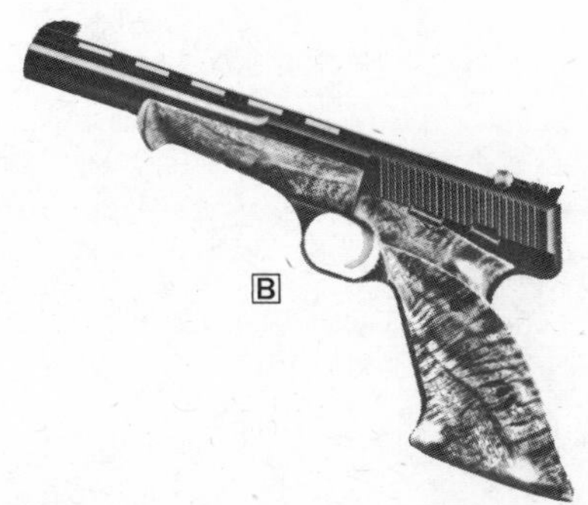

[A] BROWNING 22 AUTO CHALLENGER PISTOL
Caliber: 22 LR, 10-shot magazine.
Barrel: 4½ inches or 6¾ inches.
Length: 8⅞" over-all (4½" bbl.). **Weight:** 35 oz. (4½" bbl.).
Stocks: Select walnut, hand checkered, wrap-around.
Features: Steel frame, manual stop-open latch (automatic after last shot); gold plated grooved trigger; trigger pull adjustment screw on rear face of frame.
Sights: ⅛" non-glare blade front; frame-mtd. rear, screw adj. for w. & e.
Price: Blued, either bbl. **$79.50** Engraved and gold inlaid. . **$254.50**

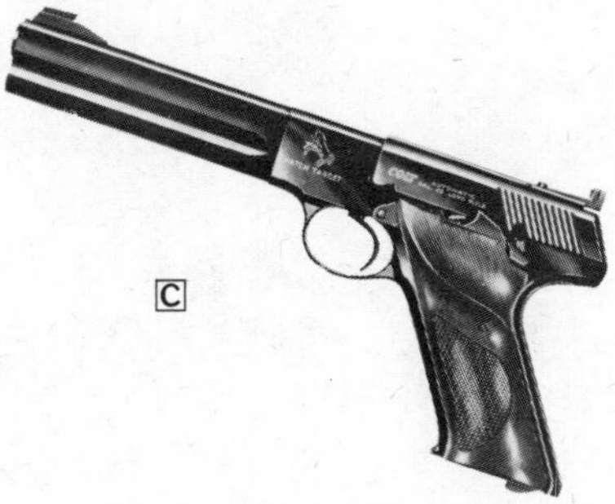

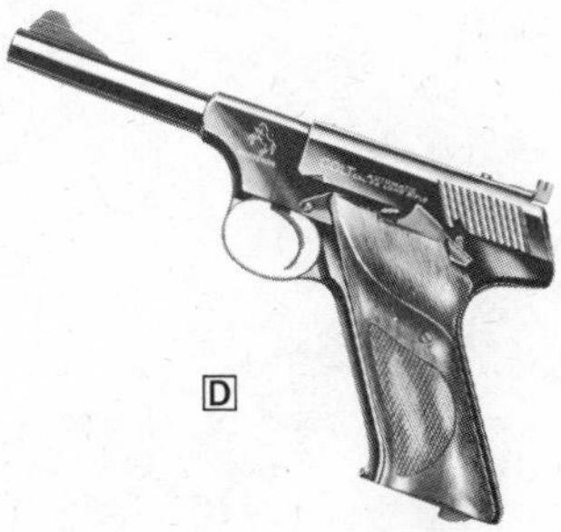

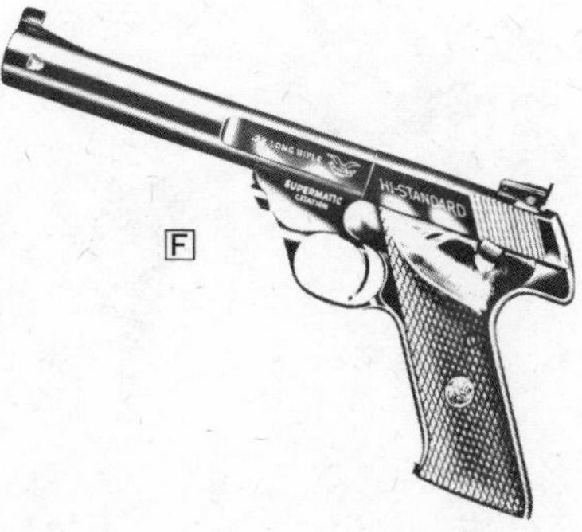

[B] BROWNING 22 AUTO MEDALIST PISTOL
Caliber: 22 LR, 10-shot magazine.
Barrel: 6¾", med.-heavy vent. rib.
Length: 11⅛" over-all. **Weight:** 46 oz. less weights.
Stocks: Full wrap-around thumbrest of select checkered walnut; matching fore-end. Left hand grips available.
Features: Dry-fire mechanism permits practice without mechanical harm. Fore-end holds variable weights. Trigger adj. for weight of pull and backlash.
Sights: ⅛" undercut removable blade front; rear frame-mtd., has micrometer clicks adj. for w. and e. Sight radius, 9½".
Price: Blued. . . . . . **$134.50** Engraved and gold inlaid. **$334.50**

[C] COLT WOODSMAN MATCH TARGET AUTO PISTOL
Caliber: 22 LR, 10-shot magazine.
Barrel: 4½ inches, 6 inches.
Length: 9 inches (4½" bbl.). **Weight:** 40 oz. (6" bbl.), 36 oz. (4½" bbl.).
Stocks: Walnut with thumbrest; checkered.
Features: Wide trigger, automatic slide stop.
Sights: Ramp front with removable undercut blade; ⅛" standard, 1/10" on special order; Colt-Elliason adjustable rear.
Price: Colt Blue only **$115.50**

[D] COLT WOODSMAN SPORT and TARGET MODEL
Caliber: 22 LR, 10-shot magazine.
Barrel: 4½ inches, 6 inches.
Length: 9 inches (4½" bbl.). **Weight:** 30 oz. (4½" bbl.), 32 oz. (6" bbl.).
Stocks: Walnut with thumbrest; checkered.
Features: Wide trigger, automatic slide stop.
Sights: Ramp front with removable blade, adjustable rear.
Price: Colt Blue only **$100.00**

COLT TARGETSMAN
Same as Woodsman S&T model except: 6" bbl. only; fixed blade front sight, economy adj. rear; without auto. slide stop. **$82.50**

[E] COLT NAT'L MATCH 45 and 38 SPECIAL GOLD CUP AUTOS
Caliber: 45 ACP or Wad Cutter; 38 Spec. W.C. 5-shot magazine.
Barrel: 5", with new design bushing.
Length: 8½ inches. **Weight:** 37 oz.
Stocks: Checkered walnut, gilt medallion.
Features: Arched or flat housing; wide, grooved trigger with adj. stop; ribbed-top slide, hand fitted, with improved ejection port.
Sights: Patridge front, Colt-Elliason rear adj. for w. and e.
Price: Colt Royal Blue **$175.00**

[F] HI-STANDARD SUPERMATIC STANDARD CITATION
Caliber: 22 LR, 10-shot magazine.
Barrel: 5½" bull weight.
Length: 10 inches (5½" bbl.). **Weight:** 42 oz. (5½" bbl.).
Stocks: Checkered walnut with or w/o thumbrest, right or left.
Features: Adjustable trigger pull; anti-backlash trigger adjustment; double acting safety; rebounding firing pin. Back & front straps stippled.
Sights: Undercut ramp front; click adjustable square notch rear.
Price: 5½" bull barrel **$110.00**

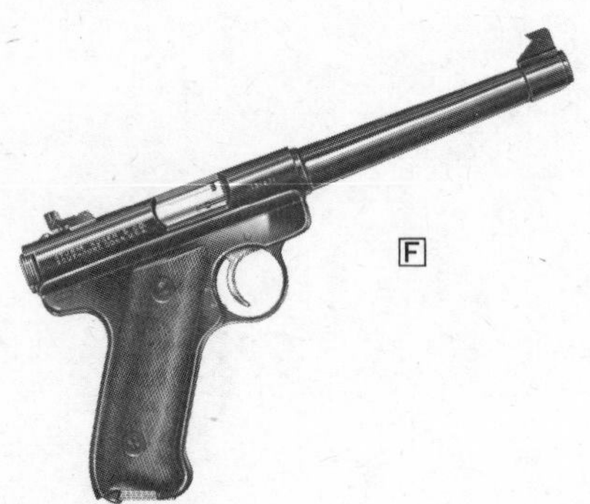

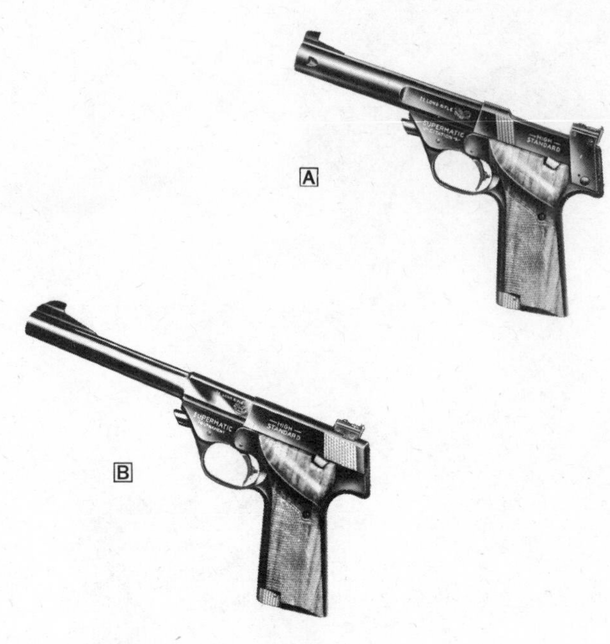

A HI-STANDARD S'MATIC CITATION MILITARY AUTO
Caliber: 22 LR, 10-shot magazine.
Barrel: 5½" bull, 7¼" fluted.
Length: 9¾ inches (5½" bbl.). **Weight:** 44½ oz.
Stocks: Checkered walnut with or w/o thumbrest, right or left.
Features: Same as regular Citation plus military style grip, stippled front- and backstraps, positive magazine latch.
Sights: Undercut ramp front; frame mounted rear, click adj.
Price: Either bbl. length **$110.00**

B HI-STANDARD S'MATIC TOURNAMENT MILITARY AUTO
Caliber: 22 LR, 10-shot.
Barrel: 5½" bull, 6¾" tapered.
Length: 9¾" (5½" bbl.). **Weight:** 45 oz.
Stocks: Checkered walnut, thumbrest for either hand.
Features: Military type grip; 5½" bbl. notched for stabilizer; non-adj. trigger; positive magazine safety; otherwise like regular Citations.
Sights: Ramp-mounted undercut front blade, adj. rear on slide.
Price: Either bbl. length **$90.00**

C HI-STANDARD (*ISU) OLYMPIC AUTO PISTOL
Caliber: 22 Short, 10-shot magazine.
Barrel: 6¾" round tapered, with stabilizer.
Length: 11¼". **Weight:** 40 oz.
Stocks: Checkered walnut w or w/o thumbrest, right or left.
Features: Integral stabilizer with two removable weights. Trigger adj. for pull and anti-backlash; Citation grade finish.
Sights: Undercut ramp front; click adj., square notch rear.
Price: Blued **$125.00**
*Complies with all International Shooting Union regulations.

D HI-STANDARD (*ISU) OLYMPIC MILITARY AUTO
Caliber: 22 Short, 10-shot magazine.
Barrel: 6¾" round tapered, with stabilizer.
Length: 11 inches. **Weight:** 40½ oz.
Stocks: Checkered walnut w or w/o thumbrest, right or left.
Features: Integral stabilizer with two removable weights; adj. trigger with anti-backlash screw. Grip as on military 45.
Sights: Undercut ramp front; frame mounted rear, click adj.
Price: Blued **$130.00**

E HI-STANDARD SUPERMATIC TROPHY MILITARY AUTO
Caliber: 22 LR, 10-shot magazine.
Barrel: 5½" heavy, 7¼" fluted.
Length: 9¾ inches (5½" bbl.). **Weight:** 44½ oz.
Stocks: Checkered walnut with or w/o thumb rest, right or left.
Features: Grip duplicates feel of military 45; positive action mag. latch; front- and backstraps stippled. Adj. trigger, anti-backlash screw.
Sights: Undercut ramp front; frame mounted rear, click adj.
Price: Either bbl. length **$125.00**
Accessories for Hi-Standard Supermatics
Stabilizers (furnished on Olympics) **$5.50**
2 oz. wgt., **$2.00.** 3 oz. wgt., **$2.50.** Extra magazines **$4.75** to **$6.50**

F RUGER Mark I TARGET MODEL AUTO PISTOL
Caliber: 22 LR only, 9-shot magazine.
Barrel: 6⅞" or 5½" bull barrel (6-groove, 14" twist).
Length: 10⅞ inches (6⅞" bbl.). **Weight:** 42 oz. with 6⅞" bbl.
Stocks: Checkered hard rubber.
Features: Rear sight mounted on receiver, does not move with slide; wide, grooved trigger. Muzzle brake (fits Mark I Target only) $6.00 extra.
Sights: ⅛" blade front, micro click rear, adjustable for w. and e. Sight radius 9⅜" (with 6⅞" bbl.).
Price: Blued, either barrel length.......................... **$67.50**
Price: Checkered walnut panels with left thumbrest........... **$71.50**

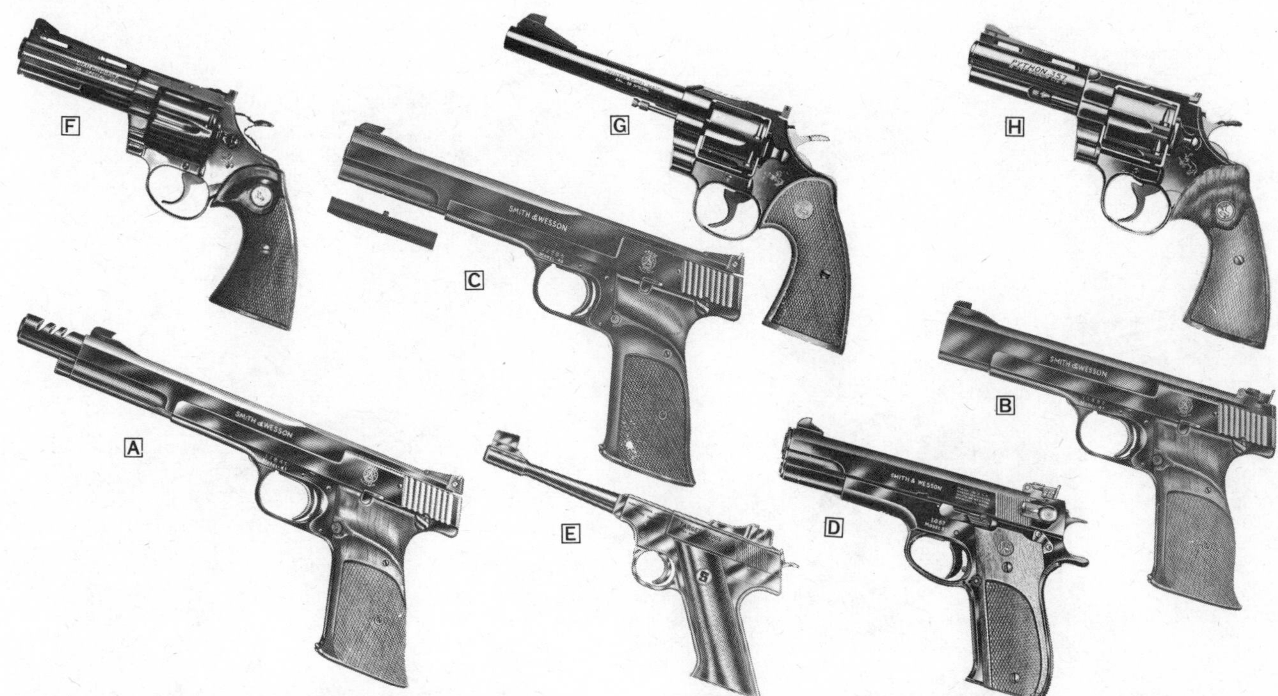

A SMITH & WESSON 22 AUTO PISTOL Model 41
Caliber: 22 LR or 22 S, 10-shot clip.
Barrel: 5″ or 7⅜″, sight radius 9⁹⁄₁₆″ (7⅜″ bbl.).
Length: 12″, incl. detachable muzzle brake, (7⅜″ bbl. only).
Weight: 43½ oz. (7⅜″ bbl.).
Stocks: Checkered walnut with thumbrest, usable with either hand.
Features: ⅜″ wide, grooved trigger with adj. stop; wgts. available to make pistol up to 59 oz.
Sights: Front, ⅛″ Patridge undercut; micro click rear adj. for w. and e.
Price: S⅞W Bright Blue, satin matted bbl., either caliber....**$120.00**

B SMITH & WESSON 22 MATCH HEAVY BARREL Model 41
Caliber: 22 LR, 10-shot clip.
Barrel: 5½″ heavy, without muzzle brake. Sight radius, 8″.
Length: 9″. **Weight:** 44½ oz.
Stocks: Checkered walnut with modified thumbrest, usable with either hand.
Features: ⅜″ wide, grooved trigger; adj. trigger stop.
Sights: ⅛″ Patridge on ramp base. S&W micro click rear, adj. for w. and e.
Price: S&W Bright Blue, satin matted top area.............**$120.00**

S & W 22 AUTO HEAVY BARREL EFS Model 41
Same as Model 41 Heavy Barrel but with extendible ⅛″ front sight. Without muzzle brake or weights. Blued...................**$132.00**

C SMITH & WESSON 22 AUTO PISTOL Model 46
Caliber: 22 LR only, 10-shot clip.
Barrel: 5″, 7″, or 5½″ heavy.
Length: 10⁹⁄₁₆″ (7″ bbl.). **Weight:** 42 oz. (7″ bbl.).
Stocks: Checkered nylon with modified thumbrest, usable with either hand.
Features: ⅜″ wide, grooved trigger; adj. trigger stop.
Sights: Front, ⅛″ Patridge undercut on 7″; ⅛″ ramp on 5″. Micro click rear adj. for w. and e.
Price: S&W Satin Blue....**$102.50** 5½″ Heavy Barrel....**$108.00**

SMITH & WESSON CONVERSION KIT
Converts Models 41 and 46 from 22 Short to 22 LR and vice versa. Consists of barrel, slide, magazine, slide stop and recoil spring.
Price, parts only **$57.75**
Price, factory installed and tested **66.00**
Price, 5½ heavy bbl. only with sights for M41 or M46........ **33.00**

D SMITH & WESSON 38 MASTER Model 52 AUTO
Caliber: 38 Special (for Mid-range W.C. with flush-seated bullet only). 5-shot magazine.
Barrel: 5″.
Length: 8⅝″. **Weight:** 41 oz. with empty magazine.
Features: Top sighting surfaces matte finished. Locked breech, moving barrel system; checked for 10-ring groups at 50 yards. Coin-adj. sight screws. Dry firing permissible if manual safety on.
Stocks: Checkered walnut.
Sights: ⅛″ Patridge front, S&W micro click rear adj. for w. and e.
Price: S&W Bright Blue.................................**$180.00**

E STERLING TARGET "CUP" SERIES AUTO PISTOL
Caliber: 22LR, 10-shot magazine.
Barrel: 4½″, 6″, and 8″.
Length: 9″ (4½″ bbl.). **Weight:** 36 oz. (4½″ bbl.).
Stocks: Checkered plastic.
Features: Adjustable trigger and balance weights; sear lock safety.
Sights: ⅛″ blade front; Click adj. square notch rear.
Price: Blued (M283) **$105.00**
Price: Blued with 6″ tapered barrel (M284) **105.00**

. . . Target Revolvers

F COLT DIAMONDBACK REVOLVER
Caliber: 22 S, L or LR, or 38 Special, 6 shot.
Barrel: 2½″ or 4″, with ventilated rib.
Length: 8⅜″ (4″ bbl.). Weight: 26 oz. (2½″ bbl.), 29 oz. (4″ bbl.).
Stocks: Checkered walnut, target type, squ3re butt.
Features: Ventilated rib; grooved, crisp trigger; swing-out cylinder; wide hammer spur.
Sights: Ramp front, adj. notch rear.
Price: Colt Blue **$125.00**

G COLT OFFICERS MODEL MATCH REVOLVER
Caliber: 22 LR or 38 Special, 6 shot.
Barrel: 6 inches.
Length: 11¼″. **Weight:** 43 oz. (22 cal.), 39 oz. (38 cal.).
Stocks: Checkered walnut, square butt.
Features: Grooved trigger, wide hammer spur, hand fitted swing-out cyl. action.
Sights: Undercut ⅛″ removable blade front, adjustable rear.
Price: Blued **$143.00**

H COLT NEW POLICE PYTHON REVOLVER
Caliber: 357 Magnum (handles all 38 Spec.), 6 shot.
Barre!: 2½″, 4″ or 6″, with ventilated rib.
Length: 9¼″ (4″ bbl.). Weight: 41 oz. (4″ bbl.).
Stocks: Checkered walnut, target type ,square butt.
Features: Ventilated rib; grooved, crisp trigger; swing-out cylinder; wide hammer spur.
Sights: ⅛″ ramp front, adj. notch rear.
Price: Colt Royal Blue........**$175.00** Nickeled........**$200.00**

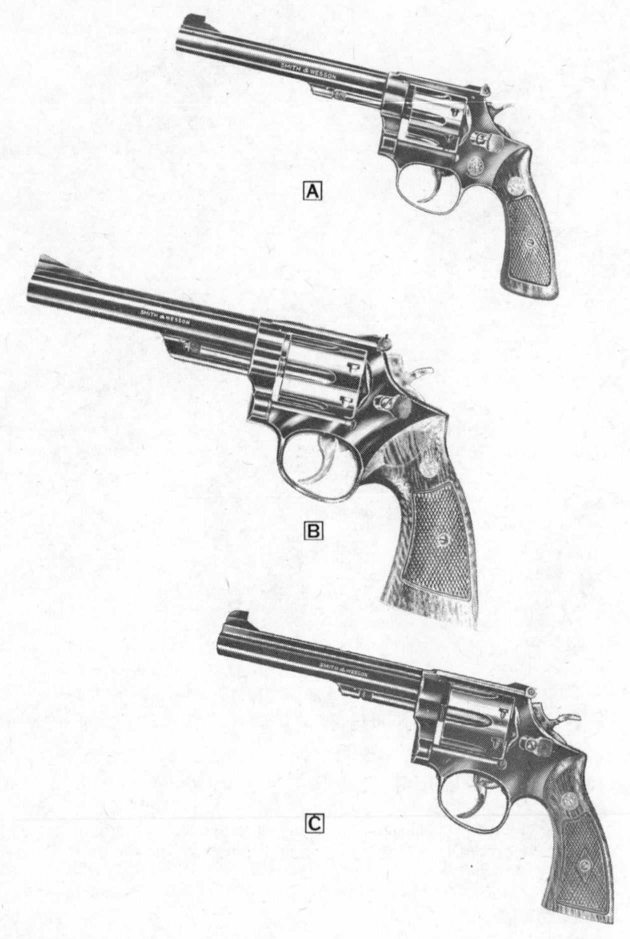

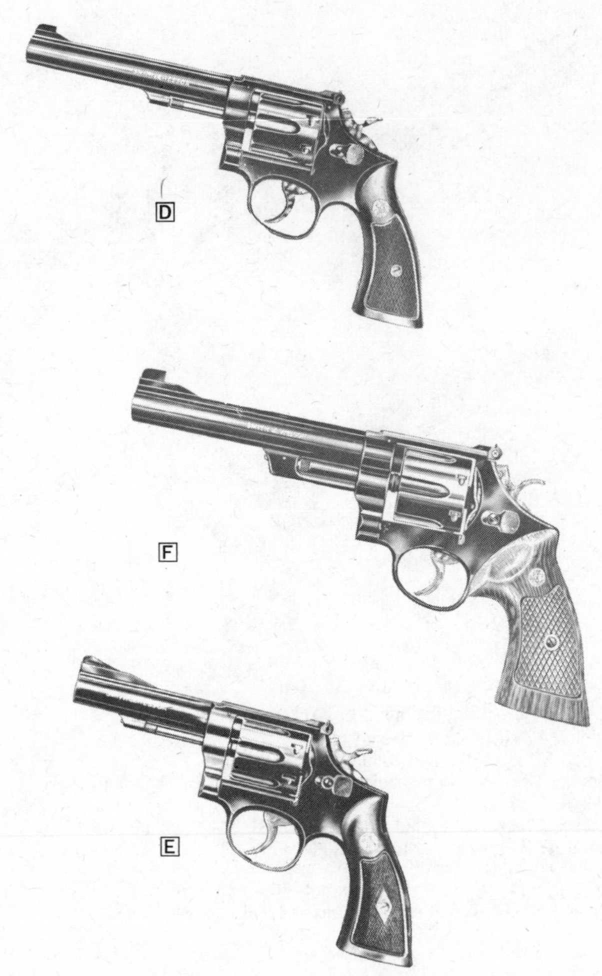

A SMITH & WESSON 1953 Model 35, 22/32 TARGET
Caliber: 22 S, L or LR, 6 shot.
Barrel: 6 inches.
Length: 10½ inches. **Weight:** 25 oz.
Stocks: Checkered walnut, Magna.
Sights: Front, 1/10" Patridge, micro click rear, adjustable for w. and e.
Price: Blued **$97.00**

B SMITH & WESSON 22 CENTER FIRE MAGNUM Model 53
Caliber: Rem. 22 Jet and 22 S, L, LR with inserts. 6 shot.
Barrel: 4", 6" or 8⅜".
Length: 11½" (6" bbl.). **Weight:** 40 oz.
Stocks: Checkered walnut, target.
Features: Grooved tangs and trigger, swing-out cylinder revolver.
Sights: ⅛" Baughman Quick Draw front, micro click rear, adjustable for w. and e.
Price: Blued **$132.00**
Price: Extra cylinder for 22 RF. (fitted) **33.00**

C SMITH & WESSON MASTERPIECE TARGET MODELS

Model:	K-22 (M17).	K-22 (M48).
Caliber:	22 LR, 6 shot.	22 RF Magnum, 6 shot.
Barrel:	6", 8⅜".	4", 6" or 8⅜".
Length:	11⅛" (6" bbl.).	11⅛" (6" bbl.).
Weight:	38½ oz. (6" bbl.).	39 oz. (6" bbl.).
Model:	K-32 (M16).	K-38 (M14).
Caliber:	32 S&W Long, 6 shot.	38 S&W Special, 6 shot.
Barrel:	6 inches.	6", 8⅜".
Length:	11⅛ inches.	11⅛ inches.
Weight:	38½ oz. (loaded).	38½ oz. (6", loaded).

Features: All Masterpiece models have: checkered walnut, Magna stocks; grooved tang and trigger; ⅛" Patridge front sight, micro. adj. rear sights. Swing out cylinder revolver.
Price: Blued, all calibers **$98.00**

D SMITH & WESSON K-38 MASTERPIECE Single Action
Same as the M14 K-38 Masterpiece except single action only, and is supplied with target type hammer and trigger. Price, blued... **$109.00**

E SMITH & WESSON COMBAT MASTERPIECE REVOLVER
Caliber: 38 Special (M15) or 22 LR (M18), 6 shot.
Barrel: 4" (2" available in 38 Spec.).
Length: 9⅛" (4" bbl.). **Weight:** Loaded, 22, 36½ oz., 38 (2" bbl.) 30 oz.
Stocks: Checkered walnut, Magna. Grooved tangs and trigger.
Sights: Front, ⅛" Baughman Quick Draw on ramp, micro click rear, adjustable for w. and e.
Price: Blued **$89.00**

F SMITH & WESSON 1955 Model 25, 45 TARGET
Caliber: 45 ACP and 45 AR, 6 shot.
Barrel: 6½" (heavy target type).
Length: 11⅞ inches. **Weight:** 45 oz.
Stocks: Checkered walnut target. Tangs and target trigger grooved, checkered target hammer.
Features: Tangs and trigger grooved; target trigger and hammer standard. Swing-out cylinder revolver.
Sights: ⅛" Patridge front, micro click rear, adjustable for w. and e.
Price: Blued **$126.50**

SMITH & WESSON ACCESSORIES
Target hammers with low, broad, deeply-checkered spur, and wide-swaged, grooved target trigger. For all frame sizes, $4.25 (target triggers not available for small frames). Target stocks: for large-frame guns, $9.10 to $10.45; for med.-frame guns, $7.15-$9.10: for small-frame guns, $6.05. These prices applicable only when specified on original order.
As separately-ordered parts: target hammers and triggers, $7.15; stocks, $8.25-$13.75.

[A] BROWNING HI-POWER 9mm AUTOMATIC PISTOL
Caliber: 9mm Parabellum (Luger), 13-shot magazine.
Barrel: $4\frac{21}{32}$ inches.
Length: 7¾ inches over-all. **Weight:** 32 oz.
Stocks: Walnut, hand checkered.
Features: External hammer with half-cock safety, thumb and magazine safeties. A blow on the hammer cannot discharge a cartridge; cannot be fired with magazine removed.
Sights: Fixed front; rear adj. for w.
Price: Blued **$108.50**

[E] BROWNING RENAISSANCE HI-POWER 9mm AUTOMATIC
Same as Browning Hi-Power 9mm Auto except: fully engraved, chrome plated, polyester pearl grips **$284.50**

[B] BROWNING 22 AUTO NOMAD PISTOL
Caliber: 22 LR, 10-shot magazine.
Barrel: 4½ inches or 6¾ inches.
Length: 8⅞″ over-all (4½″ bbl.). **Weight:** 34 oz. (4½ bbl.).
Stocks: Novadur plastic, checkered, wrap-around.
Features: Steel frame; thumb safety; bbls. interchangeable via lock screw on front of frame.
Sights: ⅛″ non-glare blade front; frame-mtd. rear, screw adj. for w. & e.
Price: Blued, either bbl. **$67.50**

[C] COLT GOVT. MODEL 45 & SUPER 38 AUTO PISTOL
Caliber: 45 ACP, 7 shot; 38 Super Auto, 9 shot.
Barrel: 5 inches.
Length: 8½ inches. **Weight:** 39 oz.
Stocks: Checkered Coltwood. Grooved trigger.
Features: Grip and thumb safeties; grooved trigger and hammer; arched mainspring housing.
Sights: Fixed, glare-proofed ramp front, square notch rear.
Price: Blued .... **$115.50** Nickeled **$133.00**

COLT CONVERSION UNIT
Permits the 45 and 38 Super Automatic pistols to use the economical 22 LR cartridge. No tools needed. Adjustable rear sight; 10-shot magazine. Designed to give recoil effect of the larger calibers. Not adaptable to Commander models. Blue finish **$70.00**

[D] COLT COMMANDER AUTO PISTOL
Caliber: 45 ACP, 7 shot; 38 Super Auto, 9 shot; 9mm Luger, 9 shot.
Barrel: 4¼ inches.
Length: 8 inches. **Weight:** 26½ oz.
Stocks: Checkered Coltwood.
Features: Grooved trigger and hammer spur; arched housing; grip and thumb safeties.
Sights: Fixed, glare-proofed ramp front, square notch rear.
Price: Blued **$115.50**

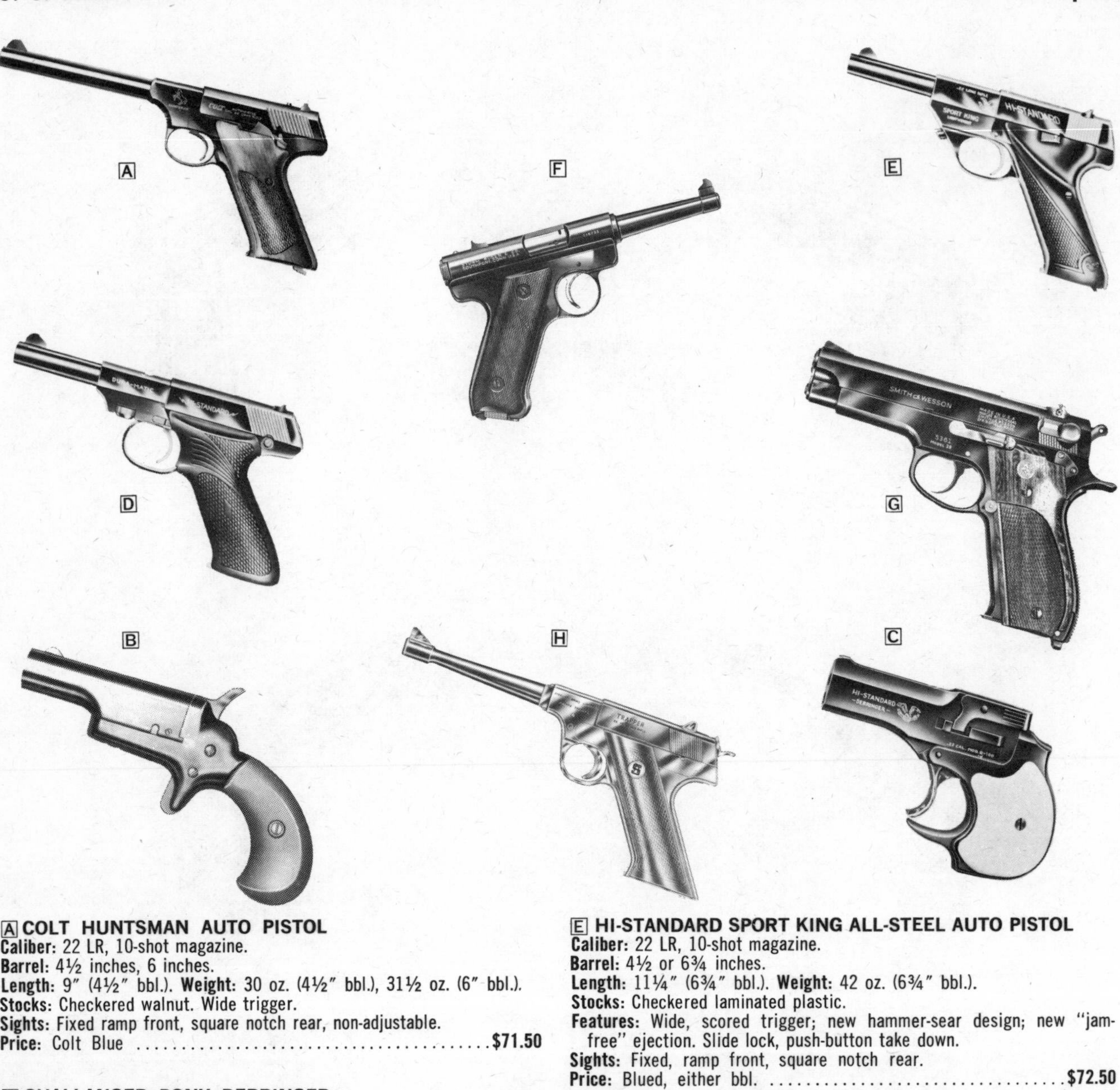

[A] COLT HUNTSMAN AUTO PISTOL
Caliber: 22 LR, 10-shot magazine.
Barrel: 4½ inches, 6 inches.
Length: 9″ (4½″ bbl.). **Weight:** 30 oz. (4½″ bbl.), 31½ oz. (6″ bbl.).
Stocks: Checkered walnut. Wide trigger.
Sights: Fixed ramp front, square notch rear, non-adjustable.
Price: Colt Blue $71.50

[B] CHALLANGER PONY DERRINGER
Caliber: 22 Short, single-shot.
Barrel: 2½″, side swing, blued.
Length: 4$\frac{15}{16}$″ overall. **Weight:** 7¾ oz.
Stocks: Brown plastic, smooth.
Features: Fixed open sights, stud trigger, auto. ejection, single action, storage case.
Price: Gold frame (M2204) $19.95
Price: Nickel frame, white plastic grips (M2205) 21.95
Price: 14K Gold frame, white plastic grips (M2206) 29.95

[C] HI-STANDARD MODEL D-100 and DM-101 DERRINGER
Caliber: 22 S, L or LR; 22 Rimfire Magnum. 2 shot.
Barrel: 3½″, over and under, rifled.
Length: 5 inches. **Weight.** 11 oz.
Stocks: Smooth ivory plastic.
Features: Hammerless, integral safety hammerblock, all steel unit is encased in a black, anodized alloy housing. Recessed chamber. Dual extraction. Top break, double action.
Sights: Fixed, open.
Price: $45.00

[D] HI-STANDARD DURA-MATIC AUTO PISTOL
Caliber: 22 LR, 10-shot magazine.
Barrel: 4½ or 6½ inches.
Length: 9 inches (4½″ bbl.). **Weight:** 32 oz. (4½ bbl.).
Stocks: Checkered plastic grips. Grooved trigger.
Features: Non slip trigger, interchangeable bbls., moulded target grips.
Sights: Fixed, ramp front, square notch rear.
Price: Blued $64.50

[E] HI-STANDARD SPORT KING ALL-STEEL AUTO PISTOL
Caliber: 22 LR, 10-shot magazine.
Barrel: 4½ or 6¾ inches.
Length: 11¼″ (6¾″ bbl.). **Weight:** 42 oz. (6¾″ bbl.).
Stocks: Checkered laminated plastic.
Features: Wide, scored trigger; new hammer-sear design; new "jam-free" ejection. Slide lock, push-button take down.
Sights: Fixed, ramp front, square notch rear.
Price: Blued, either bbl. $72.50

[F] RUGER STANDARD MODEL AUTO PISTOL
Caliber: 22 LR, 9-shot magazine.
Barrel: 4¾ or 6 inches.
Length: 8¾″ (4¾″ bbl.). **Weight:** 36 oz. (4¾″ bbl.).
Stocks: Checkered hard rubber.
Sights: Fixed, wide blade front, square notch rear.
Price: Blued $47.50
Price: With checkered walnut grips 53.50

[G] SMITH & WESSON 9mm MODEL 39 AUTO PISTOL
Caliber: 9mm Luger, 8-shot clip.
Barrel: 4 inches.
Length: 7$\frac{7}{16}$″. **Weight:** 26½ oz., without magazine.
Stocks: Checkered walnut.
Features: Magazine disconnector, positive firing pin lock and hammer-release safety; alloy frame with lanyard loop; locked-breech, short-recoil double action; slide locks open on last shot.
Sights: ⅛″ serrated ramp front, adjustable rear.
Price: Blued........... $100.00 Nickeled........... $108.00

[H] STERLING "CUP" SERIES AUTO PISTOL
Caliber: 22LR, 10-shot magazine.
Barrel: 4½″ (Heavy) or 6″ (tapered).
Length: 9″ (4½″ bbl.). **Weight:** 36 oz. (4½″ bbl.).
Stocks: Checkered plastic.
Sights: Fixed ramp (6″ bbl.) or blade (4½″ bbl.) front. Square notch rear.
Features: Interchangeable safety (4½″ bbl.).
Price: Blued (M286) 6″ $69.00
Price: Blued (M285) 4½″ 49.95

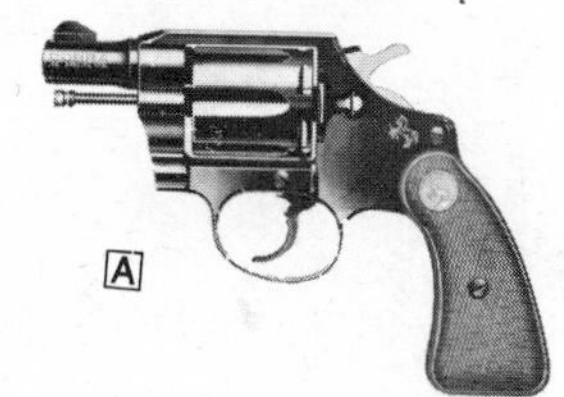

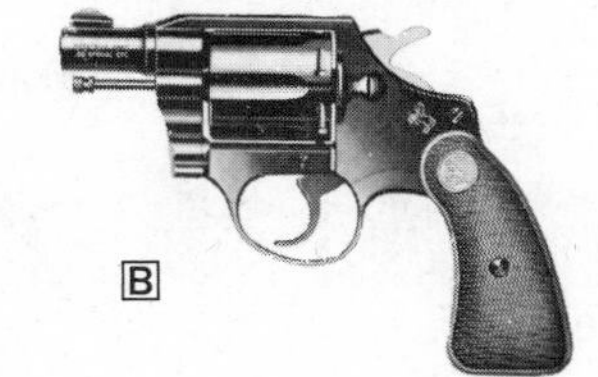

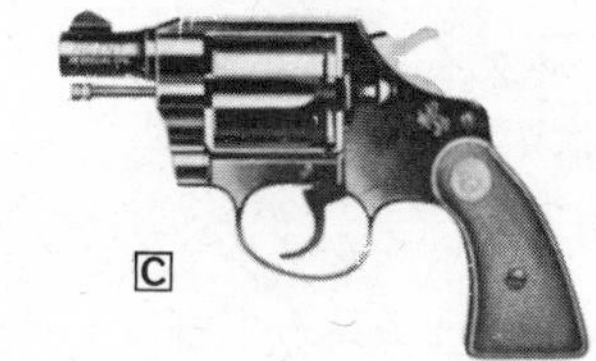

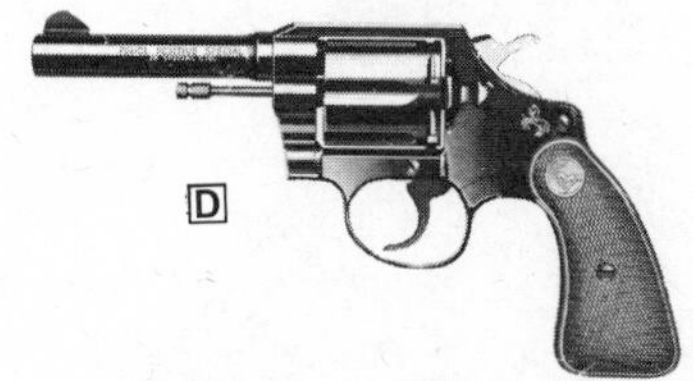

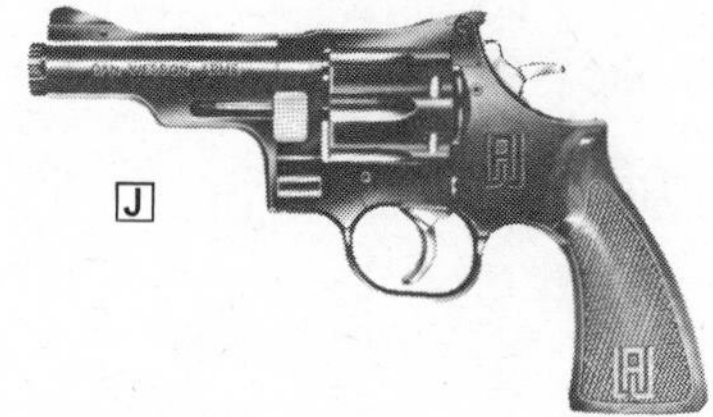

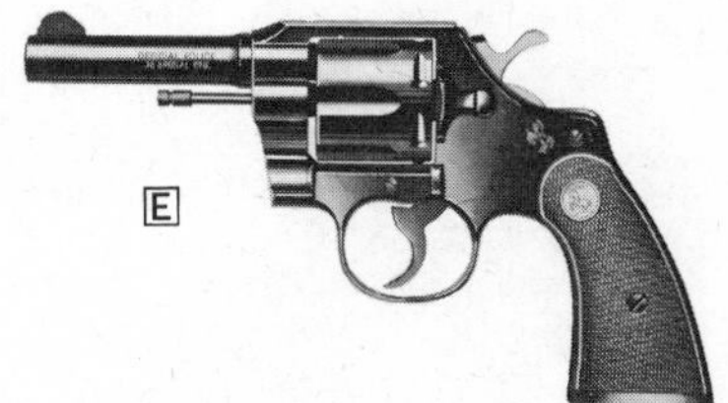

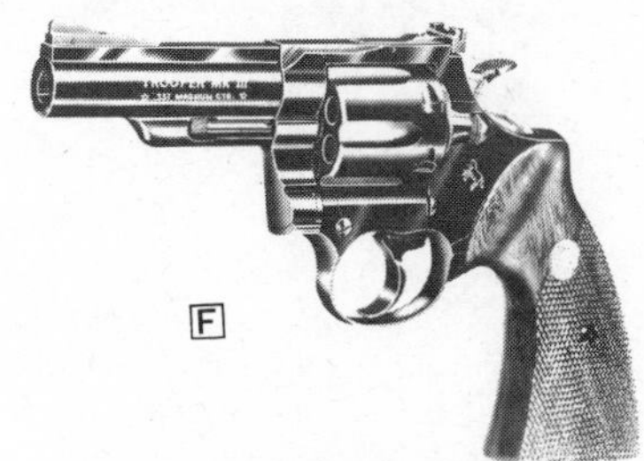

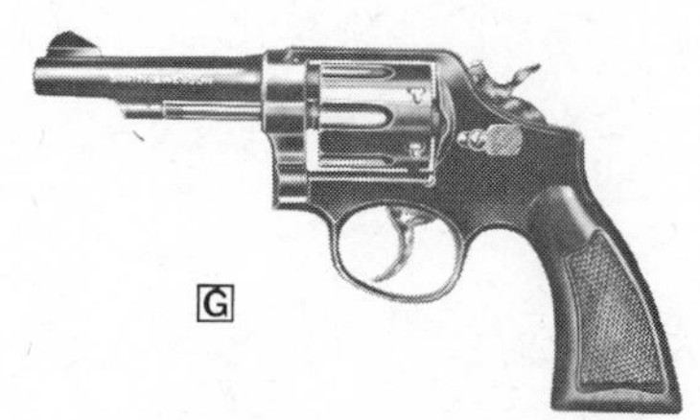

[A] COLT DETECTIVE SPECIAL
Caliber: 32 New Police or 38 Special, 6 shot.
Barrel: 2″, 3″ (32 NP available in 2″ only).
Length: 6¾″ (2″ bbl.). **Weight:** 21 oz. (2″ bbl.).
Stocks: Checkered walnut, round butt. Grooved trigger.
Sights: Fixed, glare-proofed ramp front, square notch rear.
Price: Blued ....**$93.50** Nickeled **$107.50**
Price: Blued, 38 Spec., 2″, with hammer shroud installed..... **99.50**
Price: Nickeled, 38 Spec., 2″, with hammer shroud installed.. **114.25**

[B] COLT COBRA REVOLVER
Caliber: 22 LR, 32 New Police or 38 Special, 6 shot.
Barrel: 2″, 3″ (22 LR available in 3″ only. 4″ available in 38 Spec. only).
Length: 6¾″ (2″ bbl.). **Weight:** 15 oz. (2″ bbl.), 17 oz. (4″ bbl.).
Stocks: Checkered walnut, round butt. Grooved trigger.
Sights: Fixed, glare-proofed ramp front, square notch rear.
Price: Blued ....**$98.00** Nickeled **$112.70**
Price: Blued, 38 Spec. With hammer shroud installed........ **104.00**

[C] COLT AGENT REVOLVER
Caliber: 38 Special, 6 shot.
Barrel: 2″ (Twist, 1-16) .
Length: 6¾″. **Weight:** 14 oz.
Stocks: Checkered walnut, round butt. Grooved trigger.
Sights: Fixed, glare-proofed ramp front, square notch rear.
Price: Blued...**$98.00** With a hammer shroud installed...**$104.00**

COLT HAMMER SHROUD
Facilitates quick draw from holster or pocket. Hammer spur projects just enough to allow for cocking for single action firing. Fits only Colt Detective Special, Cobra and Agent revolvers. Factory installed on new guns, $5, or as a kit for installation. Blued only..............**$6.00**
Factory installed on your gun (listed above). Blued only...... **7.50**

[D] COLT POLICE POSITIVE SPECIAL REVOLVER
Caliber: 32 New Police or 38 Special, 6 shot.
Barrel: 4″, 5″. (32 NP available in 4″ only).
Length: 8¾″ (4″ bbl.). **Weight:** 23 oz. (38 cal.).
Stocks: Checkered walnut, round butt. Grooved trigger.
Sights: Fixed, glare-proofed ramp front, square notch rear.
Price: Blued ....**$93.50** Nickeled, 4″ bbl. only.......**$107.50**

[E] COLT OFFICIAL POLICE REVOLVER
Caliber: 38 Special, 6 shot.
Barrel: 4″, 5″ and 6″.
Length: 9¼″ (4″ bbl.).
Weight: 35 oz. (38 cal., 6″ bbl.).
Stocks: Checkered walnut, square butt. Also available in round butt 4″ bbl. 38 Spec.
Sights: Fixed, glare-proofed ramp front, square notch rear.
Price: Blued .....**$110.00** Nickeled (38 cal. 4 only).....**$126.50**

[F] COLT TROOPER MK III REVOLVER
Caliber: 38 Special or 357 Magnum, 6-shot.
Barrel: 4″, 6″ (357 only).
Length: 9¼″ (4″ bbl.). **Weight:** 40 oz. (4″ bbl.), 39 oz. (6″ bbl.).
Stock: Checkered walnut, square butt. Grooved trigger.
Sights: Fixed ramp front with ⅛″ blade, adj. notch rear.
Price: Blued **$135.50.** With wide spur hammer and target stocks **$142.00**

[G] SMITH & WESSON M&P Model 10 REVOLVER
Caliber: 38 Special, 6 shot.
Barrel: 2″, 4″, 5″ or 6″
Length: 9″ (4″ bbl.). **Weight:** 30½ oz. (4″ bbl.).
Stocks: Checkered walnut, Magna. Round or square butt.
Sights: Fixed, ⅛″ ramp front, square notch rear.
Price: Blued.............**$76.50** Nickeled.............**$84.50**

SMITH & WESSON 38 M&P Heavy Barrel Model 10
Same as regular M&P except: 4″ ribbed bbl. with ⅛″ ramp front sight, square rear, square butt, wgt. 34 oz.
Price: Blued.............**$76.50** Nickeled.............**$84.50**

[H] SMITH & WESSON 38 M&P AIRWEIGHT Model 12
Caliber: 38 Special, 6 shot.
Barrel: 2 or 4 inches.
Length: 6⅞″ inches. **Weight:** 18 oz. (2″ bbl.)
Stocks: Checkered walnut, Magna. Round or square butt.
Sights: Fixed, ⅛″ serrated ramp front, square notch rear.
Price: Blued.............**$79.00** Nickeled.............**$87.00**

[J] DAN WESSON MODEL 12 REVOLVER
Caliber: 357 Magnum, 6-shot.
Barrel: 2½″, 4″, 5″ or 6″ interchangeable.
Length: 9″ (4″ bbl.). **Weight:** 30 oz. (4″ bbl.).
Stock: Three sets of stocks supplied in varying size, angle and style.
Sights: Two adj. rear sights (target or combat) supplied. ⅛″ front sight adj. for E.
Features: Wide spur (⅜″) hammer; barrel shroud offered in aluminum or steel for weight and balance preference. Tools supplied for barrel and grip changing.
Price: Blue (approx.) **$125.00**

A SMITH & WESSON 1953 Model 34, 22/32 KIT GUN
Caliber: 22 LR, 6 shot.
Barrel: 2 inches, 4 inches.
Length: 8 inches (4" bbl. and round butt). **Weight:** 22½ oz. (4" bbl.).
Stocks: Checkered walnut, round or square butt.
Sights: Front, ⅒" serrated ramp, micro. click rear, adjustable for w.&e.
Price: Blued............**$90.00** Nickeled............**$98.00**

B SMITH & WESSON Model 51 22/32 KIT GUN
Same as Model 34 except chambered for 22 WRF Magnum; 3½" barrel; weight, 24 oz. Choice of round or square butt.
Price: Blued............**$96.00** Nickeled...........**$104.00**

SMITH & WESSON KIT GUN AIRWEIGHT (Model 43, not illus.)
Same as M34 except 3½" barrel, square butt; weight 14¼ oz. 22LR.
Price: Blued............**$96.00** Nickeled...........**$104.00**

C SMITH & WESSON 32 HAND EJECTOR Model 30
Caliber: 32 S&W Long, 6 shot.
Barrel: 2", 3", 4".
Length: 8 inches (4" bbl.). **Weight:** 18 oz. (4" bbl.).
Stocks: Checkered walnut, Magna.
Sights: Fixed, ⅒" serrated ramp front, square notch rear.
Price: Blued............**$76.50** Nickeled............**$84.50**

SMITH & WESSON TERRIER Model 32 REVOLVER
Same as 32 Hand Ejector except: 38 S&W cal.; 2" bbl. only; 5 shots.
Price: Blued............**$76.50** Nickeled............**$84.50**

D SMITH & WESSON 41 M&P Model 58 REVOLVER
Caliber: 41 Magnum, 6 shot.
Barrel: 4 inches.
Length: 9¼ inches. **Weight:** 41 oz.
Stocks: Checkered walnut, Magna.
Sights: Fixed, ⅛" serrated ramp front, square notch rear.
Price: Blued............**$96.00** Nickeled...........**$104.00**

E SMITH & WESSON 41 MAGNUM Model 57 REVOLVER
Caliber: 41 Magnum, 6 shot.
Barrel: 4", 6" or 8⅜".
Length: 11⅜ inches (6" bbl.). **Weight:** 48 oz. (6" bbl.).
Stocks: Oversize target type checkered Goncala Alves wood and target hammer. Tang and target trigger grooved.
Sights: ⅛" red ramp front, micro. click rear, adj. for w. and e.
Price: S&W Bright Blue or Nickel........................**$165.00**

F SMITH & WESSON 44 MAGNUM Model 29 REVOLVER
Caliber: 44 Magnum, 44 Special or 44 Russian, 6 shot.
Barrel: 4", 6½", 8⅜".
Length: 11⅞" (6½" bbl.). **Weight:** 47 oz. (6½" bbl.), 43 oz. (4" bbl.).
Stocks: Oversize target type, checkered Goncala Alves. Tangs and target trigger grooved, checkered target hammer.
Sights: ⅛" red ramp-front, micro. click rear, adjustable for w. and e.
Price: S&W Bright Blue or Nickel........................**$165.00**

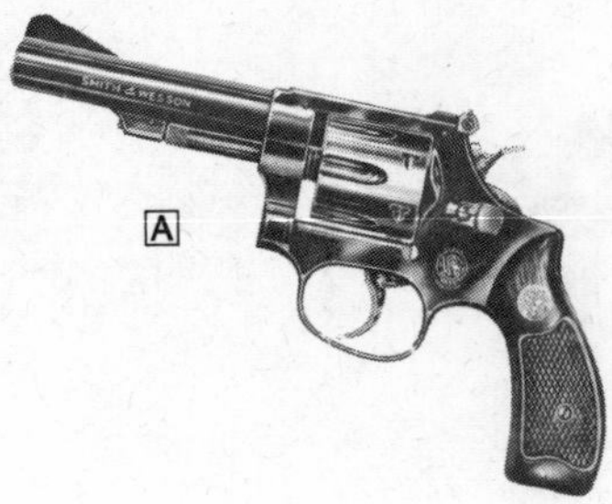

A

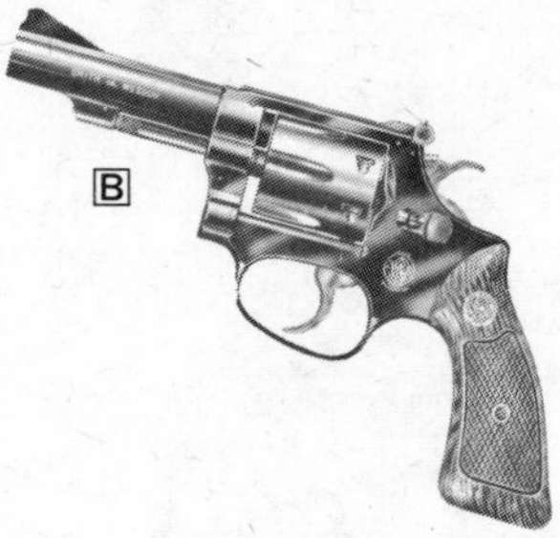

B

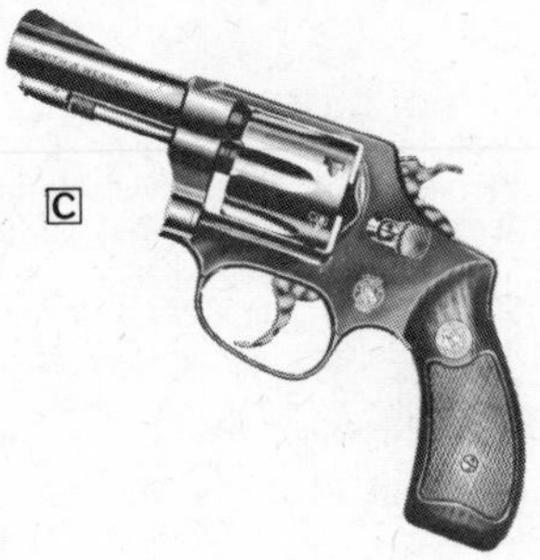

C

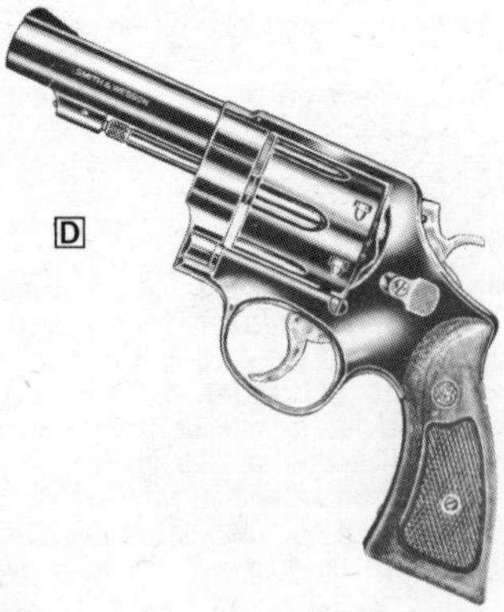

D

E

F

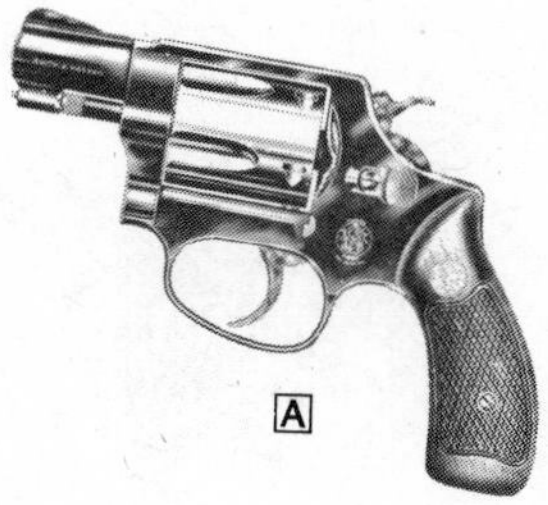

A

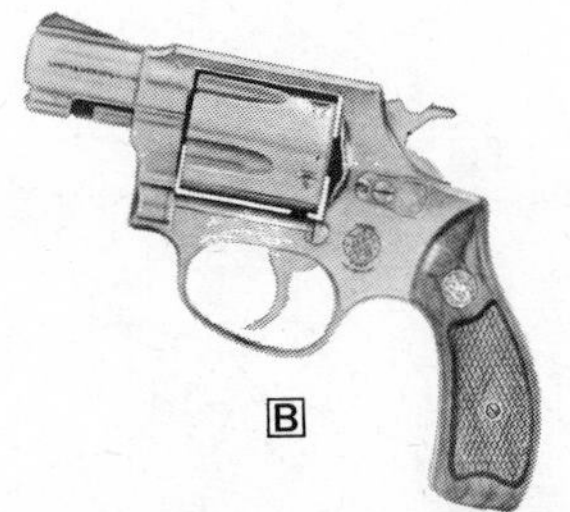

B

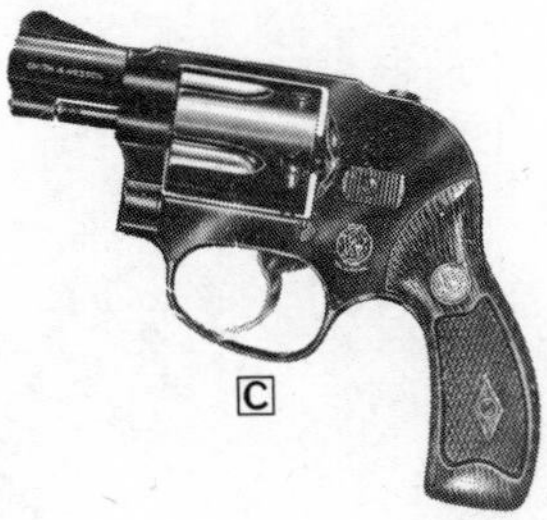

C

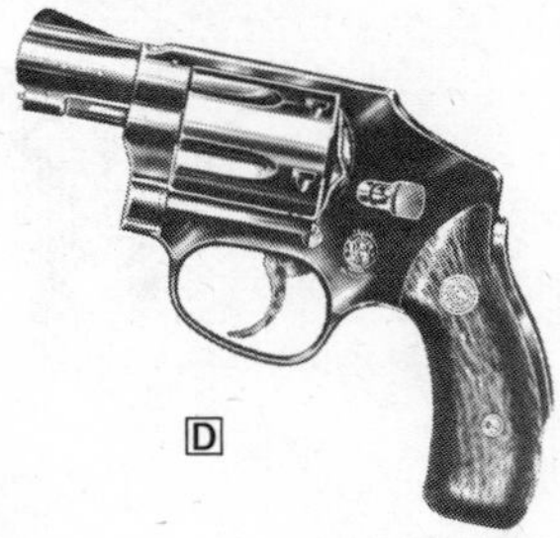

D

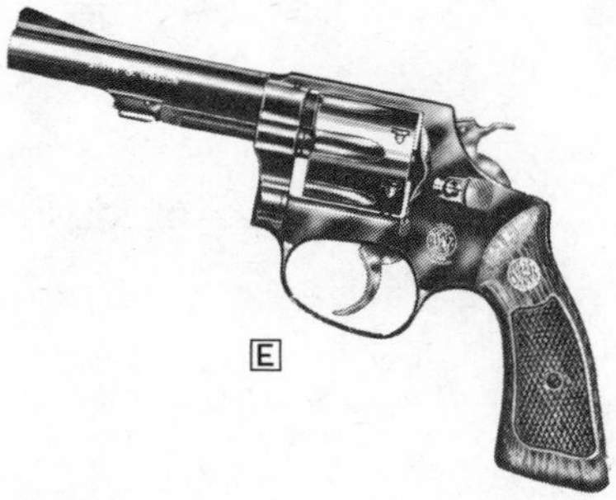

E

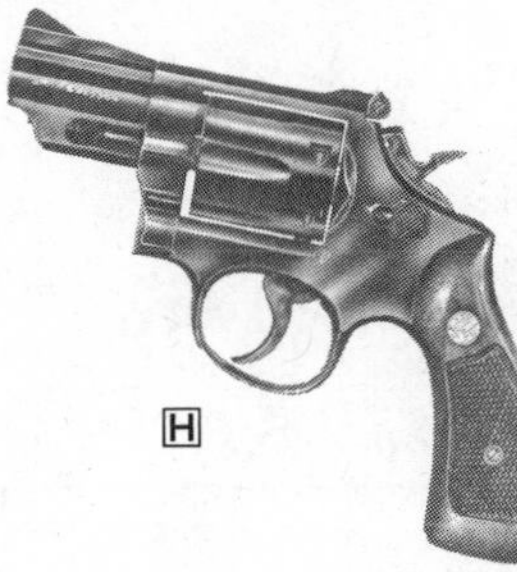

H

G

F

A SMITH & WESSON 38 CHIEFS SPECIAL & AIRWEIGHT
Caliber: 38 Special, 5 shot.
Barrel: 2 inches, 3 inches.
Length: 6½ inches (2" bbl. and round butt). **Weight:** 19 oz. (2" bbl.; 14 oz. AIRWEIGHT).
Stocks: Checkered walnut, Magna. Round or square butt.
Sights: Fixed, 1/10" serrated ramp front, square notch rear.
Price: Blued std. M-36...**$76.50** standard weight..**$84.50**
Price: Blued AIR'W M-37.. **79.00** AIRWEIGHT...... **87.00**

B SMITH & WESSON CHIEFS SPECIAL STAINLESS Model 60
Same as Model 36 except: 2" bbl. and round butt only.
Stainless steel..**$100.00**

C SMITH & WESSON BODYGUARD Model 38 REVOLVER
Caliber: 38 Special; 5 shot, double action revolver.
Barrel: 2 inches.
Length 6⅜ inches. **Weight:** 14½ oz.
Features: Alloy frame; integral hammer shroud.
Stocks: Checkered walnut, Magna.
Sights: Fixed, 1/10" serrated ramp front, square notch rear.
Price: Blued.............**$79.00** Nickeled.............**$87.00**

SMITH & WESSON BODYGUARD Model 49 REVOLVER
Same as Model 38 except steel construction. Weight 20½ oz.
Price: Blued.............**$78.50** Nickeled.............**$86.50**

D SMITH & WESSON CENTENNIAL Model 40 & AIRWEIGHT Model 42 REVOLVERS
Caliber: 38 Special, 5 shot.
Barrel: 2 inches.
Length: 6½". **Weight:** 19 oz. (Standard weight), 13 oz. (AIRWEIGHT).
Stocks: Smooth walnut, Magna.
Sights: Fixed 1/10" serrated ramp front, square notch rear.
Price: Blued, standard wgt...**$82.50** Nickeled, standard weight **$90.50**
Price: Blued AIRWEIGHT.... **88.00** Nickeled, AIRWEIGHT..... **96.00**

E SMITH & WESSON 32 & 38 REGULATION POLICE
Caliber: 32 S&W Long (M31), 6 shot. 38 S&W (M33), 5 shot.
Barrel: 2", 3", 4". (4" only in 38 S&W).
Length: 8½ inches (4" bbl.).
Weight: 18¾ oz. (4" bbl., in 32 cal.), 18 oz. (38 cal.).
Stocks: Checkered walnut, Magna.
Sights: Fixed, 1/10" serrated ramp front, square notch rear.
Price: Blued.............**$76.50** Nickeled.............**$84.50**

F SMITH & WESSON HIGHWAY PATROLMAN Model 28
Caliber: 357 Magnum and 38 Special, 6 shot.
Barrel: 4 inches, 6 inches.
Length: 11¼ inches (6" bbl.). **Weight:** 44 oz. (6" bbl.).
Stocks: Checkered walnut, Magna. Grooved tangs and trigger.
Sights: Front, ⅛" Baughman Quick Draw, on plain ramp. micro click rear, adjustable for w. and e.
Price: S&W Satin Blue, sandblasted frame edging and barrel top **$98.00**
Price: With target stocks............................... **105.00**

G SMITH & WESSON 357 MAGNUM Model 27 REVOLVER
Caliber: 357 Magnum and 38 Special, 6 shot.
Barrel: 3½", 5", 6", 8⅜".
Length: 11⅜" (6" bbl.). **Weight:** 44 oz. (6" bbl.).
Stocks: Checkered walnut, Magna. Grooved tangs and trigger.
Sights: Any S&W target front, micro click rear, adjustable for w. and e.
Price: S&W Bright Blue or Nickel........................**$143.00**

H SMITH & WESSON 357 COMBAT MAGNUM Model 19
Caliber: 357 Magnum and 38 Special, 6 shot.
Barrel: 2½", 4", 6".
Length: 9½ inches (4" bbl.). **Weight:** 35 oz.
Stocks: Checkered Goncala Alves, target. Grooved tangs and trigger.
Sights: Front, ¼" Baughman Quick Draw on 2½" or 4" bbl., ⅜" Patridge on 6 bbl., micro click rear adjustable for w. and e.
Price: S&W Bright Blue or Nickel........................**$132.00**

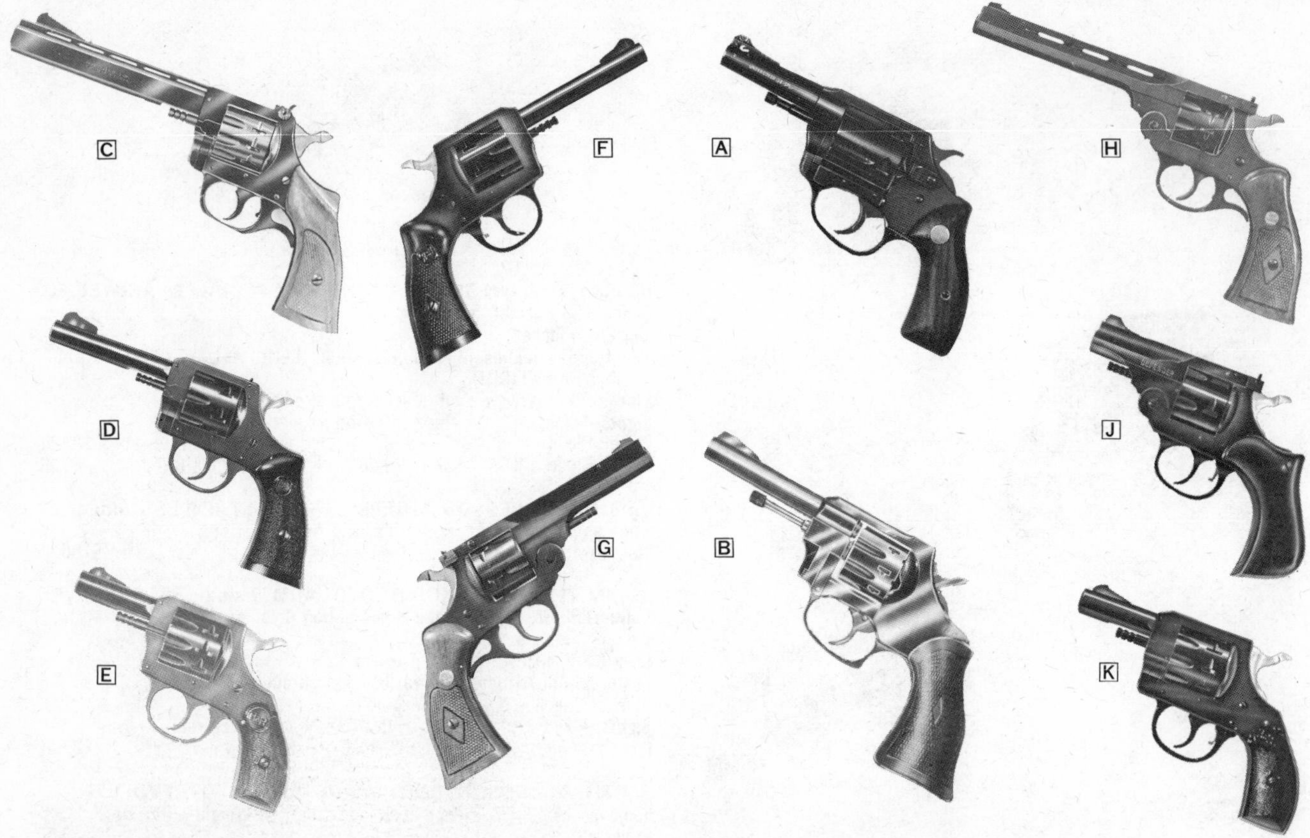

A CHARTER ARMS "UNDERCOVER 2" REVOLVER
Caliber: 38 Special, 5 shot.
Barrel: 2" or 3.
Length: 6¼" (round butt). **Weight:** 16 oz.
Features: Wide trigger and hammer spur.
Stocks: Smooth walnut, round or square butt available.
Sights: Fixed; matted ramp front, ⅛" wide blade.
Price: Polished Blue $75.23
Price: With checkered, finger-rest bulldog grips.............. 81.68

B FIREARMS INTERNATIONAL REGENT
Caliber: 22 LR, 8-shot or 32 S&W Long, 6-shot.
Barrel: 3", 4" or 6" round (2½" or 4" in 32 S&W Long).
Weight: 28 oz. (4" bbl.).
Features: Swing-out cylinder, recessed for cartridge rims.
Stocks: Checkered composition.
Sights: Fixed; ramp front.
Price: Blued, 22 LR $34.95
Price: Blued, 32 S&W Long 39.95

C H&R Model 939 Ultra "Side-Kick" REVOLVER
Caliber: 22 S, L or LR, 9 shot.
Barrel: 6", target weight with ventilated rib.
Weight: 33 oz.
Features: Swing-out, safety rim cylinder; safety lock and key.
Stocks: Checkered walnut with thumbrest.
Sights: Ramp front; rear adjustable for w. and e.
Price: H&R Crown-Luster Blue $62.50

D HARRINGTON & RICHARDSON Model 732 Guardsman
Caliber: 32 S&W or 32 S&W Long, 6 shot.
Barrel: 2½" or 4", round barrel.
Weight: 23½ oz. (2½" bbl.), 26 oz. (4" bbl.).
Features: Swing-out cylinder with auto. extractor return. Pat. safety rim cylinder. Grooved trigger.
Stocks: Checkered, black Cycolac.
Sights: Blade front; adjustable rear on 4" model.
Price: Blued..**$47.50** Chromed (Model 733) 2½" bbl. only..**$52.50**

E HARRINGTON & RICHARDSON Model 900 REVOLVER
Caliber: 22 S, L or LR, 9 shot.
Barrel: 2½", 4" or 6" round bbl.
Weight: 20 oz. (2½" bbl.), 26 oz. (6" bbl.).
Features: Snap-out cylinder; simultaneous push-pin extraction; coil springs; safety rim cylinder; Round-grip frame with 2½" bbl.
Stocks: Checkered, black Cycolac.
Sights: Fixed, blade front, square notch rear.
Price: Blued $41.50

F HARRINGTON & RICHARDSON Model 622 REVOLVER
Caliber: 22 S, L or LR, 6 shot.
Barrel: 2½", 4" or 6" round bbl.
Weight: 22 oz. (2½" bbl.).
Features: Solid steel, square-built frame; snap-out cylinder; simultaneous push-pin ejection; non-glare finish on frame; coil springs.
Stocks: Checkered black Cycolac.
Sights: Fixed, blade front, square notch rear.
Price: Blued, 2½", 4" or 6" bbl. $36.50

G HARRINGTON & RICHARDSON Model 926 REVOLVER
Caliber: 22 S, L, or LR, 9 shot.
Barrel: 4". **Weight:** 31 oz.
Features: Top-break, double or single action.
Stocks: Checkered walnut.
Sights: Fixed front, read adj. for w.
Price: Blued $62.50

H HARRINGTON & RICHARDSON SPORTSMAN Model 999 REVOLVER
Caliber: 22 S, L or LR, 9 shot.
Barrel: 6", top-break (16" twist), integral vent. rib.
Length: 10½". **Weight:** 30 oz.
Features: Wide hammer spur; rest for second finger.
Stocks: Checkered walnut, semi-thumbrest.
Sights: Front adjustable for elevation, rear for windage.
Price: Blued $67.50

J HARRINGTON & RICHARDSON Model 925 "Defender"
Caliber: 38 S&W, 5 shot.
Barrel: 2½" or 4".
Weight: 22 oz. (2½" bbl.), 31 oz. (4" bbl.). **Length:** 9" (4" bbl.)
Features: Top-break double action, push pin extractor.
Stocks: Smooth walnut, birdshead style (2½" bbl.) or square butt (4" bbl.).
Sights: Rear with windage adj., front adj. for elevation, 4" bbls. only.
Price: H&R Crown Luster Blue $62.50

K HARRINGTON & RICHARDSON Model 929 "Side-Kick"
Caliber: 22 S, L or LR, 9 shot.
Barrel: 2½", 4" or 6".
Weight: 26 oz. (4" bbl.).
Features: Swing-out cylinder with auto. extractor return. Pat. safety rim cylinder. Grooved trigger. Round-grip frame.
Stocks: Checkered, black Cycolac.
Sights: Blade front; adjustable rear on 4" and 6" models.
Price: Blued, 2½", 4" or 6" bbl. $47.50
Price: Chromed (Model 930), 4" bbl. 52.50

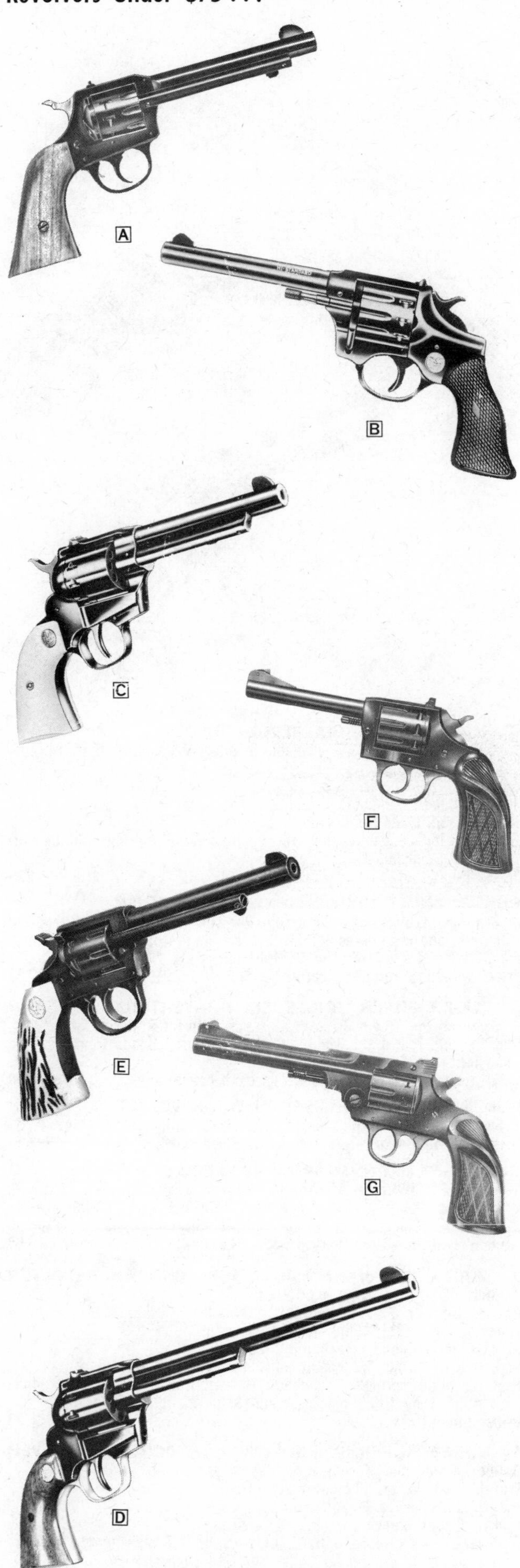

[A] HARRINGTON & RICHARDSON Model 949 FORTY-NINER
Caliber: 22 S, L or LR, 9 shot.
Barrel: 5½" round with ejector rod.
Weight: 31 oz.
Features: Contoured loading gate; wide hammer spur; single and double action. Western type ejector-housing.
Stocks: One-piece smooth walnut, frontier style.
Sights: Round blade front, adj. rear.
Price: H&R Crown-Luster Blue **$47.50**

[B] HI-STANDARD SENTINEL DELUXE REVOLVER
Caliber: 22 S or LR, 9 shot.
Barrel: 2⅜, 4 or 6 inches.
Length: 9" (4" bbl.). **Weight:** 19½ oz. (4" bbl.).
Frame: Rigid, one-piece. Swing-out, counterbored cylinder.
Features: Rebounding hammer with automatic safety block; one-stroke spring loaded ejection. Grooved trigger.
Stocks: Checkered grips. Snub has birdshead grip.
Sights: Fixed, ramp front, square notch rear.
Price: Blued . . . . **$65.00** Nickeled **$70.00**

[C] HI-STANDARD DOUBLE-NINE REVOLVER
Caliber: 22 S or LR, 9 shot.
Barrel: 5½", dummy ejector housing fitted.
Length: 11 inches. **Weight:** 27¼ oz.
Stocks: Stag ivory finish plastic. (Ebony with nickel only.)
Features: Western styling; rebounding hammer with auto. safety block; spring-loaded ejection, gold anodized trigger guard and back strap.
Sights: Blade front; movable notch rear.
Price: Blued . . . . **$70.00** Nickeled **$75.00**

[D] HI-STANDARD LONGHORN REVOLVER
Same as Double-Nine except: 9½" bbl. only; smooth walnut grips; wgt. 35 oz.; over-all 15". Blued **$75.00**

[E] IVER JOHNSON MODEL 50A SIDEWINDER REVOLVER
Caliber: 22 S, L, LR, 8 shot.
Barrel: 6 inches.
Length: 11¼". **Weight:** 31 oz.
Features: Wide spur hammer, half-cock safety, scored trigger, Flash Control cylinder, recessed shell head, push rod ejector.
Stocks: Plastic Stag Horn.
Sights: Fixed, blade front.
Price: Blued. **$42.50**

[F] IVER JOHNSON TARGET MODEL 57A REVOLVER
Caliber: 22 S or LR, 8 shot, double action.
Barrel: 4½", 6".
Length: 10¾" (6" bbl.). **Weight:** 30½ oz. (6" bbl.).
Features: Flash Control cylinder, adj. mainspring.
Stocks: Checkered thumbrest, Tenite: (walnut, **$5.80,** checkered walnut, **$9.20** extra).
Sights: Adjustable Patridge type.
Price: Blued, in flocked case. **$39.95**

IVER JOHNSON TARGET MODEL 55A REVOLVER
Same as Model 57A except without adjustable sights. Price, blued, in flocked case. **$36.75**

IVER JOHNSON CADET Model 55SA
Same as Model 55 except with 2½" barrel only, rounded tenite grips; weight 24 oz. Price, blued, in flocked case. **$36.75**
Also available in 32 or 38 S&W caliber, 5 shot. **37.50**

[G] IVER JOHNSON MODEL 67 VIKING REVOLVER
Caliber: 22 S or LR, 8 shot.
Barrel: 4½" or 6", chrome-lined heavy.
Length: 9½" (4½" bbl.). **Weight:** 34 oz. (6" bbl.).
Features: Cyl. front recessed for Flash Control, chambers also recessed for cartridge rims. Matted top, wide trigger. "Hammer-the-Hammer" action.
Stocks: Checkered, thumbrest plastic.
Sights: Adjustable Patridge type.
Price: Blued **$49.95**

IVER JOHNSON VIKING 67S SNUB REVOLVER
Same as M67 Viking except has 2¾" barrel, smooth rounded stocks, 7" over all, weighs 25 oz. (target stocks available). **$49.95**
Also available in 32 and 38 S&W caliber, 5 shot. **50.75**

IVER JOHNSON TRAILSMAN 66 REVOLVER
Same as M67 Viking but with rebounding hammer. 6" bbl. only.
Price: **$47.50**

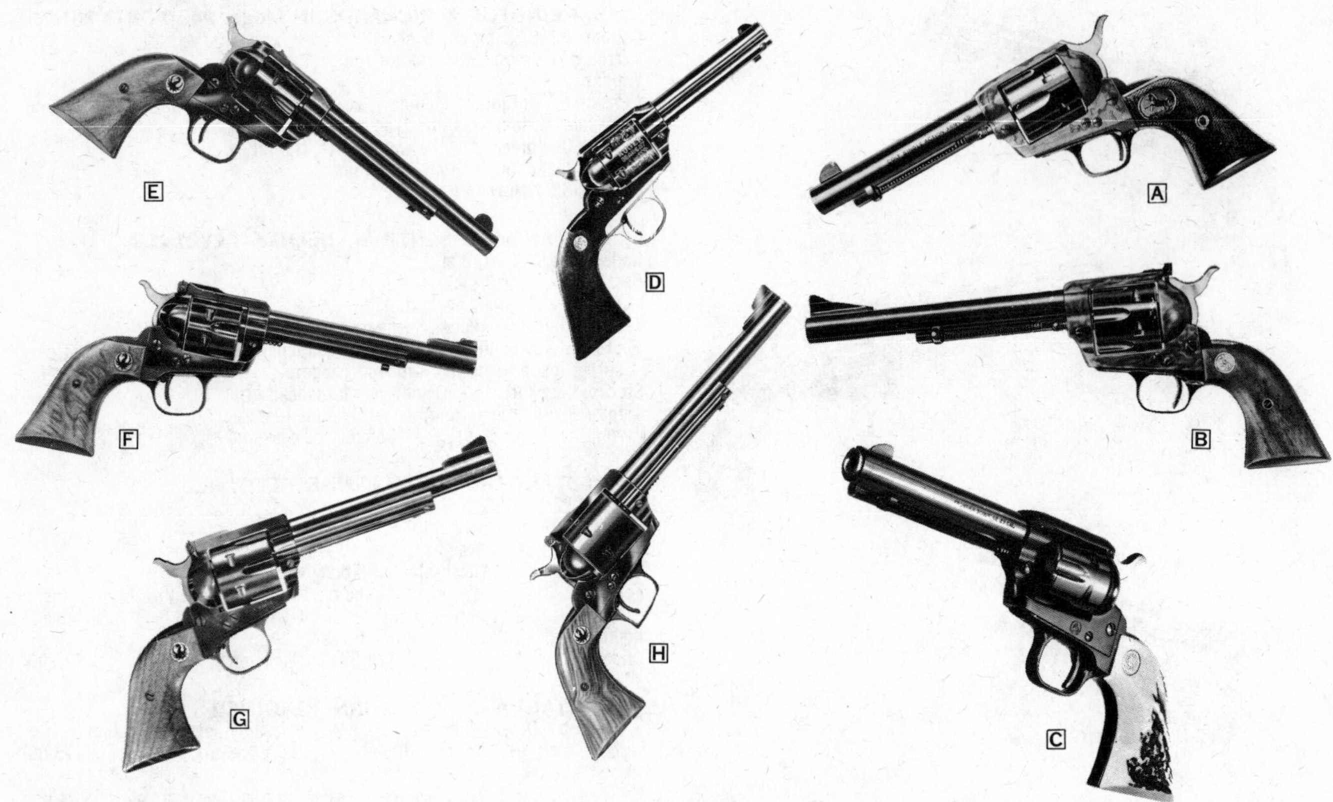

[A] COLT SINGLE ACTION ARMY REVOLVER
Caliber: 357 Magnum or 45 Colt, 6 shot.
Barrel: 4¾", 5½" or 7½". (357 Mag. 5½" only).
Length: 11½" (5½" bbl.). **Weight:** 40 oz. (5½" bbl.).
Stocks: Checkered hard rubber. (Walnut stocks $5.00 extra).
Sights: Fixed. Grooved top strap, blade front.
Price: Blued and case hardened in color **$175.00**
Price: Nickel with walnut stocks **207.25**
Price: Buntline Spec., cal. 45 only. 12 bbl., st'd. stocks **200.00**

[B] COLT SINGLE ACTION ARMY—NEW FRONTIER
Same specifications as standard Single Action Army except: flat-top frame; high polished finish, blue and case colored; ramp front sight and target rear adj. for windage and elevation; smooth walnut stocks with silver medallion **$210.00**

COLT SINGLE ACTION FRONTIER SCOUT REVOLVER
Caliber: 22 S, L, LR, 6 shot.
Barrel: 4¾" or 9½" (Buntline), steel.
Length: 9⁵⁄₁₆" (4¾" bbl.); 14¾" (9½" bbl.).
Weight: 24 oz. (4¾" bbl.); 28½ oz. (9½" bbl.).
Stocks: Black checkered composition.
Sights: Blade front, fixed notch rear.
Features: Alloy frame; blued finish. Walnut stocks $5.00 extra.
Price: 4¾" bbl. ......**$71.50** Blued, 9½" Buntline......**$82.50**

[C] COLT FRONTIER SCOUT '62 REVOLVER
Same as "K" Scout except "Midnight Blue" only, "Staglite" stocks, wgt. 30 oz., Price, 4¾" bbl. ....**$82.50** 9½" Buntline....**$93.50**

COLT FRONTIER SCOUT NICKEL REVOLVER
Same as Standard Frontier Scout except: heavier frame, walnut stocks. Weight 30 oz. Price, 4¾" bbl. **$93.50**
Price: 9½" Buntline **$104.50**

COLT FRONTIER SCOUTS with Dual Cylinders
Same as regular Frontier Scouts except: furnished with two interchangeable cylinders; one chambered for 22 LR; the other for 22 RF Magnum.
Frontier Scout **$83.50** Nickel Scout **$105.50** "62" Scout **$94.50**
Frontier Buntline **94.50** Nickel Buntline **116.50** "62" Buntline **105.50**

[D] RUGER BEARCAT REVOLVER
Caliber: 22 S or LR, 6 shot.
Barrel: 4" round, fixed blade front sight.
Length: 8⅞ inches. **Weight:** 17 oz.
Stocks: Genuine walnut with medallion.
Sights: Fixed; Patridge front, square notch rear.
Features: Alloy solid frame, patented Ruger coil-spring action; non-fluted, engraved cylinder.
Price: Blued **$44.00**

[E] RUGER SINGLE SIX REVOLVER
Caliber: 22 S, L or LR; also available in 22 RF Magnum; 6 shots.
Barrel: 5½" (6 groove, 14" twist).
Length: 10⅞". **Weight:** 36 oz.
Stocks: Smooth walnut.
Sights: Fixed; blade front, square notch rear.
Features: Independent firing pin in frame; coil springs throughout; recessed chambers.
Price: Blued **$64.25**

RUGER SINGLE SIX CONVERTIBLE REVOLVER
Same as regular Single Six except furnished with two interchangeable cylinders: one chambered for 22 S, L or LR; the other for 22 RF Magnum. Choice of 5½", 6½" or 9½" barrel.
Price: with 5½" or 6½" barrel....**$69.50** 9½" barrel....**$78.00**

[F] RUGER SUPER SINGLE SIX CONVERTIBLE REVOLVER
Same as the Single Six except: frame with integral ribs, which protect the adj. rear sight, similar to the Blackhawk; blade front sight on ramp base. 5½" or 6½" bbl.
With extra 22 Magnum cylinder in cloth pouch............. **$78.00**

RUGER 30 CARBINE BLACKHAWK REVOLVER
Same as the 357 Magnum except 7½" bbl. only (6 groove, 20" twist), weight 44 oz., 13⅛" over-all. Blued only............ **$98.50**

RUGER 357 MAGNUM—9MM/38 SPECIAL CONVERTIBLE BLACKHAWK
Same as the 357 Magnum except furnished with interchangeable cylinders for 9mm Parabellum and 38 Special cartridges..... **$110.00**
9mm cylinder, fitted to your 357 Blackhawk............ **16.00**

[G] RUGER 357 or 41 MAGNUM BLACKHAWK REVOLVER
Caliber: 41 or 357 Magnum, 6 shot.
Barrel: 4⅝" or 6½" (6-groove, 16" twist).
Length: 12⅛" (6½" bbl.). **Weight:** 39 oz.
Stocks: Smooth genuine walnut.
Sights: Ramp front ⅛", micro click rear adj. for w. and e.
Features: Coil springs throughout, flat-top frame, long sight radius, floating alloy firing pin in frame. Solid frame.
Price: Blued **$98.50**

[H] RUGER SUPER BLACKHAWK 44 MAGNUM REVOLVER
Caliber: 44 Magnum, 6 shot. Also fires 44 Spec.
Barrel: 7½" inches (6-groove, 20" twist).
Length: 13⅜ inches. **Weight:** 48 oz.
Stocks: Smooth genuine walnut.
Features: Large grip solid frame of steel; square-back guard; flat top-strap; non-fluted cylinder; wide, serrated trigger; wide-spur hammer.
Price: **$125.00**

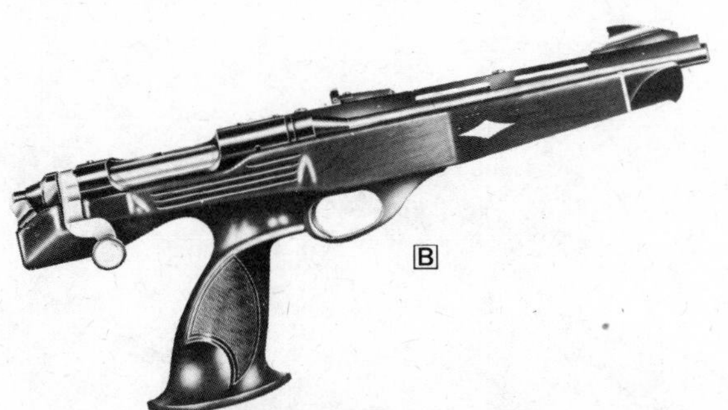

[A] CHALLENGER HOPKINS & ALLEN M-L BOOT PISTOL
Caliber: 36 or 45, single shot percussion.
Barrel: 6 inch octagonal, regular or gain twist.
Length: 13 inches. **Weight:** 34 oz.
Stocks: Smooth walnut, birdshead style.
Features: Underhammer lockwork; match trigger.
Sights: Fixed blade front, adj. rear.
Price: **$39.95**

[C] **MERRILL SPORTSMAN'S SINGLE SHOT**
Caliber: 22S, L, LR, 22WMR, 22WRF, 22 Rem. Jet, 22 Hornet, 117 K Hornet, 357, 38 Spl., 256 Win. Mag., 45 Colt/410 (3").
Barrel: 9", hinged type break-open. Semi-octagon.
Length: 10½". **Weight:** 54 oz.
Stocks: Smooth walnut with thumb & heel rest.
Sights: Front 125" blade, square notch rear adj. for w. & e.
Features: .355" rib on top, grooved for scope mounts, auto. safety, cocking indicator, hammerless.
Price: **$129.50**
Price: Extra bbls. ..... **$35.00** Wrist rest attachment **7.95**

[B] **REMINGTON MODEL XP-100 Bolt Action Pistol**
Caliber: 221 Fireball, single shot.
Barrel: 10½ inches, ventilated rib.
Length: 16¾ inches. **Weight:** 60 oz.
Stocks: Brown nylon one-piece, checkered grip with white spacers.
Features: Fits left or right hand, is shaped to fit fingers and heel of hand. Grooved trigger. Rotating thumb safety, cavity in fore-end permits insertion of up to five 38 cal., 130-gr. metal jacketed bullets to adjust weight and balance. Included is a black vinyl, zippered case.
Sights: Fixed front, rear adj. for w. and e. Tapped for scope mount.
Price: Including case **$99.95**

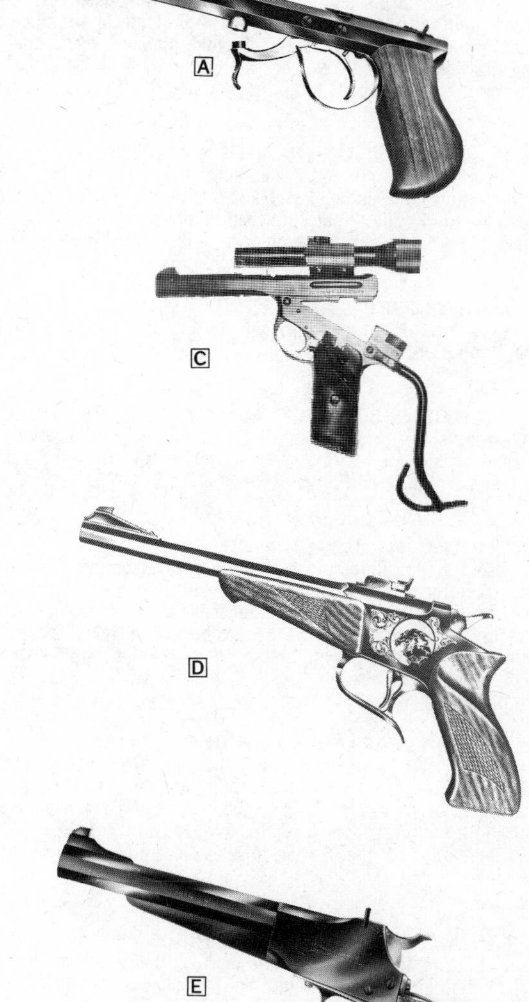

[D] **THOMPSON-CENTER ARMS CONTENDER**
Caliber: 22 S, L, LR, 22 WMR, 22 Rem. Jet, 22 Hornet, 38 Spl, 357 Mag.
Barrel: 8¾", 10", tapered octagon. Single shot.
Length: 13¼" (10" bbl.). **Weight:** 43 oz. (10" bbl.).
Stocks: Select checkered walnut grip and fore-end, with thumb rest. Right or left hand.
Sights: Under cut blade ramp front, rear adj. for w. & e.
Features: Break open action with auto-safety. Single action only. Interchangeable bbls., both caliber (rim & center fire), and length. Grooved for scope. Engraved frame.
Price: Blued **$135.00**
Price: Extra bbls. .... **$36.00** Fitted Walnut case **29.50**
Price: Bushnell Phantom scope base **5.00**

[E] **TINGLE BLACK POWDER M1960 PISTOL**
Caliber: 40, single shot, percussion.
Barrel: 8", 9", 10" or 12" octagon.
Length: 11¾ inches. **Weight:** 33 oz. (8" bbl.).
Stocks: Walnut, one piece .
Features: 6-groove bbl., easily removable for cleaning; 1-in-30 twist.
Sights: Fixed blade front, w. adj. rear.
Price: **$64.95**
Price: With detachable shoulder stock, **$19.50** extra.

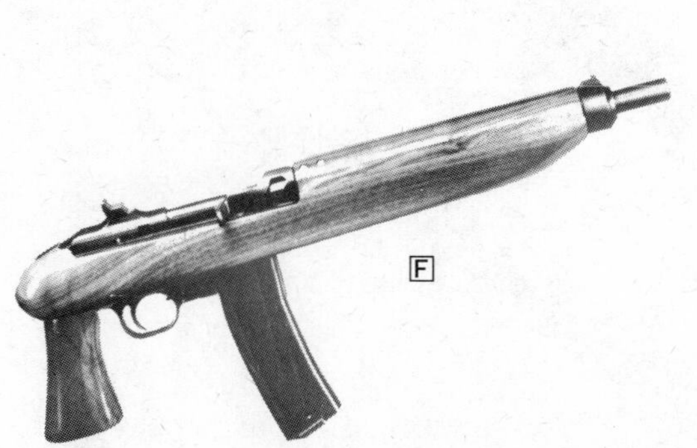

[F] **UNIVERSAL ENFORCER AUTO CARBINE**
Caliber: 30 M1 Carbine, 30-shot magazine.
Barrel: 10¼" with 12-groove rifling.
Length: 17¾". **Weight:** 4½ lbs.
Stocks: American walnut with handguard.
Features: Uses surplus 5- or 15-shot magazine. 4½-6 lb. trigger pull.
Sights: Gold bead ramp front. Peep rear adj. for w. and e. 14" sight radius.
Price: Blue finish **$129.95**
Price: Nickel plated finish **149.95**
Price: Gold plated finish **175.00**

Rifles in this section include autoloaders, pump, lever, and bolt action designs, wherein the bulk of the design/manufacturing process is of United States origin. To the great variety of designs is added an even greater variety of cartridges for which these rifles are chambered. If the user is a handloader, the combinations become limitless. Proper selection of a cartridge/rifle combination can hardly be covered in a paragraph (books sometimes fail to cover the subject), but selection of the appropriate cartridge is a good first step. The type of action, and the choice of manufacturer can then be left to taste and pocketbook.

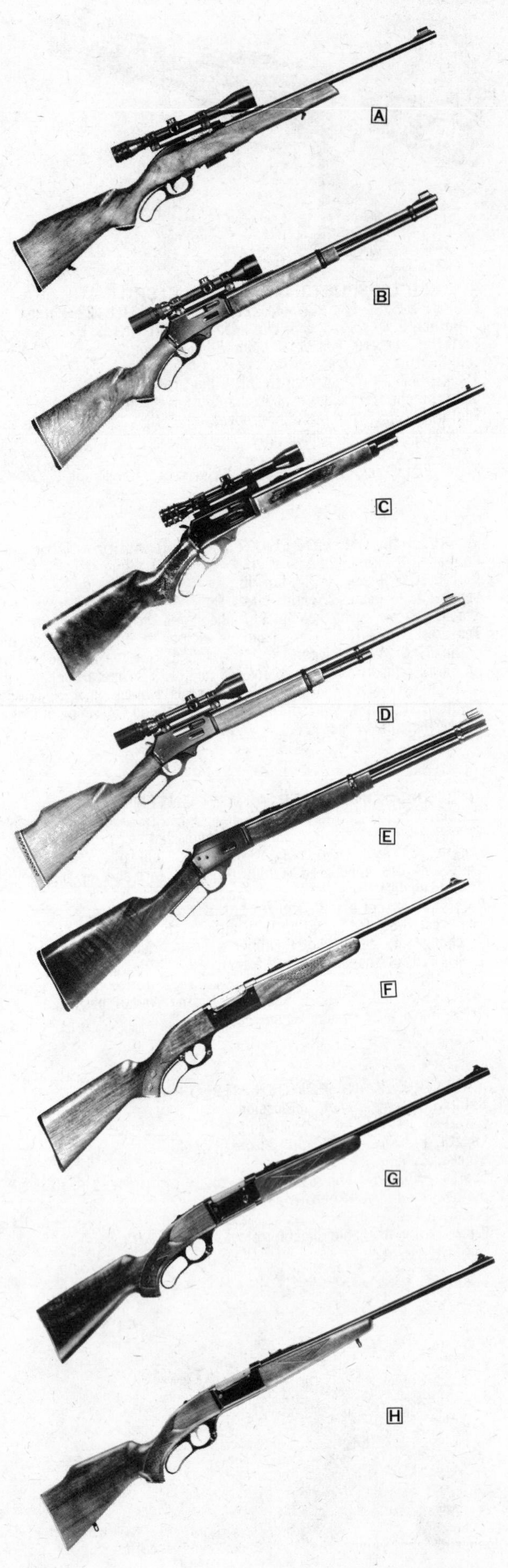

A MARLIN 62 LEVERMATIC LEVER ACTION RIFLE
4-shot detachable clip, 20" Micro-Groove bbl. Open rear sight; ramp front sight with hood. One-piece p.g. walnut stock; whiteline buttplate and grip cap. Engine turned bolt; gold plated trigger. Leather strap and swivels included. Weight 6½ lbs., 39" over-all. Cal 30 U.S. Carbine **$74.95**

B MARLIN 336C LEVER ACTION CARBINE
6-shot, full length magazine. Solid top receiver sand blasted for non-glare; slide ejection. 20" Micro-Groove bbl. Bead front sight; open rear. Offset hammer spur furnished at no charge. Gold plated trigger. Walnut p.g. stock and fore-end. Wgt. 7 lbs. 38½" over-all. Cal. 30-30. .... **$99.95**

MARLIN 336T L.A. CARBINE
Same as 336C except: straight stock; cal. 30-30 only. Brass saddle ring. Wgt., about 7 lbs. **$99.95**

C GLENFIELD 30 LEVER ACTION CARBINE
Same as Marlin 336 Carbine except: 4-shot, ⅔ magazine. 20" bbl., walnut finish stock with semi-beavertail fore-end. 38½" over-all, wgt. 7 lbs. Cal. 30-30 only **$94.95**

D MARLIN 444 MAGNUM RIFLE
Same as 336 Carbine except: 4-shot, ⅔ magazine. Tapped for scope and receiver sights. 24" bbl. of special steel. Lyman folding leaf rear sight adj. for w. & e.; hooded ramp blade front. Walnut straight grip Monte Carlo stock with fluted comb, Marlin recoil pad; detachable sling swivels and carrying strap. Wgt. 7½ lbs., 42¼" over-all. Cal. 444 Magnum **$129.95**

E MARLIN 1894 LEVER ACTION CARBINE
10-shot, full length magazine. Solid top receiver; side ejection. 20" Micro-Groove barrel. Bead front sight; open rear. Offset hammer spur furnished at no charge. Gold plated trigger. Walnut straight grip stock and fore-end. Wgt. approx. 6 lbs. 37½" over-all. Caliber .44 Magnum. A re-creation of the Marlin M1894 discontinued in 1917. Available September '69. .... **$99.95**

F SAVAGE 99E LEVER ACTION RIFLE
5-shot rotary mag. 20" bbl. Cocking indicator on tang, safety on right side of receiver. Walnut-finished checkered stock (13½"x1½"x2½"). Ramp front sight with step adj. sporting rear. Tapped for scope mounts. Wgt. 7 lbs., 39¾" over-all. Calibers: 300 Savage, 243 and 308 Winchester **$119.95**

SAVAGE 99F LIGHTWEIGHT CARBINE
Same as 99E except: 22" lightweight bbl. Damascened bolt, gold plated trigger. Improved sear mechanism, tang safety locks trigger and lever. Mag. indicator on left side. Select walnut stock with checkered p.g. and fore-end, steel buttplate. Gold bead ramp front, folding semi-buckhorn rear. Wgt. 6½ lbs., 41¾" over-all. Cals. 300 Sav., 243, 284, and 308 Win. **$147.50**

G SAVAGE 99C LEVER ACTION CLIP RIFLE
Similar to M99F except: Detachable staggered clip magazine with push-button ejection (4-shot capacity; 3 in 284). Wgt. about 6¾ lbs., 41¾" over-all with 22" bbl. Cals. 243, 284, 308 .... **$147.50**

H SAVAGE 99DL CARBINE
Same as 99F except: High comb Monte Carlo stock; anodized aluminum buttplate; slim fore-end; sling swivels. Wgt. 6¾ lbs., 41¾" over-all. Cals: 300 Sav., 243, 284 and 308 Win. **$149.95**

SAVAGE 99-PE PRESENTATION GRADE RIFLE
Full hand-engraved, including tang and lever; game scenes on action. Choice American walnut Monte Carlo stock, hand checkered. Weight, 6¾ lbs., 22" bbl. Tapered for top mount. 243, 284, 308 Win. . . **$360.00**

A SAVAGE 99-DE CITATION GRADE RIFLE
Slightly less luxurious than Presentation Grade, same cals. . . **$285.00**

B SEARS 54 LEVER ACTION CARBINE
Solid frame, 6-shot tubular mag. 20" bbl. Half-cock hammer safety. Walnut straight grip stock with nickelplated checkered steel buttplate; metal tipped fore-end (13⅛"x1⅞"x2⅝"). Bead front sight on ramp; open notch rear windage adj. Tapped for receiver sights and Sears 3x scope and #784 side mount. Wgt. 6½ lbs., 37¾" over-all. Cal. 30-30 only **$79.99**

C WESTERN FIELD 740 LEVER ACTION CARBINE
6-shot full length mag., 20" bbl., solid top receiver, side ejection. Walnut stock and fore-end, fluted comb; recoil pad, 1" leather sling strap with swivels. Hammer spur for cocking with scope mounted. Open rear, beaded front sight. Wgt. 7½ lbs., 38½" over-all. Cal. 30-30 only. **$81.95**

D WINCHESTER 88 LEVER ACTION RIFLE
Hammerless, rotating 3-lug front-locking bolt. Side ejection, cross-bolt safety. Solid frame with one-piece p.g. stock (13¾"x1½"x2⅝"), basket-weave checkered. Short stroke, fast operating lever. 22" round bbl. Bead front sight on ramp, with cover; folding leaf rear. Tapped for scope mounts; 4-shot detachable magazine, (3-shot in 284). Weight 7¼ lbs., 42½" over-all. Calibers: 243 Win., 284 Win., (10" twist), 308 Win., (12" twist) **$147.95**
Extra 4-shot magazine **4.95**

E WINCHESTER 88 CARBINE
Similar to 88 rifle. Same stock dimensions. No checkering, bbl. band on fore-end. 39½" over-all, bbl. 19". 7 lbs. **$137.95**

F WINCHESTER 94 LEVER ACTION CARBINE
Solid frame, 6-shot tubular magazine. 20" bbl. Walnut-finished straight grip stock and fore-end (13"x1¾"x2½"). Bead front sight on ramp with removable cover; open rear. Tapped for receiver sights. Weight 6½ lbs., 37¾" over-all. Cals. 30-30, (12" twist), 32 Special (16" twist). **$93.95**

WINCHESTER 94 44 MAGNUM CARBINE
Similar to 94 lever action, except 10-shot magazine, wgt. 6⅛ lbs. and 38" twist. **$99.95**

WINCHESTER 94 ANTIQUE CARBINE
Same as M94 except: color case-hardened and scrolled receiver, brass-plated loading gate and saddle ring. 30-30 only **$99.95**

G WINCHESTER MODEL 94 CLASSIC RIFLE
Solid frame, 26" octagon bbl., 8-shot tubular mag. Gold-plated loading gate, scroll-engraved receiver, metal fore-end tip, sling ring straight grip, high gloss semi-fancy walnut stock. 43¾ over-all, wgt. 8 lbs. In 30-30 only (12" twist) **$129.95**

WINCHESTER MODEL 94 CLASSIC CARBINE
Similar to 94 Classic Rifle, except: 6-shot capacity, 20" octagon bbl., 37¾" over-all, 7 lbs. 30-30 only **$129.95**

WINCHESTER 94 CLASSIC MATCHED SET
One rifle and one carbine with consecutive serial numbers. . **$284.90**

H WINCHESTER GOLDEN SPIKE COMMEMORATIVE 94
Similar to M94 Classic carbine, except receiver and tang commemorative engraved, receiver, upper and lower tang and twin barrel bands gold plated. A special Centennial medallion struck by the U. S. Mint is imbedded in the stock **$119.95**

L WINCHESTER THEODORE ROOSEVELT COMMEMORATIVES
Similar to M94 Classics, except receiver and tang commemorative engraved, crescent buttplate, half pistol grip and contoured lever, receiver, fore-end cap, and upper tang are plated in white gold. Commemorative medal imbedded in stock. Rifle has two-thirds (6-shot) magazine and weighs 7½ lbs. Price rifle or carbine. **$134.95**
Matched set with consecutive numbers **294.90**

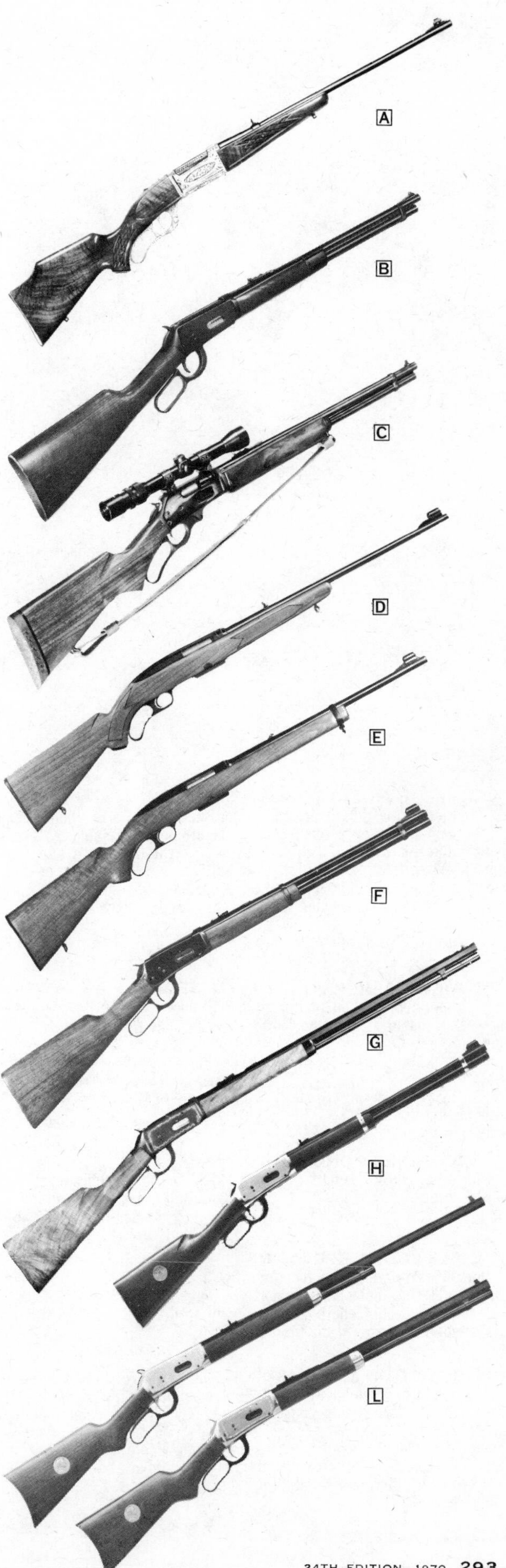

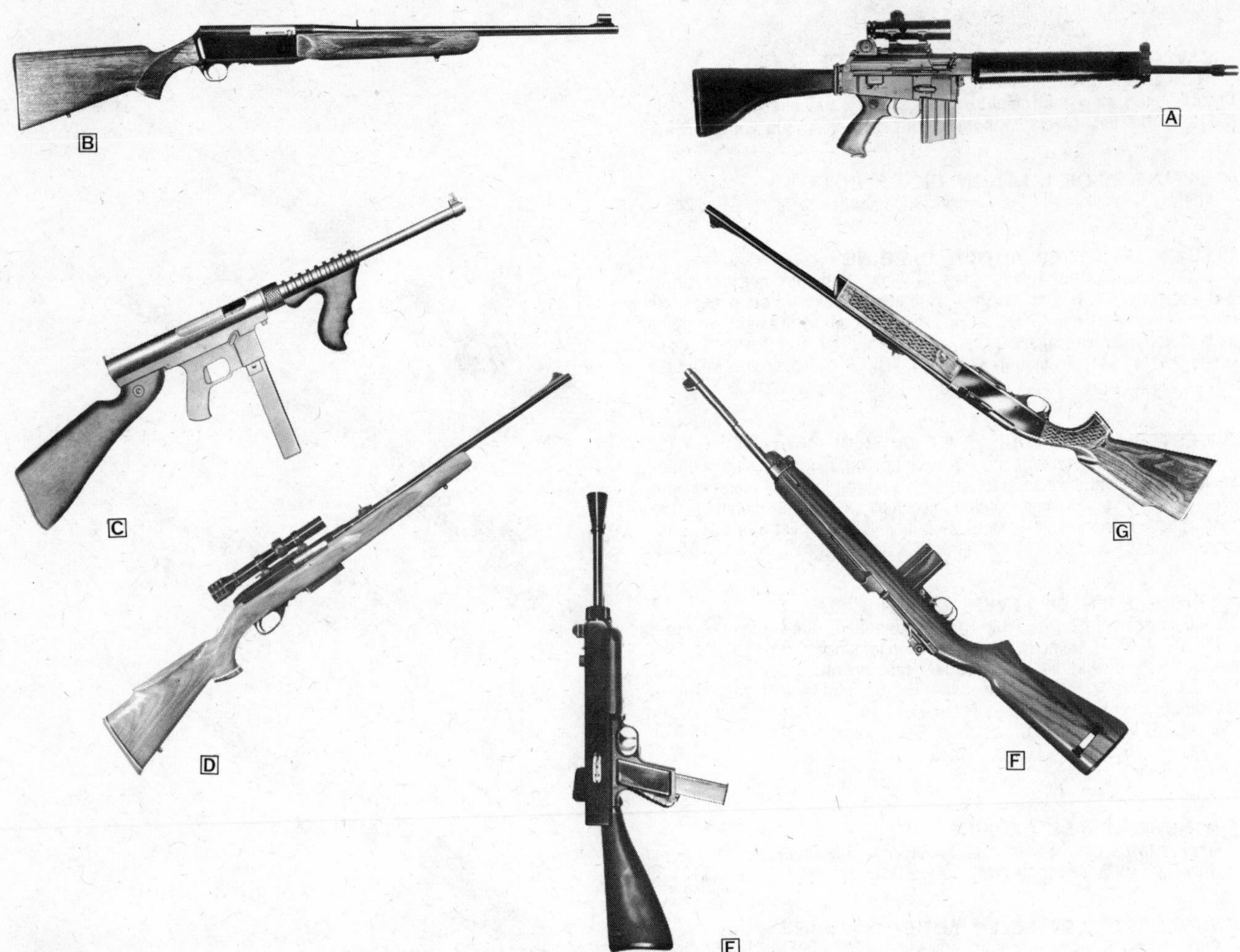

A ARMALITE AR-180 SPORTER CARBINE
Semi-automatic, gas operated carbine, cal. .223. Barrel, bolt, recoil buffer unit and stock assembled as straight-line unit, minimizes barrel jump on recoil. Over-all 38", bbl. 18¼", weight 6½ lbs. Flip-up "L" type sight adj. for w.&e., post front adj. for e. Safety lever on both sides of receiver. Nylon folding stock, phenolic fiber-glass heat dissipating fore-end. Flash-hider compensator. Price includes two 5-rd. magazines **$237.00**
3 power (2.75x20mm) telescope available with mounts..... **68.75**

B BROWNING HIGH-POWER AUTO RIFLE
Gas-operated semi-automatic rifle. Bolt locks via 7-lug, rotary-head bolt. Detachable 5-shot trap-door mag., 22" bbl. with adjustable folding-leaf rear sight and hooded ramp front. French walnut p.g. stock (13⅝"x2"x1⅝") and fore-end, with hand checkering. Wgt. 7⅜ lbs., 43½" over-all. Cals. 270, 308, 243 Win., and 30-06. Grade I..**$174.50**
Grade II. Same as Grade I except hand-rubbed, selected French walnut stock, and receiver hand engraved.......... **$189.50**

BROWNING MAGNUM AUTO RIFLE
Same as the standard caliber model, except weighs 8½ lbs., 45¼" over-all, 24" bbl., 3rd mag., Cals. 7mm Mag., 300 Win. Mag. and 338 mag. Grade I......**$189.50** Grade II......**$204.50**

C EAGLE "APACHE" CARBINE
Recoil operated semi-automatic rifle, handles the 45 ACP cartridge from a 30-shot detachable magazine. Only 4 moving parts. Over-all length 36½", bbl. length 16½", weight 9 lbs. Protected post front sight, aperture rear. Black finish.......... **$129.95**

D HARRINGTON & RICHARDSON 360 ULTRA AUTOMATIC
Gas-operated, semi-auto rifle. Side ejection, recessed bolt face, manual bolt stop. Sliding trigger guard safety. 3-round detachable box mag., 22" bbl. Open adj. rear sight, gold bead ramp front. Receiver tapped for scope. One-piece American walnut Monte Carlo stock, roll-over cheekpiece; checkered pistol grip and fore-end. 43½" over-all, wgt. 7½ lbs. Cals. 243, 308.......... **$189.00**

E J & R 68 SEMI-AUTOMATIC CARBINE
Recoil operated carbine fires from a closed bolt. Cal. 9mm parabellum, 30-shot staggered box magazine. 28½" over-all, 16¼" bbl., wgt. 7 lbs. unloaded. Sights: protected blade front; fixed peep rear. High impact plastic stock and fore-end.
Aircraft aluminum receiver.......... **$149.95**

F PLAINFIELD MACHINE CO. CARBINE
Newly manufactured gas-operated cal. 30 M1 Carbine which duplicates size and appearance of popular GI model, including click adj. rear sight. Glossy finish stock. 18" bbl. Wgt. 5½ lb. 35½" over-all. mag., 22" Douglas bbl. Open adj. rear sight, gold bead ramp front. Metal or wood handguard.......... **$105.00**
Paratrooper. With telescoping wire stock, front vertical hand grip.......... **$125.00**
Plainfielder. With Monte Carlo checkered sporting stock (also available with no checkering, at $6.00 less).......... **$125.00**

REMINGTON 742 WOODMASTER AUTO RIFLE
Gas-operated "Power-Matic" action reduces recoil. Rotary multiple lug breechbolt locks into 22" bbl., fully encloses cartridge. Hammerless, solid frame, side ejection. Gold bead front sight on ramp; step rear sight with windage adj. Walnut p.g. stock (13⅜"x1⅝"x2$^1/_{16}$") and fore-end, deluxe checkered 4-shot detachable magazine, Wgt. 7½ lbs. 42" over-all. Cals: 243 Win., 6mm Rem., 280 Rem., 308 Win. and 30-06. .... **$159.95**
Extra 4-shot magazine.......... **5.25**
Sling strap and swivels (installed).......... **9.10**
Peerless (D) and Premier (F) grades.......... **$575.00 and 1250.00**
Premier with gold inlays.......... **1950.00**

G REMINGTON 742 BDL WOODSMASTER
Same as 742 except: "stepped" receiver, Monte Carlo stock with cheekpiece (right or left), whiteline spacers, basket-weave checkering on p.g. and fore-end, black fore-end tip, RKW finish. (13$^5/_{16}$"x1⅝"x1$^{13}/_{16}$"x2½"). Cals. 30-06, 308.......... **$179.95**

REMINGTON 742 CARBINE
Same as M742 except: 18½" bbl., 38½" over-all, wgt. 6¾ lbs. Cals: 30-06, 308 Win.......... **$159.95**

[A] RUGER 44 AUTOLOADING CARBINE
Gas-operated, cal. 44 Magnum. 18½" bbl. 4-shot tubular magazine and one-piece walnut p.g. stock (13⅜"x1⅝"x2½"). Sourdough front, folding leaf rear sights. Crossbolt safety. Magazine release button. Receiver tapped for scope mounts. Weight 5¾ lbs., 37" over-all **$115.00**
Model 44-RS Deluxe, with built-in receiver sight, carbine stock and swivels **$125.00**

[B] RUGER 44 SPORTER CARBINE
Same as Ruger autoloader except: sporter stock with Monte Carlo comb, flat buttplate; full pistol grip with cap; longer streamlined fore-end, relieved for fingertips; sling swivels. Cal. 44 Magnum.... **$120.00**

[C] UNIVERSAL 1000 AUTOLOADING CARBINE
Gas operated, hammerless. 5-shot magazine. 18" bbl., 12-groove rifling. Walnut stock inletted for "issue" sling and oiler; handguard; forward one-piece swivel and bayonet stud; front blade sight with protective wings, adj. rear aperture. Crosslock safety. Wgt. 5½ lbs., 35½" over-all. Cal. 30 M1............................... **$116.95**
Universal also offers other versions of their basic M1000 Carbine, including two models handling the 256 cartridge, at prices ranging from .... **$129.95** to **$175.00**

[D] UNIVERSAL 1020 TEFLON CARBINE
Same as the 1000 Carbine but has soft, dull Teflon finish said to be self-lubricating, water and scuff resistant. Available in black, tan, blue, green and olive colored finishes, with a high finish American walnut Monte Carlo Stock........................... **$149.95**

[E] WINCHESTER 100 AUTOLOADING RIFLE
Gas-operated with cam action rotating bolt. Hammerless, solid frame; side ejection and crossbolt safety. Tapped for scope mounts. One piece walnut p.g. stock (13¾"x1½"x2⅝"), semi-beavertail fore-end, basket-weave checkered; 22" bbl. Bead front and folding leaf rear sights. 4-shot detachable magazine (3-shot in 284). Wgt. 7¼ lbs., 42½" over-
Cals. 243, 284 (10" twist), and 308 (12" twist)........... **$159.95**
Extra magazine **4.95**

WINCHESTER 100 AUTOLOADING CARBINE
Similar to 100 Autoloading rifle, with same stock dimensions. No checkering. Bbl. band on fore-end. 39½" over-all. Bbl. 19". Wgt. 7 lbs. Cals. 243, 284 (10" twist), and 308 (12" twist).............. **$149.95**
Extra magazine **4.95**

[D]

[F] REMINGTON 760 GAMEMASTER SLIDE ACTION
Hammerless, solid frame, side ejection rifle. Rotary multiple-lug breechbolt locks into 22" bbl., fully encloses cartridge. Trigger must be released and action fully closed for each shot. Checkered walnut RKW finish p.g. stock (13⅜"x1⅝"x2$\frac{1}{16}$") and for-end; black fore-end tip, non-slip buttplate, all with white spacers. Cross-bolt safety. Gold bead front sight on matted ramp, open sporting rear. Tapped for scope mounts. 4-shot detachable magazine. Wgt. 7½ lbs. 42" over-all. Cals.: 6mm Rem., 243, 270, 308 Win., 30-06...................... **$139.95**
Sling strap and swivels (installed)...................... **9.10**
Extra 4-shot clip.................................... **4.50**

[G] REMINGTON 760 BDL GAMEMASTER
Same as 760 except: "stepped receiver," Monte Carlo stock with cheekpiece (right or left), whiteline spacer, basket-weave checkering on p.g. and fore-end, black fore-end tip, RKW finish. (13$\frac{5}{16}$"x1⅝"x 1$\frac{13}{16}$"x2½"). Cals. 270, 30-06, 308....................... **$159.95**

REMINGTON 760 GAMEMASTER CARBINE
Same as M760 except has 18½" barrel. Wgt. 6¾ lbs., 38½" over-all. Cals: 308 Win., and 30-06........................... **$139.95**
Also in Peerless (D) and Premier (F) grades....... **$575** and **1250.00**
(F), with gold inlay................................... **1950.00**

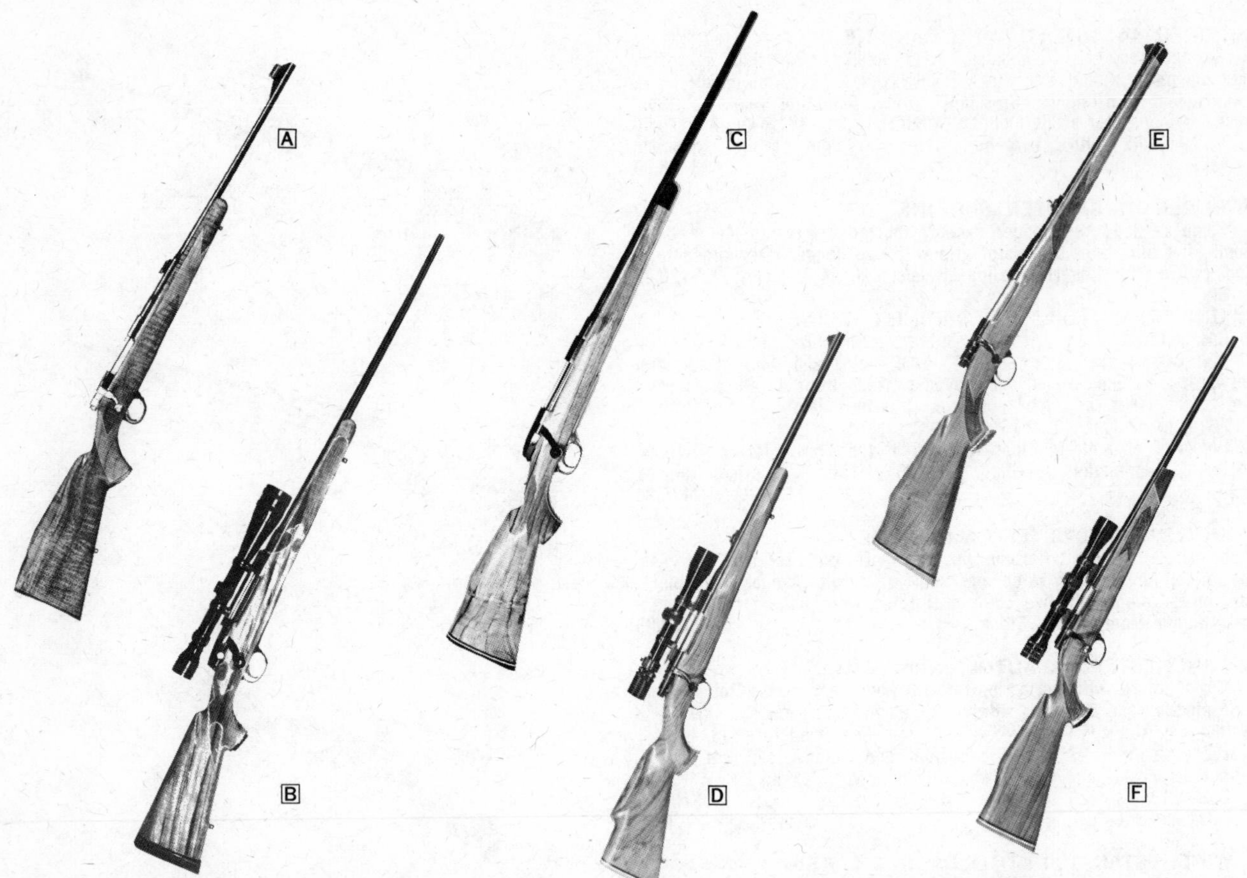

[A] BROWNING HIGH POWER RIFLE Safari Grade
Short and medium Sako or standard Mauser action with hinged floorplate, hand engraved. 3-position sliding safety. Grooved factory adjusted trigger; engraved trigger guard. Checkered walnut p.g. stock, Monte Carlo comb and cheekpiece, 13⅝"x1⅝"x1⅝"x2⅜". Swivel eyelets fitted. 22" lightweight or 24" heavyweight bbls. specifically contoured for each caliber. Hooded ramp front sight, removable adj. folding leaf rear sight. Cals: 222, 222 Mag., 22-250 or 243 (heavy bbl.) without sights; 243, 270, 284, 30-06 or 308 sights optional. Wgt. 6⅛ to 6¾ lbs. (light bbl.), 43" over-all. .... **$219.50 to $237.50**
Heavy bbl. available in 222, 222 Mag., 22-250 or 243. Wgt. 7½ to 7¾ lbs. 45" over-all .... **$219.50 to $227.50**
Also available in 7mm Rem., 300 Win., 300 H&H, 308 Norma, 338 Win., 375 H&H and 458 Win. Magnum calibers. 24" bbl., wgt. 8¼ lbs., 45" over-all including recoil pad **$244.50**

BROWNING HIGH POWER RIFLE Medallion Grade
Same cals. as Safari. Figured walnut stock with skip-line checkering, rosewood grip cap and fore-end tip. Hand engraved receiver and bbl., high-polish blue. Polished bolt, bolt sleeve, bolt handle. Gold plated trigger. All except 458 are without sights.
All Short and medium action models **$354.50**
30-06 and 270 calibers **367.50**
Magnum calibers **374.50**
458 Magnum **379.50**

BROWNING HIGH POWER RIFLE Olympian Grade
Same as Medallion except with finest figured walnut stock; 32-line checkering with hand carved scroll borders; gold initial medallion inset into grip cap. Receiver, floorplate and trigger guard satin-chrome finished. Engraved with animal scenes.
All short and medium action models **$594.50**
30-06 and 270 calibers **617.50**
Magnum calibers **624.50**
458 Magnum **629.50**

[B] CHAMPLIN PREMIER RIFLE
Six locking lugs hold the jewelled bolt at both ends of the tri-rail action. Has checkered bolt knob, 24" octagon bbl., Redfield scope mts., Canjar adj. trigger. Hand inletted oil finished select Claro walnut stock (13½"x1"x⅝"x½") of Monte Carlo design has ebony fore-end tip, black Pachmayr recoil pad, steel p.g. cap, det. sling swivels. Cals. 270, 30-06, 7mm Rem. and 300 Win. Mag. Choice of RH or LH action **$636.56**

[C] CHAMPLIN CUSTOM CROWN RIFLE
Similar to the Premier except: stock built to order, 22 line checkering, optional checkered steel p.g. cap, round or dragoon style trigger guard. Choice of high-gloss or non-glare blueing, barrel length and recoil pad style. Customers name engraved on bbl. **$850.00**
Other modifications and changes are offered such as tapered octagon barrel with integral quarter-rib, ramp and sling swivels, one or three-leaf sights and many more.

[D] HARRINGTON & RICHARDSON 300 BOLT ACTION
Mauser Supreme bolt action with hinged floorplate, adj. trigger, sliding safety. 22" bbl., adjustable rear sight, gold bead ramp front; receiver tapped for scope. American walnut stock, hand checkered p.g. and fore-end, Monte Carlo comb, roll-over cheekpiece. Sling swivels. Wgt. 7¾ lbs., 42½" over-all. Cal. 22-250, 243, 270, 308, 30-06 (5-shot), 7mm Rem. Mag., 300 Win. Mag. (3-shot) **$215.00**
With Ultragon barrel, $12 extra, 22-250 and 30 cals.
Model 330, same as M300 except: stock w/o fore-end or p.g. caps; spacers; no checkering on fore-end. Monte-Carlo stock. No swivels. Not available in 22-250 or Mag. cals. **$145.00**

[E] HARRINGTON & RICHARDSON 301 ULTRA CARBINE
Similar to M300, except: Mannlicher style stock (no roll-over cheekpiece) metal fore-end tip. 18" bbl., 39" over-all, wgt. 7¼ lbs. **$230.00**

[F] HARRINGTON & RICHARDSON 317 ULTRA WILDCAT
Sako bolt action, adj. trigger, sliding thumb safety, receiver dovetailed for scope. 20" barrel. Hand polished, hand checkered walnut p.g. stock, capped fore-end and p.g. Monte Carlo comb. Wgt. 5¼ lbs., 38½" over-all. Cals. 223 Rem. and 17/223 Mag. (handloads), 6 shot. **$235.00**
With Ultragon rifled bbl., cal. 223 only **247.00**

HARRINGTON & RICHARDSON 317 PRESENTATION GRADE
Similar to above, except special selected walnut stock, basketweave checkering on p.g. and fore-end **$425.00**

[A] HARRINGTON & RICHARDSON 370 ULTRA MEDALIST
Mauser Supreme bolt action, 24" heavy varmint-target bbl. Receiver and bbl. tapped for scope and metallic sights. Fully adj. trigger, receiver drilled and tapped for sight or scope. Oil finished, hand rubbed walnut p.g. stock, roll-over comb, semi-beavertail fore-end, recoil pad and adj. swivels. Target scope ribbed base optional at extra cost. Wgt. 9½ lbs., 44¾" over-all. Cals. 22-250, 6mm Rem., and 243, 5 shots. **$235.00**

[B] ITHACA LSA-55 BOLT ACTION RIFLE
Available in cals. 243, 308, 22-250 & 6mm. 23" bbl., 42½" over-all, wgt. approx. 6½ lbs. Hand checkered selected walnut Monte Carlo stock (13⅝" pull) with palm swell; sling swivels. Removable rear sight adj. for w. & e. Ramp front sight. Adjustable single-stage trigger. Receiver has integral scope mounting bases and detachable box magazine. **$159.95**

ITHACA LSA-55 DELUXE BOLT ACTION
Same as the std. except rollover cheekpiece, fore-end tip and pistol grip cap of rosewood with white spacers.......... **$199.95**

[C] MOSSBERG 800 BOLT ACTION RIFLE
4-shot mag. with hinged floorplate. Recessed bolt face; 6 locking lugs. Top thumb safety. 22" AC-KRO-GRUV bbl. Gold bead ramp front, adj. folding leaf rear sight. Monte Carlo cheekpiece walnut stock, checkered and carved, with whiteline spacers, sling swivels. Wgt. 6½ lbs., 42" over-all. Cals. 22-250, 243, 308.......... **$105.50**

MOSSBERG 800SM SCOPED RIFLE
Same as M800 except has Mossberg M84 4x scope. Wgt. 7½ lbs. **$128.00**

MOSSBERG 800D DELUXE RIFLE
Super grade M800 with special finish and Monte Carlo rollover-comb stock. Wgt. 6¾ lbs.......... **$170.00**

MOSSBERG 800V TARGET-VARMINT RIFLE
Model 800 with heavy 24" barrel, target scope bases, no iron sights. Cals. 243 and 22-250 only. 44" over-all, wgt. about 9½ lbs.... **$119.00**

MOSSBERG 800M MANNLICHER RIFLE
Same as M800 except has one piece Mannlicher style stock, flat bolt handle, 20" bbl., 40" over-all and weighs 6½ lbs...... **$135.00**

[D] MUSKETEER RIFLES AND CARBINE
FN Mauser Supreme bolt actions; U.S.-made checkered walnut, cheekpiece Monte Carlo p.g. stock and fore-end, sling swivels included. 24" 12-groove bbl. has a "Williams Guide" open sight adj. for w. & e. Action tapped for scope and iron sights; adj. trigger; sliding thumb safety; hinged floorplate. Wgt. 7 lbs., 44½" over-all. Cals. 243, 270, 30-06, 308, (4-shot) and 264, 308 Norma, 300 Win. and 7mm magnums (3-shot). F.I., importer.......... **$145.00**

Barreled actions.......... **$100.00**

With full length Mannlicher style stock in cals. 30-06, 308 Norma and 300 Win. Magnums.......... **$160.00**

[E] RANGER ARMS TEXAS MAVERICK RIFLE
All grades in cals. 22-250, 243, 6mm Rem., & 308. Choice of 22" or 24" bbl. and right or left hand stock and action. English or Claro walnut Monte Carlo stock (13⅝" pull) with cheekpiece, skip-line checkering, recoil pad, sling swivel studs, rosewood p.g. cap with maple spacer, polyvinyl epoxy finish. Wgt. 7¾ lbs.

Stateman's Grade has minimum coverage checkering, standard grade and finish barrel **$325.00**

Senator's Grade has medium coverage checkering, premium grade standard finish barrel **$375.00**

Governor's Grade has full coverage checkering, premium grade deluxe polish barrel, hand honed and lapped action with jeweled bolt body and knurled bolt knob **$425.00**

RANGER ARMS TEXAS MAGNUM RIFLE
Same as the Maverick except in 270, 30-06, 7mm, 300 and 358 Norma Magnum calibers. Optional 24" or 25½" bbls. Wgt. 8¼ lbs. Stateman's **$325.00.** Senator's **$375.00** and Governor's **$425.00**

[F] RANGER ARMS BENCH REST RIFLE
Single shot in choice of left or right hand models. Cals. 222 or 22-250. Thumb hole stock of laminated walnut strips with wide beavertail fore-end. 24" stainless steel bbl. Wgt. 11¾ lbs. 13½" pull. **$500.00**

[G] REMINGTON 660 BOLT ACTION CARBINE
Monte Carlo stock, checkered p.g. and fore-end (14"x1⅞"x2"). Brass-bead ramp-blade front sight, "U" notch adj. rear. Forward angled bolt, 2-position safety. Capacity 5 rds. in 6mm Rem., 243, 308; 222 Rem. Barrel 20", over-all 38¾". Wgt. 6½ lbs. **$119.95**

Sling and swivels (installed).......... **9.10**

[H] REMINGTON 660 MAGNUM CARBINE
Same as 660 Carbine except has laminated beech and walnut stock with recoil pad and quick-detachable swivels; strap supplied. 4-shot capacity in cals. 6.5mm and 350 Rem. Mag. **$149.95**

[J] REMINGTON 700 ADL BOLT ACTION RIFLE
Walnut, RKW finished p.g. stock, impressed checkering, with Monte Carlo comb and cheekpiece (13⅜"x$1\frac{11}{16}$"x$2\frac{5}{16}$"); blind magazine. Adj. trigger. Gold bead front sight on ramp, removable step-adj. rear sight with windage screw. Bolt handle checkered top and bottom. Cals. 222, (24" bbl., 43½" over-all). 6-shot; 22-250 (24" bbl., 43½" over-all), 6mm Rem., 243 and 308 Win. (22 bbl., 41½" over-all), 270 Win., 30-06, (22" bbl., 42½" over-all), 5-shot. 7 lbs.......... **$134.95**

264 or 7mm Mag., 4-shot 24" stainless steel bbl., 44½" over-all, recoil pad, 7½ lbs. **$149.95**

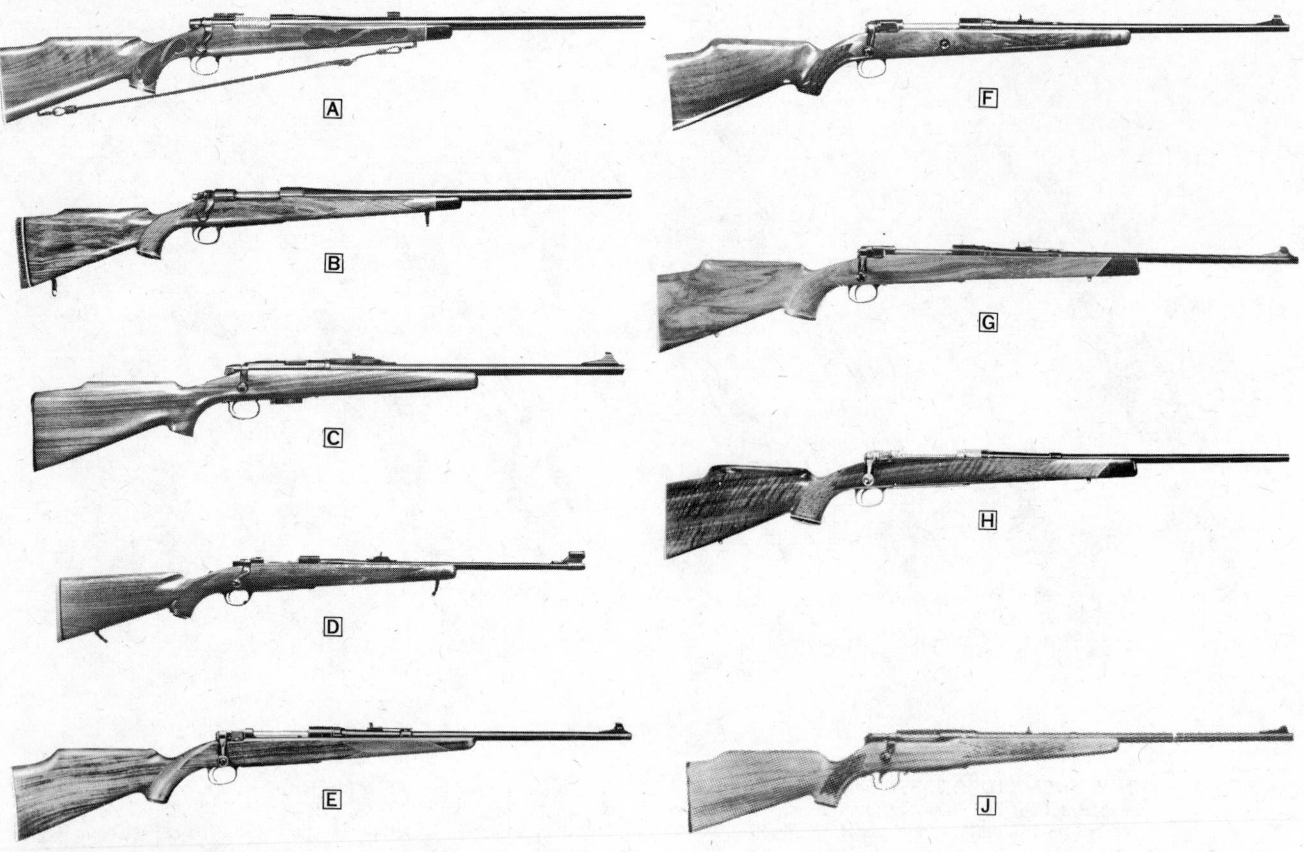

REMINGTON 700 BDL BOLT ACTION RIFLE
Same as 700-ADL except: fleur-de-lis checkering; black fore-end tip; white line buttplate and fore-end tip spacers; quick release hinged floorplate; matted-top receiver; 1" sling and quick detachable swivels. Hooded ramp front sight................................**$154.95**
6.5 Rem. Mag., 350 Rem. Mag., 264, 300 Win. or 7mm Rem. Mag., 4-shot, 264, 300 & 7mm has stainless steel bbl., 44½" over-all, recoil pad, 7½ lbs...............................**$169.95**
375 H&H or 458 Win. Mag., 4-shot, 26" bbl., 46½" over-all, recoil pad, 9 lbs. ....**$ 329.95**
Peerless Grade.........**$600** Premier Grade......... **1200.00**

A **REMINGTON 700 BDL VARMINT**
Same as 700 BDL, except: 24" heavy bbl., 43½" over-all, wgt. 9 lbs. Cals. 222, 223, 22-250, 6mm Rem., 243...................**$169.95**

B **REMINGTON 700C CUSTOM RIFLE**
Same as the 700BDL except choice of 20", 22" or 24" bbl. with or without sights. Jewelled bolt, with or without hinged floor plate. Select American walnut stock is hand checkered. Has rosewood fore-end & grip cap. Hand lapped barrel. 16 weeks for delivery after placing order. **$334.95**
Optional extras: recoil pad **$12.00**, oil finish **$13.75** and left hand cheekpiece **$25.00.**

C **REMINGTON 788 BOLT ACTION RIFLE**
4-shot detachable mag. in cals. 22-250, 6mm Rem., 243, 30-30, 308 and 44 Mag. 5-shot in 222. Walnut finished Monte Carlo hardwood stock (13⅝"x2⅝"x1⅞") with p.g. Bbl. 22" except 222 (24"). Sights; front blade on ramp, open rear, screw adj. for w. & e. Rear-sight mounting holes correct for target scope block. Receiver tapped for scope and receiver sights. Weighs 7 lbs. (44 Mag.); 7¼ lbs. (6mm, 243, 30-30, 308); 7½ lbs. (222, 22-250)..........**$89.95**

REMINGTON 788 LEFT HAND BOLT ACTION
Same as 788 except cals. 6mm & 308 only and left hand stock and action. **$94.95**
Sling strap and swivels, installed **$5.40.** Extra Mag.......**$ 4.50**

D **RUGER 77 BOLT ACTION RIFLE**
Cals. 22-250, 6mm Rem., 243 & 308. Short stroke bolt on one-piece construction with two locking lugs. Adj. trigger, hinged 5-shot magazine. 22" bbl., 1" tip-off type rings supplied as standard. Checkered American walnut stock (13¾"x2⅛"x1⅝") with p.g. cap; sling swivel studs and recoil pad. 42" over-all; Wgt. 6½ lbs............**$160.00**
With iron sights **175.00**

RUGER 77 MAGNUM RIFLE
Cals. 284 Win. (5-shot), 6.5mm or 350 Rem. Mag. (3-shot). Otherwise same as standard cal. 77. (Available in late 1969) Price to be announced.

SAVAGE 110 E BOLT ACTION RIFLE
Cals. 30-06, 243, 308 (4-shot) & 7mm Rem. Mag. (3-shot). 20" (7mm, 24") bbl., walnut finished hardwood stock (13½"x1⅝"x1½"x 2½") with checkered p.g. and fore-end with Monte Carlo comb. Hard rubber butt plate (7mm, recoil pad). Gold bead front sight on removable ramp; step elevator rear, tapped for peep or scope sights. Wgt. 6¾ lbs. (7mm, 7¾ lbs.); 40½" over-all (20" bbl.).....**$110.00**
7mm Mag. **122.50**
Model 110-EL same except left hand action........... **115.00**
7mm Mag. **127.50**

E **SAVAGE 100D BOLT ACTION RIFLE**
Same as the 110E except: 22" bbl. (24", 22-250, 6 Mag. cals.); walnut stock; aluminum butt plate (magnum, recoil pad); folding semi-buckhorn rear sight (22-250 no sights); 22-250 weighs 8 lbs.; Cals. 30-06, 22-250, 243, 270 & 308....................**$132.95**
7mm Rem., 264, 300 & 338 Win. Mag. **137.95**
Model 110DL same except left hand action............. **142.95**
Magnum calibers **147.95**

F **SAVAGE 110C BOLT ACTION RIFLE**
Same as the 110D except: Detachable 4-shot box magazine. Not available in 22-250....................................**$137.95**
Model 110CL same except left hand action............. **142.95**

G **SAVAGE 110 PREMIER GRADE RIFLE**
Same as the Model 110D except: selected French walnut stock with roll-over cheekpiece, skip-line hand checkered p.g. and fore-end. Rosewood fore-end tip and butt cap with white spacers. Sling swivel studs. Folding leaf rear sight. Right or left hand action. Wgt. 7 lbs., 7¾ in 7mm. Cal. 243 and 30-06.........................**$225.00**
Same in 7mm Rem. Mag. with 24" stainless steel bbl. **237.50**

H **SAVAGE 110-PE PRESENTATION GRADE RIFLE**
Similar to M110 Premier Grade except: choice French walnut stock; receiver, trigger guard and floor plate fully engraved, right or left hand action. 243-30-06 **$345.00,** 7mm Rem. Mag. **$355.00**

SAVAGE 110 Barreled Act'ons. Same as used in 110MC & 110 Magnum. No stock or sights. Right-hand action, 22-250, 243, 270, 308, 30-36......**$89.00;** 7mm Rem., 264, 300, 338 Win..........**$ 99.65**
With left-hand action, standard calibers **$93.00,** magnums..**103.65**
Actions only. Write to Savage for price.

J **SAVAGE 340 CLIP REPEATER**
Bolt action, 4-shot clip rifle. 225 Win. 222 Rem. (24" bbl.) or 3-shot 30-30 (22" bbl.). Walnut p.g. stock with fluted comb, white spacers, checkering on p.g. and fore-end. 13½"x1½"x2½". Ramp front sight with gold bead; folding stepped rear. Thumb safety. Wgt. about 6½ lbs., 42" over-all (24" bbl.).................**$79.95**

A SEARS 53 BOLT ACTION RIFLE

Hinged floorplate. Walnut finished Monte Carlo stock with checkered p.g. and fore-end. Tapped for receiver sights and scope mounts. Bolt face encloses cartridge head; bolt handle flat on underside. Serrated trigger. 3-position thumb safety on bolt head. White metal bead front sight on ramp. Semi-buckhorn folding rear adj. for elevation. Wgt. about 6¾ lbs. Cals. 243, 308, 270 and 30-06 (5-shot, 22" bbl., 42⅜" over-all). **$119.99**

300 Win. Mag. (4-shot, 24" bbl., 44½" over-all, recoil pad).. **129.99**

B SEARS 53 TED WILLIAMS RIFLE

Same as Sears 53 except: 270 and 30-06 only; 22" bbl., 10" twist, 42⅜" over-all, wgt. 6¾ lbs. Wide trigger. American walnut stock, Monte Carlo comb, checkered p.g. and fore-end (13⅝"x1⅜"x1¾"x 2⅜"). Recoil pad, black fore-end tip, 1" detachable swivels and sling, medallion on p.g., engine turned bolt, scrolled floor plate..... **$165.00**

C SMITH & WESSON BOLT ACTION RIFLES

All have Mauser 3-lug actions, hinged magazine floor-plates, jewelled bolts, single-stage trigger. Silver bead ramp front & open sporting rear sights, sling swivels. Available in cals. 270, 30-06, 308 & 243 with 23¾" 4-groove bbls. (243 has 6). 5-shot mag.

Model C has walnut stock with high-gloss plastic finish, checkered p.g. and fore-end (illustrated).......... **$192.50**

Model B has Monte Carlo stock.......... **202.50**

Model A has cheekpiece, rosewood p.g. cap and fore-end tip with white spacers **215.50**

Model D has full length (Mannlicher type) stock.......... **221.00**

Model E has full length Monte Carlo stock.......... **225.00**

All models are available with oil finished, instead of plastic, stocks in cal. 30-06. Deduct $17.00 from prices.

D WEATHERBY MARK V BOLT ACTION RIFLE

Designed especially for the Weatherby Magnum cartridge line, the Mark V action features: nine locking lugs; low-lift (54°) bolt handle; counter-bored bolt face and bbl. breech fully enclose the cartridge; three gas ports; streamlined, shrouded bolt sleeve; cocking indicator; adj. trigger; hinged floorplate and thumb safety. Barrels have cold-swaged rifling and are profiled in proportion to caliber. Deluxe checkered walnut Monte Carlo stock with high luster finish, recoil pad. 13½" pull. Sights are optional extras. Cals: 224, 22-250 (4-shot, 6½ lbs., 43¼" over-all, 24" bbl., 14" twist).......... **$299.50**

With 26" semi-target bbl. **309.50**

Cals., 257, 270, 300, (12" twist), 240, 7mm 30-06 (10" twist) 3-shot, 7¼ lbs., 44½" over-all 24" bbl. **$329.50**

Cal. 340 (3-shot 8½ lbs., 46½" over-all, 26" bbl., 10" twist) **339.50**

Cal. 378 (13½" pull, 2-shot, 8½ lbs., 46½" over-all, 26" bbl., 12" twist) **$425.00**

Cal. 460 (California Mesquite stock, 13⅞" pull, 2-shot, 10½ lbs., 46½" over-all. 26" bbl., 16" twist, muzzle brake).......... **$495.00**

Calibers 240, 257, 270, 7mm and 300 WM, or 30-06 may be ordered with 26" bbls. for $10.00 extra. 378s with muzzle brake, $37.50 extra.

WEATHERBY MARK V RIFLE Left Hand

Available in all Weatherby calibers except 224 and 22-250. Complete left handed action; stock with cheekpiece on right side. Prices are $10 higher than right hand models except the 460 WM is unchanged.

WESTERN FIELD 770 BOLT ACTION RIFLE

Mauser-type action with recessed bolt head and locking lugs; side safety locks trigger; non-slip bolt handle; 4-shot magazine capacity. Hand finished French walnut stock; p.g. and fore-end are hand checkered. Hooded front ramp, adjustable open rear sights. Sling swivels included. Cals. 270, 30-30. 42" over-all. **$135.00**

E WESTERN FIELD 780 BOLT ACTION RIFLE

Mauser-type action. Monte Carlo stock with cheekpiece, checkered p.g. and fore-end, whiteline spacers, 1" sling swivels. Gold bead front ramp, adj. folding leaf rear sight. 22" bbl., 42" over-all. Cals. 243, 308 .... **$96.95**

WESTERN FIELD M-780

Super grade with roll-over cheek piece stock of American walnut with rosewood p.g. cap and fore-end tip, white line spacers, cushion rubber buttplate. Cal. 308 or 243 Win. **$165.00**

F WINCHESTER 70 STANDARD RIFLE

Bolt action; wide adj. trigger; 3-position safety on fully enclosed bolt head. Red cocking indicator. Recessed bolt face. Engine-turned bolt. Floating swaged bbl. with hooded bead front sight, adj. open rear. Action tapped and sights removable for scope mounting. Walnut stock with Monte Carlo comb and cheekpiece (13½"x1¾"x1½"x2⅛"), checkered p.g. and fore-end, sling swivels. Cals. 222, 22-250, 225, 243, 270, 30-06 ,308, 6-shot (222, 4-shot), wgt. 7½ lbs., 42½" over-all, 22" bbl., 10" twist (225, 222 and 22-250 have 14" twist, 308 has 12"). **$162.95**

G WINCHESTER 70 AFRICAN

Same as M70 Standard except: 458 Win. Mag. only. 4-shot; open rear sight. 22" non-floating heavy bbl. 14" twist. Stock measures 13½"x1⅜"x1¾"x2⅜", has black plastic fore-end tip and grip cap; wgt. 8½ lbs., recoil pad and special rear sight.......... **$334.95**

[A] WINCHESTER 70 DELUXE RIFLE
Same as M70 Standard except: presentation-checkered semi-fancy walnut stock, ebony p.g. cap and fore-end tip with white spacers, knurled bolt knob, non-slip rubber buttplate. 225, 243, 270, 30-06, 300 Win. Mag. (recoil pad)............................**$324.95**

[B] WINCHESTER 70 MANNLICHER
Same as M70 Standard except: 19″ barrel bedded full-length in Mannlicher-style stock of American walnut with Monte Carlo profile and raised cheek-piece. Length 39½″ over-all, weight about 7 lbs. Available in 243, 270, 308 Win. or 30-06..................**$229.95**

[C] WINCHESTER 70 MAGNUM RIFLE
Same as M70 Standard except with recoil pad and in these magnum cals.: 7mm Rem., 264, 300, 338 Win., 375 H&H, 3-round mag. capacity. Wgt. 7¼ lbs. (8½ lbs. in 375), 24″ bbl., 44½″ over-all. R.H. twist: 9″ in 264, 9½″ in 7mm, 10″ in 300, 338, 12″ in 375...........**$117.95**

[D] WINCHESTER 70 VARMINT RIFLE
Same as M70 Standard except: 222 Rem., 22-250, 225 and 243 only, target scope blocks, no sights, 24″ heavy bbl., 14″ twist in 22-250, and 225, 10″ twist in 243. 44½″ over-all, 9¾ lbs. Stock measures 13½″x9/16″x15/16″x⅜″ from bore line....................**$117.95**

1969 Standard, Magnum and Varmint 70s feature: New anti-cramp bolt; stainless steel follower; black chromed steel guard and floorplate. Newly designed stocks have wider cheekpieces, slimmer fore-ends, new grip caps.
DeLuxe, Target and African 70s have some of these new features.

Winchester 70 Barreled Actions. No stock, sights or scope blocks; receivers tapped and plugged. **Standard:** 222 Rem., 22-250, 225, 243, 270, 308, 30-06....**$118.90; Magnum;** 264, 7mm Rem., 300 Vin., 338......**$132.50; Varmint:** 22-250, 225, 243......**$132.50; Target:** 308, 30-06....................................**$164.35**

[E] WINCHESTER 670 BOLT ACTION CARBINE
Similar to Winchester 70. Sliding, 2-position safety; recessed bolt face; red cocking indicator; wide, serrated trigger; ramp front sight and adj. open rear (both easily detachable for scope-only use). Monte Carlo stock (13½″x1¾″x1½″x2⅛″), checkered p.g. and fore-end. 19″ floating bbl. 10″ twist. Wgt. 6¾ lbs., 39½″ over-all. Cals. 243, 270, 30-06 ....**$114.95**

WINCHESTER 670 BOLT ACTION RIFLE
Same as 670 carbine except: 22″ bbl., wgt. 7 lbs., 42½″ over-all. Cals. 225 (14″ twist), 243, 270, 30-06 (10″ twist)...........**$119.95**

WINCHESTER 670 MAGNUM
Same as 670 rifle except: 24″ bbl., wgt. 7¼ lbs., 44½″ over-all. Recoil pad. Cals. 264 Mag. (9″ twist), 300 Win. Mag. (10″ twist) **$134.95**

[F] WINCHESTER 770 BOLT ACTION RIFLE
Available in cals. 222 (3-shot), 22-250, 243, 270, 30-06 & 308 (4-shot). 42½″ over-all, 22″ bbls. Walnut stock (13½″x1¾″x2⅛″x 1½″) with Monte Carlo, undercut cheekpiece, fluted comb, checkered p.g., with caps and fore-end, sling swivels. Ramp-and-hood front and sporting rear sights are detachable. Wgt. 7½ lbs. 10″ (243, 270, 30-06), 12″ (308) and 14″ (222, 22-250), twist..............**$139.95**

WINCHESTER 770 MAGNUM BOLT ACTION
In cals. 264, 7mm Rem. and 300 Win. (3-shot) Magnum. Same as the 770 except: rubber recoil pad, 24″ bbl., 44½″ over-all; wgt 7¼ lbs. 9″ (264), 9½″ (7mm) & 10″ (300) twist...............**$154.95**

[G] WINSLOW BOLT ACTION RIFLES
FN Supreme actions, Douglas barrels, custom treatment of metal and wood in 3 stock types and in 7 grades. Made in all popular cartridges.
Regal Grade Plainsmaster, with more extensive checkering, roll-over comb, ivory and ebony inlays..........................**$390.00**
Regent, Regimental, Crown, Emperor and Imperial Grades in ascending order of carving, engraving and inlaying, to........... **$3,500.00**
Regal grade Varmint with Bushmaster stock in custom calibers 17/222, 17/222 Mag. and 17/223. Priced from.............**$430.00**
Extra, for magnum calibers **10.00**

A ARMORY C-H HI-WALL RIFLE
A modernized version of the Winchester hi-wall, using investment cast 4340 chrome-moly receiver. Suitable for the heaviest high-intensity cartridges. Through-bolted stock. Adj. trigger. No sights. Any caliber, to order. Complete rifle, with Monte-Carlo, p.g. stock......... **$179.50**
Barreled action **120.00**
Action only **69.50**

B HARRINGTON & RICHARDSON 158 TOPPER RIFLE
Single shot, takedown, side lever break-open rifle. Auto. ejector. Walnut finished stock and fore-end; recoil pad. 22″ bbl. Lyman folding adj. rear and ramp front sights. Wgt. 5¼ lbs., 37½″ over-all. Cal. 30-30 .... **$39.95**
Extra interchangeable 20 ga., 26″ Mod. choke shotgun bbl... **15.00**

C CHALLENGER HOPKINS & ALLEN HERITAGE
Single shot, underhammer percussion muzzle loader. Straight grip walnut stock and fore-end. Curved buttplate, inset cap box and extended trigger guard of brass. 32″ octagonal bbl., uniform or gain twist rifling. Blade front sight and both open and peep rear sights. Barrel and action blued. 8½ lbs. Cals. 36 or 45........ **$99.95**
Offhand Deluxe. Plain version of the Heritage........ **87.95**

D CHALLENGER HOPKINS & ALLEN BUGGY CARBINE
Single shot, underhammer percussion muzzle loader. Straight grip walnut stock and fore-end, flat buttplate, 20″ octagonal bbl. All metal parts blued. Blade front sight, open adj. rear. Wgt. 5½ lbs. Cals. 36 or 45........ **74.50**

CHALLENGER HOPKINS & ALLEN DEER STALKER
.58 Cal. muzzle loading underhammer percussion rifle. 32″ octagonal bbl., 1 turn in 72″, .575 bore uses .580 gr. slug. Wgt. approx. 9½ lbs. **$139.95**

CHALLENGER HOPKINS & ALLEN 45 TARGET
Single shot, underhammer percussion muzzle loader. Heavy 32″ octagonal bbl., straight grip walnut stock. Blade front, open rear sight. Cal. 45 only........ **$84.95**

E CHALLENGER HOPKINS & ALLEN MINUTEMAN
Muzzle-loading, Kentucky-style flintlock rifle. 39″ octagonal bbl. brass-mounted stock of maple, walnut or cherry. 55″ over-all. Cals. 36 or 45. .... **$179.50**
Same, except percussion ignition........ **179.50**

CHALLENGER HOPKINS & ALLEN OVER & UNDER RIFLE
Fire the first barrel and rotate the breech and the second barrel comes up ready to fire. Each barrel has its own set of sights targeted to the same point of impact. 45 cal. with walnut stock and crescent butt-plate. 28″ blued octagonal barrels. 43″ over-all. Wgt. 8½ lbs. **$139.95**

G RUGER NUMBER ONE SINGLE SHOT
Dropping block underlever action with internal hammer, selectable full ejector or extractor, tang safety. Trigger adj. for weight, travel, and overtravel. Two piece checkered walnut p.g. stock for scope use, with recoil pad. Choice of semi-beavertail or sporting fore-end. Sling swivels (on barrel band with sporting fore-end). Bbl. 26″ (24″ 375HH, 45-70 & 458). Barrel scope mount (1″ rings) furnished, open sights an optional extra. Cals. 222, 22-250, 243, 6mm Rem., 270, 30-06, 7mm Rem. Mag. (7x57, 280, 264, 6.5 Rem. Mag., .300 Win Mag., 375H&H, 45-70 & 458 Mag. available on non-cancellable special order). 42″ over-all (26″ bbl.). Wgt. 7¾ to 8¼ lbs........ **$265.00**
For gold bead front and folding leaf rear add $15.00.
For sporting fore-end add........ **$ 20.00**
Rifle in 375H&H, 458 Mag. & 47-50 with sights and sporting fore-end **$280.00**
Barreled action in standard, magnum or special order calibers without sights. **$140.00**

H SHARPS 78 SINGLE SHOT
Falling block underlever action with internal hammer; extract adaptable to any type cartridge rim (i.e. rimmed, semi-rimmed, rimless or belted). Breech block safety is selective from manual to automatic. Classic style lever interchanges with optional extra loop or continental (English) lever. Trigger is a combination single stage (adj. for pull, sear engagement and over-travel and set trigger. Single stage adjusts from a pull of 2 to 5 lbs., set adjusts from 4 oz. to ¼ oz. Choice of barrel lengths (26″ to 36″), weights and contours. Tapped for scope mounts. Sights are an optional extra. Forearm available in two lengths and styles. Walnut stock with rubber butt plate is standard with optional extra choices of woods, cheekpieces, butt-plates and checkering. Cals. available from 17 through 50 with several new "Sharps" calibers plus old Sharps cals. in modern loads. Weighs from 6¾ lbs. to 16 lbs. (Std. unit with 30″ No. 2 bbl. weighs about 7¾ to 8¼ lbs.).
Deluxe Grade I Std. or Lightweight........ **$295.00**
Premier Grade II Std. or Lightweight........ **399.50**
Custom grades from **$495.00** to **$5,000.00.**

SHARPS GOLDEN SPIKE CENTENNIAL MODEL 78
A commemorative model (Series A) available in 50-70 cal. with 30″ bbl. only. Features hand checkered fancy walnut stocks, engraved receiver and cartridge well traps, inlaid pistol grip caps. Priced Grade III, **$495.00**; Grade VI, **$1,250.00** and Grade VIII, **$2,500.00.**

F TINGLE M-1962 MUZZLE LOADING TARGET RIFLE
A half-stock percussion target rifle of 36 or 44 cal., 52″ twist. 32″ octagon hook-breech bbl. is easily removed. Blade front and V notch adj. rear sight. One-piece walnut stock, concave cheekpiece, brass fittings. Double set triggers. Coil spring lock. Right or left hand models. Wgt. 10 lbs. 48″ over-all........ **$129.95**

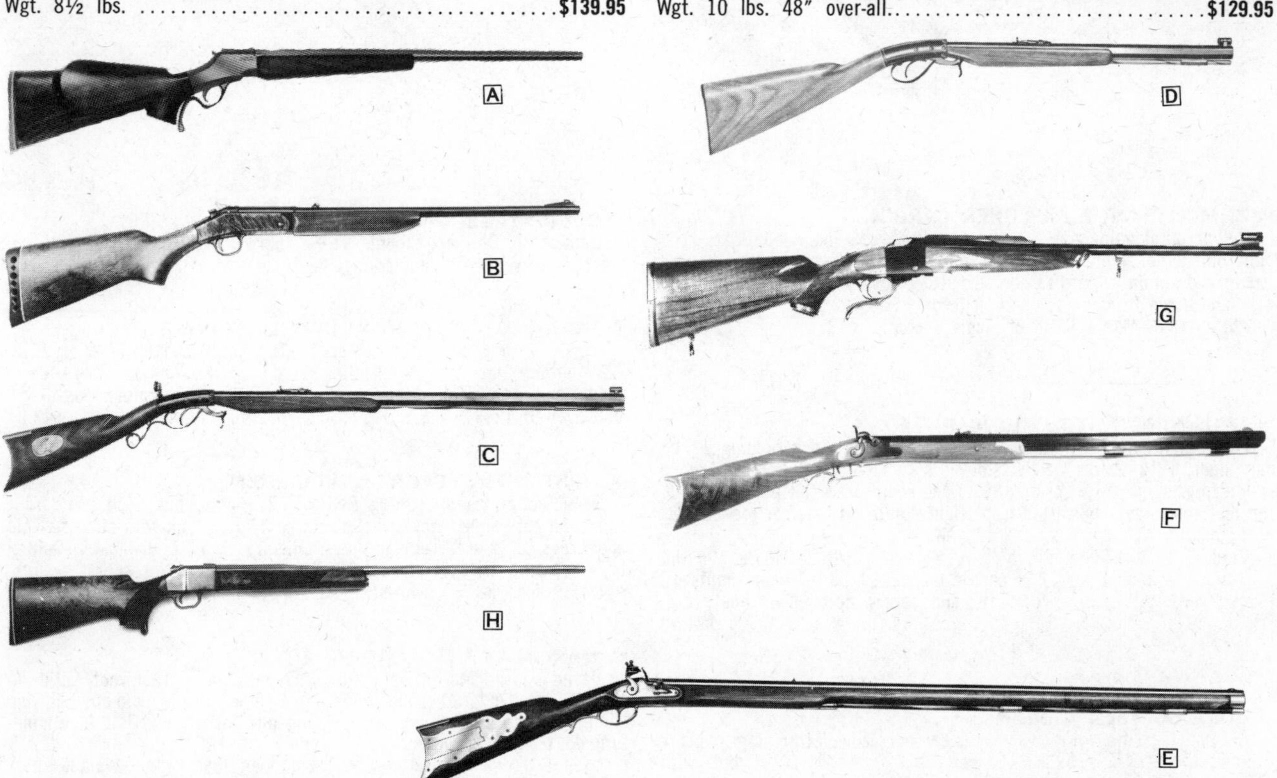

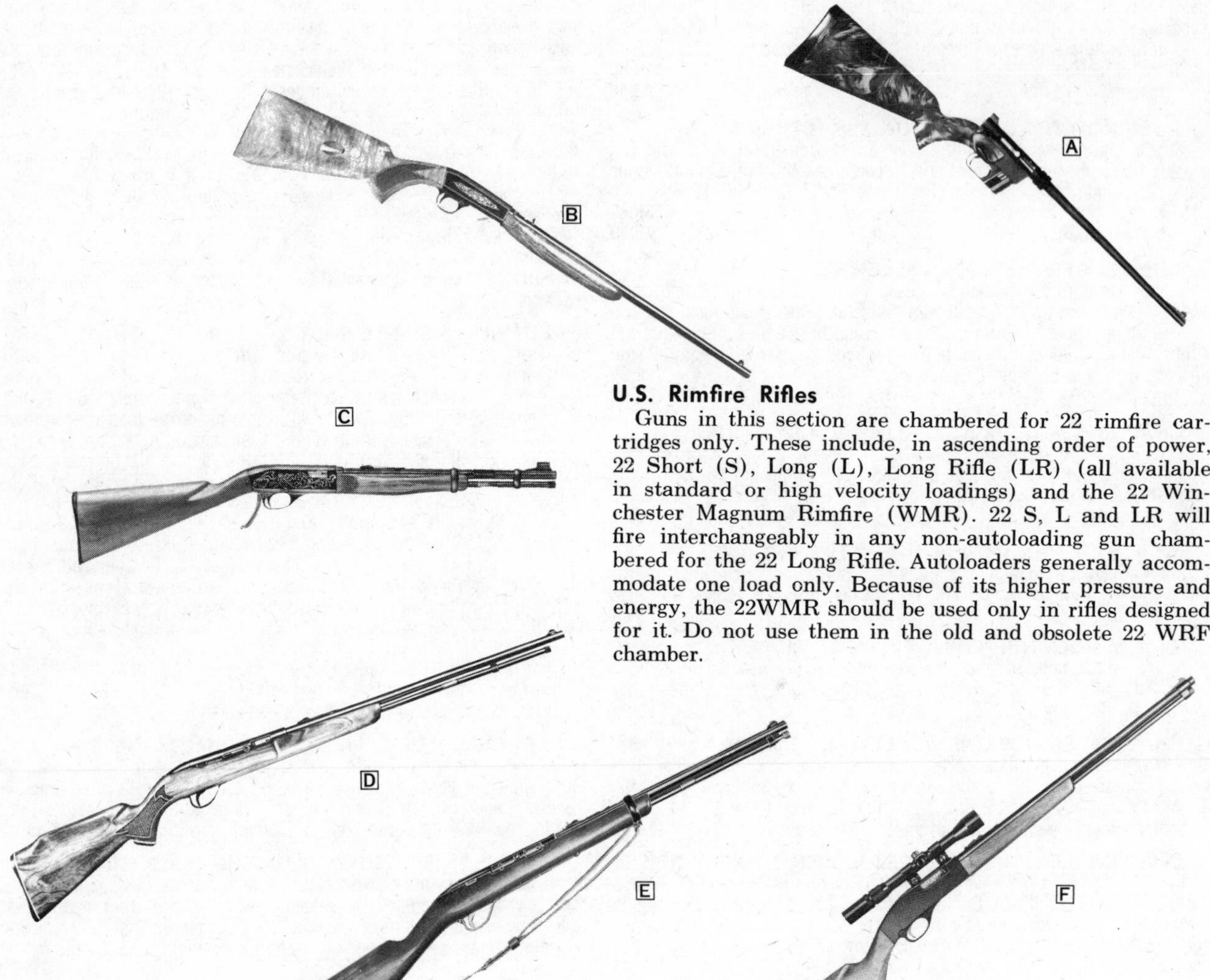

U.S. Rimfire Rifles

Guns in this section are chambered for 22 rimfire cartridges only. These include, in ascending order of power, 22 Short (S), Long (L), Long Rifle (LR) (all available in standard or high velocity loadings) and the 22 Winchester Magnum Rimfire (WMR). 22 S, L and LR will fire interchangeably in any non-autoloading gun chambered for the 22 Long Rifle. Autoloaders generally accommodate one load only. Because of its higher pressure and energy, the 22WMR should be used only in rifles designed for it. Do not use them in the old and obsolete 22 WRF chamber.

A ARMALITE AR-7 EXPLORER CARBINE

8-shot autoloading cal. 22 LR rifle. Wgt. 2¾ lbs., and floats. 16" alloy bbl. (steel lining), alloy receiver; moulded fiberglass stock houses barrel and action when disassembled. 16½" over-all when stowed. Peep rear and blade front sight. Over-all length, 34½" **$49.95**
With walnut Monte Carlo cheekpiece stock **64.50**

B BROWNING AUTOLOADING RIFLE

Lightweight auto with tubular magazine in buttstock holding 11 LR cartridges, 19¼" barrel easily removed with fore-end. Checkered French walnut p.g. stock (13¾"x1 3/16"x2⅝") and semi-beavertail fore-end. Folding leaf rear sight; gold bead front sight. Engraved receiver grooved for scope mount. Wgt. 4¾ lbs., 37" over-all.
Grade I.... **$91.50** Grade II.... **$141.50** Grade III.... **$251.50**
Grade I available for 22 S cartridges, 22¼" barrel, mag. holds 16 rounds. Grooved receiver or left hand safety optional without cost. Price **$91.50**

COLT COLTEER CARBINE

Autoloading rifle with 15-shot tubular magazine. Straight grip black walnut stock (13¾"x1⅝"x2¼") beavertail fore-end. 19½" bbl. with hooded gold bead front sight with notch rear adj. for w. and e. Receiver grooved for Tip-Off mount. Cross-bolt safety. Wgt. 4¾ lbs.. 37" over-all. 22 LR only **$65.00**

C COLT STAGECOACH CARBINE

Similar to Colteer except: 16½" bbl., 33¾" over-all. Scroll engraved receiver, with saddle ring. 22 LR only **$75.00**

D HI-STANDARD SPORT-KING DELUXE RIFLE

22 LR, L or S tubular autoloader. Mag. holds 15 LR, 17 L or 22 S. 22¼" round tapered barrel. Checkered p.g. stock with Monte Carlo comb, semi-beavertail fore-end. Open sights, slide safety. Wgt. 5½ lbs., over-all 42¾" **$49.95**

E HI-STANDARD SPORT-KING CARBINE

Same action as Sport-King Deluxe. 18¼" bbl. has bead post front and open rear sight. Western-style straight grip stock with sling swivels and brass buttplate. Tubular mag. holds 17 S, 14 L or 12 LR. Golden trigger guard, trigger and safety. Receiver grooved for scope mounts. Wgt. 5½ lbs., 38½" over-all **$49.95**

F MARLIN 49 AUTOLOADING RIFLE

Based on the Marlin 99 action this rifle has a rustproof solid-top receiver, grooved for scope mounting, with a manual hold-open device (similar to the GI carbine) for cleaning and inspection. Bolt is engine-turned; trigger is gold plated. Tubular magazine holds 19 22 LR cartridges. Front ramp, step-adjustable open rear sights. Walnut stock with white-line spacers at grip cap and buttplate. 40½" over-all; weight, about 5½ lbs. 22 LR only. **$59.95**
With Marlin 300 4x scope as illustrated **67.75**

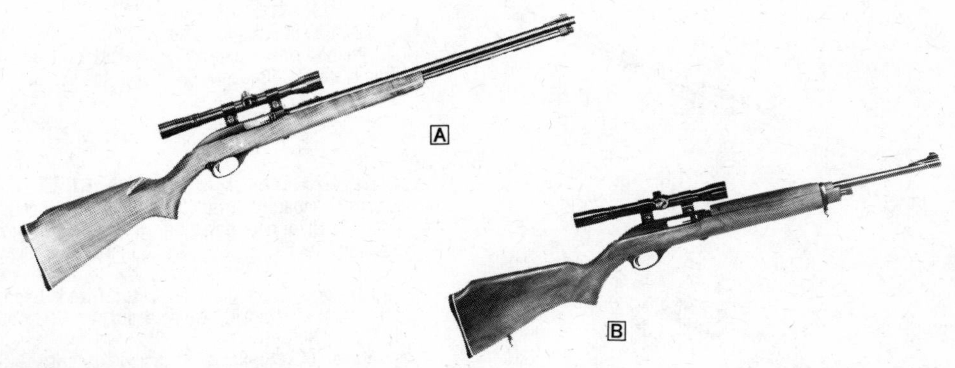

A MARLIN 99C AUTOLOADING RIFLE
19-shot auto rifle with tubular mag. 22" bbl. with open rear and hooded ramp front sights. Walnut Monte Carlo p.g. stock. Crossbolt safety. Tapped for receiver sights, grooved for Tip-Off mounts. 40½" over-all, wgt. 5½ lbs. Cal. 22 LR only **$49.95**
With Marlin 300 4x scope as illustrated **59.25**

B MARLIN 99 M1 CARBINE
Same as the Marlin 99 rifle except: Walnut handguard with band; removable rear sight, ramp front cover; swivels. 18" barrel, 37" over-all, wgt. 4¾ lbs. 9-shot tubular magazine **$49.95**
With Marlin 300 4x scope as illustrated **59.25**

MARLIN 989 M2 CARBINE
Clip magazine version of the Marlin 99 M1 Carbine. Cal. 22 LR. Two 7-shot clips **$49.95**
With Marlin 300 4x scope **59.25**

C GLENFIELD 60 AUTOLOADER
19-shot tubular mag., 22-cal. auto rifle. 22" bbl., chrome-plated trigger. Receiver grooved for Tip-Off mounts. Monte Carlo stock of American hardwood. 22 LR only **$42.95**

D GLENFIELD 70 CARBINE
22-cal. autoloader similar to Model 60 except 18" bbl. and 8-shot clip loading. Sling swivels **$42.95**

E MOSSBERG MODEL 350K RIFLE
Autoloading rifle with 7-shot, 3-way clip that handles 22 S, L or LR. Walnut p.g. stock with cheekpiece and Monte Carlo comb. 23½" "AC-KRO-GRUV" barrel. Sling swivels. Open rear sight, bead front. Tapped for peep sight, grooved for scope mount. Wgt. about 6 lbs., 43½" over-all. **$48.35**

F MOSSBERG MODEL 351K RIFLE
Autoloading rifle with one-piece walnut stock, Monte Carlo comb. Tubular magazine in buttstock holds 15 LR cartridges. Open rear and bead front sights. Receiver grooved for scope mount. 24" "AC-KRO-GRUV" barrel. Wgt. 6 lbs., 43" over-all. Cal. 22 LR only. Price . . **$49.45**

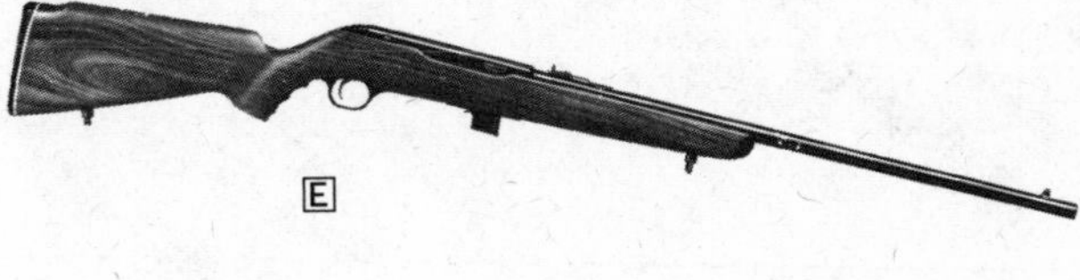

MOSSBERG MODEL 351C CARBINE
Same as Mossberg 351K except: 18½" bbl., bbl. band, sling swivels; wgt. 5½ lbs., 38½" over-all. **$51.65**

G MOSSBERG MODEL 352K CARBINE
Autoloading rifle with 18½" "AC-KRO-GRUV" barrel. 7-shot, 3-way clip handles 22 S, L or LR. Walnut pistol grip stock with Monte Carlo comb. Hinged moulded fore-end forming a 5" hand grip. Open rear and bead front sights. Sling on left side of stock. Grooved for scope mount. Wgt. 5lbs., 38" over-all. **$48.35**

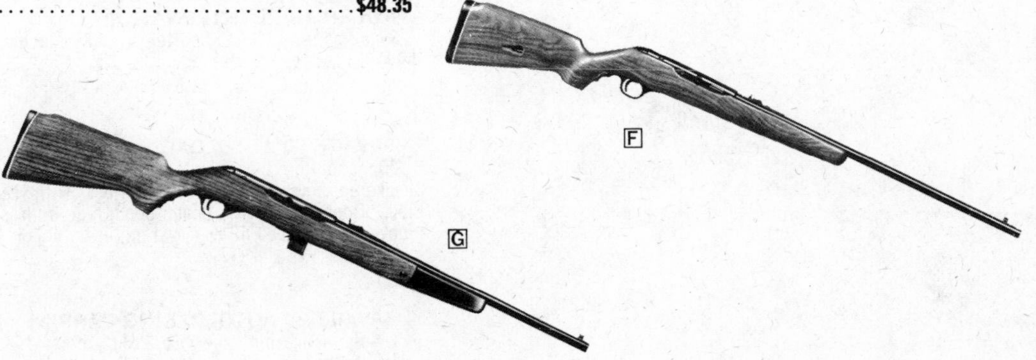

A NOBLE 285 AUTO RIFLE
22-cal. autoloading rifle with round 22" bbl. Tubular mag. holds 15 LR. Walnut finish p.g. stock. Ramp front and adj. open rear sights. Top thumb safety. Receiver grooved for Tip-Off mount. Wgt. 5½ lbs. 40" over-all. **$39.95**

B REMINGTON 552A AUTO RIFLE
An autoloading rifle designed to "match" the Model 742 big game rifle in style and handling. Uses all 22 rimfires without adjustment; capacity 15 LR, 17 L or 20 S in tubular magazine. 23" barrel, full size walnut stock, Crossbolt safety with positive disconnection of hammer and trigger; spent case deflector fitted. Bead front and step-adjustable rear sights, receiver grooved for Tip-Off mount. Wgt. about 5¾ lbs., 42" over-all. **$64.95**
Model 552GS. Same as above except 22 Short only.......... **76.95**

REMINGTON 552 BDL AUTO RIFLE
Same as Model 552A except: p.g. cap, checkered grip and fore-end, ramp front and fully adjustable rear sights. RKW finish.......... **$74.95**

REMINGTON 552C CARBINE
Same as Model 552A except: 21" barrel, wgt. 5¼ lbs., 40" over-all. **$64.95**
Sling and swivels (installed).......... **7.50**

C REMINGTON NYLON 66 AUTO RIFLE
An ultra-lightweight autoloading rifle with moulded, checkered Mohawk Brown Nylon stock and diamond-inlaid fore-end. Tubular mag. in stock holds 14 LR. 19⅝" barrel Open rear and blade front sights. Grooved for Tip-Off mount. Thumb safety on top of grip. Wgt. 4 lbs., 38½" over-all **$49.95**
With Apache Black stock, chromed bbl. and action.......... **54.95**
Model 66GS. Same as M66 except 22 Short only.......... **59.95**
Sling strap & swivels, installed.......... **5.40**

D REMINGTON MODEL 550 AUTOLOADER
Auto rifle, tubular mag. holds 22 S, 17 L, 15 LR interchangeably. Walnut p.g. stock. 24" round tapered barrel. Thumb safety. Receiver grooved for scope mounts. Wgt. 6¼ lbs. Open rear and bead front sights. Over-all 43½". Cal. 22 S, L, or LR.......... **$59.95**

RUGER 10/22 AUTO CARBINE
22 LR carbine with a 10-shot rotary, detachable magazine that fits flush with the stock. Bolt hold-open latch. Crossbolt safety. American walnut stock. Receiver tapped for scope mounts. Ivory bead front sights, folding-leaf rear. 37" over-all, 18½" bbl., wgt. 5 lbs. **$54.50**

E RUGER 10/22 AUTO SPORTER
Same as 10/22 Carbine except: Sporter style Monte Carlo stock with straight buttplate, p.g. cap, fluted fore-end and sling swivels **$64.50**

RUGER 10/22 INTERNATIONAL
Same as the 10/22 Sporter except: Mannlicher style (full length) stock **$64.50**

F SAVAGE 60 AUTOLOADING RIFLE
20" bbl., top tang safety. Tubular magazine takes 15 22 LR ctgs. Checkered walnut Monte Carlo stock with semi-beavertail fore-end. Blade front sight with bead, open rear with step elevator. Receiver grooved for scope. 40½" over-all; wgt. about 6 lbs.......... **$59.50**

G SAVAGE 90 AUTOLOADING CARBINE
Tubular magazine takes 10 22 LR ctgs. 16½" bbl., Walnut Monte Carlo stock with sling swivels. Receiver grooved for scope. 37½" over-all; wgt. about 5¼ lbs.......... **$54.50**

[A] SEARS MODEL 3T AUTO RIFLE
Autoloading rifle with tubular magazine holding 21 S, 17 L or 15 LR. Shoots all three interchangeably. 20½" round bbl. 16" twist. Crossbolt safety; burnished bolt handle, trigger and mag. cap. Walnut finished p.g. stock. Ramp front and step adjustable rear sights. Receiver grooved for scope mount. Wgt. 5 lbs., 39" over-all **$39.99**

[B] SEARS TED WILLIAMS 3T AUTO
Same as 3T except: Magazine cap, bolt handle and trigger are nickel plated; fluted walnut stock, checkered p.g. and fore-end, p.g. cap; white line buttplate spacer **$62.50**

[C] SEARS TED WILLIAMS 34 AUTO CARBINE
Solid frame autoloading rifle with tubular mag., holds 25 S or 17 LR. 21" bbl. with open rear and blade front sights. Hammerless action grooved for Tip-Off mount. Cross-bolt safety. Walnut p.g. stock with Monte Carlo comb, white spacer buttplate, straight grip, inset initial plate: semi-beavertail fore-end. Wgt. about 5½" lbs., 39" over-all. Cal. 22 S, L, or LR **$60.00**

[D] STEVENS 88 AUTOLOADING RIFLE
Tubular magazine takes 15 22LR ctgs. 22" bbl., 40½" over-all; wgt. about 6 lbs. Top tang safety. Walnut finished hardwood stock with checkering. Receiver grooved for scope **$47.50**

[E] WEATHERBY MARK XXII RIFLE
A semi-automatic 22-cal. rifle with 24" contoured barrel. 3-leaf folding rear, ramp front sights. Walnut p.g. stock with Monte Carlo comb and cheekpiece, high polish finish. Rosewood p.g. cap and fore-end tip with white line spacers. Single pin release for quick takedown. Shotgun type safety on rear tang. Action can be converted to single shot by thumb-operated lever. Grooved for Tip-Off mount. 42½" over-all, wgt. 6 lbs. **$119.50**

[F] WESTERN FIELD MODEL 836 RIFLE
Autoloading rifle with tubular mag. holding 22 S, 17 L or 15 LR. Shoots all three interchangeably. 20" round bbl. Grooved for Tip-Off mount. One-piece walnut finished p.g. stock. Bead front and step adjustable rear sights. Flash shield over action port protects shooter. Thumb safety. 40" over-all **$45.95**

WESTERN FIELD MODEL 850 RIFLE
Autoloading rifle with 3-way clip hold 7 22 S, L or LR cartridges. 18½" bbl. Thumb operated safety. Bead front, step adjustable rear sights. Streamline walnut finished p.g. stock. 39" over-all **$38.99**

[G] WESTERN FIELD MODEL 846 RIFLE
Autoloading rifle with tubular mag. holding 15 LR cartridges. 18½" round bbl. Crossbolt safety. Walnut finish p.g. stock and fore-end. Plastic buttplate. Bead front and step adjustable rear sights. Wgt. 5¼ lbs. Caliber: 22 LR only. 38½" over-all. **$46.95**

[H] WINCHESTER 290 AUTO RIFLE
Autoloading rifle with tubular mag. holding 21 S, 17 L and 15 LR. 20½" bbl. (16" twist). With square post on ramp front and square notch adj. rear. Walnut finished p.g. stock and fore-end (13⅝"x1¾"x 2¾"). Receiver grooved for Tip-Off scope mounts. Cross lock safety in front of trigger guard. Engine turned bolt. 39" over-all, wgt. 5 lbs. Cal. 22 . . . . **$56.95**

WINCHESTER 290 DELUXE
Same as M290 except: Selected walnut stock with Monte Carlo comb (drop 2¼"), cheekpiece, white spacer, basket-weave checkering, swivels. Gold-plated trigger and safety. **$75.95**

WINCHESTER 190 AUTO RIFLE
Same as M290 except: No checkering, pistol grip cap or buttplate spacer **$47.95**
M190 auto carbine. Same as M190 Rifle, except with barrel band, swivels **$49.95**

BROWNING T-BOLT T-1 REPEATING RIFLE
Straight pull, hinged bolt action rifle. 5-shot clip with single shot adapter. Thumb safety locks trigger and bolt. 22" bbl. Blade ramp front and fully adj. peep rear. Receiver grooved for Tip-Off mount. One-piece walnut p.g. stock (13½" x 1[15]/16" x 3"). Wgt. 5½ lbs. 39¼" over-all. Available with either right-hand or left-hand bolt. Cal. 22 LR (S and L also, with single-shot adapter) **$59.75**

[A] BROWNING T-BOLT T-2 REPEATING RIFLE
Same as T-1 except: 24" bbl.; stock of figured walnut with checkered p.g. and fore-end; wgt. 6 lbs.; 41¼" over-all **$79.75**

[B] HARRINGTON & RICHARDSON 865 PLAINSMAN RIFLE
5-shot clip mag. with exclusive ejector. Thumb safety 22" bbl. Monte Carlo stock in walnut finish. Open rear and blade front sight. Grooved for scope or rear peep sight. Bolt action. 39" over-all, wgt. 5 lbs. Cal. 22 S, L or LR **$37.95**

[C] MARLIN 81-C RIFLE
Bolt action rifle. Tubular mag. holds 26 S or 18 LR. Thumb safety. 22" Micro-Groove bbl. Bead front sight. Walnut p.g. stock with Monte Carlo comb. Grooved for Tip-Off mount. Gold plated trigger. 40½" over-all, wgt. 6 lbs. Cal. 22 S, L or LR **$46.95**
Marlin 300 4x20 scope **13.95**

[D] MARLIN 80-C BOLT ACTION RIFLE
Bolt action rifle. Clip mag. version of the 81-C. 8-shots. Wgt. 5½ lbs. Cal. 22 S, L or LR **$44.95**
Marlin 300 4x20 scope **13.95**

GLENFIELD 20 BOLT ACTION REPEATER
Similar to Marlin 80-C, except: Walnut finish stock, without Monte Carlo, conventional rifling **$36.95**

[E] MARLIN 980 BOLT ACTION RIFLE
22 RF Magnum bolt action rifle. 8-shot clip mag. Thumb safety. 24" Micro-Groove alloy steel bbl. Open rear sight, ramp front sight with hood. Walnut p.g. stock, Monte Carlo comb. Swivels and leather carrying strap. Grooved for Tip-Off mount. Gold plated trigger. 43" over-all, wgt. 6 lbs. **$48.95**
With Marlin 500 3x-7x Variable scope as illustrated **60.50**

[F] MOSSBERG MODEL 342K CARBINE
Bolt action carbine with 3-way adjustable 7-shot clip. 18" "AC-KRO-GRUV" barrel, thumb safety. Walnut-finished p.g. stock, Monte Carlo comb. Hinged moulded fore-end forming a 5" hand grip. Adj. open rear and bead front sights. Sling on left side of stock. Grooved for scope mount. Wgt. 5 lbs. Over-all 38". Caliber S, L or LR **$38.80**

MOSSBERG 340K RIFLE
Same as 342K Carbine except: 24" "AC-KRO-GRUV" bbl. Does not have hinged fore-end. Sling swivels. Tapped for peep sight. Wgt. 6½ lbs., 43½" over-all **$38.80**

MOSSBERG 340B RIFLE
Same as Model 340K except has hooded ramp front sight with bead and aperture, and Mossberg S330 peep with ¼-minute clicks for w. and e. **$48.95**

[G] MOSSBERG 346K RIFLE
Hammerless bolt action rifle with 24" "AC-KRO-GRUV" bbl. Tubular mag. holds 25 S or 18 LR. Thumb safety. Walnut finished p.g. stock with cheekpiece and Monte Carlo comb. Adjustable open rear sight, sporting Front. Grooved and tapped for scope or peep. Detachable sling swivels. Grooved for scope mount. 43½" over-all, wgt. 6½ lbs. **$43.35**

[H] MOSSBERG MODEL 640K CHUCKSTER
Hammerless bolt action rifle. Cal. 22 Magnum rimfire. 24" "AC-KRO-GRUV" barrel. Thumb safety and grooved trigger. Open rear and post front sight. Walnut p.g. stock with cheekpiece and Monte Carlo comb. Sling swivels. 5-shot clip. Wgt. 6 lbs., 44¾" over-all **$48.35**

[J] REMINGTON 581 RIFLE
Bolt action, 5-shot box mag., with 24" bbl. Thumb safety, 6 locking lugs at rear of bolt. Receiver grooved for scope mounts. Bead front, screw adj. open rear sights. Full size Monte Carlo stock. 42⅜" over-all, wgt. 5¼ lbs. 22 S, L, LR **$44.95**
Sling swivels & strap, installed **5.40**
Available in left hand model **49.95**

REMINGTON 582 RIFLE
Same as M581, except: tubular mag. under bbl. holds 20 S, 15 L 14 LR. Wgt. 5½ lbs. **$49.95**

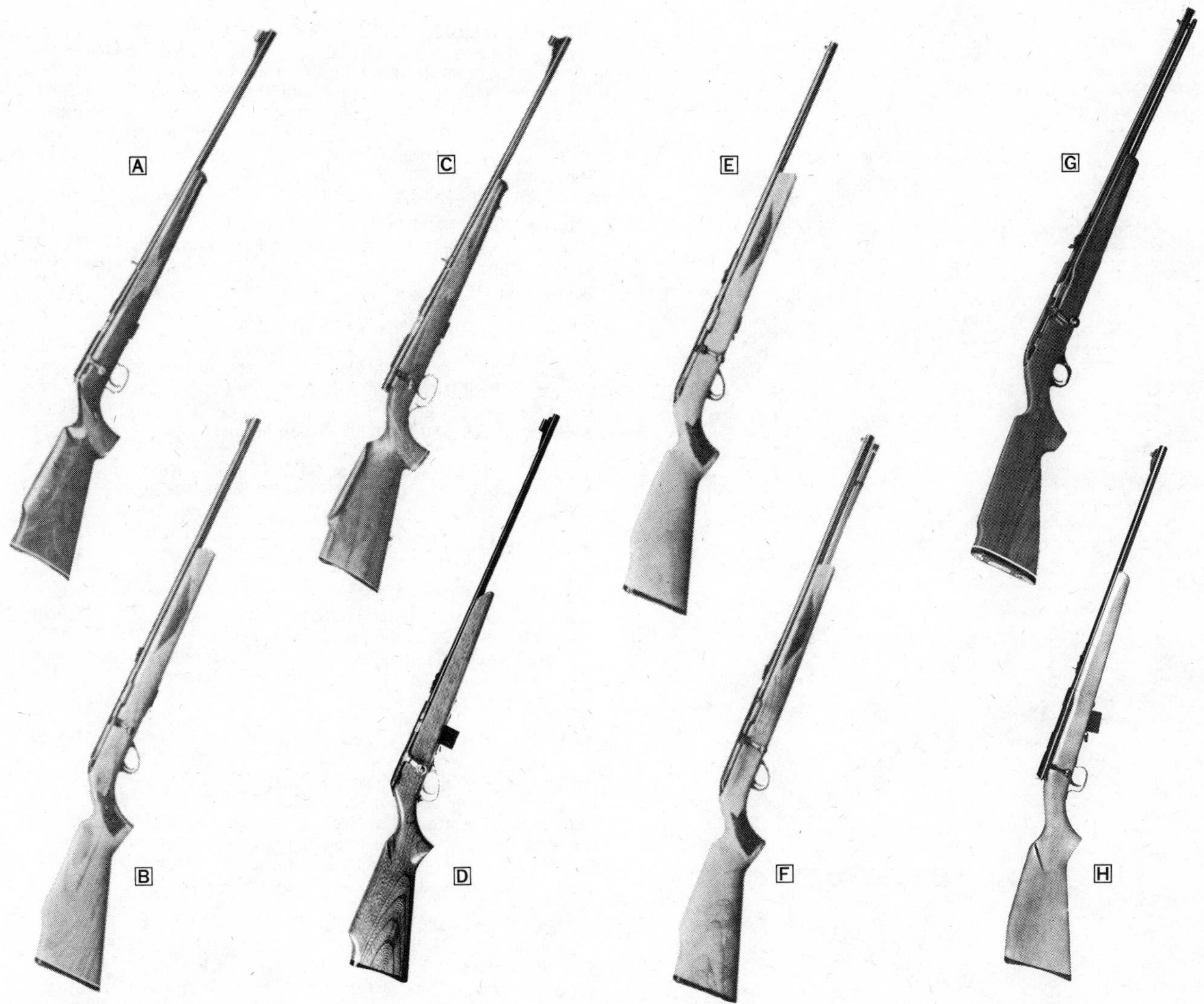

A SAVAGE 164 BOLT ACTION RIFLE
4-shot clip mag. with a 24″ bbl. Single stage adjustable trigger. Hand checkered walnut stock with cheekpiece and schnabel fore-end. Receiver grooved for scope. 42″ over-all; wgt. 6 lbs. Chambered for 22 LR only **$87.50**
Also in cal. 22 RF Magnum (4-shot mag.) as the 164M **92.50**

B SAVAGE 65 RIFLE
Bolt action rifle, cal. 22 S, L or LR; 5-shot clip, 20″ lightweight bbl. Thumb safety locks trigger. Recessed bolt face, double extractors. Monte Carlo walnut stock. Ramp front sight, open rear sight with elevator; grooved for scope mount. Wgt. 5 lbs. 39″ over-all **$42.50**
Available chambered for 22 WMR as 65M **46.50**

C SAVAGE ANSCHUTZ 54 SPORTER
Bolt action 5-shot repeater based on the Match 54 action. Detachable magazine. Trigger adjustable for weight of pull and travel. Wing safety locks firing pin and bolt. 22½″ barrel. Front sight hooded bead on ramp, rear adj. folding leaf, receiver grooved and tapped for scope. Checkered French walnut p. g. stock, with roll-over comb, schnabel fore-end, sling swivels. 22 LR only. Wgt. 6¾ lbs. **$142.50**

D SEARS MODEL 2 RIFLE
Bolt action rifle with 8-shot clip, independent thumb safety, 20¾″ bbl., gold bead front sight, open rear sight. Monte Carlo fluted comb p.g. stock, walnut finished. Sling swivels. Receiver grooved for scope mount. Wgt. 6 lbs., 40½″ over-all. Cal. 22 S, L or LR **$32.99**
Available chambered for 22 WRM as Model 2M **39.99**
With tubular mag. holding 19 S, 15 L, or 13 LR as Model 2T . . **37.99**

E STEVENS 34 RIFLE
Bolt action 22 rifle, 5-shot clip, floating bbl., thumb safety. Recessed bolt face. Fluted comb stock with full pistol grip; walnut-finished; corrugated buttplate. Open rear, post front sights. 4¾ lbs., 20″ bbl. 39″ over-all **$38.50**
Available chambered for 22 WMR as 34M **42.50**

F STEVENS 46 RIFLE
Tubular magazine bolt action 22 rifle; capacity, 22 S, 17 L, 15 LR. Otherwise same as M34 . . . . **$41.50**

G WESTERN FIELD MODEL 842 RIFLE
Bolt action repeating rifle with tubular mag. holding 25 S or 18 LR. Thumb safety. 24″ round bbl. Walnut p.g. stock with Monte Carlo comb; buttplate with white line spacer. Bead front and step adjustable open rear sights. Grooved for Tip-Off mount. Weight 6¼ lbs., 43½″ over-all. Caliber: 22 S, L, LR **$39.99**

WESTERN FIELD MODEL 830 BOLT ACTION RIFLE
Same as Model 842 except 7-shot clip mag. Wgt. 6 lbs. **$33.99**

WESTERN FIELD MODEL 822 BOLT ACTION RIFLE
Same as Model 830 except chambered for the 22 RF Magnum cartridge. 5-shot clip mag. Sling swivels furnished. 44¾″ over-all . . **$42.99**

H WINCHESTER 131 BOLT ACTION REPEATER
Seven-shot mag., walnut finish Monte Carlo stock (13½″x1½″x2½″). Red cocking and safety indicators. Bead-post front sight on ramp, adj. rear. Wgt. 5 lbs. 40″ over-all, 20¾″ barrel. 22 S, L, and LR. **$38.95**

WINCHESTER 141 BOLT ACTION REPEATER
Similar to 131, except tubular magazine in stock, holds 19 shorts, 15 longs, 13 long rifles **$41.95**

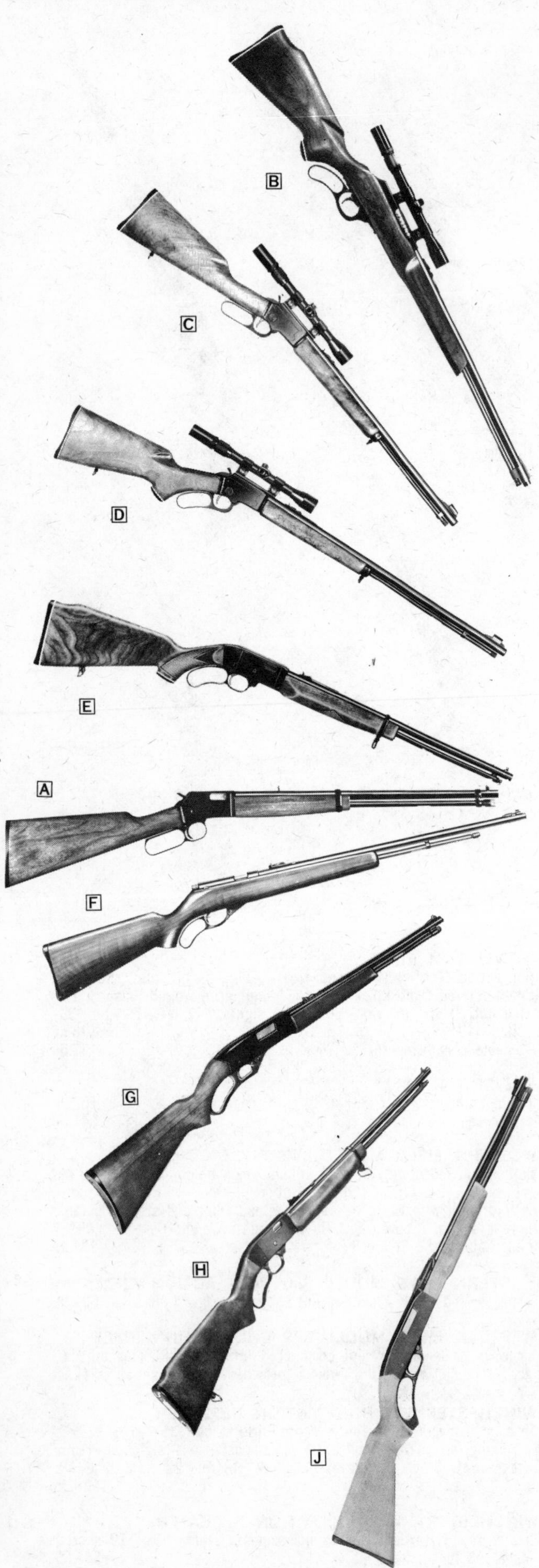

A BROWNING BL-22 LEVER ACTION RIFLE
Tubular magazine holds 22S, 17L or 15LR. Visible Hammer. 20" bbl. Short throw lever travels through an arc of only 33 degrees and carries trigger with it. Disconnect system prevents firing until lever and breech are fully closed. Walnut straight stock and fore-end. Adj. folding leaf rear and raised bead front sights. Receiver grooved for rifle scope. 36¾" over-all, wgt. 5 lbs. Grade I............**$67.50**
Same, except Grade II with gold plated trigger, hand engraved receiver with scroll design..............................**$84.50**

ITHACA 49R SADDLEGUN REPEATER
Lever action carbine with 20" bbl., tubular mag. Cal. 22LR only. Checkered walnut stock, open sights (rear adj. for w. & e.). Rebounding hammer safety, mag. cap. 15 LR. Wgt. 5½ lbs., over-all 37½" **$49.95**

B MARLIN 57M MAGNUM LEVER ACTION
24" Micro-Groove bbl. rifle, 15-shot tubular magazine for 22 WMR cartridges. Walnut stock with Monte Carlo cheekpiece. Open rear and hooded ramp front sights. Wide trigger. Adapter included for Tip-Off mount. 43" over-all, wgt. 7 lbs..............................**$72.95**
With Marlin 500 3X-7X variable scope as illustrated........ **83.50**

C MARLIN 39 LEVER ACTION MOUNTIE CARBINE
Similar to Model 39-A rifle, but with 20" Micro-Groove bbl., straight grip stock. Magazine holds 21 S or 15 LR. 36" over-all, wgt. 6 lbs. **$94.95**
With Marlin 500 3X-7X variable scope as illustrated........**106.00**

D MARLIN 39-A RIFLE
Lever action rifle. Tubular magazine holds 26 S or 19 LR. Visible hammer. 24" Micro-Groove bbl. Gold plated trigger. Micro-Groove rifling. Walnut p.g. stock and fore-end with swivels. Open rear and hooded ramp front sights. Tapped for peep sights. Tip-Off mount adapter and offset hammer spur included. 40" over-all, wgt. 6¾ lbs. Cals: 22 S, L or LR...**$94.95**
With Marlin 500 3X-7X variable scope as illustrated........**106.00**

E MOSSBERG 402 PALOMINO CARBINE
Hammerless lever action carbine with tubular magazine (20 S, 15 L, 13 LR). Walnut Monte Carlo stock, beavertail fore-end. Receiver has removable sideplate; non-glare top finish, grooved for scope mounts. Open rear and bead front sights. 20" round bbl. Grooved trigger. Wgt. 4¾ lbs., 36½" over-all. Cal. 22 S, L or LR................**$62.65**

F NOBLE 275 LEVER ACTION RIFLE
Hammerless, tubular magazine repeater rifle (21 S, 15 LR) with one-piece walnut stock (13½"x1¾"x2¾"), serrated hard rubber buttplate. Short-throw lever, visible straight-line loading. Thumb safety. Patridge type ramp front sight. Open notch rear adj. for elevation. Receiver grooved for Tip-Off scope mount. 24" bbl., 42" over-all, wgt. about 5½ lbs. Cal. 22...**$49.95**

G SEARS MODEL 5 LEVER ACTION RIFLE
Hammerless repeating lever action rifle with tubular magazine holding 21 S and 15 LR ctgs., interchangeably. Receiver grooved for Tip-Off mounts. Cross-bolt safety in front of trigger guard. Walnut finished hardwood p.g. stock. Nickel trigger. Tapered post front sight on ramp; notch rear adj.: for elevation. 20½" bbl., 16" twist, 39" over-all, wgt. about 5 lbs. Cal. 22.......................................**$49.99**
Same, except 5M, cal. 22 WRM, 11 shot.................. **54.99**

H WESTERN FIELD MODEL 865 CARBINE
A short-throw, lever action carbine with tubular magazine holding 20 S, 15 L or 13 LR. 20" round tapered barrel. Walnut finished p.g. stock with Monte Carlo comb; beavertail fore-end; sling swivels and barrel band. Bead front and step adjustable open rear sights. Wgt. 4¾ lbs., 36½" over-all......................................**$53.95**

J WINCHESTER 250 RIFLE
Lever action rifle with tubular magazine (21 S, 17 L or 15 LR). 20½" bbl., 1 in 16" twist; square post front sight on ramp and square notch adj. rear. Walnut finished p.g. stock and fore-end (13⅝"x1¾"x2¾"). Receiver grooved for Tip-Off scope mounts. Cross lock safety in front of trigger guard. Trigger disconnects when lever is moved. Engine turned bolt. Cal. 22, 39" over-all, wgt. 5 lbs. **$59.95**
Same, except M255, cal. 22 WRM, 11-shot.............. **67.95**

WINCHESTER 250 DELUXE
Same as M250 except: Selected walnut stock with Monte Carlo comb (drop 2¼"), cheekpiece, white spacer, basket-weave checkering, swivels; gold-plated trigger and safety **$79.95**
Same, except M255 DL, cal. 22 WRM, 11 shot............**$85.95**

WINCHESTER 150 LEVER ACTION CARBINE
Same as M250 except straight stock (no p.g.), no checkering or spacers. With barrel band and swivels......................**$53.95**

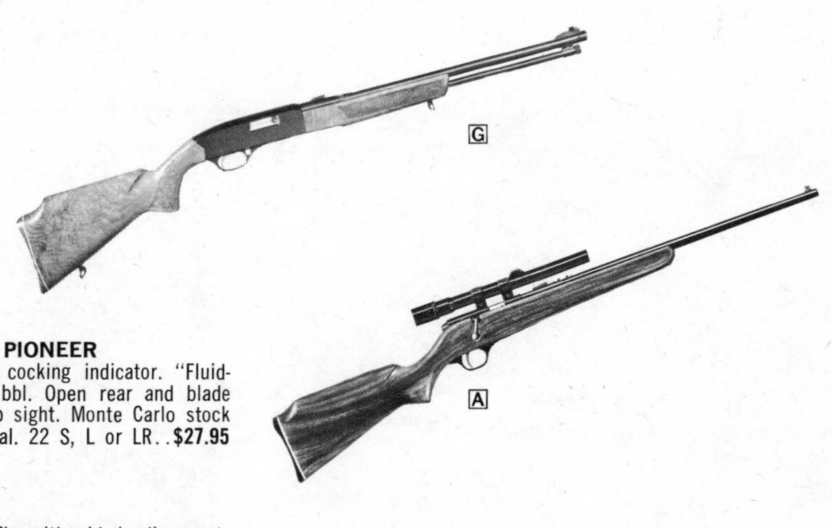

A HARRINGTON & RICHARDSON 750 PIONEER
Single shot rifle. Self cocking bolt with cocking indicator. "Fluid-Feed" loading platform. Thumb safety 22" bbl. Open rear and blade front sights. Grooved for scope or rear peep sight. Monte Carlo stock in walnut finish. Wgt. 5 lbs., 39" over-all. Cal. 22 S, L or LR. . **$27.95**

B HI-STANDARD SPORT-KING RIFLE
Tubular magazine 22 cal. slide action rifle with side-loading port, holds 24 S, 19 L or 17 LR. Checkered Monte Carlo stock, semi-beaver-tail grooved fore-end. Steel-to-steel breech lock-up. Receiver grooved for Tip-Off mount, 24" barrel. 5½ lbs., 41¾" over-all. **$59.95**

C NOBLE 235 PUMP RIFLE
Slide action rifle with tubular magazine (21 S or 15 LR). Hammerless. Thumb safety. 24" bbl. Walnut p.g. stock (13½"x1¾"x2¾") and grooved slide handle. Open rear sight adj. for elevation, bead front sight on ramp. Receiver grooved for Tip-Off mount. Wgt. 5½ lbs., 42" over-all. Cal. 22 S or LR. **$45.95**

D REMINGTON 572 FIELDMASTER PUMP RIFLE
Solid frame, slide action rifle. Tubular magazine holds 20 S or 14 LR, removes to convert to single shot. Streamlined hammerless action. 24" bbl. Cross-bolt safety. Genuine walnut p.g. stock, grooved slide handle. Open rear and bead front sights. Grooved for Tip-Off mount. Wgt. 5½ lbs. 42" over-all. Cal. 22 S, L or LR. **$64.95**

Model 572 BDL Same as the 572 except: p.g. cap, RKW finish, checkered grip and fore-end, ramp front and fully adjustable rear sights. **$74.95**

Model 572 SB Similar to the 572, but has smoothbore bbl. choked for 22 LR shot cartridges. **$74.95**

Sling and swivels, installed. **7.50**

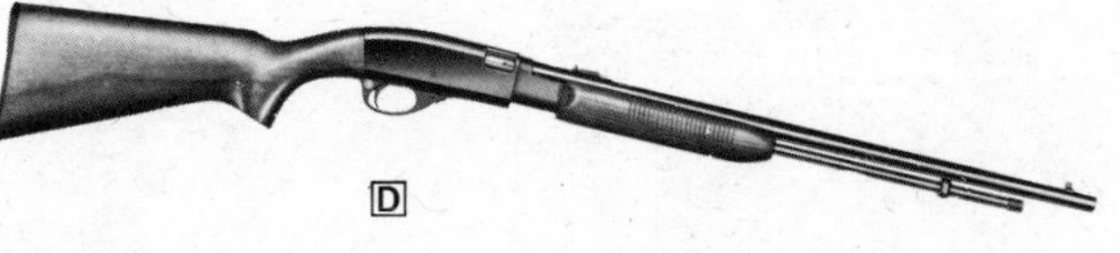

E SEARS MODEL 4T PUMP RIFLE
Hammerless slide action holding 21 S, 17 L, 15 LR ctgs. 20½" bbl. with post front sight on ramp, adj. open rear. Crossbolt safety. Walnut finish stock. 39" over-all, wgt. 5 lbs. **$54.99**

F WINCHESTER 270 PUMP ACTION
Slide action hammerless rifle with tubular magazine; holds 21 S, 17 L and 15 LR. Grooved for Tip-Off mount. Square post front sight on ramp; square notch rear adj. for w. and e. Cross lock safety on trigger guard. Engine turned bolt. 20½" bbl., 1 in 16" twist. Walnut finished hardwood stock (13⅝"x1¾"x2¾") with checkered fore-end. 39" over-all, wgt. 5 lbs. Cal. 22 S, L or LR. **$61.95**

Same, except M275, cal. 22 WRM, 11 shot. **67.95**

G WINCHESTER 270 DELUXE
Same as M270 except: Selected walnut stock with Monte Carlo comb (drop 2¼"), cheekpiece, white spacer, basket-weave checkering, swivels; gold-plated trigger and safety. **$79.95**

Same, except M275 DL, cal. 22 WRM, 11 shot. **85.95**

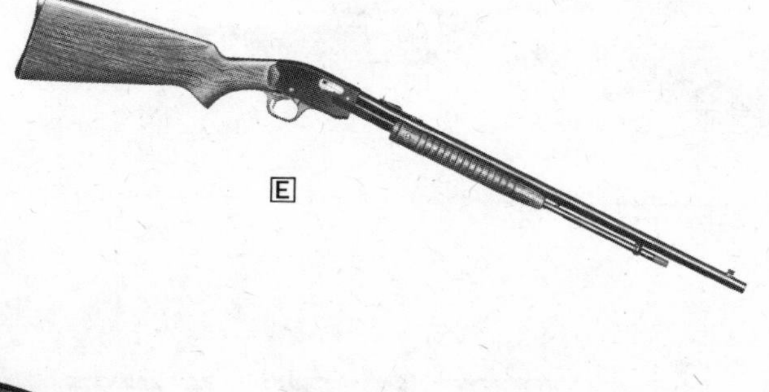

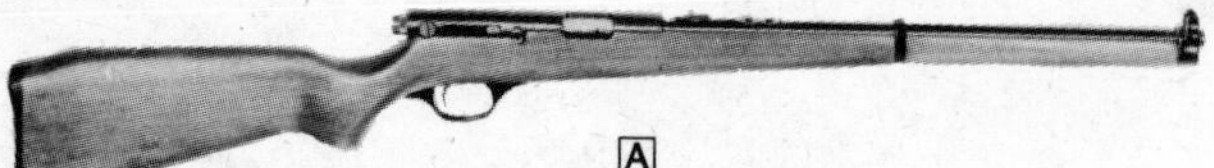

[A] HARRINGTON & RICHARDSON 755 SAHARA
Single shot rifle with automatic extraction, ejection and cocking. 18″ bbl. with protected front and adj. rear sight. Thumb safety. Mannlicher style, walnut finish p.g. stock with Monte Carlo comb. Wgt. 4 lbs., 36″ over-all. Cal. 22 S, L or LR.....................**$26.95**

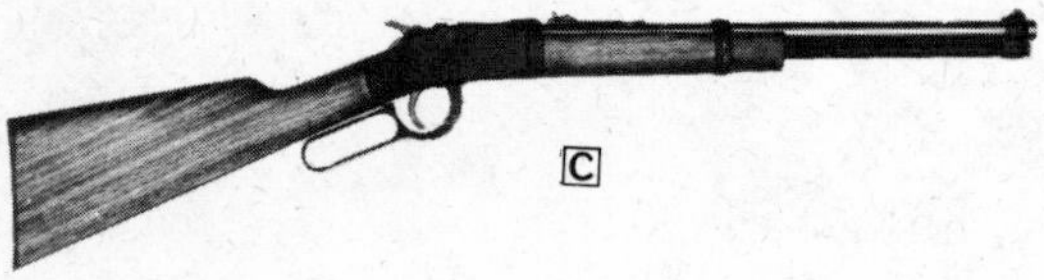

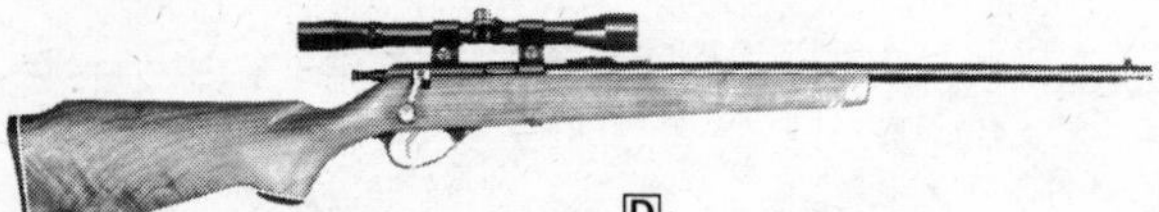

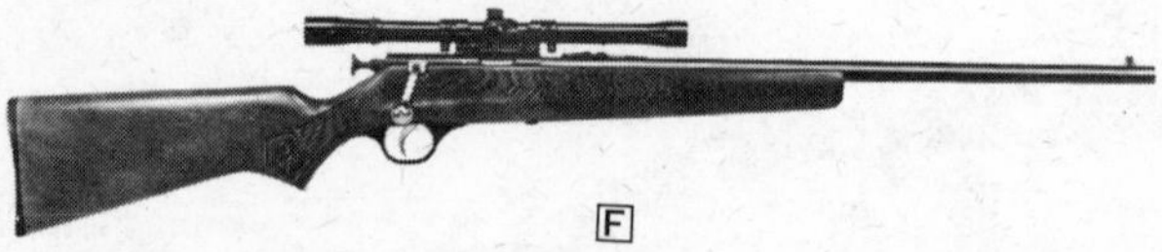

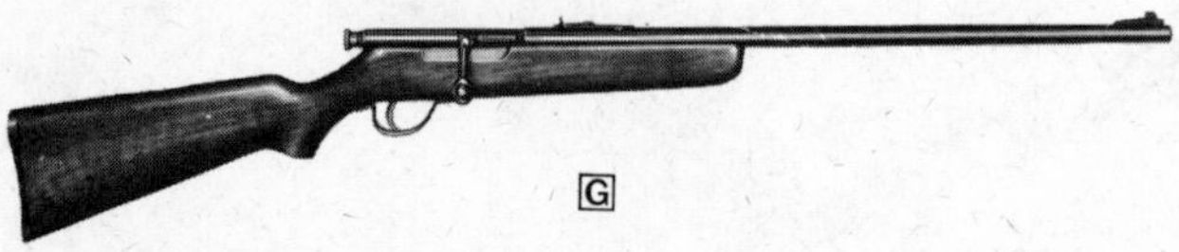

[B] HARRINGTON & RICHARDSON 760 RIFLE
Same as Sahara except: Blade dovetail front sight; Monte Carlo half-length stock; wgt. 4 lbs.............................**$22.95**

[C] ITHACA 49 SADDLEGUN
Single shot, lever action (Martini type) for 22 S, L, LR. Rebounding hammer safety, 18″ button rifled bbl. Walnut stock and fore-end. Wgt. about 5½ lbs., over-all 34½″...........................**$29.95**
Ithaca 49 Saddleguns are also available in a shortened stock, boy's model at $26.95, chambered for the 22 RF Magnum at **$34.95**; with a finely figured walnut stock; sling and swivels at **$39.95**; with extra fancy figured walnut stock with gold-shield inlay; owner's name engraved at no extra charge; receiver is hand engraved by Ithaca's master engraver; gold-plated hammer and trigger, for **$150.00**; or the same in 22 RF Magnum, **$150.00**

[D] MARLIN 101 SINGLE SHOT RIFLE
Single shot bolt action rifle. 22″ Micro-Groove bbl. Walnut finished p.g. stock with Monte Carlo comb. Adjustable rear and bead front sights. Grooved for Tip-Off mount. Cocking piece must be pulled before rifle can be fired. White line spacers. 40″ over-all, wgt. 4½ lbs. Cal. 22 S, L or LR...**$28.95**
Marlin 300 4x20 scope............................... **13.95**

[E] GLENFIELD MODEL 10 RIFLE
Similar to the Marlin 101 except standard walnut finish pistol grip stock..**$24.95**

[F] MOSSBERG M320B RIFLE
Hammerless, single shot, bolt action rifle with 24″ AC-KRO-GRUV bbl. Auto. thumb safety. Walnut finished stock with Monte Carlo comb. Hooded ramp front with bead and aperture, and peep rear with ¼-minute clicks for w. and e. **$39.35**

[G] NOBLE MODEL 222 SINGLE SHOT PIFLE
Single shot bolt action rifle, designed for young shooters. Barrel and receiver made from one piece of steel. Must be manually cocked after bolt is closed. 22″ round bbl.; peep rear sight, interchangeable with V-notch, adj. for w. & e. Walnut finished stock. 13¾″ x 1½″ x 2⅝″). Weight about 5 lbs., 38″ over-all. Cal. 22 S, L or LR..........**$22.50**

[H] REMINGTON 580 SINGLE SHOT RIFLE
Single shot bolt action 22-cal. rifle. American walnut stock, 24″ bbl. with bead front sight, adj. open rear. 6 rear-located locking lugs. Automatic thumb safety. Double extractors. Receiver grooved for Tip-Off mount. Wgt. 5 lbs., 42⅜″ over-all......................**$34.95**

REMINGTON 580 SB
Same as 580 except smoothbore bbl.....................**$39.95**

[J] CHALLANGER 2268 FRONTIERSMAN RIFLE
Single shot lever action (Martini type) for 22S, L or LR. Positive lock hammer safety, 18″ bbl., walnut finish stock and fore-end. Wgt. approx. 5½ lbs., 34″ over-all. Blade front & adj. notch rear sights. Blued finish **$28.95**
Also available in 22RF Magnum (M2269) **$33.95**; with gold plated hammer & trigger in 22S, L or LR (M2271) **$33.95**; or in 22RF Magnum (M2272) **$38.95**.

A

B

C

D

E

F

G

J

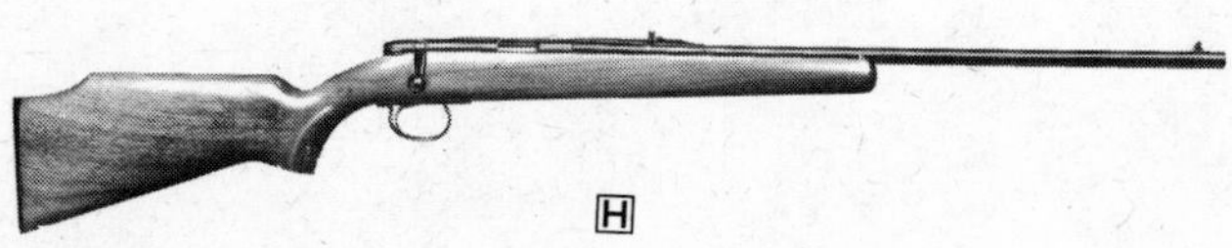
H

C

D

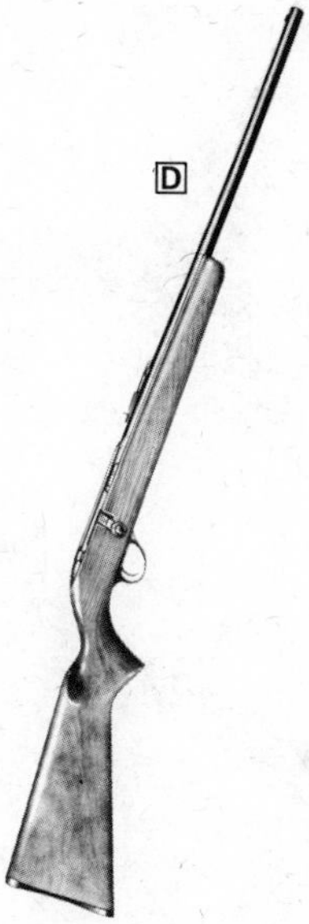

B

E

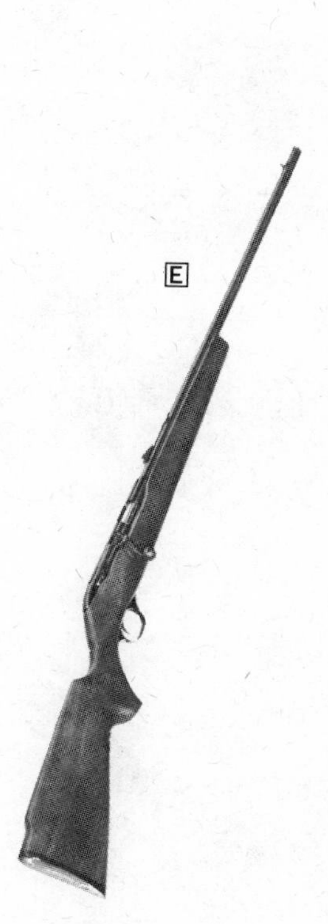

A

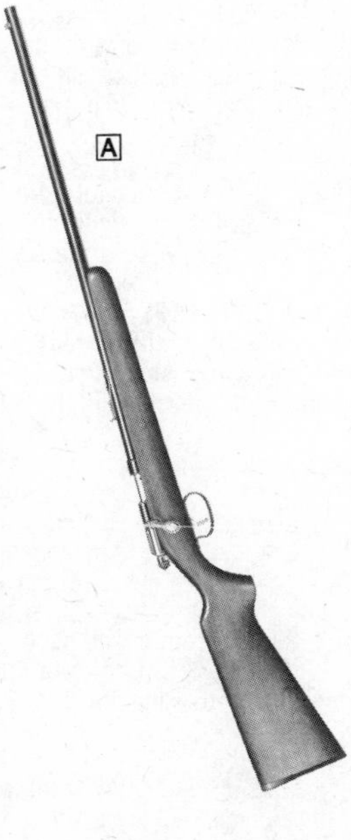

F

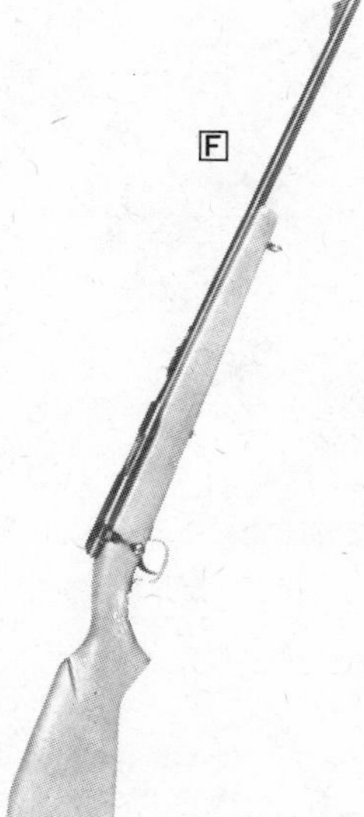

A REMINGTON 514A SINGLE SHOT RIFLE
Single shot bolt action rifle. Positive thumb safety. 24″ round bbl. Walnut-finish p.g. stock. Open rear and bead front sights. Wgt. 4¾ lbs. 41″ over-all. Cal. 22 S, L or LR.......................**$26.95**
Model 514BR. Youth Model. 12½″ stock, 40″ over-all....... **26.95**

B SAVAGE 63 BOLT ACTION CARBINE
Bolt action single shot rifle with a 18″ tapered bbl. Cocks on opening. Automatic safety. Bolt lugs lock in bbl. extension. One-piece, full length, walnut finish stock with sling swivels and corrugated butt-plate (14″ pull). Hooded ramp front and open rear sight with adj. for elevation. Grooved for Tip-Off mount. Wgt. 4 lbs., 36″ over-all. Cal. 22 S, L or LR..**$26.95**
Also available chambered for the 22 RF Magnum as the 63M. **29.95**

C SEARS MODEL 1 SINGLE SHOT RIFLE
Bolt action self-cocking rifle, with cocking indicator automatic thumb safety, bead front sight, adj. rear. Walnut finished birch p.g. stock. 20¾″ bbl., 40″ over-all, wgt. 5 lbs. Receiver grooved for scope mount. Cal. 22..**$20.99**

D STEVENS 73 RIFLE
Single shot bolt action 22 rifle. Safety goes on automatically when bolt is opened. 20″ bbl., 14″ buttstock; wgt. 4¾″ lbs., 38½″ over-all. Walnut-finished p.g. stock. Cal. 22 S, L or LR.............**$23.95**
Available as Youth's Model, **73Y,** with 12½″ stock......... **23.95**

E WESTERN FIELD MODEL 815 RIFLE
Hammerless bolt action single shot rifle. 24″ round bbl. with 8-groove rifling. Automatic safety; straight line loading platform. Walnut finished p.g. stock with Monte Carlo comb; 13″ pull. Bead front and step adj. rear sight; receiver-grooved for scope mount. Weight 5¾ lbs., 43½″ over-all...**$22.94**

F WINCHESTER 121 BOLT ACTION RIFLE
Single shot. Safety engages automatically when bolt is lifted. Red cocking indicator. Receiver grooved for scope mounts. Semi-Monte Carlo, walnut-finished stock 13½″x1½″x2½″. Bead front, adj. rear sights. Wgt. 5 lbs., 40″ long, 20¾″ barrel. 22 S, L, LR.........**$23.95**

WINCHESTER 121 BOLT ACTION YOUTH RIFLE
Similar to 121 Standard, but with stock 12¼″x1½″x2¼″, 38¾″ over-all. Wgt. 5 lbs. 22 S, L. LR...........................**$23.95**

WINCHESTER 121 BOLT ACTION DELUXE RIFLE
Similar to 121 Standard except: fluted comb, ramp front sight, sling swivels, deluxe trigger mechanism. 22 S, L, LR.............**$27.95**

A ANSCHUTZ 1411 MATCH 54 RIFLE

Bolt action single shot target rifle. Bbl. 27½"x1⁵⁄₁₆" dia. Polished action has double locking lugs. Wing type safety locks both bolt and firing pin. Short firing pin travel. Adj. trigger. French walnut prone-style American stock with Monte Carlo comb, cast-off cheekpiece. Checkered p.g., adj. rubber buttplate. Beavertail fore-end has swivel rail and adj. swivel. Receiver grooved for micro. sights. Bases for globe front sight and target scopes. Wgt. 11 lbs. 46" over-all. Cal. 22 LR. No sights **$155.00**

Left hand stocked model without sights **167.00**

B ANSCHUTZ 1413 SUPER MATCH 54 RIFLE

Same as the 1411 Match except: International type stock with thumb-hole. Adj. palm shelf on p.g. Aluminum Schutzen hook buttplate with horizontal, vertical and lateral adjustments. New yoke-type adj. palm rest. Wgt. 15½ lbs., 50" over-all. Without sights **$325.00**

Left hand stocked model without sights **335.00**

C ANSCHUTZ 1410 SUPER MATCH 54 RIFLE

Same as the 1413 Match except: Aluminum hook plate adjusts vertically only, no palm shelf or palm rest **$227.50**

Left hand stocked model without sights **238.50**

D ANSCHUTZ 1408 MATCH 54 TARGET RIFLE

Very similar to M1411, except: Built to meet International Shooting Union standard rifle requirements. Wgt. 10 lbs. with sights; 26" hand-lapped bbl., ⅞" diam., adj. 500 gram (1.1 lb.) trigger, with replacement spring to convert to 3 lb. pull. Rubber buttplate, adj. vertically. Receiver grooved for Anschutz micrometer sight (adaptable to Redfield International and Olympic). Checkered fore-end and pistol grip. Without sights. Cal. 22 LR only **$155.00**

Left hand stocked model, without sights **167.00**

E SAVAGE ANSCHUTZ 64 MATCH RIFLE

Bolt action single shot target rifle. Bbl. 26"x1¹⁄₁₆" dia. Bases for front sight and target scopes. Action grooved for micro. sights. Slide safety, adj. trigger. Monte Carlo stock with cheekpiece and deeply fluted, high comb. Contoured checkered p.g., adj. rubber buttplate. Beavertail fore-end has swivel rail and adj. swivel. Wgt. 7¾ lbs., 44" over-all. Cal. 22 LR rimfire. Without sights **$79.50**

Left hand stocked model without sights **89.50**

F M64-S, with Redfield Olympic sight **$99.75**; left hand model **$109.75**

7 lb. M64 may be ordered, at the same price, to conform with Canadian match regulations or for those who desire a lighter rifle.

SAVAGE ANSCHUTZ MARK 10 TARGET RIFLE

Similar to M 64 except: bbl. 26"x1³⁄₁₆" dia. Walnut-finished stock with cheekpiece, thumb groove, adj. fore-end hand stop and swivel. Fixed buttplate, no blocks for target scope. Wgt. 8½ lbs. Right hand only. Price **$59.95**

ANSCHUTZ Optional Sight Equipment

International micro. sight (⅙-minute click) adj. for w. and e.; slide-on bases fit receiver grooves, adj. for eye relief; interchangeable 1.1mm and 1.2mm peep sight discs. Price $41.80. Rubber eyeshade, slips onto peep sight disc, price $1.80. Globe protects front sight and controls light (sight inserts not included), $9.00. Front sight post-type inserts, set of 5, $1.65; aperture-type, set of 10, $3.30. Complete front and rear sight set includes all items above plus mounting tool .. **$49.75**

G MOSSBERG 144-LS TARGET RIFLE

Bolt action, 7-shot clip. Thumb safety. 26" heavy bbl. Walnut p.g. target type stock with cheekpiece and high comb. Adj. trigger. Mossberg S-331 ¼-minute rear and Lyman 17A front sights. Grooved for Tip-Off mounts. Sling swivels, adj. hand stop. Wgt. 8 lbs., 43" over-all. Cal. 22 LR **$62.45**

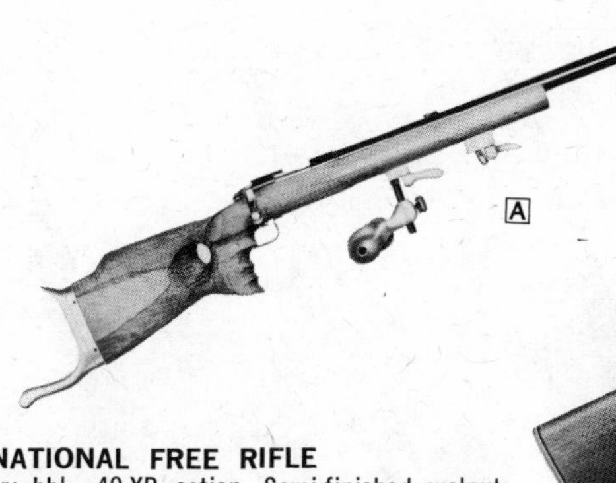

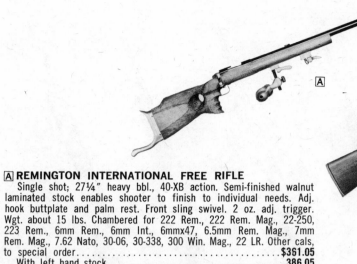

A REMINGTON INTERNATIONAL FREE RIFLE
Single shot; 27¼" heavy bbl., 40-XB action. Semi-finished walnut laminated stock enables shooter to finish to individual needs. Adj. hook buttplate and palm rest. Front sling swivel. 2 oz. adj. trigger. Wgt. about 15 lbs. Chambered for 222 Rem., 222 Rem. Mag., 22-250, 223 Rem., 6mm Rem., 6mm Int., 6mmx47, 6.5mm Rem. Mag., 7mm Rem. Mag., 7.62 Nato, 30-06, 30-338, 300 Win. Mag., 22 LR. Other cals, to special order **$361.05**
With left hand stock **386.05**

REMINGTON 40-XB RANGEMASTER TARGET Rimfire
Bolt action single shot. Loading platform gives straight-line feed. Trigger click adj. for weight of pull. 28" standard or heavy bbl. Walnut p.g. stock with high comb and beavertail fore-end. Adj. swivel base and removable fore-end stop. Redfield Olympic receiver and front sights. Scope blocks. Cal. 22 LR only. Wgt. without sights: Standard, 10 lbs.; Heavy, 12 lbs. 50½" over-all. Either model, no sights **$169.95**
With Redfield sights **204.95**

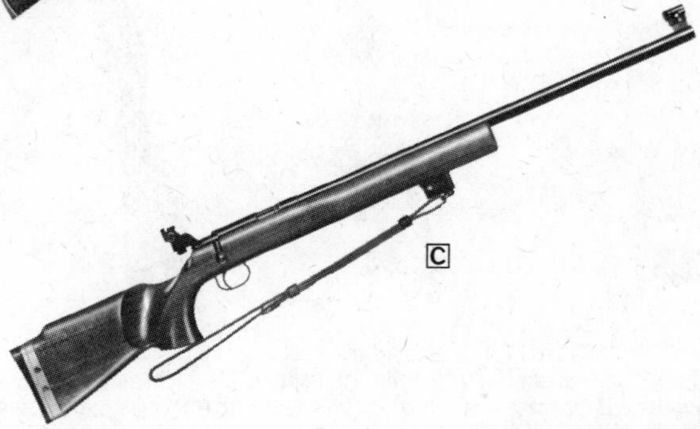

B REMINGTON 40-XB RANGEMASTER TARGET Centerfire
Same as 40-XB Rimfire except: 27¼" bbl., chambered for 222, 222 Mag., 223, 22-250 (14" twist); 6x47mm, 6mm International (12" twist); 6mm Rem. (10" or 12" twist); 6.5mm Rem. Mag., 7mm Rem. Mag. (9" twist); 7.62 Nato 30-06, 30-338, 300 Win. Mag. (10" twist). 2-ounce trigger, $40 extra. Wgt. 11¼ lbs. Heavy, 9¾ lbs. Standard. Single shot. **$224.95**
Factory accuracy requirements (MOA): 222, 222 Mag., 223—.45; 22-250, 6x47mm —.55; 6mm Int., 6mm Rem.—.60; 6.5x55mm —.70; 7mm Mag., 7.62—.75; 30-06, 30-338 — 1.00. 300 Win. Mag. — not available.
Repeating model (5-shot, clip slots) in 222, 222 Rem. Mag., 223, 6x47mm, 6mm Int., 6mm Rem., 22-250, 7.62 . . . . **$244.95**
Extra for stainless steel bbls. **20.00**

C REMINGTON 540X MATCH TARGET RIFLE
Bolt action, single shot; 22LR; 26" bbl.; wgt. 8 lbs., 2 oz. Thumb safety; tapped for iron sights, scope mounts, rear sight bracket. Stock has 12¾" to 15½" pull, 4-way adj. butt-plate & thumb cuts. . . . . **$ 89.95**
With Redfield No. 63 front & 75 rear sights **109.95**
For sling strap with front swivel block assembly installed add **6.95**

D WINCHESTER 52D BOLT ACTION TARGET RIFLE
Cal. 22 LR, single shot. No sights, tapped for front sight base and receiver sight; scope blocks fitted. Walnut target stock with full length accessory channel and adj. bedding device (13⅝"x¼"x¾" with std. wgt. bbl., from line of bore). Non-slip rubber butt pad. Choice of 28" std. wgt. (9¾ lbs.) or heavy bbl. (11 lbs.). 46" over-all **$159.95**

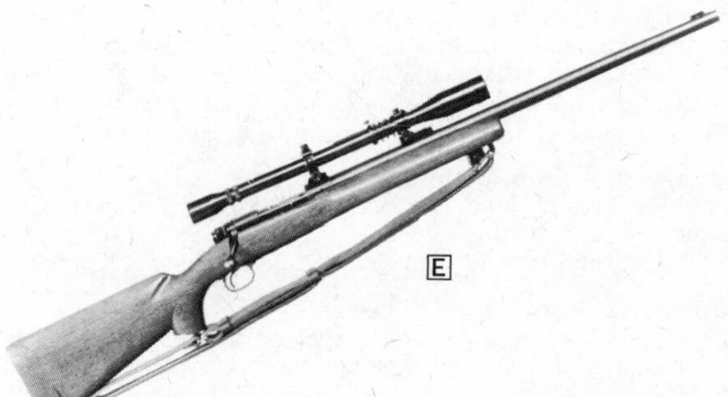

WINCHESTER 52D BARRELED ACTIONS
No stock or sights. Receiver and bbl. tapped for blocks. Standard or heavy bbl **$123.30**

E WINCHESTER MODEL 70 TARGET RIFLE
Marksman walnut stock with high comb, beavertail fore-end; (13¼"x ½"x⅞" from line of bore), adj. front swivel base, aluminum hand stop. No sights; scope bases mounted on bbl. Tapped for front sight base and receiver sight. Serrated rubber butt pad. Clip slot in receiver. Cal. 308, 30-06, 5-shot, 10¼ lbs., 24" free-floating heavy bbl.. (10" twist), 44½" over-all **$204.95**

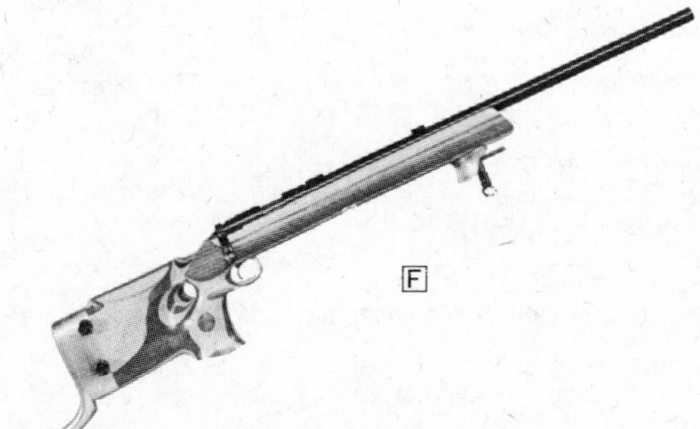

F WINCHESTER 52 INTERNATIONAL MATCH RIFLE
Single shot in 22LR. 44½" over-all; 28" heavy bbl., wgt. 13½ lbs. 1 in 16" twist. Features adj. hand stop and trigger. Receiver tapped for sights and scope bases, scope blocks are included, sling attachment. Laminated thumb-hole stock with butt plate assembly complete with hook and rubber butt-plate. Adj. for cant, horizontal and vertical movement. Has full length accessory track. Aluminum trigger guard with trigger adj. holes. Palm rest assembly, fore-end stop assembly with felt base, detachable swivel and clamping bar. **$350.00**
With Kenyon Trigger, installed **385.00**

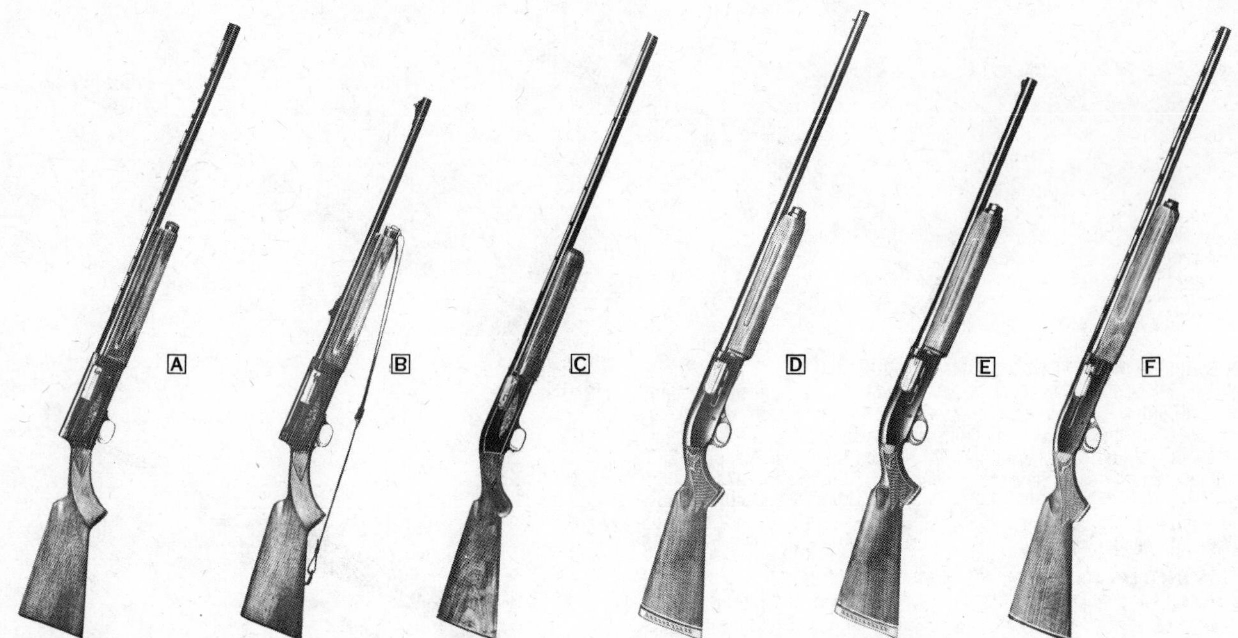

[A] BROWNING AUTO-5 Standard
Gauge: 12 only (5-shot; 3-shot plug furnished). 2¾" chambers.
Action: Recoil operated autoloader; takedown; extra bbls. interchange without factory fitting; mag. cut-off; cross-bolt safety (left-hand available).
Barrel: 26" (Cyl., Imp. Cyl.); 28" (Mod., Full); 30", 32". (Full). Matted top, medium bead sight.
Stock: 14¼"x1⅝"x2½". French walnut, hand checkered half-pistol grip and fore-end.
Weight: 7¾ to 8¼ lbs., depending on barrel.
Features: Receiver hand engraved with scroll designs and border; double extractors; bbl. and guide ring forged together.
Price: ....**$184.75** With vent. rib............**$199.75**

Browning Auto-5 Light 12, 20 and Sweet 16
Same as Std. Auto-5 except: 26" bbls. (Skeet boring in 12 & 20 ga., Cyl., Imp. Cyl., Mod. in 16 and 20 ga.); 28" bbls. (Skeet in 12 ga., Full in 16 ga., Mod., Full); 30" (Full in 12 ga.). Gold plated trigger. Wgt. 12 ga. 7¼ lbs., 16 ga. 6¾ lbs., 20 ga. 6⅜ lbs..............**$194.75**
Price: With vent. rib. Wgt. 12 ga. 7½ lbs., 16 ga. 6⅞ lbs., 20 ga. 6½ lbs. **$209.75**

Browning Auto-5 Magnum 12
Same as Std. Auto-5 except: chambered for 3" magnum shells (also handles 2¾" magnum and 2¾" HV loads). 28" Mod., Full; 30" and 32" (Full) bbls. 14"x1⅝"x2½" stock. Recoil pad. Wgt. 8¾ lbs.
Price: ....**$194.75** With vent. rib. Wgt. 9 lbs....**$209.75**

Browning Auto-5 Magnum 20
Same as Magnum 12 except barrels 28" Full or Mod., or 26" Full, Mod. or Imp. Cyl. 7 lbs....................................**$194.75**
With ventilated rib, 7½ lbs........................... **209.75**

[B] Browning Auto-5 Buck Special
Same as Std. A-5 except: 24" bbl. choked for slugs, gold bead front sight on contoured ramp, rear sight adj. for w.&e. Wgt. (12 ga.) 7⅝ lbs.
Price: **$204.75**

Browning Auto-5 Light 12, 16, 20 or 12 Buck Special
Same as Std. Buck Special except: with gold trigger and of less weight. Wgt. 12 ga., 7 lbs.; 16 ga., 6⅜ lbs.; 20 ga., 6 lbs. 2 oz.; 3" Magnum 12, 8¼ lbs.
Price: **$214.75**
All Buck Specials are available with carrying sling, detachable swivels and swivel attachments for $6.00 extra.

Browning Auto-5 Standard Trap
Same as the Auto-5 Standard except: Stock (14⅜"x1⅜"x1¾"). 30" vent. rib bbl. (Full). Wgt. 8¼ lbs...........................**$199.75**

Browning Auto-5 Light Trap
Same as Standard Trap except: Wgt. 7¾ lbs............**$209.75**

Browning Auto-5 Light Skeet
Same as Light Standard except: 12 and 20 ga. only, 26" or 28" bbl. (Skeet). Wgt. 6¼-7¼ lbs.............................**$194.75**
With vent. rib. Wgt. 6⅜-7½ lbs....................... **209.75**

[C] BROWNING DOUBLE AUTOMATIC
Gauge: 12 only (2-shot).
Action: Short recoil autoloader; takedown. Trigger guard safety.
Barrel: Twelvette: 26" (Mod., Imp. Cyl., Cyl., or Skeet); 28" (Mod., Skeet and Full); 30" (Full). Twentyweight: 26½" (all chokes).
Stock: Hunting and Skeet, 14¼"x1⅝"x2½". Trap, 14⅜"x1⅜"x1¾". French walnut, hand checkered, full p.g.
Weight: Twelvette, 6⅞ lbs.; Twentyweight, 6 lbs.
Features: Soft recoil; visible side loading; shoots all 2¾" loads without adjustment; hand engraved receiver, black and gold finish; crisp, gold plated trigger. Safety in rear of trigger guard, convenient to either hand. Low, ¼" wide vent. rib optional.
Price: Twelvette, matted bbl.....**$229.50** Vent. rib. bbl...**$244.50**
Price: Twentyweight, matted bbl. **244.50** Vent. rib. bbl... **259.50**
Price: Extra Twentyweight bbls., matted rib................ **73.50**
Vent. rib. **88.50**
Price: Extra Twelvette bbls., matted rib.................... **83.50**
Vent. rib **98.50**

[D] HI-STANDARD SUPERMATIC DELUXE AUTOS
Gauge: 12 or 20 (5-shot; 3-shot plug furnished).
Action: Gas operated autoloader (12 ga. 2¾", 20 ga. 3" chambers).
Barrel: 12 gauge, 30" (Full), 26" (Imp. Cyl.), 12 and 20 gauge, 28" (Mod. or Full). Plain barrel.
Stock: 14"x1½"x2½". Walnut, checkered p.g. and semi-beavertail fore-end. Recoil pad. 20 ga. guns have longer fore-end with sloped front.
Weight: 7½ lbs. (12 ga.). 47¾" over-all (12, 28").
Features: 12 ga. uses all 2¾" shells, 20 ga. all 2¾" or 3" shells, including rifled slugs, without adjustment.
Price: Field....**$154.95** Special, with adj. choke (27" bbl.)...**$162.95**
Price: Deluxe Rib, checkered stock, vent. rib, w/o adj. choke **179.95**
Price: Sheckered stock, vent.-rib, adj. choke............... **187.95**
Price: Duck, 3" Magnum 12 ga., 30" Full, recoil pad........ **169 95**
With vent. rib. bbl................................ **189.95**

[E] Hi-Standard Supermatic Deer Gun
Same as Supermatic Auto except: 12-ga. only, 22" plain bbl., Cyl. bore, with rifle sights. Checkered walnut stock and fore-end, recoil pad. Receiver tapped for aperture sight. 41¾" over-all, 7¾ lbs. **$169.95**

[F] Hi-Standard Supermatic Skeet
Same as Supermatic DeLuxe except: 26" Skeet choke bbl.; all external parts high polished; internal parts super finished; better grade American walnut stock (no recoil pad) and fore-end with cabinet finish. Weight about 7½ lbs.................................**$189.95**

Hi-Standard Supermatic Trap
Same features as Supermatic Skeet except: 30" full choke barrel; stock (14⅜"x1½"x1⅞"); recoil pad. Wgt. 8 lbs. 12 ga. only..**$194.95**

ITHACA MODEL 300 AUTOMATIC

Gauge: 12, 2¾" chambers.
Action: Recoil-operated; takedown; interchangeable barrels.
Barrel: Roto-Forged; (Full), 28" (Full or Mod.), 26", Imp. Cyl.).
Stock: 14"x1½x2⅝". Checkered walnut p.g., fluted fore-end.
Weight: About 7 lbs.
Features: Positive cross-bolt safety, automatic magazine cutoff permits changing loads without unloading magazine.
Price: **$139.95**

ITHACA MODEL 900 DELUXE AUTOMATIC

Gauge: 12, 2¾" chambers.
Action: Recoil-operated; takedown; interchangeable barrels, cross-bolt safety.
Barrel: Roto-Forged; 30" (Full), 28" (Full or Mod.), 26" (Imp. Cyl.), all with vent rib.
Stock: 14"x1½"x2⅝". Hand checkered walnut with white spacers at p.g. and buttplate.
Weight: About 7 lbs.
Features: Gold-plated trigger, hunting scene on receiver is deep etched and gold-filled. Gold-plated name plate inlaid in stock.
Price: **$169.95**

[A] REMINGTON 1100 SMALL GAUGE

Same as 1100 except: 28 ga. 2¾" (5-shot) or 410, 3" (except Skeet, 2½" 4-shot). 45½" over-all. Available in 25" bbl. (Full, Mod., or Imp. Cyl.) only.
Price: Plain bbl......... **$174.95** With vent. rib........ **$199.95**

REMINGTON 1100 MATCHED PAIR SKEET

Same as 1100SA Skeet except: 28 and 410 ga. With hard vinyl trunk-type gun case. Identical matched pair numbers in gold scroll on receiver.. **$495.00**

[B] REMINGTON MODEL 1100 AUTO

Gauge: 12, 16, 20 (5-shot); 3-shot plug furnished.
Action: Gas-operated autoloader.
Barrel: 26" (Imp. Cyl.), 26" Mod. in 12 and 20 ga. only), 28" Mod., Full), 30' Full in 12 ga. only.
Stock: 14"x1½"x2½" American walnut, checkered p.g. and fore-end.
Weight: 12 ga. 7½ lbs., 16 ga. 7¼ lbs., 20 ga. 7 lbs. 20 ga. available with mahogany stock, about 6¾ lbs.; 48" over-all (28" bbl.).
Features: Quickly interchangeable barrels within gauge. Matted receiver top with scroll work on both sides of receiver. Crossbolt safety.
Price: .... **$164.95** With vent. rib............ **$189.95**

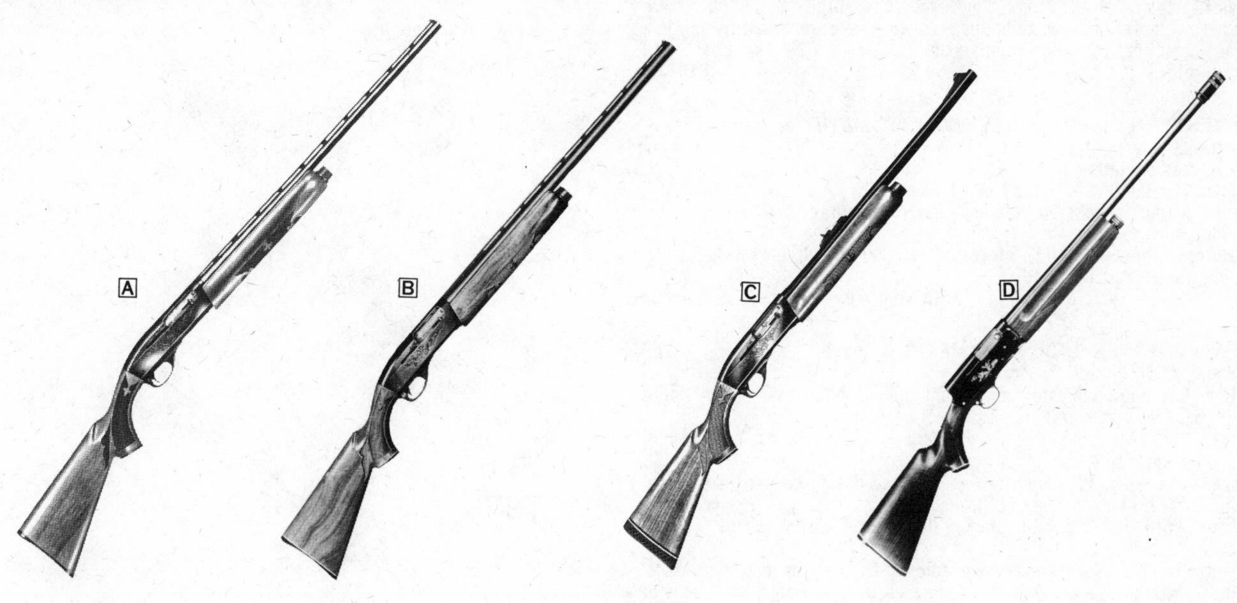

Remington 1100 Magnum

Same as 1100 except: chambered for 3" magnum loads. Available in 12 ga. (30 Full) or 20 ga. (28 Full). 14"x1½"x2½" stock with recoil pad. Wgt. 7¾ lbs.................................... **$179.95**
With vent. rib.. **204.95**

[C] REMINGTON 1100 Deer Gun

Same as 1100 except: 12 ga. only, 22" bbl. (Imp. Cyl.), rifle sights adjustable for w. and e.; recoil pad with white spacer. Weight 7¼ lbs. **$184.95**

Remington 1100D Tournament Auto

Same as 1100 Standard except: vent. rib, better wood, more extensive engraving **$550.00**

Remington 1100F Premier Auto

Same as 1100D except: select wood, better engraving..... **$1250.00**
With gold inlay **1950.00**

Remington 1100 SA Skeet

Same as the 1100 except: 26" bbl., special skeet boring, vent. rib, ivory bead front and metal bead middle sights. 14"x1½"x2½" stock. 20 and 12 ga. only. Wgt. 7½ lbs.
Price: ......**$194.95** 1100 SB (better grade walnut)...... **$219.95**
For Cutts Comp add................................ **25.00**

Remington 1100 TB Trap

Same as the 1100 except: better grade wood, recoil pad. 14⅜"x1⅜"x1¾" stock. Wgt. 8¼ lbs. 12 ga. only. 28" (Mod., Full) or 30" (Mod., Full) vent. rib bbl. Ivory bead front and white metal middle sight.
Price:.......... **$229.95** With Monte Carlo stock........ **$239.95**

Remington 1100 Extra bbls.: Plain **$45.45.** Vent. rib **$68.15.** Vent. rib Skeet **$72.40.** Vent. rib Trap **$72.40.** Deer bbl. **$54.50.** Skeet, with cutts comp. **$94.47.** Available in the same gauges and chokes as shown on guns.

[D] SAVAGE MODEL 750-AC AUTOMATIC

Gauge: 12 only (5-shot; 3-shot plug furnished).
Action: Recoil operated autoloader; takedown; friction ring adj. for loads.
Barrel: 26", plain with Savage Adj. Choke.
Stock: 14"x1¾"x2⅝". Checkered walnut, p.g., fluted fore-end.
Weight: 7¼ lbs. Over-all length 45½".
Features: Decorated alloy receiver, matted top, damascened bolt. Crossbolt safety. Trigger and safety brightly plated. Adj. Choke has click settings from Full to Cyl.
Price: **$154.95**

Savage Model 750

Same specifications as Model 750-AC except: 26" Imp. Cyl. or 28" Mod. or Full barrel without Adj. Choke.................. **$149.95**

[A] Sears Ted Williams 300 Auto
Same as the M75 except: 12 and 16 ga. 12 ga. 27" bbl. (var. choke), 16 ga. 28" bbl. (Mod or Full). Alloy scroll-etched receiver, nickel-plated trigger. Interchangeable barrels for 16 ga. (28", Mod. or Full) $49 extra. Wgt. 12 ga. 7⅛" lbs., 16 ga. 7 lbs. 48⅝" over-all (28" bbl.). 16 ga. .... **$150.00** 12 ga. **$155.00**

Sears 300 Auto
Same as Williams 300 except has walnut finished stock, no vent. rib. In 12 ga., 2¾" chamber only, with variable choke **$124.99**

UNIVERSAL AUTO WING SHOTGUN
Gauge: 12 only (5-shot; 3-shot plug furnished). 2¾" chamber.
Action: Recoil operated autoloader; takedown; extra bbls. interchange without factory fitting; cross-bolt safety.
Barrels: 26", 28" or 30" (Imp. Cyl., Mod., & Full). Vent. rib, Ivory bead front & middle sights.
Stock: 14¼"x1⅝"x2½". Walnut checkered, full p.g. and grooved fore-end.
Weight: About 7 lbs.
Price: **$139.95**

[B] UNIVERSAL DUCK WING SHOTGUN
Same features as Auto Wing except: exposed metal parts are coated with Teflon - S camouflage olive green to avoid reflection; retard rust or corrosion and resist scratches. 28" or 30". Full choke only. **$164.95**

[C] WESTERN FIELD MODEL 600 AUTOMATIC
Gauge: 12 only.
Action: Gas operated, take-down.
Barrel: 30" (Full), 28" (Mod.) or 26" (Imp. Cyl., vent. rib model only).
Stock: Walnut, checkered fore-end and p.g. with cap.
Weight: Not available.
Features: Cross-bolt safety at rear of trigger guard; engraving on receiver; recoil pad installed.
Price: .... **$144.95** With vent. rib **$164.95**

[D] WINCHESTER 1400 AUTOMATIC
Gauge: 12, 16 and 20 (3-shot).
Action: Gas operated autoloader. Front-locking 4-lug rotating bolt locks in bbl. Alloy receiver. Push button action release.
Barrel: 26" (Imp. Cyl.), 28" (Mod., Full), 30" (Full, 12 ga. only). Metal bead front sight.
Stock: 14"x1⅜"x2⅜". American walnut, new-design checkered p.g. and fore-end; fluted comb, p.g. cap, recoil pad.
Weight: With 26" bbl., 20 ga. 6½ lbs., 16, 12 ga. 6¾ lbs.; 46⅝" over-all.
Features: Self-compensating valve adjusts for std. or magnum loads. Bbls. interchangeable without fitting. Crossbolt safety in front of trigger guard.
Price:............ **$154.95** With vent. rib............ **$179.95**

Winchester 1400 Auto Deer Gun
Same as M1400 except: 12 ga. only, 42⅝" over-all with 22" bbl. specially bored for rifled slugs. Ramp front sight, adj. open rear. Stock: 14"x1½"x2⅜". Wgt. 6½ lbs........................... **$164.95**

[E] WINCHESTER 1400 AUTO TRAP
Same as M1400 except: 12 ga. only, 51" over-all with 30" full choke bbl. Stock: 14⅜"x1⅜"x1⅞". Wgt., 8¼ lbs. Metal, middle, red front sights. **$204.95.** With Monte Carlo stock (14⅜"x1½"x2⅛"x 1½"). Extended rib.................................. **$214.95**

Winchester 1400 Auto Skeet
Same as M1400 except: 12 and 20 ga. only, 26" bbl., Skeet choke, wgt. 7½ lbs. Stock: 14" x 1½" x 2½". Metal, middle, red front sights. 46⅝" over-all................................. **$204.95**

Winchester 1400 Extra Barrels: Field, 12, 16, 20 ga. **$34.95**; with vent. rib **$65.95**; Deer Gun **$45.95**; Trap, Skeet............. **$76.95**

Winchester Recoil Reduction Stocks
Spring-loaded, compressible plastic stock (12-ga. only) for M12, 1200, 1400. Drop at comb increased ⅛" on Field models with vent. rib, and on Skeet model. Trap model unchanged. Weight increases ¾ lb. on Field models only.
Ordered with Skeet or trap models, additional............ **$ 5.00**
Ordered with Field models, additional.................. **10.00**
Not available for Deer Gun, Trap w/o Monte Carlo, or Pigeon Grade.

Winchester 1400 field model available in a left-hand version in 12 ga. 28" Mod. only **$159.95.** With vent. rib **$184.95.** Skeet **$209.95** and Trap **$219.95.**

Winchester 1400 with interchangeable choke tubes which are screwed into the barrel and tightened with supplied wrench. Available in 12, 16 and 20 ga. (28") Mod. tube. **Price:** Field **$164.95,** Vent. **$189.95.** Also, L. H. in 12 ga. only plain **$169.95.** L. H. Vent. **$194.95.** Extra tubes in Full, Mod. or Imp. Cyl. **$4.95.** Wrench **$1.50.**

[A] HARRINGTON & RICHARDSON 440 PUMP
Gauge: 12, 20 (3" chamber), 16 (2¾"). 4 shots.
Action: Hammerless, side ejecting, slide action.
Barrel: 26" (Mod. or Full), 12, 16 or 20, 28" (Full), 12 only.
Stock: Walnut p.g. stock and fore-end recoil pad.
Price: **$104.95**

HARRINGTON & RICHARDSON 442 PUMP
Same as the 440 except: 12 ga. (3") 28" Full and 20 ga. (3") 26 Mod. only. Vent. rib., checkered p.g. and fore-end **$139.95**

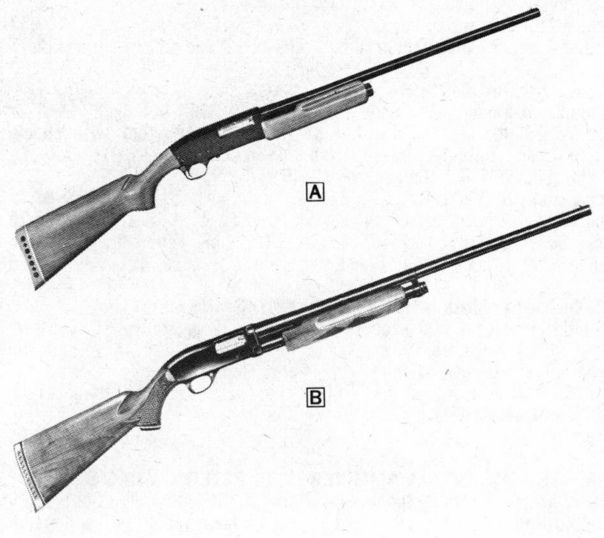

[B] HI-STANDARD FLITE-KING DELUXE PUMP GUNS
Gauge: 12, 20, 28 and 410 (6 shots; 3-shot plug furnished).
Action: "Free-falling" slide action.
Barrel: 12 ga., 30" (Full); 12, 20 ga., 28" (Mod. or Full), 26" (Imp. Cyl.); 410, 26" (Full).
Stock: 14"x1½"x2½". Walnut, checkered p.g. and fore-end. Recoil pad except: 410 & Skeet guns.
Weight: 12 ga. 7¼ lbs., 20, 410 ga. 6 lbs.
Features: Side ejection.
Price: Field **$104.95**
Price: 12 ga., with adj. choke, 27" bbl.................... **112.95**
Price: De Luxe Rib, with vent. rib, w/o adj. choke.......... **129.95**
Price: 12 and 20 ga., as above with adj. choke............. **137.95**
Price: Brush, 12 ga. only with 20" cyl. bbl., grooved fore-end. adj. rifle sights. Stock (14⅜"x1½"x1⅞") 39¾" over-all...... **$119.95**
Price: Brush Deluxe, 12 ga. only with 20" cyl. bbl., checkered p.g. and f.e., sling swivels with sling, adj. peep sight........ **$139.95**

Hi-Standard Flite-King Skeet
Same as Flite-King DeLuxe except: No recoil pad; 26" Skeet choke bbl.; all external parts high polished; internal parts super finished; better grade American walnut stock (14"x1½"x2½") and fore-end with cabinet finish. Wgt. 12 ga. 7½ lbs., 20, 6¼ lbs., 410 ga. 6 lbs. **$139.95**

Hi-Standard Flite-King Trap
Same features as Flite-King Skeet except: 30" full choke; (14⅜"x 1½"x1⅞") has recoil pad. About 7¾ lbs. 12 ga. only...... **$154.95**

[C] ITHACA MODEL 37 FEATHERLIGHT
Gauge: 12, 16, 20 (5-shot; 3-shot plug furnished).
Action: Slide; takedown; bottom ejection.
Barrel: 26", 28", 30" in 12 ga. 26" or 28" in 16 or 20 ga. (Full, Mod. or Imp. Cyl.).
Stock: 14"x1⅝"x2⅝". Checkered walnut capped p.g. stock and fore-end.
Weight: 12 ga. 6½ lbs., 16 ga. 6 lbs., 20 ga. 5¾ lbs.
Features: Ithaca Raybar front sight; decorated receiver; crossbolt safety; action release for removing shells.
Price: ......**$109.95** With vent. rib stock (14"x1½"x2½"). **$134.95**

Ithaca Model 37 De Luxe Featherlight
Same as Model 37 except: checkered stock with p.g. cap; beavertail fore-end; recoil pad. Wgt. 12 ga. 6¾ lbs.
Price:.................... **$124.95**....With vent. rib **$149.95**

Ithaca Model 37 Supreme
Same as Model 37 except: hand checkered beavertail fore-end and p.g. stock, Ithaca recoil pad and vent. rib.................. **$189.95**
37 Supreme also with Skeet (14x1½"x2½") or Trap (14½"x1½"x 1⅞") stocks at no extra charge. Other options available at extra charge.

[D] Ithaca Model 37 Deerslayer
Same as Model 37 except: 26" or 20" bbl. designed for rifled slugs; sporting rear sight, Raybar front sight; rear sight ramp grooved for Redfield long eye relief scope mount. Sling swivels. 12, 16 or 20 gauge **$129.95**
Price: With checkered stock, beavertail fore-end and recoil pad. **139.95**
Price: As above with special select walnut stock.......... **149.95**

[E] MOSSBERG MODEL 500 PUMP GUN
Gauge: 12, 16, 20; 3" (6-shot; 3-shot plug furnished).
Action: Slide, takedown; safety on top of receiver.
Barrel: 26" (Imp. Cyl.), 28" (Full or Mod.), 30" (Full), 12 ga. only. Also 12 ga. 18½" cylinder, for police only).
Stock: 14"x1½"x2½". Walnut p.g., extension fore-end. Recoil pad. 13 oz. steel plug furnished for use with Magnum barrel.
Weight: 12 ga. 6¾ lbs., 45¼" over-all (26" bbl.).
Features: Easy interchangeability of barrels; side ejection; disconnecting trigger makes doubles impossible; straight-line feed.
Price: Standard barrel **$87.75**
Price: C-lect Choke, 3" Mag., 24" Slugster bbls. **93.25**
Price: Extra barrel, 2¾" chamber **20.75**
Price: Extra Magnum, C-Lect Choke or Slug. bbl. **27.00**

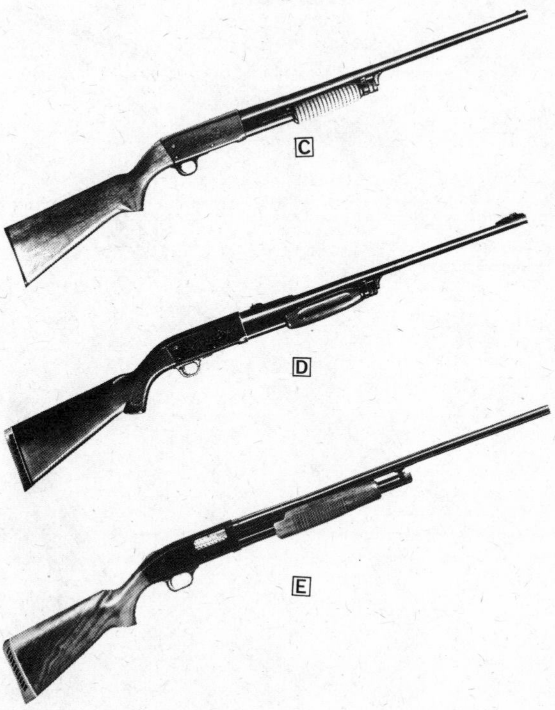

Mossberg Model 500 Super Grade
Similar to the Model 500 except: vent. rib bbls. in 12 ga. (2¾") or 20 ga. (3"); 26" (Skeet), 28" (Mod., Full), and 30" Full (12 ga. only) 2¾" or 3" mag. Checkered p.g. and fore-end stock with fluted comb and recoil pad (14"x1½"x2½").
Price: 12 or 20 ga. $107.95
Price: 12 ga. 3" Magnum or C-Lect choke 12 and 20 ga..... 112.75

Mossberg Model 500E
Similar to Model 500 except: 410 bore only, 26" bbl. (Full, Mod. or Imp. Cyl.); holds six 2¾" or five 3" shells. Walnut stock with checkered p.g. and fore-end, fluted comb and recoil pad (14"x1¼"x2½"). Weight about 5¾ lbs., length over-all 46".
Price: Standard barrels ....$ 87.75
Price: C-Lect Choke barrel 93.25
Price: Super Grade, 26" Full, Mod., or Skeet bbl., vent rib.... 107.45
Price: Super Grade, C-Lect Choke and vent rib.............. 112.75

[A] Mossberg Model 500ATR Pigeon Grade
Similar to Model 500 except: Trap gun in 12 ga. only, 30" vent rib bbl. (Full only), decorated receiver of forged lightweight alloy. Bolt and carrier engine-turned. Walnut Monte Carlo stock, custom checkered p.g. and fore-end with recoil pad (14½"x1½"x1½"x2"). Length over-all, 49¾", wgt. about 7¾ lbs.
Price: $134.00

MOSSBERG 500AA ANNIVERSARY PIGEON GRADE
Similar to the 500 Super Grade except: 12 ga. only. Gold inlay, roll-engraved receiver and selected, hand checkered American walnut stock and fore-end. All with red bead front and middle sights. Receiver and p.g. cap with "50th Anniversary" emblem.......$150.00

[B] NOBLE 66 PUMP GUNS
Gauge: 12 ga. (3" chamber), 16 ga. (2¾" chamber). 6-shot, 3-shot plug furnished.
Action: Slide, solid frame, side ejection, tang safety.
Barrel: 28" (Mod. or Full)
Stock: Walnut p.g. (13¾" x 1¾" x 2¾"), with impressed checkering.
Weight: About 7½ lbs. 48" over-all.
Features: Key Lock, protects against unauthorized use. Damascened bolt.
Price: M66XLP ....$ 86.92
With Vary-Check Choke, checkered grip recoil pad, as M66 CLP 93.79
With vent. rib, checkered grip recoil pad, as M66 RLP.... 109.06
Same as M66 RLP, with Vary-Check Choke, as M66 RCLP... 115.94

[C] NOBLE 166L DEERGUN
Same as Model P66XLP except: 24" rifled slug bbl. guaranteed to shoot 3" groups at 100 feet. Hard rubber buttplate. Sling swivels and detachable carrying strap. Lyman adj. peep rear sight and post ramp front. Wgt. 7⅜ lbs., 44" over-all.........................$101.40

[D] & [E] NOBLE 602 AND 70 SERIES PUMP GUNS
Gauge: 20 (as 602 Series), 410 (as 70 Series), 3" chambers, 5-shot; 3-shot plug furnished.
Action: Slide, solid frame; tang safety; side ejection.
Barrels: 20 ga., 28", 410 26" (Mod. or Full).
Stock: Walnut, p. g. (13¾" x 1½" x 2⅝"), impressed checkering on fore-end.
Weight: About 6½ lbs. (20 ga.), 6 lbs. (410 ga.) 48" over-all (20 ga.).
Features: Key Lock protects against unauthorized use. Damascened bolt.
Price: M602XLP $86.92
With Vary Choke, recoil pad, checkered grip, as M602 CLP, ...$93.79
With vent rib, recoil pad, checkered grip, as M602 RLP, ...$109.06
Same as RLP Models with Vary Choke, as RCLP..........$115.94
Same as RCLP Models, with alloy bbls. wgt. about 4½ lbs., as M662, 20 ga. only..........$113.75 Vent. rib..........$135.75
410 ga. 70XL **$84.68**, 70CL, **$90.57**, 70RL **$106.85**, and 70RCL **$113.06.**

[F] REMINGTON 870 WINGMASTER PUMP GUN
Gauge: 12, 16, 20 (5-shot; 3-shot wood plug. 12 oz. Vari-Weight steel plug furnished in 12 ga.).
Action: Takedown, slide action.
Barrel: 12, 16, 20 ga., 36" (Imp. Cyl.); 28" (Mod. or Full); 23 and 20 ga., 26"(Mod.), 12 ga., 30" (Full).
Stock: 14"x1⅝"x2½". Checkered walnut, p.g.; fluted extension fore-end; fitted rubber recoil pad.
Weight: 7 lbs., 12 ga. (7¾ lbs. with Vari-Weight plug); 6¾ lbs., 16 ga.; 6½ lbs., 20 ga. 48½" over-all (28" bbl.).
Features: Double action bars, crossbolt safety. Receiver machined from solid steel. Hand fitted action.
Price: Plain bbl..........$109.95 Vent. rib..........$134.95
Price: Riot gun, 18" or 20" Riot bore.................... 99.95
Price: Riot gun, 20" Imp. Cyl., rifle sights................ 109.95

[G] Remington 870 Magnum
Same as M870 except: 3" chamber, full choke. Plain bbl.; 12 ga., 30" or 20 ga., 28". Vent. rib bbl.; 12 ga., 30", 20 ga., 28" or 30.". Recoil pad. Wgt. 12 ga. 8 lbs. 20 ga. 7½ lbs.
Price: Plain bbl..........$129.95 Vent. rib bbl..........$154.95

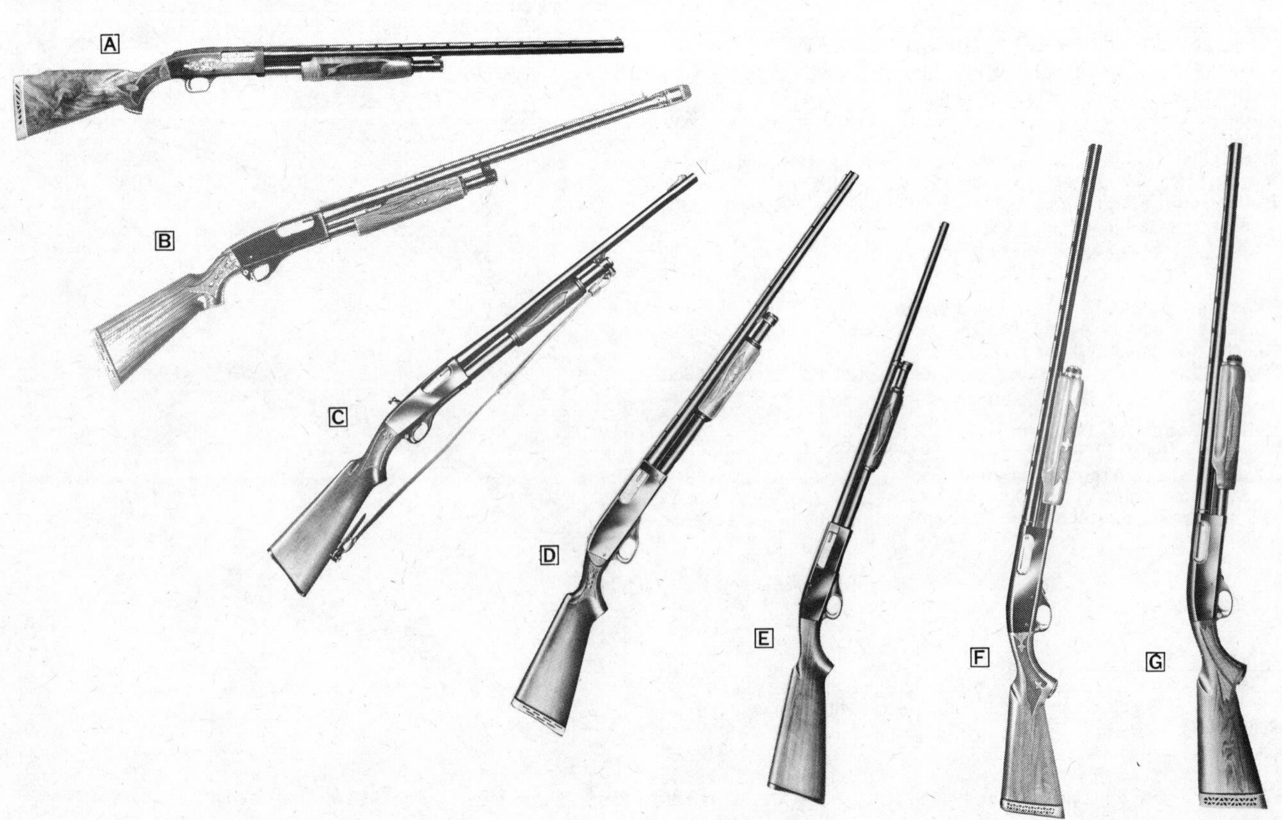

A Remington Model 870 Brushmaster Deluxe
Carbine version of the M870 with 20" bbl. (Imp. Cyl.) for rifled slugs. 40½" over-all, wgt. 6½ lbs. Recoil pad. Adj. rear, ramp front sights $129.95

Remington Model 870 Standard Deer Gun
Same as Brushmaster except: lacquer finish, no checkering or grip cap; short fore-end $109.95

B Remington 870 SA Skeet
Same as the M870 except: 26" bbl. Skeet bored. Vent. rib with ivory front and white metal middle beads. 14"x1⅝"x2½" stock with rubber recoil pad. 12 or 20 ga. only $139.95
870 SC (better grade and finish of walnut. Hand checkering) 214.95
Add **$25.00** for Cutts comp.

C Remington 870 TB Trap
Same as the M870 except: 12 ga. only, 28" (Mod. Full) or 30" (Mod., Full) vent. rib. bbl., ivory front and white metal middle beads. Special sear, hammer and trigger assy. 14⅜"x1½"x1⅞" stock with recoil pad. Hand fitted action and parts. Wgt. 8 lbs......... $174.95
With Monte Carlo stock 184.95
870 TC (better Hand checkering) 249.95
With Monte Carlo stock 259.95

Remington 870D Tournament
Same as 870 except: better walnut, hand checkering. Engraved receiver & bbl. Vent.-rib. Stock dimensions to order............ $525.00

Remington 870F Premier
Same as M8700, except select walnut, better engraving.... $1250.00
With gold inlays 1950.00

Remington 870 Extra Barrels
Plain **$35.70.** Vent. rib **$58.75.** Vent. rib Skeet **$61.55.** Vent. rib Trap **$61.55.** With rifle sights **$46.10.** Available in the same gauges and chokes as shown on guns.

D SAVAGE MODEL 30 PUMP GUN
Gauge: 12, 20 and 410, 5-shot (410, 4-shot) 3-shot plug furnished. All gauges chambered for 3" Magnum shells.
Action: Slide, hammerless, take-down; side ejection; cross-bolt safety.
Barrel: Vent. rib. 12, 20 ga., 26" (Imp. Cyl.); 28" (Mod. or Full); 12 ga., 30" (Full); 410, 26" (Mod. or Full).
Stock: 14"x1½"x2½". Walnut, checkered p.g., grooved extension fore-end, recoil pad.
Weight: 7 lbs. (410, 6¼ lbs.). Over-all 49½" (30" bbl.).
Features: Decorated lightweight receiver; gold plated trigger and safety; damascened bolt. Stainless steel front and middle bead sights.
Price: $107.50

Savage Model 30-L
Same as M30 except: 12 ga. only, 3" chamber, left-hand action and safety: 26" (Imp. Cyl.), 28" (Mod. or Full), 30" (Full) bbls. **$104.50**

Savage Model 30-T
Same specifications as 12 ga. M30 except: 30" Full choke bbl. with 3" chamber; Monte Carlo stock with trap dimensions (14⅝"x1½"x 1½"x2¼"). Recoil pad. Over-all 50". 8 lbs................. $112.50

E SEARS MODEL 200 PUMP GUN
Gauge: 12, 16 and 20 (3" chamber) (5-shot; 2-shot plug installed).
Action: Slide, front-locking rotating bolt.
Barrel: 28" Full or Mod., 26" Imp. Cyl. 12 ga only.
Stock: Walnut finished buttstock and fore-end; recoil pad.
Weight: About 6½ lbs.; 48⅝" over-all (28" bbl.).
Features: Alloy receiver, non-glare serrated top; cross-bolt safety. Interchangeable bbls., no special tools required, $24 extra.
Price: $79.99
Price: 20 gauge with 27" barrel and variable choke........... 84.99
Price: 410 gauge with 26" barrel (Full) 69.99

Sears Ted Williams 200 Pump
Same as Standard 200 except: 12 and 20 ga. only; vent. rib; 3-shot capacity; engine-turned bolt, checkered p.g. and fore-end; p.g. cap, whiteline spacers and name plate. Wgt. 12 ga. 6⅞ lbs., 20 ga. 6⅝ lbs. **$115.00.** With var. choke. **$120.00.** 410 ga. 26" (Full), wgt. 6 lbs. as M21 .... $95.00

F SEARS MODEL 21 PUMP GUN
Gauge: 20 and 410 (5-shot; 3-shot plug furnished).
Action: Solid frame pump, short stroke; cross-bolt safety.
Barrel: 20 ga. 28" (Full, Mod.), 410 26" (Full).
Stock: Walnut finish, p.g. 14½"x1½"x2½", recoil pad.
Weight: About 6 lbs.
Features: Handles both 2¾" and 3" loads; LH safety available.
Price: 20 ga. .... **$68.50** 410 ga. **$65.50**
Price: 20 ga. with 27" bbl. and adj. choke.................. 73.50

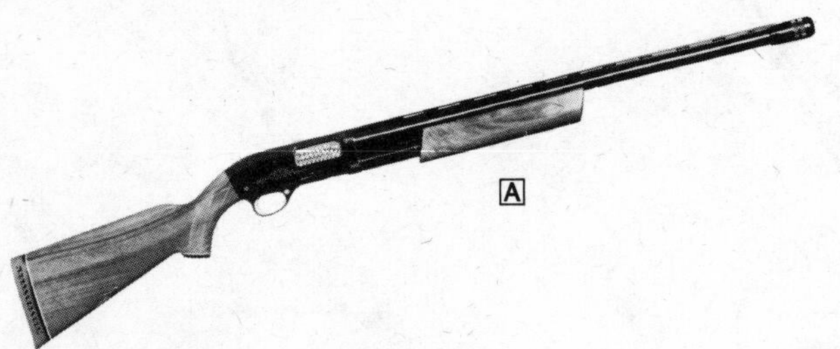

A

A SEARS TED WILLIAMS MODEL 21 PUMP GUN

Gauge: 410 (5-shot; 3-shot plug furnished).
Action: Solid frame pump, short stroke; cross-bolt safety.
Barrel: 26" (Full). Vent. rib.
Stock: 14½"x1½"x2¼". Checkered walnut, p.g., white line recoil pad and p.g. cap. Inset initial plate.
Weight: About 6 lbs.
Features: Engine turned bolt; LH safety available; handles both 2½" and 3" loads; brass bead front and middle sight.
Price: **$92.50**

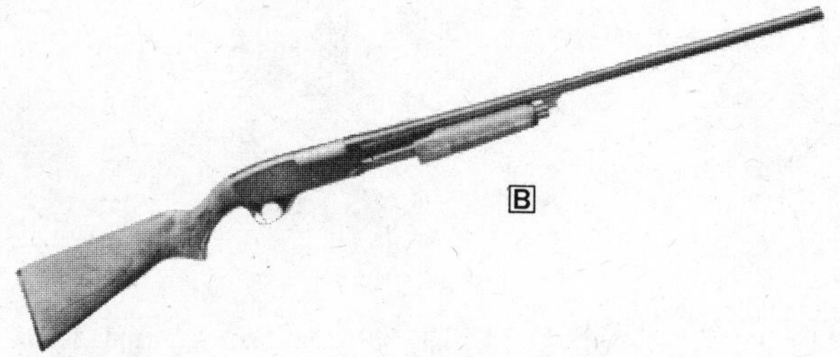

B

B STEVENS MODEL 77 PUMP SHOTGUN

Gauge: 12, 16, 20, 410, 5-shot (410, 4-shot); 3-shot plug furnished. All but 16 ga. chambered for 3" Mag.
Action: Slide, solid frame; side ejection; crossbolt safety.
Barrel: Plain. 12, 16, 20 ga. 26" (Imp. Cyl.); 28" (Mod. or Full); 12 ga. 30" (Full); 410, 26" (Mod. or Full).
Stock: 14"x1½"x2½". Full p.g., grooved extension fore-end.
Weight: 6¾ lbs. (410, 6¼ lbs.)
Features: Alloy steel receiver. Over-all 49½" (30" bbl.).
Price: **$86.95**

Stevens Model 77-AC
Same as Model 77 except: with Savage Adjustable Choke and recoil
Price: **$93.50**

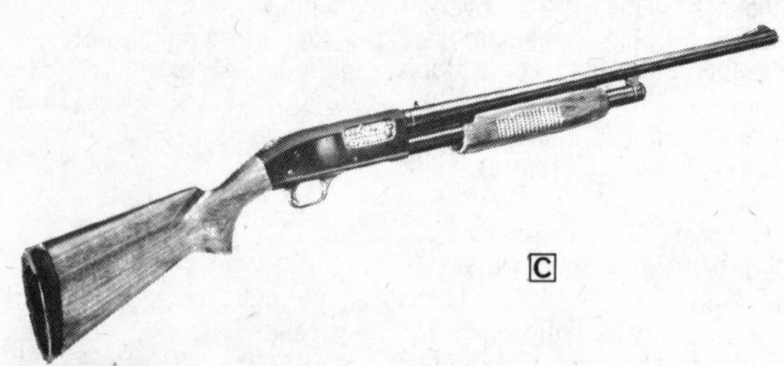

C

C WESTERN FIELD 550 PUMP SHOTGUN

Gauge: 12, 20 and 410.
Action: Slide action, takedown: top tang safety.
Barrel: 12 ga., 30" (Full), 28" (Mod.). 20 ga., 28" (Ful or Mod.). 410, 26" (Full).
Stock: Walnut finished p.g. stock, plastic buttplate, serrated fore-end.
Weight: Not available.
Features: Straight-line feed, interchangeable bbls., trigger disconnector prevents doubling.
Price: .... **$72.95** 410 (with rubber buttplate).... **$81.95**
As above, but with variable choke in 12 or 20 ga. only...... **86.95**
Slug gun with 24 bbl. without choke...................... **87.95**
Magnum 12 ga., 30" bbl. (Ful choke)..................... **87.95**
Trap gun, 30" (Full) bbl., vent. rib and trap stock, 12 ga. only **121.95**
Vent rib models available, fixed or variable choke as above.. **99.75**
to **102.95**

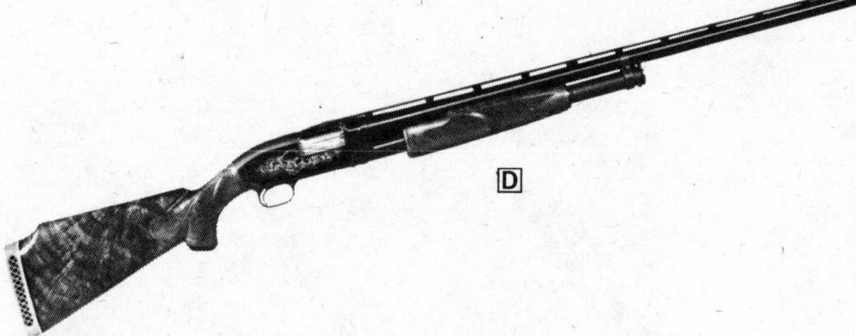

D

D WINCHESTER 12 SUPER PIGEON PUMP GUN

Gauge: 12 only, 6-shot (2-shot plug installed).
Action: Slide, one-piece receiver, takedown, side ejection.
Barrel: 26", 28", 30", floating vent. rib, any standard choke.
Stock: Full fancy American walnut, dim. to order within mfg. limits, hand-finished, "A" checkering or carving (see Win. catalog), Monte Carlo, cheekpiece or offset avail. at extra charge.
Features: Receiver engraved, "1A," "1B," or "1C" type (see Win. catalog). Working parts hand fitted.
Weight: 7¾ lbs.
Price: **$875.00**

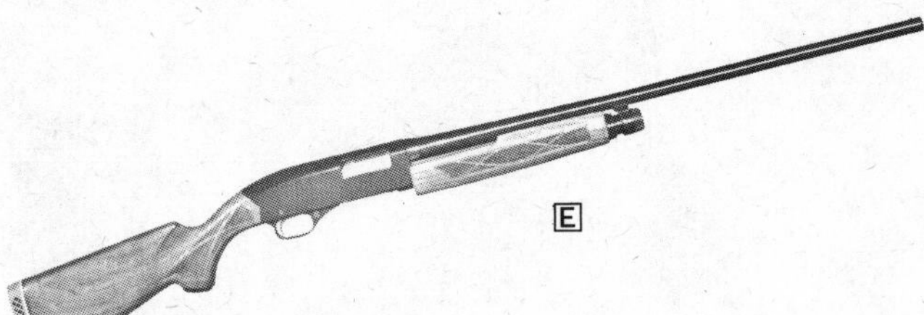

E

E WINCHESTER 1200 FIELD PUMP GUN

Gauge: 12, 16 and 20 (5-shot; 3-shot plug installed).
Action: Slide; front locking 4-lug rotating bolt locks into bbl. Alloy receiver, cross-bolt safety in front of trigger guard. Take-down.
Barrel: 26" (Imp. Cyl.), 28" (Mod., Full) and 30" Full (12 ga. only). Metal bead front sight.
Stock: 14"x1⅜"x2⅜". American walnut with new-design checkered p.g. and fore-end; fluted comb, recoil pad. Steel p.g. cap.
Weight: 12 ga. 6½ lbs. with 26" bbl. 46⅝" over-all.
Price:.................. **$109.95** With vent. rib......... **$134.95**

Winchester 1200 Skeet
Same as M1200 except: 12 and 20 ga., 26" vent. rib bbl., b. t. fore-end, metal, middle red front sights...................... **$194.95**

Winchester 1200 Trap
Same as M1200 except: 12-ga. only, 30" Full choke vent. rib bbl., 50⅝" over-all. 14⅜"x1⅜"x1⅞" stock with recoil pad, b. t. fore-end. Metal, middle, red front sights.......................... **$194.95**
With Monte Carlo stock, 13⅜"x1½"x2⅛"x1½".......... **204.95**

Winchester 1200 Field 3" Magnum
Same as 1200 except: 12 and 20 ga. only, 2¾" or 3" shells, 28" and 30" full choke bbls., 7¾ lbs. with 28" bbl., 48⅝" over-all.
Price:.................. **$129.95** With vent. rib........ **$154.95**

Winchester 1200 Deer Gun
Same as M1200 except: 12 ga. only, 22" bbl. bored for rifled slugs; rifle-type sights, rear adj. for e. only.................... **$119.95**

Winchester 1200 Extra Barrels: Field and Riot w/o sights, 12, 16, 20 ga. **$32.95.** Field with vent. rib, 12, 16, 20 ga. **$63.95.** Riot with sights and Deer Gun, 12 ga. **$43.95.** Trap, 12 ga., Full choke 30" only, Skeet, 12, 20 ga. 26" only............................... **$74.95**
Winchester 1200 with interchangeable choke tubes which are screwed into the barrel and tightened with supplied wrench. Available in 12, 16 and 20 ga. (28") Mod. tube. Price: Field **$1 9 95** Vent. rib **$144.95.** Extra tubes in Full, Mod. or Imp. Cyl. **$4.95.** Wrench **$1.50.**

Winchester Recoil Reduction Stocks
Spring-loaded, compressible plastic stock (12-ga. only) for M12, 1200, 1400. Drop at comb increased ⅛" on Field models with vent.-rib, and on Skeet model. Trap model unchanged. Weight increases ¾ lb. on Field models only.
Ordered with Skeet or trap models, additional............. **$ 5.00**
Ordered with Field models, additional.................... **10.00**
Not available for Deer Gun, Trap w/o Monte Carlo, or Pigeon Grade.

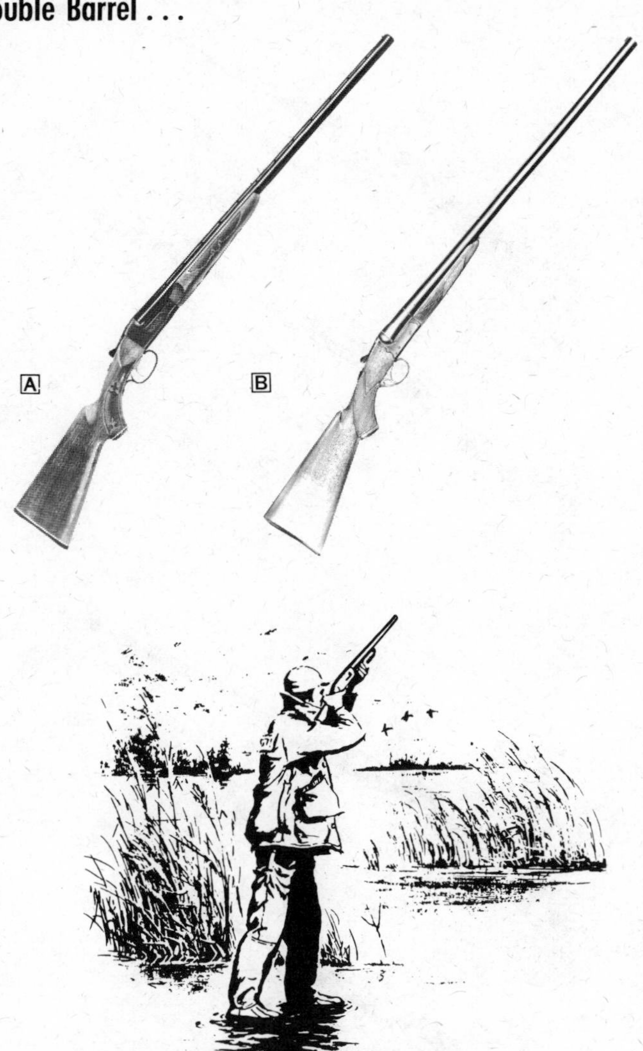

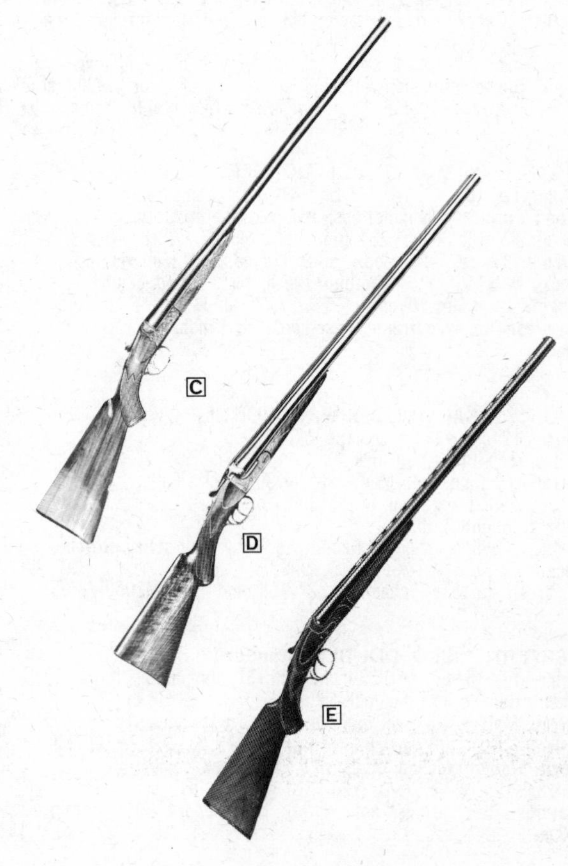

A FOX MODEL B-SE Double
Gauge: 12, 16, 20, 410 (20, 2¾" and 3"; 410, 2½" and 3" shells).
Action: Hammerless, takedown; non-selective single trigger; auto. safety. Automatic ejectors.
Barrel: 12, 16, 20 ga. 26" (Imp. Cyl., Mod.); 12, 16, 20 ga. 28" (Mod., Full); 12 ga. 30" (Mod., Full); 410, 26" (Full, Full). Vent. rib on all.
Stock: 14"x1½"x2½". Walnut, checkered p.g. and beavertail fore-end.
Weight: 12 ga. 7 lbs., 16 ga. 6¾ lbs., 20 ga. 6½ lbs., 410 ga. 6¼ lbs.
Features: Decorated, satin black finish frame; white bead front and middle sights.
Price: **$155.00**
Also available with double triggers, case hardened frame, without white line spacers and auto, ejectors as Model B.............**$130.00**

B ITHACA SKB 100 GRADE FIELD DOUBLE
Gauge: 12 and 20.
Action: Top lever, hammerless, boxlock, automatic safety, single selective trigger, non-automatic extractor.
Barrel: 12 ga. 26" (Imp. Cyl., Mod.). 28" (Imp. Cyl., Mod. or Mod., Full), 30" Mod., Full), 2¾" chambers. 20 ga. 28" (Mod., Full). 25" (Imp. Cyl., Mod.), 3" chambers
Stock: 14"x1½"x2⅝". Walnut, checkered p.g. and fore-end, p.g. cap, fluted comb.
Weight: 7 lbs. (12 ga.); 6 lbs. (20 ga.).
Features: Automatic safety. Chrome lined action and barrels.
Price: **$159.95**

C Ithaca SKB 200E Deluxe Field Grade Double
Same as 100 Grade Field except: automatic selective ejectors, bead middle sight and scroll engraving on receiver, beavertail fore-end. White line spacers. Not avail. in 28" 12 ga. (Imp. Cyl., Mod.). Gold plated trigger and nameplate **$209.95**

Ithaca SKB 200E Skeet Grade
Same as 200E Deluxe Field Grade except: recoil pad, non-auto. safety. Bbls. 26" 12 ga. or 25" 20 ga. (Skeet, Skeet). Wgt. 7⅜ lbs.
Price: **$219.45**

D NOBLE MODEL 420 Double
Gauge: 12, 16, 20, 28, 410 (2¾" chambers).
Action: Hammerless, top lever opening, double triggers, auto. safety. Etched hunting scene on frame.
Barrel: 12, 16, 20 ga. 28" (Mod., Full); 12, 16, 20, 28 ga. 26" (Imp. Cyl., Mod.), 410 (Mod., Full). Matted rib.
Stock: 14"x1⅝"x2⅝". Walnut, checkered p.g. and fore-end.
Weight: About 6-6⅞ lbs. 44¾" over-all (28" bbls.).
Features: Double lug locks and cross-bolt lock to bbl. extension.
Price: **$109.95**

NOBLE MODEL 450E DOUBLE
Gauge: 12, 16, 20 (2¾" chamber).
Action: Demi-block with triple lock, with automatic selective ejectors, double triggers.
Barrels: 28" (Mod. & Full)
Stock: Hand checkered Circassion Walnut with p.g. beavertal fore-end.
Weight: About 6⅞ lbs., 44¾" over-all.
Features: Recoil pad, hand engraved action, gold inlay on top lever. Front and middle bead sight.
Price: **$139.17**

E MARLIN L. C. SMITH FIELD DOUBLE
Gauge: 12.
Action: Sidelock, double trigger.
Barrel: 28" (Mod. & Full).
Stock: Select walnut with capped p.g. checkered, (14"x1½"x2½").
Weight: 6¾ lbs.
Features: Vent. rib, standard extractors,top auto. tang safety.
Price: **$300.00**

[A] SEARS DOUBLE BARREL GUN
Gauge: 12, 16, 20, 410. (20 and 410, 3" chambers).
Action: Hammerless, takedown. Double trigger, auto. safety.
Barrel: 12 ga. 30" (Full, Mod.); 16, 20 ga., 28", (Full, Mod.); 12, 20 ga., 26" (Mod., Imp. Cyl.); 410 ga., 26" only (Full and Full).
Stock: 14"x1⅝"x2⅝", walnut finished, p.g.
Weight: 7½ lbs. (12 ga.), 7 lbs. (16 ga.), 6½ lbs. (20 ga.), 6 lbs. (410).
Features: Black epoxied frame; bbl. and bbl. lug forged in one piece.
Price: **$79.99**
Also available in 12 or 20 ga., 28" (Mod. and Full), with vent. rib, single non-selective trigger, auto ejectors, checkered walnut stock and semi-beavertail fore-end, satin finish, scroll decorated frame... **$139.99**

[B] STEVENS MODEL 311 DOUBLE
Gauge: 12, 16, 20, 410 (20 and 410, 3" chambers).
Action: Top lever, hammerless; double triggers safety.
Barrel: 12, 16, 20 ga. 26" (Imp. Cyl., Mod.); 12, 16, 20 ga. 28" (Mod., Full); 12 ga. 30" (Mod., Full); 410 ga. 26" (Full, Full).
Stock: 14"x1½"x2½". Walnut finish, p.g., fluted comb.
Weight: 7-6¼ lbs. Over-all 45¾" (30" bbl.).
Features: Box type frame, case-hardened finish.
Price: **$94.50**

[C] UNIVERSAL DOUBLE WING DOUBLE
Gauge: 12 and 20, 3" chambers.
Action: Top break, boxlock.
Barrel: 26" (Imp. Cyl., Mod.); 28" or 30" (Mod., Full).
Stock: Walnut p.g. and fore-end, checkered.
Weight: About 7 lbs.
Features: Double triggers; Recoil pad. Beavertail style fore-end.
Price: **$129.95**
Price: 10 ga. 3½" chamber 32" Full and Full (M2030)...... **149.95**

WESTERN FIELD DOUBLE Standard
Gauge: 12, 16, 20, 410 (20 and 410, 3" chambers).
Action: Hammerless, boxlock frame.
Barrel: Matted rib, white metal bead front sight. 12 ga. 30" (Mod., Full), 16 ga., 20 ga., 28" (Mod., Full), 410 ga. 26" (Mod., Full).
Stock: Walnut-finished birch, full p.g., fluted comb.
Weight: 12, 16 ga. 7 lbs.; 20, 410 ga. 6½ lbs.
Features: Coil springs, auto safety, black epoxy finish action.
Price: **$86.99**

[D] Western Field Double Deluxe
Same as Standard except: 12 and 20 ga. only; non-selective single trigger; satin chrome finished receiver; 28" bbls. (Mod., Full) with vent. rib. 20 ga. has 3" chambers. Select walnut p.g. stock, checkered, white-line spacers, recoil pad **$139.95**

WINCHESTER 21 Custom Double Gun
12, 16 or 20 ga. Almost any choke or bbl. length combination. Matted rib, 2¾" chambers, rounded frame, stock of AA-grade full fancy American walnut to customer's dimensions; straight or p.g., cheekpiece, Monte Carlo and/or offset; field. Skeet or trap fore-end.
Full fancy checkering, engine-turned receiver parts, gold plated trigger and gold oval name plate (optional) with three initials **$1,200.00**

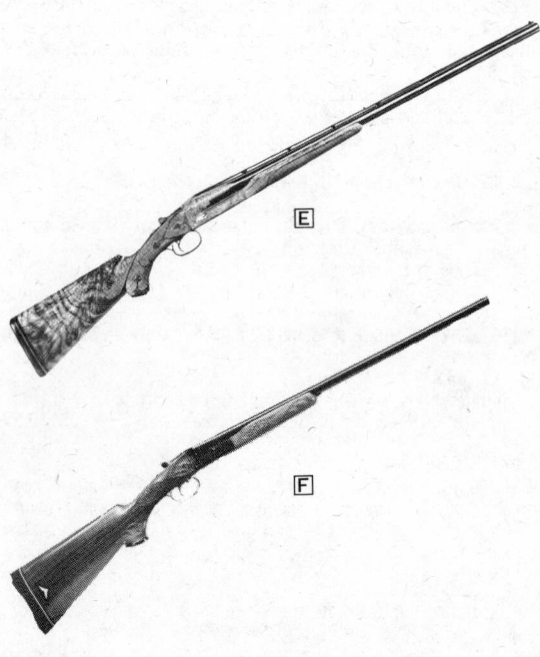

Winchester 21 Pigeon grade
Same as Custom grade except: 3" chambers, available in 12 and 20 ga.; matted or vent. rib, leather covered pad (optional); style "A" stock carving and style "6" engraving (see Win. catalog); gold inlaid p.g. cap, gold nameplate or 3 gold initials in guard........ **$2,750.00**

[E] Winchester 21 Grand American
Same as Custom and Pigeon grades except: style "B" stock carving, with style "6" engraving, all figures gold inlaid; extra pair of bbls. with beavertail fore-end, engraved and carved to match rest of gun; full leather trunk case for all, with canvas cover.......... **$3,750.00**

[F] WINSLOW DOUBLE SHOTGUNS
Gauge: 12, 20.
Action: Top lever, hammerless, single trigger, tang safety.
Barrels:
Stock: Walnut, p. g., recoil pad with white line spacer.
Weight:
Features: Custom treatment of metal and wood.
Price: From **$495.00** to **$595.00** pictured.

A BROWNING SUPERPOSED Standard
Gauge: 12 & 28, 2¾" chamber; 20 & 410, 3" chamber. Any combination of Full, Imp. Mod., Mod., Imp. Cyl., Skeet, and Cyl. chokes.
Action: Takedown; single selective gold plated trigger; automatic ejectors, manual safety combined in thumb piece with bbl. selector mechanism. Actions in proportion to gauge.
Barrels: 12, 20, 28 and 410 ga., 26½" or 28", vent. rib. Solid raised rib available on special order. Steel bead front sight.
Stock: 12 ga. 14¼"x1⅝"x2½"; 20, 28 and 410 14¼"x1½"x2⅜". French walnut, hand rubbed finish, 20-line hand checkering on semi-p.g. and fore-end. Deluxe models have fancier, finer checkering.
Weight: With 28" bbls. 12 ga. 7¾ lbs.; 20 ga. 6¾ lbs.; 28 ga. 6⅜ lbs.; 410 ga. 6½ lbs.
Features: Grade 1, blued steel with hand engraved scroll and rosette designs. Pigeon and Diana grades, steel in silver gray tone with hand engraved game scenes showing greater artistic design with each successive grade. Midas grade has specially blued steel with deeply hand carved background and hand engraved 18K gold-inlaid game birds.
Price: Grade 1, 12 or 20 ga.....**$420.00** 28 or 410 ga.....**$455.00**
Price: (28 & 410 ga. only) Pigeon Grade **$665.00,** Diana **$875.00,** Midas **$1,225.00**

Browning Superposed Magnum 12
Same as Browning Standard 12 ga. Superposed except 3" chambers; 30" (Full and Full or Full and Mod.) barrels. Stock, 14¼"x1⅝"x2½" with factory fitted recoil pad. Weight 8 lbs. Grade 1 **$425.00** Pigeon **$645.00,** Diana **$855.00,** Midas **$1,200.00.**

B Browning Superposed Lightning
Same as Standard except: 7-7¼ lbs. in 12 ga. 6-6¼ lbs. in 20 ga. Grade 1 **$435.00,** Pigeon **$645.00,** Diana **$855.00,** Midas **$1200.00**

Browning Superposed Lightning Trap 12
Same as Browning Lightning Superposed except: semi-beavertail fore-end and ivory sights; stock, 14⅜"x1⅜"x1¾". 7¾ lbs. 30" (Full & Full, Full & Imp. Mod. or Full and Mod.). Grade 1 **$445.00,** Pigeon **$655.00,** Diana **$865.00,** Midas **$1,215.00.**

Browning Superposed "New Model" Skeet
Same as the Superposed Lightning except: full pistol grip stock; recoil pad; beavertail fore end and front and center ivory sights.
Price: GD-I, 12 or 20 ga. only..........................**$430.00**

C Browning Superposed BROADway Trap 12
Same as Browning Lightning Superposed except: ⅝" wide vent. rib; stock, 14⅜"x1⅜"x1¾". 30" or 32" (Imp. Mod, Full; Mod., Full; Full, Full). 8 lbs. with 32" bbls. Grade 1 **$465.00,** Pigeon **$675.00,** Diana **$885.00,** Midas **$1,235.00.**

Browning Superposed Standard Skeet
Same as Superposed Standard except: 26½" or 28" bbls. (Skeet, Skeet). Wgt. 6½-7¾ lbs. 12 and 20 ga. Grade 1 **$430.00;** (28 and 410 ga.) **$465.00,** Pigeon **$675.00,** Diana **$885.00,** Midas **$1,235.00**

Browning Superposed Lightning Skeet
Same as Standard Skeet except: 12 and 20 ga. only. Wgt. 6-7¼ lbs. Grade 1 **$445.00,** Pigeon **$655.00,** Diana **$865.00,** Midas **$1,215.00**

D Browning Superposed Super-Light
Gauge: 12, 2¾" chamber, 20 ga., 3" chamber.
Action: Boxlock, top lever, single selective trigger. Bbl. selector combined with manual tang safety.
Barrels: 26½" (Mod. & Full, or Imp. Cyl. & Mod.)
Stock: Straight grip (14¼" x 1⅝" x 2½") hand checkered (fore-end and grip) French walnut.
Weight: 6 lbs., 8 oz. (12) & 7 oz. 20).
Features: Slender, tapered solid rib. Hand rubbed finish, engraved receiver.
Price:. **$465.00**

Browning Superposed Combinations
Standard and Lightning models are available with these factory fitted extra barrels: 12 and 20 ga., same gauge bbls.; 12 ga., 20 ga. bbls.; 20 ga., extra sets 28 and/or 410 gauge; 28 ga., extra 410 bbls. Extra barrels may be had in Lightning weights with Standard models and vice versa. Prices range from **$700.00** (12, 20 ga., one set extra bbls. same gauge) for the Grade 1 Standard to about **$2,010.00** for the Midas grade in various combinations, all as cased sets.

E ITHACA MX-8 TRAP GUN
Gauge: 12 only, 2¾" chambers.
Action: Boxlock type, single non-selective trigger; interchangeable trigger-hammer group offers choice of firing order.
Barrel: 30" or 32", especially bored for international clay target shooting. High concave vent rib has 5" ramp.
Stock: Custom, finely checkered (oiled or lacquer finish) European walnut, interchangeable with other models, 9 available including Monte Carlo.
Weight: About 8 lbs.
Features: Ventilated middle rib has additional vent ports for maximum heat dissipation, better balance and smoother swing.
Price **$1,500.00**
Extra trigger-hammer group **75.00**
Extra stock **85.00**

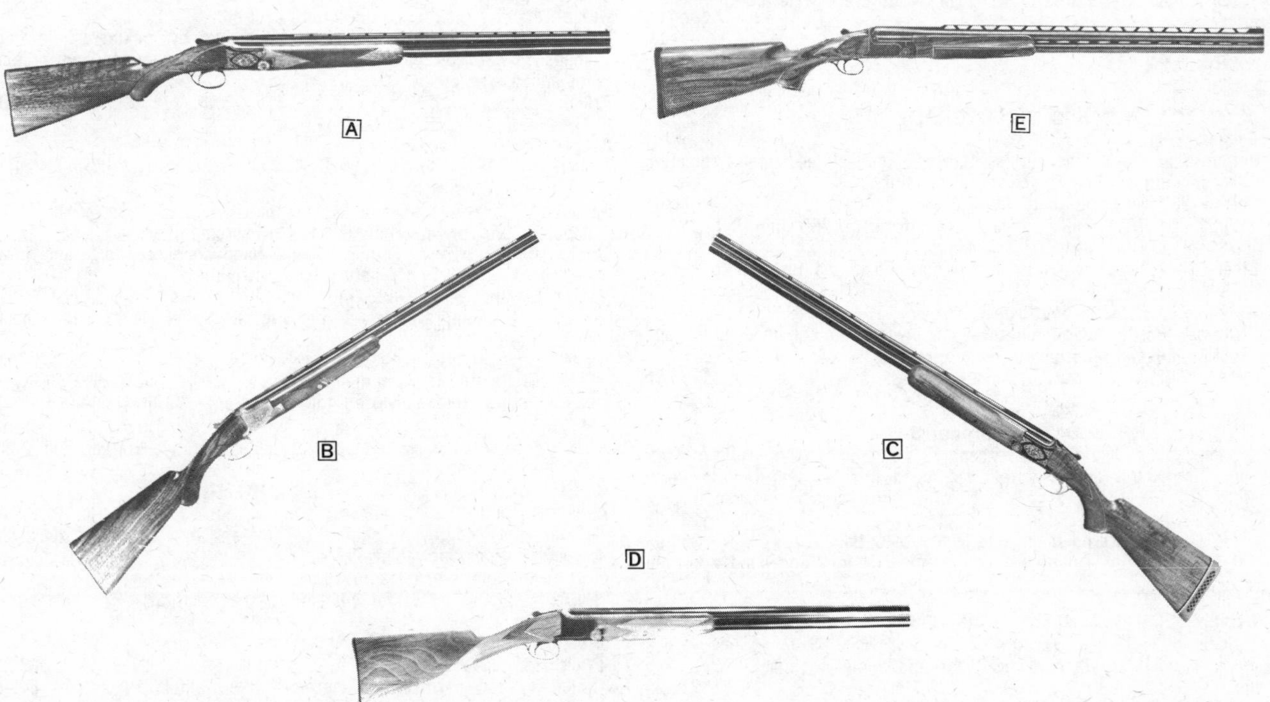

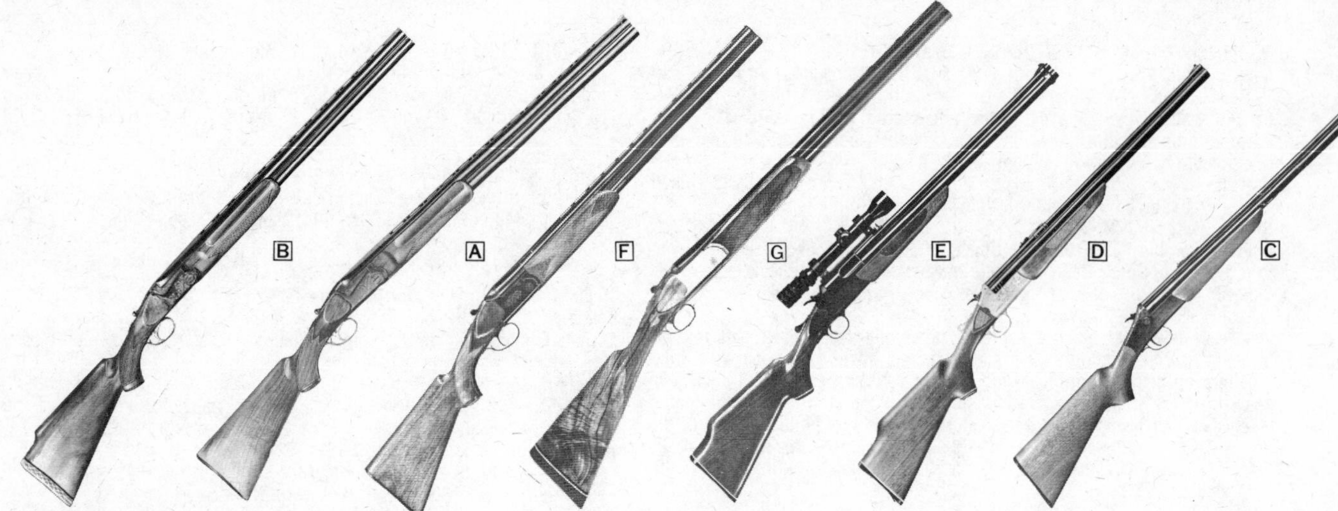

ITHACA COMPETITION I TRAP O/U
Gauge: 12 only, 2¾" chambers.
Action: Boxlock type, interchangeable hammer-trigger group. Single non-selective trigger, specify choice of firing order.
Barrel: 29¼", upper Full; lower, Imp.-Mod., vent rib has concave surface with deep cuts.
Stock: Interchangeable, 6 standard (1$\frac{3}{16}$" to 1½" at comb x1⅜" to 1⅞" at heel) and 3 Monte Carlo (1⅜" to 1$\frac{9}{16}$"x1⅜" to 1$\frac{9}{16}$") of walnut; all have 14½" pull. Fore-end has slight taper and finger groove for firm grip.
Weight: About 7¾ lbs.
Features: Extra trigger-hammer groups are available to change firing sequence and/or trigger pull. Custom stocks also available.
Price: **$825.00**
Extra trigger-hammer group **75.00**
Extra stock **85.00**

ITHACA COMPETITION I SKEET O/U
Gauge: 12 only, 2¾" chambers.
Action: Boxlock type, interchangeable hammer-trigger group. Single non-selective trigger.
Barrel: 2/¾" (Skeet & Skeet). Vent rib has concave surface with deep cuts.
Stock: 14½x1½""x2⅜", interchangeable walnut, custom stocks available.
Weight: About 7¾ lbs.
Features: Extra trigger-hammer groups to change firing order and/or weight of pull. Leather faced recoil pad has bevelled heel that will not catch. Extra stocks interchange for different style and dimension.
Price: **$900.00**
Extra trigger-hammer group **75.00**
Extra stock **85.00**

[A] ITHACA SKB 500 FIELD GRADE O-U
Gauge: 12, 20.
Action: Top lever, hammerless, boxlock; gold-plated single selective trigger; automatic ejectors, non-auto safety.
Barrel: 26" vent. rib (Imp. Cyl., Mod.); 28" (Imp. cyl., Mod. or Mod., Full); 30" (Mod., Full); 12 ga., 2¾" chambers. 26" (Imp. Cyl., Mod.); 28" (Mod., Full); 20 ga., 3" chambers.
Stock: 14"x1½"x2⅝". Walnut, checkered p.g. and fore-end, p.g. cap, fluted comb.
Weight: 7½ lbs. (12); 6½ lbs. (20).
Features: Border scroll engraved receiver. Chrome lined bbls. and action. Regular front sight.
Price: **$239.95**

[B] Ithaca SKB 600 Trap Grade O-U
Same as 500 Field Grade except 30" bbl. (Imp. Mod., Full, or Full, Full), fine scroll engraved receiver; bead middle sight; Monte Carlo stock (14½"x1½"x1½"x2"), p.g. white line spacer and recoil pad. Wgt. 7¾ lbs. **$283.95**
Field Grade 600, no recoil pad or Monte Carlo **269.95**
Trap Grade 700, select walnut oil finished stock and band engraved receiver **$395.00**

Ithaca SKB 600 Skeet Grade O-U
Same as 600 Trap except: 26" or 28" bbls. (Skeet, Skeet), stock (14"x1½"x2⅝"), standard buttplate and whiteline spacer. Wgt. 7½ lbs. **$279.95**
Skeet Grade 700, select walnut oil finished stock and band engraved receiver **$395.00**

[C] SAVAGE MODEL 24-S O-U
Gauge: Top bbl. 22 S, L, LR; bottom bbl. 410 or 20 ga., 3" chambers.
Action: Side lever opening; hammer has spur for bbl. selection. Separate extractors.
Barrel: 24"; top rifled; Full choke shotgun bbl. below.
Stock: 14"x1½"x2½". Walnut finish, p.g., corrugated buttplate.
Weight: 6¾ lbs. Over-all 40".
Features: Open rifle sights, rear adj. receiver grooved for scope mount.
Price: , ... **$58.50**
With top bbl. for 22 RF Magnum **58.50**

[D] Savage Model 24-DL
Same specifications as Model 24-S except: two-way top lever opening, select walnut stock with Monte Carlo comb and beavertail fore-end, white line spacers, checkered; satin black, decorated receiver, trigger guard and lever **$72.50**
With top bbl., for 22 RF Magnum **72.50**

[E] Savage Model 24-V
Same as Model 24-DL except: 222 Rem. and 20 ga. only; satin-black frame and trigger; barrel band; folding leaf rear sight; rec. tapped for scope (scope base $2 extra) **$89.50**
With 4x scope as Model 24 V/S **119.95**

SAVAGE MODEL 330 O/U
Gauge: 12, 2¾" chambers.
Action: Top lever, break open. Selective single trigger, auto safety locks trigger, coil springs.
Barrel: 26" (Mod. & Imp. Cyl.), 28" or 30" (Mod. & Full).
Stock: 14"x1½"x2½"). Walnut, checkered p.g. and fore-end, hard rubber plate.
Weight: About 7 lbs., 46½" (30" bbl.) over-all.
Features: Monoblock locking rails are engaged by locking shield that snaps forward as gun is closed. This shield overlaps the breech for added strength.
Price: **$199.50**

[F] SAVAGE MODEL 440 O-U
Gauge: 12, 2¾" chambers.
Action: Top lever, break open. Non selective single trigger, auto. safety, all coil springs.
Barrel: 26" (Skeet & Skeet or Mod. & Imp. Cyl.), 28" (Mod. & Full), 30" (Mod. & Full), all with vent rib and hard-chrome lined.
Stock: 14"x1½"x2½". French walnut, hand checkered p.g. and fore-end, hand rubbed finish, hard rubber buttplate.
Weight: 6½ lbs., length 42½"-46" over-all.
Features: Hand engraved steel receiver. Simple extractors. Fast hammer fall.
Price: **$237.50**
Trap Grade 440-T, with manual safety, extra wide trap style vent. rib, extractors, semi-beavertail fore-end, Monte Carlo stock and recoil pad. **$285.00**
Deluxe Grade 444, with ejectors, single selective trigger and semi-beavertail fore-end **$289.50**

[G] CHAMPLIN OVER & UNDER SHOTGUN
Gauge: 12 only, 2¾" Chambers.
Action: Fully engraved, choice of frosted or color case hardened, specifications not yet available.
Barrel: Any length or choke desired. Vent rib.
Stock: Custom made to customers specifications with choice of straight or p.g.
Weight: Average 7 to 8 lbs.
Price: **$642.50**
Deluxe Grade, with finer engraving and walnut **847.50**
Custom Grade, with engraving by one of America's foremost engravers **$1,100.00** and up.

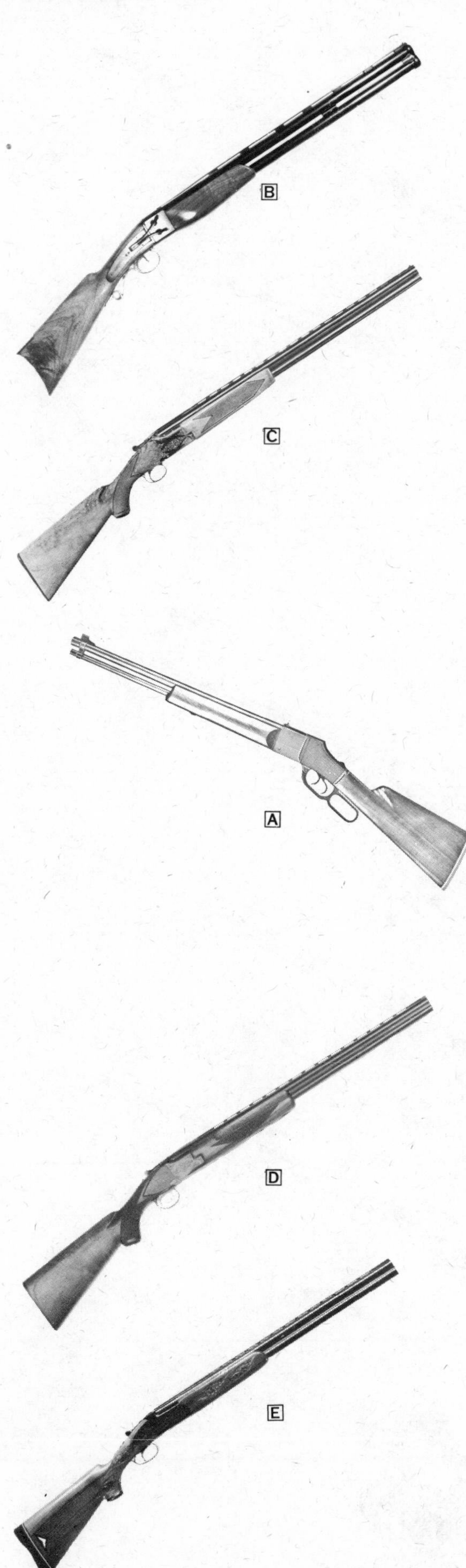

[A] STAGGS-BILT O-U RIFLE SHOTGUN
Gauge: Top bbl. 20 ga., 3" chamber; bottom 30-30 Win.
Action: Top break lever, hammerless. Two triggers.
Barrels: 19⅞"; top mod. choke, bottom rifled.
Stock: Straight-grip walnut with recoil pad (13¾"x1 5/16(x2 1/16").
Weight: 6½ lbs., 36" over-all.
Features: Leaf rear and sourdough front sights, cam-operated dual-extractor.
extractor. Shotgun-type positive sear lock safety. All coil springs.
Price: **$99.50**

[B] TINGLE MUZZLE LOADING O-U M1965 SHOTGUN
Gauge: 10 or 12.
Barrels: 30" over and under, open bores; easily removed for cleaning.
Stock: Walnut (beavertail fore-end).
Features: Barrels, lock and trigger plate blued; buttplate and trigger guard brass. Mule-ear side hammers. Double triggers.
Weight: 8½ lbs., 46" over-all.
Price: With ventilated rib **$169.95**

UNIVERSAL OVER WING O/U SHOTGUN
Gauge: 12, 20. 3" chamber.
Action: Top lever, hammerless, box lock, double triggers.
Barrel: 26" vent. rib (Imp. Cyl., & Mod.); 28" or 30" (Mod. & Full). Front & Middle sights.
Stock: 14"x1½"x2⅝". Walnut, checkered p.g. and fore-end. Recoil Pad.
Weight: 7½ lbs. (12); 6½ lbs. (20).
Price: **$199.95**
With single-trigger, engraved receiver and fancier stock . . . **249.95**

[C] WINCHESTER 101 OVER-UNDER Field Gun
Gauge: 12 and 28, 2¾"; 20 and 410, 3".
Action: Top lever, break open. Manual safety combined with bbl. selector at top of receiver tang.
Barrel: Vent. rib 26" 12, 26½", 20 and 410 (Imp. Cyl., Mod.), 28" Mod & Full), 30" 12 only (Mod. & Full). Metal bead front sight. Chrome plated chambers and bores.
Stock: 14"x1½"x2½". Checkered walnut p.g. and fore-end; fluted comb.
Weight: 12 ga: 7¾ lbs. Others 6¼ lbs.; 44¾" over-all (28" bbls.).
Features: Single selective trigger, auto ejectors. Hand engraved receiver.
Price: 12 or 20 ga. **$325.00**
Price: 28 or 410 ga. **340.00**

Winchester 101 Trap Gun
Same as the 101 Field gun except: Metal front and middle bead sights. 30" (Full & Full) bbl. only. 14⅜"x1⅜"x1⅞" stock with 1¼" pitch down and recoil pad. 12 ga. only **$330.00**
With Monte Carlo stock (14⅜"x1⅜"x1⅜x1⅞"), 30" or 32", Full and Full or Imp. Mod. and Full **340.00**

Winchester 101 Single Barrel Trap Gun
Same as M101 Trap except: Single bbl. 34" (Full), 32" (Full) or 32" (Imp.-Mod.) Vent.-rib. 12 ga. only. Monte Carlo stock **$325.00**

Winchester 101 Combination Trap Set
Same as M101 Trap except: Single bbl. 32" or 34" (Full) and extra over-under bbls. 30" or 32" (Imp.-Mod. & Full). Includes fitted trunk case **$525.00**
3-bbl. set: 32" single bbl. (Full), 32" single bbl. (Imp.-Mod.), and 32" over-under bbls. (Imp.-Mod. & Full) **$700.00**

[D] Winchester 101 Skeet
Same as M101 except: 12 ga., 26" bbls., 20, 26½", 12, 20, 28 & 410, 28". Bored Skeet and Skeet only **$325.00**

Winchester M101 Combination Skeet Set
Same as M101 20 ga. Skeet except: Includes Skeet bbls. in 410 & 28 ga. Vent. ribs match 20 ga. frame. With fitted trunk case . . **$700.00**

Winchester 101 Magnum Field Gun
Same as 101 Field Gun except: chambers 3" Magnum shells; 12 & 20 ga. 30" (Full & Full) bbls. only; hand-engraved receiver, select French walnut stock with fluted comb, hand-checkered pistol grip and beavertail fore-end with recoil pad **$325.00**

[E] WINSLOW OVER-UNDER SHOTGUNS
Gauge: 12, 20.
Action: Top-lever sidelock, hammerless, single trigger, tang safety.
Barrel: Vent. rib.
Stock: Walnut, p. g., recoil pad with white line spacer.
Weight: NA.
Features: Custom treatment of metal and wood.
Price: From **$495.00** to **$695.00** (pictured).

[A] H & R TOPPER MODELS 158 and 198
Gauge: 12, 16, 20 and 410. (3" chamber).
Action: Takedown. Side lever opening. External hammer, auto ejection. Case hardened frame.
Barrel: 12 ga., 28", 30", 32", 36"; 16, 20 and 410 ga., 28". (Full choke). 12, 20 ga. available 28" (Mod.).
Stock: Walnut finished hardwood; p.g., recoil pad. (14"x1¾"x2½").
Weight: 5 to 6½ lbs., according to gauge and bbl. length.
Features: Self-adj. bbl. lock; coil springs throughout; automatic rebound hammer.
Price: M158 .... $35.95
Model 198. Chrome frame, ebony stock. 410 only, 28" bbl.... 39.95

H & R TOPPER JR. MODEL 490
Like M158 except ideally proportioned stock for the smaller shooter. Can be cheaply changed to full size. 20 or 410 ga., 26" bbl. (Mod.) $35.95

[B] H & R TOPPER BUCK MODEL 162
Same as M158 except 12 ga. 24" cyl. bored bbl., adj. Lyman peep rear sight, blade front $39.95
Weight: 6¼ lbs.; over-all 47".
Features: Cross bolt safety; push-button action release.

[C] ITHACA 66 SUPERSINGLE
Gauge: 12, 20, 410 (3" chamber).
Action: Non-takedown; under lever opening.
Barrel: 12, 20 ga. 28" (Mod., Full); 12 ga., 30" (Full), 410, 26" (Full).
Stock: Straight grip walnut-finish stock and fore-end.
Weight: About 7 lbs.
Features: Rebounding hammer independent of the lever.
Price: $34.95
With vent. rib, 20 ga. only 49.95

Ithaca 66 Supersingle Youth
Same as the 66 Standard except: 20 (26" Bbl., Mod.) and 410 ga. (26" Bbl., Full) shorter stock with recoil pad $36.95
With vent. rib, 20 ga. only 51.95

[D] ITHACA MODEL 66 RS SUPERSINGLE Buckbuster
Same as the Model 66 Standard except: 12 and 20 ga. only, 22" bbl. with rifle sights, designed to shoot slugs $42.95

[E] ITHACA 4E GRADE SINGLE BARREL TRAP GUN
Gauge: 12 only.
Action: Top lever break open hammerless, dual locking lugs.
Barrel: 30" or 32", rampless rib.
Stock: (14½"x1½"x1⅞"). Select walnut, checkered p.g. and beavertail fore-end, p.g. cap, recoil pad. Monte Carlo comb, cheekpiece. Cast-on, cast-off or extreme deviation from standard stock dimensions $100 extra. Reasonable deviation allowed without extra charge.
Features: Frame, top lever and trigger guard engraved. Gold name plate in stock.
Price: Custom made: Write factory for price.

Ithaca 5E Grade Single Barrel Trap
Same as 4E except: Vent. rib bbl., better wood, more extensive engraving, and gold inlaid figures. Custom made: Write factory for price.

Ithaca $3000 Grade Ejector
Same as 5E except: Special wood, better engraving, figures inlaid in green and yellow gold and platinum, gold plated trigger.

[F] SAVAGE MODEL 220L SINGLE
Gauge: 12, 16, 20, 410 (12, 20 and 410, 3" chambers).
Action: Side lever break open; automatic top tang safety; hammerless; auto. ejector.
Barrel: 12 ga. 30"; 16, 20 ga. 28"; 410 ga. 26". Full choke only.
Stock: 14"x1½"x2½". Walnut, p.g. full fore-end.
Weight: About 6 lbs. Over-all 46" (30" bbl.).
Features: Unbreakable coil springs; satin black finish.
Price: $46.50

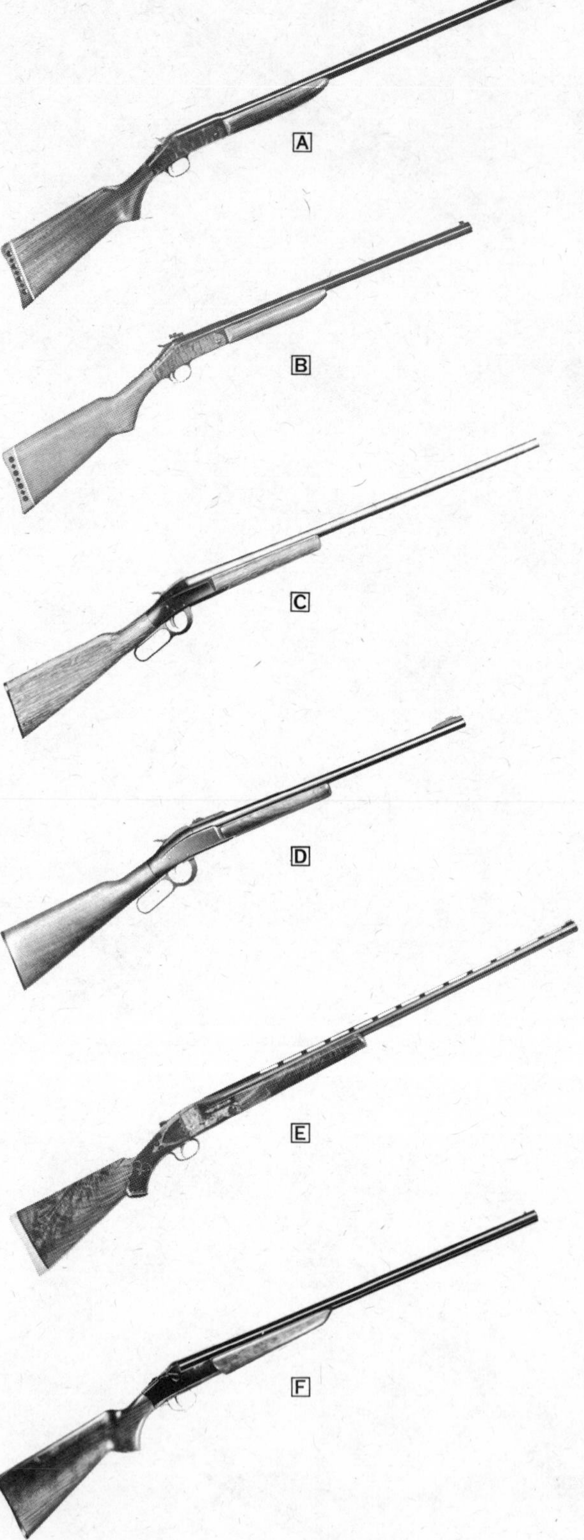

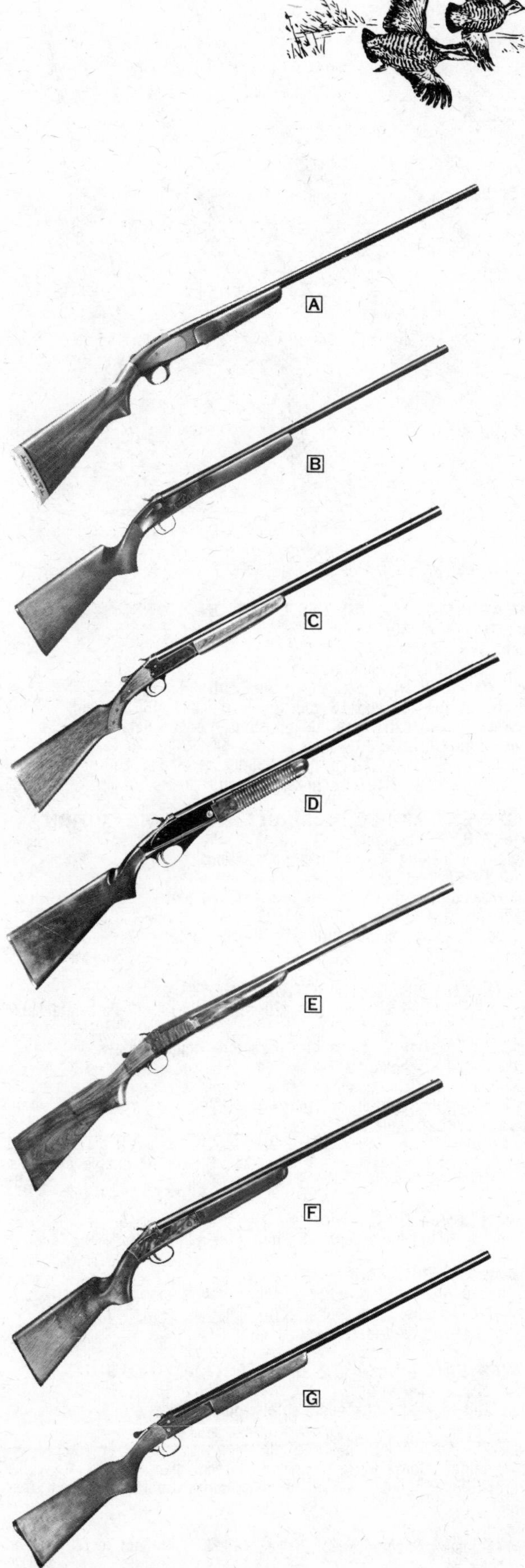

A SEARS SINGLE BARREL GUN
Gauge: 12, 16, 20, 410 (All 3″ ex. 16 ga.).
Action: Side button release. External hammer, auto. ejector, coil springs.
Barrel: 12 ga., 30″, 36″; 16 and 20 ga., 28″; 410, 26″. Full choke only.
Stock: 14″x1½″x2½″. Walnut finish hardwood, p.g.
Weight: About 7 lbs. 36″ bbl. 7½ lbs.
Features: Wide cocking lever; decorated frame.
Price: .... **$32.99** 36″ bbl. **$33.99**
Youth's Model. 12½″ stock with recoil pad; 20 ga. 26″ bb., Mod. choke, or 410 ga., 26″ bbl., Full choke. Wgt. about 6½ lbs.
Price: **$33.99**

B STEVENS MODEL 940 Single Barrel Gun
Gauge: 12, 16, 20, 28, 410 (12, 20 and 410, 3″ chambers).
Action: Side lever break open; hammer; auto. ejector.
Barrel: 12 ga. 28″, 30″, 32″, 36″; 16, 20, 28 ga. 28″; 410 ga. 26″. Full choke only.
Stock: 14″x1½″x2½″. Walnut finish, p.g.
Weight: About 6 lbs. Over-all 42″ (26″ bbl.).
Features: Satin black, decorated frame, low rebounding hammer.
Price: 26″ to 32″ bbls. .... **$35.50** 36″ bbl.......... **$37.50**

Stevens M940 Youth's Gun
Same as Model 940 except: 26″ bbl., 20 ga. Mod. or 410 Full, 12½″ stock with recoil pad. Wgt. about 5½ lbs. **$37.50**

C Stevens M94-C
Similar to M940 except: top lever opening, case hardened finish, checkered p.g......... **$37.50** 12 ga. 36″ bbl........ **$39.50**

D STEVENS MODEL 95 SINGLE SHOT
Gauge: 12 and 20 (2¾″ or 3″).
Action: Push-button opening, spring operated extractor.
Barrel: 12 ga., 28″ (Mod.), 30″ o r32″ (Full). 20 ga. 28″ (Full).
Stock: Full p.g. and fluted comb, walnut finish; fore-end deeply grooved (14″x1½″x2½″).
Weight: 7¼ lbs. Over-all 44″-48″.
Features: Streamlined solid frame, rebounding external hammer.
Price: **$32.50**

E UNIVERSAL SINGLE WING SHOTGUN
Gauge: 12 only, 3″ chamber.
Action: Top break, takedown, external hammer.
Barrel: 28″, full or mod. choke.
Stock: Walnut, p.g.
Weight: About 7 lbs.
Features: Beavertail fore-end. Automatic ejection.
Price: **$41.50**

F WESTERN FIELD 100 Single Barrel Gun
Gauge: 12, 16, 20, 410 (410, 3″ chamber).
Action: Hammerless; thumb slide break open.
Barrel: 12 ga., 30″; 16, 20 ga., 28″; 410 ga., 26″. All Full choke.
Stock: Walnut finished, p.g., recoil pad. 13¾″x1½″x2¼″.
Weight: 6¼ to 7 lbs.
Features: Automatic safety, auto ejector.
Price: **$36.99**
Also available as Youth's Model. 12½″ stock, 20 or 410 gauge. Wgt. 6 lbs., 41″ over-all................................ **$37.99**

G WINCHESTER MODEL 370 Single Barrel
Gauge: 12, 20, 410 (3″ chamber); 16, 20 and 28 (2¾″).
Action: Top break, takedown, external hammer.
Barrel: 12 ga., 30″, 32″, 36″; 16 ga., 30″, 32″; 20 and 28 ga., 28″; 410 ga., 26″. Full choke only.
Stock: Hardwood p.g. (14″x1⅜″x2⅜″), full fore-end.
Weight: 5½ to 6¼ lbs. Over-all 48¼″ (32″ bbl.).
Features: Auto. ejection, rebounding hammer. Top snap opens left or right.
Price: .... **$37.95** **Price:** 12 ga. 36″ bbl......... **$38.95**
Also available as Youth's Model. 12½″ stock, 20 or 410 ga. Wgt. 5½ (410) or 6 lbs., 26″ bbl., 40¾″ over-all................ **$38.95**

A MARLIN GOOSE GUN BOLT ACTION
Gauge: 12 only, 3-shot (3" chamber).
Action: Takedown bolt action, thumb safety, detachable clip.
Barrel: 36", Full choke.
Stock: Walnut, p.g., recoil pad, leather strap & swivels.
Weight: 7¼ lbs., 57" over-all.
Features: Double extractors, tapped for receiver sights. Swivels and leather carrying strap. Gold-plated trigger.
Price: **$59.95**

Glenfield Model 50 Bolt Action
Same as the Marlin Goose Gun except: 12 and 20 ga., 3". No sling or swivels. Recoil pad on 12 ga. Bbls. 12 ga. 28", 20 ga. 26" (Full). Wgt. 6¾ lbs., 49" over-all (28" bbl.).......... **$48.95**

B MOSSBERG MODEL 183K BOLT ACTION
Gauge: 410, 3-shot (3" chamber).
Action: Bolt; top-loading mag.; thumb safety.
Barrel: 25" with C-Lect-Choke.
Stock: Walnut finish, p.g., Monte Carlo comb.
Weight: 5½ lbs. 44½" over-all.
Features: Moulded trigger guard with finger grooves.
Price: **$44.95**
Also available in 410 ga. with 24" bbl., detachable Full and Mod. choke tubes, as M183D.......... **$42.95**

C MOSSBERG MODEL 395K BOLT ACTION
Gauge: 12, 3-shot (3" chamber).
Action: Bolt; takedown; detachable clip.
Barrel: 28" with C-Lect-Choke.
Stock: Walnut finish, p.g. Monte Carlo comb; recoil pad.
Weight: 6¾ lbs. 47½" over-all.
Features: Streamlined action; top safety; grooved rear sight.
Price: **$54.95**
Also available in 20 ga. 3" chamber 28" bbl. 6¼ lbs., as M385K, **$50.50**, and in 16 ga. 28" bbl., 6¾ lbs., as M390K.......... **$53.85**

MOSSBERG MODEL 395S BOLT ACTION
Same as Model 395K except 24" barrels with adjustable folding leaf rear sight and ramp front, for use with slugs. Sling supplied.. **$56.85**

D SEARS BOLT ACTION 410
Gauge: 410, single shot, 3" chamber.
Action: Top loading, self-cocking bolt.
Barrel: 24", Full choke.
Stock: Walnut finished hardwood, p.g., corrugated buttplate.
Weight: 4¾ lbs. 43" over-all.
Features: Automatic thumb safety.
Price: **$24.99**
Same, except a repeater with 3-shot detachable clip. Wgt. 5½ lbs. **$32.99**
Also available with 5-shot tubular mag. (3-shot plug furnished), non-automatic safety. Wgt. 6 lbs. 44½" over-all.......... **$44.99**

E SEARS MODEL 140 BOLT ACTION
Gauge: 12, 16 or 20; 3-shot.
Action: Self-cocking bolt.
Barrel: 25", with adj. choke.
Stock: Walnut finished, p.g., corrugated buttplate.
Weight: 7½ lbs. (12 and 16 ga.); 7 lbs. (20 ga.); 46" over-all.
Features: Double extractors; thumb safety; 2-shot detachable clip.
Price: 12 ga. ....**$42.99** 16 ga. ....**$41.99** 20 ga. **$39.99**
Price: w/o adj. choke, 12 ga. (Full) **$38.99** 20 ga. (Full)..... **36.99**
Price: 12 ga. only, 20" Cyl. choke, with rifle sights.......... **42.99**

F STEVENS MODEL 51 SINGLE SHOT BOLT ACTION
Gauge: 410, 3" chamber.
Action: Top loading, streamlined bolt action.
Barrel: 24" Full choke.
Stock: Walnut finish, checkered fore-end and p.g.
Weight: About 4¾ lbs. Over-all 43½".
Features: Band extractor, automatic thumb safety.
Price: **$35.25**

G STEVENS 58 BOLT ACTION SHOTGUN
Gauge: 12, 16, 20 2¾" chambers. 20 ga. also in 3". (2-shot detachable clip).
Action: Self-cocking bolt; double extractors; thumb safety.
Barrel: 25", Full choke.
Stock: Walnut finish, checkered fore-end and p.g., recoil pad.
Weight: 7-7½ lbs. Over-all 46" (43½" in 410)
Features: Crisp trigger pull.
Price: **$49.75**
Also available in 410 ga., 3" chamber, 3-shot detachable clip, 5½ lbs. **$41.50**

Stevens 58AC Bolt Action
Same as Model 58 except: 25" bbl. with Adj. Choke.......... **$53.50**

Stevens 59 Bolt Action
Same as Model 58 410 ga. except: tubular mag. holding five 3" or six 2½" shells; 3-shot plug furnished; no recoil pad. Wgt. 6 lbs. 24" bbl., 44½" over-all.......... **$49.95**

H WESTERN FIELD 172 BOLT ACTION SHOTGUN
Gauge: 12 (3" chamber).
Action: Self-cocking bolt. Thumb safety, double locking lugs, detachable clip.
Barrel: 28" adj. choke, shoots rifled slugs.
Stock: Walnut, Monte Carlo design, p.g., recoil pad.
Features: Quick removable bolt with double extractors, grooved rear sight.
Price: **$42.95**
M175 Same as above except 20 ga., **$39.95** Without recoil pad and adj. choke **$34.95**

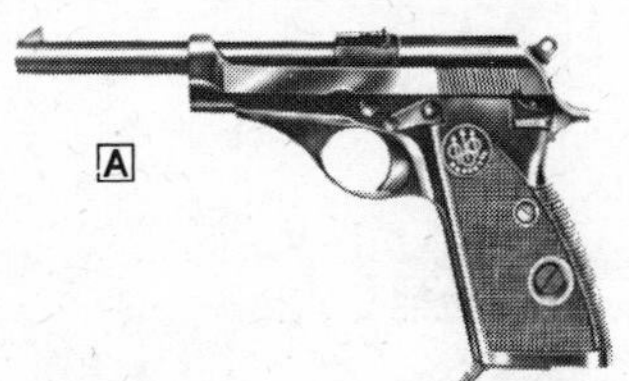
A

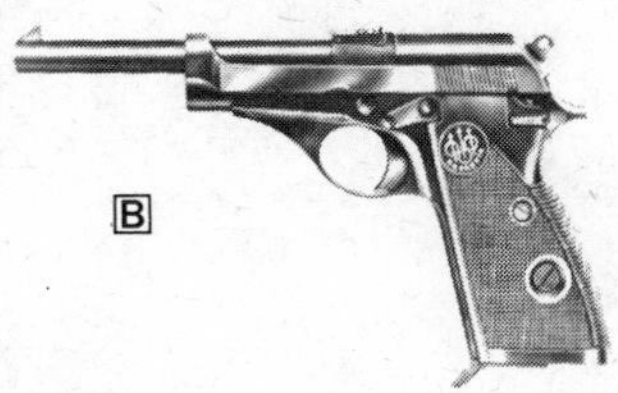
B

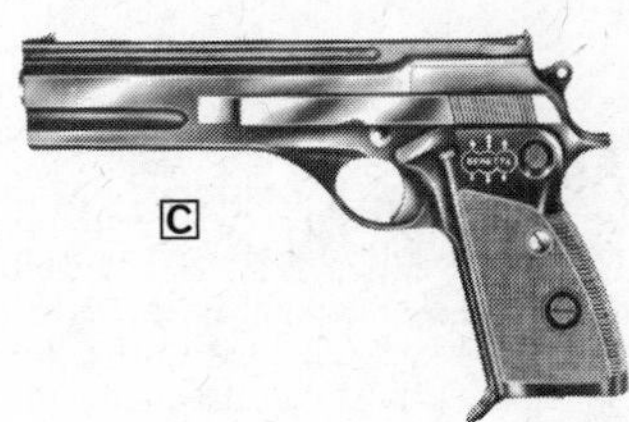
C

D

E

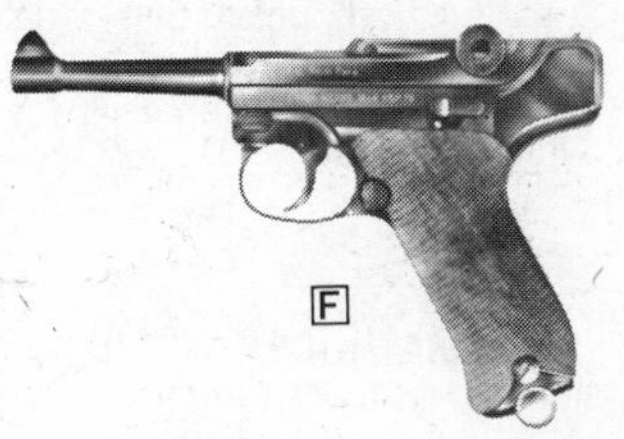
F

A BERETTA JAGUAR AUTO PISTOL
6" bbl. with an over-all length of 8¾". Wgt. approx. 19 oz. 10-shot magazine with finger spur. 22 LR only. Two piece wrap-around plastic grips are checkered. Adj. rear sight, external hammer, thumb lever safety. Slide stays open on the last shot. Blued. From Galef. **$69.95**

B BERETTA PUMA AUTO PISTOL
External-hammer auto pistol. 32 Auto. 10-shot magazine with finger spur. 6" bbl., weighs approx. 19 oz., 9½" over-all. Adj. rear sight, thumb lever safety, wrap-around plastic checkered grips. Blued. From Galef. **$69.95**

C BERETTA SABLE AUTO PISTOL
Cal. 22 LR, 10-shot magazine with finger spur. 6" bbl., 8¾" over-all, wgt. approx. 26 oz. Adj. rear sight, 3 blade front sight. Crossbolt safety, external hammer. Wrap-around checkered plastic grips. Blued. From Galef. **$87.00**

D BERETTA BRIGADIER AUTO PISTOL
Military and police auto pistol in 9mm Luger (Parabellum) caliber. Single action, external hammer, side safety. 4½" barrel, 31 oz., 8" over-all. Fixed sights. Black plastic wrap-around grips, 8-shot capacity. Slide stays open on last shot. From Galef. Blued........... **$117.50**

E ERMA BABY MODEL PISTOLEN
Made in 32 and 380 auto., 6-shot magazine and 2¾" barrel, this toggle-bolt pistol is reminiscent of the Luger design. Blue-black finish; checkered walnut grips; sidelock safety. Length 5¼" over-all, weight about 19 oz. L. A. Distributors, importer.................... **$89.95**

F ERMA KGP70 AUTO PISTOL
9MM version of the P-08. 8-shot magazine. Checkered walnut grips. Toggle-bolt stays open on last shot. Fixed barrel with double action feature and falling block thumb safety lever. Open notch rear and blade front sight. Weighs 38½ oz., 4⅜" bbl., 8½" over-all. Blued. L. A. Distributors, importer........................ **$129.95**

[A] ERMA FB1 PISTOL
Lightweight (14 oz.) 25-caliber pistol has 6-shot magazine. 5⅜" over-all with 2½" barrel, all steel frame with walnut grips and thumb safety. Blued finish. LA Distributors, importer................ **$39.95**

[B] ERMA 22 PISTOLEN
22 version of the famous Model P-08. 8-shot magazine takes 22 LR. Checkered walnut grips. Familiar toggle-bolt stays open on last shot. Open notch rear and blade front sight. 9" over-all, wgt. 36 oz. with a 4⅝" bbl. Blued. L. A. Distributors, importer................ **$49.95**

ERMA 22 "NAVY" PISTOLEN
Similar to Erma 22 Luger, except with 12" barrel, walnut fore-end, adj. rear sight. 16½" over-all, 48 oz. LA Distributors, importer.. **$99.95**

GAUCHO AUTOMATIC PISTOL
All steel construction with either 5" or 6½" barrel, this 22 LR pistol has a 10-shot magazine, adjustable rear sight and hand-checkered wood grips. Length over-all 10½" (6½" barrel), weight 30 oz. Blued finish. Firearms International, importer............... **$59.95**

[C] HK-4 AUTO PISTOL
Harrington & Richardson offer a new import, the HK-4, a light autoloading pistol (17 oz.) in 22, 25, 32 and 380 caliber. Any of these may be easily changed to the other calibers by switching bbls. and/or magazines. Magazine- and thumb safeties; double action on the first shot; quick takedown and dustfree construction are features. Cased, with barrels and magazines for all four calibers............ **$110.00**

LA FURY PISTOL
8-shot autoloader with thumb safety, walnut grips, gold-plated trigger, fixed sights, high-luster blue. Cal 25. LA Distributors, importer. Blued .... **$29.95** Chrome.............. **$31.25**

[D] LLAMA MODEL IXA AUTO PISTOL
45 ACP cal. Blued finish, ribbed slide, broad hammer spur and adj. square notch rear and blade front target sights. 7-shot magazine. Wgt. 2 lbs. 6 oz., 5⅜" high, 8½" over-all, 5" bbl. Thumb and grip safeties. Stoeger, importer............................... **$78.95**

LLAMA MODEL VIII AUTO PISTOL
Same as above except: Super cal., 9-shot, 2 lbs. 6½ oz.... **74.95**

[E] LUGER 22 AUTO PISTOL
This fixed barrel, solid alloy wrame, toggle joint action pistol is a 22 LR version of the famous P-08. Weighing 30 oz. it has a 12-shot capacity with one round in the chamber. Action remains open after last shot and as magazine is removed. 4½" barrel. Grip and balance are identical to the P-08. Stoeger, importer **$69.95**

[F] MAB AUTOLOADING PISTOL
Uses a rotary unlocking system, exposed hammer. 8 or 15 shot magazine, thumb safety, fixed sights. Blued finish. Cal. 9mm, wgt. 38 oz. Mars Equipment, importers....................... **$109.00**

[G] MAUSER HSc AUTO PISTOL
This commercial model is made in West Germany by the original Mauser organization. In cals. 32 (8-shot) and 380 (7-shot) Auto. Pistol is 6⅜" over-all, with a 3⅜" bbl. and weighs 23 oz. Features exposed hammer spur, double action with thumb safety lever and magazine disconnect safety. Also, walnut checkered grips, blued finish and fixed sights. Interarms, importer.......................... **$96.00**

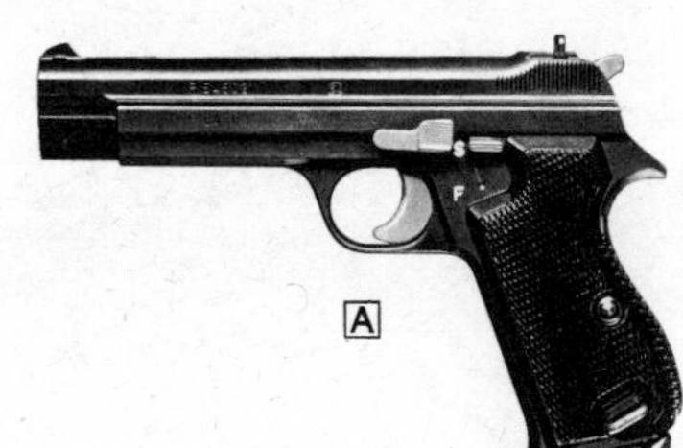

A

[A] SIG 210 AUTOMATICS
Available in 22 LR, 7.65 Luger or 9mm Luger, 8-shot 4¾" bbl., 8½" over-all, wgt. approx. 34 oz. Double pull trigger. Fixed notch rear, blade front sights. Grooved wooden grips. Thumb safety. Polished blue finish. Imported by Grieder, Benet Arms Co., & Casanova Guns......**$220.00**
With checkered hard rubber grips and matte finish....... **197.00**
Conversion unit, available with all components necessary to convert to cal. 22...**$100.00**

SIG 210 TARGET AUTOMATICS
Same as the M210 except: 7.65mm and 9mm only. 6" bbl., adj. target trigger, micro. rear sight adj. for w. and e.; adj. front sight. Hard rubber grips and matte finish. Wgt. 38⅓ oz., 9⅔" over-all..**$249.00**
Same, but with 4¾" bbl............................. **225.00**

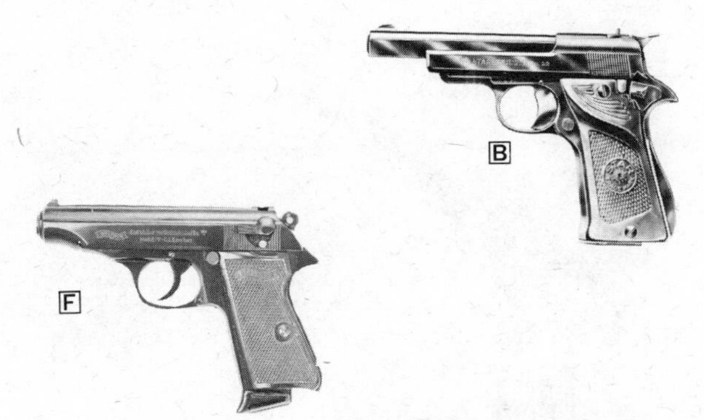

B

F

[B] STAR MODEL FR AUTO PISTOL
All feature quick takedown, thumbrest grips, checkered backstrap, thumb- and half-cock safeties. 22 LR, 10-shot magazine; extra mag. furnished at prices shown. F.I., importers. Standard, 5" bbl. 26 oz. Fixed sights.
Blued....**$59.95** Chromed....**$69.95** Chromed, engr. ..**$94.95**
Star Sport, same as the "FR" except: 6" bbl., 28 oz., adj. sights.
Blued.............**$59.95** Chromed.............**$69.95**

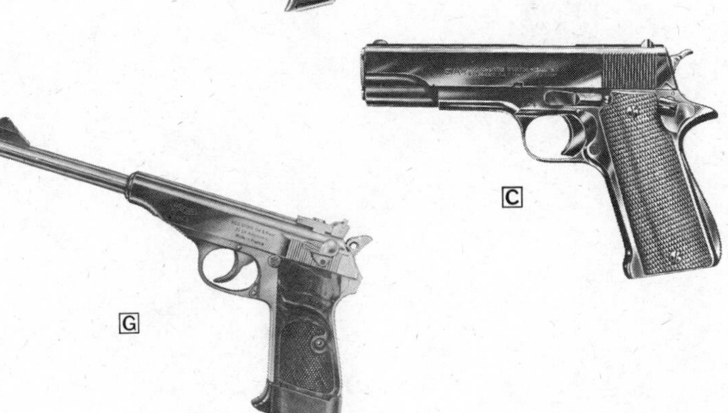

C

G

[C] STAR MODEL A, B & P AUTOS
Based on the U. S. Pistol, M1911A1 short recoil system with half-cock and thumb safeties, exposed hammers, these pistols feature 9-shot (.38 Super Model A & 9MM Para. Model B) and 7-shot (45ACP Model P) magazines. Weigh approx. 2 lbs. 6 oz., have 5" bbl., and are 8½" over-all. They have checkered walnut grips, fixed sights and are blued. F. I., importer.............................**$89.95**

[D] UNIQUE CORSAIR AUTO PISTOL
Has thumb and magazine safeties as wel as a half-cock position on the exposed hammer. Thumbrest checkering plastic grips, adj. sights. 6" bbl., 9⅛" over-all, wgt. 26 oz., blued, 10-shot. Cal. 22 LR. F. I., importer. **$65.95**

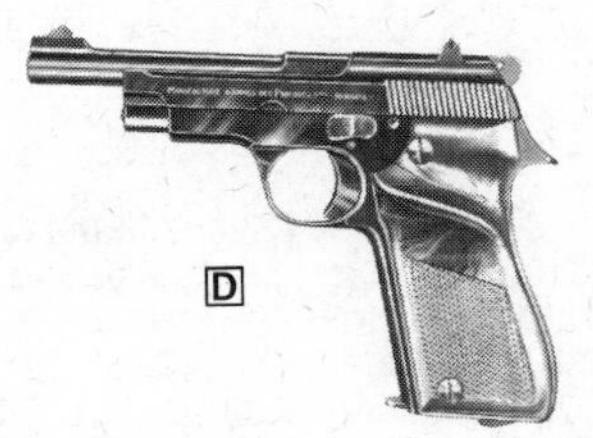

D

[E] WALTHER P-38 AUTOMATIC PISTOL
This commercial model is made in W. Germany of lightweight alloys, in polished blue finish. Weight 27½ oz., 8⁷⁄₁₆", over-all; 4¹⁵⁄₁₆" barrel. Safety locks firing pin, blocks action and drops the hammer; signal pin indicating when chamber is loaded; single or double action, external hammer. 8-shot magazine (2 furnished), checkered plastic grips and lanyard swivel are standard. Interarms, importer...........**$140.00**
Same but with matte finish **106.00**
Same but in 22 LR cal. with matte finish **132.00**

E

[F] WALTHER MODEL PP PISTOL
A line of pocket auto pistols that feature an exposed hammer, double or single action. Indicator pin shows if chamber is loaded. Bbl. length, 3⅞"; wgt., 23 ozs., over-all, 6⁵⁄₁₆", Mag. capacity, 8 shots except 380 cal. holds 7. Cals. 32 or 38. Blued. Interarms.....**$96.00**

[G] WALTHER SPORT MODEL PISTOL
Basically the Walther PP in 22 LR, this pistol offers a longer barrel (6"), click rear sight, thumb rest grips, extension mag. Interarms, importer. **$120.00**

A HAMMERLI INTERNATIONAL AUTO PISTOLS 206-207

Adj. precision trigger set for 2 lbs. 7⁷⁄₁₆" bbl., high speed action, micro. rear sight adj. for w. and e. ⅛" front sight. Muzzle brake and bbl. wgt. standard. Thumbrest, checkered grips. 22 S or LR **$215.00**

Model 207, same as 206 except: adj. French walnut grips made to ISU rules **$245.00**

B HAMMERLI INTERNATIONAL AUTO PISTOLS 208-209-210

M208 is like the M206 but has 6" bbl., is without muzzle brake, and has a 3-lb. trigger pull. Designed for Ladies Matches, it weighs only 35 oz. Price .... **N.A.**

M209 is like the M206 but offers several advanced features: 6 gas ports over chamber permit adj. of leakage for balancing to various cartridge brands or types; new combination muzzle brake and new light bolt for less jar. Cal. 22 Short only.

M209, standard walnut grips .... **N.A.**

M210, adj. walnut grips .... **N.A.**

Regular grips with thumbrest and checkering **$15.00.** Adj. grips with checkering **$40.00.** Magazine for cal. 22 S or LR **$9.00.** Additional wgt. **$6.00.** Muzzle brake **$4.00.** Grieder, importer.

C HAMMERLI MATCH PISTOLS 104-105

Single shot pistol has 5-lever set-trigger, adj. to fractions of an ounce. Round 11⅛" bbl. Micro. rear sight with click adj. for w. and e. ⅛" front sight. Selected French walnut grips with adj. shelf, trigger-finger ramp and custom finish. Martini action. Cal. 22 LR. Imported by Grieder **$255.00**

Model 105, same as 104 except: octagonal bbl. and deep blue finish **$320.00**

D SARMCO MTS 2-1 MATCH PISTOL

Olympic Match single shot free pistol, 22 LR. Adj. wrap-around grips, hand-carved from Circassian walnut, have an adj. heel rest. Double-set pin-type trigger with built-in shock absorber, adj. to fractions of an ounce. Sights have micro. adjustments and are detachable. Wgt. 3 lbs. Comes with a complete set of cleaning and adjusting tools, extra sights, oil can, in fitted, cushioned hardwood carrying case. Imported by Sarmco; custom order only, 4 months delivery **$395.00**

E SARMCO MTS Margolin Pistol

Automatic target pistol with 6-shot magazine, cal. 22 LR. Blued, checkered target stocks with adj., removable, heel rest. Both trigger pull and trigger travel adj., both sights adj. Rear is on bridge, (7½" radius), does not move in firing. Wgt. 37 oz., 6.3" bbl. Extra sights, muzzle brake, two weights, adj. heel rest, tools, spare magazine, cleaning equipment supplied in cushioned hardwood case. Imported by Sarmco **$150.00**

Also as MTS 1-1, an improved version in 22 Short caliber, with special thumb-hole stock, otherwise as the Margolin above. Custom order only, 4 mos. delivery **$275.00**

F WALTHER OSP RAPID FIRE MATCH PISTOL

A newly designed pistol, complying with International Rules. 22 Short only; 5-shot magazine. Simple barrel take-down; bolt held open after last shot. Weight, about 41 oz., 11⅞" over-all. 5¾" bbl. Supplied with spare magazine, barrel weight, cleaning rod, brush and wrench. Interarms, importer **$189.50**

Also, as the GSP in 22 LR cal. **$189.50**

A ARMINIUS REVOLVERS
Double-action revolver with swing-out cylinder, simultaneous ejection. Free-floating firing pin. Fixed sights, checkered composition grips. Cals. 22 S, L, LR with 2", or 4" or 6" bbls. LA Distributors, importer. $41.50
Also, in 32 cal. with 2" or 4" bbl...................... 46.50

B ASTRA CADIX REVOLVERS
Double action revolvers with adj. rear sight; shrouded ejector rod; one piece checkered stocks and swing out cylinder. Cals. 22 LR (9 shots) or 38 Spec. (5 shots) with 4" or 6" bbl. Wgt. 25 to 27 oz., blued, F. I., importer................................$64.50

C DAKOTA REVOLVERS
Single action revolvers with case hardened receivers; brass trigger guard and backstrap; fixed sights; floating firing pin and one-piece smooth walnut grips. 4⅝", 5½, or 7½" barrels ($2.25 extra for 7½") in 22 rimfire, 22 WMR, 357 Magnum or 45 Colt caliber. Intercontinental Arms. $89.75
With extra 22 WMR cylinder........................... 97.20
Also as Super Dakota in 41 and 44 Magnum calibers, 5½" and 7½" bbls. with flat-top frame, adj. sights front and rear, long magnum grip, square-back guard................................$99.75

D Dakota Engraved Models Identical to $89.75 models above, and in same calibers, but heavily engraved in scroll and floral pattern on frame, cylinder and hammer. Guard and straps polished bright brass, frame finished bright, rest blue. One-piece smooth walnut grips.
4⅝" and 5½" bbls.........$165.00   7½"........$175.00

C

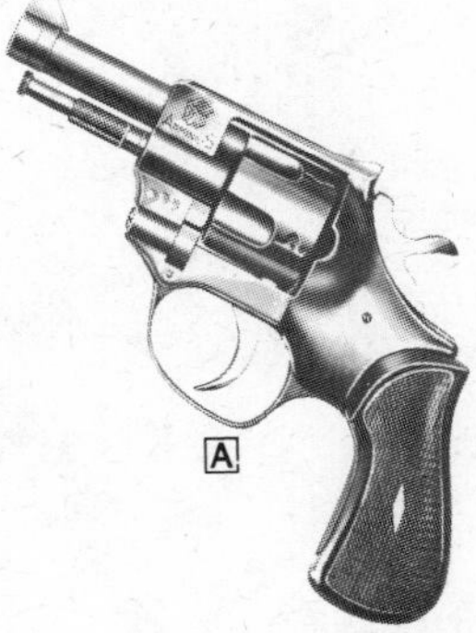

A

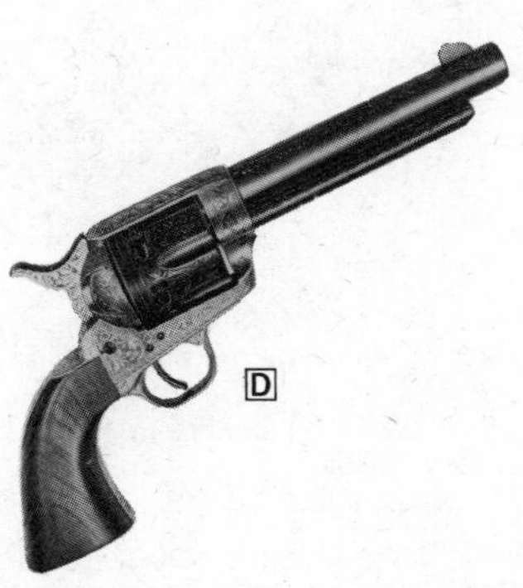
D

E

B

E DEPUTY 22 SINGLE ACTION REVOLVER
6-shot, loading and ejection through loading gate. 4¾" bbl. Fixed front sight, notch rear. Black satin finish, checkered walnut grips. 22 S, L, LR. LA Distributors, importer.......................$39.95
Also, as the Adjusto with adj. target sights............... 47.95
Available as Deputy Combo with interchangeable cylinder for 22WMR $49.95
Also, as the Adjusto with adj. target sights............... 59.95
The Deputy is also available as a 6-shot single action revolver in 357 Magnum. Satin black finish, except for color case-hardened frame; walnut grips $75.25

F HAWES WESTERN MARSHAL REVOLVERS
Single action, frontier style 6-shot revolvers made in 45 Long Colt, 357 or 44 Mag. Moulded stag grips, floating firing pin, 5½" barrel, fixed sights. All working parts of steel, blue finish over-all. Weight, 40 oz. $84.95
As above, but with an extra cylinder compatible with the barrel, 357 Mag./9mm, 44 Mag/44-40, 45 Colt/45ACP.............$96.95
As above but in 22 S, L or LR cal....$49.95   22 WMR.... 52.95
With both 22 cal. cylinders...................................$61.95

G HAWES MONTANA MARSHAL REVOLVERS
Same as Western Marshal except: solid brass backstrap and trigger guard, hand-rubbed rosewood grips.........................$94.95
As above, but in 22 cal. rimfire.......................... 59.95

H HAWES TEXAS MARSHAL
Same as Western Marshal except: revolver is fully chromed with black or white Pearlite grips............................$94.95
As above, but in 22 cal. rimfire.......................... 64.95

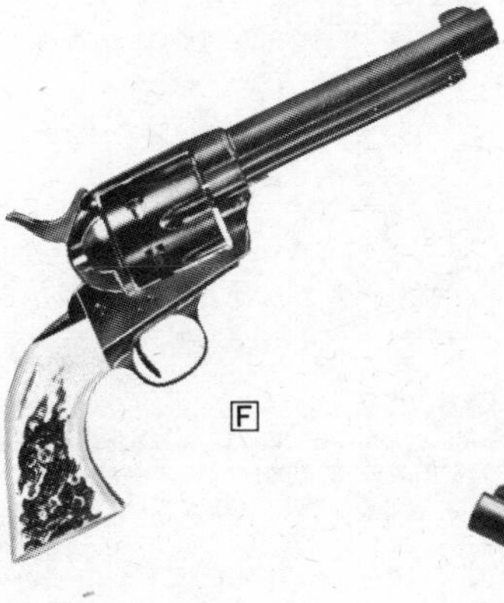

F

G

H

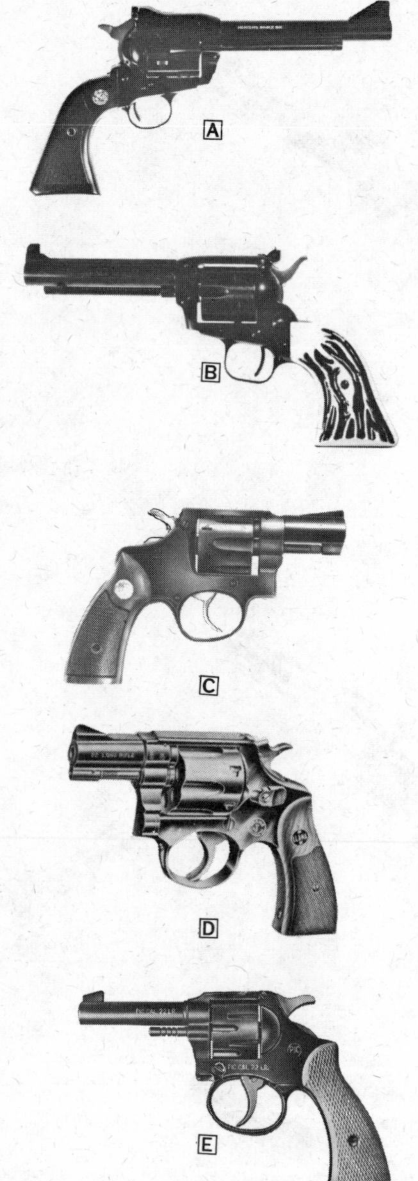

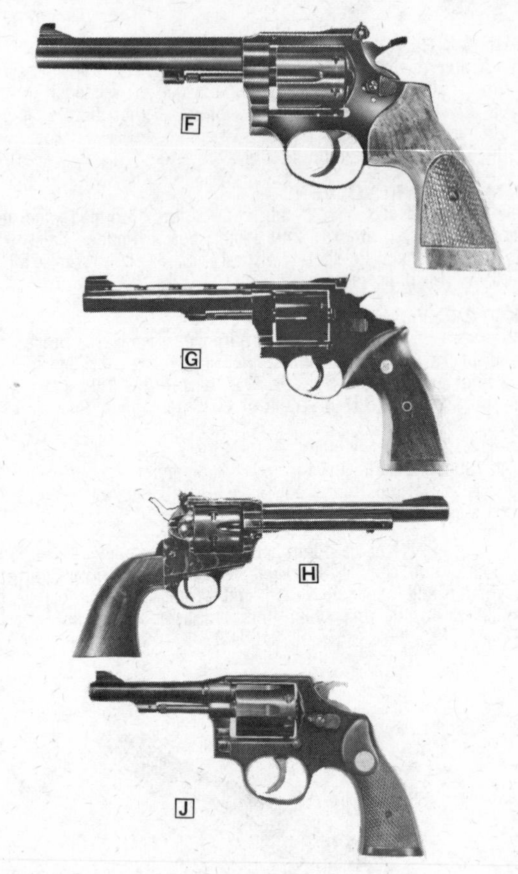

HERTER'S 22 GUIDE REVOLVER
Double action, swingout style, 8-shot 22 rimfire, 4" or 6" bbls. Checkered plastic grips. Fixed sights.
Blued ....**$29.65** Chromed **$34.05**

A HERTER'S POWERMAG REVOLVER
Single action, frontier-style 6-shot revolver made in Herter's own 401 Powermag caliber. Cartridges and ctg. components available from them. 6½" bbl. 12½" over-all. Extra-long grips, adj. rear and ramp front sights. **$58.30**

HERTER'S CUSTOM GRADE SUPER REVOLVER
Same as the Powermag except in 357 Mag. or 44 Mag. cal. **$65.95**

B HERTER'S WESTERN SINGLE ACTION
22 rimfire, 6-shot single action revolver with 5" bbl., plastic stag-horn grip, blade front sight, rear adj. for w & e. Blued.......**$27.45**

C I.N.A. TIGER REVOLVERS
5 shot, walnut grips, swing-out cylinder. 2¼" or 3¼" barrel. Weight 13 oz. (2¼" bbl.) 38 Spl. Firearms I. & E. Corp., importer.
Blued................**$49.50** Nickeled...............**$54.95**
Gold plated (2¼" barrel only).......................... **70.75**
Same, only 32 S&W Long, 6 shot cylinder.
Blued................**$43.50** Nickeled...............**$49.95**
Gold plated (2¼" barrel only) **63.75**

D LLAMA MARTIAL 22 REVOLVER
A match revolver in 22 LR cal. with 6" vent. rib bbl. Micro rear sight adj. for w. and e. Wide, grooved trigger and hammer. Recessed cyl. Target style, checkered walnut grips. Wgt. 26 oz. Stoeger, agents. **$65.00**

LLAMA MARTIAL 38 REVOLVER
Similar to the Martial 22 above except 38 Spl. cal., 4" (29 oz.) or 6" bbl. **$65.00**
Llama Martials also available in chrome plated finish **$79.95** or engraved with blue finish **$94.95.**

E PIC BIG SEVEN REVOLVER
7-shot, 22 LR double-action revolver has standard size frame, 3½" barrel with blue-black finish on metal parts. Cylinder drops out for loading. Checkered walnut grips. Precise Import Corp., importer **$17.95**

ROSSI REVOLVERS
22 LR (7-shot), 32 S&W Long and 38 spl. (6-shot) revolvers with swing-out cylinders, simultaneous ejection. 2" or 3" bbls. in 22, 3" in 32. Wgt.: 22, 11½ oz. (3" bbl.), 32, 19 oz. 7" over-all. In presentation case. F. I., importers. 22 LR, 2" or 3" bbl., nickel-plated only..**$38.25**
32 S & W, 4" bbl. blue or nickel plated finish............ **60.50**
38 Spl., 4" bbl., blue or nickel plated finish.............. **60.50**

F J. P. SAUER DELUXE REVOLVER
6-shot swing-out cylinder double action revolver. With adj. rear sight, checkered walnut grips, wide trigger and hammer spur. Cal. 38 S&W Spl. or 22 LR with 4" or 6" bbl. 11⅛" over-all, wgt. about 39 oz. (6"). Blued. Hawes National, importer.....................**$104.95**

J. P. SAUER CUSTOM REVOLVER
Same as above except with walnut thumbrest target grips and vent. rib. **$119.95**

SOLINGEN LIBERTY CHIEF REVOLVER
6-shot revolvers with swing-out cylinder, simultaneous ejection. Fixed sights, adj. trigger, checkered, rounded walnut grips. Cal. 38 Spl., 16½" over-all (2" bbl.) Solingen Cutlery, importers.
Blued **$59.95**

G STALLION SINGLE ACTION REVOLVER
6-shot, loading and ejection through loading gate. Cals. 22 LR or 22 WMR, 5½" or 6½" bbl., 11⅝" over-all (6½"), wgt. 2 lbs., 6 oz. Rear sight adj. for w.&e., ramp front. Smooth walnut grips with interior fastening. Blued. Galef, importer...................**$87.00**

H MASTER TARGET REVOLVER
Double action revolver with adj. micro. rear and Patridge front sights. Checkered walnut over-size grips, trigger and hammer spur. Cal. 38 S&W Special with 2", 4", or 6" bbl. 11⅛" over-all and wgt. approx. 39 oz. (6" bbl.). Blued. L.A. Distributors, importer **$54.95**

J TAURUS REVOLVER
Swing-out cylinder, checkered grips, fixed sights. Cal. 38 Spl., 4" round bbl., 6-shot. Wgt. 32 oz. Blued or nickel. F. I., importer..**$60.50**

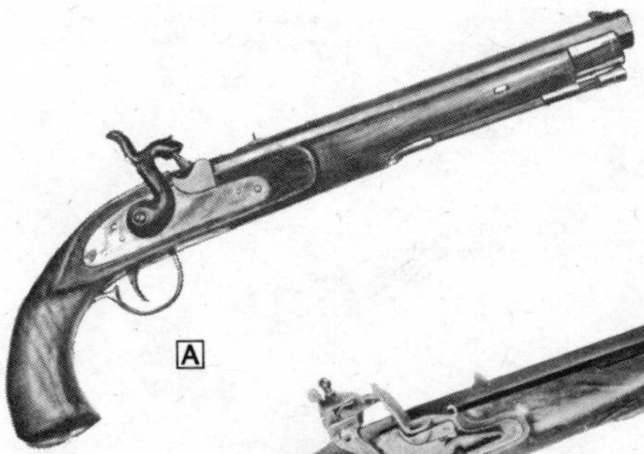

A DIXIE KENTUCKY PERCUSSION PISTOL
Muzzle-loading caplock single shot with 9" octagonal rifled barrel, cal. 40. Maple stock, brass furniture, open sights. Black powder only **$62.50**
Same as above except flintlock **69.50**
Dixie shows numerous other flintlock and percussion revolvers and pistols in their catalog 118 cost $1.00 post paid.

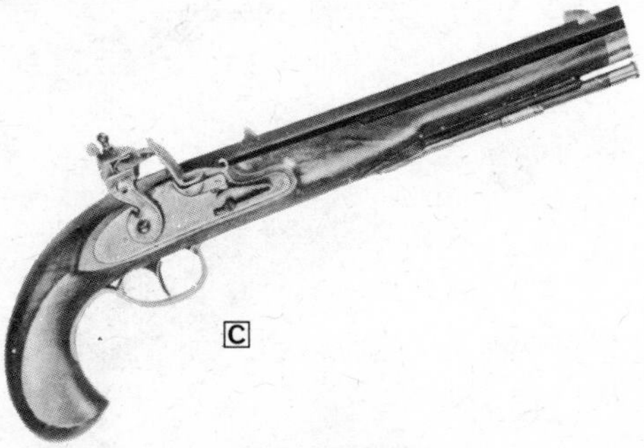

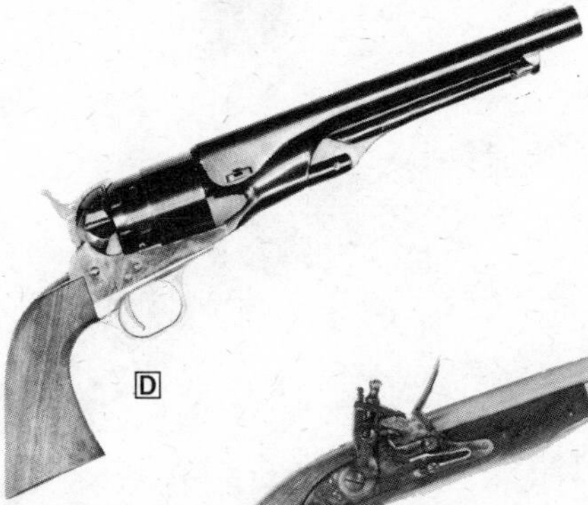

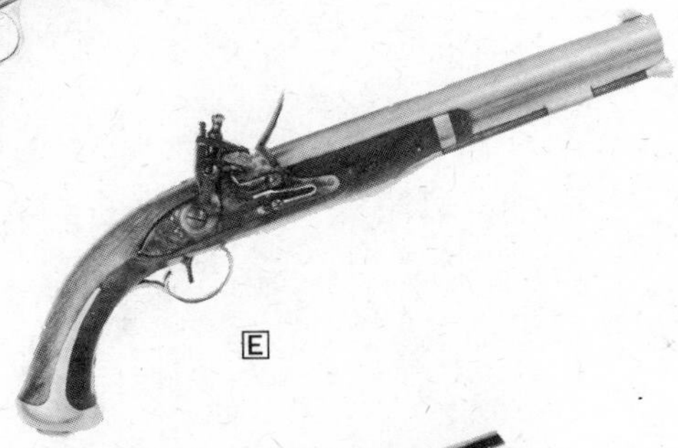

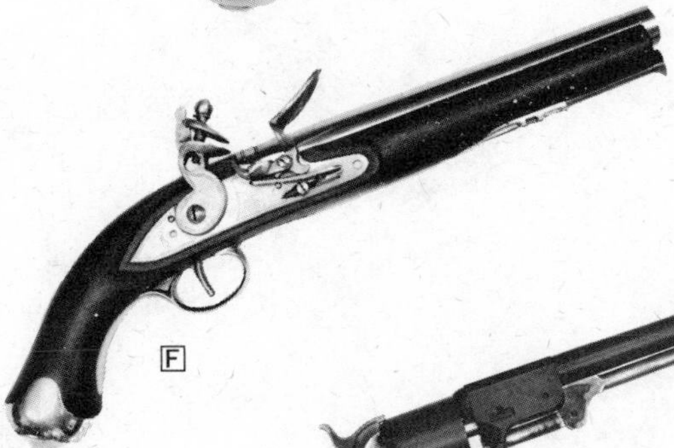

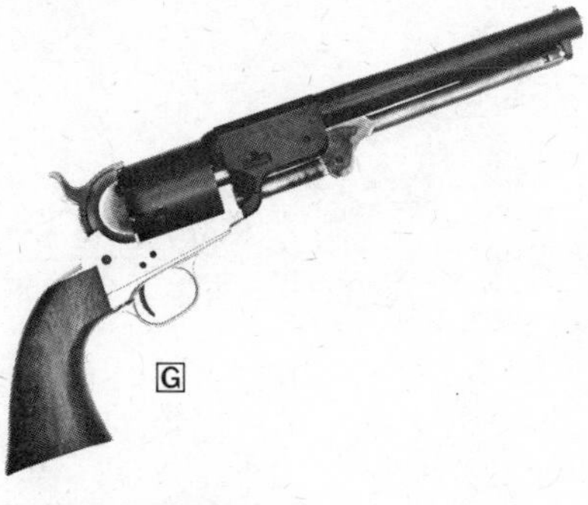

B HAWES FAVORITE PISTOL
Replica of the famous Stevens Favorite tip-up target pistol, with chrome frame and blued 8" barrel, moulded checkered white plastic grips. Fires 22 S, L or LR single-shot. Weight, 20 oz.; length 12" over-all **$32.95**
Deluxe model with smooth walnut grips **39.95**

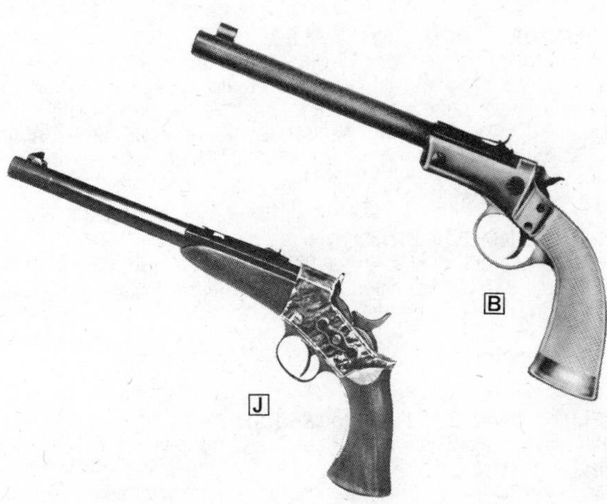

C KENTUCKIAN FLINTLOCK or PERCUSSION PISTOL
A single shot pistol designed for black powder only. 9½" octagon barrel, caliber 44, rifled. Brass front and steel rear sights are dove-tailed into barrel. Case hardened, engraved lockplate. Trigger guard, barrel cap, ramrod tip and thimbles solid brass. Polished one-piece full-length stock of select walnut. Weight about 40 oz.; 15½" over-all. Imported by Intercontinental Arms. Either form **$59.95**

D MARS EQUIPMENT 44 ARMY
Exact replica of Colt's 1860 Army revolver. Caliber 44, using .451" round ball, black powder and caps. 8" round barrel, walnut stocks, blue finish with case hardened frame. Weight, 44 oz. **$89.95**
Similar in 36 cal. Navy, brass mounted **49.95**

E MARS EQUIPMENT FLINTLOCK PISTOLS
Replica of the Harpers Ferry, model 1805. 16" over-all, 10" bbl., 54 cal. rifled bore. Varnished wood, brass mountings. Case hardened lock-plate marked with eagle, "U.S." and "Harpers Ferry 1807" **$99.95**
Also, Virginia model similar to the M-1805 but with swivel ramrod and shorter grip. Marked "Virginia" and "Richmond 1812" **$99.95**

F MARS EQUIPMENT BRITISH FLINTLOCK PISTOL
A replica of the British cavalry weapon of the Geoge III period. 69 caliber, smoothbore, for BLACK POWDER ONLY. Full length walnut fin-ished stock, steel barrel (9") and lock, brass fittings. Lock is marked "TOWER" and GR under a crown. Weight about 3½ lbs., 15¼" over-all **$39.95**

G NAVY ARMS 1861 COLT REVOLVER
A replica of the Colt 1861 Navy, 36 caliber percussion revolver. 7½" blued steel barrel; case hardened frame; brass back strap and trigger guard; one-piece walnut grips. Wgt. 41 oz., 13" over-all. **$80.00**
In presentation walnut case with powder flask, bullet mould and capper at **$125**. Engraving extra; **$60, $80, $120,** depending on style.

H NAVY ARMS 1860 ARMY REVOLVER
A percussion Army revolver, a copy of the 1860 Colt, with a pol-walnut grips. Cal. 36 or 44 . . . . **$45.00**
NAVY ARMS SHOULDER STOCK of highly polished walnut, fits all Navy Arms percussion revolvers **$30.00**

NAVY ARMS "YANK" AND "SHERIFF'S" REVOLVERS
Replicas of the Colt 1851 Navy revolver. Caliber 36, percussion. 7½" octagon barrel (Yank only); case hardened frame and loading lever; silver plated backstrap and trigger guard **$90.00**
Also available as Sheriff's model, with barrel length to customer order, with or without loading lever. Special order only **$90.00**
Engraved Yanks, **$60, $80, $120** extra, depending on style.

J NAVY ARMS ROLLING BLOCK PISTOL
Exact copy of Remington Number 3 rolling block pistol. Cal. 357 Magnum, with blued steel barrel, case-hardened frame, and walnut stock. Cased with accessories **$125.00**

NAVY ARMS KENTUCKY PISTOL
Flintlock, with rifled steel barrel, blued. Case hardened, engraved lockplates. Cal. 44, 15½" over-all. Navy Arms, importer.... $80.00

A NAVY ARMS 1858 NEW MODEL ARMY REVOLVER
A replica of the Remington 44 caliber Civil War percussion revolver. 8" octagon barrel; brass trigger guard; two-piece walnut grips. Weight 46 oz., 13¾" over-all. Blued.... $90.00
Also available in 36 caliber with 7⅜" barrel.... 90.00
Engraving extra; **$70, $90, $130,** depending on style.
Navy also supplies a full line of M.L. accessories, cappers, pouches, holsters, flasks and moulds. Brochure on request.

B RENEGADE PERCUSSION MODEL
Double barreled pistol, rifled, in 36 or 44 caliber, for black powder only. 8¼" blued barrels; case hardened frame. Sideplates, hammers, brass trigger guard and brass buttcap engraved. Proofed with 30% overload, certificate furnished. Weight 32 oz. Intercontinental Arms. $39.95

C REPLICA ARMS 44 DRAGOON
6-shot 44-cal. replica of the 2nd Dragoon Model percussion muzzle-loading revolver. 7½" bbl., blued and case-hardened. Square-back brass trigger guard. For black powder use.... $104.50
Flask 19.95

D REPLICA ARMS 1861 NAVY-1860 ARMY
36-cal., 6-shot black powder percussion Navy revolver, duplicating the Colt 1861 Navy. Frame, lever and hammer are case-hardened, rest of metal is blued. Iron or brass back strap is cut for stock.... $89.95
Same, but 44-cal. Army 89.95
Shoulder stock, either.... 35.00

E REPLICA ARMS WALKER REVOLVER
A replica of the big Walker Colt, this caplock gun weighs about 4½ lbs., measures 15¾" over-all. 6-shot. Case-hardened frame, hammer and lever; brass trigger guard. Cylinder has rolled engraving scene. 44 caliber, for black powder only. 9" octagon-round bbl. Left hand twist. From Replica Arms.... $115.00
Walker powder flask.... 19.95
Walker mould, single cavity.... 11.50
Walker tool 3.00
Cased, with all accessories.... 188.50

F REPLICA ARMS TEXAS PATERSON of 1836
Cal. 36 round ball only 6", 7½", 9" or 12" bbls. 11 groove, slow right hand twist. 17" over-all with 12" bbl. Folding trigger; smooth walnut grips. Case-hardened frame and hammer. Notch in hammer is rear sight, brass blade post front. 5-shot, blued, engraved cyl., for black powder only. From Replica Arms **$104.50.** With 12" bbl., **$109.50**
Paterson powder flask... **$20.00** Mould 12.50
Capper .... 12.00 Rod 1.50

G REPLICA ARMS BABY DRAGOON of 1848
Cal. 31, 5-shot. 4", 5", 6" octagon bbl. revolver, 10⅜" (6" bbl.) over-all, wgt. 25 oz. Case-hardened frame. Square brass trigger guard and back strap. One-piece smooth walnut grips. Notched hammer rear and post front sights. Polished blue finish, etched cyl. For black powder only. From Replica Arms.... $76.25
Brass bullet mould, double cavity.... 11.50
Powder flask, small.... 9.50

H REPLICA ARMS WELLS FARGO REVOLVER
Like the Baby Dragoon except: made with 3", 4", 5" or 6" bbl. without loading lever.... $73.00

J NAVY ARMS DERRINGER
A shooting replica of the sharps 4-barrel pistol. Polished brass frame; 2⅝" blued steel bbls. Black plastic carved grips. Spur trigger. Barrels move forward for loading, firing pin rotates to each bbl. position. 22 Short only. Weight 10 oz., 5" over-all.... $40.00
Also available in presentation walnut case at **$45.00.**

A BRONCO 22 RIFLE
Ultra lightweight single shot 22 featuring a swing-out chamber, skeletonized 1-pc. receiver and p.g. stock, push-button safety. Wgt. 3½ lbs. F. I., importer $14.95

B ERMA M22 CARBINE
A close copy of the U.S. M1 in 22 LR. 10-shot mag., 17¾" barrel, 35⁵⁄₁₆" over-all, original type sights. Receiver grooved for scope. 15-shot mag. also available at extra cost. 5¾ lbs. LA Distributors, importers $69.95

C FRANCHI CENTENNIAL AUTOLOADING RIFLE
A semi-automatic rifle with tubular magazine in the buttstock holds 11 22 L R cartridges (16 Shorts in Gallery model) Push-button cross-bolt safety, receiver grooved for scope mounting. Quick takedown feature. 21" barrel with gold bead ramp front and step adjustable open rear sights. Stock is walnut with checkered p.g. and finger-grooved semi-beavertail fore-end. Weight 5 lbs., 2 oz., 39" over-all. Stoeger, importer .... $ 86.95
Deluxe model with fully engraved receiver 124.95

D GEVARM E1 AUTOLOADING RIFLE
Carbine style take down rifle. Detachable 8 shot clip, cal. 22 LR. 19½" bbl. (6 grooves, 17½" twist). Reversible spring guide. Striker bar on breechblock, fires from open bolt, automatic ejection. Receiver grooved for Tip-Off mounts. Blade front sight, open adj. rear. Bolt handle safety. French walnut two-piece p.g. stock and fore-end, p.g. cap. 36⅞" over-all. Under 21" taken down. Gevelot, Canada, importers, U.S. dists., Blumenfeld Co $73.70

E GEVARM A3 AUTOLOADING SPORTER
Same as E1 except 19½" bbl., tunnel front sight with 5 interchangeable inserts, tangent sliding leaf rear. French walnut one-piece p.g. stock, schnabel-type fore-end tip $92.40

HERTER'S G-90 22 AUTO RIFLE
Tubular magazine holds 12 22 LR; side safety, bolt holds open on last shot, 20" bbl. Walnut p.g. stock and fore-end. Receiver grooved for tipoff scope mounts.. Blade front sight, adj. rear. 40½" over-all, 5¾ lbs. Herter, importers $39.55
With 4x scope and mount 50.55

F NAVY ARMS 66 RIFLE
Lever action 22 rimfire rifle built to resemble the Winchester 66. Full length tubular magazine, 14 LR capacity, brass frame and butt-plate. 18" blued bbl. Blade front sight, open leaf rear. Straight-grip walnut-finish stock, not checkered. 39½" over-all, wgt. 7 lbs. Navy Arms, importer $120.00

G SARMCO MODEL TZ-17 RIFLE
5-shot bolt action hunting carbine in 22 LR. Walnut half-p.g. stock, adj. trigger pull, blade front sight, open tangent adj. rear. Wgt. 5.9 lbs. Sarmco, importer $70.00

STEYR CUSTOM CARBINE
A bolt action rimfire repeater with detachable 5-shot clip magazine; safety on bolt with indicator; action is hand honed and grooved for Tip-Off mount. Double stage adj. trigger. Open leaf rear sight, hooded ramp front. Walnut full length stock with checkered p.g. and fore-end; sling swivels. Wgt. 5¾ lbs., 38½" over-all. Cal. 22 LR Stoeger, importer $140.00
with double set trigger $150.00

TRADEWINDS MODEL 311A RIFLE
Bolt action 22 LR repeater with detachable 5-shot clip magazine; sliding safety on receiver locks trigger and bolt handle. Open 3-leaf rear sight, hooded ramp front; receiver grooved for scope mounting. Monte Carlo walnut stock with checkered p.g. and fore-end; sling swivels. Wgt. 6 lbs., 41¼" over-all. Tradewinds, importer $84.50
5-shot clip .... $4.75   10-shot clip 5.75

H TRADEWINDS AUTOLOADING RIFLE
Detachable 5-shot mag., 23¾" bbl. cal. 22 LR. Bead front sight, 3-leaf folding rear. Receiver grooved for scope mounts. Walnut p.g. stock with cheekpiece, schnabel fore-end. 41½" over-all, 5¾ lbs. Tradewinds, importer $89.50

J WALTHER KKJ—22 RF & HORNET SPORTER
Bolt action sporting rifle, cal. 22 LR, 22 WMR or 22 Hornet. 22" barrel; 5-shot detachable clip magazine; open rear sight adjustable for w. and e. and bead front sight. Checkered Monte Carlo walnut p.g. stock (13⅞"x1⅜"x1¾"x2½"). Cross-bolt safety, receiver grooved for tip-off mounts. 41⅛" over-all, wgt. 6 lbs. Double set triggers $10 extra. Interarms, importers $144.00
22 Hornet or 22 RF Magnum calibers 144.00

[A] ALASKAN BOLT ACTION RIFLES
Made in Belgium, these rifles are available in three styles. Magnum rifles are chambered for 338, 300 Win. 7mm Rem. and 300 Weatherby. All have Monte Carlo stock of French walnut; p.g. and fore-end checkered and capped with rosewood; sling swivels and recoil pad attached. 24" barrel on rifles, 20" barrel on Magnum Carbine which has full length Mannlicher stock. No sights. Standard rifle can be had in 30-06, 243 or 7x57 but does not have recoil pad. Skinner's Sportsmans Supply, importer ....**$200.00** to **$225.00**

[B] BSA MONARCH DELUXE RIFLES
Available in 222, 243, 270, 308, 30-06 and 7mm Mag. BSA rifles feature a fully adjustable trigger, a bolt head that encloses the cartridge and is in turn enclosed by the barrel extension, a gas-proof cocking piece, hinged floorplate, silent safety with cocking indicator, integral scope dovetails, and a checkered, walnut stock with cheekpiece and recoil pad. Weight about 6¼ lbs. From Galef. **$149.95**

BSA MONARCH DELUXE VARMINT RIFLE
Same as Monarch DeLuxe except has heavy barrel, and made in 222 Rem. or 243 Win. only. About 8½ lbs. From Galef...........**$169.95**

[C] CETME-SPORT AUTO RIFLE
5-shot autoloader with unusual roller and cam breech-locking mechanism. Available with wood or steel (with bipod) fore-end. Flip-up aperture rear sight, protected blade front. Muzzle brake, carrying sling, spare mag., cleaning kit furnished. Cal. 308, 17¾" 4-groove bbl. (9.4" twist), 40" over-all, 10½ lbs. Cannot be converted to full auto. fire. Mars Equipment, importers..........................**$229.95**
Scope mounts with 1" or 26mm rings.................. **12.00**
20-shot magazine.................................... **9.50**

CONTINENTAL ARMS RIFLE
Bolt action rifle with hinged floorplate has Siemens Martin barrel; integral half rib with express rear, hinged hooded front ramp sights; swivel holder. Stock is of French walnut, checkered fore-end and p.g. with trap in grip cap; horn or ebony tip. Available in 338, 458 Win. Mag.; 244, 375 H&H, 8x68S, 416 Rigby, 505 Gibbs or custom chambered in other calibers. Continental Arms, importer.........**$450.00**

[D] CONTINENTAL ARMS DOUBLE RIFLE
Boxlock action, engraved with single selective trigger and auto. ejectors. Blade front and express rear sights. Straight two-piece stock with checkered p.g. and fore-end. Chambered for 270 Win., 30-40, 8x57JRS, 303, 30-06, 375 H&H, 450 500, 450 Nitro Express, 465 or 470 Rigby. Continental Arms, importer. Write for prices.

[E] FN SUPREME RIFLE
Available in all popular calibers, incl. Magnums. 24" barrel (22" in 308). Checkered Monte Carlo p.g. stock of French walnut. Streamlined bolt sleeve; 5-shot magazine (3-Mag., 4-243, 308); sliding side safety; hinged floorplate; adjustable trigger. Hooded ramp front and Tri-Range rear sights; tapped for scope. Weight about 7¾ lbs., 44½" over-all. Firearms International, importer. Standard calibers...**$254.50**
Supreme in 264, 300 Win., 7mm Mag., 220 Swift. **278.50**
Supreme bbld. action, std..**$133.50** Action only **83.50**
Supreme bbld. action, Mag. **157.50** Action only ..**89.50** to **96.75**
Supreme benchrest actions; single shot; solid bottom, no magazine or trigger ....**$82.25** to **$94.50**

[F] FERLACH DOUBLE RIFLE
Anson & Deeley engraved, silvered action, treble lock with Greener cross bolt. 22", 24" or 26" bbls., all popular calibers from 7x57mm to 300 Win. Mag. Two triggers each settable. Auto. safety and ejectors. Circassian walnut checkered p.g. stock and fore-end, with cheekpiece, horn p.g. cap and buttplate; ramp front sight and express rear. Wgt. 7½-8 lbs. Flaig's, importer. **$1,000.00**

[G] FERLACH DOUBLE O-U RIFLE
Like the Ferlach side-by-side double rifle except: double Greener 4-lock action, calibers 270 to 458 Win., matted-rib bbls. Left- or right-hand cheekpiece stock. 8½-9½ lbs. Flaig's, importer. ..**$1,100.00**
Other rifles and drillings available. Write for catalog.

[A] HERTER'S MARK J9 RIFLES

Bolt action sporters with BSA-type (British) action. Hooded, gas-diverting cocking piece, recessed bolt face encloses cartridge head, side safety, integral dovetail scope mount bases, fully adjustable trigger, hinged floorplate. Monte Carlo p.g. stock. Q.D. swivels, ramp front sight, adj. rear. 23½" bbl., about 6¼ lbs., all popular calibers, including Magnums. Custom Supreme Grade.... **$98.95.** With Douglas bbl. **$114.95**

Same, except without sights.. **$94.55.** With Douglas bbl... **109.95**

Same with sights, in Mannlicher stock.......... **109.95**

Same, except Presentation grade. Has selected wood stock, checkered and flared p.g. and fore-end, both capped with black plastic and white spacers........ **$107.75.** With Douglas bbl.......... **$123.95**

Same, except without sights.. **$103.35** With Douglas bbl... **1'8.95**

Bbld. actions, polished & blued **$71.45.** With Douglas bbl... **87.95**

Action only, in the white specify length or cartridge...... **55.50**

Varmint Model, with heavier stock, beavertail fore-end.... **118.95**

Same, without sights.......... **113.95**

HERTER MARK J9 RIFLES

Similar to U9 Models except: Based on improved Mauser type action (with adj. trigger), low-scope safety, integral scope mounting blocks on receiver. Cals. 22-250, 243, 6mm, 264, 270, 7mm Rem. Mag., 308, 30-06, 300 Win. Mag. Custom Grade.......... **$87.95**

Without sights **83.50**

Same, with Mannlicher stock.. **$96.75.** With varmint stock.. **96.75**

Same, Presentation Grade, checkered choice walnut stock, roll-over comb, black fore-end tip and p.g. cap with white-line spacers.. **96.75**

Without sights.......... **91.25**

Bbld. actions, blued.......... **63.50**

Actions, in the white (short).. **$49.95.** Long.......... **50.95**

[B] HUSQVARNA LIGHTWEIGHT RIFLES Series 4100

Mauser-type rifle in 243, 6.5x55, 270, 308, 30-06 with 20½" bbl. 41½" over-all. Adj. open rear, hooded ramp front sights; receiver tapped for peep and scope sights. Oiled French walnut stock with cheekpiece, checkered grip and fore-end. Hinged floorplate. Sling swivels. Wgt. about 6½ lbs. Tradewinds. **$175.00**

Series 4000, same as S-4100, but has high, Monte Carlo stock with cheekpiece. **$182.50**

Series 3000 Crown Grade, same as S-4000 but 23¾" bbl., 44¾" over-all; stock has ebonite p.g. cap and fore-end with white spacers; jeweled bolt. Wgt. about 7¼ lbs. Same cals. plus 7mm Magnum.

Monte Carlo stock. **$198.50**

Series 456-458, same as S-4000 except with full length stock, and not available in 6.5x55. Straight-comb stock. **$198.50**

With Monte Carlo. **210.00**

Presentation Rifle, same as Crown Grade except specially selected Monte Carlo stock; adjustable trigger; engraved action, guard and bbl. breech. Wgt. 7½ lbs. Cals. 7mm Magnum, 30-06, 270 and 243, 44" over-all **$410.00**

[C] HUSQVARNA 6000 IMPERIAL RIFLES

Same as S-3000 Crown Grade rifles except: Select European walnut Monte Carlo stock with cheekpiece, high gloss finish, 3-leaf folding rear sight and adjustable trigger. 243, 270, 308, 30-06 and 7mm Rem. Mag. Tradewinds, importer. **$257.50**

[D] HUSQVARNA 7000 IMPERIAL RIFLES

Same as S-4000 lightweight rifles except: Select European walnut Monte Carlo stock with cheekpiece, high gloss finish. Fully adjustable trigger, 3-leaf folding rear sight. 243, 270, 308 and 30-06 calibers. Tradewinds, importer. **$227.50**

HUSQVARNA ACTIONS & BBLD. ACTIONS

Same actions used in HVA rifles. 5-shot std., 3-shot in magnums; hinged floorplate, sliding safety at rear of bolt handle. Wgt. 2½ lbs., 8¾" over-all. Polished blue. Specify length. **$82.50**

Barreled actions (same calibers as in Crown Grade) std. 23¾", lightweight 20½". Tradewinds, importer. **$119.95**

[E] INTERNATIONAL BOLT ACTION RIFLE

British made Mauser-type action with jeweled bolt and hinged floorplate. Magazine holds 5 rounds, 3 in mag. cals. 24" barrel chambered for 243, 270, 308 Win., 30-06, 22-250 or 7mm Rem. Mag. Equipped with Williams ramp front and open mid sights. Monte Carlo stock of French walnut; checkered, capped p.g. and rosewood fore-end tip; sling swivels and Pachmayr recoil pad attached. Weight, 7½ lbs., 44" over-all. International Distributors, importer **$169.50**

[F] MANNLICHER SCHOENAUER RIFLES AND CARBINES

Made in carbine style with 20" bbl. (18¼" in 6.5mm), wgt. about 7½ lbs. In rifle style with sporter stock and 22" bbl., wgt. 7½-8 lbs. Carbine comes in 243, 6.5mm, 7mm, 270, 30-06, 308 and 358 Win. cals.; rifle in 243, 270 and 30-06 only. Hooded ramp front sight and folding leaf rear. Dummy sideplate aids fitting scope mount; tapped for Steyr mount. 5-shot rotary magazine. Spooned bolt handle. Walnut stock with medium high Monte Carlo comb, checkered p.g. (with cap and white spacer) and fore-end; rifle has black fore-end tip with white spacer; sling swivels. Adjustable single- or double-set trigger. From Stoeger. **$340.00**

Magnum model rifles available in 257 Weatherby, 264 Win., 338 Win. and 458 Win. with single trigger. **$370.00**

Alpine Carbine available with high grade, hand carved wood, hand engraving, in 243 and 30-06. .... **$540.00**

[G] PARKER-HALE MAUSER RIFLE

Imported by JANA International, the 1200 Super series bolt action rifle has adj. trigger; hinged floorplate; hooded ramp front and folding middle sight; receiver tapped for scope mounts; sling swivels with sling and recoil pad. Monte Carlo stock with checkered p.g. and fore-end. Contrasting color fore-end tip and p.g. cap, both with white line spacers. 22" bbl. 43" over-all, wgt. 7½ lbs. Cal. 243, 270, 30-06, 308 Win. (5 shot). **$149.95**

7mm Rem. Mag. 300 Win. Mag. or 308 Norma Mag......... **159.95**

PRESENTATION RIFLE, same as the 1200 Super except with French walnut stock, fully scroll engraved action, trigger guard and magazine floor plate. Also, no sights. Std. Cals. **$199.95.** Mag. Cals..... **$209.95**

VARMINT RIFLE, same as the 1200 Super except with a glass bedded free floating 24", 4 lb. target bbl., target scope base blocks. Wgt. 9½ lbs. In cals. 22/250, 6mm Rem & 243............ **$169.95**

SAKO FINNBEAR RIFLE

3-lug, long L-61 action, bolt handle safety lug, cold-swaged barrel, recessed bolt face. Checkered walnut stock with Monte Carlo comb, recoil pad and sling swivels. Calibers: 264, 270, 7mm Rem. Mag., 30-06, 338, and 300 Win. Mag. Firearms Int., importer. **$220.30**

Also available in Deluxe grade with French walnut stock, skipline checkering, contrasting grip cap and fore-end tip, engraved trigger guard and floorplate, recoil pad. **$309.10**

L-61 barreled action **141.95**

L-61 action only **96.45**

B SAKO "FINNWOLF" RIFLE

Hammerless lever action rifle with a gear-operated, short-throw lever. Solid frame with side ejection; detachable 4-shot box magazine; cross-bolt safety behind trigger. One-piece walnut stock (13¾"x1½"x 2⅝") with Monte Carlo cheekpiece, fluted comb, checkered p.g. and fore-end; sling swivels, checkered plastic buttplate and p.g. cap. 23½" bbl. has bead front sight on hooded ramp; no rear sight. Mount blocks for 1" Tip-Off mounts. Wgt. about 7 lbs., 42¼" over-all. Cals. 243 and 308. F.I., importer **$235.95**

C SAKO FORESTER RIFLE

Sako L579 medium-length action and a cold formed Swedish 23" steel barrel (12-groove, 1-12" twist), made in 22-250, 243 and 308 cal. Features include: integral, tapered-dovetail scope blocks; Sako adjustable trigger; hinged floorplate and Dual-Range rear sight (optional). Monte Carlo walnut stock, checkered at p.g. and fore-end. Over-all, 42". Weight 6½ lbs. F.I., importers **$198.65**

With Mannlicher stock 20" bbl., 39" over-all **224.35**

Deluxe grade. Same extras as Sako Vixen Deluxe......... **284.60**

Heavy barrel model (8 lbs.), 243 or 22-250 cal., less front sight. **220.75**

L579 action, medium and benchrest only **87.75**

L579 barreled action **131.05**

Heavy barreled action, 243 or 22-250 cal. only. **141.95**

D SAKO VIXEN RIFLE

Using the L-461, shortest of Sako actions, otherwise it is like the Sako Forester. Three styles: Sporter, 23½" bbl.; Mannlicher, 20" bbl. and Heavy Barrel, 23½", no front sight. Calibers: Rem. 222, 223 and 222 Magnum. Firearms International, importer.

Sporter, weight 6½ lbs., 43⅜" over-all **$192.55**

Mannlicher, weight 6½ lbs., 40" over-all **208.55**

Heavy barrel, weight 8 lbs., 43⅜" over-all **206.00**

Sporter also available in deluxe grade with French walnut stock, skip-line checkering, contrasting grip cap and fore-end tip, engraved trigger guard and floor plate; recoil pad **$265.65**

Sako L461 barreled action **$124.45**. Heavy bbld. action ... **$128.95**

L461 action, short and benchrest only **83.35**

E SCHULTZ & LARSEN 68DL RIFLE

A 4-lug bolt action rifle with tubular receiver, 24" bbl., adj. trigger; thumb safety; hinged floorplate. Walnut Monte Carlo stock (13½" pull) with checkered p.g. and fore-end; white line recoil pad and grip cap; 1" swivels. 44½" over-all, 7½ lbs. Without sights. Cal. 264 Win., 7x61 S&H, 7mm Rem., 308 Norma 300 Win., 338 Win. Magnum; 22-260, 243 Win., 6mm Rem., 6.5x55, 270 Win., 308 Win. Fessler, importer. **$485.00**

Same except 458 Win. Mag. **588.00**

F SHIKAR BOLT ACTION RIFLE

A sporter weight rifle with select walnut p.g. stock, basket-weave checkered on p.g. and fore-end. Contrasting wood fore-end tip, recoil pad, both with white-line spacers. Without sights. Cals. 243, 270, 7mm Rem. Mag., 30-06, 308 and 300 Win. Mag. LA Distributors, importer. **$249.50**

STEYR-MANNLICHER MODEL SL RIFLE

Receiver is machined from solid steel and has a detachable 5-shot rotary-drum magazine. Bolt has six locking lugs, cocking indicator and recessed face. Open rear, hooded ramp front sights. Safety locks bolt and sear. Choice of single- or double-set trigger. Monte Carlo stock, checkered p.g. and fore-end, epoxy finished. Available in 222 Rem., 222 Rem. Mag., or 223. Weight 6¼ lbs. Stoeger, importer.... **$195.00**

Carbine with full-length Mannlicher stock................ **205.00**

Target rifle with 26" heavy bbl., without sights.......... **205.00**

STEYR-MANNLICHER MODEL L RIFLE

Similar to Model SL, but with long action for caliber 22-250 Rem., 225 or 243 Win. **$195.00**

Chambered for 308 Win. **213.95**

Target rifle with 26" heavy bbl., without sights.......... **205.00**

Carbine with full-length Mannlicher stock................ **205.00**

Carbine chambered for 308 Win........................ **224.00**

STEYR-MANNLICHER MODEL M RIFLE

Similar to Model L, but cals. 7x57, 270 or 30-06........ **$240.00**

Carbine with full-length Mannlicher stock................ **250.00**

STEYR-MANNLICHER MODEL S RIFLE

Similar to Model M, but in cals. 7MM Rem. Mag., 257 Wby., 264 Win. Mag., 300 HH Mag., 338 Win. Mag., 375 HH Mag., & 458 Win. Mag. **$265.00**

G TRADEWINDS "HUSKY" LIGHTWEIGHT RIFLE

HVA action. 21½" Swedish steel barrel with hammer-forged bore. Bead front and fixed rear sights. Italian walnut stock, hand checkered, with Monte Carlo comb; cal. 22-250, 243, 270, 7mm Mag., 30-06. About 6½ lbs., 43" over-all.. **$157.75**

H TRADEWINDS 600 VARMINT RIFLE

Short HVA action has 23¾" medium-wgt. barrel in cals. 222 Rem., 222 Rem. Mag., 22-250, 223, 243 and 308 Win. No sights, tapped for standard scope mounts. 4 shot (3 in 22-250, 243 or 308) detachable box magazine, adjustable double set trigger. Monte Carlo European walnut stock with cheekpiece, checkered p.g. and fore-end. About 6¾ lbs. Tradewinds, importer. Test target accompanies rifle. **$169.50**

Same as above except with adj. single trigger, steel trigger guard, front sight and folding rear sight........................ **$172.50**

TRADEWINDS ACTION & BBLD. ACTIONS

Same actions used in the series 600 rifles. 4-shot std., 3-shot in magnums; hinged floorplate, sliding safety at rear of bolt handle, adjustable double set trigger. Weight 2½ lbs., 7⅞" over-all. Polished blue. Specify length. **$89.95**

Barreled actions (same calibers as Series 600 rifles) with 23¾" barrel. 30¾" over-all. Weight 4¾ lbs. **$129.95**

Brevex Magnum Mauser action. Hardened and heat-treated chrome-vanadium steel receiver, internal release on hinged floorplate, single stage trigger. For caliber 378 Weatherby, 404 Jeffreys & 416 Rigby. Weight 3¼ lbs., 9½" over-all, delivered in the white. Tradewinds, importer. **$160.00**

[A] BSA MARTINI-INTERNATIONAL MK III 22 RIFLE

Made by Birmingham Small Arms Co., the MK III features the Martini action; new free floating barrel press-fitted into action and locked in place by two cross bolts. Available in left or right hand cheekpiece models, the loading port and sight base are also reversed for southpaw shooters. 29″ barrel, 12 or 14½ lbs. Trigger adjustable from ½ to 3½ lb. pull. Dovetail base on action for tube sight mounting, regular bases on bbl. for scope mounts. Al Freeland, importer.

Without sights, light or heavy model **$210.00**

Available with Parker-Hale, Freeland or Redfield International sights at extra cost.

[B] PARKER-HALE 1200 TX TARGET RIFLE

Cal. 7.62mm NATO (308 Win.), 5-shot magazine. 26″ free floating (1″ dia.) glass bedded bbl. Mauser '98 action (commercial) with adj. single stage trigger and triple (trigger, bolt & sear) locking sliding thumb safety. Oil finished walnut target stock (13³⁄₁₆″x1¹¹⁄₁₆″x1¹⁵⁄₁₆″) has high comb beavertail fore-end, full p.g. recoil pad and adj. hand stop. 46¾″ over-all, wgt. 10½ lbs. Jana International, importer. —Price to be announced.

[C] HAMMERLI-TANNER MATCH RIFLE

Designed for 300 meter competition, this heavy (16¼ lbs.) single shot "free" rifle is available in most popular centerfire calibers. Barrel length 29½″. Micrometer click rear sight has variable aperture and is adjustable for w. and e.; globe front sight has 4 inserts. Walnut thumbhole stock has adjustable palm rest and sling swivel; buttplate adjusts to any position. Available only on special order with 6- to 10-month delivery. H. Grieder, importer **$590.00**

SARMCO OLYMPIC MATCH TARGET RIFLE

Bolt action center- and rimfire rifles, made to order only to insure meeting latest Olympic and I.S.U. regulations. Delivery time, 4 mos. Double set trigger, adj. from ½-lb. to 3.3 lbs.; ⅙-minute aperture rear sight; detachable hooded front sight. Palm rest, buttplate, swivel, sling, stock angle, butt length are all adj. Russian walnut thumbhole stock, thumbrest pistol grip, cheekpiece, hook buttplate and detachable hooks. Tools, cleaning equipment and accessories (including extra sights) in fitted walnut case, contained with the rifle in a plush-lined carrying-storage case.

Strela, wgt. 15.2 lbs., 22LR cal. **$395.00**
Zenith, wgt. 17.2 lbs. 7.62mm Russ. cal. **550.00**

[D] SCHULTZ & LARSEN 61 MATCH RIFLE

22 LR single shot bolt action rifle meeting International Match requirements. Has a 28″ free-floating bbl., globe front sight with removable inserts. Micro. peep rear sight with removable iris discs, adj. for w. and e. 32″ sight radius. 2 adj. buttplates furnished for offhand and prone positions. Adj. palm rest. Walnut thumbhole stock with cheekpiece and adj. handrest. Full length rail under stock to adj. forward sling swivel, hand stop and palm rest. Choice of trigger systems: adj. "hair"; adj. double pull or slack trigger (4-14 oz.); or adj. double pull (3-4 lbs.). 49″ over-all; wgt. approx. 16½ lbs. Fessler, importer. **$565.00**

SCHULTZ & LARSEN 62 MATCH RIFLE

Same as the S&L 61 except: for centerfire calibers. 4-lug bolt action, 27½″ bbl., 33½″ sight radius; 50″ over-all; wgt. approx. 17 lbs. Cal. 6.5x55 Swedish, 7.62 Nato, or any other standard caliber. Fessler, importer. **$585.00**

[E] WALTHER KKS-D STANDARD 22 MATCH RIFLE

A bolt action single shot rifle with double locking lugs; wing safety on bolt; light trigger pull; 25.6″ bbl. and 44″ over-all. Walnut stock with checkered p.g. and fixed sling attachment on fore-end. Globe front sight, aperture rear sight adj. for w. & e. Wgt. 8½ lbs.; cal. 22 LR. Interarms, importer **$114.50**

As the KKM Matchmaster; like the KKS-D except: adj. trigger pull. Checkered fore-end also; rubber butt with dove-tail bar; slide bar on fore-end with adj. sling attachment, two extra front sight inserts. Wgt. 10 lbs. **$119.50**

As the KKM-11; same features as the KKM except: with adj. alloy hook buttplate plus regular buttplate and adj. palm rest. Wgt. 12 lbs., 44½″ over-all **$139.50**

As the KKM International; same as the KKM-11 except: 28″ heavy tapered bbl. (heavier bbl. without taper available). Heavy walnut stock with thumbhole and adj. hand shelf. 8 sight inserts incl. Wgt. 15½ lbs. (with straight bbl. 17 lbs.), 46″ over-all................... **$198.50**

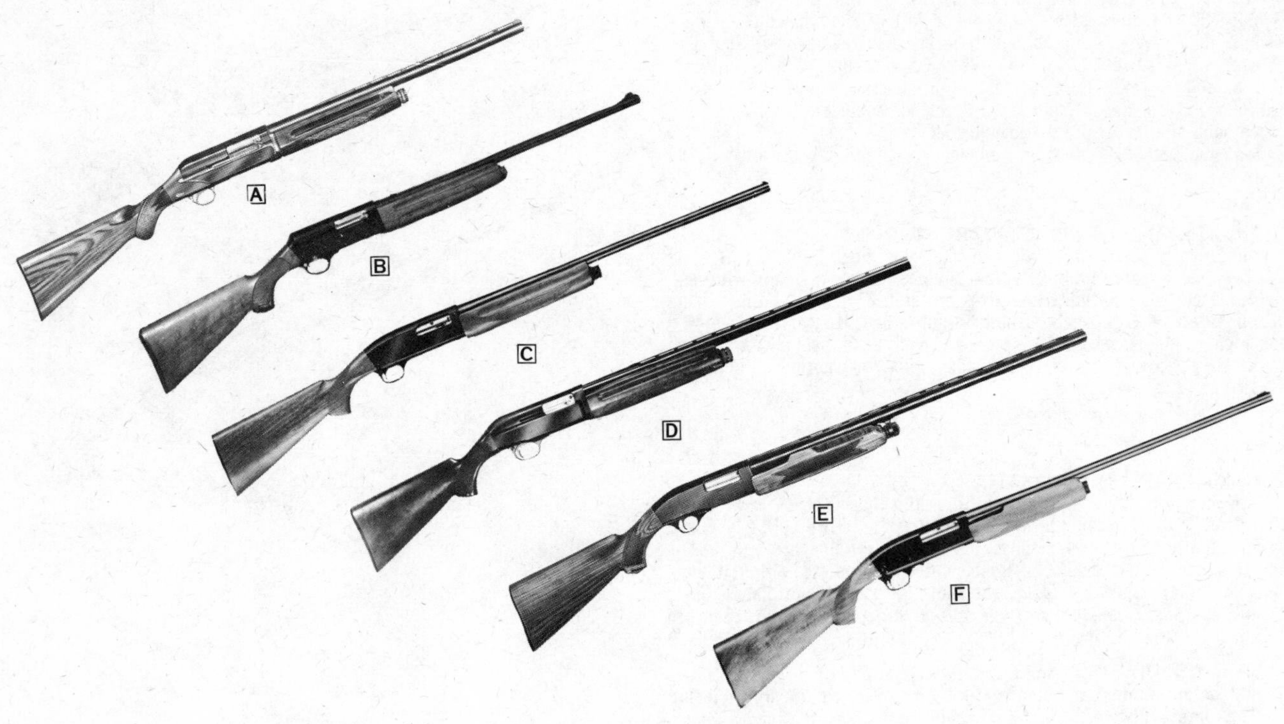

BERETTA AL-2 AUTOMATIC SHOTGUN

Gas-operated in 12 or 20 ga., 2¾" chambers. 28" Full or Mod., 26" Imp. Cyl. chokes, ventilated-rib interchangeable barrels. Hand-checkered p.g. walnut stock (14⅛"x1½"x2½") and fore-end. 3-shot mag. can be emptied without working shells through action. Engraved receiver. Crossbolt safety. Wgt. 7¼ lbs. Garcia, importer....**$200.00**

Also with middle bead as the AL-2 Skeet (12ga. 26", Skeet) and AL-2 Trap (14⅜"x1⅜"x1¾") 12 ga. 30" Full...............**$210.00**

Extra barrels **80.00**

A BREDA AUTOMATIC SHOTGUNS

Italian made in 12 or 20 ga., 2¾" or 3" chambers. Magazine holds four 2¾" or three 3" shells; extension tube (extra) for 7 shots. Nickel-chrome steel barrel with vent. rib or plain has muzzles threaded for "Quick Choke" tubes; 24½" length. Barrel bore, breech and bolt assembly are hard chromed. Auto. magazine cut-off; push-button holds carrier latch in loading position; depressing cartridge retaining lever unloads magazine. Adjustable stock of Italian walnut has checkered p.g. and beavertail fore-end, 14"x2½"x1⅝". Continental Arms, importer ....**$169.50 to $194.50**

B FRANCHI AUTOMATIC SHOTGUNS

Made in 12 and 20, 2¾" chamber. These Stoeger imports have alloy receivers, chrome-lined bbls., auto. cut-off, 4-shot cap., walnut checkered pistol grip and fore-end. Adj. friction piece sets recoil for standard on hi-vel. loads. 24" or 26" (Imp. Cyl.), 28" (Full or Mod.) or 30" Full (12 only). Wgt. 12, 6¼ lbs., 20, 5 lbs. Plain bbl. **$164.95** • Vent. rib bbl. **$191.95** • 3" Magnum models in 12 (32") or 20 (28") Full, with steel receivers and recoil pads. Wgt. 12, 8¼ lbs. 20, 6 lbs. Plain bbl. 12, **$185.95** • 20, **$175.95** • Vent. rib bbl. 12, **$212.95** • 20 **$202.95**

The Hunter. Same as the Standard except: vent. rib only; engraved receiver, high finish select walnut stock, chromed trigger. **$221.95**

Slug Gun, 12 or 20, 22" Cyl. bbl. with blade front and rear sight adj. for w. and e.; sling swivels. 12 ga., choice of steel or alloy receiver. 20 ga., alloy only **$201.95**

Dynamic 12. Same as the Standard except: 12 only, steel receiver, chromed breech bolt and lifter, **$169.95** • With vent. rib. **$201.95** • Skeet Gun, **$201.95** • Slug Gun..........................**$201.95**

Wildfowler. Same as Standard Mag. except: ventilated rib bbl. 20 has alloy receiver. 12, **$253.95** • 20......................**$249.95**

Eldorado. Same as the Standard except: vent. rib only. Receiver scroll engraved; gold plated trigger, chromed breech bolt. Also made with 3" (magnum) chambers in 12 (32") or 20 (28") Full choke bbls. **$324.95**

Other highly decorated Franchis, Crown **$750**, Diamond **$1,000** and Imperial **$1,200.00.**

Extra bbls. Plain **$48.** (Mag. **$55**), Vent. rib. (V.R. Mag. **$75**). Slug or Skeet **$68.**

C LA SALLE AUTOMATIC SHOTGUNS

12-gauge, 2¾" chambers, 30" or 28" full choke bbl., 28" modified or 26" imp. cyl. barrel, chromed bore. Magazine has 3-shot capacity. Wgt., about 6½ lbs. Custom grade has checkered walnut pistol grip stock and fore-end. F-I, Importer..........................**$169.95**

Extra interchangeable chrome lined bbl.................. **34.80**

D TRADEWINDS H-150 & H-170 AUTO SHOTGUNS

Light alloy receiver, 5-shot tubular magazine. 12 gauge only, 2¾"; 26" (Imp. Cyl.), 28" (Mod. or Full), 30" (Full). Select Italian walnut stock, p.g. and fore-end hand checkered. Wgt. 6¾ lbs. Ramp-mounted bead front sight....**$159.95** H-170, Same except vent. rib....**$179.95**

Deluxe 200 series, same as 170 except engraved receiver **$227.50** • Trap model (14⅜"x1⅜"x1⅞"), 30" bbl. **$227.50**

E BERETTA SL-2 SLIDE ACTION SHOTGUN

Slide action 12 ga., 2¾" chambers. 28" Full or Mod., 26" Imp. Cyl,. ventilated rib interchangeable barrels. Hand-checkered walnut p.g. stock (14⅛"x1½"x2³⁄₁₆") and fore-end. 3-shot magazine can be emptied without working shells through action. Crossbolt safety. Wgt. 7¼ lbs. Garcia, importer **$185.00**

Extra barrels **72.00**

F LA SALLE SLIDE ACTION SHOTGUNS

Made by Manufrance with a light alloy receiver, French walnut stock and fore-end with new waterproof finish, 14"x1⅝"x2¼". plain or chromed interchangeable barrels, oversized crossbolt safety head. Made in 12 or 20 ga. (3" chamber) with 26" (Imp. Cyl.), 28" (Mod. or Full) bbls. Also with 3" chambers in 12 ga. (30"). Full choke bbls. Standard model with plain stock and grooved fore-end, **$97.95.** Custom model with checkered pistol grip and fore-end and chrome plated bore in 12 ga. and 12 ga. magnum only. F. I., importers **$137.95**

Extra barrel, plain........**$18.00** Chrome lined........**$33.70**

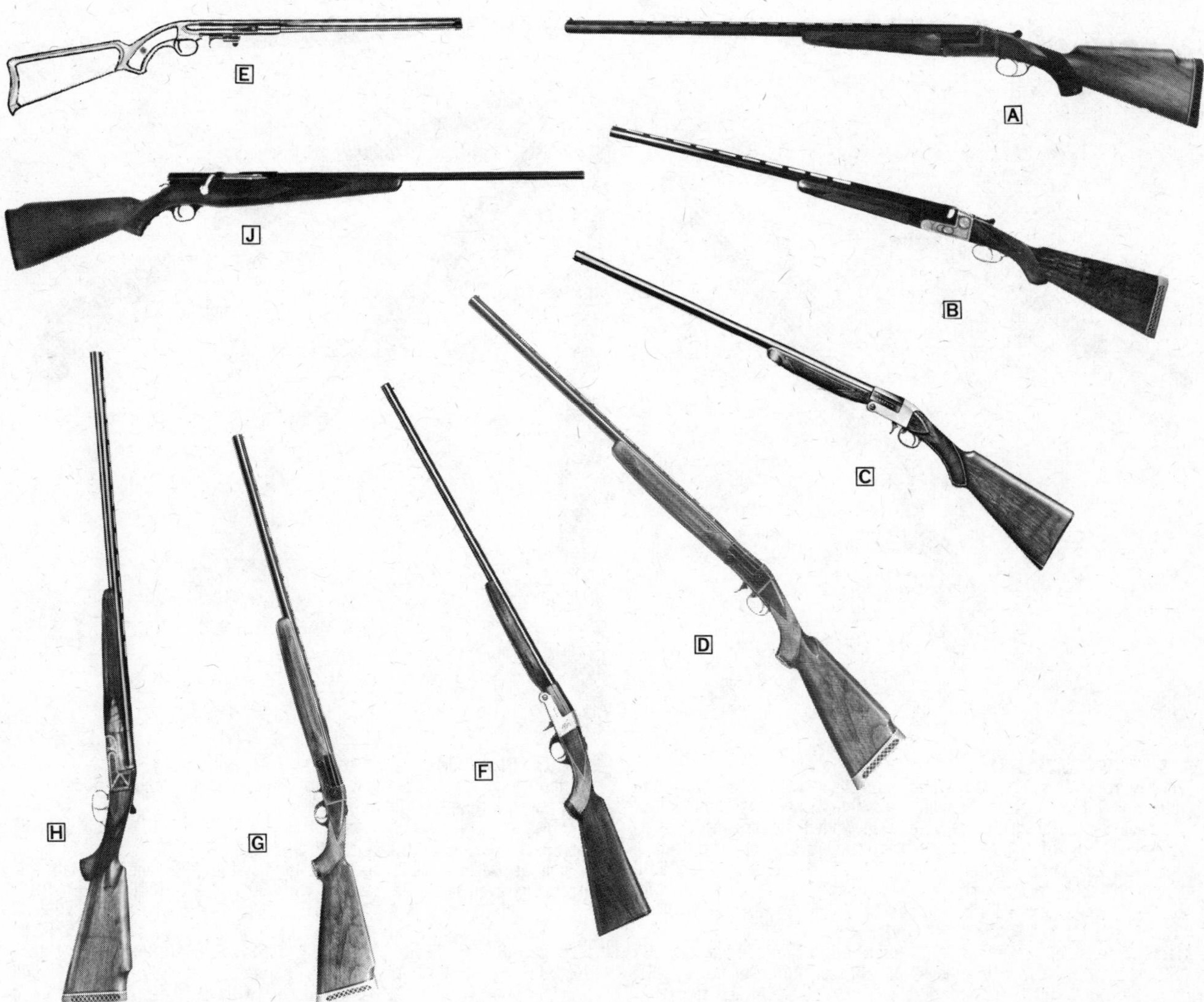

A A & F SINGLE BARREL TRAP GUN
Made in Italy, this 12 ga. gun has a vent. rib barrel, checkered walnut p.g. stock with Monte Carlo comb, and recoil pad. Abercrombie and Fitch, importer **$395.00**

B ATLAS SINGLE BARREL TRAP GUN
30" or 32" vent. rib barrel of Boehler steel; chromed bore; 12 gauge only. Checkered walnut Monte Carlo stock (14½"x1⅜"x1⅞"x2¼") and beavertail fore-end; recoil pad; engraved action and auto. ejector, weighs about 8 lbs. **$365.00**
With custom engraving, gold trigger and gold lettering **425.00**

C BERETTA FS-1 FOLDING SHOTGUN
This hammerless single is made in 12 (30"), 20 (28"), 28 or .410 ga. (26") full choke bbl.; stock has checkered walnut grip and fore-end, the latter permanently attached. Barrel is made in Beretta mono-bloc construction. Cocks on opening; crossbolt safety in trigger guard. Wgt. from 4½ lbs. (410) to 5½ lbs. (12 ga.). Garcia, importer. **$65.00**

D BERETTA TR-1 MONTE CARLO TRAP SHOTGUN
12 ga. only, 2¾" chambers, 32" single barrel trap-choked, with vent rib. Crossbolt safety, auto. ejector. Engraved receiver. Checkered Monte Carlo p.g. stock of European walnut (14⅜"x1⅜"x1¾") with beavertail fore-end and trap-style recoil pad. Bbl. release in front of guard. Front and middle bead sights. Garcia, importer. Wgt. about 8¼ lbs. **$160.00**
Also, with extended vent rib as the TR-2 .... **$175.00**

E BRONCO 410 SHOTGUN
Lightweight single shot (3" chamber), featuring swing-out chamber, skeletonized 1-pc. receiver and p.g. stock, push-button safety. 4½ lbs. F. I., importer **$19.95**

F COMPANION FOLDING SHOTGUN
Monobloc receiver is machined from solid stock and satin chrome-plated. Available in 12, 20 and 410 ga. (3" chambers) and 16 or 28 ga. (2¾") with 28" (Full) barrel (30" Full also in 12 ga., 26" Full only in 410). European walnut stock (14"x1½"x2⅝") has checkered fore-end and capped p.g., plastic buttplate. Weight 4½ to 5½ lbs. Galef, importer **$49.95**
With vent. rib **54.95**

CHARLES DALY SUPERIOR GRADE TRAP GUN
12 ga. (2¾"), 32" (Full) Vent rib (4⁄10") bbl., double beads. Scroll engraved receiver is nickel finished. Manual safety, auto ejector, recoil pad. Checkered Monte Carlo p.g. stock and beavertail forearm with Greener type lock. Daly, importer **$329.50**

J DICKSON BOLT ACTION SHOTGUN
.410 (3") Spanish made weighs 5½ lbs. 3-snot capacity. 25" full choke bbl. Checkered p.g. and fore-end. Sliding thumb safety. American Import, importer **$32.50**

KREIGHOFF SINGLE BARREL TRAP
12 ga. (2¾") 32" or 34" (Full) vent. rib bbls. Internal parts are hardened heat treated steel. Mechanical trigger, short hammer fall. Monte Carlo stock with checkered p.g. and grooved beavertail fore-end. Thumb safety. Wgt. about 8½ lbs. Europa, importer. (Standard) **$750.00**
Also, San Remo grade, **$1,150.00**; Monte Carlo grade, **$2,750.00**; Crown grade, **$2,850.00** and Super Crown grade, **$3,150.00**.
Extra bbls. **$295.00**

G MONTE CARLO TRAP GUN
Made in Italy, this single barrel 12 ga. trap gun has a 32" vent. rib barrel; engraved, blued receiver with automatic extractor and gold-plated trigger. Monte Carlo stock has recoil pad and hand-checkered p.g. and fore-end. Weight 8¼ lbs. Galef, importer **$149.95**

ROSSI SINGLE BARREL SHOTGUN
Available in all gauges with 29" full-choked barrel and 2¾" chamber, except 3" 410. Tip-up action has exposed hammer; stock has checkered p.g. Made in Brazil. Firearms International, importer . . **$29.95**

H STOEGER 27 TRAP GUN
Boxlock action, single bbl., double under-locking lugs, Greener type crossbolt, ejector, has no safety. 12 ga., 30" (Imp. Mod.) or 32" (Full) chrome lined bbl. (Full), with vent. rib. Checkered Monte Carlo p.g. stock (14½"x1⅜"x2⅛"), with beavertail fore-end. 49" over-all, wgt. 8¼ lbs. Stoeger Arms Corp., importer **$449.50**

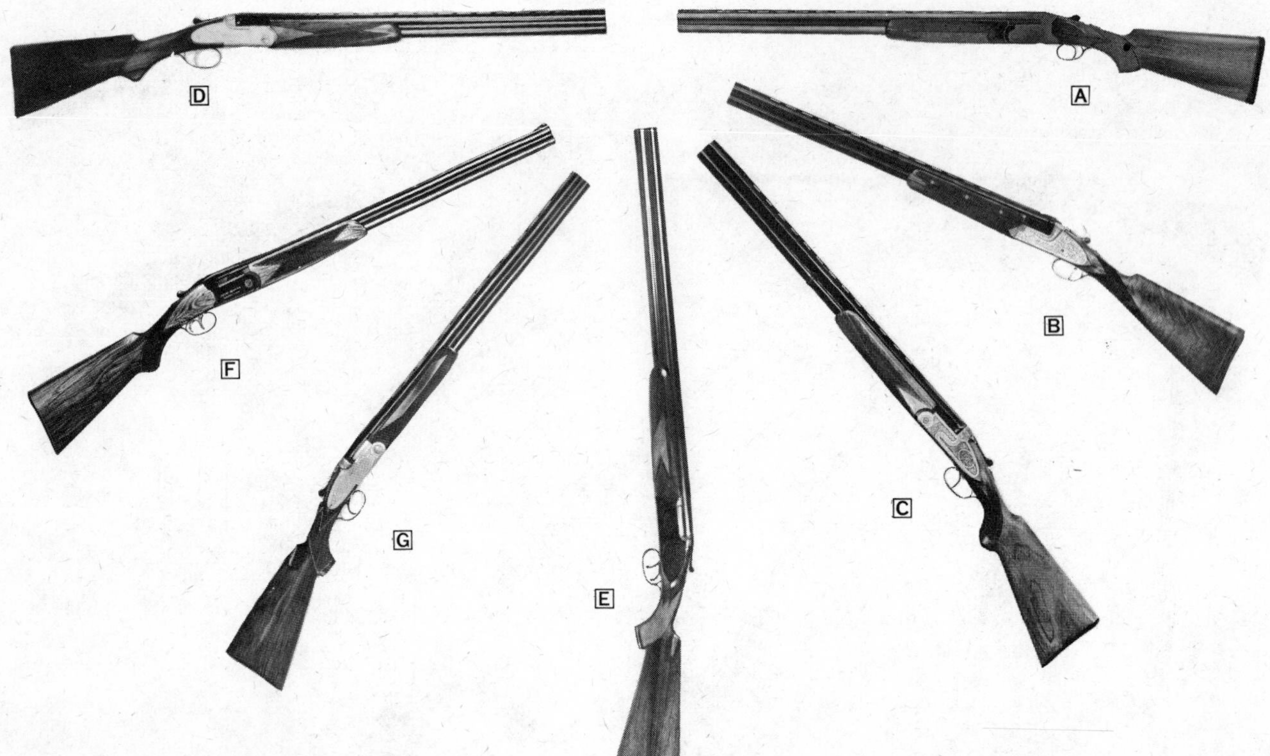

A A & F PERAZZI O-U
Made in Italy, this 12 ga. features interchangeable stocks for Trap or Field, and interchangeable double or single trigger assemblies. All models have vent. ribs, hand-checkered p.g. walnut stocks with beavertail fore-ends, bright-finished actions. Abercrombie & Fitch, importer.
Trap, with 29" bbl., parallel rib, wgt. 7½ lbs. **$875.00**
Pigeon, 28" bbl., tapered rib, wgt. 7¼ lbs. **875.00**
Skeet, 26" bbl., tapered rib, wgt. about 7 lbs. **950.00**

B ATLAS GRAND PRIX OVER-UNDER
Merkel-type sidelock action, fully engraved, 12 or 20 gauge, 26" or 28" vent. rib barrels in choice of chokes. Auto. ejectors, SST, straight or p.g. stock to order; about 7¼ lbs. Atlas, importer. From .... **$700.00** up

C ATLAS MODEL 750 OVER-UNDER
Merkel-type action, highly engraved; 12, 16 or 20 gauge, vent. rib barrels 26" or 28" in standard chokes; non-ejector, non-selective single trigger. Straight or p.g. stock, hand checkered (14½"x1½"x2½"), 6¼-7 lbs. Atlas, importer **$245.00**
Same as M750 but 3" Magnum in 12 or 20 ga. **245.00**
Same as M750 but 30" bbls., and auto ejectors **265.00**

D ATLAS MODEL 87 OVER-UNDER
Similar to M750 but p.g. stock only (14"x1½"x2½"), silvered or case-hardened action. Atlas, importer **$230.00**
Same, but in 3" Magnum (as M95) **235.00**
Same, but boxlock action, 26" bbls. only, double triggers, and 3" in 28 or 410 ga. only (as M65) **$195.00**
Same, but with non-selective ST (as M65-ST) **225.00**

ATLAS 150 SERIES OVER-UNDER SHOTGUN
12 and 20 ga. Bbls. 26" (IC & M or Skeet), 28" (M & F), 30" (F & extra F). Vent. rib. Boxlock action with crossbolt. Chromed bores, silver-plated or case-hardened engraved receiver. Single non-selective triggers. Straight or p.g. stock, checkered. Wgt. 6½-7¼ lbs. Atlas Arms, importer .... **$275.00** With ejectors **$325.00**
With better engraving, as the M160 .... **295.00**
M160 with auto-ejectors, as the M180 (12 ga. only) **345.00**

E BAIKAL MODEL IJ-12 O-U SHOTGUN
Available in 12 ga. (2¾") only, this Russian made shotgun has 28" barrels (Mod. & Full) with chrome-plated chambers and bores, and raised solid rib. Top lever action has full barrel width locking plate and non-auto., top tang safety. Stock has hand-checkered p.g. and fore-end. Weight 7¼ lbs. Finley-Moody, importers **$175.00**

F BERETTA BL-1 OVER-UNDER SHOTGUN
Low-profile Monoblock boxlock action, 12 ga., with 30" or 28" M&F or 26" IC&M chrome-moly steel barrels. Double triggers, front trigger hinged, w/o ejectors. Walnut p.g. stock (14¼"x1⅝"x2½", 2" pitch down) and fore-end hand checkered. Auto safety, 2¾" chambers. Ramp front sight, 4 fluorescent inserts. Wgt. 7 lbs. Garcia, importer **$190.00**
Extra bbls. **110.00**

Beretta BL-2 O-U
Selective single trigger version of BL-1. Trigger selector located on upper tang, integral with safety **$235.00**
Extra bbls. **110.00**

Beretta BL-3 DeLuxe O-U Shotgun
Same as Beretta BL-2, but with gold-plated SST, and ventilated-rib barrel. Engraved receiver. 12 ga., with 30" or 28" M&F or 26" IC&M chrome-lined barrels. Wgt. 7⅛ lbs. **$265.00**
3" Mag., 30" M&F barrels, 7⅜ lbs. **$265.00**
20 ga., (3") or 28 ga. (2¾"), 28" M&F or 26" IC&M barrels, stock 14¼"x1½"x2⅜", 2¼" pitch down, 6 lbs. **$265.00**
up 14⅜"x1⅜"x1¾", 1½" pitch down, with p.g. cap and contoured recoil pad. Wgt 7¼ lbs. **$285.00**
coil pad. Wgt. 7¼ lbs. **$275.00**
Skeet, 12 (2¾"), 28 (2¾") or 20 (3") ga., 26" S1 & 2 barrels. Stock (12 ga.) 14¼"x1⅝"x2½" (20 ga.) 14¼"x1½"x2⅜"; both with 2" pitch down. Wgt. (12) 7 lbs.; (20) 6 lbs. **$285.00**
Extra bbls. Field **$130.00**. Trap or Skeet **$138.00**

Beretta BL-4 DeLuxe O-U Shotgun
Similar to BL-3, with addition of selective auto. ejectors, extensive receiver engraving, deluxe hand checkering ...... **$325.00** to **$460.00**
Extra bbls. Field **$160.00** Trap or Skeet **$170.00**

Beretta BL-5 Premium O-U Shotgun
Same as BL-4, except fully engraved receiver, specially selected walnut stock and fore-end, capped p.g. .... **$440.00** to **$460.00**
Extra bbls. Field **$177.00** Trap or Skeet **$187.00**

G BERETTA SO2 PRESENTATION OVER-UNDER SHOTGUN
Sidelock action, special chrome-nickel receiver, Boehler anti-rust barrels. All interior parts chromed. Receiver, tangs, screws, lever, guard, fore-end release, safety and standing breech scroll engraved, with a silver pigeon inlaid in the top lever. Trigger, safety and top lever checkered. 12 ga., ventilated rib barrels only, Skeet and trap models available. 26" Imp. Cyl. & Mod. or 28" Mod. & Full standard. Other borings to order without extra cost. Straight or p.g. stocks, perfectly matched from one-piece selected European walnut (14½"x1⅜"x 2³⁄₁₆"). Double triggers standard. Wgt. from about 7¼ lbs. Garcia, importer **$870.00**
Same, Model SO3, profusely scroll and relief engraved, fancy selected walnut **$1,000.00**
Same, Model SO4, sidelocks are hand detachable, more elaborate engraving, full grain walnut stock and fore-end .... **$:,200.00**
Same, Model SO5, gold Crown Grade symbol inlaid into top lever. Built to customer's complete specifications if desired, the whole virtually hand-made **$1,600.00**
All SO series Presentation Models may be had with stocks to customer's specifications (at small or no extra charge) or with selective or non-selective single trigger at little or no extra cost.
For extra bbls. ordered with gun, add to price of gun: SO-2, **$335**; SO-3, **$360**; SO-4, **$410**; & SO-5, **$440**.

[A] BRETTON OVER-UNDER SHOTGUN
Made in France, this 12 ga. shotgun weighs only 4½ lbs. Receiver is of heat-treated Dural; steel barrels may be unscrewed and replaced with 16 ga. or slug barrels. Continental Arms, importer **$285.00**
Deluxe engraved model **365.00**

[B] BRNO OVER-UNDER SHOTGUNS
Made in Czechoslovakia, available in 12 or 16 ga. only. Simple design has 25 fewer parts; all parts interchange without hand fitting. Double-single trigger (rear trigger acts as selector). Skeet (illustrated), trap or field grades available. Continental Arms, importer **$210.00**

[C] CONTINENTAL ARMS OVER-UNDER SHOTGUNS
The Nikko (illustrated) is a Japanese made gun available in either 12 or 20 gauge. Boxlock action is hand engraved; jeweled frame, automatic ejectors and lugs. Barrels of hard-chromed vanadium steel with vent. rib. Oil finished, checkered p.g. stock and fore-end which is completely detachable **$285.00**
Other high-grade shotguns are available from Continental. These are made in Belgium and have engraved boxlock actions; 4-way locking system; single selective trigger; selective ejectors and vent. rib. Available in all gauges for 12 through 28.
Royal Crown grade . . . . **$ 975.00**
Imperial Crown grade **1250.00**

[D] CHARLES DALY OVER-UNDER SHOTGUNS
12 ga., 2¾" (3" mag. in 30" F&F), 20 (3"), 28 ga. (2¾") or 410 (3") chambers. Boxlock action, scroll engraved; firing pins quickly removable. Auto safety (manual on Skeet & Trap models), combined with bbl. selector; auto. selective ejectors. Single selective inertia type gold-plated trigger. Checkered walnut semi-pistol grip stock and fore end (14"x1½"x2½"). Recoil pad on magnums. Vent. rib bbls. with steel bead. 20 ga. in 26" (IC&M); 28" (M&F). 12 ga. in 26" (Skt., & Skt., IC&M, plus M&F in 28" only), 30" (M&F or F&F). Wt. 12 ga. 7⅜ lbs.) 20 ga. 6¾ lbs.; in 28" bbls. (12 or 20 ga.) **$329.00**
28 or 410 gauge **349.00**
12 ga., 3" mag., F&F, 30" bbls., 8 lbs. **335.00**
Superior Grade. Same as Field Grade except: figured walnut, full p.g. stock with p.g. and grooved fore-end; special checkering **$349.00**
28 or 410 gauge **369.00**
Superior Skeet. Same as Superior Grade except: 12 or 20 gauge; 26" & 28" bbls., manual safety. Skeet and Skeet bored **$349.00**
28 or 410 gauge **369.00**
12 or 20 ga. with Selexor* **369.00**
Superior Trap. Same as the Superior Skeet except: 12 ga. 30", M&F, IM&F or F&F. Manual safety. Standard trap stock (14⅜"x1⅜"x1¾") or Monte Carlo (14⅜"x1½"x1½"x2½") with recoil pad **$349.00**
With Monte Carlo stock **359.00**
With Selexor* (M. C. only) **379.00**
With ½" wide (Flat-Top) vent. rib. With or w/out M. C. stock **389.00**
Venture Grade. Similar to Field Grade except: 12 or 20 ga. (2¾" chambers) only, 28" (Mod. & Full) or 26" (Mod. & Imp. Cyl.) barrels with vent rib, single non-selective trigger and non-auto. safety. Weight, about 7 lbs. **$249.00**

CHARLES DALY DIAMOND GRADE OVER-UNDER
Same as Daly Superior Grades except finest French walnut, more extensive checkering and a fully engraved receiver, guard, etc. **$575.00**
* Selexor: Allows either automatic selective ejection or extraction. A button on each side of the receiver provides control. RH button for lower bbl. or LH button for the upper.

[E] DICKSON GRAY EAGLE O-U
Zoli boxlock action, auto. safety, double triggers, 3" chambers. In 12, 20 ga., 26" bbl. (Imp. Cyl. & Mod.), 28" (Mod. & Full). Wgt. about 7 lbs. (12 ga.), 6 lbs., 20 ga. Vent. rib. Hand checkered walnut p.g. stock and beavertail fore-end (14"x1½"x2½"). American Import Co. **$215.00**

[F] FERLACH O-U TURKEY GUN
Boxlock action, Greener cross bolting, top snap, double triggers, Boehler steel bbls., 22" or 24". Top bbl., 12, 16 or 20 gauge; lower, 22 Hornet, 222 Rem., 243 257, 6.5x55, 270, 7x57, 30-06. Engraved action, Circassian stock, hand checkered at p.g. and fore-end. About 6½ lbs. Flaig's importer. **$525.00**
Write for catalog of drillings and combination guns.

[G] FI M69 OVER-UNDER SHOTGUN
12 ga. (2¾" vent. rib bbls. in 30" (F&M, F&F), 28" (F&M) & 26" (IC&M). Also, 20 ga. (3") in 28" (F&M) & 26" (IC&M). Hammerless, double trigger, thumb safety. Walnut stock with checkered p.g. and forearm. FI, importer **$189.50**

[H] FOREVER YOURS O-U SHOTGUNS
Ferlach-made, Anson & Deeley 4-lock type action, double Greener cross-bolt, Boehler proof steel barrels, ventilated rib, auto ejectors, double triggers, engraved action, checkered Circassian walnut pistol grip stock & split fore-end. Available with or without cheekpiece. Horn p.g. cap and buttplate. Weight 7-7½ lbs. Available in standard gauges, chokes and barrel lengths. Imported by Flaig's, **$675.00.** With single set trigger. **$750.00**

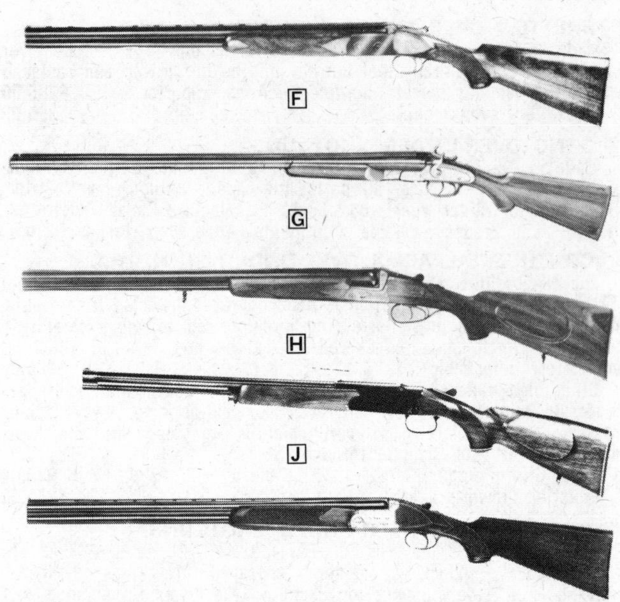

A FRANCHI FALCONET OVER & UNDER

Italian-made, this shotgun features easy-cocking action, short, fast hammer fall. Walnut stock, checkered pistol grip and fore-end; 14¼"x 1⅜"x2¼", pitch down 2¾"; stocks or order within limits (¼" in comb hgt., ½" in pull). Skeet stock, 14¼"x1⅝"x2½". Trap, 14⅜"x 1½"x1⅞". 12 Gauge only with vent. rib, single selective trigger and automatic ejectors. Field model has automatic safety. Field—26" (Imp. Cyl. & Mod.), 28" (Mod. & Full), or 30" (Mod. & Full). Skeet—26" (Skeet #1 & #2); Trap—30" (Mod. & Full) bbls. Chromed bores, engraved receiver. Stoeger.

Falconet Ebony (12 & 20) **$269.95**, Buckskin (12 & 20) **$279.95**, Silver (12 only) **$289.95**. Standard Skeet (12 only) **$374.95** or Std. Skeet with 12 and 20 ga. bbls. **$574.95**. Standard Trap. **$374.95** or Super Trap **$450.00**. Imperial Grade **$935.00**, Pigeon Grade **$1000.00** or Monte Carlo Grade **$1,300.00**.

B HERTER'S S 27 DELUXE ROYAL GRADE

Chambered for 12 ga. Choice of barrel lengths and chokes. Weight with 28" barrels 7 lbs., 12 oz. Available with 5/16" deluxe ventilated rib. **$168.95**

C KRIEGHOFF MODEL 32 OVER-UNDER

The Europa Corp. imports this near-duplicate of the old Remington 32. A three-way safety (manual, auto or inoperative) and Boehler special steel bbls. are standard on all M32's. Made in 12 and 20 only, with selective single trigger, ejectors and ventilated rib, the M32 is available as a Skeet or field gun with 28" bbl. or as a trap gun (30" bbls.) at **$595.00.** • Other bbl. lengths and chokes to order, as is a Monte Carlo stock. The San Remo grade, with fancier walnut and relief engraving, is **$995.00.** • The Monte Carlo carries extra fancy wood, elaborate engraving and silver inlays, Monte Carlo stock at **$2,650.00.** • The Crown Grade is like the Monte Carlo but has gold inlays, at **$2,750.00.** • The Super Crown, like the Crown, has both gold and silver inlaid figurines, at **$3,000.00.** Extra bbls. with standard borings .... **$275.00** to **$295.00**

D LAMES OVER-UNDER SHOTGUN

Boxlock action is hand engraved, all parts are blued except single selective trigger which is gold plated. European walnut stock has hand-checkered p.g. and fore-end. Available in 12 ga. only, with 26" (Imp. Cyl. & Mod.), 28" (Imp. Cyl. & Mod. or Mod. & Full), 30" and 32" (Mod./Imp. and Full or Full and Full). LA Distributors, importer **$329.95**

LAURONA OVER-UNDER SHOTGUN

Boxlock 12 ga. shotgun has vent. rib barrels choked Mod. and Full. Stock has checkered p.g. and fore-end. Twin-single triggers. Receiver is lightly engraved. Mars Equipment, importers.............. **$199.00**

E RICHLAND ARMS 844 OVER-UNDER SHOTGUN

Boxlock action of nickel-chrome steel, blued, non-selective single trigger and simple extractors. Stock (14"x1⅝"x2¼") of European walnut with checkered p.g. and fore-end. Barrels of English Vickers steel, 12 ga. only, 30" (Full & Full) 7 lbs., 3 oz., 28" (Mod. & Full) 7 lbs., or 26" (Imp. Cyl. & Mod.) 6¾ lbs.......................... **$189.50**

F RICHLAND 828 OVER-UNDER

Casehardened receiver. Rosette engraving. Walnut stock (1½"x 2¼"x14¼") has skip-line hand checkering with matching quick-detachable fore-end. Ventilated rib. Non-selective single trigger. Plain extractors, non-automatic safety. Sliding bolt cross lock. In 28 ga. (2¾" chamber) with 28" (F&M) or 26" (IC&M) barrels. Weighs 5¼ lbs. (26"). **$268.00**

G ROSSI OVERLAND EXPOSED HAMMER DOUBLE

12 ga. (3") with 28" & 20" (F&M, IC&M)) bbls; 20 ga. (3") with 26" and 20" (F&M) bbls. and 410 (3") 26" (F&F) bbls. Double triggers and hammers. Semi pistol grip stock and beavertail fore-end. Thumb lever release, bead front sight. F. I., importer.................... **$75.00**

SAUER 66 OVER-UNDER

Based on the Purdey-System with Holland and Holland type removable sidelocks. Has a single selective trigger, selective automatic ejectors and the field model features an automatic slide safety. Krupp-Special steel barrels with ventilated rib, ivory front and middle bead, a selected fancy walnut stock (14¼"x1½"x2¼") with p.g., ventilated recoil pad and fine line hand checkering. Available in three grades of engraving. 12 ga. only (other gauges to be announced later). Barrel length and choke: 26" (IC&M) 28" (F&M) 30" (F&M). Wgt. 7¼ lbs. Weatherby, importer. Grade I **$495.00,** Grade II **$595.00** & Grade III **$695.00.**

Trap model available with special trap stock and ventilated rib. 30" and 32" (F&F, F&M). Grade I **$550.00,** Grade II **$650.00** and Grade III, **$750.00.**

Skeet with 26" (S&S) barrels. Grade I **$550.00,** Grade II **$650.00** & Grade III **$750.00.**

H SAUER BBF OVER-UNDER RIFLE-SHOTGUN

Stock (14½"x1⅝"x2¾") made of selected walnut, with p.g., cheekpiece and hand checkering, and is built in the classic tradition. The trigger guard is steel. 16 ga. (2¾"). Rifle barrel: 222, 243, 30-30, 30-36 and 7x65R. Barrel length: 25"; Krupp-Special gun barrel steel; Shotgun barrel full choke; rifle barrel hammer-forged; matted rib; bead front sight; folding leaf rear sight. Blitz action with Kersten lock; centrally guided firing pins; front trigger for rifle barrel designed as adjustable single-set trigger; sear safety manually operated by slide on upper tang. Wgt. 61 lbs. Weatherby, importer.

Standard Model (with arabesque engravings on action and fine hand checkering) **$550.00**

De Luxe Model (with Scotch checkering on selected walnut stock, white line spacers at p.g. and butt plate, and hunting scene engravings on action). **$645.00**

VOERE O-U RIFLE-SHOTGUN

Available in 20 ga., 3" chamber, over 222, 222 Mag. or 223 rifle caliber. 23⅝" barrels with simple extractor and folding rear and blade front sights. Single trigger. Locking lever is pushed left for cocking, right to open the breech. Walnut cheekpiece stock; checkered p.g. and fore-end; white spacers at grip cap and buttplate. Sling swivels attached. Weight, 6½ lbs.; length, 40" over-all. L. A. Distributors, importer **$219.95**

J ZOLI SILVER SNIPE OVER-UNDER

Purdey type boxlock action with crossbolt, 12 or 20 ga. (3" chambers); satin chrome-plated receiver, single selective trigger, simple extractors and auto. safety. Chrome-lined barrels with vent rib; 30" (12 ga. only, Mod. & Full), 28" (Mod. & Full), or 26" (Imp. Cyl. & Mod.). Walnut stock (12 ga., 14⅜"x1⅜"x2 1/16"; 20 ga., 14 5/16"x1⅝"x 2 9/16") with checkered p.g. and fore-end, plastic buttplate. Weight about 6½ lbs. Galef, importer.......................... **$229.95**

Trap, Skeet models have non-auto. safety, wide non-glare vent. rib and suitable stock dimensions, 2¾" chambers............. **$259.95**

ZOLI GOLDEN SNIPE OVER-UNDER

Same as Silver Snipe except selective auto. ejectors...... **$274.95**
Trap, Skeet models **304.95**

AYA SIDELOCK DOUBLE
A true, quick removable sideblock action with gold-plated mechanism, single selective trigger and selective automatic ejectors is available in 12 (2¾") and 20 ga. (3"). Barrels 26" (Imp. Cyl. & Mod.), 28" (Mod. & Full) or 30" (Mod. & Full, 12 ga. only) have vent. rib. Hand-checkered p.g. stock with beavertail fore-end. Weight 7¼ and 6½ lbs., respectively. F.I., importer **$300.00**

AYA YEOMAN DOUBLE
Available in 12 ga. only, 28" (Mod. & Full) barrel with 2¾" chambers. Hand-checkered p.g. and beavertail fore-end stock. Two triggers, simple extractors, and top tang safety. Weight 7 lbs., 44½" over-all. F.I., importer **$125.00**

AYA 410 DOUBLE
Similar to the Yeoman, but in 410 only. 26" (Mod. & Full or Full & Full) barrel, 3" chambers. Straight checkered stock and field type fore-end. Weight 4¾ lbs., 42⅜" over-all. **$150.00**

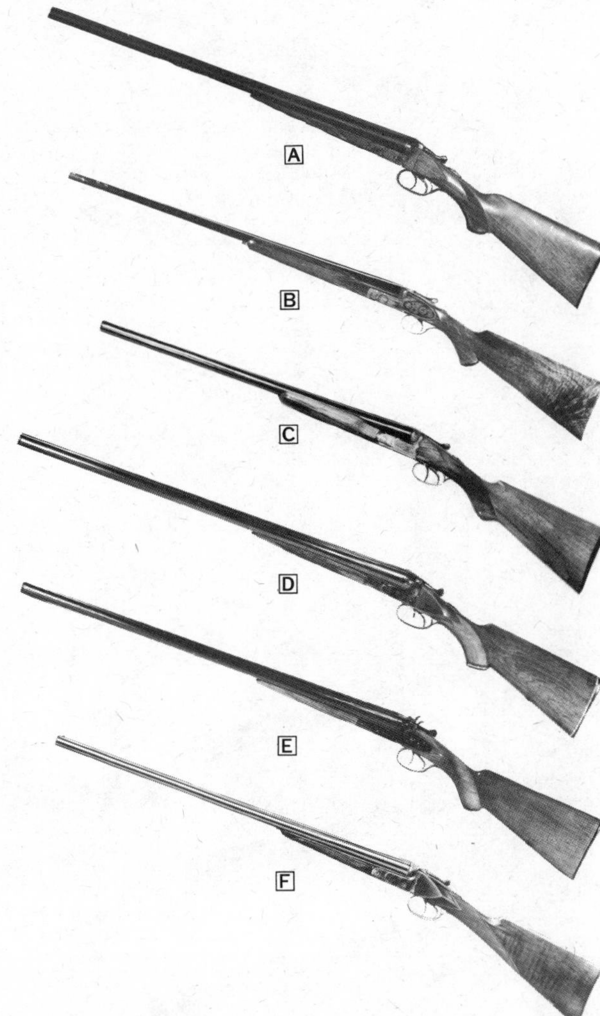

A&F KNOCKABOUT DOUBLES
Made in Italy to A&F's specifications, the Mark I Knockabout is a side-by-side, in 12 (26" or 28" bbls.), 20, 28 or 410 (26"). All gauges have double triggers, plain extractors, color case-hardened action and checkered walnut p.g. stock and fore-end. About 6½ lbs. (12 ga.); 5½ lbs. (20 ga.); 5¼ lbs. (28, 410). 12 or 20 ga., **$150.** 28 and 410 **$25.00** higher. The Mark II is similar to the Mark I, but has vent. rib, ejectors and a beavertail fore-end. 12 and 20 gauge, **$259.50.** The Mark III is a 12, 20 or 28 ga. over-under with single trigger, vent. rib, engraved action with antique silver finish. 26" and 28" barrels only, with choice of choke. Weight, 6¾ lbs. (12 ga.); 5½ lbs. (20 ga.).
12, 20 ga. **$289.50,** 28, 410 ga. **$297.50**

A **A&F ZANOTTI SHOTGUN**
A custom made side-by-side double in 12 ga. (26" Mod. & Imp. Cyl. or 28" Mod. & Full); 20 and 28 ga. (26" Mod. & Imp. Cyl). 12 ga. has semi-p.g. walnut stock and beavertail fore-end; 20 and 28 ga. have straight grip and slim fore-end. All have single non-selective triggers, ejectors, gold stock inlay for initials, etc. Abercrombie & Fitch, importer.
12 or 20 gauge.......... **$675.00** 28 gauge........... **$750.00**

B **A&F FINEST QUALITY SHOTGUNS**
Abercrombie & Fitch import the famous Purdey, Holland & Holland, Boss and Westley Richards shotguns. All are custom-made and hand-finished and, while A&F carries a few models in stock, guns ordered with custom specifications usually require 1 to 2 years for delivery. All have full side locks, single or double triggers and ejectors. Westley Richards side-by-side doubles start at **$900.,** the others at **$2800.;** over-under models start at **$3400.**

C **ATLAS 200 SERIES DOUBLE GUNS**
12, 16, 20, 28 and 410 ga., 26". (Imp. Cyl. and. Mod.), or 26" and 28" (Mod. and Full), bbls. Engraved Anson & Deeley-type action. Vickers steel bbls. with chromed bores. Walnut stock with checkered semi-p.g. and beavertail fore-end. Wgt. approx. 6-7 lbs. Double trigger. . **$180.00** M204 with single trigger **$210.00.** M206 with single trigger, auto ejectors **$230.00.** Note: 410, 28 ga. in M200 only.
M208 Magnum same as M200 except 12 or 20 ga., 3" chambers, **$185.00;** with single non-seleceive trigger................ **$195.00**

ATLAS 145 DOUBLE SHOTGUN
Similar to M200 except: Vent. rib, choice of p.g. or straight stock, full hand engraving, entire gun of nickel-chrome steel. 12 & 20 ga. only. Atlas Arms, importer............................ **$290.00**
With two sets of bbls., 26" (Skeet 1 & 2); 28" (M & F).... **395.00**

ATLAS 500 MAGNUM DOUBLE SHOTGUN
Similar to M200 Magnum except; 10 ga., 3½ chambers, 32" bbls. (F & F); 12, 20 ga., 3" chambers, 28" (M & F). Vent. rib, double triggers, recoil pad. Action especially built for magnum loads. Atlas Arms, importer **$210.00**

ATLAS 300 DOUBLE SHOTGUN
12 and 20 ga., 26" bbls. ((IC & M); 28" (M & F). Holland & Holland type sidelock action with Purdey-type lock. Hand engraved, auto ejectors. Superior walnut stock, checkered on p.g. and fore-end. Non-selective single trigger. Wgt. 7¼ lbs. (12 ga.). 6¼ lbs. (20 ga.). Atlas Arms, importer................................... **$440.00**
Model 310, with single selective trigger................. **485.00**

D **BAIKAL MODEL IJ-58 DOUBLE**
Made in Russia, this shotgun uses a triple-locking system, top lever action with non-auto safety. 28" barrels (Mod. & Full) have chrome-plated chambers and bores, raised solid rib. Stock has hand-checkered p.g. and fore-end. 16 ga. (2¾") only. Weight 6¾ lbs. Finley-Moody, importers **$116.00**
As Model IJ-54 in 12 ga. (2¾") with auto. safety and cocking indicators. Weight 7½ lbs. **$140.00**

E **BAIKAL MODEL BM-20 HAMMER DOUBLE**
Russian made, this triple-locking system, top lever action shotgun has exposed hammers. 20 ga. (2¾"), 28" barrels are choked Mod. and Imp. Cyl. with chrome-plated chambers and bores, solid rib. Stock p.g. and fore-end are hand checkered. Weight 6½ lbs. Finely-Moody, importers **$92.00**

BERETTA GR-2 DOUBLE
Greener type boxlock action, engraved receiver, coil mainsprings. Folding front trigger, auto. safety. Walnut hand-checkered stock (14"x 1½"x2½", 2¼" pitch down) and semi-beavertail fore-end. 12 ga., 2¾" chambers, 30" or 28" (M&F), 26" (IC&M) barrels. 20 ga., 2¾" chambers, 28" (M&F) or 26" (IC&M) barrels. 7⅛ lbs.................. **$260.00**
Extra bbls. **125.00**

BERETTA GR-3 DOUBLE
Same as GR-2 except single selective trigger........... **$280.00**
12 ga. Magazine (3" chambers), 30" M&F barrels, stock 14"x1½"x 2½", (2½" pitch down), recoil pad, 8 lbs. **$280.00**
Extra bbls. **130.00**

BERETTA GR-4 DOUBLE
Same as GR-3 except fully hand-engraved receiver, selective auto. ejectors, full p.g. stock with grip cap. 12 ga., 2¾"......... **$335.00**
Extra bbls. **180.00**

F **BERNARDELLI GAMECOCK DOUBLES**
Boxlock action, double underlugs, case-hardened with light engraving; plain extractors, double triggers, auto. safety. Checkered straight grip walnut stock and fore-end (14"x1½"x2¼"). 12 or 20 ga. with 25" bbls., 2¾" chambers (IC, M), 28" (M, F), wgt. 6-6½" lbs. Stoeger, importer **$205.00**
Deluxe Gamecock, like above except: sideplate action, engraved, chrome-lined bbls., selected fancy wood..................... **$295.00**
Premier Gamecock, similar to Deluxe, except auto-ejectors, non-selective single trigger, Greener-type cross bolt, 3" chambers. . **$390.00**

BERNARDELLI ITALIA HAMMER DOUBLES
Made from modern steel, but with old-style external hammers. 12 ga. only 30" chrome-lined bbls. (M, F), 2¾" chambers. Action has Greener-type crossbolt, double triggers, engraved sideplates, double underlugs, half-cock safety. Checkered fancy walnut stock and fore-end. Stoeger, importer.................................... **$194.80**
Brescia model, similar to Italia except: 12 ga., 28" or 30" bbls., 20 ga., 26" bbls. (IC, M)............................... **$140.00**

[A] CONTINENTAL ARMS DOUBLE GUNS

The Centaure is a hand made Belgian shotgun with triple locking lugs and side clips. French walnut stock, hand-checkered p.g. and fore-end. 12 ga., 30" barrels only **$137.50**

Supra De Luxe Model 5 is a better quality gun made in Belgium. Boxlock action with Greener cross-bolt and engraved game scene. Available in all gauges and barrel lengths from 26" to 32"; Skeet, trap and field models **$395.00**

Model 62 is like the Model 5 but also in 12 ga. Magnum; vent. rib; Anson Deeley boxlock action, engraved; selective auto. ejectors; horn grip cap and buttplate **$495.00**

Model 40 is like the Model 5 but chambered for 10 ga. Magnum; double underlugs; 32" barrel full-choke; double triggers; weight about 10 lbs. **$495.00**

The best quality sidelock gun (illustrated) is hand made in Belgium and has engraved locks, double triggers and a straight buttstock with hand checkering at the wrist and fore-end. Available singly or in matched pairs, each **$2500.00**

[B] CHARLES DALY EMPIRE GRADE DOUBLE

12 ga., 2¾" (3" in 30" F&F), 16 ga. 2¾ or 20 ga. (3) chambers, 26" (IC&M), 28" (M&F) and 30" (F&F) bbls. with tapered, raised vent rib. Boxlock action, double locking lugs and triggers; auto safety. Blued receiver is engraved. Walnut, checkered pistol grip stock and beavertail fore-end; recoil pad on magnum model. Wgt., 12 ga. 7¼ lbs., 16 ga. 6½ lbs., 20 ga., 6¼ lbs. in 28" bbls. **$236.00**

DARNE DOUBLE BARREL SHOTGUN

The unique action whose protruding double "ears," pulled rearward, slide the entire breechblock back exposing the chambers for loading. All models have raised ribs, French walnut checkered pistol grip and fore-end stocks, (14¼"x1⅝"x2½") double triggers and selective ejectors. Stoeger, importer. Bird Hunter in 12 or 20 ga., 25½" bbls. (Imp. Cyl. & Mod.). Wgt. approx. 6¼ lbs. (12)—5¾ lbs. (20) .... **$220.00** • Pheasant Hunter De Luxe. Same as the Hunter except: 12 ga. 28" (Mod. & Full), fancy wood and engraving, **$297.00** • Quail Hunter Supreme. Same as the Deluxe but in 20 or 28 ga. only, 25½" (Imp. Cyl. & Mod.) bbls. Elaborate hand engraved action, hard-chromed bores, carrying strap and swivels. **$387.00**

[C] DAVIDSON 63B DOUBLE SHOTGUN

12, 16, 20, 28, 410 ga. Anson & Deeley crossbolt action (28 & 410 w/o crossbolt). Automatic tang safety. Manual extractors. Brushed nickel finish, engraved. 28 ga., 25" bbls. (IC & M); 410, 25" (F & F); 12, 16, 20 gauges; 26", 28", 30" bbls., all popular chokes. Front and middle bead sights. Spanish walnut p.g. stock hand checkered, with grip cap, white-line spacers. Davidson, importers. ...... **$ 99.50**

Magnum, 12 and 20 ga., 3" chambers, 26", 28", 30" bbls... **119.50**

Magnum, 10 ga., 3½" chambers, 32" bbls. (F & F)........ **149.50**

Model 63BDL. A deluxe version of the Model 63B with select walnut stock, 18 line checkering and more receiver engraving. 20 ga. (Mod. & Full or Imp. Cyl. & Mod.) 2¾" chambers, weight 6 lbs. 7 oz. or 410 (Full & Full) 3" chambers, 5 lbs. 11 oz. **$109.50**

12 ga. with single trigger **124.50**

DAVIDSON 69SL SIDELOCK DOUBLE

12 ga. (2¾") with 30", 28" (M&F) or 26" (IC&M) bbls. Also 20 ga. (2¾") with 28" (M&F) or 26" (IC&M) bbls. Checkered walnut p.g. stock and forearm with white-line spacers. Nickel finish, engraved detachable sideplates with cocking indicators. Automatic safety, manual extractors, gold plated trigger, two brass sighting beads. Wgt. 7 lbs. (12 ga.) Davidson, importer **$129.50**

[D] DICKSON COMPACT DOUBLE

Anson & Deeley type action, case-hardened receiver, auto-safety, single trigger. Hand-checkered walnut p.g. stock (14"x1$\frac{9}{16}$"x2½"). 12 ga., 28" (M&F, IC&M), 3" chambers. Wgt. about 6 lbs. 12 oz. Standard Extractors, vent. rib, rubber recoil pad. American Import Co., importer. **$145.00**

DICKSON FALCON MAGNUM DOUBLE

Scroll-engraved Anson & Deeley type action, Holland type extractors, raised matted rib, auto. safety, double triggers. Checkered p.g. stock and beavertail fore-end. Recoil pad. 32" bbls., Full and Full, 3½" chambers, 10-gauge Magnum. American Import Co....... **$148.50**

DICKSON FALCON DOUBLE SHOTGUN

Same as Magnum 10 except: 12 or 20 ga. in 28" M&F, or 26" IC, 3" chambers. Black plastic butt plate and p.g. cap with white spacers. American Import Co. **$108.50**

DIXIE BREECH-LOADING HAMMER DOUBLES

Of modern Belgian, Italian or Spanish manufacture, proofed for heaviest smokeless powder loads, these double guns are available in 12, 16, 20 and 410 ga., regular or Magnum with 28" to 32" barrels. Case-hardened frames with modest engraving. Straight, semi-pistol or full pistol-grip halfstocks, some with checkered grip and fore-end, some smooth. Dixie Gun Works, importers.......... **$110 to $125.00**

[E] FERLACH COMPANION DOUBLE GUN

12, 16, 28 (2¾" chambers), 20, 410 (3" chambers). Choice of bbl. lengths and chokes. Anson & Deeley action, two triggers, auto. ejectors, semi-beavertail fore-end. Circassian walnut stock of standard dimensions, checkered p.g. cap, cheekpiece optional. Choice of recoil pad or horn buttplate. 6½-7 lbs. Flaig's, importer. **$500.00**

[F] KRIEGHOFF AMERICAN DRILLING

Blitz action, engraved receiver. Shotgun locks are auto-cocking with indicators. Rifle lock cocks by moving tang-mounted slide forward. Split extractors lift rifle case higher than shotshells. Wide black nylon trigger guard. Stock has checkered p.g. and beavertail fore-end, Pachmayr recoil pad. Gun comes with 22 WMR insert barrel fitted inside right shotgun tube. Available in double 12 ga. over 30-06 or 7mm Mag. 25" barrels, 41" over-all; weight, 7 lbs. Harry Owens, importer **$945.00**

Extra insert barrel for 22 LR........................ **24.00**

[G] MATADOR II DOUBLES

An improved version of F.I.'s popular side-by-side. Available in 12 ga. (2¾" chamber) and 20 ga. (3" chamber) only with 26" (Imp. Cyl. & Mod.), 28" (Mod. & Full) or 30" Mod. & Full (12 ga. only) vent. rib bbls. Walnut stock with checkered pistol grip and beavertail fore-end. Has double underlocks; bushed floating firing pins; color case-hardened receiver; selective auto. ejectors and single selective trigger; auto. safety. Wgt. 7¼ lbs. in 12 ga., 6½ lbs. in 20 ga. 44½" over-all (28" bbls.) **$210.00**

[A] MERCURY MAGNUM DOUBLES
10 (3½"), 12 or 20 ga. (3") magnums. 12 and 20 ga. have 28" (F&M) brazed rib bbls., 10 ga. in 32" F&F. Triple-lock Anson & Deeley type action with double triggers, front hinged; auto safety, extractors; safety gas ports; engraved frame. Walnut, checkered pistol grip stock and beavertail fore-end; (14"x1⅝"x2¼") with recoil pad. Wgt. 12 ga., 7¼ lbs., 20 ga., 6½ lbs. 45" over-all. Tradewinds, importer...... **$134.50**
10 ga., 10⅛ lbs., 49" over-all **159.95**

[B] P.O.S. 10 GAUGE MAGNUM DOUBLE
Made in Spain, this shotgun uses Anson & Deeley top lever type action, Purdey type locks. Case hardened action, checkered Spanish walnut p.g. stock, with recoil pad, beavertail fore-end. 32" (Full) bbls., 3½" chambers. Wgt. 11 lbs. Sloans Sporting Goods Co., importer. **$150.00**

PREMIER DOUBLE BARREL SHOTGUNS
The Continental model is an exposed hammer side-lock gun with two triggers available in 12, 16, 20 or 410. All have 26" barrels choked Mod. & Full except 410, 26". French walnut stock (14"x1⅝"x 2½") checkered at p.g. and fore-end. Length 44½" over-all;; weight about 7 lbs. Ed Paul's Sporting Goods, importer **$131.25**
Ambassador model is similar to above except: hammerless side-lock action with auto. safety on tang. **$144.30**
Brush King has a boxlock action and is fitted with 22" barrels choked Mod. and Imp. Cyl. available in 12 or 20 ga. only. Length 39" over-all; weight about 6 lbs. **$113.95**
Other models and grades are available. Write importer for catalog.

[C] RICHLAND ARMS SHOTGUNS
Imports from Spain and Italy. The 200 is a demibloc side-by-side double with auto. safety, two triggers, long beavertail fore-end, walnut p.g. stock with cheekpiece and recoil pad. 12, 16, 20, 28 or 410 ga. 410 and 20 ga. with 3" chambers, others 2¾". 30", 28", 26" or 22" (20-ga. only) bbls., all standard chokes..................... **$129.50**
202 is the 200 with extra set of 12 or 20 ga. bbls......... **179.50**
711 is a 10-ga., 3½" chambered long range double with 32" F&F bbls. **$149.50**
Same, 3" chambers 12 ga., 30" F&F bbls................ **139.50**
707 is a lightweight (6½ lbs.) 20 ga. Magnum double with improved forcing cones, chokes and borings for 80%-85% patterns with 4's. 26" (IC&M), 28" (M&F) or 30" (F&F) bbls. Checkered walnut p.g. stock, beavertail fore-end, recoil pad.......................... **$179.50**
707-2, with two sets of barrels. 30" (M&F) & 26" (IC&M).. **249.50**

[D] SANDERSON SHOTGUNS
Illustrated is the Classic Bird Gun, M200 S-I, a lightweight double in 28 (4½ lbs.) to 12 gauge (6 lbs.); standard 2¾" or 2" chambers, with barrels from 25" up. The walnut stock has a straight grip and classic fore-end. Auto ejectors, hinged front trigger and engraved action. **$425.00** up. 2" and 2½" shells are available from Sanderson.
Belgian-made Neumann shotguns imported by Sanderson include the 10 gauge Magnum double from **$385**; 12, 20 and 410 3" doubles from **$249.50** and 20 gauge bird guns.

[E] WEBLEY & SCOTT 700, 701, 702 DOUBLE GUNS
12 or 20 ga. Anson & Deeley action, boxlock. hammerless, top lever, no extension, solid tumbler, auto. safety. 26" bbls. (Mod. & Imp. Cyl.), 28" (F. or M. & F., M., I.P.), 30" (Full & Ful, Mod. or Imp. Cyl.). Straight or semi-pistol grip stock, hand checkered (14⅝" x1½"x2¼"). Custom fitting, recoil pad, single non-selective trigger, optional at extra cost. About 6¾ lbs. (12-28") to 5¾ lbs. in 20x28". Service Armament Co., importers.
Model 700, light scroll engraving, selected French walnut..**$375.00**
Model 702, more scroll engraving, better French walnut.... **550.00**
Model 701, profusely scroll engraved, fancy French walnut.. **750.00**
Write for information on other W&S guns; from........... **30.00**

SAUER ROYAL SIDE BY SIDE
Anson & Deeley action with Greener cross bolt; double underlocking lugs; single selective trigger; automatic slide safety; side firing pin indicators. Krupp-Special steel barrel with ivory bead, matted rib. Fine arabesque engraving on grey case hardened action. Selected walnut stock (14¼"x1½"x2¼") with fine line hand checkering. White spacers at p.g. cap and ventilated recoil pad. The beavertail fore-end is furnished with a patented spring snap. 12 ga. (2¾") with 28" & 30" (F&M) bbls. 20 ga. (3") with 28" (F&M) & 26" (IC&M) bbls. Wgt. 12 ga., approx. 6½ lbs.; 20 ga. approx. 6 lbs. Weatherby, importer. **$345.00**

[F] SAUER DRILLING 3000-E RIFLE-DOUBLE SHOTGUN
Finest walnut is used for the modified Monte Carlo stock (14½"x 1⅝"x2¾") with p.g., cheek-piece, sling swivels, metal trigger guard and fore-end with checkering. Features a patent spring snap. 12 ga. bbls. chambered for 2¾" shells. Calibers of rifle barrels: available in 222, 243, 30-30, 30-06 and 7x65R. 25" bbl. Krupp-Special gun barrel steel; matted rib; bead front sight; automatically operated folding leaf rear sight; right barrel modified, left barrel full choke; rifle barrel hammer-forged. Blitz action with Greener cross bolt; double underlocking lugs; separate rifle cartridge extractor; front trigger acts as set trigger, adjustable fo pull; vertical firing pin indicators; Greener side safety mechanism locks all 3 bbls.; sear slide safety on upper tang locks right shotgun barrel when firing rifle barrel. Wgt. 6½ to 7¼ lbs., depending on rifle caliber. Weatherby, importer.
3000-E Standard Model (with arabesque engravings on action and fine line hand checkering)................................ **$625.00**
3000-E De Luxe Model (with Scotch checkering on selected walnut stock, white spacers at p.g. and butt plate and hunting scene engravings on action)...................................... **$715.00**

SAUER ARTEMIS SIDE BY SIDE
12 ga. (2¾") with 30" & 38" (F&M) bbls. 20 ga. (3") with 28" (F&M) & 26" (IC&M) bbls. With Holland and Holland type removable side-locks with double sear safeties and automatic selective ejectors. Stock (14¼"x1½"x2¼") and beavertail fore-end, with fine line hand checkering, are made of highly figured walnut. Krupp-Special steel barrels with ivory bead front sight, Greener cross bolt, double under locking lugs, automatic slide safety and single selective trigger. Weight about 6½ lbs. Weatherby, importer. Grade I (with fine line engraving) **$1,295.00**
Grade II (with full English arabesque engraving),....... **1,495.00**

[G] ZEPHYR WOODLANDER II DOUBLE
Precision bored and choked bbls. have flat-matted rib, Anson & Deeley type boxlock action with double underlugs, gold plated double triggers and game-scene engraving. Spanish walnut stock with checkered pistol grip and fore-end (14"x1⅝"x2½"). Automatic safety. 12 or 20 ga., 25" (Imp. Cyl. & Mod.), 28" (Mod. & Full) or 12 ga. (30") or 410 (25"), Full & Full bbls. 6¼ lbs. to 7¼ lbs. Plain extractors, but with Greener type crossbolt, epoxy finished stock. Stoeger, importer. **$139.95**

[H] ZEPHYR STERLINGWORTH II DOUBLE
Similar to the Woodlander except: genuine sidelock action with double sears, 2¾" chamber in 12 and 28 ga., 3" chamber in 20. 12 ga. 25" (Imp. Cyl. & Mod.), 28" (Mod. & Full); 20 ga. (28"), Full & Full, 28 ga. (25"), Mod. & Full bbls. Greener type crossbolt, epoxy finished stock.. **$169.95**

ZEPHYR VICTOR SPECIAL DOUBLE
12 ga. (2¾") with 30", 28" (F&M) and 25" (IC&M) bbls. Anson & Deeley type box lock action, double triggers, plain extractors. Checkered walnut p.g. stock (14"x1⅝"x2½") and forearm. Wgt. 7 lbs. (25" bbl.). **$110.95**

[J] ZOLI SILVER HAWK DOUBLE
Modified Anson & Deeley boxlock action with Purdey triple locks, 12 or 20 ga. (3" chambers); satin chrome-plated receiver with light engraving; double triggers, plain extractors, auto. safety, pins indicate loaded chambers. Chrome-lined barrels, 26" (Imp. Cyl. & Mod.), 28" (Mod. & Full); in 12 ga. only, 30" (Mod. & Full) and 32" (Full & Full). European walnut stock (14⅜"x1⅜"x2$\frac{5}{16}$"), hand-checkered fore-end and p.g. with cap, plastic buttplate. Weight about 6¼ lbs. Galef, importer **$179.95**

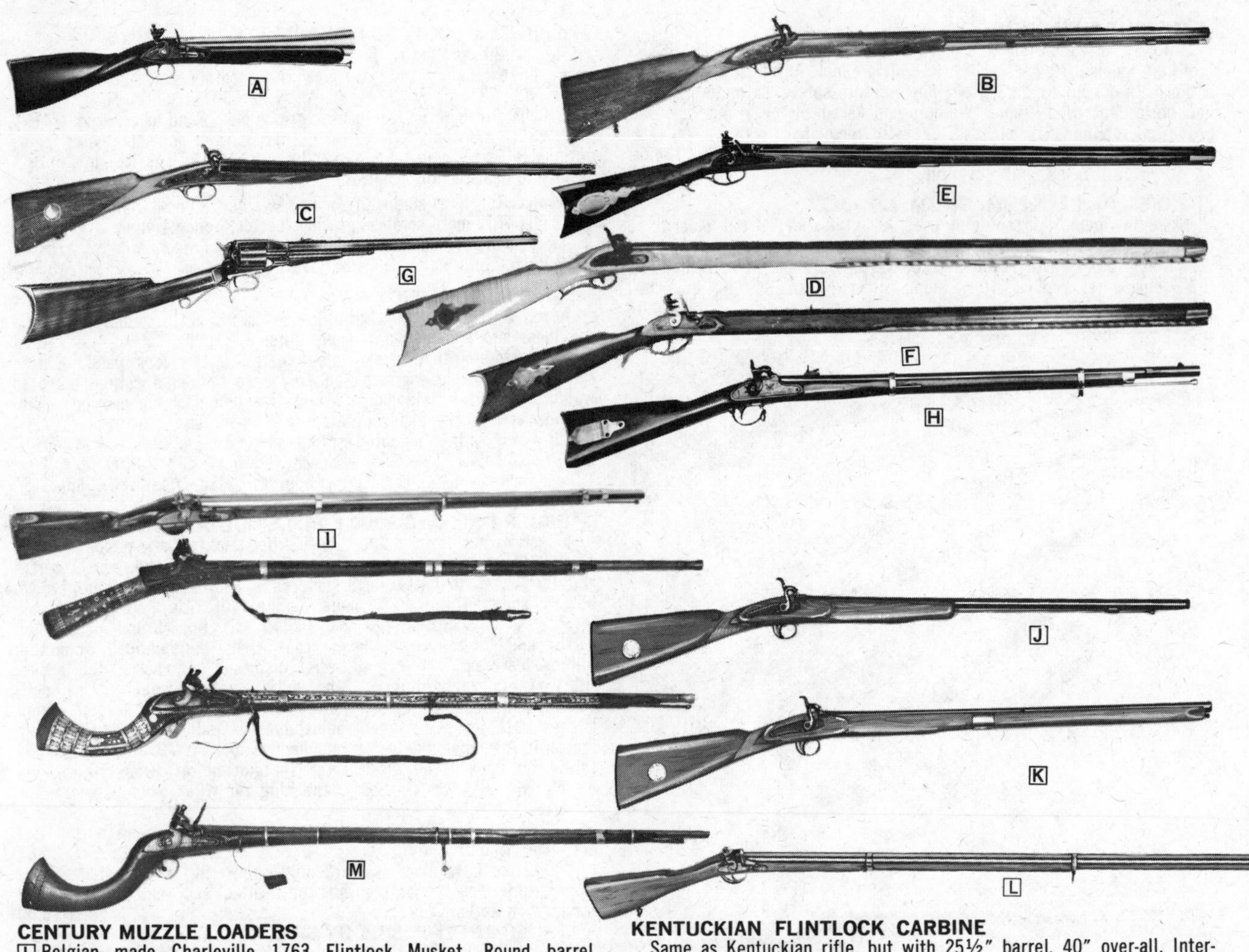

CENTURY MUZZLE LOADERS

[I] Belgian made Charleville 1763 Flintlock Musket. Round barrel, 45" long smooth bore, 69 caliber. Stock walnut finished wood, brass barrel bands and trigger guard. Overall length 60". Weight 8½ lbs. Proof tested for black powder by Belgian Official Proof House. Century Arms Importers **$99.50** [J] Percussion action ⅔ stock, 28" blued barrel. Checkered pistol grip. Weight 3½ lbs. Ramrod, patch box. **$19.50.** Flintlock action. **$29.50.** [K] Percussion action, full length stock. 28" blued barrel. Checkered pistol grip. Weight: 4 lbs. Ramrod, patch box **$24.50.** Flintlock action **$34.50.** [L] Also, Military flintlock model, 50" barrel 12 ga. Ramrod **$54.50.** [M] Antique rifles—Genuine antiques, made over a century ago, no two alike. **$99.00.**

[A] COACH GUARD BLUNDERBUSS

A close copy of the flintlock muzzleloaders used against highwaymen. Metal parts blued, wooden stock has polished, ebonized finish. Proof tested. Mars Equipment, importers.................... **$99.95**

[B] DIXIE HALFSTOCK RIFLE

Percussion lock 40-cal. rifle, 32" round bbl., 6 grooves. Checkered stock and fore-end, open sights, wood ramrod in two thimbles. Steel furniture. Wgt. about 7½ lbs. **$62.50**

[C] DIXIE PERCUSSION SHOTGUNS

Newly made in Belgium from old parts. Most have cap boxes. Barrels average 32". 6 lbs., single shot, 410 to 32 ga. **$24.95**

Similar, except double barrel, about 20 ga., 8 lbs.......... **$59.95**

[D] DIXIE SQUIRREL RIFLE

Percussion cap 40-cal. rifle with 40" bbl., 48" twist, six lands. Full length hard maple stock, stained and varnished, with patchbox. Brass furniture. Kentucky rifle sights, two, "candy-striped" cleaning rods furnished. Wgt., about 10 lbs. For black powder only. Dixie Gun Works, importer. **$139.50**

Flintlock version **149.50**

Double set triggers (installed by purchaser).............. **8.50**

[E] KENTUCKIAN FLINTLOCK RIFLE

Built in the image of the early Pennsylvania "Kentuckies." Fullstock, 33½" octagonal barrel, 44 caliber. Weight about 6¼ lbs., over-all 48". Engraved lockplate and brass patchbox, solid brass furniture, open sights, hardwood ramrod. Intercontinental Arms, importer..... **$125.00**

Also available in percussion **125.00**

KENTUCKIAN FLINTLOCK CARBINE

Same as Kentuckian rifle, but with 25½" barrel, 40" over-all. Intercontinental Arms, importer. **$125.00**

Also available in percussion **125.00**

[F] KENTUCKIAN FLINTLOCK RIFLE

A modern cal. .40 version of the Pennsylvania-Kentucky. Blued 40" octagon barrel, 13/16" across the flats, 6 lands. Case-hardened, engraved lockplate, European walnut full-length stock with patchbox, brass furniture. Black powder only. 55" over-all, wgt. about 10 lbs. Dixie Gunworks, importers. Percussion model.................... **$164.50**

Flintlock model **169.50**

[G] NAVY ARMS CARBINE

6-shot revolving carbine based on the Remington 44 Army revolver. 16" or 18" bbl., buckhorn rear sight, adjustable silver blade front. Straight grip wooden stock, curved metal buttplate, scrolled trigger guard. Navy Arms, importers............................ **$125.00**

ROSSI TRADE MUSKET

Inexpensive black powder percussion muzzle-loader. Brass bands, full length p.g. stock, steel ramrod. 36" round barrel, 5 lbs. F. I., importer **$15.95**

STOEGER FLINTLOCK ARMS

M4910 is a red-painted full-stocked 12 ga. single shot, 51" bbl., fittings are brass. 9¼ lb. **$69.95**

M6475 is ⅞ stocked in walnut, with 14 ga., 36" barrel....... **59.95**

M5033 is a half-stock double in 14 gauge, bbls. 31", straight-grip walnut stock. 7 lbs. **$106.95**

M4957B is a checkered half-stock single bbl., 33" long in 14 gauge, iron fittings, 6 lbs. **$62.95**

M6494 is 34" bbld. 4 gauge of 9¾ lbs., with hook buttplate and ⅞-stock with metal bands. **$71.95**

M6475W is a plain ⅞-walnut stock in 14 gauge, with 36" single bbl. Iron fittings, 7½ lbs. **$59.95**

[H] ZOUAVE RIFLE

A percussion muzzle-loading rifle, cal. 58, that duplicates the Civil War Remington Model 1863. Walnut ⅞-length stock with steel ramrod, sling swivels and brass patchbox in stock. Case-hardened lock, blued 33" barrel and brass furniture. Bead front and open rear sights. Wgt. 9½ lbs., 52" over-all. Navy Arms, importer.............. **$100.00**

Zouave Carbine, 22" bbl. **100.00**

A rifle made to similar specifications is offered by Mars Equipment. **$99.95**

Guns in this section are compression powered by: A) disposable CO_2 cartridge; B) by hand pumping of air; C) by cocking a spring which compresses air. This air is released when the trigger is pulled. Calibers are 177 (BB or pellet) and 22 pellet, except for Sheridan rifles, these using a special form of 20-cal. bullet. Pellet guns are usually rifled, those for BBs only are not; 177-cal. rifles can shoot BBs also, of course.

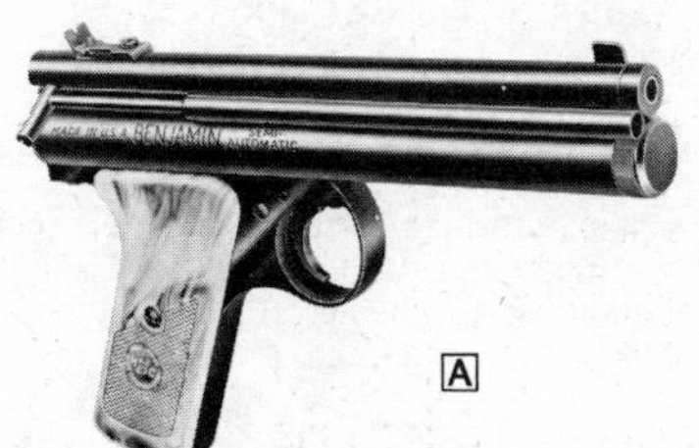

A

BENJAMIN 262 SUPER CO² ROCKET (not illus.)
Caliber: 22, single shot.
Barrel: 5¾", rifled bronze liner.
Length: 9¼". **Weight:** 3 lbs.
Power: Standard CO² cylinder, 2-stage power.
Features: Plastic stocks. Adj. rear sight. Fingertip safety. Target outfit includes pellets, Bell target and paper targets, one CO² cartridge; $4.00 extra.
Price: **$27.00**

D

A BENJAMIN 422 SEMI-AUTOMATIC PISTOL
Caliber: 22, 10-shot.
Barrel: 5 9/16", rifled bronze liner.
Length: 9". **Weight:** 2 lbs.
Power: Standard CO² cylinder. Muzzle velocity about 400 fps.
Features: Trigger and hammer safeties, checkered plastic thumbrest grips, adj. rear sight, blade front.
Price: Blued **$27.50**

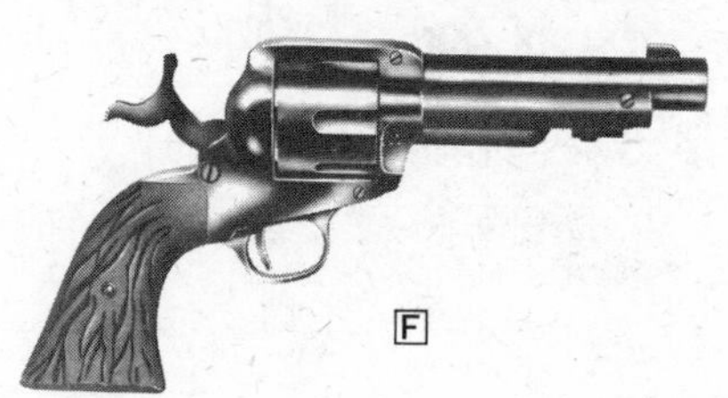

F

B BENJAMIN SUPER S. S. TARGET PISTOL SERIES 130
Caliber: BB, 22 and 177; single shot.
Barrel: 8 inches; BB smoothbore; 22 and 177, rifled.
Length 11". **Weight:** 2 lbs.
Power: Hand pumped.
Features: Bolt action; fingertip safety; adj. power.
Price: M130, BB.. **$32.00** M132, 22.. **$32.00** M137, 177.. **$32.00**

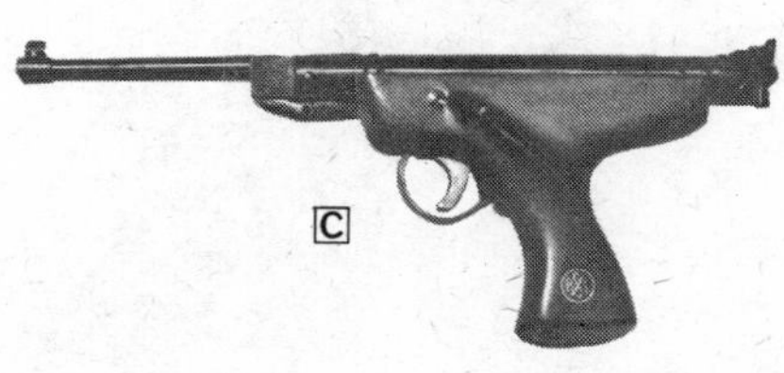

C

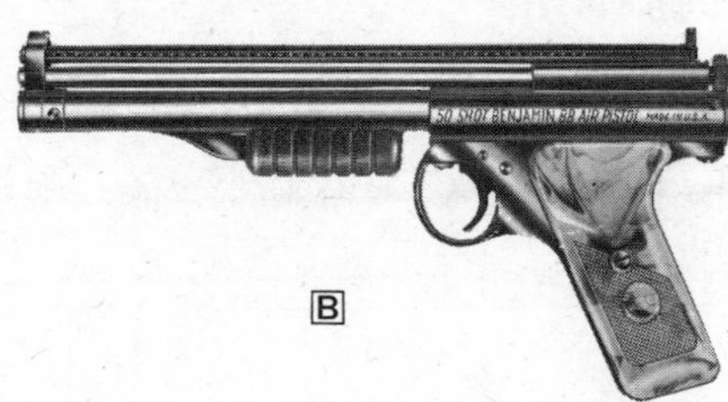

B

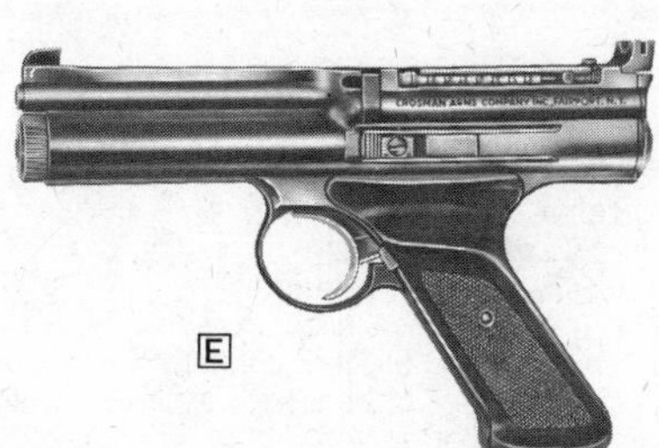

E

C BSF MATCH EXPORT PISTOL
Caliber: 177 single shot
Barrel: 7" rifled
Length: 15¾ inches. **Weight:** 2 lbs. 10 oz.
Power: Spring (barrel cocking).
Features: One piece walnut grip with thumb-rest. Adjustable trigger. Bead front, rear adjustable for w. and e. Air Rifle Hdqtrs, importer.
Price: **$34.50**

D CROSMAN 130 PISTOL
Caliber: 22, single shot.
Barrel: 8", rifled.
Length: 10 inches. **Weight:** 26 oz.
Power: Hand pumped.
Features: Moulded plastic grips. Cross-lock safety. Self-cocking action. Enclosed loading chamber.
Price: **$26.95**

E CROSMAN 600 SEMI-AUTOMATIC PISTOL
Caliber: 22, 10-shot.
Barrel: 5¼ inches, button rifled.
Length: 9½ inches. **Weight:** 40 oz.
Power: Crosman Powerlet CO² cylinder.
Features: Thumbrest plastic grips; adj. rear sight; thumb safety; ammo-count magazine.
Price: **$34.50**

F CROSMAN SINGLE 6 CO² REVOLVER
Caliber: 22, 6-shot.
Barrel: 4¾ inches, button rifled.
Length: 10⅜ inches. **Weight:** 24 oz.
Power: Crosman Powerlet CO² cylinder.
Features: Single-action. Frontier styling, staghorn style grips. Long-spur hammer for fanning.
Price: **$22.95**

CROSMAN 45 REVOLVER
Caliber: BB, 18-shot.
Barrel: 4¾ inches, smoothbore.
Length: 10⅜ inches. **Weight:** 34 oz.
Power: Crosman Powerlet CO² cylinder.
Features: Single-action. "Peacemaker" styling and feel, staghorn plastic grip, long-spur hammer, tubular spring-fed magazine.
Price: **$22.95**

A CROSMAN MARK I TARGET PISTOL
Caliber: 177, single shot.
Barrel: 7¼ inches, button rifled.
Length: 10⅝ inches. **Weight:** 43 oz.
Power: Crosman Powerlet CO^2 cylinder.
Features: New system provides same shot-to-shot velocity, adj. from 300- to 400 fps. Checkered thumbrest grips, right or left. Patridge front sight, rear adj. for w. & e. Adj. trigger.
Price: 22 or 177 .... **$27.95**

CROSMAN MARK II TARGET PISTOL
Same as Mark I except 22 cal. **$27.95**

C DAISY 179 SIX GUN
Caliber: BB, 12-shot.
Barrel: Steel lined, smoothbore.
Length: 11½ inches. **Weight:** NA.
Power: Spring.
Features: Forced feed from under-barrel magazine. Single action, molded wood grained grips.
Price: **$8.95**

E DAISY CO^2 200 AUTOLOADING PISTOL
Caliber: BB, 175-shot semi-auto.
Barrel: 7½ inches, steel-lined, smoothbore.
Length: 11 5/32", sight radius 9". **Weight:** 24 oz.
Power: Daisy CO^2 cylinders, 8½ grams (100 shots) or 12 grams (160 shots).
Features: 175-shot magazine; constant full power; valve system eliminates gas leakage; checkered thumbrest stocks; undercut ramp front sight and adjustable rear.
Price: **$23.95**

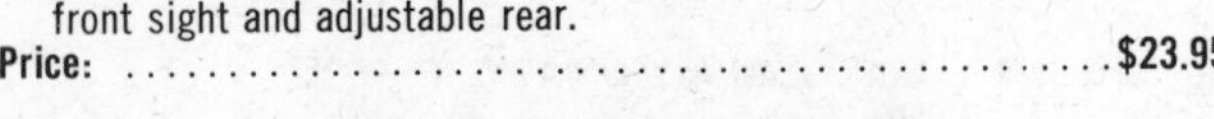

G

DIANA 5 TARGET PISTOL
Same as the Hy-Score 815 except: Air Rifle HQ degreases, inspects, test fires, adjusts, sights-in and repackages **$34.50**
Without accurizing 29.95

DIANA 6 TARGET PISTOL
Same as the Hy-Score 816 but with accurizing done as described above **$57.50**
Without accurizing 49.95

G CROSMAN 45 AUTO REPEATER
Caliber: 22, 6-shot.
Barrel: 4¾", 10 lands, r.h. (1-16) twist, button rifled.
Length: 8". **Weight:** 45 oz.
Power: Crosman Powerlet CO^2 cylinder.
Features: Authentic functional recoil and slide action, sights adj. for w. and e. Velocity 370fps.
Price: **$39.95**

B CROSMAN 38 TARGET REVOLVER M9
Caliber: 22, 6-shot.
Barrel: 6 inches, rifled.
Length: 11 inches. **Weight:** 38 oz.
Power: CO^2 Powerlet cylinder.
Features: Double action, revolving cylinder. Adj. rear sight.
Price: **$34.95**

CROSMAN 38 COMBAT REVOLVER
Same as 38 Target except 3½" bbl., 38 oz. **$34.95**

D DAISY 177 BB PISTOL
Caliber: BB, 150-shot.
Barrel: Formed steel, smoothbore.
Length: 10⅜ inches. **Weight:** NA.
Power: Spring.
Features: Gravity feed, adjustable rear sight, molded plastic thumbrest grips.
Price: **$8.95**

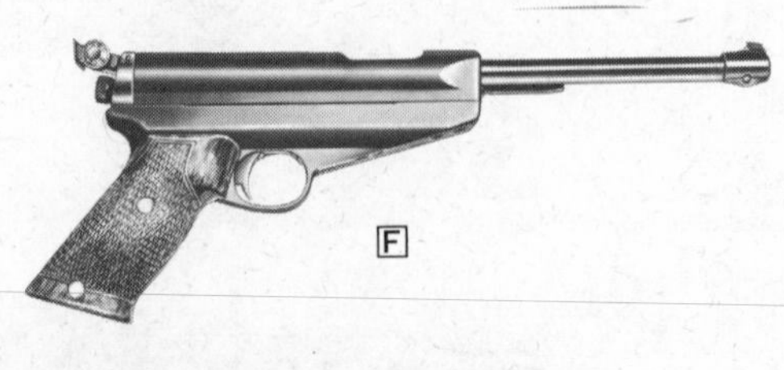

F

F FEINWERKBAU 65 TARGET PISTOL
Caliber: 177, single shot.
Barrel: 7½", rifled, fixed to receiver.
Length: About 15". **Weight:** 42 oz.
Power: Spring, cocked by left-side lever.
Features: Recoiless operation, may be set to give recoil; Micro. rear sight, 14" radius. Adj. trigger; normal 17.6 oz. pull can be raised to 48 oz. for training. Checkered, thumbrest target grips. Air Rifle Hdqtrs. or Daisy, importer.
Price: **$144.50**

[A] HAMMERLI MASTER CO^2 TARGET PISTOL
Caliber: 177, single shot.
Barrel: 6.7", rifled, 12 grooves, R.H.
Length: 16". **Weight:** 38 oz.
Power: 8g. or 12g. CO^2 cyl., 40-60 plus shots.
Features: Easy manual loading; residual gas vented automatically; 4-way adj. trigger; ramp front sight, ⅞" blade (other widths avail.), micro-click rear; sight radius adj. 11½" to 13⅜". Bbl.- and grip weights available, $4 and $3.50.
Price: **$54.00**

A

B

[B] HAMMERLI SINGLE TARGET PISTOL Model 452
Caliber: 177, single shot.
Barrel: 5.2 inches, rifled.
Length: 12 inches. **Weight:** 34 oz., including CO^2 cylinder.
Power: Standard CO^2 cylinder.
Features: Auto spring loader; adj. trigger; valve permits emptying CO^2 cylinder. Micrometer adj. rear sight. ⅛" blade front sight on ramp. H. Grieder, importer. Price incl. 10 CO^2 cylinders, 100 pellets.
Price: **$41.00**

[C] HEALTHWAYS ML 175 CO^2 AUTOMATIC PISTOL
Caliber: BB, 100-shot repeater.
Barrel: 5¾", smooth.
Length: 9½". **Weight:** 28 oz.
Power: Standard CO^2 cylinder.
Features: 3 position power switch. Automatic ammunition feed. Positive safety.
Price: **$19.95**

HEALTHWAYS MA22 CO^2 AUTOMATIC PISTOL
Same as Healthways ML175 except rifled 22 cal. bbl., rear sight adj. for w. and e., cap. 50 lead balls. **$24.00**

C

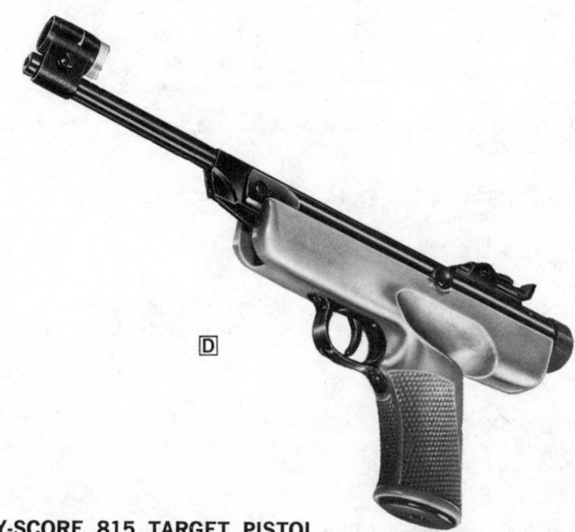

D

HY-SCORE 815 TARGET PISTOL
Same as Hy-Score M816 except: without recoil-less system; is slightly shorter and lighter; has fixed aperture front sight. In plastic case. Also in 22 cal. **$29.95**

[D] HY-SCORE 816 M TARGET PISTOL
Caliber: 177, single shot.
Barrel: 7" precision rifled.
Length: 16 inches. **Weight:** 50 oz.
Power: Spring, bbl. cocking.
Features: Recoil-less firing, adj. trigger. Hooded front sight with 3 apertures, click adj. rear with 4 apertures. Plastic thumbrest target grips.
Price: In plastic case **$49.95**

HY-SCORE 814 JUNIOR PISTOL
Caliber: 177 darts, BBs, single shot.
Barrel: Smoothbore.
Length: About 10 inches. **Weight:** N.A.
Power: Spring, compressed by screwing in breech plug.
Features: Checkered wooden grips.
Price: Blued **$5.95**

A HY-SCORE 802 AUTOLOADING PISTOL
Caliber: 22, 6-shot repeater.
Barrel: 10¼ inches, rifled.
Length: 10¼ inches. **Weight:** 30½ oz.
Power: Spring.
Features: Thumbrest target grips. Recoil comparable to standard target pistols. 3-pound trigger pull. Shutter type loading.
Price: Blued **$29.95.** M800, same except single shot.......... **$24.95**

LUFT PISTOLE 210 TARGET
Caliber: 177, single shot.
Barrel: 4¾" rifled.
Length: 8". **Weight:** 45 oz.
Power: Spring.
Features: Same size, weight & shape as a standard auto. pistol. Simulated slide lifts, cocking the gun, as the breech is loaded. Navy Arms, importer.
Price: **$17.50**

B MARKSMAN REPEATER PISTOL
Caliber: 177, 20-shot repeater.
Barrel: 2½ inches, smoothbore.
Length: 8¼ inches. **Weight:** 24 oz.
Power: Spring.
Features: Thumb safety. Uses BB's, darts or pellets. Repeats with BB's only.
Price: Black finish **$9.95**

C SEARS CO^2 SINGLE ACTION REVOLVER
Caliber: 22, 6-shot.
Barrel: 4¾", rifled.
Length: 10 5/16". **Weight:** 42 oz.
Power: CO^2 Powerlet cylinder.
Features: Plastic staghorn grips; long-spur hammer with positive safety.
Price: **$18.75**

E WALTHER MODEL LP2
Caliber: 177, single shot.
Barrel: 9.4", rifled.
Length: 12.8" **Weight:** 20 oz.
Power: Spring-air.
Features: Recoil-less operation, cocking in grip frame. Micro-click rear sight, adj. for w. & e. 4-way adj. trigger. Plastic thumbrest grips; wood grip at extra cost. Interarms, importer.
Price: **$72.00**

F WALTHER MODEL 53 PISTOL
Caliber: 177, single shot.
Barrel: 9⅜", rifled.
Length: 12¼". **Weight:** 42 oz.
Power: Spring.
Features: Micrometer rear sight. Interchangeable rear sight blades. Adj. trigger. Target grips. Bbl. weight available at extra cost. Interarms, Alexandria, Va.
Price: **$38.00**

G WEBLEY AIR PISTOLS

Model:	**Junior**	**Premier**
Caliber:	177	177 or 22
Barrel:	6⅛"	6½"
Weight:	24 oz.	33 oz.
Power:	Spring, barrel cocking	Same
Sights:	Adj. for elev.	Adj. for w.&e.
Trigger:	Fixed	Adj.
Price:	**$19.95**	**$27.50**

Features: Come with cardboard storage case, pellets, spare washer. Service Armament, importer.

H WINCHESTER 363 TARGET PISTOL
Caliber: 177, Single shot.
Barrel: 7" rifled.
Length: 16". **Weight:** 3 lbs.
Power: Spring, barrel cocking.
Features: Recoil-less firing, adj. double pull type trigger, hooded front sight with 3 apertures, click adj. rear sight. Plastic thumbrest target grips. M.V. 378 fps.
Price: **$49.95**

J WINCHESTER 353 TARGET PISTOL
Caliber: 177 or 22, single shot.
Barrel: 7" rifled.
Length: 16". **Weight:** 2 lbs. 11 oz.
Power: Spring, barrel cocking.
Features: Plastic thumbrest target grips. Adj. double pull trigger, Micro rear sight, detachable bead front with hood. M.V. 378 fps.
Price: **$29.95**

[A] ANSCHUTZ 250 TARGET RIFLE
Caliber: 177, single shot.
Barrel: 18½", rifled, one piece with receiver.
Length: 45". **Weight:** 11 lbs. with sights.
Power: Spring, side-lever cocking, 11 lb. pull.
Features: Recoilless operation. Two-stage adj. trigger. Checkered walnut p.g. stock with Monte Carlo comb & cheekpiece; adj. buttplate; accessory rail. Air Rifle Hdqtrs., importer.
Price: Without sights **$145.00**
Add **$22.50** for utility aperture sights or **$42.50** for premium aperture sights.

BAVARIA/WISCHO 55N SPORTING RIFLE
Caliber: 177 or 22, single shot.
Barrel: 16½", rifled.
Length: 40½". **Weight:** 6.4 lbs.
Power: Spring (barrel cocking).
Features: High velocity (728 fps in 177, 590 fps in 22) and accuracy combined with rapid loading, can be reloaded in 5 seconds. Stock is of walnut with checkered p.g. and buttplate. Open rear, bead front sights; receiver grooved for scope mounting. Trigger is adjustable. Air Rifle Hdqtrs, importer.
Price: **$56.50**

[B] BSA METEOR SUPER
Caliber: 177 or 22, single-shot.
Barrel: 18½", rifled.
Length: 42". **Weight:** 6 lbs.
Power: Spring, bbl. cocking.
Features: Beechwood Monte Carlo stock, recoil pad. Adjustable single-stage trigger. Bead front, adjustable rear sight. Positive relocation of barrel for same zero shot to shot. Galef, importer.
Price: **$39.95**

[C] BENJAMIN 3030 CO^2 REPEATER
Caliber: BB only.
Barrel: 25½", smoothbore, takedown.
Length: 36". **Weight:** 2 lbs. 13 oz.
Power: Standard CO^2 cylinder.
Features: Bolt action. 30-shot repeater with permanent-magnet, shot-holder ammo feed.
Price: **$25.50**

[D] BENJAMIN SERIES 3100 SUPER 100 SHOT RIFLES
Caliber: BB, 100-shot; 22, 85-shot repeater.
Barrel: 23", rifled or smoothbore.
Length: 35". **Weight:** 6 lbs.
Power: Hand pumped.
Features: Bolt action. 100-shot, piggy back full view magazine. Bar V adj. rear sight. Walnut-finished p.g. stock.
Price: M3100, BB . . . . **$38.50** M3120, 22 rifled **$38.50**
Also available with custom stock at $3 extra.

[E] BENJAMIN SERIES 362 SUPER CO^2 SINGLE SHOT
Caliber: 22 only.
Barrel: 23", rifled.
Length: 35". **Weight:** 6 lbs.
Power: Standard CO^2 cylinder. 2 power settings.
Features: Bolt action. Bronze-lined steel bbl. Adj. rear sight. Walnut-finished stock. Two-stage power.
Price: **$31.50**
Also available with custom stock at $3 extra.

[F] BENJAMIN SERIES 340 RIFLE
Caliber: 22 and 177 pellets or BB; single shot.
Barrel: 23", rifled.
Length: 35". **Weight:** 6 lbs.
Power: Hand pumped.
Features: Bolt action, walnut stock and pump handle. Adj. V sight.
Price: M340, BB . . **$35.95** M342, 22 . . **$35.95** M347, 177 . . **$35.95**
Available with custom stock at $3 extra.

[G] CROSMAN M-1 CARBINE
Caliber: BB, 22-shot.
Barrel: Smoothbore, steel.
Length: 35⅝". **Weight.** 4½ lbs.
Power: Spring.
Features: Patterned after U.S. M1 carbine, uses slide action cocking, military type adj. sights. Hardwood stock.
Price: **$19.95**

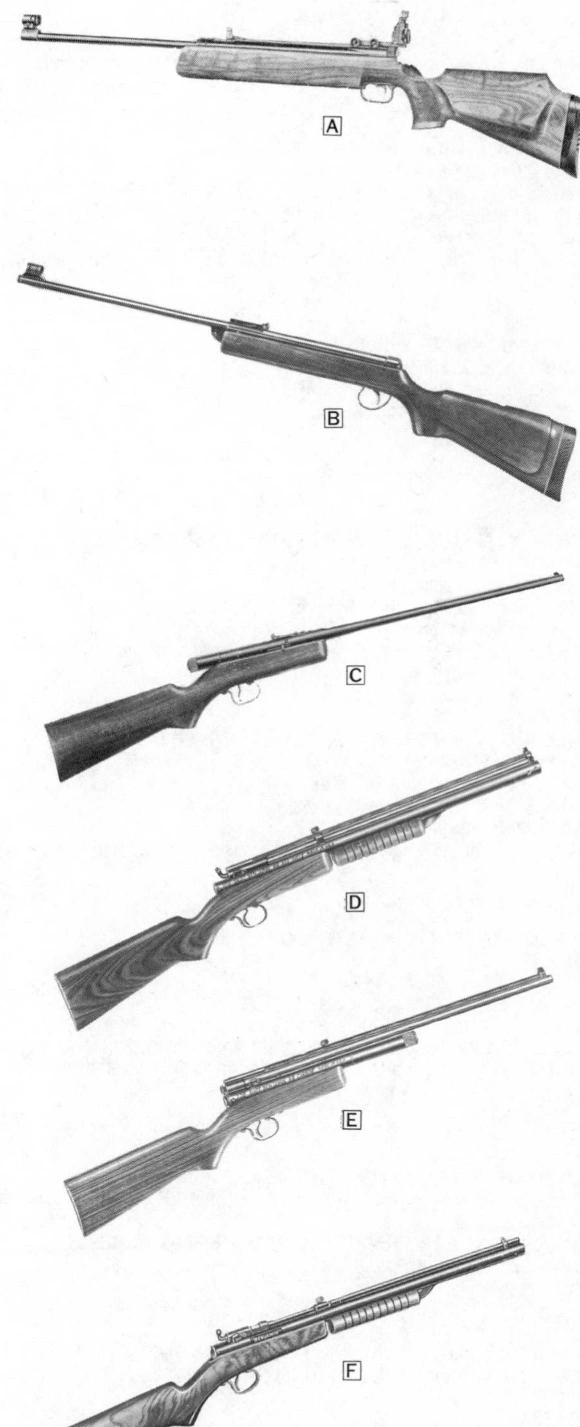

A CROSMAN 99 REPEATER RIFLE
Caliber: 22, 14-shot.
Barrel: 19½ inches, button rifled steel.
Length: 40 inches. **Weight:** 5 lbs. 10 oz.
Power: Crosman Powerlet CO^2 cylinder.
Features: Lever action pellet rifle with swing-arm loading principle; has size and balance of firearm counterparts. Two-stage power selector. Adj. rear sight.
Price: **$37.50**

B CROSMAN 1400 RIFLE
Caliber: 22, single shot.
Barrel: 19½ inches, rifled steel.
Length: 35 inches. **Weight:** About 6 lbs.
Power: Hand pumped.
Features: Bolt action. Air-Trol valve prevents air lock from over-pumping. Adj. trigger, left or right hand safety.
Price: **$36.95**

C CROSMAN 160 RIFLE
Caliber: 22, single shot.
Barrel: 21 inches, button rifled steel.
Length: 40 inches. **Weight:** 5⅜ lbs.
Power: 2 Crosman Powerlet CO^2 cylinders.
Features: Bolt action. Monte Carlo stock, hard rubber butt plate. Adj. receiver sight. Turning cross-lock safety.
Price: **$41.50**

D CROSMAN 166 LEVER ACTION REPEATER
Caliber: BB, 30-shot.
Barrel: 17 inches, smoothbore steel.
Length: 34 inches. **Weight:** 3 lbs. 8 oz.
Power: Crosman Powerlet CO^2 cylinder.
Features: Magnetic swing-loading feed. External hammer with safety notch. Adj. open rear sight.
Price: **$21.95**

E CROSMAN V-350 SLIDE ACTION RIFLE
Caliber: BB, 22-shot.
Barrel: 16 inches, smoothbore steel.
Length: 34¾ inches. **Weight:** 3½ lbs.
Power: High compression spring.
Features: Sliding bbl. cocks and loads. Visual loading magazine. Adj. open rear sight.
Price: **$16.95**

F CROSMAN PELLMASTER 700
Caliber: 22
Barrel: 18 inches, rifled steel.
Length: 36¾ inches. **Weight:** 4 lbs.
Power: Crosman Powerlet CO^2 cylinder.
Features: One stroke cocking and safety knob, hooded post front and adjustable rear sight, high Monte Carlo comb walnut finished hardwood stock. Uniform velocity from shot to shot, designed for NRA 10 meter competition.
Price: **$27.95**

CROSMAN PELLMASTER 707
Same as Pellmaster 700 exvept 177 cal. and BB........... **$27.95**

G CROSMAN POWERMASTER 760 REPEATER RIFLE
Caliber: 177 pellets, or BB, 180 shot.
Barrel: 19½ inches.
Length: 35 inches. **Weight:** 4 lb. 2 oz.
Power: Hand pumped.
Features: Velocity over 550 fps. Power choice. Hardwood stock, solid steel barrel, safety, sights adj. for w. and e.
Price: **$22.95**

H CROSMAN TRAPMASTER SHOTGUN
Gauge: .380 inch, chambers Crosman CO^2 shotshells.
Action: One-stroke, side cocking single shot.
Barrel: 28″ true cylinder bore, full length rib.
Stock: 14¼″x1″x2″, contoured hardwood, walnut finished.
Weight: 6¼ lbs. 46″ over-all.
Power: Crosman Giant CO^2 Powerlet.
Features: Pattern is about 14″ dia. at 40 feet (effective range). Plastic shotshells contain about 55 No. 8 pellets. Looks and feels like other shotguns.
Price: **$49.95**

CROSMAN CO^2 SKEET SET
Includes Trapmaster shotgun, box of 25 reusable plastic break-away targets, 100 shotshells, 10 giant Powerlets and Skeet trap with remote foot release **$89.95**

A B C D E F G H

[A] DAISY 21 DOUBLE BARREL RIFLE
Caliber: BB, 48-shot.
Barrel: 23½ inches, smoothbore.
Length: 37¾ inches. **Weight:** 4½ lbs.
Power: Spring, barrel cocking.
Features: Two barrels and triggers; automatic safety; beaded front ramp and open rear sights.
Price: **$23.95**

[B] DAISY 25 PUMP GUN
Caliber: BB, 50-shot.
Barrel: 18 inches, smoothbore.
Length: 37 inches. **Weight:** NA.
Power: Pump cocking spring.
Features: Ramp front and adj. rear sights. BBs are spring-force fed.
Price: **$16.95**

[C] DAISY 1894 SPITTIN' IMAGE CARBINE
Caliber: BB, 40-shot.
Barrel: 17½ inches, smoothbore.
Length: 35 inches.
Power: Spring.
Features: Cocks halfway on forward stroke of lever, halfway on return.
Price: **$19.49**
Price: With 4X Scope, as M3894 .... **26.95**
Price: With fluted receiver, cocking lever, saddle ring, loading port, fore-arm cap and contoured butt plate, as 3030 .... **$21.49**

[D] DAISY 99 TARGET SPECIAL RIFLE
Caliber: BB, 50-shot.
Barrel: 18 inches, smoothbore.
Length: 36 inches.
Power: Spring.
Features: Wood stock, beavertail fore-end; sling; hooded front sight with four insert apertures, adj. aperture rear.
Price: **$19.95**

[E] DAISY RIFLES

Model:	**96**	**95**	**111**	**102**	**1776**
Caliber:	BB	BB	BB	BB	BB
Barrel:	18″	18″	18″	13½″	13½″
Length:	36″	35⅛″	35″	30½″	30½″
Power:	Spring	Spring	Spring	Spring	Spring
Capacity:	700	700	700	500	500
Price:	**$16.95**	**$12.95**	**$11.95**	**$8.95**	**$9.95**

Price: Model 96 with 4X scope, as M496 .... **$24.45**
Features: 96 has M.C. stock and oversize fore-end; 95 stock is wood, fore-end plastic; 111 and 1776 have plastic stocks; 102 has wood stock; 1776 has sighting tube w/aperture and is gold finished.

[F] DAISY HIGH POWER RIFLES

Model:	**160**	**220**	**230**	**250**
Caliber:	177 & BB	177	22	22
Barrel:	12″	14½″	15¾″	15¾″
Rifled:	No	Yes	Yes	Yes
Length:	33″	36″	38″	38″
Weight:	3 lbs.	3¾ lbs.	5 lbs.	5½ lbs.
Power:	Spring	Spring	Spring	Spring
Price:	**$16.45**	**$22.95**	**$27.95**	**$32.95**

Features: All are barrel cocking with beechwood stocks. 160 and 220 have bead front and adj. rear sights. 230 and 250 have blade front and adj. rear target sights.

[G] DAISY CO_2 300 REPEATER
Caliber: BB, 5-shot semi-auto.
Barrel: 22 inches, smoothbore.
Length: 37⅞ inches. **Weight:** 2 lbs. 14 oz.
Power: Daisy 8.5 or 12 gram CO_2 cylinder.
Features: Free-style stock, cross-bolt safety, 200 shot magazine capacity, blade front daj: open rear sights, receiver grooved for scope.
Price: **$31.49**
Price: With 4X scope, as CO_2 3300 .... **38.95**

[H] DAISY 572 SPITTIN' IMAGE SLIDE ACTION RIFLE
Caliber: BB, 45-shot.
Barrel: 22½ inches, smoothbore.
Length: 42¼ inches.
Power: Spring.
Features: Pump-cocking, cross-bolt safety, takedown bbl., adj. rear sight, under bbl. magazine, wood-grained stock and fore-end.
Price: **$21.95**
Price: With 4X scope, as 2572 .... **29.45**

[J] DAISY 2299 QUICK SKILL RIFLE KIT
Caliber: BB, 50-shot
Barrel: 24 inches, smoothbore.
Length: 37⅝ inches (adult stock). **Weight:** 3¼ lbs.
Power: Spring.
Features: Kit includes rifle, shooting glasses, ammo, official targets and instruction manual. No sights, meant for instinct shooting instruction.
Price: **$25.95**

[A] DAISY VL SHOOTING SYSTEM
Caliber: 22VL caseless ctg., single shot.
Barrel: Solid steel, 6 lands and grooves 1 in 16" twist.
Length: 38 inches. **Weight:** 51 lbs.
Power: Fires 29 gr. bullet at 1,150 fps.
Features: Cartridge has no case or primer. Action has no firing pin or ejector. Cocking by recessed lever. Ignition is by air released under high pressure causing friction to ignite material at base of bullet. Also has auto. safety, plastic wood finished stock with checkered p.g. and fore-end. Rear sight adj. for w. & e.; blade front.
Price: Model 0002 .... **$39.95**

PRESENTATION VL
Same as above but with walnut stock, storage gun case with foam cushion lining, brass wall hangers and 300 rounds of ammunition. Model 0003. .... **$125.00**

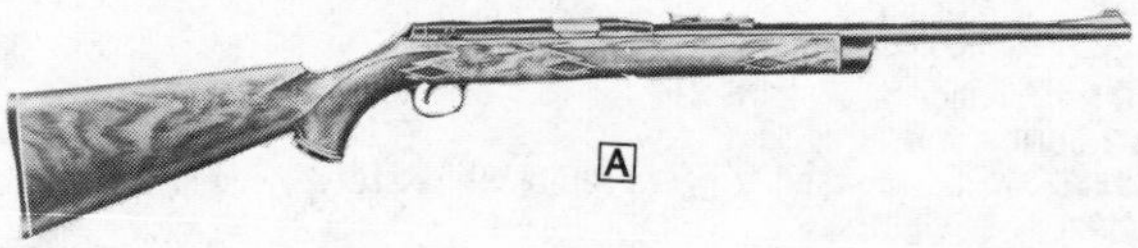

DIANA 60 TARGET RIFLE
Caliber: 177, single shot.
Barrel: 18", rifled.
Length: 43½". **Weight:** 9½ lbs. with sights and detachable bbl. sleeve.
Power: Spring (barrel cocking).
Features: Recoil-less type action, no jar. Micro. aperture rear sight, globe front with 4 inserts. Two-stage, adj. trigger, pull less than 1 lb. Checkered walnut p.g. stock with Monte Carlo comb & cheekpiece, rubber buttplate. Air Rifle Hdqtrs., importer.
Price: **$118.50**
Add $19.00 for Tyrolean Stock.

[B] DIANA 65 TARGET RIFLE
Same as the M60 except weighs 11 lbs., has adj. stock length; M.V. 50 fps., double trigger, (Available about July 1969).
Price: **$169.75**

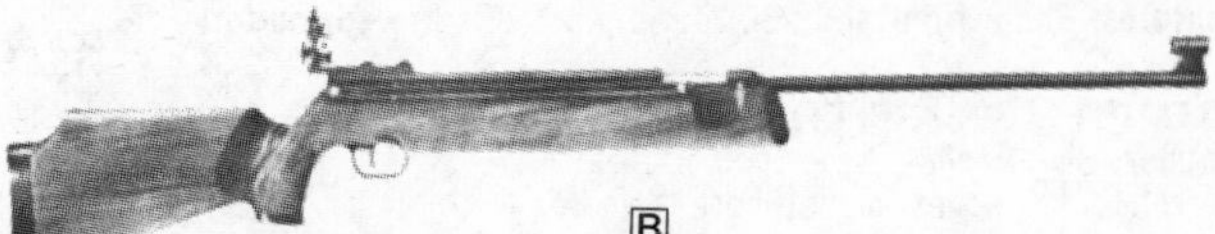

[C] FEINWERKBAU 150 MATCH RIFLE
Caliber: 177, single shot.
Barrel: 19½" rifled steel, one piece with receiver.
Length: 42". **Weight:** 9¾ lbs.
Power: Hand cocked by side lever. Less than 10 lbs. pull required.
Features: Barrel and receiver recoil together, independent of stock, to eliminate felt recoil, are locked up when gun is cocked. Micro. rear peep sight, globe front with inserts. Trigger fully adj. Muzzle velocity 575 fps. Checkered walnut stock with Monte Carlo cheekpiece, palmswell p.g. Daisy or Air Rifle Hdqtrs., importers.
Price: 150S (9 lb. Std.) **$169.75**; 150SL (L.H.) **$188.75**; 150ST (Tyrol. stock), 150STL (L.H. Tyrol. stock) **$199.50**

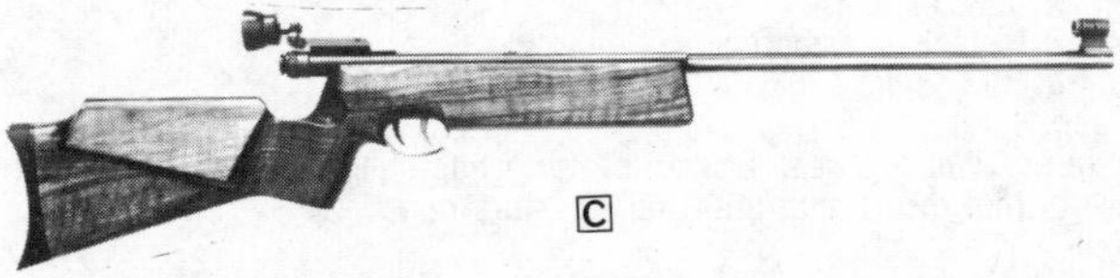

[D] FEINWERKBAU 110 RIFLE
Same as F'bau 150 except: has slight recoil effect; 20" bbl., 640 fps. M.V. Available from A.R.H. or Daisy.
Price: M110 Std. (9 lbs.) or M110D (11 lbs.) **$144.50**

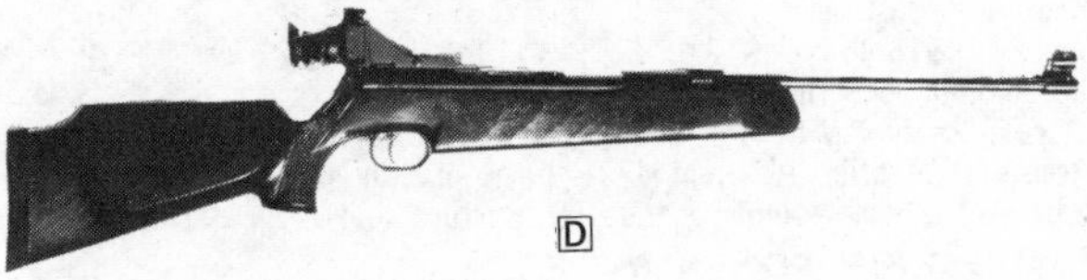

[E] HAMMERLI CO² MATCH RIFLE Model 472
Caliber: 177, single shot.
Barrel: 23¼", rifled steel.
Length: 41½". **Weight:** 9 lbs. 11 oz.
Power: Standard CO_2 cylinder or CO_2 Powerlets.
Features: Walnut p.g. stock with Monte Carlo comb and cheekpiece; adj. trigger; curved rubber buttplate. Micrometer rear sight, globe front sight. H. Grieder, importer.
Price: **$124.00**

M471 Junior Same except has bbl. post front sight and bbl. mounted rear sight, no pad, weight 6 lbs. **$74.00**

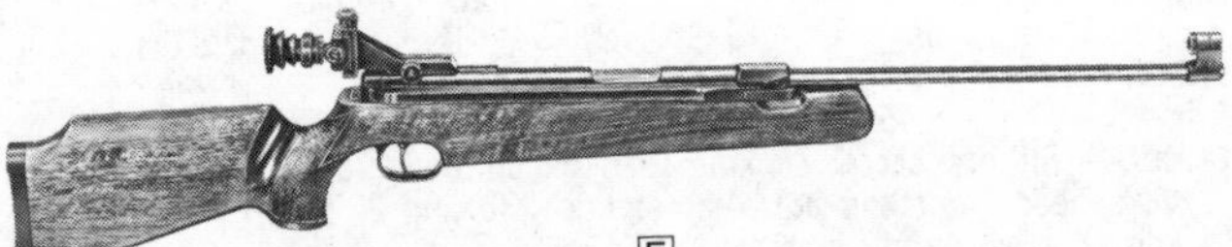

[F] HEALTHWAYS PLAINSMAN MC22 AUTO RIFLE
Caliber: 22, 75-shot.
Barrel: 20½ inches, rifled for round lead balls.
Length: 41 inches. **Weight:** 4½ lbs.
Power: CO_2 (8- or 12-gram cylinder).
Features: Up to 50 shots automatically with 12-g. cylinder; no cocking, pumping, etc. Full size p.g. wood stock.
Price: **$35.00**

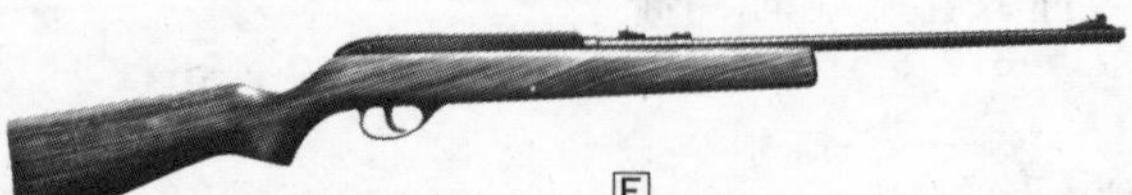

[G] **Plainsman MX175.** Same as MC22 except 175" smoothbore for BBs; weighs 8 oz. less. **$30.00**

HY-SCORE 809M TARGET RIFLE
Caliber: 22, single shot.
Barrel: 19 inch rifled.
Length: 44 inches. **Weight:** 7 pounds.
Power: Spring, bbl. cocking.
Features: Adj. target receiver sight, aperture front with 4 inserts, in addition to open adj. middle sight also with 4 apertures.
Price: **$64.95**

A

B

C

D

E

F

G

[A] HY-SCORE RIFLES

Model:	808	806	813	801	807
Caliber:	177	177	22	22	22
Barrel:	12″	14½″	14¼″	15¾″	17⅜″
Rifled:	No	Yes	Yes	Yes	Yes
Length:	33″	36½″	36½″	38½″	41¾″
Weight:	3 lbs.	3¾ lbs.	4 lbs.	5 lbs.	5 lbs. 14 oz.
Power:	Spring	Spring	Spring	Spring	Spring
Price:	**$14.95**	**$19.95**	**$25.95**	**$29.95**	**$39.95**

Features: All are barrel cocking. All have adj. sights and regular triggers except 807, which has an adj. trigger. Staeble 2.2X scope and mt. available for all but 808, **$14.95.**

M813 and scope available at a combination price of **$33.40**
M801 available as 801M with click adj. receiver sight....... **$49.95**

[B] HY-SCORE 810M OLYMPIC INTERNATIONAL RIFLE

Caliber: 177, single shot.
Barrel: 19¼″ 12-groove rifled.
Length: 44″. **Weight:** 9½ lbs.
Power: Spring (barrel cocking).
Features: Full cheekpiece, Monte Carlo stock, hand checkered; grooved fore-end, curved rubber buttplate. Adj. target receiver sight (includes 4 apertures), hooded front sight (includes 4 inserts).
Price: **$99.95**

M810SM SUPER MATCH

As above but with weight increased to 14 lbs., bbl. locking device, adj. stock, replaceable mainspring, MV 650 fps, accuracy tested: ¼″ spread at 33′ **$169.95**

[C] PIC MINUTEMAN M77 RIFLE

Caliber: 177; 22, single shot.
Barrel: 14″, 6- and 10-groove rifled.
Length: 36″. **Weight:** 3¼ lbs.
Power: Spring (barrel cocking).
Features: Adj. sights, grooved for scope, light wood p.g. stock., finger-grooved fore-end.
Price: 177.............. **$13.50** **Price:** 22.............. **$14.00**
With 4x tip-off mount scope **$5.50** extra.

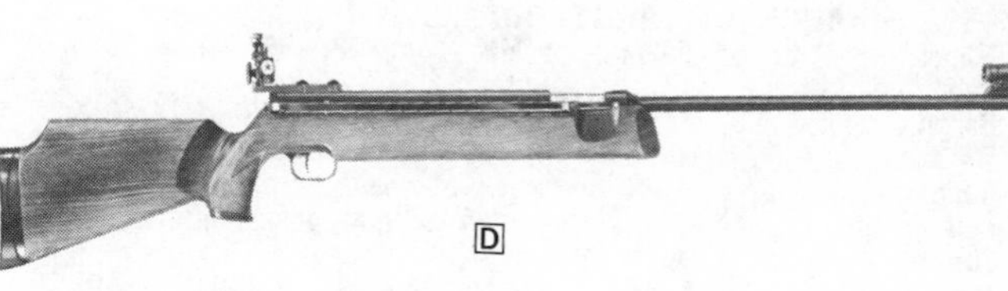

[D] SAVAGE-ANSCHUTZ 250 TARGET RIFLE

Caliber: 177, single shot.
Barrel: 18½″, rifled steel fixed to receiver, movable compression cylinder.
Length: 45″ **Weight:** 11 lbs. with sights.
Power: Hand cocked by side lever, about 11 lbs. cocking effort.
Features: Recoiless shooting via oil damper and compensating piston. Two-stage trigger adj. for finger length. French walnut, Monte Carlo stock and beavertail fore-end; checkered p.g. with Wundhammer swell. Accepts Anschutz target sights.
Price: Without sights **$145.00**

[E] SHERIDAN BLUE AND SILVER STREAK RIFLES

Caliber: 5mm (20 cal.), single shot.
Barrel: 18½″, rifled.
Length: 37″. **Weight:** 5 lbs.
Power: Hand pumped (swinging fore-end).
Features: Rustproof barrel and piston tube. Takedown. Thumb safety. Mannlicher type walnut stock.
Price: Blue Streak .... **$38.75** Silver Streak **$39.75**
Sheridan accessories: Intermount, a base for ⅜″ Tip-Off scope mounts, **$6.75**; Sheridan-Williams 5DSH receiver sight, **$7.00**; Model 22 Targetrap, **$12.50**; Model 38 Targetrap **$30.00**; Sheridan 5mm pellets, **$2.50** for 500.

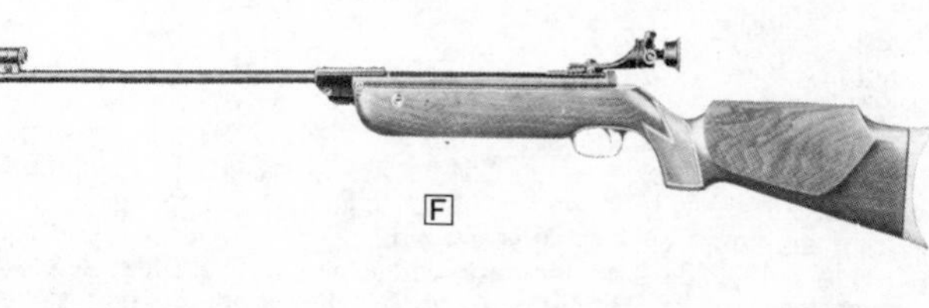

[F] WALTHER LG 55-M RIFLE

Caliber: 177, single shot.
Barrel: 16″, rifled.
Length: 41⅜″. **Weight:** 9 lbs. (9.7 lbs. with bbl. sleeve).
Power: Spring (barrel cocking).
Features: Micro. click adj. receiver sight, globe target front, 3 inserts. Walnut cheekpiece Monte Carlo, checkered p.g. stock. Tyrolean stock $10 extra. Interarms, importers.
Price: **$96.00**
Double set triggers available with any LG 55-M for $12 extra.

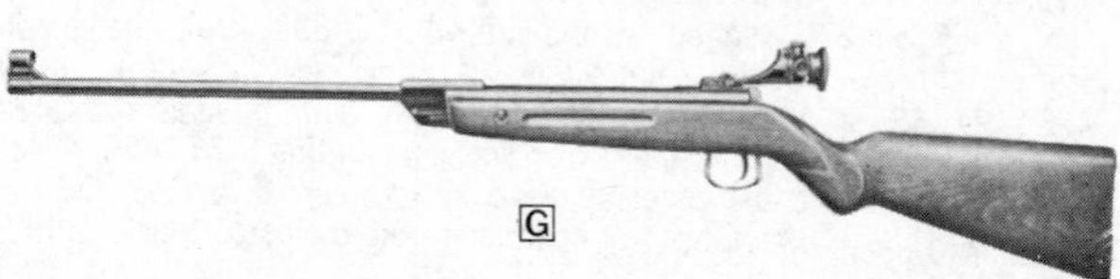

[G] WALTHER LG 53-ZD RIFLE

Caliber: 177, single shot.
Barrel: 16″, rifled.
Length: 41⅜″. **Weight:** 6 lbs.
Power: Spring (barrel cocking).
Features: Micro. click adj. receiver sight; globe front with 3 inserts. Adj. trigger. Checkered p.g. stock. Interarms and other importers.
Price: **$68.00**

A WEBLEY AIR RIFLES

Model:	Jaguar	Falcon	Mark III
Caliber:	177	177, 22	177, 22
Barrel:	NA.	17¼″	18½″
Length:	37″	41½″	43½″
Weight:	4 lbs.	6 lbs.	6 lbs.
Power:	spring	spring	spring
Sights:	open, adj.	open, adj.	globe front
Price:	**$27.50**	**$39.95**	**$75.00**

Features: Wooden p.g. stocks. Receivers grooved for scope mounts. Jaguar comes with target holder, target cards, 500 pellets, 12 darts, oil. Mk III is lever-cocking, others bbl.-cocking. Service Armament, importer.

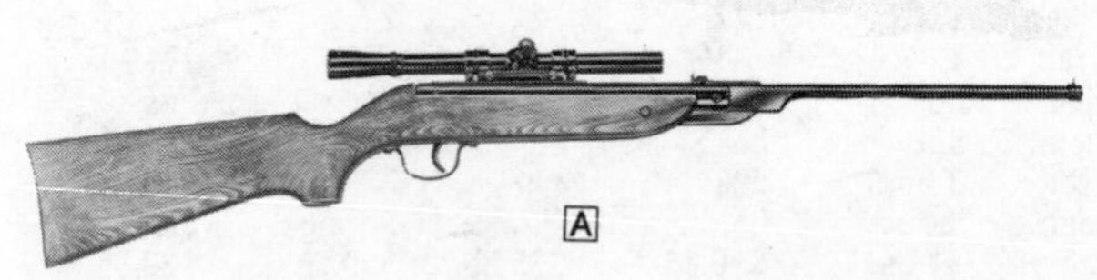
A

B WEIHRAUCH 30 & 50 SERIES RIFLES

Model:	30 M-II	30S	50 M-II	50S	50 E
Caliber:	177	177	177	177	177
Barrel:	16⅞″	16⅞″	18½″	18½″	18½″
Trigger:	fixed	fixed	fixed	adj.	adj.
Length:	40″	40″	43½″	43½″	43½″
Wgt., lbs.:	5½	5½	7	7	7¼
Price:	**$36.50**	**$44.50**	**$44.50**	**$49.95**	**$56.50**

Features: All are rifled and spring-operated by single stroke cocking. Post and ramp front sights (except 50S and 50E have globe fronts with 4 inserts). Open click rear sights, adj. for w. & e., except 30 Mk-11 has lock-screw windage. Walnut finished stocks. 50E has cheek-piece, checkering, ¾″ sling swivels. MV of all 660-67 fps. Air Rifle Hdqtrs., importer.

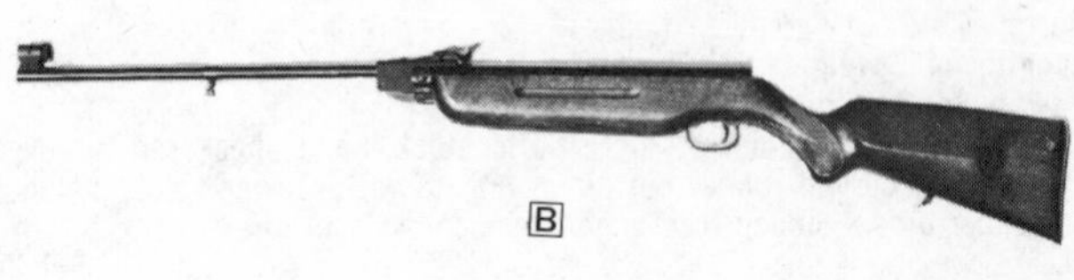
B

C WEIHRAUCH 35 TARGET RIFLES

Model:	35	35L	35E
Caliber:	177	177	177
Barrel:	19½″	19½″	22″
Wgt. lbs.:	7½	7½	8
Rear sight:	open	open	open
Front Sight:	All with globe and 4 interchangeable inserts.		
Power:	All with spring (barrel cocking).		
Price:	**$67.50**	**$74.50**	**$89.95**

Features: Trigger fully adj. and removable. Open rear sight click adj. for w. and e. P.g. high comb stock with beavertail fore-end, walnut finish, except 35E have checkered walnut with standard cheekpiece. 35L has Tyrolean cheekpiece stock. Air Rifle Hdqtrs., importer.

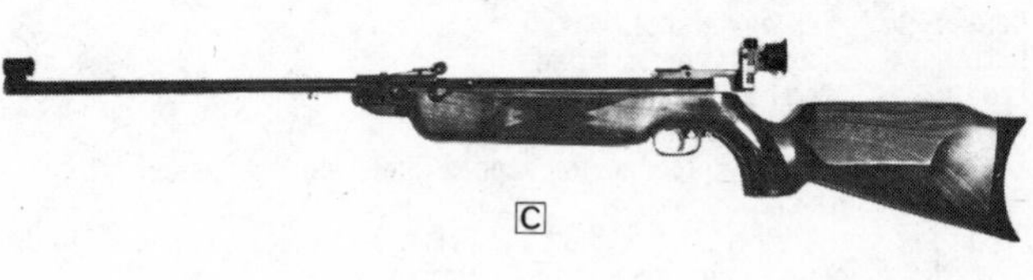
C

F WEIHRAUCH 55 TARGET RIFLES

Model:	55SF	55SM	55MM	55MM	55MM-L	55T
Caliber:	177	177	177	177	177	177
Barrel:	18½″	18½″	18½″	18½″	18½″	18½″
Wgt. lbs.:	7¼	8½	8½	7½	8½	8½
Rear Sight:	open	aperture	aperture	open	aperture	aperture
Front Sight:	All with globe and 4 interchangeable inserts.					
Power:	All with spring (bbl. cocking) .600 fps					
Price:	**$64.50**	**$78.50**	**$94.50**	**$84.50**	**$109.50**	**$109.50**

Features: Trigger fully adj. and removable. Micrometer rear sight adj. for w. and e., on all but 55SF and 55MM. P.g. high comb stock with beavertail fore-end, walnut finish stock on 55SF, SM. Walnut stock on 55MM, Tyrolean stock on 55T. Air Rifle Hdqtrs., importer.

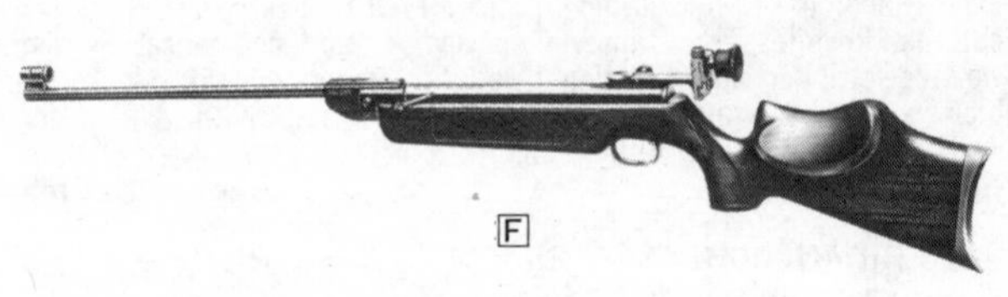
F

G WINCHESTER AIR RIFLES

Model	416	422	423	425
Calibers:	177	177	177	22
Length:	33″	36″	36″	38″
Wgt. lbs.:	2¾	3¾	4	5
Velocity, fps:	363	480	480	543
Price:	**$15.95**	**$22.95**	**$27.95**	**$32.95**

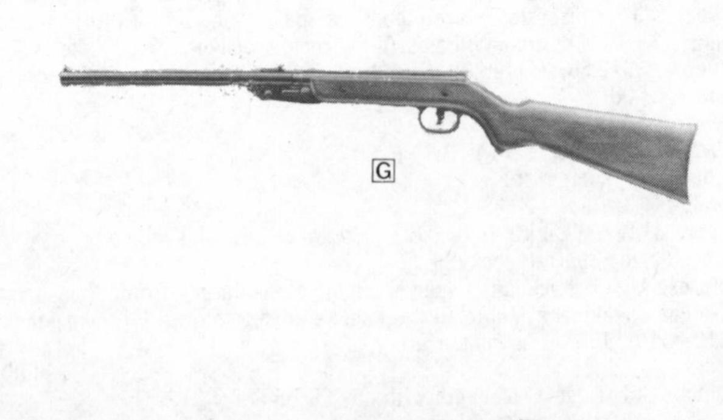
G

H WINCHESTER HIGH POWER AIR RIFLES

Model	427	435	450	333
Caliber:	22	177	177	177
Length:	42″	44″	44½″	43¼″
Wgt. lbs.:	6	6½	7¾	9½
Velocity, fps:	660	693	693	576
Price:	**$39.95**	**$54.95**	**$84.95**	**$169.95**

Features: All are rifled, except 416 (smoothbore), and spring operated by single stroke cocking. **Triggers:** 416, 422 & 423—double pull type triggers. 425, 427 & 435—adjustable double pull type triggers. 333—two stage trigger adj. for wgt., pre-travel & sear-off. **Front sights:** 416 & 422—bead post front sights; 423—blade front sight with ramp. 425 & 427—hooded front sights; 450 & 333—interchangeable front sight assemblies. **Rear Sights:** 416, 422 & 423—adj. screw, 425, 427, 435 & 450—Adj. micro., 333—Adj. diopter. Also, 425, 427, 435 & 450 have dovetail bases for scope mounting. 435, 450 & 333 have rubber butt pads, cheekpieces & checkered p.g. areas. 333 has an auto. safety, when bbl. is open and red indicator when bbl. is closed.

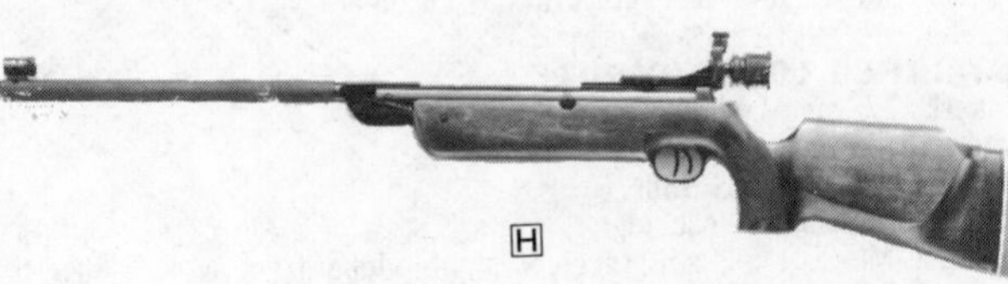
H

Micrometer Receiver Sight

Receiver Sights

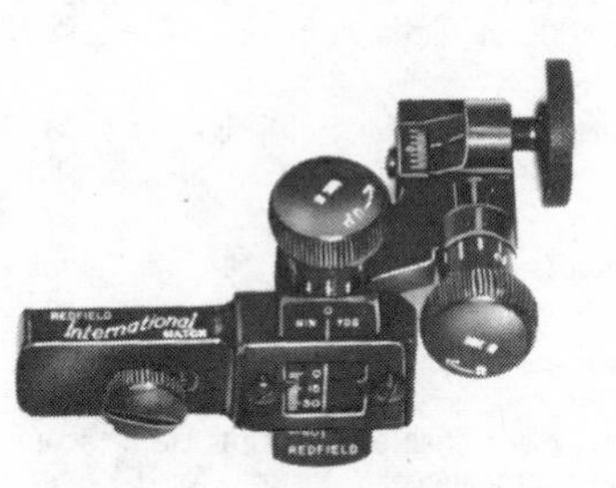

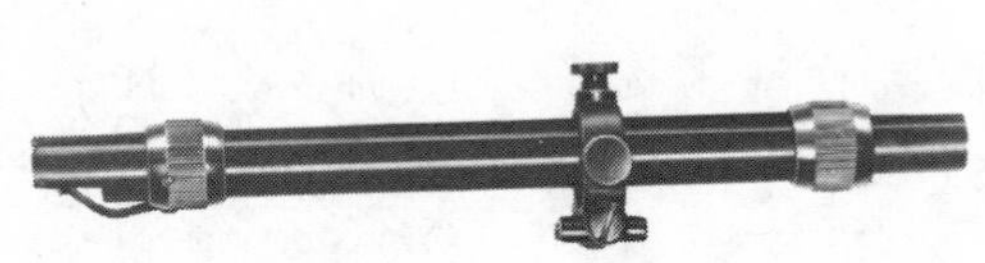

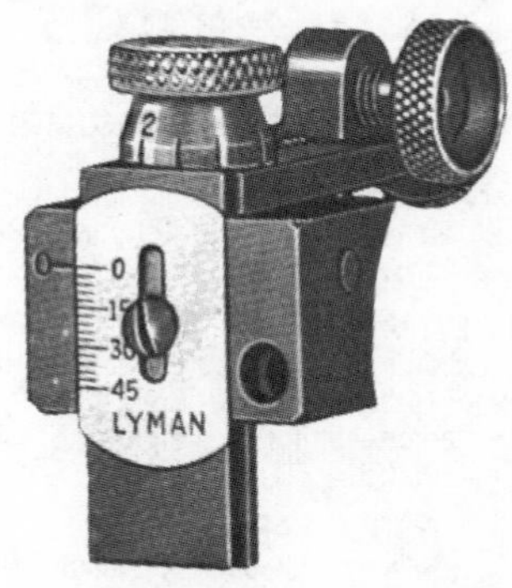

INTERNATIONAL GUNS INC.
Handles the complete line of Parker-Hale (British) metallic sights. Write for catalog.

LYMAN No. 48
¼-min. clicks for w. & e. Any disc. Target or Stayset (hunting) knobs. Quick release slide, adjustable zero scales. Made for almost all modern big-game rifles. Price: **$17.50** With long slide....... **$19.50**

LYMAN No. 57
¼-min. clicks. Target or Stayset knobs. Quick release slide, adjustable zero scales. Made for almost all modern rifles. Price...... **$9.50**

LYMAN No. 60
¼-min. clicks for w. and e. Extension arm permits choice of 3 positions of eye relief. Designed for use on medium-weight, small bore target rifles. Price....... **$9.75**

LYMAN No. 66
Fits close to the rear of flat-sided receivers, furnished with target or Stayset knobs. Quick release slide, ¼-min. adj. For most lever or slide action or flat-sided automatic rifles. Price....... **$9.50**

LYMAN No. 524 HI-LO EXTENSION RECEIVER-SIGHT
Apertures above and below for metallic and scope lines of sight. ¼-min. adj. For Win. 52 Sporter, 52 Standard (old and new), 52 Heavy Barrel (target and marksman stocks); Rem. 40X. Price....... **$19.50**

REDFIELD TROPHY
Aluminum construction. Staff detaches for scope use. Point-blank screw returns sight to same zero position. Features hunter-type knobs with coin slots, ¼-min. clicks. For most popular rifles. Price.... **$10.95**

REDFIELD MICRO-STEEL
Made entirely of machined tool steel. ¼-min. micrometer click adj. with Hunter knobs. Quick detachable staff. Made for many centerfire rifles....... **$14.95**

REDFIELD No. 75
For Junior Target rifles. ¼-min. clicks for w. and e. Quick detachable extension, adj. to two positions. Available in two heights, scope or standard. For 75HW—Win. 75: 75HG and SG—Sav. 19; 75HV and SV—Stev. 416, Sears Ranger; 75HM and SM—Mossberg, master actions; 75HB and SB—Ballard; 75HR and SR—Win. SS, High Wall action only; Walnut Hill and 417; 75RT—Rem. 513T; 75RS—Rem. 513S; 75RX—Rem. 521. Price....... **$16.95**

REDFIELD INTERNATIONAL MATCH
Spring loaded windage and elevation adjustments eliminate lost motion or backlash. Large adjusting screws. ¼-min. click values. Base and ⅞" disc. Fits same base as Olympic. Price....... **$32.95**
With base and "Sure-X" disc (see Sight Attachments). Price.. **$44.85**

REDFIELD INTERNATIONAL MARK 8
⅛-min. click adj. for windage and elevation distinguishes the Mark 8 which has all of the refinements of Redfield's International Match. Equipped with standard base and ⅞" disc. Price....... **$39.95**
With base and Sure-X disc (see Sight Attachments). Price.. **$51.85**

REDFIELD OLYMPIC
Elevation, windage, and extension adjustments. New elevation compensation. ¼-min. click. Base and ⅞" disc. Made for practically all target rifles. Price....... **$24.95**
Extra bases. Price....... **3.95**
With base and Sure-X disc (see Sight Attachments). Price.... **$36.85**

TRADEWIND SNAP-SHOOTER
Micrometer click elevation adjustment, sliding windage adjustment with locking screws. Designed to fit rear scope mount holes in Husqvarna HVA and FN Mauser actions. Price....... **$9.50**

WILLIAMS "FOOLPROOF"
Internal click adjustments. Positive locks. For virtually all rifles, plus Win., Rem. and Ithaca shotguns. Price....... **$12.00**
Add .50 for Twilight aperture. Extra shotgun aperture...... **2.00**

B-SQUARE SPRINGFIELD
For 03A3. Windage and elevation by means of allen screws. Locks on dovetail. Wrench furnished. Price....... **$5.00**

B-SQUARE SMLE (LEE-ENFIELD)
For No. 4 and Jungle carbine. No drilling or tapping required. 3/32" disc furnished. Price....... **$3.95**

BURTON ROUGH SERVICE
Adj. for w. & e. Mounts with two 6-40 screws. For most rifles.. **$8.75**

BUEHLER
"Little Blue Peep" auxiliary sight used with Buehler and Redfield scope mounts. Price....... **$3.35**
Mark IV front sight for above....... **.95**

FREELAND TUBE SIGHT
Uses Unertl 1" micrometer mounts. Complete with bases for 22-cal. target rifles, inc. 52 Win., 37, 40X Rem. and BSA Martini. Price.. **$42.50**

KUHARSKY AUXILIARY
Fits onto B&L or Kuharsky mounts to give emergency sighting. Includes peep rear and post front sights; extension rail slides forward for increased sight radius. Price....... **$9.95**

LYMAN No. 40
Mounts on left side of receiver. By releasing locking lever, slide can be adjusted for elevation. Slot in aperture permits horizontal alignment. Target disc. for Sav. 40, 45, 340, 342, Stevens 58, 322, 325, Marlin 55, Moss. 185K and H&R 349. Price....... **$6.50**

LYMAN No. 53
Shotgun receiver sight, mounts compactly near rear of receiver. For most Win., Rem., Sav., Marlin, Mossberg, J. C. Higgins and Ithaca shotguns. Price....... **$4.40**

LYMAN No. 55
Located at rear of receiver; compact, easily adjusted. For almost all low-priced bolt action rifles. Price....... **$4.40**

REDFIELD RECORD
Aluminum construction with detachable staff for scope use. Adj. by means of locking screws. Point-blank screw returns sight to zero position. For most rifles. Price....... **$7.95**

REDFIELD RE-22
1965 model for all dovetail-grooved 22 rifles (takes place of SS sights). Adj. for w. and e....... **$7.95**

REDFIELD RE-SG
Shotgun receiver sight; mounts compactly at rear of receiver. Fits most shotguns by use of slotted base installed on receiver wall. Price....... **$9.95**

REDFIELD RE-24
For Savage M24's over-under rifle-shotgun....... **$9.95**

REDFIELD X-TUBE
For use with Redfield Olympic or International Match rear sights. Front telescope-type mount attaches to scope block. Price.... **$24.95**

WILLIAMS 5-D SIGHT
Low cost sight for shotguns, 22's and the more popular big game rifles. Adjustment for w. and e. Fits most guns without drilling or tapping. Also for Br. SMLE. Price....... **$7.00**

WILLIAMS ACE-IN-THE-HOLE PEEP
Auxiliary sight that slips into the Williams QC scope mount. Adj. for w. and e. Price....... **$2.50**

WILLIAMS GUIDE
Receiver sight for .30 M1 Car., M1903A3 Springfield, Savage 24's, Savage-Anschutz rifles and Wby. XXII. Utilizes military dovetail; no drilling. Double-dovetail W. adj., sliding dovetail adj. for E. Price. **$7.00**

Sporting Leaf and Tang Sights

HOPKINS & ALLEN NUMRICH MUSKET SIGHT
Three-way rear leaf sight designed for 58 cal. muzzle loading military rifles. Fixed V-notch for 50-yard range, flip-up aperture for 100 yards and V-notch for 200 yards. Particularly suited to Springfield and Zouave rifles. Price....................................... **$4.95**

LYMAN No. 16
Middle sight for barrel dovetail slot mounting. Folds flat when scope or peep sight is used. Sight notch plate adjustable for e. White triangle for quick aiming. 3 heights; A—.400" to .500", B—.345" to .445", C—.500" to .600". Price.................................. **$2.95**

MARBLE FALSE BASE
New screw-on base for most rifles replaces factory base. ⅜" dovetail slot permits installation of any Marble rear sight. Can be had in sweat-on models also. Price **$2.00**

MARBLE FOLDING LEAF
Flat-top or semi-buckhorn style. Folds down when scope or peep sights are used. Reversible plate gives choice of "U" or "V" notch. Adjustable for elevation. Price..................... **$4.50 — $5.96**
Also available with both w. and e. adjustment.............. **$4.90**

MARBLE SPORTING REAR
With white enamel diamond, gives choice of two "U" and two "V" notches of different sizes. Adjustment in height by means of double step elevator and sliding notch piece. For all rifles; screw or dovetail installation. Price .... **$4.30—$5.50**

MARBLE SPORTING REAR
Single step elevator. "U" notch with white triangle aiming aid. Lower priced version of double step model. Price.................... **$2.30**

O.S.E. WINDAGE OPEN REAR
Screw set windage adjustment of .025" per graduation. Dovetail installation, choice of short or long base and flat top or semi-buckhorn. Full w. & e. adjustment with use of O.S.E. Adjustable height front sight. Original Sight Exchange. Price, open rear only................. **$3.95**

REDFIELD SEMI-BUCKHORN FOLDING LEAF
Semi-buckhorn sight for dovetail slot mounting. Sturdy spring holds sight in upright position. No. 47L .375"-.475"; No. 47H .375"-.562" high. Price **$4.45**

REDFIELD FLAT TOP FOLDING LEAF
Same as above except flat top style. No. 46L .375"-.475"; No. 46H .375"-.562" high. Price **$4.45**

REDFIELD SEMI-BUCKHORN SPORTING REAR
Reversible sighting plate gives choice of "U" notch or "V" notch. Five-step elevator. Fits standard dovetail slot. No. 49L for most rifles, No. 49S for 22's and carbines. Semi-buckhorn. Price............ **$4.45**

REDFIELD FLAT TOP SPORTING REAR
Same as above except flat top style. No. 48L for most rifles, No. 48S for 22's and carbines. Price................................ **$4.45**

WILLIAMS GUIDE
Open rear sight with w. and e. adjustment. Bases to fit most military and commercial barrels. Choice of square "U" or "V" notch blade, $^3/_{16}$", ¼", $^5/_{16}$", or ⅜" high.................................. **$5.00**
Extra blades, each................................... 1.25

Globe Target Front Sights

FREELAND SUPERIOR
Furnished with six 1" plastic apertures. Available in 4½"-62½" lengths. Made for any target rifle. Price with base............. **$16.00**
Price with 6 metal insert apertures...................... 19.00

FREELAND JR
Same as above except standard dovetail mounting, various heights. Price with base and 6 plastic apertures..................... **$14.00**
Price with 6 metal insert apertures....................... 17.00

FREELAND TWIN SET
Two Freeland Superior or Junior Globe Front Sights, long or short, allow switching from 50 yd. to 100 yd. ranges and back again without changing rear sight adjustment. Sight adjustment compensation is built into the set; just interchange and you're "on" at either range. Set includes base and 6 plastic apertures. Twin set (long or short). **$28.00**
Price with 6 metal apertures.......................... 32.00
Price, Junior Twin Set (long or short) plastic apertures...... 26.00
Price, Junior Twin Set (long or short) metal apertures....... 30.00

FREELAND MILITARY
Short model for use with high-powered rifles where sight must not extend beyond muzzle. Screw-on base; six plastic apertures. Price **$15.00**
Price with 6 metal apertures............................ 18.00

LYMAN No. 17A
7 interchangeable inserts which include 4 apertures, one transparent amber and two posts .050" and .100" in width. Price........... **$3.75**

LYMAN No. 17A XNB
For Springfield 03 and 03A3. Replaces issue front sight and barrel band. With seven inserts. Price.............................. **$6.00**

LYMAN 77
Similar to M17A, except mounts to a separate base, is quickly detachable. Base **$1.50.** Sight........................... **$5.00**

REDFIELD Nos. 63 and 64
For rifles specially stocked for scopes where metallic sights must be same height as scopes. Instantly detachable to permit use of scope. Two styles and heights of bases. Interchangeable inserts. No. 64 is ¼" higher. With base, Price................................ **$7.95**

REDFIELD No. 65
1" long, ⅝" diameter. Standard dovetail base with 7 aperture or post inserts which are not reversible. For any rifle having standard barrel slot. $^{13}/_{32}$" height from bottom of base to center of aperture. No. 65NB same as above with narrow base for Win. 54 N.R.A., 70, and Savage 40, 45, and 99 with ramp front sight base. Price........... **$5.95**

REDFIELD No. 66
Replaces entire removable front sight stud, locked in place by screw in front of barrel band. ¾" from bottom of base to center of aperture. For Spgfld. 1903. Price.................................... **$5.95**

REDFIELD No. 68
For Win. 52, heavy barrel, Sav. 19 and 33, and other rifles requiring high front sight. $^{17}/_{32}$" from bottom of base to center of aperture. Standard dovetail size only. Price.............................. **$5.95**

REDFIELD OLYMPIC
Detachable. 10 inserts—5 steel, sizes .090", .110", .120", .140", .150"; one post insert, size .100"; four celluloid, sizes .090", .110", .120", .140". Celluloid inserts in clear, green, or amber, with or without cross hairs. For practically all rifles and with any type rear sight. Fits all standard Redfield, Lyman, or Fecker scope blocks. With base, Price. **$15.90**

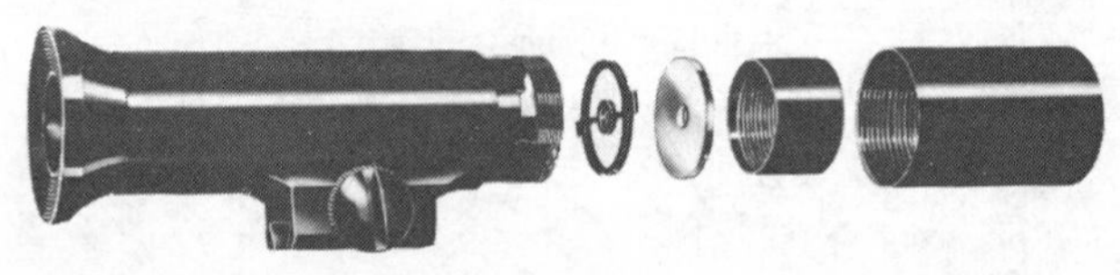

REDFIELD INTERNATIONAL SMALLBORE FRONT (Illustrated)
Similar to Olympic. Drop-in insertion of eared inserts. Outer sleeve prevents light leakage. Two-step base allows quick forward-backward change between 100 and 50 yards........................ **$18.90**
with standard base and inserts......................... 17.90

REDFIELD INTERNATIONAL MILITARY BIG BORE
Same as International Match except tube only 2¼" long. For 30 cal. use. **$17.90**

REDFIELD 285 S RAMP
No. 285 ramp designed for 22's fits without drilling by use of dovetail filler block. Redfield Sourdough, gold tip and ivory bead front sights fit dovetail slot on ramp. Short, streamlined design. Price without front sight.. **$3.25**

WOMACK DUAL RANGE
Instant change from 50 to 100 yards by rotating front knurled sleeve ½ turn. Choice of 6" or 10" length. Price, including 6 apertures, base and screws... **$21.00**

Ramp Sights

JAEGER
Band type with detachable hood, gold or ivory bead. When ordering, give height and muzzle diameter. Price **$7.95**

LYMAN SLIP-ON RAMP AND FRONT SIGHT
No soldering or brazing necessary, has tapered hole. Inside dia. .550″ to .640″. Removable hood. Price for ramp, sight and hood . . **$8.20**

LYMAN SCREW-ON RAMP AND SIGHT
Used with 8-40 screws but may also be brazed on. Heights from .110″ to .350″. Price with sight **$4.95**

MARBLE COUNTOUR RAMP
For late model Rem. 725, 740, 760, 742. 9/16″ between mounting screws. Price **$4.50**

MARBLE RAMPS
Available in either screw-on or sweat-on style. 5 heights; 3/16″, 5/16″, 3/8″, 7/16″, 9/16″. Standard 3/8″ dovetail slot. Price **$4.25**
Hoods for above ramps **1.00**

PEDERSON "REX"
Offered as the "Rex" ramp, this is a hoodless type without barrel band. Heights available are 1/4″ to 9/16″. Blued or in the white, and without sights. Price **$2.50**

REDFIELD SWEAT-ON RAMPS
Standard 3/8″ dovetail with screw for holding position while sweating. 5/16″, 3/8″, or 9/16″ high, 3 3/8″ over all. Price, without hood . . **$4.95**

REDFIELD SCREW-ON RAMPS
Same as sweat-on except has two screws for mounting. Price, without hood **$4.95**
Hoods for above ramps **1.00**

WILLIAMS SHORTY RAMP
Companion to "Streamlined" ramp, about 1/2″ shorter. Screw-on type, it is furnished in 1/8″, 3/16″, 9/32″, and 3/8″ heights without hood only. Price **$3.50**

WILLIAMS STREAMLINED RAMP
Hooded style in screw-on or sweat-on models. Furnished in 9/16″, 7/16″, 3/8″, 5/16″, 3/16″ heights. Price with hood **$5.50**
Price without hood **4.50**

WILLIAMS SHOTGUN RAMP
Designed to elevate the front bead for slug shooting or for guns that shoot high. Diameters to fit most 12, 16, 20 ga. guns. Fastens by screw-clamp, no drilling required. Price, with Williams gold bead . **$3.50**
Price, without bead **2.75**

Front Sights

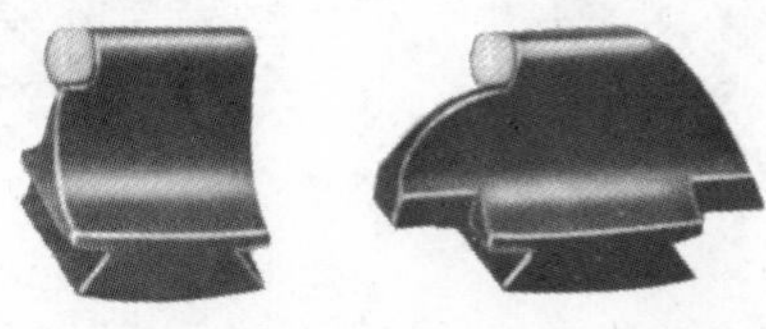

LYMAN BLADE & DOVETAIL SIGHTS
Made with gold, silver or red beads 1/16″ to 3/32″ wide and in varying heights for most military and commercial rifles . . from **$1.70** to **$2.00**

LYMAN No. 22
Ivory bead front sight for Savage 24 series. O-U. Price **$2.50**

MARBLE STANDARD
Ivory, red, or gold bead. For all American made rifles. 1/16″ wide bead with semi-flat face which does not reflect light. Specify type of rifle when ordering **$1.90**

MARBLE-SHEARD "GOLD"
Show up well even in darkest timber. Shows same color on different colored objects; sturdily built. Medium bead. Various models for different makes of rifles so specify type of rifle when ordering. Also made for 30 or 9 mm Lugers, Colt's Single Action Army, Bisley Model, with plain sight or any other Colt's or S & W revolver with stationary front sight. Price **$3.20**

MARBLE COUNTOURED
Same contour and shape as Marble-Sheard but uses standard 1/16″ or 3/32″ bead, ivory, red or gold. Specify rifle type **$2.20**

O.S.E. ADJUSTABLE HEIGHT FRONT
Screw adjustment gives .025″ change in height for each turn. 5 models give adjustments from .260″ to .880″. Fits 3/8″ dovetail barrel or ramp slots. White or gold bead. Original Sight Exchange. Price . **$2.95**

REDFIELD SOURDOUGH PATRIDGE
Gold face set at 45° angle; blackened, it serves as a target sight. Blade or dovetail styles; width .070″. Square block of phosphor bronze inlaid to provide visibility in poor light. Price **$3.45**

REDFIELD-CARBINE BLADE TYPE
Sourdough patridge, ivory bead or gold tip, 1/16″ only. For Win., Sav., Krag, Spgfld., Rem. Price **$3.45**

REDFIELD IVORY BEAD OR GOLD TIP
1/16″. For practically all rifles, carbines, pistols and revolvers. Price **$2.45**

REDFIELD FULL BLOCK
For Springfield 03 (not 03A3) in Sourdough, 1/16″ gold or ivory bead. **$4.45.** Mauser Dovetail—For narrom Mauser and other European dovetail slots. Sourdough, gold or ivory bead. **$2.45—$3.45.** De Luxe Ramp Blades—Sourdough, 1/16″ gold or ivory bead. Price **$2.00**

TRADEWIND SNAP-SHOOTER
Silver inlay post. Fits 3/8″ dovetail; height, 33/64 from bottom of dovetail. Price **$1.50**

WILLIAMS BRILLIANT BEAD
Large bright bead. In .250″ and .340″ base widths; 7 heights from .260″ to .538″. Price **$3.25**

WILLIAMS IVORY & GOLD BEAD
Has flat sides. Made for Williams .250″ ramps. Also available in .340″ width, 1/16″ and 3/32″ bead sizes. 10-heights **$2.25**

WILLIAMS GUIDE BEAD SIGHT
Fits all shotguns. 1/8″ ivory, red or gold bead. Screws into existing sight hole. Various thread sizes and shank lengths **$1.75**

Handgun Sights

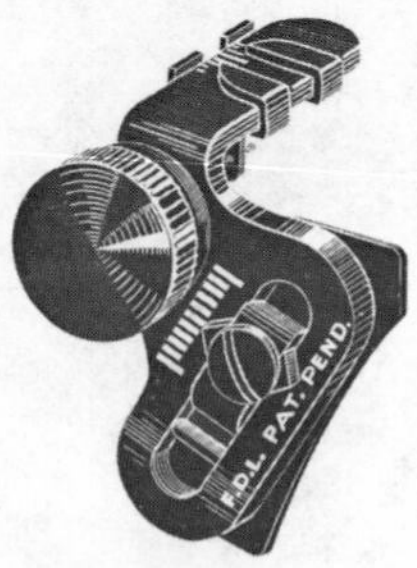

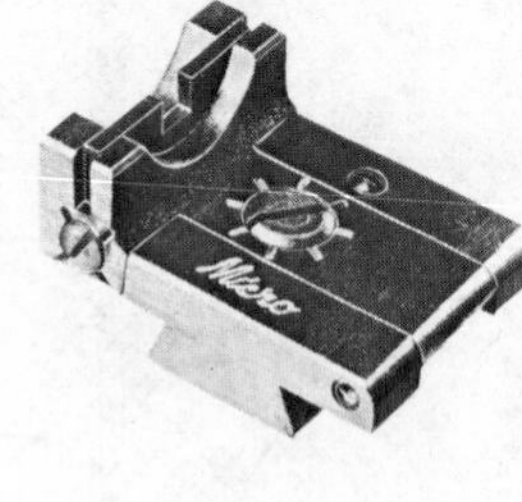

Left—FDL revolver sight.
Above—Micro handgun sight.

BO-MAR DE LUXE
Gives ⅜" w. and e. adjustment at 50 yards on Colt Gov't 45, sight radius under 7". For Colt, Hi-Standard, Ruger and S&W autos. Uses existing dovetail slot. Has shield-type rear blade. **$16.00**

BO-MAR LOCK-UP RAMP
For Colt 38, 45 autos. Has locking barrel feature which positions and centers the barrel in relation to the slide to assure free functioning and barrel lock-up. To be installed by competent pistolsmith only. **$22.50**

BO-MAR HIGH STANDARD RIB
Full length, 8¾" sigh radius, for all bull barrels and military. Slide alteration required. **$30.00**

BO-MAR LOW PROFILE RIB
Streamlined rib with front and rear sights; 7⅞" sight radius. Brings sight line closer to the bore than standard or extended sight and ramp. Weighs 4 oz. Made for Colt Gov't 45, Super 38, and Gold Cup 45 and 38. .... **$28.00**
Extended sight and ramp, 8⅛" radius, 5¾ oz. **34.00**
Rib & tuner—inserted in Low Profile Rib—accuracy tuner. Adjustable for barrel positioning. **39.95**

BO-MAR FRONT SIGHTS
⅛" tapered post, made for Colt, Hi-Standard, Ruger and S&W autos. .... **$3.00—$4.00**

F.D.L. WONDERSIGHT
Micrometer rear sight for Colt and S&W revolvers. 1-min. clicks for windage. Sideplate screw controls elevation.................. **$4.95**

HEG TRIANGLE REAR
Standard has small blade, w. & e. adj. gives ½" at 50 yds. for Colt, High-Standard and Luger target guns....................... **$10.00**

HEG TRIANGLE REAR DELUXE
As above but extends sight radius slightly and has over-size blade for least distraction.................................... **$12.00**

HEG PISTOL RIB
Made for 45-cal. autos. Must be installed by gunsmith. Adds 3¾ oz. to slide. Made in two models. With std. 7 7/16" radius and the extended 8 11/16" radius **$25.00**

MICRO
Click adjustable w. and e. rear with plain or undercut front sight in 1/10", ⅛", or 5/32" widths. Standard model available for 45, Super 38 or Commander autos. Low model for above pistols plus Colt Service Ace. Also for Ruger with 4¾" or 6" barrel. Price for sets.......... **$15.50**
Price with ramp front sight........................... **18.50**

MICRO
Non-adjustable sight set for 45 auto.................... **$7.50**

Shotgun Sights

FOR DOUBLE BARREL SHOTGUNS (PRESS FIT)
Marble 214—Ivory front bead, 11/64".... **$1.00; 215**—same with .080" rear bead and reamers.... **$2.95. Marble 220**—Bi-color (gold and ivory) front bead, 11/64" and .080 rear bead, with reamers.... **$3.95; Marble 221**—front bead only.... **$1.90. Marble 223**—Ivory rear .080.... **$1.00. Marble 224**—Front sight reamer for 214-221 beads.... **$0.75; Marble 226**—Rear sight reamer for 223.......................... **$0.75**

FOR SINGLE OR DB SHOTGUNS (SCREW-ON FIT)
Marble 217—Ivory front bead 11/64"..**$1.20**; with tap and wrench..**$2.50**
Marble 218—Bi-color front, 11/64".... **1.60**; with tap and wrench...**3.05**
Marble 223T—Ivory rear .080........**1.60**; with tap and wrench.. **3.05**
Marble Bradley type sights 223BT—⅛", 5/64" and 11/64" long. Gold, Ivory or Red bead **$1.60**

MARK FRONT SIGHT
Screw-on type, with bead to fit plain bbls., and ribs ¼", 5/16", ⅜" and ½" wide. Precision Gun Sight Company.................**$3.50**

POLY-SIGHT
Luminous bead ramp front and aperture rear, connected and supported by a 12" bridge, for use on shotguns with slugs or buckshot. Adj. for windage, elevation. Not for break-open guns. Price, including installation at Poly-Choke Co., and postage **$36.70**

SLUG SITE
A combination V-notch rear and bead front sight made of adhesive-backed formed metal approx. 7" over-all. May be mounted, removed and re-mounted as necessary, using new adhesive from the pack supplied. **$5.00**

Sight Attachments

BARRETT IRIS SIGHTING DISC
For all American extension receiver sights. Standard model includes rubber eye guard...**$13.50**
With rotating colored filters............................ **16.75**

FREELAND LENS ADAPTER
Fits 1⅛" O.D. prescription ground lens to all standard tube and receiver sights for shooting without glasses. Price without lens..**$10.50**
Price lens ground to prescription....................... **11.50**

MERIT ADAPTER FOR GLOBE FRONT SIGHTS
An Iris Shutter Disc with a special adapter for mounting in Lyman or Redfield globe front sights. Price..........................**$9.00**

MERIT IRIS SHUTTER DISC
Eleven clicks give 12 different apertures. No. 3 and Master, primarily target types, .022" to .125"; No. 4, ½" dia. hunting type, .025" to .155". Available for all popular sights. The Master Disc, with flexible rubber light shield, is particularly adapted to extension, scope height, and tang sights. All Merit Deluxe models have internal click spring; are hand fitted to minimum tolerance. Price..............**$8.00—$11.00**
Master..............**$10.00**   Master Deluxe.......... **13.00**

MERIT LENS DISC
Similar to Merit Iris Shutter (Model 3 or Master) but incorporates provision for mounting prescription lens integrally. Lens may be obtained locally, or prescription sent to Merit. Sight disc is 7/16" wide (Mod. 3), or ¾" wide (Master). Lens, ground to prescription, **$7.60.** Standard tints, **$9.10.** Model 3 Deluxe.....................**$13.00**
Master Deluxe **$16.00**

REDFIELD VARD (Variable Diopter)
For shooters with visual problems. By adjusting the focus ring to focus the lens system at a point between the front sight aperture and the bull and controlling the size of the iris diaphragm, a crisp sharp high-contrast sight picture can be achieved. Provision is made for a prescription lens holder for shooters whose requirements exceed the focus capability of the VARD. Comes with smoke-gray filter. Front thread is 9/32—32NS and will fit International and Olympic sights now being produced. Older O/I sights with 7/32 thread will be converted at the plant for $3.45 on request. Maximum magnification is 1.3X. Use of the VARD adds approximately 1.5" to the sight. Extension attaching bases listed allow the sight to move forward 1.5" to accommodate for this extra length. Prices: VARD-IRIS Combination with filter **$39.95**
Iris Diaphragm only with filter......................... **19.95**
Prescription lens holder **1.95**
Set of 3 filters—Yellow, Sage Green and Gray............ **3.95**

REDFIELD SURE-X SIGHTING DISC
Eight hole selective aperture. Fits any Redfield target sight. Each click changes aperture .004". Price.........................**$7.95**

REDFELD SIGHTING DISCS
Fit all Redfield receiver sights. .046" to .093" aperture. ⅜", ½" and ⅞" O.D. Price, each.................................**$ .95**

WILLIAMS APERTURES
Standard thread, fits most sights. Regular series ⅜" to ⅝" O.D., .050" to .125" hole. "Twilight" series has white reflector ring. .093" to .125" inner hole. Price, regular series..**$.75.** Twilight series..**$1.25**
New wide open 5/16" aperture for shotguns fits 5-D and Foolproof sights. Price **$2.00**

MERIT OPTICAL ATTACHMENT
For revolver and pistol shooters. Instantly attached by rubber suction cup to regular or shooting glasses. Any aperture .020" to .156". Price, **$8.00.** Deluxe (swings aside)..........................**$10.00**

HUNTING, TARGET◆ AND VARMINT◆ SCOPES

Maker and Model	Magn.	Field at 100 Yds. (feet)	Relative Bright-ness	Eye Relief (in.)	Length (in.)	Tube Diam. (in.)	W&E Adjust-ments	Weight (ozs.)	Other Data	Price
American Inst. Corp.										
Tamron Imperial	2¾	44	58.4	3½	10¼	1	Int.	8½	Dot or post $5.50 extra on 1" models.. Range finder reticle $10 extra on the variable. All reticles self-centering.	$49.50
Tamron Imperial	4	30	64	3½	11½	1	Int.	9½		59.50
Tamron Imperial	3-9	39-13	157-18	3½	12½	1	Int.	14¼		89.50
Westerner Pistol	1½	23		12-20	7⅞	.75	Int.	5½		24.50
Bausch & Lomb										
Custom Baltur A	2½	43	64	3¼	12¼	1	Ext.	9½	Must be used with B&L or other adj. mount. Baltur A, Balfor A, come with crosshairs. Dot $10 extra. Tapered crosshairs and tapered post $5 extra for Balfor A. Variable scopes have tapered crosshair only.	49.95
Custom Balfor A	4	30	56	3¼	12¼	1	Ext.	9		59.95
Custom Balvar 5	2½-5	40-20	164-41	3½	12¾	1	Ext.	9½		79.95
Custom Balvar 8A	2½-8	40-12½	256-25	3½	12¾	1	Ext.	10½		99.95
Trophy Baltur B	2½	42	164	3	12⅛	1	Int.	11		49.95
Trophy Balfor B	4	30	64	3	11⅞	1	Int.	11	Centered reticle. CH; dot, $10 extra; tapered CH or post, $5 extra. Adj. ½ MOA.	59.95
Trophy Balsix B	6	20	36	3	11⅞	1	Int.	10¾		69.95
Trophy Balvar 8B	2½-8	40-12½	207-20	3½	11⅞	1	Int.	12½		99.95
Browning										
22 Scope	4	24	56	2½-4	9⅜	.75	Int.	6¼	22 Scope w/mount $43.95. Crosshair standard on all models. Post optoinal at no extra cost on 4x (1"). Fine or medium cross-hair optional at no extra cost on 1" Variable Scope. Choice of 2, 3 or 4 minute dot on 4 x (1"), $10 extra. Choice of post or 3-1 minute dot on Variable Scope, $10 extra.	32.95
Browning	4	31	61	3¼-4½	11¼	1	Int.	10¼		59.95
Browning	2-7	44-16	241-20	3-4½	11¼	1	Int.	11½		94.95
Bushnell										
Scopechief IV	2¾	43	58	4	10	1	Int.	8½	Scopechief models have Command Post reticle with Magnetic Control Ring. Constantly centered reticles in Scopechiefs, Customs and Banners. Integral mounts $10 extra on Scopechiefs. Phantoms intended for handgun use.	49.50
Scopechief IV	4	32	64	3¾	11¾	1	Int.	10½		59.50
Scopechief IV	6	20	40	4	12½	1	Int.	11½		69.50
Scopechief IV	1½-4½	78-26	216-23	4¼-3¼	9¼	1	Int.	7¾		74.50
Scopechief IV	2½-8	44-15	160-16	4-3¼	11	1	Int.	11		84.50
Scopechief IV	3-9	39-13	160-18	3¾-3¼	11½	1	Int.	12¼		89.50
Scopechief 22	3-8	30-12	55-6	2½	11	⅞	Int.	7½	Mount rail. Similar 4x at $14.95.	19.95
Custom M	2½	49	64	4¼	10½	1	Int.	7¾		37.50
Custom M	4	27	64	3¾	11½	1	Int.	9¾		44.50
Custom M	6	19	40	3¼	13	1	Int.	10¾		47.50
Custom M	3-9	35-12½	159-18	3¾-3	12¼	1	Int.	12½		64.50
Custom 22	3-7	29-13	28-5	2	10	⅞	Int.	6½	Mount rail. Similar 4x at $10.95.	15.95
Banner	2½	45	64	4¼	10½	1	Int.	8		29.50
Banner	4	30	64	4	11¾	1	Int.	10		36.50
Banner	6	19½	29	3¾	13¼	1	Int.	10½		39.50
Banner	1½-4½	63-28	169-25	4¼-3¼	10	1	Int.	10¼		46.50
Banner	3-9	39-13	115-13	3¾-3	11¼	1	Int.	12		49.50
Phantom	1 1/3	24	441	6-17	7⅝	⅞	Int.	5		24.50
Phantom	2½	10	100	7-16	9¼	⅞	Int.	5½		34.50
Collins										
Bulittco	2½	40	164	3	11¼	1	Int.	9½	One-piece duralumin tube with oilproof rubber packings at lens/metal joints. Nitrogen filled.	34.95
Bulittco	4	30	64	3	11¼	1	Int.	9½		36.95
Bulittco	6	20	28	3	11¼	1	Int.	9½		38.95
Colt										
Coltmaster Jr.	4	30			12½	.75	Int.	7	Coltmaster Jr. scopes have tip-off mounts.	10.75
Coltmaster Jr.	6	20			14½	.75	Int.	8		13.75
Davis Optical										
Spot Shot 1½"	10, 12, 15, 20, 25, 30	10-4		2	25	.75	Ext.		Focus by moving non-rotating obj. lens unit. Ext. mounts included. Recoil spring $3.50 extra.	89.50
Spot Shot 1¼"	10, 12, 15, 20	10-6		2	25	.75	Ext.			69.50
Habicht										
4 S-D	4	30	64	3¼	11	1.18	Int.	13	From Del-Sports. With e. only, $62.75. With light alloy tube. (27mm), mounting rail, $69.75; same, e. only, $65.75.	63.90
Herter's										
Perfect	1	100	256	3-5	9¾	1	Int.	10¼	A variety of reticles including dots and rangefinders available in different scopes at small price increase. Hudson Bay rimfire scopes: 4x, $15.98; 6x, $16.98; 3-9x, $24.95.	32.95
Mark II	2¾	44	58	3½	10¼	1	Int.	8½		25.95
Mark IV	4	30	64	3½	11½	1	Int.	9½		28.48
Mark VI	6	20	38	3½	12¾	1	Int.	10½		30.95
Mark VIII	8	15½	22	3½	12½	1	Int.	14½		38.49
Mark IA	3-9	14-41	157-18	3½	12½	1	Int.	14½		49.95
Mark XXI	4-12	11½-34	100-14	3½	13¼	1	Int.	12½		49.95
Hy-Score										
No. 467	4	26	14	1¾	12	.75	Int.	7¼	Alloy tubes. Weather and fog-proof. 400 series scopes are made in Japan.	8.95
No. 469	6	19	6	1¾	12	.75	Int.	7½		11.95
Model 461-466	2½	35	64	3	9⅞	1	Int.	8		19.95
Model 462-468	4	28	64	3	11⅝	1	Int.	10		19.95
Model 463	6	22	28.1	3	11¾	1	Int.	10		20.95
Vari-Power 464	3-9	36-16	126-12	3¼	12½	1	Int.	14		29.95
Vari-Power 471	3-9	35-14	193-18	3¼	12½	1	Int.	14		36.95
Jason										
860	4	27¼	64	3½	12	1	Int.	9	Constantly centered reticles, ball-bearing click stops, nitrogen filled tubes, coated lenses.	19.95
864	6	17½	28	3¼	12	1	Int.	9		21.95
861	3-9	31½-12	112-12	3	13¼	1	Int.	13¾		29.95
865	3-9	31½-12	177-19	3	13½	1	Int.	15¼		34.95

SCOPES & MOUNTS

Hunting, Target and Varmint Scopes—Continued

Maker and Model	Magn.	Field at 100 Yds. (feet)	Relative Bright-ness	Eye Relief (in.)	Length (in.)	Tube Diam. (in.)	W&E Adjust-ments	Weight (ozs.)	Other Data	Price
Leupold										
M8	2	25	100	8-18	8.45	1	Int.	7.25		46.50
M8	3	43	45	3.85	10.13	1	Int.	8.25	Constantly centered reticles; in addition to the crosshair reticle the post, tapered (CPC) and duplex reticles are optional at no extra cost. Dot reticle $10.00 extra. 2x suitable for handguns and Win. 94.	59.50
M8	4	30	50	3.85	11.50	1	Int.	9.00		59.50
M8	7½	14	32	3.60	12.60	1	Int.	12.75		74.50
M8	10	10	16	3½	13	1	Int.	13¾		94.50
M8	12	9	11	3½	14½	1	Int.	14		99.50
Vari-X II	2-7	42-18	144-17	3.7-4.12	11.00	1	Int.	10.75		79.50
Vari-X II	3-9	30.5-13	208-23	3.5-4.12	12.60	1	Int.	13.75		89.50
Lyman										
All-American	2½	43		3¼	10½	1	Int.	8¾	2, 3, or 4 minute dot reticle $10 extra. Choice of standard CH, tapered post, or tapered post and CH reticles. All-weather reticle caps. All Lyman scopes have new Perma-Center reticle which remains in optical center regardless of changes in W. & E.	49.50
All-American	3	35		3¼	11	1	Int.	9		49.50
All-American	4	30		3¼	12	1	Int.	10		59.50
All-American	6	20		3¼	13⅞	1	Int.	12¼		67.50
◆All-American	8	14		3¼	14⅜	1	Int.	13		84.50
◆All-American	10	12		3¼	15½	1	Int.	13½		84.50
◆Super Targetspot	10, 12, 15, 20, 25, 30	12, 9.3, 8.9, 5.6, 4.3, 4	86%	2-1⅞	24-24⅜	.75	Ext.	24¼-25	Non-rotating objective lens focusing. ¼ MOA click adjustments. Sunshade, $2 extra. Steel case, $9 extra. 5 different dot reticles, $10.00 extra.	135.00
Marlin										
300	4	23	25	1½	11¾	⅞	Int.	9	Coated lenses, non-magnifying reticles. Tri-Post reticle. A 4x Glenfield M200, suitable for 22 rifles, and with ½-minute adj., is $8.00.	13.95
500	3-7	24-10	49-16	1¾	12	⅞	Int.	9½		16.95
600	3	29	144	3½	12½	1	Int.	10		32.95
700	5	20	64	3½	12½	1	Int.	11		34.95
800	1½-5	55-19	256 49	3½	11⅜	1	Int.	13½		42.95
900	3-9	35-12	169-19	3¼	12¾	1	Int.	14		44.95
Glenfield 400	4	28	64	3½	12	1	Int.	9		20.00
Nickel										
Supra	2½	42	72	3½	11½	1.18	Int.	7½		75.00
Supra	4	33	30	3½	11½	1.18	Int.	8		75.00
Supra	4	32	81	3½	11¼	1.18	Int.	9	¼ MOA click adjustments. Steel or alloy tubes. Weatherproof reticle caps. Crosshair, post and c.h. or post and cross-bar reticles are standard. New "Diflex" coated lenses. Continental Arms Co.	85.00
Supra	6	21	36	3½	12½	1.18	Int.	9		85.00
◆Supra Varminter	6	24	56	3¼-5	12¼	1.18	Int.	11½		89.50
Supra Vari-Power	1-4	66.5-27.3	153-28	3½	10½	1.18	Int.	13.1		115.00
Supra Vari-Power	1½-6	60-21.6	176-36	3½	12	1.18	Int.	14.8		140.00
Supra Vari-Power	2½-6	38-21	125-36	3½	11¾	1.18	Int.	11		125.00
Supra Vari-Power	2½-9	42-15.6		3½	14½	1.18	Int.	17.3		160.00
Supra Vari-Power	4-10	30-12	100-18.5	3½	12½	1.18	Int.	12½		135.00
Pacific										
2.5x Supreme	2½	36		3½	11¾	1	Int.	10	All Pacific scopes have constantly centered reticles, coated lenses and ¼ MOA adj. Nitrogen filled. Choice of crosshair or post and crosshair.	27.95
4X Supreme	4	31		3½	12½	1	Int.	12		36.95
6x Supreme	6	20		3½	11½	1	Int.	11		33.95
3-9x Supreme	3-9	34-14		3½	12½	1	Int.	13		52.95
Precise Imports										
NR-15	4	23	14	2	11	.75	Int.	6¾		7.95
20257	3-7	23-13	43-8	3	11½	.75	Int.	7½	Price with mount.	13.95
20265	2½	32	164	3¾	12	1	Int.	9.6	All scopes have constantly centered reticle.	24.95
20244	4	29	64	3½	12	1	Int.	9		24.95
20249	3-9	36-13	177-19	3	13⅓	1	Int.	15		39.95
20260	10	12.2	16	3	12½	1	Int.	10½		29.95
Realist										
Apache	4	30	6	2	12½	.75	Int.	7		9.95
Apache	6	20	4	2	13¾	.75	Int.	8	Scope price includes mount. Constantly centered reticles in Riflescopes. CH or P&CH standard. Dot $10 extra. Sunshades available $6.95 — $8.95. Nitrogen processed. Aluminum construction.	12.50
Riflescope	2½	44	66	3-5	10½	1	Int.	8		49.75
Riflescope	4	31	73	3-5	12⅜	1	Int.	9		57.50
Riflescope	6	20	38	3-5	14	1	Int.	10		59.50
Brushscope	1½-4½	65-26	225-49	3-5	11	1	Int.	11½		69.50
Riflescope	3-9	34-12	144-16	3-5	13¼	1	Int.	11		89.50
Camputer	6	20	38	3-5	14⅝	1	Int.	18	Supplied with special mounts and range cams for most popular rifles and calibers.	119.50
Auto/Range	4	31	73	3-5	11	1	Int.	17		119.50
	1½-4½	65-26	225-49	3-5	12¼	1	Int.	17		129.50
	3-9	34-12	144-16	3-5	12¾	1	Int.	17		129.50

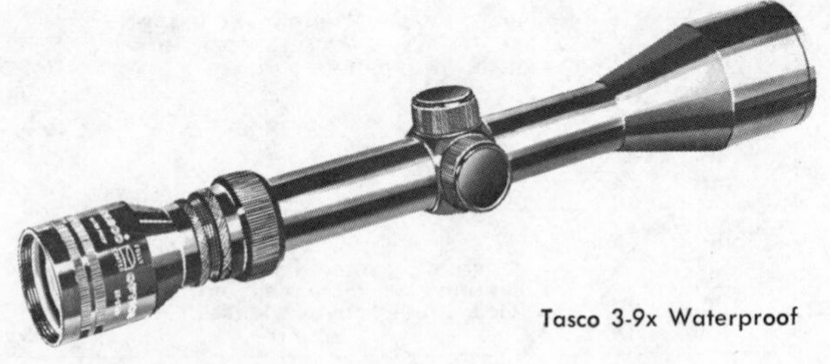

Tasco 3-9x Waterproof

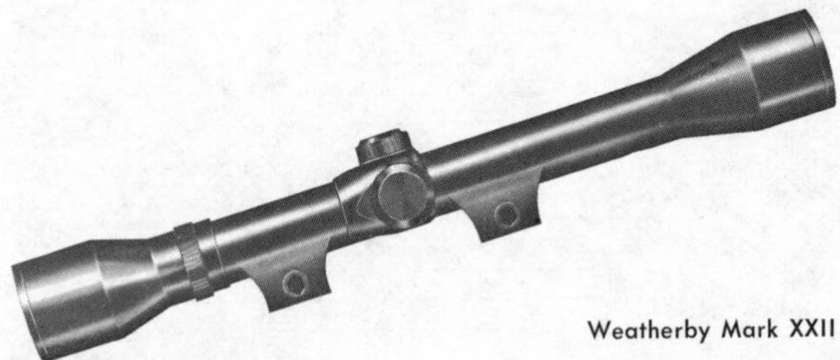

Weatherby Mark XXII

Hunting, Target and Varmint Scopes—Continued

Maker and Model	Magn.	Field at 100 Yds. (feet)	Relative Bright-ness	Eye Relief (in.)	Length (in.)	Tube Diam. (in.)	W&E Adjust-ments	Weight (ozs.)	Other Data	Price
Redfield										
Frontier	2.3	18	100	6-10	10⅜	.75	Int.	6	Frontier models are for Win. M94, Rem. 600, mount forward of the receiver.	39.95
Frontier	2	30	144	6-10	11½	1	Int.	8.5		59.95
Sportster 4X	3.9	24.5	27	3-3¾	9½	.75	Int.	6¼		39.95
Magnum 2¾X	2¾	42.5	64	3-3¾	10⅜	1	Int.	8	Constantly centered reticles; scratchproof Tuf-Coat finish; W. & E. dials adjustable to zero; weatherproof sealed. Reticle same size at all powers. Add $20 for Accu-Range, $10 for dot (not avail. in Frontiers or Sportsters). 12X has separate parallax adj. knob, ¼" clicks.	59.95
Magnum 4X	4	31	61	3-3¾	11⅜	1	Int.	9¾		64.95
Magnum 6X	6	20	46.7	3-3¾	13¼	1	Int.	11¼		84.95
Magnum 12X	12	10	13.7	3-3¾	14⅞	1	Int.	13.5		119.95
Magnum Variable	1-4	85-30	289-31	3½	9¾	1	Int.	10¼		89.95
Magnum Variable	2.3-7	44-16	182-20	3-3¾	11¾	1	Int.	11½		99.95
Magnum Variable	3.3-9.1	37.5 12.5	159-19	3-3¾	12¾	1	Int.	12½		109.95
Magnum Variable	4-12	28-9	100-12	3-3¾	13⅞	1	Int.	14		129.95
3200 Target	12, 16, 20, 24,	6½, 5¼, 4, 3¾	9, 6, 3¼, 2¼	2½	23¼	1	Int.	21	Mounts solidly. Extra fine CH, $10.	169.95
Sanders										
Bisley 2½x20	2½	42	64	3	10¾	1	Int.	8¼	Alum. alloy tubes, ¼" adj., coated lenses. Two other scopes are also offered: a 3-9x at $52.50, and a 6x45 at $42. Rubber lens covers (clear plastic) are $2.50; with amber-colored lenses, $3.50. Choice of reticles in CH, PCH, 3-post.	34.00
Bisley 4x33	4	28	64	3	12	1	Int.	9		38.00
Bisley 6x33	6	19	28	3	12½	1	Int.	9½		40.00
Bisley 8x33	8	18	16	3¼	12½	1	Int.	9½		42.00
Bisley 10x33	10	12½	10	2½	12½	1	Int.	10¼		44.00
Bisley 8x45	8	18	30	3¼	12½	1	Int.	11¼		44.00
Bisley 5-13x40	5-13	29-10	64-9	3	14	1	Int.	14		56.50
Savage										
2520	2½	43		3	10¾	1	Int.	8.5	Coated lenses, duralumin tubes.	31.50
0433	4	30		3	12	1	Int.	10	Reticles permanently centered.	37.50
3833	3-8	35-13		3	11½	1	Int.	12		59.75
2037	3-7	25-14		2	11¼	.875	Int.	8	For 22 rifles; price includes mounts.	14.95
0420	4	25½		2	11½	.75	Int.	8.5		9.75
0620	6	17½		2	11½	.75	Int.	8.5		12.50
Scope Instruments										
2650	2½	32	164	3½	11½	1	Int.	10		24.95
2652	4	29	64	3¼	11½	1	Int.	9½	Constantly centered reticles—CH or post. Nitrogen filled. Yellow haze filter.	24.95
2654	6	21	28	3	11½	1	Int.	9½		27.50
2658	3-9	29-13	113-12	3	13¼	1	Int.	14¼		37.50
2656	3-9	29-12	177-19	3½	13¼	1	Int.	16		39.95
Sears										
No. 53801	4	30		2	11½	.75	Int.	6	First three scopes for 22's only, complete with rings for grooved receivers. Crosshair or post and crosshair reticle. Big game scopes come with mount rings. Bases available to fit almost all H.P. rifles. Fixed crosshair reticle remains in center regardless of adjustment. No. 53824 for Sears M54 & Win. M94. Mounts w/adj. included.	12.50
No. 53802	4	28		2	11½	.75	Int.	8		8.99
No. 53803	3-6	30-16					Int.	6½		13.99
No. 53824	3	37		3-6	10⅜	1	Int.	8½		34.99
No. 53821	4	30		3¼	11¼	1	Int.	12		40.00
No. 53827	2½-8	37-14		3-5	13¼	1	Ext.	11		59.99
No. 53901	1				8	1	Int.	8½		49.75
Southern Precision										
562	2½	40	144	3½	12	1	Int.	9¼	Centered reticles, CH or post. All elements sealed.	21.95
564	4	30	64	3½	12	1	Int.	9¼		23.95
566	6	21	28	3¼	12	1	Int.	9¼		23.95
Stoeger										
4x	4	30	64	3	12	1	Int.	9	CH only. ½" clicks. Obj. tube diam. 1½" in fixed powers, 1⅞" in variable.	24.95
6x	6	20	28	3	12¾	1	Int.	9		29.95
8x	8	16	25	3	12	1	Int.	13		35.95
3x-9x	3-9	38-11	170-20	3	11½	1	Int.	12¾		46.95
Swift										
Grizzly	2½	32	159	3	11.7	1	Int.	8.5	Dot, tapered post & CH or Rangefinder reticles available on all but Zoom & Game, $2.50 extra. Rangefinder optional on Zoom & Game. All have self-centering reticles.	24.00
Stag	4	28½	64	3	11.7	1	Int.	8.5		24.50
Gamescope	4	30	64	3	11.7	1	Int.	9		36.00
Bighorn	6	18½	28	3	11.7	1	Int.	8.5		27.50
Yukon	2½-8	32½-13	164-16	3	13¼	1	Int.	11.3		38.00
Zoomscope	2½-8	41-15½	256-25	3½	12½	1	Int.	16.1		67.50

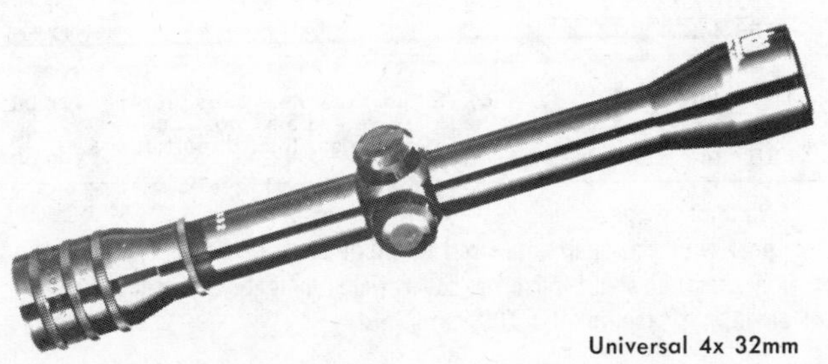
Universal 4x 32mm

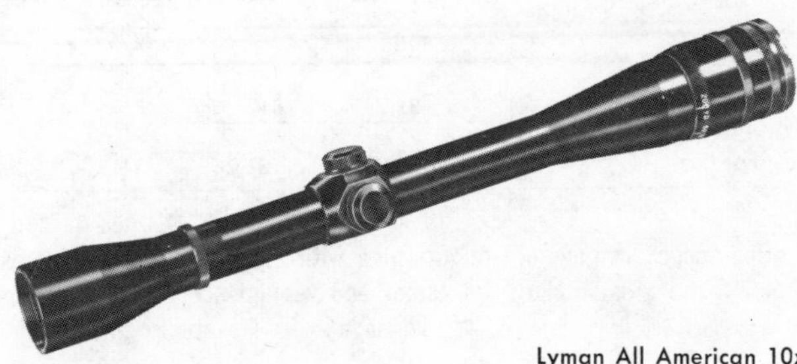
Lyman All American 10x

Hunting, Target and Varmint Scopes—Continued

Maker and Model	Magn.	Field at 100 Yds. (feet)	Relative Bright-ness	Eye Relief (in.)	Length (in.)	Tube Diam. (in.)	W&E Adjust-ments	Weight (ozs.)	Other Data	Price
Tasco										
Zoom Target	3-7	28-12	130-24	2¼	12	⅞	Int.	9½	Lens covers furnished. Constantly centered reticles. Write the importer, Tasco, for data on complete line.	19.95
Pistol Scope	1½	23	216	19	8⅝	⅞	Int.	7½		19.95
Sniper	2-5	36-18	150-24	3¼	11¼	1	Int.	10		29.95
Super Marksman	3-9	35-14	266-29	3.2	12⅜	1	Int.	12½		39.95
Tops										
4X	4	28½	64	3	11½	1	Int.	9½	Hard-coated lenses, nitrogen filled, shock-proof tested. Write Ed Paul, importer, for data on complete line.	23.95
8X	8	14½	16	3	13	1	Int.	10		29.95
3X-9X	3-9	33-15	175-19	3	12¾	1	Int.	14		39.95
Tradewinds										
TW-4	4	31	81	3¼	10.8	1	Int.	11	Lightweight dural tubes. Dot reticles same price, leather scope caps included. Tradewinds, Inc., importer.	54.50
TW-VARI	2.5-8	35.4-14.8	100-20.25	3¼	12¼	1	Int.	12.7		69.50
TW-Zoom	1.5-4	62-28	144-20	3¼	9.7	1	Int.	11.6	Diamond Dot reticle.	57.50
United										
Golden Hawk	4	30	64		11⅞	—	Int.	9½		44.50
Golden Grizzly	6	18½	44		11⅞	1	Int.	11	Anodized tubes, nitrogen filled. Write United for data on complete line.	55.00
Golden Falcon	4-9	29½-14	100-20		13½	1	Int.	12¼		89.50
Golden Plainsman	3-12	33-12½	169-11		13½	1	Int.	12¾		110.00
Unertl										
Falcon	2¾	40	75.5	4	11	1	Int.(1')	10	Black dural tube in hunting models. (2 oz. more with steel tube.)	50.00
Hawk	4	34	64	4	11¾	1	Int.(1')	10.5		54.00
Condor	6	17	40	3-4	13½	1	Int.(1')	12		68.00
◆1" Target	6,8,10	16-10	17.6-6.25	2	21½	.75	Ext.	21	Dural ¼ MOA click mounts. Hard coated lenses. Non-rotating objective lens focusing.	67.00
◆1¼" Target	8,10,12,14	12-6	15.2-5	2	25	.75	Ext.	25		90.00
◆1½" Target	8,10,12,14 16,18,20,24	11.5-3.2		2¼	25½	.75	Ext.	31		105.00
◆2" Target	8,10,12,14 16,18,24 30,36		22.6-2.5	2¼	26¼	1	Ext.	44		145.00
◆Varmint, 1¼"	6,8,10,12	14.1-7	28-7.1	2½	19½	.875	Ext.	26	¼ MOA dehorned mounts. With target mounts.	92.00 95.00
◆Ultra Varmint, 2"	8,10, 12,15	12.6-7	39.7-11	2½	24	1	Ext.	34	With dehorned mount. With calibrated head.	115.00 132.00
◆Small Game	4,6	25-17	19.4-8.4	2¼	18	.75	Ext.	16	Same as 1" Target but without objective lens focusing.	49.00
◆Vulture	8 10	11.2 10.9	29 18½	3-4	15⅝ 16⅛	1	E or I	15½	Price with internal adj. Price with ¼ MOA click mounts.	82.00 98.00
◆Programer 200	8,10,12,14 16,18,20,24 30,36	11.3-4	39-1.9		26½	1	Ext.	45	With new Posa mounts.	192.00
Universal										
Deluxe UC	2½	32	172	3½	12	1	Int.	9¼	Aluminum alloy tubes, centered reticles, coated lenses. Similar Standard series available at lower cost.	24.95
Deluxe UE	4	29	64	3½	12	1	Int.	9		24.95
Deluxe UG	6	17½	28	3¼	12	1	Int.	9		26.95
Deluxe UL	3-9	34-12	177-18	3	12¾	1	Int.	15¼		42.95
Weatherby										
Mark XXII	4	25	50	2½-3½	11¾	⅞	Int.	9¼	Focuses in top turret.	29.50
Imperial	2¾	47½	90	3¼-5	10½	1	Int.	9¼	¼ MOA adj. for e., 1 MOA for w. in all models. Reticles: CH, post and CH, Lee Dot or Open Dot ($12.50 extra).	69.50
Imperial 4x	4	33	81	3¼-4½	11⅛	1	Int.	10¼		79.50
Imperial 6x	6	21½	62	3¼-4½	12½	1	Int.	12⅜		89.50
Imperial Variable	2-7	48-17¾	324-27	4.3-3.1	11 3/16	1	Int.	12	A second line of scopes, identical to the Imperials except that they have no internal adjustments, is available at $20 less.	99.50
Imperial Variable	2¾-10	37-14.6	296-22	4½-3½	12½	1	Int.	14⅛		109.50
Weaver										
K1.5	1½	56		3-5	9¾	1	Int.	7		29.50
K2.5	2½	43		3-6	10⅜	1	Int.	8½		37.50
K3	3	37		3-6	10⅜	1	Int.	8½		37.50
K4	4	31		3-5½	11¼	1	Int.	9½		45.00
K6	6	20		3-5	13⅝	1	Int.	11	Crosswires, post, rangefinder or Dual X reticle optional on all K and V scopes (except no RF in K1½, post in K8, 10, 12, or RF in V22). Dot $7.50 extra in K and V models only. Objective lens on K8, K10, K12, V9 and V12 focuses for range.	52.50
K8	8	15		3-5	15⅜	1	Int.	12¼		57.50
K10	10	12		3-5	15½	1	Int.	12½		59.50
K12	12	10		3-5	15¾	1	Int.	12½		72.50
V4.5	1½-4½	54-21		3-5	10	1	Int.	8½		55.00
V7	2½-7	40-15		3-5	11⅝	1	Int.	10½		62.50
V9	3-9	33-12		3-5	13	1	Int.	13		69.50
V12	4-12	24-9		4	13		Int.	13		79.50
V22	3-6	30-16		2	12½	.875	Int.	6½		14.95
C4	4	28		2	11⅞	.750	Int.	7		9.75
C6	6	18		2	12⅜	.750	Int.	8		12.50
Zeiss										
Diatal D	4	31.5	64	3⅛	10½	1.18	Int.	11	Alloy tubes. Leather caps furnished. Turret dials not calibrated. Carl Zeiss, Inc., importer.	135.00
Diatal D	6	21	49	3⅛	12½	1.18	Int.	13½		147.00
Diavari D	1½-6	60-21	161-36	3⅛	12¼	1.18	Int.	16¼		199.00

◆Signifies target and/or varmint scope.

Hunting scopes in general are furnished with a choice of reticle—crosshairs, post with crosshairs, tapered or blunt post, or dot crosshairs, etc. The great majority of target and varmint scopes have medium or fine crosshairs but post or dot reticles may be ordered.

W—Windage E—Elevation MOA—Minute of angle or 1" (approx.) at 100 yards, etc.

TELESCOPE MOUNTS

Maker, Model, Type	W and E Adjust.	Scopes	Suitable for	Price
Bausch & Lomb				
Custom One Piece (T)	Yes	B&L, other 1" scopes.	Most popular rifles.	30.90—**36.90**
Custom Two Piece (T)	**Yes**			**22.90**
Trophy (T)	**No**	1". With int. adj.		**19.90**
Browning				
One Piece (T)	W only	1" split rings	Browning FN rifles.	**22.70**
One Piece (T)	No	3/4" split rings	Browning 22 semi-auto	**4.50**
One Piece Barrel Mount Base	No	Groove mount	22 rifles with grooved receiver.	**6.50**
Two Piece	No	3/4" ring mount.	For Browning T-bolt 22	**6.00**
B-Square Co.				
Mono-Mount	**No**	Leupold M8-2x (mounts ahead of action)	M94 Win. M1 Carbine.	**11.50** **9.50**
Buehler				
One Piece (T)	W only	3/4" or 1" solid rings; 7/8", 1" or 26mm split rings. 4" or 5" spacing.	All popular models.	**Solid rings—19.60** **Split rings—24.25**
One Piece "Micro-Dial" Universal	Yes	Same. 4" ring spacing only.	Most popular models.	**Solid—24.85 Split—29.50**
Two Piece (T)	W only	Same. Rings for 26.5—27mm adjust to size by shims.	Rem. 700, 721, 722, 725; Win. 70, 52; FN; Rem. 37; Mathieu; Schultz & Larsen; Husq.	**Solid—19.60** **Split—24.25**
One Piece Pistol Base	W only	Uses any Buehler rings.	S&W K, Colt and Ruger.	**Base only—10.50**
One Piece (T)	W only	Same.	Rem. 600 rifle and XP100 pistol.	**Base only—10.50**
Bushnell				
Universal (T)	W only	1" split rings	All rifles with top of action tapped for 6/48 screws. Two steel 6/48 studs are screwed into receiver holes, eliminating conventional base. Rings drop over studs, are held by opposing screws which give rough windage adj. Economy mount set,	**14.95** **9.75**
Dual Purpose	No	Phantom	V-block bottoms lock to chrom-moly studs seated in two 6-48 holes.	**5.00**
Rigid	No	**Phantom**	Heavy loads in Colt, S&W, Ruger revolvers, **Rem. XP100, Ruger Hawkeye.**	**5.00**
94 Win.	No	Phantom	M94 Win., end of bbl. clamp or center dovetail.	**5.00**
Collins				
Bulittco (T)	E only	1" split rings	Rimfire rifles with grooved receivers.	**4.98**
Conetrol				
One Piece (T)	W only	1" solid or split rings.	Sako dovetail bases (12.95);	**Solid rings—19.85**
Two Piece (T)	W only	Same.	Sako dovetail bases ($12.95); for S&K bases on M1 Carb., SMLE 4 & 5, $9.90. **Hunter bases, 9.95; solid rings, 5.90; split rings, 9.90.**	**Split rings—25.85**
Griffin & Howe				
Standard Double Lever (S)	No	All standard models.	All popular models. (Garand $37.50; Win. 94 $30.00).	**30.00**
E. C. Herkner Echo (S)	No	All standard models.	All popular models. Solid or split rings.	**14.50—19.75**
Heym				
QD Low Claw Type (T)	W only	1" and 26mm split rings.	Most bolt action rifles. Frank & Walter Klepeis, importer.	**23.50**
Holden				
Ironsighter (T)	No	1" split rings	Many popular rifles. Rings have oval holes to permit use of iron sights.	**14.95**
International Guns Inc. handles the complete line of Parker-Hale (British) Roll-Over and other scope mounts.				
Jaeger				
QD, with windage (S)	W only	7/8", 1", 26mm; 3 heights.	All popular models.	**34.00**
QD Magnum Mount (S)	W only	Same.	Same. 4 7/8" between rings.	**42.00**
QD Railscope Mount	W only		For scopes with dovetail rib	**34.00**
Jaguar				
QD Dovetail (T)	No	1", 26mm and 26½mm rings.	For BSA Monarch rifle (Galef, importer).	**16.95**
Kesselring				
Standard QD (T)	W only	3/4", 7/8", 1", 26mm—30mm split or solid rings.	All popular rifles, one or two piece bases.	**12.50-20.00**
See-Em-Under (T)	**W only**	**Same.**	Rem. 760, 740, 788, Win. 100, 88, Marlin 336	**16.50**
QD Dovetail (T)	W only	1", 26mm.	Steyr 22, Sako, B.S.A., Brno, Krico	**16.50**
Kwik-Site (T)	No	1" split rings	Fits Weaver type bases. Mounts scope high to permit iron sight use.	**11.95**
Lehman				
Featherweight (T)	No	1", 26mm split rings.	Uses target type dovetail bases.	**Split— 9.00** **Extra bases— 1.50**

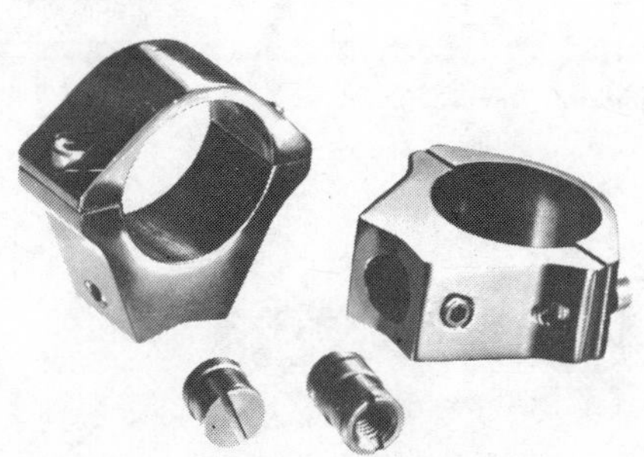

Left—Bushnell lightweight economy mount. Right—Holden Ironsighter.

TELESCOPE MOUNTS—Continued

Maker, Model, Type	W and E Adjust.	Scopes	Suitable for	Price
Leupold				
Detacho (T)	No	1" only.	All popular rifles. Instantly detachable, leaving W. & E. adjustable peep sight available.	13.50
			Bases for Rem. 600 series	9.95
			Bases for Win. M94 and Rem. XP100.	5.00—7.50
M3 (T)	Yes	1" only.	Rem. 700, 740, Win. 70, 88, 100, Wby. Mark V, FN, others. Bases reversible to give wide latitude in mounting.	24.50
Lyman All-American				
Tru-lock (T)	No	¾", ⅞", 1", 26mm, split rings.	All popular post-war rifles, plus Savage 99, 98 Mauser. One or two piece bases.	9.50
Marlin				
One Piece QD (T)	No	1" split rings	Most popular models. Glenfield model. 5.00.	6.95
Mashburn Arms				
Positive Zero (T)	With or w/o W	All standard models.	All popular models, solid or two-piece base, solid or split rings.	17.50—32.50
Numrich				
Side mount	No	1" split rings	M1 carbine.	6.95
Pachmayr				
Lo-Swing (S)	Yes	¾", ⅞", 1", 26mm solid or split loops.	All popular rifles. Scope swings aside for instant use of iron sights.	20.00
Lo-Swing (T)	Yes	¾", ⅞", 1", 26mm split rings.	Adjustable base. Win. 70, 88; Rem. 721, 722, 725, 740, 760; Mar. 336; Sav. 99.	25.00
Precise Imports				
M-21 (rings only)	No	1" tube; not over 32mm obj.	Fit Weaver bases.	3.95
M-22 (rings only)	No	1" tube; 40mm obj. scopes		3.95
Realist				
V lock QD (T)	No	1" split rings.	Most popular rifles.	10.50
Redfield				
JR-SR (T)	W only	¾", 1", 26mm.	Low, med. & high, split rings. Reversible extension front rings for 1". 2-piece bases for Mannlicher Schoenauer and Sako. JR-SR comes with integral folding peep sight.	19.90—43.85
Swing-Over (T) base only	No	1". (Not for variables.)	Standard height split rings. Also for shotguns.	14.95
JR-IER (T) base only	W only	Intermediate Eye Relief scopes.	Uses standard Redfield rings.	8.95
Ring (T)	No	¾" and 1"	Split rings for grooved 22's.	5.95—9.95
S&K				
Insta-Mount (T) base only	No	Takes Conetrol, Weaver, Herter or United rings.	M1903, A3, M1 Carbine, Lee Enfield #3, #4, #5, P14, M1917, M98 Mauser, FN Auto, AR-15.	5.75-15.75
Conventional rings and bases	No	1" split rings	Most popular rifles.	18.35
Sako				
QD Dovetail (T)	W only	1" or 26mm split rings.	Sako, or any rifle using Sako action. 3 heights and extension rings available. Firearms International, importer.	18.95—22.50
Savage				
Detachable (T)	No	1" split rings.	Most modern rifles. One or two piece bases.	9.75-10.25
No. 40 (S)	No	1"	For Savage 340	3.00
Tasco				
700(T) and 800(S) series	No	1" split rings, regular or high.	Many popular rifles. Swing mount, 9.95.	4.50—10.45
M722	No	Split rings.	For 22s with grooved receivers.	3.00
Tradewinds				
Two Piece (T)	W only	26mm or 1" split rings.	Husqvarna, HVA rifles, actions. Scope removable w/o changing sighting. Tradewinds, imp.	14.95—18.95
Unertl				
Posa (T)	Yes	¾", ⅞", 1" scopes	Unertl target or varmint scopes.	25.00—26.00
¼ Click (T)	Yes	¾", 1" target scopes	Any with regular dovetail scope bases.	23.00—24.00
Dehorned Varmint (T)	Yes	¾", ⅞", 1" scopes	Same, less base.	20.00—23.00
Weaver				
Detachable Mount (T & S)	No	¾", ⅞", 1", 26mm.	Nearly all modern rifles. Extension rings, 1" **$11.00**	9.75
Type N (S)	No	¾" scopes only.	Same. High or low style mounts.	2.00
Pivot Mount (T)	No	¾", 1", 26mm.	Most modern big bore rifles.	12.50
Tip-Off (T)	No	¾", ⅞".	22's with grooved receivers.	2.00, 3.00
Tip-Off (T)	No	1". two-piece	Same. Adapter for Lee Enfield—**$1.75**	8.00
Williams				
Offset (S)	No	¾", ⅞", 1", 26mm solid, split or extension rings.	Most rifles (with over-bore rings, **$17.50**). Br. S.M.L.E. (round rec.) **$2.50** extra.	15.00
QC (T w/peep)	No	Same.	Same. Add $8.25 for micro. windage ring.	20.00
QC (T w/o peep)	No	Same.	Most 22 rifles, plus Mar. 36, 39, 93, 336, Sav. 23D, Win. 05, 07, 10.	17.50
QC-TM-B22	No	Same.	For Browning 22 autoloader and Rem. 241.	17.50

(S)—Side Mount **(T)—Top Mount.** 22mm = ⅞" 25.4mm = 1" 26mm = 1.18" 26.5mm = 1.045"

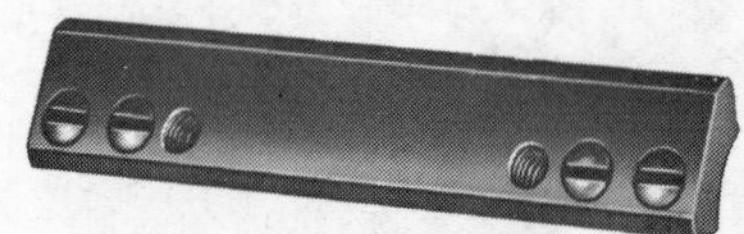

Weaver detachable side-mount

SPOTTING SCOPES

BAUSCH & LOMB BALSCOPE Sr.—60mm objective. 20X. Field at 100 yds. 11.1 ft. Relative brightness, 9. Wgt., 48 oz. Length closed, 16⁷⁄₁₆". Rapid prismatic focusing ... **$115.00**
- Also 15X, 30X, and 60X eyepieces, each ... **25.00**
- Triple eyepiece turret (without eyepiece) ... **18.95**
- Combination auto window/camera tripod adaptor ... **24.95**
- Carrying case ... **20.95**
- Tele-Master camera adapter ... **32.95**

BAUSCH & LOMB BALSCOPE ZOOM—15X to 60X variable power. 60mm objective. Field at 1000 yds. 150 ft. (15X) to 37½ feet (60X). Relative brightness 16 (15X) to 1 (60X). Wgt., 48 oz., 16¹¹⁄₁₆" overall. Integral tripod lug. Straight eyepiece ... **$149.50**
- With 45° eyepiece ... **159.50**

BAUSCH & LOMB BALSCOPE 20—40mm objective. 20X. Field at 100 yds., 7.5 ft. 15⅜" over-all, Wgt., 22 oz. ... **$24.95**

BAUSCH & LOMB BALSCOPE 10—30mm objective. 10X. Field at 100 yds., 7.5 ft. 10¼" over-all, weight, 9 oz. ... **$9.95**

BUSHNELL SPACEMASTER—60mm objective, 25X. Field at 100 yds., 10.5 ft. Relative brightness, 5.76. wgt., 39 oz. Length closed, 15¼". Prism focusing, sliding sunshade ... **$95.00**
- 15X, 20X, 25X, 40X and 60X eyepieces, each ... **22.50**
- 20X wide angle eyepiece ... **27.50**

BUSHNELL SPACEMASTER 45°—Same as above except: Wgt., 43 oz., length closed 16¼". Eyepiece at 45° ... **$99.50**

BUSHNELL SENTRY—50mm objective. 20X. Field at 100 yds., 13.1 ft. Relative brightness, 6.25. Eye relief, ½". Wgt., 24 oz. Length closed, 13" ... **$54.50**
- Also 32X and 48X eyepieces, each ... **19.50**

BUSHNELL ZOOM SPOTTER—40mm objective. 9X-30X var. power .. **$29.50**

BUSHNELL ELECTRO-ZOOM—40mm obj., 12X-40X var. power ... **$49.50**

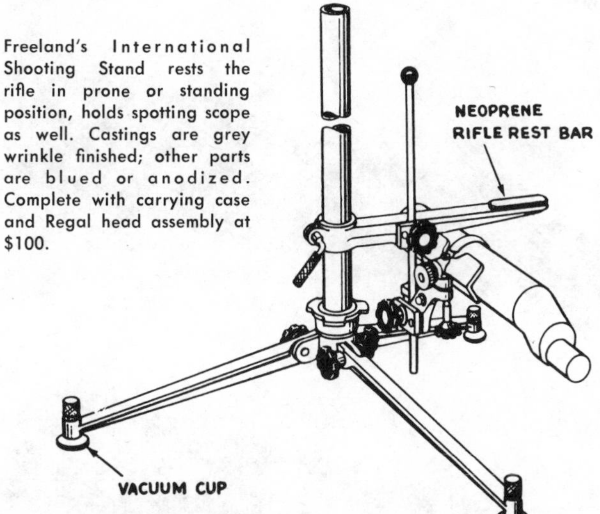

Freeland's International Shooting Stand rests the rifle in prone or standing position, holds spotting scope as well. Castings are grey wrinkle finished; other parts are blued or anodized. Complete with carrying case and Regal head assembly at $100.

HY-SCORE MODEL 460—60mm objective. 15X, 20X, 25X, 40X and 60X eyepieces included. Field at 100 yds. 15.8 to 3.2 ft. Length closed 11". Wgt., 35 oz. With tripod and case ... **$182.00**

PACIFIC ZOOM—60mm objective, 15X to 50X variable. Field at 100 yds., 7½-3½ ft. Aluminum body. With adj. tripod ... **$94.50**

PACIFIC 15x60—60mm objective, 5 eyepieces (15X, 20X, 30X, 40X, 50X), adj. tripod. 100-yd. field, 12-3¼ ft. ... **$89.50**

PRECISE IMPORTS, T-15—60mm objective, 15X to 30X zoom scope. About 15" long, weighs approximately 6 lbs. with adj. tripod. ... **$49.95**

PRECISE IMPORTS, T-19—60mm objective, interchangeable eyepieces of 15X, 20X, 30X, 40X, 60X. Sliding sunshade. Weighs about 6 lbs. with adj. tripod. ... **$69.95**

SATURN RANGER—60mm objective. 20X. Field at 100 yds., 10.4 ft. Relative brightness, 9. Eye relief, ⁹⁄₁₆". Wgt., 33 oz. Length closed, 15⁵⁄₁₆". Spiral adjustment of eyepiece. Chilford Arms ... **$54.50**

SATURN SCOUT—44mm objective. 20X. Field at 100 yds., 6.7 ft. Relative brightness, 4.84. Eye relief, ½". Wgt., 23 oz. Length closed, 13". Draw tube plus spiral focusing. Chilford Arms ... **$29.50**

SOUTHERN PRECISION MODEL 549—60mm objective and 5 eyepieces from 15X to 60X; extensible sunshade and folding tripod. Closed, 14¾", Wgt., 4¼ lbs. ... **$79.50**

SOUTHERN PRECISION MODEL 550 — 60mm objective and 4 turret-mounted eyepieces from 20X to 60X; ext. sunshade and folding tripod. Closed, 16¼", wgt., 5½ lbs. with tripod (included) ... **$75.00**

SOUTHERN PRECISION ZOOM MODEL 547 — 60mm objective, 25X to 50X; ext. sunshade folding tripod. Closed, 18", wgt. 4½ lbs. with tripod (included) ... **$69.50**

SOUTHERN PRECISION MODEL 546—50mm objective, 25X. Folding tripod, leather case included. Closed, 13", wgt. 3 lbs. ... **$27.00**

SWIFT TELEMASTER M841—60mm objective. 15X to 60X variable power. Field at 1000 yards 160 feet (15X) to 40 feet (60X). Wgt. 3.4 lbs. 17.6" over-all ... **$135.00**
- Tripod for above ... **30.50**
- Photo adapter ... **10.95**
- Case for above ... **23.00**

SWIFT MODEL 821—60mm objective. 15X, 20X, 30X, 40X and 60X eyepieces included. Field at 100 yds., 158 to 32 ft. 18" tripod with friction clutch adj. handle. Length 13½" (without sunshade). 6 lbs. ... **$96.00**

SWIFT MODEL 822—40mm objective. 20X eyepiece, tripod adapter, sunshade and dust cap. Length closed 10". Wgt. 27 oz. ... **$46.50**

TASCO 8TOZ—60mm objective. 20X to 60X variable power. Field at 1000 yards 158 feet (16X) to 40 feet (50X). Wgt. 4½ lbs. 18" over-all ... **$79.95**

UNERTL RIGHT ANGLE—63.5mm objective. 24X. Field at 100 yds., 7 ft. Relative brightness, 6.96. Eye relief, ½". Wgt., 41 oz. Length closed, 19". Push-pull and screw-focus eyepiece. 16X and 32X eyepieces $18 each. ... **$110.00**

UNERTL STRAIGHT PRISMATIC — Same as Unertl Right Angle except: straight eyepiece and wgt. of 40 oz. ... **$92.00**

UNERTL 20X STRAIGHT PRISMATIC — 54mm objective. 20X. Field at 100 yds., 8.5 ft. Relative brightness, 6.1. Eye relief, ½". Wgt., 36 oz. Length closed, 13½". Complete with lens covers ... **$74.00**

UNERTL TEAM SCOPE—100mm objective. 15X, 24X, 32X eyepieces. Field at 100 yds. 13 to 7.5 ft. Relative brightness, 39.06 to 9.79. Eye relief, 2" to 1½". Weight, 13 lbs. 29⅞" overall. Metal tripod, yoke and wood carrying case furnished (total weight, 80 lbs.) ... **$450.00**

WEATHERBY—60mm objective, 20X-45X zoom ... **$93.50**
- With fixed power eyepiece ... **85.00**
- Tripod for above ... **14.95**

SCOPE ATTACHMENTS

DAVIS TARGETEER—Objective lens/tube units that attach to front of low power scopes, increase magnification to 8X. 1¼" lens, **$25,** 1½" lens ... **$29.50**

HERMANN DUST CAPS—Connected leather straps, hand made, natural color. For all popular scopes. ... **$4.00**

LEE TACKHOLE DOTS—Various size dots for all scopes. Price ... **$7.50—$15.00**

LYMAN HAZE FILTER—For morning and late afternoon hunting. Filters out blue and violet rays allowing only the best part of the spectrum to transmit through your telescope lenses. For all reflescopes ... **$2.75**

PGS SCOPE SHIELDS—Flexible rubber, usable at front and rear, protect scopes from snow or rain. Made for all scopes. ... **$3.95**

PREMIER RETICLES—Various size dots for all scopes, also special reticles to order. Price—**$7.00** to **$18.50.** **PREMIER WEATHER CAPS**—transparent, high light transmission. For all popular scopes. Price **$3.50.** Special sizes ... **$5.00**

RING MOUNTS—Custom made for German-type claw bases. Don's Gun Shop.

STORM KING LENS CAPS—A hinged glass-and-rubber protector set (2), made in various sizes for all scopes. May be unhinged or sighted through. Anderson Gun Shop. Per pair ... **$2.95**

VISS'S SUPREME LENS COVERS — Hinged protectors for most scope models, front and rear lenses shielded. E. D. Vissing Co. Per pair, postpaid. ... **$4.95**

SPOTTING SCOPE STANDS

DAVIDSON MARK 245 — Bipod adjustable for elevation, 9½"-14½". Side mount with two straps. Black crinkle finish. Length folded 16½". Price ... **$23.95**

FREELAND ALL ANGLE—Tripod adjustable for elevation. Left or right side mount with worm drive clamp. Folding legs. Clamps available for any scope tube size. Black, gray, or green crinkle finish. Price. ... **$20.75**
- Also 12" 18", 24" extensions available. ... **$3.00-5.00**

FREELAND OLYMPIC—Bipod adjustable for elevation. All angle mount with padded worm drive clamp. Folding legs. Clamps available for any scope tube size. Black, grey, or green crinkle finish. Price ... **$23.75**
- Also 12", 18", 24" extensions available. ... **$3.00-5.00**
- Zoom head for tripod or bipod. ... **$10.00**

FREELAND REGAL BIPOD—Choice of saddle or zoom head. All adjustment knobs are oversize for easy adjusting. Large "ball" carrying knob. Gray or green finish. ... **$26.75**
- Above with stability weight. ... **33.25**
- Extensions 12"-24" ... **$3.00-5.00**

O. S. E.—Tripod adjustable for elevation. Top mount with worm drive rubber-covered clamp. Folding legs. Clamps available for any scope tube size. Black or green crinkle finish. Price ... **$13.95**

Chokes & Brakes

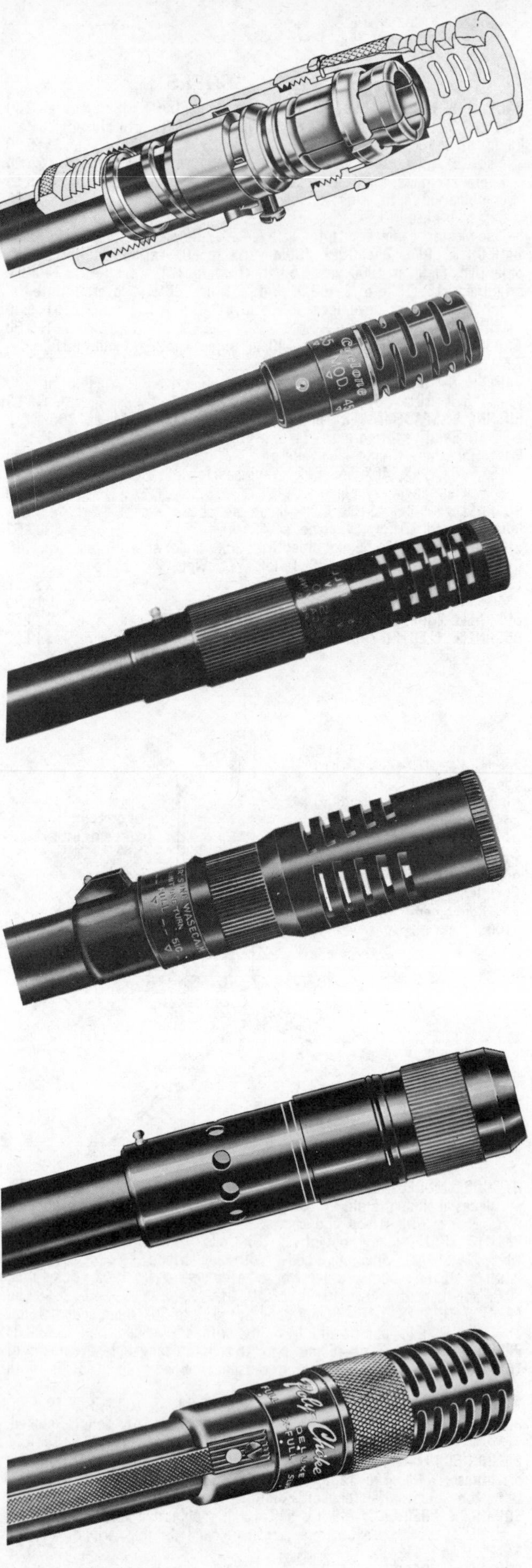

Adjustomatic Choke

The Adjustomatic, made by the Hartford Gun Choke Co., of Newington, Conn. is conventional in appearance, size, length, weight and choice of choke settings, but unique in that it can be set to automatically give a tighter choke on subsequent shots than that of the setting selected for the first shot. It is simply controlled by a reset button. If desired, it can be set to give any pattern of a manually adjusted choke for continuous shooting. For 12, 16 or 20 gauge, $29.95 installed at the factory or by a qualified agent.

Cyclone Choke

The Cyclone Choke is a small-diameter manually set design, available with either Standard non-slotted sleeve, Regular ventilated sleeve or Duo-Vent sleeve in 12, 16 or 20 gauge. The Duo-Vent features staggered self-cleaning slots around the choke area to give maximum recoil reduction. All model Cyclones have settings for total "Pattern Control," are three inches long, and weigh from 3 oz. in 12 gauge to 2½ oz. in 20 gauge. Prices, installed at the Hartford Gun Choke Co., are: Standard, $21.70; Regular, $24.70; Duo-Vent, $27.70.

Emsco Choke

E. M. Schacht of Waseca, Minn., offers the Emsco, a small diameter choke which features a precision curve rather than a taper behind the 1½" choking area. 9 settings are available in this 5 oz. attachment. Its removable recoil sleeve can be furnished in dural if desired. Choice of three sight heights. For 12, 16 or 20 gauge. Price installed, $21.95. Not installed, $16.50.

Vari-Choke

Herter's, Inc., supplies the Vari-Choke, which features a ball-bearing micro-click adjustment of the pattern sleeve, rather than the spring system used by others. This model has 8 choke settings, from Full to Improved Cylinder. With Recoil Eliminator, price is $15.95 installed; without Eliminator, $12.25.

Lyman CHOKE

The LymanCHOKE is similar to the Cutts Comp in that it comes with fixed-choke tubes or an adjustable tube, with or without recoil chamber. The adjustable tube version sells for $21.95 with recoil chamber, $19.50 without, in 12, 16 or 20 gauge.

Lyman also offers a Single-Choke Adaptor at $12.25 installed. This permits use of any of the Cutts Comp tubes or an adjustable choke tube, with or without recoil chamber. If recoil chamber is desired, add $2.45.

Poly-Choke

Poly-Choke Co., Inc., now is offering the Deluxe Signature Poly-Choke. It provides 9 choke settings (marked in 24 karat gold) to cover the complete pattern range as well as handle rifled slugs. It comes in two versions, the standard at $24.95, and the ventilated model at $27.95 installed. Fits 12, 16, 20 or 28 gauge. The Poly-Choke has been on the market for more than 30 years and is still gaining popularity.

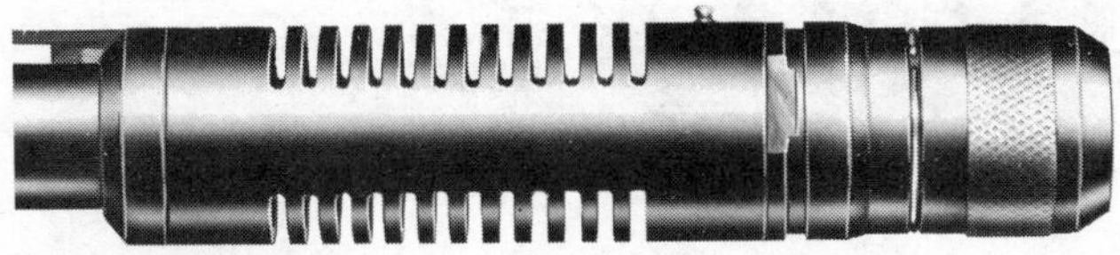

Cutts

Cutts Compensator

The Cutts Compensator is one of the oldest variable choke devices available. Manufactured by Lyman Gunsight Corporation, it is available with either a steel or aluminum body. A series of vents allows gas to escape upward and downward, reducing recoil without directing muzzle blast toward nearby shooters.

For the 12-ga. Comp body, six fixed-choke tubes are available: the Spreader — popular with Skeet shooters; Improved Cylinder; Modified; Full; Superfull, and Magnum Full. Full, Modified and Spreader tubes are available for 16, 20, 28, and .410, and an Adjustable Tube, giving Full through Improved Cylinder chokes, is offered in 12, 16, 20 and 28 gauges.

Barrel adaptors in various internal diameters are available at $1.00 to permit exact fitting of Cutts Expansion Chambers.

The Comp body with wrench and adaptor sells for $13.00; Comp Tubes are $3.25 each, steel or aluminum, and the Adjustable Tube is $9.75. Factory installation is $7.00, plus transportation.

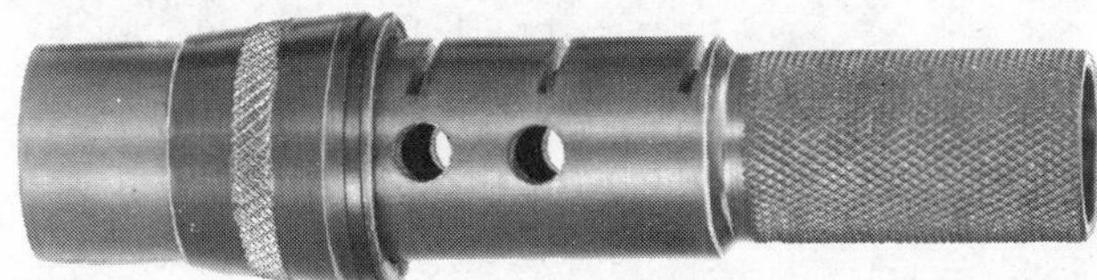

Jet-Away

Jet-Away Choke

Arms Ingenuity Corp., makers of the Jet-Away, say that this device controls patterns through partial venting of the powder gases which normally enlarge patterns. The Jet-Away has a series of three slots in the top of the tube and a sliding control sleeve. When the sleeve is in its rearward position, all slots are uncovered, the maximum of gas is vented and patterns are densest. To obtain more open patterns, the sleeve is moved to cover one or more slots. In 12 or 20 gauge only, the Jet-Away is made ol aluminum, weighs 3 ozs. $24.95 installed.

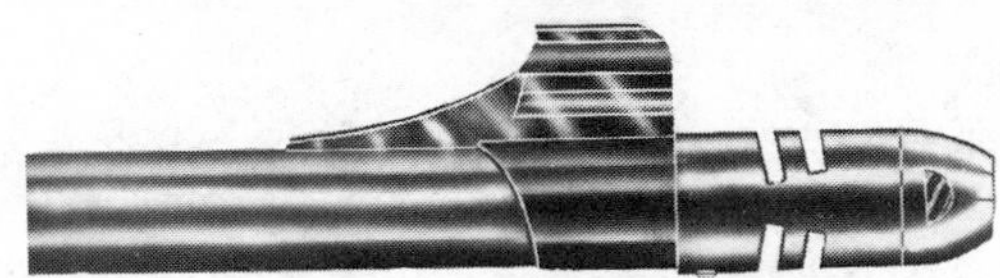

Herter's

Herter's Rifle Recoil Eliminator

The Recoil Eliminator is a metal tube—115/16" long and 7/8" diam. in the standard model, same length and 1 1/8" diam. in target type — which is screwed to the muzzle. Angled ports direct escaping gas upward and rearward, reducing recoil and muzzle jump. The target model has a shield to prevent muzzle blast from annoying nearby shooters. Weights are 2 oz. and 3 oz. re¬pectively. Made for calibers 25 to 32. Price of standard, $2.50; $5.50 installed. Target, $3.50 and $6.50.

Dahl

Dahl Muzzle Blast Controller

Only 1½" long by ¾" in diameter, this device is claimed to reduce recoil up to 40%. An outer sleeve, threaded onto the gun muzzle, is threaded on the inside to accept a machined plug which is bored through for bullet passage. Gas behind the bullet is bled off through slots in the plug, swirled through a number of tiny passages while contained by the sleeve, and then vented upward, this final action somewhat offsetting muzzle jump. Standard model, $12; Deluxe $14. 2" long Streamlined, no flaps. Custom, $15. Installation, $5.

The 1½" collet length is fully backed-up to prevent blown patterns arising from the springiness and vibration found in unsupported collet sleeves. A U.S. patent (No. 2,977,702) was obtained on this feature some time ago.

Rex

Rex Sha-Cul Rifle Muzzle Brake

C. R. Pedersen & Son engineered the Rex Sha-Cul muzzle control tube to cut down recoil and blast. The manufacturers state that the device helps eliminate bullet wobble, thus aiding accuracy. 3" long and 13/16" in diam., the Sha-Cul can accommodate all calibers from 22 to 458. It requires ½" of barrel thread to install. Sold on an "unconditional money-back guarantee," the price is $17.50, plus $3.50 installation.

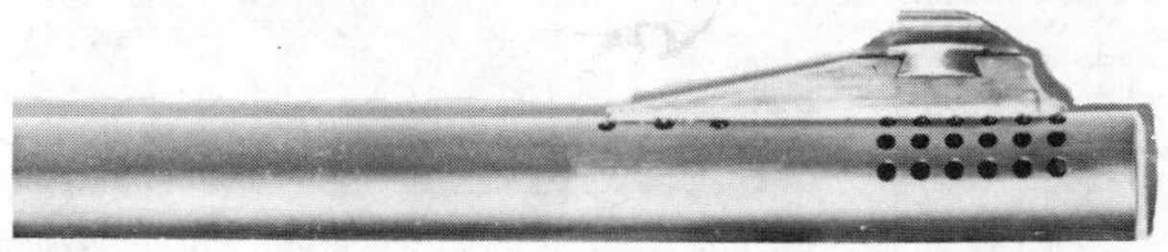

Pendleton

Pendleton Dekicker

This Dekicker is unusual in that it is not a separate tube added onto a rifle muzzle but is machined into the barrel itself. Obviously, it cannot be installed by the customer. It must be sent to J. F. Mutter's Pendleton Gunshop, where a section of the bore a short distance behind the muzzle is relieved into an expansion chamber. Exit holes drilled at precise locations vent gas to lower apparent kick. Because metal is removed instead of being added, there is a small decrease in gun weight.

Installation, including barrel polishing, is $35 in calibers from the 220 Swift to 358 Magnum; $40 for 375 to 458; $40 for 460 Weatherby and large single barrel express calibers.

The Arms Library for

COLLECTOR • HUNTER • SHOOTER • OUTDOORSMAN

A selection of books—old, new and forthcoming—for everyone in the arms field, with a brief description by . . . RAY RILING

ballistics and handloading

The Bullet's Flight, from Powder to Target, by F. W. Mann. Ray Riling Arms Books Co., Phila., Pa. 1965. A reprint of the very scarce original work of 1909. Introduction by Homer S. Powley, 384 pp. illus. $9.95.
One of the best known and scholarly-developed works on basic ballistics.

Cartridges of the World, by Frank C. Barnes, John T. Amber ed., Gun Digest Co., Chicago, Ill., 1969. 8½"x11", 378 pp. Profusely illus. Paperbound. $6.95.
The second edition of a comprehensive reference for hunters, collectors, handloaders and ballisticians. Covering over 1000 cartridges, loads, components, etc., from all over the world.

Centerfire American Rifle Cartridges, 1892-1963, by Ray Bearse, A. S. Barnes & Co., S. Brunswick, N.J., 1966. 198 pp., illus. $15.00.
Identification manual covering caliber, introduction date, origin, case type, etc. Self-indexed and cross-referenced. Headstamps and line drawings are included.

Centerfire Pistol and Revolver Cartridges, by H.P. White, B. D. Munhall and Ray Bearse. A. S. Barnes, N.Y., 1967. 85 pp. plus 170 pp., illus. $10.00
A new and revised edition covering the original Volume I, Centerfire Metric Pistol and Revolver Cartridges and Volume II, Centerfire American and British Pistol and Revolver Cartridges, by White and Munhall, formerly known as Cartridge Identification.

Complete Guide to Handloading, by Phil Sharpe. Funk & Wagnalls, N. Y. C., 1953 (3rd ed., 2nd rev.). 734 pp., profusely illustrated, numerous line and halftone charts, tables, lists, etc., $10.00.
The bible of handloaders ever since its first appearance in 1937, but badly dated now.

Condensed Professional Loading and Reloading Data, by Herter & Herter. Publ. by the authors, Waseca, Minn., 3rd ed., 1966. 459 pp., illus., paperbound. $4.50.
Full data on all cartridge forms and voluminous coverage of handloading in all aspects.

Handbook for Shooters and Reloaders, by P. O. Ackley. Priv. publ., Salt Lake City, 1962-1965. Illus. Vol. I, 567 pp., $8.00; Vol. II, 495 pp., $8.00. The two volumes, special at $15.00.
Storehouse of technical information on ammunition and its use by a noted authority, with supplemental articles by other experts. Ballistic charts plus loading data for hundreds of cartridges, standard and wildcat.

Handloader's Digest, *ed.* by John T. Amber. Gun Digest Co., Chicago, 1968. 320 pp., well illus. Paperbound. $4.95.
The fourth and latest edition of a popular and comprehensive reference work on reloading, with articles by leading experts on ammunition.

Home Guide to Cartridge Conversions, by Geo. C. Nonte, Jr., Stackpole Books, Harrisburg, Pa., 1967. 404 pp., illus. $8.95.
A new, revised and enlarged ed. of instructions, charts and tables for making ammunition no longer available, or which has become too expensive on the commercial market.

Hornady Handbook of Cartridge Reloading. Hornady Mfg. Co., Grand Island, Nebr., 1967. 360 pp., illus. $3.50.
Handloader's reference, with much detail on projectiles, ballistics, etc., on many popular U.S. and imported firearms. An excellent new work with particularly needed ballistic detail.

The Identification of Firearms and Forensic Ballistics, by G. Burrard. A. S. Barnes, New York, 1962. 217 pp., illus. $3.95.
A standard, reliable, authoritative English work in the criminal-legal field of ballistics.

Interior Ballistics, How a Gun Converts Chemical Energy to Projectile Motion, by E. D. Lowry. Doubleday and Co., N.Y., 1968. 168 pp., including index and bibliography., illus. with 4 halftones and 17 line drawings. $4.50.
An introduction to the history of small arms and weapons relative to the science of internal ballistics, especially for the layman and student.

Lyman Handbook No. 44. Lyman Gunsight Corp., Middlefield, Conn., 1967. $3.50
Latest edition of a favorite reference for ammunition handloaders, whether novice or veteran.

Manual of Pistol and Revolver Cartridges, by Hans A. Erlmeier and Jakob H. Brandt. J. E. Erlmeier Verlag, Wiesbaden, Germany, 1967. This is Volume I and covers Centerfire, Metric Calibers. 271 pp., including a bibliography; well illus. in halftone and line. $18.00.
A reference work of international status, listing cartridges by calibers and alphabetically, for rapid reference. The text is in both German and English language. A Volume II Centerfire, American and British Calibers is contemplated.

Methods in Exterior Ballistics, by F. R. Moulton. Dover Publ., N.Y.C., 1962. 257 pp., paper covers, $1.75.
A standard work on the mathematics of advanced theoretical and experimental exterior ballistics.

The NRA Handloader's Guide. Ashley Halsey, Jr., ed. Nat'l Rifle Assn., Washington, D.C., 1969. 312 pp., illus., paperbound. $5.00.
Revised edition of a reloading handbook, based on material published in *The American Rifleman.*

Pocket Manual for Shooters and Reloaders, by P. O. Ackley. Publ. by author, Salt Lake City, Utah, 1964. 176 pp., illus., spiral bound. $3.25.
Good coverage on standard and wildcat cartridges and related firearms in popular calibers.

Principles and Practice of Loading Ammunition, by Lt. Col. Earl Naramore. Stackpole Books, Harrisburg, Pa., 1954. 915 text pages, 240 illustrations. $14.95.
Actually two volumes in one. The first part (565 pp.) deals with ballistics and the principles of cartridge making—and the chemistry, metallurgy, and physics involved. The second part (350 pp.) is a thorough discussion of the mechanics of loading cartridges. 1967 printing.

Shooter's Bible Reloader's Guide, 2nd ed., by R. A. Steindler. Shooter's Bible, Inc., S. Hackensack, N.J., 1968. 220 pp., fully illus. $3.95.
Comprehensive coverage of technology and methods of handloading all types of small arms ammunition. This is a useful work.

Shotgun Ballistics for Hunters, by R. B. Boughan. Barnes, N.Y.C., 1965. 159 pp., illus. $6.50.
Analysis of shotgun ballistics as applied to getting good performance in target and game shooting.

Small Arms Ammunition Identification Guide. Panther Publ., Boulder, Colo., 1968. 151 pp., illus., paperbound. $3.00.
Facsimile of a U.S. Army text on cartridge identification, which includes data on foreign ammunition used in Vietnam and elsewhere.

Small Arms Design and Ballistics, by Col. T. Whelen. 1945. Stackpole Books, Harrisburg, Pa. Vol. I, 352 pp., Vol. II, 314 pp., both illus. Each, $6.00.
Authoritative technical data on firearms. Vol. I covers design, function, and operation. Vol. II deals with interior and exterior ballistics.

Speer Manual for Reloading Ammunition No. 7. Speer, Inc., Lewiston, Idaho, 1966. 382 pp., illus. $2.95.
A popular manual on handloading, with authoritative articles on loading, ballistics, and related subjects. Decorated paper wrappers.

Why Not Load Your Own? by Col. T. Whelen. A. S. Barnes, New York, 1957, 4th ed., rev. 237 pp., illus, $5.95.
A basic reference on handloading, describing each step, materials and equipment. Loads for popular cartridges are given.

The Winchester-Western Ammunition Handbook. Thomas Nelson & Sons, N.Y.C., 1964. 185 pp., illus. $1.95.
Called the world's handiest handbook on ammunition for all types of shotguns, rifles and handguns. Full of facts, photographs, ballistics and statistics.

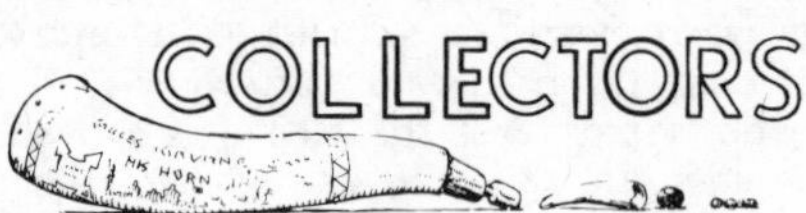

COLLECTORS

Accoutrement Plates, North and South, 1861-1865, by Wm. G. Gavin. Geo. Shumway, York, Pa., 1963. 236 pp., 220 illus. $12.00.
The 1st detailed study of Civil War belt buckles and cartridge box insignia. Dimensions, materials, details of manufacture, relative and dollar values given.

The Age of Firearms, a Pictorial History, by Robert Held and Nancy Jenkins. Harper & Bro., N.Y.C., 1957, 192 pp., elegantly and profusely illus. $7.50.
A graphic history of firearms, particularly interesting for the average person with an interest in arms.

Air Guns, by Eldon G. Wolff. Milwaukee Public Museum, Milwaukee, Wis., 1958. 198 pp., illus. Paper, $6.00.
A scholarly and comprehensive treatise, excellent for student and collectors' use, of air gun history. Every form of arm is described, and a list of 350 makers is included.

The American Bayonet, 1776-1964, by A. N. Hardin, Jr. Geo. Shumway, York, Pa., 1964. 252 pp., profusely illus. $20.00.
First comprehensive book on U. S. bayonets of all services, a standard reference for collectors. All bayonets made for long arms are described in full detail, with outstanding photographs, and historical development of principal types. Full references and bibliography.

American, British & Continental Pepperbox Firearms, by Jack Dunlap. H. J. Dunlap, Los Altos, Calif., 1964. 279 pp., 665 illus. $15.00.
Comprehensive history of production pepperpots from early 18th cent. through the cartridge pepperbox. Variations are covered, with much data of value to the collector.

American Engraved Powder Horns, by Stephen V. Grancsay. Originally published by The Metropolitan Museum of Art, at N.Y.C., 1945. The 1st reprint publ. by Ray Riling Arms Books Co., Phila., Pa. 1965. 96 pp. plus 47 full-page plates. $13.50.

A study based on the J. H. Grenville Gilbert collection of historic, rare and beautiful powder horns. A scholarly work by an eminent authority. Long out of print and offered now in a limited edition of 1000 copies.

American Knives, the First History and Collectors' Guide, by Harold L. Peterson. Scribner's, N.Y.C., 1958. 178 pp., well illus. $4.95.

A timely book to whet the appetite of the ever-growing group of knife collectors.

American Polearms, 1526-1865, by R. H. Brown. N. Flayderman Co., New Milford, Conn., 1967. 198 pp., 150 plates. $14.50.

Concise history of pikes, spears, and similar weapons used in American military forces through the Civil War.

American Socket Bayonets, 1717-1873, by D. B. Webster, Jr. Museum Rest. Service, Ottawa, Can. 1964. 48 pp., 60 illus. paperbound. $1.50.

Concise account of major types, with nomenclature, characteristics, and dimensions. Line drawings.

The American Sword 1775-1945, together with *American Silver Mounted Swords 1700-1815,* by Harold L. Peterson. Ray Riling Arms Books Co., Phila., Pa., 1965. 287 and 78 pp. illus. $16.00.

An authoritative survey of the swords worn by the uniformed forces of the United States from the Revolution to the close of World War II, plus the rare reprint of "Silver Mounted Swords" from the exhibition at the Corcoran Gallery of Art. Limited stock.

Ancient Armour and Weapons in Europe, by John Hewitt. Akademische Druck- u. Verlagsanstalt, Graz, Austria, 1967. 3 vols., 1151 total pp., illus. $50.00.

Reprint of a renowned British work first published 1855-1860; covers armor, weapons, military history and tactics through the 17th century.

Antique Pistols, by S. G. Alexander, illus. by Ronald Paton. Arco Publ. Co., New York, 1963. 56 pp., 12 color plates. $15.00.

The large 8-color plates show 14 examples of the pistol-maker's art in England and U.S.A., 1690-1900. Commentary on each by a knowledgeable English collector.

Archaeology of Weapons, by R. E. Oakeshott. F. A. Praeger, New York, 1960. 359 pp., illus. $10.

A scholarly treatise on arms and armor from prehistory to the age of chivalry. It presents a full, accurate, most readable account of the development and use of weapons through this period.

Armes a Feu Francaises Modeles Reglementaires, by J. Boudriot. Paris, 1961-1968. 4 series of booklets; 1st and 2nd series, 5 booklets; 3rd and 4th, 6 booklets. Each series, $6.75, $9.75, $10,75, $11.75, resp.

Detailed survey of all models of French military small arms, 1717-1861, with text in French and fine scale drawings. Each series covers a different period of development; the last covers percussion arms.

Armes Blanches Militaires Francaises, by Christian Aries. P. Petitot, Paris, 1968. Unpaginated, paperbound, 9 volumes. $9.50 per vol., $84.00 complete.

Pictorial survey of French military swords, in French text and line drawings in exact detail. The classifications in the various volumes are the author's own and do not follow any specific sequence. The work must be used as a complete set for maximum benefit.

Le Armi da Fuoco Portatili Italiane, dalle Origini al Risorgimento, by Gen. Agostino Gaibi. Bramante Editrice, Milan, Italy, 1962. 527 pp., 320 illus. (69 in color), in slip case. $65.00

A magnificently produced volume covering Italian hand firearms from their beginning into the 18th cent. Italian text. Superb illus. of historic weapons, engraving, marks, related equipment. A companion book to *Armi e Armature Italiane.*

Armi E Armature Europee, by B. Thomas-O. Gamber-H. Schedelmann, Bramante Editrice, Milano, Italy, 1965. 246 pp., magnificently illus., mainly in full color. $40.00. Ed. ltd. to 1600 copies.

Italian text version of *Arms and Armor of Europe* by the same authors in German text. Text and commentary cover 50 pp., and there are 196 pp. of illus.

Armi e Armature Italiane, Fino al XVIII Secolo, by Aldo Mario Aroldi. Bramante Editrice, Milan, Italy, 1961. 544 pp., profusely illus. (much in color). In slip case, $65.00.

A luxurious work on the golden age of Italian arms makers through the 18th cent., emphasizing body and horse armor, edged weapons, crossbows, early firearms. Italian text. Beautiful and scholarly work for the advanced collector.

Armi E Armature Orientali, by Gianni Vianello, Bramante Editrice, Milano, Italy, 1966. 423 pp. Magnificently illustrated, mainly in full-color tip-ins. $56.00 with slip case. Ed. ltd. to 1600 copies.

A new addition to a notable series of fine books in the arms and armor field. The introduction is 68 pp., 105 pp. of commentary on the 250 pp. of illus.

Arming the Troops, by Paul C. Boehret. Publ. by the author at Chalfont, Pa., 1967. 39 pp., illus. $7.50. The same in paper wrappers $5.00.

A catalog of arms makers of the early years of U.S. history, from 1775 to 1815.

The Armourer and his Craft, by Charles ffoulkes. Frederick Ungar Publ. Co., N.Y., 1967. 199 pp., illus. $18.50.

Standard British reference on body armor, 11th-16th cent.; covering notable makers, construction, decoration, and use. 1st ed. 1912, now reprinted.

Armourers Marks, by D. S. H. Gyngell. Thorsons, Ltd., England, 1959. 131 pp., illus. $6.95.

Some of the marks of armourers, swordsmiths and gunsmiths of almost every foreign country.

Arms and Armor, by Vesey Norman. Putnam's, N.Y.C., 1964. 128 pp., 129 illus. $3.98.

Authoritative, compact coverage of European armor and weapons prior to the age of firearms. Excellent illus., many in color.

Arms & Armor from the Atelier of Ernst Schmidt, Munich, by E. Andrew Mowbray, compiler. Mowbray Co., Providence, R.I., 1967. 168 pp., well illus. $11.95.

Principally a compilation of plates from the extremely rare Schmidt catalog displaying the famous replicas of medieval armor and weapons made in his shop from about 1870 to 1930. Limited edition.

Arms and Armor in Colonial America, 1526-1783, by H. L. Peterson. Crown, New York, reprint ed., 1964. 350 pp., illus. $3.95.

Well-organized account of arms and equipment used in America's colonization and exploration, through the Revolutionary period.

Arms and Armour, 9th to 17th Century, by Paul Martin. C.E. Tuttle Co., Rutland, Vt., 1968. 298 pp., well illus. $15.00.

Beautiful illustrations and authoritative text on armor and accessories from the time of Charlemagne to the firearms era.

Arms and Armour of the Western World, by B. Thomas, O. Gamber & H. Schedelmann. McGraw Hill, N.Y.C., 1964. 252 pp., illus. (much in color), $27.50.

Museum quality weapons and armor shown and described in a magnificent book, which gives the association of specimen arms with the men and events of history. Superb photographs in color. Pub. 1963 in German as "Die Schönsten Waffen . . ." price $25.00.

Arms Collection of Colonel Colt, by R. L. Wilson. Herb Glass, Bullville, N.Y., 1964. 132 pp., 73 illus. Lim. deluxe ed., $16.50; trade ed., $6.50.

Samuel Colt's personal collection is well-described and photographed, plus new technical data on Colt's arms and life. 51 Colt guns and other revolving U.S. and European arms are included.

The Art of the Gunmaker, by J. F. Hayward; Vol. I, 1500-1660; Vol. II, 1660-1830. St. Martin's Press, New York, 1962-64. Vol. I: 303 pp. plus 64 pp. of illus., $15.00; Vol. II: 352 pp., 220 illus., $18.50.

Comprehensive survey of firearms development and ornamentation by leading makers in Europe and the U.S. Prepared by a museum expert with excellent illus., this book offers valuable new information.

Arts of the Japanese Sword, by B. W. Robinson. Chas. E. Tuttle Co., Rutland, Vt., 1961. 110 pp. of descriptive text with illus., plus 100 full page plates, some in full color. $10.00.

An authoritative work, divided into 2 parts—the first on blades, tracing their history to the present day; the second on mounts and fittings. It includes forging processes; accounts of the important schools of swordsmiths; techniques employed, plus a useful appendix on care and cleaning.

Ballard Rifles in the H. J. Nunnemacher Coll., by Eldon G. Wolff. Milwaukee Public Museum, Milwaukee, Wisc., 2nd ed. 1961. Paper, 77 p. plus 4 pp. of charts and 27 plates. $2.50.

A thoroughly authoritative work on all phases of the famous rifles, their parts, patent and manufacturing history.

Basic Documents on U.S. Martial Arms, commentary by Col. B. R. Lewis, reissue by Ray Riling, Phila., Pa., 1956 and 1960.

Rifle Musket Model 1855. The first issue rifle of musket caliber, a muzzle loader equipped with the Maynard primer, 32 pp. $2.00.

Rifle Musket Model 1863. The typical Union muzzle-loader of the Civil War, 26 pp. $1.25.

Breech-Loading Rifle Musket Model 1866. The first of our 50 caliber breechloading rifles, 12 pp. $1.25.

Remington Navy Rifle Model 1870. A commercial type breech-loader made at Springfield, 16 pp. $1.25.

Lee Straight Pull Navy Rifle Model 1895. A magazine cartridge arm of 6mm caliber. 23 pp. $2.75.

Breech-Loading Rifle Musket Model 1868. The first 50-70 designed as such. 20 pp. $1.50.

Peabody Breech-Loading Arms (five models)—27 pp. $2.25.

Ward-Burton Rifle Musket 1871—16 pp. $2.00.

Springfield Rifle, Carbine & Army Revolvers (cal. 45) Model 1873 including Colt and Smith & Wesson hand arms. 52 pp. $2.25.

U.S. Magazine Rifle and Carbine (cal. 30) Model 1892 (the Krag Rifle) 36 pp. $2.50.

Bayonets, an Illustrated History and Reference Guide, by F. J. Stephens. Arms and Armour Press, London, 1968. 76 pp., stiff paper wrappers, 134 photographs. $3.75.

A general historical survey of all categories of the weapon, from the U.S. and many other countries.

Bilderatlas zum Grundriss der Waffenlehre, by K.T. vonSauer. Pawlas, Nurnberg, Germany, 1968. Paper folder containing 28 pp. text and 26 plates. $7.50.

Facsimile of an 1869 set of plates depicting military rifles of Germany, with explanatory pamphlet in German text.

The Book of the Continental Soldier, by Harold L. Peterson. Stackpole Books, Harrisburg, Pa., 1968. 287 pp., of large format profusely illus. with halftone, line, and including art work by H. Charles McBarron, Jr., Clyde A. Risley and Peter Copeland. $12.95.

A thorough and commendable work in every pertinent aspect. Covers in satisfying detail every facet of the soldier's existence.

Book of the 22, by Richard Arnold. Barnes & Co., N.Y.C., 1962. 188 pp., illus., $2.95.

Authoritative data for the 22 rifleman and pistoleer, detailing arms of this caliber in use throughout the world, history of the weapons and cartridges.

Bowie Knives, by R. Abels. Pub. by the author, N.Y.C., 1960. 48 pp. profusely illus. Paper covers. $2.00.

A booklet showing knives, tomahawks, related trade cards and advertisements.

Brass Spikes & Horsehair Plumes: A Study of U.S. Army Dress Helmets, 1872-1903, by Gordon Chappell, Arizona Pioneers Hist. Soc., Tucson, Ariz. 1966. 50 pp., illus. Paper covers. $2.00.

Historical monograph on military headgear of the period.

The Breech-Loader in the Service, 1816-1917, by Claud E. Fuller, N. Flayderman, New Milford, Conn., 1965. 381 pp., illus. $14.50.

Revised ed. of a 1933 historical reference on U.S. standard and experimental military shoulder arms. Much patent data, drawings, and photographs of the arms.

A voluminous work that covers handloading—and other things—in great detail. Replete with data for all cartridge forms.

British Military Bayonets from 1700 to 1945, by R.J.W. Latham. Arco Publ. Co., N.Y.C., 1969. 94 pp., illus. $8.50.

History and identification catalog of British bayonets, with fine illustrations, marks, dimensions, and equipment of various British army units.

British Military Firearms 1650-1850, by H. L. Blackmore. Arco Publ. Co. Inc., New York, 1962. 296 pp. and 83 plates of photographs, line drawings, appendices and index. $10.00.

This excellent work admirably and authoritatively covers the subject in every detail. Highly recommended.

British Military Swords, From 1800 to the Present Day, by J. W. Latham, Crown Publishers, N.Y., 1967, 91 pp., illus. $3.95.

Survey of British swords used by various branches of the Army, with data on their manufacture, specifications, and procurement.

British Pistols and Guns, 1640-1940, by Ian Glendenning. Arco Publ. Co., N.Y., 1967. 194 pp., photos and drawings. $7.50.

Historical review of British firearms, with much data and illustration of furniture and decoration of fine weapons.

The British Soldier's Firearm, 1850-1864, by C. H. Roads. Herbert Jenkins, London, 1964. 332 pp., illus. $12.50.

Detailed account of development of British military arms at the acme of the muzzle-loading period. All models in use are covered, as well as ammunition.

The Canadian Gunsmiths 1608-1900, by S. James Gooding. Museum Restoration Service, Canada, 1962. 322 pp., illus. $17.50.
Comprehensive survey of the gunmakers of Canada and the products of their skill, from early settlement to the age of the breech-loader.

Cartridge Headstamp Guide, by H. P. White and B. D. Munhall. H. P. White Laboratory, Bel Air, Md., 1963. 263 pp., illus. $10.00.
An important reference on headstamping of small arms ammo, by manufacturers in many countries. Clear illus. of 1936 headstamps of every type.

Cartridges, by H. C. Logan, Standard Public., Inc., Huntington, W. Va., 1948. 204 pp., illus. $2.98, Deluxe First ed. $10.00.
"Pictorial digest of small arms ammunition," with excellent line illus. and competent text for collectors of obsolete ammunition. In very limited supply, being the scarce out-of-print and best original edition.

Cartridges for Collectors, by Fred A. Datig. Borden Publishing Co., Alhambra, Calif., Vol. I (Centerfire), 1958; Vol. II (Rimfire and Misc. Types, 1963; Vol. III (Additional Rimfire, Centerfire, and Plastic), 1967. Each of the three volumes 176 pp., well illus. and each priced at $7.50.
Vol. III supplements the first two books and presents 300 additional specimens. All illus. are shown in full-scale line drawings.

Civil War Carbines, by A. F. Lustyik. World Wide Gun Report, Inc., Aledo, Ill., 1962. 63 pp., illus. paper covers. $2.00.
Accurate, interesting summary of most carbines of the Civil War period, in booklet form, with numerous good illus.

Civil War Collector's Encyclopedia, by Francis A. Lord. Stackpole Books, Harrisburg, Pa., 1963. 384 pp., 350 illus. $17.95.
A reference work on Civil War relics, for museums, students, writers, and collectors of Union and Confederate items. Identifies arms, uniforms, accoutrements, ordnance material, currency, postage, etc. Many patent drawings. Lists of manufacturers and vendors, North and South, are given.

Civil War Guns, by Wm. B. Edwards. Stackpole Books, Harrisburg, Pa., 1962. 464 pp., over 400 illus. $15.00.
Comprehensive survey of Civil War arms, identification data, procurement procedures, and historical data. Important information on replicas, imitations, and fakes.

Classic Bowie Knives, by Robert Abels. R. Abels, Inc., N.Y., 1967. 97 pp., illus. with numerous fine examples of the subject. $7.50.
A nostalgic story of the famous blades, with trade adverts on them, and photos of users.

The Collecting of Guns, ed. by Jas. E. Serven. Stackpole Books, Harrisburg, Pa., 1964. 272 pp., illus. $24.50.
A new and massive compendium of gun lore for serious collectors by recognized experts. Separate chapters cover major categories and aspects of collecting. Over 600 firearms illus. Handsomely designed, deluxe binding in slip case. Reprint of 1966, $5.95.

Collector's Guide to American Cartridge Handguns, by DeWitt E. Sell. Stackpole Books, Harrisburg, Pa., 1963. 234 pp., illus. $3.98.
Catalogs the important U.S. makers in its field, with histories of the firms and their production models. Photos, descriptions and features of many older and current handguns are included.

Collectors' Guns, by Don Myrus. Arco Publ. Co., Inc., New York, 1962. 128 pp., illus. $3.50.
The fascinating story of firearms—from the early hand cannon to the Peacemaker—with over 200 rare photographs and illus.

Collector's Item Sears, Roebuck Catalog. The Gun Digest Co., Chicago, Ill., 1969. 730 pp., profuse illus. including 45 pp. of old guns. Paperbound. $6.95.
A reprint of the 1908 Sears catalog, destined to be a treasured replica for the archives of history.

Colt Firearms from 1836, by James E. Serven. Foundation Press, Santa Ana, Calif., 1964. 398 pp., illus. $17.95.
5th edition of a comprehensive work on Colt guns, with much historical data, patents, drawings and photographs of the various models. Most complete and reliable work on its subject.

Colt Gun Book, by Lucian Cary. Arco Publ. Co. Inc., New York, 1961. 142 pp., profusely illus. $3.50.
A Colt picture book, showing the guns and the men who used them, with much data on the noted outlaws and touching on the inventor.

Colt's Variations of the Old Model Pocket Pistol, 1848 to 1872, by P. L. Shumaker. Borden Publishing Co., Alhambra, Calif., 1966. A reprint of the 1957 edition. 150 pp., illus. $6.00.
A useful tool for the Colt specialist and a welcome return of a popular source of information that had been long out-of-print.

The Complete Book of Gun Collecting, by Charles E. Chapel. Coward-McCann Inc., N.Y.C., 1960. 222 pp., illus. $4.50.
Answers hundreds of questions for the beginner, and is a reference for the advanced collector and student of firearms. It covers hand cannon of the 14th century to arms of the present day.

Confederate Arms, by Wm. A. Albaugh III, and E. N. Simmons. Stackpole Books, Harrisburg, Pa., 1957. 278 pp., illus. $12.50.
Contains much heretofore unpublished information on the arms and associated material of the Confederacy.

Confederate Handguns, by Wm. A. Albaugh III. Hugh Benet Jr., and Edw. N. Simmons. Geo. Shumway, York, Pa., 1963. 272 pp., 125 illus. $16.00.
Every known true Confederate pistol and revolver is described and illus., with the story of its maker and procurement by the C.S.A. Much new information. Includes listing of C. W. makers and dealers, information on replicas and fakes. Indispensable to the collector and student of these arms and their period.

The Crossbow, by Sir Ralph Payne-Gallwey, Bramhall House, New York, 1968. A reprint in facsimile. 328 pp., well illus. including appendices and a treatise on Oriental bows. $4.95.
The standard, respected work on medieval and later military and sporting crossbows—their construction, history and management.

Cut and Thrust Weapons, by E. Wagner. Spring Books, London, 1967. 491 pp., line drawings. $17.50.
English translation of a survey of European edged weapons, their traditions, manufacture, and use.

Digest of Patents Relating to Breech-Loading and Magazine Small Arms (1836-1873), by V. D. Stockbridge, Washington, 1874. Reprinted 1963 by E. N. Flayderman, Greenwich, Conn. 180 pp., 880 illus. $12.50.
An exhaustive compendium of patent documents on firearms, indexed and classified by breech mechanism types. Valuable reference for students and collectors.

Duelling Pistols, by J. A. Atkinson. Stackpole Books, Harrisburg, Pa. 144 pp., illus. (incl. color plates), $12.95.
Account of duelling practice in Great Britain, with data on various types of pistols, their makers, and their users. Memorable duels are recalled, and a bibliography is included.

Early American Gunsmiths 1650-1850, by H. J. Kauffman. Bramhall House, N.Y., 1968. 2nd reprint. 94 pp., illus. $1.98.
A record of the men and the arms they made.

Early Percussion Firearms, by Lewis Winant. Wm. Morrow & Co., Inc., N.Y.C., 1959. 292 pp., illus. $2.98.
A history of early percussion firearms ignition—from Forsyth to Winchester 44-40, from flintlocks of the 18th century to centerfires. Over 230 illus. of firearms, parts, patents, and cartridges—from some of the finest collections here and abroad.

English, Irish and Sottish Firearms, by A. Merwyn Carey. Arco Publishing Co., Inc., N.Y., 1967. A reprint. 121 pp., illus. in line and halftone. $6.50.
Out-of-print since 1954, this work covers the subject from the middle of the 16th century to the end of the 19th.

English Pistols & Revolvers, by J. N. George. Arco Publ. Co., Inc., N.Y.C., 1962. 256 pp., 28 plates. $6.00.
The 2nd reprinting of a notable work first publ. in 1938. Treats of the historical development and design of English hand firearms from the 17th cent. to the present. A much better book than the former reprint, particularly as to clarity of the tipped-in plates.

European & American Arms, by Claude Blair, Batsford, London, and Crown Publ., N.Y.C., 1962, 192 pp., 9" x 12". Profusely and magnificently illus. $6.95.
A complete visual encyclopedia on all sorts of arms of Europe and America with over 600 photographs of pieces from nearly all the major collections of Western Europe, America, and Russia, from about 1100 to 1850. A splendid text describes histroical and technical developments.

European Armour in the Tower of London, by A.R. Dufty. H.M. Stationery Office, London, England, 1968. 17 pp. text, 164 plates. $12.60.
Pictorial record of almost 400 pieces of armor, helmets, and accouterments in the famous Tower of London collection.

European Arms & Armour, by Chas. H. Ashdown. Brussel & Brussel, N.Y., 1967. A reprint. 384 pp., illus. with 42 plates and 450 drawings. $5.95.
Historical survey of body armor up to the era of gunpowder, with some coverage on weapons and early firearms.

European Arms and Armour, Wallace Collection, by Sir James Mann. The Wallace Collection, London, 1962. 2 vols., 714 pp., 208 plates. $9.75.
A new edition of the catalog of an important British collection, containing historical notes and fine illus. Vol. I, on armor; Vol. II on arms of all types and accessory equipment.

The Evolution of the Colt, by R. L. Wilson, R. Q. Sutherland, Kansas City, Mo., 1967. 54 pp., illus. $3.00.
Pictures the fine Colt arms of the publisher from percussion to cartridge. Includes a Colt bibliography.

Famous Guns from the Smithsonian Collection, by H. W. Bowman. Arco Publ. Co., Inc., New York, 1967. 112 pp., illus. $3.50.
The finest of the "Famous Guns" series.

Famous Guns from the Winchester Collection, by H. W. Bowman. Arco Publ. Co., N.Y.C., 1958 and later. 144 pp., illus. Paperbound. 75¢.
The gems of the hand and shoulder arms in the great collection at New Haven, Conn.

'51 Colt Navies, by N. L. Swayze. Gun Hill Publ. Co., Yazoo City, Miss., 1967. 243 pp., well illus. $15.00.
The first major effort devoting its entire space to the 1851 Colt Navy revolver. There are 198 photos of models, sub-models, variations, parts, markings, documentary material, etc. Fully indexed.

Firearms, by Howard Ricketts. G. P. Putnam's Sons, N.Y.C., 1962. 128 pp., illus., slip case, $5.95.
An entertaining and colorful summary of the development and use of firearms. Excellent illus. of collectors' arms and related history.

Firearms Curiosa, by Lewis Winant. Ray Riling, Philadelphia, Pa. 2nd and deluxe reissue 1961, 281 pp., well illus. $8.50.
Two reissues publ. by Bonanza Books, N.Y., 1965. Same size as above, $2.98. A smaller size, 1968. $1.98.
An important work for those with an interest in odd, distinctive and unusual forms and firing

Firearms in England in the Fourteenth Century, by T.F. Tout. Geo. Shumway, York, Pa., 1958. 58 pp., illus., paper covers. $4.00.
Reprint of a 1911 monograph on the history and manufacture of early British firearms, by a distinguished historian.

The Flintlock, Its Origin and Development, by Torsten Lenk; J. T. Hayward, Editor. Holland Press, London, 1964. 192 pp., 134 illus. $6.95.
First English-text version of the 1939 Swedish work termed "the most important book on the subject." Original illus. are reproduced, and a new index and bibliography complete this valuable book.

Flintlock Pistols, by F. Wilkinson. Stackpole Books, Harrisburg, Pa., 1968. 75 pp., illus. $4.95.
Illustrated reference guide by a British authority, covering 17th-19th century flintlock pistols.

The Francis Bannerman Catalog. Francis Bannerman Co., N.Y.C., 1965. 262 pp., large format, paperbound. $5.00.
The 1965 release of a famous arms firm, used over the years by most arms collectors. Also available: a reprinting of a 1903 Bannerman catalog, 118 pp., well illus., $3.00.

The French Army in America, by E. P. Hamilton. Museum Restoration Service, Ottawa, 1967. 108 pp., illus. $3.00.
Concise historical coverage, illus. with contemporary documents and manual-of-arms plates. Text in English and French. Paper wrappers.

French Military Weapons, 1717-1938, by James E. Hicks. N. Flayderman & Co., New Milford, Conn. 1964. 281 pp., profusely illus. $9.50.
A valuable reference work, first publ. 1938 as *Notes on French Ordnance,* this rev. ed. covers hand, shoulder, and edged weapons, ammunition and artillery, with history of various systems.

The Fuller Collection of American Firearms, by H. L. Peterson. Eastern National Park & Monument Assn., 1967. 63 pp., illus. $2.50.
Illustrated catalog of principal military shoulder arms in the collection. Decorated paper wrappers.

The Gatling Gun, by Paul Wahl & D. R. Toppel. Arco Publ., N.Y.C., 1965. 168 pp., illus. $4.95.
History of the famed rapid-fire weapon used by many of the world's armies and navies from 1861.

German Submachine Guns and Assault Rifles. WE, Inc., Old Greenwich, Conn., 1967. 161 pp. $5.95.
Aberdeen Proving Ground reports on over 50 models of World War II German rapid-fire weapons are reprinted.

Die Geschichtliche Entwicklung Der Handfeuerwaffen, by M. Thierbach, Akademische Druck, Graz, Austria, 1965. Vol. I, 590 pp., German text; Vol. II, 36 plates. $37.00.
The famous German work on history and development of firearms, accessories and ammunition, first published in 1886 in Dresden.

A Glossary of the Construction, Decoration and Use of Arms and Armor in all Countries and in all Times, by Geo. C. Stone, Jack Brussel, New York, 2nd reprint, 1966. 694 pp., illus. $9.95.
The outstanding work on its subject, authoritative and accurate in detail. The major portion is on oriental arms.

The Gun and its Development, by W. W. Greener. Bonanza Books, N.Y., 1967. A reprint. 804 pp., profusely illus. $7.95.
A facsimile of the famous 9th edition of 1910. Covers history and development of arms in general, with emphasis on shotguns.

The Gun Collector's Handbook of Values, by C.E. Chapel. Coward-McCann, N.Y.C., 1968. 398 pp., illus. $10.00.
The 8th rev. ed. of the best-known values reference for collectors, with prices for 1969-1970.

Gunmakers of Indiana, by A.W. Lindert. Publ. by the author, Homewood, Ill., 1968, 3rd ed. 284 pp., illus. Large format. $15.00.
An extensive and historical treatment, illus. with old photographs and drawings.

Guns of the Old West, by C. E. Chapel. Coward-McCann Inc., N.Y.C., 1961. 306 pp., illus. $4.95.
A definitive book on American arms that opened the frontier and won the West. Shows arms, rare pictures, advertisements, and pertinent associated material.

Guns Through the Ages, by Geoffrey Boothroyd. Sterling Publ. Co., N.Y.C., 1962. 192 pp., illus. $1.69.
A detailed illustrated history of small arms from the invention of gunpowder to today. Covers ignition methods, proof marks, fakes, ammo, etc. Bibliography.

Haandskydevaabens Bedommelse, by Johan F. Stockel. Udgivet Af Tojuhusmuseet, Copenhagen, Denmark. 2nd.limited reprint, 1966. Vol. I, 397 pp. plus 6 plates, Vol. II, 1080 pp. illus., Both $20.00.
Printed in Danish but considered by scholars to be the finest and most complete source for the "marks" and "touches" of gunmakers. Both are well illus.

Handbuch Der Waffenkunde, by Wendelin Boeheim. Akademische D. u. V., Graz, Austria, 1966. 694 pp., illus. $14.00.
One of the famous works of 1890—long out-of-print. Now in a new printing. German text. Historical weapons and armor from the Middle Ages through the 18th century.

Die Handfeuerwaffen, by Rudolf Schmidt. Vienna, Austria, 1968. Vol. I, text 225 pp., Vol. II, 76 plates. $20.00.
Reprint of an important 1875 German reference work on military small arms, much prized by knowledgeable collectors. The fine color plates in Vol. II show detailed and exploded views of many longarms and handguns.

Hawken Rifles, The Mountain Man's Choice, by John D. Baird. Baird Publ., Pence, Ind., 1968. 95 pp., illus. $15.00.
Covers the rifles developed for the Western fur trade. Numerous specimens are described and shown in photographs.

Henry Deringer's Pocket Pistol, by John E. Parsons. Morrow, N.Y.C., 1952. Over 70 illustrations. $7.50.
An excellent and complete account of this famous maker, coupled with an extensive story on Deringer's imitators, the later cartridge derringers, etc.

Hints to Riflemen, by H. W. S. Cleveland. Distributor, Robert Halter, New Hope, Pa., 286 pp., illustrated. $6.50.
A reprint of the original 1864 edition, to which *Practical Directions for the Use of the Rifle* has been added.

A History of the Colt Revolver, by C. T. Haven and F. A. Belden. Bonanza Books, N.Y., 1967. A reprint. 711 pages large format, profusely illus. in line and halftone. $8.95.
A great and massive work, including details on other Colt arms from 1836 to 1940. A must for every Colt collector.

A History of Firearms, by W. Y. Carman. Routledge & Kegan Paul Ltd., London, England, 1955. 207 pp., illus. $4.50.
A concise coverage, from earliest times to 1914, with emphasis on artillery.

A History of Firearms, by H. L. Peterson. Chas. Scribner's Sons, N.Y.C., 1961. 57 pp., profusely illus. $3.50.
From the origin of firearms through each ignition form and improvement to the M-14. Drawings by Daniel D. Feaser.

History of Modern U.S. Military Small Arms Ammunition, by F. W. Hackley, W. H. Woodin and E. L. Scranton. Macmillan, N.Y.C., 1967. 315 pp., 8½"x11", over 500 exact-scale drawings and 100 photos. $25.00.
A superb work based on years of research by the capable authors. Covers cartridges for handguns, rifles and machine guns; miscellaneous, experimental and unidentified rounds, etc.

A History of Spanish Firearms, by James D. Lavin. Arco Co., New York, 1965. 304 pp., illus. $9.95.
This history, beginning with the recorded appearance of gunpowder in Spain, traces the development of hand firearms through their golden age — the eighteenth century — to the death in 1825 of Isidro Soler. Copious reproductions of short and long arms, list of gun makers and their "marks" a glossary, bibliography and index are included.

A History of Weaponry, by Courtlandt Canby, Hawthorne Books, Inc., New York, 1963. 112 pp., illus. $2.98.
From the caveman's club to the M-14 rifle, from Greek fire to the ICBM.

The History of Winchester Firearms 1866-1966, ed. by T. E. Hall and P. Kuhlhoff, Winchester-Western Press, New Haven, Conn., 1966. 159 pp., illus. $10.00.
Called the collector's item of the century, this 3d ed. of Geo. R. Watrous' work rises to new glory in its scope and illustrations. Beautifully produced, with a slip case showing old hunting scenes by A. B. Frost and Frederic Remington. Limited ed.

Identifying Old U.S. Muskets, Rifles & Carbines, by Col. A. Gluckman. Stackpole Books, Harrisburg, Pa., 1965. 487 pp., illus. $10.00.
Collector's guide to U.S. long arms, first publ. 1959. Numerous models of each type are described and shown, with histories of their makers.

An Introduction to British Artillery in North America, by S. J. Gooding. Museum Rest. Serv., Ottawa, 1965. 54 pp., illus., Paperbound, $1.50.
Concise account of such equipment used in America 1750-1850.

Japanese Armour, by L. J. Anderson. Stackpole Books, Harrisburg, Pa., 1968. 84 pp., illus. $4.95.
British reference on museum quality armor made by the Myochin and Saotome families between the 15th and 20th centuries.

Japanese Polearms, by R. M. Knutsen. Holland Press, London, 1963. 271 pp., well-illus. Line drawings and photos. $18.00.
Each category of Japanese spear is described and illus. in this hist. treatment, including schools of spear and sword fencing. Lists leading makers and glossary.

Japanese Sword Blades, by Alfred Dobree. George Shumway, York, Pa., 1967. 39 pp., illus., in paper wrappers. $4.50.
A two-part monograph, reprinted from a notable work.

The Kentucky Rifle, by J. G. W. Dillin. Geo. Shumway, York, Pa., 1967. 5th ed. 202 pp., illus. $20.00.
A respected work on the long rifles developed in colonial days and carried by pioneers and soldiers. Much information of value to collectors and historians. Limited ed.

Longrifles of North Carolina, by John Bivins, Jr. Geo. Shumway, York, Pa., 1968. 200 pp., profusely illus. $24.00.
Historical survey of North Carolina gunmakers and their production during the 18th and 19th centuries. Over 400 gunsmiths are included. Fine photographs.

Longrifles of Note, by Geo. Shumway, Geo. Shumway, York, Pa., 1967. 90 pp., illus. Paper covers. $3.95.
A review of 35 fine American long rifles, with detailed illustrations showing their art work, plus descriptive material.

The Luger Pistol, by Fred A. Datig. Privately published, Los Angeles, Calif., 1962. 328 pp. well-illus. $8.50.
Larger, revised ed. of the story behind the most famous pistol of all time.

Manhattan Firearms, by Waldo E. Nutter, Stackpole Books, Harrisburg, Pa., 1958. 250 pp., illus., in halftone. $10.00.
Complete history of the Manhattan Firearms Mfg. Co., and its products. Excellent specialized reference.
A very small number of copies, bound in full leather, autographed and numbered, are available. $25.00.

The Mantons: Gunmakers, by W. Keith Neal and D. H. L. Back, Walker & Co., New York, 1966. 300 pp., illus. $25.00.
Well-documented account of the life and work of John and Joseph Manton, and others of the British gunmakers. A long list, with serial numbers, etc., of Manton guns, is included.

The Manufacture of Armour and Helmets in 16th Century Japan by Sakakibara Kozan. Holland Press, London, 1963. 156 pp., 32 pp. of illus. $20.00.
Important reference on styles and steps of making Japanese armor, first publ. Tokyo, 1800. Eng. trans., revised by H. R. Robinson of Tower of London Armouries.

Master French Gunsmiths' Designs reproduced in facsimile with preface notes by S. V. Grancsay. Greenberg, N.Y.C., 1950. 22 pp. text plus 15 pp. illus. $8.50.
Originally published in a limited ed. @ $15.00. Available only from Ray Riling.

Metal Uniform Insignia of the US Army in the Southwest, 1846-1902, by S. B. Brinckerhoff, Arizona Pioneers Hist. Soc., Tucson, Ariz., 1965. 28 pp., illus. Paper covers. $1.00.
Monograph on buttons, badges, buckles, and other uniform insignia.

Metallic Cartridges, T. J. Treadwell, compiler. The Armoury, N.Y.C., 1959. Unpaginated. 68 plates. Paper, $2.95. Cloth, $5.95.
A reduced-size reproduction of U.S. Ordnance Memoranda No. 14, originally publ. in 1873, on regulation and experimental cartridges manufactured and tested at Frankford Arsenal, Philadelphia, Pa.

Military Arms of Canada, by Upper Canada Hist. Arms Soc. Museum Restoration Serv., West Hill, Ont., 1963. 43 pp., illus. $1.50.
Booklet cont. 6 authoritative articles on the principal models of Canadian mil. small arms. Gives characteristics of each, makers, quantities produced.

Military Edged Weapons of the World, 1880-1965, by H. A. Maeurer. Mauerer, College Pt., N.Y., 1967. 151 pp., illus. $4.50.
Various swords, blades, etc., in a private collection are dimensioned, described, and photographed. A guide for collectors. Paper wrappers.

Military Headgear in the Southwest, 1846-1890, by S. B. Brinckerhoff, Arizona Pioneers Hist. Soc., Tucson, Ariz., 1963. 16 pp., illus. Paper covers. $1.00.
Historical monograph, reprinted from the journal *Arizoniana*. With bibliography.

Military Sharps Rifles and Carbines, by R. E. Hopkins. Hopkins, Campbell, Calif., 1967. 141 pp., illus. $11.50.
A guide to the principal types, with photographs, patent data, technical details, etc.

More Single-Shot Rifles, by James J. Grant. Wm. Morrow & Co., Inc., N.Y.C., 1959. 332 pp., illus. $7.50.
In this new work, a companion book to the author's *Single-Shot Rifles*, will be found new facts on U.S. and other single shot arms. 19 pages from a German catalog are featured, plus patent drawings of Borchardt, Farquharson, Henry and others.

Louis Napoleon on Artillery: The Development of Artillery from the 14th to the 17th Century, by W. Y. Carman, Arms and Armour Press, Middlesex, England, 1967. 24 pp., illus. Paper covers. $2.75.
A reprinting of rare original material—10 finely engraved plates, with 70 drawings, on the development of artillery, plus brief text.

The New Highland Military Discipline, by Geo. Grant. Museum Restoration Service, Ottawa, 1967. 32 pp., illus. $1.50.
Reprint of a Scottish drill manual, regimental history, with illus. contemporary and modern. Paper wrappers.

The 9-pdr. Muzzle Loading Rifle, by J. D. Chown. Museum Restoration Service, Ottawa, 1967. 32 pp., Illus. $1.50.
Reprint of an early Canadian artillery manual, with historical notes. Paper wrappers.

Notes on Canadian Shotshells, by N. Krevosheia and A. M. Provick, compilers. N. Krevosheia, Edmonton, Canada, 1967. Paper wrappers, 32 pp., illus. $2.00.
An illustrated handbook for collectors with line drawings and photos of domestic, contract, export and miscellaneous shells and their boxes, etc.

One Hundred Great Guns, by Merrill Lindsay. Walker & Co., N.Y., 1967. 379 pp., fine color illus. $14.95.
Deluxe illus. history of firearms, covering all principal types of small arms and their makers. Bibliography.
A super-deluxe edition is available at $75.00.

Oriental Armour, by W. R. Robinson, Walker and Co., New York, 1967. 257 pp., illus. $12.50.
The author traces the evolution of Oriental armor from ancient times to the period in which it was finally discarded.

BOOKS

The Original Mauser Magazine Sporting Rifles. Shooter's Bible, S. Hackensack, N.J. 56 pp., illus., paperbound. $1.00.
Facsimile reprint of a Mauser firearms brochure, with English text.

The Peacemaker and Its Rivals, by John E. Parsons. Morrow, N.Y.C., 1950. 140 pp., illustrated. Appendix, bibilography, and index. $7.50.
Detailed history and development of the Single Action Army Colt, with an over-all study of the six-shooter's significance in American history.

The Pennsylvania-Kentucky Rifle, by Henry J. Kauffman. Bonanza Books, N.Y., 1968. A reprint. 374 pp., illus. $3.95.
A classic work first publ. in 1960 on early long rifles. Makers, descriptions, and manufacturing methods are covered.

Photographic Supplement of Confederate Swords, by Wm. A. Albaugh III. Wm. A Bond, Vernon, Tex., 1963. 205 pp., 300 photos. $6.95.
Over 200 specimens of C. W. edged weapons are shown, with data on their owners and makers. Useful for collectors and students.

The Powder Flask Book, by Ray Riling. Bonanza Books, N. Y. 1968. A reprint. 520 pp., large format, profusely illus. First re-issue of the 1953 original ed. $9.95. A limited number of the originals are available for inscription and autograph at $50.00.
Covers the literature on flasks, their makers, and users—hunters, shooters and the military—as well as showing the arms, cased or not, short and long. A relative price listing for collector advantage is included.

The Rampant Colt, by R.L. Wilson. Thomas Haas, Spencer, Ind., 1969. 107 pp., well illus. $10.00.
Study of Samuel Colt's coat-of-arms and the rampant colt figure used on Colt firearms and in advertising.

Rapiers, by Eric Valentine. Stackpole Books, Harrisburg, Pa., 1968. 76 pp., 58 photos., 3 drawings. $4.95.
A desirable monograph, first on its subject, to be publ. in English. Covers methods of authentication, renovation, cleaning and preservation.

Remington Handguns, by C. L. and C. R. Karr. Crown, N.Y.C., 3rd ed., 1956, 60 plates, 166 pp. $2.49.
An enlargement of their fine first edition, the Karrs have added 12 new illustrations and considerable text material. Valuable and informative. The standard reference on Remington pistols.

The Remington Historical Treasury of American Guns, by Harold L. Peterson. Thomas Nelson & Sons, N.Y.C., 1966. 199 pp., illus. $1.95.
A historical saga woven into first-rate Americana through the facts and details of the Remington firm and their products.

The Revolver, Its Description, Management, and Use, by P. E. Dove. Arms and Armour Press, London, 1968. 57 pp., 6 engravings, stiff paper wrappers. $3.75.
A facsimile reprint of a rare classic, dealing principally with the Adams revolver compared to the qualities of the Colt.

Revolving Arms, by A. W. F. Taylerson, Walker and Co., New York, 1967. 123 pp., illus. $8.50.
A detailed history of mechanically-rotated cylinder firearms in Europe and the U.S. Primarily on handguns, but other types of revolving guns are included.

Rifled Infantry Arms, by J. Schon; trans. by Capt. J. Gorgas, USA. Dresden, 1855; facsimile reprint by W. E. Meuse, Schuylersville, N.Y., 1965. 54 pp., illus. $2.50.
Reprint of classic essay on European military small arms of the mid-19th century. Paper covers.

The Rifled Musket, by Claud E. Fuller. Stackpole Books, Harrisburg, Pa., 1958. 302 pp., illus. $10.00.
The authoritative work of the late Claud E. Fuller and basically an account of the muskets whose model dates fell within the Civil War years—1861, 1863 and 1864. Part Two treats of the contract muskets. Some reproduced material, notably Bartlett & Gallatin's "Digest of Cartridges," is almost wholly illegibile, as is much of an 1860 Ordnance Dept. report.

G. Roth Aktiengesellschaft. Horn Co., Burlington, Vt., 1968. 28 pp., illus., paperbound. $2.50.
Reprint of a German cartridge catalog of 1913, with drawings and dimensions.

Royal Sporting Guns at Windsor, by H.L. Blackmore. H.M. Stationery Office, London, England, 1968. 60 pp. text, 52 plates. $9.54.
Catalog of the most decorative and interesting guns in the Royal Armoury collection at Windsor Castle.

Russian Pistols in the 17th Century, by L. Tarassuk. Geo. Shumway, York, Pa., 1968. 35 pp. plus plates. $4.00.
Monograph on museum quality Russian handguns of the 17th century. Fine, detailed photographs.

Samuel Colt Presents, R. L. Wilson, compiler. Wadsworth Atheneum, Hartford, Conn., 1961. 293 pp., profusely illus. $10.00.
Showing and describing a profusion of rare and super-rare museum-quality Colt arms exhibited at the Atheneum, it is one of the most important and desirable books on rare Colt arms.

Samuel Colt's New Model Pocket Pistols, by S. G. Keogh. Priv. publ., 1964. 31 pp., 20 illus., paperbound. $3.00.
"The story of the 1855 Root model revolver," with detailed classification data and descriptions. Well-illus.

The Samurai Swords, by J. M. Yumoto. Tuttle Co., Rutland, Vt., 1958. 191 pp., illus. $4.50.
Detailed information on evaluation of specimens, including origin and development of the Japanese blade.

Savage Automatic Pistols, by James R. Carr. Publ. by the author, St. Charles, Ill., 1967. A reprint. 129 pp., illus. with numerous photos. $6.50.
Collector's guide to Savage pistols, models 1907-1922, with features, production data, and pictures of each. A reprint of the circa 1912 Savage promotional and instructive booklet titled *It Banishes Fear* is recommended to accompany the above. Paper wrappers, 32 pp. $1.50.

Schuyler, Hartley & Graham Catalog. Publ. by Norm Flayderman, Greenwich, Conn., 1961. 176 pp., illus. $9.50.
A reprint of a rare 1864 catalog of firearms, military goods, uniforms, etc. An extensive source of information for Civil War collectors.

The Sharps Rifle, by W. O. Smith. Morrow, N.Y.C., 1943, reprinted 1965. 138 pp., illus. $8.50.
Study of America's first successful breech-loader patented 1848, with information on its history, development, and operation.

Shosankenshu, by H. L. Joly. Holland Press, London, 1963. Unpaginated. $12.50.
List of Japanese artists' names and kakihan found on sword furniture by the late European authority. Completed in 1919, previously unpubl., this is a facsimile of Joly's MS. and line drawings. Lists nearly 3,000 names.

Single Shot Rifles, by Frank de Haas. The Gun Digest Assn., Chicago, Ill., 1968. 288 pp. within decorated paper wrappers, profusely illus. $7.95.
A comprehensive analysis of over 55 significant single shot rifles and actions, replete with mechanical details. Biographies of the inventors, history, pertinent dates and design commentary included.

Single-Shot Rifles, by James J. Grant. Wm. Morrow & Co., N.Y.C., 4th printing 1964. 385 pp., illus. $8.50.
A detailed study of these rifles by a noted collector.

Small Arms, by Frederick Wilkinson, Hawthorne Books, Inc., New York, 1966. 256 pp., illus. $4.95.
A history of small firearms, techniques of the gunsmith, equipment used by combatants, sportsmen and hunters.

Small Arms and Ammunition in the United States Service, 1776-1865, by B.R. Lewis. Smithsonian Inst., Washington, D.C., 1968. 338 pp. plus 52 plates. $8.50.
2nd printing of a distinguished work for historians and collectors. A limited number of deluxe, signed and numbered copies (1st reprinting 1960) are available in full leather and gilt top at $25.

Small Arms Makers, by Robert Gardner. Bonanza Books, N.Y., 1963. 378 pp., illus. with marks and touches in line. $5.95.
A massive directory of makers of firearms, edged weapons, crossbows and polearms, with over 13,000 entries. A useful reference.

Smith and Wesson 1857-1945, by Robert J. Neal and Roy J. Jenks. A. S. Barnes and Co., Inc., N.Y.C., 1966. 500 pp., illus. with over 300 photos and 90 radiographs. $25.00.
A long-needed book, especially for knowledgeable enthusiasts and collectors. Covers an investigation of the series of handguns produced by the Smith and Wesson Company.

The Soldier's Manual, by J. H. Nesmith. (First publ. in Philadelphia in 1824.) Geo. Shumway, York, Pa., 1963. 108 pp., frontis, and 11 color plates. $13.50.
Facsimile reproduction of an important early American militia drill manual, covering exercises with musket, pistol, sword, and artillery. The color plates depict accurately the picturesque uniforms and accoutrements of elite militia corps of Phila. and vicinity. Intro. by Anne S. K. Brown traces the origin of the text matter and the early engravers.

Sporting Guns, by Richard Akehurst. G.P. Putnam's Sons, New York, N.Y., 1968. 120 pp., excellently illus. and with 24 pp. in full color. $5.95.
One of the noted Pleasures and Treasures series. A nostalgic tracing of the history of shooting, and of the guns and rifles used by the sportsman.

Springfield Muzzle-Loading Shoulder Arms, by C.E. Fuller. F. Bannerman Sons, N.Y.C., reprinted 1968. 176 pp., illus. $12.50.
Long-awaited reprint of an important 1930 reference work on weapons produced at Springfield Armory, 1795-1865, including ordnance reports, tables, etc., on flintlock and percussion models.

The Story of Allen and Wheelock Firearms, by H. H. Thomas. C. J. Krehbiel, Cincinnati, 1965. 125 pp., illus. $6.50.
Brief history of the Allen & Wheelock guns produced in mid-19th century, and their maker. Well illus. with descriptions of specimens.

The Story of Pope's Barrels, by Ray M. Smith. Stackpole Books, Harrisburg, Pa., 1964., 211 pp., illus. $10.00.
Detailed account of the achievements and life of Harry M. Pope, master rifle bbl. maker.

Superimposed Load Firearms 1360-1860, by D. R. Baxter. Privately printed for the author in Hong Kong, 1966. $22.00. Foreword by Keith Neal. Ltd. ed., 500 copies only.
Excellently illustrated with photographs, diagrams, figures and patent drawings. Covers over-under arms of all countries, and a list of gunmakers and inventors is included.

Sword, Lance and Bayonet, by Charles ffoulkes and E. C. Hopkinson. Arco Publishing Co., N.Y., 1967. 145 pp., well illus. in line and halftone. $7.50.
A facsimile reprint of the first attempt at a consecutive account of the arms, both general and official use, since the discarding of armor.

The Sword and Same, by Arai Hakuseki & Inaba Tsurio. C. E. Tuttle, Rutland, Vt., 1963. 235 pp., illus. $17.50.
Translation of classic Japanese treatise on the sword, circa 1700. Contains much curious sword-lore, with notes and illus. by the late H. L. Joly.

The 36 Calibers of the Colt Single Action Army, by David M. Brown. Publ. by the author at Albuquerque, N.M., 1965. 222 pp., well-illus. $9.95.
Edited by Bev Mann of *Guns Magazine*. This is an unusual approach to the many details of the Colt S.A. Army revolver. Halftone and line drawings of the same models make this of especial interest.

Treasury of the Gun, by H. L. Peterson, Crown Publishing Co.'s reprint, N.Y.C., 1965. 252 pp. profusely illus., some in color. $7.95.
A beautiful production, presenting a new high in authoritative text. Virtually every significant type of firearm of the past 650 years is shown.

Underhammer Guns, by H. C. Logan. Stackpole Books, Harrisburg, Pa., 1964. 250 pp. illus. $10.00.
A full account of an unusual form of firearm dating back to flintlock days. Both American and foreign specimens are included.

U.S. Martial and Semi-Martial Single-Shot Pistols, by C. E. Chapel, Coward-McCann Inc., N.Y.C., 1962. 352 pp., over 150 illus. $7.50.
Describes in detail all single shot martial pistols used by the US. armed forces and by military units of the states. A definitive guide.

United States Martial Pistols and Revolvers, by Col. Arcadi Gluckman. Stackpole Books, Harrisburg, Pa., 1939; 3rd printing, 1959. 249 pp. plus appendices and 29 plates. $7.95.
The models from 1799 to 1917 are fully described and identified, including arms of secondary classification and of contract makers.

U.S. Military Firearms, 1776-1956, by Maj. Jas. E. Hicks. J. E. Hicks & Son. La Canada, Calif., 216 pp., incl. 88 pages of fine plates. $12.50.
Covering 180 years of America's hand and shoulder weapons. The most authoritative book on this subject. Packed with official data.

U.S. Sword Bayonets, 1847-1865, by R. V. Davis, Jr. Priv. prt., Pittsburgh, Pa., 1963. 36 pp., 17 pl., paper. $4.00.
Histories, production data, and good photos of U. S. military sword bayonets of Civil War era.

Weapons, by E. Tunis. World Publishing Co., N.Y.C., 1954. 153 pp., a large book, well-illus. $4.95.
A pictorial history of arms with complementing narrative. Coverage: from the first tied stone thrown by pre-historic man to super bombs.

Weapons of the British Soldier, by Col. H. C. B. Rogers. Seeley Service & Co., London, 1960. 259 pp., illus. in line and halftone plus full color frontis. $5.50.
The story of weapons used by the British soldier throughout the ages, and the many developments in personal arms during the course of history.

The Webley Story, by Wm. C. Dowell, Skyrac Press, Leeds, Eng. 337 pp., profusely illus. $18.00.
Detailed study of Webley pistols and revolvers, covering over 250 specimens. This important reference also gives detailed listing of English small arms cartridge patents through 1880.

The Whitney Firearms, by Claud Fuller. Standard Publications, Huntington, W. Va., 1946. 334 pp., many plates and drawings. $8.50.
An authoritative history of all Whitney arms and their maker. Highly recommended. Exclusive with Ray Riling Arms Book Co.

Winchester—The Gun That Won the West, by H. F. Williamson. Combat Forces Press, Washington, D. C., 1952. Later eds. by Barnes, N. Y. 494 pp., profusely illus. $4.95.
A scholarly and essential economic history of an honored arms company, but the early and modern arms introduced will satisfy all but the exacting collector.

The Winchester Book, by Geo. Madis. Publ. by the author, Dallas, Tex., 1961. 378 pp., illus. $15.00.
Covers the famous Winchester line in great detail, with many illus. Contains much new information for the collector.

GENERAL

The Adaptable Black Bear, by J. R. Matson. Dorrance & Co., Phila., Pa., 1967. 147 pp., illus. $4.00.
Complete picture of the black bear, its adaptation to environment, habits, disposition and behavior in the wild.

Age of Great Guns, by Frank E. Comparato. Stackpole Books, Harrisburg, Pa. 1965. 386 pp. illus. $11.95.
Of cannon kings and cannoneers who forged the fire-power of artillery. A highly acclaimed work of importance to artillery enthusiasts.

Air Gun Batteries, by E. G. Wolff. Public Museum, Milwaukee, Wisc., 1964. 28 pp., illus., paperbound. 75¢.
Study of discharge mechanisms on reservoir air guns.

The Album of Gunfighters, by J. Marvin Hunter and Noah H. Rose, Warren Hunter, Helotes, Texas, 1965. 4th printing. 236 pp., wonderfully illus., with spectacular oldtime photos. $15.00.
For the serious gunfighter fan there is nothing to equal this factual record of the men-behind-the-star and the human targets that they faced.

American Bird Decoys, by W. J. Mackey Jr. Dutton, N.Y.C., 1965. 256 pp., illus. $10.00.
The history and fine points of decoys for all gamebird species, with much data for collectors and hunters.

American Indian Tomahawks, by Harold L. Peterson. Museum of the American Indian Heye Foundation, N.Y.C., 2nd printing 1969. Paper covers, 142 pp., text plus 314 photographs. $9.95.
A notable contribution to the collecting field. An appendix, "The Blacksmith Shop" by Milford G. Chandler is included.

The American Rifleman Magazine, Author and Subject Index, Vol. II, Wesley R. Burrell, compiler. W. R. Burrell, Galesburg, Michigan, 1962. Paper covers, 63 pp., $4.95.
Covers every article in the 1951-1960 issues of *The American Rifleman*. A valuable tool for location of material published in those years.

Americans and their Guns, compiled by Jas. B. Trefethen, ed. by Jas. E. Serven, Stackpole Books, Harrisburg, Pa., 1967. 320 pp., illus. $9.95.
The National Rifle Association of America story through nearly a century of service to the nation. More than a history—a chronical of help to novice and expert in the safe and proper use of firearms for defense and recreation, as well as a guide for the collector of arms.

The Anatomy of Firearms, by R. L. Wallack. Simon & Schuster, N.Y.C., 1965. 320 pp., illus. $6.95.
Guide to guns of all types, ammunition, ballistics, repairs and adjustments, and related topics.

Animals in Africa, by Peter and Philippa Scott. Clarkson N. Potter, N.Y., 1963. Profusely, magnificently illus. Unpaginated. Large format. $7.95.
The enchanting story, in words and pictures, of a journey by the authors through the National Parks of Kenya to Murchison Falls Park in Uganda. Over 180 pictures in black-and-white, 20 in full color.

AR15, M16 and M16A1 5.56MM Rifles, by D. B. McLean. Normount Armament Co., Forest Grove, Ore., 1968. Unpaginated, illus., paperbound. $3.50.
Descriptions, specifications, and operation of various models are given in text and numerous illustrations.

Archery, by C. J. Longman and H. Walrond. Frederick Ungar Co., N.Y., 1967. 534 pp., illus. in line and halftone. $12.00.
Reproduction of a standard, important British reference work, first publ. in 1894, on the history, uses and techniques of archery.

Arco Gun Book, ed. by Larry Koller. Arco Publ. Co. Inc., N.Y.C., 1962. 397 pp., illus. $7.50.
A concise encyclopedia for arms collectors, shooters and hunters.

Armour, by Viscount Dillon. Geo. Shumway, York, Pa., 1968. 75 pp., illus., paperbound. $4.00.
Facsimile of British monographs titled *An Elizabethan Armourer's Album* and *Armour Notes.*

Armour and Weapons, by Paul Martin. Herbert-Jenkins, London, England, 1969. 308 pp., very well illus. $13.00.
Authoritively traces the development of armor for horse and man, and includes contemporary weapons. 240 black-and-white and 20 fine color plates. A fine new work.

Armoured Fighting Vehicles, by Malcolm McGregor, Walker & Co., New York, 1967. 56 pp., illus. $15.00.
Describes 12 tanks and armored cars, representative of those used in the two World Wars. The illustrations in full-color are true scale drawn from actual models.

The Art of Archerie, by Gervase Markham. A reprint of the 1634 original, publ. in London. Geo. Shumway, York, Pa., 1968. 172 pp. $12.00.
This classic treatise, written to keep alive the art of archery in warfare, treats with the making of longbows and their use. A scholarly introduction to the new issue by S. V. Grancsay adds an enlightening historical perception.

The Art of Shooting, by C. E. Chapel. Barnes, N.Y.C., 1960. 424 pp., illus. $3.95.
A comprehensive, simplified guide to every aspect of pistol, revolver, and rifle shooting. A history of rifle development is included.

The Art of Survival, by C. Troebst. Doubleday & Co., Garden City, N.Y. 1965. 312 pp. illus. $5.95.
Narratives of devices of survival in difficult terrain or circumstances and evaluation of rescue and life-saving procedures.

The Art of the Decoy: American Bird Carvings, by Adele Earnest. Clarkson N. Potter, Inc., N.Y.C., 1966. $10.00.
The origin of a lost art explained, plus some data on the most famous carvers. Over 106 black-and-white photos, 35 line drawings and an 8-page insert in full color.

Baron von Steuben and his Regulations, by Joseph R. Riling, Ray Riling Arms Books Co., Philadelphia, Penna., 1966. 207 pp., illus. $12.50.
A documented book on this great American Major General and the creation by him of the first official "Regulations." Includes the complete facsimile of these regulations.

Be Expert with Map and Compass, by B. Kjellstrom. Stackpole Books, Harrisburg, Pa., 1967. A reprint. 136 pp., plus practicing compass and protractor. Well illus. in line. $3.95.
Newly revised ed. of the *Orienteering Handbook*. A detailed and helpful work for the outdoorsman.

Better ways of Pathfinding, by R. S. Owendoff. Stackpole, Harrisburg, Pa., 1964. 96 pp., illus. $2.95.
Practical methods of finding one's way in unfamiliar areas, using maps, compass, and the sky.

Bring Your Own Wilderness Doctor, by Dr. E. Russel Kodet and Bradford Angier. Stackpole Books, Harrisburg, Pa., 1968. 127 pp., illus. in line drawings. $3.95.
Called the "outdoorsman's emergency manual" it offers security of knowing what to do best—in case of the worst.

A Bibliography of Military Books up to 1642, by Maurice J. D. Cockle. A new reprint of the Holland Press, London, 1965. 320 pp., illus. $15.00.
Describes the important military books from the invention of gunpowder to subject date. A standard reference.

Birds in Our Lives, ed. by A. Stefferud and A. L. Nelson. Gov't. Prtg. Office, Washington, D. C. 20402, 1966, 576 pp., 80 drawings, 372 photos. $9.00.
61 authors have contributed to this great book, the illus. by Bob Hines. A successful effort to bring any and all readers an appreciation of—and an interest in—the part birds play in their lives.

Black Powder Snapshots, by Herb Sherlock. Standard Publications, Huntington, W. Va. 50 pp., illus. $2.98.
Deluxe large volume containing 23 major Sherlock drawings and 95 punchy, marginal sketches.

The Book of the American West, ed. by Jay Monaghan. Julian Messner, New York, 1963. 608 pp., 200 illus. (many in color). $9.95.
A special chapter on frontier firearms is a feature of this massive work. 10 experts on Western hist. in as many fields of study contributed to the book. Illus. include works by the best contemporary artists.

The Book of the American Woodcock, by Wm. G. Sheldon, Ph.D. University of Mass. Press, Amherst, 1967. 227 pp., bibliography, appendices and index. $8.50.

Boys in the Revolution, by Jack Coggins, Stackpole Books, Harrisburg, Pa., 1967. 96 pp., illus. $4.50.
Young Americans tell their part in the war for independence—what they did, what they wore, the gear they carried, the weapons they used, the ships they sailed on, the campaigns in which they fought.

The Bowmen of England, by D. Featherstone. C. N. Potter, Inc., N. Y., 1967. 200 pp., illus. in line and halftone. $4.50.
The English longbow—its birth, tactical use, years of victory and decline in war. For the serious student and collector.

Buxton's Guide—Foreign Firearms. John S. Herold, Greenwich, Conn., 1963. 300 pp., 745 illus. Paperbound, $2.95.
Lists modern rifles, handguns and shotguns from European and other countries, by makers, including illus., descriptions and prices.

The Camping Manual, compiled by Fred Sturges, Stackpole Books, Harrisburg, Pa., 1967. 160 pp., illus. $3.95.
An excellent refresher on the fundamentals, with a digest of the newest methods and latest advice for those who want to enjoy camping more.

Cannonade—Great Artilley Actions of History, by Fairfax Downey. Doubleday & Co., N.Y. 381 pp., illus. $6.50.
A splendid history of artillery, one sure to please the student, the ordnance man, gun-minded readers generally.

Carbine Handbook, by Paul Wahl. Arco Publ. Co., N.Y.C., 1964. 80 pp., illus., $5.00; paperbound, $3.95.
A manual and guide to the U.S. Carbine, cal. .30, M1, with data on its history, operation, repair, ammunition, and shooting.

Carbines Cal. .30 M1, M1A1, M2 and M3, by D.B. McLean. Normount Armament Co., Forest Grove, Ore., 1964. 221 pp., well illus., paperbound. $3.00.
U.S. field manual reprints on these weapons, edited and reorganized.

A Colt Bibliography, by G.M. Lord. Privately produced by the author, Bothell, Wash., 1968. 32 pp., mimeographed stapled sheets. $3.00.
Lists articles, books, etc., of interest to the Colt collector, gunsmith and or historian.

Complete Book of Rifles and Shotguns, by Jack O'Connor. Harper & Bros., N.Y.C., 1961. 477 pp., illus. $6.95.
A splendid two-part book of encyclopedic coverage on every detail of rifle and shotgun.

Complete Book of Shooting, by Jack O'Connor et al. Outdoor Life—Harper & Row, N.Y.C., 1965. 385 pp., illus. $5.95.
Fundamentals of shooting with rifle, shotgun, and handgun in the hunting field and on target ranges.

The Daggers and Edged Weapons of Hitler's Germany, by Maj .J. P. Atwood. Publ. privately for the author in Berlin, Germany, 1965. 240 pp. illus. New edition, 1967. $15.00.
Lavishly illus. with many plates in full color, this is an outstanding production, easily the best information (for the collector) on the subject.

Daggers and Fighting Knives of the Western World: From the Stone Age Until 1900, by Harold L. Peterson, Walker and Co., New York, 1967. 256 pp., illus. $7.50.
The only full-scale historical and analytical work on this subject, from flint knives of the stone age to British and American naval dirks.

Design and Development of Fighting Vehicles, by R. M. Ogorkiewicz. Doubleday, N.Y.C., 1968. 208 pp. plus 174 plates. $7.95.
A review of design and engineering problems of battle tanks and other armored vehicles since World War II, with evaluations of tank design.

Die Handwaffen, by Werner Eckardt and Otto Morawietz. H. G. Schulz, Hamburg, 1957. 265 pp., 15 plates, 175 illus. $10.00.
An important work (in German) on German Service arms from their beginnings through World War II. A symposium on the subject—ancient, obsolete, semi-modern and modern.

BOOKS

The Duel: a History of Duelling, by Robert Baldick. Clarkson N. Potter, Inc., N.Y.C., 1965. 212 pp. illus. $8.50.
All phases of the duel, from trial by combat to recent times, together with accounts of famous encounters. Illus. with contemporary drawings and photos.

Encyclopedia of Firearms, ed. by H. L. Peterson. E. P. Dutton, N.Y.C., 1964. 367 pp., 100 pp. of illus. incl. color. $13.50.
Fine reference work on firearms, with articles by 45 top authorities covering classes of guns, manufacturers, ammunition, nomenclature, and related topics.

Encyclopedia of Modern Firearms, Vol. I, compiled and publ. by Bob Brownell, Montezuma, Iowa, 1959. 1057 pp. plus index, illus. $20.00. Dist. by the Gun Digest Co.
Massive accumulation of basic information on nearly all modern arms pertaining to "parts and assembly." Replete with arms photographs, exploded drawings, manufacturers' lists of parts, etc.

Explosives and Demolitions, U.S. Field Manual 5-25, Normount Armament Co., Forest Grove, Ore. 215 pp., illus., paperbound. $4.00.
A reprint of the Army FM dated 14 May 1959.

Firearms, by H. L. Blackmore. E. P. Dutton, N.Y.C., 1964. 160 pp., well-illus., paperbound. $1.75.
Firearms history from its beginnings to recent times. Fine photographs of museum-quality arms.

Firearms, by Walter Buehr. Crowell Co., N.Y.C., 1967. 186 pp., illus. $5.95.
From gunpowder to guided missile, an illustrated history of firearms for military and sporting uses.

Firearm Silencers, by D. B. McLean. Normount Armament Co., Forest Grove, Ore., 1968. 123 pp., illus., paperbound. $4.00.
The history, design, and development of silencers for U.S. military firearms.

Firearms, Traps & Tools of the Mountain Men, by Carl P. Russell. A. A. Knopf, N.Y., 1967. 448 pp., illus. in line drawings. $12.50.
Detailed survey of fur traders' equipment in the early days of the west.

The Fireside Book of Guns, by Larry Koller. Simon & Schuster, N.Y.C., 1959. 284 pp., illus. in artistic photography and full-color plates. $12.95.
On all counts the most beautiful and colorful production of any arms book of our time, this work adequately tells the story of firearms in America—from the first explorers to today's sportsmen.

Four Studies on the History of Arms, by Arne Hoff, et al. Tojhusmuseet, Copenhagen, 1964. 145 pp., illus., paperbound. $6.75.
A Danish museum publication containing in English text scholarly monographs on arms topics of historic interest.

Free for the Eating, by Bradford Angier, Stackpole Books, Harrisburg, Pa., 1966. 191 pp., illus. $4.95.
Discusses and illustrates 100 wild plants and 300 ways to use them.

More Free for the Eating, Wild Foods, by Bradford Angier, Stackpole Books, Harrisburg, Pa., 1969. 192 pp., illus. $4.95.
A sequel to *Free for the Eating,* being a nature-study cookbook with an additional 200 ways to prepare common wild plants.

The A. B. Frost Book, by Henry M. Reed. Charles E. Tuttle Co., Rutland, Vermont, 1967. 149 pp., of large format with over 70 plates, 44 in color, and many line drawings. $20.00.
A collection of the sketches, drawings and paintings by a famous outdoor artist (1851-1928). Includes his noted sporting and shooting masterpieces.

Fundamentals of Small Arms, U.S. TM9-2205. Normount Armament Co., Forest Grove, Ore. 236 pp., illus., paperbound. $3.50.
Reprint of the U.S. Army technical manual dated 7 May 1952.

Game Animals, by Leonard Lee Rue III. Harper & Row, N. Y., 1968. 655 pp., incl. appendix and index. Illus. with maps and photos. $6.50.
A concise guide to and field book of North American species.

Gas, Air and Spring Guns of the World, by W. H. B. Smith. Stackpole Books, Harrisburg, Pa., 1957. 279 pp., well illus. $10.00.
A detailed, well-documented history of the air and gas gun industry throughout the world. It includes ancient and modern arms, and it devotes a chapter to accurate velocity tests of modern arms.

German Infantry Weapons, ed. by D.B. McLean. Normount Armament Co., Forest Grove, Ore., 1966. 191 pp., illus., paperbound. $3.00.
World War II German weapons described and illustrated, from military intelligence research.

German Mauser Rifle, Model of 1898, by Coombes & Aney. F. Bannerman, N.Y.C., 1921. 20 pp., illus., paperbound. $1.50.
Reprint of a pamphlet describing a famous military rifle, its bayonets, ammunition, and accessories.

German Tanks of World War II, by F.M. Von Senger und Etterlin. Stackpole Books, Harrisburg, Pa., 1969. 176 pp., nearly 300 photos and drawings. Large format. $11.95.
A fully illustrated and definitive history of German armoured fighting vehicles, 1926-1945. Written in English.

German Weapons-Uniforms-Insignia 1841-1918, by Maj. J. E. Hicks. J. E. Hicks & Son, La Canada, Calif., 1958. 158 pp., illus. $6.00.
Originally published in 1937 as *Notes on German Ordnance 1841-1918,* this new edition offers the collector a wealth of information gathered from many authentic sources.

The Golden Guide to Guns, by Larry Koller. Golden Press, N.Y.C., 1966. 160 pp., illus., paperbound, pocket-size. $1.00.
Introduction to rifles, shotguns, and handguns for all uses. Profusely illus., much in color.

Great American Guns and Frontier Fighters, by Will Bryant, Grosset & Dunlap, New York, 1961. 160 pp., illus. $3.95.
Popular account of firearms in U.S. history and of the events in which they played a part.

Great Weapons of World War II, by J. Kirk and R. Young. Bonanza Books, N.Y., 1968. 348 pp., profusely illus. The latest reprint. $4.95.
Covers, in text and picture, great and powerful weapons, planes, tanks as well as small arms, miscellaneous arms and naval attack vessels.

The Gun Digest, 1944 First Annual Edition, ed. by John T. Amber. Follett Publ. Co., Chicago, Ill., 1944, 1963. 162 pp., illus., paperbound. $2.95.
Reprint edition of the prized first edition of *The Gun Digest.* Many useful articles on small arms and their uses.

Gun Digest, 23rd ed., 1969, ed. by John T. Amber. Gun Digest Co., Chicago, Ill., 1968, 416 pp., profusely illus. $4.95.
Known as the world's greatest gun book because of its factual, informative data for shooters, hunters, collectors, reloaders and other enthusiasts. Truly of encyclopedic importance. Decorated paper wrappers.

Gun Digest Treasury, ed. by J. T. Amber, 3rd edition, 1966. Gun Digest Co., Chicago, Ill. 416 pp., illus. Paperbound $4.95, Hardbound $7.95.
The best from 20 years of the GUN DIGEST, selected from the annual editions.

Gun Trader's Guide, by Paul Wahl, Shooter's Bible, Inc., New York, 1968. 5th rev. ed. 220 pp., 8"x10", profusely illus. Paperbound. $3.95.
Complete guide to the identification of modern firearms and giving their current market values.

The Gunfighter, Man or Myth?, by Joseph G. Rosa, Oklahoma Press, Norman, Okla., 1969. 229 pp., illus., (including weapons). $5.95.
A well-documented work on gunfights and gunfighters of the West and elsewhere. Great treat for all gunfighter buffs.

The Gunner's Bible, by Bill Riviere. Doubleday, N.Y.C., 1965. 192 pp., illus. Paperbound. $1.95.
General guide to modern sporting firearms and their accessories, for all shooters.

Gunology, by P. M. Doane. Winchester-Western, N.Y.C., 1968. 64 pp., illus., paperbound. $2.95.
A comprehensive course for professional sporting arms salesmen. Of great help to the arms man are the hundreds of questions on arms and hunting.

Guns, by Dudley Pope. Delacorte Press, N.Y.C., 1965. 256 pp., illus. $14.95.
Concise history of firearms, stressing early museum-quality weapons. Includes small arms as well as artillery, naval, and airborne types. Fine photographs, many in color.

Guns & Ammo 1969 Annual. Geo. Martin, ed. Petersen Publ. Co., Los Angeles, Calif., 1968. 368 pp., illus. Paperbound, $3.95; hard cover, $5.95.
Coverage of contemporary firearms and ammunition, with articles of interest to gun enthusiasts.

Guns Annual for 1969, edited by Jerome Rakusan. Publishers Development Corp., Skokie, Ill., 1968. 122 pp., well illus., decorated paper wrappers. $1.50.
An annual publication describing and illustrating firearms available in current markets, plus articles by experts in the field of collecting, shooting, ammunition, etc.

Guns Illustrated 1970, edited by Mitch Westra. The Gun Digest Co., Chicago, Ill., 1969. 224 pp., profusely illus. $2.95.
Complete guide to modern firearms, air guns, scopes, and related equipment; copious illustrations, specifications, and prices.

Guns and Rifles of the World, by Howard L. Blackmore, The Viking Press, New York, 1965. 290 pp. 1042 halftone and line illustrations. $30.00.
One of the finest books to come out of England. Covers firearms from the handgun to air, steam, and electric guns.

Guns and Shooting, by Maj. Sir Gerald Burrard. Barnes & Co., N.Y.C., 1962. 147 pp. $1.95.
Expanded from the author's earlier *In the Gunroom,* this contains 153 often-asked questions on shotguns and rifles, with authoritative answers covering guns, ammunition, ballistics, etc.

Guns and Shooting, a Bibliography, by R. Riling. Greenberg, N.Y.C., 1951. 434 pp., illus. $20.00.
A selected listing, with pertinent comment and anecdote, of books and printed material on arms and ammunition from 1420 to 1950.

The Guns of Harpers Ferry, by S.E. Brown Jr. Virginia Book Co., Berryville, Va., 1968. 157 pp., illus. $12.50.
Catalog of all known firearms produced at the U.S. armory at Harpers Ferry, 1798-1861, with descriptions, illustrations and a history of the operations there.

Hatcher's Notebook, by Maj. Gen. J. S. Hatcher. Stackpole Books, Harrisburg, Pa., 1952. 2nd ed. with four new chapters, 1957. 629 pp., illus. $10.00.
A dependable source of information for gunsmiths, ballisticians, historians, hunters, and collectors.

A History of Knives, by Harold L. Peterson. Charles Scribner's Sons, N.Y.C., 1966. 64 pp., illus. $3.50.
The fine drawings of Daniel D. Feaser combine with the author's commendable text to produce an important work. From the earliest knives of prehistoric man through the evolution of the metal knife.

A History of War and Weapons, 449 to 1660, by A. V. B. Norman and D. Pottinger. Thomas Y. Crowell Co., N.Y., 1966. 224 pp., well illus. with sketches. $6.95.
An excellent work for the scholar on the evolution of war and weapons in England. Many sketches of arms and weapons of all sorts add importance.

The History of Weapons of the American Revolution, by Geo. C. Neumann. Harper & Row, N.Y., 1967. 373 pp., fully illus. $15.00.
Collector's reference covering long arms, handguns, edged and pole weapons used in the Revolutionary War.

Home in Your Pack, by Bradford Angier, Stackpole Books, Harrisburg, Pa., 1965. 192 pp., illus. $4.50.
An outdoorsman's handbook on equipment, woodcraft, and camping techniques.

How to Build Your Home in the Woods, by Bradford Angier, Stackpole Books, Harrisburg, Pa., 1967. 310 pp., illus. $6.00.
Detailed instructions on building cabins, shelters, etc., with natural materials. How to obtain food from nature, and how to live in the wilderness in comfort.

How to Defend Yourself, your Family, and your Home, by Geo. Hunter. David McKay, N.Y.C., 1967, 307 pp., illus. $6.95.
The only book available for the public at large that advocates their ownership of firearms—including handguns. Covers laws of self-defense, setting up home protection, and much else.

How to Live in the Woods on $10.00 a Week, by Bradford Angier, Stackpole Books, Harrisburg, Pa., 1959. 269 pp., illus. $5.00.
Modern-day homesteading explained by an expert; where to go and how to achieve freedom and comfort on today's frontiers.

Indian and Oriental Armour, by Lord Egerton of Tatton. Stackpole Books, Harrisburg, Pa., 1968. 178 pp., well illus., some in color. $14.95.
New edition of a rare work which has been a key reference for students of the subject, plus a creditable source on Oriental history.

Instinct Shooting, by Mike Jennings. Dodd, Mead & Co., N.Y.C., 1959. 157 pp., 20 line drawings, illus. $3.75.
All about Lucky McDaniel and his surprisingly successful discovery of a new aerial shooting technique, one which will let almost anyone, novices *preferred,* hit flying targets with only minutes of instruction.

Introduction to Muzzle Loading, by R. O. Ackerman. Publ. by the author, Albuquerque, N.M., 1966. 20 pp., illus. with author's sketches. $1.50.
This booklet, in paper wrappers, will be Book No. 1 of a projected series. Contains a glossary of muzzle loading terms, and is aimed at the novice.

Ironmaker To The Confederacy, by C. B. Dew. Yale Univ. Press, New Haven, 1966. 345 pp., illus. $10.00.
History of Joseph R. Anderson's Tredegar Iron Works in Richmond, Va., which produced weapons and military equipment essential to the Confederacy's armed forces.

Japanese Infantry Weapons, ed. by D.B. McLean. Normount Armament Co., Forest Grove, Ore., 1966. 241 pp., well illus., paperbound. $3.50.
Survey of World War II Japanese weapons, based on military intelligence research.

The Japanese Sword and Its Fittings, by members of the Japanese Sword Society of New York. Cooper Union Museum, N.Y.C., 1966. Paper covers. 26 pp. of text plus many illus. $3.50.
The authoritative text in the form of a catalog describing the illus. of items in the possession of members of the society.

Johnson Rifles and Light Machine Guns, ed. by D.B. McLean. Normount Armament Co., Forest Grove, Ore., 1968. 55 pp., illus., paperbound. $2.00.
Manual on the only recoil-operated auto-loading rifle issued to U.S. forces.

Knife Throwing as a Modern Sport, by H. K. McEvoy and C. V. Gruzanski. Charles C. Thomas, Springfield, Ill., 1965. 57 pp., illus. $4.50.
For first time, a concise, easy-to-read and complete story on this modern sport.

A Knight and His Armour, 95 pp., $2.95.
A Knight and His Castle, 108 pp., $2.95.
A Knight and His Horse, 96 pp., $3.25.
A Knight and His Weapons, 95 pp., $2.95.
A series planned for young readers, by R. E. Oakeshott. Lutterworth Press, London, 1966. All illus. Of interest to adults as well.

Mexican Military Arms, The Cartridge Period, by James B. Hughes, Jr. Deep River Armory, Inc., Houston, Texas, 1967. 135 pp., photos and line drawings. $4.50.
An interesting and useful work, in imprinted wrappers, covering the period from 1866 to 1967.

The Minute Men, by J.R. Galvin. Hawthorn Books, N.Y.C., 1967. 286 pp. $6.95.
History of the colonial militia to the beginning of the Revolutionary War, including data on the battles of Lexington and Concord.

Modern ABC's of Bow and Arrow, by G. H. Gillelan. Stackpole Books, Harrisburg, Pa., 1967. 160 pp., illus. $4.95.
Survey of techniques for beginners and experts in target archery as well as bowhunting.

Modern ABC's of Guns, by R. A. Steindler. Stackpole Books, Harrisburg, Pa. 1965. 191 pp., illus. $4.95.
Concise lexicon of today's sporting firearms, their components, ammution, accessory equipment and use.

The New Wildfowler, ed. by Noel M. Sedgwick, et al. Herbert Jenkins, London, 1961. 311 pp., illus. in black & white and color. $6.50.
Replete with all the modern details of a great sport, including material on guns, decoys, rigging, etc.

L. D. Nimschke, Firearms Engraver, by R. L. Wilson. John J. Malloy, publisher, Teaneck, N.J., 1965. *Quanto,* 107 pp., profusely illus. $17.50.
Showing a wide variety of designs, initials and monograms and ever-so-many portions of collectors' arms. A thoroughly interesting work for the collector and an inspiration to the engraver.

No Second Place Winner, by Wm. H. Jordan, publ. by the author, Shreveport, La. (Box 4072), 1962. 114 pp., illus. $5.00.
Guns and gear of the peace officer, ably discussed by a U.S. Border Patrolman for over 30 years, and a first-class shooter with handgun, rifle, etc.

The Other Mr. Churchill, by Macdonald Hastings. Dodd Mead, N.Y.C., 1965. 336 pp., illus. $1.98.
Important biography of a great London gunmaker and forensic ballistics expert, who contributed much to the color and excellence of British firearms tradition.

Pageant of the Gun, by Harold L. Peterson. Doubleday & Co., Inc., Garden City, N. Y., 1967. 352 pp., profusely illus. $5.95.
A storehouse of stories on firearms, their romance and lore, their development and use through 10 centuries. A most satisfying history of firearms chronologically presented.

Picture Book of the Continental Soldier, by C.K. Wilbur. Stackpole Books, Harrisburg, Pa., 1969. 96 pp., well illus. $4.95.
A wealth of detailed material in text and fine drawings, depicting Revolutionary War weapons, accouterments, field equipment, and the routine of the soldier's life. Included are artillery, edged weapons, muskets, rifles, powder horns, etc.

Pistols, Rifles and Machine Guns, by W.G.B. Allen. English Universities Press, London, 1953. 178 pp., illus. $4.50.
A straightforward explanation of the principles that govern the operation of small arms, in simple, non-technical language.

Pocket Guide to Archery, by H.T. Sigler. Stackpole Co., Harrisburg, Pa., 1960. 96 pp., illus. $2.95.
Useful introduction to the subject, covering equipment, shooting techniques, and bow hunting of small game and deer.

Redbook of Used Gun Values, Guns Magazine, Skokie, Ill., 1967. 130 pp. $2.50.
Rev. ed. for 1969. A guide to buying and selling; used pistols, rifles, shotguns. Handy pocket size in imprinted covers.

Rifleman and Pistolman, by L. B. Escritt, Arco Publ. Co., Inc., N.Y.C., 1962. 156 pp., illus. $3.50. First publ. in England 1955.
A first class work on the use and maintenance of rifled weapons. Principles of ballistics and other complex issues are carefully discussed.

Round Shot and Rammers, by H. L. Peterson. Stackpole Books, Harrisburg, Pa., 1969. 128 pp., illus. $9.95.
Artillery in America through the Civil War years, with much detail on manufacture, history, accessory equipment, and use of all types of cannon. Fine line drawings show the guns, their equipment, and the men who used them.

Second World War Combat Weapons, by Hoffschmidt & Tantum. WE, Inc., Old Greenwich, Conn., 1968. 212 pp., illus. $7.95.
German weapons, vehicles, and projectiles illustrated and described. First of a 7-vol. series.

Secret Fighting Arts of the World, by J. F. Gilbey. Tuttle, Rutland, Vt., 1963. 150 pp., illus. $3.75.
20 chapters on advanced techniques of unarmed combat, described in anecdotal form.

Shooter's Bible, No. 60. John Olson, ed. Shooter's Bible Inc., S. Hackensack, N.J., 1969. 576 pp., illus. $3.95.
An annually-published guide to firearms, ammunition, and accessories.

Shooter's Bible Game Cook Book, by Geraldine Steindler. Follett Publ. Co., Chicago, Ill. 1965. 224 pp., illus., cloth, $6.95; paper, $3.95.
Full information on preparing game for the table, including recipes and methods of field-dressing.

Shooter's Bible Gun Trader's Guide, by Paul Wahl. Shooter's Bible, S. Hackensack, N.J., 5th edition, 1968. 220 pp., illus., paperbound. $3.95.
Revised guide to market values of modern firearms, with identification data on U.S. and imported guns.

Shooting Muzzle Loading Hand Guns, by Charles T. Haven. Guns Inc., Massachusetts, 1947. 132 pp., illus. $6.50.
A good summary of shooting methods, both contemporary and modern. Duelling with M.L. handguns is also covered.

Shooting Preserve Management: The Nilo System, by Edw. L. Kozicky and John Madson, Winchester-Western Press, 1966. 312 pp., illus. $4.95.
A highly comprehensive treatment on game and preserve operations that is destined to be the "bible" for shooting preserve operators—or those aspiring. An extensive bibliography is included.

The Shorebirds of North America, by Peter Matthiesen, ed. by Gordon Stout, with species accounts by R. S. Palmer. Viking Press, N.Y.C., 1967, 288 pp., 32 6-color plates, 10"x14", $22.50. De Luxe ltd. ed., extra bound, $50.00.
A magnificent book, probably the outstanding work on the shorebirds of the nothern western world. 32 chapters cover 59 species. The illustrations are superb.

Sketch Book 76: The American Soldier 1775-1781, by R. Klinger and R. A. Wilder, Arlington, Va., 1967. 53 pp., illus. Paper covers. $2.50.
Sketches, notes, and patterns compiled from a study of clothing and equipment used by the American foot soldier in the Revolutionary War.

Skills for Taming the Wilds, by Bradford Angier, Stackpole Books, Harrisburg, Pa., 1967. 320 pp., illus. $6.95.
A handbook of woodcraft wisdom, by a foremost authority, showing how to obtain maximum comfort from nature.

Small Arms Lexicon and Concise Encyclopedia, by Chester Mueller and John Olson. Stoeger Arms, So. Hackensack, N.J., 1968. 312 pp., 500 illus. $14.95.
Definitions, explanations, and references on antiques, optics, ballistics, etc., from A to Z. Over 3,000 entries plus appendix.

Small Arms of the World, by J. E. Smith and W. H. B. Smith. Stackpole Books, Harrisburg, Pa., 1966. 735 pp., profusely illus. $17.95.
New up-dated and broadened 8th ed. of a famous classic. Military weapons—from Argentina to Yugoslavia—with detailed data on recognizing, appraising, loading, operating, stripping, assembling; covers evolution, handguns, carbines, rifles, auto rifles, machine guns and SMGs.

Stoeger Gun Parts Catalog, compiled and published by Stoeger Arms Corporation, South Hackensack, N.J., 1968. 416 pp., illus. $2.00.
A mail-order catalog listing over 1000 parts for pistols, rifles and shotguns, domestic and foreign. Includes gunsmith tools and accessories.

Stories of the Old Duck Hunters and Other Drivel, by Gordon MacQuarrie and compiled by Zack Taylor. Stackpole Books, Harrisburg, Pa., 1967. 223 pp., illus. $5.95.
An off-beat relaxing and enjoyable group of 19 best-remembered outdoor stories, previously publ. in magazines.

Submachine Guns Caliber .45, M3 and M3A1, U.S. FM23-41 and TM 9-1217. Normount Armament Co., Forest Grove, Ore., 1967. 141 pp., illus., paperbound. $3.00.
Reprint of two U.S. Army manuals on submachine guns.

Swords & Daggers, by Frederick Wilkinson. Hawthorn Books, N.Y., 1968. 256 pp., well illus. $5.95.
Good general survey of edged weapons and polearms of collector interest, with 150 pp. of illustrations and descriptions of arms from Europe, Africa and the Orient.

Swords of Hitler's Third Reich, by Major J.R. Angolia, F.J. Stephens, Essex, England, 1969. Over 100 pp., well illus. $8.50.
A comprehensive work on the swords of the German Army, Navy, Air Force, SS, Police, Fire Dept., and many other government departments—plus belts, hangers, and accouterments—all described and illus.

Teaching Kids to Shoot, by Henry M. Stebbins. Stackpole Books, Harrisburg, Pa. 1966. 96 pp. illus. $2.95.
Designed for parents and leaders who want to develop safety conscious firearms-users.

Tear Gas Munitions, by T. F. Swearengen, Charles C. Thomas, Springfield, Ill., 1966. 569 pp., illus. $34.50.
An analysis of commercial (riot) gas guns, tear gas projectiles, grenades, small arms ammunition, and related tear gas devices.

Textbook of Small Arms, 1929. Reprint of an official British publ. Holland Press, London, 1961. 427 pp., illus. $12.50.
Reprint in facsimile of an official prime source on military rifles, swords, bayonets, revolvers, grenades, machine guns, cartridges, ballistics, etc.

The Thompson Gun, publ. by Numrich Arms, West Hurley, N. Y., 1967, 27 pp., illus., paper covers. $1.95.
A facsimile reprint, excellently done, of a 1923 catalog of Thompson sub-machine guns.

Thompson Submachine Guns, compiled from original manuals by the publ. Normount Armament Co., Forest Grove, Oregon, Ill., 1968. Over 230 pp., well illus., many exploded views. Paper wrappers. $4.00.
Five reprints in one book: Basic Field Manual, Cal. 45, M1928AI (U.S. Army); Cal. 45, Model 1928, (for British); Cal., 45 (U.S. Ordnance); Model MI, Cal., 45 (U.S. Ordnance) and Ultra Modern Automatic Arms (Auto-Ordnance Corp.).

The Tournament, its Periods and Phases, by R. C. Clephan. Frederick Ungar Co., N.Y., 1967. A reprint. 195 pp., illus. with contemporary pictures plus half-tones of armor and weapons used by contestants. $16.50.
A rare and eagerly-sought work, long out-of-print. A scholarly, historical and descriptive account of jousting.

A Treatise of Artillery, by John Muller. Museum Restoration Service, Ottawa, Canada, 1965. 216 pp., plus many plates. $17.50.
A creditable reprint of a famous and excellent original work of the third ed. of 1780, printed in London. This reprint limited to 850 numbered copies. The plates should be highly useful to the artillery buff.

Use and Maintenance of the Browning "Hi-Power" Pistol, (No. 2 Mk 1 and Commercial Models), by D.B. McLean. Normount Armament Co., Forest Grove, Ore., 1966. 48 pp., illus., paperbound. $1.50.
Covers the use, maintenance, and repair of various Browning 9mm parabellum pistols.

Walther Pistols and Rifles, by W. H. B. Smith, et al. Stackpole Books, Harrisburg, Pa., 1962. 172 pp., illus. $5.00.
Revised, enlarged ed. of the work first publ. in 1946. Full information on all Walther products including operation, stripping, ammunition, etc.

Warriors' Weapons, by Walter Buehr. Crowell Co., N.Y.C., 1963. 186 pp., illus. $5.95.
Illustrated history of pre-gunpowder arms, from stone ax to crossbow and catapult.

Weapons of the American Revolution, and Accoutrements, by Warren Moore. Funk & Wagnalls, N.Y., 1967. 225 pp., fine illus. $10.00.
Revolutionary era shoulder arms, pistols, edged weapons, and equipment are described and shown in fine drawings and photographs, some in color.

The Weapons Merchants, by Bernt Engelmann. Crown Publ., Inc., N. Y., 1968. 224 pp., illus. $4.95.
A true account of illegal traffic in death-dealing arms by individuals and governments.

Weapons and Tactics, Hastings to Berlin, by Jac Weller, St. Martin's Press, New York, 1966. 238 pp., illus. $6.00.
Primarily on the infantry weapons of today, with basic data on those of the past.

Weapons of War, by P. E. Cleator. Crowell Co., N.Y.C., 1968. 224 pp., illus. $5.95.
A British survey of warfare from earliest times, as influenced by the weapons available for combat.

Wild Game Cookbook, by L.E. Johnson. Benjamin Co., N.Y.C., 1968. 160 pp. $1.95.
Recipes, sauces, and cooking hints for preparation of all types of game birds and animals.

The Wild Turkey, its History and Domestication, by A. W. Schorger, Univ. of Oklahoma Press, Norman, Okla., 1966. 625 pp., illus. $10.00.
Detailed coverage of habitats, characteristics, breeding, and feeding of the American wild turkey. Bibliography.

Wilderness Cookery, by Bradford Angier. Stackpole Books, Harrisburg, Pa., 1967. 256 pp., illus. $4.95.
An excellent work, one that will be of big interest to hunters, fishermen, campers, et al.

Wildwood Wisdom, by Ellsworth Jaeger. The Macmillan Company, New York, N.Y. 1964. 491 pp. well-illus. by author. $5.95.
An authoritative work, through many editions; about all there is to know about every detail for the outdoorsman.

Williams 1968-69 Blue Book of Gun Dealing. Williams Gun Sight Co., Davison, Mich., 1968. 76 pp., illus., paperbound. $2.50.
Suggested price ranges for many models of rifles, shotguns, handguns, sights, etc., with other useful information for the gun trader.

The World of the White-Tailed Deer, by L. L. Rue III. J. B. Lippincott Co., Phila., 1967. A reprint. 137 pp., fine photos. $4.95.
An eminent naturalist-writer's account of the year-round activities of the white-tailed deer.

The World's Assault Rifles (and Automatic Carbines), by D. D. Musgrave and T. B. Nelson. T. B. N. Enterprises, Alexandria, Va., 1967. 546 pp., profusely illus. $17.50.
High velocity small-bore combat rifles are shown and described in much detail, arranged by type and nationality. A companion volume to *The World's Submachine Guns,* by Nelson and Lockhoven.

The World's Submachine Guns (and Machine Pistols), by T. B. Nelson and H. B. Lockhoven. T. B. N. Enterprises, Alexandria, Va., 1962. 739 pp., profusely illus. $15.50.
The 2nd printing (1964) of the first work with descriptive data on all significant SMGs to date, arranged by national origin. A glossary in 22 languages is included. It is a companion volume to the *The World's Assault Rifles* by Musgrave and Nelson.

Antique Firearms: Their Care, Repair and Restoration, by Ronald Lister. Crown Publ., New York, 1964. 220 pp., 66 plates, 24 fig. $2.98.
A workshop manual for collectors and gunsmiths, giving correct procedures for every step in preserving firearms.

Checkering and Carving of Gun Stocks, by Monte Kennedy. Stackpole Books, Harrisburg, Pa., 1962. 175 pp., illus. $10.00.
Rev., enlarged clothbound ed. of a much sought-after, dependable work.

Complete Guide to Gunsmithing, by C. E. Chapel. Barnes & Co., N.Y.C., 1962. 479 pp., illus. $6.95.
2nd rev. edition, known earlier as *Gun Care and Repair,* of a comprehensive book on all details of gunsmithing for the hobbyist and professional.

Firearms Blueing and Browning, by R. H. Angier. Stackpole Books, Harrisburg, Pa. 151 pp., illus. $5.00.
A useful, concise text on chemical coloring methods for the gunsmith and mechanic.

Gun Engraving Review, by E. C. Prudhomme, G. E. R. Publ. Co., Shreveport, La., 1965. 150 pp., profusely illus. (some in color.) $21.95.
Excellent examples of the gun engraver's art to serve as a guide to novice or expert. Selection of tools, techniques and a directory of engravers is given.

Gunsmithing, by Roy F. Dunlap. Stackpole Books, Harrisburg, Pa., 714 pp., illus. $10.00.
Comprehensive work on conventional techniques, incl. recent advances in the field. Valuable to rifle owners, shooters, and practicing gunsmiths.

Gunsmithing Simplified, by H. E. Macfarland. Washington, D.C., 1950, A. S. Barnes, N.Y.C., 1959. 303 pp., illus. $6.95.
A thorough dependable concise work with many helpful short-cuts.

Gunstock Finishing and Care, by A. D. Newell. Stackpole Books, Harrisburg, Pa. A new printing, 1966. 473 pp. illus. $9.50.
Amateur's and professional's handbook on the selection, use and application of protective and decorative coatings on gun stocks.

Home Gun Care & Repair, by P. O. Ackley. Stackpole Books, Harrisburg, Pa., 1969. 191 pp., illus. $5.95.
Basic reference for safe tinkering, fixing, and converting rifles, shotguns, handguns.

HOW . . . by L. Cowher, W. Hunley, and L. Johnston. NMLR Assn., Indiana, 1961. 107 pp., illus. Paper covers. $2.95.
This 1961 rev. ed., enlarged by 3 chapters and additional illustrations, covers the building of a muzzle-loading rifle, target pistol, and powder horn, and tells how to make gunflints.

How To Convert Military Rifles. Williams Gun Sight Co., Davison, Mich., 1968. 76 pp., illus., paperbound. $1.50.
Manufacturer's catalog and handbook on altering military rifles for sporting use.

Introduction to Modern Gunsmithing, by H. E. MacFarland. Stackpole Books, Harrisburg, Pa., 1965. 320 pp., illus. $6.95.
Up-to-date reference for all gunsmiths on care, repair, and modification of firearms, sights, and related topics.

Lock, Stock and Barrel, by R. H. McGrory. Publ. by author at Bellmore, N.Y., 1966. Paper covers. 122 pp., illus. $3.00.
A handy and useful work for the collector or the professional with many helpful procedures shown and described on antique gun repair.

Make Muzzle Loader Accessories, by Robert H. McCrory. R. H. McCrory, Bellmore, N.Y., 1967. 28 pp., paper wrappers, illus. with sketches. $1.50.
A capably executed handbook on how to make a powder horn, capper, nipple wrench, loading block and spring vise.

The Modern Kentucky Rifle, How to Build Your Own, by R. H. McCrory. McCrory, Wantagh, N.Y., 1961. 68 pp., illus., paper bound. $3.00.
A workshop manual on how to fabricate a flintlock rifle. Also some information on pistols and percussion locks.

Professional Gunsmithing, by W. J. Howe. Stackpole Books, Harrisburg, Pa., 1968 reprinting. 526 pp., illus. $10.00.
Textbook on repair and alteration of firearms, with detailed notes on equipment and commercial gunshop operation.

Restocking a Rifle, by Alvin Linden. Stackpole Books, Harrisburg, Pa., 1969. 138 combined pp., of text. Well illus. Large format. $9.95.
A re-issue in one volume of the 3 earlier Linden instruction guides on: Stock Inletting; Shaping; Finishing of the Springfield, Enfield and Winchester M70 rifles.

handguns

Automatic Firearm Pistols, by Elmer Swanson. N.E. Swanson, Secaucus, N.J., 1955. 210 pp., illus. $10.00.
Catalog of U.S. and foreign-made automatic pistols, with illustrations, descriptions, and prices.

Automatic Pistols, by H. B. C. Pollard, WE, Old Greenwich, Conn. 1966. 110 pp., illus. $5.00.
A facsimile reprint of the scarce 1920 original. Covers historical development of military and other automatics, shooting, care, etc.

Book of Pistols & Revolvers, by W. H. B. Smith. Stackpole Books, Harrisburg, Pa., 1968. 758 pp., profusely illus. $14.95. Buy with Book of Rifles and both are $19.95.
Rev. and enlarged, this encyclopedic reference, first publ. in 1946, continues to be the best on its subject.

Combat Shooting for Police, by Paul B. Weston. Charles C. Thomas, Springfield, Ill., 1967. A reprint. 194 pp., illus. $7.50.
First publ. in 1960 this popular self-teaching manual gives basic concepts of defensive fire in every position.

Fired In Anger, by Robt. Elman. Doubleday, Garden City, N.Y., 1968. 416 pp., illus. with 250 photos. $7.95.
Describes and illustrates the personal handguns used by famous and infamous Americans, including soldiers, outlaws and historical figures.

Gil Hebard Guns, Gil Hebard, Knoxville, Ill. Catalog No. 18, 1967. 220 pp., illus. Paperbound. $1.00.
Outstanding sales catalog of handgunner's needs, plus excellent articles by pistol experts on sport and target shooting.

The Handbook of Handgunning, by Paul B. Weston. Crown Publ., N.Y.C., 1968. 138 pp., illus. with photos. $4.95.
"New concepts in pistol and revolver shooting," by a noted firearms instructor and writer.

Handbuch der Faustfeuerwaffen, by Gerhard Bock and W. Weigel. J. Neumann-Neudamm, Melsungen, Germany, 1968. 4th and latest ed., 724 pp., including index. Profusely illus. $21.00.
A truly encyclopedic work in German text on every aspect of handguns. Highly recommended for those who read German.

Handgunner's Guide, by Chic Gaylord. Hastings House, N.Y.C., 1960. 176 pp., illus. $2.98.
From choosing a handgun to the psychology of gun-fighting, including drawing and firing for speed and accuracy.

Japanese Hand Guns, by F.E. Leithe. Borden Publ. Co., Alhambra, Calif., 1968. Unpaginated, well illus. $8.50.
Identification guide, covering models produced since the late 19th century. Brief text material gives history, descriptions, and markings.

The Luger Pistol (Pistole Parabellum), by F. A. Datig. Borden Publ. Co., Alhambra, Calif., 1962. 328 pp., well illus. $8.50.
An enlarged, rev. ed. of an important reference on the arm, its history and development from 1893 to 1945.

Lugers Unlimited, by F. G. Tilton, World-Wide Gun Report, Inc., Aledo, Ill., 1965. 49 pp., illus. Paper covers. $2.00.
An excellent monograph about one of the most controversial pistols since the invention of hand firearms.

Luger Variations, Vol. I, by Harry E. Jones. H. E. Jones, Torrance, Calif., 1967. 304 pp., well illus. $12.00.
A 3rd reprinting of an important work on Luger handguns, first publ. in 1959. Many variants of the arm are shown in fine photographs, and each is fully described.

The Mauser Self-Loading Pistol, by Belford & Dunlap. Borden Publ. Co., Alhambra, Calif. Over 200 pp., 300 illus., large format. $12.50.
The long-awaited book on the "Broom Handles," covering their inception in 1894 to the end of production. Complete and in detail: pocket pistols, Chinese and Spanish copies, etc.

Modern Pistol Shooting, by P.C. Freeman. Faber & Faber, London, England, 1968. 176 pp., illus. $4.00.
How to develop accuracy with the pistol. Fine points in technique are covered, with information on competitive target shooting.

The "Parabellum" Automatic Pistol, the English version of the official DWM handbook on Luger pistols. Normount Armament Co., Forest Grove, Oregon, Ill., 1968. 42 pp., illus. Paper wrappers. $1.00.
A user's handbook, a reference work for collectors. A reprint of the original detailed instructions on use, disassembly and maintenance. Includes three folding plates.
Pistol and Revolver Guide, by George Nonte. Stoeger Arms Corp., So. Hackensack, N.J., 1967. 192 pp., well illus. Paper wrappers. $3.95.
A history of the handgun, its selection, use and care, with a glossary and trade directory.
Pistols, A Modern Encyclopedia, by Stebbins, Shay, & Hammond. Stackpole Co., Harrisburg, Pa., 1961. 380 pp., illus. $4.98.
Comprehensive coverage of handguns for every purpose, with material on selection, ammunition, and marksmanship.
Pistols of the World, by Claude Blair. Viking Press, N.Y.C., 1968. 206 pp., plus plates. $30.00.
Authoritive review of handguns since the 16th century, with chapters on major types, manufacture, and decoration. Fine photographic illustrations.
The Revolver, 1818-1865, by Taylerson, Andrews, & Frith. Crown Publ., N.Y.C., 1968. 360 pp., illus. $7.50.
Noted British work on early revolving arms and the principal makers, giving production data and serial numbers on many models.
The Revolver, 1865-1888, by A.W.F. Taylerson. Crown Publ., N.Y.C., 1966. 292 pp., illus. $3.49.
Detailed study of 19th-century British and U.S. revolvers, by types and makers, based on study of patent records.
Sixguns by Keith, by Elmer Keith. Stackpole Co., Harrisburg, Pa., 1968 (reprint of 1961 edition.) 335 pp., illus. $12.95.
Long a popular reference on handguns, this work covers all aspects, whether for the shooter, collector or other enthusiasts.
System Mauser, A Pictorial History of the Model 1896 Self-Loading Pistol, by J. W. Breathed, Jr., and J. J. Schroeder, Jr. Handgun Press, Chicago, Ill., 1967. 273 pp. Well illus. with photos of the arms, factory manual repros., etc. $9.95.
A distinguished coverage of the subject, of high interest to collectors and students or those using the pistol. A 1st ed., limited to 1000 numbered copies.
10 Shots Quick, by Daniel K. Stern. Globe Printing Co., San Jose, Calif., 1967. 153 pp., photos. $8.50.
History of Savage-made automatic pistols, models of 1903-1917, with descriptive data for shooters and collectors.
Browning Hi-Power Pistols. Normount Armament Co., Forest Grove, Ore., 1968. 48 pp., illus., paperbound. $1.50.
A handbook on all models of Browning Hi-Power pistols, covering their use, maintenance and repair.

African Hunting, by Wm. C. Baldwin. Abercrombie & Fitch Library, N.Y., 1967. 451 pp., illus. $12.95.
Limited printing of a much-desired book giving vivid accounts of big game hunting exploits in Africa. First publ. in 1863.
African Rifles and Cartridges, by John Taylor. Stackpole Books, Harrisburg, Pa. 431 pp., illus. $7.50.
Complete and detailed information on all cartridges and rifles for African game, by one who hunted there for 30 years. Highly recommended.
After Wild Sheep in the Altai and Mongolia, by Prince Demidoff. Abercrombie & Fitch Library, N.Y., 1966. 324 pp., with photographs and drawings. $10.00.
Limited printing of a famous British work of 1900, on hunting big game in Asia. Long out-of-print.
American Partridge & Pheasant Shooting, by Frank Schley. Abercrombie & Fitch Library, N.Y.C., 1968. 238 pp., illus. $7.95.
Facsimile of an American sporting classic work, including detailed engravings of game birds.
The American Sportsman, by Elisha J. Lewis. Abercrombie & Fitch Library, N.Y., 1967. 510 pp., illus. $10.95.
Limited issue of a scarce classic American work on the hunting field, first publ. in 1851.
The Art of Hunting Big Game in North America, by Jack O'Connor. Alfred A. Knopf, N.Y., 1967. 404 pp., line drawings and photos. $8.95.
A complete book on the subject, from tracing the origin of game on this continent to the various techniques practised in the sport on different species. Rifles and cartridges discussed at length.
The Art of Wing Shooting, by W.B. Leffingwell. Abercrombie & Fitch Library, N.Y.C., 1968. 190 pp., illus. $7.95.
An outstanding treatise on shotgun marksmanship, first publ. 1894, with explicit drawings on techniques of leading the target.
Asian Jungle, African Bush, by Charles Askins. Stackpole Books, Harrisburg, Pa., 1959. 258 pp., illus. $10.00.
A where-to-go and how-to-do guide for game-rich Indo-China. The African section deals with game, the use of various arms and ammo on specific species.
Bell of Africa, by W. D. M. Bell, with foreword and introduction by Wally Taber and Col. T. Whelen. N. Spearman and Holland Press, London, 1960. 236 pp., illus. $4.75.
On elephants and the hunter, extracted from Bell's own papers, it includes an appendix on rifles and rifle shooting.
Big Game Hunting in the West, by Mike Cramond. Mitchell Press, Vancouver, B.C., Can., 1965. 164 pp., illus. $5.95.
Accounts of hunting many species of big game and predators are given plus a section on rifles, equipment, and useful tips for the field.
Bird Hunting Know-How, by D.M. Duffey. Van Nostrand, Princeton, N.J., 1968. 192 pp., illus. $5.95.
Game-getting techniques and sound advice on all aspects of upland bird hunting, plus data on guns and loads.
Bowhunting for Deer, by H. R. Wambold. Stackpole Books, Harrisburg, Pa., 1964. 160 pp., illus. $5.95.
Useful tips on deer, their habits, anatomy, and how-when-where of hunting, plus selection and use of tackle.
Buckshot and Hounds, by C. J. Milling. A. S. Barnes, N.Y., 1967. 132 pp., illus. $4.95.
Deer-driving methods and traditions of the South and West, with present-day adaptations described.
Calling All Game, by Bert Popowski. Stackpole Books, Harrisburg, Pa., 1952, 306 pp. Illus. $4.95.
Practical methods of attracting game, from quail to moose, using artificial decoys and calls.
Charles Morgan on Retrievers, ed. by Ann Fowler and D.L. Walters. Abercrombie & Fitch, N.Y.C., 1968. 168 pp., illus. $12.50.
Based on years of success in schooling hunting dogs, this work gives full details of an expert's proven methods to guide experienced trainers.
Complete Book of Hunting, by Clyde Ormond. Harper & Bros., N.Y.C., 1962. 467 pp., well-illus. $6.95.
Part I is on game animals, Part II is on birds. Guns and ammunition, game, habitats, clothing, equipment, etc., hunters' tips are discussed.
Crow Shooting, by Bert Popowski. A. S. Barnes and Co., N.Y.C., 1946. (4th printing 1957). 216 pp., illus. $5.00.
Practical and entertaining, telling how to locate roosts, build blinds and employ cover; the use of various decoys for shooting with rifle or shotgun.
The Deer Hunter's Bible, by Geo. Laycock. Doubleday, Garden City, N.Y., 1963. 154 pp., illus., paperbound. $1.95.
Handy summary of deer hunting lore, by an expert. Guns, loads, bowhunting, care of venison, field techniques are covered.
The Deer Hunter's Guide, by F. E. Sell. Stackpole Books, Harrisburg, Pa., 1964. 192 pp., illus. $5.00.
Western hunting lore for rifle- and bow-hunter, with data on woodcraft, trail signs, venison, and trophies, etc.
The Deer of North America, edit. by W. P. Taylor. Stackpole Books, Harrisburg, Pa., 1956. 668 pp., illus. incl. full-color plates. $12.50.
Leading authorities in all parts of the deer range have contributed their intimate studies of the animal.
Duck Hunting, by J. G. MacKenty. Barnes, N.Y.C., 1953, rev. ed. 1965. 192 pp., well-illus. $4.95.
New edition of a long-accepted standard reference on every phase of duck hunting in America.
Elephant Hunting in East Equatorial Africa, by Arthur H. Neumann. Abercrombie & Fitch Library, N.Y., 1966. 455 pp., illus. $12.50.
Limited ed. of a rare hunting book, first publ. in 1898 and difficult to locate. An account of 3 years' ivory hunting under Mt. Kenia . . . the Lorogi Mountains . . . and Lake Rudolph. Over 60 illus.
The End of the Game, by P. H. Beard. Viking Press, N.Y.C., 1965. 256 pp., fine illus. $12.95.
Account of recent changes in African game country and decline of the game population.
Game for the Sporting Rifle, by Henry Tegner, Herbert Jenkins, London, Eng., 1963. 191 pp., illus. $4.00.
The game birds, animals, and varmints of Britain are described and illus., together with advice on proper guns and hunting methods, trophies, etc.
Game Bird Hunting, by F. P. Rice & J.I. Dahl. Outdoor Life—Harper & Row, N.Y.C., 1965. 190 pp., illus. $3.95.
Survey of North American game birds of all types, written by a noted scholar and a hunter of wide experience.
Game Bird Hunting in the West, by Mike Cramond. Mitchell Press, Vancouver, B.C., Can., 1967. 246 pp., illus. $5.95.
Identification and hunting methods for each species of waterfowl and upland game birds, plus a section on shotgun types, equipment, and related subjects for the hunter.
Game Shooting, by Robert Churchill (revised by Macdonald Hastings), Stackpole Books, Harrisburg, Pa., 1967. 252 pp., illus. $8.95.
A welcome reappearance of standard reference that pioneered game shooting techniques.
Good Hunting, by Jas. L. Clark, Univ. of Oklahoma Press, Norman, Okla., 1966. 242 pp., illus. $5.95.
Fifty years of collecting and preparing habitat groups for the American Museum.
The Great Arc of the Wild Sheep, by J. L. Clark. Univ. of Oklahoma Press, Norman, Okla., 1964. 247 pp., illus. $6.95.
Every classified variety of wild sheep is discussed, as found in North America, Asia & Europe. Numerous hunting stories by experts are included.
Great True Hunts, ed. by Peter Barrett. Prentice-Hall, Englewood Cliffs, N.J., 1967. 278 pp., illus. $4.95.
Big game hunting stories from *True* magazine, telling of hunting exploits of famous men around the world.
The Grizzly Bear, edited by B. D. and E. Haynes, Univ. of Oklahoma Press, Norman, Okla., 1966. 386 pp., illus. $5.00.
Collected stories about various encounters with the grizzly by mountain men, settlers, naturalists, scouts and others.
Grizzly Country, by Andy Russell. A.A. Knopf, N.Y.C., 1968. 302 pp., illus. $6.95.
Many-sided view of the grizzly bear and his world, by a noted guide, hunter and naturalist.
Guns & Ammo for Hunting Big Game, by Elmer Keith; John Lachuk, Ed. Petersen Publ. Co., L.A., 1965, reprinted 1967. 384 pp., illus. $4.95.
An expert on firearms and wildlife writes on hunting subjects, including guns, ammunition, and how to hunt various species of American game.
Honker, by C. S. Williams. Van Nostrand. N.Y.C., 1967. 192 pp., illus. $7.50.
A wealth of information for the hunter and conservationist, on geese exclusively — their habits, gunning techniques, ecology, etc.
How to Hunt Whitetail Deer, by L.A. Anderson. Funk & Wagnalls, N.Y.C., 1968. 116 pp., illus. $5.95.
Useful reference for deer hunters, both novice and experienced, giving basic information and valuable pointers.
How to Hunt Small Game, by L.A. Anderson. Funk & Wagnalls, N.Y.C., 1968. 160 pp., well illus. $5.95.
All-inclusive, concise work on its subject by a capable authority.
A Hunter's Wanderings in Africa, by Frederick Courteney Selous. Abercrombie & Fitch Library, N.Y., 1967. 455 pp., illus. $11.95.
Limited ed. of a rare and much-sought original work of 1881. A world-famous big game hunter tells of his African exploits.
Hunting in Africa, by Frank C. Hibben, Hill and Wang, New York, N. Y., 1962. 236 pp., illus. $5.00.
18 true stories about exotic and dangerous African animals and the tracking and hunting of them.
Hunting Dog Know-How, by D. M. Duffey. Van Nostrand, Princeton, N.J., 1965. 177 pp., illus. $5.95.
Covers selection, breeds, and training of hunting dogs, problems in hunting and field trials.

BOOKS

Hunting Our Biggest Game, by C. Ormond. Stackpole Books, Harrisburg, Pa., 1956. 197 pp., illus. $5.00.
Written for trophy hunters—bear, moose, elk, caribou, mountain sheep, and goat. Filled with useful information for that hunt-of-a-lifetime.

Hunting Our Medium Size Game, by Clyde Ormond. Stackpole Books, Harrisburg, Pa., 1958. 219 pp., illus. $5.00.
Covers deer, whitetails and mules; black bear; antelope; coyotes; bobcats and cougar. Included are sections on equipment, use of rifles, and care of venison.

Hunting Pronghorn Antelope, by Bert Popowski. Stackpole Books, Harrisburg, Pa., 1959. 227 pp., illus. $6.50.
Covers habits, habitat, hunting, equipment, care of meat and trophies.

Hunting the Whitetail Deer, by Tom Hayes. Barnes, N.Y.C., 1960, rev. ed. 1966. 259 pp., illus. $4.95.
Hunter's manual of practical information on rifles, ammunition, deer habits, woodcraft and hunting technique.

Hunting with Bow and Arrow, by George Laycock and Erwin Bauer. Arco Publ. Co., Inc., N.Y.C., 1966. $2.50.
A practical guide to archery as a present-day sport. Mentions equipment needed and how to select it. Illus. instructions on how to shoot with ease and accuracy.

Jack O'Connor's Big Game Hunts, by Jack O'Connor. E. P. Dutton, N.Y.C., 1963. 415 pp., illus. $4.95.
26 detailed chronicles of successful trips for big game, selected from *Outdoor Life.*

Krider's Sporting Anecdotes, edited by Milnor H. Klapp. Abercrombie & Fitch Library, N.Y., 1966. 292 pp., illus. $8.00.
Limited issue of the much-wanted work on Philadelphia's renowned gunsmith, John Krider, publ. first in 1853. A rich fund of knowledge on upland shooting, dogs and match shooting, etc.

Living Off the Country, by B. Angier. Stackpole Books, Harrisburg, Pa., 1959. 241 pp., illus. $5.00.
In a simple and entertaining manner the author explains how to live off nature when emergency arises and how to stay alive in the woods.

Modern ABC's of Bird Hunting, by Dave Harbour, Stackpole Books, Harrisburg, Pa., 1966. 192 pp., illus. $4.95.
From city's edge to wilderness this gives the occasional hunter the quickest way on how to increase his bag. Covers all game birds of the U.S. or Canada.

The New Hunter's Encyclopedia, edited by Leonard Miracle and James B. Trefethen, plus specialized articles by over 60 outstanding contributors. Stackpole Books, Harrisburg, Pa. 1966. 1131 pp., profusely illus. with 2047 photos, diagrams, drawings and full-color plates. $24.95.
A massive work covering every detail of every sort of hunting in the U.S., Canada and Mexico.

Nove Secoli Di Armi Da Caccia, by L. G. Boccia. Editrice Edam, Firenze, Italy, 1967. 181 pp., illus. with many fine photos of superb museum quality in full color. $15.00.
In Italian text, a historical survey of hunting weapons of Italian origin and their makers.

On Your Own in the Wilderness, by Col. T. Whelen and B. Angier. Stackpole Books, Harrisburg, Pa., 1958. 324 pp., illus. $5.00.
Two eminent authorities give complete, accurate, and useful data on all phases of camping and travel in primtive areas.

The Puma, Mysterious American Cat, by S. P. Young and E. A. Goldman, Dover Publ., N.Y., 1964. 358 pp., illus. Paper covers. $2.25.
A two-part work: the first on the history, economic status and control; the second on classifications of the races of the puma.

Records of North American Big Game, 1964 Edition, comp. by Boone & Crockett Club. Holt, Rinehart & Winston, New York, 1964. 398 pp., illus. $15.00.
Standard reference on hunting trophies and record specimens of every species, also data on scoring methods, care of specimens, hunting stories. Replaces 1958 edition.

The Rifle and Hound in Ceylon, by Samuel White Baker. Abercrombie & Fitch Library, N.Y., 1967. 422 pp., well illus. $12.95.
Limited printing of a classic description of elephant-hunting, deer-coursing and elk-hunting in the East. First published in the 1850s.

Records of North American Big Game, compiled by the Records Committee of the Boone and Crockett Club, Holt, Rinehart and Winston, N.Y.C. 3d printing of the 1964 edition. 398 pp., well illus., and with color frontis. $15.00.
The 5th issue of the famous useful series, and the largest and most complete.

Safari, by Elmer Keith. Safari Publ., La Jolla, Calif., 1968. 166 pp., illus. $7.95.
Guide to big game hunting in Africa, with anecdote and expert advice on hunting many species of game. Information on guns, ammunition, equipment, and planning the safari is included. Fine photographs.

A Sporting chance . . . , by D. P. Mannix. E. P. Dutton & Co., N. Y., 1967. 248 pp. illus. with 50 photos. $6.95.
Unusual methods of hunting the exotic species from hounds to falcons. Inspiring reading for those desiring to get away from the commonplace.

Sporting Guns, by Richard Akehurst. G.P. Putnam's Sons, N.Y.C., 1968. 120 pp., illus. $5.95.
History of shooting and of the guns and rifles developed to meet the hunter's needs, with anecdotes of the hunting field.

The Sportsman's Companion, by Lee Wulff. Harper & Row, N.Y.C., 1968. 413 pp., illus. $11.95.
Compendium of writings by various experts on hunting and fishing for American game. A useful reference for the outdoorsman.

Three Years' Hunting & Trapping in America and the Great Northwest, by J. Turner-Turner. Abercrombie & Fitch Library, N.Y.C., 1967. 182 pp., illus. $10.95.
Reprint of an 1888 account of a determined quest for valuable furs in one of the world's least hospitable regions.

Travel & Adventure in Southeast Africa, by F.C. Selous. A&F Press, N.Y.C., 1967. 522 pp., illus. $11.95.
New edition of a famous African hunting book, first published in 1893.

The Treasury of Hunting, by Larry Koller. Odyssey Press, N.Y.C., 1965. 251 pp., illus. $7.95.
Concise accounts of all types of hunting in the U.S. Excellent illustrations, many color photographs taken in various hunting fields.

Trophy Heads, by John W. Moyer. Ronald Press, N.Y.C., 1962. 258 pp., well-illus., in slip case. $16.00.
Valuable reference for trophy hunters. Describes the animals, measurements, care of specimens in the field.

The Upland Game Hunter's Bible, by Dan Holland. Doubleday, N.Y.C., 1961. 192 pp., illus. Paper covers. $1.95.
Hunter's manual on the principal species of American upland game birds and how to hunt them.

The Varmint and Crow Hunter's Bible, by Bert Popowski. Doubleday & Co., N.Y.C., 1962. 185 pp., 150 illus. Paper covers. $1.95.
Hunting and trapping techniques described by a well-known authority. Chapters on woodchucks, crows, foxes, snakes, guns, etc.

Wild Fowl Decoys, by Joel Barber. Dover Publ., N.Y.C., 1954. 156 pp., 134 illus., paperbound. $3.00.
A fine work on making, painting, care and use of decoys in hunting, recently reprinted. Full data on design and construction.

Wildfowling At A Glance, by R.W. Coykendall, Jr. Stackpole Books, Harrisburg, Pa., 1968. 94 pp., illus. $2.95.
Covers wildfowl hunting in America, including ducks, decoys, dogs, boats, and blinds.

RIFLES

Big Game and Big Game Rifles, by John Taylor. Herbert Jenkins, London, 4th printing, 1958. 215 pp. with frontis. and tables. $3.50.
Pondoro's well known and popular African work. Rifles described for all big game with data on the arm, its sights, trajectories, etc.

The Big-Game Rifle, by Jack O'Connor, Alfred A. Knopf, N.Y.C., 1951. 371 pp., plus XI pp. Well illus. $8.95.
Discusses construction, purpose and use for all types of big game as well as ammo., sights, accessories, etc.

The Book of Rifles, by W. H. B. Smith. Stackpole Books, Harrisburg, Pa., 1963 (3rd ed.). 656 pp., profusely illus. $12.50.
An encyclopedic reference work on shoulder arms, recently up-dated. Includes rifles of all types, arranged by country of origin. Buy with Book of Pistols & Revolvers and both are $19.95.

The Book of the Springfield, by E. C. Crossman (1932) and R. F. Dunlap. Stackpole Books, Harrisburg, Pa., 1951. 567 pp., illus. $6.00.
Rev. and enlarged ed., brought up-to-date by Dunlap, and covering military sporting and target rifles using the 30-06 cartridge, their metallic and telescopic sights, ammunition, etc.

The Boy's Book of Rifles, by C. E. Chapel. Coward-McCann, N.Y.C., 1948, rev. ed., 1960. 274 pp., illus. $3.95.
For all young men of Boy Scout age at every phase of small-caliber marksmanship and safe gun handling. It tells how to qualify for NRA medals and Scout Merit Badges for Marksmanship.

Boy's Single-Shot Rifles, by Jas. J. Grant, William Morrow & Co., Inc., New York, 1967. 608 pp., illus. $6.00.
A wealth of important new material on an ever-popular subject, authoritatively presented. By the author of *Single Shot Rifles* and *More Single Shot Rifles.*

The Breech-Loading Single-Shot Match Rifle, by N. H. Roberts and K. L. Waters. D. Van Nostrand Co., Princeton, N.J., 1967. 293 pp., fine photos. $12.50.
Account of the Schuetzen rifle in America, with material on famous shooters, gunsmiths, ammunition, and related topics.

Garand Rifles MI, MIC, MID, by Donald B. McLean. Normount Armament Co., Forest Grove, Oregon, Ill., 1968. Over 160 pp., 175 illus., paper wrappers. $3.00.
Covers all facets of the arm: battlefield use, disassembly and maintenance, all details to complete lock-stock-and-barrel repair, plus variations, grenades, ammo., and accessories; plus a section on 7.62mm NATO conversions.

How to Select and Use Your Big Game Rifle, by Henry M. Stebbins. Combat Forces Press, Washington, 1952. 237 pp., illus. $6.50.
Concise valuable data on rifles, old and new—slide action, lever, semi automatic, and single shot models are covered.

The Lee-Enfield Rifle, by E. G. B. Reynolds. Arco Publ. Co., N.Y., 1968. 224 pp., drawings and photos. $9.50.
New U.S. edition of a standard reference on models and modifications of the famous British military rifle.

Mister Rifleman, by Col. Townsend Whelen and Bradford Angier. Petersen Publ. Co., L.A., 1965, reprinted 1967. 377 pp., well illus. $4.95.
Autobiography of the late Col. Whelen, noted firearms authority, with supplementary material. Much on marksmanship and hunting techniques.

The Modern Hunting Rifle, by Tom Hayes. A. S. Barnes, New York, 1963. 304 pp., illus. $1.98.
Guide to selection of rifles for hunting large and small game, U.S. and foreign. Chapters on loads, bullets, sights, etc.

Notes on Sporting Rifles, by G. Burrard, E. Arnold and Co., London, England, 1953. 4th ed. rev., 183 pp., illus. $4.00.
A British book on large-bore big game rifles, particularly those for Indian and African shooting. Contains the noted "Hodsock Ballistic Tables," recomputed by O. Western.
Recreating the Kentucky Rifle, by Wm. Buchele, Geo. Shumway, Publ., York, Pa., 1967. 83 pp., illus. $10.00. Ltd. ed., 500 copies.
A delightful work covering historical development, design, raw materials, tools and supplies for making the rifle, etc. Separate folded plans included.
The Rifle Book, by Jack O'Connor. Random House (Knopf), N.Y.C., 1948. 3rd ed., 1964. 338 pp., illus. $8.95.
A definitive work, out-of-print until recently, which covers actions, design, ammunition, sights and accessories.
Rifles, a Modern Encyclopedia, by H. M. Stebbins. Stackpole Books, Harrisburg, Pa., 1958. 376 pp., well illus. $15.00.
An excellently prepared work covering rifles for every use on target and game. Every associated rifle phase is included, for the youth to the user-expert on big game.
A limited number of deluxe copies, bound in full leather, autographed and numbered, are available. $25.00.
Shooting the Percussion Rifle, by R. O. Ackerman. Publ. by the author, Albuquerque, N.M., 1966. 19 pp., illus. in line by the author. Paper wrappers, $1.50.
This well prepared work is Book No. 2 of a projected series. This one gives basic information on the use of the muzzle-loading rifle.
Small Bore Target Shooting, by H. G. B. Fuller. Herbert Jenkins, London, 1964. 264 pp., well illus. $5.50.
Authoritative English work, covering rifle types, buying hints, ammunition, accessories, and range technique.
Sniper Rifles of Two World Wars, by W. H. Tantum IV. Museum Restoration Service, Ottawa, Can., 1967. 32 pp., illus. $1.50.
Monograph on high-accuracy rifles used by troops in World Wars I and II and in Korea. Paper wrappers.
The Sporting Rifle and Its Use in Britain, by Henry Tegner. Herbert Jenkins, London, 1962. 190 pp., illus. $4.00.
British hunting methods and equipment described by an expert, including guns, ammunition, field equipment, dogs, and stalking.
Springfield Rifles, M1903, M1903AI, M1903A3, M1903A4, compiled by the publ. Normount Armament Co., Forest Grove, Ore., 1968. Over 115 pp., illus., paper wrappers. $2.50.
Routine disassembly and maintenance to complete ordnance inspection and repair; bore sighting, trigger adjustment, accessories, etc.
Twenty-Two Caliber Varmint Rifles, by C. S. Landis. Stackpole Books, Harrisburg, Pa., 1947. 521 pp., profusely illustrated. $7.50.
A vast amount of data on the many wildcat 22's, including numerous scale drawings of cartridges and chambers.

American Partridge and Pheasant Shooting, Frank Schley. Abercrombie & Fitch Library, N.Y., 1967. 222 pp., illus. with detailed engravings of game birds. $7.95.
Limited printing of the rare sporting classic of 1877, considered for years the most important book available on the use of the scattergun.
The Art of Wing Shooting, by Wm. B. Leffingwell. Abercrombie & Fitch Library, N.Y., 1967. 192 pp., illus. $7.95.
Limited issue of a practical treatise on the use of the shotgun, first publ. in 1894. Contains a wealth of period anecdotes.
Automatic and Repeating Shotguns, by R. Arnold. Barnes & Co., N.Y.C., 1960. 173 pp., illus. $2.95.
Their history and development, with expert professional advice on choosing a gun for clay target shooting, game shooting, etc.
Clay Pigeon Marksmanship, by Percy Stanbury and G. L. Carlisle. Herbert Jenkins, London, 1964. 216 pp., illus. $5.00.
Handbook on learning the skills, with data on guns & equipment and competition shooting at all types of clay targets; by two eminent British writers.
Field, Skeet and Trapshooting, by C. E. Chapel. Revised ed. Barnes & Co., N.Y.C., 1962. 291 pp., illus. $6.95.
A useful work on shotgun shooting, including gun types, ammo, accessories, marksmanship, etc.
Game Shooting, by Robert Churchill. (Rev. by M. Hastings.) Stackpole Books, Harrisburg, Pa., 1967. 252 pp., drawings and photos. $8.95.
A recent revision of the 1955 British treatise on modern shotguns and their use in the hunting field.
Gough Thomas's Gun Book, by G. T. Garwood. A. & C. Black, London, England, 1969. 160 pp., illus. $6.00.
Excerpts of articles on the shotgun published in *Shooting Times,* by a noted British authority. Wide-ranging survey of every aspect on the shotgun, its use, behavior, care, and lore.
Hartman on Skeet, by Barney Hartman. D. Van Nostrand Co., Princeton, N.J., 1967. 143 pp., illus. $8.95.
A champion shooter's explanation of Skeet shooting techniques, covering the fine points mastered by experts.
Mastering the Shotgun, by R. A. Knight. E. P. Dutton & Co., N. Y., 1967. 123 pp. illus. with 65 drawings and photos. $4.95.
A down-to-earth commonsense guide, teaching how to hit what you aim at in the field, at skeet and at trap shooting.
The Modern Shotgun, by Maj. Sir Gerald Burrard. A. S. Barnes & Co., N.Y.C., 1961. In 2 vols., 1074 pp. Cased, $8.95.
Completely reliable and authoritative on the shotgun and its ammunition in every aspect.
Parker, America's Finest Shotgun, by P. H. Johnson. Outlet Book Co., Inc., N. Y., 1968. 260 pp., illus. $1.98.
An account of a great sporting arm—from post Civil War until 1947, when it was sold to Remington. Values, models, etc.
Shooting For Beginners, by E. N. Barclay. Percival Marshall & Co., London, 1963. 74 pp., illus. $1.75.
Concise introduction to British techniques and customs in shotgunning for game birds.

The Shot Gun, by T. D. S. & J. A. Purdey. A. & C. Black, London, Eng., 1962. 144 pp., illus. with photos and diagrams. $2.50.
Revised 3rd ed. of a well-known British work for all scattergunners by two members of the notable gunsmith family. Covers the gun and its use in the field, at traps, and for skeet.
The Shotgun Book, by Jack O'Connor. Alfred A. Knopf, N.Y., 1965. 332 pp., plus index, illus. with line and photos. $8.95.
The definitive, authoritative book with up-to-date chapters on wildfowling, upland gunning, trap and Skeet shooting. It includes practical advice on shotgun makes, models and functions, as well as data on actions, gauges, barrels, loads, chokes. pellets and ballistics.
The Shotgunner's Book, by Col. Charles Askins. Stackpole Books, Harrisburg, Pa., 1958. 365 pp., illus. $8.50.
Concise coverage of everything from design and manufacture to shooting form and ammunition.
Shotguns and Shooting, by E. S. McCawley Jr. Van Nostrand, N.Y.C., 1965. 146 pp., illus. $2.98.
Lucid coverage of shotgun development, various types, ammunition, and related subjects. Covers gun care, safety, and use in hunting fields or on skeet or trap ranges.
Shotguns by Keith, by E. Keith. Stackpole Books, Harrisburg, Pa., 1967. 307 pp., illus. A new edition, $7.95.
Guns and their accessories from history to ornamentation, their ammunition, and the practical use of American, English and European arms.
Skeet Shooting with D. Lee Braun, Robt. Campbell, ed. Grosset & Dunlap, N.Y., 1967. 160 pp., illus. $4.95.
Thorough instructions on the fine points of Skeet shooting.
Sure-Hit Shotgun Ways, by F. E. Sell, Stackpole Books, Harrisburg, Pa., 1967. 160 pp., illus. $5.95.
An expert with the scatter gun uncomplicates its effective use in every field, gives quick-skill methods for the sportsman.

IMPORTANT NOTICE TO BOOK BUYERS

Books listed above may be bought from Ray Riling Arms Books, 6844 Gorsten St., Phila., Pa. 19119; Norm Flayderman, Squash Hollow, RFD 2, New Milford, Conn. 06776 or Rutgers Gun Books, 127 Raritan Ave., Highland Park, N. J. 08904. Send full payment with order and include postage as applicable, or request C.O.D. shipment if for U.S. delivery only. (Post Office makes extra charge for CODs.) U.S. buyers add 25c for orders less than $10. Canadian buyers add 30c per book in U.S. funds for uninsured shipment, or 60c per book if insured. If other than U.S. funds are sent add current conversion percentage. Foreign buyers must remit in U.S. funds or add ample bank collection charges to foreign checks. Add 60c per book, uninsured (any additiional or actual post will be billed later), or 75c for a registered shipment up to 11 lbs. (CODs not permitted to Canada or foreign countries.) Penna. shipments must include current sales tax. Book lists (new and used), when available, 50c (free with order). Arms Library listings show current prices; if lower prices prevail at time of order a credit or refund will be issued. If prices are higher, a notice will be sent. *Always order from the latest* GUN DIGEST.

Shooting Publications

Write directly to the sources noted for titles listed and ask for their latest catalog. Do not order from the GUN DIGEST.

A Joint Resolution—A 4-page statement by the National Police Officers Assn. and the National Shooting Sports Foundation, outlining the role of firearms in U.S. history and voicing their stand against ill-planned restrictive gun laws. Free.[1]

Basic Pistol Marksmanship—Textbook for basic pistol courses. 25¢[2]

Basic Rifle Marksmanship—Textbook for basic rifle courses. 25¢ ea.[2]

The Elk—125-page report on the hunting and management of this game animal, more properly called *wapiti*. Extensive biblio. $1.00.[4]

Free Films—Brochure listing outdoor movies available to sportsmen's clubs. Free.[1]

The Gun Law Problem—Information about firearms legislation. Free.[2]

Handloading Made Easy—A leaflet answering the neophyte's questions about reloading. Free from National Reloading Mfgr's. Assn., 433 Silas Deane Hwy., Weathersfield, Conn. 06109

How to be a Crack Shot—A 14-page booklet detailing everything necessary to becoming an outstanding shot. Free.[3]

Fundamentals of Claybird Shooting—A 39-page booklet explaining the basics of Skeet and trap in non-technical terms. Many diagrams. 25¢ ea.[4]

Handbook on Small Bore Rifle Shooting—80-page booklet, with pictures and diagrams, tells in detail what the beginner should know about marksmanship, equipment, aiming, firing positions, care of the rifle, etc. 25¢.[1]

Hunter Safety Instructor's Guide—How to conduct an NRA Hunter Safety Course. 25¢ ea.[2]

Hunting and Shooting Sportsmanship—A 4-page brochure defining the "true sportsman" and giving information on the outdoor field. Free.[1]

Junior Rifle Handbook—Information about the NRA junior program with short instruction course. (25 copies issued to each new affiliated junior club without charge.) 25¢ ea.[2]

NRA Hunter Safety Handbook—Textbook for students. 10¢ ea.[2]

National Shooting Preserve Directory—Up-to-date listing of small game preserves in the U.S. and Canada. Free.[1]

Ranger Targets— To be used in qualifying for the NRA Ranger emblem; supplied free in reasonably large quantities.[1]

Shooting's Fun for Everyone—The why, when, where, and how of riflery for boys and girls. 20 pp. 5¢ ea.[1]

Trap or Skeet Fundamentals—Handbooks explaining fundamentals of these two sports, complete with explicit diagrams to start beginners off right. Free.[3]

25 Foot Shooting Program—Complete information on a short range shooting program with CO^2 and pneumatic rifles and pistols. 35¢[2]

What Every Parent Should Know When a Boy or Girl Wants a Gun—Straightforward answers to the 15 questions most frequently asked by parents. 8 pp. 5¢ ea.[1]

The Cottontail Rabbit—56-page rundown on America's most popular hunting target. Where to find him, how to hunt him, how to help him. Bibliography included. $1.00 ea.[4]

For the Young Hunter—A 32-page booklet giving fundamental information on the sport. Single copies free, 15¢ each in bulk.[4]

Gray and Fox Squirrels—112-page paperbound illustrated book giving full rundown on the squirrel families named. Extensive bibliography. $1.00 ea.[4]

How to Have More Pheasant Hunting—A 16-page booklet on low cost hunting, including data on in-season stocking and how to start a small preserve. 25¢.[1]

The Mallard—80-page semi-technical report on this popular duck. Life cycle, laws and management, hunting—even politics as they affect this bird—are covered. Bibliography. $1.00 ea.[4]

NRA Booklets—Ranging from 12 to 36 pages, these are articles on specific arms or arms types. Titles available are: Sighting In; The 45 Automatic; The M1 Rifle; Telescopic Sights; Metallic Sights; Duck Hunting; U.S. Cal. 30 Carbine; Remodeling the 03A3; Remodeling the 303 Lee-Enfield; Remodeling the U.S. 1917 Rifle; M1903 Springfield Rifle; Military Rifles and Civil War Small Arms, 50¢ ea. Gun Cabinets, Racks, Cases & Pistol Boxes, 75¢. Deer Hunting, $1.00.[2]

Under the heading of "Range Plans" are 15 booklets priced from 10¢ to $1.00. All are described in an order form pamphlet available from the NRA.

NRA Firearms & Ammunition Fact Book—352-page book of questions and answers, ballistic charts and tables, descriptions of firearms and ammunition. NRA, Washington, D.C., 1964. $2.00 ea. ($1.75 to NRA members).

NRA Firearms Assembly Handbook, Volumes I and II—Articles describing the assembly and disassembly of various arms. Vol. I, 160 pp., covers 77 guns, Vol. II, 176 pp., 87 guns. Illustrated with exploded-view and supplementary drawings. NRA, Washington, D.C., 1960 and 1964. $3.50 ea. (2.50 to NRA members).

NRA Firearms Handling Handbook—21 major articles on the proper useage of most types of small arms available to civilians. Illus. NRA, Washington, D.C., 1962, 80 pp. $2.75 ($1.75 to NRA members).

NRA Gun Collectors Handbook—20 feature articles on all phases of gun collecting, plus a listing of all important museums. NRA, Washington, D.C., 1959. 48 pp., illus. $2.50 ($1.50 to NRA members).

NRA Handloader's Guide—Enlarged & Revised. A successor to the *NRA Illustrated Reloading Handbook*, this excellent new work covers all aspects of metallic-case and shotshell reloading. Washington, D. C., 1969, fully illus. $5.00 (NRA members, $4.00).

NRA Hunters Handbook—51 major pieces, 18 shorter ones. NRA, Washington, D.C., 1960. 72 pp., illus. $3.00 ($2.00 to NRA members).

NRA Illustrated International Shooting Handbook—18 major articles detailing shooting under ISU rules, training methods, etc. NRA, Washington, D.C., 1964. $2.50 ea. ($1.50 to NRA members).

NRA Illustrated Shotgun Handbook—50 articles covering every phase of smoothbore shooting, including exploded views of many shotguns. NRA, Washington, D.C. 1964. 128 pp. $3.00 ea. ($2.00 to NRA members).

NRA Questions and Answers Handbook—150 queries and replies on guns and shooting. NRA, Washington, D.C., 1959. 46 pp. with index, illus. $2.50 ($1.50 to NRA members).

NRA Shooters Guide—40 articles of high interest to shooters of all kinds. Over 340 illus. NRA, Washington, D.C., 1959. 72 pp., $3.00 ($2.00 to NRA members).

NRA Shooting Handbook—83 major articles plus 35 shorts on every phase of shooting. NRA, Washington, D.C., 1961. 224 pp., illus. $4.50 ($3.50 to NRA members).

Principles of Game Management—A 25-page booklet surveying in popular manner such subjects as hunting regulations, predator control, game refuges and habitat restoration. Single copies free, 15¢ each in bulk.[4]

The Ring-Necked Pheasant—Popular distillation of much of the technical literature on the "ringneck." 104-page paperbound book, appropriately illustrated. Bibliography included. $1.00 ea.[4]

Start A Gun Club—All of the basic information needed to establish a club with clay bird shooting facilities. 24 pp. 50¢[1]

Where To Shoot Muzzle Loaders In The U.S.A.—Publ. for black powder burners, and lists more than 100 muzzle loading clubs. 10¢.[1]

The White-Tailed Deer—History, management, hunting—a complete survey in this 108-page paperbound book. Full bibliography. $1.00 ea.[4]

Wingshooter's Handbook—A 24-page booklet of information useful to both beginning and veteran shotgunners. Free from Poly-Choke, Dept. W4, Hartford, Conn.

You and Your Lawmaker—A 22-page citizenship manual for sportsmen, showing how they can support or combat legislation affecting shooting and outdoor sports. 10¢ ea.[2]

[1]National Shooting Sports Foundation, Inc. 1075 Post Road, Riverside, Conn. 06878

[2]National Rifle Association of America, 1600 Rhode Island Ave., Washington, D. C. 20036

[3]Remington Arms Company, Dept. C—Bridgeport, Conn. 06602

[4]Olin Mathieson Conservation Dept., East Alton, Ill. 62024

Publishers: Please send review copies to John T. Amber, P.O. Box 0, Chicago, Ill. 60690

PERIODICAL PUBLICATIONS

Alaska Sportsman
Alaska Northwest Pub. Co., Box 4-EEE, Anchorage, Alaska 99503. $6.00 yr. Hunting and fishing articles.

American Field†
222 W. Adams St., Chicago, Ill. 60606. $9.00 yr. Field dogs and trials, occasional gun and hunting articles.

The American Rifleman (M)
National Rifle Assn., 1600 Rhode Island Ave. N.W., Wash., D.C. 20036. $5.00 yr. Firearms articles of all kinds.

The American Sportsman Quarterly (Q)
239 Great Neck Rd., Great Neck, N.Y. 11021. $18.00 yr.

Argosy
Popular Publ., Inc., McCall St., Dayton 1, Ohio. $5.00 yr.

Army (M)
Assn. of the U.S. Army, 1529 18th Ave. N.W., Wash., D.C. 20036. $6.00 yr. Occasional articles on small arms.

Deutsches Waffen Journal
Journal-Verlag Schwend GmbH, Postfach 340, Schwabisch Hall, Germany. $8.00 yr. Antique and modern arms, their history, technical aspects, etc.

Ducks Unlimited, Inc. (M)
P.O. Box 66300, Chicago, Ill. 60666.

The Field†
The Harmsworth Press Ltd., 8 Stratton St., London W.I., England. $27.00 yr. Hunting and shooting articles.

Field & Stream
Holt, Rinehart and Winston, Inc., 383 Madison Ave., New York, N.Y. 10017. $4.00 yr. Warren Page on firearms plus hunting and fishing articles.

Fishing and Hunting Guide
Fishing and Hunting Guide Ltd., P.O. Box 48, Dolton, Ill. 60419. $3.00 yr.

Fur-Fish-Game
A. R. Harding Pub. Co., 2878 E. Main St., Columbus, Ohio 43209. $3.50 yr. "Gun Rack" column by M. H. Decker.

Gunfacts Magazine
Hazard Publications, Inc., Box 9335, Arlington, Va. 22209. $9.00 yr.

The Gun Report
World Wide Gun Report, Inc., Box 111, Aledo, Ill. 61231. $6.00 yr. For the gun collector.

Gun Week†
Sidney Printing & Publishing Co., P.O. Box 150, Sidney, Ohio 45365. $4.00 yr. U.S. and possessions; $4.50 yr. Canada; $6.00 yr. foreign. Tabloid paper on guns, hunting, shooting.

Guns & Ammo
Petersen Pub. Co., 8490 Sunset Blvd., Los Angeles, Calif. 90069. $5.00 yr. Guns, shooting, and technical ballistics articles.

Guns
Guns Magazine, 8150 N. Central Park Ave., Skokie, Ill. 60076 $7.50 yr. Articles for gun collectors, hunters and shooters.

Guns and Game*
Stanco Sports Library, Inc., 261 Fifth Ave., New York, N.Y. 10016. $3.00 yr., $4.00 foreign. Technical and general articles.

Guns & Hunting*
Maco Publishing Co., Inc., 1790 Broadway, New York, N.Y. 10019. $6.00 yr. Gun collecting, shooting and hunting articles.

Guns Review
Ravenhill Pub. Co. Ltd., Low Hall Rd., Horsforth, Leeds, England. $6.50 yr. For collectors and shooters.

Gun World
Gallant Publishing Co., 116 E. Badillo, Covina, Calif. 91722. $5.00 yr. For the hunting, reloading and shooting enthusiast.

The Handgunner (M)
U.S. Revolver Assn., 59 Alvin St., Springfield, Mass. $3.50 yr. General handgun and competition articles.

The Handloader Magazine*
Dave Wolfe Pub. Co., Box 3482, Rte. 4, Peoria, Ill. 61614. $4.00 yr.

Hobbies
Lightner Pub. Co., 1006 S. Michigan Ave., Chicago, Ill. 60605. $5.00 yr.; Canada $6.00; foreign $6.50. Collectors departments.

International Shooting Sport*
Union Internationale de Tir, 62 Wiesbaden-Klarenthal, Klarenthalerstr., Germany. $3.60 yr., p.p. For the International target shooter.

The Journal of the Arms & Armour Society (M)
F. Wilkinson (Secy.), 40 Great James St., Holborn, London WC1, England. $4.00 yr. Articles for the collector.

Law and Order
Law and Order Magazine, 72 W. 45th St., New York, N.Y. 10036. $4.00 yr. Articles on weapons for law enforcement.

Muzzle Blasts (M)
National Muzzle Loading Rifle Assn.; P.O. Box 67, Friendship, Ind. 47021. $6.00 yr. For the black powder shooter.

National Rifle Assn. Journal (British)
Natl. Rifle Assn. (BR.), Bisley Camp, Brookwood, Surrey, England.

National Wildlife*
Natl. Wildlife Fed. Inc., 381 W. Center St., Marion, O. 43302. $5.00 yr. w/Assoc. membership.

New Zealand Wildlife (Q)
New Zealand Deerstalkers Assoc. Inc., P.O. Box 263, Wellington, N.Z. $2.00 U.S. and Canada, elsewhere on application. Hunting and shooting articles.

Ordnance* (M)
American Ordnance Assn., Transportation Bldg., Wash., D.C. 20006. $8.00 yr. $7.00 to members. Occasional articles on small arms and related subjects.

Outdoor Life
Popular Science Pub. Co., 355 Lexington Ave., New York, N.Y. 10017. $4.00 yr. Arms column by Jack O'Connor.

Outdoor World*
Preston Publications Inc., 1645 Tullie Circle, N.E., Atlanta, Ga. 30329. $5.75 yr. Conservation and wildlife articles.

Police*
Charles C Thomas, Publisher, 301-327 E. Lawrence Ave., Springfield, Ill. 62703. $9.50 yr. Articles on identification, etc.

Police Times (M)
7777 N.E. 3rd Court, Miami, Fla. 33138.

Popular Mechanics
Hearst Corp., 575 Lexington Ave., New York, N.Y. 10022. $4.00 yr., $4.50 Canada, $6.00 foreign. Hunting and shooting articles.

Precision Shooting
Precision Shooting, Inc., Winthrop, Maine 04364. $4.50 yr. For all advanced shooters. Journal of the N.B.R.S.A.

The Rifle Magazine*
Dave Wolfe Publishing Co., Rt. 4, Box 3482, Peoria, Ill. 61614. $4.00 yr.

The Rifleman (Q)
National Smallbore Rifle Assoc., 113 Southwark St., London S. E. 1, England. $7.00 (5 yrs.). Data on British Matches and International Matches, and technical shooting articles.

Rod and Gun in Canada
Rod and Gun Pub Corp., 1475 Metcalfe St., Montreal 2, P.Q., Canada. $3.00 yr., $5.00 2 yrs., out of Canada, postage $1.00 p. yr. extra. Regular gun and shooting articles.

Saga
Gambi Public., 333 Johnson Ave., Brooklyn, N.Y. 11026. $5.00 yr. U.S., $5.50 Canada.

The Shooting Industry
Publisher's Dev. Corp., 8150 N. Central Pk., Skokie, Ill. 60076. $7.00 yr. 9 times a year.

The Shooting Times (England)†
Braywick House, Braywick Rd., Maidenhead, Berks., England. Rates on application. Game shooting and firearms articles.

Shooting Times
Peoria Journal-Star, Inc., Box 1500, War Memorial Dr., Peoria, Ill., 61601. $5.00 yr. Gun ads plus articles on every gun activity.

The Shotgun News‡
Snell Publishing Co., Columbus, Nebr. 68601. $3.00 yr. Sample copy 50¢. Gun ads of all kinds.

The Skeet Shooting Review
National Skeet Shooting Assn., 212 Linwood Bldg., 2608 Inwood Rd., Dallas, Tex. 75235. $6.00 yr. Scores, averages, skeet articles.

Sporting Goods Business
7 E. 43rd, New York, N.Y. 10017. Trade journal.

The Sporting Goods Dealer
2018 W. Washington Ave., St. Louis, Mo. 63166. The sporting goods trade journal.

Sports Afield
The Hearst Corp. 57th St. at 8th Ave., New York, N.Y. 10019 $4.00 yr. Pete Brown on firearms plus hunting and fishing articles.

Sports Age Magazine
P.O. Box 67, Minneapolis, Minn. Trade journal.

Sports Illustrated†
Time, Inc., 540 N. Michigan Ave., Chicago, Ill. 60611. $7.00 yr. Articles on the current sporting scene.

Trap & Field
Review Pub. Co., 1100 Waterway Blvd., Indianapolis, Ind. 46202. $7.00 yr. Scores, averages, trapshooting articles.

True
Fawcett Publ., Inc., Fawcett Bldg., Greenwich, Conn. 06830. $5.00 yr. U.S., Poss., and Canada; $7.00 yr. All other countries.

Valor
Natl. Police Offic. Assoc., Natl. Police Academy Bldg., 1890 S. Trail, Venice, Fla. 33595. $5.00 yr.

Wildlife Review (Q)
Fish & Wildlife Branch, Dep't of Rec. and Conservation. Parliament Bldgs., Victoria, B.C. $1.00 2 yrs.

* Published bi-monthly
† Published weekly
‡ Published twice per month
M Membership requirements; write for details.
Q Published Quarterly.

ARMS ASSOCIATIONS IN AMERICA AND ABROAD

Alabama Gun Collectors Assn.
Miss Betty Voss, 2326 Cahaba Rd., Birmingham, Ala. 35223
Alamo Arms Collectors
Bill Brookshire, 410 Rector, San Antonio, Tex. 78216
Amateur Trap Shooting Assn.
P.O. Box. 246, Vandalia, O. 45377
American Military Inst.
Box 568, Washington, D.C. 20044
American Ordnance Assn.
R. E. Lewis, 616 Transportation Bldg., Washington, D.C. 20006
American Reloaders Assn.
Dean Grennell, Box 4007, Covina, Calif. 91722
American Single Shot Rifle Assn.
Dr. John P. May, 13 E. Prospect Ave., Mt. Prospect, Ill. 60056
American Society of Arms Collectors, Inc.
Rob. F. Rubendunst, 6550 Baywood Ln., Cincinnati, O. 45224
Antique Arms Coll. Assn. of Conn.
A. Darling, 35 Stanley St., New Haven, Conn. 06511
Arapahoe Gun Collectors
Bill Rutherford, 3268 S. Downing, Englewood, Colo.
Arizona Gun Collectors
Mike Welker, 1940 E. Clarendon, Phoenix, Ariz. 85016
Arkansas Gun & Cartridge Coll. Club
M. Cutrell, 2006 E. 7th, Pine Bluff, Ark. 71601
Ark-La-Tex Gun Collectors Assn.
Harry King, 414 Mohawk Trail, Shreveport, La. 71107
Armor & Arms Club
Secretary S. V. Grancsay, Metropolitan Museum of Art, N. Y., N. Y. 10028
Arms Collectors of the Southwest
Robert Kuban, Box 543, Yuma, Ariz.
Arms and Armour Society of London
F. Wilkinson, 40 Great James St., Holborn, London, W.C.I.
Barberton Gun Collectors Assn.
R. N. Watters, 1108 Bevan St., Barberton, O.
Bay Cities Arms Coll. Assn.
P. Oldham, 8714 Hollywood Blvd., Los Angeles, Ca. 90069
Bay Colony Weapons Collectors
Carl Majesky, 42 Cabot Rd., Danvers, Mass.
Bayou Gun Club
G. Rountree, 2101 Easter Ln., New Orleans, La. 70114
Boone & Crockett Club
400 Forbes Ave., Pittsburgh, Pa.
Calif. Muzzle Loader Assn.
A. Moore, 3960 Palos Verdes Dr. N., Palos Verdes Estates, Ca. 90274
Carolina Gun Collectors Assn.
J. Marshall, P.O. Box 787, Wilmington, N.C. 28401
Central Illinois Gun Collectors Assn., Inc.
Paul Peterson, 1251 South East, Jacksonville, Ill.
Central Indiana Gun Coll. Assn.
Paul E. Daughterty, 421 E. Washington St., Hartford City, Ind. 47348
Central Ohio Gun and Indian Relic Coll. Assn.
Coyt Stookey, 134 E. Ohio Ave., Washington C.H., O. 43160
Central Penn Antique Arms Assn.
W. Motter, 27 Donald Ave., Middletown, Pa. 17057
Central States Gun Collectors Assn.
Chas. J. Versluls, 701 Broadway, Waterloo, Ia. 50703
Chippewa Valley Weapons Collectors
J. M. Sulllvan, 504 Ferry St., Eau Claire, Wis. 54701
Chisholm Trail Antique Gun Coll. Assn.
L. Smith, 2233 Bella Vista, Wichita, Kans. 67203
Connecticut Gun Guild
R. Harris, P.O. Box 67, Cornwall Bridge, Conn. 06754
Cowtown Gun Traders & Collectors
W. Morgan, 1401 Jacksboro Hwy., Ft. Worth, Tex.
Crawfordsville Gun Club, Inc.
Rob. J. K. Edmonds, R.R. 2, Crawfordsville, Ind. 47933
Cumberland Valley Arms Collectors Assn.
N. Naylor, Rte. #2, Hagerstown, Md. 21740
Dallas Gun Collectors Assn.
D. Jackson, 8603 Angora, Dallas, Tex. 75218
Delaware Antique Arms Collectors
C. Landis, 2408 Duncan Rd., Wilmington, Del. 19808
Dixie Arms Collectors
Ruth Greecy, 1509 W. 7th, Hattiesburg, Miss. 39401
Dixie Gun Collectors Assn.
Albert E. Lewis, Box 6027, Daytona Beach, Fla.
Eastern Iowa Gun and Cartridge Collectors Assn.
F. Fitzpatrick, 305 N. Eliza St., Maquoketa, Ia. 52060
Edwardsville, Ill. Gun Collectors
A. W. Stephensmeler, 317 N. Grand Bl., St. Louls, Mo. 63103
Egyptian Gun Collectors Assn. Inc.
George W. Harlow, 312 Main St., Mt. Vernon, Ill. 62864
Experimental Ballistics Associates
Ed Yard, 110 Kensington, Trenton, N. J. 08608
Florida Gun Collectors Assn.
G.J. Levy, P.O. Box 186, Hialeah, Fla. 33010
Forks of the Delaware Weapons Assn.
John F. Scheid, 348 Bushkill St., Easton, Pa. 18042
Fort Dearborn Frontiersmen
Art Pardi, 434 W. Hickory, Lombard, Ill. 60148
Fort Lee Arms Collectors
W. E. Sammis, R.D. 776 Brookridge Dr., Valley Cottage, N. Y. 10989
Fox Valley Arms Fellowship, Inc.
Bruce Eckersberg, P.O. Box 301, Palatine, Ill. 60067
Four State Collectors Assn.
M. G. Wilkinson, 915 E. 10th, Pittsburgh, Kan. 66762
Georgia Arms Collectors
James F. Watterson, 2915 Paces Lake Ct., N.W., Atlanta, Ga. 30339
Great Lakes Weapons Coll. Assn., Inc.
E. Warnke, 7207 So. 36th St., Franklin, Wis. 53132
Historical Firearms Soc. of South Africa
"Minden" 11 Buchan Rd., Newlands, Cape Town, South Africa
Houston Gun Collectors Assn.
C. McKim, 5454 Stillbrooke, Houston, Tex. 77035
Hudson-Mohawk Arms Collectors Assn., Inc.
Bennie S. Pisarz, R.D. 2, Ilion, N.Y. 13357
Illinois Gun Collectors
P. E. Pitts, P.O. Box 1524, Chicago, Ill. 60690
Illinois State Rifle Assn.
2800 N. Milwaukee Ave., Chicago, Ill. 60618
Indian Territory Gun Collectors Assn.
Tom C. DeHart, P.O. Box 4491, Tulsa, Okla. 74104
International Cartridge Coll. Assn., Inc.
A. D. Amesbury, 4065 Montecito Ave., Tucson, Ariz. 85711
Iroquois Arms Collectors Assn.
Dennis Freeman, 14144 McNeeley Rd., Akron, N. Y. 14001
Jefferson State Arms Collectors
Art Chipman, 2251 Ross Lane, Medford, Ore. 97501
Jersey Shore Antique Arms Collectors
Bob Holloway, 1755 McGalliard Ave., Trenton, N. J. 08610
John Hunt Morgan Gun Coll. Assn.
Ray Van Hook, No. 3 Emily St., Parls, Ky. 40361
Kentuckiana Arms Coll. Assn.
John F. Harder, Box 1776, Louisville, Ky. 40201
Kentucky Gun Collectors Assn.,
Ben Johnson, Box 64, Owensboro, Ky. 42301
Lakeshore Gun Collectors
R. N. Watters, 1108 Bevan St., Barberton, Ohio 44203
Lancaster Muzzle Loading Rifle Assn.
Robert Rambo, R. D. #1, Cochranville, Pa. 19330
Les Arquebusiers de France,
M. Moy, 68 rue Ledru-Rollin, 94-Saint-Maur-des-Fosses, France
Little Fort Gun Collectors Assn.
Ernie Robinson, P.O. Box 194, Gurney, Ill. 60031
Long Island Antique Gun Coll. Assn.
R. W. Karl, 72 E. 17th St., Huntington Station, N.Y. 11746
Los Angeles Gun & Ctg. Collectors Assn.
F. H. Ruffra, 1254 9th St., Santa Monica, Calif.
Lower Canada Arms Collectors Assn.
Secretary, P.O. Box 1162, St. B, Montreal 101, Quebec, Can.
Maple Tree Gun Coll. Assn.
E. P. Hector, Meriden Rd., Lebanon, N.H. 03766
Maryland Arms Coll. Assn., Inc.
H. R. Moale, 2602 Hillcrest Ave., Baltimore, Md. 21234
Massachusetts Arms Collectors
John J. Callan, Jr., 15 Montague St., Worcester, Mass. 01603
Maumee Valley Gun Collectors Assn.
J. Jennings, 3450 Gallatin Rd., Toledo, O. 43606
Memphis Antique Weapons Assn.
F. Dauser, 3429 Jenkins, Memphis, Tenn. 38118
Memphis Gun Collectors Assn.
T. C. Lee, Jr., 166 Picardy Pl., Memphis, Tenn. 38111
Meramec Valley Gun Collectors
L. W. Olson, Star Route, St. Clair, Mo.
Michigan Gun Collectors Assn.
W. H. Heid, 8914 Borgman Ave., Huntington Woods, Mich. 48070
Michigan Rifle & Pistol Assn.
John W. Novitch, 124 Moss Ave., Highland Park, Mich. 48023
Mid-State Arms Coll. & Shooters Club
B. Pisarz, R.D. 2, Ilion, N.Y. 13357
Midwest Gun Collectors Assn.
James Tregg, RR #1, Spring Bay Rd., East Peoria, Ill. 61611
Minnesota Weapons Coll. Assn., Inc.
W. Nemitz, P.O. Box 5098, Minneapolis, Minn. 55406
Mississippi Gun Collectors Assn.
Mrs. J. E. Swinney, Box 1332, Hattiesburg, Miss. 39401
Mississippi Valley Gun & Cartridge Coll. Assn.
Mel Sims, Viola, Ill.
Missouri Valley Arms Collectors
A. D. McCall, 1902 Meadow Ct., Harrisonville, Mo. 64701
Montana Arms Collectors Assn.
Chris Sorensen, 175 6th Ave., W.N. Kalispell, Mont. 59901
Muzzle Loaders' Assn. of Great Britain
D. R. Hawkes, 12 Monument Green, Weybridge, Surrey, Eng.
National Bench Rest Shooters Assn., Inc.
Bernice McMullen, 607 W. Line St., Minerva, O. 44657
National Muzzle Loading Rifle Assn.
Box 67, Friendship, Ind. 47021
National Police Officers Assn. of America
Natl. Police Academy Bldg., 1890 So. Trail, Venice, Fla. 33595
National Reloading Mfrs. Assn., Inc.
Robert Matt, 433 Silas Deane Highway, Wethersfield, Conn. 06109
National Rifle Assn.
1600 Rhode Island Ave., Washington, D.C. 20036
National Rifle Assn. (British)
Bisley Camp, Brookwood, Surrey, England
National Shooting Sports Fdtn., Inc.
Charles Dickey, 1075 Post Rd., Riverside, Conn. 06878
National Skeet Shooters Assn.
George W. White, 212 Linwood Bldg., 2608 Inwood Rd., Dallas, Tex. 75235
Nebraska Gun & Cartridge Collectors
E. M. Zalud, 710 West 6th St., North Platte, Neb. 69101
New Hampshire Arms Collectors Inc.
James Tillinghast, Box 5, Marlow, N. H. 03456
New Jersey Arms Collectors Club, Inc.
D. Blake, 82 Southgate Rd., Murray Hill, N.J. 07974
New Mexico Gun Collectors Assn.
P. Strober, 8906 Cordova Ave. N.E., Albuquerque, N.M. 87121
New York State Arms Collectors Assn., Inc.
Marvin Salls, R. D. 1, Ilion, N. Y. 13357
New Zealand Deerstalkers Assn.
I. D. Wright, P.O. Box 263, Wellington, New Zealand
Niagara Arms Collectors
Box 948, Beamsville, Ont., Canada
North Alabama Gun Coll. Assn.
H. Attaya, Jr., 5624 Woodridge St., Huntsville, Ala. 35802
Northeastern Ohio Gun Coll. Assn.
John T. Kanne, 1715 Walnut Blvd., Ashtabula, O.
Northern California Historical Arms Coll. Assn.
John L. Moss, 156 Mirada Dr., Daly City, Ca. 94015
Northern Indiana Gun Collectors Assn.
Joe Katona, 16150 Ireland Rd., Mishawaka, Ind. 46544
Northern Tier Antique Gun Collectors
Cliff Breidinger, Trout Run, Pa.
North-South Skirmish Assn.
F. Schoch, 1247 Croyden Rd., Lyndhurst, Ohio 44124
Ohio Gun Collectors Assn., Inc.
Mrs. C. D. Rickey, 130 S. Main St., Prospect, O. 43342
Old Fort Gun Collectors Assn.
Jim Hemminger, Box 156, Van Buren, Ark.
Ontario Arms Collectors Assn.
P. Peddle, 174 Ellerslie Ave., Willowdale, Ont., Canada
Oregon Arms Coll. Assn. Inc.
Dan Scherlie, 204 N.E. 47th, Portland, Ore. 97213
Paso Del Norte Gun Collectors Assn.
Ken Hockett, 1216 Mescalero, El Paso, Tex. 79925
Patch & Ball Gun Collectors
J. Falerias, 1417 Raspberry Ln., Flint, Mich. 48507
Pelican Arms Collectors
B. Thompson, 9142 Cefalu Dr., Baton Rouge, La. 70811
Penn-Mar-Va Antique Arms Soc.
T. Wibberley, 54 E. Lincoln Ave., Hagerstown, Md. 21740
Pennsylvania Antique Gun Collectors Assn.
S. B. Smullen III, R. D. 4, Narcissa Rd., Norristown, Pa. 19401
Pennsylvania Gun Collectors Assn.
Arch Waugh, RD 2, Washington, Pa. 15301
Pikes Peak Gun Collectors Guild
Charles Cell, 406 E. Uintah St., Colorado Springs, Colo. 80903
Pioneer Gun Collectors Assn.
J. O. Wingate, 4611 Cherokee, Amarillo, Tex. 79109
Potomac Arms Collectors Assn.
N. Henry, 709 Brantford, Silver Spring, Md. 20904
Presque Isle Gun Collectors Assn.
James Welch, 156 E. 37th St., Erie, Pa. 16506
Quad City Arms Coll. Assn.
A. Squire, 1845 W. 3rd St., Davenport, Ia. 52802
Redlands Arms Collectors
Harold W. Cleveland, 140 The Terrace, Redlands, Calif.
Royal Oak Gun Collectors
Margaret Parker, 13143 Borgmann, Huntington Woods, Mich. 48070

Sabine Gun Collectors Club
Mrs. J. Nugent, Rt. 1, Box 176-B, Orange, Tex. 77630
San Bernardino Valley Gun Collectors
F. Schaperkotter, 2697 Acacia Ave., San Bernardino, Cal. 92405
San Fernando Valley Arms Coll.
L. Campbell, 232 S. 6th, Valinda, Cal. 91744
San Gabriel Valley Arms Collectors
J. Mandeville, 16831 Holton, Valinda, Cal. 91744
Santa Barbara Antique Arms Coll. Assn., Inc.
Henry Ealand, 3011 Paseo Del Refugio, Santa Barbara, Calif. 93454
Sauk Trail Gun Collectors
Pete Carlock, R.F.D., Prophetstown, Ill. 61277
Shasta Arms Collectors Assn.
L. C. Lacey, Box 715, Project City, Cal. 96079
Shooting Sports Assn., Inc.
Dan Fales, 1075 Post Rd., Riverside, Conn. 06878
Smoky Mountain Gun Collectors Assn.
W. Brundage, 111 Dixie Ln., Oak Ridge Tenn. 37830
Solomon Valley Gun Collectors
Frank Wheeler, Box 230, Osborne, Kan. 67473
Somerset Rifle & Pistol Club
J. Richard Ross, 2 Stein Bldg., Somerset, Pa. 15501
South Carolina Arms Coll. Assn.
J. W. McNelley, 3215 Lincoln St., Columbia, S.C. 29201
Southern California Arms Collectors Assn.
Frank E. Barnyak, 4204 Elmer Ave., No. Hollywood, Cal. 91602
Southern Indiana Gun Collectors Assn., Inc.
Harold M. McClary, 509 N. 3rd St., Boonville, Ind. 47601
Sporting Arms and Ammunition Manufacturers' Inst.
420 Lexington Ave., N. Y., N. Y. 10017
Stark Gun Collectors, Inc.
Lester C. Brown, 1632 Pontius Pl. N.E. Canton, O.
Stratford Gun Collectors Assn., Inc.
F. Santora, 351 Grovers Ave., Bridgeport, Conn. 06605
Tampa Bay Gun Collectors Assn.
Col. Emmet M. Jeffreys, 401 49th St., N., St. Petersburg, Fla. 33710
Tennessee Gun Collectors Assn., Inc.
M. H. Parks, 3556 Pleasant Valley Rd., Nashville, Tenn. 37204
Texas Gun Collectors Assn.
Nancy Pabst, 225 W. Gramercy, San Antonio, Tex. 78212
Tippecanoe Gun and Cartridge Collectors Club
Leonard Ledman, RR 12, Box 212, Lafayette, Ind.
Tri-State Gun Collectors
Laurence Stombaugh, 2223 Makin Dr., Lima, O. 45804
Two Lick Valley Gun Collectors
Zenas Hoover, 222 Phila. St., Indiana, Pa. 15701
U. S. International Trap and Skeet Assn.
Box 1437, Huntington Beach, Ca. 92647
U. S. Revolver Assn.
Stanley A. Sprague, 59 Alvin St., Springfield, Mass. 01104
Utah Gun Collectors Assn.
S. Gerald Keogh, 875 20th St., Ogden, Utah 84401
Vermont Gun Coll. Assn.
C. E. Reynolds, 25 Simpson Ct., So. Burlington, Vt. 05403
Virginia Arms Collectors & Assn.
W. H. Bacon, 4601 Sylvan Rd., Richmond, Va. 23225
Wabash Valley Gun Collectors Assn., Inc.
Mrs. Betty Baer, 1002 Lincoln Pk. Ave., Danville, Ill. 61832
Waco Gun Collectors
C. V. Pruitt, 4021 N. 26th, Waco, Tex.
Washington Arms Collectors, Inc.
L. A. Funk, 9404 Woodland Rd., Puyallup, Wash. 98371
Westchester Arms Collectors Club, Inc.
F. E. Falkenbury, Jr., 75 Hillcrest Rd., Hartsdale, N. Y. 10530
Western Illinois Gun Collectors Assn.
Verne Geer, 421 Pearl, Macomb, Ill.
Willamette Valley Arms Coll. Assn.
M. Brooks, 2110 W. 20th, Eugene, Ore. 97405
Wisconsin Gun Collectors Assn., Inc.
S. Cibulka, 2556 N. 70th St., Wauwatosa, Wis. 53213
Wyoming Gun Collectors
Bob Funk, 224N. 2W., Riverton, Wyo. 82501

New M-16 Training Round

Device 3F67A, a 5.56mm training cartridge, has been developed under contract for the Marine Corps by the Naval Training Device Center, Orlando, Florida. The cartridges are being manufactured by Remington. This device will be used for scoring against an "aggressor" target, which drops upon being hit by the training cartridge. The 5.56mm training cartridge, which can be fired from an M-16 rifle, fires a 5-gr. bullet at a muzzle velocity of 1040 fps. In contrast, the standard 5.56mm cartridge fires a 55-gr. bullet at a velocity of 3300 fps. Muzzle energy is 1,330 ft. lbs.—about 100 times more powerful than the training cartridge.

The major requirement placed upon the training cartridge is that its energy shall not exceed 12 ft. lbs. and shall maintain a minimum energy of 12 inch/ounces at 200 feet. The bullet is partially hollow, being closed at the heel and open at the nose. Its accuracy is about 10½" extreme spread at 50 yards. The point of impact is two to three inches below the point of aim with regular loads. When fired at a few feet for penetration into a 20% gelatin, the bullet went in 3-4", but at 50 yards the penetration is only two inches. The bullet channel in the gelatin is clear.

By comparison, a 22 Short, 29-gr. lead bullet, fired with a muzzle velocity of 900 fps at the eight-inch gelatin block, shows complete penetration, accompanied by radial fracturing along the entire length of the bullet channel. The 5-gr. bullet, when fired into soft plywood at 50 yards, penetrates about 0.2", then bounces off. At a few feet from the muzzle, the bullet penetrates its length and remains stuck in the plywood. The bullet will not operate the M-16 rifle in automatic or semi-automatic firing, thus making it necessary to pull the bolt and eject the cartridge. 12-ft. lb muzzle energy makes the bullet dangerous and possibly lethal at extremely close ranges. It is intended to be fired at targets only, and safety precautions must be exercised. Servicemen in the vicinity should wear bulletproof vests and safety goggles. If, by accident, someone is hit by the bullet, recovery chances are good because of the non-radial feature of the bullet.

Allen Cohen, Project Engineer

Smokeless Powder Equivalent?

"Look on the end flap of a box of shotgun shells," says Ted McCawley, public relations manager for Remington Arms Company, Inc., "and you'll find a series of letters and numbers which are used to describe the load inside. The meaning of most of these symbols is obvious to experienced shooters — or so it would seem anyway. For example, a box of Remington shotgun shells might be marked 'SP-12-6 3¾ - 1¼-6.' The 'SP12-6' means 12 gauge plastic shells with number 6 shot; '3¾ - 1¼-6' means that the shells are loaded with powder equivalent to 3¾ drams and 1¼ ounces of number 6 shot. 'Simple enough,' you say, but is it? What does powder equivalent to 3¾ drams really mean?

"In the old days of black powder in shotguns," continues McCawley, "the strength of a load was defined more by the amount of powder used than by the generally inaccurately known velocity of the shot charge. This led to the designation of loads by powder charge weight. The avoirdupois dram was a unit of convenient size, being 1/16 of an ounce. Hence loads were defined by the number of drams of black powder which they contained and were called 3-dram or 4-dram, etc., loads.

"Of course the old-timers couldn't carry a scale around with them for loading so a scoop of the correct volume to give a known weight of powder was needed. This also was tied in with the fact that the earliest smokeless powders were supposed to be made to load on a basis of equal bulk or volume with black powder. In other words, a shell loaded with a 3-dram black powder scoopful of smokeless powder would give the same ballistics as a similar shell loaded with the same scoopful of black powder.

"A standard 3-dram charge cup was developed by the Union Metallic Cartridge Company which held 3 drams (82 grains) of black powder. This cup was 1.125" long by 0.625" in diameter. As smokeless powders developed beyond the stage mentioned in the preceding paragraph, they no longer even approximated a 'bulk for bulk' performance with black powder. However, the old designations for the 'strength' of a load persisted.

"Shooters had a good idea of just how heavy a 3-dram load was, so that it became customary to load smokeless powder to give ballistics equivalent to those of the black powder load being duplicated. Hence the smokeless powder load was designated as a '3-dram equivalent' load.

"This designation is an interesting carry-over from the early days of the shotgun and, of course, bears very little relation to the original loads. However, it is a convenient shorthand familiar to most shooters and is useful as long as the background and limitations of the expression are understood."

Directory of the Arms Trade

AMMUNITION (Commercial)

Alcan Shells, Inc., 3640 Seminary Rd., Alton, Ill. 62002
Amron Corp., 525 Progress Ave., Waukesha, Wis. 53186
Cascade Cartridge Inc., See Omark
Federal Cartridge Co., 2700 Foshay Tower, Minneapolis, Minn. 55402
Frontier Cartridge Co., Inc., Box 906, Grand Island, Neb. 68801
Omark-CCI, Inc., Box 660, Lewiston, Ida. 83501
Remington Arms Co., Bridgeport, Conn. 06602
Service Armament, 689 Bergen Blvd., Ridgefield, N.J. 07657
Speer-DWM, Box 641, Lewiston, Ida. 83501
Super-Vel Cartridge Co., Box 40, Shelbyville, Ind. 46176
Weatherby's, 2781 E. Firestone Blvd., South Gate, Calif. 90280
Winchester-Western, East Alton, Ill. 62024

AMMUNITION (Custom)

AMCOA, 1805 S. Federal Blvd., Denver, Colo. 80219
Ammodyne, Box 1589, Los Angeles, Calif. 90053
Bill Ballard, 118½ Clark Ave., Billings, Mont. 59102
Jerry & Betty Bird, Box 10183, Corpus Christi, Tex. 78410
Caldwell's Loading Serv., 1314 Monroe Dr., N.E., Atlanta, Ga. 30306
Russell Campbell, 219 Leisure Dr., San Antonio, Tex. 78201
Cumberland Arms, 1222 Oak Dr., Manchester, Tenn. 37355
Custom Ammo & Gunsmithing, 390 S. Main, Moab, Utah 84532
E. W. Ellis Sport Shop, RFD 1, Box 139, Corinth, N.Y.
Ellwood Epps, 80 King St., Clinton, Ont., Canada
Dan Farley, 1551 Prescott Lane, Springfield, Ore. 97477
Steve Filipiak, 1270 So. Raleigh, Denver, Colo. 80219
R. H. Keeler, 1304 S. Oak, Port Angeles, Wash. 98362
Paul J. Kopsch, 718 Foster Park Rd., West, Lorain, Ohio 44653 (KTW tungsten bullets)
Dean Lincoln, 390 S. Main, Moab, Utah 84532
Mansfield Gunshop, Box 83, New Boston, N.H. 03070
Man-Tol Shells, Box 134, Bunnell, Fla. 32010
Maryland Reloading Service, 835 Beaver Dam Rd., Beltsville, Md.
Merlo Custom Reload Serv., Box 964, Great Falls, Mont. 59401
Merrill Reloading Service, Box 249, Libertyville, Ill. 60048
Midland Stamp Co., Box 2202, Memphis, Tenn. 38102 (pistol ammo only)
F. H. Miles, P.O. Drawer 509, Bedford, Va. 24523 (custom cases)
Modern Gun Craft, 18 Charles, E. Norwalk, Conn. 06855
Montana Custom Handloads, 408 S. Bozeman, Bozeman, Mont. 59715
Moody's Reloading Serv., 2108 Broadway, Helena, Mont. 59601
Northwest Shooters Supply, Box 508, Baker, Ore. 97814
Numrich Arms Corp., 203 Broadway, W. Hurley, N.Y. 12491
Robert Pomeroy, 45 Wyoming, Waterbury, Conn. 06706 (custom shells)
RDH Ammunition Inc., 1805 S. Federal Blvd., Denver, Colo. 80219
Ray's Custom Loads, 920 Pepper Dr., El Cajon, Calif.
Reloading Service, Midland Ave., Washington, N.J. 07882
Sanders Cust. Gun Serv., 2358 Tyler Lane, Louisville, Ky. 40205
Shooter's Service & Dewey, Inc., Clinton Corners, N.Y. 12514
Shot Shell Components, 365 So. Moore, Lakewood, Colo. 80226
Super Vel Cartridge Corp., Shelbyville, Ind. 46176
James C. Tillinghast, Box 568, Marlow, N.H. 03456
Tri-Test Munitions Co., 1330 Laura Lane, Lake Bluff, Ill. 60044
True-Blue Co., 1400 E. Palmer Ave., Glendale, Calif. 91205 (blanks)
"W" Cases, Rte. 1, Box 1018, Carnation, Wash. 98014
Wagner's Gunroom, 284 E. Main, Ashland, O. 44805
Walmax Inc. (See True-Blue)
Wanda Cartridge Co., P.O. Box 45901, Houston, Tex. 77045
Gene West, 137 Baylor, Pueblo, Colo. 81005

AMMUNITION (Foreign)

Abercrombie & Fitch, Madison at 45th St., New York, N.Y. 10017
Ammodyne, Box 1859, Los Angeles, Calif. 90053 (RWS)
Canadian Ind. Ltd. (C.I.L.), Box 10, Montreal, Que., Canada
Centennial Arms Co., 3318 W. Devon Ave., Chicago, Ill. 60645 (Hirtenberg, Austrian)
Colonial Ammunition Co., Box 8511, Auckland, New Zealand
DWM, Speer Prods. Inc., Box 641, Lewiston, Ida. 83501
Gevelot of Canada, Box 1593, Saskatoon, Sask., Canada
Hudson, 52 Warren, New York, N. Y. 10007
Hy-Score Arms Co., 200 Tillary, Brooklyn, N.Y. 11201
Imperial Chemical Ind., 488 Madison Ave., N.Y., N.Y. 10022
S. E. Lazlo, 200 Tillary, Brookyn, N.Y. 11201
NORMA-Precision, South Lansing, N.Y. 14882
Oregon Ammo Service, Box 19341, Portland, Ore. 97219
Stoeger Arms Corp., 55 Ruta Ct., So. Hackensack, N.J. 07606
James C. Tillinghast, Box 568, Marlow, N.H. 03456

ANTIQUE ARMS DEALERS

Robert Abels, 157 E. 64th St., N.Y., N.Y. 10021 (Catalog $1.00)
Ed Agramonte, 41 Riverdale Ave., Yonkers, N.Y. 10701
Antique Firearms Co., 206 Wilshire Blvd., Wilson, N.C. 27893
F. Bannerman Sons, Inc., Box 26, L.I., Blue Point, N.Y. 11715
Wm. Boggs, 1783 E. Main, Columbus, Ohio 43205
Donnin's Arms Museum, 12953 Biscayne Blvd., N. Miami, Fla. 33161
Ellwood Epps Sporting Goods, 80 King St., Clinton, Ont., Canada
Farris Muzzle Guns, 1610 Gallia St., Portsmouth, Ohio 45662
A. A. Fidd, Diamond Pt. Rd., Diamond Pt., N.Y. 11338
N. Flayderman & Co., Squash Hollow, New Milford, Conn. 06776
Herb Glass, Bullville, N.Y. 10915
Gold Rush Guns, Shop 1, 1567 California St., San Francisco, Calif. 94109
Gold Rush Guns, Shop 2, P.O. Box, Afton, Va. 22920
Goodman's for Guns, 1101 Olive St., St. Louis, Mo. 63101
Griffin's Guns & Antiques, R.R. 4, Peterboro, Ont., Canada
The Gun Shop, 6497 Pearl Rd., Cleveland, O. 44130
Heritage Firearms Co., 1 Danbury Rd., Rte. 7, Wilton, Conn. 06897
Ed Howe, 2 Main, Coopers Mills, Me. 04341
Jackson Arms, 6209 Hillcrest Ave., Dallas, Tex. 75205
Jerry's Gun Shop, 9220 Ogden Ave., Brookfield, Ill. 60513
Lever Arms Service, 771 Dunsmuir, Vancouver 1, B.C., Canada
Wm. M. Locke, 3607 Ault Pk. Rd., Cincinnati, O. 45208
Charles W. Moore, R.D. 2, Schenevus, N.Y. 12155
Museum of Historical Arms, 1038 Alton Rd., Miami Beach, Fla. 33139
National Gun Traders, Inc., Box 776, Miami, Fla. 33135
New Orleans Arms Co., Inc., 240 Chartres St., New Orleans, La. 70130
Old West Gun Room, 10855 San Pablo Ave., El Cerrito, Cal. 94530
Paramount Sporting Goods, 15 Henry Rd., Bombay-1, India (replicas)
Pioneer Guns, 5228 Montgomery, Norwood, O. 45212
Powell & Clements Sporting Arms, 210 E. 6th St., Cincinnati, O. 45202
Glode M. Requa, Box 35, Monsey, N.Y. 10952
Martin B. Retting Inc., 11029 Washington, Culver City, Calif. 90230
San Francisco Gun Exch., 74 Fourth, San Francisco, Calif. 94103
Santa Ana Gunroom, 1638 E. 1st St., Santa Ana, Calif. 92701
Ward & Van Valkenburg, 402-30th Ave. No., Fargo, N. Dak. 58102
M. C. Wiest, 234 N. Tulane Ave., Oak Ridge, Tenn. 37830
Yeck Antique Firearms, 579 Tecumseh, Dundee, Mich. 48131

BULLET & CASE LUBRICANTS

Alpha-Molykote Corp., 65 Harvard, Stamford, Conn. 06904 (Type U)
Birchwood-Casey Co., Inc., 7900 Fuller Rd., Eden Prairie, Minn. 55343
Bullet Pouch, Box 4285, Long Beach, Calif. 90804 (Mirror-Lube)
Chopie Tool & Die Co., 531 Copeland, La Crosse, Wis. 54601 (Black-Solve)
Cooper-Woodward, Box 972, Riverside, Cal. 92502 (Perfect Lube)
Green Bay Bullets, 233 N. Ashland, Green Bay, Wis. 54303 (EZE-Size case lube)
Herter's, Inc., Waseca, Minn. 56903 (Perfect Lubricant)
Javelina Rifle Supply, Box 337, San Bernardino, Cal. 92402 (Alox beeswax)
Jet-Aer Corp., 165 3rd St., Paterson, N.J. 07514
Lehigh Chemical Co., Box 120, Chestertown, Md. 21620 (Anderol)
Lenz Prod. Co., Box 1226, Sta. C, Canton, O. 44708 (Clenzoil)
Lyman Gun Sight Corp., Middlefield, Conn. 06455 (Size-Ezy)
Micro Shooter's Supply, Box 213, Las Cruces, N. Mex. 88001 (Micro-Lube)
Nutec, Box 1187, Wilmington, Del. 19899 (Dry-Lube)
Pacific Gunsight Co., Box 4495, Lincoln, Neb. 68504
Phelps Rel. Inc., Box 4004, E. Orange, N.J. 07019
RCBS, Inc., Box 1919, Oroville, Calif. 95965
SAECO Rel. Inc., P.O. Box 778, Carpinteria, Cal. 93013
Scientific Lubricants Co., 3753 Lawrence Ave., Chicago, Ill. 60625
Shooters Accessory Supply (SAS), Box 250, N. Bend, Ore. 97459
Wilkins & Schultz Inc., Box 334, Barrington, Ill. 60010 (Sure Mark)

CHOKE DEVICES & RECOIL ABSORBERS

A & W Engineering, 6520 Rampart St., Houston, Tex. 77027 (shotgun diverter)
Arms Ingenuity Corp., Box 1, Weatogue, Conn. 06089 (Jet-Away)
Contra-Jet, 7920 49th Ave. So., Seattle, Wash. 98118
Dahl's Gun Shop, Rt. 2, Billings, Mont. 59101
Edwards Recoil Reducer, 269 Herbert St., Alton, Ill. 62002
Emsco Chokes, Waseca, Minn. 56093
Hartford Gun Choke Co., Inc., Russell Rd., Newington 11, Conn.
Herter's, Inc., Waseca, Minn. 56093. (Vari-Choke)
Lyman Gun Sight Co., Middlefield, Conn. 60455 (Cutts Comp.)
C. R. Pedersen & Son, Ludington, Mich. 49431 (Sha-Cul Brake)
Pendleton Dekickers, 1200 S. W. Hailey Ave., Pendleton, Ore. 97801
Poly-Choke Co., Inc., Box 296, Hartford, Conn. 06101
St. Louis Precision Products, 902 Michigan Ave., St. Louis, Mich. 48880 (Gun-Tamer)

CHRONOGRAPHS AND PRESSURE TOOLS

A & W Eng., 6520 Rampart St., Houston, Tex. 77027 (press. tool)
American Craftsmen, 12645 La Cresta Dr., Los Altos Hills, Calif. 94022
Avtron, P. O. Box 132, Stanton, Calif. 90680
B-Square Co., Box 11281, Ft. Worth, Tex. 76110
Chrondek Electronics, Inc., 3027 Enterprise, Costa Mesa, Calif. 92626
Chronograph Specialists, P.O. Box 132, Stanton, Calif. 90680
Herter's, Waseca, Minn. 56093
ITCC, 2879 Cinnabar, Phoenix, Ariz. 85028
Micro-Sight Co., 242 Harbor Blvd., Belmont, Calif. 94002 (Techsonic)
Oehler Research, P.O. Box 9135, Austin, Tex. 78756
York-Cantrell, 30241 Rosebriar, St. Clair Shores, Mich. 48082 (press. tool)

CLEANING & REFINISHING SUPPLIES

ADSCO, Box 191, Ft. Kent, Me. 04743 (stock finish)
Ed Agramonte, 41 Riverdale Ave., Yonkers, N.Y. 10701 (Ed's cold blue)
Allied Products Co., 734 N. Leavitt, Chicago, Ill. 60612 (Cor-O-Dex)
Ammodyne, Box 1589, Los Angeles, Cal. 90053 (Gun Kote)
Backus Co., 411 W. Water St., Smethport, Pa. 16749 (field gun-cleaner)
Birchwood-Casey Chem. Co., 7900 Fuller Rd., Eden Prairie, Minn. 55343 (Anderol, etc.)
Bisonite Co., Inc., Box 84, Buffalo, N.Y. 14217
Jim Brobst, 31 S. 3rd, Hamburg, Pa. 19526 (J-B Compound)
Geo. Brothers, Great Barrington, Mass. 01230 (G-B Linspeed Oil)
Browning Arms, Rt. 4, Box 624-B, Arnold, Mo. 63010
Bullet Pouch, Box 4285, Long each, Cal. 90804 (Mirror Lube)
Burnishine Prod. Co., 8140 N. Ridgeway, Skokie, Ill. 60076 (Stock Glaze)
Chopie Tool & Die Co., 531 Copeland, La Crosse, Wis. 54601 (Black-Solve)
Clenzoil Co., Box 1226, Sta. C, Canton, O. 44708
Commercial Chemical Co., Inc., Box 711, Houston, Tex. (bore oil)
Corrosion Reaction Consultants, Inc., Dresher, Pa. 19025 (Mask)
Custom Industries, 18900 Detroit Ave., Lakewood, O. 44107
Dex-Kleen, Box 509 Des Moines, Ia. 50302 (gun wipers)
Dri-Slide, Inc., Industrial Park, Fremont, Mich. 49412
Forty-Five Ranch Enterpr., Box 1080, Miami, Okla. 74354
Frye Industs., Box 1244, Laguna Beach, Cal. 92652
Fur Fame Bait Co., Route 1, Lindsay, O. 43442 (U.S. Bbl. Blue)
Gun-All Products, Box 244, Dowagiac, Mich. 49047
Percy Harms Corp., 7349 N. Hamlin, Skokie, Ill. 60076
Hell Mtn. Gun Shop, R.D. 2, Lebanon, N.J. 08833 (Moose Milk)
Hi-Speed Patch, 1488 N. Glen, Fresno, Calif. 93728 (oiled patches)
Frank C. Hoppe, P.O. Box 97, Parkesburg, Pa. 19365
Hunting World, 247 E. 50th St., N.Y., N.Y. 10022 (P-H Safari Kit)
Jet-Aer Corp., 165 3rd St., Paterson, N.J. 07514 (blues & oils)
LPS Res. Labs. Inc., 2050 Cotner Ave., Los Angeles, Calif. 90025
Carl Lampert Co., 2639 So. 31st St., Milwaukee, Wis. 53215 (gun bags)
Lehigh Chem. Co., Box 120, Chestertown, Md. 21620 (Anderol)
LEM Gun Spec., Box 31, College Park, Ga. 30022 (Lewis Lead Remover)
Liquid Wrench, Box 10628, Charlotte, N.C. 28201 (pen. oil)
Lynx-Line Gun Products, Box 3985, Detroit, Mich. 48227
Marble Arms Co., 1120 Superior, Gladstone, Mich. 49837
Mill Run Prod., 1360 W. 9th, Cleveland, O. 44113 (Brite-Bore Kits)
Mint Luster Cleaners, 1102 N. Division, Appleton, Wis. 54911
Mistic Metal Mover, Inc., 19 E. Peru St., Princeton, Ill. 61356
Mitchell Chemical Co., Wampus Lane, Milford, Conn. (Gun Guard)
New Method Mfg. Co., Box 175, Bradford, Pa. 16701 (gun blue)
Numrich Arms Co., West Hurley, N.Y. 12491 (44-40 gun blue)
Nutec, Box 1187, Wilmington, Del. 19899 (Dry-Lube)
Outers Laboratories, Onalaska, Wis. 54650 (Gunslick kits)
Glen A. Pemberton, 260 Macedon Center Rd., Fairport, N.Y. 14450
Polyform Mfg. Corp., Box 305, Escondido, Calif. 92025
R.E.I., 101 Wolpers, Park Forest, Ill. 60466 (whale oil lube)
Radiator Spec. Co., Charlotte, N.C. 28201 (liquid wrench)
Realist Inc., N. 93 W. 16288 Megal Dr., Menomonee Falls, Wis. 53051
Rice Prod. Co., Box 2531, Palm Beach, Fla. 33480
Riel & Fuller, 423 Woodrow Ave., Dunkirk, N.Y. 14048 (anti-rust oil)
Rig Products Co., Box 279, Oregon, Ill. 61061 (Rig Grease)
Rocket Chemical Co., Inc., 5390 Napa St., San Diego, Calif. 92110 (WD-40)
Rusteprufe Labs., Box 333, Sparta, Wis. 54656
Seatex Corp., 6400 Westpark Dr., Houston, Tex. 77027
Service Armament, 689 Bergen Blvd., Ridgefield, N. J. 07657 (Parker-Hale)
Sheldon's Inc., Box 508, Antigo, Wis. 54409 (shotgun brushes)
Shirtpocket Gun Rod, 1518 Alabama St., Vallejo, Calif. 94594
Shooters Specialties, Box 264, LaMirada, Calif. 90638 (Schukra rod)
Silicote Corp., Box 359, Oshkosh, Wis. 54901 (Silicone cloths)
Silver Dollar Guns, 7 Balsam St., Keene, N.H. 03431 (silicone oil)
A. D. Soucy, Box 191, Ft. Kent, Me. 04743 (stock finish)
Sportsmen's Lus., Inc. Box 732, Anoka, Minn. 55303 (Gun Life lube.)
Sun Ray Chemicals, 371-30th Ave., San Francisco, Calif. 94121
Taylor & Robbins, Box 164, Rixford, Pa. 16745 (Throat Saver)
C. S. Van Gorden, 120 Tenth Ave., Eau Claire, Wis. 54701 (Instant Blue)
W&W Mfg. Co., Box 365, Belton, Mo. 64012 (shotgun cleaner)
Webber Gage Division, 12900 Triskett Rd., Cleveland, O. 44111 (Luger oil)
H. M. Whetstone & Co., 282 St. George St., St. Augustine, Fla. 32084
Williams Gun Sight, 7389 Lapeer Rd., Davison, Mich. 48423 (finish kit)
Winslow Arms Co., P.O. Box 578, Osprey, Fla. 33595 (refinishing kit)
Woodstream Corp., P.O. Box 327, Lititz, Pa. 17543 (Mask)

COMPONENTS—BULLETS, POWDER, PRIMERS

Accuracy Bullet Co., 2443 41st St., San Francisco, Calif. 94116 (Perfecast bullets)
Alcan, 3640 Seminary Rd., Alton, Ill. 62002
Bahler Die Shop, Box 336, Florence, Ore. 97439 (17 cal. bull.)
Lee Baker, Box 65786, Los Angeles, Calif. 90000 (17 cal. bull.)
Barnes Bullets Inc., 318 Rosevale Rd., Grand Junction, Colo. 81501
Martin Burklow, 938 Windsor, Bristol, Tenn. 37620
Bitterroot Bullet Co., Box 412, Lewiston, Ida. 83501
Centrix, 2116 N. 10th Ave., Tucson, Ariz. 85705
Curry Bullet Co., 4504 E. Washington Blvd., Los Angeles, Calif. 90022
Division Lead, 7742 W. 61 Pl., Summit, Ill. 60502
DuPont, Explosives Dept., Wilmington, Del. 19898
Dan Farley, 1551 Prescott Lane, Springfield, Ore. 97477 (17 cal. bull.)
Forty Five Ranch Enterprises, Box 1080, Miami, Okla. 74354
Joe F. Frye, 3657 Oakley Ave., Memphis, Tenn. 38111 (cast bullets)
Ernest L. Gardiner, Box 1682, Rockford, Ill. 61110
G. J. Godwin, 863 Plymouth, E. Bridgewater, Mass. 02333 (cast bullets)
Green Bay Bullets, 233 No. Ashland, Green Bay, Wis. 54303 (lead)
Frank A. Hemsted, Box 281, Sunland, Calif. 91040
Hercules Powder Co., 910 Market St., Wilmington, Del. 19899
Herter's Inc., Waseca, Minn. 56093
Hi-Precision Co., Box 121, Orange City, Ia. 51041
B. E. Hodgdon, Inc., 7710 W. 50th Hwy., Shawnee Mission, Kans. 66202
Crawford H. Hollidge, Cotuit Rd., Marston Mills, Mass. 02648
Hornady Mfg. Co., Box 1848, Grand Island, Neb. 68801
N. E. House Co., Middletown Rd., E. Hampton, Conn. 06424
Jurras Munition Corp., Box 163, Shelbyville, Ind. 46176
Kenru Reloading Serv., 166 Normandy, Rochester, N.Y. 14619
L. L. F. Die Shop, 1281 Highway 99 North, Eugene,Ore. 97402
Lyman Gun Sight Corp., Middlefield, Conn. 06455
Markell, Inc., 4115 Judah St., San Francisco, Calif. 94112
Meyer Bros., Wabasha, Minn. 55981 (shotgun slugs)
Miller Trading Co., 20 S. Front St., Wilmington, N.C. 28401
Norma-Precision, So. Lansing, N.Y. 14882
Northridge Bullet Co., 9025 Parthenia, Northridge, Calif.
Northwest Shooters Supply, Box 508, Baker, Ore.
Nosler Bullet Co., Box 671, Bend, Ore. 97701
Oregon Ammo Service, Box 19341, Portland, Ore. 97219
Robert Pomeroy, 45 Wyoming Ave., Waterbury, Conn. 06706
Rainbow Prod., P.O. Box 75, Wishram, Wash. 98673 (bullets)
Remington-Peters, Bridgeport, Conn. 06602
Jim Russell, 10115 N. Central, Indianapolis, Ind. 46280
S. W. M. Bullet Co., 1122 S. Cherry St., Port Angeles, Wash. 98362 (17 cal.)
Sanderson's, 724 W. Edgewater, Portage, Wis. 53901 (cork wad)
Sierra Bullets Inc., 10532 S. Painter Ave., Santa Fe Springs, Calif. 90670
Sisk Bullet Co., Box 398, Iowa Park, Tex. 76367
Speedy Bullets, Box 1262, Lincoln, Neb. 68501
Speer Products Inc., Box 641, Lewiston, Ida. 83501
C. H. Stocking, Hutchinson, Minn. 55350 (17 cal. bullet jackets)
Sullivan Arms Corp., 5204 E. 25th, Indianapolis, Ind. 46218
Super-Vel Cartr. Corp., 129 E. Franklin St., Shelbyville, Ind. 46176
Taylor Bullets, P.O. Box 21254, San Antonio, Tex. 78221
True-Blue Co., 1400 E. Palmer Ave., Glendale, Calif. 91205 (blanks)
James C. Tillinghast, Box 568, Marlow, N.H. 03456
Vitt & Boos, Sugarloaf Dr., Wilton, Conn. 06897
Walker Machine Tool, 4804 Pinewood Rd., Louisville, Ky. 40218
Walmax, Inc., 1400 E. Palmer Ave., Glendale, Calif. 91205 (blanks)
L. D. Whitmer, 318 Basin St., Navarre, O. 44662
Winchester-Western, New Haven, Conn. 06504
Chas. Wissel, Box 312, New Paltz, N.Y. 12561
F. Wood, Box 386, Florence, Ore. 97439 (17 cal.)
Xelex Ltd., Hawksbury, Ont., Canada (powder)
Zero Bullet Co., 7254 Farnum, Inkster, Mich. 48141

CUSTOM GUNSMITHS AND CUSTOM GUN WORK

A & M Rifle Co., Box 1713, Prescott, Ariz. 86301
Ace Sports Center, 1590 York Ave., New York, N.Y. 10028
Franz Achleithner, Main St., Margaretville, N.Y. 12455
P. O. Ackley, P.O. Box 17347, Salt Lake City, Utah 84117
R. E. Anderson, 706 S. 23rd St., Laramie, Wyo. 82070
Arms Divs., M. R. Co., 968 Radcliffe Rd., Baltimore, Md. 21204
Bacon Creek Gun Shop, Cumberland Falls Rd., Corbin, Ky.
Bain and Davis Sptg. Gds., 599 W. Las Tunas Dr., San Gabriel, Calif. 41776
Barber's Southpaw Conversions, 26 N.W. 2nd, Portland, Ore. 97209
Barta's, Rte. 1, Cato, Wis. 54206
Bayer's Gun Shop, 213 S. 2nd, Walla Walla, Wash. 99362
Bennett Gun Works, 561 Delaware Ave., Delmar, N.Y. 12054
Irvin L. Benson, Saganaga Lake, Ontario, Canada
Gordon Bess, 708 River St., Canon City, Colo. 81212
Al Biesen, West 2039 Sinto Ave., Spokane, Wash. 99201
Jack Blurton, Ramsey, Ill. 62080

Boone Mountain Trading Post, Averyville Rd., St. Marys, Pa. 15857
Bortmess Arms Co., Box 1008, Bradenton, Fla. 33505
Bruce Betts, 26 Rolla Gardens Dr., Rolla, Mo. 65401
T. H. Boughton, 410 Stone Rd., Rochester, N.Y. 14616
L. H. Brown, Rte. 2, Airport Rd., Kalispell, Mont. 59901
George Bunch, 7735 Garrison Rd., Hyattsville, Md. 20784
Tom Burgess, 13906 E. 4th Ave., Opportunity, Wash. 99216 (metalsmithing only)
Butler's Gun Repair Shop, Poultney, Vt. 05764
Gus Butterowe, 4000 Cedar Springs Rd., Dallas, Tex. 75219
Caldwell Gun Shop, 5056 Roseville, No. Highlands, Calif. 95660
Campbell Gun Shop, Inc., 2721 E. Gunnison, Colo. Sprgs., Colo. 80909
Dick Campbell, 1445 S. Meade, Denver, Colo. 80219
Carl's Gun Shop, 37 Breton, Ste. Therese de Blainville, Ont., Can. (Antique)
Carl's Powder Keg, 14331 Clark St., Riverdale, Ill. 60627
Carpenter's Gun Works, Rte. 32, Plattekill, N.Y. 12568
Carter Gun Works, 2211 Jefferson Pk. Ave., Charlotteville, Va. 22903
Cassell's Gun Shop, 201 Grace Ave., Worland, Wyo. 82401
Ray Chalmers, 18 White Clay Dr., Newark, Del. 19711
Chicago Gun Center, 3109 W. Armitage, Chicago, Ill. 60647
Chuck's Custom Gun Stocks, P.O. Box 1123, Frederick, Md. 21701
Kenneth E. Clark, 18738 Highway 99, Madera, Calif. 93637
Consolidated Armslube, 905 Spruce Ave., Alamagordo, N. Mex. 88310
Philip R. Crouthamel, 817 E. Baltimore, E. Lansdowne, Pa. 19050
Custom Rifle Shop, 4550 E. Colfax Ave., Denver, Colo. 80220
Jim Cuthbert, 715 S. 5th St., Coos Bay, Ore. 97420
Dahl's Gunshop, Rt. 2, Billings, Mont. 59101
Albert Daniels, 2339 So. St. Louis, Chicago, Ill. 60623
Dave's Gun Shop, 3994 Potters Rd. West, Ionia, Mich. 48846
Dee Davis, 5658 So. Mayfield, Chicago, Ill.
Joe E. Dillen, 1206 Juanita S.W., Massillon, Ohio 44646
Don's Gun Shop, 128 Ruxton Ave., Manitou Springs, Colo. 8029,
Charles Duffy, Williams Lane, W. Hurley, N.Y. 12491
Bill English, 4411 S. W. 100th, Seattle, Wash. 98146
Ellwood Epps, 80 King St., Clinton, Ont., Canada
Ermas Firearms, Steelville, Mo. 65565
Ken Eyster, Heritage Gunsmiths Inc., R. 2, Centerburg, O. 43011
N. B. Fashingbauer, Box 366, Lac Du Flambeau, Wis. 54538
Ted Fellowes, 9245-16th Ave., S.W., Seattle, Wa. 98106 (muzzle loaders)
Loxley Firth Firearms, R. D. 4, Baldwinsville, N.Y. 13027
Marshall F. Fish, Westport, N.Y. 12993
Jerry Fisher, 1244—4th Ave. West, Kalispell, Mont. 59901
Flagler Gun Clinic, Box 8125, West Palm Beach, Fla. 33402 (Win. A2 Conv.)
Freeland's Scope Stands, 3737—14th Ave., Rock Island, Ill. 61201
Fred's Gun Shop, 7860 W. Jewell, Lakewood, Colo. 80227
Frederick Gun Shop, 10 Elson Drive, Riverside, R.I. 02915
Frontier Gunshop, 3584 Mt. Diablo Blvd., Lafayette, Calif. 94549
Fuller Gunshop, Cooper Landing, Alas. 99572
Geo. M. Fullmer, 2499 Mavis St., Oakland, Cal. 94501 (metal work)
Gibbs Rifle Products, Viola, Ida. 83872
Gillman Brothers, Upper High Crest Dr., High Crest Lake, Butler, N.J. 07405
A. R. Goode, 3306 Sellman Rd., Adelphi, Md. 20783
E. M. Greashaw, S. Centerville, RR 2, Sturgis, Mich. 49091
Griffin & Howe, 589-8th Ave., New York, N.Y. 10017
Dale M. Guise, Rt. 2, Box 239, Gardners, Pa. 17324
Gunsports Co., P.O. Box 4283, Hamilton, Ont., Canada
H & R Custom Gun Serv., 68 Passaic Dr., Hewitt, N.J. 07421
Harkrader's Cust. Gun Shop, Box 475, Christiansburg, Va. 24073
Bob Harris, 307 Park, Marietta, Ga. 30062
Elden Harsh, Rt. 4, London, O. 43140
Rob't. W. Hart & Son, 401 Montgomery St., Nescopeck, Pa. 18635 (actions, stocks)
Hal Hartley, Box 147, Blairs Fork Rd., Lenoir, N.C. 28654
Iver Henriksen, 1211 So. 2nd, Missoula, Mont. 59801
Edw. O. Hefti, 300 Fairview, College Sta., Tex. 77840
Wm. Hobaugh, Box 657, Philipsburg, Mont. 59858
E. H. Hoffman, Woodstock, Va. 22664
Huckleberry Gun Shop, 10440 Kingsbury Rd., Delton, Mich. 49046 (rust blueing)
Ernest Hurt, Box 1033, Muskogee, Okla. 74401
Independent Machine & Gun Shop, 1416 N. Hayes, Pocatello, Ida. 83201
Jackson's, Box 416, Selman City, Tex. 75689
Paul Jaeger, 211 Leedom, Jenkintown, Pa. 19046
Jerry's Gun Shop, 9220 Ogden Ave., Brookfield, Ill. 60513
Jerry's Gun Shop, 1527 N. Graceland Ave., Appleton, Wis. 54911
Jerry's Gun Shop, Rte. 3, Twin Falls, Ida. 83301
Jim's Gun Shop, 715 So. 5th St., Coos Bay, Ore. 97420
John's Gun Repair, 104 Avondale, Jackson, Mich. 49203
Johnson Automatics Assoc., Inc., Box 306, Hope Valley, R.I. 02832
Bob Johnson, 1730 Sprague, Spokane, Wash. 99200
Johnson's Gun Shop, 6267 Blackstone, Fresno, Calif. 93726
Johnson's Kenai Rifles, Box 6208, Annex Br., Anchorage, Alaska 99502
Keener Gun Works, 8529 Reseda Blvd.. Northridge, Calif. 91324
Kennedy Gun Shop, Rt. 6, Clarksville, Tenn. 37040
Monte Kennedy, R.D. 2, Kalispell, Mont. 59901
Kennon's Custom Rifles, 5408 Biffle, Stone Mtn., Ga. 30083
Kerr Sport Shop, Inc., 9584 Wilshire Blvd., Beverly Hills, Calif. 90210
Kess Arms Co., 3283 N. Green Bay Ave., Milwaukee, Wis. 53212
Kesselring Gun Shop, Box 350, Rt. 1, Burlington, Wash. 98233
Klein's Sporting Goods, 4540 W. Madison, Chicago, Ill. 60624
Knights Gun Store, Inc., Jennings & Vickey, Ft. Worth, Tex. 76104
Ward Koozer, Box 18, Walterville, Ore. 97489
R. Krieger & Sons, 34923 Gratiot, Mt. Clemens, Mich. 48043
Lacy's Gun Service, 2200 Park Rd., Charlotte, N.C. 28203
Harry Lawson Co., 3328 N. Richey Blvd., Tucson, Ariz. 85716
Ledel, Inc., Main and Commerce Sts., Cheswold, Del. 19936
LeFever Arms Co., R.D. 1, Lee Center, N.Y. 13363
Max J. Lindauer, R.R. 1, Box 114, Washington, Mo. 63090
Robt. L. Lindsay, Box 805, Gaithersburg, Md. 20760
Llanerch Gun Shop, 2800 Township Line, Upper Darby, Pa. 19083
Loven Firearms, Rte. 82, Millbrook, N.Y. 12545
J. L. Lyden, 1516 Chelton Ave., Pittsburgh, Pa. 15226
McCormick's Custom Gun Bluing, 4936 E. Rosecrans Ave., Compton, Calif. 90221
Harry McGowen, Rt. 3, St. Anne, Ill. 60964
R. J. Maberry, 511 So. K, Midland, Tex. 79701
Harold E. MacFarland, Star Route, Box 84, Cottonwood, Ariz. 86326
Maryland Gun Exchange, Rt. 40 W., RD 5, Frederick, Md. 21701
Mashburn Arms Co., 112 W. Sherman, Oklahoma City, Okla. 73102
Mathews & Son, 10224 S. Paramount Blvd., Downey, Calif. 90241
Maurer Arms, 2366 Frederick Dr., Cuyahoga Falls, Ohio 44221
Middaugh's Nodak, 318 2nd St., Bismarck, N.D. 58501
Mike's Musket Shop, 5126 Victoria Dr., Vancouver 16, B.C., Canada
Mile-Hi Gun Shop, 84 N. Main, Bellingham, Mass. 02019
Robert U. Milhoan & Son, Rt. 3, Elizabeth, W. Va. 26143
Miller Gun Works, Central P.O. Box 619, Naha, Okinawa
Earl Milliron, 1249 N.E. 166th Ave., Portland, Ore. 97230
Mills Custom Stocks, 401 N. Ellsworth, San Mateo, Calif. 94401 (antique)
Morton Gun Works, 2115 Sante Fe St., Wichita Falls, Tex. 76309
J. R. Nation, 9627 Massridge, Dallas, Tex. 75238
Natl. Gun Traders, Inc., Box 776, Miami, Fla. 33135
Clayton N. Nelson, 1725 Thompson Ave., Enid, Okla. 73701
Newman Gunshop, 119 Miller Rd., Agency, Ia. 52530
Nu-Line Guns, Inc., 3727 Jennings Rd., St. Louis, Mo. 63121
O'Brien Rifle Co., 324 Tropicana No. 128, Las Vegas, Nev. 89109
Pachmayr Gun Works, 1220 S. Grand Ave., Los Angeles, Calif. 90015
Charles J. Parkinson, 116 Wharncliffe Rd. So., London, Ont., Canada
George Pearsall, 514 N. State, Chicago, Ill. 60610
Pendleton Gunshop, 1200 S.W. Hailey Ave., Pendleton, Ore. 97801
C. R. Pedersen & Son, Ludington, Mich. 49431
Al Petersen, Box 8, Riverhurst, Sask., Canada
A. W. Peterson Gun Shop, Rt. 1, Box 1510, Mt. Dora, Fla. 32757 (ML rifles, also)
Purcell's Gunshop, 915 Main St., Boise, Idaho 83702
R & M Serv. (Molezzo), 9882 E. Manning, Selma, Calif. 93662
Fred Renard, Rte. 1, Symsonia, Ky. 42082
Lloyd Resor, Union City, Ind. 47390
Royal Arms, Inc., 10064 Bert Acosta, Santee, Calif. 92071
Sam's Gun Shop, 25 Squam Rd., Rockport, Mass. 01966
Sanders Custom Gun Serv., 2358 Tyler Lane, Louisville, Ky. 40205
Sandy's Gun Repair, Rockport, Ill. 62370
Saratoga Arms Co., R.D. 3, Box 387, Pottstown, Pa. 19464
Roy V. Schaefer, 965 W. Hilliard Lane, Eugene, Ore. 97402
George Schielke, Washington Crossing, Titusville, N.J. 08560
Schuetzen Gun Works, 1226 Prairie Rd., Colorado Springs, Colo. 80909
Schumaker's Gun Shop, 208 W. 5th Ave., Colville, Wash. 99114
Schwartz Custom Guns, 9621 Coleman Rd., Haslett, Mich. 48840
Schwarz's Gun Shop, 41-15th St., Wellsburg, W. Va. 26070
Joseph M. Sellner, 117 Florence Ave., Piscataway, N.J. 08854
Shebal's Gun Shop, Corn. 14th & Lacey, Fairbanks, Alaska 99701
Shilen Rifles, Inc., 4510 Harrington Rd., Irving, Tex. 75060
Harold H. Shockley, Box 355, Hanna City, Ill. 65126 (hot bluing & plating)
Shooters Service & Dewey Inc., Clinton Corners, N.Y. 12514
Shooters Supply, 2507 Smith, Houston, Tex. 77006
Walter Shultz, R.D. 3, Pottstown, Pa. 19464
Simmons Gun Spec., 700 Rogers Rd., Olathe, Kans. 66061
Simms Hardware Co., 2801 J St., Sacramento, Calif. 95816
Skinner's Gun Shop, Box 941, Juneau, Alaska 98801
Markus Skosples, 1119-35th St., Rock Island, Ill. 61201
Jerome F. Slezak, 9109 Kennedy Ave., Cleveland, O. 44104
John Smith, 912 Lincoln, Carpentersville, Ill. 60110
K. E. Smith, 8766 Los Choches Rd., Lakeside, Calif. 92040
Smitty's Gunshop, 308 S. Washington, Lake City, Minn. 55041
Clifford K. Snider, 132 W. 25th St., Hamilton, Ont., Canada
Snapp's Gunshop, 6911 E. Washington Rd., Clare, Mich. 48617
R. Southgate, Rt. 2, Franklin, Tenn. 37064 (new Kentucky rifles)
Sportsmens Equip. Co., 915 W. Washington, San Diego, Calif. 92103
Ikey Starks, 1058 Grand Ave., So. San Francisco, Calif. 94080
Keith Stegall, Box 696, Gunnison, Colo. 81230
Suter's House of Guns, 401 N. Tejon, Colorado Springs, Colo. 80902
Swanson Custom Firearms, 1051 Broadway, Denver, Colo. 80203
Armand D. Swenson, 3223 W. 154th St., Gardena, Calif. 90242
Sycamore, Box 505, Borough Hall Sta., Jamaica,L.I., N.Y. 11424
T-P Shop, 212 E. Houghton, West Branch, Mich. 48661
Talmage Ent., 1309 W. 12th St., Long Beach, Calif. 90813
Taylor & Robbins, Box 164, Rixford, Pa. 16745
Theno's Gun Shop, Box 273, Issaquah, Wash. 98027
Tom's Gunshop, 600 Albert Pike, Hot Springs, Ark. 71901
John Torell, P.O. Box 615, Evergreen, Colo. 80439
C. Hunt Turner, 618 S. Grove, Webster Groves, Mo. 63119 (shotguns only)
Roy Vail, R. 1, Box 8, Warwick, N.Y. 10990
J. W. Van Patten, Box 145, Foster Hill, Milford, Pa. 18337
R. M. Verner, 263 Kurtz Rd., Marietta, Ga. 30060
Walker Arms Co., R. 2, Box 38, Selma, Ala. 36701
Harold Waller, 1288 Camillo Way, El Cajon, Calif. 92021

R. A. Wardrop, Box 245, Mechanicsburg, Pa. 17055
J. E. Warren, Box 72, Eastham, Mass. 02642
Watertown Shooting Supplies, Box 233, Watertown, Conn. 06795
M. G. Watts, 5627 Euclid, Kansas City, Mo. 64130
Weatherby's, 2781 Firestone Blvd., South Gate, Calif. 90280
Weber Rifle Actions, Box 515, Woodbridge, Calif. 95258
Wells Sport Store, 110 N. Summit St., Prescott, Ariz. 86301
R. A. Wells, 3452 N. 1st, Racine, Wis. 53402
Robert G. West, 6626 S. Lincoln, Littleton, Colo. 80120
Western Stocks & Guns, 2206 E. 11th, Bremerton, Wash. 98310
O. Wheeler, 405 W. 10th St., Holden, Mo. 64040
M. C. Wiest, 234 N. Tulane Ave., Oak Ridge, Tenn. 37830
Williams Gun Sight Co., 7389 Lapeer Rd., Davison, Mich. 48423
Lou Williamson, 401 Wanda Way, Hurst, Tex. 76053
Wilson Gun Store Inc., R.D. 1, Rte. 225, Dauphin, Pa. 17018
Charles Winczer, 1590 York Ave., N.Y., N.Y. 10028
Lester Womack, Box 506, Grand Canyon, Ariz. 86023
W. H. Womack, 2124 Meriwether Rd., Shreveport, La. 71108
Wyatt's Custom Gunshop, Kosciusko, Miss. 39090
Yorktown Custom Arms, 2727 W. Market, Akron, O. 44313
Russ. Zeeryp, 1026 W. Skyline Dr., Morristown, Tenn. 37814

DEALERS IN COLLECTORS' CARTRIDGES

Antique Arsenal, 365 So. Moore St., Lakewood, Colo. 80226
C. G. Battles, 215 Magyar, Wellington, O. 44090
J. A. Belton, 52 Sauve Rd., Ste. Philomene, Quebec, Canada
Peter Bigler, 291 Crestwood Dr., Milltown, N.J. 08850
Cameron's, 16690 W. 11th Ave., Golden, Colo. 80401
Carter Gun Works, 2211 Jefferson Pk. Ave., Charlottesville, Va. 22903
Gerry Coleman, 163 Arkell St., Hamilton, Ont., Canada
Chas. E. Duffy, Williams Lane, West Hurley, N.Y. 12419
Ellwood Epps, 80 King St., Clinton, Ont., Canada
Ed Howe, 2 Main St., Coopers Mills, Me. 04341
Walt Ireson, 47 Chedoke Ave., Hamilton, Ont., Canada
Jackson Arms, 6209 Hillcrest Ave., Dallas, Tex. 75205
Keokuk, 616 Kingsley Dr., Loves Park, Ill. 61111
McDaneld & Wheeler, Box 230, Osborne, Kans. 67473
Miller Bros., Rapid City, Mich. 49676
Oregon Ammo Service, Box 19341, Portland, Ore. 97219 (catlg. $1.00)
Martin B. Retting Inc., 11029 Washington, Culver City, Calif. 90230
Perry Spangler, 519 So. Lynch, Flint, Mich. 48503 (list 35c)
Jon Taylor House of Cartridges, 12 Cascade Bay, Brandon, Manit., Can.
Ernest Tichy, 365 S. Moore, Lakewood, Colo. 80226
James C. Tillinghast, Box 568, Marlow, N.H. 03456 (list 50c)
Wilkins Gun Shop, 1060 N. Henderson, Galesburg, Ill. 61401 (list 50c)

ENGRAVERS, ENGRAVING, TOOLS

Emma C. Achleithner, Main St., Margaretville, N.Y. 12455
E. Averill, Rt. 1, 60 Chestnut St., Cooperstown, N.Y. 13326
Joseph Bayer, Sunset Ave., Sunset Hill, RD 1, Princeton, N.J. 08540
Sid Bell, Box 188, Tully, N.Y. 13159
Weldon Bledsoe, 6812 Park Place Dr., Fort Worth, Tex. 76118
Max E. Bruehl, 4956 Elston Ave., Chicago, Ill. 60630
Creative Carvings Inc., R.D. 2, Tully, N.Y. 13159
Bill Dyer, 503 Midwest Bldg., Oklahoma City, Okla. 73102
Ken. Flood, 63 Homestead, Stratford, Conn. 06497
Jos. Fugger, c/o Griffin & Howe, 589-8th Ave., N.Y., N.Y. 10017
G & R Tackle Co., Wm. H. Mains, 2895 Seneca St., Buffalo, N.Y. 14224
Donald Glaser, 1520 West St., Emporia, Kans. 66801
Arnold Griebel, 4724 N. Keystone Ave., Chicago, Ill. 60630
Griffin & Howe, 589-8th Ave., N.Y., N.Y. 10017
F. R. Gurney, 8503 87th Ave., Edmonton, Alberta, Can.
Neil Hartliep, Box 733, Fairmont, Minn. 56031
Frank E. Hendricks, Rt. 2, Box 189J, San Antonio, Tex. 78228
L. C. Hoyt, 321 E. Minnesota St., Indianapolis, Ind. 46225
Paul Jaeger, 211 Leedom, Jenkintown, Pa. 19046
Charles H. Jerred, 853 W. 1st St., Fulton, N.Y. 13069
Robert C. Kain, Newfane, Vermont 05345 (American 50 guns)
Lance Kelly, P.O. Box 1072, Pompana Beech, Fla. 33061
Wm. H. Mains, 2895 Seneca St., Buffalo, N.Y. 14224
Rudy Marek, Rt. 1, Box 1A, Banks, Ore. 97106
S. A. Miller, Central P.O. Box 619, Naha, Okinawa
Frank Mittermeier, 3577 E. Tremont Ave., New York, N.Y. 10465
Charles Namiot, 48 W. 48th St., New York, N.Y. 10036
Albin Obiltschnig, Ferlach, Austria
Stan Ozias, 1225 South St., Wrentham, Mass. 02093
Pachmayr Gun Works, Inc., 1220 S. Grand Ave., Los Angeles, Calif. 90015
Hans Pfeiffer, 2005 Washington, Maywood, Ill. 60153
E. C. Prudhomme, 302 Ward Bldg., Shreveport, La. 71101
R. E. I. Engravings, 101 Wolpers, Park Forest, Ill. 60466
John R. Rohner, Sunshine Canyon, Boulder, Colo. 80302
Robert P. Runge, 94 Grove St., Ilion, N.Y. 13357
Shooters Specialties,Box 264, La Mirada, Calif. 90638
Lester Smith, Box 3129, C. Reece Br., Johnson City, Tenn. 37601
Russell J. Smith, 231 Springdale Rd., Westfield, Mass. 01085
Robt. Swartley, 2800 Pine St., Napa, Calif. 94559
Ray Viramontez, 209 Tellfair Ave., Albany, Ga. 31705
Floyd E. Warren, Rt. 3, Box 87, Cortland, O. 44410
John E. Warren, P.O. Box 72, Eastham, Mass. 02642
John Westby-Gibson, 612 84th St., N.W., Bradenton, Fla. 35505
A. A. White Engr., P.O. Box 68, Manchester, Conn. 06040

GAME CALLS

Black Duck, 1735 Davis, Whiting, Ind. 46394
Burnham Bros., Box 100-C, Marble Falls, Tex. 78654
Green Head Co., 342-2nd St., La Salle, Ill. 61301
Faulk's, 616 18th St., Lake Charles, La. 70601
Lohman Mfg. Co., 320 E. Spring, Neosho, Mo. 64850
M. L. Lynch, 306 Edgewood Blvd., Birmingham, Ala. 35209
Mallardtone, 2901 16th St., Moline, Ill. 61265
Ed. Mehok, 1737 Davis Ave., Whiting, Ind. 46394
Phil. S. Olt Co., Box 550, Pekin, Ill. 61554
Penn's Woods Call Co., Box 41, Delmont, Pa. 15626
Scotch Game Call Co., 60 Main St., Oakfield, N.Y. 14125
Sport-Lore, Inc., 1757 Cherry St., Denver, Colo. 80220
Johnny Stewart Wildlife Calls, Box 1909, Waco, Tex. 76703
Weems Wild Calls, Box 7261, Ft. Worth, Tex. 76111
Wightman Electronics, Box 989, Easton, Md. 21601
Wildlife Prod. Inc., Prof. Bldg., East Perkins Ave., Sandusky, Ohio 44870 (Lectro Hunter)
Tex Wirtz Ent., Inc., 1925 W. Hubbard St., Chicago, Ill. 60622

GUN CASES, CABINETS AND RACKS

A.R.C. Electronics Inc., 15302 So. Illinois Ave., Paramount, Calif. 90723
Amer. Safety Gun Case Co., Holland, Mich. 49424
Aremac Co., 101 N. Verity Parkway, Middletown, O. 45042
Artistic Wood Specialties, 828 N. Wells, Chicago, Ill. 60610
Morton Booth Co., Box 123, Joplin, Mo. 64802
Brewster Corp., Old Lyme, Conn. 06371
Browning Arms Co., Rt. 4, Box 624-B, Arnold, Mo. 63010
Castle Sptg. Gods., Inc., 498 Nepperhan Ave., Yonkers, N.Y. 10701
Challanger Gun Case Co., 105-23 New York Blvd., Jamaica, N.Y. 11433
Coladonato Bros., Box 156, Hazleton, Pa. 18201
Dutton's, Rte. 8, Box 508, Jacksonville, Fla. 32216 (single rack)
Ellwood Epps Sporting Goods, Clinton, Ont., Canada
Ferrell Co., Rte. 3, Gallatin, Tenn. 37066 (Redi-Rack)
Fiber Prod. Mfg. Co., 601 W. 26th St., New York, N.Y. 10001
Gun-Ho Case Mfg. Co., 501 Robert St., St. Paul, Minn 55101
B. E. Hodgdon, Inc., 7710 W. 50 Hiway, Shawnee-Mission, Kans. 66202
Hoegh Slimline Case Co., Box 952, La Crescent, Minn. 55947
Ithaca Gun Co., Box 700, Ithaca, N.Y. 14850
J-K Imports, Box 403, Novato, Cal. 94947 (leg 'o mutton case)
Kolpin Bros. Co., Inc., Box 231, Berlin, Wis. 54923
Lock, Stock & Barrel, 26 Carver's Green, Chaska, Minn. 55318
Marble Arms Corp., 1120 Superior, Gladstone, Mich. 49837
National Sports Div., 19 E. McWilliams St., Fond du Lac, Wis. 54935
Paul-Reed, Inc., P.O. Box 227, Charlevoix, Mich. 49720
Penguin Assoc. Inc., Box 97, Parkersburg, Pa. 19365
Precise Imp. Corp., 3 Chestnut, Suffern, N.Y. 10901
Pretto Cabinet Co., 1201 E. Walnut, Oglesby, Ill. 61348
Protecto Plastics, Inc., Box 37, Wind Gap, Pa. 18091
Richland Arms Co., 321 W. Adrian, Blissfield, Mich. 49228
Saf-T-Case, Box 10512, Dallas, Tex. 75207
San Angelo Die Castings, Box 984, San Angelo, Tex. 76901
Buddy Schoellkopf, 148 Fordyce St., Dallas, Tex. 75207
Sile Distr., 7 Centre Market Pl., New York, N.Y. 10013 (leg o'mutton case)
Stearn Mfg. Co., Div. & 30th St., St. Cloud, Minn. 56301
Supreme Products, 815 Morgan Dr., #301, Los Angeles, Calif. 90049 (automobile)
Sure Shoot'n, Box 195, Jacksonville, Ill. 62650 (leg o'mutton case)
Universal Auto Gun Rack Co., 215 S. Oak Cliff Blvd., Dallas, Tex. 75208
Western Holder Co., Box 33, Menomonee Falls, Wis. 53051
Western Products Co., Box 771, Laredo, Tex. 78040 (racks)
Woodstream Corp., Box 327, Lititz, Pa. 17543
Yield House, Inc., RFD, No. Conway, N.H. 03860

GUN PARTS, ANTIQUE

Bannerman, F., Box 26, Blue Point, Long Island, N.Y. 11715
Shelley Braverman, Athens, N.Y. 12015 (obsolete guns)
Carter Gun Works, 2211 Jefferson Pk. Ave., Charlottesville, Va. 22903
Dixie Gun Works, Inc., Hwy 51, South, Union City, Tenn. 38261
Ellwood Epps Sporting Goods, 80 King St., Clinton, Ont., Canada
Golden Eagle, 36 E. Brown St., West Haven, Conn. 06516 (list 25c)
International Gunmakers, 12315 Newburgh, Livonia, Mich. 48150
Edw. E. Lucas, 32 Garfield Ave., Old Ridge, N.J. 08857 (45-70)
R. M. Marek, Rt. 1, Box 1-A, Banks Ore. 97106 (cannons)
Thomas I. Mazzola, 6937 54th Ave., Maspeth, N.Y. 11378
Numrich Arms Co., West Hurley, N.Y. 12491
Robert Patton, Box 13155, San Antonio, Tex. 78213 (Obsolete Win.)
A. Sheldon Rich, 114 Franklin St., Revere, Mass. 02151
Norman S. Romig, 910 Fairmount Ave., Trenton, N.J. 08629
S&S Firearms, 88-21 Aubrey Ave., Glendale, N.Y. 11227
H. M. Schoeller, 569 S. Braddock Ave., Pittsburgh, Pa. 15221 (ML)
Rob. Thompson, 844-14th Ave., So., Clinton, Ia. 52732 (Win. only)
R. M. Verner, 263 Kurtz Rd., Marietta. Ga. 30060
C. H. Weisz, Box 311, Arlington, Va. 22210

GUN PARTS, U. S. AND FOREIGN

Badger Shooter's Supply, Owen, Wisc. 54460
Shelley Braverman, Athens, N.Y. 12015
Philip R. Crouthamel, 817 E. Baltimore, E. Lansdowne, Pa. 19050
Charles E. Duffy, Williams Lane, West Hurley, N.Y. 12491
Federal Ordnance Inc., P.O. Box 36032, Los Angeles, Calif. 90036
Greeley Arms Co., Inc., 223 Little Falls Rd., Fairfield, N.J. 07006
Gunner's Armory, 186 Dartmouth St., San Francisco, Calif. 94124
H&B Gun Corp., 1228 Fort St., Lincoln Park, Mich. 48166
Hudson Sporting Goods Co., 52 Warren St., New York, N.Y. 10007
Hunter's Haven, Zero Prince St., Alexandria, Va. 22314
Inter-American Co., P.O. Box 8022, Sacramento, Calif. 95818
Bob Lovell, Box 401, Elmhurst, Ill. 60126
Numrich Arms Co., West Hurley, N.Y. 12491
Potomac Arms Corp. (see Hunter's Haven)
Powder Horn, Box 545, Pt. Pleasant, N.J. 08742
Reed & Co., Shokan, N.Y. 12481
Martin B. Retting, Inc., 11029 Washington, Culver City, Cal. 90230
Santa Barbara of America, Ltd., P.O. Box 925, So. Houston, Tex. 77587 (barrels and barreled actions)
Sarco, Inc., 192 Central, Stirling, N.J. 07980
R. A. Saunders, 3253 Hillcrest Dr., San Antonio, Tex. 78201 (clips)
Schmid & Ladd, 14733 Hwy. 19 So., Clearwater, Fla. 33516
Shooters Specialties, Box 264, LaMirada, Calif. 90638
Clifford L. Smires, R.D., Columbus, N.J. 08022 (Mauser)
Spokane Sporting Goods, 1702 N. Monroe, Spokane, Wash. 99205
N. F. Strebe, 4926 Marlboro Pike, S.E., Washington, D.C. 20027
Tilden Mfg. Co., 607 Santa Fe Dr., Denver, Colo. 80204

GUNS (Foreign)

Abercrombie & Fitch, Madison at 45th, New York, N.Y. 10017
Adanac Sporting Goods, 505 Bellingham Ntl. Bk. Bldg., Bellingham, Wash. 98225
Alaskan Rifles, Box 941, Juneau, Alaska 99801
American Import Co., 1167 Mission St., San Francisco, Calif. 94103
Armi Fabbri, Casella 206, Brescia, Italy
Atlas Arms, Inc., 2704 N. Central, Chicago, Ill. 60639
Benet Arms Co., 1567 California, San Francisco, Calif. 94109
Blumenfeld Co., 80 W. Virginia Ave., Memphis, Tenn. 38100
Browning Arms Co., Rt. 4, Box 624-B, Arnold, Mo. 63010
Centennial Arms Corp., 3318 W. Devon, Chicago, Ill. 60645
Century Arms Co., 3-5 Federal St., St. Albans, Vt. 05478
Continental Arms Corp., 697 Fifth Ave., New York, N.Y. 10022
W. H. Craig, Box 927, Selma, Ala. 36701
Charles Daly, Inc., 88 Chambers St., New York, N.Y. 10007
Dave's House of Guns, 9130 Viscount Row, Dallas, Tex. 75247
Davidson Firearms Co., 2703 High Pt. Rd., Greensboro, N.C. 27403 (shotguns)
Dixie Gun Works, Inc., Hwy 51, South, Union City, Tenn. 38261 ("Kentucky" rifles)
Eastern Firearms Co., 790 S. Arroyo Pkwy., Los Angeles, Calif. 91105
Europa Corp., P.O. Box 48-1367, Miami, Fla. 33148
J. Fanzoj, P.O. Box 25, Ferlach, Austria 9170
R. C. Fessler & Co., 1634 Colorado Blvd., Los Angeles, Calif. 90041
Finlandia Firearms, 1524 Cabrito Rd., Van Nuys, Calif. 91406 (Tikka)
Firearms Imp. & Exp. Co., 251 S.W. 22nd Ave., Miami, Fla. 33135 (I.N.A.)
Firearms International, 4837 Kerby Hill Rd., Washington, D.C. 20022
Flaig's Lodge, Millvale, Pa. 15209
Freeland's Scope Stands, Inc., 3737 14th Ave., Rock Island, Ill. 61201
J. L. Galef & Son, Inc., 85 Chambers, New York, N.Y. 10007
Garcia Sptg. Arms Corp., 329 Alfred Ave., Teaneck, N.J. 07666
Gevarm (see Blumenfeld Co.)
Gevelot of Can. Ltd., Box 1593, Saskatoon, Sask., Canada
Gold Rush Guns, 1567 California, San Francisco, Calif. 94109 (SIG)
H. F. Grieder, Box 487, Knoxville, Ill. 61448 (Hammerli)
Harrington & Richardson Arms Co., 320 Park Ave., Worcester, Mass. 01610 (HK pistol)
Hawes Firearms Co., 8222 Sunset Blvd., Los Angeles, Calif. 90046
Healthways, Box 45055, Los Angeles, Calif. 90061
Herter's, Waseca, Minn. 56093
Imperial Arms, 3318 W. Devon, Chicago, Ill. 60645
Interarmco, 10 Prince, Alexandria, Va. 22313 (Walther)
Interarms Ltd., 10 Prince St., Alexandria, Va. 22313 (Mauser)
Intercontinental Arms, 10927 W. Pico, Los Angeles, Calif. 90064
International Firearms Co., Ltd., Montreal 1, Que., Canada
International Distr., Box 7566, Miami, Fla. 33155
Ithaca Gun Co., Box 700, Ithaca, N.Y. 14850 (Perazzi)
Italguns, Via Leonardo da Vinci 36, 20090 Trezzano, Milano, Italy
J-K Imports, Box 403, Novato, Cal. 94947 (Italian)
Jana Intl. Co., Box 1107, Denver, Colo. 80201
Guy T. Jones Import Co., 905 Gervais St., Columbia, S. Car. 29201
L. A. Distributors, 4 Centre Market Pl., New York, N.Y. 10013
L&A Gun Brokerage, 484 Lake Park Ave., Oakland, Calif. 94610 (Handi-Gun)
Jos. G. Landmann, 2308 Preetz/Holstein, W. Germany (JGL)
S. E. Laszlo, 200 Tillary St., Brooklyn, N.Y. 11201
Lever Arms Service, 771 Dunsmuir, Vancouver 1, B.C., Canada
Liberty Arms Corp., Box 306, Montrose, Calif. 91020
Mars Equipment Corp., 3318 W. Devon, Chicago, Ill. 60645
McKeown's Guns, R.R. 1, Pekin, Ill. 61554
Navy Arms Co., 689 Bergen Blvd., Ridgefield, N.J. 07657
Omnipol, Washingtonova 11, Praha 1, Czechoslovakia
Harry Owen, 11955 Salem Dr., Granada Hills, Calif. 91344
Pachmayr Gun Works, 1220 S. Grand Ave., Los Angeles, Calif. 90015 (Fabbri)
Parker-Hale, Whittall St., Birmingham 4, England
Ed Paul Sptg. Goods, 172 Flatbush Ave., Brooklyn, N.Y. 11217 (Premier)
Precise Imp. Corp. (PIC), 3 Chestnut, Suffern, N.Y. 10901
Premier Shotguns, 172 Flatbush Ave., Brooklyn, N.Y. 11217
Replica Arms Co., Box 640, Marietta, O. 45750
Richland Arms Co., 321 W. Adrian St., Blissfield, Mich. 49228
Sanderson's, 724 W. Edgewater, Portage, Wis. 53901
Savage Arms Corp., Westfield, Mass. 01085 (Anschutz)
Service Armament, 689 Bergen Blvd., Ridgefield, N.J. 07657 (Greener Harpoon Gun)
Simmons Spec., Inc., 700 Rogers Rd., Olathe, Kans. 66061
Skinner's Gun Shop (see Alaskan Rifles)
Sloan's Sprtg. Goods, Inc., 88 Chambers St., New York, N.Y. 10001
Solingen Cutlery, Box 306, Montrose, Calif. 91020
Sportex Intl. Ltd., 4807 Van Noord Ave., Sherman Oaks, Calif.
Stoeger Arms Co., 55 Ruta Ct., S. Hackensack, N.J. 07606
Tradewinds, Inc., P.O. Box 1191, Tacoma, Wash. 98401
Universal Firearms Corp., 3746 E. 10th Ct., Hialeah, Fla. 33013
Valor Imp. Corp., 159 S.E. 10th, Hialeah, Fla. 33011
Voere (see L.A. Distributors)
Waffen-Frankonia, Box 380, 87 Wurzburg, W. Germany
Weatherby's, 2781 Firestone Blvd., So. Gate, Calif. 90280 (Sauer)
Dan Wesson Arms, 293 So. Main, Monson, Mass. 01057
Zavodi Crvena Zastava, 44 Gavrila Principa St., Belgrade, Yugosl.

GUNS (Pellet)

Air Rifle Hq., Grantsville, W. Va. 26147
Benjamin Air Rifle Co., 1525 So. 8th St., St. Louis, Mo. 63104
Continental Arms Corp., 697 5th Ave., New York, N. Y. 10022
Crosman Arms Co., Inc., Fairport, N.Y. 14450
Daisy Mfg. Co., Rogers, Ark. 72756 (also Feinwerkbau)
Fanta Air Rifles, Box 8122, La Crescenta, Calif. 91214
J. L. Galef & Son, Inc., 85 Chambers St., New York, N.Y. 10007 (B.S.A.)
H. F. Grieder, Box 487, Knoxville, Ill. 61448 (Hammerli)
Healthways, Box 45055, Los Angeles, Calif. 90061
Gil Hebard Guns, Box 1, Knoxville, Ill. 61448
Hy-Score Arms Co., 200 Tillary St., Brooklyn, N.Y. 11201
Interarmco, 10 Prince, Alexandria, Va. 22313 (Walther)
International Dist., Box 7566, Miami, Fla. 33155 (Hammerli-Master)
Kerrco, Inc., Box 368, Hastings, Nebr. 68901
Marksman Products, Box 25396, Los Angeles, Calif. 90025
Precise Imports Corp. (PIC), 3 Chestnut, Suffern, N.Y. 10901
Sears, Roebuck & Co., 825 S. St. Louis, Chicago, Ill. 60607
Service Armament, 689 Bergen Blvd., Ridgefield, N.J. 07657 (Webley, Jaguar)
Sheridan Products, Inc., 3205 Sheridan, Racine, Wis. 53403
Solingen Cutlery, Box 306, Montrose, Calif. 91020
Stoeger Arms Corp., 55 Ruta Ct., S. Hackensack, N.J. 07606 (Peerless)
Stuart Distr. Co., 6 Riverside Dr., Baltimore, Md. 21221
Dan Wesson Arms, 293 S. Main, Monson, Mass. 01057

GUNS, U.S.-made

Agawam Arms Co., 916 Suffield St., Agawam, Mass. 01001
Ed Agramonte, 41 Riverdale Ave., Yonkers, N.Y. 10701
Amer. Craftsmen, Inc., 12645 La Cresta Dr., Los Altos Hills, Calif. 94022
Apache Arms Co., 225 W. University Dr., Tempe, Ariz. 85281
ArmaLite, 118 E. 16th St., Costa Mesa, Calif. 92627
Champlin Firearms, Inc., Box 3191, Enid, Okla. 73701
Charter Arms Corp., 265 Asylum, Bridgeport, Conn. 06610
Colt's, 150 Huyshope Ave., Hartford, Conn. 06102
Eagle Gun Co., 2921 Main St., Stratford, Conn. 06497
Firearms Intl. Corp., 4837 Kerby Hill Rd., Washington, D.C. 20022
Golden Age Arms Co., 158 W. New England, Worthington, O. 43085
Harrington & Richardson, Park Ave., Worcester, Mass. 01610
High Standard Mfg. Co., 1817 Dixwell Ave., Hamden, Conn. 06514
Ithaca Gun Co., Ithaca, N.Y. 14850
Iver Johnson Arms & Cycle Works, Fitchburg, Mass. 01420
Kent Firearms Ltd., Inc., 14 E. Woodland Ave., Springfield, Pa. 19064
MBAssociates, Box 196, San Ramon, Calif. 94583
Marlin Firearms Co., 79 Willow, New Haven, Conn. 06502
Merrill Co., Inc., Box 187, Rockwell City, Ia. 50579
O. F. Mossberg & Sons, Inc., 7 Grasso St., No. Haven, Conn. 06473
Navy Arms Co., 689 Bergen Blvd., Ridgefield, N.J. 07657
Noble Mfg. Co., Inc., S. Main St., Haydenville, Mass. 01039
Numrich Arms Corp., W. Hurley, N.Y. 12491
Plainfield Machine Co., Inc., Box 281, Dunellen, N.J. 08812
Powder Horn, Box 545, Pt. Pleasant, N.J. 08742
Ranger Arms Co., Box 704, Gainesville, Tex. 76240 (Texan Mag.)
Remington Arms Co., Bridgeport, Conn. 06602
Savage Arms Corp., Westfield, Mass. 01085
Sears, Roebuck & Co., 825 S. St. Louis, Chicago, Ill. 60607
Sharps Arms Co., 5448 Riley Lane, Salt Lake City, Utah 84107
Smith & Wesson, Inc., Springfield, Mass. 01101
Staggs Enterprises, 3240 E. Camelback Rd., Phoenix, Ariz. 85018 (O/U rifle-shotgun)
Sterling Arms Ltd., 2215 Elmwood Ave., Buffalo, N.Y. 14216
Sturm, Ruger & Co., Southport, Conn. 06490

Thompson-Center Arms, Box 2405, Rochester, N.H. 03867 (Contender pistol)
Tingle, 1125 Smithland Pike, Shelbyville, Ind. 46176 (muzzleloader)
Universal Firearms Corp., 3746 E. 10th Ct., Hialeah, Fla. 33013
Ward's, 619 W. Chicago, Chicago, Ill. 60607 (Western Field brand)
Weatherby's, 2781 E. Firestone Blvd., South Gate, Calif. 90280
Dan Wesson Arms, 293 So. Main St., Monson, Mass. 01057
Western Auto, 2107 Grand Ave., Kansas City, Mo. 64108
Winchester Repeating Arms Co., New Haven, Conn. 06504
Winslow Arms Co., P.O. Box 578, Osprey, Fla. 33595

GUNSMITH SCHOOLS

Colorado School of Trades, 1545 Hoyt, Denver, Colo. 80215
Lassen Junior College, 11100 Main St., Susanville, Calif. 96130
Oregon Technical Institute, Klamath Falls, Ore. 97601
Penn. Gunsmith School, 812 Ohio River Blvd., Pittsburgh, Pa. 15202
Trinidad State Junior College, Trinidad, Colo. 81082

GUNSMITH SUPPLIES, TOOLS, SERVICES

Adams & Nelson Co., 4125 W. Fullerton, Chicago, Ill. 60639
Alamo Heat Treating Co., Box 55345, Houston, Tex. 77055
Alley Supply Co., Box 458, Sonora, Calif. 95370
American Edelstaal, Inc., 350 Broadway, New York, N.Y. 10013
Anderson Gunshop, 1203 Broadway, Yakima, Wash. 98902 (tang safe)
Armite Labs., 1845 Randolph St., Los Angeles, Cal. 90001 (pen oiler)
Atlas Arms Inc., 2704 N. Central, Chicago, Ill. 60639
B-Square Co., Box 11281, Ft. Worth, Tex. 76110
Benrite Co., 353 Covington, San Antonio, Tex. 78220
Brown & Sharpe Mfg. Co., Precision Pk., No. Kingston, R.I. 02852
Bob Brownell's, Main & Third, Montezuma, Ia. 50171
W. E. Brownell, 1852 Alessandro Trail, Vista, Calif. 92083 (checkering tools)
Maynard P. Buehler, Inc., 17 Orinda Hwy., Orinda, Calif. 94563 (Rocol lube)
Burgess Vibrocrafters, Inc. (BVI), Rte. 21, Grayslake, Ill. 60030
M. H. Canjar, 500 E. 45th, Denver, Colo. 80216 (triggers, etc.)
Centerline Prod. Box 14074, Denver, Colo. 80214
Chicago Wheel & Mfg. Co., 1101 W. Monroe St., Chicago, Ill. 60607 (Handee grinders)
Christy Gun Works, 875 - 57th St., Sacramento, Calif. 95819
Clymer Mfg. Co., 14241 W. 11 Mile Rd., Oak Park, Mich. 48237 (reamers)
Colbert Die Cast Co., 10107 Adella, South Gate, Calif. 90280 (Panavise)
A. Constantine & Son, Inc., 2050 Eastchester Rd., Bronx, N.Y. 10461 (wood)
Dayton-Traister Co., 7028 164th St., S.W., Edmonds, Wash. 98020 (triggers)
Dem-Bart Co., 3333 N. Gove St., Tacoma, Wash. 98407 (checkering tools)
Die Supply Corp., 3173 E. 66th St., Cleveland, O. 44127
Wm. Dixon, Inc., Box 89, Newark, N.J. 07101
Dremel Mfg. Co., P.O. Box 518, Racine, Wis. 53401 (grinders)
Chas. E. Duffy, Williams Lane, West Hurley, N.Y. 12491
Dumore Co., 1300 - 17th St., Racine, Wis. 53403
E-Z Tool Co., 918 Douglas, Des Moines, Ia. 50313 (lathe attachment)
Edmund Scientific Co., 101 E. Gloucester Pike, Barrington, N.J. 08007
F. K. Elliott, Box 785, Ramona, Calif. 92065 (reamers)
Foredom Elec. Co., Rt. 6, Bethel, Conn. 06801 (power drills)
Forster Appelt Mfg. Co., Inc., 82 E. Lanark Ave., Lanark, Ill. 61046
Keith Francis, Box 343, Talent, Ore. 97540 (reamers)
G. R. S. Corp., Box 1157, Boulder, Colo. 80302 (Gravermeister)
Gold Lode, Inc., P.O. Box 31, Addison, Ill. 60101 (gold inlay kit)
Grace Metal Prod., Box 67, Elk Rapids, Mich. 49629 (screw drivers, drifts)
Gopher Shooter's Supply, Box 246, Faribault, Minn. 55021 (screwdrivers, etc.)
The Gun Case, 11035 Maplefield SE., El Monte, Calif. 91733 (triggers)
H. & M., 24062 Orchard Lake Rd., Farmington, Mich. 48024 (reamers)
Hartford Reamer Co., Box 134, Lathrop Village, Mich. 48075
R. E. Hutchinson, Burbank Rd., Sutton, Mass. 01527 (engine turning tool)
O. Iber Co., 626 W. Randolph, Chicago, Ill. 60606
The Joplings, Box 483, Bellevue, Neb. 68005
Kasenite Co., Inc., 3 King St., Mahwah, N.J. 07430 (surface hrdng. comp.)
Lea Mfg. Co., 238 E. Aurora St., Waterbury, Conn. 06720
Lock's Phila. Gun Exch., 6700 Rowland Ave., Philadelphia, Pa. 19149
Marker Machine Co., Box 426, Charleston, Ill. 61920
Viggo Miller, P.O. Box 4181, Omaha, Neb. 68104
Miller Single Trigger Mfg. Co., Box 69, Millersburg, Pa. 17061
Frank Mittermeier, 3577 E. Tremont, N.Y., N.Y. 10465
Moderntools Corp., Box 407, Dept. GD, Woodside, N.Y. 11377
Karl A. Neise, Inc., 5602 Roosevelt Ave., Woodside, N.Y. 11377
P & C Tool Co., Box 22066, Portland, Ore. 97222
P.G.E. Products, 6700 Rowland Ave., Philadelphia, Pa. 19100
Palmgren, 8383 South Chicago Ave., Chicago, Ill. 60167 (vises, etc.)
C. R. Pedersen & Son, Ludington, Mich. 49431
Penn Ind., Box 8904, Philadelphia, Pa. 19135 (contour gauge)
Ponderay Lab., 210 W. Prasch, Yakima, Wash. 98902 (epoxy glass bedding)
Redford Reamer Co., Box 6604, Detroit, Mich. 48240
Richland Arms Co., 321 W. Adrian St., Blissfield, Mich. 49228
Riley's Supply Co., Box 365, Avilla, Ind. 46710 (Niedner buttplates, caps)
Roderick Arms & Tool Corp., 110 2nd St., Monett, Mo. 65708
Rob. A. Saunders, 3253 Hillcrest Dr., San Antonio, Tex. 78201 (45 conversion kit)
Schuetzen Gun Works, 1226 Prairie Rd., Colo. Springs, Colo. 80909
Shaw's, 1655 S. Euclid Ave., Anaheim, Calif. 92802
Shebal's Gun Shop, 14th & Lacey, Fairbanks, Alaska 99701
Shooters Specialties, Box 246, La Mirada, Calif. 90638
Silken Compass Cutter Co., Box 242, Oceanside, N.Y. 11592
A. D. Soucy Co., Box 191, Fort Kent, Me. 04743 (ADSCO stock finish)
L. S. Starrett Co., Athol, Mass. 01331
T.D.C., Box 42072, Portland, Ore. 97242
Timney Mfg. Co., 5624 Imperial Hwy., So. Gate, Calif. 90280 (triggers)
Stan de Treville, Box 2446, San Diego, Calif 92112 (checkering patterns)
Twin City Steel Treating Co., Inc., 1114 S. 3rd, Minneapolis, Minn. 55415
Vanguard Arms Corp., Box 46566, Los Angeles, Calif. 90046 (45 single-actions)
Ward Mfg. Co., 500 Ford Blvd., Hamilton, O. 45011
Will-Burt Co., Box 160, Orrville, O. 44667 (vises)
Williams Gun Sight Co., 7389 Lapeer Rd., Davison, Mich. 48423
Wilson Arms Co., Box 364, Stony Creek, Branford, Conn. 06405
Wilton Tool Corp., 9525 W. Irving Pk. Rd., Schiller Park, Ill. 60176 (vises)
Woodcraft Supply Corp., 71 Canal St., Boston, Mass. 02114
Wright Gun & Tool Co., Box 245, Bloomsburg, Pa. 17815

HANDGUN ACCESSORIES

B. L. Broadway, 1503 Jasper, Chula Vista, Calif. 92011 (machine rest)
Case Master, 4434 N.W. 35 Ct., Miami, Fla. 33142
Central Specialties Co., 6030 N. Northwest Hwy., Chicago, Ill. 60631
John Dangelzer, 3056 Frontier Pl., N.E., Albuquerque, N.M. 87106 (flasks)
Bill Dyer, 503 Midwest Bldg., Oklahoma City, Okla. 73102 (grip caps)
R. S. Frielich, 396 Broome St., New York, N.Y. 10013 (cases)
Hunt Eng., 1211—17th St., Yucaipa, Calif. 92399 (Multi-Loader)
R. G. Jensen, 16153½ Parthenia, Sepulveda, Calif. 91343 (auxiliary chambers)
Matich Loader, Box 958, So. Pasadena, Calif. 91030 (Quick Load)
Pachmayr, 1220 S. Grand, Los Angeles, Calif. 90015 (cases)
Platt Luggage, Inc., 2301 S. Prairie, Chicago, Ill. 60616 (cases)
Jules Reiver, 4104 Market St., Wilmington, Del. 19899 (cases)
Sportsmen's Equipment Co., 415 W. Washington, San Diego, Calif. 92103
M. Tyler, 1326 W. Britton, Oklahoma City, Okla. 73114 (grip adaptor)

HANDGUN GRIPS

Beckelhymer's, Hidalgo & San Bernardo, Laredo, Tex. 78040
Belmont Products, 415—2nd Ave. N., Twin Falls, Ida. 83301
Caray Sales Co., 2044 Hudson St., Ft. Lee, N.J. 07024
Cloyce's Gun Stocks, Box 1133, Twin Falls, Ida. 83301
Crest Carving Co., 401 S. Cypress St., La Habra, Calif. 90631
Enforcer Prod. Div., Caray Sales Co., 2044 Hudson St., Fort Lee, N.J. 07024
Fitz, Box 49797, Los Angeles, Calif. 90049
Herret's, Box 741, Twin Falls, Ida. 83301
Mershon Co., Inc., 1230 S. Grand Ave., Los Angeles, Calif. 90015
Mustang Grips, 13830 Hiway 395, Edgemont, Calif. 92508
Safety Grip Corp., Box 456, Riverside St., Miami, Fla. 33135
Sanderson Custom Pistol Stocks, 17695 Fenton, Detroit, Mich. 48219
Jay Scott, 81 Sherman Place, Garfield, N.J. 07026
Sile Dist., 7 Centre Market Pl., New York, N.Y. 10013
Sports, Inc., 5501 Broadway, Chicago, Ill. 60640 (Franzite)
John W. Womack, 3006 Bibb St., Shreveport, La. 71108

HOLSTERS & LEATHER GOODS

Berns-Martin, Box 335, Elberton, Ga. 30635
Bianchi Holster Co., 212 W. Foothill Blvd., Monrovia, Calif. 91016
Edward H. Bohlin, 931 N. Highland Ave., Hollywood, Calif. 90038
Boyt Co., Box 1108, Iowa Falls, Ia. 51026
E. A. Brandin Saddle Co., Rte. 2, Box 243-A, Monroe, La. 71201
Brauer Bros. Mfg. Co., 817 N. 17th, St. Louis, Mo. 63106
Browning Arms Co., Rt. 4, Box 624-B, Arnold, Mo. 63010
J. M. Bucheimer Co., Box 30, Frederick, Md. 21701
Cole's Acku-Rite, Box 25, Kennedy, N.Y. 14747
Colt's, 150 Huyshope Ave., Hartford, Conn. 06102
Daisy Mfg. Co., Rogers, Ark. 72756
Eugene DeMayo & Sons, Inc., 2795 Third Ave., Bronx, N.Y. 10455
Filmat Enterpr., Inc., 287 Market St., East Paterson, N.J. 07407
Flintrop Arms Co., 4034 W. National Ave., Milwaukee, Wis. 53215
Goerg Ent., 3009 S. Laurel, Port Angeles, Wash. 98362
Don Hume, Box 351, Miami, Okla. 74354
The Hunter Co., 1215 12th St., Denver, Colo. 80204

George Lawrence Co., 306 S. W. First Ave., Portland, Ore. 97204
S. D. Myres Saddle Co., Box 9776, El Paso, Tex. 79988
Pony Express Sport Shop, 17460 Ventura Blvd., Encino, Calif. 91316
Red Head Brand Co., P.O. Box 10956, Dallas, Tex. 75207
R. E. Roseberry, 810 W. 38th, Anderson, Ind. 46011
Safariland Leather Products, 1946 S. Myrtle Ave., Monrovia, Calif. 91016
Safety Speed Holster Co., 910 So. Vail, Montebello, Calif. 90641
San Francisco Gun Exchange, 75 Fourth St., San Francisco, Calif. 94103
Buddy Schoellkopf Products, Inc., 148 Fordyce, Dallas, Tex. 75207
Seventrees, Ltd., 315 W. 39 St., New York, N.Y.
Sile Distr., 7 Centre Market Pl., New York, N.Y. 10013
Smith & Wesson Leather Co., P.O. Box 1125, Monrovia, Cal. 91016
Tandy Leather Co., 1001 Foch, Fort Worth, Texas 76107
Basil Tuller, 29 Germania St., Galeton, Pa. 16922 (Protektor Prod.)
Western Products Co., Box 771, Laredo, Tex. 78040
Whitco, Box 1712, Brownsville, Tex. 78520 (Hide-A-Way)
Wolfram Leather Co. (See Smith & Wesson Leather Co.)
Woodland Sport and Gift Shop, Box 107, Mayfield, N.Y. 12117

HUNTING, CAMP GEAR, CLOTHING, ETC.

Abercrombie & Fitch, 45th & Madison Ave., N.Y., N.Y. 10017
Alaska Sleeping Bag Co., 701 N.W. Dawson Way, Beaverton, Ore., 97005
Alp Sport of Colorado, Box 1081, Boulder, Colo. 80302
Alpine Hut, Box 1456, Wenatchee, Wash. 98801
Armour Star Lite Foods, Box 4309, Chicago, Ill. 60680
Eddie Bauer, 417 E. Pine St., Seattle, Wash. 98122
L. L. Bean, Freeport, Me. 04032
Bear Archery Co., R.R. 1, Grayling, Mich. 49738 (Himalayan backpack)
Belgo-American Co., 5468 S. Ridgewood Ct., Chicago, Ill. 60615
Bernzomatic Corp., 740 Driving Pk. Ave., Rochester, N.Y. 14613 (stoves & lanterns)
Big Beam, Teledyne Co., 290 E. Prairie St., Crystal Lake, Ill. 60014 (lamp)
Thos. Black & Sons, 930 Ford St., Ogdensburg, N.Y. 13669 (ctlg. 25c)
Camouflage Mfg. Co., Box 16373, Jacksonville, Fla. 32216
Camp and Trail Outfitters, 112 Chambers St., N.Y., N.Y. 10007
Camp Trails, 3920 W. Claredon, Phoenix, Ariz. 85019 (packs only)
Challanger Mfg. Co., Box 550, Jamaica, N.Y. 11431 (glow safe)
Coleman Co., Inc., 250 N. St. Francis, Wichita, Kans. 67201
Colorado Spts. Corp., Box 5544, Denver, Colo. 80217
Converse Rubber Co., 392 Pearl St., Malden, Mass. 02148 (boots)
Corcoran, Inc., Zero Canton Street, Stoughton, Mass. 02072
Dana Safety Heater, J. L. Galef & Son, Inc., 85 Chamber St., N.Y. N.Y. 10007
DEER-ME Prod. Co., Box 345, Anoka, Minn. 55303 (tree steps)
Dunham's Footwear, RFD 3, Brattleboro, Vt. 05301 (boots)
Edmont-Wilson, 1300 Walnut St., Coshocton, O. 43812 (gloves)
Fabrico Mfg. Corp., 1300 W. Exchange, Chicago, Ill. 60609
Filmat Enterpr., Inc., 287 Market St., East Paterson, N.J. 07407 (field dressing kit)
Game-Winner, Inc., 2940 First Natl. Bk. Bldg., Atlanta, Ga. 30303
Gander Mountain, Inc., Box 248, Wilmot, Wis. 53192
George & Son 424 S.W. Washington, Portland, Ore. 97204
Gerry Mountain Sports, Inc. (see Colorado Sports)
Gokey, 94 E. 4th St., St. Paul, Minn. 55101
Greenford Products, Inc., 64 Old Orchard, Skokie, Ill. 60076 (heaters & ranges)
Gun Club Sportswear, Box 477, Des Moines, Ia. 50302
Gun-Ho Case Mfg. Co., 501 Robert St., St. Paul, Minn. 55101
Hawthorn Co., Div. of Kellwood Co., New Haven, Mo. 63068 (tents)
Highland Outfitters, Box 121, Riverside, Calif. 92501
Herter's Inc., Waseca, Minn. 56093
Himalayan Ind., Box 950, Monterey, Calif. 93950
Bob Hinman, 1217 W. Glen, Peoria, Ill. 61614
Holubar, Box 7, Boulder, Colo. 80301
Humphrey Prod., P.O. Box 2008, Kalamazoo, Mich. 49003 (camping equipment)
Hunt Mfg. Co., 216 W. Ontario, Chicago, Ill. 60610 (Power Starting Amplifier)
Hunting World, 247 E. 50th St., New York, N.Y. 10022
Kelty Pack, Inc., Box 3645, Glendale, Calif. 91201
Kigel Textile Co., 118 N. St. Clair St., Toledo, O. 43604
Peter Limmer & Sons, Box 66, Intervale, N.H. 03845 (boots)
Marble Arms Corp., 1120 Superior, Gladstone, Mich. 49837
Mid-Western Sport Togs, Berlin, Wis. 54923
Moor & Mountain, 14 Main St., Concord Center, Mass. 01742
National Sports Div., 19 E. McWilliams St., Fond du Lac, Wis. 54935
Nimrod & Wayfarer Trailers, 500 Ford Blvd., Hamilton, O. 45011
Charles F. Orvis Co., Manchester, Vt. 05254 (fishing gear)
Paulin Infra-Red Prod. Co., 1600 S. Waterloo, Cleveland, O. 44110 (Coleman stove conv.)
Portablind, Box 3221, Lubbock, Tex. 79410 (hunting high seat)
Powerwinch Corp., 184 Garden St., Bridgeport, Conn. 06605
Primus-Sievert, 47 Larkin St., Stamford, Conn. 06906 (stoves)
Thomas Quinn, 2650 S. University Village, Seattle, Wash. 98105
Raemco, Box 882, Somerville, N.J. 08876 (stoves)
Ray-O-Vac, 212 E. Washington, Madison, Wis. 53703 (lanterns & flash lights)
Recreational Equip., Inc., 423 Pike St., Seattle, Wash. 98101
Red Head Brand Co., P.O. Box 10956, Dallas, Tex. 75207
Red Wing Shoe Co., Rte. 2, Red Wing, Minn. 55066
Refrigiwear, Inc., 71 Inip Dr., Inwood, L.I., N.Y. 11696
Reliance Prod. Ltd., 1830 Dublin Ave., Winnipeg 21, Man., Can. (tent peg)
SS&G Inc., P.O. Box 246, Layton, U. 84041 (packs)
Safari Mfg. Co., Inc., 843 10th, Worthington, Minn. 56187 (cartop trunk)
Buddy Schoellkopf, Inc., 148 Fordyce St., Dallas, Tex. 75207
Seater Heater, Inc., 2031 W. Calle Placida, Tucson, Ariz. 85705
Servus Rubber Co., 1136 2nd St., Rock Island, Ill. 61201 (footwear)
Smith & Stone, 50 St. Clair Ave. W., Toronto, Ont., Can.
Sport Chalet, Box 626, La Canada, Calif. 91011
Sportsgear, Inc., 4909 Fremont Ave. So., Minneapolis, Minn. 55409 (pack sack & port. chair)
Sportsmen Prod. Inc., Box 1082, Boulder, Colo. 80302 (snowshoes)
Star-Fire, Inc., Box 1057, Escondido, Calif. 92025 (butane torch)
Stearns Mfg. Co., Division & 30th St., St. Cloud, Minn. 56301
Sterno Inc., 105 Hudson St., Jersey City, N.J. 07302 (camp stoves)
Burt Stumpf, 408 Morrison Ave., Waterloo, Ill. 62298 (Easy-Way hunting vest)
10-X Mfg. Co., 100 S.W. 3rd St., Des Moines, Iowa 50309
Thermos Div., KST Co., Norwich, Conn. 06361 (Pop Tent)
Therm'x Corp., Inc., 1268 Folsom St., San Francisco, Calif. 94103
Norm Thompson, 1805 N.W. Thurman St., Portland, Ore. 97209
Trailblazer, Redwine Co., 170 University Dr., Athens, Ga. 30602
Trailwise-The Ski Hut, 1615 University Ave., Berkeley, Calif. 94703
Travel Industries, Box 108, Oswego, Kan. 67356 (Dreamer pickup fleet)
Trigg Mfg. Co., Box 850, Danville, Ky. 40422 (clothing)
Trimline Campers, 7426 W. Capitol Dr., Milwaukee, Wis. 53216
U-C-Lite Mfg. Co., 290 E. Prairie St., Crystal Lake, Ill. 60014 (Big beam car- and hand-flashlights)
Eug. Usow Mfg. Co., 227 So. Seeley Ave., Chicago, Ill. 60612 (clothing)
Ute Mountain Corp., Box 3602, Englewood, Colo. 80110 (Metal Match)
Utica Duxbak Corp., Utica, N.Y. 13502
Visa-Therm Prod., Inc., P.O. Box 486, Bridgeport, Conn. 06601 (Astro/Electr. vest)
Vogt. Mfg. Co., 100 Fernwood Ave., Rochester, N.Y. 14621 (fluorescent belt)
Waffen-Frankonia, Box 380, 87 Wurzburg, W. Germany
Walle-Hawk Corp., Box 1024, Burlington, Vt. 05401 (survival kit)
Ward Mfg. Co., 500 Ford Blvd., Hamilton, O. 45015 (trailers)
Weinbrenner Shoe Corp., 2025 N. Summit Ave., Milwaukee, Wis. 53202
Wilson & Co. Campsite Foods, Prudential Plaza, Chicago, Ill. 60601
Wisconsin Shoe Co., 1039 So. Second, Milwaukee, Wis. 53204
Woods Bag & Canvas Co., Ltd., 16 Lake St., Ogdensburg, N.Y. 13669
Woodstream Corp., Box 327, Lititz, Pa. 17543 (Hunter Seat)
Woolrich Woolen Mills, Woolrich, Pa. 17779
Zeus Portable Generator Co., 12435 Euclid Ave. Cleveland, O. 44106

HUNTING KNIVES, AXES AND HATCHETS

Adanac Sporting Goods, 505 Bellingham Natl. Bk. Bldg., Bellingham, Wash. 98225
B.H.S. Mfg. Co., Box 24, Troy, Mich. 48084 (pocket axe)
L. L. Bean, Freeport, Maine 04032
Bear Archery Co., R.R. 1, Grayling, Mich. 49738
Buck Knives, Inc., 6588 Federal Blvd., San Diego, Calif. 92114
W. R. Case Knives, 20 Russell Blvd., Bradford, Pa. 16701
Challanger Mfg. Co., 105-23 New York Blvd., Jamaica, N.Y. 11433
Clyde E. Fischer, Rt. 1, Box 170-M, Victoria, Tex. 77901
Gerber Legendary Blades, 14200 S.W. 72nd St., Portland, Ore. 99223
Gutman Cutlery Co., Inc., 3956 Broadway, New York, N.Y. 10032
KA-BAR Cutlery, Inc., 5777 Grant Ave., Cleveland, O. 44105
W. Kneubuhler, P.O. Box 327, Pioneer, O. 43554
Len Co., Box 101, Brooklyn, N.Y. 11214
MAC Intl. Corp., 333 N. Michigan, Chicago, Ill. 60601
Marble Arms Corp., 1120 Superior, Gladstone, Mich. 49837
W. F. Moran, Jr., Rt. 5, Frederick, Md. 21701
Morseth Sports Equipment, Clinton, Wash. 98236
O. A. Nordlund, Lewistown, Penna. 17044
Lee E. Olsen Knife Co., 7 Joy St., Howard City, Mich. 49329
Plumb Inc., 4837 James St., Philadelphia, Pa. 19137
Randall-Made Knives, Box 1988, Orlando, Fla. 32802
Ruana Knife Works, Box 574, Bonner, Mont. 59823
Russell Belt Knives, 1313 Snowdon St., Ottawa 8, Ont., Canada
Sanders, 2358 Tyler Lane, Louisville, Ky. 40205 (Bahco)
Skatchet, Inc., P.O. Box 302, Springfield, Va. 22150
Tru-Balance Knife Co., 2110 Tremont Blvd., Grand Rapids, Mich. 49504
True-Temper, 1623 Euclid, Cleveland O. 44100
W-K Knives, P.O. Box 327, Pioneer, O. 43554
Western Cutlery Co., 5311 Western Ave., Boulder, Colo. 80302

LOAD TESTING & CHRONOGRAPHING

Carter Gun Works, 2211 Jefferson Pk. Ave., Charlottesville, Va. 22903
Custom Ballistics' Lab., 3354 Cumberland Dr., San Angelo, Tex. 76901
Horton Ballistics, North Waterford, Me. 04267
Hutton Rifle Ranch, Topanga, Calif. 90290 (daily fee range also)
Jurras Co., Box 163, Shelbyville, Ind. 46176
Kennon's, 5408 Biffle, Stone Mountain, Ga. 30083
Plum City Ballistics Range, RFD 1, Box 128, Plum City, Wis. 54761
R & M Chronograph Serv., 9882 E. Manning, Selma, Calif. 93662
Shooters Service & Dewey, Inc., Clinton Corners, N.Y. 12514 (daily fee range also)
H. P. White Lab., Box 331, Bel Air, Md. 21014

METALLIC SIGHTS

B-Square Eng. Co., Box 11281, Ft. Worth, Tex. 76110
Bo-Mar Tool & Mfg. Co., Box 168, Carthage, Tex. 75633
Maynard P. Buehler, Inc., 17 Orinda Highway, Orinda, Calif. 94563
Chicago Gun Center, 3109 W. Armitage, Chicago, Ill. 60647
Christy Gun Works, 875 57th St., Sacramento, Calif. 95819
Clerke Technicorp., 2054 Broadway Ave., Santa Monica, Calif. 90404
Art Cook Supply, Rte. 2, Box 123B, Laurel, Md. 20810 (Illum. gunsight)
Firearms Dev. Lab., Box 278, Scotts Valley, Calif. 95060
Freeland's Scope Stands, Inc., 3734-14th Ave., Rock Island, Ill. 61201
P. W. Gray Co., Fairgrounds Rd., Nantucket, Mass. 02554 (shotgun)
Hi-Lo Sights, P.O. Box 131, Lyndon Station, Wis. 53944
International Guns, 66 Warburton Ave., Yonkers, N.Y. 10701
Lyman Gun Sight Corp., Middlefield, Conn. 06455
Marble Arms Corp., 1120 Superior, Gladstone, Mich. 49837
Merit Gunsight Co., P.O. Box 995, Sequim, Wash. 98382
Micro Sight Co., 242 Harbor Blvd., Belmont, Calif. 94002
Original Sight Exchange Co., Box J, Paoli, Pa. 19301
C. R. Pedersen & Son, Ludington, Mich. 49431
Precision Gun Sight Co., Box 2143, West Hartford, Conn. 06117 (shotgun)
Redfield Gun Sight Co., 1315 S. Clarkson St., Denver, Colo. 80210
Schwarz's Gun Shop, 41 - 15th St., Wellsburg, W. Va. 26070
Simmons Gun Specialties, Inc., 700 Rodgers Rd., Olathe, Kans. 66061
Slug Site Co., 3835 University, Des Moines, Ia. 50311
Stokes Ent., 5290 Long Beach Blvd., Long Beach, Calif. 90805
Wm. Tell Gun Sight, Inc., Rte. 1, Wilder, Ida., 83676
Trius Prod., Box 25, Cleves, O. 45002 (bi-ocular)
Williams Gun Sight Co., 7389 Lapeer Rd., Davison, Mich. 48423
W. H. Womack, 2124 Meriwether Rd., Shreveport, La. 71108

MISCELLANEOUS

Adhesive Flannel, Forest City Prod., 722 Bolivar, Cleveland, O. 44115
Archery, Bear Co., R.R. 1, Grayling, Mich. 49738
Arms Bookseller, Norm Flayderman, RFD 2, Squash Hollow, New Milford, Conn. 06776
Arms Bookseller, Rutgers, Mark Aziz, 127 Raritan Ave., Highland Park, N.J. 08904
Barrel Band Swivels, Phil Judd, 83 E. Park St., Butte, Mont. 59701
Barrel Bedding Device, W. H. Womack, 2124 Meriwether Rd., Shreveport, La. 71108
Bedding Kit, Bisonite Co., Box 84, Buffalo, N.Y. 14217
Bedding Kit, Fenwal, Inc., 400 Main St., Ashland, Mass. 01721
Bench Rest Pedestal, Jim Brobst, 31 S. 3rd St., Hamburg, Pa. 19526
Bench Rest Stands, Suter's, 401 Tejon, Colorado Springs, Colo. 80902
Binocular/Camera Harness, Jack Worsfold Assoc., Box 25, Forest Hill, Md. 21050
Bootdryers, Backgaard & Butler, 1939 Waukegan Rd., Glenview, Ill. 60025
Bore Collimator, Alley Supply Co., Box 458, Sonora, Calif. 95370
Bore Collimator, Collins Co., Box 40, Shepherdsville, Ky. 40165
Bore Lamp, Spacetron, Inc., Box 84, Broadview Ill. 60155
Borescope, Eder Inst. Co., 2293 N. Clybourn, Chicago, Ill. 60614
Borescope, J. G. Mundy, 1008 MacDade Blvd., Collingdale, Pa. 19023
Bore Sighter, Rifleman's Bore Sighter Co., P.O. Box 3292, Saginaw, Mich. 48601
Breech Plug Wrench, Swaine Machine, 195 O'Connell, Providence, R.I. 02905
Can Thrower, Trius Prod., Box 25, Cleves, O. 45002
Capper, Muzzle-Loading, Pat Burke, 3339 Farnsworth Rd., Lapeer, Mich. 48446
Cartridge Boxes, Llanerch Gun Shop, 2800 Township Line, Upper Darby, Pa. 19083
Cartridge Box Labels, Milton Brynin, Box 162, Fleetwood Sta., Mt. Vernon, N.Y. 10552
Cartridge Box Labels, Peterson Label Co., 58 Harrison Brook Drive, Basking Ridge, N.J. 07920
Cartridge Box Labels, General Mail Order Co., Box 16, Syosset, N.Y. 11791
Cartridge Box Labels, Jasco, Box 49751, Los Angeles, Calif. 90049
Case Gauge, Plum City Ballistics Range, Box 128, Plum City, Wis. 54761
Chrome Brl. Lining, Marker Mach. Co., Box 426, Charleston, Ill. 61920
Clamp-On Choke, Penn Atlantic Supply, Inc., 47 W. State St., Doylestown, Pa. 18901
Color Hardening, Alamo Heat Treating Co., Box 55345, Houston, Tex. 77055
Contour Gauge, Penn. Ind., Box 8904, Philadelphia, Pa. 19135
Cronoscope, Wein Prod. Inc., P.O. Box 34647, Palms, Calif. 90034
Crossbows, Midwest Crossbow Co., 9043 So. Western, Chicago, Ill. 60620
Crow Caller, Wightman Elec. Inc., Box 989, Easton, Md. 21601
Custom Bluing, J. A. Wingert, 124 W. 2nd St., Waynesboro, Pa. 17268
Decoys, Deeks, Inc., Box 2309, Salt Lake City, Utah 84114
Decoys, Sports Haven Ltd., Box 19323, Portland, Ore. 97219
Decoys, Tex Wirtz Ent., Inc., 1925 W. Hubbard St., Chicago Ill. 60622
Decoys, Woodstream Corp., Box 327, Lititz, Pa. 17543
Distress Flares, Marsh Coulter Co., Box 333, Tecumseh, Mich. 49286
Dog House, Canine Pal Sales, 421 E. 39th Ave., Gary, Ind. 46409 (portable)
Double Hand Trap, Melco Wood Prod., Geneva, N.Y. 14456
Dry Firing Aid, Pitman Industries, Box 325, Pitman, N.J. 08071
Ear-Valv, Sigma Eng. Co., 11320 Burbank Blvd., N. Hollywood, Cal. 91601
Electric Heater, Dampp-Chaser, Inc., Box 1610, Hendersonville, N.C. 28739
Emergency Food, Chuck Wagon Foods, Micro Dr., Woburn, Mass. 01801
Flares, Colt Industries, Huyshope Ave., Hartford, Conn. 06102
Flares, Goble Assoc., Box 1057, Escondido, Calif. 92025
Flat Springs, Alamo Heat Treating Co., Box 55345, Houston, Tex. 77055
Folding Cup, Bob Lane Co., Box 333, Branford, Conn. 06405
Game Hoist, Flanders Mfg. Co., Box 33363, Houston, Tex. 77033
Game Hoist, PIC, 3 Chestnut, Suffern, N.Y. 10901
Game Scent, Pete Rickard, Box 26, Cobleskill, N.Y. 12043 (Indian Buck lure)
Gas Pistol, Penguin Assoc., Inc., Box 97, Parkesburg, Pa. 19365
Gun Bedding Kit, Resin Div., Fenwal, Inc., 400 Main St., Ashland, Mass. 01601
Gun Lock Chain, Lundy Corp., 1123-24 Davenport Bk. Bldg., Davenport, Ia. 52801
Gun Lok, 4780 Old Orchard Trail, Orchard Lake, Mich. 48034
Gun Socks Covers, East-Tenn Mills, Inc., Box 1030, Johnson City, Tenn. 37601
Hearing Protector, American Optical Co., Mechanic St., Southbridge, Mass. 01550
Hearing Protector, David Clark Co., 360 Franklin St., Worcester, Mass. 01601
Hearing Protector, Curtis Safety Prod. Co., Box 61, Webster Sq. Sta., Worcester, Mass. 01603
Hearing Protector, Ray-O-Vac, 212 E. Washington, Madison, Wis. 53703
Hearing Protector, Sanitizer Bath, Graco Pharm. Co., 172 W. Main St., Meriden, Conn. 06450
Hollow Pointer, Goerg Ent., 3009 S. Laurel St., Port Angeles, Wash. 98362
Hugger Hooks, Roman Products, Box 891, Golden, Colo. 80401
Hunting Blind, Sports Haven Ltd., Box 19323, Portland, Ore. 97219
Insert Barrels, (22 RF), H. Owen, 11955 Salem Dr., Granada Hills, Calif. 91344
Leather Rest-Bags, B. Tuller, 29 Germania, Galeton, Pa. 16922
Magazine Clip (Colyer), Great Northern Trading Post, 13001 Hwy. 65 N.E., Rte. 4, Anoka, Minn. 55303
Magazine Clips, Rob't. A. Saunders, Box 260, San Antonio, Tex. 78201
Miniature Guns, C. H. Stoppler, 1426 Walton Ave., N.Y., N.Y. 10459
Nipple Wrenches, Chopie Tool & Die Co., 531 Copeland Ave., La Crosse, Wis. 54601
Optical Attach., Three V Prod., 3007 Rochester St., Arlington, Va. 22213
Pell Remover, A. Edw. Terpening, 838 W. Darlington Rd., Tarpon Springs, Fla. 33589
Pressure Testg. Machine, York-Cantrell, Inc., 30241 Rosebriar, St. Clair Shores, Mich. 48082
Recoil Pads, etc., Mershon Co., Inc., 1230 S. Grand, Los Angeles, Cal. 90015
Recoil Pads, Pachmayr Gun Works, 1220 S. Grand Ave., Los Angeles, Cal. 90015
Recoil Pads, Supreme Prod., 815 Morgan Dr., No. 301, Los Angeles, Calif. 90049
Recoil Reducer, J. B. Edwards, 269 Herbert St., Alton, Ill. 62002
Retriev-R-Trainer, Scientific Prod. Corp., 5417A Vine St., Alexandria, Va. 22310
Rifle Rests, E. L. Beecher, 2155 Demington Dr., Cleveland Hgts., O. 44106
Rifle Rests, Cole's Acku-Rite Prod., Box 25, Kennedy, N.Y. 14747
Rifle Rests, Frontier Arms, Inc., Box 2593, Cheyenne, Wyo. 82001
Rifle Rests, E-N Gun Prod., 1015 Van Hoy Ave., Winston-Salem, N.C. 27104
Rifle Rests, Harris Engr., Inc., Box 305, Fraser, Mich. 48026 (bipods)
Rifle Rests, The Gun Case, 11035 Maplefield, El Monte, Cal. 91733
Rifle Rests, Ten Ring Mfg. Co., Box 157, New City, N.Y. 10956 (Rifle-Mate)
Rifle Rests, W. H. Womack, 2124 Meriwether Rd., Shreveport, La. 71108
RIG, NRA Scoring Plug, Rig Prod. Co., Box 279, Oregon, Ill. 60161
Rubber Cheekpiece, W. H. Lodewick, 2816 N. E. Halsey, Portland, Ore. 97232
Safe-T-Shell, Inc., 4361 Woodhall Rd., Columbus, O. 43221 (shotgun)
Safeties, Doc Line Co., 18440 John R. St., Detroit, Mich. 48203
Safeties, Williams Gun Sight Co., 7389 Lapeer Rd., Davison, Mich. 48423
Salute Cannons, Naval Co., Rt. 611, Doylestown, Pa. 18901
Scope Safeties, W. H. Lodewick, 2816 N.E. Halsey, Portland, Ore. 97232
Score Booster, R. D. Stam, 25 Ridge View Dr., E. Rochester, N.Y. 14445
Sharpening Stones, Russell's Arkansas Oilstones, P.O. Box 474, Fayetteville, Ark. 72701
Shell Cracker, Stoneco, Inc., 5401 No. Federal Blvd., Denver Colo. 80200
Shooting Coats, 10-X Mfg. Co., 100 S. W. 3rd, Des Moines, Iowa 50309
Shooting/Testing Glasses, Davis Aircraft Prod., Scudder & Woodbine, Northport, L.I., N.Y. 11768
Shooting Glasses, M. B. Dinsmore, Box 21, Wyomissing, Pa. 19610
Shooting Glasses, Mitchell's, Box 539, Waynesville, Mo. 65583
Shooting Ranges, Shooting Equip. Inc., 4616 W. 20th St., Chicago, Ill. 60650
Shotgun Recoil Kit, CHB, 3063 Hiram, Wichita, Kan. 67217
Shotgun Sight, bi-ocular, Trius Prod., Box 25, Cleves, O. 45002

Shotshell Pouches, Filmat Enterpr., Inc., 287 Market St., East Paterson, N.J. 07407
Silver Grip Caps, Bill Dyer, 503 Midwest Bldg., Oklahoma City, Okla. 73102
Slide Safety (Mausers), Doc Line Co., 18440 John R., Detroit, Mich. 48203
Snap Caps, Filmat, 287 Market, East Paterson, N.J. 07407
Snowshoes, Sportsmen Prod. Inc., Box 1082, Boulder, Colo. 80302
Springfield Safety Pin, B-Square Co., P.O. Box 11281, Ft. Worth, Tex. 76110
Springs, W. Wolff Co., Box 232, Ardmore, Pa. 19003
Stock-Lo-Kater, Earl Pellant, 1716 N. Serrano, Hollywood, Cal. 90027
Swivels, Michaels, P.O. Box 13010, Portland, Ore. 97213
Swivels, Sile Dist., 7 Centre Market Pl., New York, N.Y. 10013
Swivels, Williams Gun Sigght Co., 7389 Lapeer Rd., Davison, Mich. 48423
Taxidermy, Jack Atcheson, 2309 Hancock Ave., Butte, Mont. 59701
Taxidermy, Jonas Bros., 1037 Broadway, Denver, Colo. 80203
Taxidermy, Knopp Bros., N. 6715 Division St., Spokane, Wash. 99208
Taxidermy, Mac's, 201 N. Grand Ave., Waukesha, Wis. 53186
Teenuts, Dot Product Supply Co., 10544 Lunt Ave., Rosemont, Ill. 60018
Tree Stand Co., 23 Main St., Matawan, N.J. 07747
Triggers, Canjar Rifle Acc., 500 E. 45th St., Denver, Colo. 80216
Trigger Guards, Michaels, P.O. Box 13010, Portland, Ore. 97213
Trigger Shoe, Flaigs, Babcock Blvd., Millvale, Pa. 15209
Trigger Shoe, Pacific Gun Sight Co., Box 4495, Lincoln, Neb. 68504
Trigger Shoe, Melvin Tyler, 1326 W. Britton, Oklahoma City, Okla. 73114
Trophies, L. G. Balfour Co., Attleboro, Mass. 02703
Trophies, Blackinton & Co., 140 Commonwealth, Attleboro Falls, Mass. 02763
Trophies, F. H. Noble & Co., 535 W. 59th St., Chicago, Ill. 60621
Trap, claybird, Deerback Prod., 8239 Hayle Ave., Dallas, Tex. 75227
Trap, claybird, Outers Lab., Inc., Onalaska, Wis. 54650
Trap claybird, Trius Prod., Box 25, Cleves, O. 45002
Truck tie-downs, Aardvark Ind., 1115 Blue Lakes Blvd. No., Twin Falls, Ida. 83301
Worldhunting info., Jack Atcheson, 2309 Hancock Ave., Butte, Mont. 59701

MUZZLE LOADING BARRELS OR EQUIPMENT

Luther Adkins, Box 281, Shelbyville, Ind. 46176 (breech plugs)
Jesse F. Booher, 2751 Ridge Ave., Dayton, Ohio 45414
G. S. Bunch, 7735 Garrison, Hyattsville, Md. 20784 (flask repair)
Pat Burke, 3339 Farnsworth Rd., Lapeer, Mich. 48446 (capper)
Challanger Mfg. Co., 105-23 New York Blvd., Jamaica, N.Y. 11433 (H.&A. guns)
Cherry Corners Gun Shop, Rte. 1, Lodi, Ohio 44254
Earl T. Cureton, Rte. 6, 7017 Pine Grove Rd., Knoxville, Tenn. 37914 (powder horns)
John N. Dangelzer, 3056 Frontier Pl. N.E., Albuquerque, N. Mex. 87106 (powder flasks)
Ted Fellowes, 9245 16th Ave. S.W., Seattle, Wash. 98106
International Gunmakers, 12315 Newburgh Rd., Livonia, Mich. 48150
JJJJ Ranch, Wm. Large, Rte. 1, Ironton, Ohio 45638
J. Lewis Arms Mfg., 3931 Montgomery Rd., Cincinnati, Ohio 45212 (pistol)
Log Cabin Sport Shop, R.D. 1, Lodi, Ohio 44254
Jos. W. Mellott, 334 Rockhill Rd., Pittsburgh, Pa. 15243 (barrel blanks)
W. L. Mowrey Gun Works, Inc., Box 711, Olney, Tex. 73674
Numrich Corp., W. Hurley, N.Y. 12491 (powder flasks)
Penna. Rifle Works, 319 E. Main St., Ligonier, Pa. 15658 (ML guns, parts)
H. M. Schoeller, 569 So. Braddock Ave., Pittsburgh, Pa. 15221
C. E. Siler, 9 Sandhurst Dr., Asheville, N.C, 28806 (flint locks)

PISTOLSMITHS

Alamo Heat Treating, Box 55345, Houston, Tex. 77055
Allen Assoc., 7448 Limekiln Pike, Philadelphia, Pa. 19138 (speed-cock lever for 45 ACP)
Bain and Davis Sptg. Gds., 559 W. Las Tunas Dr., San Gabriel, Cal. 91776
Behlert & Freed, Inc., 33 Herning Ave., Cranford, N.J. 07016 (short actions)
R. M. Champlin, Stanyan Hill, Wentworth, N.H. 03282
F. Bob Chow, Gun Shop, 3185 Mission, San Francisco, Calif. 94110
J. E. Clark, 7424 Broadacres Rd., Shreveport, La. 71109
Custom Gunshop, 33 Herning Ave., Cranford, N.J. 07016
Alton S. Dinan, Jr., P.O. Box 6674, Canaan, Conn. 06018
Dan Dwyer, 915 W. Washington, San Diego, Calif. 92103
Dy-Bro Products, 410 E. Linn, Marshalltown, Ia. 50158
Giles' 45 Shop, Rt. 1, Box 41A, Odessa, Fla. 33556
Gil Hebard Guns, Box 1, Knoxville, Ill. 61448
Larry S. Krause, 5628 Winchester, Chicago, Ill. 60636
Macs Accuracy Serv., 3260 Lakewood So., Seattle, Wash. 98144 (45 ACP)
Rudy Marent, 9711 Tiltree, Houston, Tex. 77034 (Hammerli)
Match Arms Co., 831 Mary St., Springdale, Pa. 15144
Modern Gun Craft, 18 Charles St., E. Norwalk, Conn. 06855
Pachmayr Gun Works, 1220 S. Grand Ave., Los Angeles, Calif. 90015
R. L. Shockey, 1614 S. Choctaw, E. Reno, Okla. 73036
Sportsmens Equipmt. Co., 915 W. Washington, San Diego, Calif. 92103
Armand D. Swenson, 3223 W. 145th St., Gardena, Calif. 90249
Whitney Inc., 6742 Tampa Ave., Reseda, Calif. 91335

REBORING AND RERIFLING

A & M Rifle Co., Box 1713, Prescott, Ariz. 86301
P. O. Ackley, P.O. Box 17347, Salt Lake City, Utah 84117
Bain & Davis Sptg. Gds., 559 W. Las Tunas Dr., San Gabriel, Calif. 91776
Carpenter's Gun Works, Rt. 32, Plattekill, N.Y. 12568
Fuller Gun Shop, Cooper Landing, Alaska 99572
Ward Koozer, Box 18, Walterville, Ore. 97489
Les' Gun Shop, Box 511, Kalispell, Mont. 59901
Nu-Line Guns, 3727 Jennings Rd., St. Louis, Mo. 63121
Al Petersen, Riverhurst, Saskatchewan, Canada
Schuetzen Gun Works, 1226 Prairie Rd., Colorado Springs, Colo. 80909
J. Hall Sharon, Box 106, Kalispell, Mont. 59901
Smith's Gun Shop, Box 486, East Tawas, Mich. 48730
Snapp's Gunshop, 6911 E. Washington Rd., Clare, Mich. 48617
R. Southgate, Rt. 2, Franklin, Tenn. 37064 (Muzzleloaders)
J. W. Van Patten, Box 145, Foster Hill, Milford, Pa. 18337

RELOADING TOOLS AND ACCESSORIES

Acme Industries, 625 W. Lawrence, Appleton, Wis. 54911
Air Speed Loader Co., 2670 S. W. Georgian Pl., Portland, Ore. 97201
Alcan Co., Inc., 36400 Seminary Rd., Alton, Ill. 62002
Alpha-Molykote Corp., 65 Harvard, Stamford, Conn. 06904
Anchor Alloys, Inc., 966 Meeker Ave., Brooklyn, N.Y. 11222 (chilled shot)
Anderson Mfg. Co., Royal, Ia. 51357 (Shotshell Trimmers)
Aurands, 229 E. 3rd St., Lewistown, Pa. 17044
Automatic Reloading Equipment, Inc., P.O. Box 1248, Newport Beach, Calif. 92663
B-Square Eng. Co., Box 11281, Ft. Worth, Tex. 76110
Bahler Die Shop, Box 386, Florence, Ore. 97439
Bair Machine Co., Box 4407, Lincoln, Neb. 68504
Belding & Mull, P.O. Box 428, Philipsburg, Pa. 16866
Belmont, 415—2nd Ave. N., Twin Falls, Ida. 83301 (lead cutter, etc.)
Blackhawk Small Arms Amm., C2274 POB, Loves Park, Ill. 61111
Brown Precision Co., 5869 Indian Ave., San Jose, Calif. 95123
Bobill Prod., 2316 Maple Leaf Dr. E., Jacksonville, Fla. 32211
Bonanza Sports, Inc., Rt. 4, Box 278, Faribault, Minn. 55021
C-H Tool & Die Corp., Box L, Owen, Wis. 54460
California Wholesale Co., 24712-6th St., San Bernardino, Cal. 92410 (Shelpac)
Capital Enterprises, Box 121, Verona, N.J.
Carbide Die & Mfg. Co., Box 226, Covina, Calif. 91722
Carter Gun Works, 2211 Jefferson Pk. Ave., Charlottesville, Va. 22903
Cascade Cartridge, Inc., (See Omark)
Chellife Corp., R.D. 1, Box 260 A1, Felton, Del. 19943
Container Development Corp., 415 Monroe, Watertown, Wis. 53094
Cooper Engineering, 612 E. 20th, Houston, Tex. 77008
Cooper-Woodward, Box 972, Riverside, Calif. 92502 (Perfect Lube)
Del-Hart Ent., 2759 W. Broadway, Los Angeles, Cal. 90041
Design & Development Co., 1002 N. 64th St., Omaha, Neb. 68132
Clarence Detsch, 135 Larch Rd., St. Mary's, Pa. 15857 (bullet dies)
Division Lead Co., 7742 W. 61st Pl., Summit, Ill. 60502
Dom Enterprises, 3985 Lucas, St. Louis, Mo. 63103
Dy-Bro Products, 410 E. Linn, Marshalltown, Ia. 50158
Eagle Products Co., 9666 Remer St., So. El Monte, Cal. 91733
Em-Ge Items, 3126 Lucas St., St. Louis, Mo. 63103
W. H. English, 4411 S. W. 100th, Seattle, Wash. 98146 (Paktool)
Excel, Inc., 9375 Chestnut St., Franklin Pk., Ill. 60131
Fall Sales Co., Box 833, Paradise, Calif. 95969
Fitz Grips, Box 49797, Los Angeles, Calif. 90049 (Fitz Flipper)
Flambeau Plastics, 801 Lynn, Baraboo, Wis. 53913
Fordwad Inc., 4322 W. 58th St., Cleveland, O. 44109
Forster-Appelt Mfg. Co., Inc., 82 E. Lanark Ave., Lanark, Ill. 61046
Full Ed'z Creel Co., 717 W. 9th St., Cheyenne, Wyo. 82001
Earl Gibbs, 1620 Sheridan Blvd., Denver, Colo. 80214
Gopher Shooter's Supply, Box 246, Faribault, Minn. 55021
The Gun Clinic, 81 Kale St., Mahtomedi, Minn. 55115
H & H Sealants, Box 448, Saugerties, N.Y. 12477 (Loctite)
H & S Mfg. Co., 2514 Morse, Chicago, Ill. 60645
Hart Products, 401 Montgomery St., Nescopeck, Pa. 18635
Heatbath Mfg. Co., P.O. Box 78, Springfield, Mass. 01101
Frank A. Hemsted, Box 281, Sunland, Cal. 91040 (swage dies)
Henniker Machine Co., Henniker, N.H. 03242
Hensley & Gibbs, Box 10, Murphy, Ore. 97533
E. C. Herkner Co., Box 5007, Boise, Ida. 83702
Herter's, Inc., RR1, Waseca, Minn. 56093
B. E. Hodgdon, Inc., 7710 W. 50 Hiway, Shawnee Mission, Kans. 66202
Hollywood Reloading, Inc., 6116 Hollywood Blvd., Hollywood, Calif. 90028
Hulme Firearm Serv., Box 83, Millbrae, Calif. 94030 (Star case feeder)
Independent Mach. & Gun Shop, 1416 N. Hayes, Pocatello, Ida. 83201
JASCO, Box 49751, Los Angeles, Calif. 90049

Javelina Products, Box 337, San Bernardino, Cal. 92402 (Alox beeswax)
Jay's Sports Inc., Menomonee Falls, Wis. 53051 (powd. meas. stand)
Jim's Custom Gun Repair, 1901 Metz, Oregon, Ohio 43616 (primer seating device)
Kenru Reloading Serv., 166 Normandy, Rochester, N.Y. 14619
Kexplore, Box 22084, Houston, Tex. 77027
Kuharsky Bros., 2425 W. 12th, Erie, Pa. 16500 (primer pocket cleaner)
Lachmiller Eng., 6445 San Fernando Rd., Glendale, Calif. 91201
Lee Engineering, Rt. 2, Hartford, Wis. 53027
Leon's Reloading Service, 3945 No. 11 St., Lincoln, Neb. 68521
L. L. F. Die Shop, 1281 Highway 99 N., Eugene, Ore. 97402
Ljutic Industries, 918 N. 5th Ave., Yakima, Wash. 98902
Lock's Phila. Gun Exch., 6700 Rowland, Philadelphia, Pa. 19149
Lyman Gun Sight Corp., Middlefield, Conn. 06455
Paul McLean, 2670 Lakeshore Blvd., W., Toronto 14, Ont., Canada (Universal Cartridge Holder)
McKillen & Heyer, 3871 Kirtland, Willoughby, O. 44094 (case gauge)
Mayville Eng. Co., Box 267, Mayville, Wis. 53050 (shotshell loader)
Merit Gun Sight Co., P.O. Box 995, Sequim, Wash. 98382
Minnesota Shooters Supply, 1915 E. 22nd St., Minneapolis, Minn. 55404
Jack Moffett, 726 Fugate Ave., Charlotte, N.C. 28205
Murdock Lead Co., Box 5298, Dallas, Tex. 75222
National Lead Co., Box 831, Perth Amboy, N.J. 08861
Normington Co., Rathdrum, Ida. 83858 (powder baffles)
John Nuler, 12869 Dixie, Detroit, Mich. 48239 (primer seating tool)
Ohaus Scale Corp., 29 Hanover Rd., Florham Park, N.J. 07932
Omark-CCI, Inc., Box 660, Lewiston, Ida. 83501
Pacific Gun Sight Co., Box 4495, Lincoln, Neb. 68504
C. W. Paddock, 1589 Payne Ave., St. Paul, Minn. 55101 (cartridge boxes)
Parke Precision Prod., 842 Crestfield Dr., Duarte, Calif. 91010
Vernon Parks, 104 Heussy, Buffalo, N.Y. 14220 (loaders bench)
Leland Pauly, Camptonville, Calif. 95922
Perfection Die Co., 1614 S. Choctaw, El Reno, Okla. 73036
Penn Ind., Box 8904, Philadelphia, Pa. 19135
Phelps Reloader Inc., Box 4004, E. Orange, N.J. 07019
Plum City Ballistics Range, Box 128, Plum City, Wis. 54761
Pollard Prec. Prod., 23032 Strathern St., Canoga Park, Calif. 91304
Ponsness-Warren, Inc., Box 186, Rathdrum, Ida. 83858
Potter Eng. Co., 1410 Santa Ana Dr., Dunedin, Fla. 33528
Powd-R-Horn, 3802 W. Augusta, Phoenix, Ariz. 85021
Powder-Keg, 811 N.E. 14th Ct., Ft. Lauderdale, Fla. 33304
Marian Powley, 103 Farmstead Lane, Glastonbury, Conn. 06033
Precision Reloaders, 6249 Fern Lane, Paradise, Cal. 95969
R & K Plastic Industries Co., 3891 W. 150th St., Cleveland, O. 44111
RCBS, Inc., Box 1919, Oroville, Calif. 95965
Randall Reloads, 8314 Courtland Dr., Rockford, Mich. 49341
Raymor Industries, 5856 So. Logan Ct., Littleton, Colo. 80120 (primer mag.)
Redco, Box 15523, Salt Lake City, Utah 84115
Redding-Hunter, Inc., 114 Starr Rd., Cortland, N.Y. 13045
Remco, 1404 Whitesboro St., Utica, N.Y. 13502 (shot caps)
Rifle Ranch, Rte. 1, Prescott, Ariz. 86301
Rochester Lead Works, Rochester, N.Y. 14608 (leadwire)
Roman Prod., Box 891, Golden, Colo. 80401
Rotex Mfg. Co. (see Texan)
Ruhr-American Corp., So. East Hwy. 55, Glenwood, Minn. 56334
SAECO Rel. Inc., P.O. Box 778, Carpinteria, Calif. 93013
Savage Arms Co., Westfield, Mass. 01085
Scientific Lubricants Co., 3753 Lawrence Ave., Chicago, Ill. 60625
Shelpac, 24712 6th, San Bernardino, Cal. 92410
Shoffstalls Mfg. Co., 744 Ellis Place, E. Aurora, N.Y. 14052
Shooters Accessory Supply, Box 250, N. Bend, Ore. 97459 (SAS)
Shooters Serv. & Dewey, Inc., Clinton Corners, N.Y. 12514 (bullet spinner)
Sil's Gun Prod., 490 Sylvan Dr., Washington, Pa. 15301 (K-spinner)
Jerry Simmons, 713 Middlebury St., Goshen, Ind. 46526 (Pope de- & recapper)
Sport Ammo Corp., 8407 Center Dr., Minneapolis, Minn. 55432 (mini-kit tool)
Star Machine Works, 418 10th Ave., San Diego, Calif. 92101
Strathmore Gun Spec., Box 308, Strathmore, Calif. 93267
Sullivan Arms Corp., 5204 E. 24th St., Indianapolis, Ind. 46218
Swanson Co. Inc., 2205 Long Lake Rd., St. Paul, Minn. 55112 (Safari loader)
Tecto, 1625 Washington N.E., Minneapolis, Minn. 55418
Texan Reloaders, Inc., P.O. Box 5355, Dallas, Tex. 75222
Three V Prod., 3007 N. Rochester, Arlington, Va. 22213
United Sports & Mfg., 1371 4th Ave., New Kensington, Pa. 15068
VAMCO, Box 67, Vestal, N.Y. 13850
W. S. Vickerman, 505 W. 3rd Ave., Ellensburg, Wash. 98926
Wm. B. Vincent, Jr., R. 2, Hillsdale, Mich. 49242 (bushings)
Wanda Cartr. Co., P.O. Box 45901, Houston, Tex. 77045 (plastics)
Ward Sptg. Gds Store, 405 Court St., Clay Center, Kans. 67432
Weatherby, Inc., 2781 Firestone Blvd., South Gate, Calif. 90280
Webster Scale Mfg. Co., Box 188, Sebring, Fla. 33870
Whit's Shooting Stuf, 2121 Stampede Ave., Cody, Wyo. 82414
Wilkins & Schultz Inc., Box 334, Barrington, Ill. 60010
L. E. Wilson, Inc., Box 324, Cashmere, Wash. 98815
Xelex, Ltd., Hawksbury, Ont., Canada (powder)
Zenith Ent., Rt. 1, Box 52z, Del Mar, Calif. 92014
A. Zimmerman, 127 Highland Trail, Denville, N.J. 07834 (case trimmer)

RIFLE BARREL MAKERS

A & M Rifle Co., P.O. Box 1713, Prescott, Ariz. 86301
P.O. Ackley, P.O. Box 17347, Salt Lake City, Utah 84117
Apex Rifle Co., 7628 San Fernando, Sun Valley, Calif. 91352
Christy Gun Works, 875 57th St., Sacramento, Calif. 95819
Clerke Technicorp., 2054 Broadway Ave., Santa Monica, Calif. 90404
Cuthbert Gun Shop, 715 So. 5th, Coos Bay, Ore. 97420
G. R. Douglas, 5504 Big Tyler Rd., Charleston, W. Va. 25312
Federal Firearms Co., Inc., Box 145, Oakdale, Pa. 15071 (Star bbls., actions)
Gibbs Rifle Prod., Viola, Ida. 83872
A. R. Goode, 3306 Sellman Rd., Adelphi, Md. 20783
Hart Rifle Barrels, Inc., RD 2, Lafayette, N.Y. 13084
Wm. H. Hobaugh, Box 657, Philipsburg, Mont. 59858
Intern'l Gunmakers, 12315 Newburgh Rd., Livonia, Mich. 48150
Jim's Gun Shop, 715 So. 5th St., Coos Bay, Ore. 97420
Johnson Automatics, Box 306, Hope Valley, R.I. 02832
Les' Gun Shop, Box 511, Kalispell, Mont. 59901
L. E. Nauman, 1048 S. 5th, Douglas, Wyo. 82633
Nu-Line Guns, Inc., 3727 Jennings Rd., St. Louis, Mo. 63121
Numrich Arms, W. Hurley, N.Y. 12491
SS & D, Inc., Clinton Corners, N.Y. 12514 (cold-formed bbls.)
Sanders Cust. Gun Serv., 2358 Tyler Lane, Louisville, Ky. 40205
J. H. Sharon, Box 106, Kalispell, Mont. 59901
Ed Shilen Rifles, 4510 Harrington Rd., Irving, Tex. 75060
Bliss Titus, 70 E. 2nd No., Heber City, Utah 84032
Walker Machine Tool Co., 4804 Pinewood Rd., Louisville, Ky. 40218
M. G. Watts, 5627 Euclid, Kansas City, Mo. 64130
Wilson Arms, Box 364, Stony Creek, Branford, Conn. 06405

SCOPES, MOUNTS, ACCESSORIES, OPTICAL EQUIPMENT

Alley Supply Co., P.O. Box 458, Sonora, Calif. 95370 (Scope collimator)
American Import Co., 1167 Mission, San Francisco, Calif. 94103
Anderson Gun Shop, 1203 Broadway, Yakima, Wash. 98902 (lens cap)
Bausch & Lomb Inc., 635 St. Paul St., Rochester, N.Y. 14602
Bennett, 561 Delaware, Delmar, N.Y. 12054 (mounting wrench)
Browning Arms, Rt. 4, Box 624-B, Arnold, Mo. 63010
Maynard P. Buehler, Inc., 17 Orinda Highway, Orinda, Calif. 94563
Bullitco, Box 40, Shepherdsville, Ky. 40165 (Scope collimator)
D. P. Bushnell & Co., Inc., 639 Bushnell Bldg., Pasadena, Calif. 91107
Chilford Arms Mfg. Co., 9 First St., San Francisco, Calif. 94105
Kenneth Clark, 18738 Highway 99, Madera, Calif. 93637
Collins Co., Box 40, Shepherdsville, Ky. 40165 (Scope collimator)
Colt's, Hartford, Conn. 06102
Compass Instr. & Optical Co., Inc., 104 E. 25th St., New York, N.Y. 10010
Conetrol, Hwy 123 South, Seguin, Tex. 78155
Continental Arms Corp., 697-5th Ave., New York, N.Y. 10022 (Nickel)
Davis Optical Co., P.O. Box 6, Winchester, Ind. 47934
Del-Sports, Main St., Margaretville, N.Y. 12455 (Kahles)
Diana Imports, Main St., Margaretville, N.Y. 12455 (Habicht)
Don's Gun Shop, 128 Ruxton, Manitou Springs, Colo. 80829 (claw mtg. rings)
Duo-Gun Prod., 3213 Partridge Ave., Oakland, Calif. 94605 (mount)
Firearms International, 4837 Kerby Hill Rd., Washington, D.C. 20022
Flaig's, Babcock Blvd., Millvale, Pa. 15209
Freeland's Scope Stands, Inc., 3734 14th, Rock Island, Ill. 61201
Bert Friedberg & Co., 820 Mission St., San Francisco, Cal. 94103
Griffin & Howe, Inc., 589-8th Ave., New York, N.Y. 10017
E. C. Herkner Co., Box 5007, Boise, Idaho 83702
H. J. Hermann Leather Co., Box 136, Pittstown, N.J. 08867 (lens cap)
Herter's Inc., Waseca, Minn. 56093
J. B. Holden Co., Box H-1495, Plymouth, Md. 48170 (Iron sighter)
Hy-Score Arms Corp., 200 Tillary St., Brooklyn, N.Y. 11201
Paul Jaeger, 211 Leedom St., Jenkintown, Pa. 19046 (Nickel)
Jana Intl. Co., Box 1107, Denver, Colo. 80201
Jason Empire, 1211 Walnut, Kansas City, Mo. 64106
Kesselring Gun Shop, Box 350, Rt. 1, Burlington, Wash. 98283
Kuharsky Bros., 2425 W. 12th St., Erie, Pa. 16500
Kwik-Site, 27367 Michigan, Inkster, Mich. 48141 (rings)
T. K. Lee, Box 2123, Birmingham, Ala. 35201 (reticles)
E. W. Lehman, 3821 Albatross St., San Diego, Calif. 92103
E. Leitz, Inc., 468 Park Ave., So., New York, N.Y. 10016
Leupold & Stevens Instruments, Box 25347, Portland, Ore. 97225
Jake Levin and Son. Inc., 1211 Walnut. Kansas City, Mo. 64106
Lyman Gun Sight Corp., Middlefield, Conn. 06455
Marble Arms Co., 1120 Superior St., Gladstone, Mich. 49837
Marlin Firearms Co., 79 Willow St., New Haven, Conn. 06502
Mashburn Arms Co., 112 W. Sheridan, Oklahoma City, Okla. 73102
O. F. Mossberg & Sons, Inc., 7 Grasso Ave., North Haven, Conn. 06473
Numrich Arms, West Hurley, N.Y. 12491
Nydar Div., Swain Nelson Co., Box 45, Glenview, Ill. 60025 (shotgun sight)
Original Sight Exchange Co., Box J, Paoli, Pa. 19301
PGS, Peters' Inc., 622 Gratiot Ave., Saginaw, Mich. 48602 (scope shields)
Pachmayr Gun Works, 1220 S. Grand Ave., Los Angeles, Calif. 90015
Pacific Gun Sight Co., Box 4495, Lincoln, Neb. 68504
Ed Paul's Sptg. goods, Inc., 172 Flatbush Ave., Brooklyn, N.Y. 11217 (Tops)
Pickering Co., 2110 Walnut, Unionville, Mo. 63565
Precise Imports Corp., 3 Chestnut, Suffern, N.Y. 10901 (PIC)
Premier Reticles, Perry, W. Va. 26844

Realist, Inc., N. 93 W. 16288, Megal Dr., Menomonee Falls, Wis. 53051
Redfield Gun Sight Co., 1315 S. Clarkson St., Denver, Colo. 80210
S & K Mfg. Co., Box 247, Pittsburgh, Pa. 16340 (Insta-mount)
Sanders Cust. Gun Serv., 2358 Tyler Lane, Louisville, Ky. 402305 (MSW)
Savage Arms, Westfield, Mass. 01085
Scope Inst. Co., 25-20 Brooklyn-Queens Expressway West, Woodside, N.Y. 11377
Sears, Roebuck & Co., 825 S. St. Louis, Chicago, Ill. 60607
Selsi Co., 40 Veterans Blvd., Carlstadt, N.J. 07072
Southern Precision Inst. Co., 710 Augusta St., San Antonio, Tex. 78215
Southwest Cutlery, 1309 Olympic, Montebello, Calif. 90640 (lens cap)
Stoeger Arms Co., 55 Ruta Ct., S. Hackensack, N.J. 07606
Swift Instruments, Inc., 952 Dorchester Ave., Boston, Mass. 02125
Tasco, 1075 N.W. 71st, Miami, Fla. 33138
Tradewinds, Inc., Box 1191, Tacoma, Wash. 98401
Trueline Instruments, Box 1357, Englewood, Colo. 80110
John Unertl Optical Co., 3551-5 East St., Pittsburgh, Pa. 15214
United Binocular Co., 9043 S. Western Ave., Chicago, Ill. 60620
Universal Firearms Corp., 3746 E. 10th Ct., Hialeah, Fla. 33013
Vissing Co., Box 437, Idaho Falls, Idaho 83402 (lens cap)
H. P. Wasson, Box 181, Netcong, N.J. 07857 (eyeglass apertures)
Weatherby's, 2781 Firestone, South Gate, Calif. 90280
W. R. Weaver Co., 7125 Industrial Ave., El Paso, Tex. 79915
Williams Gun Sight Co., 7389 Lapeer Rd., Davison, Mich. 48423
Carl Zeiss Inc., 444 Fifth Ave., New York, N.Y. 10018 (Hensoldt)

STOCKS (Commercial and Custom)

W. S. Abe, 5124 Huntington Dr., Los Angeles, Calif. 90032
R. E. Anderson, 706 So. 23rd St., Laramie, Wyo. 82070
G. & S. Bartlett, 23004 W. Lancaster Rd., Lancaster, Calif. 93534
John Bianchi, 212 W. Foothill Blvd., Monrovia, Calif. 91016 (U. S. carbines)
Al Biesen, West 2039 Sinto Ave., Spokane, Wash. 99201
E. C. Bishop & Son Inc., Box 7, Warsaw, Mo. 65355
Wm. Buchele, 2832 Sagamore Rd., Toledo, O. 43606 (ML only)
Cadmus Ind., 6311 Yucca St., Hollywood, Calif. (U. C. carbines)
Calico, 1648 Airport Blvd., Windsor, Calif. 95492 (blanks)
Chuck's Custom Gun Stocks, P.O. Box 1123, Frederick, Md. 21701
Mike Conner, Box 324, Cedar Crest, N.M. 87008
Crane Creek Gun Stock Co., Box 268, Waseca, Minn. 56093
Crest Carving Co., 401 S. Cypress St., La Habra, Calif. 90631
Charles De Veto, 1087 Irene Rd., Lyndhurst, O. 44124
Reinhart Fajen, Box 338, Warsaw, Mo. 65355
N. B. Fashingbauer, Box 366, Lac Du Flambeau, Wis. 54538
Ted Fellowes, 9245 16th Ave. S. W., Seattle, Wash. 98106
Clyde E. Fischer, Rt. 1, Box 170-M, Victoria, Tex. 77901
Jerry Fisher, 1244—4th Ave., Kalispell, Mont. 59901
Flaig's Lodge, Millvale, Pa. 15209
Horace M. Frantz, Box 128, Farmingdale, N.J. 07727
Freeland's Scope Stands, Inc., 3734 14th Ave., Rock Island, Ill. 61201
Frontier Gunshop, 3584 Mt. Diablo Blvd., Lafayette, Calif. 94549
Aaron T. Gates, 3229 Felton St., San Diego, Calif. 92104
Dale Goens, Box 224, Cedar Crest, N.M. 87008
Gould's Myrtlewood, 1692 N. Dogwood, Coquille, Ore. 97423
Rolf R. Gruning, 315 Busby Dr., San Antonio, Tex. 78209
Gunstocks-Rarewoods, Haleiwa, Hawaii 96712
Gunwoods (N.Z.) Ltd., Box 18505, New Brighton, Christchurch, New Zealand (blanks)
Hank's Stock Shop, 1500 Mill Creek Rd., Ukiah, Calif. 95482
Harper's Custom Stocks, 959 Lombrano St., San Antonio, Tex. 78207
Harris Gun Stocks, Inc., 12 Lake St., Richfield Springs, N.Y. 13439
Elden Harsh, Rt. 4, London, O. 43140
Hal Hartley, Box 147, Blairsfork Rd., Lenoir, N.C. 28654
Hayes Gunstock Service Co., 914 E. Turner St., Clearwater, Fla. 33516
Edward O. Hefti, 300 Fairview, College Sta., Tex. 77840
Herter's Inc., Waseca, Minn. 56093
Howard's, Box 1133, Twin Falls, Ida. 83301
Hurst Custom Gunstocks, 917 Spotswood Ave., Norfolk, Va. 23517
Jackson's, Box 416, Selman City, Tex. 75689 (blanks)
Paul Jaeger, 211 Leedom ST., Jenkintown, Pa. 19046
Bob Johnson, 1730 E. Sprague, Spokane, Wash. 99200
I. D. Johnson, Rt. 1, Strawberry Point, Ia. 52076 (blanks)
Monte Kennedy, R.D. 2, Kalispell, Mont. 59901
Dale M. Larsen, Box 123, Niagara, Wis. 54151
Leer's Gun Barn, Rt. 3, Sycamore Hills, Elwood, Ind. 46036
LeFever Arms Co., Inc., R.D. 1, Lee Center, N.Y. 13363
J. L. Lyden, 1516 Chelton, Pittsburgh, Pa. 15226
Maryland Gun Exchange, Rt. 40 W., RD 5, Frederick, Md. 21701
Maurer Arms, 2366 Frederick Dr., Cuyahoga Falls, O. 44221
Leonard Mews, 6116 Hollywood Blvd., Hollywood, Calif. 90028
Robt. U. Milhoan & Son, Rt. 3, Elizabeth, W. Va. 26143
Mills (D.H.) Custom Stocks, 401 N. Ellsworth Ave., San Mateo, Calif. 94401
Nelsen's Gun Shop, 501 S. Wilson, Olympia, Wash. 98501
Niemiec's Gun Shop, 7507 Lillian Lane, Highland, Cal. 92346 (blanks)
Oakley and Merkley, Box 2446, Sacramento, Calif. 95801 (blanks)
Ernest O. Paulsen, Chinook, Mont. 59523 (blanks)
Peterson Mach. Carving, Box 1065, Sun Valley, Calif. 91352
Roberts Wood Prod., 1400 Melody Rd., Marysville, Calif. 95901
L. B. Rothschild, 4504 W. Washington Blvd., Los Angeles, Calif. 90016
Royal Arms, Inc., 10064 Bert Acosta Ct., Santee, Calif. 92071
Sanders Cust. Gun Serv., 2358 Tyler Lane, Louisville, Ky. 40205 (blanks)
Saratoga Arms Co., R.D. 3, Box 387, Pottstown, Pa. 19464
Roy Schaefer, 965 W. Hilliard Lane, Eugene, Ore. 97402 (blanks)
Shaw's, 1655 S. Euclid Ave., Anaheim, Calif. 92802
Thomas Shelhamer, Rt. 3, Box 189A, Dowagiac, Mich. 49047
Walter Shultz, R.D. 3, Pottstown, Pa. 19464
Sile Dist., 7 Centre Market Pl., New York, N.Y. 10013
Ed Sowers, 8331 DeCelis Pl., Sepulveda, Calif. 91343
Sportsmen's Equip. Co., 915 W. Washington, San Diego, Calif. 92103 (carbine conversions)
Stag Custom Stocks, 1430 So. Gilbert St., Fullerton, Calif. 92633
Keith Stegall, Box 696, Gunnison, Colo. 81230
Stinehour Rifles, Box 84, Cragsmoor, N.Y. 12420
J. R. Sundra, 683 Elizabeth St., Bridgeville, Pa. 15017
Swanson Cust. Firearms, 1051 Broadway, Denver, Colo. 80203
V. S. Swenson, Rt. 1, Ettrick, Wis. 54627
D. W. Thomas, Box 184, Vineland, N.J. 08360
Roy Vail, Rt. 1, Box 8, Warwick, N.Y. 10990
John E. Warren, Box 72, Eastham, Mass. 02642
Weatherby's, 2781 Firestone, South Gate, Calif. 90280
Western Stocks & Guns, Inc., 2206 E. 11th, Bremerton, Wash. 98311
Orland Wheeler, 405 W. 10th St., Holden, Mo. 64040
Joe White, Box 8505, New Brighton, Christchurch, N.Z. (blanks)
Fred Wranic, 6919 Santa Fe, Huntington Park, Calif. 90255 (mesquite)
Paul Wright, 4504 W. Washington Blvd., Los Angeles, Calif. 90016
Wyatt's Gunshop, Kosciusko, Miss. 39090

SURPLUS GUNS, PARTS AND AMMUNITION

Allied Arms Ltd., 655 Broadway, New York, N.Y. 10012
B. P. Caldwell, Jr., 211 E. Chicago Ave., Chicago, Ill. 60611
Century Arms, Inc., 3-5 Federal St., St. Albans, Vt. 05478
W. H. Craig, Box 927, Selma, Ala. 36701
Cummings Intl. Inc., 41 Riverside Ave., Yonkers, N.Y. 10701
Eastern Firearms Co., 790 S. Arroyo Pkwy., Pasadena, Calif. 91105
Fenwick's, P.O. Box 38, Weisburg Rd., Whitehall, Md. 21161
Hudson Sptg. Goods, 52 Warren, New York, N.Y. 10007
Hunter's Lodge, 200 S. Union, Alexandria, Va. 22313
Inter-American Imp.-Exp. Co., P.O. Box 8022, Sacramento, Calif. 95818
International Guns, Inc., 66 Warburton Ave., Yonkers, N.Y., 10701
Kadet's Arsenal, 7388 N. Center, Mentor, O. 44060
Klein's Sporting Goods, 4540 W. Madison, Chicago, Ill. 60624
Lever Arms Serv., 771 Dunsmuir St., Vancouver, B.C., Canada
Mars Equipment Corp., 3318 W. Devon, Chicago, Ill. 60645
National Gun Traders, 251-55 W. 22nd, Miami, Fla. 33135
P & S Sales, Box 155, Tulsa, Okla. 74102
Plainfield Ordnance Co., Box 281, Dunellen, N.J. 08812
Potomac Arms Corp., Box 35, Alexandria, Va. 22313
Ruvel & Co., 707 Junior Terr., Chicago, Ill. 60613
Service Armament Co., 689 Bergen Blvd., Ridgefield, N.J. 07657
Z. M. Military Research Co., 9 Grand Ave., Englewood, N.J. 07631

TARGETS, BULLET & CLAYBIRD TRAPS

Black Products Co., 13513 Calumet Ave., Chicago, Ill. 60627
Bunnerlight Target Co., Box 2756, Tampa, Fla. 33601 (timer)
Caswell Target Carriers, Box 344, Anoka, Minn. 55303
Cole's Acku-Rite Prod., Box 25, Kennedy, N.Y. 14747 (Site Rite targets)
Detroit Bullet Trap Co., 2233 N. Palmer Dr., Schaumburg, Ill. 60172
Dupont Target Co., Dupont, Ind. 47231 (motorized target carrier)
Gopher Shooter's Supply, Box 246, Faribault, Minn. 55021 (Lok-A-Leg target holders)
Hamlin Products, 2741 Wingate Ave., Akron, O. 44314
Hits, Inc., P.O. Box 415, Branford, Conn. 06405 (life size coin op.)
L & M Cork Products, Mokena, Ill. 60448 (bullet target)
Laycock Inc., P.O. Box 55, Tampa, Fla. 33601 (Bunner light)
Murray G-D Scope Target, 648 E. Meyer Blvd., Kansas City, Mo. 64131
National Target Co., 7050 Spring Pl., N.W., Washington, D.C. 20012
Outers Laboratories, Inc., Onalaska, Wis. 54650 (claybird traps)
Peterson Label Co., 58 Harrison Brook Dr., Basking Ridge, N.J. 07920 (paste-ons)
Police Ordnance, P.O. Box 1980, Costa Mesa, Calif. 92626 (Multi-Rotating target system)
Product Masters, 816-15th Ave. N., Minneapolis, Minn. 55411 (stands)
Ranger Arms Co., Box 704, Gainesville, Tex. 76240 (paper targets)
Realistic Target Corp., (See HITS)
Remington Arms Co., Bridgeport, Conn. 06602 (claybird traps)
Scientific Prod. Corp., 5417A Vine St., Alexandria, Va. 22310 (Targeteer)
Sheridan Products, Inc., 3205 Sheridan, Racine, Wis. 53403 (traps)
Shooting Equip. Inc., 4616 W. 20th St., Chicago, Ill. 60650 (electric range)
Sterling-Fleischman Inc., 176 Penna Ave., Malvern, Pa. 19355
Time Products Co., 355 Burlington Rd., Riverside, Ill. 60546 (target patches)
Trius Prod., Box 25, Cleves, O. 45002 (claybird, can thrower)
Valentine Equip. Co., 2630 W. Arthington, Chicago, Ill. 60612 ("Crazy Quail" clay target game)
Winchester-Western, New Haven, Conn. 06504 (claybird traps)
Wisler Western Target Co., 205 2nd St., San Francisco, Calif. 94105 (NRA targets)
X-Ring Prod. Co., Outers Lab., Onalaska, Wis. 54650 (traps)

GLOSSARY FOR GUNNERS

Action Breech mechanism of a gun, by which it is loaded and unloaded.

Air Space Space in a loaded cartridge case not occupied by powder or bullet base.

Anvil In a primer or cartridge case, a fixed point against which the priming mixture is compressed, and thereby detonated, by the action of the firing pin.

Ball Earlier term for "bullet," and still used in some military terminology.

Ballistics Science of projectiles in motion.

Barrel The part(s) of a gun through which passes the bullet or shot, traveling from breech to muzzle.

Base Wad Compressed paper or other material inside a shotshell, varying in size and form.

Battery Cup Type of shotshell ignition form in which the cap or primer is held.

Belted Case Cartridge case with a band or belt at base, just ahead of extractor groove, and on which case (otherwise "rimless") positions in rifle chamber. See "Headspace."

Black Powder A mixture of charcoal, sulphur and saltpeter used as a propellant. Gives off much smoke when burned. See "Smokeless Powder."

Bore The inside of the barrel of a gun.

Bore Diameter In rifled arms, the diametrical measurement between tops of lands.

Breech Bolt The part of a breech that resists the rearward force of the combustion that occurs when a cartridge is fired.

BT Boat-tail, referring to the base taper given certain bullets to give them greater efficiency at long ranges.

Bullet The projectile *only,* not to be applied to the cartridge, which see. See also "Ball."

Bullet Mould Metallic device with a cavity(s) into which molten lead (or lead alloy) can be poured and allowed to harden into the projectile.

Caliber Bore or groove diameter expressed (in English) in decimals of an inch, otherwise in the metric system. Frequently compounded to indicate powder capacity of cartridge case; to show date of adoption; to show case length or to show proprietor, etc. E.g., 30-40, 30-06, 8x57mm or 375 Holland & Holland.

Cannelure Circumferential groove(s) around a bullet or cartridge case. In the latter refers to extractor groove, in lead bullets the lubrication grooves, in jacketed bullets the expansion point and/or where case is crimped.

Caplock Used of a muzzleloading gun whose ignition system employs a percussion cap, a small thimble-like metal cup containing a detonating mixture. This cup, placed on a "nipple," transmits flame to the powder charge when struck by the gun's hammer.

Cartridge A complete round of ammunition, made up, simply, of a cartridge case, primer, bullet (or shot) and powder.

Cartridge Case Commonly, the brass or copper envelope that contains powder, primer and projectile, but applicable to shotshells, too, whether of all brass (not common), paper and metal or plastic and metal.

CF Centerfire (cartridges); those ignited by means of (generally) a separate and replaceable primer.

Chamber That part of the bore, at the breech, formed to accept the cartridge.

Choke The constriction of a shotgun bore at the muzzle to various degrees, designed to control pellet charge spread at the target.

Chronograph An instrument which measures the velocity of a projectile.

Clip See "Magazine."

Cordite A nitroglycerine smokeless powder used mainly in Great Britain.

Crimp The bending inward of the case mouth perimeter, in order to grip and hold the bullet, or to keep the shot in a paper case intact.

Cylinder In a revolver, a cartridge container that rotates (generally) around an axis parallel to and below the barrel.

Die In handloading ammunition, any of a number of tools used to size bullets or cases, seat bullets, etc.

Drams Equivalent Term used to indicate that a certain charge of smokeless powder gives ballistics equal to a stated volumetric charge of black powder.

Drift The bullet's movement to right or left, away from the line of the bore, caused by bullet rotation or spin.

Drilling A three-barrel gun, popular in Europe, which usually combines smoothbore and rifled barrels.

Ejector Correctly the device(s) at the barrel breech or within the action that forcibly expels the fired case from the gun. See "Extractor."

Energy In bullets, the amount of work done, at given ranges, expressed in foot pounds.

Erosion More or less gradual wearing away of rifling by combustion gas, heat and bullet friction.

"Everlasting" Case Brass cartridge case made from heavy stock, intended for extended reloading life.

Extractor Device that removes or partially removes the fired cartridge case from the chamber. See "Ejector."

Firing Pin A part of the action, actuated by the trigger, that hits the primer and fires the cartridge.

Flintlock Used of a muzzleloading gun fired by means of a piece of flint, held in the hammer or "cock" jaws, striking against a steel "frizzen." Incandescent particles of steel scraped from the frizzen fall into a "pan" holding powder. This ignited powder flames through the "touch-hole," thus firing the main charge.

Follower A metal platform in a clip or magazine that pushes the cartridges upward at the proper angle for feeding into the chamber.

Gas Check A cup (usually copper) used on the base of a lead bullet to protect it from hot powder gases.

Gauge Unit of bore measurement in shotguns, determined by the number of solid lead round balls, of the bore diameter, obtainable from one pound of lead. E.g., 12 gauge means a bore of such size that 12 balls of that size make a pound of lead.

Gilding Metal A copper-zinc alloy used as bullet jacket material; usually 5% to 10% zinc.

Grooves Spiral cuts in a bore which cause the bullet to spin as it travels down the barrel.

Groove Diameter In rifled arms, the diametrical measurement between bottoms of grooves.

Group Number of shots fired into a target (number and range optional), usually with one sight setting.

Hammer A part of the action (in some guns) actuated by the trigger. The hammer drives the firing pin against the primer, thus igniting the cartridge powder charge.

Hang-fires Cartridges which fire as long as several seconds after firing pin strikes primer.

H.P. Hollow point, a design feature of certain bullets. See "Mushroom."

Headspace For rimmed cartridges, the distance from the face of the breechblock to the barrel seat for the forward surface of the case rim. For a rimless bottleneck cartridge, the distance from the face of the breechblock to a predetermined point on the shoulder of the chamber. For rimless straight cartridges, the distance from the face of the breechblock to the shoulder or ledge in the chamber. Belted cases headspace on the forward edge of the belt.

Lands That portion of the bore remaining after the rifling or grooves have been cut.

Leading Lead deposited on bore by bullets passing through.

Magazine Device or reservoir to hold extra cartridges, of many types and names. "Clip," once reserved for the slender metal strip from which cartridges are stripped into a magazine well, now refers to separate, detachable magazines also, as with those for autoloading pistols, many rifles and shotguns.

Matchlock An early form of firearm in which the priming charge was ignited by a cord or "match" of slow-burning material.

M.C. Metal Case, a form of bullet completely covered forward with copper or copper alloy (usually) jacket. Generally a military bullet type, and also termed "solids," and F.M.J. (full metal jacketed).

Mid-Range Usually used in connection with trajectory, referring to a point midway between muzzle and target or game.

Misfires Cartridges which do not fire when firing pin strikes primers.

MRT Mid Range Trajectory. See above.

Mushroom The capacity of certain bullets to expand on or after impact, also the term given to some soft point or hollow point bullets. See "S.P." and "H.P."

Muzzle End of barrel opposite to breech; point from which bullet or shot leaves barrel.

Muzzle-Loader Gun loaded through the front end of the bore, using loose powder and ball (or shot) or paper cartridges.

M.E. Muzzle Energy. See "Energy."

M.V. Muzzle Velocity. See "Velocity."

Nipple On muzzle-loading guns, the small metal cone at the rear of the barrel (or cylinder) through which the flame from the percussion cap passes to ignite the powder charge.

Ogive The radius of the curve of the nose of a bullet, usually expressed in calibers.

O.P.E. Open Point Expanding, a term for bullets of hollow point form made by Western Cartridge Co.

Over-bore Capacity Condition in which the volume of a cartridge case exceeds the amount of powder which can most efficiently be burned.

Pan See "Flintlock."

Paradox Smoothbore gun in which the final few inches of barrel are rifled to increase efficiency of round ball or bullet use. Also called "Explora" and "Fauneta" guns by Westley Richards.

Patching, Cloth Used to form a gas seal around the projectile (round ball or conical bullet) of a muzzle-loading gun and engage the rifling.

Pattern Of pellets from a shotgun, usually expressed as so many pellets within a 30-inch circle at 40 yards.

Percussion Cap Small metallic cup containing fulminating material that explodes when struck by gun's hammer. See "Nipple."

Pistol Said by some to derive from Pistoia, an early gun making center in Italy. Any small, concealable, short-barreled (2″-10″) hand weapon, generally *not* a revolver.

Pressure The gas pressure generated in a cartridge on its being fired, usually expressed in (greatest) pounds per square inch (p.s.i.).

Primer In a centerfire cartridge, the small cup containing a detonating mixture, which is seated in a recess in the base of the case. In a rimfire, a similar mixture inside the folded rim of the case.

Proprietary Cartridge One developed and sold exclusively by one business organization.

Ramrod Rod, of wood or metal, used to force home the projectile in a muzzle-loading gun and sometimes to hold cleaning implements.

Rebated Rim Type of cartridge case rim smaller in diameter than the case is at a point just forward of the extractor groove.

Recoil The backward thrust of a gun caused by the reaction to the powder gases pushing the bullet forward.

Revolver A multi-shot handgun, using a revolving cylinder as a cartridge container.

RF Rimfire cartridges. Those containing their primer mixture in the rim, which is where they are struck by the firing pin.

Rifling Spiral grooving cut into the bore of rifles and handguns to impart spin to their bullets, thus assuring point-on flight and accuracy.

Rim The projecting edge of the base or "head" of certain cartridges.

Rook Cartridge Low powered cartridge developed in England for shooting pest birds and animals.

Shot Lead or lead-alloy spheres used as projectiles in smoothbore guns.

Shotgun A smoothbore gun using cartridges loaded with shot.

Shoulder The sloping portion of a bottleneck cartridge case that joins the body and neck.

Sizing In handloading cartridges, sizing (or resizing) brings the fired cartridge case back to the (full or partial) dimensions of the new or unfired case. Bullets are also sized.

Smokeless Powder Gunpowder which gives off almost no smoke when burned. See "Black Powder." Usually made by nitrating and otherwise chemically treating purified cotton waste.

S.P. Soft Point, a term used for bullets with partial metal jacketing, having some lead exposed at the front.

Trajectory Curved path of bullet in flight, a parabola.

Twist Angle of the rifling relative to the axis of the bore. Usually uniform, and expressed in turns or part-turns in so many inches. Less common, "progressive" or "gain" twist, usually starting at a rate at breech that becomes gradually faster.

Velocity Projectile speed, usually measured in feet per second (f.p.s.) at the muzzle and other distances such as 100 yards, 200 yards, etc.

Vent Orifice through the nipple.

Wad A disc of paper, felt, plastic or other material used in shotshells; sometimes in metallic cases, too, but not commonly today.

a. Filler Wad—placed between the powder and card or Nitro wad to cushion the shot from the thrust of the hot powder gases, and to bring the shot to the proper height for correct crimping.

b. Over-powder Wad—placed between powder and filler wads, sometimes called Nitro wads.

c. Top Wad—thin card placed on top of the shot in roll crimp shells—star crimp shells do not require a top wad.

d. Base Wad—these are permanently built into the shell at the base to hold the paper tube to the brass and give added support to the thin brass wall.

Wheel-lock Used of a muzzleloading gun fired by means of a piece of flint or pyrites, held in the hammer jaws, which is held over a serrated steel wheel. This wheel, set in motion by a tensioned spring, protrudes through the bottom of the "pan" (wherein powder has been placed) and bears against the flint. Sparks are created, as in the flintlock, and the gun is fired by a flame passing through the touch-hole.

Wildcat Cartridge designed by a private experimenter; not available as a factory-loaded round.

WCF Winchester Center Fire.

WRF Winchester Rim Fire.

Zero That sight setting which gives bullet group desired, and from which subsequent changes in sight settings will be made.

Colt's No. 1 All-Metal Derringer, caliber 41 Rimfire, in De Luxe Grade.

NEW! GUN DIGEST 1970
WHERE-TO-BUY-IT-DIRECTORY

Firearms, Ammunition, Accessories and Gunsmithing Services

Alabama

Albertville . . . Crickett Hall
Alexander City . . . City Home & Auto
Alexander City . . . Ray Voss
Andalusia . . . Ye Old Gun Shoppe
Anniston . . . Anniston Sporting Goods
Anniston . . . Carter Gun Shop
Anniston . . . Tornado Supply
Atmore . . . Rex's Sporting Goods
Bay Minette
Builders Hardware & Supply
Bessemer . . . Long Lewis Hdwe. Co.
Bessemer . . . Traywick Sporting Goods
Birmingham . . . Lovemans
Birmingham . . J. L. Quick & Son Co.
Birmingham . . . Stewarts Sport Shop
Birmingham . . . The Gun Shop
Centre . . . Tabs Sporting Goods
Childersburg . . . Limbaugh Hardware
Clanton . . . Western Auto Assoc. Store
Coden . . . Olde Fort Alabama
Columbia . . . Orr's Gun Shop
Columbiana
Western Auto Assoc. Store
Cullman . . . Mary Carter Paint Store
Cullman . . . Harold Mayo's Gun Shop
Decatur . . . Garrison Boats & Motors
Decatur . . . Sandline & Sons
Decatur . . . Wiley Sales Co.
Dothan . . . Pake McKeen
Dothan . . . Target Arms Company
Enterprise . . . Joe C. Jones Hardware
Enterprise . . . Moose Hope Sports Shop
Florence . . . Roberts Hardware
Gadsden . . . Schwartz Gun Shop
Gadsden . . . Fred Singtons
Georgiana . . . Jim Johnson Sons
Guntersville
Paul's Stop & Swap Gun Shop
Huntsville . . . House of Guns
Huntsville . . . Hutchens
Huntsville . . . Johns Guns & Camping
Huntsville . . . Wiley Sales Co.
Jasper . . . Parkland Hdwe. Co.
Mobile . . L. G. Adams Sporting Goods
Mobile . . . B & W Sport Shop
Mobile . . . Brannan Sporting Goods
Mobile . . . Downtown Hardware
Mobile . . . Eugene Thoss Jr. & Sons
Montgomery
Montgomery Sporting Goods Co.
Montgomery . . Relfe Shotshell Supply
Montgomery . . . The Gun Shop
Montgomery . . . Woolco Dept. Store
Opelika . . . Penny's Store
Phenix City . . . Davis Sporting Goods
Prichard . . Eddie's Pawn & Gun Shop
Russellville
W. R. Alsbrooks Guns & Ammo
Russellville Dependable Service Center
Saraland . . . Coastal Hdwe. & Supply
Scottsboro . . . W. J. Word
Selma . . . Benderskys
Sheffield . . . Martin Marine
Sylacauga Arnold Hardware & Supply
Talledega . . . Barton Co., Inc.
Tuscaloosa . . . Circle Wood Gun Shop
Tuscaloosa . . . Hanly's Pawn Shop
Tuscaloosa . . Allen Jemison Hardware
Tuscaloosa . . . Mack's Bait Shop
Tuscaloosa . . . Pake McKeen
Tuscaloosa . . . Woolco Dept. Store

Alaska

Anchorage . Bob Seaman's Sport Shop
Anchorage . . . Caribou Ward
Anchorage . . Custom Bluing Gun Shop
Anchorage . . . Great Northern Guns
Anchorage . . . Gun & Ammo Shop
Anchorage . . . Howard's Gun Shop
Anchorage
Mountain View Sport Center, Inc.
Anchorage . . . J. C. Penney
Clear . . . O. A. Mooney & Sons
Cordova . . . Karl's Gun Shop
Fairbanks . . Frontier Sporting Goods
Fairbanks . . . Penska's Outdoor Store
Fairbanks . . . Shebal's Gun Shop
Juneau . . . Brownie's Gun Shop
Juneau . . . Skinner's Gun Shop
Juneau . . . Totem Bay Associates
Ketchikan . . . Tongass Trading Co.
Palmer . . . Kosloskys
Sitka . . . Tackle Shop

Arizona

Douglas . . . Frank Fair Sporting Goods
Flagstaff . . . Andy's Sporting Goods
Flagstaff . . . Babbitt Bros. Trading Co.
Glendale . . . Sport Center
Globe . . . Unique Sporting Goods
Kingman . . . Central Commercial Co.
Mesa . . . M&S Sporting Goods
Mesa . . Mesa Hdwe. & Sporting Goods
Mesa . . . Petersons Sporting Goods
Mesa . . . O. S. Stapley Co.
Nogales . . . Ace Electric
Nogales . . . Brackers Dept. Store
Phoenix . Bohn's Handloading Supplies
Phoenix . . . Jewel Box Loan
Phoenix . . . Quillens Gun Shop
Phoenix . . . Stop & Swap
Prescott . . . Prescott Gun & Tackle
Prescott . . . Rifle Ranch
Prescott . . . The Sportsmans Shop
Scottsdale . . . Averys
Scottsdale . . Gunsmoke Sports Center
Show Low . . . A & A Sporting Goods
Tucson . . . Lathrop's
Tucson . . . Steinfelds
Tucson . . . Super City Dept. Store
Winslow . . . Hutch's Sporting Goods
Yuma . . . Frank's Gun Shop
Yuma . . . Marine & Sport Supply
Yuma . . . Mesa Sport Shop
Yuma . . . Starlite Gun Shop

Arkansas

Batesville . . . Airport Sports Mart
Batesville . . . Parks Hdwe. Co.
Benton . . . Smith's House of Guns
Camden . . . Lloyd's Bait Shop
Crossett . . . Jordans Sporting Center
Crossett . Homer Pierce Sporting Goods
De Queen . . . Wilson Hardware
Des Arc . . . Eddin's Hardware
DeWitt . . . Bill's True Value Hardware
De Witt . . . Schall Horn Hdwe.
Earle . . . Bruce's Repair Shop
El Dorado . . Cawvey Fix It Shop, Inc.
El Dorado . . . Lewis Sporting Goods
Fayetteville . . . Park's Place
Forrest City . . . Havens
Ft. Smith . . Midwest Hdwe & Supply
Harrison . . . Holt, Inc.
Heber Springs . . . George's Sport Shop
Helena . . . C. E. Mayer Co.
Hope . . . La Grone Williams Hdwe.
Hot Springs . . . Bob's Gun Shop
Hot Springs . . . Albert Pike Supply Co.
Jonesboro
Charlie Keller's Sporting Goods
Lake Village . Livingston Sport Center
Little Rock . . . Blass Park Plaza
Little Rock . . Pfeiffers Sporting Goods
Little Rock . . Star Sporting Goods Co.
Magnolia . . . Olive Sporting Goods
Malvern . . . Quality Hardware
Mc Ghee . . . The Sportsman's Center
Mena . . . Ellis Goss Hdwe.
Mountain Home The Sportsman's Shop
Newport Farm & Ranch Sporting Goods
North Little Rock . . . R. E. Phillips Co.
North Little Rock
Razorback Shooters Supply
Paragould . . . Pete Gregory Hdwe.
Paris . . . Paris Hardware
Pine Bluff . . . Arkansas Worm Ranch
Pine Bluff . . . Grady Newton, Inc.
Prescott . . . Prescott Hdwe. Co.
Russellville . . . Rush Sporting Goods
Searcy . James For Guns-Western Auto
Siloam Springs
Blackie's Army-Navy Store
Springdale . . . Jack's Loading Supplies
Springdale . Laymans Shopping Center
Star City . . . Beesons
Stuttgart . . . Macks Sport Shop
Trumann . . . Dudley Hardware
West Memphis . . . Ray's Electric
West Memphis . . Sportsmans One Stop

California

Alameda . . . Alameda Sporting Goods
Alhambra . . . Butler Bros.
Alpine . . . Alpine Trading Post
Alturas . . . Ingrahams Hdwe.
Anaheim . . . Elz Fargo Gun
Anaheim . . . Gemco
Anaheim . . . Gun Refinishing & Repair
Anaheim . . . Sportsmans Workshop
Anaheim . . . Wisser Sporting Goods
Anderson . . . Army Navy Store
Anderson . . . Bert's Sporting Goods
Apple Valley . . Valley Sporting Goods
Arcata . . . A. Brizard, Inc.
Arlington . . Stewart's Sporting Goods
Artesia . . . Leach's Sporting Goods
Auburn . . . G. E. Lukens & Sons, Inc.
Azusa . . . Bill's Sporting Goods
Bakersfield . . Snider's Sporting Goods
Bakersfield . . . Vincent's, Inc.
Barstow . . . Platt's Gift & Sport Shop
Bellflower Shenk Bros. Sporting Goods
Bell Gardens
Newport Koch Hdwe & Sports
Berkeley . . . Earl E. Buchanan
Beverly Hills . . . Kerrs Sport Shop
Bishop . . . Brucks Sporting Goods
Bishop . . . Mac's Sporting Goods
Blythe . . . Farm Fresh Sporting Goods
Blythe . . . Imperial Hdwe. Co.
Brawley . . . Imperial Hdwe. Co.
Bridgeport
Eatons Redwood Sporting Goods
Bridgeport . . . Ken's Sporting Goods
Burbank . . . Humes Sporting Goods
Burney . . . Vaughn's Sporting Goods
Calexico . . . Imperial Hdwe. Co.
Camarillo Camarillo Sporting Goods
Cambell . . . Heller's Camp
Canoga Park . . Canoga Sporting Goods
Carmichael . . . Bicks Sporting Goods
Carmichael . Lombard Sporting Goods
Cayucos . . . Stovnis Sporting Goods
Ceres . . . Bilson Sport Shop
Chester . . . M. D. Ayoob Dept. Store
Chico . . . A. Barth Sporting Goods
Chico . . . Chico Gun Shop
Cloverdale . . . Glenns Rifle Shop
Clovis . . . Preuss Gun Shop
Colusa
Chick Montgomery Sports Equipment
Compton . . . Woody's Sporting Goods
Concord . . . Concord Sports & Service
Concord . . . Diablo Sports Center
Corcoran . . . F. G. Gross Hdwe Co.
Corcoran . . . Woody's
Corona . . . Stutsman Sporting Goods
Costa Mesa . . . Grant's Surplus
Costa Mesa . . . F. W. Woolworth Co.
Covina . . . Chick's Sporting Goods
Culver City . . . Sportsman's Exchange
Cypress . . The Powderhorn Gun Shop
Davis . . . Cookes Gunsmithery
Delano . . . Delano Hdwe.
Del Paso Heights . Al's Sporting Goods
Dinuba . . . Woodhouse Cyclery
Dos Palos . . . Roberts
Downey . . . Matheus & Sons
Downey . . . The Sportsmans Supply
Duarte . . . Campers Haven
Duarte . . . Harry's Gun Shop
Dunsmuir . . . Big Sporting Goods
El Centro . . . Ace Sporting Goods
El Centro . . . Imperial Hdwe. Co.
El Cajon
Stanley Andrews Sporting Goods Co.
Encino Pony Express Sport Shop, Inc.
Escalon . . . Ray's Sporting Goods
Esparto . . . Esparto Gun Shop
Eureka . . . Bucksport Sporting Goods
Eureka
Steelhead Louie Sporting Goods
Fairfield . . . Fairfield Sport Shop
Fall River Mills
Summers Sporting Goods
Folsom . . . W. M. Rumsey
Fontana . . . Lazio's Sporting Goods
Ft. Bragg Tom Cooney Sporting Goods
Fortuna . . . Grunert Sporting Goods
Fremont . . . Alameda Sporting Goods
Fremont . . . K-Sports
Fresno . . . Advance Reloading Supplies
Fresno . . . Hanoians Sporting Goods
Fresno . . . Herb Bauer Sporting Goods
Fresno . . . Johnson's Gun Shop
Fresno . . . Roos Atkins
Fresno . . . Vettling Sporting Goods
Fullerton . . . Neal's Sporting Goods
Garberville . . . The Tackle Shop
Garden Grove . . Grove Sporting Goods
Gilroy . . . Jim's Sport Shop
Gilroy . . . Ray's Sportland
Glendale . . . Alaskan African Arms
Glendale . . . Cornwall & Kelty
Granada Hills Wm. Gammill Gunsmith
Grass Valley . . . General Gunsmithing
Grass Valley . . . Tom's Gun Shop
Gridley . . . Bromer Hardware Inc.
Guerneville . . . Ferenz Sport Shop
Hanford . . . Sports Center
Hanford . . . Tulare Sports Center
Hawthorne . . . Perry's Sporting Goods
Hayward . . . G and H Sports Center
Hayward . . . Skaggs Hardware
Hemet . . . Jim Cain Sporting Goods

Hollister .... The Outdoorsman
Hollywood Brass Rail Sporting Goods
Hollywood Hollywood Gun Shop, Inc.
Holtville .... Imperial Hdwe. Co.
Indio .... Imperial Hdwe. Co.
Indio .... The Outdoorman
Inglewood ... AB & S Sporting Goods
Inglewood .... Cole's
Inglewood ..... Mel's Sporting Goods
La Crescenta .... Liberty Arms Corp.
La Crescenta
Viking Leather Specialties
La Fayette ...... Frontier Gun Shop
Laguna Beach
Bill & Al's Sporting Goods
La Habra ..... A & A Athletic Supply
La Habra ... Johnson's Guns & Ammo
Lakeport ..... Pete's Sporting Goods
Lakewood .... Butler Bros.
Lakewood
Lakewood Center Sporting Goods
La Mesa ..... La Mesa Sporting Goods
Lancaster ...... The Gun Shop, Inc.
Lancaster .... Rowell's Shoe
Lemon Grove
Berry's Lemon Grove Sptg. Goods
Lemoore .... Lowes
Livermore .... Minoggios Sport Center
Long Beach .... Shore Sporting Goods
Long Beach . Thompson's Sptg. Goods
Los Alamitos . Harrison Sporting Goods
Los Angeles .. Blaine's Sporting Goods
Los Angeles .... FEDCO
Los Angeles .... G. W. Arms Sales Co.
Los Angeles ..... King's Gun Works
Los Angeles Lees Sportsmans Exchange
Los Angeles .... New York Hdwe.
Los Angeles .... Pachmayr Gun Works
Los Angeles
Richey's Cameras & Sporting Goods
Los Angeles .... Sportsmen's Den
Los Banos ..... San Luis Sport Shop
Los Gatos ...... Wild Cat Sport Shop
Marysville .. Gordons Sporting Goods
Marysville .... Randolph's
Marysville ..... Ray Gouge Firestone
Merced ...... Whitehouse Gun Shop
Middletown .... The Corner Store
Midway City ...... Crest Carving Co.
Modesto .... Argonaut Gun Shop
Modesto ...... Ed. F. Lacque & Sons
Modesto .... Turners Hardware
Mojave .... Carol's Dept. Store
Montebello ...... The Outdoorsman
Monterey ..... Rasmussen & Moody
Montrose .... Solingen Cutlery
Morgan Hill ... Squeri Bros. Hardware
Mountain View .... Eddys Sport Shop
Mt. Shasta .... Bob's Gun Shop
Napa .... Georges Gun Shop
Napa .... Glaziers Supply Store
Napa .... Yates Cochrane
National City
J. N. Weisser Sporting Goods
Nevada City .... Alpha Hardware Co.
Norco ..... L. C. Davidson Company
N. Sacramento .... Swarts Hardware
Norwalk ..... Western Gun Exchange
Novato .... Jim's Sport Shop
Oakland .... Grand Auto Stores
Oakland .... Reilly's Gun Shop
Oakland .... Siegles Guns
Oakland .... Simon Hardware
Oceanside . Johnson's Sporting Goods
Ojai .... Messer's Sports Center
Ontario ... Bumsteads Sporting Goods
Orange .... Fowler Gun Room
Orland .... Buckes
Oroville .... Curriers Appliance
Oroville .... R. C. B. S., Inc.
Oxnard ...... Oxnard Sporting Goods
Oxnard ..... Sportsmen's Exchange &
Western Gun Traders
Oxnard .... Walker's Gun Shop
Pacifica ...... Pacifica Sports Center
Pacific Beach
Jim & John's Sporting Goods
Palmdale ..... Gibbs Sporting Goods
Palm Springs ..... Frontier Gun Shop
Palo Alto .... Spiro's Sport Shop
Palo Alto .... Stanford Sport Shop
Paradise .... Edd Marty Chaplin
Pasadena .... Harrys Gun Shop
Paso Robles .... Halls Sporting Goods
Paso Robles ... Paso Robles Mercantile
Petaluma .... Mike's Gun Shop
Pittsburg .... Imperial Gun Shop
Placerville ...... Placerville Hardware
Pleasant Hill .... Hogan's Stores, Inc.
Pomona ... Beamon's Sporting Goods
Pomona .... Pomona Gun Shop
Pomona .... Rod Gun & Hobby Shop
Porterville .... Sportsman
Quincy ...... Mike's Sporting Goods
Red Bluff ...... Army & Navy Store
Red Bluff .... Bob's Sport Shop
Redding .... Army-Navy Stores, Inc.
Redding .... Vern's Sportshop
Redlands .. Pratt Bros. Sporting Goods
Redondo Beach
Shooters-Hunters-Reloaders
Redondo Beach .... Sportsville U.S.A.
Redwood City .... B & D Sport Shop
Rio Dell . Grundmans Sporting Goods
Rio Vista .... Oilwell Materials
Riverside ... Bob Stewart's Gun Shop
Riverside .. Pratt Bros. Sporting Goods
Riverside ... Threshers Sporting Goods
Rosemead .... Parry's Sporting Goods
Sacramento ...... Christy Gun Works
Sacramento ..... Ed's Sporting Goods
Sacramento ..... Murphy's Gun Shop
Sacramento .... Jack Shauls
Sacramento .... Simms Hardware Co.
Sacramento .... Tower of Sports
Salinas .... Sherwood Sport Shop
Salinas ..... Stan Lisk Sporting Goods
Salinas ..... Star Fish Sporting Goods
San Andreas .... Treats General Store
San Bernardino .. Gene's Trading Post
San Bernardino ..... Hunters Supply
San Bernardino .. P Q Sporting Goods
San Bernardino
Pratt Bros. Sporting Goods
San Bruno ... Ellingson's Sport Center
San Clemente ..... Harry's Gun Shop
San Diego .... Frontier Gun Shop
San Diego .... Krasne's Gun Shop
San Diego ...... Pacific Surplus, Inc.
San Diego
Stanley Andrews Sporting Goods Co.
San Fernando .... Ed Sowers Custom
Gun Stocks & Shooting Supplies
San Francisco .. Abercrombie & Fitch
San Francisco ...... Joe Cuneo Guns
San Francisco
Park Prosidio Sporting Goods
San Francisco ... Fred Rush Gunshop
San Francisco
San Francisco Gun Exchange
San Gabriel . Bain & Davis Sptg. Goods
San Gabriel ..... Jeffs Sporting Goods
San Jose . Guerra Bros. Sporting Goods
San Jose .... The Gun Exchange
San Jose .... Paul's Custom Rifles
San Jose ...... Reed Sporting Goods
San Jose .... F. Schilling & Son
San Leandro .... Jim's Bait Shop
San Leandro ...... Kodiak Gun Shop
San Leandro .... The Traders
San Luis Obispo
Stewart & Sons Gun Dealers
San Mateo ... Ellingsons Sport Center
San Rafael ...... Western Sport Shop
Santa Ana .... Neal's Sporting Goods
Santa Ana .... Santa Ana Gun Room
Santa Barbara
All-American Sporting Goods Co., Inc.
Santa Barbara .... J. J. Jenkins
Santa Barbara .... Ott's
Santa Clara ... Cope & McPhetres, Inc.
Santa Cruz .... Grays Gun
Santa Cruz .... Sportsman's Shop
Santa Fe Springs .... Paul Purdum
Santa Maria ...... Farmers Hardware
Santa Maria .... Glenn Roemer Hdwe.
Santa Monica .... Ames Guns
Santa Monica ... Bay Sporting Goods
Santa Rosa Joseph Cuneo Sport Shop
Santa Rosa ..... Lou's Sporting Goods
Santa Rosa ..... Perkins Sport Shop
Santa Susana . Simi Valley Gun Service
Scotia .... A. Brizard, Inc.
Seaside .... A to Z Sport Center
Sebastopol .... The Rifleman
Sonoma .... Ed. Peterson, Inc.
Sonora .... Alley Supply
Sonora .... The Sportsman
South Gate
Weatherby's Sporting Goods
Stockton .... Davenport Arms Co.
Stockton . So. McKinley Bargain Store
Stockton
Reloading & Ammunition Shop
Stockton .... Turner Hdwe. Co.
Studio City
Early & Modern Firearms Co., Inc.
Suison .... Paul's Boat Harbor
Sunland ...... Shawnee Sports Center
Sunnyvale .... Ted's Gun Shop
Susana Knolls .... Cienega Gun Shop
Susanville .... Millar Hardware
Susanville .... The Sportsman
Taft .... Taft Sporting Goods
Tahoe Valley ..... The Outdoorsman
Topanga .... Hutton Rifle Ranch
Torrance .... Torrance Cycle
Tulare .... Linder Hardware Co., Inc.
Tulelake .... Tulelake Hardware
Turlock .... Bilson Sport Shop
Turlock .... Turner Hardware Co.
Ukiah .... Palace Sport
Upland ..... Ralph's Sporting Goods
Vallejo .... Al's Sport Shop
Van Nuys ...... Barkley's Gun Shop
Van Nuys .... Butler Bros.
Ventura
All American Sporting Goods Co., Inc.
Ventura .... Shaffers
Victorville ..... Victorville Hardware
Visalia .... Cross Horlock Co.
Visalia .... Dale's Sporting Goods
Watsonville ...... Valley Sport Shop
Weaverville .. Walters Sporting Goods
West Covina .... The Gun Room
Westwood .... Lassen Sport Shop
Whittier .... The Accuracy Shop
Whittier .... Hinshaw's Dept. Store
Williams .... The Boat Fair
Willow Creek
L. E. Blasch Sporting Goods
Willows .... Valley Firestone
Willows ..... Willows Sporting Center
Woodlake ...... Boas Minnow Farm
Woodlake ... Woodlake Hardware Co.
Woodland ... Georges Sporting Goods
Woodland .... Henigan and Shull
Yreka .... Bish's Gun Shop
Yreka .... Don's Sporting Goods
Yuba City .... Bromer Hardware, Inc.
Yucaipa .... Olive's Gun Shop

Colorado

Arvada .... Al's Sporting Goods
Arvada .... Sportline Gun Dept.
Aurora .... Arlans
Aurora .. Gart Bros. Sport Goods Co.
Aurora .... Sports Villa
Boulder ... Arapahoe Sporting Goods
Boulder .... Gamelines, Inc.
Canon City ...... Jimmy's Sport Shop
Climax .... Leighton Co., Inc.
Colorado Springs
Blick Sporting Goods Co.
Colorado Springs Campbell's Gun Shop
Colorado Springs
Dave Cook Sporting Goods Co.
Colorado Springs Suters House of Guns
Cortez ..... Howards Sporting Goods
Craig .... Craig Sports
Delta .... Murphy's Sport Shop
Denver .... Ace Sporting Goods
Denver Dave Cook Sporting Goods Co.
Denver ..... Gart Bros. Sport Goods
Denver .... Martins Gun Shop
Denver .... Rhine Products Corp.
Denver .... Sports Villa
Englewood ..... Arapahoe Gun Shop
Englewood .. Gart Bros. Sport Goods
Englewood .... Sivey's
Ft. Collins .. Ed Deans Sporting Goods
Ft. Collins .... House of Guns
Ft. Morgan .... Coast To Coast Store
Ft. Morgan ..... The Clatworthy Co.
Glenwood Springs
Bob's Sporting Goods
Glenwood Springs
Van's Highway Shop
Grand Junction
L. Cook Sporting Goods
Grand Junction .... Rod & Gun Shop
Greeley ... Jones Co. Sporting Goods
Greeley .... Sargents Sport Shop
Gunnison ..... Mac's Marine Service
Hotchkiss .... Stengel's Gunshop
Lakewood . Lakewood Sporting Goods
Littleton
Andrews Ammunition and Arms
Littleton .... B & H Ski
Longmont . Arapahoe Sporting Goods
Loveland .... Draper Drugs
Naturita .... Naturita Shooting Shop
Pueblo .... Johnson Hardware
Rifle .... The Sports Shop
Salida .... The Magnum
Salida .... Tuttles Trading Post
Sterling . Dollerschell's Sporting Goods
Sterling .... RL's Gun Sales & Service
Sugar City . Ye Gunne Butcher Shoppe
Westminster . Denver Sporting Goods
Westminster .... Gambles
Westminster Westminster Sptg. Goods
Wheatridge .... Sports Unlimited

Connecticut

Bridgeport Dick's Sport and Cycle Shop
Bridgeport .... Pasieka Bros.
Bridgeport .... People's Hardware
Bridgeport ..... Sportmens Den, Inc.
Danbury .... Jade Custom Guns
Darien .... Bob's Guns Division
Darien .... Darien Sport Shop
Deep River ... Johnny's Sport Center
East Hartford A. V. Bryant, Gunsmith
Glastonbury Glastonbury Sport Center
Groton ... Campbell's Sporting Goods
Guilford .... Pioneer Gunshop
Hamden .... Cook, Newton & Smith
Hamden .... Piscitellis Gun Shop
Ledyard .... Chappy's Gun Shop
Manchester .... Banville's Gun Center
Manchester .... Nassiff Arms Co.
Marion ... Elwood V. Tainter & Sons
Middletown .. Middlesex Sport Center
Monroe .... Sports World
New Britain .. Hoffman's Sport Center
New Britain .. Young's Guns & Ammo
New Canaan ...... Bob's Sports, Inc.
New Haven .... Antique Guns & Parts
New Haven .... New England Armory
New London .... J. L. Raub
New Milford .... Valley Sport Center
New Preston .... Antique Armory
North Canton . D. R. Custer Gunsmith
North Haven .... Lal's Gunshop, Inc.
Norwalk .... Sportland, Inc.
Norwich . Campbell's Sporting Goods
Norwich ... Walenda's Studio of Guns
Oakville ..... Midway Sporting Goods
Old Saybrook Middlesex Sport Goods
Orange ..... Yankee Gun Shop, Inc.
Portland .... Zah's Sport Shop
Putnam .... Bob Racine Sports
Ridgefield ..... Safari Outfitters, Ltd.
Rockville .... Fire Arms, Inc.
Roxbury .... J. Dewey Gun Co.
Sandy Hook .. Garrison Firearms, Inc.
Seymour ...... Seymour Sport Shop
Shelton .... The Gun Rack
Stamford .... Bob's Sports, Inc.
Stamford .... George A. Pecot

Stamford .... Village Sport Shop
Stratford .... Stan's Gun Shop
Stratford .... Stratford Gun Shop
Torrington ..... Frank's Sport Store
Torrington ..... Sportsmens Paradise
Torrington ...... Sport Traders, Inc.
Uncasville . Fort Shantok Trading Post
Warehouse Point . C. Ray Boudman, Jr.
Watertown Watertown Shooters Supply
West Hartford .... Clapp & Treat, Inc.
Willimantic ...... Nassiff Arms, Inc.
Windsor .... Victor A. Positano
Windsor .... Townline Marine
Winsted .... William Rosgen
Wolcott ..... Anzes Fire Arms Supply
Woodbury . Judson Darrow Gunsmith

Delaware

Dover .... Buchanan Service
New Castle .... Miller Gun Shop
Seaford ...... Y & M Sporting Goods
Smyrna ..... Smyrna Sporting Goods

District of Columbia

Washington .... Atlas Sport Shop

Florida

Apopka .... BJP, Inc.
Arcadia .... Tinsley's Feed Store
Boynton Beach .. Boynton Gun Shop
Bradenton Wm. Henry Sporting Goods
Clearwater .... The Big Store
Cocoa ..... Belk-Lindsey Dept. Store
Clearwater Hayes Gunstock Service Co.
Dade City ...... Dade City Hardware
Dania ...... H. M. Nierling Gunsmith
Daytona .... Buck's Gun Shop
Deland .... Angevine Gun Shop
Deland . Nordmann's Hdwe. & Supply
Delray Beach .... Rods and Guns
Eau Gallie ... Southern Gun Exchange
Eau Gallie . Eau Gallie Gun-Pawn Shop
Ft. Myers .... Bulls Eye Sport
Ft. Myers .... Davis Gun Sales
Fort Walton Beach
Vernon Gun Consulting
Frostproof .... Allison T. French
Reloading Supplies
Gainesville .... Gulf Hardware
Gainesville ..... Rice Grose Hardware
Gainesville .... The Rancher
Haines City .... Buff Sales Co.
Havana .... Moreland's Gunshop
Hollywood .... Chira's
Hollywood .... Hollywood Gun
Hollywood ... Jones Equipment Co.
Hollywood ...... Tom's Gun Shop
Inglis . Backwater Sportsmen Club, Inc.
Jacksonville .... Skip's Gun Shop
Jacksonville .... Towers Hardware
Key West .... Charlie's Gun Shop
Kissimee .. Tom Addison's Gun Shop
Lake Geneva ...... Slim's Fish-N-Stuff
Lake Wales .... Bill's Gun Shop
Live Oak .... Mack's Sport Shop
Mango .... Frank Wm. Coutcher
Marianna .. Russell Sports Distributors
and Gun Shop
Miami .... Bensons Loan Co.
Miami .... Peter Bataskov Firearms &
Shooting Supplies
Miami .... Bullseye, Inc.
Miami .... Century Arms
Miami .... Europa Corporation
Miami ... Flagler Jewelry & Loan Co.
Miami .... National Gun Traders
Miami .... Seminole Gun Shop
Miami .... Southern Gun Distribs.
Miami .... Tamiami Gun Shop
Miami .... The Fix-It Swap Shop
Miami .... The Gun Shop, Inc.
Miami Shores ... The Gun Shop, Inc.
Miami ...... Traeger Bros. & Assocs.
Mt. Dora ... A. W. Peterson Gunshop
Naples ...... Sunshine Ace Hardware
Nokomis . John W. Norman, Gunsmith
Ocala .... Marion Hardware Co.
Ocala .... Pasteur's Sport Shop
Opa-Locka
Art Lawson Custom Firearms, Inc.
Orlando .... Gun Traders
Orlando .... Triggermart
Palatka ...... Motes Hardware Store
Palatka . Taylor's Westgate Ace Hdwe.
Panama City .. C & G Sporting Goods
Parker .... Rush Gun Shop
Panama City
Montin Hardware & Sporting Goods
Pensacola ..... Biggs Sporting Goods
Pensacola .... Pennys
Plant City . Plant City Growers Assoc.
Riviera Beach Custom Gunsmiths, Inc.
St. Petersburg ... Kenneth D. Clothier
St. Petersburg . Gulfshore Sport Center
St. Petersburg .... Bill Jackson
St. Petersburg .... Ed. Maier
Sanford ..... Robson Sporting Goods
Sarasota
Alton Horne Custom Gunsmith
Sarasota .... Tucker Sporting Goods
Starke .... Starke Builders Supply
Stuart .... McDonald Repair
Tallahassee .... Downtown Hardware
Tallahassee .... F. M. Poggie
Tampa .... Jesse E. Harpe
Tampa .... Kenfix Company
Tampa .... Pioneer Tire Co., Inc.
Tarpon Springs . John K. Gentry & Son
Titusville ... Belk-Lindsey Dept. Store
Warrington .... Gator Sport Shop
Wildwood ...... Clarence L. Howard

Georgia

Albany
Albany Sporting Supply Co., Inc.
Albany ...... City Loan & Music Co.
Albany Owens Sporting Goods & Hdwe.
Albany .... The Albany Gun Shop
Ashburn .... Barker Hardware
Athens .... Athens Firearms, Inc.
Atlanta Atlanta Armory Company, Inc.
Atlanta .... Bates Hardware
Atlanta . Brooklyn Loan & Jewelry Co.
Atlanta .... Deans, Inc.
Atlanta .... King Hardware Co.
Atlanta Everett Roach Sporting Goods
Atlanta .... Surplus Guns, Inc.
Atlanta .... The Gun Room, Inc.
Augusta .... Frye's Guns
Augusta ..... Georgia Sporting Goods
Bainbridge ... Frank's Gun-Sport Shop
Bainbridge .... Jakes Pawn Shop
Barnesville .... Keadle Hardware
Blakely .... Foster's Gun Shop
Cairo .... Roddenberry Hardware Co.
Cartersville ..... Abercrombie's, Inc.
Cedartown ... Casey's Sporting Goods
Chickamauga .... Tri-State Arms
Claxton .... Kicks Sports Center
Columbus . Citizen Jewelry & Loan Co.
Columbus .... Richardson Home
Columbus .... The Accuracy Gunshop
Cordele .... The Gun Shop
Cornelia .... Modern Gun Shop
Covington . White's Tire & Auto Supply
Cumming Holbrook Hardware & Supply
Dalton .... Lackey Marine
Decatur .... The Gun Corral
Decatur .... Sportsmens Paradise
Donalsonville
Hatcher Sporting Goods Co.
Doraville .... Old Sarge Army Surplus
East Point .... The Gun Room
Fitzgerald . Western Auto Assoc. Store
Forsyth .... Chambers Sporting Goods
Gainesville .... Stancil Martin Sports
Greensboro .... P & S Pawn Shop
Hartwell
James J. Morsey Custom Gunstocker
Kathleen .... Whites Gunshop
Kingsland ..... Bush Sporting Goods
Lawrenceville
Western Auto Assoc. Store
Mableton ... Mableton Sporting Goods
Macon .... Averys
Macon ..... R. L. Dunn Hardware Co.
Macon ...... Weaver's Sporting Goods
Macon Westgate Firearms & Accessories
Macon .... Willingham, Inc.
Marietta The Mountain View Gun Shop
McDonough Sportsman Gun Shop, Inc.
Milledgeville .... Cooks
Milledgeville
Frank Hines Sporting Goods
Montezuma ... Tindol Sporting Goods
Moultrie .... Baell Mercantile Co.
Newnan .... Johnson Hardware Co.
Nicholls .... Bickley Farm Supply
Pinehurst .... Raymond E. Davis Guns
Rentz
Ronnie Horne's Handloaders Supply
Rome .... Owens Hardware Co.
Rossville .... Peerless, Inc.
Savannah .... Cranmans
Savannah .... Ed's Reblueing
Savannah ...... Stubbs Hardware Co.
Smyrna .... Home & Hobby Hardware
Statesboro
W. C. Akins & Son Hdwe. Co.
Statesboro ..... Roy Smith's Gunshop
Summerville .. Summerville Gun Shop
Swainsboro .... The Sports Shop
Tennille .... McMaster Supply Co.
Thomaston . O. W. Jones & Sons Hdwe.
Thomasville ..... Knapp Hardware Co.
Thomasville .. Vaughns Sporting Goods
Valdosta .... The Sports Center
Warner Robins
Blackwater Sporting Goods
Waycross ...... Mayo Bros. Hardware
Waycross .... Okefenokee Gun Service
Waycross .... The Sport Shop
Waynesboro ..... Goodyear Tire Co.

Hawaii

Honolulu ... Honolulu Sporting Goods
Honolulu ..... King's Sporting Goods

Idaho

Blackfoot ... Alaskan Sporting Goods
Blackfoot .... Just's Army Store
Blackfoot .... Sam's Sport Center
Boise .... Grand Central Market
Boise .... Gerald K. King
Boise .... Moons Gun & Tackle
Boise .... Purcell Sporting Goods
Boise .... Skaggs Drug Center
Boise .... The Bon Marche
Burley .... Morgan Hardware
Caldwell ...... Becker Hardware Co.
Caldwell ...... Pennywise Drug Store
Coeur D'Alene
Lighthouse Sporting Goods
Emmett .... Dill's Sporting Goods
Gibbonsville .... Broken Arrow
Grangeville ...... Western Outfitters
Idahoe Falls .... Bon Marche
Idaho Falls .... Bukys Village
Idaho Falls .. Northway Sports Center
Idaho Falls .... The Mart
Idaho Falls
The Outdoorsman Sporting Goods
Idaho Falls .... Woodys, Inc.
Kooskia .... Brownie's Service
Lewiston .... L&B Supply
Lewiston .. LoLo Sporting Goods, Inc.
Lewiston .... Reed Hardware Co.
Lewiston .... Warrens Sport Shop
Moscow .... Tri-State Store
Mountain Home .... Gem State Loan
Nampa ..... Herb Carlson Sport Shop
Nampa .... Ken's Jewelry & Loan
Nampa .... Pennywise Drug Store
Pierce ...... X. E. Durante Hardware
Pocatello . Bistline Lumber & Hardware
Pocatello ... Crockett Sporting Goods
Pocatello .... Freddy's Sport Shop
Pocatello .... Getty's Sport Center
Pocatello .... Pocatello Gun Shop
Pocatello ...... Roy's Sporting Goods
Pocatello ...... Sam's Loan & Jewelry
Pocatello ..... Sunset Sporting Goods
Rexburg .... Rainbow Sport Shop
Rexburg .. Thompson Sporting Goods
Rigby .... Marv's Sport Shop
Rupert .... Western Auto Store
St. Anthony .... Ives Sporting Goods
Salmon .... Buckhorn Gun Shop
Salmon .... Havemann Hardware
Salmon ...... Lock, Stock and Barrel
Sand Point .... The Pastime
Twin Lakes Blue Lakes Sporting Goods
Twin Falls .... Gerrish Sporting Goods
Twin Falls ..... Pennywise Drug Store
Twin Falls .... Red's Trading Post
Twin Falls . West Point Sporting Goods

Illinois

Abingtdon ..... Winkless Sport Center
Addison .... Puccini's
Alton ..... Klump Boat & Motor Co.
Alton .... Wittel's & Co.
Anna .. Union County Sporting Goods
Anna .... A. W. Walter Jr. & Co.
Antioch Gibbs & Jensen Sporting Goods
Aurora .... Arenkills Loan Bank
Aurora .... Aurora Main Store, Inc.
Aurora .... Crosby's Sport Shop
Aurora ... Lake States Gun Exchange
Aurora . Precision Shooters Supply Co.
Barrington ... Darkens Sporting Goods
Bartonville .. Ed Rebbec's Sport Shop
Belleville .... Belleville Hardware
Belleville .... Kiefer Stocks
Belvidere ...... Garrigan's Sport Shop
Berwyn .... Mages Sport Center
Bloomington
J. Howard Rose Sporting Goods
Blue Island Blue Island Gun Shop, Inc.
Broadview . Hildebrand Sporting Goods
Brookfield .... Jerry's Gun Shop
Cairo .... Metheny's Gun Shop
Calumet City ... Arco Sporting Goods
Calumet City
Calumet Marine & Sports Supply
Canton
Duryea's Trading & Sporting Goods
Carbon Cliff
Carbon Cliff Bait & Tackle Shop
Carbondale .... C & F Boats & Motors
Carbondale .... Jim's Sporting Goods
Carbondale ..... Veath's Sports Mart
Casey .... Stifal Hardware
Centralia .... Dwight F. Cross
Centralia .... Hanseman Gun Shop
Centralia 20th Century Sporting Goods
Champaign ..... Bailey & Himes, Inc.
Champaign Curly's Gun and Pawn Shop
Chester .... Parker Hardware
Chicago .... Abercrombie & Fitch
Chicago ..... Chicago Archery Center
Chicago .... Chicago Gun Center
Chicago .... Clip Master
Chicago . Community Discount Center
Chicago
Gabby Hartnett Recreation, Inc.
Chicago .... Gitter & Siovic, Inc.
Chicago Jack Gundlach Sporting Goods
Chicago .... H. Harris
Chicago ... Henry's Sport & Bait Shop
Chicago .... Hi-Way Sport Shop
Chicago .. Klein's Sporting Goods, Inc.
Chicago .... Mages Sporting Goods
Chicago .... Marshall Field & Co.
Chicago . Marquette Sports Equipment
Chicago ...... Roseland Sports Center
Chicago ...... Sam Santo Sport Store
Chicago .... Scaramuzzo & Sons
Chicago N. H. Schulkin Sporting Goods
Chicago .... Sevic Sport Shop
Chicago .... Simmon's Sport Shop
Chicago ..... Sportsman's Center, Inc.
Chicago .... Superior Sport Store
Chicago .... Varsity Sporting Goods
Chicago .... Vim Sports Co., Inc.
Chicago .... Wielgus Sport Shop
Chicago .... E. H. Winkler

Chicago Heights . Vicari's Gunshop, Inc.
Chicago Ridge
Chicago Ridge Gun & Range, Inc.
Cicero .... Cicero Sporting Goods
Cicero .... Novak Sporting Goods
Clinton .... Rolofson Sporting Goods
Collinsville .... L. J. Williams, Jr.
Crystal Lake
Dave's News & Sport Store, Inc.
Danville .... Bott's Sporting Goods
Danville
Cleve Alexander Sporting Goods
Decatur .... Bill Dotsons, Inc.
Decatur .... Frank's Sport Shop
Decatur ..... Ray Myers Sports Center
Decatur .... Rupert's Sport Shop
Deerfield .... Custom Load
Deerfield
Deerfield Bicycle & Sport Shop
DeKalb .... Tommy's Sport Shop
Des Plaines
Johnson Sporting Goods Co., Inc.
Dixon .... D. C. Long's Sportsman
Dundee .. Fox Valley Rifle Range, Inc.
Du Quoin ..... Maclin Westside Drug
East Peoria ... K. C. Fish & Sports Co.
Edwardsville .... Kriege Hardware
Effingham . Vogt Bros. Sporting Goods
El Dorado . El Dorado Sporting Goods
Elgin .... Keeney Sporting Goods
Elgin .... Sportsman's Lodge
Elk Grove Elk Grove Village Sports, Inc.
Elmhurst ... Chipain's Sporting Goods
Elmhurst ... Elmhurst Pro Sport Shop
Evanston
Angler's Supply & Sporting Goods
Evergreen Park
Klein's Sporting Goods, Inc.
Flora .... Gambles
Forest Park
Ray Hanson's Favorite Sport Shop
Fox Lake ..... Homan Sporting Goods
Fox Lake ...... Lechner's Tackle Box
Franklin Park
Bell's Gun & Sport Shop, Inc.
Freeport .... Ciganek Sporting Goods
Freeport ... Freeport Sporting Goods
Freeport
Messing & Becker Sporting Goods
Galesburg . Dom's Sporting Goods Co.
Galesburg .... Nelson Sporting
Galesburg .. Gale Ward Athletic Goods
Geneseo .... Cherry's Sporting Goods
Geneva .... Geneva Sport Shop
Glencoe .... Ray's Sport Shop
Glen Ellyn . Glen Sport & Camera Shop
Glen Ellyn .... The Powder Horn
Glenwood . Bill's Trap & Skeet Supply
Granite City .. Fahnster Tire & Supply
Greenville ...... Main Tire & Battery
Hanover .... Sullivan's Hardware
Harvard .... Carlson's Sporting Goods
Harvard .... Re-Bild Gun Shop
Havana .... Zempel Hardware
Henry .... Perdew Gun Shop
Herrin .... Church Sporting Goods
Highland .... Broadway Tire
Highland Park Greenwald's Sport Shop
Highland Park
Highland Park Sport Shop, Inc.
Hillside .. Klein's Sporting Goods, Inc.
Hoffman Estates .. Omega Sport Shop
Hoopeston . Country Shooters Supply
Jacksonville .... D&D Sports Center
Jacksonville ... Gene's Sporting Goods
Jacksonville . Spaulding Sporting Goods
Jerseyville .... Norton Hardware
Joliet
Bowl Rite Bowling & Sporting Goods
Joliet .... Stukel's World of Sports
Joliet .... AH. Swanson Co.
Kankakee .... Hank's Sporting Goods
Kankakee
Salkeld & Sons Sporting Goods
Kewanee
Breedlove Sports & Hardware Store
Knoxville .... Gil Hebard Guns
La Grange .... Lockhart's Sport Shop
Lake Forest .... Koppens
Lake Zurick ..... Village Sport Center
Lanarle .... Kroll Repair Service
Lansing .... Lansing Hardware
Lemont .. Southwest Shooters Supply
Libertyville .... Suburban Sportsman
Lincoln .... Vic's Sports
Lincoln .... Werth Gun Shop
Lombard ...... Lombard Sport Shop
Loves Park ... Blackhawk Small Arms
Lyndon .... Johnson Roller Mill
Lyons
Midwest Sporting Goods Co., Inc.
Macomb .... Dannys
Macomb ...... Feathers Sport Center
Markham .... Ed Shirley's Sports
Mattoon .... Bob's Gun Shop
Mattoon
Oakley & Son Cycle Hobby & Marine
Mattoon .... Paullins
McHenry .... Ernie's Sport Center
McHenry ...... McHenry Gun Center
Melrose Park ... Mages Sporting Goods
Melrose Park .... Mercury Sports
Melrose Park
Rubin Sporting Goods Co., Inc.
Melrose Park Suburban Sporting Goods
Millstadt
Broken "L" Gun & Saddle Shop
Monmouth . Mitchell's Sporting Goods
Morris .... Redfern Hardware
Morton .... Sander's Gun Shop
Morton Grove ... Dempster All Sports
Morton Grove
L&B Schulkin Sporting Goods
Mt. Carmel ...... E. D. Walter Sports
Mt. Prospect Maxon Shooter's Supplies
Mt. Prospect
Randhurst Sports Chalet, Inc.
Mt. Prospect .... Wille, Inc.
Mundelein .. Suburban Sportsman, Inc.
Murphysboro Bowers & Sons Hardware
Naperville .... Master Shooters
Naperville ..... Naperville Sport Shop
New Berlin ...... Bernie's Gun Shop
Newton .... Franke Recreation Parlor
Niles .... Klein's Sporting Goods, Inc.
Normal ..... Gibson's Sporting Goods
Northbrook
Stark's Northbrook Sports Center
Northfield ... Bess Hardware & Sports
Oak Lawn .... Associated Guns
Oak Lawn
Oak Lawn Gun & Sports, Inc.
Oak Lawn .... Sundeen Guns
Oak Park .... Breit & Johnson
Oak Park .... Cunningham-Reilly, Inc.
Olney .. Bauman True Value Hardware
Olney .... Richland County Tire
Oregon .... Doeden's
Palatine .... Pro Sport Center
Paris .... Steffeys
Park Forest ... Sports & Hobbies, Inc.
Park Ridge .... Blyth Enterprises, Inc.
Pekin .... Bob's Rod & Gun Shop
Pekin ... Buckley Brothers Sport Shop
Pekin .... Shipman Sport Center
Peoria .... Hinman Outfitters
Peoria ...... Jack's Hunter's Supplies
Peoria ...... Keenan Sporting Goods
Peoria Heights .. Heights Hardware Co.
Pinckneyville ... Hicks Trading Station
Pinckneyville .. Mann's Sporting Goods
Plainfield .... Van's Gun Shop
Pontiac ...... Shepherd's Pet Shop & Sporting Goods
Princeton ... Ky-Wa Acres Sport Shop
Quincy .... Merkel's, Inc.
Quincy ...... Snowhill's Sports Shop
Rantoul .... Litchfield Hardware
Richmond .... Oakdale Sports
Riverdale .... Chuck's Gun Shop
Roberts .... Harold's Firearms
Rockford Humpal Sporting Goods Co.
Rockford . McNames Gun Repair Shop
Rockford Mortenson's Sporting Goods
Rockford Rockford Sports Center, Inc.
Rockford .... Sterns
Rock Island .... 44th Street Bait Shop
Rock Island ... Freelands Scope Stand
Rolling Meadows ...... Sports Chalet
Round Lake .... Avon Hardware, Inc.
Round Lake . Cross Sport & Gun Shop
Sandwich
R. G. Seitzinger Sporting Goods
Savanna .... Pitts Sport Store
Shabbona .... Carter's Gun Shop
Shabbona .... T & J Shop
Shelbyville ... Rose Center Rifle Shop
Sparta ...... Henderson's Equipment
Springfield ...... Sportsman's Center
Sterling ...... Rock River Sport Shop
Streator .... Christoff's Hardware
Sycamore ...... Hagen Ace Hardware
Toulon .... John's Gun Room
Urbana .. Lorry's Favorite Sport Shop
Vandalia .... The Sports Center
Villa Park
Community Discount Center, Inc.
Watseka .... G & M Sports Center
Wauconda .... Dorkens For Sports
Wauconda .... Herb's Sport Shop
Waukegan .. Downtown Sports Center
Waukegan .... Grand Sporting Goods
Waukegan .... Shaw Bros. Gun Center
Waukegan .... Smoke 'N Gun
Wheaton .... Wheaton Sport Shop
Wilmette Wilmette Bicycle-Sport Shop
Winnetka .... Fred's Bicycle Shop
Woodstock .... P. O. Knuth Company
Wyanet .. Hickory Grove Hunting Club

Indiana

Anderson .... Gun Barn
Aurora .... Kennedy Sporting Goods
Avilla .... Riley's, Inc.
Bloomington .... Schmalz Dept. Store
Bloomington
University Sporting Goods
Boonville .... Addingtons
Brazil .... Clarks Sporting Goods
Chesterton .... Jack's Gun Shop
Columbus .... Marlin Sporting Goods
Columbus ..... Ron's Reloading Shop
Columbus Thompson's Sporting Goods
Connersville
Knight's Custom Gun Shop
Corydon ... Lamon & Davis Hardware
Crawfordsville ... Ben Hur Sport Shop
Crown Point . R. E. Safford Enterprise
Dyer ... Schereville Bait & Sport Shop
East Chicago .... J. P. Davis & Co.
Edwardsport Edwardsport Lumber Co.
Elkhart ..... Berman Sporting Goods
Elkhart . Sportsman's Enterprises, Inc.
Evansville .... B&S Sporting Guns
Evansville .... Beards Sporting Goods
Evansville Gus Doerner Sporting Goods
Evansville .... Franklin Drug Co.
Evansville .... Rajo Gun Shop
Ft. Wayne .. Buchwald Sporting Goods
Ft. Wayne . Cashman's Sporting Goods
Frankfort . Conkright Sporting Goods
Galveston
J. L. Jones Firearms & Ammunition
Gary ..... Broadway Sports & Marine
Gary .... Griffin Sport & Marine, Inc.
Goshen .... Goshen Rod & Gun Shop
Goshen .... Phil's Sporting Goods
Greensburg Doerflinger Sporting Goods
Griffith .... Blyth's Sport Shop
Hammond .... The Sportsman's Store
Hartford ...... Suite Sporting Goods
Indianapolis Broad Ripple Sports Shop
Indianapolis . Em-Roe Sporting Goods
Indianapolis ..... Shaw's Gulf Service
Indianapolis . Vonnegut Hardware Co.
Kokomo .... The Gun Room
LaFayette .... A. F. Herbst
Lafayette ...... The Sportsman, Inc.
Lafayette .... Trader Horn Co.
La Porte ... Bob's Custom Handloads
La Porte .... La Porte Sporting Goods
Lawrenceburg ... Triangle Sport Shop
Lawrenceburg ... Triangle Sport Shop
Linton .... Wright's Bait Shop
Madison ...... Bill's Sporting Goods
Marysville ... Marysville Hardware Co.
Michigan City ..... Bob's Sport Shop
Muncie Dick's Antique & Modern Arms
Muncie .... Dustin Waymire
Muncie .... Kirk's Sporting Goods
Muncie .... Retz Sporting Goods
Muncie .... Sheward's Gun Repair
New Albany .... Bush Keller Co.
New Albany .... Combs Custom Guns
New Castle ...... Ramrod Gun Shop
North Manchester ... Schutz Brothers
North Vernon . J. R. Greathouse & Son
Osgood .... Gloyd Hardware
Paolt .... Boule Sporting Goods
Peru .... Yentes Sporting Goods
Plymouth ..... Don's Sporting Goods
Rensselaer .... Hudsons
Richmond
Cooper & Evans Sporting Goods
Richmond .... Phil's Sport Shop
Rochester .... Baileys Hardware
Rockport ... Schoenfeld Rexall Drug
St. Paul
Settle's Antique & Modern Firearms
Seymour .... Stewarts Appliance
Shelbyville .... Cartridge Cabin
Speedway City Vonnegut Hardware Co.
Syracuse .. Wawasee Sportsman Center
Terre Haute . McMillan Sporting Goods
Terre Haute .. Paitsons Bros. Hardware
Terre Haute .... Poffs Sporting Goods
Valparaiso .... Bernard Gotaut
Valparaiso .... Johnstons Sports
Veedersburg .... J. C. Sport Shop
Vincennes .... Tresslars
Vincennes .. Vanmeter Sporting Goods
Winchester ..... Keener Sports Store
Winchester .... Sports Center

Iowa

Ames .... Long's Specialties
Ames .... Nims Sportsman
Ames .... Woods Shooting Supply
Anamosa .... R. L. Flaucher & Son
Aurelia .... Menetee Hardware
Boone ...... Red Fox Sporting Goods
Britt .... Kreitinger Hardware
Burlington .... Dehner Seed
Burlington .... Lloyds Surplus
Carroll ..... Uptown Sporting Goods
Cedar Falls ...... Olsen's Boat House
Cedar Rapids .... Coast To Coast Store
Cedar Rapids .... Drews
Centerville .... Favorite Sports
Charles City .. Monroe Sporting Goods
Cherokee .... Doors Sport Service
Clarinda .... Campbell Farm
Clear Lake Clarks Sport & Hobby Shop
Clinton .... Lateke Marina
Clinton .... R. D. Letch Co.
Corning .... Ashenfelter Leather
Council Bluffs .... Peoples Dept. Store
Creston .... Dreys Sporting Goods
Davenport ... Cratons Sporting Goods
Davenport ... Credit Island Sport Shop
Davenport .... Don's Sport Shop
Davenport .. Kunkel's Sporting Goods
Decorah ...... Lange Sporting Goods
Denison ..... Denison Sporting Goods
Des Moines .... Betts & Son Hardware
Des Moines .... Central Hardware Co.
Des Moines
Des Moines Pawn-Sporting Goods
Des Moines .... Gun Craft
Des Moines .... Hog Gun Shop
Des Moines ..... Ted Holm Gun Sales
Des Moines
Hopkins Sporting Goods, Inc.
Des Moines .... Jay's Sales Co.
Des Moines .... Thode Sporting Goods
Dubuque ...... Central Hardware Co.
Dubuque .... Junie's Tri-State

Dubuque
Bob Zehentner's Sporting Goods
Emmetsburg Johnsons Sporting Goods
South English .... Slates Service
Estherville .... Lees Sport Shop
Evans Dale .... Cedar Sport Shop
Fairfield ....The Sport Shop
Farmington .... Bob's Shop
Ft. Dodge Kautzky Sporting Goods Co.
Ft. Dodge .... Nordquist Sports
Ft. Madison .... Burgunds
Glenwood ......Coast To Coast Store
Grinnell .... Harry's Sport Shop
Grundy Center .. John High Hardware
Independence ...Coast To Coast Store
Independence
Freeman's Sporting Goods
Iowa City John Wilson Sporting Goods
Laurens ......Laurens 5 To 1 Store
Leon .. Leon Concrete & Bldg. Supply
Le Mars ....Adler Sporting Goods
Manchester .... Cassel & Cassel
Manchester . Hawkers Sporting Goods
Manchester ....Saunders
Maquoketa ..Casady's Sporting Goods
Marengo ..Style & Economy Clothiers
Marshalltown .. Hays Sporting Goods
Marshalltown ..... Turners Gunshop
Mason City .Bobs Shooters Supply Co.
Mason City ...Decker Sporting Goods
Mason City .... Greischar
Muscatine ....Carlisle Sporting Goods
Muscatine ... Safley's Sporting Goods
Mystic .... Hampton's Gun Shop
Newton ....Coast To Coast Store
Oelwein ....Coast To Coast Store
Osceola .... Clark Sporting Goods
Oskalooza .... Firestone
Oskaloosa ....Upton & Colville
Perry ....Al's Sporting Goods
Perry .... Walt's Sport Shop Inc.
Sac City .... Art's Sports
Shell Rock ....Pruin Body Shop
Sioux City .... Olson Sporting Goods
Sioux City ...... Riverside Hardware
Spencer ....Sportsmans
Storm Lake .....Coast to Coast Store
Waterloo .... Coburn Sporting Goods
Waterloo ....Winder Sport Shop, Inc.
Waverly .... Dales Sport Shop
Waverly .... Sportsmen's Corner
Webster City ... Jones Sporting Goods

Kansas

Abilene .... R. H. V. Store
Arkansas City ..Arkche Supp. & Serv.
Ashland ....Sportsmans Supply
Atchinson ....Rudolph's
Chanute ....Sportsmans Supply
Clay Center ... Ward's Sporting Goods
Coffeyville ....Frazee's Firestone
Coffeyville .... Schille's
Colby .... Pratt Hardware
Columbus ....Hurst Firestone
Concordia
F. D. Everitt & Son Hardware
Dodge City Pennington Sporting Goods
Downs ....181 Gun Shop
Emporia .... Emporia Sport Shop
Eureka .... Gambles
Ft. Scott .... Central Gun Shop
Garden City
Western Kansas Sporting Goods
Goodland ...McClure Sporting Goods
Goodland .....Myers Sporting Goods
Great Bend ...Brant's Sporting Goods
Great Bend ..... Field & Lake Sports
Great Bend .... Gibsons Products
Great Bend ...Phillips Sporting Goods
Hopewell .... Curtis Gun Shop
Hoxie .... Mickey Hardware
Hugoton .... Floyds Hardware
Hutchinson ... Boren Sporting Goods
Hutchinson ...... Reno's Ace Hdwe.
Independence . Kansan Boat & Marine
Iola ....Wilson Hdwe.
Junction City Ski's Shooting Supplies
Junction City ....Waters, Inc.
Kansas City ....Gateway
Kansas City ....Schrader's Sport Shop
Kansas City .. Smitty's Boats & Motors
Lawrence .....Ernst & Son Hardware
Lawrence ... Wilson Supply & Service
Leavenworth ....Gateway
Leoti ....Y & S Camper Sales
Liberal .... Chaffin Hardware
Manhattan Smith Bros. Sporting Goods
Mankato .... McCarthy Hardware Co.
Merriam .... B. E. Hodgon
Newton .... Graber's Hardware
Norton .... Horneys
Oberlin .... Guinns
Ogden ....Main St. Pawn
Ottawa .... Brown Hardware Co.
Overland Park .... Lucky's
Parsons .....Farran's Sporting Goods
Phillipsburg .... Finkbeiner's
Russell Friesen Army & Sporting Goods
St. Francis ......St. Francis Hardware
Salinas .... Cleves Marine
Scott City ....Bryan's, Inc.
Scott City ...... Claycomb-McDaniel
Topeka ....G. F. Y.
Topeka ....Maverick Gun Works
Topeka ..... Topeka Sporting Goods
Ulysses ....Gish Sporting Goods
Wathena .... Kaelins
Wellington .... Cooley's
Wellington .... Lawrence Drug
Wellington .Wellington Sporting Goods
Wichita ...... Hesse Sporting Goods
Wichita .... Lewis Bros.
Wichita ..Wichita Sporting Goods Co.
Winfield ..... Hyter Sporting Goods
Winfield ....Shooters Supply

Kentucky

Ashland .... Jay's Loan Co.
Bardstown .... Swap Shop
Berea .... Coffey's Gun Shop
Bowling Green
Aspley & Aspley Hardware
Brandenberg
Brandenberg Sporting Goods
Campbellsville .... Crabtrees
Covington .... Egelston Maynard
Elizabethtown .... Surplus, Inc.
Fulton ....Bennett Electric Co.
Fulton .... Railroad Salvage Co.
Glasgow .... Bob's Gun & Tackle
Glasgow .... Sports Shop
Greenville .... E. A. Cohen & Sons
Hazard ....Sterling Hardware
Henderson .... Paynes
Henderson .. Reynolds Sporting Goods
Hopkinsville ...Cayce Yost Hardware
Independence ... Cleveland Gun Shop
Lexington J. T. Barrick Sporting Goods
Lexington ....Phillip Gall & Son
Lexington .... Rosenberg Bros.
Liberty .... Reid's Gun Shop
Louisville Blue Grass Shooters Supply
Louisville ....S. E. Davis Co.
Louisville ....Davis & Son, Inc.
Louisville .... Sutcliffe
Louisville .... The Oakwood
Louisville .... Tinsley Gun
Louisville Umberger's Sporting Goods
Loyall .... Harco Distributors
Madisonville . Arnold Sporting Goods
Mayfield Look of Sky Sporting Goods
Mayfield ..... W. Kentucky Hatchery
Maysville ...... Maysville Sport Shop
Melbourne .... Jack's Sports Shop
Middlesboro .. Middlesboro Hardware
Moorehead ....Perry Hardware
Owensboro .... Cox Gun Shop
Owensboro .... L. Mahlinger
Paducah ... Ray Gage Sporting Goods
Paducah ....Jones Marine
Paducah .... Sportsmans Paradise
Paris ..... Ben Cohen Sporting Goods
Plesor Ridge Park
Sumners Sporting Goods

Louisiana

Abbeville ....Landry Stores
Alexandria Briston Marine–Hardware
Bastrop ...... Alan's Sporting Goods
Bastrop .... Bastrop Feed
Baton Rouge .... Bonfanti
Baton Rouge .... Sport Shop
Baton Rouge Steinberg's Sports Center
Bogalusa .... Land Of Sports
Bunkie .... Kenards
Crowley ..... Morrows Sports Center
De Ridder .... Kerns
Eunice .... Johnson, Inc.
Gonzales ....Gonzales Sport Shop
Houma ....Jones Sporting Goods
Jena . Jimmy Wallace Sporting Goods
Lafayette .... Southern Arms
Lafayette .... The Sportsman
Lake Charles .... Buster Keaton, Inc.
Lake Charles ..... E&M Sports Center
Lake Charles ...... House For Sports
Lake Providence ....Schneider's, Inc.
Manx .... Boyens Hardware
Minden ....Goodwill Hardware
Monroe ...... Gene's Sporting Goods
Monroe ....Haddad Hardware
Monroe ....Hunt & Whitaker
Morgan City .Spanish Trail Arms, Inc.
Natchitoches .....Deblieux & McCain
New Iberia ....Comptons
New Orleans .... Crescent Gun
New Orleans .. New Orleans Arms Co.
New Orleans .... Rolands
New Orleans .... Security Co.
Shreveport .... Arms Center
Shreveport .... Evans Sporting Goods
Shreveport . Harbuck Sporting Goods
Shreveport ....Lorants
Shreveport ....Otto Sport Center
Shreveport .... Turbocraft, Inc.
Shreveport W. H. Womack Riflesmith
Sterlington .... DeFee's
Tallulah .... Crawford Feed
Tallulah .... Johnson's Firestone
Thibodaux .... N. J. Gaubert
Ville Platte .... G. Ardoin & Co.
Westwego ....Coulon's

Maine

Ashland ...... Ashland Hardware Co.
Auburn ....Higgins Sport Center
Augusta .... Ft. Western Tire Co.
Bangor .... W. T. Grant & Co.
Bangor .... Morrison's Gun Shop
Bangor .... F. L. Wight Co, Inc.
Belfast ....Hall Hardware Co.
Belfast .... Home Furnishing Co.
Belfast .... Wm. B. Keswick
Biddeford ..... Major Frank R. Irving
Brunswick ....Atlantic Tire & Supply
Brunswick .... MacIntosh Outfitters
Brunswick ......Pelletier's Outfitters
Caribou .... Briggs Hardware Co.
Caribou .... Nelson & Page
Dixfield .... Drury's Gun Shop
Dover, Foxcroft . Western Auto Store
East Orland .... R. W. Neider
East Wilton ....Rolfe Maingas
Ellsworth .... Maddock's Sport Shop
Ellsworth ... H. F. Wescott Hardware Co., Inc.
Fairfield ....Joseph's Outlet
Farmington .... Pearson's
Fort Kent ..... A. J. Neadeau & Son
Fort Kent .... A. D. Soucy Co.
Freeport ...... Freeport Hardware Co.
Greenville ....Sander's Store
Halldwell .... H. L. Nilson
Houlton .... Almon H. Fogg Co.
Houlton .... Rod & Gun
Kennebunk ...... R. W. Libby & Son
Kittery .... Kittery Trading Post
Kittery ..Tom Taylor Sporting Goods
Kittery ....Webber's Sporting Goods
Lewiston .... Wise Pawn Shop
Lincoln ....Lincoln Sport Shop
Livermore Falls ...... Ed's Gun Shop
Livermore Falls
C. H. Newcomb Sporting Goods
Madawaska .. Madawaska Sport Shop
Milford .... Gun-Craft
Millinockett
Hikel Bros. Sporting Goods
Milo .... Milo Sport Shop
Norway ....Woodman's
North Windham .Sebago Trading Post
Old Town ......Ross Sporting Goods
Pittsfield ....White's Gun Shop
Portland ...... Carl's Sporting Goods
Portland
Porteous Mitchell Sporting Shop
Portland .... Tommy's Hardware Co.
Portland ......Whitmore's Gun Shop
Presque Isle ..... Roy's Army & Navy
Rockland .... H. H. Cree & Co.
Rumford ....Hamannes
Rumford .... Rumford Surplus
Saco .... Kennedy's Tackle
Saco .... King's Fly Shop
Skowhegan ....Cross Hardware
South Waterford Yankee Gunsmith Co.
Topsham ....Dick's Gun Repair
Waterville .... W. T. Grant Co.
Westbrook .... Knight's Hardware
Westbrook ....Paul's Gun Shop
Westbrook Tom Taylor Sporting Goods
Winslow ..... Proctor & Bowie Co.
Winthrop .... Audette's
Wiscassett .... Flood's Hardware
Wiscassett .... Harvey's Gun Shop

Maryland

Annapolis .... Bataskou Firearms
Baltimore ..... Baltimore Gunsmiths
Baltimore . Edmondson Hardware Co.
Baltimore .... Miller's Guns
Baltimore National Sporting Goods Co.
Baltimore ...... Peltzer's Sport Shop
Baltimore ....Schreiber & Jones
Bethesda .... The Sportsman
Brooklyn Park Marvin's Sport City, Inc.
Chevy Chase ...... Colony Arms Co.
Chillum .... Apple Hardware, Inc.
Cumberland .... Sport Shoppe
Denton .... Will's Sporting Goods
Easton .... Shanahan & Wrightson
Elkton .... Herbert F. DeWitt, Inc.
Elkton .... Elkton Supply Co.
Essex ...... Bayside Sporting Goods
Essex .... Marvin's Sport City, Inc.
Frederick ... Maryland Gun Exchange
Frederick ....Shipleys Inc.
Frostburg .... Prichard Corp.
Gaithersburg ....Robert L. Lindsay
Garrison Maryland Sporting Goods, Inc.
Hillcrest Hights
Marvin's Sport City, Inc.
Indian Head
Indian Head Sportmen's Den
Jefferson ....The Trading Post
Laurel ....Voss Sporting Goods
LaValle .... LaValle Sport Center
Mt. Ranier .... Bob's Gun Shop
Oakland .... Carroll's Sport Shop
Ocean City .. Elliott's Sports Marina
Pasadena ..... Bart's Sporting Goods
Quantico .... Dave's Sport Shop
Riverdale .... Atlas Sport Store
Rockville ....Custom Gun Service
Rockville .... Rockville Trading Post
Salisbury .... Morris O. Hammond
Silver Springs .... Atlantic Guns
Silver Springs . Potomac Trading Post
Towson ....Ponentos Supplies
Towson ....Valley Gun Shop
Upperco .... Duffy's Gun Room
Upper Marlboro ..... Bud's Gun Shop
Woodbine ... Carroll Shooters Supply
Worton . Robt. Elliott Sporting Goods

Massachusetts

Agawam .... Agawam Assocs.

Andover .... Dana's Sport Shop
Arlington ...... Holovak & Coughlin
Athol .... Epquoig Firearms
Attleboro .... Klebe Sport Shop
Ayer .... New England Arms
Bedford .... Jordan Marsh
Beverly .... Johnny Appleseed
Billerica .... Quirion's Rod & Gun
Boston .... Giordani Bros.
Boston .... Ivanhoe Sports Center
Boston .... Jordan Marsh Co.
Boston .... Kirkwood Bros.
Boston ... Bob Smith Sporting Goods
Brockton .... A. C. Grady Co.
Brockton .... Mammoth Marts
Brockton .... Sports World
Brockton .... Wetzell's
Burlington ...... Middlesix Gun Serv.
Buzzards Bay Red Top Sporting Goods
Cambridge .... Harvard Gun Shop
Cambridge .... Lechmere Sales
Cambridge ...... Roach Hardware Co.
Canton .... Cline's Gun Room
Chelmsford .J. E. Dominicis Gunsmith
Chicopee .... Kenneth R. Stich
Concord .... Macone Sporting Goods
Dalton .... Dalton Gun Shop
Dedham .. Dedham Sportsmen Center
Dedham .... Lechmere Sales
Dighton .... Carr's Trading Post
East Longmeadow .... The Gun Barrel
East Springfield . Thomason Gun Shop
Fall River .... Al Dexter's
Fall River ... Russ Gold Sporting Co.
Falmouth .... Gun & Tackle
Fitchburg .... Jake's Sport Center
Fitchburg ...... Peter Whitney Guns
Framingham .... Bretts
Framingham . Lew Horton Sport Shop
Franklin
Franklin Reservoir Sport Center
Gardner ..... General Sporting Goods
Greenfield .... Clark Sport Shop
Greenfield .... Geo. R. Jonelunas
Groton .... Frank's Sport Shop
Holland ...... Holland Sports Marina
Holyoke .... Ward Two
Hyannis .... Puritan Clothing
Lawrence .... Al's Rod & Gun
Lawrence .... Tom's Gun & Sport
Leominster .... The Sport Mart
Leominster . Werner's Sporting Goods
Littleton .... Frank's Sport Shop
Littleton Nashoba Valley Sport Center
Lowell .... Schulman's
Lynn .... Jerry's, Inc.
Lynn .... Pennyworth's
Malden .... Day's Sporting Goods
Marlboro .... The Gun Shop
Mattapoisett .. Capeway Sport Center
Maynard .... Victor Brociner
Medford .... Bernie Gould Guns
New Bedford .... McGees
New Bedford ... Smith Athletic Store
Newburyport . Chas. A. Carroll & Co.
Newburyport ... Narrow's Gun Shop
North Adams ... Bill's Sporting Goods
North Adams .. Center Sporting Goods
North Dartmouth . .Smith Mills Sports
Norwell .... Bradberry's
Norwood .... Ortin's Sport Shop
Norwood ...... Sandell's Sport Center
Orleans .... Goose Hummocks
Pittsfield ..... Ernie's Sporting Goods
Pittsfield . Dick Moon Sporting Goods
Pittsfield ... Pittsfield Sporting Goods
Plainville .... Custom Sporting Goods
Plymouth ..... M&M Sporting Goods
Salem .... Salem Army-Navy
Seekonk ..... Thompsons Sport Shop
Shrewsbury .... Underwood Arms
Somerville .... Detras
South Dartmouth .... J. M. Arsenault
Springfield .... Blair's Range
Still River ...... Bucky's Sport Shack
Stoneham .... Al's Gun Shop
Stoughton .... Corcoran's
Stoughton ... Stoughton Trading Post
Sudbury .... H. P. Stratemeyer
Swansea ..... Thompson's Sport Shop
Taunton ... Pierce Taunton Hardware
Townsend .... The Trading Post
Tyngsboro .... Forest Marine Co.
Wakefield .... Mike's Gun Shop
Waltham .... Scott's Surplus
Ware .... Sporting Goods & Blrds.
Wareham .... American Arms Co.
Watertown .... Ivanhoe Sports Center
Westboro .... Hawill's
West Boylston .... Never Fail Products
Worcester ..... Ivanhoe Sports Shop
Worcester ... MacBen Sporting Goods
Worcester .... The Fair
Worcester .... The Rod & Gun

Michigan

Ada .... Gilmore's Sporting Goods
Adrian .... W. Johnson Service
Adrian .... Mau Mee
Adrian .... Noveskys
Allegan .... Stone's Sport Shop
Alma .... Don Elsea Sports
Alma .... Van Attens
Alpena ...... Alpena Sporting Goods
Alpena .... Neuman's Tire
Ann Arbor
Ann Arbor Arms & Sporting Goods
Ann Arbor ...... Fox Tent & Awning
Armada .... Mac's Firearms
Auburn ..... Auburn Hts. & Hardware
Baldwin .... Eds Sport Shop
Battle Creek .... Frosty's
Battle Creek .... Lakeview Hardware
Battle Creek ...... Marine-Gun Shop
Bay City .... Breen's Sport Shop
Bay City .... Leo D. Goddeyne
Bay City .... Jennison Hardware
Beaverton .... Morris Hardware
Beaverton .... White's
Bedford .... Bedford Bait Shop
Benton Harbor .... Gardner's
Big Rapids .... Grunst Bros.
Bridgman .... Al's Sport Center
Bridgeman .... Daves All Sport
Buchanan .... Allen Hardware
Buchanan .... Sullivan Bros.
Cadillac .... Johnson Hardware
Cedar Springs
Log Cabin Sporting Goods
Charlotte .... Munger's Sports
Clare .... Grove Brothers
Clarkston ...... Lawson's Gun Shop
Clio .... Water Wonderland
Comstock Park
Comstock Park Sports & Hobby
Crystal Falls ...... Bauman Sports Inc.
Davison ...... Williams Gun Sight Co.
Dearborn .... Kenneth J. Budney
Dearborn .... Nichols Sport
Dearborn .... Wyoming Hardware
Dearborn .... Zims Sports
Detroit .... B&M Firearms
Detroit .... "EPPS"
Detroit .... Gell's Sporting Goods
Detroit .... Griswold Sporting Goods
Detroit .... Gun Rack
Detroit .... Maurie's Gun Serv.
Detroit .... Stephen T. Milford
Detroit .... Neumann's Gun Shop
Detroit .... Wessel Gun Service
Eaton Rapids ..... Appleby Gun Shop
Eaton Rapids .. Keeler's Trading Post
Escanaba .... Jerry's Sport City
Farmington . Budde's Sport Shop, Inc.
Fennville ...... Dickinson's Hardware
Ferndale .... Greakes Sporting Goods
Flint .... Art Beauchamp
Flint ...... Allsports Sporting Goods
Flint .... C-W Arqunco Co.
Flint .... Flint Tent & Awning
Flint .... Goods Sporting Goods
Flushing .... Central Distributors
Fremont .... Sherman Sport Shop
Gaylord .... Marzof's Alphorn
Gibraltar .... Dick's Gun Shop
Grand Haven . Hoby Bell's Sport Shop
Grand Rapids ... Al & Bob Sport Inc.
Grand Rapids ...... Bobs Gun Shop
Grand Rapids . Buikema Sport Center
Grand Rapids .... Custom Gun Shop
Grand Rapids .. Davis Bros. Gun Shop
Grand Rapids ... Godwin Sport Shop
Grand Rapids .. Kent Block Hardware
Grand Rapids Olsen Bros. Sport Center
Grand Rapids ...... Peck's Bait Shop
Grand Rapids ..... Roy's Sport Shop
Grand Rapids .... Wurzburg's
Greenville ... Daniel's Sporting Center
Greenville ...... Jack's Bait & Tackle
Grosse Pt. .... Detroit Gun Sight
Grosse Pointe Park ... B. McDaniel Co.
Hamtrack .... Jack Roy's Gun Shop
Harbor Spring ..... Harbor Gun Shop
Haslett .... William C. Roege, Jr.
Hastings .... Leary's Sport Ctr.
Hazel Park .... Gun Bugs Haven
Hillman .... Hillman Hdwe.
Hillsdale .... Tolan's Gun Shop
Holland .... Bobs Sport Shop
Holland .... Main Auto Supply
Holland .... Prins Gun Shop
Holland .... Superior Sport Store
Holly .... Cliff Dreyer
Houghton Lake Hgts ... Tuck's Hdwe.
Indian River ...... Northland Sports
Ionia .... Tom's Tackle Shop
Iron Mt .... Bert & Harvey's
Iron Mt .... Izzys Ski & Sport
Iron Mt .... Smittys Spt. Gds.
Ironwood .... Ben's Rod & Gun Shop
Jackson .. Beach & Heuman Sptg. Gds.
Jonesville .... H & S Hobby Shop
Kalamazoo ... Eastwood Plaza Sports
Kalamazoo
Miller & Boardman Sporting Goods
Kalamazoo .... Schau Powell, Inc.
Kalkaska .... Vallaro Sport Shop
Keego Harbor ...... Briggs Sptg. Gds.
Lambertville .... Wolverine Arms
Lansing ... Beck Bros. Sport Shop, Inc.
Lansing .... Britton's Sport Store
Lansing ..... McCloud's Gunsmithing
Lansing .... Norton's Firearms
Lansing .... Sportland
Lansing .... Vander Voort's
Lakeview .... Lakeview Sport
LaPeer .... LaPeer Hardware
Lincoln Park .... Hoods Gun Shop
Linwood .... Bid Pen Sptg. Gds.
Livonia .... Gell's Civilian PX
Ludington ..... C. R. Pederson & Son
Ludington .... Tuck Sport Shop
Mancelona .... Rays Sport Shop
Manistee ..... Freidrich Sport Shop
Marquette .... Gibb's Sptg. Splys.
Marshall .... Marshall Sport Shop
Menominee .... Lou's Sport Shop
Michigan Center O'Briens Trading Post
Midland .... Al's Sport Shop
Monroe .... Cooks Sportland
Morley .... Franks Sport Shop
Mt. Clemens ...... R. Krieger & Sons
Mt. Clemens .... Prevost Spt. Gds.
Munising .... Madigan Bros.
Muskegon .... The Outdoorsman
Newberry .... Dukes Sport Shop
New Buffalo .... Al's Gun Shop
Niles .... James Kehrer Guns
Novi .... Trickey's
Owosso ...... Johns Sports & Marine
Owosso .... Shippee & Smith
Paw Paw .... Sportsman's Corner
Pentwater ... Bob Maynards Gun Shop
Petoskey .... Bremmeyer Bain Co.
Pontiac ..... S. C. Rogers Sptg. Goods
Pontiac .... Simms Bros.
Pontiac .... Ralph E. White
Port Huron .... Docks Sptg. Gds.
Port Huron .... Northgate Sports Ctr.
Rochester ... Harold Freeborn & Son
Saginaw .... Moreley Bros.
Saginaw .... Peters Gun Shop
Saginaw .... Sam's
Saginaw .... Shea's Allsports
Saginaw .... Smith Hardware
Saginaw .... Vic's Sport Shop
St. Clair Shores .... Dunhams, Inc.
St. Johns .... Allen Dean Sport Center
St. Johns .... A. R. Dean Hrdwe.
Sawyer .... Peterson's Gunshop
Scottville .... Scott's Sport Store
Southfield .... Dunhams, Inc.
Southfield .... M. T. Sportsman Center
South Haven .... McKimmies, Inc.
Spruer .... Wills Gunshop
Sturgis .... Sportsarama
Sturgis .... Sturgis Sporting Goods
Traverse City ..... Hampels Gun Shop
Traverse City ..... Vaneenaam Hdwe.
Union City .... E. W. Merchants
Union Lake .... Dunhams, Inc.
Union Lake .... Simms Bros.
Utica .... Heide & Kidd
Warren .... Gell's Sptg. Goods
White Cloud .... Bob Osborne
White Hall .... Duck Lake Gun
Whitehall ..... Vern Scholl Sport Shop
Wyandotte ... G. C. Reloading Service
Wyandotte .... Ken's Gun Shop
Wyoming .... Bentley's Gun Shop

Minnesota

Alexandria .... Sports Center
Anoka ..... Great North Trading Post
Austin .... Dugans Sport Shop
Bagley .... Northland Sport Ctr.
Baudette .... Gambles
Bemidji .... Coast to Coast Store
Bemidji .... Lakeland Sptg. Goods
Brainerd .... King's Sptg. Goods
Breckenridge ...... Scheel's Hardware
Caledonia .... Coast to Coast Store
Calidonia ...... Otterson's Reloading
Deerwood ..... Deerwood Sport Shop
Detroit Lakes ... Coast to Coast Store
Detroit Lakes ...... Lake Sport Shop
Duluth .... Pike Lake Gamble
Duluth .... Reliable Co.
East Grand Forks Giese Hardware Co.
Ely .... Coast to Coast Store
Eveleth ...... Arrow Head Gun Shop
Fairmont ..... Coast to Coast Store
Fairmont .... Mahowald's
Faribault .... Mahler Hardware
Faribault .... Mahowald's Sptg. Goods
Farmington Farmington Shooters Sply.
Fergus Falls ..... Ottertail Ski & Sport
Fergus Falls .... Vores
Forrest Lake Bob Johnson's Sptg. Gds.
Fridley .... Traders Den
Hastings .... Gamble Store
Hibbing .... Big V Dept. Store
Hibbing .... Guy's Sptg. Goods
Hibbing .... Hyde Supply
Hutchinson .... Quade, Inc.
International Falls . Riley's Sptg. Goods
International Falls .... Totem Pole
Little Falls .... Pap's Sport Shop
Long Prairie .... Vic's Sports
Mahtowa
Arrowhead Ammunition-Firearms
Mankato .... Mahowald's
Marshall ...... Kenney's Sport Shop
Minneapolis .... Christys
Minneapolis .... Corries
Minneapolis .... Donaldsons
Minneapolis .... George's Gunsmithing
Minneapolis . Golden Valley Sports Ctr.
Minneapolis .... Guns Unlimited
Minneapolis .... Larson-Olson Co.
Minneapolis ...... Lloyd's Sport Shop
Minneapolis ...... Lyndale Hardware
Minneapolis . Minneapolis Outlet Store
Minneapolis .... Northland Sports
Minneapolis .. Ostroms Sporting Goods
Minneapolis .... Warner Hdwe.
Montevideo .... Gordy's Camera
Moorehead .... Sportland, Inc.

Moorhead .. Valley Gun & Sport Shop
Morris .... Cruze Electric
Mound .... W. S. Candell Co.
Mountain Lake ..... Jungas Hardware
New Brighton .. Twin Ski Sptg. Goods
New Ulm .... Retzlaff Hdwe.
North St. Paul ...... Olson Hardware
Ortonville ...... Coast to Coast Store
Owatonna ...... Bjoraker Sport Shop
Owatonna ..... Johnsons Sport Shop
Pelican Rapids ... Coast to Coast Store
Pipestone .... Strobers Marine
Ray .... Westerburg Gun Shop
Red Wing .... Carlsons Sport
Redwood Falls Nelson Schjaastad Hdwe.
Rochester .... Dale's Gun Shop
Rochester .... Dayton's
Robbinsdale .... Coast to Coast Store
Rochester .... Frerich's Hdwe.
St. Cloud .... Pap's Sport Shop
St. Cloud . Centennial Hdwe.-Spt. Shop
St. Cloud .... Scheel's Hardware
St. Cloud .... Thielman's
St. Louis Park .... Christys
St. Paul ..... Dolan Sporting Goods
St. Paul ...... Joos Bait & Sptg. Goods
St. Paul .... Larry's Live Bait
St. Paul .... Russell Bait Store
St. Paul .... Virales Sport Ctr.
Shakope ... Great North Trading Post
Staples .... Anderson's Hdwe.
Stillwater .... Stillwater Surplus
Taylors Falls .... Rivard's Sptg. Goods
Thief River Falls . Coast to Coast Store
Tracy .... Rignell Ace Hdwe.
Virginia .... Biss Repair Shop
Wadena .... Coast to Coast Store
Wadena .... Merickel Lumber
Wadena .... Wadena Hdwe.
Watseka .... Herter's
Wells .... Gun Exchange
West St. Paul
Suburban Hardware & Marine
Willmar .... Bill's Gun & Tackle
Willmar .... Nelson Hdwe.–Sptg. Gds.
Winona Blackhawk Shooters/Trappers
Winona .... Graham & McGuire
Winona .... Out-Dor Store
Worthington .... Coast to Coast Store
Worthington .. B. Lundgren Sptg. Gds.
Worthington .... Rickbeil's Hdwe.

Mississippi

Aberdeen ...... City Sporting Goods
Batesville .... Mize Hardware
Biloxi .... Pat O'Neal's Buy & Sell
Brookhaven .... Davis Sporting Goods
Clarksdale Compassi Sptg. Gds. & Hdwe.
Cleveland .... Dunlap's Hardware
Columbus . Chick Sharp Sporting Gds.
Corinth .... Clausel Brothers
Durant .... Waller Hardware
Greenville .... Riverside Hardware Co.
Greenwood ...... Glovers Spt. Goods
Grenada ..... Collins Sporting Goods
Gulfport .... Loflin's Gun Shop
Hattiesburg ... Hattiesburg Hardware
Hattiesburg ..... Smokie's Spt. Gds.
Jackson .... Barfield Hardware Co.
Jackson .... Tatum Brown
Kosciusko .... Attala Sporting Center
Lauderdale ... La Geose's Gun Repair
Laurel .... Sid's Trading Post
Laurel .... Frank Gardner
Laurel .... Thaxton's Sporting Goods
Lucedale .... R. F. Ratliff, Jr.
Meridian ...... Hammond Gun Shop
Meridian .... Maxey's
Natchez .... Rex Sptg. Gds.
Natchez .... The Sport Center
Pascagoula .... City Pawn & Gun Shop
Pascagoula .... Monti Market
Pascagoula .... Sportsman Center
Port Gibson .. Claiborne Hardware Co.
Sardis .... Hearn's Trading Post
Starkville .... Smith Hdwe. Co.
Vicksburg .... The Sport Shop
Winona .... Shooks
Yazoo City ...... Planter's Hdwe. Co.

Missouri

Advance Richmond Hardware & Lumber
Ballwin .... Depco Sport Supplies
Bel Ridge . Bailey's Outdoor Supply Co.
Bethany ...... B & J Sporting Goods
Brookfield
Beach's Sporting Goods Corp.
Cabool .... Durnell Sports Shop
Cameron .... Hawkins Store
Cape Girardeau ... Beards Sport Shop
Cape Girardeau Southern Boat & Motor
Carthage .... Carthage Hdwe.
Chaffee .... Whitaker Hardware
Chillicothe .... Frost Hdwe.
Clayton .... Kelly Sptg. Goods
Creve Coeur .... Essen Hardware
Dexter .... Chrisman Hdwe.
Edina ...... Patterson & Rose Hdwe.
Elvins .... Edgar Sporting Goods
Fenton .... Dennis Hdwe.
Gladstone ...... George Rogers, Guns
Hermann .... Gosen's Sptg. Goods
Independence . Maywood Sptg. Goods
Jackson .... L. C. Jenkins
Jefferson City Goodins Sporting Goods
Jonesburg .. Taynor's Sporting Goods
Joplin .... Carlson's Hdwe.
Kansas City .... Bargain City
Kansas City .. R. S. Bar Gun Collection
Kansas City .... Binting Hardware Co.
Kansas City ...... C. R. Specialty Co.
Kansas City .... R. S. Elliott Arms Co.
Kansas City .... Gateway Sptg. Goods
Kansas City ... J. S. Palmer, Gunsmith
Kansas City ...... Parkview-Gem Inc.
Kansas City .... Troost Gun Shop
Kirkwood ...... Casey's Sport Stores
Kirkwood ..... Central Hardware Co.
Kirkwood ..... Kip's Sporting Goods
Lebanon
Pearce Home & Auto Supply, Inc.
Lebanon .... Perry's Firestone
Lees Summit Seerban Yamaha & Sports
Lexington .. Pat's Army & Sptg. Goods
Liberty .... Boggess Hardware
Liberty ...... C. & C. Sporting Goods
Maryville .. B. & W. Sporting Goods Co.
Memphis .... Gundys Gun Shop
Merigold .... Hoyt C. Daves
Mexico .... Graf & Sons
Moberly .... Connorstire
New Hampton
C.C. Wilson Discount Sporting Gds.
Neosho .... Hickory Hill Ranch
North Kansas City .... Guns Inc.
Overland .... American Arms
Poplar Bluff ..... 303 Sporting Goods
Raytown .... The Sport Spot
Richland Gunrunner Gun & Saddle Co.
Rockport .. Opp & Prime Sptg. Goods
Rolla ...... Bruce A. Betts, Gunsmith
Rolla . Twitty True Value Home Center
St. Charles .... Faerber Sptg. Goods
St. Clair .... Custom Gunworks
St. James .... Plemmons Hardware
St. Joseph ... Hatfield Sporting Goods
St. Joseph .. Harry Heiten Sptg. Goods
St. Joseph .... Mr. B. Hardware
St. Louis .... A.A.A. Sptg. Goods
St. Louis .... Cassani Sptg. Goods
St. Louis ...... Central Hardware Co.
St. Louis .... Ernie's Gun Shop
St. Louis . Floyd's Auto & Home Sply.
St. Louis .... Goodmans for Guns
St. Louis .... K's Sporting Goods
St. Louis ... Kay's Photo & Optical Co.
St. Louis . Tom Mc Gregor Sptg. Goods
St. Louis .... National Sptg. Goods
St. Louis .... Nu-Line Sptg. Gds.
St. Louis .... Tom's Guns
Salem .... Malone's Sptg. Goods
Sedalia .... Cash Hardware
Springfield .... Consumer's Hardware
Springfield Jay Key & Gun Shop Service
Springfield .... Plaza Hardware
Sullivan .... Bruce's Gunshop
Summit .... J. Scott Jr.
Trenton .... Dean's Gun Shop
Trenton .... Guns
Villa Ridge
Farmers Wayside Stores, Inc.
Warrenton .... Eagle Point Farm
Wellston
Pearlman's Sporting Goods, Inc.
Willow Springs ...... Dave's Gun Shop

Montana

Billings .... Qs Sport Shop
Billings .... Reiters Marina
Billings .... Rerneking Gun Shop
Billings .... Scheel's Hardware Co.
Bozeman .... The Beaver Pond
Bozeman .... The Powder Horn
Butte ...... Franks Gun & Cycle Shop
Butte ...... Fran Johnson Sport Shop
Butte .... Phil Judd Hardware, Inc.
Butte .... Lucky Bug Shop
Butte .... The Sportsmen of Butte
Columbia Falls O'Neal Sporting Goods
Cut Bank
Davenport & McAlpine Hardware
Dillon ...... Sneed's Sporting Goods
Fort Benton ...... Harry's Gun Shop
Glasgow .... D. & G. Sport Center
Glasgow .... Jim's Husky Super Stop
Glasgow .... Tag-Markle
Glendive .... Coast to Coast Store
Glendive .... The Beer Jug
Great Falls .... Alsports Supply
Great Falls ...... Coast to Coast Store
Great Falls . Great Falls Sporting Goods
Great Falls .... Morris Sporting Goods
Great Falls .... Osco Drug 931
Hardin .... Clarence Beck
Havre ...... Bing & Bob's Sport Shop
Havre .... Buttreys
Helena .... Army Navy Stores
Helena .... The Four Seasons
Kalispell ...... Capps Sporting Goods
Kalispell .... Gamble Store
Kalispell .... Kalispell Mercantile Co.
Kalispell ..... Read's Sporting Goods
Lewistown .... Don's
Lewiston .... The Sport Center
Lewiston .... Van's Sport Center
Libby .... Sports Center
Libby ... The Caribou Sporting Goods
Livingston .... R. E. Dickensheets
Miles City .... The Sports Center
Missoula All American Sporting Goods
Missoula ..... Mau-Jones Sptg. Goods
Missoula ... Missoula Merchantile Co.
Missoula ... Playmore Sporting Goods
Missoula ..... Spears Sporting Goods
Missoula .... Bob Ward & Sons
Plentywood ..... Smith Farm Supply
Polson .... Polson Sports Center
Rudyard .... Sanvik Bros. Inc.
Shelby .... Hardware Hank
Shelby .... S. & Q. Hardware
Sunburst .... Big Sky Blue Shop

Nebraska

Alliance .. Professional Gun Shops, Inc.
Auburn .... Heskell Implement
Beatrice .... Uhl's Sporting Goods
Bellevue .... Woodle Hardware
Blair ..... Scheffler's Sporting Goods
Broken Bow .... Coast to Coast Store
Columbus .... Carlson's Gunshop
Columbus .... Persons Sport Shop
Crofton . Marlon Smith-Gambles Dealer
David City .... Vern's Gun Shop
Fairbury .... Bedlan's Sporting Goods
Falls City .... Lorenzo's Shoe
Fremont .... Baker's Sporting Goods
Fremont ...... Bennett's Gun Shop
Fremont ..... Thompson's Sport Shop
Grand Island .... Dubs Inc.
Hastings .... Sporting Goods, Inc.
Holbrook ... H. D. Minnick Hdwe. Co.
Holdrege ... Hilsabeck Sporting Goods
Kearney . Pollat's Sportsman Hangout
Lexington .... Ed's Sptg. Gds.
Lincoln .... Central Gun Inc.
Lincoln .... Golds
Lincoln .... Gun Rack
Lincoln .... Lawlors
Lincoln ... Western Gun & Supply Co.
Madison .... W. A. Lafleur & Son
McCook .... Joe Moskal Sptg. Gds.
McCook .... Rutts Store
Norfolk .... Gambles Store
No. Platte .... Boldt's Rod & Gun
No. Platte ... Glenary Gun & Gift Shop
No. Platte ... Young's Sporting Goods
Ogallala .... Coast to Coast Stores
Omaha .... Bahnsen's, Inc.
Omaha .... Brandeis
Omaha .... Canfields Dept. Store
Omaha .... Guncraft
Omaha .... Gun Haven
Omaha Mertz & Sons Dealers-Gunsmiths
Omaha Mondo's Sptg. Goods & Service
Omaha ...... Moneymaker Guncraft
O'Neill ...... Montgomery Hardware
Plattsmouth .. W. A. Swatek Hardware
Sidney ... Haworth Hdwe. & Sptg. Gds.
Sidney .... Reads Army Store, Inc.
Scotts Bluff
Lordino's Sports Products
Scotts Bluff ...... Sports Center, Inc.
Scotts Bluff ... Valley Sporting Goods
Trenton .... Trenton Sptg. Goods
Valentine .... Sandhills Sports Center
Wakefield ..... Fullerton Lumber Co.
Wayne .... Coast to Coast Store
Wisner .... Becker Hardware
York ...... Toms & Sons Sptg. Goods

Nevada

Boulder City ...... M. & T. Gun Sales
Elko ... Wallace's Western Sportsman
Fallon .... Fallon Sptg. Goods
Gardnerville ...... The Outdoorsman
Hawthorne .... A. J. Park Gunshop
Las Vegas ..... Christensen Shooters
Supply & Spt. Gds.
Las Vegas .... The Outdoorsman
Las Vegas .... Vegas Gun Traders
Las Vegas .... Vegas Village Dept.
Lovelock .... Davins
Reno .... Markfore
Reno .... Mount Rose Sporting Goods
Reno .... The Sportsman
Sparks .... Block Sporting Goods
Sparks ...... Greenbrae Sports Center
Sparks .... Saturn Sports, Inc.
Tonopah ... Wolfe's Desert Hdwe. Co.
Winnemucca .... C. B. Brown
Winnemucca .... The Reliable Co.
Yerington .... The Westerner
Zephyr Cove ...... The Outdoorsman

New Hampshire

Bartlett .... The Bartlett Trading Post
Bethlehem .... H. & H. Outdoorland
Berlin .... King's
Bradford . Dickie's Bait & Tackle Shop
Center Ossipee
The Gun Rack and Sport Shop
Colebrook ... Ducrets Sporting Goods
Concord . Frank & Bob's Supermarket
Concord ...... Haggett's Sport Shop
Concord .... Mickey Finn, Inc.
Derry .... Derry Trading Post
Derry . Great Northern Sports Center
Plymouth .... Ted Guinnan's Dugout
Dover .... Neal Hardware, Inc.
Exeter .... Vic's Market
Grafton .... Brewster's Guns
Groveton .... Emerson & Son, Inc
Sptg. Gds. & Hdwe.
Hampton .... K. & H. Firearms Co.
Hampton Falls .... R. P. Merrill & Son
Hanover .... Campion's Inc.
Hillsboro .... Halladay's Store
Hookset .... Riley's Sport Shop
Keene .... Gunsmith Association
Keene .... Vernon W. Maine

Keene ... Silver Dollar Guns
Keene ... Zimmerman's
Kingston ... Kingston Outboard Corp.
Laconia ... Paugus Bay Sptg. Gds. Co.
Laconia ... Shooters Service & Supply
Lancaster ... Connary's Sptg. Goods
Lebanon ... Welch's Jewelry
Manchester ... Mickey Finn, Inc.
Manchester ... Hanks Sport Ctr.
Manchester ... Lynch's
Manchester ... Bob Marks Sport Shop
Manchester ... J. J. Moreau
Manchester ... Ted's Sport Shop
Marlow ... Sand Pond Gun Shop
Milan ... Rays Gun Shop
Montvernon ... Reed B. Parks
Nashua ... Family Sports Center
Nashua ... Bob Marks Sports
Newport ... Bob's Sport Shop
Newport ... Rody's Gun Shop
No. Conway ... Robertson Store
No. Haverhill ... The Green Store
Pittsfield ... Volpe's Store
Plymouth ... Joe's Gun Shop
Portsmouth
Automotive & Electronics Supplies
Rochester ... Hooper & Carrigan
Troy ... Gus Adamson
Whitefield ... The Fournier Store
Wolfeboro ... Lakes Region Sports

New Mexico

Albuquerque ... H. Cook Sptg. Goods
Albuquerque ... M & W Sptg. Goods
Clovis ... Foster's Gun Shop
Clovis ... Wades Sptg. Goods
Deming ... White's Assoc. Store
Farmington ... Ross Sptg. Goods
Gallup ... Gallup Sptg. Goods
Hobbs ... Vandiver Hdwe.
Las Cruces ... Funk's
Las Cruces ... Gibson Products
Las Cruces ... Van Noys
Las Vegas ... Fur, Fin & Feather
Portales ... Nation's Gun Shop
Roswell ... House of Guns
Roswell ... Maxwell's
Roswell ... Wilsons
Santa Fe ... Tianos Sptg. Goods
Silver City ... E. Cosgrove, Inc.
Truth or Consequences
Zaid Fandey Sptg. Gds.

New Jersey

Asbury Park ... Bob Kislin's Sptg. Goods
Audubon ... Polly Bros. Inc.
Belleville ... Sportsmans Haven
Bellmawr ... The Sportsman's Lair
Belvidere ... Jackson's Sptg. Goods
Blackwood ... Jay's Sports Center
Bound Brook ... Efinger Sporting Goods
Bridgeton ... Busnardo's Sport Center
Camden ... G & P Archery
Collingswood ... Curriden's, Inc.
Dayton ... Dayton Gun Shop
Denville ... Denville Boat
Elizabeth ... Ross Sport Shop, Inc.
Elizabeth ... Solomon's Inc.
Flemington ... Al's Gun Repair
Flemington ... Hunterdon Sptg. Goods
Fords ... Zud Supply Co.
Frenchtown ... Art's Sport Shop
Garfield ... S. Meltzer & Sons
Glassboro ... Bob's Little Sport Shop
Hackettstown County Line Sport Shop
Harrington Pk. ... Roehr's Gun Shop
Highland Park Paul Tellier Guns & Amm.
Highland Park
Rutgers Gun & Boat Center
Hope ... Walker's Sporting Goods
Jersey City ... Cajo's Gun-A-Rama
Keansburg ... Yaqui Arms
Kearny ... Raven Rock Arms Co.
Kenvil ... Ammerman Sptg. Gds.
Lakewood ... S-M-A-R-T Services
Ledgewood
Ledgewood Outdoorsman, Inc.
Lindenwold ... Willis Sport Ctr.
Lumberton ... Staley's Gun Repair
Manasquan ... D. and H. Sport Shop, Inc.
Maple Shade ... Fellowship Gun Shop
Medford Lakes ... The Outdoorsman
Milltown ... Herman Treptow
Millville ... Jim Bolton Sport Shop
Millville ... Millville Sport Center
Monclair ... George H. Mc Carthy
Montvale Standard Target Amm. Reload
Mt. Ephraim ... Woodland Gun House
Mt. Holly ... Checker Auto Supply
Mullica Hill ... Oscar C. Jenkins
New Milford ... The Arms & Amm. Shop
Newton ... Gun Repair Service
Nutley ... Frank L. Samara Jr.
Oldbridge ... Edward E. Lucas
Paramus ... Morsan Paramus, Inc.
Paramus ... Ramsey Outdoor Stores
Paterson ... Paterson Rod & Gun
Pequannock ... Sportsmen's Den
Perth Amboy ... Fishkin Bros.
Phillipsburg ... Falks Dept Store 7
Pine Brook ... Wrights Gun Service
Piscataway ... Sportsman's Den
Pt. Pleasant ... The Sports Shop
Pomona ... Bernard J. Korsak
Pompton Plains Livingston Sport Center
Quinton ... Smith Gun Shop
Ramsey ... Ramsey Outdoor Stores
Red Bank ... Kislins
Ridgefield ... Service Armament Co.
Roseland ... P. J. O'Hare
Saddle Brook ... R. J. Enoree
Saddle Brook Targeteers Sporting Goods
Salem ... G. W. Cawman & Son
Scotch Plains ... Ray's Sport Shop
Secaucus ... Old Mill Trap & Skeet
Toms River ... Ficket's Gun Shop
Trenton ... Russo Rod & Gun Shop
Union ... Morsan Union, Inc.
Union ... Rosenberg's Gun Shop, Inc.
Union City ... Transfer Sta. Sptg. Goods
Vineland ... George Haughey, III
Vineland ... Petes Gun Shop
Wail ... Guy's Sport Shop
Washington ... Hi-Way Sport Shop
Washington ... Washington Sptg. Goods
West New York ... Levy's Inc.
Woodbine Colorado Sportsmans Center
Wyckoff Tom Norman's Sport Shop, Inc.
Yardmille ... Harry's Sporting Goods

New York

Albany ... Jim Maher's Sptg. Gds.
Albany ... Ressus Sptg. Goods
Albany ... Taylor & Vadney, Inc.
Amherst ... Al. Dekdebrunn
Amsterdam ... Guns
Amsterdam ... John E. Larrabee, Inc.
Astoria ... Sea & Land Spts. Co.
Auburn ... Byrn's Sptg. Gds.
Auburn ... Bob Nolan's Sptg. Gds.
Auburn ... Pearson's Spts.
Babylon ... Babylon Sport Center
Babylon ... Bill Boyce
Baldwin ... Norman Richman
Baldwinsville ... Firth's Firearms Co.
Ballston Spa ... Wurster Sptg. Gds.
Batavia ... Batavia Marine
Batavia ... Salway's Hdwe.
Batavia ... Trading Post
Bayshore ... Al's Guns Supplies
Bay Shore ... Gem Gun Shop
Bethpage ... Gun Gallery, Inc.
Binghamton ... Allen's Sport Shop
Binghamton ... Chenango Valley Shop
Binghamton ... Dick's Sport Shop
Binghamton ... Parks Gun Shop
Brewerton ... Brewerton Shop
Brewster ... John Knapp Sptg. Ctr.
Brockport ... Sportsmans Shop
Bronx ... Cromwells
Bronx ... Franks Sport Shop
Bronx ... Westchester Trading Co.
Brooklyn ... Ambrose Outdoor Store
Brooklyn ... Fortway Camera
Brooklyn ... Goodwear Sptg. Gds.
Brooklyn ... John & Al
Brooklyn ... Meteor Arms Inc.
Brooklyn ... Mandall Supplies Corp.
Brooklyn ... Ed Paul's Sptg. Gds.
Brooklyn ... Triangle Stores
Buffalo ... Allsport, Inc.
Buffalo ... Angert Auto Parts
Buffalo ... Downtown Gun Shop
Buffalo ... Dick Fisher, Inc.
Buffalo ... G & R Tackle Co.
Buffalo ... Outdoor Store
Buffalo ... H. L. Peters, Inc.
Buffalo ... Ted's Sport Shop
Canadaiqua ... Cole & Rae's, Inc.
Canastota ... Blakes Lee's Gun Shop
Carthage ... Lloyd's Gun Shop
Cassville ... Wm. J. Byers III
Castile ... Castile Gun Shop
Chestertown ... Beecher Brainard
Clarence ... Neubrand's Guns
Clayton ... Steele's Shop
Clinton Cors ... J. Dewey Service
Cohocton ... Ed. Hart's Guns
College Point ... G & G Gunsmiths
Copiague ... Lou's Arms
Corning ... National Sporting Gds.
Corona ... Jerome Kritz Serv.
Cortland ... Hines Service
Cuba ... Cuba Gun Shop
Deer Park ... Galaxy Firearms Co.
Delmar ... Thomas V. Corrigan
Dunkirk ... Lakeshore Sptg. Gds.
Dunkirk ... Walt's Sptg. Gds.
Elma ... Guy's Guns
Elmira ... Bensen, Jessup & Knapp, Inc.
Essex ... Al's Tackle Shop
Farmingdale ... Magnum Gun Co.
Farmingdale Morsan Farmingdale, Inc.
Flushing ... B & B Sptg. Gds. Co.
Flushing ... Empire Sport Shop
Freeport ... Fishing Hole
Freeville ... Hughes Guns
Fulton ... B & T Sport Shop
Fulton ... F. O. Stanton
Garnerville ... Zugibie Bros.
Geneva ... Harmon's Sport Shop
Glen Cove ... Lemp's Gun Shop
Glens Falls ... Goldstock's Sptg. Gds.
Gouverneur ... H. H. Loomis
Gowanda ... Western Store
Grand Island ... I. Rubin
Greenvale ... Greenvale Sport Shop
Hamburg ... Art Pfeiffer
Hammondsport ... Roy Jacobs
Harrison ... Harrison Sport Shop
Hempstead ... Hempstead Store
Hempstead ... Robin Hood Store
Henrietta ... Genesee Valley Shop
Herkimer ... C & D Sport Shop
Herkimer ... Maddy's Guns
Hicksville ... Mid Island Sports
Hillsdale ... Hillsdale Sport Shop
Holcomb ... Creekside Gun Shop
Hornell ... Scotts Gun Shop
Hornell ... Southern Tier Hobby
Horseheads ... Ray Hotchkiss Sptg. Gds.
Horseheads ... Wilkens Gulf Service
Hudson ... Steiner's Spts. Cntr.
Hudson Falls ... Juckett Sptg. Gds.
Hudson Falls ... Moran's Sptg. Gds.
Huntington ... Guns & Ammo Shop
Ithaca ... Gees Sport Shop
Ithaca ... Pearson's Sports
Ithaca ... Stone's Guns
Jamestown ... John W. Bollman
Jamestown ... Collins Sport Shop
Jamestown ... Lundquist Hdwe. Co.
Johnson City ... Southside Hdwe.
Johnstown ... Klena Bros.
Johnstown ... Lizio's Gun Shop
Kenmore ... Fred Hoffman Sports
Kenmore ... Loaders Lodge
Kingston ... Potter Bros.
Kingston ... Spada's Sport Shop
Kingston ... Jack L. Williamson
Kirkland ... Kirkland Armory
La Grangeville ... Kanuk Enterprises
Larchmont ... Clark & Finney
Lawtons ... Keoppen Gun Shop
Levittown ... Colonial Firearms, Inc.
Liberty ... Berner's Sptg. Gds.
Lisbon ... H. Bill Gray
Liverpool ... Wayne D. Burgess
Livingston Manor ... Willowemoc Shop
Lockport ... Cabin Range
Lockport ... John F. Collins
Lockport ... Dick Cummings Sptg. Gds.
Lockport ... Regan's Sptg. Gds.
Macedon ... Dean R. Newcomb
Mahopac ... Tom Kat, Inc.
Malone ... East End Hardware
Massena ... W. L. Smith, Inc.
Medford ... Phil Primrose
Medina ... Medina Trading Post
Melville ... Sportorama
Merrick ... The Outdoorsman
Middleton ... Gun Center
Middletown ... Bob Lounsbury
Middletown ... Royal Coachman, Inc.
Middleville ... W. Canada Spt. Shop
Mineola ... Mineola Guns, Inc.
Monroe ... Smith & Strebel Co.
Mt. Kisco ... C. S. Daum Sptg. Gds.
Mt. Vernon ... Fisherman's Center
Nanuet ... Lombard's
Newark ... Gerry's Trading Post
Newburgh ... Conover's Sptg. Gds.
Newburg ... M. C. Kinney Corp.
Newburgh ... Shapiro Sptg. Gds.
New Hartford ... Mohawk Trading Post
New Hyde Park ... Jericho Canvas Co.
New Rochelle ... Allen Sport Shop, Inc.
New Rochelle ... Parker Dist.
New York ... Abercrombie & Fitch
New York ... Continental Arms Corp.
New York ... Hermans
New York ... Harry Moss & Son
New York ... Wm. Mills & Son, Inc.
New York ... Paragon Sptg. Gds.
New York ... Rex Firearms Inc.
Newport ... Wm. H. Wheatley
New York ... Zirmo Co.
Niagara Falls ... Stanley Hohenstein
Niagara Falls ... John Di Salvo Sptg. Gds.
Norfolk ... Don's Guns
North Dartmouth. Ray Pease Sptg. Gds.
Northport ... Bowman's Sptg. Gds. Co.
North Syracuse ... Sports Mart Inc.
North Tonawanda ... Otto Walther & Son
Northville ... Rulison's Sport Shop
Odessa ... Odessa Hrdwe.
Ogdensburg ... Sports Mart
Olean ... Adams Sptg. Gds.
Olean ... Bluementhals
Olean ... Hopkins Sptg. Gds.
Oneonta ... Bill's Sport Shop
Oneonta ... Floyd's Gun Shop
Oneonta ... Stevens Hrdwe. Inc.
Oswego ... Ontario Sptg. Gds.
Oswego ... Oswego Guns
Palmyra ... Jim's Sports Un.
Parish ... Breckheimers
Parishville ... Harry Caringi Shop
Patchoque ... Royal Fishing Tackle
Pearl River ... Art Hoffmeyer
Penn Yan ... Ron's Gun Shop
Phelps ... De Vito's Sptg. Gds.
Phelps ... Tate's Sptg. Gds.
Pine Bush ... Town & Country Corp.
Plattekill ... Carperter's Works
Plattsburgh ... Larkin Camera
Plattsburgh ... Ray's Gun Shop
Port Jervis ... Deer Park Gun Shop
Port Jervis ... Tri State Sply.
Poughkeepsie ... Arlington Sptg. Gds.
Poughkeepsie ... Big Indian Gun Shop
Poughkeepsie ... M. Douglas Campbell
Poughkeepsie ... John N. Lucas
Poughkeepsie ... Wolf's Sport Shop
Prospect ... Prospect Reloaders Supply
Ravena ... Sportsmen's Trading Post
Remsen ... Robert Ainley
Rensselaer ... Jerry's Gun Exchange
Riverhead ... Edward's Disc. Ctr.
Riverhead ... Riverhead Sports, Inc.
Rochester ... ABC Sport Shop

Rochester . Commercial Sptg. Gds. Co.
Rochester .... Robt. W. Eve Guns
Rochester .... Dick Fischer, Inc.
Rochester .... Gun Shop
Rochester ....S. J. Hunting Lodge
Rochester .... Naum Bros, Inc.
Rochester ...... Slim's Sport Supply
Rome ....Mike's Sport Shop
Rome .... Wells Boat Shop
Rome ...... Dick Wilson's Sptg. Gds.
Saratoga Springs .. Savard's Gun Shop
Saratoga Springs ....R. W. Walton
Schaghticoke ....Beecroft's Gun Shop
Schenectady .. Goldstock's Sptg. Gds.
Schenectady ....Guns
Seneca Falls .... Hadley's Hrdwe.
Seneca Falls .....Moulton's Sptg. Gds.
Sherrill .... Sykes Sales
Sidney ....Marcy's Sport Shop
Silver Creek ... Frank Chiappone Store
Silver Creek ....Stoll's Gun Shop
Smithtown .... Smithtown Spts. Inc.
Sodus ....Cooks
Sparrow Bush .... Phil Bob Sptg. Gds.
Spencerport ... Big Ridge Sport Shop
Spring Valley ...... Palmach Shooters
Staten Island .... Harry Kaplan
Staten Island ......Nick's Gun Repair
Syracuse ....Gem Spt. Supply Co.
Syracuse ....W. T. Grant Co.
Syracuse ......Mulligan's Sport Shop
Syracuse .... Reliable Loan Co.
Syracuse .... Vad's Sport Shop
Ticonderoga ...... David Avery Guns
Tonawanda .... Dick Fischer, Inc.
Tonawanda ...... Seeger's Gun Shop
Tonawanda .... Sportsman's Paradise
Tonawanda .... E. L. Sweet & Son
Troy ....Andy's Sptg. Gds. Inc.
Troy ....Tigars Sptg. Gds.
Utica ....Highland Gun Shop
Wantagh .... Voehringers
Wantagh ....Woodside Studios
Warsaw .... W. W. Griffith Oil Co.
Waterloo .... Jarvis Auto Supply
Watertown ....W. W. Conde Hdwe.
Watertown ......Seaway Sport Shop
Watervliet .... Gun Shop
Waverly .... Jim's Sptg. Gds.
Wawarsing ....Geary's Sport Shop
Webster ....J. R. Rieger
Wellsville .... Carter Hardware
W. Hurley ......Numrich Arms Corp.
Westport .... Marshall F. Fish
Westport .... 'Trader' Robinson
West Sand Lake ... Miller's Gun Works
West Seneca .... Al. Dekdebrunn
White Plains .... Clark & Finney
White Plains .... Maletown, Inc.
White Plains .... Shooter's Shop
Wolcott .... Pettit's Gun Shop
Yonkers .... Ed. Agramonte, Inc.
Yonkers .... Vic De Mayos Inc.

North Carolina

Albemarle .... Lowder Hdwe. Co.
Albemarle ..... Stanley Hardware Co.
Albemarle ..... Bill Tobias Gun Shop
Asheville .... Don's Gun Shop
Asheville .... Doug's Gun Shop
Asheville .... Finkelsteins Inc.
Asheville ....Hunting & Fishing Splys.
Beech Creek .... Patrick's
Bostic .... F. E. Biggerstaff
Charlotte .... Builders Hdwe. Co.
Charlotte ..... Carolina Police Supply
Charlotte ....Collias-Lawing & Co.
Charlotte .... Collins Dept. Store
Charlotte .... Faul & Crymes, Inc.
Charlotte ....The Sportsman Inc.
China Grove ....Guns
Concord ..... Ritchie Hdwe. Co. Inc.
Conover ....Charlies Bait Shop
Davidson .... Dancy Arms
Durham .... Durham Sptg. Gds.
Elizabeth City ... Froggy's Sport Shop
Ellerbe ....Horton's
Fayetteville .Cumberland Pawn & Loan
Fayetteville ..... A. K. Mc Callum Co.
Fayetteville ..... Pine State Gun Shop
Franklin ...... Macon County Hdwe.
Gaston .... Carsons Spt. Gds.
Gastonia .... Akers Center Hdwe.
Gastonia ....Franklin Hdwe.
Gastonia ....Southern Supply Co.
GoldsboroMcBride & Herring Sptg. Gds.
Goldsboro ...... Music & Sports, Inc.
Greensboro
Dockery Lumber & Hardware
Greensboro ....Phipps Hardware
Greensboro .. Southside Hardware Co.
Greenville ....H. L. Hodges
Hazelwood .... Cline Bradley Co.
Hendersonville
Sherman's Sporting Goods
Hickory ......Clark Tire & Auto Sply.
Hickory .... Hickory Sptg. Gds. Co.
Hickory ... The Sportsman of Hickory
Hickory .... Walter Motors, Inc.
High Point ....Beeson Hdwe. Co.
Jacksonville ... Boom Town Furn. Co.
Jacksonville . Furniture Fair Sptg. Gds.
Kannapolis ....Ritchie Hdwe. Co.
Kings Mountain .....Phifer Hdwe. Co.
Lenoir ....Winkler Gun Shop
Long Beach ...... Save-U-Stores, Inc.
Morgantown ..... The Hobby Center
New London ....Pickler Arms Co.
Newport .... Eubanks & Co.
North Wilksboro ..... Swaffords, Inc.
Raleigh .... Hackneys, Inc.
Raleigh .... Hill's Inc.
Raleigh .... Thornes, Inc.
Raleigh .... Village Pharmacy
Roanoke Rapids
Harris Joyner Sptg. Gds.
Robbins .... Central Hardware
Rocky Mount ......Jim's Sport Shop
Rocky Mount .Joyners Athletic House
Salisbury ......Goodman's Gun Shop
Salisbury .... Salisbury Sptg. Gds.
Sanford ....Carolina Sptg. Gds.
Sanford .... Doyce Gregson
Sanford .... Mann's Hardware
Spring Lake ...... Woody's Gun Shop
Statesville ....Adams Sptg. Goods
Valdese ....Major Electric Co.
Wadesboro .... Cowick Porter Hdwe.
Walnut Cove .... Reynolds Gun Shop
Williamston . Griffin's Shooting Center
Wilmington .. Miller Trading Company
Wilson .... Stephens Hdwe.
Winston-Salem ... Bocock-Stroud Co.
Winston-Salem .... Ken's Gun Shop
Winston-Salem ... Pleasants Hdwe. Co.
Winston-Salem .. Wilson-Pleasants Co.
Zebulon ....J. W. Perry Jr. Store

North Dakota

Bismarck .... Roy's Gun Shop
Bismarck ......Sioux Sporting Goods
Columbus .... Miller Hardware
Cooperstown ...Tims Oil & Supply Co.
Devils Lake ....Gerrells
Edgeley ...... Ron's Sales and Service
Fargo .... Als Sport Shop
Fargo .... A. Beckers Sporting Goods
Fargo ....Scheels Our Own Hardware
Garrison .... Robinson Sport Shop
Grand Forks .....Tremys Sport Shop
Jamestown ...Gun & Reel Sport Shop
Leeds .... Miller Drug
Minot ....Dakota Firearms
Minot .... Gun Schmidt
Minot .... Harvey Enterprizes
Minot .... Northland Sptg. Gds.
Minot .... Northwest Sporting Goods
Minot ....Saunders
Riverdale ... Riverdale Sporting Goods
Rugby .... Bucks Sport Shop
Williston ....Coast to Coast
Williston .... Pangers Sporting Goods

Ohio

Akron ....Boyles Hunting
Albany .... Coe's
Alliance ......Alliance Gun Exchange
Alliance ......Dicken & Marshall, Inc.
Ashland .... D. E. Satterfield
Ashtabula ....William Limback
Athens .Swearigen Sporting Goods Inc
Aurora ....Joseph Prenosil
Austintown . .Sportsmans Trading Post
Avon ......Avon Hardware, Gunshop
Barbberton .... A. E. Bechter
Baltic .... Levi Yoder
Bedford ...... Bedford Gun & Tackle
Bellefontaine ....Paul Wammes
Bellevue ... Fennwood Shooting Park
Bucyrus ....Parsel's Gun Shop
Butler .... Main Hardware
Cambridge .... Vance Sporting Goods
Canal Fulton
Hillview Sportsman Supply
Canton .....Buckeyee Sports Supply
Canton .... Canton Hardware Co.
Canton .... Field And Stream
Canton ...... John's Sporting Goods
Canton ....Real Live Bait
Celina ....Heckler Hardware Co.
Celina ....Whitacre Gun Shop
Chesterland ....Hart Arms Co.
Chillicothe ....John S. Cole Shooters
.... Supplies
Chillicothe .. Hornstein Hardware Co.
Cincinnati Brendamour Sporting Goods
Cincinnati
Cincinnati Gun Specialists, Inc.
Cincinnati .... Pioneer Guns
Cincinnati .. Queen City Fire Arms Co.
Cincinnati ....Shillito's
Circleville ....Pettits Sport Shop
Cleveland .... A. A. Rod & Gun Shop
Cleveland ....Abele Davis Corp.
Cleveland . Clark Gun & Supply Goods
Cleveland Cleveland Custom Gun Shop
Cleveland .... Higbee Company
Cleveland ....Nash Shooting Supplies
Cleveland .... Newman Stern Co.
Columbus . Columbus Sporting Goods
Columbus .... Daves Gun Store
Columbus .... Federated Dept. Stores
Columbus . Graceland Sporting Goods
Columbus ....Kennedy & Son
Columbus .... Linden Hardware
Columbus .. Outdoors Sporting Goods
Columbus .... Zanes Gun Rack
Coshocton . Coshocton Sporting Goods
Coshocton .... Roscoe Hardware
Crestline .... Fisher's Sporting Goods
Crestline .... Shot & Shell
Dayton ....Cole Sporting Goods
Dayton ... Dayton Gun Headquarters
Dayton .... Jim Flynn Inc.
Dayton ...... M & M Sporting Goods
East Cleveland ....Heckman Arms Co.
Eastlake .... Imperial Firearms
Elyria .... Mens Shop
Fairborn ....George's Arsenal
Fairview Park .... The Dodd Co.
Findlay .... Douglas Gun Shop
Findlay ......Jacqua Sporting Goods
Findlay .... Rose Sporting Goods
Fostoria ...... Veres Sportsman Shop
Fremont .... Bruce Custom Guns
Fremont ....Fremont Gun Store
Fremont ...... Wassermans Gun Store
Freeport . Freeport Sportsman Supply
Gallipolis ... The McKnight Davies Co.
Garrettsville .... Fays Gun Shop
Glouster .... The Economy Store
Greenfield .... Greenfield
Grove City ....Pat's Gun Repair
Hamilton .C. A. Clark's Sporting Goods
Hamilton ....Roemer Hardware
Hanoverton ... Grant Dicks Gun Shop
Heath .... Rex's Gun Shop
Huron .... Lander Company
Ironton .... Bob Linn Sporting Goods
Kenton ...... Kenton Surplus Store
Kinsman ....Virgils Gun Shop
Kinsman ....Yorktown Gun Shop
Lancaster City News & Sporting Goods
Lebanon ...Bashfords Sporting Goods
Lima ....Crows Gun Shop
London ....Thomas Hardware
Louisville ....J. B. Metzger Hardware
Lowell .... John Huges Service Station
Madison ......Erbackers Sport Center
Mansfield ....Diamond Hardware Co.
Mansfield ...... Goetz Hardware Co.
Marion .... Hintons Sport Shop
Marietta ......Hoffs Sporting Goods
Marietta ....John Yost
Marion .... Idle Hour Sports
Massillon ....Hal's Sport Shop
Maumee .... Bobs Marathon
Maumee ..... Fleegers Pro. Hardware
Medina ...Albrights Sportsmans Shop
Middletown .... Allsports Inc.
Middletown .... Roberson
Middletown
Streifthaus Sporting Goods
Milford . Charlie Grossman's Gun Shop
Mt. Blanchard
Foster Hardware & Sport Shop
Newark ......Farquhar & Steinbaugh
Newcomerstown ....Bill Heifner
New Philedelphia
Sam Bond Sportsmans Supply
North Bend ....K. & W. Gun Shop
North Lawrence .Schrader's Gun Shop
Norwalk .... P. H. Fulstow Co.
Norwood ...... Geo. C. Burrier, Guns
Norwood .... Pioneer Guns
Orrville .... Martheys Sporting Goods
Orwell .... Huntley Jewelry
Oxford .... Ronnies Bait
Painesville ... Atwells Sporting Goods
Parma ....The Gun Shop
Peebles .... Lucas Hardware
Peninsula ..... Buckeye Sports Center
Perrysburg ... Lake Erie Marine Corps.
Piqua .... Davis Gun Shop
Ravenna .... Minards Sporting Goods
Rittman .... Chief Coins
Salem ....Williams Guns and Supplies
Sandusky .... Bogert Gun Store
Sandusky . Herb's Sportsmans Supply
Scio .... Scio Pottery Museum
Seville .... Jone's Store
Sharon Center .... Stauffers Inc.
Shelby .... Shelby Sporting Goods
Springfield ....George Meek Co.
Springfield ...... Reco Sporting Goods
Tallmadge ...Yorktown Custom Arms
Thornville ..... Gary Smith-Firearms
Tiffin ....Baik Bros. Co.
Toledo .... Gedert Gun Shop
Toledo .... Gross Photo Mart Inc.
Toledo .... U. Janney
Toledo .... Lickendorfs
Toledo .... Tackle Box-Inc.
Toledo ....Trilby Sport Center
Toledo .... Van Burens Gun Shop
Trenton .... Young's Gun Shop
Troy ....Jerry Dye, Gunsmith
Troy ....Troy Sports Center
U. Heights ..... Dratler Custom Guns
Upper Sandusky ... Lees Trading Post
Upper Sandusky
V. A. Mennigen Sporting Goods
Urichsville .... Bills Gun Room
Vandalia
Miami Valley Shooting Grounds
Van Wert .... The Gunsett Co.
Van Wert ....Tex Gun & Coin Shop
Wadsworth .... Russ Bordner Inc.
Waldo ... McClarens Sportsman Store
Warren .... Elm Road Sport Shop
Warren .... Sport Land
Waverly ....Hawley's Gun Shop
Westerville ....Accent Guns
Woodsfield ....Modern Hardware
Woodsfield ..Schwalls Sporting Goods
Wooster .... Forest Atland, Gunsmith
Wooster ......Pierces Sporting Goods
Xenia ....Dan Prindle
Youngstown ...... Austintown Tool
Zanesville ....Bonifield Hardware Co.
Zanesville ...... Glossman Hardware
Zanesville .... Niebel Sporting Goods

Oklahoma

Alva ... Gibson Products
Ardmore ... Lukes
Bartlesville . Lehman's Sporting Goods
Bartlesville ... The Sport Shop
Broken Arrow ... Hoods Sales
Chandler ... Lawrence Hardware
Claremore ... Wilson Hardware
Clinton ... Shamburg Sporting Goods
Drumright ... Smitty's Gun Shop
Duncan ... Murf's
Duncan ... Woolworth Dept. Store
Enid ... Larry Black's
Enid ... Zaloudek's
Frontier City ... Service Arms
Guthrie ... Bill Nelson Sporting Goods
Guthrie ... Martin's Sporting Goods
Guymon ... Kingsland
Hartshorne ... Hartshorne Hardware
Idabel ... Idabel Hardware
Mangum ... Cox Auto Supply
McAlester ... Diamond Hardware
Miami ... Beacon Hardware
Miami ... Forty Five Ranch Ent.
Miami ... Williams Hardware
Midwest City ... Service Arms Co.
Muskogee ... Oak Gun Shop
Muskogee ... V. F. Smith Sport Shop
Norman ... Norman Import/Export
Norman ... Sports Center
Nowata ... Titsworth Motor Co.
Oklahoma City
Andy Anderson Sporting Goods
Oklahoma City ... Ed. L. Kloss
Oklahoma City ... Mashburn Amrs
Oklahoma City .S. W. Shooters Supply
Oklahoma City ... Underwater Sports
Ponca City ... Chittum Gun Shop
Sands Springs ... Service Arms
Sapulpa ... Sapulpa Sporting Goods
Shawnee ... Baptist Hardware
Stillwater ... Murphy's
Tulsa ... Davis Stores
Tulsa ... Dong's Sporting Goods
Tulsa ... Froug's Dept. Store
Tulsa ... The Sportsman

Oregon

Astoria ... Kaufman's Sport Center
Astoria ... McGregor Supply
Bend ... Bob's Sporting Goods
Bend ... Ken Cale Hardware
Chiloquin ... Kircher Hardware
Cloverdale ... Bill's Guns
Coos Bay ... Fithian's Gun Shop
Coos Bay ... Stewart Sport Shop
Coquille ... Taylor Sport Shop
Corvallis ... Nixon Sports Center
Corvallis ... Les & Bob's
Elgin ... Houser Hardware
Enterprise ... Weaver Hardware
Eugene ... Eugene Gun Shop
Eugene ... Maxon's Gun
Florence ... The Sportsman
Gold Beach ... Morrie's Outdoor
Grant's Pass
Grants Pass Sporting Goods
Grants Pass ... Milo's Sporting Goods
Gresham ... Bonnell's Sport Center
Hood River ... Franz Hardware
John Day ... John Day Hardware
Klamath Falls
Joe Green Sporting Goods
Klamath Falls ... Hal's Sport Shop
Klamath Falls ... Sierra Gun Shop
Klamath Falls ... The Gun Store
Klamath Falls ... Totem Sptg. Goods
LaGrande .. W. H. Bohenkamp Hdwe.
LaGrande ... Choates
LaGrande ... LaGrande Outdoor Sply.
LaGrande ... Zimmerman Hdwe.
Madras ... Oscar's Sptg. Goods
Medford ... Lamport Sptg. Goods
Myrtle Pt. ... Suncrest Gunstock
Newport ... B and B Sports Center
Oregon City ... Coleman Electric
Oregon City . .Oregon Cty. Sptg. Goods
Pendleton ... Coast to Coast Store
Pendleton ... Darrel's Gun Shop
Portland ... Allison & Carey
Portland ... Bazar
Portland ... Bwana Junction
Portland ... Meier & Frank
Portland ... Nick's Guns
Portland ... Roberts Gunstocks
Portland ... St. John's Sptg. Goods
Portland ... Serafin's
Portland ... The Gun Room
Portland ... The Gun Trader
Prineville ... Bill's Sport Shop
Prineville ... Ernie's Sport Shop
Roseburg ... Umpqua Gun Store
Salem ... Anderson's Sptg. Goods
Salem ... Cascade Merc. Co.
Springfield ... Fireside Sports
The Dalles ... Mer's
Tillamook ... Hawkins & James
Toledo ... B & B Sport Ctr.
Union ... Reuter Hardware
Wallowa ... Wallowa Hdwe.

Pennsylvania

Aliquippa ... Sol's Stores
Allentown ... Nestors Sporting Goods
Allentown ... Phillips Dept. Store
Altoona ... Burkett Gun Shop
Altoona ... Helsel Hardware
Altoona ... Pioneer Gun Sales
Ambridge Ambridge Army & Navy Store
Ambridge ... Sol's Stores
Andalusia ... Robert S. Kraus
Ardmore ... Eylers Sport Shop
Beaver Falls
Valley Sportsmans Supply Co.
Bedford ... Beegle's Sporting Goods
Belle Vernon ... The Gun Rack
Bellwood ... Cornmesser Hardware
Benleyville .. Bentleyville Sport Shop
Berwick ... Cons. Supply Store
Bethlehem ... Marcus Sporting Goods
Bethlehem ... F. E. Weinland Hardware
Bloomsburg ... Lamatia Sport Goods
Blue Ball ... Shirks Saddle Shop
Braddock ... Wally's Gun Shop
Bradford ... Beezer Appliance
Bradford ... Lundins Sporting Goods
Bridgeville ... Stone's Sport Center
Bristol ... Aquarium Hobby Shop
Brookville ... Chestnut Gun Shop
Brookville ... Demans
Broomall ... Gordon's Sporting Goods
Butler ... Kirkpatrick Sporting Goods
Butler ... I. G. Klugh Gun Shop
Butler ... Kopies Gun Shop
Carbondale
Mermelsteins Sporting Goods
Carlisle ... J. B. Bixler & Son
Carlisle Sheaffer Bros. Sporting Goods
Carnegie ... R & D Gun Shop
Catawissa ... Susquehanna House
Chambersburg
Gale Diehl Sporting Goods
Clarendon ... Robert P. Ferry
Clarion ... Variety Dist. Co.
Clearfield ... Grice Gun Shop
Clearfield ... Paul T. Yoder
Clifton Heights .. Antique Firearms & Military Equipment
Clifton Heights ... Brooks
Clymer ... H & H Gun Shop
Coatesville
Commonwealth Firearms & Supply
Coatesville ... East End Hardware
Columbia Uncle Nev's Sporting Goods
Connellsville . Edenbo Sporting Goods
Conshohocken ... Walt's Sport Shop
Coraopolis ... West Hills Sport Shop
Corning Height ... Polly Bros, Inc.
Crum Lynne ... Joseph D. Dvornicich
Curryville ... Burgets Hardware Co.
Dauphin ... Wilson's Gun Store
Doylestown
Meininger's Sporting Goods
Easton ... Falk's Dept. Store
Easton . Grube & Betts Sporting Goods
Edensburg ... Shopp Sporting Goods
Elizabethtown ... Tropical Treat
Elverson ... Warwick Gun Shop
Emporium ... Grimones
Ephrata ... Ernie's Sporting Goods
Erie ... Decoys Unlimited
Erie ... Erie Sport Store
Erie ... Gorenflos
Erie ... Lighthouse Arms
Erie ... Kuharsky Bros., Inc.
Erie ... The Sportman, Inc.
Fairless Hills
Lower Bucks Safety Brake, Inc.
Farrell ... Sport Center
Feasterville
E. J. Malone Sporting Goods
Ft. Loudon ... Walker's Trading Post
Franklin ... Rearm Sport Center
Girrard ... Jim's Gun Shop
Glenshaw ... Kleber's Sporting Goods
Hanover ... W. E. Sell Sporting Goods
Harrisburg
Percy Hoffman Sporting Goods
Hatboro ... Chick's Archery Supplies
Hawley ... J. W. Nichols
Herman ... Eichenlaub Sport Shop
Huntingdon ... C. H. Miller Hardware
Indiana . Markles Sporting Goods Store
Ingram ... Sam F. Simpson & Sons
Jacobus ... Smith Village
Jacobus ... Straley's
Jeannette .. Mac's Auto & Sport Store
Jenkintown ... Paul Jaeger, Inc.
Jersey Shore . National Sporting Goods
Johnstown ... W. T. Grant Co.
Johnstown Gresh's Guns & Ammunition
Johnstown ... Overdorff Bros.
Johnstown . The Swank Hardware Co.
King Of Prussia ... Brooks
Kittanning ... McConnell & Watterson
Kutztown ... Beck Sport Shop
Lancaster ... Hoak & Yarnall, Inc.
Lancaster ... Reilly Bros. & Raub
Lancaster ... Shenk Bros.
Lancaster ... The Sportsman's Den
Lansdale ... Weingartner Sport Shop
Latrobe ... Army & Navy Store
Lebanon ... Parson's Sporting Goods
Leechburg ... Service Book Store
Lehighton ... Drumbore Gun Shop
Levittown ... Gateway Gun Shop
Lewistown ... Aurand's For Sports
Lititiz ... The Lititz Sports Center
Lititz ... Wholesale Shooters Supplies
Littlestown
E. B. Geiman Sporting Goods
Lockhaven ... E. H. Draucker & Son
Logantown ... Dean's Place
Loganville ... Klinedinst & Hopper
Lyndora ... Kopies Gun Shop
Mahanoy City
Varanavage's Shooting Supplies
McClellandtown ... 21 Super Market
McKeesport ... Leonatti Bros., Inc.
McKeesport . . Shader's Sporting Goods
Meadville ... Meadville Sporting Goods
Meadville ... Robbie's Sportcenter
Meadville Selby Almon Sporting Goods
Meadville ... Wolffs
Mechanicsburg . Ritter's Hardware Co.
Milford ... Sportsman's Rendezvoos
Millvale ... Flaigs
Milton ... Milton Sports Center
Monroeville ... Jacobs Sporting Goods
Morgantown . Muehlenberg, Hardware
Mt. Joy ... Ray Knorr Sporting Goods
Mountaintop ... Davis Gun Shop
Mount Union
D. C. Goodman & Sons, Inc.
Nanticoke ... Crawford's
Nanticoke ... D & R Discount House
Natrona Heights ... Joseph Horne Co.
Nazareth ... Nazareth Sporting Goods
New Berrytown
L. Guiswhite Sporting Goods
New Bethlehem . Evans Sporting Goods
New Bethlehem . . Forrester's Antiques
New Bethlehem ... Sayer's Truck Stop
New Britain ... Arts Surplus
New Castle ... Sporting Goods Co.
New Freedom
Young & McNew Sporting Goods
New Holland .. The Sportsman's Shop
New Kensington
Jacobs Sporting Goods Co.
New Oxford ... Joe's Gun Shop
New Providence
Scott's Trap & Skeet Supplies
Norristown ... Nesters Toys
Northhampton Was Den Sporting Goods
North East ... Hogue Gun Store
Northumberland .. Andrews Hardware
Northumberland ... Gun Rack, Inc.
Oil City ... Oil City Army Store
Oil City ... Sportsmens Den
Osceola Richardson's Sportsmans Store
Philadelphia ... Brooks
Philadelphia ... Colosimo's Guns
Philadelphia
James E. Duffy, Jr. Gunsmith
Philadelphia
Locks Philadelphia Gun Exchange
Philadelphia ... M&H Sporting Goods
Pitcairn ... Esman's
Pittsburgh ... Bolton Sporting Goods
Pittsburgh ... DeBay Sports Center
Pittsburgh ... E.J.H. Gunshop
Pittsburgh ... Martin's Gun Shop
Pittsburgh ... Myers Sporting Goods
Pittsburgh ... Firearms Unlimited, Inc.
Pittsburgh ... Honus Wagner Co.
Pittsburgh ... Joseph Horne Co.
Pittsburgh ... Huch Sport Shop
Pittsburgh ... Ideal Sport Shop
Pittsburgh ... Jerry's Shooters Service
Pittsburgh ... Kaufman's
Pittsburgh .. South Hills Sports Center
Pittsburgh ... Tackle Service
Pittsburgh ... The Swap Shop
Plymouth ... F. W. Woolworth
Polk ... Roy's Gifts & Firearms
Pottstown ... A. P. Giangiacomo
Pottsville ... George Derbes
Prospect Park Prospect Sporting Goods
Punxsutawney . . Williams Sport Center
Reading . . Bill's Bait & Sporting Goods
Reading ... Boscous East
Reading ... Kagens, Inc.
Rochester ... Smith Bros. Gun Store
Sandy Lake ... Lakeview Sport Shop
St. Mary's ... Dauers Sport Shop
St. Mary's ... Smith Sport Store
Scranton ... Evers Gun Shop
Sewickley ... Dempsey's Gun Shop
Shamokin ... Jones Hardware Co.
Sharon ... Beckdol's Sporting Goods
Sharon ... Gene's Gun Repair Shop
Sharon ... The Sportsman's Shop
Sharpsburg ... L. B. Arms
Shippenville ... Bill's Sport Shop
Shippenville
Chamberlain Sporting Goods
Slippery Rock ... Big Buck Gun Shop
Somerset ... Somerset Sport Shop
Springfield ... Earl Freas
Stahlstown ... Dicks Barber
State College ... Waltz Sporting Goods
Tamaqua ... P. & B. Sporting Goods
Telford .. Indian Valley Sports Center
Telford ... Shooters Den
Tionesta . Forest County Sport Center
Titusville ... Bryan Hardware, Inc.
Titusville ... S. C. Hopkins
Tremont ... Tremont Hardware, Co.
Tyrone ... Burley Bros.
Upper Darby ... Brooks
Upper Darby ... Joffe's Gun Shop
Upper Darby ... Llanerch Gun Shop
Warren ... Farr's Sporting Goods
Warren ... Finley Sporting Goods
Warren ... Goosheven Gun Shop
Washington ... Ace Auto
Washington ... Coen Oil Co.
Washington ... National Retail Stores

Washington ... Reeves Sporting Goods
Waynesburg .... Mac's Hardware
Waynesburg . Joe Riggs Sporting Goods
West Chester ... Briggs Sporting Goods
West Chester .... The Gun Shop
West Reading .. Wiests Sporting Goods
Whitehall .... Joseph Horne Co.
Wilkinsburg . Braverman Arms Co. Inc.
Williamsport
E. L. Blair & Co Sporting Goods
Williamsport .. Handy Home & Sports
Williamsport
Harders Sporting Goods Co.
Williamsport .... Lenny's Sports
Willow Street .... Clair Frank
Willow Street ... Don Greenawalt Guns & Shooting Supplies
Windber .... Good Shooting Supplies
Wyncote .... Polly Bros.
Wyoming ..... Carey's Sporting Goods
York .... Lincoln Hiway Garage
York
C. Patterson & Son Sporting Goods
York ... Scott Stevens Sporting Goods
York .... Stonybrook Sporting Goods
York ..... Wolfgang's Sporting Goods

Rhode Island

Coventry Ctr., ... Wm. G. Gessner, Sr.
Cranston ... Champ's Custom Loading
Cranston ...... Elmwood Sport Shop
Cranston .... Quick Sports Haven
East Greenwich .... Sportsmen's Shop
East Providence ... G & M Sport Center
Hope .... Lowell Gun Shop
Newport .... Don's Sports
Newport ..... Ryan's Sporting Goods
North Kingston . Quonset Sports Haven
Portsmouth .... R. M. Keshura
Providence ... Jimmy's Custom Guns
Providence ...... Malt's Gun Service
Smithfield .... Hunting Lodge
Warwick .... Commander Bob's

South Carolina

Aiken .... Hobby House Marine
Anderson ... Anderson Hardware Co.
Anderson .... Grady's Sport
Barnwell .... 300 Gun Shop
Charleston .... Norvell's
Columbia ... Columbia Gun Exchange
Columbia .... S. B. McMasters
Dillon .... Winesett's
Easley .... Pepper Hardware
Florence .... Barringer Hardware
Greenville .... Belk Simpson
Greenville .... Putnam's
Greenwood .... Jack Ellenberg
Marion .... Manning Jolly, Jr.
Mt. Carmel .... D. J. McAllister
North Charleston ..... S & S Gun Shop
Newberry . Frank Lominack Hardware
Orangeburg ... J. W. Smoak Hardware
Spartanburg .... Hoffman Fur
Summerton .... Grayson-Elliott
Summerville .. Old River Rd. Antiques
Sumter .... Carolina Hardware
Ulmer .... Palmetto Antiques
Westminster .. Randy's Gun Exchange

South Dakota

Aberdeen ...... Coast To Coast Store
Aberdeen .... Leftys Bait
Arlington .... Maxwells
Belle Fourche Pioneer Sporting Goods
Brookings .... Bills Sport Shop
Chamberlain ...... Trusty's Gun Shop
Clark .... Kyles Hardware
Deadwood .... Olson's Gun
Deadwood .... Stearn & Shedd
DeSmet .... Ollies Auto Electric
Howard .... Dons Sporting Center
Huron .... Huron Surplus & Guns
Huron .... Mahowald Hardware
Huron .... U. S. Army Surplus
Minot ..... Saunders Sporting Goods
Mitchell .... Leader Hardware
Pierre .... Coast To Coast Store
Pierre .... Hinseys Oahe Sport Shope
Rapid City .... Du Ell Sporting Goods
Rapid City .... Robbies Gun Shop
Rapid City .... Sport Club
Rapid City .... The Powder Horn
Sioux Falls . Hunting & Fishing Supply
Sioux Falls .... Johns Sporting Goods
Sioux Falls
Olsen Marine & Sporting Goods
Sioux Falls ... West Sioux Falls Hdwe.
Valley Springs ...... Big 45 Gun Shop
Vermillion . Thompson O. K. Hardware
Watertown .... Nelson Ace Hardware
Yankton
Kennys Service & Sporting Goods

Tennessee

Bristol .... Bristol Hardware Corp.
Athens .... Cherokee Hardware
Cerro Gordo ...... Harbour Pitts Co.
Chattanooga .. Olson's Gun & Supplies
Chattanooga ... Terminal Loan Office
Chattanooga .. W. A. Wood Supply Co.
Clarksville ..... Kennedy's Gun Shop
Clarksville ... N. P. C. Sportsman Store
Cleveland .... Economy Auto Supply
Cookeville
Brown & Watson Sporting Goods
Cookeville ..... Mid-State Sport Shop
Cowan .... Sport City Sales
Crossville . Crossville Surplus & Salvage
Dickson ..... Nick's Hardware Co, Inc.
Dickson .... Roger Hamilton
Elizabethton . Mack Roller Sport Shop
Fairview .... M. T. Wallace & Son
Fayetteville ..... Goodrich Hardware
Franklin .... Sparkman-Ethridge
Gallatin .... Ed Mack Sport Center
Greenville ..... Richards Trading Post
Harriman .... Harrison Sporting Goods
Hendersonville .... Russell's Gun Shop
Hohenwald . Ray Grimes Hardware Co.
Jackson .. Ham Howse Sporting Goods
Jackson
Travis Johnson's Sporting Goods
Johnson City .... Ben's Sport Shop
Johnson City .... Londons
Kingsport Dobyn's-Taylor Hardware Co.
Kingsport .... Lynn Garden Hardware
Knoxville .... Athletic House
Knoxville
Fowler & Irick Sporting Goods
Knoxville .... Millers
Knoxville .... United Loan Co.
Knoxville .... Zayres
Lawrenceburg .... Rayfield Hardware
Leach ..... Goodsuns Sporting Goods
Lewisburg ...... Turner Auto Supply
Livingston .... Roberts Hardware
Livingston ..... Speck Bros. Hardware
Loudon .... Greer's Inc.
Maryville .... Mosers
McMinnvillee . Brown Reloading Center
McMinnville . McMinnville Boat Center
McMinnville .... Sportsman Den
Memphis .... B & B Sales Co.
Memphis ... Mid-Continent Armament
Memphis .... University Arms
Memphis .... York Arms Co.
Morristown ..... Cox Sporting Goods
Morristown .... Firestone Store
Morristown Hasson Bryan Hardware Co.
Nashville ... American Firearms, Inc.
Nashville ...... Bob's Sporting Goods
Nashville ...... Clay's Sporting Goods
Nashville ...... Gun City U.S. A. Inc.
Nashville .... Sportsman Store
Newport .... Buck's Pawn Shop
Oak Ridge ..... Oak Ridge Disc. Store
Pulaski .... Abernathy Hardware
Pulaski .... Blue Bird Sporting Goods
Santa Fe .... Leon's Gun Shop
Savannah ..... Tenn Tusky Fisherman
Sevierville ..... Carl Ownby Hardware
Shelbyvilie .... Martin & Price
Signal Mountain .... Brown Bros.
Sparta ...... Jimmy's Sporting Goods
Tullahoma .... Whit's Sport Shop
Union City .... Turner Kirkland
Wartburg .... Shannon's
Waynesboro .. Waynesboro Hardware
Whitehaven .... York Arms Co.
Winchester .... Judges Gun Shop

Texas

Abilene .... Bible Hardware
Abilene .... The Mackey Co.
Alice .... Alice Hardware Co.
Amarillo .... Amarillo Traders
Amarillo ...... H&H Sporting Goods
Amarillo .... Tom & Roy's Gun Shop
Amarillo .. Vance Hall Sporting Goods
Athens . Montgomery Sporting Goods
Atlanta .... Price Hardware Co.
Austin .... Chuck's Gun Shop
Austin ...... Chas. P. Davis Hardware
Austin E. R. Haire Custom Stockmaker
Austin .... McBride Gun Shop
Austin .... Oshmans
Austin .... Petmeckys
Bandera .... B. F. Langford
Bay City .... Denn Bros.
Bay City .... Oshmans
Beaumont .... Kyle's Inc.
Beaumont . McKnights Sporting Goods
Beeville ...... Burrows Hardware Co.
Beeville ..... Roberts & McKenzie, Inc.
Big Springs . Big Springs Hardware Co.
Borger .... Wicks Sporting Goods
Brownsville ...... J. H. Batsell & Sons
Brownsville .... Brownsville Hardware
Brownwood .... Weakley Watson
Center ..... Payne & Payne Hardware
Cleveland ...... Cleveland Hardware
Colorado City ...... Taylor Hardware
Corpus Christi
Connally's Shooters Supplies
Corpus Christi .... Oshmans
Corpus Christi ...... Texas Gun Clinic
Corpus Christi
Wehring-Matthews Hardware Co.
Cuero ... Wagner Hardware & Machine
Dallas .... Buckhorn Trading Post
Dallas .... Cullum & Boren Co.
Dallas .... Gibson
Dallas .... Ketchum & Killum
Dallas .... Bill Lundgren's Guns
Dallas .... Moore-Ehler Co.
Dallas .... Navy Exchange
Dallas
Ray's Hardware & Sporting Goods
Dallas .... Wiley's Gun
Del Rio .... Shively's Gun Shop
Del Rio .... Russell Hardware
Denison ...... Dusek Sporting Goods
Denton .... Denton Sports Center
Denton .... Pierces
Dumas .... Phillips & Sons
Eagle Pass .... Eagle Hardware
ElCampo .... The Sports Center
ElCampo . Mack J. Webb Hardware Co.
El Paso .... Beav's Sport Shop
El Paso ...... El Paso Sporting Goods
El Paso .... Firearms Inc.
El Paso .... Hellier Co.
El Paso .... Orville C. Kuberski
El Paso ...... Popular Dry Goods Co.
Falfurrias .... Forsyths
Floydada .... Kirk & Son Hardware
Ft. Worth .... B-Square Company
Ft. Worth .... Cross Gun Shop
Ft. Worth .... Knights Gun Store
Ft. Worth .... Leonard's Dept. Store
Ft. Worth .... Lowell Pruett
Ft. Worth .... Manning's Disc.
Ft. Worth .... Noble Firearms
Fredericksburg .... Probst
Fredericksburg .... The Sports Center
Freeport .... Firestone Store
Galveston .... Skains Sporting Goods
Gatesville ... Jim Miller's Army Store
Goliad .... Ramseys Inc.
Grand Prairie . Henry's Sporting Goods
Grapevine
Jess Stockwell Shooters Supply
Groves .... Keith Hardware
Hamilton
George W. Chambless Sporting Goods
Halingen .... The Sportsman
Hearne .... Gables Auto Supply
Henrietta .... Moore's Hardware
Hillsboro .... House Lumber Co.
Hondo .... Gaines Store
Houston .... Britts
Houston .... Consolidated Aero
Houston .... Deep River Armory, Inc.
Houston .... Foleys
Houston ...... Heights Tackle House
Houston .... W. A. Holt Inc.
Houston .... Houston Sport Shop
Houston .... Joskes
Houston .... Oshmans
Houston .... Texas Gun Clinic
Houston .... Zero Gun Shop
Junction .. Chenault's Sporting Goods
Katy .... Gene's Sport Shop
Kermit .... Blakes Sport Goods
Kerrville .... Chas. Schreiner Co.
Kilgore ...... Adams Sporting Goods
Kingsville ... Ed Byrne Furn. & Appl.
Laredo .... Beckelhymers
Laredo .... Guerra Hardware
Longview ..... H & T Sporting Goods
Los Saenz .. Gonzales Merchantile Co.
Lubbock .... A. Acme Pawn Shop
Lubbock .... Farmer's Exchange
Lufkin ... Abney & Medford Hardware
Lufkin .... Haygood's Sporting Goods
Marshall .... Logan & Whaley
Marshall .... Manlys
McAllen .... Broadway Hardware
McAllen .... J.B. Guthrie Co.
McAllen .... The Sportsman
McAllen .... Valley Sports Shop
Mercedes .... Borderland Hardware
Mineral Wells . . Davidson Hardware Co.
Mission Mission Hardware & Supply Co.
Monahans ..... Lyle's Sporting Goods
Nacogdoches ..... Cason Monk & Co.
Nacogdoches
Nacogdoches G. I. Supplies
New Braunfels ...... Louis Henne Co.
Odessa .... Ace Pawn Shop
Odessa ..... Roberts Hardware Supply
Odessa .... Texas Wholesale Supply
Orange .... Guns' N Gadgets
Orange .... The Sportsman Shop
Pampa .... Addington's Western Store
Paris .... Williams Sporting Goods
Pasadena ... Pasadena Sporting Goods
Pleasanton ...... Fred Krause Supply
Port Arthur .... Kens Gun Clinic
Port Arthur Wil Moritz Sporting Goods
Port Arthur
Bill Warren's Sportsmans Shop
Port Lavaca .... Oshmans
Richardson
Hank's Sporting & Shooting Supplies
Rockdale .... Spuds Gun Shop
Rosenberg
Rude & Sons Hardware & Sporting
San Angelo .... B & B Trading Co.
San Angelo . Sammons Sporting Goods
San Antonio Bowman Sporting Goods
San Antonio . Dillard's Sporting Goods
San Antonio .... Kaufmans Inc.
San Antonio .... Joskes
San Antonio .. Nagel's Sporting Goods
San Antonio .... Potchernicks
San Antonio .... Topperweins
San Antonio
Gene Toudouze Hardware Co.
San Juan .... Valley Hardware
San Saba .... San Saba Hardware
Seguin ...... Sageveil Sporting Goods
Seguin .... Vivroux Hardware Co.
Sherman .... Sanders Sporting Goods
Snyder ... Fish Newton Hardware Co.
South Houston .... K-M Shooters
Sweetwater .... Turner Hardware

Texarkana .... Riley's Sporting Goods
Texas City .... Busbee's Hardware
Texas City ...Trout's Sporting Goods
Tyler .... Mac's Gun Shop
Tyler . Bob Reynolds Custom Gunshop
Victoria .... Firestone Store
Victoria .... Zac Lentz Hardware
Victoria .... Victoria Hardware
Waco .... Cogdells
Waco .... Holt's Sporting Goods
Weslaco .... Borderland Hardware
Wichita Falls ... G & C Sporting Goods
Wichita Falls ... Holt's Sporting Goods

Utah

American Fork
Robinson Sporting Goods
Brigham City Thompson Sporting Goods
Cedar City .... Hunter Hardware
Heber City .... Ashton Pro
Lehi .... Hutch's Pro
Logan .... Al's Sporting Goods
Logan .... Sunset Sporting Goods
Magna .... Falvo's Sporting Goods
Moab .... Custom Ammo
Moab .... Miller's
Murray ...... Jerry's Sporting Center
Murray .... Trail Sports Center
Ogden .... Armstrong Sporting Goods
Ogden .... Gift House
Ogden .... Kammeyer's
Ogden .... Kent's Shooters Supply
Ogden ...... Sunset Sporting Goods
Ogden .... Williamson's Sports
Orem .... Burr's
Orem .... The Sportsman
Price .... Price Trading Co.
Provo .... Innes Sporting Goods
Provo .... Provo Sporting Goods
Roy .... Sunset Sporting Goods
St.George .... Nelson Supply
St.George .... Pickett Lumber
Salt Lake City .... Auerbach's
Salt Lake City ..... Beehive Antiques
Salt Lake City .... Chris & Dick's
Salt Lake City .. Duce Sporting Goods
Salt Lake City .... Gallenson's
Salt Lake City ...... Guns Unlimited
Salt Lake City .. Joe's Sporting Goods
Salt Lake City .... P. M. Guns
Salt Lake City ...... Red Front Store
Salt Lake City .... Shopper's Discount
Salt Lake City ... Skagg's Drug Center
Salt Lake City .... West Side Drug
Salt Lake City
Wolfe's Sportsman's Headquarters
Salt Lake City .. Zinik Sporting Goods
Tooele .... Sunset Sporting Goods
Vernal .... Sunset Sporting Goods

Vermont

Arlington .... Wisewood
Bennington
Ted DeMarco's Sporting Goods
Bennington .... Gun Rack
Brattleboro ..... Burrows Sport Shop
Brattleboro Clapp's Sporting Goods Co.
Brattleboro .... Sam's Dept. Store
Burlington .... Linden Gun Shop
Burlington .... L. P. Woods, Inc.
Enosburg Falls .... A. Brown
Fairhaven .... W. S. Lloyd
Lyndonville .... Edmund's PHC
Manchester Center ..... Cartridge Box
Morrisville .... A. Brown
Morrisville .... Thomas D. Hirchak, Jr.
New Haven Jct.
Lathrop Sporting Goods
Norich .... Devaux's Gun Shop
Rutland .... Lindholm Sport Center
Rutland .... Wilson's Sports
St.Albans .... Bushey Sporting Goods
St. Albans .... Sports Shop
St.Johnsbury .... C. H. Dana, Jr.
Shelburne .... White's
West Danville .... W. D. Hall
Windsor .... Joseph C. Meyette, Jr.
Woodstock .... W. H. Shurtleff
Woodstock .... Woodstock Sports

Virginia

Alexandria ...... Potomac Arms Co.
Alexandria .... Interarmco
Altarista .... Altarista Hardware
Annandale .... Dawson's
Arlington .... Sport Fair Inc.
Ashburn ..... Forest Farm Gun Club
Baileys Cross Roads . Atlas Sport Store
Bridgewater .. Rockingham Milling Co.
Bristol .... DeVault's
Buena Vista .... Douty Hardware
Buena Vista .... White's Hardware
Charlottesville .... Carter's Gun Works
Charlottesville . Wayne Greene's Sports
Charlottesville .... Chuck Kraft
Chase City .... Jeffrey-Lambert
Chesterfield .... Fred L. Cook, Jr.
Danville .... Booth White Sports Shop
Fairfax .... Jay Lee Sports
Falls Church .... Davis Gun Shop
Falls Church .... Kuhn's
Floyd .... Phipps
Franklin .... Whitley Hardware
Fredericksburg ..... Abels Gun Shop
Fredericksburg Fredericksburg Center
Galax .... J. C. Matthews
Galax .... Vass Kapp Hardware
Gladys .... Suddith's Gun Shop
Glen Allen .... Green Top Service
Harrisonburg ..... Landes Enterprises
Harrisonburg . Rockingham Milling Co.
Harrisonburg ... Rocking R. Hardware
Hopewell .. Carmany's Sporting Center
Keysville .... Hamner Bros.
Leesburg .... Thomas F. Stewart
Lovingston .... Eugene J. Baker
Manassas .... J. E. Rice Co.
Marion .... Robinson's
Martinsville Bryant's Sporting Center
Newport News .... Long's Sport Shop
Newport News Sherwood Hobby House
Norfolk .... Blaustein & Reich
Norton .... Nards Appliance
Petersburg ..... Dixie Sporting Goods
Poquoson ...... PoQuoson Gun Shop
Portsmouth ...... Harrell's Sport Shop
Richlands ..... Nat'l Sportsman Shop
Richmond .... Carwich Marine
Roanoke .... Colonial Gun Supply
Richmond ...... Harris Flippen & Co.
Richmond .... Sportsman's Shop
St.David's Church Kings Crossing Store
Salem .... Creasy's Gun Shop
Smithfield .... Allen P. Thacker
South Hill .... Jeffrey Lambert
Staunton ..... Worthington Hardware
Timberville ..... Rockingham Milling
Va. Beach .... Sportsman's Shop
Warrenton .... Clark Bros.
Warsaw .... Irondale
Winchester ...... Braddock Sport Shop
Winchester ..... David A. Falmestoch
Woodstock ..... Western Auto Dealer

Washington

Aberdeen .... Failors Sporting Goods
Aberdeen ...... Reiners Sports Shop
Anacortes .... Bryant's Sporting Shop
Bellevue .... Ernst Hardware
Bellevue .... Vernel Sport Shop
Bellingham .... H & H Sporting Goods
Bellingham Ira Yeager's Sporting Goods
Burlington ...... Kesselring Gun Shop
Castle Rock
Four Corners Sporting Goods
Chehalis .... Two Yard Birds
Chehalis .... Wisner's Gun Shop
Cle Elum .... Victory Sporting Goods
Colville .... Rambles Sport Shop
Deer Park .... Weber Hardware
Edmonds .... Custom Gun Service
Ellensburg
Will Strange Sporting Goods
Everett .... Everett Sport Shop
Longview .... Ed's Gun Shop
Longview .... Manchesters
Longview .... Spikes Sporting Goods
Longview .... Ted's Rifle Shop
Millwood .... Ed. Karrer's Guns
Moses Lake .... Tri State Store
Omak ...... Hendrickson Sport Shop
Oroville .... Fleishmans
Port Angeles .... Katz's Gun Shop
Port Angeles ... Mel's Sporting Goods
Port Angeles .... The Mart
Port Orchard .... Pete's Gun Shop
Raymond .... Odell's Gun Shop
Pasco .... Barrie's Sporting Goods
Puyallup .... Stoners
Renton ...... Seattle Sporting Goods
Richland .... B B & M Sporting Goods
Seattle .... Bon Marche
Seattle .... Ernst Hardware Co.
Seattle ..... Keth Peabody's Sport Inc.
Seattle .... Seattle Sporting Goods
Seattle .... Sportsman Supply Co.
Seattle .... Waffenfabrik-West
Seattle ...... Warshals Sporting Goods
Seattle .... Webbs Gun Shop
Shelton .... Guns
Spokane .... Amer. Int. Co.
Spokane .... Crescent Dept Store
Spokane .... Ed's Gun Shop
Spokane .... Sportsmans Surplus
Spokane .... Trap House
Spokane .... Two Swabbies
Sunnyside .. Amundson Hardware Co.
Sunnyside .... Killingstad Bros.
Tacoma ...... Deritis Sporting Goods
Tacoma .... Chet Paulson, Inc.
Tacoma .... Totem Guns
Toppenish .... Roeberry's Rec. Center
Walla Walla .. Brock's Sporting Goods
Walla Walla Drum Heller Hardware Co.
Walla Walla ..... Thrifty Drug Center
Wenatche .... Adams Sport Shop
Wenatchee .. Stallings, Adams, Conway
West Seattle ... Seattle Sporting Goods
Winslow ...... Anderson's Hardware
Yakima .... Anderson's Guns
Yakima .... Jerry's Gun Shop
Yakima .... Lewis & Sears
Yakima ..... Mellotte Sporting Goods
Yakima .... Ted's Sporting Goods

West Virginia

Beckley .... Keatleys Inc.
Bradshaw .... Davis Photo Service
Buckhannon A. G. Shannon's Hardware
Charleston .... The Gun Store
Dellslow .... Ed. Galasky
Elkins .... The Sport Shop
Elm Grove .... Millikens Gun Shop
Fairmont .... Lipsons
Fairmont .... The Sport Store
Ft.Ashby .... Dave's Gun Shop
Gassaway .... Byrne Hardware
Gassaway
Gassaway Hardware & Furniture
Huntington ...... Mac & Daves Loans
Keyser .... Graysons
Madision ..... Spencer's Sport Center
Marlington C. J. Richardson Hardware
Milton .... Morris Watch Shop
Morgantown .. McPhersons, Gunsmith
Moundsville ... Sullivan Gun Specialty
New Martinsville ..... Allen O. Pinner
New Martinsville ..... The Sport Shop
Nitio .... Amlo Corp.
Nitro ... Nitro Hardware & Supply Co.
Oak Hill .... New River Supply co.
Oak Hill . Roy's Loan & Sporting Goods
Parkersburg . Chancellor Hardware Co.
Philippi .... Wolfe & Co.
Princeton Douglas Sporting Goods Inc.
Richwood .... Coe's Sport Shop
Romney .... Bob Mar Sport
Shady Spring ..... Ray's Leisure Time
Spencer .... Eddie's Sport Shop
Stumptown .... Williams Gun Shop
Summersville .... Herold & Herold
Vienna .... Opha B. Poling
Webster Spring ... Damron Hardware
Weirton .... Weir Cove Sporting Goods
Wellsburg ...... Schwarz's Gun Shop
West Columbia ...... Paul Fitzgerald
Weston .... Dave's Sport Shop
Wheeling .... Banov Sports Center
Williamson ..... Alberts Loan Office
Williamson . Hatfield's Sporting Goods

Wisconsin

Antigo .... Sport Marine Inc.
Appleton ... Schieder Mayer Hardware
Baraboo .... Baraboo Sporting Goods
Baraboo ...... Premo's Service Store
Beaver Dam .... Beaver Sport Shop
Beloit .... Beloit Sport Center
Beloit .... Krueger Sport Shop
Berlin .... Cunningham Hardware
Berlin .... Curly's Sport Shop
Black Earth .... Bill's Shoe & Sport
Brandon .... Brandon Sport Shop
Brillion .... Brillion Sports
Brookfield .... Brookfield Ind.
Cashton .... Hundt Imp. Co.
Chilton .... Farm & Home Supply
Chippewa Falls ..... Bill's Sport Shop
Chippewa Falls .... Mac's Marine
Cumberland . Indian Head Sport Shop
Eagle River .... Speiss Sporting Goods
East Troy .... The Trading Post
Eau Claire ...... Outdoor Sport Shop
Edgar .... Kresbach's
Elkhorn .... Pat's Sport Shop
Fond Du Lac .... The Sport Shop
Fontana .. Fontana Army-Navy Store
Ft. Atkinson ... Lakeland Sport Shop
Franksville .... Bodven's
Glenbeulah .... Dick's Gun Shop
Green Bay ...... Bertrand Sport Shop
Green Bay .... Denis Sport Shop
Green Bay .... Gordon Bent Co.
Green Bay ..... Prange Budget Center
Hager City .... Prairie View Gun Shop
Hartford .... Johns Sport Shop
Iola .... C. Neil Krause
Iron Ridge
Earl Sportsman's Trading Post
Janesville ...... Janesville Sport Shop
Kaukana .... Dave's Sport Shop
Kenosha .... Bogard's Gun Shop
Kenosha .... Tyson's, Inc.
LaCrosse .... Bills Sport Shop
LaCrosse
Tausches Retail Hardware Inc.
Land O'Lakes .... Eberly's
Lomira .... Bill's Sport Shop
Madison .... Berg Pearson
Madison . H. H. Petrie Sporting Goods
Madison .... Rush Gun Shop
Madison . Wisc. Felton Sporting Goods
Manitowoc .... Finders Keepers
Manitowoc ... Sporting Goods Supply
Marinette ...... Marinette Sport Shop
Marshfield .... Miller's Sport Shop
Mazomanie .... W. J. Ewald
Menomonee Falls ...... Jay's Sports
Menomonee Falls .. Sports Unlimited
Menomonie .... The Sport Shop
Merrill .... Dukes Sport Shop
Milwaukee .... A. B. C. Supply
Milwaukee .... Casanovas Inc.
Milwaukee .... Dean's Sport Shop
Milwaukee .... Flintrop Arms
Milwaukee ... Johnson Sporting Goods
Milwaukee .... Ken's Gun Center
Milwaukee .... Kess Arms
Minocqua ..... Lakeland Sport Shop
Monroe .... Martins Sport Shop
New London .... Sport O Lectric
Oconomowoc
Stevens Sporting Goods, Inc.
Oshkosh .... A-1 Service
Oshkosh .... Hergert Sport Center
Oshkosh .... Joe's Sport Shop
Oshkosh ...... Spanbaur Sport Shop
Oshkosh .. Valley Arms & Equipment

Park Falls ....Scullys Inc.
Pepin .... Pepin Hardware
Peshtigo .... Pete's Sport Shop
Phillips .... Martwick's
Plymouth ....Langjahr's
Portage ....Coast To Coast Store
Portage ....Portage Sport Shop
Port Washington
Schiller's Sporting Goods
Prairie DuChein ... Richard Stark, Inc.
Racine ....Fodor's
Racine .... Higgin Sporting Goods
Racine ....The Trading Post
Reedsburg ....Fred F. Haugh
Reedsburg ....Tom's Gun Shop
Rice Lake .... Lou's Sport Shop
Richland Center .....A. H. Krouskop
Ripon ....Ripon Sport Shop
Shawano .... Fritz's Gun Repair
Shawano ....K&G Sport Shop
Solon Springs ......Al's Gun Repairs
South Milwaukee ..... N. Hints Sports
Stetsonville ....Mundt "Jeep"
Stevens Point .... Boyers Sport Marine
Stevens Point .... Sport Shop
Sturgeon Bay ... Em's Sporting Goods
Sun Prairie .... Klein's
Superior ....The Mareus Co.
Tomah ....Coast To Coast Store
Tomahawk .. Bennett Sporting Goods
Viroqua .... K&L, Inc.
Waterford ...... Jensen's Sport Shop
Watertown .. Hemp's Sporting Goods
Waukesha .... Becker Sporting Goods
Waukesha ...... Jim's Sports Heaven
Waukesha ..... Jim's Streams & Field
Wausau
Shepherd & Schaller Sporting Goods
Wausau ....The Gunsmith
Wauwatosa ..... Schelkles Gun Shop
West Allis .... Bob's Bait Shop
West Allis .... Don's Gun Shop
Wilmot .... Gander Mountain
Wisconsin Rapids .. Johnson Hills, Inc.
Wisconsin Rapids .. Perry's Sport Shop

Wyoming

Buffalo .... Sullivan's Sport Shop
Casper ....Ideen's Repair
Casper .... K. Mart 4069
Casper .... Sunset Sporting Goods
Cheyenne ..... Grand Central Market
Cheyenne ....Peoples
Cheyenne .... Tempo
Cheyenne ......The Supply Sergeant
Cody .... The Fishhook
Cody .... The Gun Hawk
Douglas .... The Saul Co.
DuBois .... Welty's General Store
Evanston ....Nevilles
Gillette .... Gambles
Gillette .... Sport Shop, Inc.
Lander .... Lander Saddlery
Laramie ......Linde's Sporting Goods
Pinedale ..Wind River Sporting Goods
Rawlins .... Birite Drug
Rawlins .... Gambles
Rawlins ...... Gene's Sporting Goods
Riverton Hartman Co. Sporting Goods
Riverton ..... The House Of Muskets
Rock Springs .. Mike's Sporting Goods
Sheridan .... Ritz Sporting Goods
Sheridan ....Sheridan Gun Shop
Torrington .... Gambles
Worland ....The Outdoorsman

Canada

Campbell River F. H. Camp, Gunsmith
Hamilton .... The Cartridge Club
Hamilton ....Gunsports Co.
Hamilton ...Snider, Custom Gunsmith
Peterborough .... Trigger Talk
Toronto ......Sole's Sporting Goods
Vancover ....Hough Custom Guns
Victoria .... Robinson's

Puerto Rico

Rio Piedras .... Sports Shop 1967

LAST MINUTE LISTINGS

Olathe, Kansas
.... Simmons Gun Specialties
Wichita, Kansas ...... The Gun Shop
Salem, Ohio .... Fisher's
Beaumont, Texas .... Oshman's

ADDITIONAL "WHERE-TO-BUY-IT" DIRECTORY LISTINGS:

Firearms and accessories are also available at most of these stores, including their catalog offices: SEARS, ROEBUCK AND CO., MONTGOMERY WARD, ALDENS, SPIEGEL, WESTERN AUTO, FED-MART, K-MART, MAY CO., OSHMAN'S, J. C. PENNEY and FEDCO.

IMPORTANT NOTICE REGARDING THE WHERE-TO-BUY-IT-DIRECTORY

The GUN DIGEST Directory of the Arms Trade has long been considered by our readers a highly important and valuable guide to those companies and individuals who offer a product—of their own manufacture or an import—to the millions of people who make up the great world of guns and shooting.

For that reason, the GUN DIGEST has been asked repeatedly to offer a directory that lists the names and towns or cities of the firearms dealers and gunsmiths throughout the United States where the extensive array of products described and illustrated in our pages can be obtained.

The enactment in the latter part of 1968 of the Federal Gun Control Act was the final stimulus we needed to compile such a listing. Today, many if not most of the products manufactured in the field of firearms and related items must be obtained from a dealer operating in the same state where the buyer resides. Ordering guns and components by mail or other common carrier is forbidden by the Gun Control Act '68 to the average individual in the great majority of cases.

Therefore, to let our millions of readers know where in their own state they may go to buy the products we show, we offer this first issue of the WHERE-TO-BUY-IT-DIRECTORY.

This new Directory is not complete, we know, for despite considerable advertising and several mailings we did not obtain 100% response. We'll do better next year, you may be sure.

To those firearms dealers and gunsmiths not represented in these pages of our new WHERE-TO-BUY-IT-DIRECTORY, our apologies, regrets, and this note: if you will get in touch with us your name and location will be included in our next edition. *There is no charge of any kind for this service.*

INDEX

to the departmental and display pages
of the GUN DIGEST--*24th Edition*